A-Z WEST MIDLANDS BIRMINGHAM

CONTENTS

REFERENCE

Motorway	M6
A Road	A38
Under Construction	
Proposed	
B Road	B4284
Dual Carriageway	
One Way Street — Traffic flow on A Roads is also indicated by a heavy line on the driver's left	➡
City Centre Ring Road & Junction Numbers	①
Restricted Access	
Pedestrianized Road	
Track / Footpath	
Cycleway (Selected)	
Railway	Station, Heritage Station, Level Crossing, Tunnel
Midland Metro — The boarding of Metro trams at stops may be limited to a single direction, indicated by the arrow.	Stop
Built Up Area	HOOPER STREET
Local Authority Boundary	
Posttown Boundary	
Postcode Boundary within Posttown	
Map Continuation	20 / Large Scale City Centre 4
Car Park (Selected)	P
Church or Chapel	†
Fire Station	■
Hospital	Ⓗ
House Numbers A & B Roads only	20 ... 40
Information Centre	𝑖
Junction Name (M6 Toll only)	BELFRY JUNCTION
National Grid Reference	⁴12
Park & Ride	Monkspath P+🚌
Police Station	▲
Post Office	★
Toilet: without facilities for the Disabled	▽
with facilities for the Disabled	▽
for exclusive use by the Disabled	▽
Viewpoint	✳ ✳
Educational Establishment	
Hospital or Hospice	
Industrial Building	
Leisure or Recreational Facility	
Place of Interest	
Public Building	
Shopping Centre or Market	
Other Selected Buildings	

SCALE

Map Pages 8-217	Map Pages 4-7
1:18103 3½ inches to 1 mile	1:9051 7 inches to 1 mile
0 ¼ ½ ¾ Mile	0 ⅛ ¼ ⅜ Mile
0 250 500 750 Metres 1 Kilometre	0 100 200 300 400 500 Metres
5.52 cm to 1 km	11.05 cm to 1 km
8.89 cm to 1 mile	17.78 cm to 1 mile

Copyright of Geographers' A-Z Map Company Ltd.

Head Office:
Fairfield Road, Borough Green, Sevenoaks, Kent TN15 8PP
Telephone: 01732 781000 (Enquiries & Trade Sales)
01732 783422 (Retail Sales)
www.a-zmaps.co.uk
Copyright © Geographers' A-Z Map Co. Ltd. 2004

Ordnance Survey®

This product includes mapping data licensed from Ordnance Survey® with the permission of the Controller of Her Majesty's Stationery Office.
© Crown Copyright 2004. All rights reserved. Licence number 100017302
EDITION 2 2004

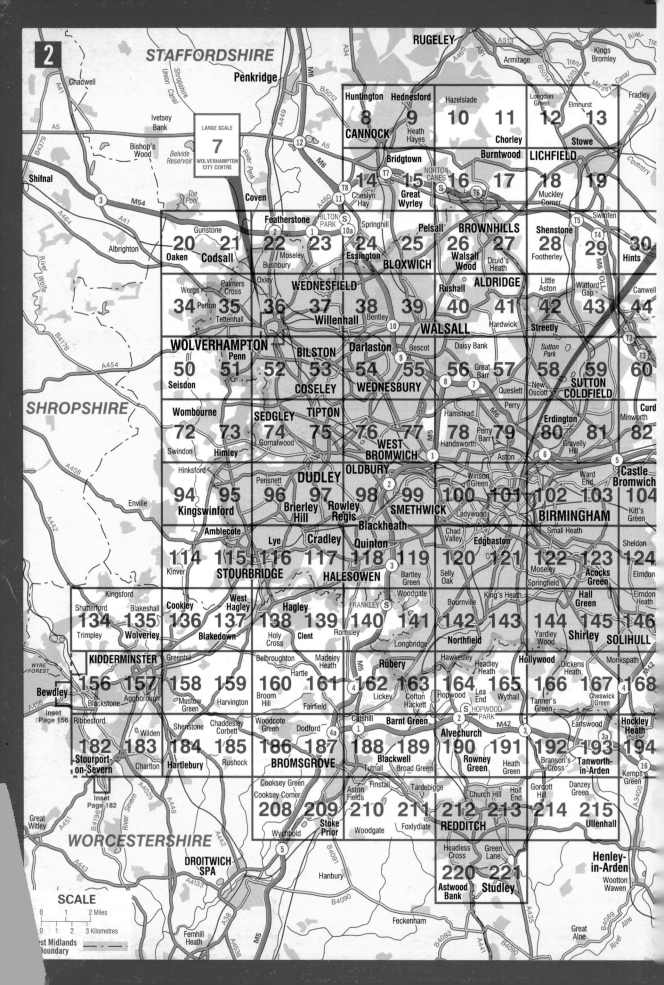

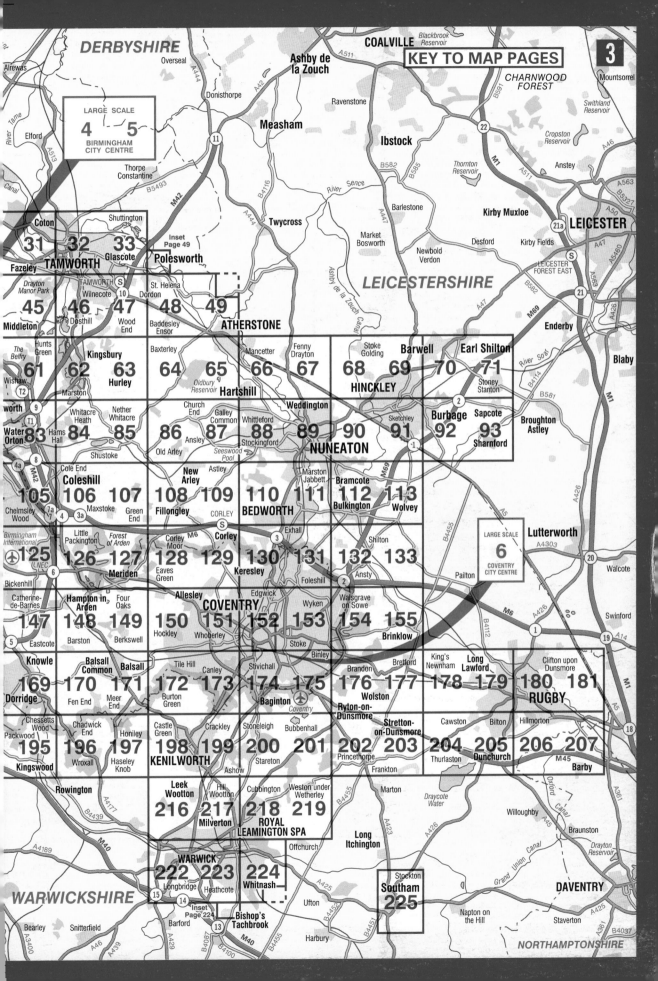

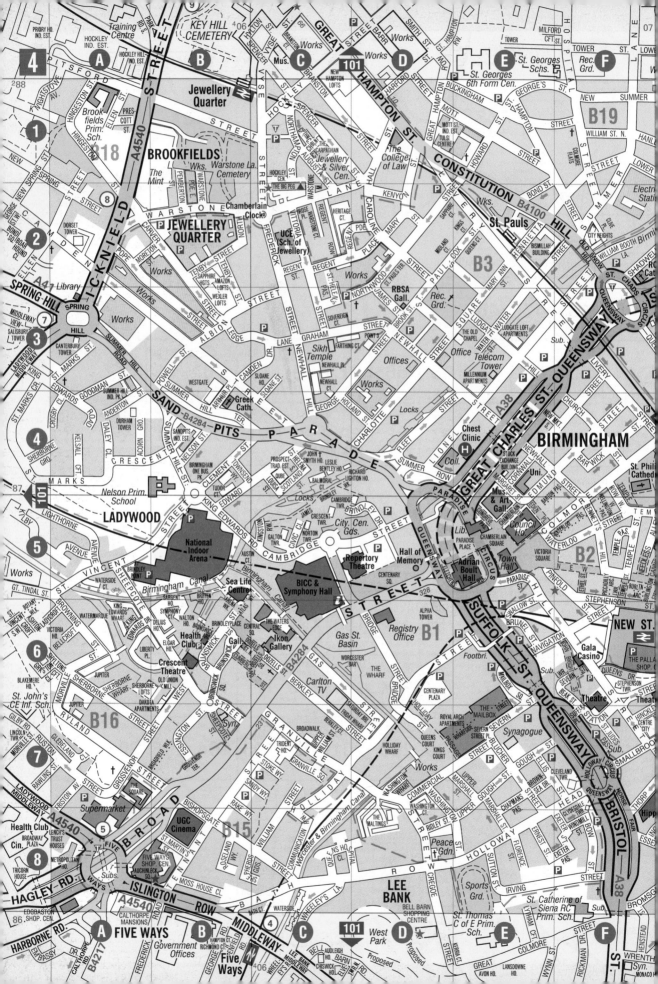

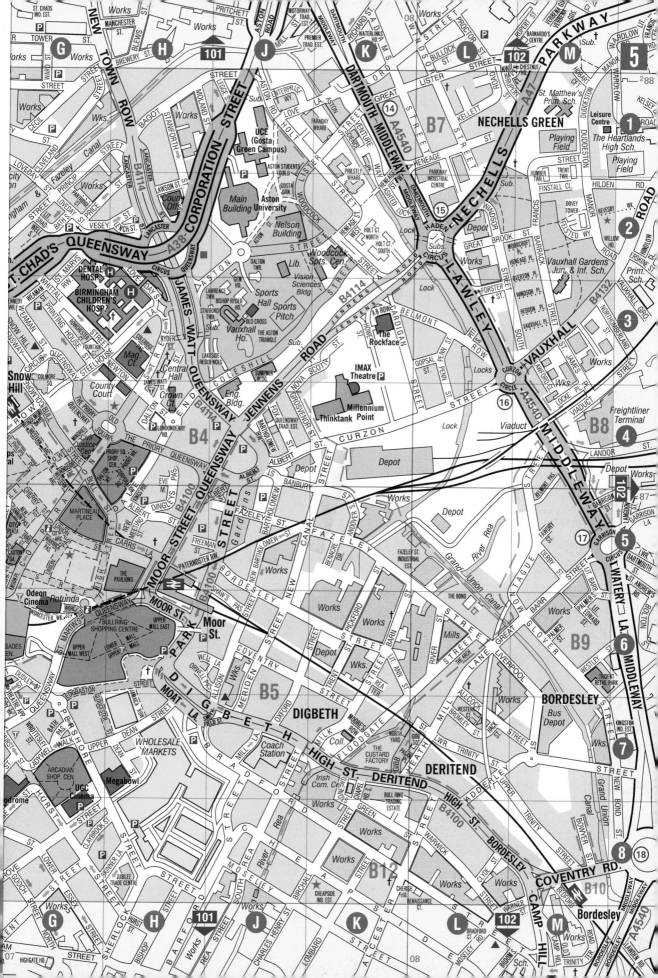

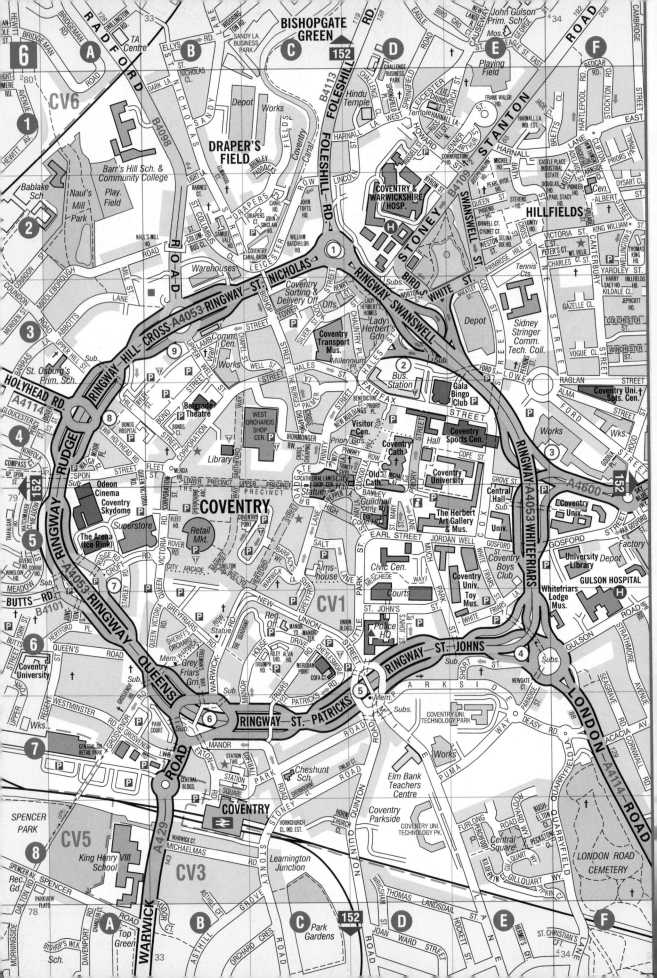

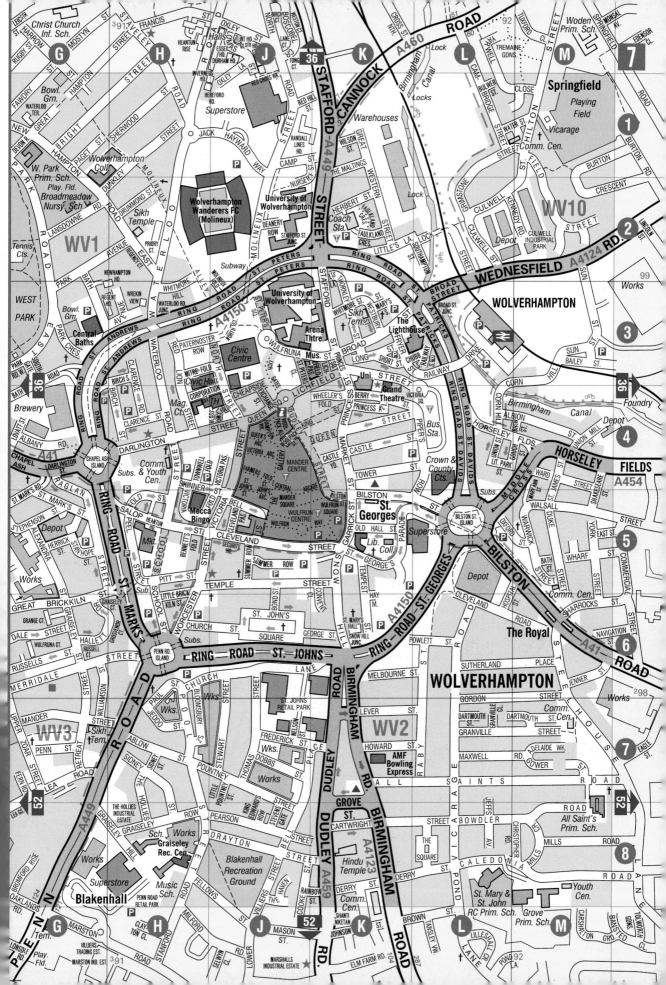

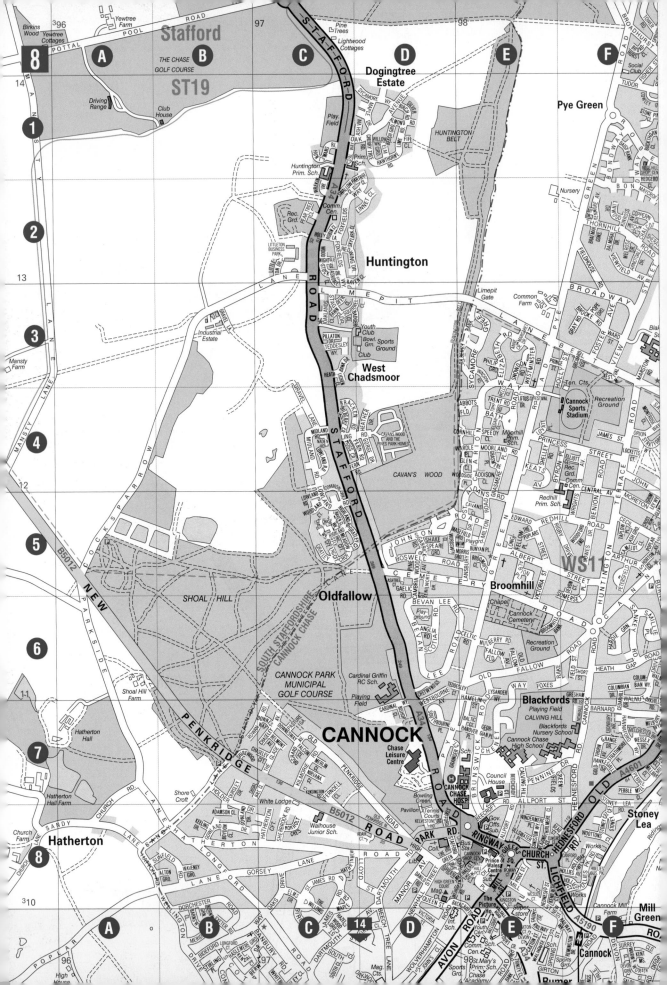

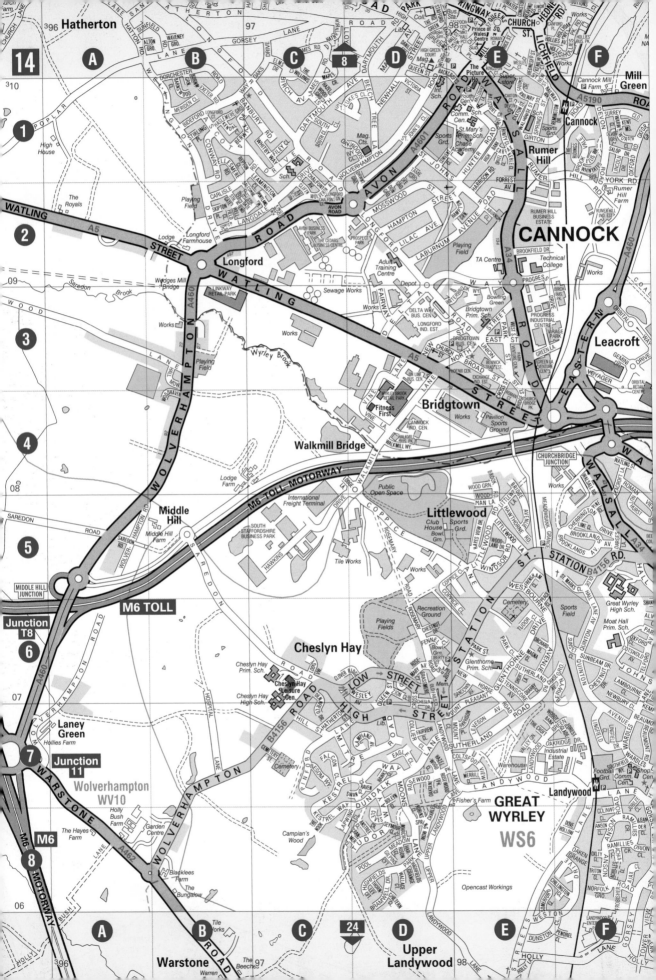

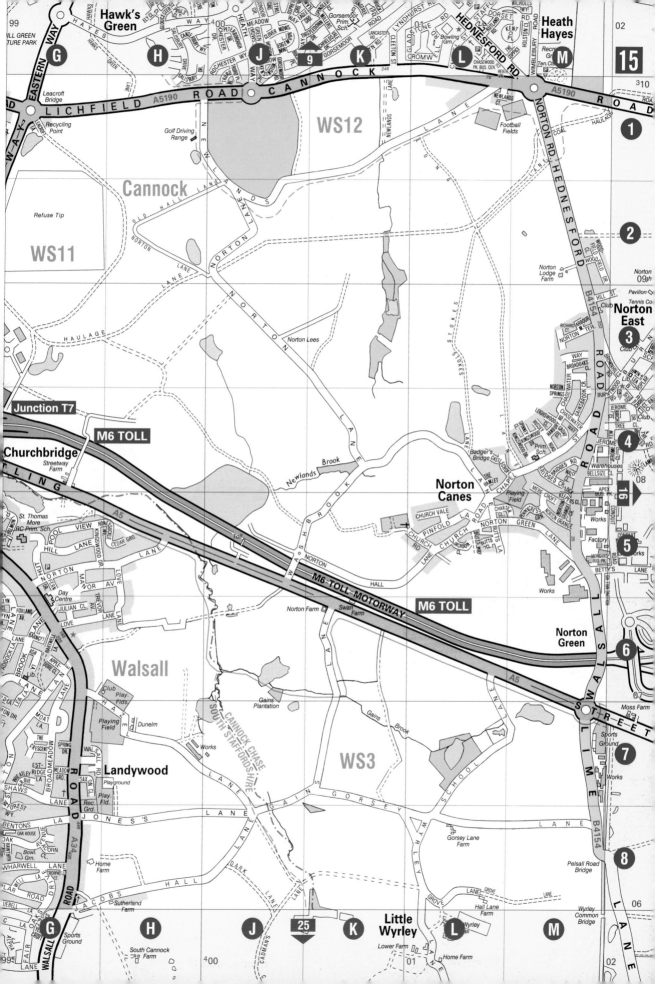

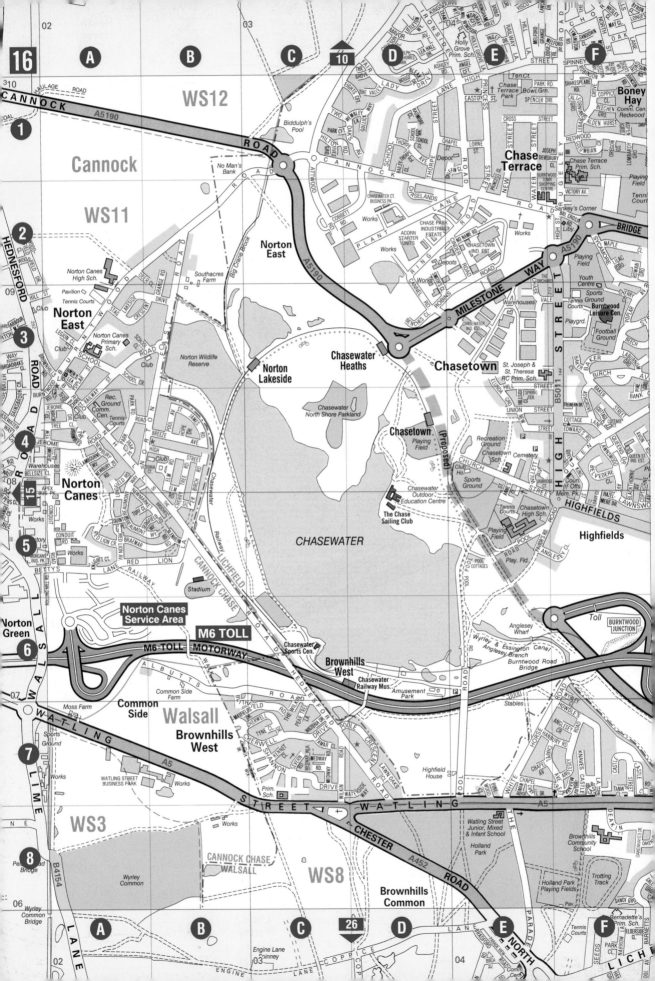

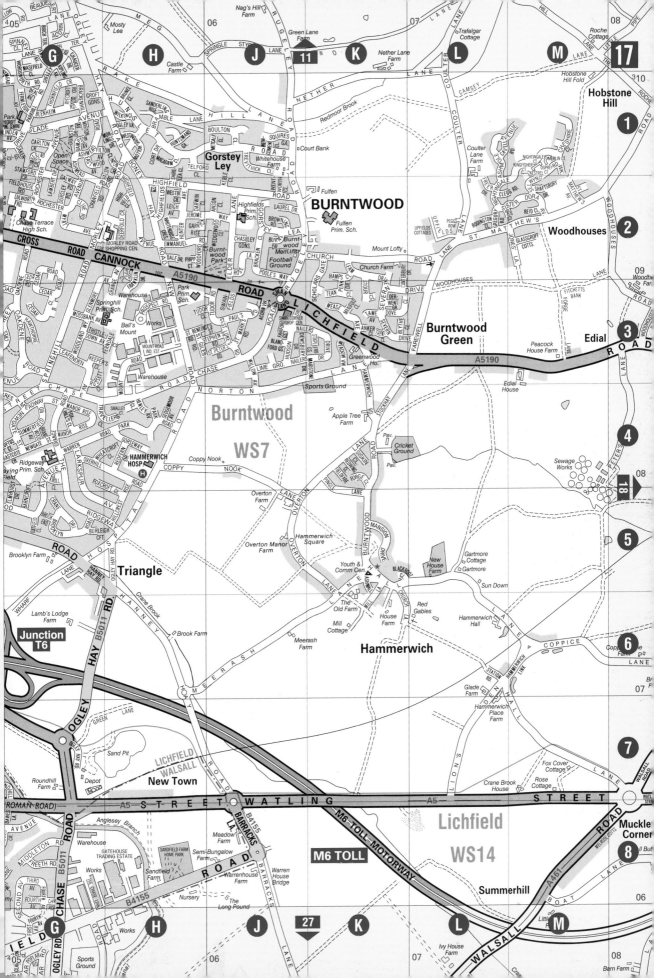

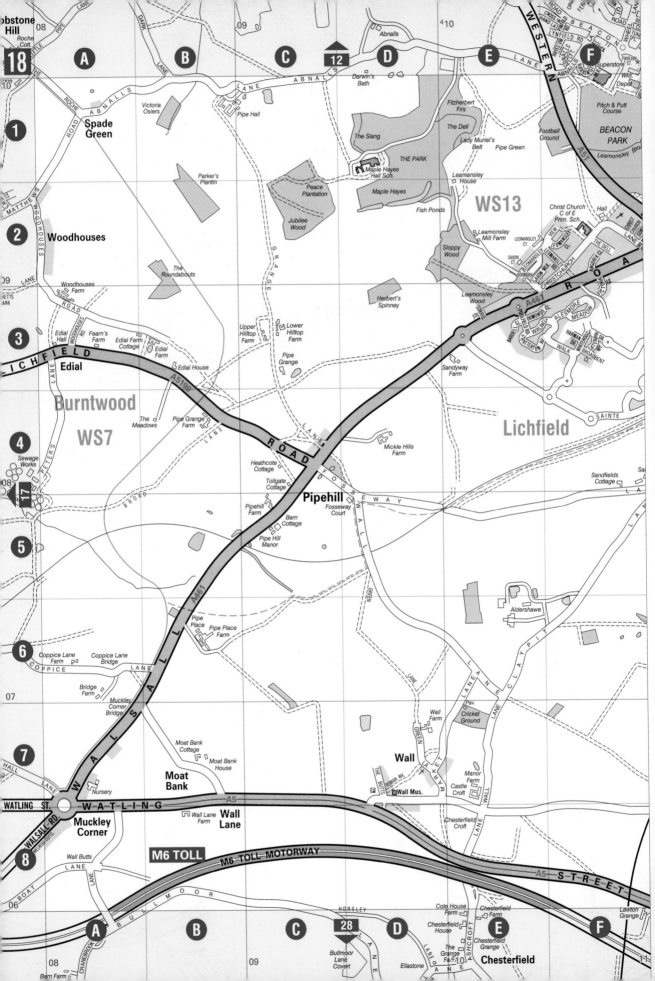

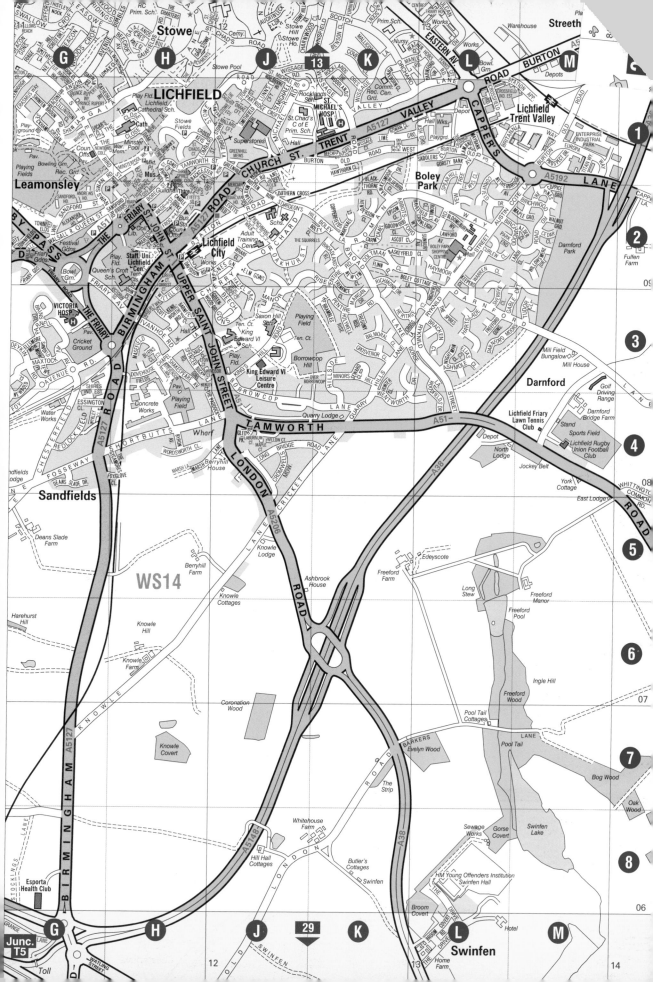

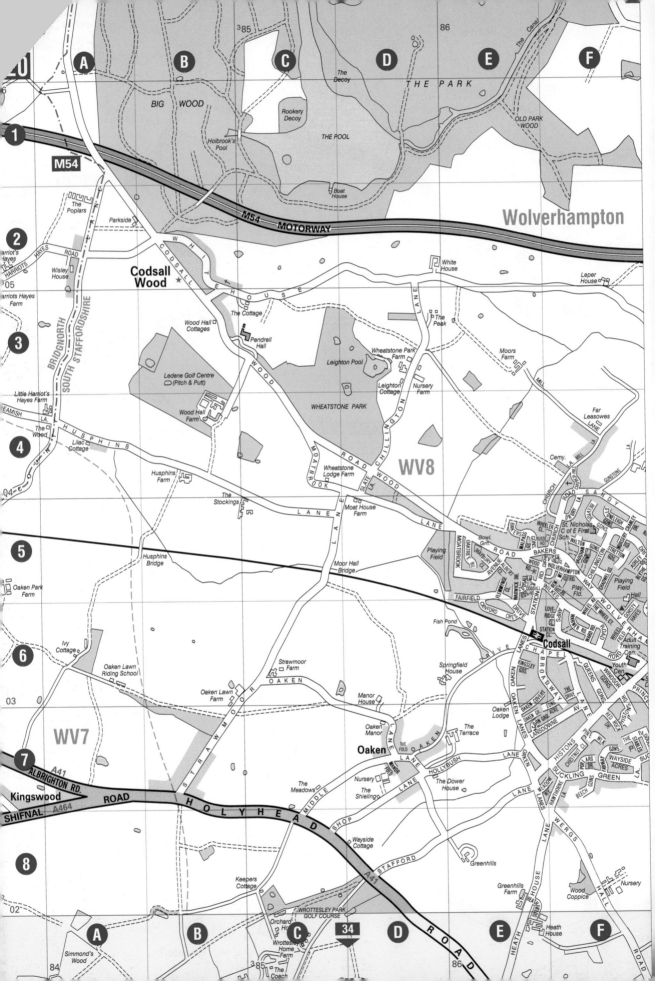

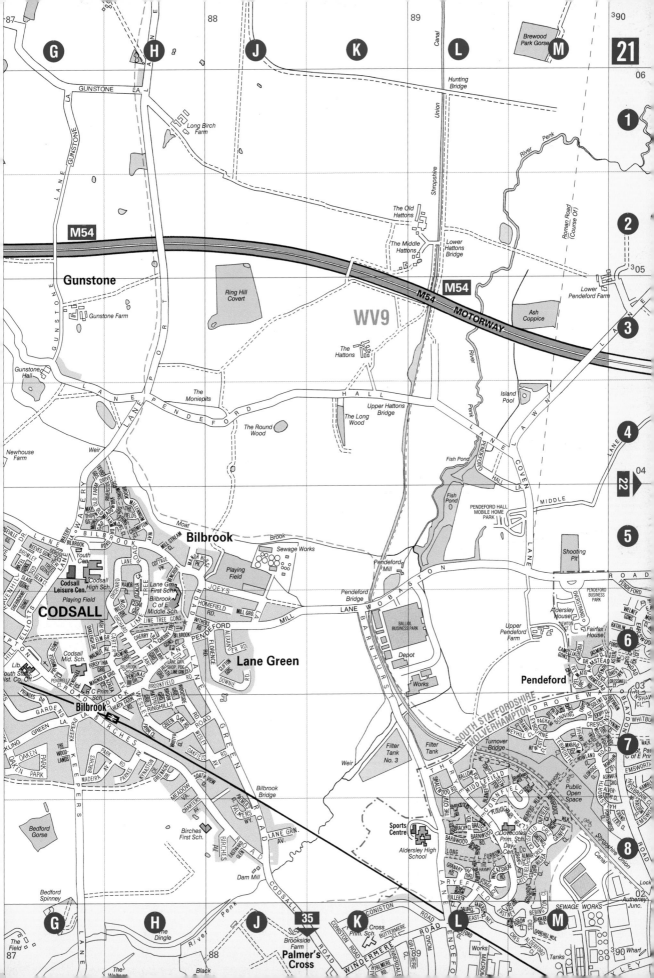

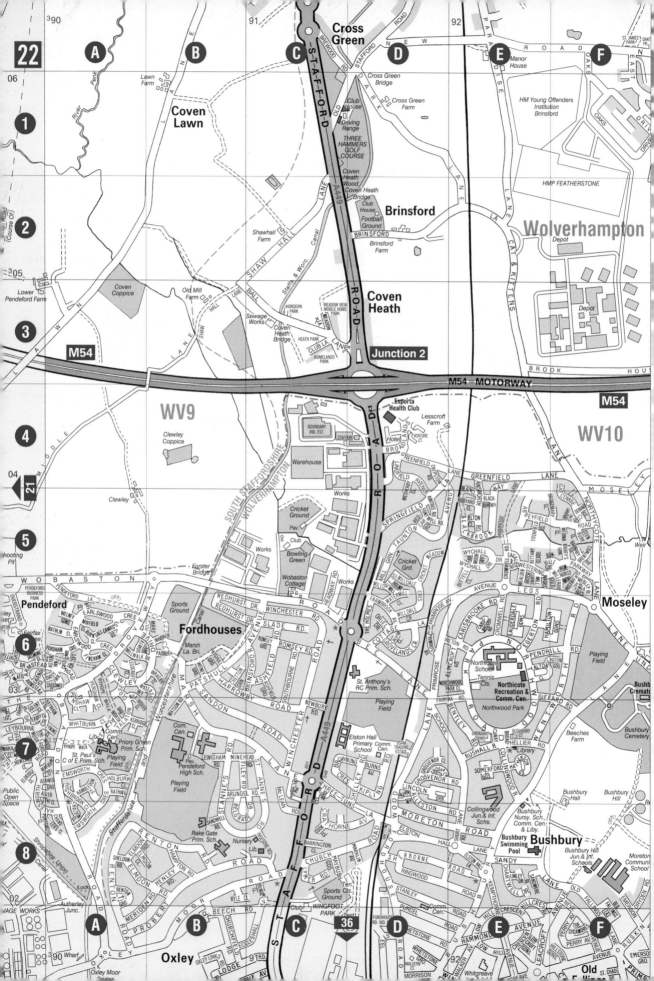

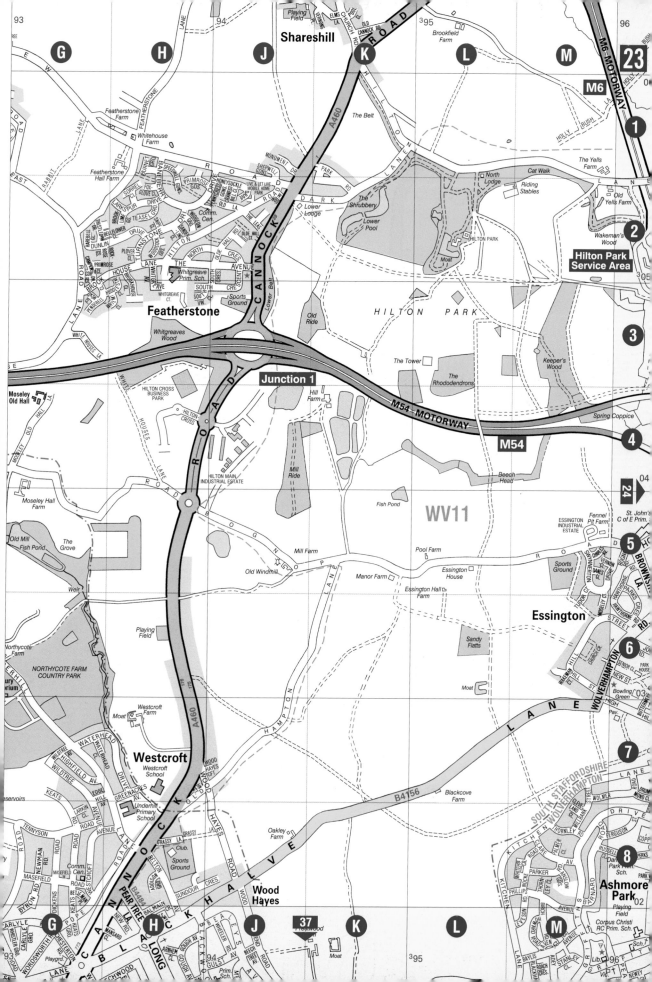

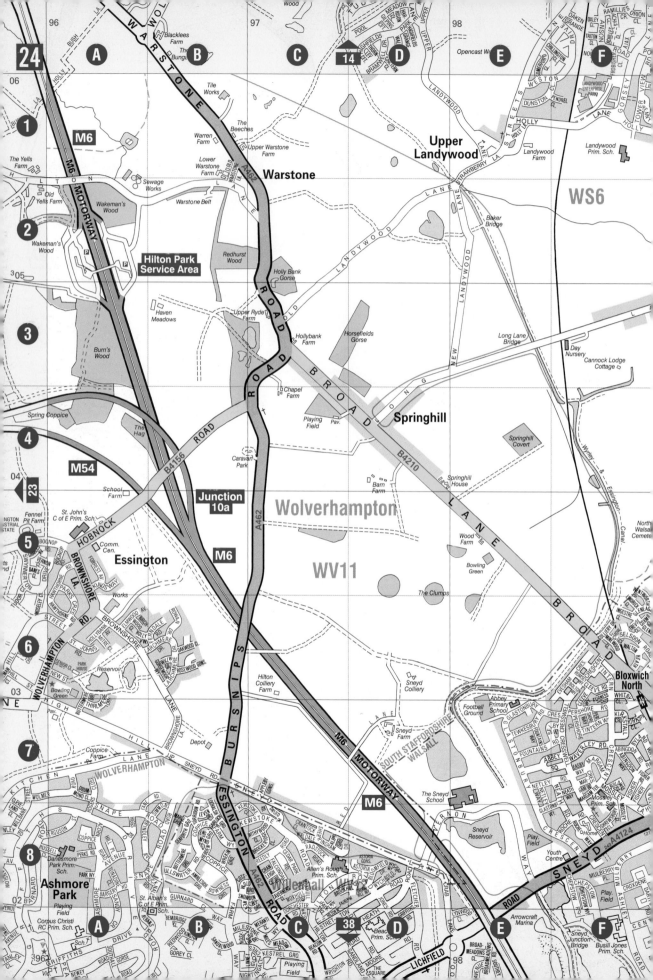

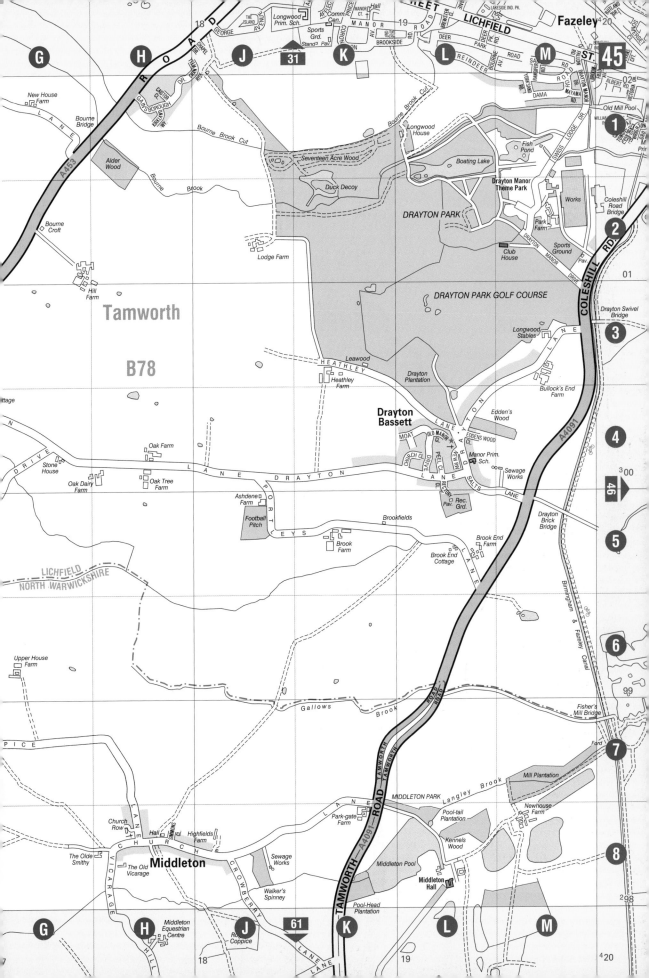

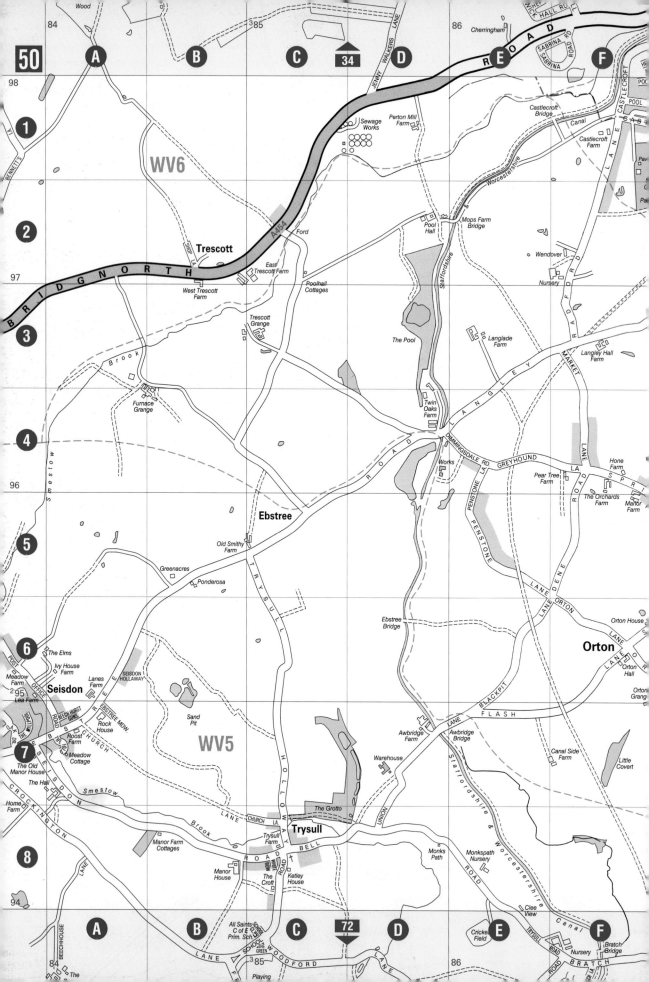

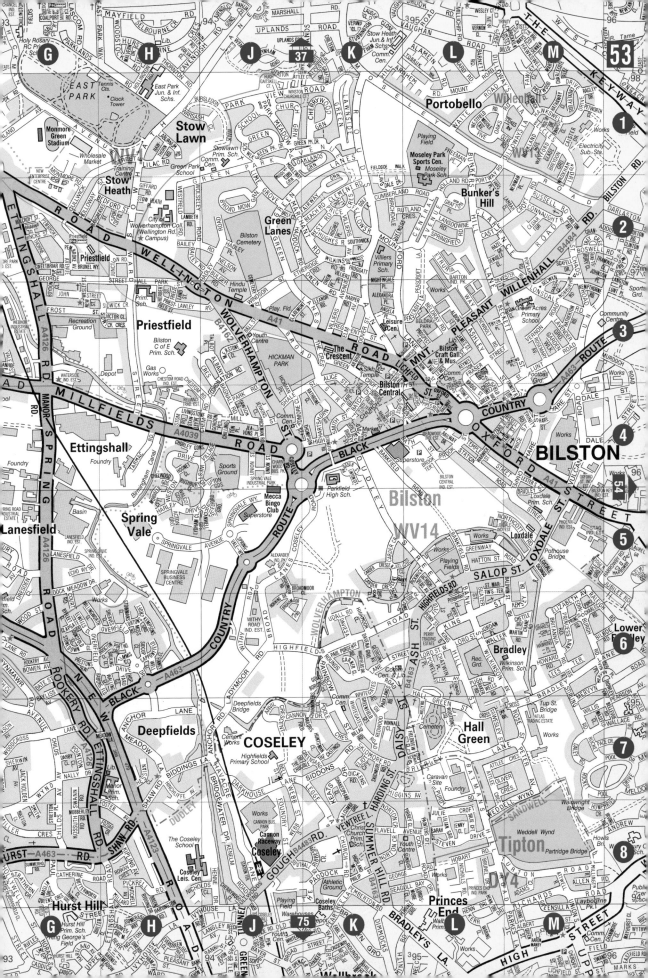

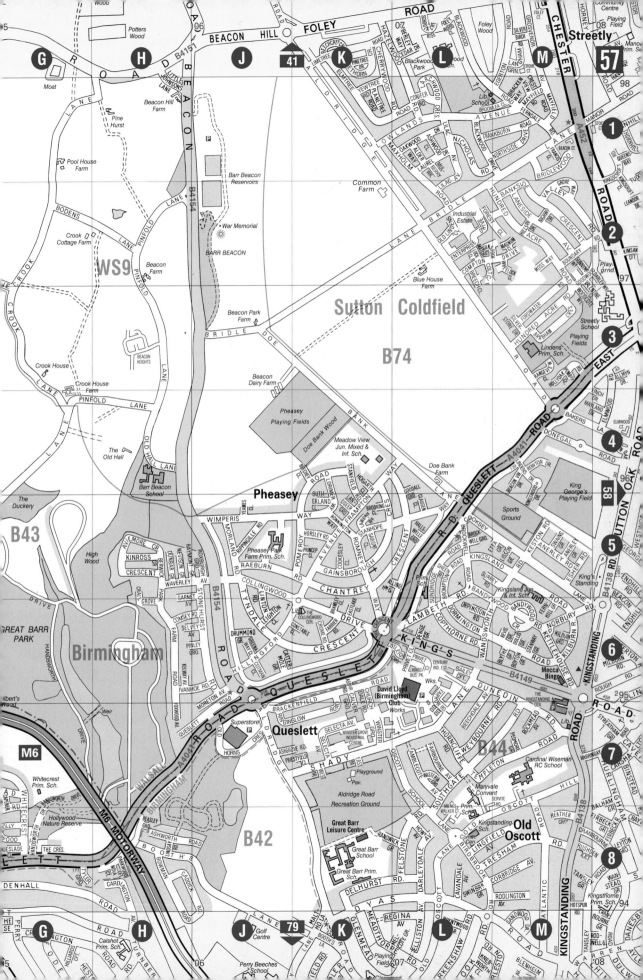

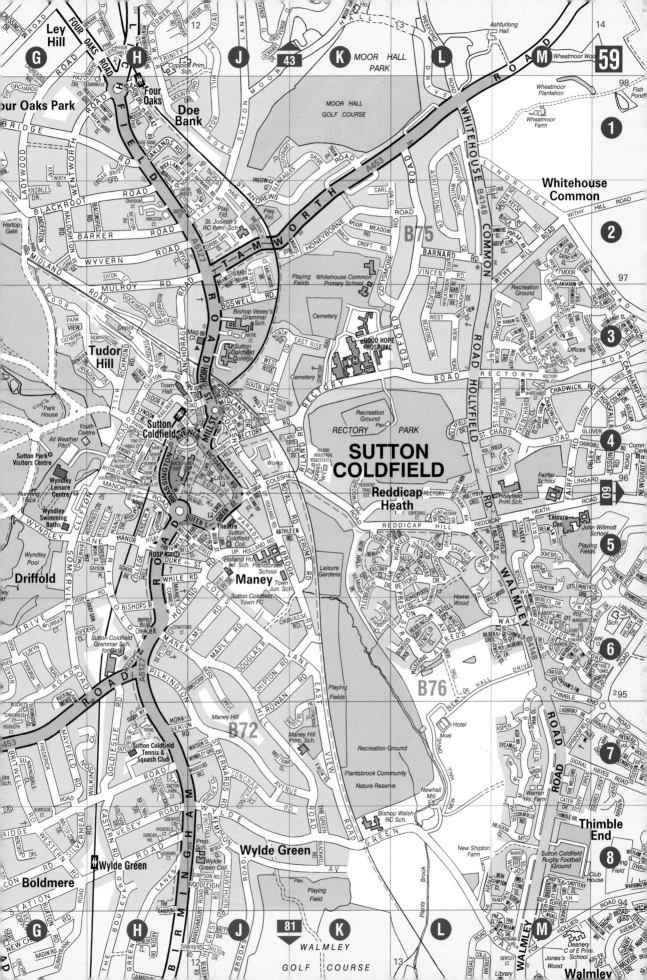

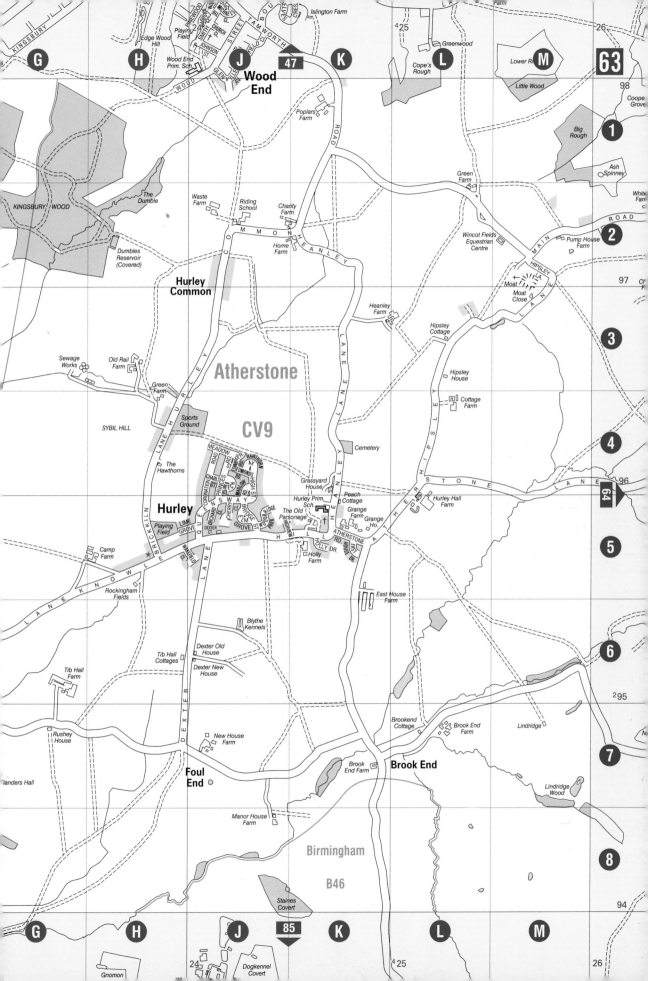

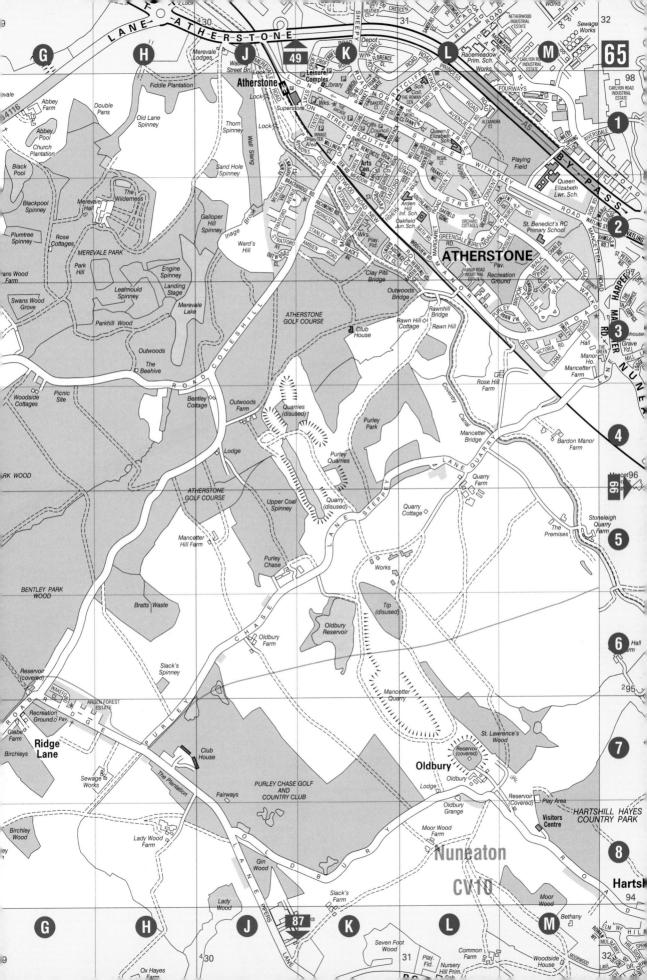

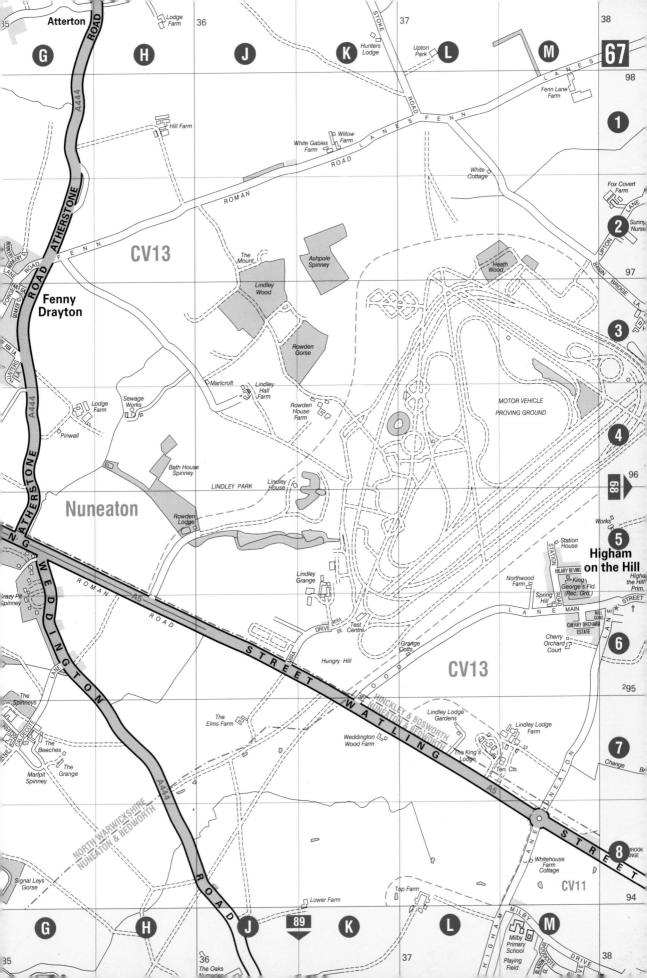

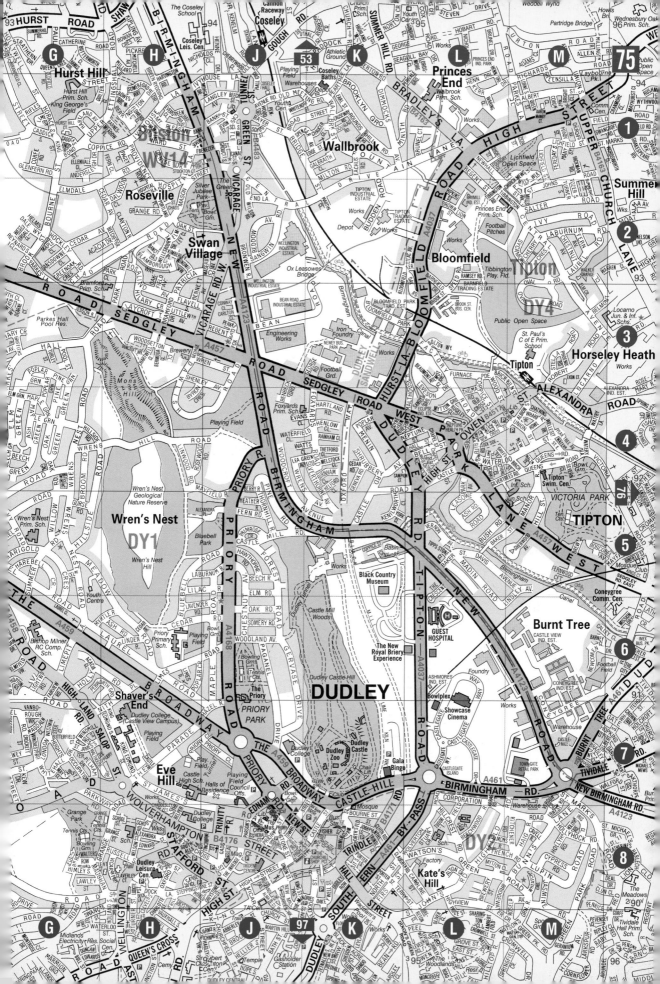

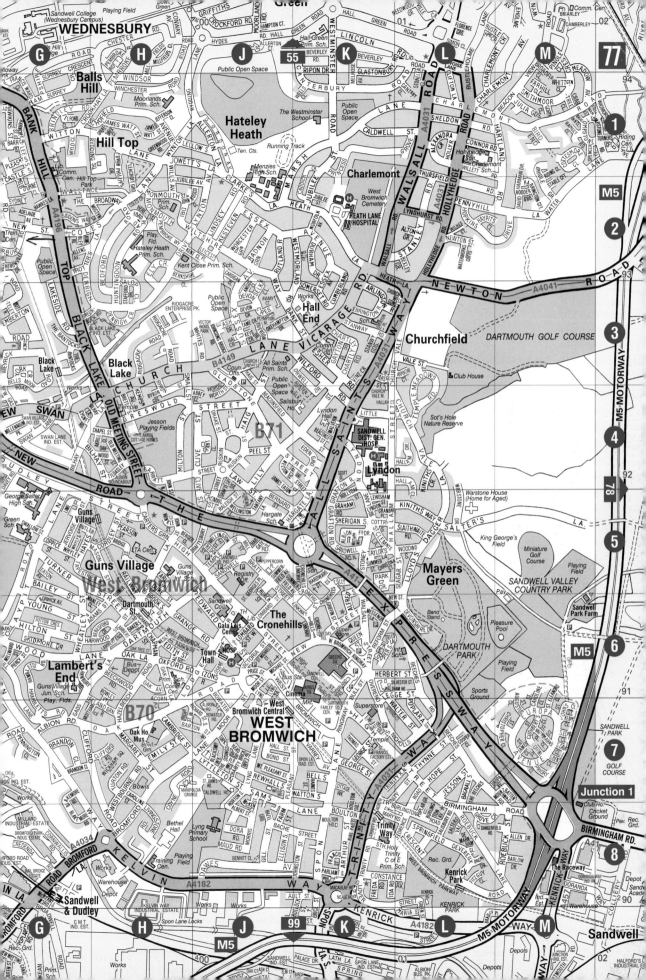

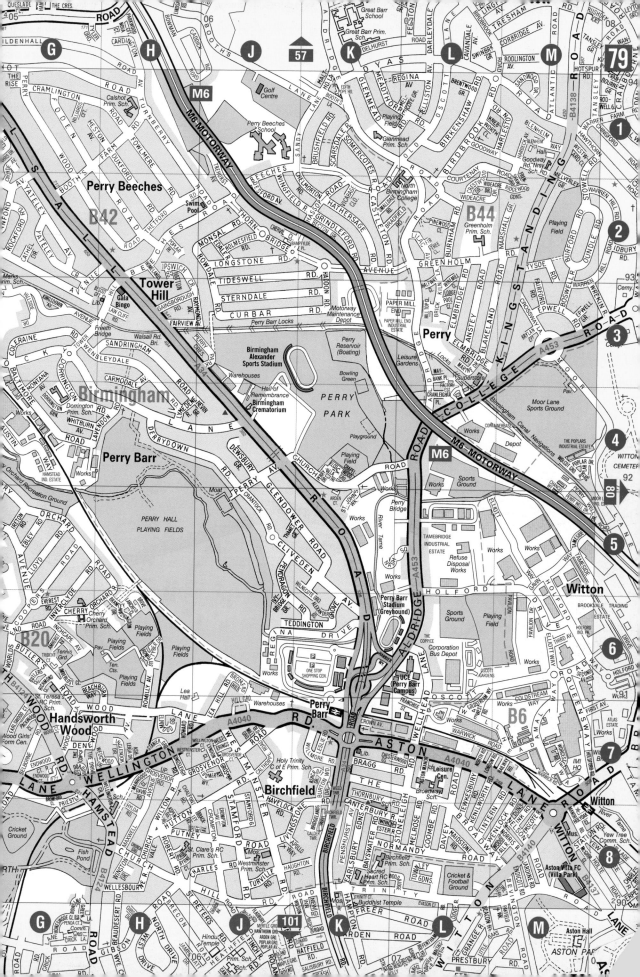

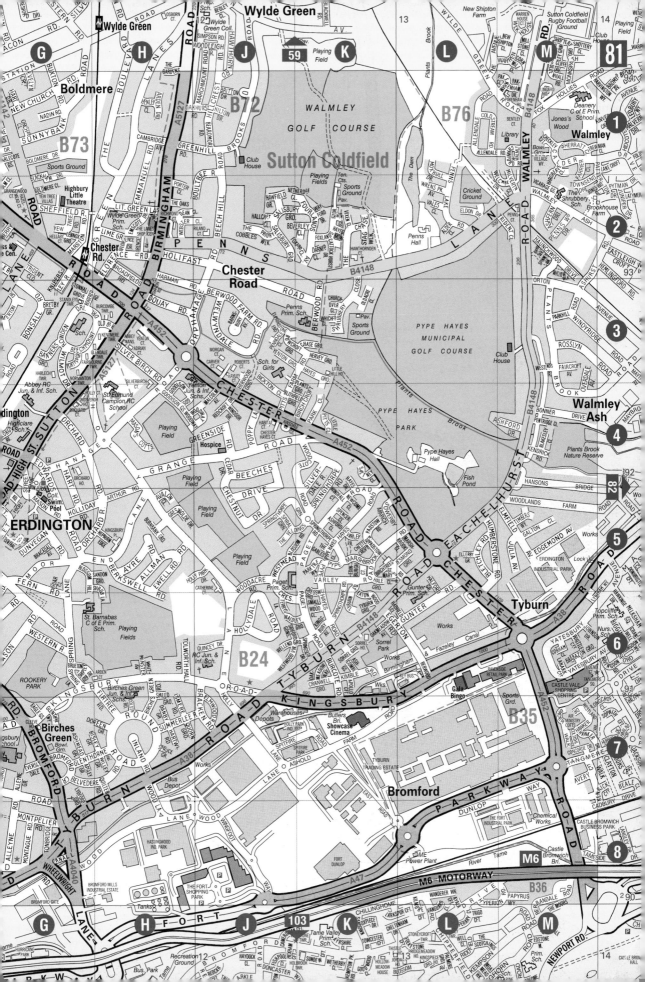

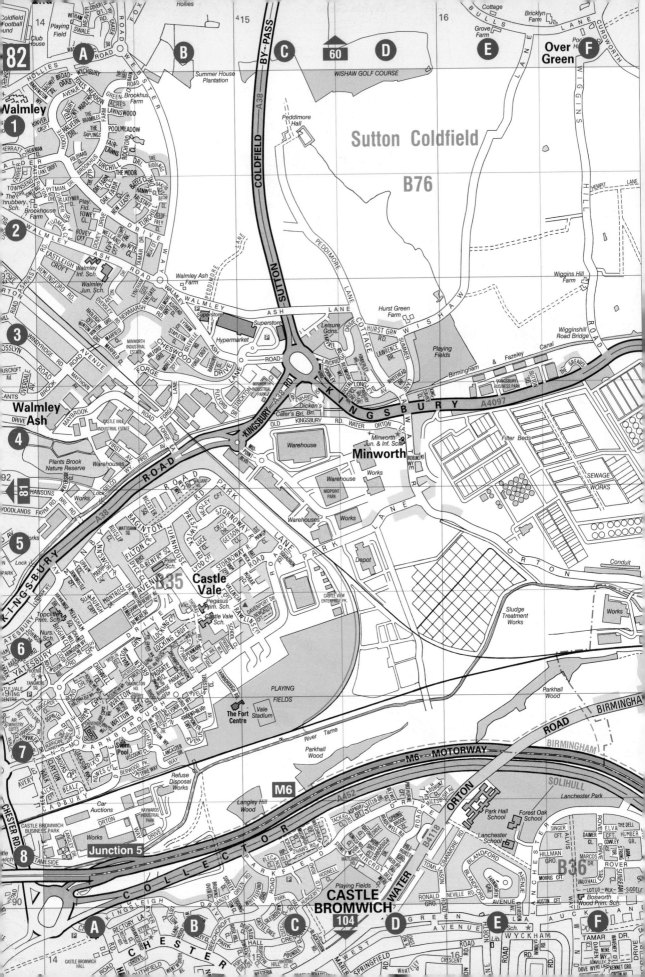

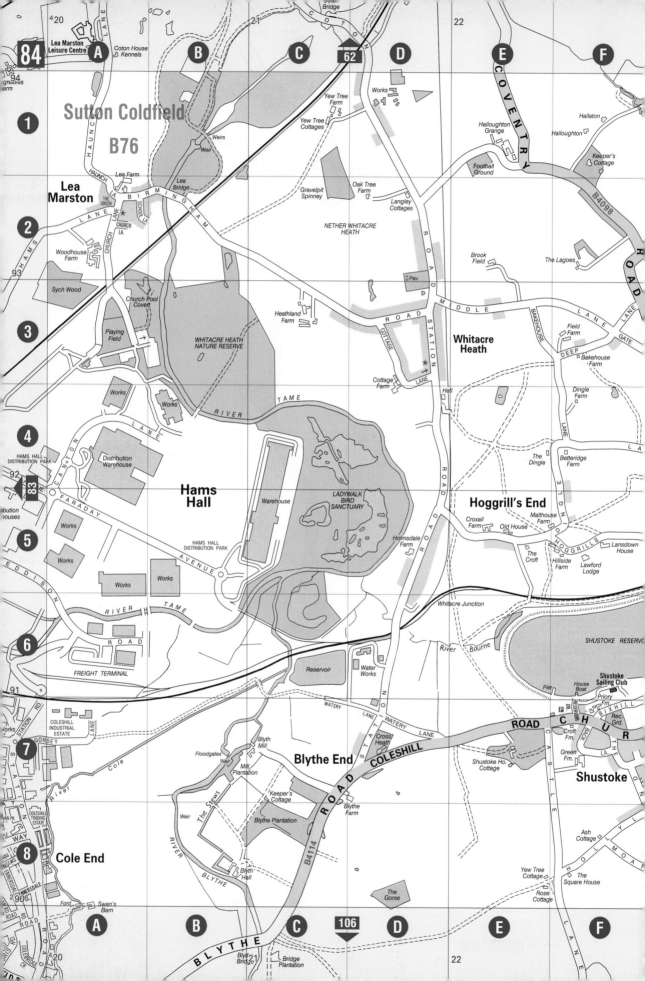

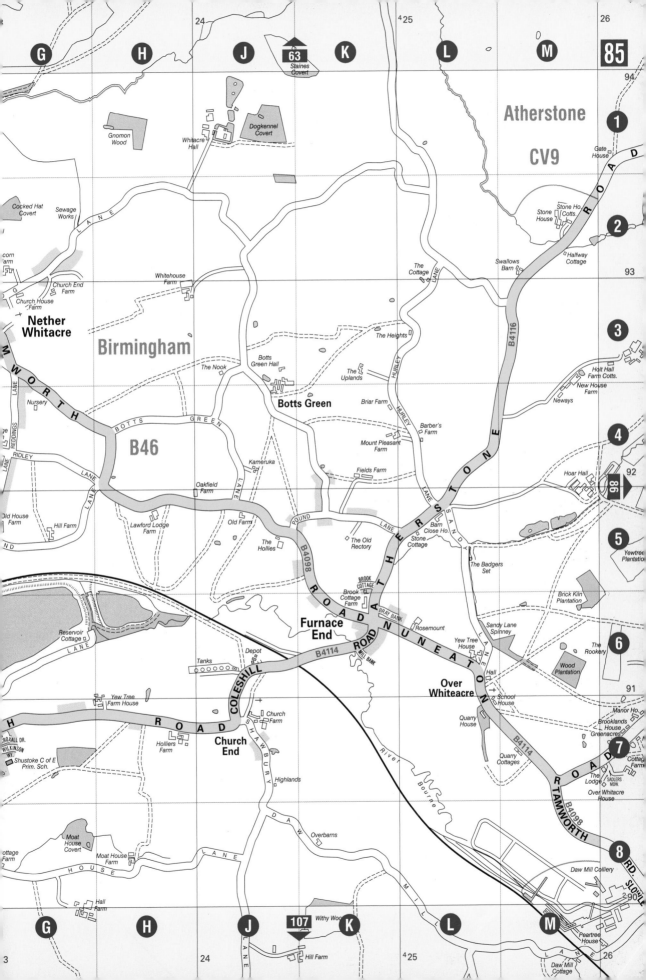

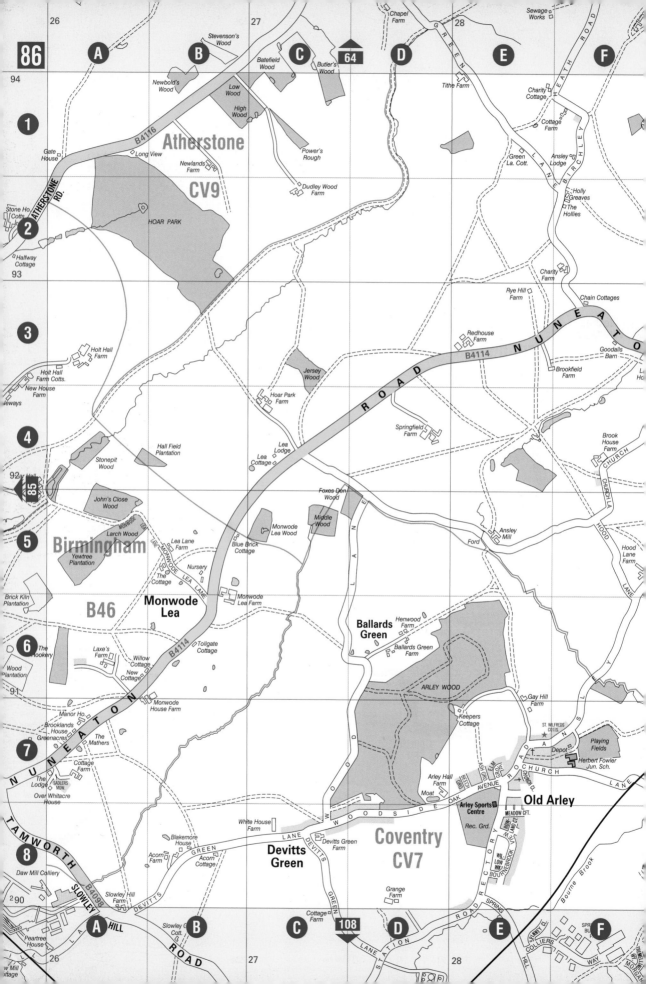

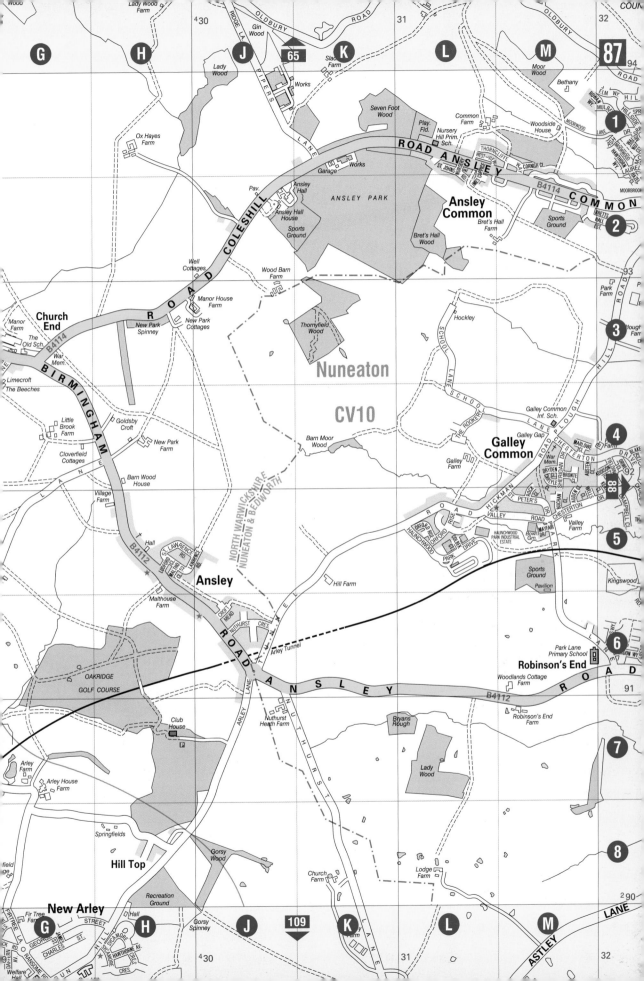

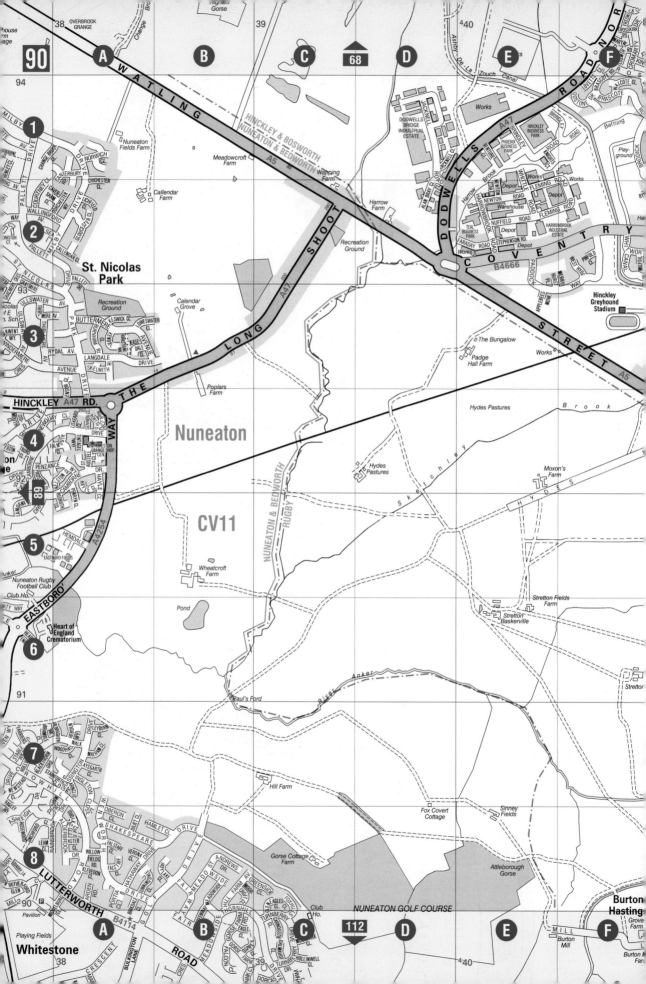

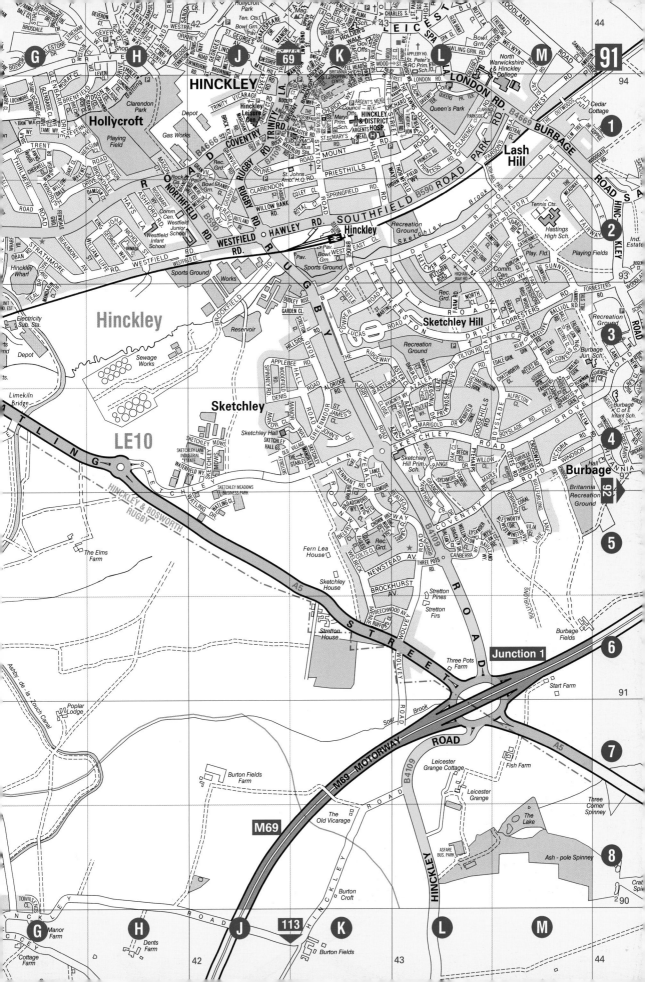

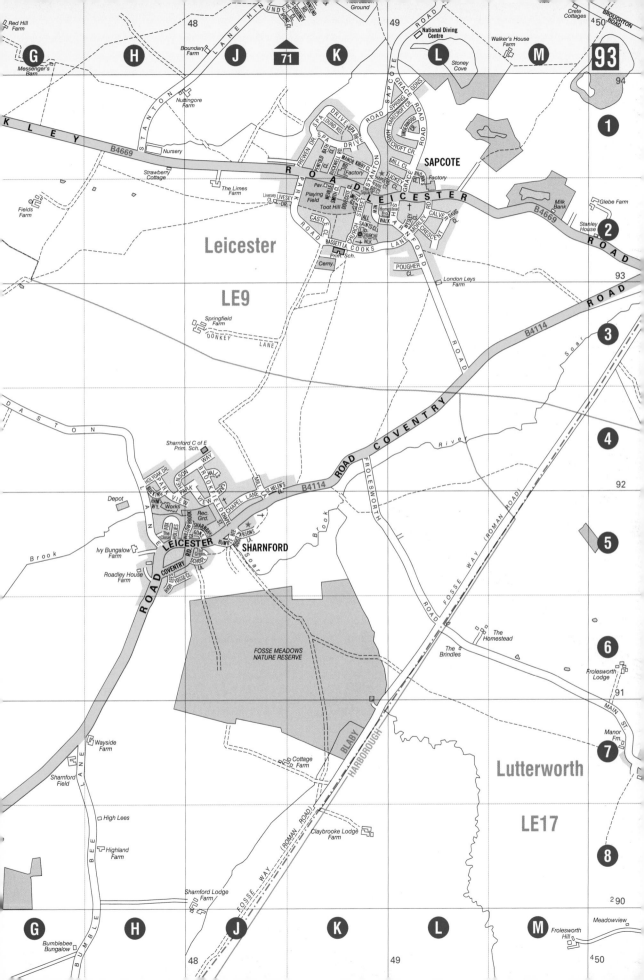

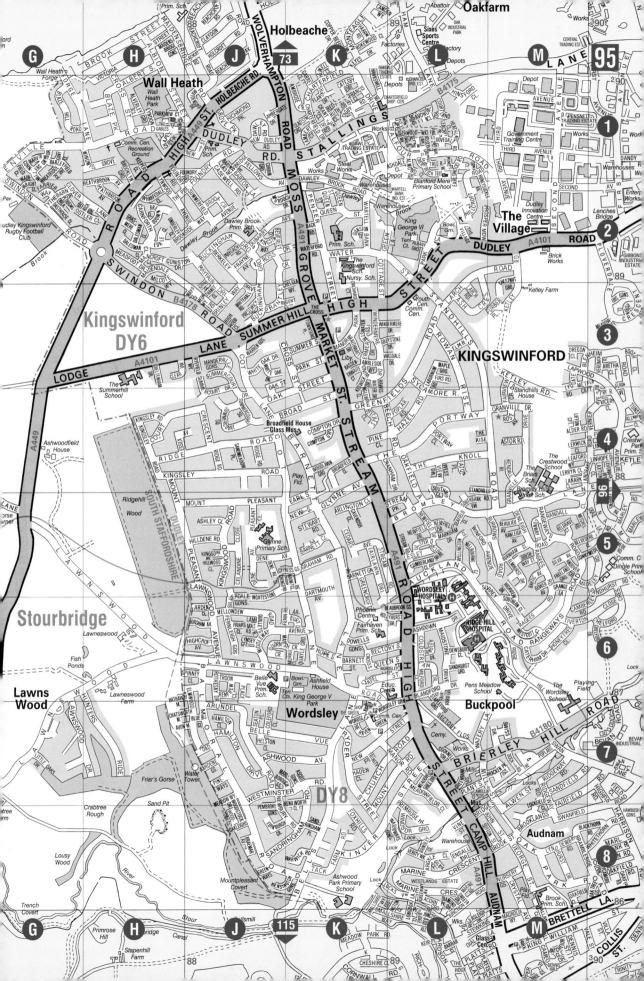

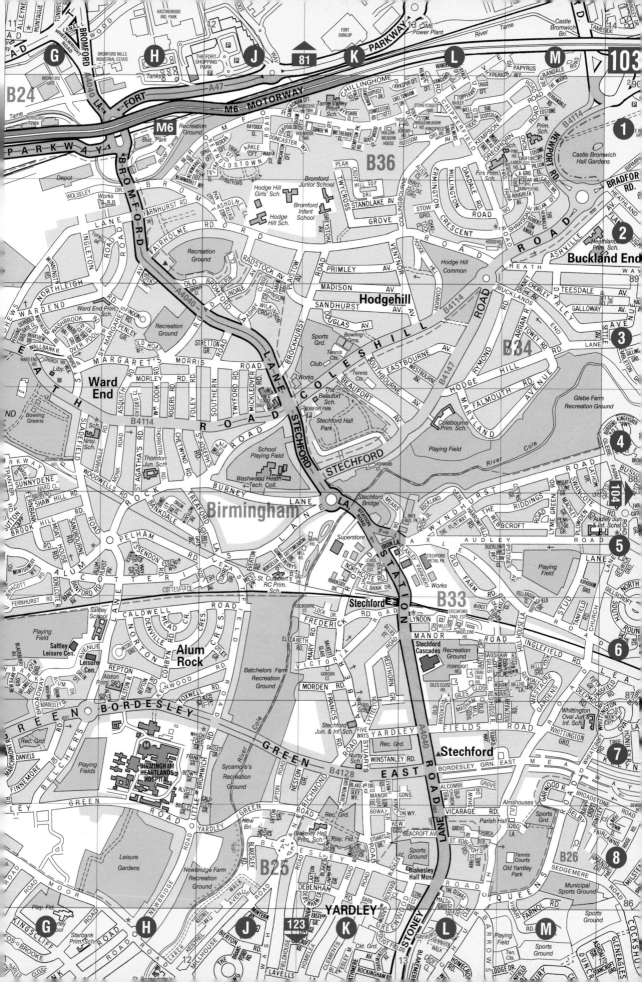

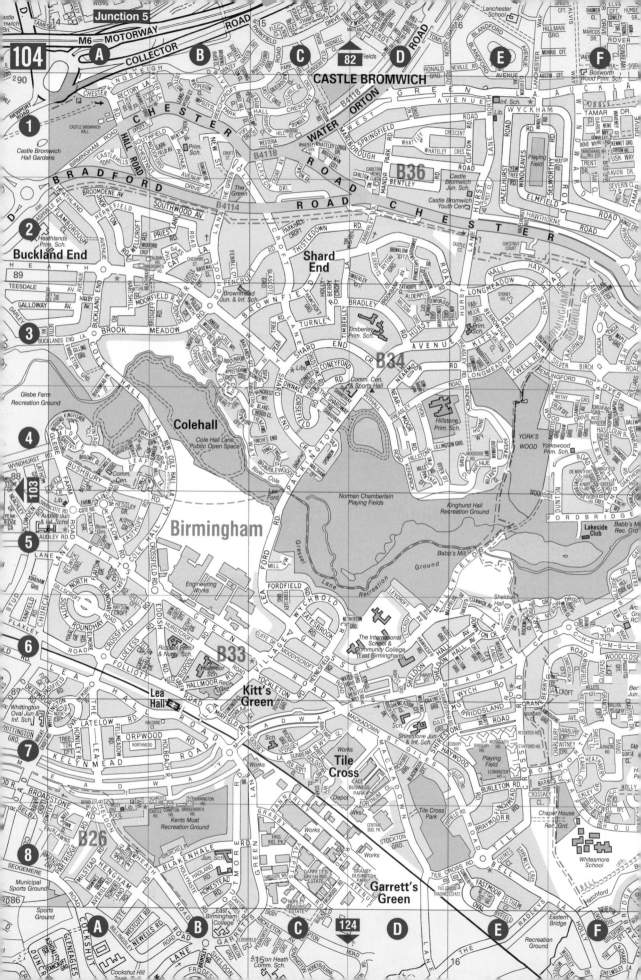

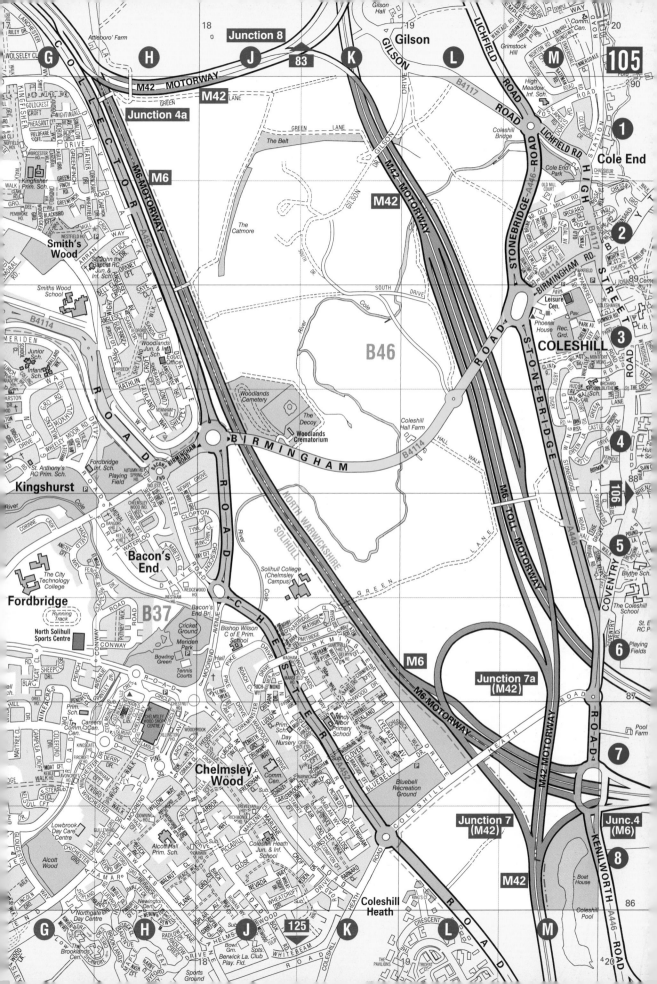

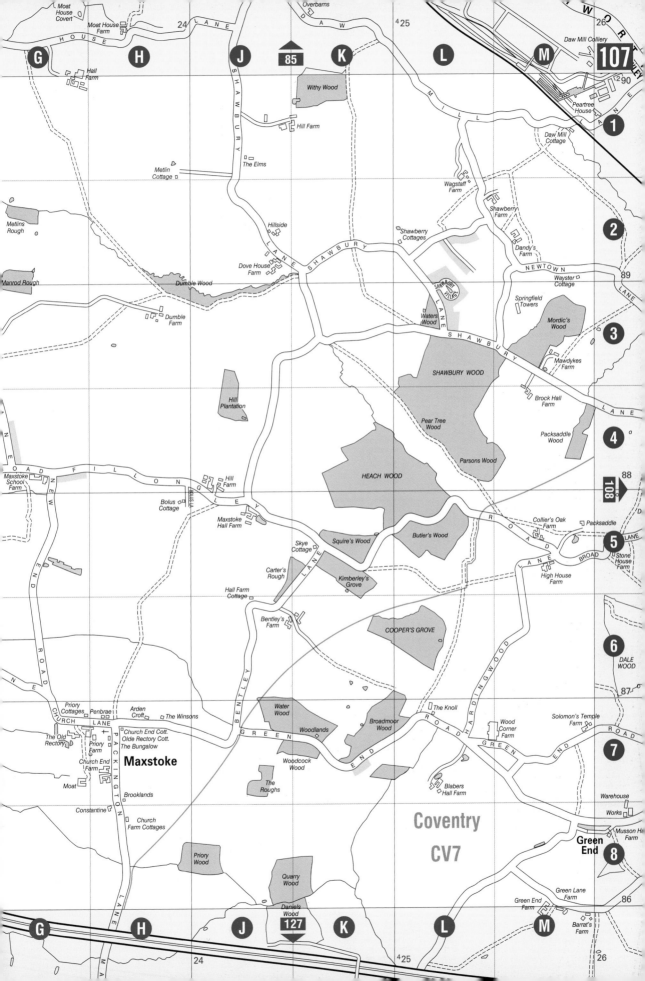

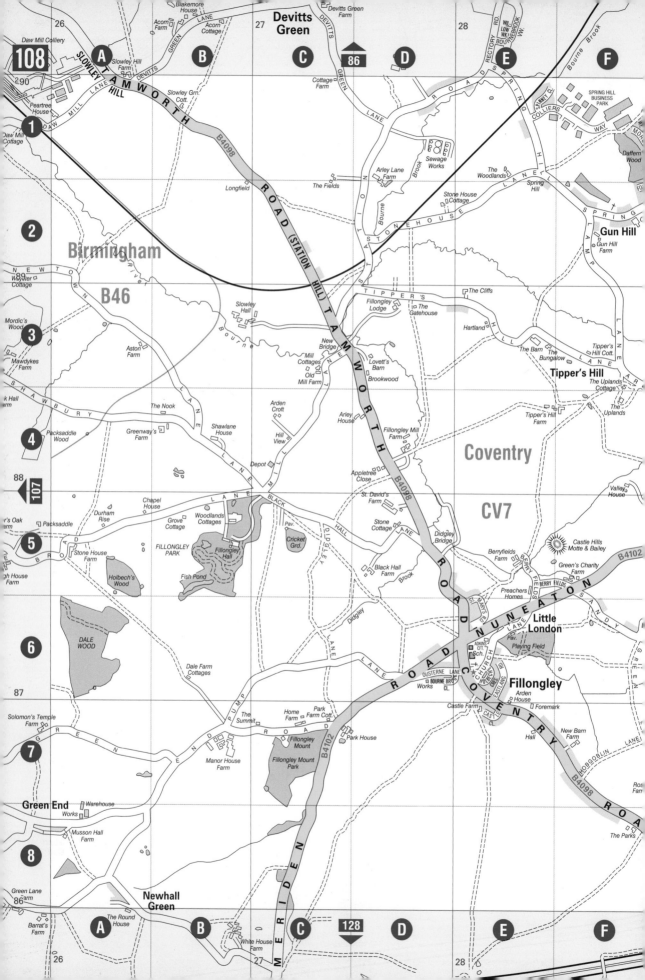

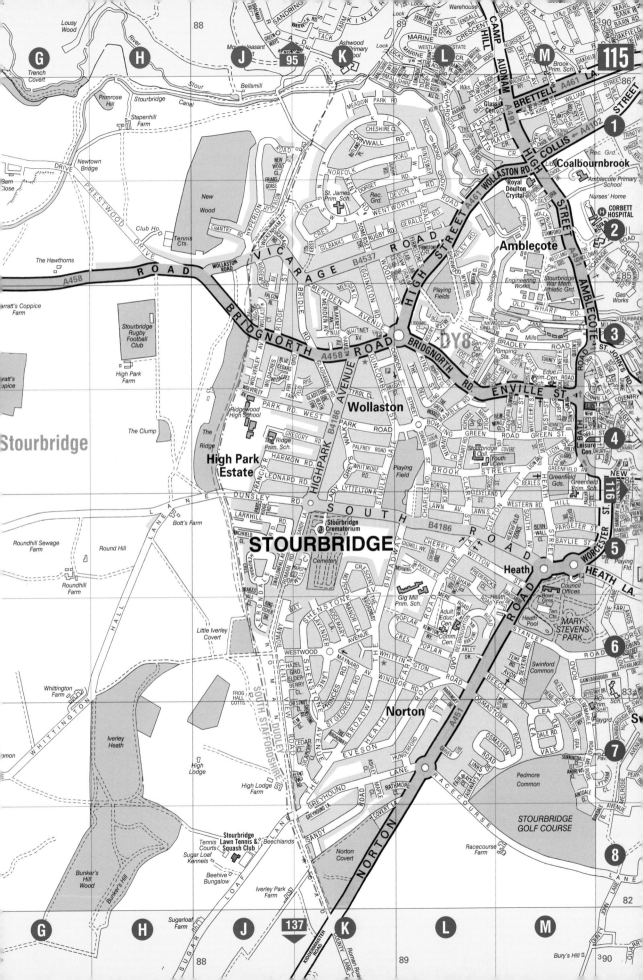

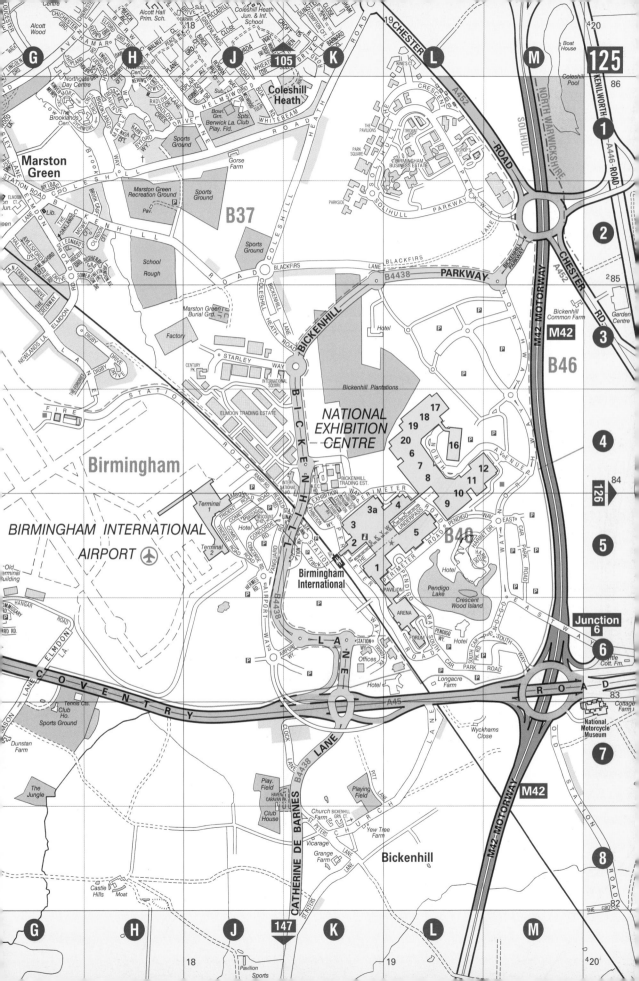

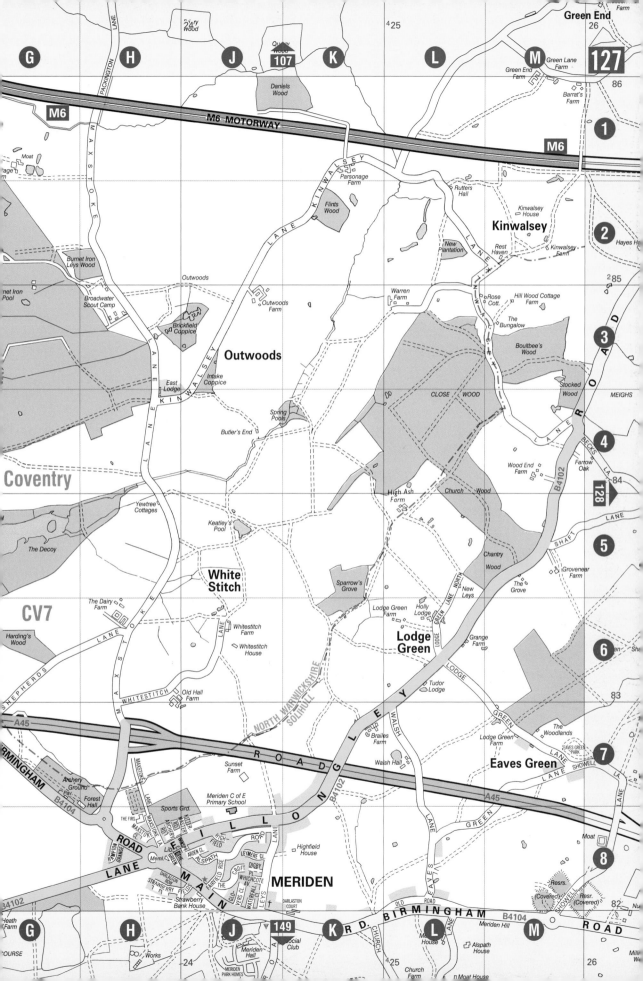

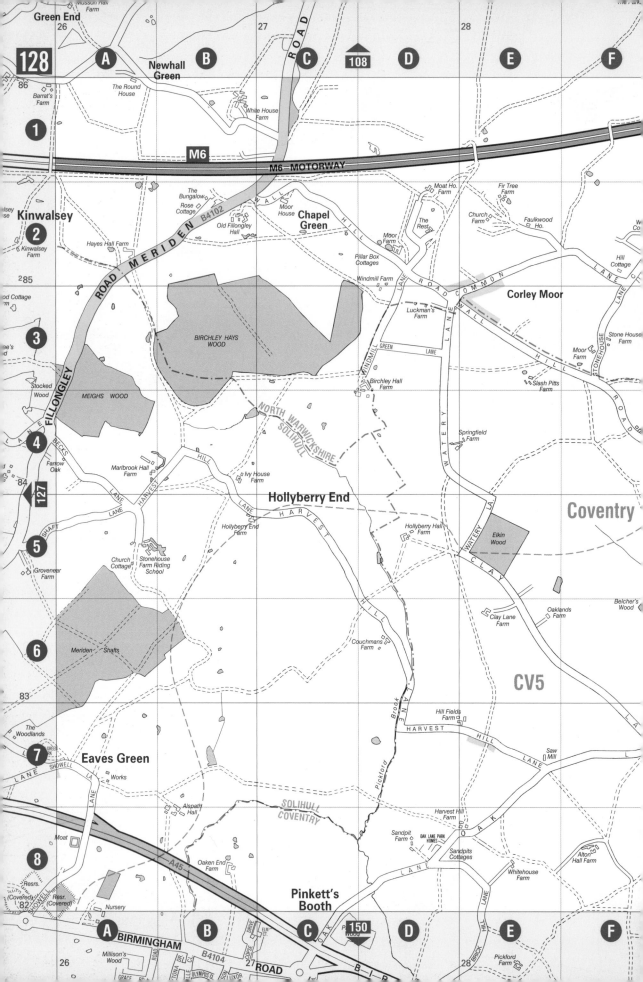

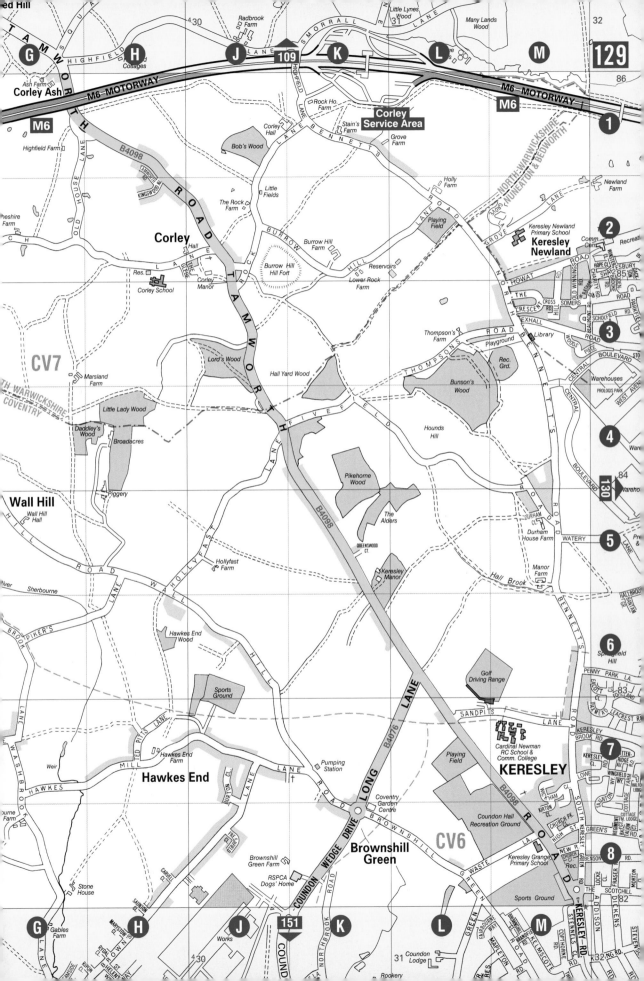

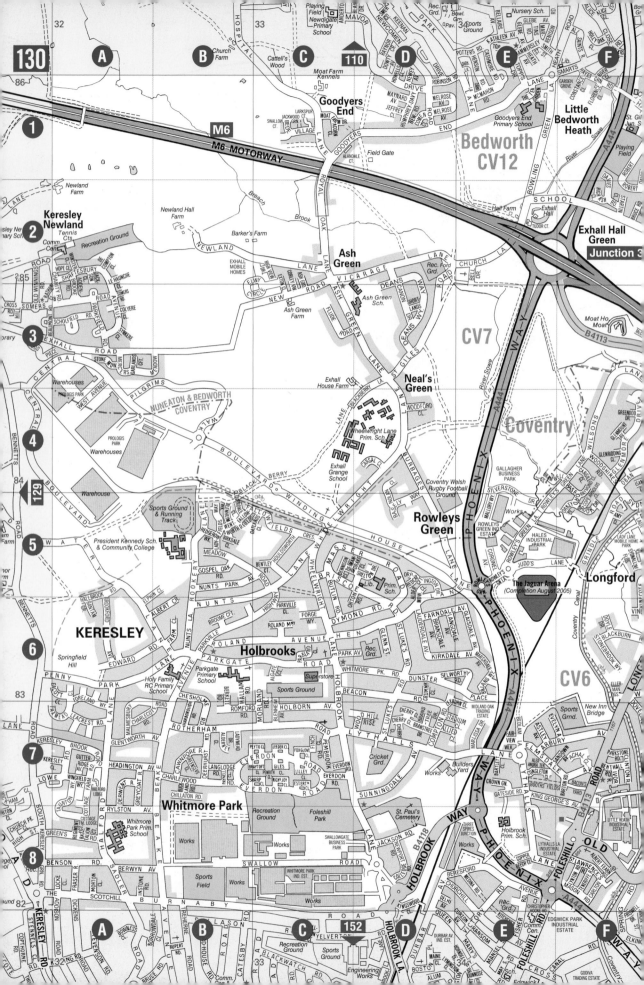

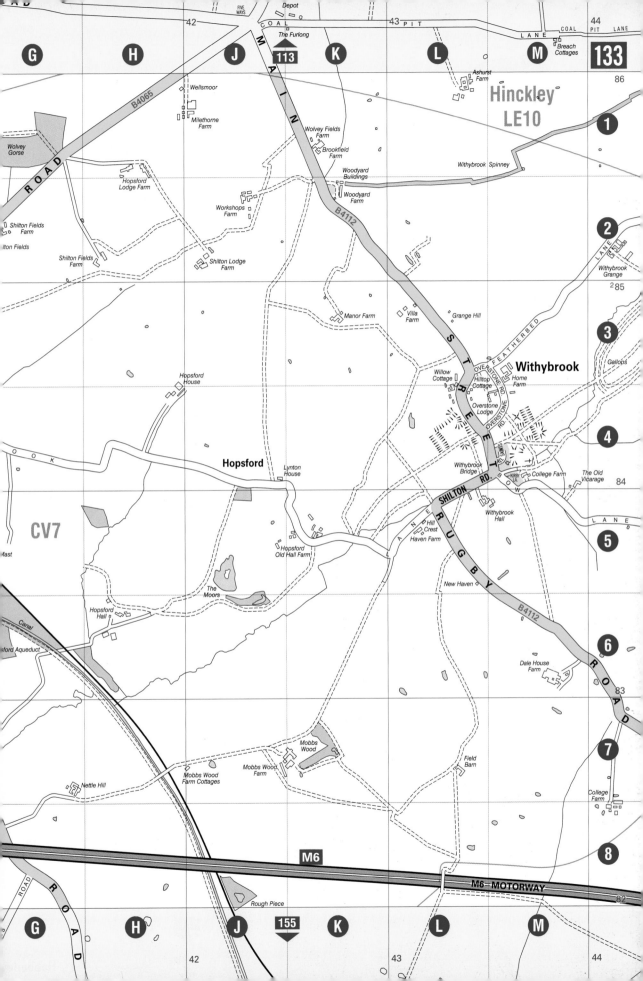

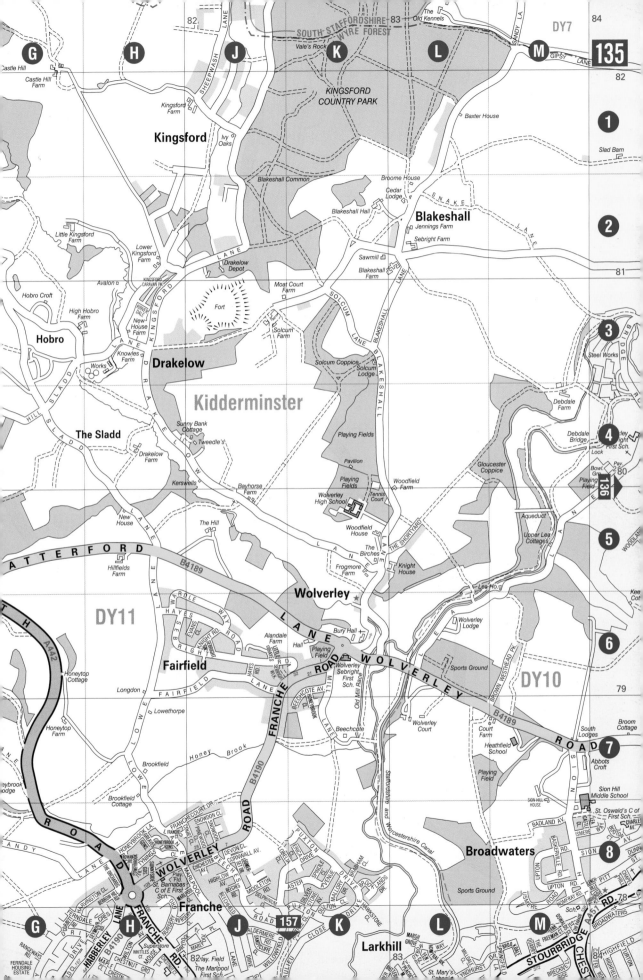

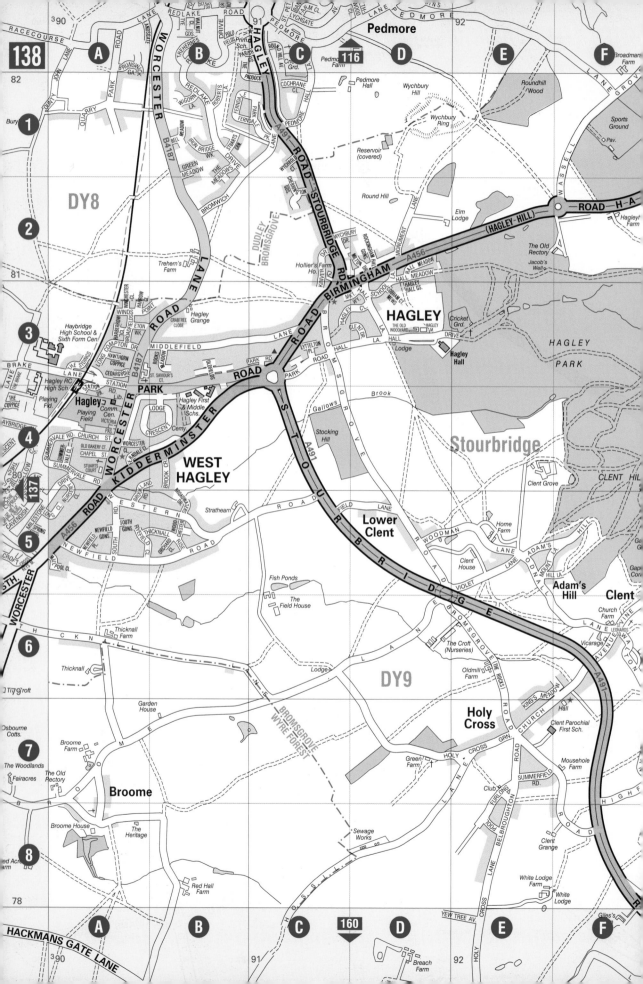

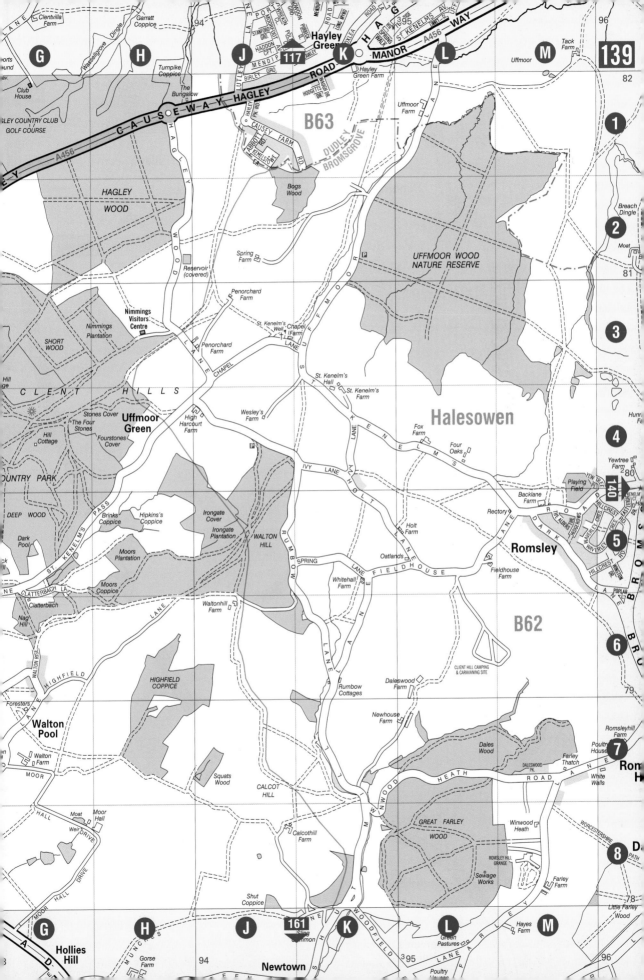

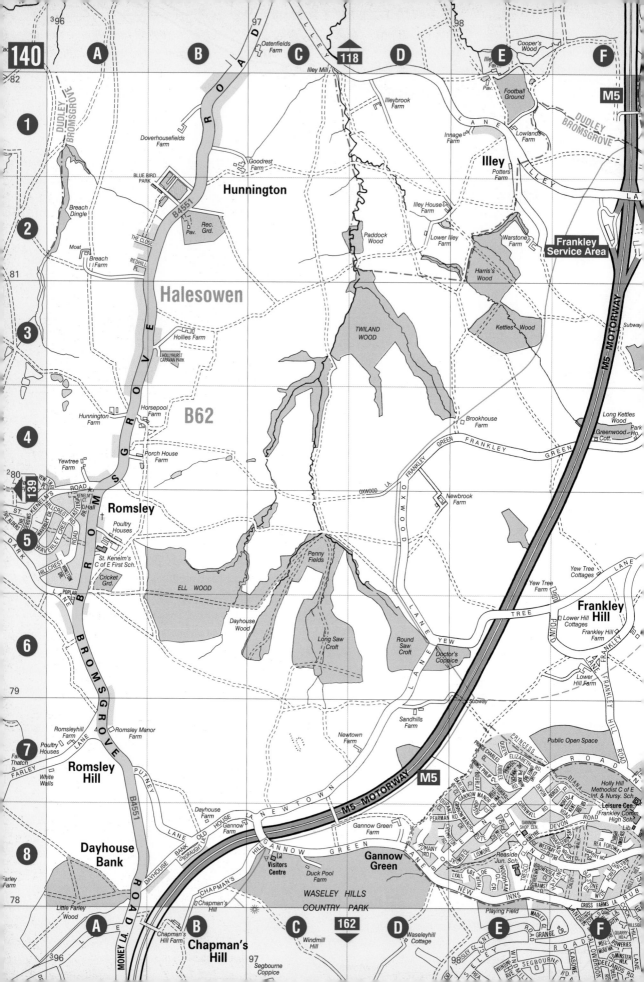

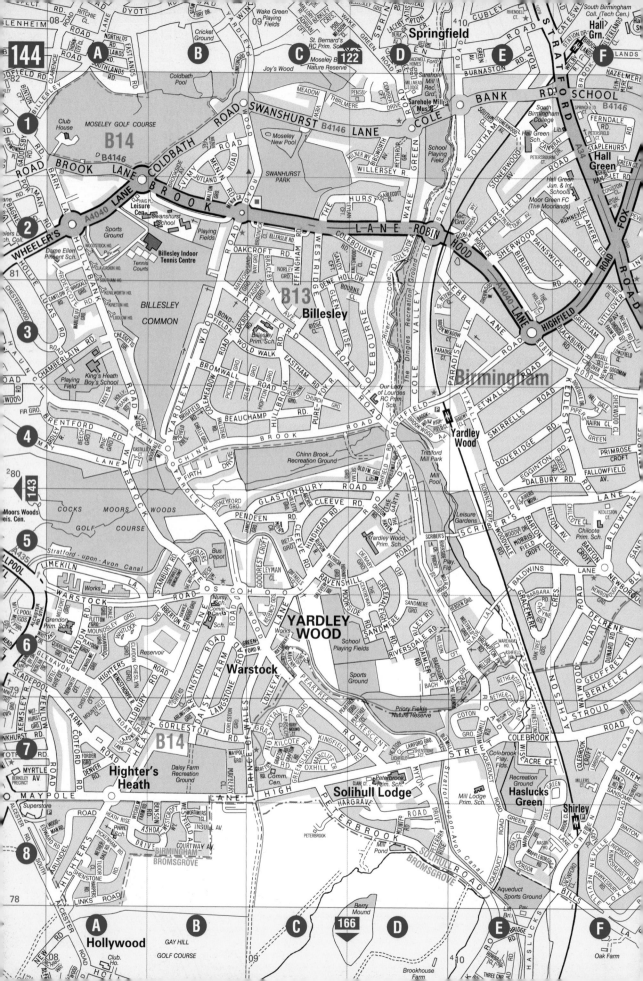

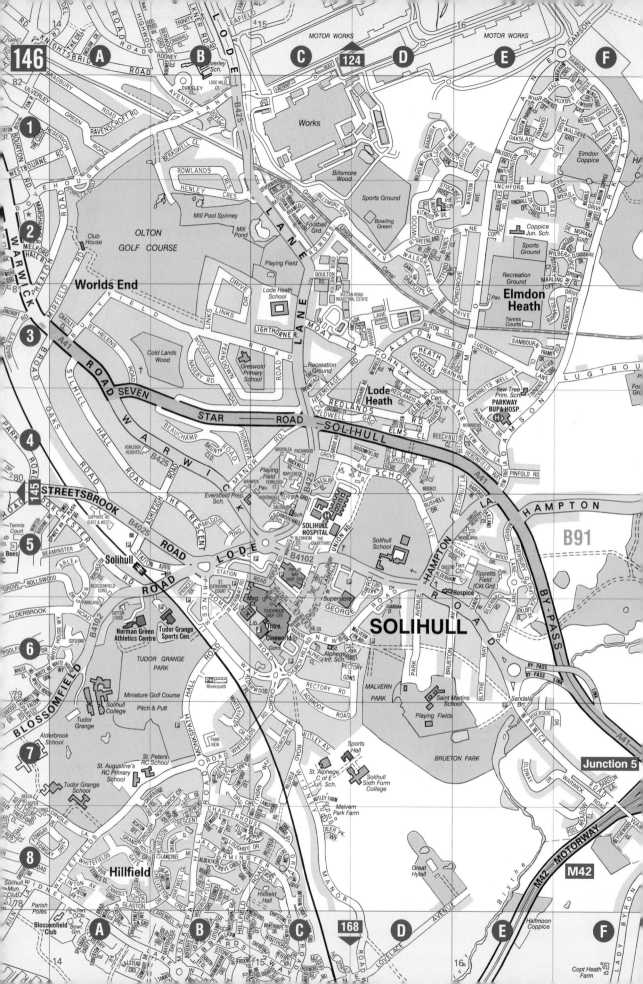

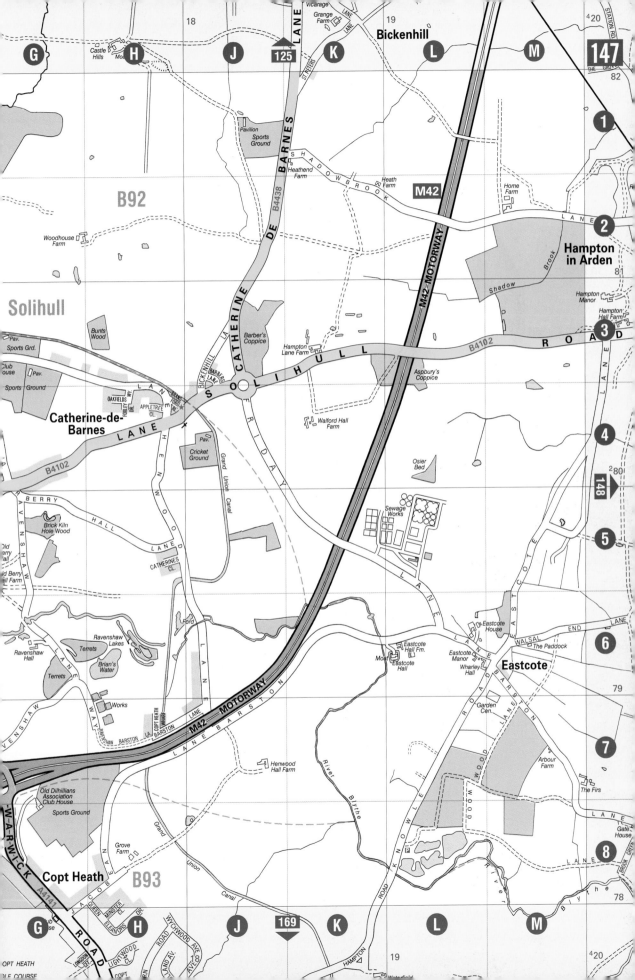

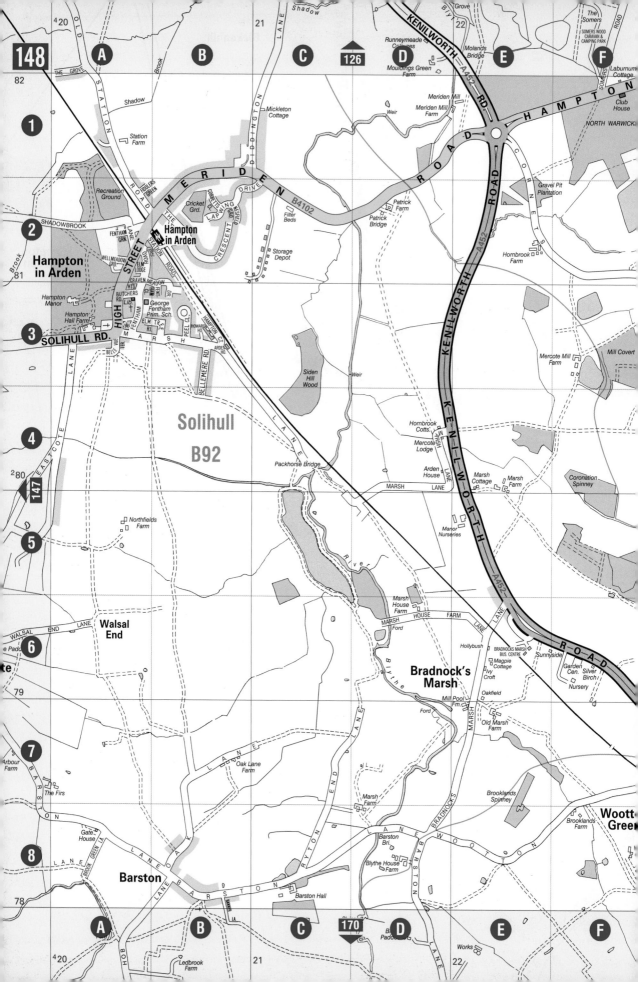

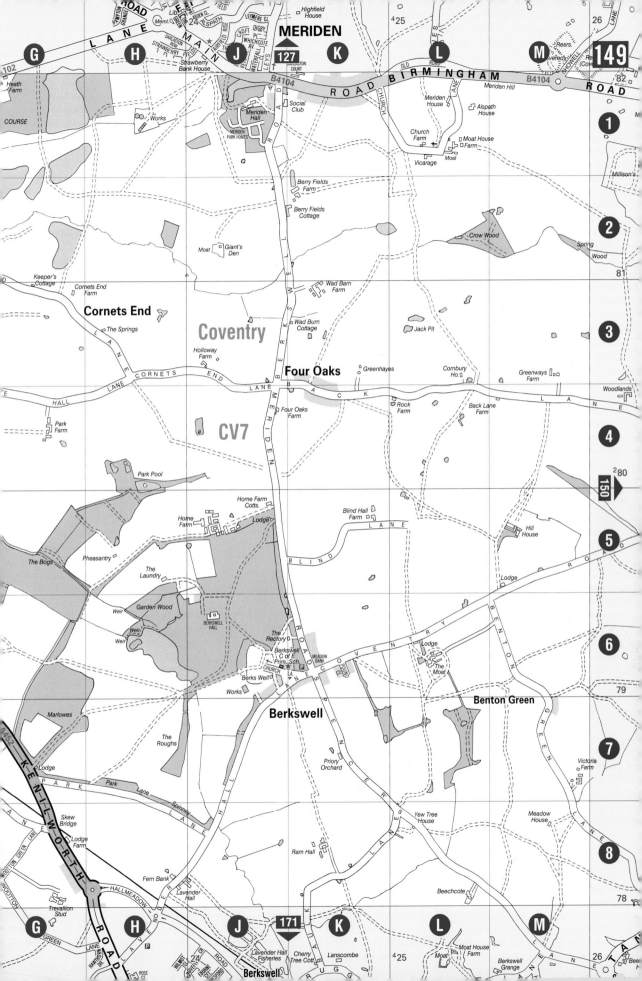

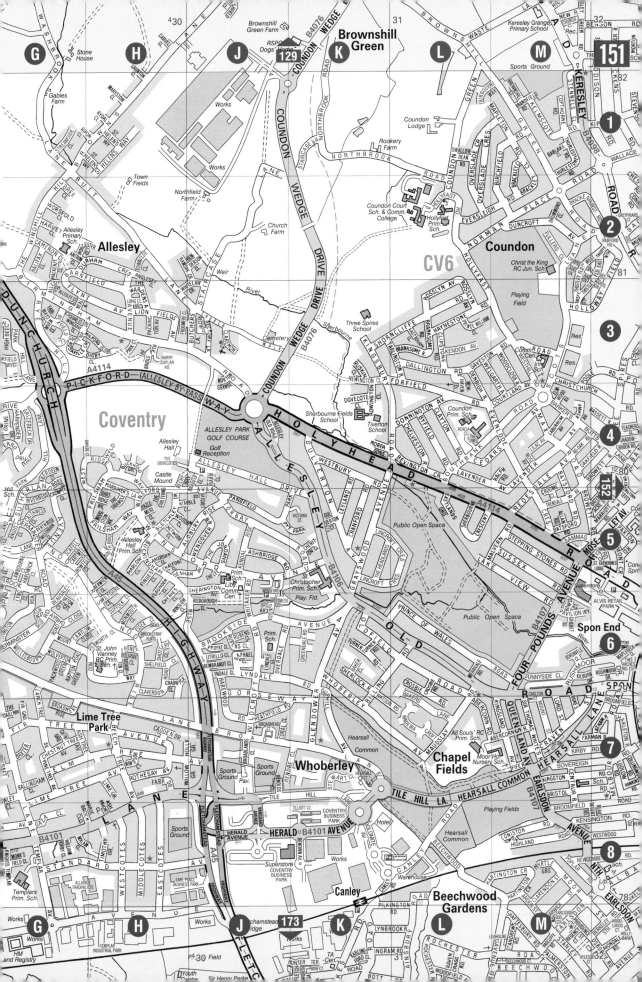

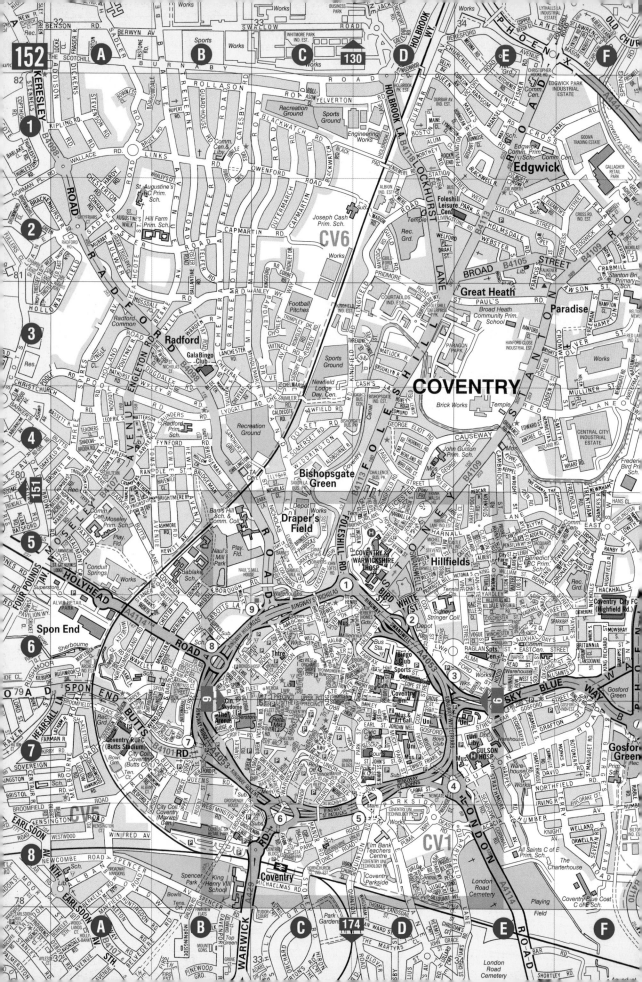

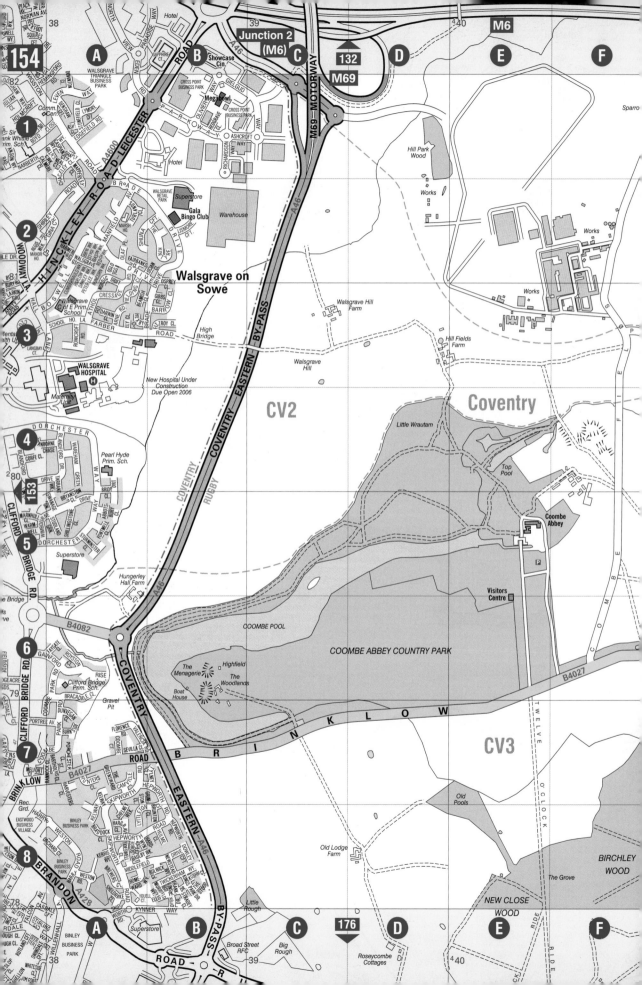

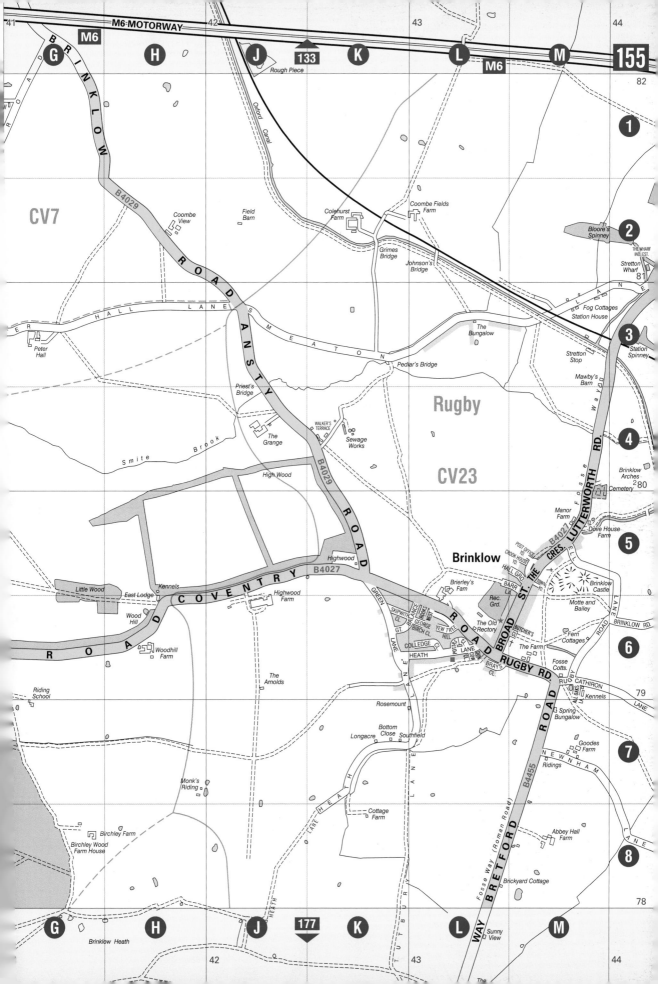

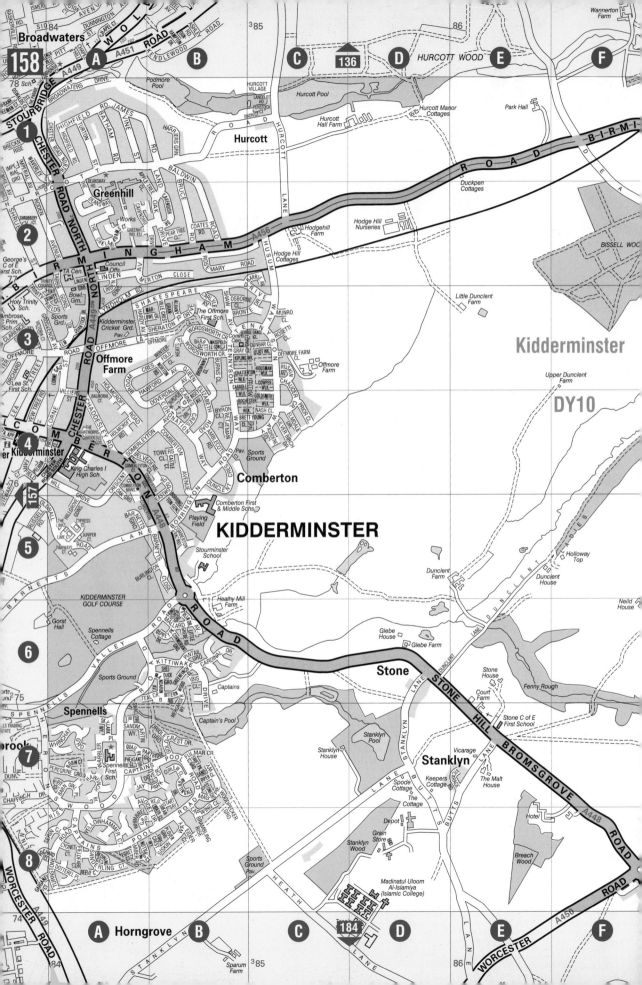

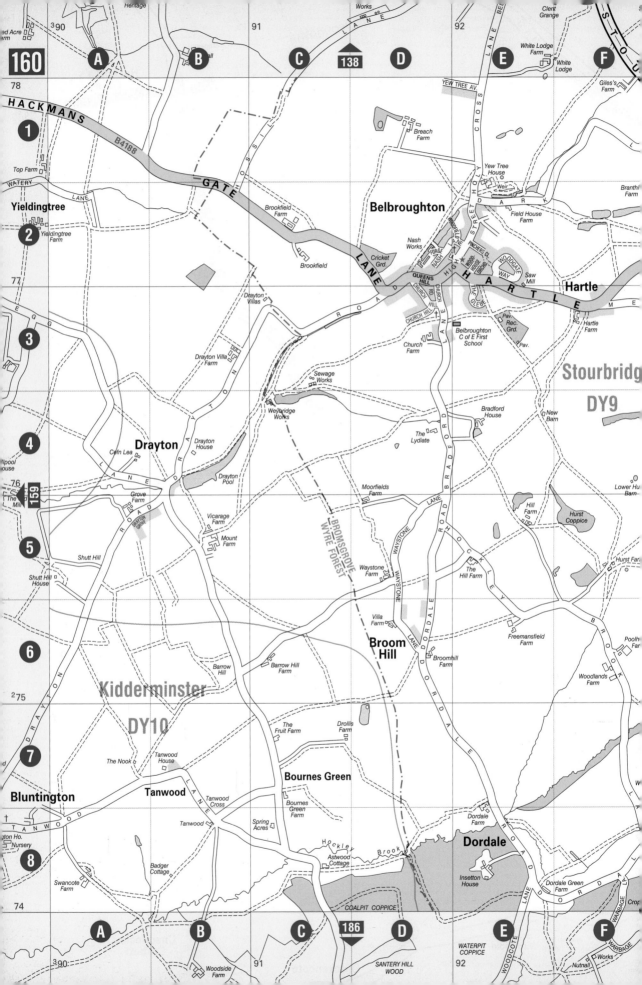

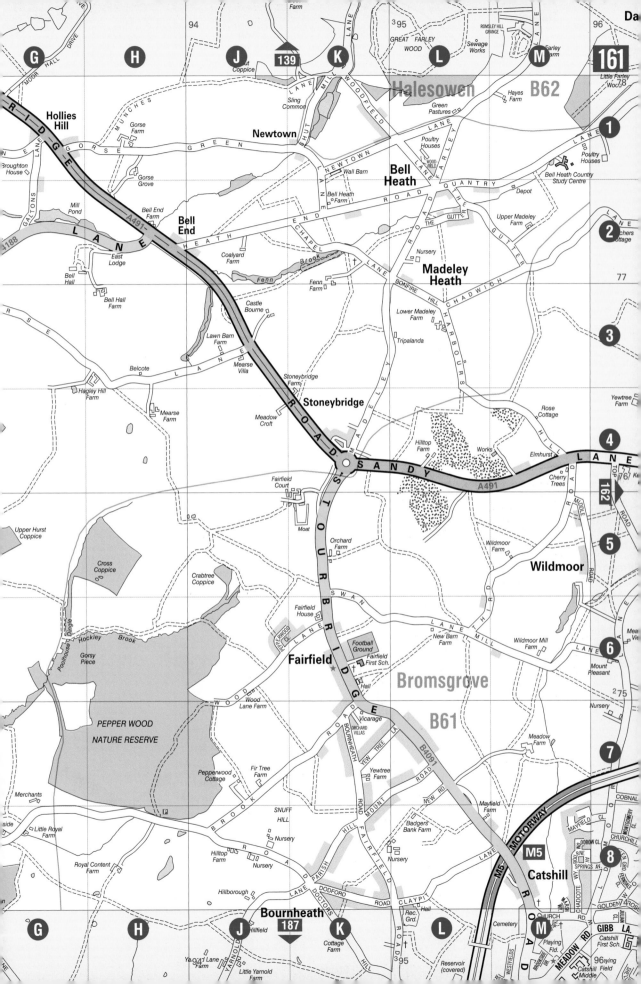

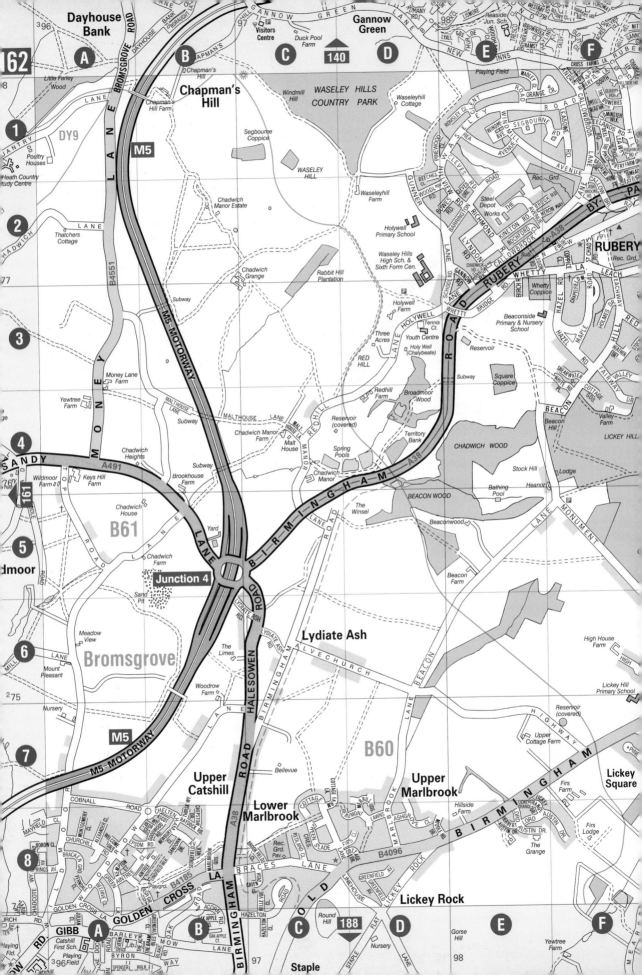

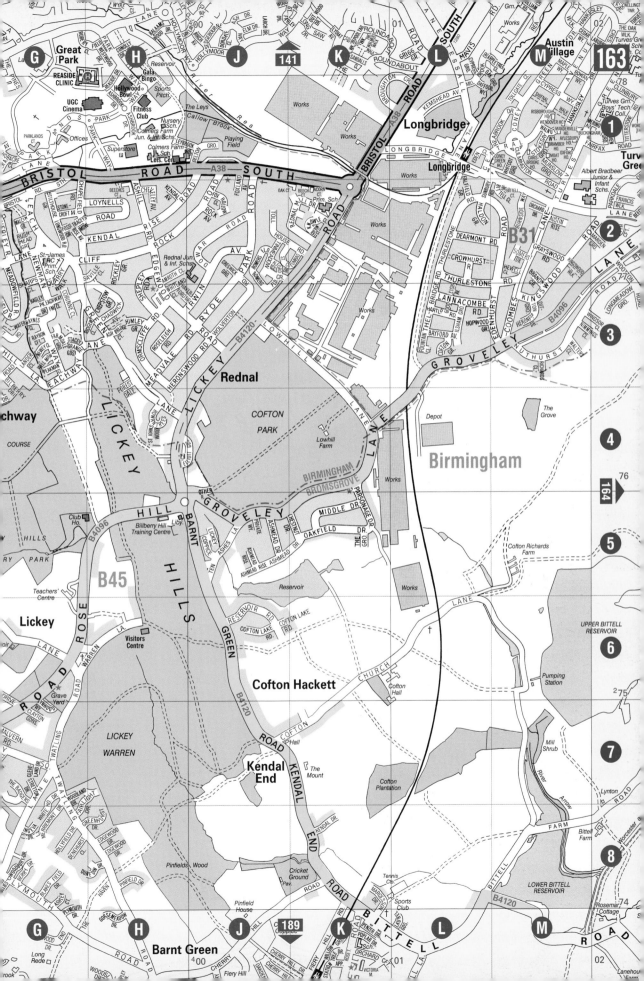

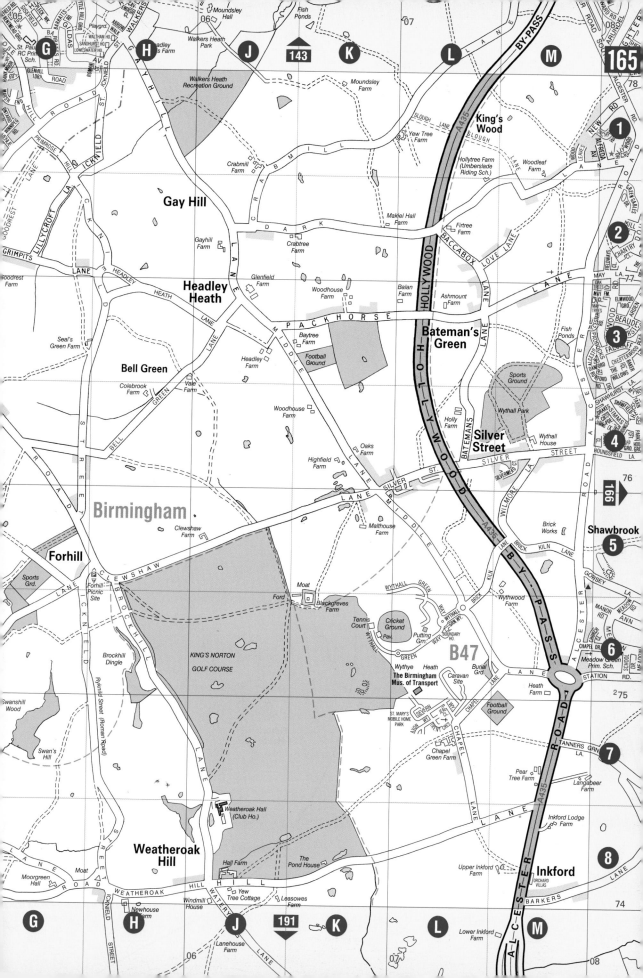

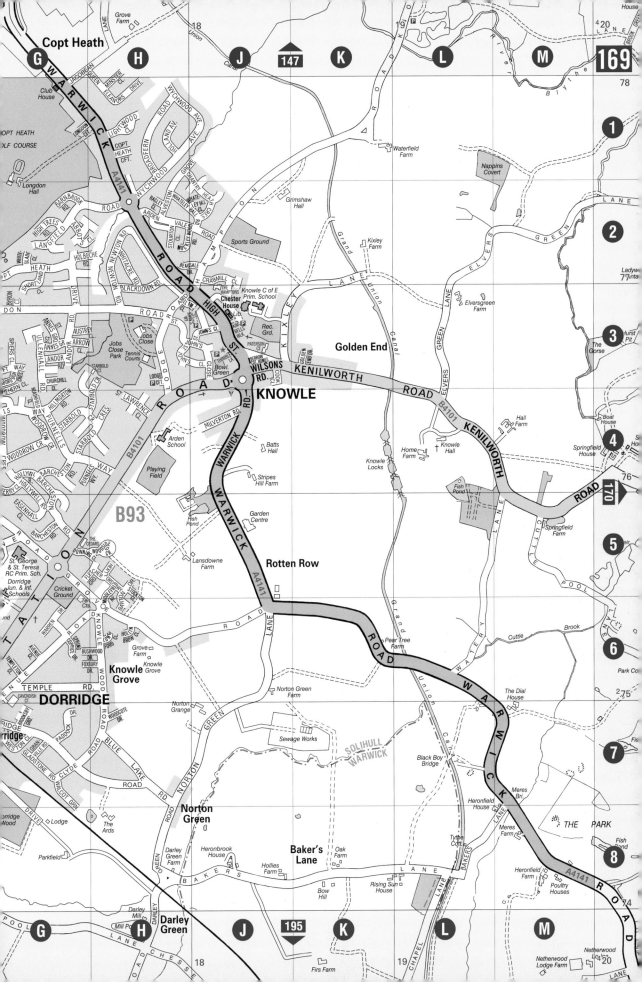

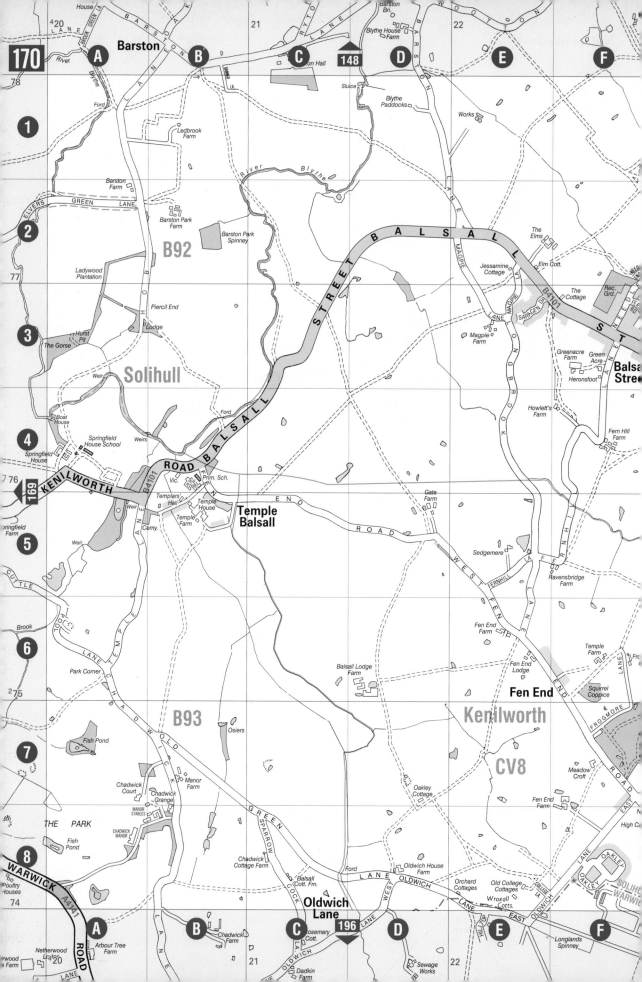

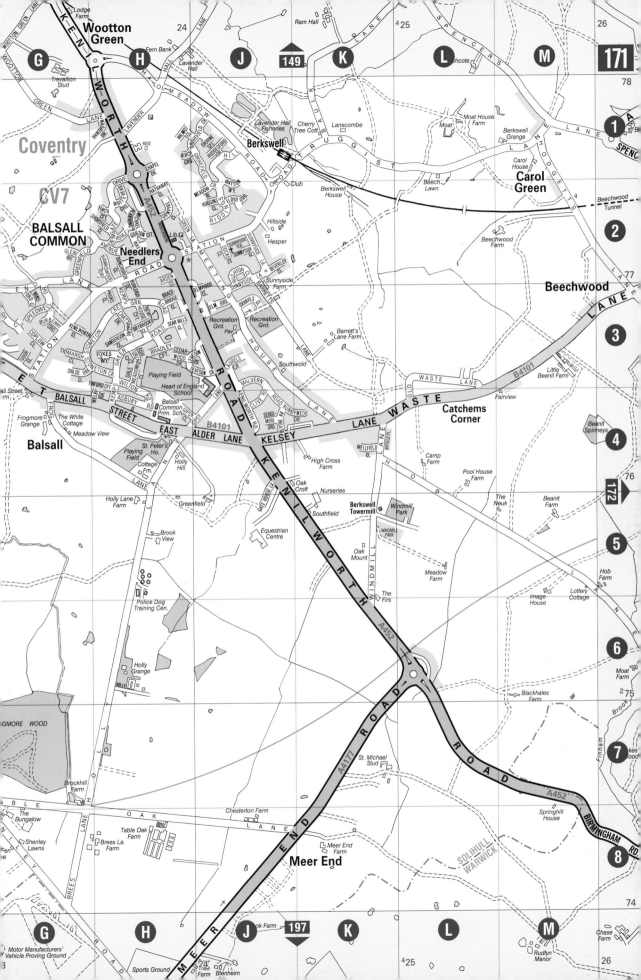

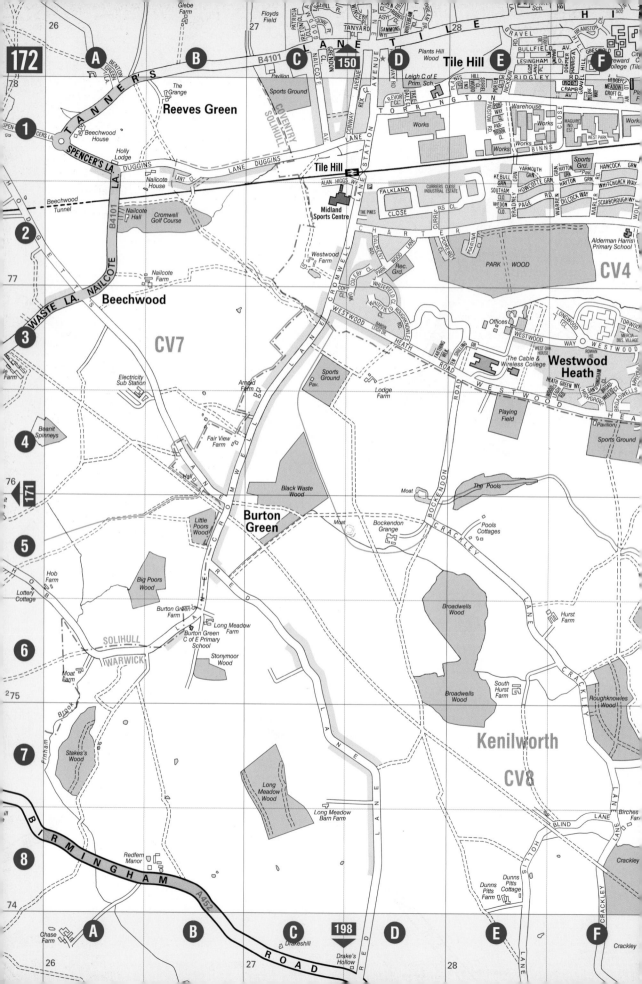

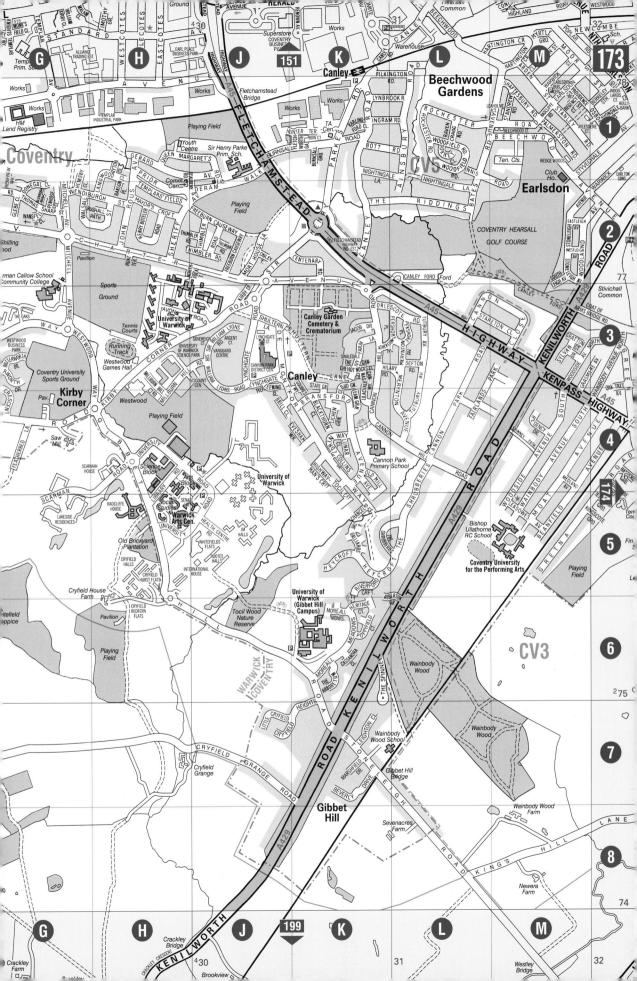

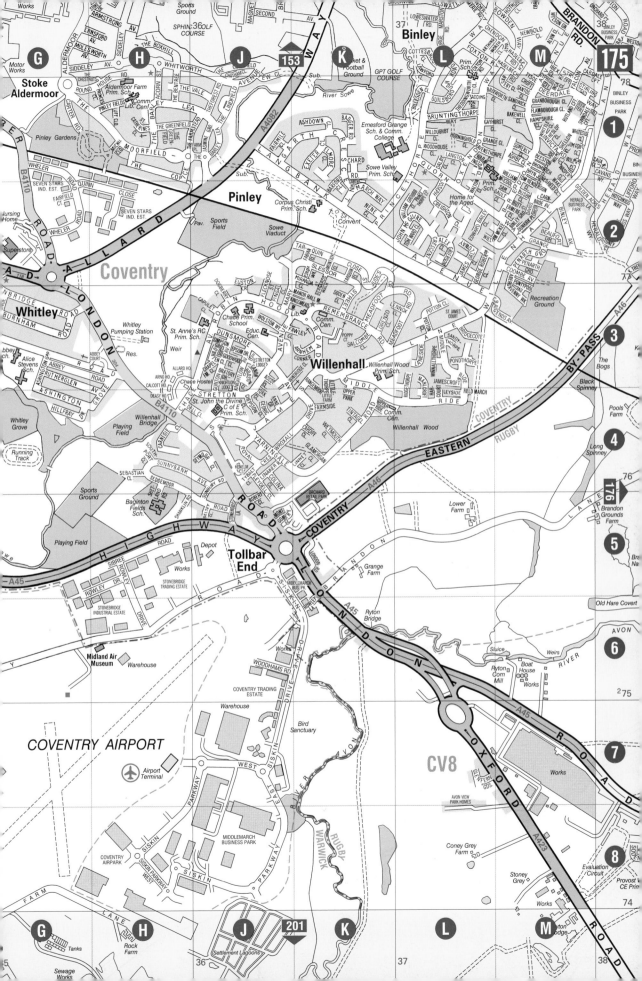

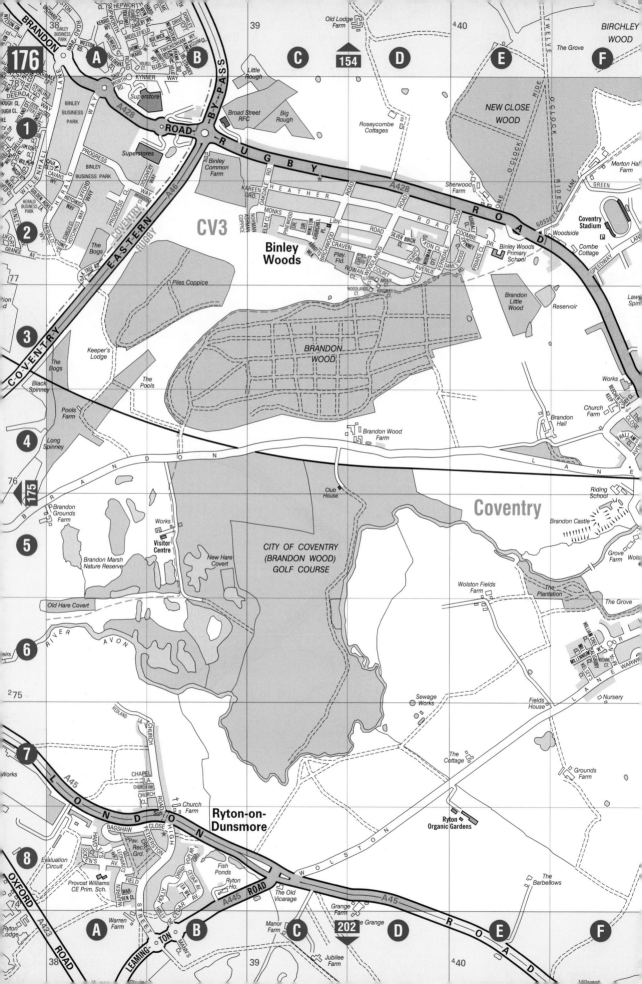

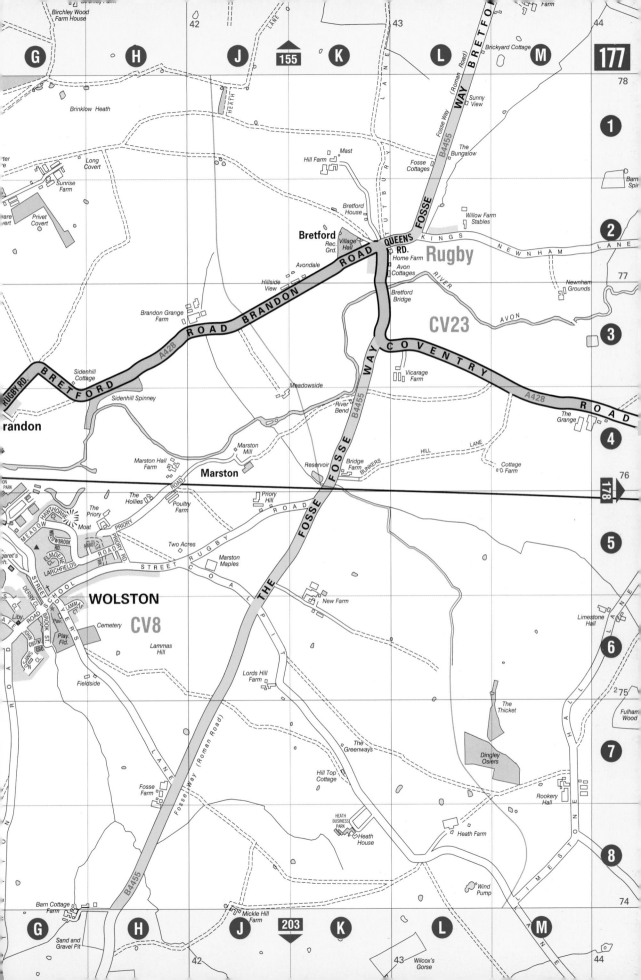

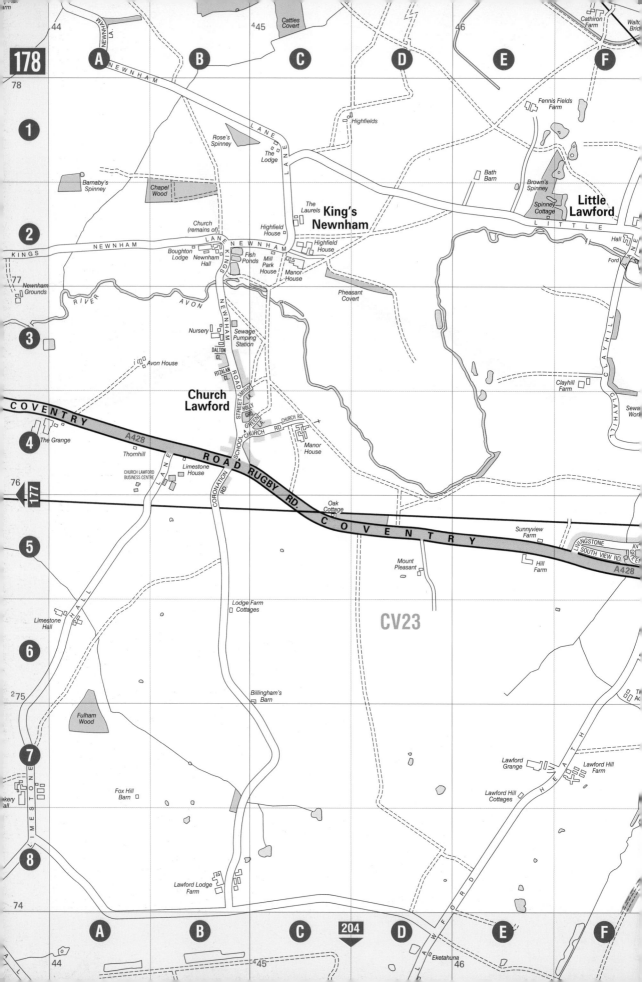

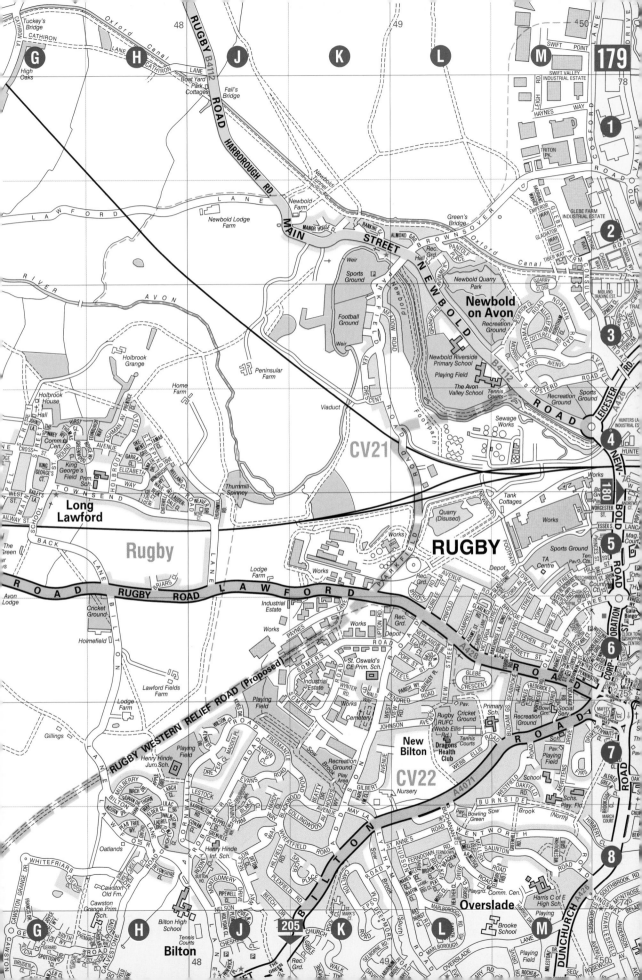

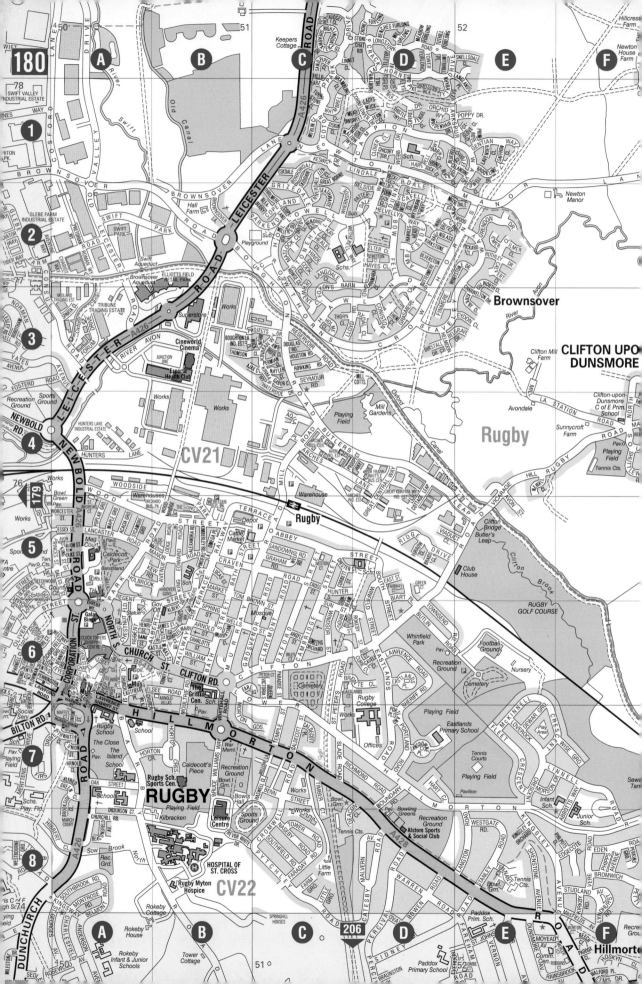

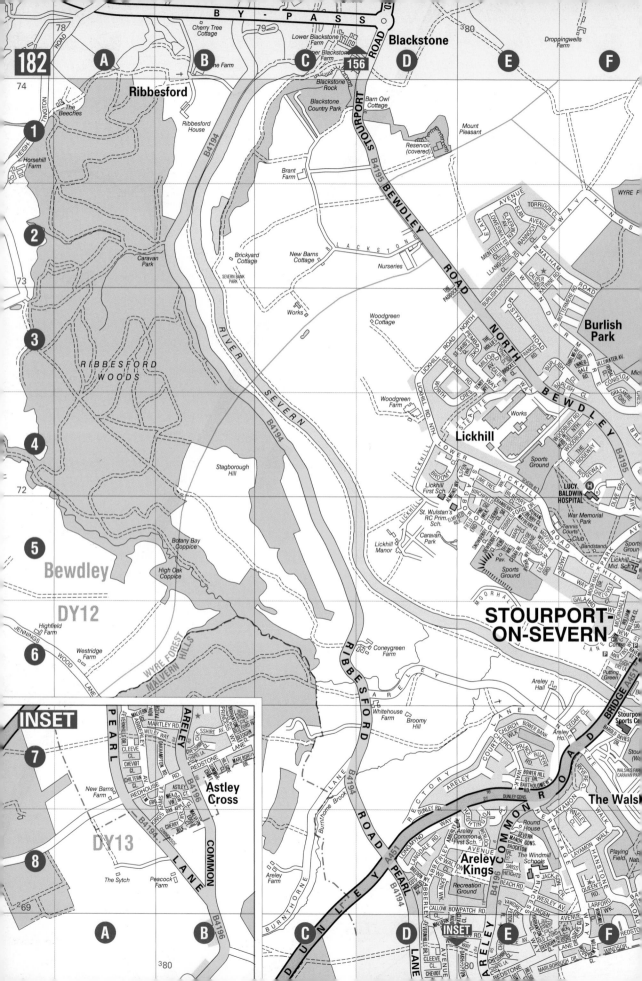

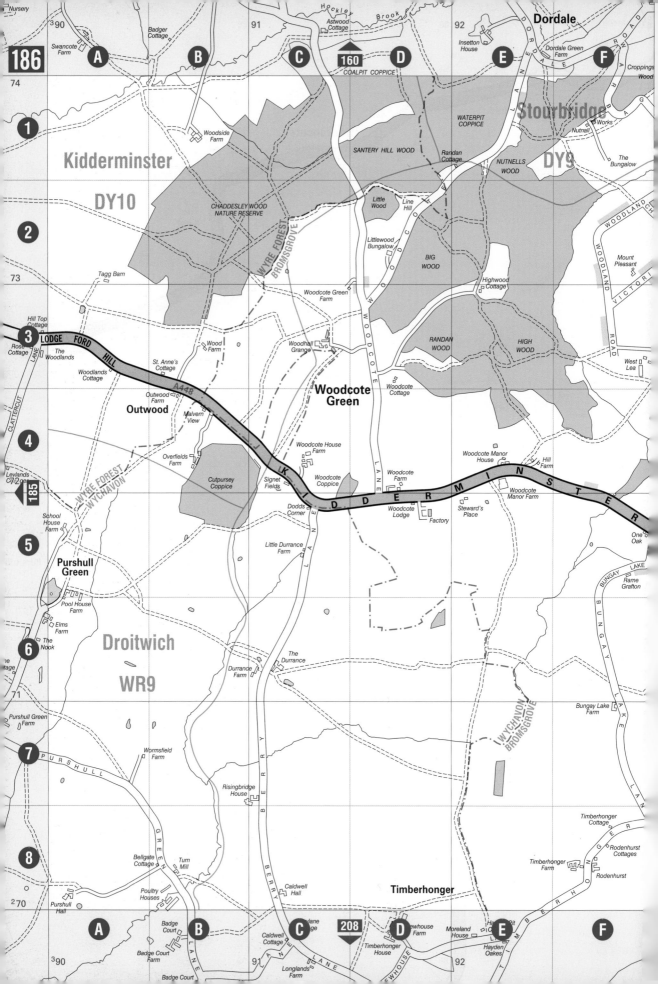

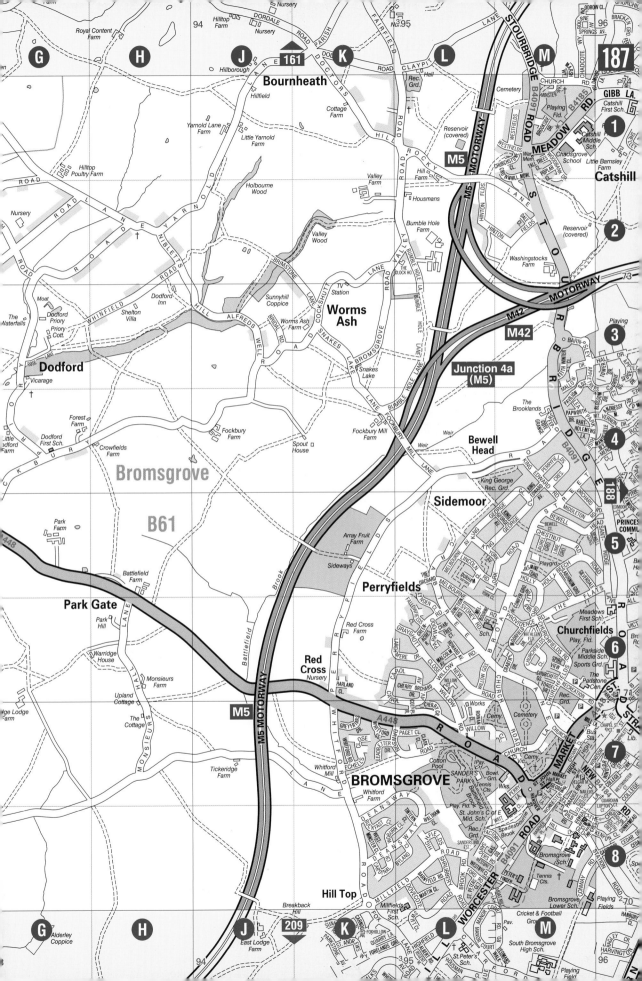

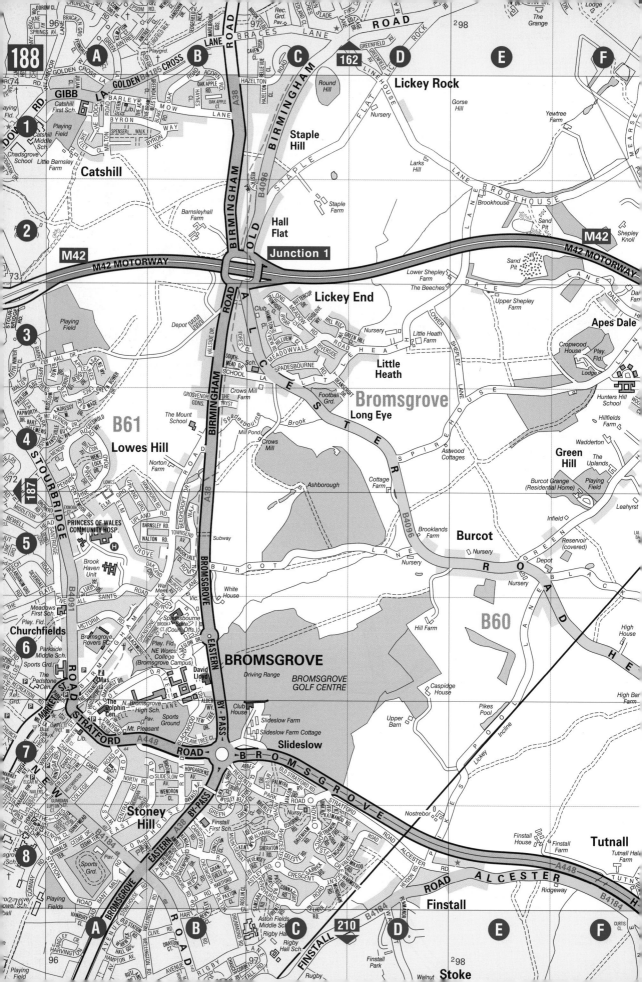

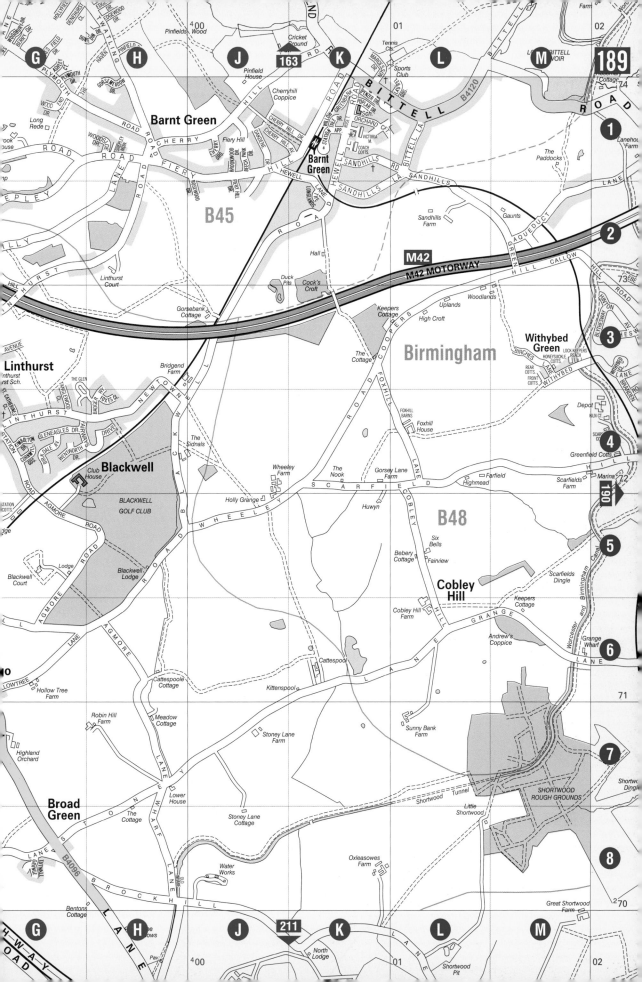

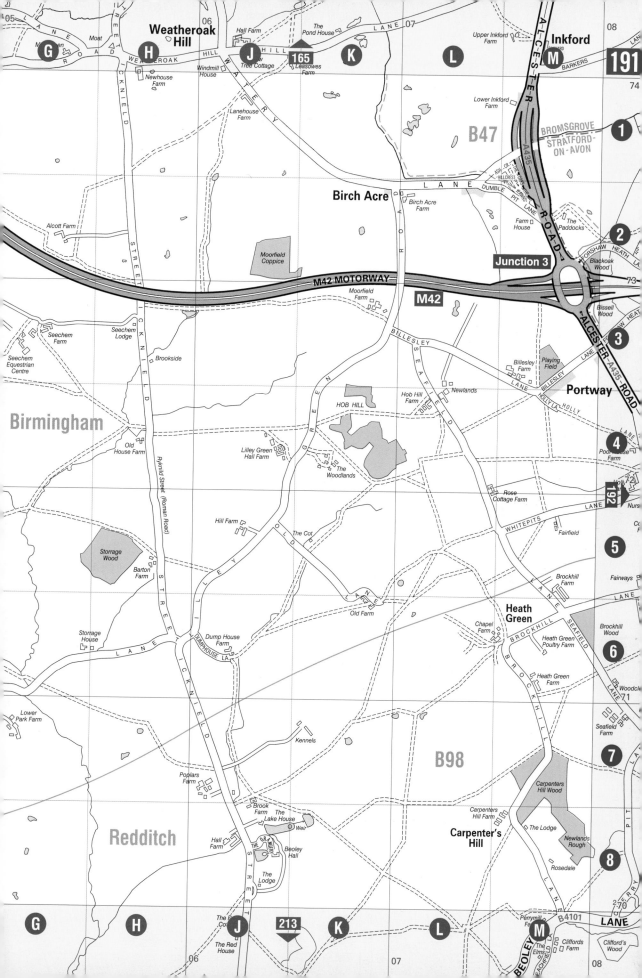

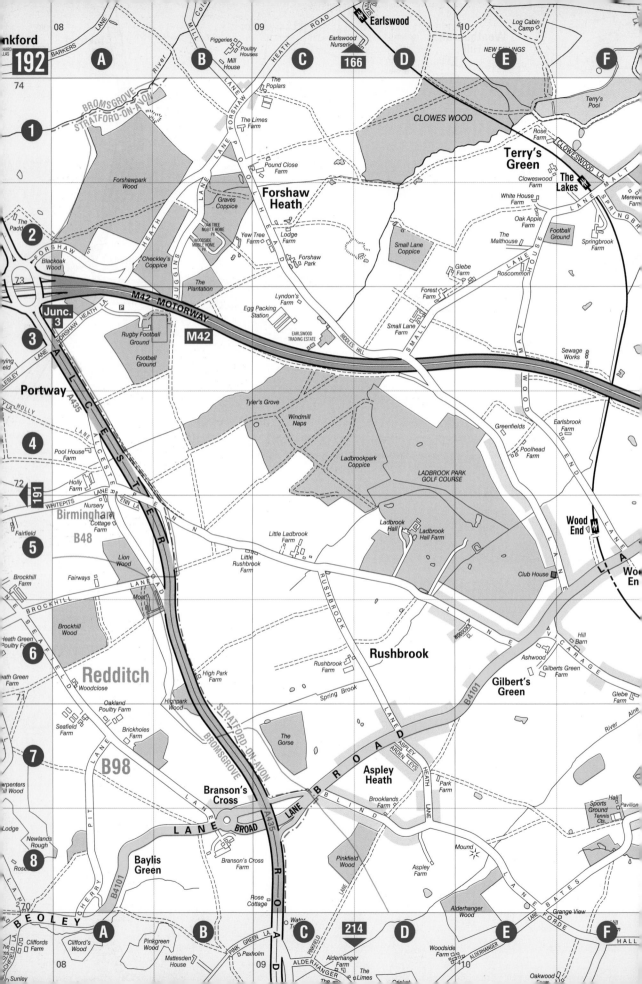

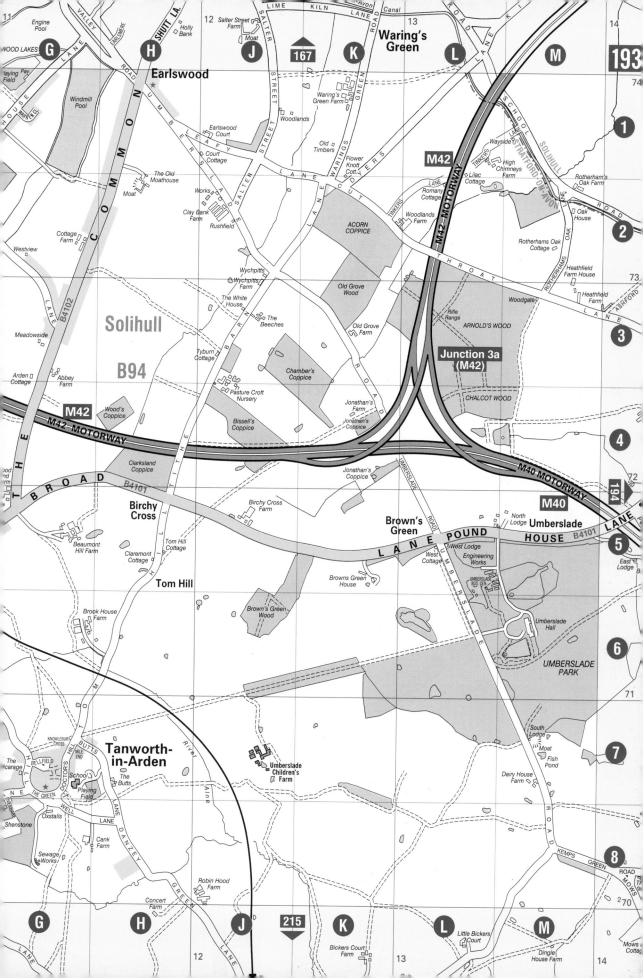

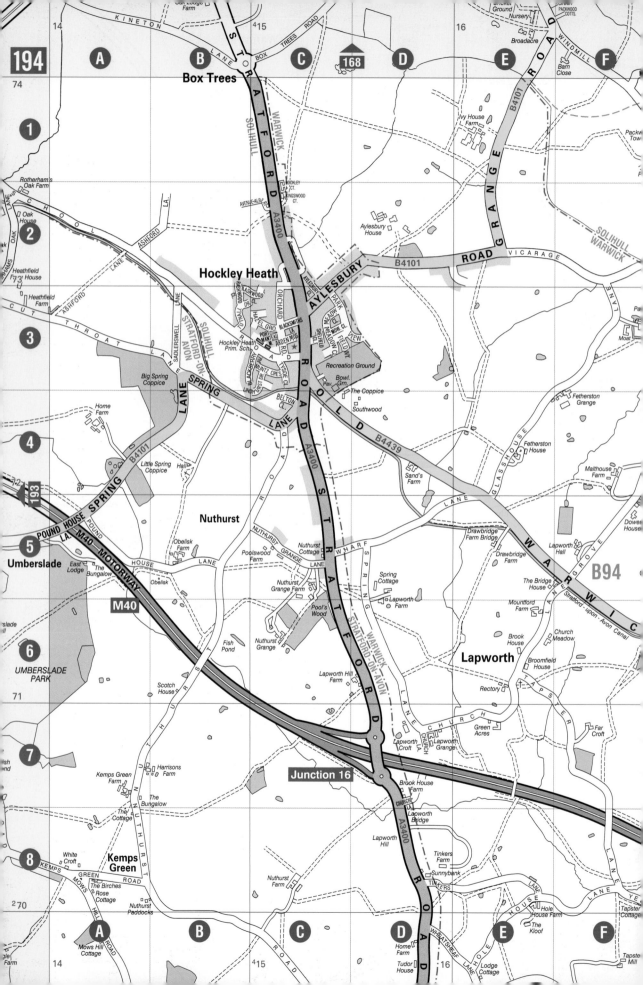

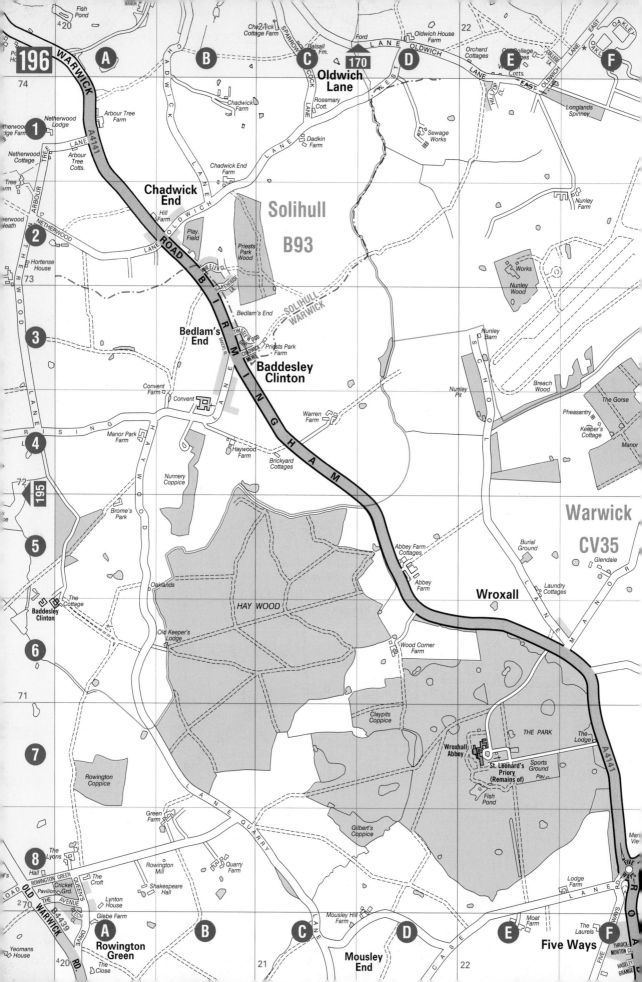

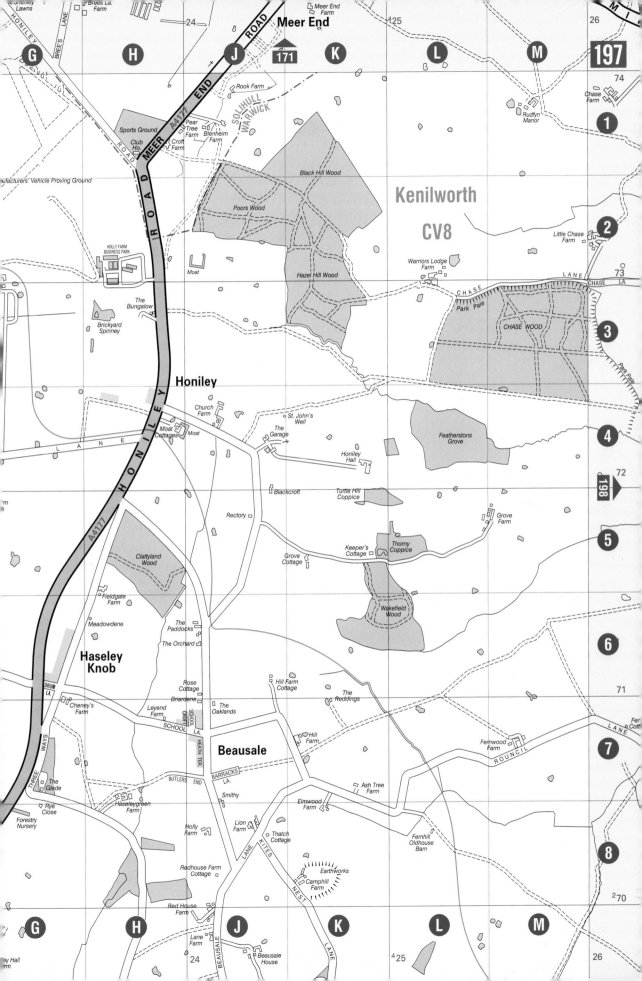

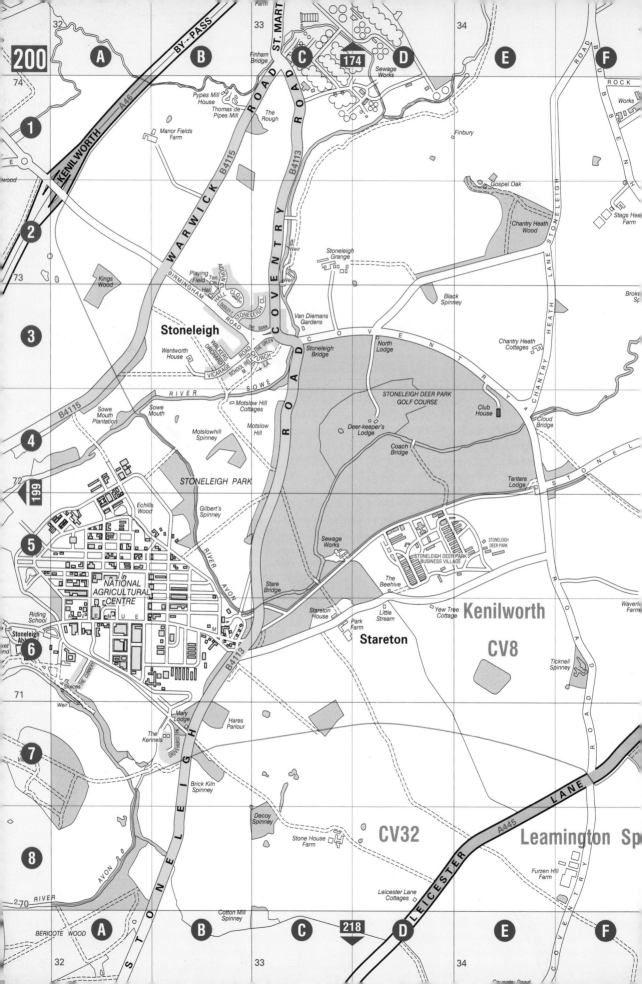

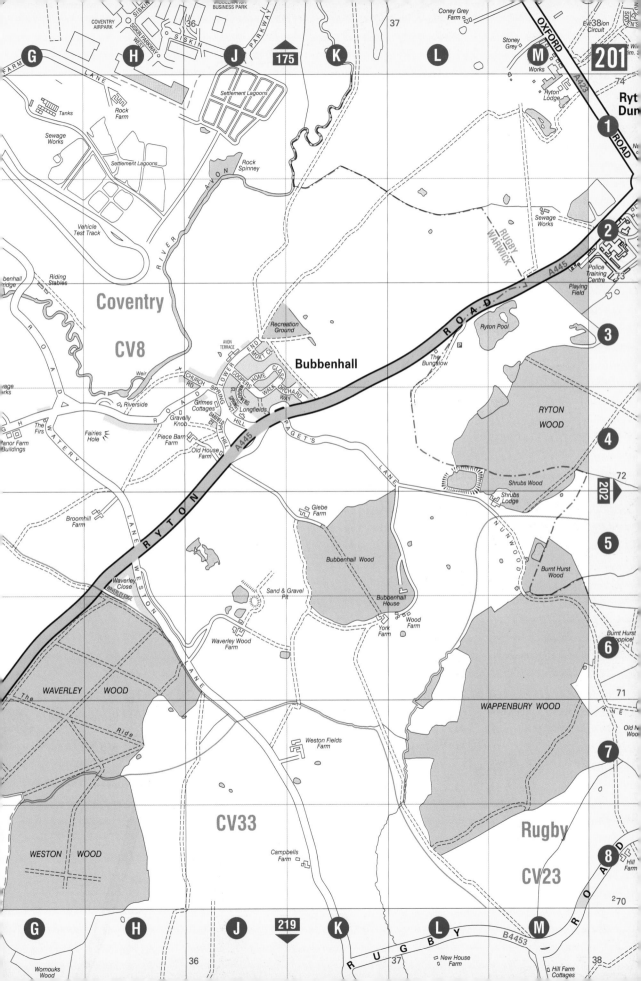

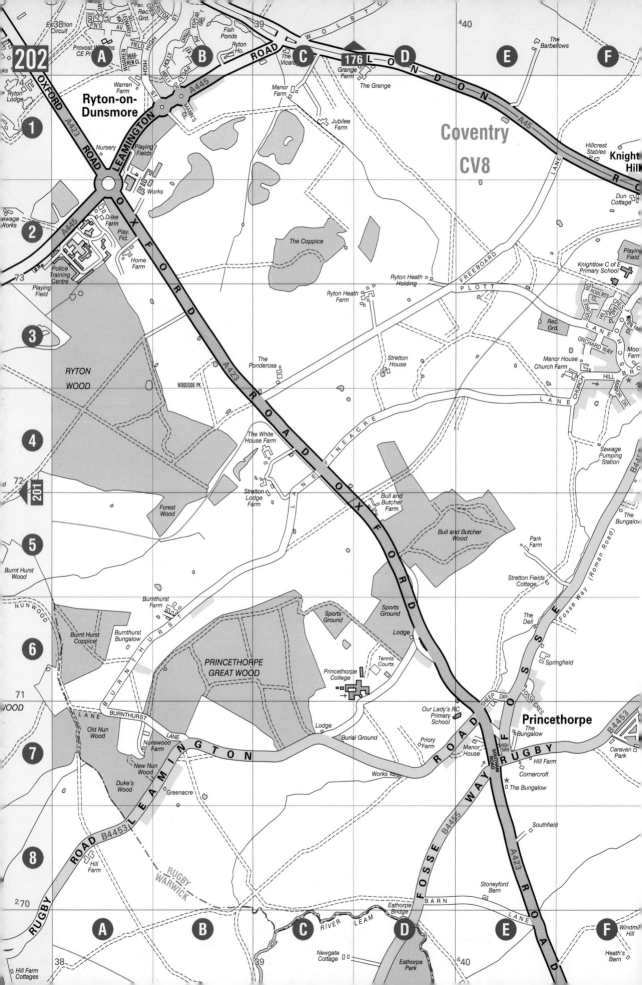

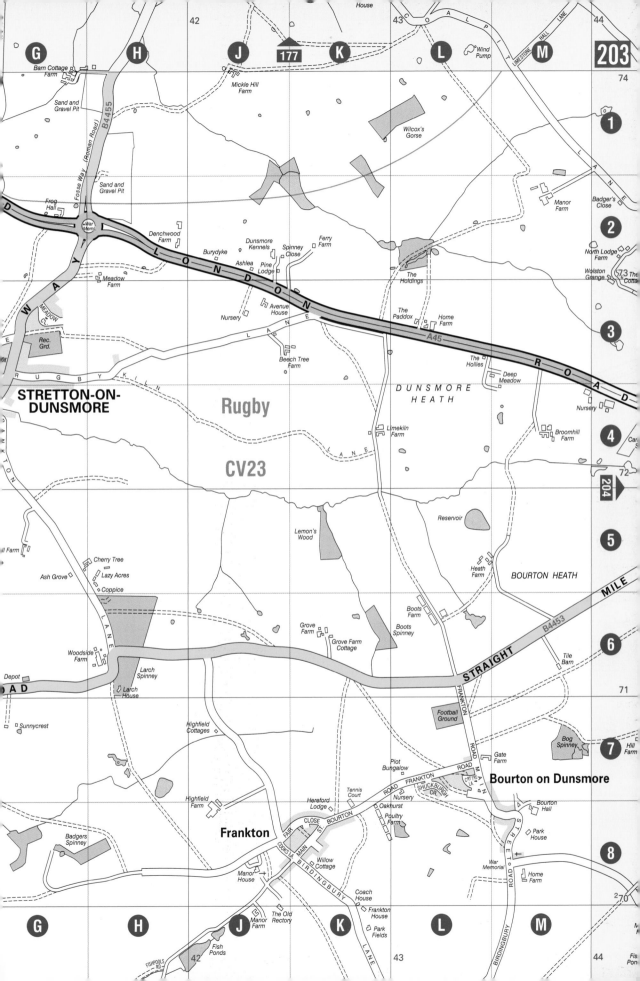

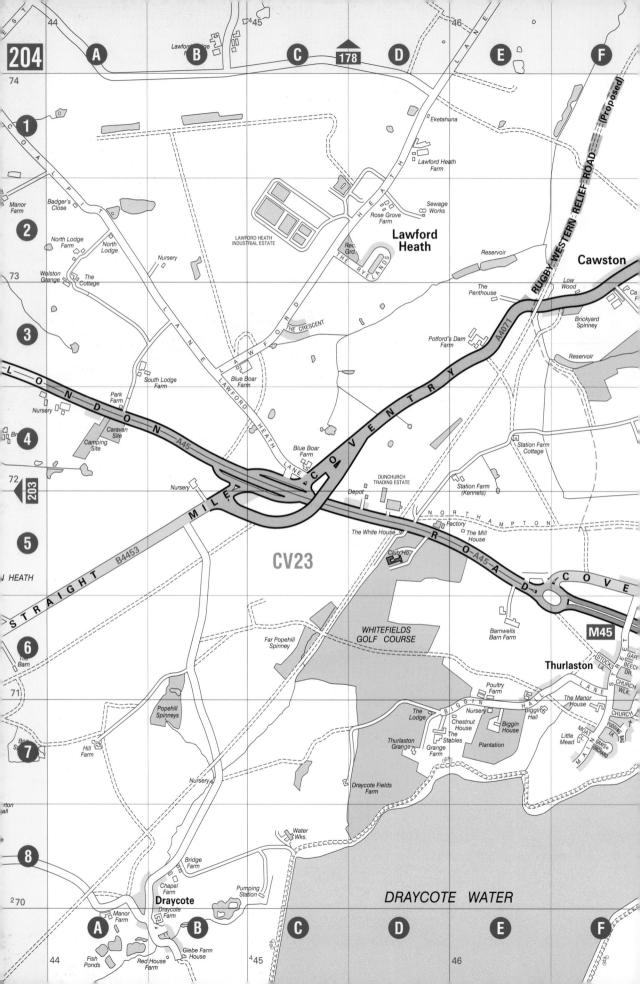

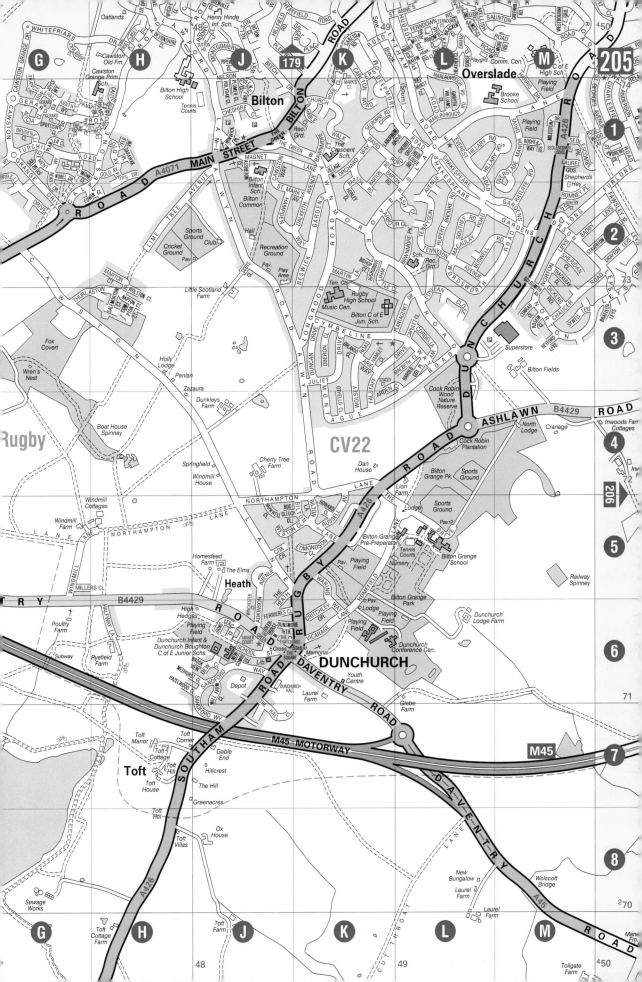

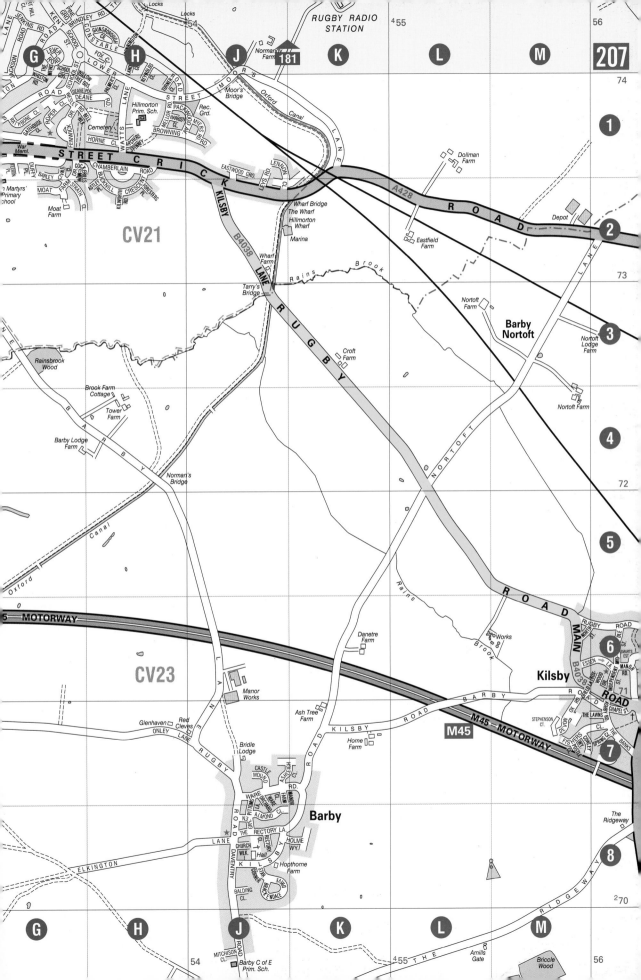

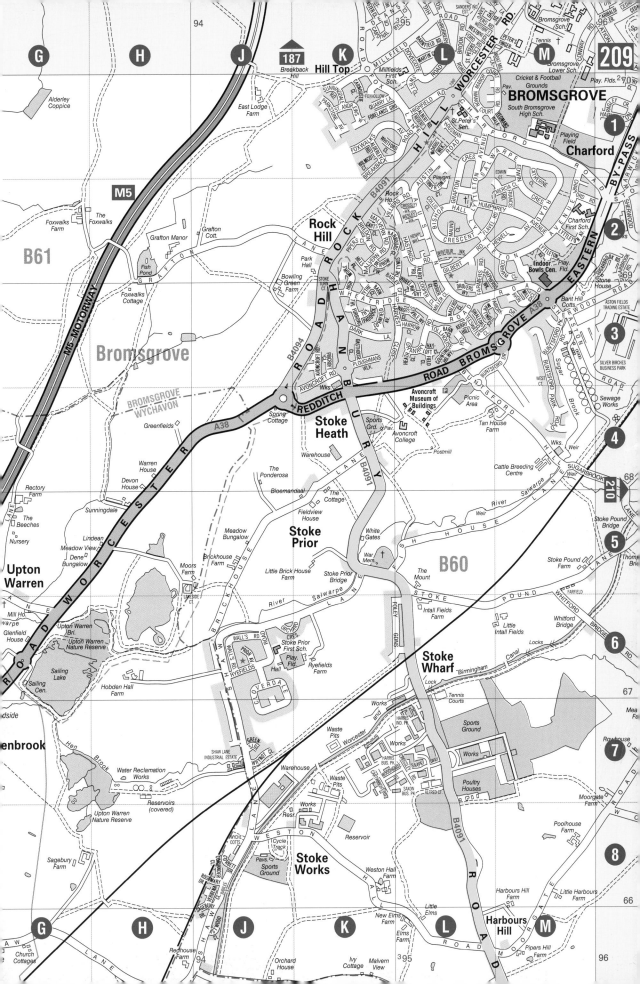

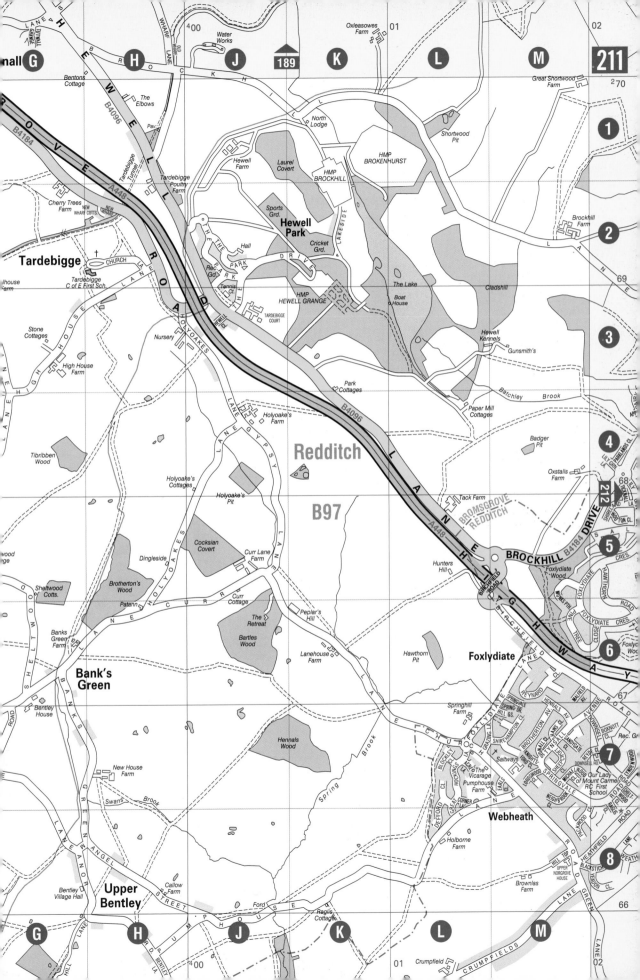

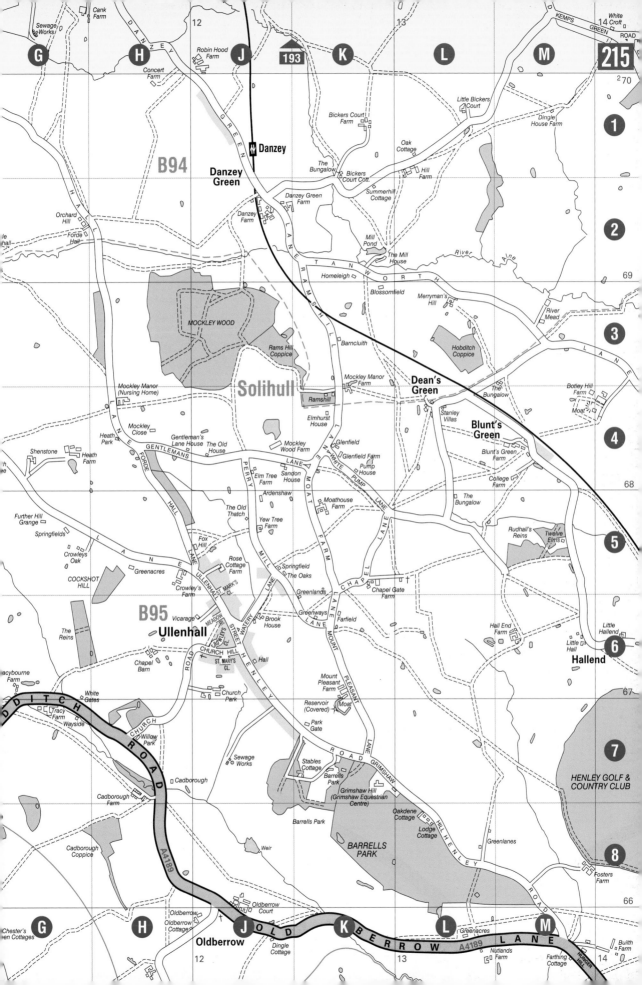

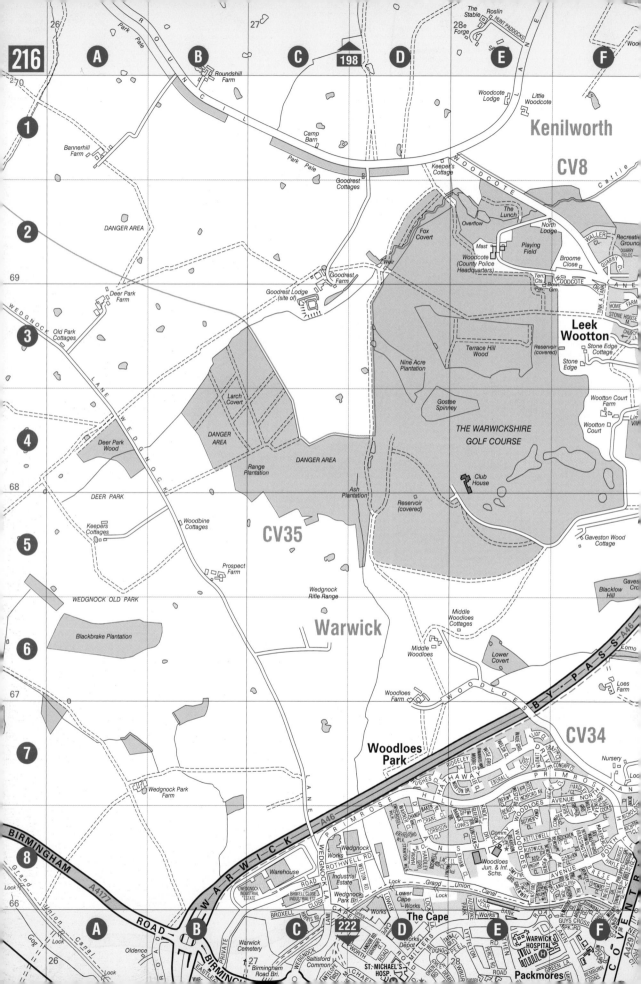

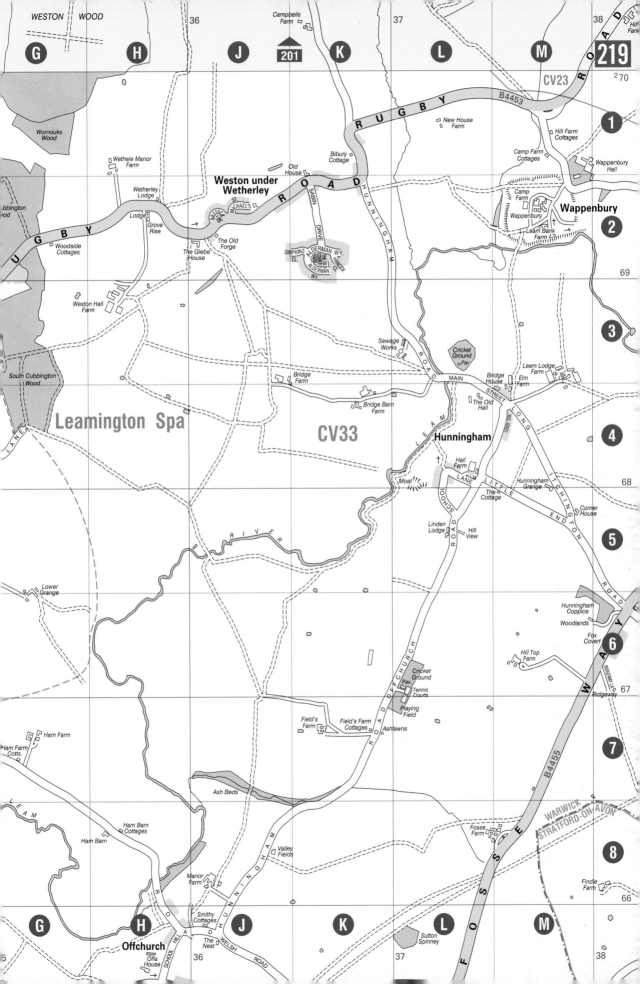

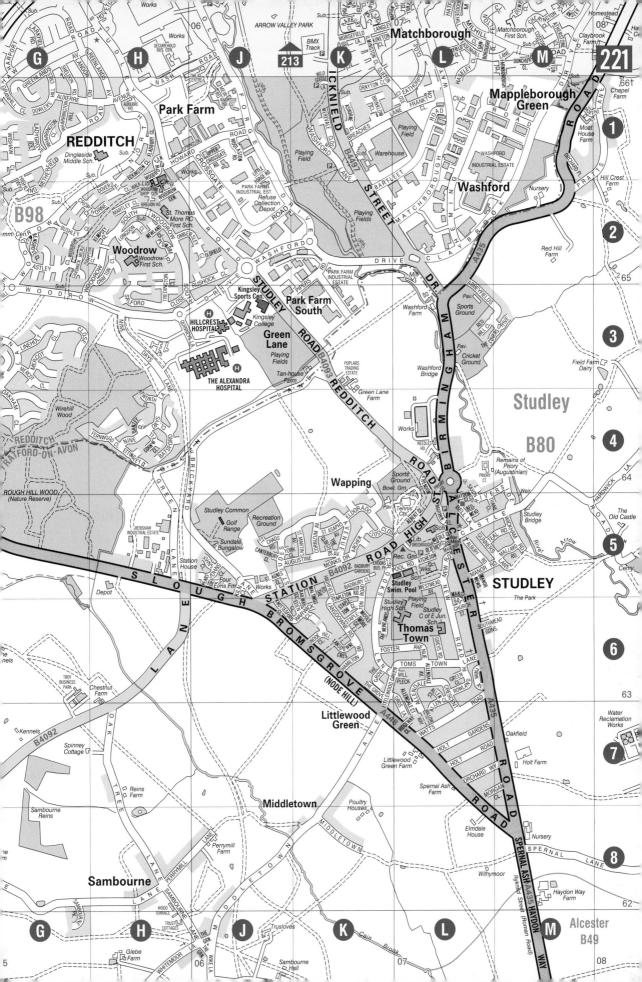

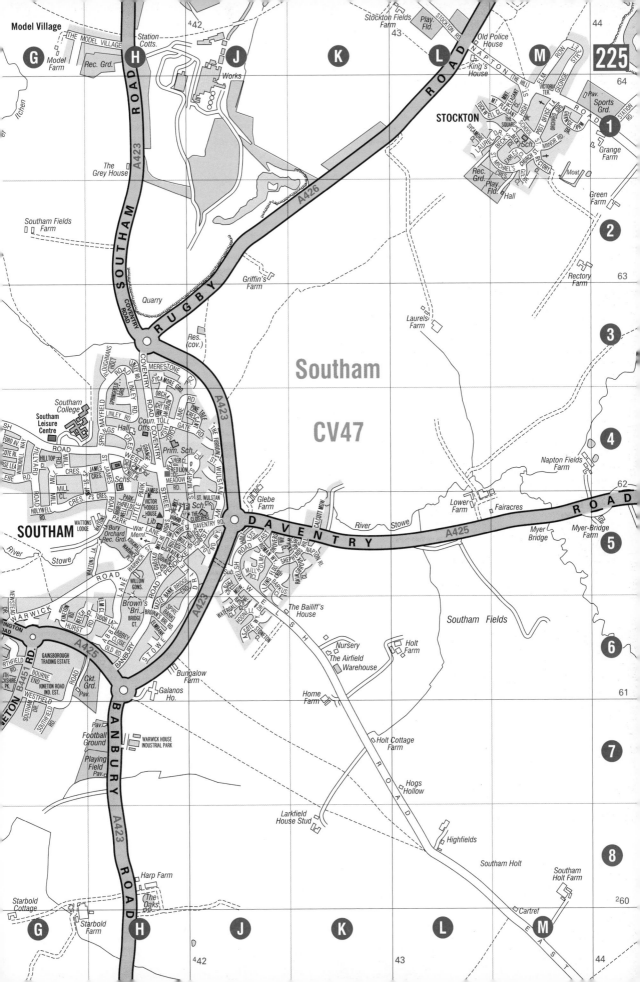

INDEX

Including Streets, Places & Areas, Industrial Estates, Selected Flats & Walkways,
Stations, Junctions and Selected Places of Interest.

HOW TO USE THIS INDEX

1. Each street name is followed by its Postcode District and then by its Locality abbreviation(s) and then by its map reference; e.g. **Abberley Av.** DY13: Stour S . . . .8D **182** is in the DY13 Postcode District and the Stourport-on-Severn Locality and is to be found in square 8D on page **182**. The page number is shown in bold type.

2. A strict alphabetical order is followed in which Av., Rd., St., etc. (though abbreviated) are read in full and as part of the street name; e.g. **Adamson Cl.** appears after **Adams Ho.** but before **Adams Rd.**

3. Streets and a selection of flats and walkways too small to be shown on the maps, appear in the index with the thoroughfare to which it is connected shown in brackets; e.g. **Abberton Ct.** *B23:* Erd . . . .7C **80** (off Dunlin Cl.)

4. Addresses that are in more than one part are referred to as not continuous.

5. Places and areas are shown in the index in **BLUE TYPE** and the map reference is to the actual map square in which the town centre or area is located and not to the place name shown on the map; e.g. **ADAMS HILL** 5E **138**

6. An example of a selected place of interest is **Alexandra Theatre** 7K **101** (6F **4**)

7. An example of a station is **Acocks Green Station (Rail)** 5J **123**

8. Junction names are shown in the index in **BOLD TYPE**; e.g. **BELFRY JUNC.** 7J **61**

9. Map references shown in brackets; e.g. **Abbotts La.** CV1: Cov . . . .6B **152** (3A **6**) refer to entries that also appear on the large scale pages **4-7**.

GENERAL ABBREVIATIONS

All. : Alley	**Cl.** : Close	**Gth.** : Garth	**Mdw.** : Meadow	**Sq.** : Square
App. : Approach	**Coll.** : College	**Ga.** : Gate	**Mdws.** : Meadows	**Sta.** : Station
Arc. : Arcade	**Comn.** : Common	**Gt.** : Great	**M.** : Mews	**St.** : Street
Av. : Avenue	**Cnr.** : Corner	**Grn.** : Green	**Mt.** : Mount	**Ter.** : Terrace
Bk. : Back	**Cott.** : Cottage	**Gro.** : Grove	**Mus.** : Museum	**Twr.** : Tower
Blvd. : Boulevard	**Cotts.** : Cottages	**Hgts.** : Heights	**Nth.** : North	**Trad.** : Trading
Bri. : Bridge	**Ct.** : Court	**Ho.** : House	**No.** : Number	**Up.** : Upper
Bldg. : Building	**Cres.** : Crescent	**Ho's.** : Houses	**Pde.** : Parade	**Va.** : Vale
Bldgs. : Buildings	**Cft.** : Croft	**Ind.** : Industrial	**Pk.** : Park	**Vw.** : View
Bungs. : Bungalows	**Dpt.** : Depot	**Info.** : Information	**Pas.** : Passage	**Vs.** : Villas
Bus. : Business	**Dr.** : Drive	**Intl.** : International	**Pl.** : Place	**Vis.** : Visitors
Cvn. : Caravan	**E.** : East	**Junc.** : Junction	**Pct.** : Precinct	**Wlk.** : Walk
C'way. : Causeway	**Ent.** : Enterprise	**La.** : Lane	**Res.** : Residential	**W.** : West
Cen. : Centre	**Est.** : Estate	**Lit.** : Little	**Ri.** : Rise	**Yd.** : Yard
Chu. : Church	**Fld.** : Field	**Lwr.** : Lower	**Rd.** : Road	
Chyd. : Churchyard	**Flds.** : Fields	**Mnr.** : Manor	**Rdbt.** : Roundabout	
Circ. : Circle	**Gdn.** : Garden	**Mans.** : Mansions	**Shop.** : Shopping	
Cir. : Circus	**Gdns.** : Gardens	**Mkt.** : Market	**Sth.** : South	

LOCALITY ABBREVIATIONS

A Grn : **Acock's Green**	Blak : **Blakedown**	Cod W : **Codsall Wood**	Frly : **Freasley**	I'ley : **Iverley**
Alb : **Albrighton**	Blox : **Bloxwich**	Coft H : **Cofton Hackett**	Frol : **Frolesworth**	Ken : **Kenilworth**
Ald G : **Alderman's Green**	Blun G : **Blunt's Green**	Col : **Coleshill**	Gall C : **Galley Common**	Ker E : **Keresley End**
A'rdge : **Aldridge**	Bly P : **Blythe Valley Park**	Cookl : **Cookley**	Gent : **Gentleshaw**	Kidd : **Kidderminster**
Alle : **Allesley**	Bod H : **Bodymoor Heath**	Cor : **Corley**	Glas : **Glascote**	Kils : **Kilsby**
A'chu : **Alvechurch**	Bold : **Boldmere**	Cose : **Coseley**	Gorn : **Gornalwood**	K'bry : **Kingsbury**
A'cte : **Alvecote**	Bord G : **Bordesley Green**	Cou : **Coughton**	Gt Barr : **Great Barr**	K Hth : **King's Heath**
Amb : **Amblecote**	B'hth : **Bournheath**	Coven : **Coven**	Gt Wyr : **Great Wyrley**	K'hrst : **Kingshurst**
Amin : **Amington**	B'vlle : **Bournville**	Cov H : **Coven Heath**	Gren : **Grendon**	K New : **King's Newnham**
Ansl : **Ansley**	Bour D : **Bourton on Dunsmore**	Cov : **Coventry**	Griff : **Griff**	K Nor : **King's Norton**
Ans C : **Ansley Common**	Bram : **Bramcote**	Crad : **Cradley**	Gun H : **Gun Hill**	K'sdng : **Kingstanding**
Ansty : **Ansty**	Bran : **Brandon**	Crad H : **Cradley Heath**	Guys C : **Guy's Cliffe**	K'wfrd : **Kingswinford**
Arb : **Arbury**	Bret : **Bretford**	C Grn : **Cross Green**	Hag : **Hagley**	Kinv : **Kinver**
Arl : **Arley**	Brie H : **Brierley Hill**	Cubb : **Cubbington**	Hale : **Halesowen**	Kitts G : **Kitt's Green**
Arm : **Armitage**	Brin : **Brinklow**	Curb : **Curborough**	Hall G : **Hall Green**	Know : **Knowle**
Ash G : **Ash Green**	B'frd : **Brinsford**	Curd : **Curdworth**	Hamm : **Hammerwich**	Lapw : **Lapworth**
Ash C : **Ashley Common**	B'gve : **Bromsgrove**	Dad : **Dadlington**	H Ard : **Hampton in Arden**	Law H : **Lawford Heath**
Asty : **Astley**	Brme : **Broome**	Dan G : **Danzey Green**	H Mag : **Hampton Magna**	Lea M : **Lea Marston**
Aston : **Aston**	Bwnhls : **Brownhills**	Darl : **Darlaston**	H Hill : **Hampton on the Hill**	Lea S : **Leamington Spa**
Aston F : **Aston Flamville**	Brow : **Brownsover**	Dic H : **Dickens Heath**	Hnbry : **Hanbury**	Leek W : **Leek Wootton**
A'wd B : **Astwood Bank**	Bubb : **Bubbenhall**	D'frd : **Dodford**	Hanch : **Hanch**	Lich : **Lichfield**
Ath : **Atherstone**	Bud : **Budbrooke**	Dord : **Dordon**	Hand : **Handsworth**	Lick : **Lickey**
Att : **Atterton**	Bulk : **Bulkington**	Dorr : **Dorridge**	Harb : **Harborne**	L End : **Lickey End**
Bad C : **Baddesley Clinton**	Burb : **Burbage**	Dost : **Dosthill**	Harb M : **Harborough Magna**	Lilb : **Lilbourne**
Bad E : **Baddesley Ensor**	Burc : **Burcot**	Dray B : **Drayton Bassett**	Hartl : **Hartlebury**	Lill : **Lillington**
Bag : **Baginton**	Burn : **Burntwood**	Dud : **Dudley**	Harts : **Hartshill**	Lit A : **Little Aston**
Bal C : **Balsall Common**	Burt G : **Burton Green**	Dunc : **Dunchurch**	Harv : **Harvington**	Lit H : **Little Hay**
Bal H : **Balsall Heath**	Burt H : **Burton Hastings**	Dunl : **Dunley**	Hase : **Haseley**	Lit L : **Little Lawford**
Bks G : **Banks Green**	Bush : **Bushbury**	Earl S : **Earl Shilton**	Hase K : **Haseley Knob**	Lit P : **Little Packington**
Barby : **Barby**	Cald : **Caldecote**	Earls : **Earlswood**	Hton : **Hatherton**	Lit W : **Little Wyrley**
Barf : **Barford**	Canly : **Canley**	E Grn : **Eastern Green**	Hatt : **Hatton**	Longb : **Longbridge**
Barn : **Barnacle**	Cann : **Cannock**	Edg : **Edgbaston**	Haz : **Hazelslade**	Longd : **Longdon**
B Grn : **Barnt Green**	Cann W : **Cannock Wood**	Elmb : **Elmbridge**	Head H : **Headley Heath**	Longf : **Longford**
Bars : **Barston**	Can : **Canwell**	Elme : **Elmesthorpe**	H'cte : **Heathcote**	Long I : **Long Itchington**
Bart G : **Bartley Green**	Cas B : **Castle Bromwich**	Elmh : **Elmhurst**	Hth H : **Heath Hayes**	Long L : **Long Lawford**
Barw : **Barwell**	Cas V : **Castle Vale**	Elm L : **Elmley Lovett**	Hed : **Hednesford**	Lwr B : **Lower Bentley**
Bass P : **Bassetts Pole**	Cath B : **Catherine-de-Barnes**	Env : **Enville**	H'ton : **Heightington**	Lwr F : **Lower Fulbrook**
Bax : **Baxterley**	Cats : **Catshill**	Erd : **Erdington**	Hen A : **Henley-in-Arden**	Lwr G : **Lower Gornal**
Beau : **Beausale**	Cau : **Caunsall**	Ess : **Essington**	High H : **Higham-on-the-Hill**	Lwr P : **Lower Penn**
Bed : **Bedworth**	Caw : **Cawston**	E'shll : **Ettingshall**	Hillm : **Hillmorton**	Low H : **Low Habberley**
Belb : **Belbroughton**	Chad C : **Chaddesley Corbett**	Exh : **Exhall**	Hillp : **Hillpool**	Loz : **Lozells**
Bntly : **Bentley**	C'wich : **Chadwich**	F'fld : **Fairfield**	Hill W : **Hill Wootton**	Lutly : **Lutley**
Ben H : **Bentley Heath**	C'wick : **Chadwick**	Fare : **Farewell**	Hilt : **Hilton**	L Ash : **Lydiate Ash**
Beo : **Beoley**	Chad E : **Chadwick End**	Faz : **Fazeley**	Himl : **Himley**	Lye : **Lye**
Berk : **Berkswell**	C Ter : **Chase Terrace**	F'stne : **Featherstone**	Hinc : **Hinckley**	Lynn : **Lynn**
Bew : **Bewdley**	Chase : **Chasetown**	Fen E : **Fen End**	Hints : **Hints**	Maj G : **Major's Green**
Bick : **Bickenhill**	Chel W : **Chelmsley Wood**	Fen D : **Fenny Drayton**	Hock : **Hockley**	Man : **Mancetter**
Bilb : **Bilbrook**	C Hay : **Cheslyn Hay**	Fill : **Fillongley**	H'ley H : **Hockley Heath**	Map G : **Mappleborough Green**
Bils : **Bilston**	C'fld : **Chesterfield**	Finh : **Finham**	Hodg H : **Hodge Hill**	Marl : **Marlbrook**
Bil : **Bilton**	Ches : **Chesterton**	Fins : **Finstall**	H'wd : **Hollywood**	Mars : **Marston**
Bin : **Binley**	Ches G : **Cheswick Green**	Foot : **Footherley**	Hon : **Honiley**	Mars G : **Marston Green**
Bin W : **Binley Woods**	Chor : **Chorley**	F'bri : **Fordbridge**	Hop : **Hopwas**	Mart : **Marton**
B'moor : **Birchmoor**	C'hll : **Churchill**	F'hses : **Fordhouses**	Hopw : **Hopwood**	Max : **Maxstoke**
Birm : **Birmingham**	Chu L : **Church Lawford**	Forh : **Forhill**	H'ham : **Hunningham**	Mer : **Meriden**
Birm A : **Birmingham Int. Airport**	Clay : **Clayhanger**	Four C : **Four Crosses**	Hunn : **Hunnington**	Midd : **Middleton**
Bis T : **Bishop's Tachbrook**	Clent : **Clent**	Four O : **Four Oaks**	Hunt : **Huntington**	M Oak : **Mile Oak**
B'dwn : **Blackdown**	Cliff : **Cliff**	Frad : **Fradley**	Hurc : **Hurcott**	Min : **Minworth**
B'hth : **Blackheath**	Clift D : **Clifton upon Dunsmore**	Fran : **Frankley**	Hurl : **Hurley**	M'path : **Monkspath**
B'wll : **Blackwell**	Cod : **Codsall**	F'ton : **Frankton**	Ism : **Ismere**	Mose : **Moseley**

Mox : **Moxley**
Muck C : **Muckley Corner**
Mus G : **Mustow Green**
Nat E C : **National Exhibition Centre**
Nech : **Nechells**
Neth : **Netherton**
Neth W : **Nether Whitacre**
New A : **New Arley**
N'bld A : **Newbold on Avon**
New O : **New Oscott**
Newt : **Newton**
N'fld : **Northfield**
Nort C : **Norton Canes**
Nun : **Nuneaton**
Nur : **Nurton**
Oaken : **Oaken**
Off : **Offchurch**
Old A : **Old Arley**
Oldb : **Oldberrow**
O'bry : **Oldbury**
Old H : **Old Hill**
Old M : **Old Milverton**
Olton : **Olton**
Out : **Outhill**
Over W : **Over Whitacre**
Oxl : **Oxley**
Patt : **Pattingham**
Pedm : **Pedmore**
Pels : **Pelsall**
Pend : **Pendeford**
Penk : **Penkridge**
Penn : **Penn**
P'ntt : **Pensnett**
P Barr : **Perry Barr**
Pert : **Perton**
Picc : **Piccadilly**
Pin : **Pinwall**
Pip : **Pipehill**
Pole : **Polesworth**
Pot M : **Potters Marston**
Prin : **Princethorpe**
Quar B : **Quarry Bank**
Quin : **Quinton**
Rad S : **Radford Semele**
Rat C : **Ratcliffe Culey**
Redd : **Redditch**
Redn : **Rednal**
Ribb : **Ribbesford**
Ridge L : **Ridge Lane**
Roms : **Romsley**
R'ley : **Roughley**
Row : **Rowington**
Row R : **Rowley Regis**
Row G : **Rowney Green**
Rubery : **Rubery**
Rugby : **Rugby**
Rus : **Rushall**
Rush : **Rushock**
Rytn D : **Ryton-on-Dunsmore**
Salt : **Saltley**
Sam : **Sambourne**
Sap : **Sapcote**
Sed : **Sedgley**
Seis : **Seisdon**
S Oak : **Selly Oak**
S End : **Shard End**
Share : **Shareshill**
Sharn : **Sharnford**
Shat : **Shatterford**
S Mag : **Sheepy Magna**
Sheld : **Sheldon**
S'fld : **Shelfield**
Shens : **Shenstone**
Shen W : **Shenstone Woodend**
Sher : **Sherbourne**
Shil : **Shilton**
Shir : **Shirley**
Shu : **Shustoke**
Shut : **Shuttington**
S Hth : **Slade Heath**
Small H : **Small Heath**
Smeth : **Smethwick**
Sol : **Solihull**
Sou : **Southam**
S'brk : **Sparkbrook**
S'hll : **Sparkhill**
Stap : **Stapleton**
Stare : **Stareton**
Stech : **Stechford**
Stir : **Stirchley**
S'ton : **Stockton**
Stoke G : **Stoke Golding**
Stoke H : **Stoke Heath**
Stoke P : **Stoke Pound**
S Prior : **Stoke Prior**
Stone : **Stone**
S'lgh : **Stoneleigh**
S'lgh P : **Stoneleigh Park**
S Stan : **Stoney Stanton**
Ston : **Stonnall**
Stourb : **Stourbridge**
Stour S : **Stourport-on-Severn**
Stourt : **Stourton**
S'hay : **Streethay**
S'tly : **Streetly**
Stret D : **Stretton-on-Dunsmore**
Stret F : **Stretton under Fosse**
Stud : **Studley**
S Cold : **Sutton Coldfield**
Swind : **Swindon**
S'fen : **Swinfen**
Tam : **Tamworth**
Tan A : **Tanworth-in-Arden**
Tard : **Tardebigge**
Tett : **Tettenhall**
Thurl : **Thurlaston**
Tid G : **Tidbury Green**
Tile H : **Tile Hill**
Tip : **Tipton**
Titt : **Titton**
Tiv : **Tividale**
Tort : **Torton**
Tres : **Trescott**
Trim : **Trimpley**
Try : **Trysull**
Tutn : **Tutnall**
Two G : **Two Gates**
Tys : **Tyseley**
Ullen : **Ullenhall**
Up Ben : **Upper Bentley**
Up Gor : **Upper Gornal**
Upton : **Upton**
U War : **Upton Warren**
Wall : **Wall**
W Hth : **Wall Heath**
Walm : **Walmley**
Wals : **Walsall**
Wals W : **Walsall Wood**
W'grve S : **Walsgrave on Sowe**
Wapp : **Wappenbury**
W End : **Ward End**
Ware : **Waresley**
Wart : **Warton**
Warw : **Warwick**
Wat O : **Water Orton**
W'bry : **Wednesbury**
Wed : **Wednesfield**
W'frd : **Weeford**
W Cas : **Weoley Castle**
W Brom : **West Bromwich**
W Weth : **Weston under Wetherley**
W'wd H : **Westwood Heath**
What : **Whateley**
W'nsh : **Whitnash**
Whitt : **Whittington**
Wig P : **Wigston Parva**
Wild : **Wildmoor**
W'hall : **Willenhall**
W'hby : **Willoughby**
Wiln : **Wilnecote**
Wim : **Wimblebury**
Win G : **Winson Green**
Wis : **Wishaw**
With : **Witherley**
Withy : **Withybrook**
Witt : **Witton**
Woll : **Wollaston**
W'cte : **Wollescote**
Wols : **Wolston**
Wolv : **Wolverhampton**
W'ley : **Wolverley**
Wlvy : **Wolvey**
Wom : **Wombourne**
Wood E : **Wood End**
Wool : **Woolscott**
Word : **Wordsley**
Wrox : **Wroxall**
Wych : **Wychbold**
Wykin : **Wykin**
W Grn : **Wylde Green**
Wyt : **Wythall**
Yard : **Yardley**
Yard W : **Yardley Wood**

3B Business Village
B21: Hand 2D 100

A

A1 Trad. Est. B66: Smeth 2B 100
Aaron Manby Ct. DY4: Tip 1M 75
Abberley B77: Wiln 7J 33
Abberley Av. DY13: Stour S ...8D 182
Abberley Cl. B63: Hale 7M 117
B98: Redd 4J 213
Abberley Ind. Cen.
B66: Smeth 4D 100
Abberley Rd. B68: O'bry 2H 119
DY3: Lwr G 5C 74
Abberley St. B66: Smeth 4D 100
DY2: Dud 1J 97
Abberton Cl. B63: Hale 6C 118
Abberton Ct. *B23: Erd 7C 80*
(off Dunlin Cl.)
Abberton Gro. B90: M'path 2B 168
Abberton Ho. *B97: Redd 5A 212*
(off Lock Cl.)
Abberton Way CV4: Canly 6K 173
Abbess Gro. B25: Yard 8L 103
Abbey, The CV8: Ken 4F 198
Abbey Cl. B60: B'gve 7C 188
B71: W Brom 4J 77
CV47: Sou 6H 225
Abbey Ct. B68: O'bry 5H 99
CV3: Cov 3H 175
CV8: Ken 5F 198
Abbey Cres. B63: Crad 5K 117
B68: O'bry 1K 119
Abbey Cft. B78: Pole 2K 49
ABBEYDALE 4G 213
Abbeydale Cl. CV3: Bin 6M 153
Abbeydale Rd. B31: N'fld 7A 142
Abbey Dr. WS3: Pels 4A 26
Abbey End CV8: Ken 5F 198
Abbeyfield Rd. B23: Erd 2D 80
WV10: Bush 5E 22
Abbeyfields Dr. B80: Stud 3L 221
Abbey Fields Swimming Pool
.......4E 198
Abbey Gdns. B67: Smeth 8L 99
Abbey Ga. CV11: Nun 5J 89
Abbey Ga. Shop. Pct.
CV11: Nun 5J 89
Abbey Grn. CV11: Nun 4H 89
Abbey Grn. Ct. B78: Pole 3K 49
Abbey Hill CV8: Ken 4F 198
Abbey Ind. Est. CV2: Cov 4M 153
Abbey La. CV47: Sou 6H 225
Abbey Mans. B24: Erd 3H 81
Abbey Rd. B17: Harb 4D 120
B23: Erd 7D 80
B63: Crad 5J 117
B67: Smeth 8K 99
B77: Glas 6D 32
B97: Redd 5E 212
CV3: Cov 3F 174
(not continuous)
DY2: Dud 3K 97
DY3: Gorn 6C 74
DY11: Kidd 3G 157
Abbey Sports Cen. 5H 89
Abbey Sq. WS3: Blox 7E 24
Abbey Stadium 2E 212
Abbey Stadium Sports Cen. 2E 212
Abbey St. B18: Hock 4G 101
CV11: Nun 4H 89
(not continuous)
CV21: Rugby 5C 180
DY3: Gorn 6C 74
WS12: Hed 2H 9
Abbey St. Nth. B18: Hock 4G 101
Abbey Trad. Cen. B97: Redd ...4E 212
Abbey Vw. B78: Pole 1B 48
Abbey Way CV3: Cov 3F 174
Abbotsbury Cl.
CV2: W'grve S 5A 154
Abbotsbury Way CV11: Nun ...2M 111
Abbots Cl. B93: Know 2G 169
WS4: Rus 3C 40
Abbots Fld. WS11: Cann 4E 8
Abbotsford Av. B43: Gt Barr 7F 56
Abbotsford Dr. DY1: Dud 2E 96
Abbotsford Rd. B11: S'brk 3B 122
CV11: Nun 1L 111
WS14: Lich 2K 19
Abbots Rd. B14: K Hth 2L 143
Abbots Way B18: Hock 3H 101
CV34: Warw 3D 222
WV3: Wolv 8L 35
Abbotswood Clo B98: Redd 6A 214
Abbott Rd. B63: Hale 1J 139
Abbotts Cl. DY13: Stour S 3K 183
Abbotts Grn. LE10: Burb 4M 91
Abbotts La. CV1: Cov ...6B 152 (3A 6)
Abbotts M. DY5: Brie H 8D 96
Abbotts Pl. WS3: Blox 8K 25
Abbotts Rd. B24: Erd 8F 80
Abbotts St. CV31: Lea S 2M 223
WS3: Blox 7K 25
Abbotts Wlk. CV3: Bin W 2C 176
CV8: Wols 5H 177
Abbotts Way CV21: Hillm 8F 180
Abdon Av. B29: W Cas 2B 142
Abeles Way CV9: Ath 7J 49
Abelia B77: Amin 6F 32
Abercorn Rd. CV5: Cov 7L 151
Aberdeen Cl. CV5: E Grn 4G 151
Aberdeen Rd. CV11: Nun 8L 89
Aberdeen St. B18: Win G 5E 100
Aberford Cl. WV12: W'hall 5D 38
Abergavenny Wlk.
CV3: Bin 2M 175
Abigails Cl. B26: Sheld 2B 124
Abingdon Cl. WV1: Wolv 7H 37
Abingdon Rd. B23: Erd 2B 80
DY2: Neth 6K 97
WS3: Blox 7F 24
WV1: Wolv 7H 37
Abingdon Way B35: Cas V 6A 82
CV11: Nun 2M 89
WS3: Blox 7F 24
Ablewell St. WS1: Wals 8M 39
Ablow St. WV2: Wolv ...1C 52 (7H 7)
Abnalls Cft. WS13: Lich 8F 12
Abnalls La. WS13: Lich 1A 18
(not continuous)
Abney Dr. WV14: Cose 8F 52
Abney Gro. B44: K'sdng 7B 58
Aboyne Cl. B5: Edg 3K 121
Ab Row B4: Birm 6M 101 (3K 5)
Acacia Av. B37: K'hrst 3F 104
CV1: Cov 8E 152 (7F 6)
Acacia Av. DY12: Bew 6C 156
WS5: Wals 5A 56
Acacia Cl. B37: K'hrst 3F 104
B69: Tiv 7B 76
DY1: Dud 6G 75
Acacia Ct. CV6: Cov 4L 151
Acacia Cres. CV12: Bed 6K 111
WV8: Bilb 5H 21
Acacia Dr. WV14: Cose 2G 75
Acacia Gro. CV21: Rugby 5A 180
WS12: Wim 6M 9
Acacia Rd. B30: B'vlle 1E 142
CV10: Nun 4E 88
CV32: Lea S 8K 217
Acacia Ter. B12: Bal H 4A 122
Acanthus Rd. B98: Redd 3M 213
Accord M. WS10: Darl 2D 54
Ace Bus. Pk. B33: Kitts G 7D 104
Acfold Rd. B20: Hand 4E 78
Achal Cl. CV6: Cov 7F 130
Acheson Rd.
B90: Hall G, Shir 7F 144
Acheston Rd. B28: Hall G 7F 144
Achilles Cl. CV34: H'cte 7M 223
WS6: Gt Wyr 8F 14
(not continuous)
Achilles Rd. CV6: Cov 2G 153
Achurch Cl. LE9: S Stan 6K 71
Ackers, The (Activity Cen.) ...3D 122
Ackleton Gdns. WV3: Wolv 2M 51
Ackleton Gro. B29: W Cas 1M 141
ACOCKS GREEN 6J 123
Acocks Green Bowl 6H 123
Acocks Green Station (Rail) ...5J 123
Acorn Cl. B27: A Grn 4H 123
B30: B'vlle 1E 142
B70: W Brom 6H 77
CV8: S'lgh 2B 200
CV12: Bed 1C 130
WS6: Gt Wyr 8G 15
WS7: C Ter 8G 11
WS11: Hth H 7J 9
Acorn Ct. B45: Redn 2K 163
CV32: Lea S 7A 218
Acorn Dr. CV22: Bil 8H 179
Acorn Gdns. B30: Stir 1G 143
Acorn Gro. B1: Birm 6H 101 (4A 4)
DY8: Word 8L 95
WV8: Cod 7E 20
Acorn Rd. B61: Cats 8B 162
B62: B'hth 1C 118
WV11: Wed 8A 24
Acorns, The B61: Cats 1A 188
Acorn Starter Units
WS7: C Ter 2D 16
Acorn St. CV3: Cov 1H 175
WV13: W'hall 7C 38
Acorn Way WS7: Burn 3J 17
Acre, The DY7: Kinv 6B 114
Acre Cl. CV31: W'nsh 5A 224
Acre Ho. DY7: Kinv 6B 114
Acre La. B97: Redd 7L 211
Acre Ri. WV12: W'hall 4B 38
Acres, The WV3: Wolv 8J 35
Acres Rd. DY5: Quar B 1D 116
Acton Cl. B98: Redd 4K 213
Acton Dr. DY3: Lwr G 6B 74
Acton Gro. B44: K'sdng 6A 58
WV14: Bils 5H 53
Adam Ct. B63: Hale 5M 117
WS11: Cann 8D 8
Adam Rd. CV6: Cov 2G 153
Adams Brook Dr.
B32: Bart G 8H 119
Adams Cl. B66: Smeth 2K 99
DY4: Tip 8M 53
Adams Ct. DY10: Kidd 2A 158
ADAMS HILL 5E 138
Adams Hill DY9: Clent 5E 138
B32: Bart G 8H 119
Adams Ho. DY11: Kidd 3J 157
Adamson Cl. WS11: Cann 8B 8
Adams Rd. WS8: Bwnhls 4G 27
WV3: Wolv 2J 51
Adams St. B7: Birm 4M 101 (1K 5)
B70: W Brom 6H 77
CV21: Rugby 6L 179
WS2: Wals 7K 39
Adam St. DY11: Kidd 4J 157
Adare Dr. CV3: Cov 1C 174
Ada Rd. B9: Birm 7B 102
B25: Yard 3H 123
B66: Smeth 6B 100
Ada Wrighton Cl.
WV12: W'hall 2C 38
Adcock Dr. CV8: Ken 4G 199
Adcote Cl. LE9: Barw 3A 70
Addenbrooke Ct. B64: Old H ...1M 117
Addenbrooke Cres.
DY11: Kidd 8G 157
(not continuous)
Addenbrooke Dr. B73: W Grn ...7H 59
Addenbrooke Pl. WS10: Darl ...2D 54
Addenbrooke Rd. B67: Smeth ...6M 99
CV7: Ker E 2A 130
Addenbrooke St. WS3: Blox 2J 39
WS10: Darl 1D 54
Addenbrook Way DY4: Tip 1D 76
Adderley Gdns. B8: Salt 4D 102
(not continuous)
Adderley Pk. Cl. B8: Salt 5E 102
Adderley Park Station (Rail) ...6D 102
Adderley Rd. B8: Salt 6C 102
Adderley Rd. Sth. B8: Salt 6C 102
Adderley St. B9: Birm ...8A 102 (7L 5)
CV1: Cov 5E 152
Adderley Trad. Est. B8: Salt ...5C 102
Addingham Cl. CV34: Warw 8E 216
Addington Way B69: Tiv 7D 76
Addison Cl. CV10: Gall C 4A 88
WS10: W'bry 7L 55
WS11: Cann 4E 8
Addison Cft. DY3: Lwr G 4A 74
Addison Gro. WV11: Wed 8H 23
Addison Pl. B46: Wat O 6H 83
WV14: Bils 2A 54
Addison Rd. B7: Nech 1C 102
B14: K Hth 2L 143
CV6: Cov 1A 152
CV22: Bil, Rugby 8K 179
DY5: Brie H 7B 96
WS10: W'bry 7L 55
WV3: Wolv 1M 51
Addison St. WS10: W'bry 7F 54
Addison Ter. WS10: W'bry 7F 54
Adelaide Av. B70: W Brom 2G 77
Adelaide Ct. CV12: Bed 7G 111
Adelaide Dr. WS12: Wim 6M 9
Adelaide Rd. CV32: Lea S 1L 223
Adelaide St. B97: Redd 5D 212
CV1: Cov 5E 152 (1F 6)
DY5: Brie H 6D 96
Adelaide Twr. *B34: S End 4C 104*
(off Packington Av.)
Adelaide Wlk.
WV2: Wolv 1E 52 (7M 7)
Adelphi Ct. *DY5: Brie H 7D 96*
(off Promenade, The)
Adey Rd. WV11: Wed 1M 37
Adkins Cft. CV7: Fill 6E 108
Adkins La. B67: Smeth 8M 99
Adkinson Av. CV22: Dunc 6J 205
Admington Rd. B33: Sheld 1C 124
Admiral Gdns. CV8: Ken 3J 199
Admiral Parker Dr.
WS14: Shens 4F 28
Admiral Pl. B13: Mose 5M 121
Admirals Way B65: Row R 7B 98
CV11: Bram 3E 112
Admiral Wlk. DY11: Kidd 1L 157
Adonis Cl. B79: Tam 2C 32
Adrian Boult Hall 7K 101 (5E 4)
Adrian Ct. B24: Erd 3H 81
Adrian Cft. B13: Mose 8C 122
Adrian Dr. LE9: Barw 2A 70
Adrians' Cl. CV9: Man 3M 65
Adria Rd. B11: S'hll 5B 122
Adshead Rd. DY2: Dud 2J 97
Adstone Gro. B31: N'fld 8M 141
Advent Gdns. *B70: W Brom 6H 77*
(off Brook St.)
Adwalton Rd. WV6: Pert 6F 34
Affleck Av. B78: M Oak 8K 31
Agenoria Dr. DY8: Stourb 4M 115
AGGBOROUGH 5L 157
Aggborough Cres.
DY10: Kidd 6L 157
Aggborough Stadium 5M 157
Agincourt Rd. CV3: Cov 2E 174
Agmore La. B60: Tard 6H 189
Agmore Rd. B60: B'wll 5G 189
Aiden Ct. WS13: Lich 2J 19
Aiden Ct. Rd. WS13: Lich 1J 19
Ainsbury Rd. CV5: Cov 1L 173
Ainsdale Cl. CV6: Ald G 5H 131
DY8: Stourb 7M 115
Ainsdale Gdns. B24: Erd 4J 81
B63: Hale 7K 117
Ainsworth Rd. B31: N'fld 7D 142
WV10: Bush 4E 22
Aintree Cl. B61: Cats 8A 162
CV6: Cov 4E 152
CV12: Bed 5H 111
DY11: Kidd 1K 157
WS12: Haz 3M 9
Aintree Dr. CV32: Lill 6C 218
Aintree Gro. B34: S End 3E 104
Aintree Rd. WV10: F'hses 5D 22
Aintree Way DY1: Dud 6E 74
Aire Cft. B31: N'fld 8B 142
Airfield Dr. WS9: A'rdge 6E 40
Air Ministry Cotts.
B35: Cas V 7M 81
Airport Way B26: Birm A 5J 125
Aitken Cl. B78: Tam 7A 32
Ajax Cl. CV21: Rugby 3B 180
WS6: Gt Wyr 8F 14
Akrill Cl. B70: W Brom 4H 77
Akrill Cott. Homes, The
B70: W Brom 4H 77
Alamein Rd. WV13: W'hall 8L 37
Alan Bray Cl. LE10: Hinc 2D 90
Alandale Av. CV5: E Grn 5E 150

Alandale Ct.—Alumwell Rd.

Alandale Ct. CV12: Bed 1C 130
Alan Higgs Way CV4: Tile H 1C 172
Alasdair Ho. B17: Harb 4B 120
Albany Cl. DY10: Kidd 3B 158
Albany Ct. *B62: Quin 2G 119*
(off Binswood Rd.)
CV1: Cov 7A 152
Albany Cres. WV14: Bils 3J 53
Albany Dr. WS12: Wim 6L 9
Albany Gdns. B91: Sol 5E 146
Albany Gro. DY6: K'wfrd 2L 95
WV11: Ess 8C 24
Albany Ho. B34: S End 2B 104
Albany Rd. B17: Harb 3C 120
CV1: Cov 8A 152
CV5: Cov 8A 152
WV1: Wolv 7B 36 (4G 7)
Albany Ter. CV32: Lea S 8L 217
Albemarle Rd. DY8: Stourb 7M 115
Albermarle Rd. DY6: K'wfrd 4A 96
Albert Av. B12: Bal H 3A 122
Albert Bean Cl. CV31: W'nsh 5A 224
Albert Clarke Dr.
WV12: W'hall 2C 38
Albert Cl. B80: Stud 5L 221
WV8: Cod 5E 20
Albert Cres. CV6: Cov 6B 130
Albert Davie Dr. WS12: Hed 5L 9
Albert Dr. B63: Hale 7M 117
DY3: Swind 7E 72
Albert Fearn Gdns. CV6: Cov 8F 130
Albert Ho. *WS10: Darl 3C 54*
(off Factory St.)
Albert Rd. B6: Aston 1K 101
B14: K Hth 2L 143
B17: Harb 4B 120
B21: Hand 8E 78
B23: Erd 6D 80
B33: Stech 7K 103
B61: B'gve 1L 209
B63: Hale 7M 117
B68: O'bry 1J 119
B78: Faz 1A 46
B79: Tam 4B 32
CV5: Alle 1A 150
DY10: Kidd 3M 157
LE10: Hinc 8K 69
WV6: Wolv 6M 35
Albert Smith Pl. B65: Row R 5A 98
Albert Sq. CV21: Rugby 6B 180
Albert St. B4: Birm 7L 101 (5H 5)
B5: Birm 6M 101
B69: O'bry 1G 99
B70: W Brom 8J 77
B97: Redd 4E 212
CV1: Cov 5E 152 (2F 6)
CV10: Nun 6E 88
CV21: Rugby 6B 180
CV32: Lea S 8J 217
CV34: Warw 2D 222
DY4: Tip 1M 75
DY5: P'ntt 2D 96
DY6: W Hth 1H 95
DY8: Stourb 4M 115
DY9: Lye 4E 116
WS2: Wals 7L 39
WS10: W'bry 7F 54
WS11: Cann 5E 8
WS12: Hed 4K 9
Albert St. E. B69: O'bry 2H 99
Albert Wlk. B17: Harb 4C 120
Albion Av. WV13: W'hall 7C 38
Albion Bus. Pk. B66: Smeth 1L 99
Albion Ct. CV11: Nun 6K 89
Albion Fld. Dr. B71: W Brom 5K 77
Albion Ho. B70: W Brom 7J 77
Albion Ind. Est. B70: W Brom 7G 77
CV6: Cov 2D 152
Albion Ind. Est. Rd.
B70: W Brom 7F 76
Albion Pde. DY6: W Hth 1H 95
Albion Pl. WS11: Cann 5E 8
Albion Rd. B11: S'brk 4D 122
B21: Hand 8D 78
B70: W Brom 7F 76
(not continuous)
B71: W Brom 1B 100
WS8: Bwnhls 1E 26
WV13: W'hall 7B 38
Albion Rdbt. B70: W Brom 5H 77
Albion St. B1: Birm 6H 101 (3B 4)
B69: O'bry 8E 76
B79: Tam 4C 32
CV8: Ken 4G 199
DY4: Tip 4M 75
DY5: Brie H 6D 96
DY6: W Hth 8H 73
WV1: Wolv 7D 36 (4L 7)
WV13: W'hall 7C 38
WV14: Bils 3L 53
Albion Ter. *B46: Wat O 6H 83*
(off St Pauls Ct.)
Albion Way WS7: C Ter 8F 10
Alborn Cres. B38: K Nor 1D 164
Albright Ho. *B69: O'bry 5E 98*
(off Kempsey Cl.)
Albrighton Ho. B20: Hand 6F 78
Albrighton Rd. B63: Hale 6L 117
WV7: Alb 7A 20
Albrighton Wlk. CV11: Nun 7A 90
Albright Rd. B68: O'bry 5K 99
Albury Rd. B80: Stud 5L 221
Albury Wlk. B11: S'brk 2A 122
Albutts Rd. WS8: Nort C 6B 16
Alcester Dr. B73: New O 6D 58
(not continuous)
WV13: W'hall 8K 37
Alcester Gdns. B14: K Hth 2L 143
Alcester Highway B98: Redd 1F 220
ALCESTER LANES END 4L 143
Alcester Rd. B13: Mose 7L 121
B47: H'wd 8A 144
B47: Wyt 1M 191
B48: Earls 3M 191
B60: Burc, L End 3C 188
B60: Fins, Tard, Tutn 8D 188
B80: Stud 5L 221
B94: Tan A 3A 192
B98: Beo 4B 214
Alcester Rd. Sth. B14: K Hth 2L 143
(not continuous)
Alcester St.
B12: Birm 1M 121 (8K 5)
B98: Redd 5E 212
Alcester Wlk. B97: Redd 5E 212
Alcombe Gro. B33: Stech 7L 103
Alcott Cl. B93: Dorr 7F 168
Alcott Gro. B33: Kitts G 6D 104
Alcott La. B37: Mars G 1F 124
Alcove, The WS3: Blox 7K 25
Aldborough La. B97: Redd 4B 212
Aldbourne Rd. CV1: Cov 4C 152
Aldbourne Way B38: K Nor 2D 164
Aldbury Ri. CV5: Cov 5H 151
Aldbury Rd. B14: K Hth 7A 144
Aldeburgh Cl. WS3: Blox 6G 25
Aldeford Dr. DY5: Brie H 1D 116
Alden Hurst WS7: C Ter 1F 16
Alder Av. DY11: Kidd 1K 157
Alderbrook Cl. B97: Redd 4B 212
DY3: Sed 8B 52
Alderbrooke Dr. CV11: Nun 8A 90
Alderbrook Rd. B91: Sol 6M 145
Alder Cl. B47: H'wd 3B 166
B76: Walm 2L 81
WS14: Lich 2M 19
Alder Coppice DY3: Sed 7C 52
Alder Ct. CV9: Ath 8K 49
Alder Cres. WS5: Wals 5B 56
Alder Dale WV3: Wolv 8L 35
Alderdale Av. DY3: Sed 6C 52
Alderdale Cres. B92: Sol 2E 146
Alder Dr. B37: Chel W 8H 105
Alderflat Pl. B7: Birm 4C 102
Alderford Cl. WV8: Pend 1M 35
Aldergate B79: Tam 4B 32
Alder Gro. B62: Quin 3E 118
Alderham Cl. B91: Sol 5D 146
Alderhanger La.
B94: Beo, Tan A 1D 214
B98: Beo 1C 214
Alderhithe Gro. B74: Lit A 6B 42
Alder La. B30: B'vlle 3C 142
CV7: Bal C 4J 171
Alderlea Cl. DY8: Stourb 7A 116
Alderley Cres. WS3: Wals 4L 39
Alderley Rd. B61: B'gve 1K 209
Alderman Bowen Leisure Cen.
6G 103
Alderman Gee Hall
CV12: Bed 5G 111
(off Dempster Rd.)
ALDERMAN'S GREEN 6H 131
Alderman's Grn. Ind. Est.
CV2: Ald G 6K 131
Alderman's Grn. Rd.
CV2: Ald G 7H 131
(not continuous)
Aldermans La. B97: Redd 3B 212
Alderman Way
CV33: W Weth 2K 219
Alder Mdw. Cl. CV6: Cov 5D 130
Aldermere Rd. DY11: Kidd 1J 157
Alderminster Cl. B97: Redd 5E 220
Alderminster Rd. B91: Sol 8B 146
CV5: E Grn 5G 151
Aldermoor La. CV3: Cov 8G 153
Aldermore Dr. B75: S Cold 3M 59
Alderney Cl. CV6: Cov 7B 130
CV11: Bram 3F 112
Alderney Gdns. B38: K Nor 8D 142
Alderpark Rd. B91: Sol 6M 145
Alderpits Rd. B34: S End 2D 104
(not continuous)
Alder Rd. B12: Bal H 5A 122
CV6: Cov 7G 131
DY6: K'wfrd 4M 95
WS10: W'bry 3G 55
WV1: Wolv 7D 36 (4L 7)
ALDERS, THE 3L 31
Alders, The B62: Roms 5M 139
CV12: Bed 7E 110
Alder's Cl. B98: Redd 6G 213
Alders Dr. B98: Redd 5M 213
Aldersea Dr. B6: Aston 2M 101
Aldersgate B78: K'bry 2D 62
CV11: Nun 6J 89
Aldershaw Rd. B26: Yard 4L 123
Aldershaws B90: Dic H 4G 167
Alders La. B79: Tam 3L 31
CV10: Nun 2A 88
Aldersley Av. WV6: Tett 2L 35
Aldersley Cl. WV6: Tett 2M 35
Aldersley High School Sports Cen.
8K 21
Aldersley Leisure Village 3M 35
Aldersley Rd. WV6: Tett 4L 35
Aldersley Stadium 3M 35
Aldersmead Rd. B31: N'fld 7C 142
Alderson Rd. B8: Salt 5F 102
Alders Rd. CV34: Warw 5D 222
Alderton Cl. B91: Sol 8B 146
Alderton Dr. WV3: Wolv 1L 51
Alderton M. CV31: Lea S 3C 224
Alder Way B60: B'gve 7B 188
B74: S'tly 1L 57
WS12: Haz 3A 10
Alderwood Pl. B91: Sol 6B 146
Alderwood Pct. DY3: Sed 8C 52
Alderwood Ri. DY3: Up Gor 4D 74
Aldgate Dr. DY5: Brie H 2C 116
Aldgate Gro. B19: Birm 4K 101
Aldin Cl. B78: M Oak 7L 31
Aldington Cl. B98: Redd 8F 212
Aldin Way LE10: Hinc 6G 69
Aldis Cl. B28: Hall G 8E 122
WS2: Wals 2G 55
Aldis Rd. WS2: Wals 2G 55
Aldrich Av. CV4: Tile H 6E 150
ALDRIDGE 3H 41
Aldridge By-Pass
WS9: A'rdge 4H 41
Aldridge Cl. B68: O'bry 5J 99
B78: B'moor 1M 47
DY8: Word 1L 115
Aldridge Rd. B44: Gt Barr 7J 57
B68: O'bry 1H 119
B74: Lit A 4M 41
B74: S'tly 8K 41
LE10: Burb 3K 91
WS4: Wals 6C 40
WS9: A'rdge 4M 41
Aldridge Sailing Club 1E 40
Aldridge St. WS10: Darl 2D 54
Aldridge Youth Theatre 3H 41
Aldrin Way CV4: Canly 4K 173
Aldwick Cl. CV32: Lill 5A 218
Aldwych Cl. WS9: A'rdge 1H 41
Aldwyck Dr. WV3: Wolv 1G 51
Aldwyn Av. B13: Mose 7M 121
Alec Wilson Sports Cen. 5H 111
Alesmore Mdw. WS13: Lich 3F 18
Alesworth Dr. LE10: Burb 5M 91
Alexander Av. LE9: Earl S 1F 70
Alexander Cl. B61: Cats 8A 162
Alexander Ct. CV34: Warw 2F 222
Alexander Gdns. B42: P Barr 6K 79
LE10: Hinc 7J 69
Alexander Hill DY5: Quar B 1F 116
Alexander Ind. Pk. WV14: Bils 5J 53
Alexander Rd. B27: A Grn 5H 123
B67: Smeth 7L 99
CV12: Bed 6J 111
WS2: Wals 7F 38
WV8: Bilb 6J 21
Alexander Ter. B67: Smeth 3M 99
Alexander Way B8: Salt 6F 102
Alexandra Av. B21: Hand 2D 100
Alexandra Ct. CV3: Cov 7G 153
CV8: Ken 5G 199
CV9: Ath 1L 65
CV21: Rugby 6B 180
(off James St.)
DY3: Gorn 6C 74
(off Redhall Rd.)
Alexandra Cres. B71: W Brom 1L 77
Alexandra Ho. B27: A Grn 7K 123
WS13: Lich 2G 19
Alexandra Ind. Est. DY4: Tip 3A 76
Alexandra M. B79: Tam 4C 32
Alexandra Pl. DY1: Dud 5H 75
WV14: Bils 3K 53
Alexandra Rd. B5: Bal H 3L 121
B21: Hand 2D 100
B30: Stir 3G 143
B63: Hale 6M 117
CV1: Cov 5F 152
CV21: Rugby 5B 180
CV31: Lea S 3A 224
DY4: Tip 4M 75
WS1: Wals 2L 55
WS10: Darl 3E 54
WV4: Penn 4A 52
Alexandra St. CV11: Nun 5H 89
DY1: Dud 8H 75
WV3: Wolv 8B 36 (5G 7)
Alexandra Ter. CV6: Cov 5C 130
Alexandra Theatre 7K 101 (6F 4)
Alexandra Wlk.
CV21: Rugby 6B 180
(off James St.)
Alexandra Way B69: Tiv 7A 76
WS9: A'rdge 4H 41
Alex Grierson Cl. CV3: Bin 2L 175
Alfall Rd. CV2: Cov 4H 153
Alford Cl. B45: Redn 2J 163
Alfreda Av. B47: H'wd 1M 165
Alfred Ct. B60: S Prior 7L 209
Alfred Grn. Cl. CV22: Rugby 7A 180
Alfred Gunn Ho. B68: O'bry 5H 99
Alfred Rd. B11: S'hll 4B 122
B21: Hand 1E 100
CV1: Cov 5F 152
Alfred Squire Rd. WV11: Wed 4J 37
Alfred St. B6: Aston 1B 102
B12: Bal H 4B 122
B14: K Hth 2M 143
B66: Smeth 2C 100
B70: W Brom 6K 77
B79: Tam 4A 32
CV21: Rugby 6M 179
WS3: Blox 8H 25
WS10: Darl 4C 54
Alfreds Well B61: D'frd 3J 187
Alfreton Cl. LE10: Burb 4M 91
Alfriston Rd. CV3: Finh 5C 174
Alfryth Ct. *B15: Edg 1J 121*
(off Lee Cres.)
Algate Cl. CV6: Cov 6C 130
Algernon Rd. B16: Edg 5D 100
Alhambra Rd. B60: B'gve 8C 188
Alice Arnold Ho. CV2: Cov 8H 131
Alice Cl. CV12: Bed 8F 110
Alice St. WV14: Bils 3K 53
Alice Wlk. WV14: Bils 4K 53
Alicia Cl. CV22: Caw 1G 205
Alison Cl. DY4: Tip 7A 54
Alison Dr. DY8: Stourb 7M 115
Alison Rd. B62: Hale 6F 118
Alison Sq. CV2: Ald G 5H 131
Allan Cl. B66: Smeth 4B 100
DY8: Word 1M 115
All Angels Wlk. B68: O'bry 5H 99
Allan Rd. CV6: Cov 5M 151
Allans Cl. CV23: Clift D 4G 181
Allans Dr. CV23: Clift D 4G 181
Allans La. CV23: Clift D 4G 181
Allard B77: Glas 7E 32
Allard Ho. CV3: W'hall 3H 175
Allard Way CV3: Bin, Cov 2G 175
Allbut St. B64: Crad H 8K 97
Allcock St. B9: Birm 8A 102 (6L 5)
DY4: Tip 1C 76
Allcroft Rd. B11: Tys 7F 122
Allenby Cl. DY6: K'wfrd 4A 96
Allen Cl. B43: Gt Barr 2E 78
B80: Stud 6L 221
Allendale Av. B80: Stud 6L 221
Allendale Ct. B80: Stud 6L 221
Allendale Cres. B80: Stud 6L 221
Allendale Gro. B43: Gt Barr 1E 78
Allendale Rd. B25: Yard 2H 123
B76: Walm 1L 81
Allen Dr. B70: W Brom 8M 77
WS10: Darl 3C 54
ALLEN END 3F 60
Allen Ho. B43: Gt Barr 2E 78
Allen Rd. DY4: Tip 8M 53
WS10: W'bry 4F 54
WV6: Wolv 6M 35
Allens Av. B18: Hock 3F 100
B71: W Brom 2G 77
Allens Cl. WV12: W'hall 4B 38
CV9: Bad E 1C 64
Allens Cft. Rd. B14: K Hth 4H 143
Allens Farm Rd. B31: N'fld 6K 141
Allen's La. WS3: Pels 7M 25
Allensmead B77: Wiln 7C 32
Allensmore Cl. B98: Redd 7M 213
Allen's Rd. B18: Hock 3F 100
Allen St. B70: W Brom 6H 77
B77: Two G 8C 32
Allerdale Rd. WS8: Clay 2E 26
Allerton Cl. CV2: Cov 7L 153
Allerton Ct. B71: W Brom 8J 55
Allerton La. B71: W Brom 1J 77
Allerton Rd. B25: Yard 2H 123
ALLESLEY 3H 151
Allesley By-Pass CV5: Cov 3H 151
Allesley Cl. B74: S Cold 3J 59
Allesley Ct. CV5: Alle 3G 151
Allesley Cft. CV5: Alle 3G 151
Allesley Hall Dr.
CV5: Alle, Cov 4J 151
Allesley Old Rd. CV5: Cov 4J 151
Allesley Rd. B92: Olton 1K 145
CV21: N'bld A 3M 179
Allesley St. B6: Aston 4L 101
Alleston Rd. WV10: Bush 7D 22
Alleston Wlk. WV10: Bush 7D 22
Alley, The DY3: Lwr G 6B 74
Alleyne Gro. B24: Erd 7G 81
Alleyne Rd. B24: Erd 8G 81
Alliance Cl. CV11: Nun 6M 89
Alliance Trad. Est.
CV4: Tile H 8G 151
Alliance Way CV2: Cov 4G 153
Allibone Cl. CV31: W'nsh 5A 224
Allied Cl. CV6: Cov 7D 130
Allingham Gro. B43: Gt Barr 5L 57
Allington Cl. WS5: Wals 1D 56
Allison St. B5: Birm 7M 101 (6J 5)
Allitt Gro. CV8: Ken 4H 199
Allman Rd. B24: Erd 5H 81
Allmyn Dr. B74: S'tly 3A 58
All Oaks La. CV23: Brin 6M 155
Allport Rd. WS11: Cann 8E 8
Allport St. WS11: Cann 8E 8
ALL SAINTS 4G 101
All Saints Av. DY12: Bew 5C 156
All Saints Cl. CV7: Withy 4M 133
LE9: Sap 2K 93
All Saints Dr. B74: Four O 7F 42
All Saints Ind. Est.
B18: Hock 4G 101
All Saints La. *CV1: Cov 4F 6*
(off Lwr. Ford St.)
CV1: Cov 6E 152
(Oxford St.)
All Saints Rd. B14: K Hth 3L 143
B18: Hock 4H 101
B61: B'gve 6A 188
CV12: Bed 8F 110
CV34: Warw 8G 217
WS10: Darl 3E 54
WV2: Wolv 1D 52 (7K 7)
All Saints Sq. CV12: Bed 6H 111
All Saints St. B18: Hock 4G 101
All Saints Way B71: W Brom 5K 77
Allsops Cl. B65: Row R 5M 97
Allton Av. B78: M Oak 8K 31
Allton Ct. B77: Glas 6E 32
Allwell Dr. B14: K Hth 7M 143
Allwood Gdns. B32: Bart G 7G 119
Alma Av. DY4: Tip 2A 76
Alma Ct. CV11: Bram 3F 112
Alma Cres. B7: Birm 5B 102
Alma Ind. Est. WS10: Darl 3C 54
Alma Pas. B17: Harb 3D 120
Alma Pl. B12: Bal H 4B 122
DY2: Dud 8J 75
Almar Ct. WV8: Pend 8M 21
Alma Rd. LE10: Hinc 8K 69
Alma St. B19: Hock 3L 101
B63: Crad 4J 117
B66: Smeth 3C 100
CV1: Cov 6E 152 (4F 6)
WS2: Wals 5K 39
WS10: Darl 3C 54
WS10: W'bry 6H 55
WV10: Wolv 6F 36
WV13: W'hall 7B 38
Alma Way B19: Loz 2K 101
Alma Works WS10: Darl 4D 54
Almeys La. LE9: Earl S 1F 70
Almond Av. CV10: Nun 3C 88
CV32: Lea S 6M 217
DY11: Kidd 1H 157
WS2: Wals 5E 38
WS5: Wals 5A 56
Almond Cl. B29: W Cas 3A 142
CV23: Barby 8J 207
WS3: Pels 7M 25
WS11: Hth H 7J 9
Almond Cft. B42: Gt Barr 3F 78
Almond Gro. CV21: N'bld A 2L 179
CV34: Warw 8G 217
WV6: Wolv 5C 36
Almond Rd. DY6: K'wfrd 1L 95
WS12: Hunt 1D 8
Almond Tree Av. CV2: Cov 7H 131
Almond Way DY13: Stour S 5D 182
LE9: Earl S 3E 70
Almsbury Ct. B26: Sheld 5C 124
Alms Ho's. WS1: Wals 1K 55
WV4: Penn 6M 51
Almshouses CV12: Bed 6J 111
CV34: Warw 3E 222
(off Castle Hill)
Alnwick Cl. WS12: Hth H 7L 9
Alnwick Ho. B23: Erd 3F 80
Alnwick Rd. WS3: Blox 5H 25
Alperton Dr. DY9: W'cte 7E 116
Alpha Bus. Pk. CV2: Cov 8K 131
Alpha Cl. B12: Bal H 3L 121
Alpha Ho. CV2: Cov 6C 130
Alpha Twr. B1: Birm 7J 101 (6D 4)
Alpha Way WS6: Gt Wyr 1G 25
Alpine Ct. CV8: Ken 3G 199
Alpine Dr. DY2: Neth 5H 97
WS12: Hed 5K 9
Alpine Ri. CV3: Cov 4A 174
Alpine Way WV3: Wolv 7J 35
Alport Cft. B9: Birm 7B 102
Alspath La. CV5: E Grn 5F 150
Alspath Rd. CV7: Mer 8J 127
Alstom Sports & Social Club
8D 180
Alston Cl. B74: Four O 7G 43
B91: Sol 3D 146
WS12: Hth H 7L 9
Alston Gro. B9: Bord G 6H 103
Alston Ho. B69: O'bry 3D 98
Alston Rd. B9: Bord G 6H 103
B69: O'bry 2E 98
B91: Sol 3D 146
Alston St. B16: Birm 7G 101
Althorpe Dr. B93: Dorr 6D 168
Althorpe Ind. Est.
CV31: Lea S 2A 224
Althorpe St. CV31: Lea S 2A 224
Alton Av. WV12: W'hall 5B 38
Alton Cl. B97: Redd 8B 212
CV2: Cov 7K 131
WV10: Bush 6E 22
Alton Gro. B71: W Brom 2L 77
DY2: Dud 8L 75
WS11: Cann 8B 8
Alton Rd. B29: S Oak 6F 120
Alum Cl. CV6: Cov 1D 152
Alum Dr. B9: Bord G 6G 103
Alumhurst Av. B8: W End 5G 103
ALUM ROCK 6H 103
Alum Rock Rd. B8: Salt 4D 102
Alumwell Cl. WS2: Wals 8H 39
Alumwell Rd. WS2: Wals 8H 39

Alvaston Cl.—Arley Dr.

Alvaston Cl. WS3: Blox ... 6J 25
ALVECHURCH ... 3B 190
Alvechurch Highway
B60: L Ash ... 6C 162
B97: Redd ... 3E 212
B98: Redd ... 3E 212
Alvechurch Ho. *B60: B'gve* ... *6B 188*
(off Burcot La.)
Alvechurch Rd. B31: Longb ... 1B 164
B63: Hale ... 7M 117
Alvechurch Station (Rail) ... 5A 190
ALVECOTE ... 3K 33
Alvecote Cotts. B79: A'cte ... 3K 33
Alvecote La. B79: A'cte ... 3K 33
Alvecote Pools Nature Reserve ... 5M 33
Alvecote Priory (remains of) ... 4L 33
Alveley Cl. B98: Redd ... 5K 213
Alverley Cl. DY6: W Hth ... 1H 95
Alverley Rd. CV6: Cov ... 3C 152
Alverstoke Cl. WV9: Pend ... 7A 22
Alverstone Rd. CV2: Cov ... 5G 153
Alverton Cl. B77: Dost ... 5C 46
Alveston Cl. B98: Redd ... 7J 213
Alveston Gro. B9: Bord G ... 7H 103
B93: Know ... 2H 169
Alveston Pl. CV32: Lea S ... 8A 218
Alveston Rd. B47: H'wd ... 2A 166
Alvia Ho. CV1: Cov ... 6C 6
Alvin Cl. B62: B'hth ... 8F 98
CV3: Bin ... 8M 153
Alvington Cl. WV12: W'hall ... 5D 38
Alvis Cl. B79: Tam ... 2M 31
Alvis Retail Pk. CV5: Cov ... 6A 152
Alvis Wlk. B36: Cas B ... 8F 82
Alwen St. DY8: Word ... 7M 95
Alwin Rd. B65: Row R ... 7B 98
Alwold Ct. B29: W Cas ... 7M 119
Alwold Rd.
B29: W Cas, S Oak ... 7M 119
Alwyn B77: Wiln ... 2E 46
Alwyn Cl. WS6: Gt Wyr ... 6F 14
Alwyn Freeman Ct.
CV7: Ker E ... *3A 130*
(off Somers Rd.)
Alwynn Wlk. B23: Erd ... 6B 80
Alwyn Rd. CV22: Bil ... 1J 205
Amal Way B6: Witt ... 7M 79
(not continuous)
Amanda Av. WV4: Penn ... 5M 51
Amanda Dr. B26: Yard ... 8A 104
Amazon Lofts B1: Birm ... 2B 4
Ambassador Ct.
CV32: Lea S ... 6M 217
Ambassador Rd.
B26: Birm A ... 5J 125
Ambell Cl. B65: Row R ... 4M 97
Amber Bus. Village
B77: Amin ... 6H 33
Amber Cl. B77: Amin ... 6H 33
Amber Ct. B77: Amin ... 6H 33
Amber Dr. B69: O'bry ... 4G 99
Ambergate Cl. B97: Redd ... 4B 212
WS3: Blox ... 6J 25
Ambergate Dr. DY6: W Hth ... 1J 95
Amber Gro. WS11: Hth H ... 6J 9
Amberley Av. CV12: Bulk ... 6C 112
Amberley Ct. B29: S Oak ... 1E 142
Amberley Grn. B43: Gt Barr ... 3E 78
Amberley Gro. B6: Witt ... 6A 80
Amberley Rd. B92: Olton ... 5M 123
Amberley Way B74: S'tly ... 8L 41
Amber Way B62: Hale ... 3B 118
Amberwood Cl. WS2: Wals ... 6D 38
Ambien Rd. CV9: Ath ... 2K 65
Ambion Way LE10: Hinc ... 8M 69
AMBLECOTE ... 2L 115
Amblecote Av. B44: Gt Barr ... 7L 57
Amblecote Rd. DY5: Brie H ... 2C 116
DY10: Kidd ... 4B 158
Ambler Gro. CV2: Cov ... 6J 153
Ambleside B32: Bart G ... 8J 119
CV2: W'grve S ... 7L 131
CV21: Brow ... 2D 180
LE9: Barw ... 2C 70
Ambleside Cl. WV14: Bils ... 6L 53
Ambleside Dr. DY5: Brie H ... 1C 116
Ambleside Gro. WV12: W'hall ... 8B 24
Ambleside Rd. CV12: Bed ... 7G 111
Ambleside Way B60: B'gve ... 8B 188
CV11: Nun ... 3L 89
DY6: K'wfrd ... 3K 95
Ambrose Cl. CV21: Rugby ... 3C 180
WV13: W'hall ... 7L 37
Ambrose Cres. DY6: K'wfrd ... 1K 95
Ambury Way B43: Gt Barr ... 1D 78
AMC Cinema ... 8G 101
Amelas Cl. DY5: Brie H ... 8A 96
Amelia Cl. CV12: Bulk ... 6C 112
Amersham Cl. B32: Quin ... 4L 119
CV5: Cov ... 5H 151
Amesbury Rd. B13: Mose ... 6L 121
Ames Rd. WS10: Darl ... 2C 54
Amethyst Ct. B92: Olton ... 8M 123
AMF Bowling
Coventry ... 6H 153
Oxley ... 3C 36
Wolverhampton ... 1D 52 (7K 7)
Amherst Av. B20: Hand ... 6G 79
Amherst Bus. Cen.
CV34: Warw ... 2B 222
Amherst Rd. CV8: Ken ... 2E 198
Amicombe B77: Wiln ... 8J 33
AMINGTON ... 5G 33
Amington Cl. B75: R'ley ... 5K 43
Amington Ind. Est. B77: Amin ... 6H 33
(not continuous)
Amington Pk. B77: Amin ... 3G 33
Amington Rd. B25: Yard ... 3H 123
B77: Tam, Amin ... 5C 32
B90: Shir ... 1G 167
Amiss Gdns. B10: Small H ... 1C 122
Amity Cl. B66: Smeth ... 4B 100
Amos Av. CV10: Nun ... 7H 89
WV11: Wed ... 2H 37
Amos-Jaques Rd.
CV12: Bed ... 5G 111
Amos La. WV11: Wed ... 2J 37
Amos Rd. DY9: W'cte ... 7F 116
Amphlett Ct. B60: B'gve ... 7A 188
Amphlett Cft. DY4: Tip ... 5B 76
Amphletts Cl. DY2: Neth ... 6L 97
Ampton Rd. B15: Edg ... 2H 121
Amroth Cl. B45: Redn ... 2H 163
Amroth M. CV31: Lea S ... 3C 224
Amwell Gro. B14: K Hth ... 6M 143
Amy Cl. CV6: Longf ... 5F 130
Anchorage Rd. B23: Erd ... 6D 80
B74: S Cold ... 3H 59
Anchor Brook Ind. Pk.
WS9: A'rdge ... 2F 40
Anchor Cl. B16: Edg ... 8E 100
B77: Amin ... 5E 32
Anchor Cres. B18: Win G ... 4F 100
Anchor Flds. DY10: Kidd ... 3M 157
Anchor Hill DY5: Brie H ... 8C 96
Anchor La. B91: Sol ... 3D 146
WV14: Cose ... 7H 53
(not continuous)
Anchor Mdw. WS9: A'rdge ... 3G 41
Anchor Pde. WS9: A'rdge ... 3H 41
Anchor Rd. WS9: A'rdge ... 3H 41
WV14: Cose ... 7J 53
Anchorway Rd. CV3: Finh ... 5A 174
Anders B79: Tam ... 3A 32
Andersleigh Dr. WV14: Cose ... 1G 75
Anderson Av. CV22: Rugby ... 1A 206
Anderson Cres. B43: Gt Barr ... 6E 56
Anderson Dr. CV31: W'nsh ... 7A 224
Anderson Gdns. DY4: Tip ... 5A 76
Anderson Rd. B23: Erd ... 3E 80
B66: Smeth ... 8A 100
B67: Smeth ... 8A 100
DY4: Tip ... 4A 76
Anders Sq. WV6: Pert ... 5E 34
Anderton Cl. B74: S Cold ... 2G 59
Anderton Ct. B13: Mose ... 7A 122
Anderton Pk. Rd.
B13: Mose ... 6A 122
Anderton Rd. B11: S'brk ... 3B 122
CV6: Ald G ... 4H 131
CV12: Bed ... 8C 110
Anderton St.
B1: Birm ... 6H 101 (4A 4)
Andover Cres. DY6: K'wfrd ... 5M 95
Andover Pl. WS11: Cann ... 5G 9
Andover St. B5: Birm ... 7M 101 (5K 5)
Andressy M. B61: B'gve ... 4A 188
Andrew Cl. CV8: Bag ... 7F 174
CV13: Stoke G ... 2D 68
WV12: W'hall ... 3D 38
Andrew Ct. B76: Walm ... 6M 59
Andrew Dr. WV12: W'hall ... 3D 38
Andrew Gdns. B21: Hand ... 7E 78
Andrew Rd. B63: Hale ... 6A 118
B71: W Brom ... 7M 55
DY4: Tip ... 8A 54
Andrews Cl. DY5: Quar B ... 1E 116
Andrews Ho. WS13: Lich ... 2G 19
Andrews Rd. WS9: Wals W ... 5H 27
Anerley Gro. B44: Gt Barr ... 5M 57
Anerley Rd. B44: Gt Barr ... 5M 57
Anfield Ct. CV31: Lea S ... 2B 224
Angela Av. B65: Row R ... 5D 98
CV2: W'grve S ... 8L 131
Angela Pl. WV14: Bils ... 3K 53
Angel Cft. WS7: C Ter ... 8E 10
Angelica B77: Amin ... 5F 32
Angelica Cl. WS5: Wals ... 6A 56
Angelina St. B12: Birm ... 1M 121
Angel Pas. DY8: Stourb ... 4A 116
Angel St. B97: Up Ben ... 8H 211
DY1: Dud ... 1H 97
WV13: W'hall ... 7A 38
Anglesey Av. B36: Cas B ... 2H 105
Anglesey Bus. Pk.
WS12: Hed ... 5L 9
Anglesey Cl. CV5: Alle ... 2H 151
WS7: Chase ... 5E 16
Anglesey Cres. WS8: Bwnhls ... 7F 16
WS12: Hed ... 4J 9
Anglesey M. WS12: Hed ... 4J 9
Anglesey Rd. WS8: Bwnhls ... 7F 16
WS13: Lich ... 7H 13
Anglesey St. B19: Loz ... 2J 101
WS12: Hed ... 4H 9
Angless Way CV8: Ken ... 6F 198
Anglian Rd. WS9: A'rdge ... 3D 40
Anglia Rd. WS11: Cann ... 6D 8
Anglo African Ind. Pk.
B69: O'bry ... 7E 76
Angorfa Cl. WS13: Lich ... 2F 18
Angus Cl. B71: W Brom ... 3J 77
CV5: E Grn ... 5G 151
CV8: Ken ... 3J 199
Angus Rd. LE9: Barw ... 3A 70
Anita Av. DY4: Tip ... 7A 76
Anita Cft. B23: Erd ... 7D 80
Ankadine Rd. DY8: Amb ... 3B 116
Anker Cl. WS7: Burn ... 3K 17
Anker Ct. CV11: Nun ... 6M 89
Ankerdine Av.
DY13: Stour S ... *8D 182*
(off Langdale Rd.)
Ankerdine Ct. B63: Hale ... 6A 118
Anker Dr. B77: Tam ... 5B 32
B79: Tam ... 5B 32
CV23: Long L ... 4H 179
Ankermoor Cl. B34: S End ... 3B 104
Ankermoor Ct. B77: Tam ... 4E 32
Ankerside B78: Pole ... 1K 49
Ankerside Shop. Cen.
B79: Tam ... 5B 32
Anker St. CV11: Nun ... 6K 89
Anker Vw. B77: Tam ... 6C 32
B78: Pole ... 1A 48
Anley Way CV6: Cov ... 3C 152
Annan Av. WV10: Bush ... 2E 36
Ann Cft. B26: Sheld ... 5D 124
Anne Cl. B70: W Brom ... 6E 76
Anne Ct. B76: Walm ... 6A 60
Anne Cres. CV3: W'hall ... 4J 175
WS11: Cann ... 3E 8
Anne Gro. DY4: Tip ... 8B 54
Anne Rd. B66: Smeth ... 2C 100
DY5: Quar B ... 8G 97
WV4: Penn ... 3B 52
Ann Rd. B47: Wyt ... 6A 166
Annscroft B38: K Nor ... 7D 142
Ann St. WV13: W'hall ... 6B 38
Ansbro Cl. B18: Win G ... 4F 100
Anscluf Rd. DY5: Brie H ... 8B 96
Ansell Dr. CV6: Longf ... 4G 131
Ansell Rd. B11: S'brk ... 3C 122
B24: Erd ... 8F 80
Ansell Way CV34: Warw ... 2D 222
ANSLEY ... 5H 87
Ansley Cl. B98: Redd ... 8M 213
ANSLEY COMMON ... 1L 87
Ansley Comn. CV10: Ans C ... 1L 87
Ansley La. CV7: Old A ... 7E 86
CV10: Ansl ... 7F 86
Ansley Rd. CV10: Nun ... 6J 87
Ansley Way B92: Sol ... 2D 146
Anslow Gdns. WV11: Wed ... 8M 23
Anslow Rd. B23: Erd ... 4C 80
Anson Av. WS13: Lich ... 1G 19
Anson Cl. CV22: Bil ... 7J 179
WS6: Gt Wyr ... 8F 14
WS7: Burn ... 2J 17
WV6: Pert ... 4E 34
Anson Ct. B70: W Brom ... 2F 76
B78: Faz ... 1B 46
Anson Gro. B27: A Grn ... 7K 123
Anson Rd. B70: W Brom ... 3E 76
WS2: Wals ... 7E 38
WS6: Gt Wyr ... 8F 14
Anson Way CV2: W'grve S ... 1M 153
Anstey Cft. B37: F'bri ... 5G 105
Anstey Gro. B27: A Grn ... 8H 123
Anstey Rd. B44: K'sdng ... 3L 79
Anston Junc. WS2: Wals ... 8E 38
Anston Way WV11: Wed ... 2K 37
Anstree Cl. WS6: C Hay ... 8D 14
Anstruther Rd. B15: Edg ... 2D 120
ANSTY ... 6D 132
Ansty Dr. WS12: Hth H ... 8K 9
Ansty Rd. CV2: Cov ... 5J 153
CV2: W'grve S ... 3M 153
CV23: Brin, Stret F ... 3J 155
Antelope Gdns. CV34: Warw ... 1C 222
Anthony Rd. B8: Salt ... 6E 102
Anthony Way CV2: Cov ... 7J 153
Anton Cl. DY12: Bew ... 4D 156
Anton Dr. B76: Walm ... 3A 82
Antony Gardner Cres.
CV31: W'nsh ... 5A 224
Antony Rd. B90: Shir ... 8H 145
Antrim Cl. CV5: Alle ... 2G 151
Antringham Gdns. B15: Edg ... 1D 120
Antrobus Rd. B21: Hand ... 8E 78
B73: Bold ... 8E 58
Anvil Cres. WV14: Cose ... 7J 53
Anvil Dr. B69: O'bry ... 3E 98
Anvil Wlk. B70: W Brom ... 5F 76
APES DALE ... 3F 188
Apex Bus. Pk. WS11: Nort C ... 4M 15
Apex Ind. Pk. DY4: Tip ... 1D 76
Apex Rd. WS8: Bwnhls ... 2C 26
Apley Rd. DY8: Woll ... 2L 115
Apollo B79: Tam ... 3M 31
Apollo Cl. WS11: Cann ... 4G 9
Apollo Cft. B24: Erd ... 6K 81
Apollo Rd. B68: O'bry ... 3J 99
DY9: W'cte ... 4G 117
Apollo Way B20: Hand ... 8K 79
B66: Smeth ... 4C 100
CV34: Warw ... 4K 223
Apperley Way B63: Crad ... 2H 117
Appian Cl. B14: K Hth ... 4L 143
B77: Two G ... 2C 46
Appian Way B90: Ches G ... 5K 167
Applebee Rd. LE10: Burb ... 3J 91
Applebees Mdw. LE10: Hinc ... 3E 90
Appleby Cl. B14: K Hth ... 4K 143
Appleby Gdns. WV11: Ess ... 7C 24
Appleby Gro. B90: M'path ... 3B 168
Appleby Ho. LE10: Hinc ... 8L 69
Applecross B74: Four O ... 8F 42
Applecross Cl. CV4: W'wd H ... 3F 172
Appledore Cl. WS6: Gt Wyr ... 6G 15
WS12: Wim ... 6L 9
Appledore Ct. WS3: Blox ... 1H 39
Appledore Dr. CV5: Alle ... 4F 150
Appledore Rd. WS5: Wals ... 1D 56
Appledore Ter. WS5: Wals ... 1D 56
Appledorne Gdns.
B34: S End ... 3B 104
Apple Gro. CV22: Bil ... 7H 179
Apple Pie La. CV10: Harts ... 6B 66
Applesham Cl. B11: S'brk ... 3D 122
Appleton Av. B43: Gt Barr ... 1D 78
DY8: Stourb ... 7A 116
Appleton Cl. B30: B'vlle ... 1E 142
Appleton Cres. WV4: Penn ... 4A 52
Apple Tree Cl. B23: Erd ... 5B 80
DY10: Kidd ... 1A 158
LE9: Barw ... 1B 70
Appletree Cl. B31: Longb ... 8M 141
B91: Cath B ... 4H 147
Appletree Gro. WS9: A'rdge ... 5H 41
WV6: Wolv ... 4C 36
Appletree La. B97: Redd ... 4A 212
Appletrees Cres. B61: B'gve ... 3M 187
Apple Wlk. WS11: Hth H ... 7J 9
Applewood Gro. B64: Old H ... 1M 117
Appleyard Cl. CV12: Bed ... 7H 111
Appollo Cinema ... 1M 223
Approach, The CV31: Lea S ... 3M 223
April Cft. B13: Mose ... 6B 122
Apse Cl. WV5: Wom ... 2F 72
Apsley Cl. B68: O'bry ... 2G 119
Apsley Cft. B38: K Nor ... 7H 143
Apsley Gro. B24: Erd ... 7G 81
B93: Dorr ... 7F 168
Apsley Ho. B64: Old H ... 7M 97
Apsley Rd. B68: O'bry ... 2G 119
Aqua Pl. CV21: Rugby ... 4C 180
Aqueduct La. B48: A'chu ... 2M 189
Aqueduct Rd. B90: Shir ... 7E 144
Aragon Dr. B73: S Cold ... 3G 59
CV34: Warw ... 3J 223
Arbor Cl. B77: Tam ... 6D 32
Arbor Ct. B71: W Brom ... 3L 77
Arboretum, The CV4: Canly ... 6K 173
Arboretum Rd. WS1: Wals ... 7M 39
Arbor Way B37: Chel W ... 8J 105
Arbour Cl. CV8: Ken ... 6H 199
CV22: Rugby ... 2K 205
Arbour Ga. WS9: Wals W ... 5H 27
Arbour M. WS11: Nort C ... 3M 15
Arbourtree Ct. WV5: Wom ... 2H 73
Arbour Tree La.
B93: Chad E ... 2M 195
Arbury Av. CV6: Cov ... 7E 130
CV12: Bed ... 6G 111
Arbury Cl. CV32: Lill ... 6A 218
Arbury Dr. DY8: Word ... 6K 95
Arbury Gth. CV10: Nun ... 6C 88
Arbury Hall ... 2D 110
Arbury Hall Rd. B90: Shir ... 1K 167
Arbury Rd. CV10: Nun ... 7C 88
Arbury Wlk. B76: Min ... 4D 82
Arcade B31: N'fld ... 5A 142
Arcade, The CV9: Ath ... 1K 65
DY3: Up Gor ... 4E 74
WS1: Wals ... 8L 39
Arcadia *B70: W Brom* ... *6J 77*
(off W. Bromwich Ringway)
Arcadian Cinema ... 8L 101
Arcadian Shop. Cen.
B5: Birm ... 8L 101 (7G 5)
Arcal St. DY3: Sed ... 2E 74
Arch, The B9: Birm ... 7A 102 (6L 5)
Archer Cl. B68: O'bry ... 4H 99
B80: Stud ... 5K 221
WS10: W'bry ... 6E 54
Archer Ct. DY9: W'cte ... 7E 116
Archer Gdns. B64: Crad H ... 8J 97
Archer Rd. B14: Yard W ... 5C 144
B98: Redd ... 5E 212
CV8: Ken ... 6E 198
WS3: Blox ... 3L 39
Archers Cl. B23: Erd ... 1D 80
(not continuous)
Archers Spinney CV21: Hillm ... 1H 207
Archery Flds. CV34: Warw ... 3F 222
Archery Rd. CV7: Mer ... 8H 127
CV31: Lea S ... 1L 223
Arches, The B10: Small H ... 1B 122
Arches Bus. Cen.
CV21: Rugby ... 4C 180
Arches Ind. Est.
CV21: Rugby ... 5D 180
Arches Ind. Est., The
CV1: Cov ... 6A 152
Arches La. CV21: Rugby ... 4C 180
Arch Hill DY10: Kidd ... 3L 157
Arch Hill St. DY2: Neth ... 4J 97
Archibald Rd. B19: Loz ... 1J 101
Arch Rd. CV2: Cov ... 4L 153
Archway, The WS4: Wals ... 6M 39
Arcot Rd. B28: Hall G ... 7F 122
Ardath Rd. B38: K Nor ... 7G 143
Ardav Rd. B70: W Brom ... 1F 76
Ardedale B90: Shir ... 1J 167
Arden Av. CV9: Ath ... 1L 65
Arden Bldgs. B93: Dorr ... 6F 168
Arden Cl. B77: Amin ... 4E 32
CV7: Bal C ... 2H 171
CV7: Mer ... 8J 127
CV22: Bil ... 4K 205
CV31: Lea S ... 4B 224
CV34: Warw ... 8G 217
DY8: Woll ... 2L 115
DY8: Word ... 6J 95
Ardencote Rd. B13: Mose ... 2A 144
Arden Ct. B24: Erd ... 6H 81
B42: P Barr ... 5K 79
B92: H Ard ... 2A 148
CV3: Bin W ... 2D 176
DY3: Lwr G ... *6D 74*
(off Chiltern Cl.)
Arden Cft. B46: Col ... 8M 83
B92: Sol ... 5C 124
Arden Dr. B26: Yard ... 2M 123
B73: W Grn ... 1H 81
B75: S Cold ... 4B 60
(not continuous)
B93: Dorr ... 7F 168
Arden Forest Est.
CV10: Ridge L ... 7G 65
Arden Gro. B19: Loz ... 1J 101
B69: O'bry ... 4G 99
Arden Ho. *B60: B'gve* ... *6B 188*
(off Burcot La.)
B92: H Ard ... 3B 148
Ardenlea Ct. B91: Sol ... 4C 146
Arden Leys B94: Tan A ... 7D 192
Arden Meads B94: H'ley H ... 3C 194
Arden Oak Rd. B26: Sheld ... 4D 124
Arden Pl. WV14: Bils ... 5B 54
Arden Rd. B6: Aston ... 1K 101
B8: Salt ... 6C 102
B27: A Grn ... 5H 123
B45: Fran ... 8G 141
B47: H'wd ... 3A 166
B67: Smeth ... 5A 100
B77: Hock ... 4F 46
B93: Dorr ... 7F 168
CV8: Ken ... 6H 199
CV11: Nun ... 8A 90
CV12: Bulk ... 7C 112
Ardens Cl. B98: Redd ... 7A 214
Arden St. CV5: Cov ... 8M 151
CV9: Ath ... 2L 65
Arden Va. Rd. B93: Know ... 2H 169
Arderne Dr. B37: F'bri ... 8G 105
Ardgay Dr. WS12: Hed ... 2F 8
Ardingley Wlk. DY5: Brie H ... 2B 116
Ardley Cl. DY2: Dud ... 1K 97
Ardley Rd. B14: K Hth ... 4A 144
Areley Comn. Rd.
DY13: Stour S ... 7B 182
Areley Ct. DY13: Stour S ... 7D 182
ARELEY KINGS ... 8E 182
Areley La. DY13: Stour S ... 6D 182
Arena B40: Nat E C ... 6L 125
Arena, The (Ice Rink)
... 7B 152 (5A 6)
Arena Theatre ... 7C 36 (3J 7)
Arena Wlk. B1: Birm ... 6B 4
Aretha Cl. DY6: K'wfrd ... 3A 96
Argent Ct. CV4: Canly ... 3J 173
Argent's Mead LE10: Hinc ... 1K 91
Argent's Mead Wlk.
LE10: Hinc ... 1K 91
Argil Cl. WV11: Wed ... 1K 37
Arguile Pl. LE10: Hinc ... 8J 69
Argus Cl. B76: Walm ... 6M 59
Argyle Av. B77: Tam ... 5D 32
Argyle Cl. DY8: Word ... 8L 95
WS4: Wals ... 6B 40
Argyle Rd. WS4: Wals ... 6B 40
WV2: Wolv ... 3B 52
Argyle St. B7: Nech ... 1C 102
B77: Amin ... 6E 32
CV21: Rugby ... 6C 180
(not continuous)
Argyle Way CV33: Bis T ... 8E 224
Argyll Ho. WV1: Wolv ... 5C 36
Argyll St. CV2: Cov ... 6G 153
Ariane B79: Tam ... 2L 31
Ariel Way CV22: Bil ... 3K 205
Arion Cl. B77: Tam ... 4D 32
Arkall Cl. B79: Tam ... 2C 32
Arkle B77: Dost ... 5D 46
Arkle Cft. B36: Hodg H ... 1J 103
B65: Row R ... 3M 97
Arkle Dr. CV2: W'grve S ... 2M 153
Arklet Cl. CV10: Nun ... 4C 88
Arkley Gro. B28: Hall G ... 2H 145
Arkley Rd. B28: Hall G ... 2H 145
Arkwright Rd. B32: Quin ... 4J 119
WS2: Wals ... 4H 39
Arlen Dr. B43: Gt Barr ... 8D 56
Arlescote Cl. B75: Four O ... 7J 43
Arlescote Rd. B92: Sol ... 7C 124
Arless Way B17: Harb ... 6A 120
Arleston Way B90: Shir ... 1L 167
Arley Cl. B69: O'bry ... 4D 98
B98: Redd ... 4K 213
DY11: Kidd ... 7G 157
Arley Ct. DY2: Neth ... 3J 97
Arley Dr. DY8: Stourb ... 6L 115

Aston St.—Balmoral Rd.

Aston St. B4: Birm 5M 101 (3H 5)
(not continuous)
DY4: Tip 2C 76
WV3: Wolv 1A 52
Aston Students Guild 1J 5
Aston Triangle, The
B4: Birm 6M 101 (3J 5)
Aston University 5M 101 (2J 5)
Aston Villa FC 8M 79
Astor Dr. B13: Mose 8C 122
Astoria Cl. WV12: W'hall 8D 24
Astoria Gdns. WV12: W'hall 8D 24
Astor Rd. B74: S'tly 8A 42
DY6: K'wfrd 4M 95
ASTWOOD BANK 8E 220
Astwood Cl. B60: S Prior 8J 209
Astwood La. B96: A'wd B 8A 220
WR9: Wych 8F 208
AT7 Sports Cen. 2G 153
Atcham Cl. B98: Redd 6M 213
Atcheson Cl. B80: Stud 5L 221
Athelney Ct. WS3: Pels 6A 26
Athelstan Gro. WV6: Pert 4F 34
Athelstan Way B79: Tam 2M 31
Athena Dr. CV34: Warw 4K 223
Athena Gdns. CV6: Cov 8G 131
ATHERSTONE 1K 65
Atherstone Arts Cen. 1K 65
Atherstone By-Pass
CV9: Ath 8H 49
Atherstone Cl. B90: Shir 7E 144
B98: Redd 8M 213
Atherstone La. CV9: Bax, Hurl 5K 63
Atherstone Leisure Complex 8K 49
Atherstone Rd. B46: Over W 5K 85
CV9: Bntly 5K 85
CV9: Hurl 5K 63
CV9: Pin 6K 49
CV9: With 7M 49
CV10: Harts 7B 66
CV13: Fen D 5G 67
WV1: Wolv 7H 37
Atherstone Station (Rail) 1J 65
Atherstone St. B77: Two G 1B 46
B78: Faz 1B 46
Atherston Pl. CV4: Canly 3K 173
Athlone Rd. WS5: Wals 1C 56
Athol Cl. B32: Bart G 1K 141
Athole St. B12: Birm 2A 122
Atholl Cres. CV10: Nun 7E 88
Athol Rd. CV2: W'grve S 3A 154
Atkins Wlk. B78: Pole 1A 48
Atkins Way LE10: Burb 2L 91
Atlantic Ct. *WV13: W'hall 8A 38*
(off Cheapside)
Atlantic Rd. B44: Gt Barr 1M 79
Atlantic Way WS10: W'bry 8E 54
Atlas Cft. WV10: Oxl 3C 36
Atlas Est. B6: Witt 7A 80
B11: Tys 4G 123
Atlas Gro. B70: W Brom 6F 76
Atlas Trad. Est. WV14: Bils 7M 53
Atlas Way B1: Birm 6B 4
Attenborough Cl. B19: Hock 4K 101
ATTERTON 1G 67
Atterton La. CV9: With 1B 66
CV13: Att 1B 66
Attingham Dr. B43: Gt Barr 7D 56
WS11: Hth H 7H 9
Attleboro La. B46: Wat O 7G 83
ATTLEBOROUGH 8K 89
Attleborough By-Pass
CV11: Nun 7K 89
Attleborough Flds. Ind. Est.
CV11: Nun 6M 89
Attleborough Rd. CV11: Nun 6K 89
Attlee Cl. B69: Tiv 7D 76
Attlee Cres. WV14: Bils 7L 53
Attlee Gro. WS11: Hth H 7J 9
Attlee Rd. WS2: Wals 5E 38
Attoxhall Rd. CV2: Cov 5L 153
Attwell Pk. WV3: Wolv 2K 51
Attwell Rd. DY4: Tip 8M 53
Attwood Cl. B8: Salt 3E 102
Attwood Cres. CV2: Cov 2J 153
Attwood Gdns. WV4: E'shll 4E 52
Attwood Rd. WS7: C Ter 1C 16
Attwood St. B63: Hale 4M 117
DY9: Lye 4F 116
Atworth Cl. B98: Redd 4H 221
Aubrey Rd. B10: Small H 1F 122
B32: Harb 2L 119
Auchinleck Dr. WS13: Lich 8J 13
Auchinleck Ho. *B16: Birm 8A 4*
(off Broad St.)
Auchinleck Sq. B15: Birm 8A 4
Auckland Dr. B36: Cas B 1F 104
Auckland Ho. B32: Quin 5M 119
Auckland Rd. B11: S'brk 2A 122
B67: Smeth 3L 99
DY6: K'wfrd 5L 95
Auden Cl. CV10: Gall C 5M 87
Auden Ct. WV6: Pert 5F 34
Audleigh Ho.
B15: Birm 1J 121 (8C 4)
Audlem Wlk. WV10: Wolv 4G 37
Audley Dr. DY11: Kidd 1G 157
Audley Rd. B33: Stech 5L 103
AUDNAM 8M 95
Audnam DY8: Word 8M 95
Augusta Pl. CV32: Lea S 1M 223
Augusta Rd. B13: Mose 5L 121
B27: A Grn 4J 123
Augusta Rd. E. B13: Mose 5M 121
Augusta St.
B18: Birm 5J 101 (1C 4)
Augustine Av. B80: Stud 5J 221
Augustine Gro. B18: Hock 3F 100
B74: Four O 4F 42
Augustines Wlk. WS13: Lich 6G 13
Augustus Cl. B46: Col 8M 83
Augustus Ct. B15: Edg 1F 120
Augustus Rd. B15: Edg 1D 120
CV1: Cov 5F 152
Augustus St. WS2: Wals 8K 39
Aulton Cres. LE10: Hinc 8H 69
Aulton Rd. B75: R'ley 6L 43
Aulton Way LE10: Hinc 8H 69
Ault St. B70: W Brom 8K 77
Austcliff Cl. B97: Redd 3D 220
Austcliff Dr. B91: Sol 1C 168
AUSTCLIFFE 4B 136
Austcliffe Holiday Home Pk.
DY10: Cookl 3B 136
Austcliffe La. DY10: Cookl 4C 136
Austcliffe Rd. DY10: Cookl 4A 136
Austen Cl. CV10: Gall C 4M 87
Austen Ct. CV32: Cubb 4E 218
Austen Pl. B15: Edg 1H 121
Austen Wlk. B71: W Brom 4K 77
Austin Cl. B27: A Grn 5K 123
CV9: Ath 2K 65
DY1: Dud 7F 74
Austin Cote La. WS14: Lich 2L 19
Austin Ct. B1: Birm 7H 101 (5B 4)
Austin Cft. B36: Cas B 8E 82
Austin Dr. CV6: Cov 2G 153
Austin Edwards Dr.
CV34: Warw 1H 223
Austin Ho. WS4: Wals 6M 39
Austin Ri. B31: Longb 2M 163
Austin Rd. B21: Hand 8C 78
B60: B'gve 2L 209
Austin St. WV6: Wolv 5B 36
AUSTIN VILLAGE 8M 141
Austin Way B42: P Barr 4G 79
Austrey Cl. B93: Know 3G 169
Austrey Gro. B29: W Cas 1A 142
Austrey Rd. DY6: K'wfrd 4A 96
Austwick Cl. CV34: Warw 8E 216
Austy Cl. B36: Hodg H 1L 103
Automotive Components Pk.
WS10: W'bry 6C 54
Autumn Berry Gro.
DY3: Sed 3E 74
Autumn Cl. WS4: S'fld 8C 26
Autumn Dr. DY3: Lwr G 5D 74
WS4: S'fld 8C 26
WS13: Lich 7K 13
Autumn Gro. B19: Hock 3J 101
Autumn Ho. B37: K'hrst 4H 105
Auxerre Av. B98: Redd 1G 221
Auxerre Ho. B98: Redd 1H 221
Avalon Cl. B24: Erd 5H 81
Avalon Rd. B60: B'gve 7C 188
Avebury Cl. CV11: Nun 7M 89
Avebury Gro. B30: Stir 2J 143
Avebury Rd. B30: Stir 1J 143
Ave Maria Cl. B64: Old H 8L 97
Avenbury Cl. B98: Redd 8M 213
Avenbury Dr. B91: Sol 5E 146
Aventine Way CV21: Rugby 2M 179
Avenue, The B27: A Grn 5J 123
B45: Rubery 2E 162
B60: B'wll 3G 189
B65: Row R 6A 98
B76: Walm 8L 59
CV3: Cov 3G 175
CV35: Row 8M 195
DY10: Blak 8H 137
DY11: Kidd 1A 184
DY11: Ware 8A 184
WV3: Wolv 1H 51
WV4: Penn 5L 51
WV10: F'stne 2H 23
WV10: Wolv 4F 36
Avenue Albert B94: H'ley H 2B 194
Avenue Cl. B7: Nech 3A 102
B93: Dorr 6G 169
Avenue M. CV8: S'lgh P 6A 200
Avenue Nth. LE9: Earl S 1G 71
Avenue Rd. B6: Aston 3M 101
B7: Nech 3M 101
B14: K Hth 1K 143
B21: Hand 7D 78
B23: Erd 5F 80
B65: B'hth, Row R 8D 98
B93: Dorr 6G 169
B96: A'wd B 8E 220
CV8: Ken 3D 198
CV11: Nun 7J 89
CV21: Rugby 5L 179
CV31: Lea S 2L 223
DY2: Dud 3F 96
WS10: Darl 3D 54
WS12: Hth H 7L 9
WV3: Wolv 7L 35
WV14: Cose 1J 75
Avenue Sth. LE9: Earl S 1G 71
Averill Rd. B26: Yard 8A 104
Avern Cl. DY4: Tip 3B 76
Aversley Rd. B38: K Nor 8D 142
Avery Ct. B68: O'bry 2H 119
CV34: Warw 3F 222
Avery Cft. B35: Cas V 7M 81
Avery Dell Ind. Est.
B30: K Nor 4H 143
Avery Dr. B27: A Grn 5J 123
Avery Ho. B16: Edg 8G 101
Avery Myers Cl. B68: O'bry 4H 99
Avery Rd. B66: Smeth 3D 100
B73: New O 7C 58
Aviary Ct. B71: W Brom 3J 77
Aviemore Cl. CV10: Nun 7G 89
Aviemore Cres. B43: Gt Barr 5H 57
Avill B77: Hock 4G 47
Avill Gro. DY11: Kidd 2J 157
Avington Cl. DY3: Sed 2D 74
Avion Cen. WV6: Wolv 5A 36
Avion Cl. WS1: Wals 2M 55
Avocet Cl. B33: Stech 6L 103
CV2: Ald G 6H 131
CV23: Brow 1C 180
Avocet Dr. DY10: Kidd 7A 158
Avon B77: Hock 4G 47
Avonbank Cl. B97: Redd 3C 220
Avon Bus. Pk. WS11: Cann 2C 14
Avon Cl. B14: K Hth 8K 143
B60: B'gve 3M 209
CV12: Bulk 3B 112
DY5: P'ntt 3B 96
WV6: Pert 6F 34
Avon Ct. B73: S Cold 4H 59
CV21: Rugby 5A 180
CV32: Lea S 6M 217
Avon Cres. WS3: Pels 8A 26
Avoncroft Ho. B37: Chel W 7G 105
Avoncroft Mus. of Buildings 4L 209
Avoncroft Rd. B60: Stoke H 4K 209
Avondale Cl. DY6: K'wfrd 1L 95
Avondale Ct. B31: N'fld 8L 141
Avondale Rd. B11: S'hll 5C 122
CV5: Cov 1A 174
CV8: Bran 4F 176
CV32: Lill 5C 218
WV6: Wolv 6M 35
Avon Dr. B13: Mose 7B 122
B36: Cas B 1F 104
WV13: W'hall 7C 38
Avon Gro. WS5: Wals 6A 56
Avon Ho. B15: Birm 1K 121 (8D 4)
DY10: Kidd 7L 157
Avon Ind. Est. CV21: Rugby 4C 180
Avonlea Ri. CV32: Lea S 7K 217
Avon Lodge CV11: Nun 4G 89
Avonmere CV21: N'bld A 2L 179
Avon M. DY8: Word 7H 95
Avon Rd. B63: Crad 4H 117
B90: Shir 8K 145
CV4: Canly 3H 173
CV8: Ken 6E 198
CV31: W'nsh 6A 224
DY8: Stourb 6M 115
DY11: Kidd 6H 157
WS3: Blox 8L 25
WS7: Chase 4F 16
WS11: Cann 2C 14
Avon St. B11: S'hll 4C 122
CV2: Cov 4H 153
CV21: Rugby 5A 180
CV23: Clift D 5E 180
CV34: Warw 2G 223
Avon Ter. CV8: Bubb 3J 201
Avon Vw. Pk. Homes
CV8: Rytn D 7L 175
Avon Wlk. LE10: Hinc 1G 91
Avon Way B47: Wyt 7L 165
Avro Way B35: Cas V 7B 82
Awbridge Rd. DY2: Neth 6J 97
Awefields Cres. B67: Smeth 5K 99
Awlmakers Gro. WS3: Blox 2J 39
Awson St. CV6: Cov 3F 152
Axborough La. DY10: Cookl 5C 136
Axcess 10 Bus. Pk.
WS10: W'bry 8E 38
Axholme Rd. CV2: Cov 5L 153
Axletree Way WS10: W'bry 3G 55
Axminster Cl. CV11: Nun 4L 89
Ayala Cft. B36: Hodg H 8L 81
Aylesbury Cl. B94: H'ley H 2C 194
Aylesbury Cres. B44: K'sdng 1A 80
Aylesbury Ho. B31: Longb 1M 163
Aylesbury Rd. B94: H'ley H 3C 194
Aylesdene Ct. CV5: Cov 1M 173
Aylesford Cl. DY3: Sed 7C 52
Aylesford Dr. B37: Mars G 2G 125
B74: Four O 4E 42
Aylesford Rd. B21: Hand 8D 78
Aylesford St. CV1: Cov 5E 152
CV31: Lea S 3A 224
Aylesmore Cl. B32: Bart G 8J 119
B92: Olton 1L 145
Aynho Cl. CV5: E Grn 6G 151
Aynsley Ct. B90: Shir 7J 145
Ayre Rd. B24: Erd 5H 81
Ayrshire Cl. B36: Hodg H 1K 103
LE9: Barw 3A 70
Ayrton Cl. WV6: Pert 5G 35
Aysgarth Cl. CV11: Nun 7A 90
Azalea Cl. LE10: Burb 4L 91
WV8: Bilb 6H 21
Azalea Dr. LE10: Burb 3L 91
Azalea Gro. B9: Bord G 7F 102
Azalea Wlk. LE10: Burb 4L 91
Aziz Isaac Cl. B68: O'bry 3H 99

B

Babbacombe Rd. CV3: Cov 4D 174
Babington Rd. B21: Hand 2E 100
Bablake Cl. CV6: Cov 1M 151
Bablake Cft. B92: Olton 8A 124
Babors Fld. WV14: Cose 6G 53
Babworth Cl. WV9: Pend 7A 22
Baccabox La. B47: H'wd 2L 165
Bacchus Rd. B18: Hock 3F 100
Bachelors Bench
CV9: Ath 2K 65
Bache St. B70: W Brom 8J 77
Bach Mill Dr. B28: Hall G 6D 144
Backcester La. WS13: Lich 1H 19
Backcrofts WS11: Cann 8D 8
Backhouse La. WV11: Wed 5J 37
Back La. B46: Shu 7F 84
B64: Crad H 8H 97
B90: Dic H 4G 167
CV7: Mer 4K 149
CV23: Long L 5G 179
CV34: Warw 3E 222
DY10: Mus G, Shens 1F 184
WS9: A'rdge 2M 41
WS14: Foot 8D 28
Back Rd. B38: K Nor 7F 142
DY6: K'wfrd 2K 95
Back St. CV11: Nun 4J 89
BACONS END 5H 105
Bacons End B37: K'hrst 4H 105
Bacon's Yd. CV6: Cov 7F 130
Badbury Cl. B80: Stud 5K 221
Badbury Gdns. B80: Stud 5K 221
Badby Leys CV22: Rugby 2M 205
BADDESLEY CLINTON 3C 196
Baddesley Clinton 6M 195
Baddesley Cl. CV31: Lea S 4D 224
BADDESLEY ENSOR 8C 48
Baddesley Rd. B92: Olton 7L 123
Baden Powell Cl.
WS15: Cann W 3F 10
Bader Rd. WS2: Wals 7F 38
WV6: Pert 6E 34
Bader Wlk. B35: Cas V 7M 81
Badger Brook La.
B96: A'wd B 8E 220
Badger Cl. B90: Ches G 5K 167
B98: Redd 6K 213
WS12: Hunt 3C 8
Badger Rd. CV3: Bin 1K 175
Badgers, The B45: B Grn 7G 163
Badgers Bank Rd.
B74: Four O 4F 42
Badgers Cl. WS3: Pels 4A 26
Badgers Cft. B62: Hale 2B 118
Badger St. DY3: Up Gor 4E 74
DY9: Lye 4E 116
Badgers Wlk. DY13: Stour S 5F 182
Badgers Way B34: Stech 4A 104
WS12: Hth H 7K 9
Badger Way B60: B'wll 4H 189
Badland Av. DY10: Kidd 8M 135
Badminton Cl. DY1: Dud 6F 74
Badon Covert B14: K Hth 7K 143
Badsey Cl. B31: N'fld 5C 142
Badsey Rd. B69: O'bry 4D 98
Baffin Cl. CV22: Bil 8L 179
Baggeridge Cl. DY3: Sed 1A 74
Baggeridge Country Pk. 3L 73
Baggeridge Country Pk. Vis. Cen.
2M 73
Baggott St. WV2: Wolv 2C 52
BAGINTON 7F 174
Baginton Cl. B91: Sol 4B 146
Baginton Rd. B35: Cas V 5A 82
CV3: Cov 3B 174
(not continuous)
Bagley Ind. Pk. DY2: Neth 5K 97
Bagley's Rd. DY5: Brie H 3C 116
Bagley St. DY9: Lye 4C 116
Bagnall Cl. B25: Yard 3K 123
Bagnall Rd. WV14: Bils 4J 53
Bagnall St. B70: W Brom 7L 77
(Beeches Rd.)
B70: W Brom 2D 76
(Shaw St.)
DY4: Tip 2D 76
(Chimney Rd.)
DY4: Tip 8C 54
(Newman Rd.)
WS3: Blox 3J 39
Bagnall Wlk. DY5: Brie H 8D 96
Bagnell Rd. B13: Mose 2M 143
Bagot St. B4: Birm 5L 101 (1H 5)
Bagot Way CV34: H'cte 6L 223
Bagridge Cl. WV3: Wolv 1H 51
Bagridge Rd. WV3: Wolv 1H 51
Bagshaw Cl. CV8: Rytn D 8A 176
Bagshawe Cft. B23: Erd 2D 80
Bagshaw Rd. B33: Stech 6L 103
Bailey Av. B77: Hock 4F 46
Bailey Cl. WS7: C Ter 1D 16
WS11: Cann 5G 9
Bailey Rd. WV14: Bils 2H 53
Baileys Ct. B65: Row R 6B 98
Bailey's La. CV23: Long L 4G 179
Bailey St. B70: W Brom 5G 77
WV1: Wolv 7E 36 (3M 7)
Bailye Cl. WS13: S'hay 8M 13
Baines La. LE10: Hinc 8K 69
Bains Dr. WS13: Lich 3G 19
Bakehouse La. B46: Neth W 3E 84
B93: Chad E 3B 196
CV21: Rugby 6M 179
Bakeman Ho. *B25: Yard 3K 123*
(off Tivoli, The)
Baker Av. CV31: Lea S 3M 223
WV14: Cose 7F 52
Baker Cl. WS7: Chase 3F 16
Baker Ho. Gro. B43: Gt Barr 2D 78
Baker Rd. WV14: Bils 6L 53
Bakers Ct. CV9: Ath 1K 65
Bakers Cft. CV9: Bad E 8C 48
Bakers Gdns. WV8: Cod 5E 20
BAKER'S LANE 8K 169
Bakers La. WS13: Lich 2H 19
B74: S'tly 4M 57
B93: Know 8J 169
CV5: Cov 6L 151
WS9: A'rdge 3H 41
Bakers M. B93: Chad E 3B 196
Baker St. B10: Small H 8D 102
B11: S'hll 5C 122
B21: Hand 1F 100
B70: W Brom 6H 77
CV6: Longf 3H 131
DY4: Tip 5L 75
(not continuous)
WS7: Chase 3F 16
Bakers Wlk. B77: Wiln 3F 46
Bakers Way WS12: Hed 4H 9
WV8: Cod 5E 20
Bakewell Cl. CV3: Bin 1M 175
WS3: Blox 6J 25
Balaams Wood Dr.
B31: Longb 8H 141
Balaclava Rd. B14: K Hth 1L 143
Bala Cl. DY13: Stour S 4G 183
Balcaskie Cl. B15: Edg 2E 120
Balcombe Ct. CV22: Hillm 1E 206
Balcombe Rd. CV22: Hillm 1D 206
Balden Rd. B32: Harb 2L 119
Balding Cl. CV23: Barby 8J 207
Baldmoor Lake Rd. B23: Erd 2F 80
Bald's La. DY9: Lye 4F 116
Baldwin Cl. B69: Tiv 7D 76
Baldwin Cft. CV6: Cov 8H 131
Baldwin Gro. WS11: Hth H 7J 9
Baldwin Rd. B30: K Nor 7G 143
DY10: Kidd 1B 158
DY12: Bew 1B 156
DY13: Stour S 5H 183
Baldwins Ho. *DY5: Quar B 1F 116*
(off Maughan St.)
Baldwins La. B28: Hall G 5E 144
Baldwin St. B66: Smeth 3B 100
WV14: Bils 5M 53
Baldwin Way DY3: Swind 7E 72
Balfour B79: Tam 5A 32
Balfour Cl. LE10: Burb 2L 91
Balfour Ct. B74: Four O 6G 43
WV6: Wolv 5M 35
(off Balfour Cres.)
Balfour Cres. WV6: Wolv 5M 35
Balfour Dr. B69: Tiv 7C 76
Balfour Ho. B16: Edg 8F 100
Balfour Rd. DY6: K'wfrd 1L 95
Balfour St. B12: Bal H 3L 121
Balham Gro. B44: K'sdng 7A 58
Balholm B62: Hale 4D 118
Balking Cl. WV14: Cose 6H 53
Ballantine Rd. CV6: Cov 3B 152
Ballarat Wlk. DY8: Stourb 4M 115
Ballard Cres. DY2: Neth 4K 97
Ballard Rd. DY2: Neth 4K 97
BALLARDS GREEN 6D 86
Ballard Wlk. B37: K'hrst 3G 105
Ballfields DY4: Tip 4D 76
Ball Ho. *WS3: Blox 1H 39*
(off Somerfield Rd.)
Ballingham Cl. CV4: Tile H 7G 151
Balliol Bus. Pk. WV9: Pend 6K 21
Balliol Ho. B37: F'bri 7F 104
Balliol Rd. CV2: Cov 5H 153
LE10: Burb 3M 91
Ball La. WV10: Cov H 3C 22
Ballot St. B66: Smeth 4B 100
BALLS HILL 1G 77
Balls Hill WS1: Wals 7M 39
Balls St. WS1: Wals 8M 39
Balmain Cres. WV11: Wed 1H 37
Balmoral Cl. B62: Hale 2B 118
CV2: Cov 3M 153
WS4: Rus 2D 40
WS14: Lich 3K 19
Balmoral Ct. B1: Birm 4C 4
CV10: Nun 4E 88
DY10: Kidd 4A 158
WS12: Cann 4G 9
Balmoral Dr. WS12: Hed 2F 8
WV5: Wom 8G 51
WV12: W'hall 2B 38
Balmoral Rd. B23: Erd 4F 80
B32: Bart G 2G 141
B36: Cas B 2G 105
B74: Four O 4F 42
DY8: Word 6J 95

West Midlands Atlas 231

Balmoral Rd.—Bath St.

Balmoral Rd. LE9: Earl S 2D **70**
WV4: Penn 4A **52**
Balmoral Vw. DY1: Dud 7E **74**
Balmoral Way B65: Row R 5D **98**
CV32: Cubb 3C **218**
WS2: Wals 5G **39**
WS7: C Ter 8E **10**
BALSALL 4H **171**
BALSALL COMMON 3H **171**
BALSALL HEATH 4M **121**
Balsall Heath Rd. B5: Bal H 2K **121**
B12: Bal H 2L **121**
BALSALL STREET 3G **171**
Balsall St. CV7: Bal C 4B **170**
Balsall St. E. CV7: Bal C 4G **171**
Balthazar Cl. CV34: H'cte 5L **223**
Baltic Cl. WS11: Cann 7E **8**
Baltimore Rd. B42: P Barr 3G **79**
Balvenie Way DY1: Dud 6F **74**
Bamber Cl. WV3: Wolv 1L **51**
Bamburgh B77: Two G 2C **46**
Bamburgh Gro. CV32: Lea S 6L **217**
Bamford Cl. WS3: Blox 6J **25**
Bamford Ho. WS3: Blox 6J **25**
Bamford Rd. WS3: Blox 6J **25**
WV3: Wolv 1A **52**
Bamford St. B77: Glas 6D **32**
Bampfylde Pl. B42: Gt Barr 2J **79**
Bampton Av. WS7: C Ter 1G **17**
Bamville Rd. B8: W End 4G **103**
Banbery Dr. WV5: Wom 5F **72**
Banbrook Cl. B92: Sol 1D **146**
Banbury Cl. DY3: Sed 3E **74**
Banbury Cft. B37: F'bri 7F **104**
Banbury Ho. B33: Kitts G 7E **104**
Banbury Rd. CV34: Warw 3J **222**
CV47: Sou 6H **225**
WS11: Cann 1C **14**
Banbury Rd. Hill
CV34: Warw 4G **223**
Banbury St. B5: Birm 6M **101** (4J **5**)
Bancroft B77: Glas 7F **32**
Bancroft Cl. WV14: Cose 2H **75**
Bandywood Cres.
B44: Gt Barr 6M **57**
Bandywood Rd. B44: Gt Barr 5L **57**
Baneberry Dr. WV10: F'stne 1H **23**
Banfield Av. WS10: Darl 2C **54**
Banfield Rd. WS10: Darl 5C **54**
Banford Av. B8: W End 5G **103**
Banford Rd. B8: W End 5G **103**
Bangham Pit Rd. B31: N'fld 3L **141**
Bangley La. B78: Hints 3D **44**
(Cranebrook Hill)
B78: Hints 1F **44**
(Waggoners La.)
Bangor Ho. B37: F'bri 5H **105**
Bangor Rd. B9: Bord G 7D **102**
Bank, The CV8: S'lgh 3C **200**
Bank Cres. WS7: Chase 4F **16**
Bankcroft CV31: Lea S 4C **224**
Bankdale Rd. B8: W End 5H **103**
Bankes Rd. B10: Small H 8E **102**
Bank Farm Cl. DY9: Pedm 8C **116**
Bankfield Dr. CV32: Lea S 8J **217**
Bankfield Rd. DY4: Tip 1C **76**
WV14: Bils 4K **53**
(not continuous)
Banklands Rd. DY2: Dud 3L **97**
Bank La. CV1: Cov 6A **152**
Bank Rd. CV9: Ath 1L **65**
DY2: Neth 3K **97**
DY3: Gorn 6C **74**
(not continuous)
Banks, The CV23: Kils 7M **207**
BANK'S GREEN 6G **211**
Banks Grn.
B97: Bks G, Up Ben 6G **211**
Bankside B13: Mose 7D **122**
B43: Gt Barr 2E **78**
WV5: Wom 2F **72**
Bankside Cl. CV3: Cov 3F **174**
Bankside Cres. B74: S'tly 2M **57**
Bankside Way WS9: A'rdge 7H **27**
Banks Rd. CV6: Cov 4A **152**
Banks St. WV13: W'hall 7A **38**
Bank St. B14: K Hth 1L **143**
B64: Crad H 8J **97**
B71: W Brom 3J **77**
CV21: Rugby 6A **180**
DY5: Brie H 6D **96**
DY9: Lye 4F **116**
WS1: Wals 8M **39**
WS12: Hth H 8L **9**
WV10: Wolv 4E **36**
WV14: Bils 6L **53**
WV14: Cose 1H **75**
Bank Ter. LE9: Barw 3A **70**
Bankwell St. DY5: Brie H 5C **96**
Banky Mdw. LE10: Burb 2A **92**
Banner La. B92: Bars 8B **148**
CV4: Tile H 5D **150**
Bannerlea Rd. B37: K'hrst 4F **104**
Bannerley Rd. B33: Sheld 8C **104**
Banners Ct. B73: S'tly 6B **58**
BANNERS GATE 5B **58**
Banners Ga. Rd. B73: S'tly 6B **58**
Banners Gro. B23: Erd 3G **81**
Banners La. B63: Crad 3K **117**
B97: Redd 4E **220**
Banner's St. B63: Crad 3K **117**
Banners Wlk. B44: K'sdng 7B **58**
Bannington Ct. WV12: W'hall 5D **38**
Bannister Rd. WS10: W'bry 7D **54**
Bannister St. B64: Crad H 8K **97**
Banquo App. CV34: H'cte 6M **223**
Banstead Cl.
WV2: Wolv 2E **52** (8M **7**)
Bantam Gro. CV6: Cov 6A **130**
Bantams Cl. B33: Kitts G 7C **104**
Bant Mill Rd. B60: B'gve 8A **188**
Bantock Av. WV3: Wolv 1M **51**
Bantock Ct. WV3: Wolv 1L **51**
Bantock Gdns. WV3: Wolv 8L **35**
Bantock House Mus. 8M **35**
Bantock Rd. CV4: Tile H 7E **150**
Bantocks, The B70: W Brom 3G **77**
Bantock Way B17: Harb 4D **120**
Banton Cl. B23: Erd 1D **80**
Bantry Cl. B26: Sheld 5C **124**
BAPTIST END 3J **97**
Baptist End Rd.
DY2: Dud, Neth 4J **97**
Baptist Wlk. LE10: Hinc 8K **69**
Barbara Rd. B28: Hall G 5E **144**
Barbara St. B79: Tam 4A **32**
Barbel Dr. WV10: Wolv 5G **37**
Barber Cl. WS12: Hth H 7L **9**
Barberry Ho. B38: K Nor 8F **142**
Barbers La. B92: Cath B 3J **147**
Barber Wlk. CV35: H Mag 2A **222**
Barbican Ri. CV2: Cov 7L **153**
Barbourne Cl. B91: Sol 2B **168**
Barbridge Cl. CV12: Bulk 7C **112**
Barbridge Rd. CV12: Bulk 6B **112**
Barbrook Dr. DY5: Brie H 2B **116**
BARBY 8J **207**
Barby La. CV22: Hillm 1F **206**
CV23: Barby 4G **207**
BARBY NORTOFT 3M **207**
Barby Rd. CV22: Rugby 7A **180**
CV23: Barby, Kils 6L **207**
Barcheston Rd. B29: W Cas 8A **120**
B93: Know 4G **169**
Barclay Ct. WV3: Wolv 7A **36**
Barclay Rd. B67: Smeth 8L **99**
Barcliffe Av. B77: Glas 6E **32**
Barcroft WV13: W'hall 6B **38**
Bardell Cl. WS13: Lich 3E **18**
Bardenholme Gdns.
DY9: W'cte 6D **116**
Bardfield Cl. B42: Gt Barr 1F **78**
Bardley Dr. CV6: Cov 3C **152**
Bardon Dr. B90: Shir 7J **145**
Bardon Rd. LE9: Barw 1B **70**
Bardon Vw. Rd. B78: Dord 2A **48**
Bardsey Cl. LE10: Hinc 8H **69**
Bard St. B11: S'hll 4C **122**
Bardwell Cl. WV8: Pend 1M **35**
Bardwell La. WS15: Longd 1J **11**
Barford App. CV31: W'nsh 7B **224**
Barford Cl. B76: Walm 5M **59**
B98: Redd 8M **213**
CV3: Bin 2K **175**
WS10: Darl 1C **54**
Barford Cres. B38: K Nor 7J **143**
Barford Hill CV35: Barf 8E **222**
Barford Ho. B5: Birm 2L **121**
Barford M. CV8: Ken 5H **199**
Barford Rd. B16: Birm 5E **100**
B90: Shir 7K **145**
CV8: Ken 6H **199**
CV34: Warw 8F **222**
CV35: Sher 8A **222**
Barford St. B5: Birm 1L **121** (8H **5**)
Bargate Dr. WV6: Wolv 5A **36**
Bargehouse Wlk. B38: K Nor 2E **164**
Bargery Rd. WV11: Wed 8A **24**
Barham Cl. B90: M'path 4A **168**
Barham Rd. B74: S Cold 2H **59**
Barker's Butts La. CV6: Cov 4M **151**
Barkers La. B47: Wyt 8M **165**
WS14: S'fen 7K **19**
Barker St. B19: Loz 2H **101**
B68: O'bry 3J **99**
BARK HILL 2B **156**
Bark Piece B32: Bart G 6J **119**
Barkus Cl. CV47: Sou 5J **225**
Barlands Cft. B34: S End 3B **104**
Barle Gro. B36: Cas B 2F **104**
Barlestone Dr. LE10: Hinc 8G **69**
Barley Cl. CV21: Hillm 1G **207**
DY3: Sed 2F **74**
WS9: A'rdge 7L **41**
WS12: Hed 4H **9**
WV8: Pend 8L **21**
Barley Ct. CV32: Lea S 7M **217**
Barley Cft. B60: Stoke H 2K **209**
WV6: Pert 6D **34**
Barleyfield LE10: Hinc 6J **69**
Barleyfield Ho. *WS1: Wals 1L 55*
(off Bath St.)
Barleyfield Ri. DY6: W Hth 1G **95**
Barleyfield Row WS1: Wals 1L **55**
Barley Lea, The CV3: Cov 1H **175**
Barley Mow La. B61: Cats 1A **188**
Barlich Way B98: Redd 7F **212**
Barling Way CV10: Nun 8H **89**
Barlow Cl. B45: Fran 7E **140**
B68: O'bry 6G **99**
B77: Amin 5E **32**
Barlow Ct. B78: K'bry 3D **62**
Barlow Dr. B70: W Brom 8M **77**
Barlow Rd. CV2: Ald G 6K **131**
WS10: W'bry 4G **55**
Barlow's Rd. B15: Edg 4D **120**
Barmoral Cl. B79: Tam 2B **32**
Barmouth Cl. WV12: W'hall 3C **38**
Barnabas Rd. B23: Erd 5F **80**
Barnaby Sq. WV10: Bush 5F **22**
Barnack Av. CV3: Cov 4B **174**
Barnack Dr. CV34: Warw 8E **216**
BARNACLE 3B **132**
Barnacle La. CV12: Bulk 8C **112**
Barnard Cl. B37: Chel W 8K **105**
CV32: Lill 6C **218**
Barnardo's Cen.
B7: Birm 4A **102** (1M **5**)
Barnard Pl. WV2: Wolv 3E **52**
Barnard Rd. B75: S Cold 2L **59**
WV11: Wed 8M **23**
Barnard Way WS11: Cann 7F **8**
Barn Av. DY3: Sed 2C **74**
Barnbridge B77: Wiln 7C **32**
Barnbrook Rd. B93: Know 2G **169**
Barn Cl. B30: Stir 3H **143**
B60: Stoke H 3L **209**
B63: Hale 7L **117**
B64: Crad H 3L **117**
B78: Dord 3M **47**
CV5: Cov 4J **151**
CV31: W'nsh 6B **224**
DY9: Lye 5C **116**
WS13: Lich 6H **13**
Barncroft B32: Bart G 8L **119**
WS6: Gt Wyr 6G **15**
WS7: Chase 5G **17**
Barncroft Rd. B69: Tiv 1A **98**
Barncroft St. B70: W Brom 1G **77**
Barne Cl. CV11: Nun 2B **112**
Barnes Cl. B37: F'bri 7E **104**
Barnes Ct. CV1: Cov 5C **152** (2B **6**)
Barnes Hill B29: W Cas 7M **119**
Barnesmeadow Pl.
WV14: Cose 1H **75**
Barnes Rd. WS14: Shens 3G **29**
Barnesville Cl. B10: Small H 1G **123**
Barnet Rd. B23: Erd 4D **80**
BARNETTBROOK 4J **159**
Barnett Cl. DY6: K'wfrd 5K **95**
WV14: Bils 5K **53**
Barnett Grn. DY6: K'wfrd 5K **95**
Barnett La. DY6: K'wfrd 4K **95**
DY8: Word 4K **95**
Barnett Rd. WV13: W'hall 8L **37**
Barnetts Cl. DY10: Kidd 5B **158**
Barnetts Gro. DY10: Kidd 5A **158**
Barnetts La. DY10: Kidd 6M **157**
WS8: Bwnhls 1F **26**
Barnett St. B69: Tiv 7A **76**
DY4: Tip 5A **76**
DY8: Word 6K **95**
Barney Cl. DY4: Tip 6M **75**
Barn Farm Cl. WV14: Bils 2A **54**
Barnfield Av. CV5: Alle 2G **151**
Barnfield Cl. WS14: Lich 3H **19**
Barnfield Dr. B92: Sol 3E **146**
Barnfield Gro. B20: Hand 4E **78**
Barnfield Rd. B61: B'gve 8L **187**
B62: B'hth 2D **118**
DY4: Tip 2L **75**
DY13: Stour S 8F **182**
WV1: Wolv 7G **37**
Barnfield Trad. Est. DY4: Tip 2L **75**
Barnfield Way WS12: Haz 3A **10**
Barnford Cl. B10: Small H 8C **102**
Barnford Cres. B68: O'bry 6H **99**
Barnfordhill Cl. B68: O'bry 6G **99**
Barn Grn. WV3: Wolv 2M **51**
BARN HILL 4C **166**
Barn Ho. B8: W End 5K **103**
Barnhurst La.
WV8: Bilb, Pend 6K **21**
Barn La. B13: Mose 2A **144**
B21: Hand 2E **100**
B92: Olton 5L **123**
CV23: Prin 8D **202**
Barn Mdw. B25: Yard 8K **103**
Barnmoor Ri. B91: Sol 2C **146**
Barn Owl Dr. WS3: Pels 5M **25**
Barn Owl Pl. DY10: Kidd 7A **158**
Barn Owl Wlk. DY5: Brie H 3C **116**
Barnpark Covert B14: K Hth 7J **143**
Barn Piece B32: Quin 5H **119**
Barnsbury Av. B72: W Grn 3J **81**
Barns Cl. WS9: Wals W 5F **26**
Barns Cft. B74: Lit A 5B **42**
Barnsdale Cres. B31: N'fld 5L **141**
Barns La. WS4: Rus 2C **40**
WS9: A'rdge 2D **40**
Barnsley Cl. CV9: Ath 2K **65**
Barnsley Hall Dr.
B61: B'gve 3M **187**
Barnsley Rd. B17: Edg 8A **100**
B61: B'gve 5B **188**
Barnstaple Cl. CV5: Alle 5F **150**
Barnstaple Rd. B66: Smeth 4B **100**
Barn St. B5: Birm 7M **101** (6K **5**)
Barnswood Cl. B63: Crad 4J **117**
WS11: Cann 1B **14**
BARNT GREEN 1K **189**
Barnt Grn. Rd. B45: Coft H 5J **163**
Barnt Green Sailing Club 6A **164**
Barnt Green Station (Rail) 1K **189**
Barn Way WS12: Wim 5M **9**
Barnwell Cl. CV22: Dunc 5J **205**
Barnwood Cl. B98: Redd 4K **213**
Barnwood Rd. B32: Quin 5M **119**
WV8: Pend 8L **21**
Baron Cl. WS7: C Ter 8E **10**
Baron Leigh Dr.
CV4: W'wd H 3D **172**
Barons Cl. B17: Harb 3A **120**
Barons Ct. B92: Sol 5C **124**
Barons Ct. Trad. Est.
WS9: Wals W 7E **26**
Barons Cft. CV3: Cov 2E **174**
CV10: Nun 5C **88**
Baron's Fld. Rd. CV3: Cov 2D **174**
Barpool Rd. CV10: Nun 5F **88**
Barrack Cl. B75: S Cold 3A **60**
Barrack La. B63: Crad 3H **117**
Barracks, The LE9: Barw 3A **70**
Barracks Cl. WS3: Blox 1L **39**
Barracks La. CV35: Beau 7J **197**
WS3: Blox 1K **39**
WS8: Bwnhls 8J **17**
Barracks Pl. WS3: Blox 1L **39**
Barracks Rd. DY13: Stour S 8J **183**
Barrack St. B7: Birm 5A **102** (2M **5**)
B70: W Brom 1G **77**
CV34: Warw 2E **222**
Barracks Way
CV1: Cov 7C **152** (5C **6**)
Barra Cft. B35: Cas V 5B **82**
Barrar Cl. DY8: Amb 1L **115**
Barras Ct. CV2: Cov 5G **153**
Barras Grn. CV2: Cov 5G **153**
Barras Grn. Bungs.
CV2: Cov 5G **153**
Barras La. CV1: Cov 6B **152** (3A **6**)
Barratts Cl. DY12: Bew 6A **156**
Barratts Cft. DY5: P'ntt 8C **74**
Barratts Ho. B14: K Hth 7L **143**
Barratts Rd. B38: K Nor 8G **143**
Barratts Stile La. DY12: Bew 6A **156**
BARR COMMON 6H **41**
Barr Comn. Cl. WS9: A'rdge 6H **41**
Barr Comn. Rd. WS9: A'rdge 6H **41**
Barrett Cl. DY10: Kidd 3B **158**
Barretts La. CV7: Bal C 3J **171**
Barrhill Cl. B43: Gt Barr 7E **56**
Barrie Av. DY10: Kidd 2C **158**
Barrie Rd. LE10: Hinc 6K **69**
Barrington Cl. WS5: Wals 6A **56**
WV10: Oxl 8C **22**
Barrington Rd. B45: Rubery 2E **162**
B92: Olton 7L **123**
CV22: Bil 7J **179**
Barr Lakes La. WS9: A'rdge 2E **56**
Barr La. CV13: High H 6A **68**
CV23: Brin 5L **155**
Bar Rd. CV3: Cov 1E **174**
Barron Rd. B31: N'fld 6B **142**
Barrow Cl. B98: Redd 6M **213**
CV2: W'grve S 3B **154**
Barrowfield Ct. CV8: Ken 5F **198**
Barrowfield La. CV8: Ken 5F **198**
Barrow Hill Rd. DY5: P'ntt 8C **74**
Barrow Ho. *B16: Edg 8F 100*
(off Meyrick Wlk.)
Barrow Rd. CV8: Ken 5F **198**
Barrows La. B26: Yard 1L **123**
(not continuous)
Barrows Rd. B11: S'brk 3C **122**
Barrow Wlk. B5: Birm 2L **121**
(not continuous)
Barrs Cres. B64: Crad H 1M **117**
Barrs Rd. B64: Crad H 2L **117**
Barrs St. B68: O'bry 5G **99**
Barr St. B19: Hock 4J **101** (1D **4**)
(not continuous)
DY3: Lwr G 6C **74**
Barry Ho. CV2: Cov 8K **131**
Barry Jackson Twr.
B6: Aston 2M **101**
Barry Rd. WS5: Wals 2C **56**
Barsby Cl. CV9: Ath 2K **65**
Barsham Cl. B5: Edg 3J **121**
Barsham Dr. DY5: Brie H 1C **116**
BARSTON 8A **148**
Barston Cl. CV6: Cov 6G **131**
Barston La. B91: Sol 7H **147**
(Ravenshaw, not continuous)
B91: Sol 7F **146**
(Warwick Rd.)
B92: Bars, H Ard 6M **147**
CV7: Bal C 8D **148**
Barston Rd. B68: O'bry 2H **119**
Bartestree Cl. B98: Redd 8M **213**
Bartholemews La.
B61: B'gve 4M **187**
Bartholomew Ct. CV3: Cov 3F **174**
Bartholomew Row
B5: Birm 6M **101** (4J **5**)
Bartholomew St.
B5: Birm 7M **101** (5J **5**)
Bartic Av. DY6: K'wfrd 5M **95**
Bartleet Rd. B67: Smeth 4K **99**
B98: Redd 2K **221**
Bartlett Cl. CV6: Cov 7E **130**
CV34: Warw 2F **222**
DY4: Tip 8B **54**
Bartley Cl. B92: Olton 7M **123**
Bartley Dr. B31: N'fld 1L **141**
BARTLEY GREEN 8K **119**
Bartley Green Leisure Cen. 8J **119**
Bartley Ho. B32: Bart G 1K **141**
Bartley Woods B32: Bart G 7H **119**
Barton Cres. CV31: Lea S 3C **224**
Barton Cft. B28: Hall G 5F **144**
Barton Dr. B93: Know 6H **169**
Barton Ind. Pk. WV14: Bils 2L **53**
Barton La. DY6: W Hth 1J **95**
Barton Lodge Rd.
B28: Hall G 5E **144**
Barton Pas. B3: Birm 5E **4**
Barton Rd. CV6: Cov 7F **130**
CV10: Nun 8J **89**
CV12: Bed 6G **111**
CV22: Bil 1K **205**
WV4: E'shll 5F **52**
Bartons Bank B6: Aston 2L **101**
Bartons Ct. CV2: Cov 5G **153**
Barton's Mdw. CV2: Cov 3H **153**
Barton St. B70: W Brom 7H **77**
Bar Wlk. WS9: A'rdge 8J **27**
BARWELL 3A **70**
Barwell Cl. B93: Dorr 5E **168**
CV32: Lea S 6M **217**
Barwell Ct. B9: Birm 7B **102**
Barwell La. LE9: Barw 4A **70**
LE10: Hinc 6L **69**
Barwell Path LE10: Hinc 7L **69**
Barwell Rd. B9: Birm 7B **102**
Barwick St. B3: Birm 6K **101** (4F **4**)
Basalt Cl. WS2: Wals 5G **39**
Basant Cl. CV34: Warw 2G **223**
Bascote Cl. B97: Redd 8B **212**
Bascote Ri. CV47: Sou 4G **225**
Basely Way CV6: Longf 5D **130**
Basford Brook Dr.
CV6: Longf 4F **130**
Basildon Wlk.
CV2: W'grve S 2A **154**
Basil Gro. B31: N'fld 5L **141**
Basil Rd. B31: N'fld 5L **141**
Basin Bri. La. CV13: Stoke G 2A **68**
Basin La. B77: Tam 6D **32**
Baskerville Rd. DY10: Kidd 8M **135**
Baskeyfield Cl. WS14: Lich 2K **19**
Baslow Cl. B33: Stech 5L **103**
WS3: Blox 6H **25**
Baslow Rd. WS3: Blox 6H **25**
Bason's La. B68: O'bry 4J **99**
Bassano Rd. B65: B'hth 8C **98**
Bassenthwaite Ct.
DY6: K'wfrd 3K **95**
Bassett Cl. B76: Walm 5L **59**
WV4: Penn 3J **51**
WV12: W'hall 5D **38**
Bassett Cft. B10: Small H 1B **122**
Bassett La. LE9: Sap 2K **93**
Bassett Rd. B63: Crad 3G **117**
CV6: Cov 4A **152**
WS10: W'bry 6J **55**
(not continuous)
Bassetts Gro. B37: K'hrst 4F **104**
BASSETT'S POLE 7B **44**
Bassett St. WS2: Wals 8H **39**
Bassnage Rd. B63: Hale 7L **117**
Batch Cft. WV14: Bils 4K **53**
Batchcroft WS10: Darl 1D **54**
Batchelor Cl. DY8: Amb 1M **115**
BATCHLEY 5B **212**
Batchley Rd. B97: Redd 5B **212**
Bateman Dr. B73: W Grn 7H **59**
Bateman Rd. B46: Col 8M **83**
Batemans Acre Sth.
CV6: Cov 5A **152**
BATEMAN'S GREEN 3L **165**
Batemans La.
B47: H'wd, Wyt 4L **165**
Bates Cl. B76: Walm 2B **82**
Bates Gro. WV10: Wolv 4G **37**
Bates Hill B97: Redd 5D **212**
Bates La. B94: Tan A 8E **192**
Bates Rd. CV5: Cov 2L **173**
Bate St. WS2: Wals 6L **39**
WV4: E'shll 6G **53**
Batham Rd. DY10: Kidd 1A **158**
Bath Av. WV1: Wolv 7B **36** (2G **7**)
Bath Cl. LE9: Sap 1K **93**
Bath Ct. B15: Birm 8J **101** (8C **4**)
B29: W Cas 2B **142**
Batheaston Cl. B38: K Nor 2D **164**
Bath Mdw. B63: Crad 4L **117**
Bath Pas. B5: Birm 8L **101** (7G **5**)
Bath Pl. CV31: Lea S 2M **223**
Bath Rd. CV9: Ath 2L **65**
CV11: Nun 4J **89**
DY4: Tip 4A **76**
DY5: Quar B 7G **97**
DY8: Stourb 4M **115**
WS1: Wals 1L **55**
WS11: Cann 4E **8**
WV1: Wolv 7B **36** (4G **7**)
Bath Row B15: Birm 8J **101** (8C **4**)
B69: O'bry 1D **98**
Bath St. B4: Birm 5L **101** (2G **5**)
CV1: Cov 5D **152** (1E **6**)
CV21: Rugby 6B **180**
CV31: Lea S 2M **223**
DY2: Dud 1J **97**
DY3: Sed 8E **52**

Bath St.—Belfry Junc.

Bath St. WS1: Wals 8L 39
WV1: Wolv 8E 36 (5M 7)
WV13: W'hall 8B 38
WV14: Bils 4L 53
Bathurst Cl. CV22: Bil 1L 205
Bathurst Rd. CV6: Cov 3A 152
Bath Wlk. B12: Bal H 4L 121
Bathway Rd. CV3: Finh 5A 174
Batmans Hill Rd. DY4: Tip 7L 53
WV14: Bils 7L 53
Batsford Cl. B98: Redd 4H 221
Batsford Rd. CV6: Cov 4M 151
Batson Ri. DY5: Brie H 1A 116
Battalion Ct. CV6: Cov 8A 130
Battenhall Rd. B17: Harb 4A 120
Battens Cl. B98: Redd 6F 212
Battens Dr. B98: Redd 5K 213
Battery Retail Pk.
B29: S Oak 7E 120
Battery Way B11: Tys 5E 122
Battledown Cl. LE10: Hinc 7H 69
Battlefield Hill WV5: Wom 2J 73
Battlefield La. WV5: Wom 3H 73
Baulk La. CV7: Berk 1K 171
Bavaro Gdns. DY5: Quar B 7G 97
Baverstock Rd. B14: K Hth 7L 143
Bawnmore Ct. CV22: Bil 1K 205
Bawnmore Pk. CV22: Bil 2L 205
Bawnmore Rd. CV22: Bil 1K 205
Baxter Av. DY10: Kidd 2L 157
Baxter Cl. CV4: Tile H 7G 151
CV9: Ath 2L 65
Baxter Ct. CV31: Lea S 2A 224
Baxter Gdns. DY10: Kidd 2M 157
BAXTERLEY 3D 64
Baxterley Grn. B76: Walm 8M 59
B91: Sol 5K 145
Baxter Rd. DY5: Brie H 7C 96
Baxters Grn. B90: Shir 1G 167
Baxters Rd. B90: Shir 1H 167
Bayer St. WV14: Cose 1J 75
Bayford Av. B26: Sheld 5C 124
B31: Longb 3L 163
Bayley Cres. WS10: Darl 1C 54
Bayley Ho. WS8: Bwnhls 3F 26
Bayley La. CV1: Cov 7D 152 (5D 6)
Bayleys La. DY4: Tip 1C 76
Bayley Twr. B36: Hodg H 1L 103
Baylie Ct. DY8: Stourb 4M 115
(off Green St.)
Baylie St. DY8: Stourb 5M 115
Baylis Av. WV11: Wed 1M 37
BAYLIS GREEN 8A 192
Bayliss Av. CV6: Longf 5G 131
WV4: E'shll 6G 53
Bayliss Cl. B31: N'fld 4B 142
WV14: Bils 2J 53
Baynton Rd. WV12: W'hall 2C 38
Bayston Av. WV3: Wolv 1L 51
Bayston Rd. B14: K Hth 5L 143
Bayswater Rd. B20: Hand 8K 79
DY3: Lwr G 6D 74
Bayton Ind. Est. CV7: Exh 2G 131
Bayton Rd. CV7: Exh 2G 131
Bayton Rd. Ind. Est.
CV7: Exh 1H 131
Bayton Way CV7: Exh 2J 131
Bay Tree Cl. B38: K Nor 1D 164
Baytree Cl. CV2: Cov 8K 131
WS3: Blox 7G 25
Baytree Rd. WS3: Blox 7G 25
Baywell Cl. B90: M'path 2A 168
Bazzard Rd. CV11: Bram 3F 112
CV12: Bram 3F 112
Beach Av. B12: Bal H 4B 122
WV14: Cose 6F 52
Beach Brook Cl. B11: S'hll 4B 122
Beachburn Way B20: Hand 6G 79
Beach Cl. B31: N'fld 8C 142
Beachcroft Rd. DY6: W Hth 8J 73
Beach Dr. B63: Hale 4A 118
Beach Rd. B11: S'hll 4B 122
DY13: Stour S 8E 182
WV14: Bils 2K 53
Beach St. B63: Hale 4A 118
Beach Trade Cen.
B12: Bal H 4B 122
Beachwood Av. DY6: W Hth 8J 73
Beacon Cl. B43: Gt Barr 8F 56
B45: Rubery 3G 163
B66: Smeth 2A 100
Beacon Ct. B43: Gt Barr 8F 56
B74: S'tly 1M 57
Beacon Dr. WS1: Wals 1A 56
Beaconfields WS13: Lich 1G 19
Beacon Gdns. WS13: Lich 8G 13
Beacon Hgts. WS9: A'rdge 3H 57
Beacon Hill B6: Aston 1L 101
B45: Rubery 4F 162
WS9: A'rdge 8J 41
Beacon Ho. B45: Rubery 2E 162
(off Callowbrook La.)
Beacon La. B45: Lick 6D 162
B60: L Ash 6D 162
DY3: Sed 8E 52
Beacon M. B43: Gt Barr 8F 56
Beacon Pas. DY3: Sed 1D 74
(off High St.)
Beacon Ri. DY3: Sed 8E 52
DY9: W'cte 5D 116
WS9: A'rdge 6H 41
Beacon Rd. B43: Gt Barr 1H 57
B44: K'sdng 5A 58
B73: Bold 8G 59
CV6: Cov 6C 130
WS5: Wals 4D 56
WS9: A'rdge 1H 57
WV12: W'hall 1C 38
Beaconsfield Av.
CV22: Rugby 8A 180
WV4: E'shll 3D 52
Beaconsfield Ct. CV11: Nun 4K 89
WS1: Wals 1B 56
Beaconsfield Cres.
B12: Bal H 4L 121
Beaconsfield Dr. WV4: E'shll 3D 52
Beaconsfield Rd. B12: Bal H 5L 121
B74: S Cold 2H 59
CV2: Cov 7H 153
Beaconsfield St.
B71: W Brom 4J 77
CV31: Lea S 2B 224
Beaconsfield St. W.
CV31: Lea S 1B 224
Beacon St. WS1: Wals 8A 40
WS13: Lich 8F 12
WV14: Cose 8F 52
Beacon Trad. Est.
WS9: A'rdge 3G 41
Beacon Vw. B45: Rubery 3F 162
WS2: Wals 7F 38
(not continuous)
Beacon Vw. Dr. B74: S'tly 4M 57
Beaconview Ho.
B71: W Brom 8M 55
Beacon Vw. Rd. B71: W Brom . . .7L 55
Beacon Way WS9: Wals W 6G 27
WS12: Wim 6M 9
Beake Av. CV6: Cov 8B 130
Beakes Rd. B67: Smeth 6M 99
Beaks Farm Gdns. B16: Edg . . .7D 100
Beaks Hill Rd. B38: K Nor 8E 142
Beak St. B1: Birm 7K 101 (6F 4)
Beale Cl. B35: Cas V 7A 82
CV33: Bis T 8E 224
Beale Ho. B16: Edg 8F 100
Beales Cnr. DY12: Bew 6B 156
Beales St. B6: Aston 1B 102
Beale St. DY8: Stourb 4M 115
Bealeys Av. WV11: Wed 1M 37
Bealeys Cl. WS3: Blox 6G 25
Bealeys Fold WV11: Wed 4K 37
(off Nicholls Fold)
Bealeys La. WS3: Blox 6G 25
Beamans Cl. B92: Olton 5A 124
Beaminster Rd. B91: Sol 5A 146
Beamish Cl. CV2: W'grve S 3A 154
Beamish La. WV8: Cod W 4A 20
Beamont Cl. DY4: Tip 3L 75
Bean Cft. B32: Bart G 6J 119
Beanfield Av. CV3: Finh 5M 173
Bean Rd. DY2: Dud 1K 97
DY4: Tip 3J 75
Bean Rd. Ind. Est. DY4: Tip 3J 75
Beans Slade Dr. WS14: Lich 4G 19
Beardmore Rd. B72: W Grn 1J 81
Bear Hill B48: A'chu 4B 190
Bear Hill Dr. B48: A'chu 3B 190
Bear La. Cl. B78: Pole 2K 49
Bearley Cft. B90: Shir 1J 167
Bearmore Rd. B64: Old H 8L 97
Bearnett Dr. WV4: Penn 7J 51
Bearnett La. WV4: Lwr P 8H 51
WV5: Wom 8H 51
Bearsdon Cres. LE10: Hinc 7H 69
BEAR WOOD 8A 100
Bearwood Ho. B66: Smeth 5A 100
Bearwood Rd. B66: Smeth 8A 100
Bearwood Shop. Cen.
B66: Smeth 8A 100
Beasley Gro. B43: Gt Barr 8H 57
Beaton Cl. WV13: W'hall 7L 37
Beaton Rd. B74: Four O 6G 43
Beatrice St. WS3: Blox 3J 39
Beatrice Wlk. B69: Tiv 7A 76
Beatty Cl. LE10: Hinc 6K 69
Beatty Dr. CV22: Bil 7K 179
Beatty Ho. DY4: Tip 1A 76
Beaty's Gdns. CV32: Lill 5A 218
Beaubrook Gdns. DY8: Word 6L 95
Beauchamp Av. B20: Hand 4F 78
CV32: Lea S 8M 217
DY11: Kidd 6J 157
Beauchamp Cl. B37: Chel W 7H 105
B76: Walm 2B 82
Beauchamp Ct. CV32: Lea S . . .8M 217
DY11: Kidd 6K 157
Beauchamp Gdns.
CV34: Warw 3H 223
Beauchamp Hgts.
DY11: Kidd 6K 157
Beauchamp Hill CV32: Lea S . . .8L 217
Beauchamp Ind. Pk.
B77: Wiln 1D 46
Beauchamp Rd. B13: Mose 4B 144
B77: Hock 4F 46
B91: Sol 4E 146
CV8: Ken 7E 198
CV32: Lea S 8M 217
CV34: Warw 1H 223
Beau Ct. WS11: Cann 8E 8
Beaudesert WS7: C Ter 8G 11
Beaudesert Cl. B47: H'wd 3A 166
Beaudesert Pk.
WS15: Cann W 3G 11
Beaudesert Rd. B20: Hand 1H 101
B47: H'wd 3A 166
CV5: Cov 8A 152
Beaudesert Vw. WS12: Haz 4A 10
Beaufell Cl. CV34: Warw 8E 216
Beaufort Av. B34: Hodg H 3K 103
CV32: Cubb 4C 218
DY11: Kidd 2G 157
Beaufort Cl. LE10: Burb 5L 91
Beaufort Dr. CV3: Bin 2M 175
Beaufort Pk. B8: W End 4K 103
Beaufort Rd. B16: Edg 8F 100
B23: Erd 7E 80
Beaufort St. B98: Redd 6E 212
Beaufort Way WS9: A'rdge 5H 41
Beaulieu Av. DY6: K'wfrd 5M 95
Beaulieu Cl. DY11: Kidd 1J 157
Beaulieu Pk. CV31: Lea S 3D 224
Beaumaris Cl. CV5: Alle 4F 150
DY1: Dud 6F 74
Beaumont Av. LE10: Hinc 2G 91
Beaumont Cl. WS6: Gt Wyr 7F 14
Beaumont Ct. CV6: Cov 5A 152
(off Beaumont Cres.)
Beaumont Cres. CV6: Cov 5A 152
Beaumont Dr. B17: Harb 5B 120
DY5: Brie H 2B 116
Beaumont Gdns. B18: Hock 3F 100
Beaumont Gro. B91: Sol 4M 145
Beaumont Lawns B60: Marl 8C 162
Beaumont Pk. B30: K Nor 5F 142
Beaumont Pl. CV11: Nun 5G 89
Beaumont Rd. B30: B'vlle 3E 142
B62: B'hth 1E 118
CV7: Ker E 3M 129
CV11: Nun 4F 88
WS6: Gt Wyr 7F 14
WS10: W'bry 5F 54
Beaumont Way WS11: Nort C . . .5A 16
Beaurevoir Way
CV34: Warw 1G 223
BEAUSALE 7J 197
Beausale Cft. CV5: E Grn 6G 151
Beausale Dr. B93: Know 2H 169
Beausale La.
CV35: Beau, Hatt 8J 197
Beauty Bank B64: Crad H 1A 118
Beauty Bank Cres.
DY8: Stourb 3L 115
Beaver Cl. WV11: Wed 4M 37
Bebington Cl. WV8: Pend 1M 35
Beccles Dr. WV13: W'hall 1M 53
Beche Way CV5: Cov 4H 151
Beckbury Av. WV4: Penn 4J 51
Beckbury Rd. B29: W Cas 8A 120
CV2: W'grve S 2M 153
Beck Cl. B66: Smeth 5A 100
Beckenham Av. B44: K'sdng 8A 58
Beckensall Cl. DY1: Dud 8H 75
Becket Cl. B74: Four O 3F 42
Beckett Cl. B98: Redd 4F 212
Beckett St. WV14: Bils 3L 53
Beckfield Cl. B14: K Hth 7L 143
WS4: S'fld 1C 40
Beckfoot Cl. CV21: Brow 1D 180
Beckfoot Dr. CV2: W'grve S . . .8M 131
Beckford Cft. B93: Dorr 6F 168
Beckman Rd. DY9: Pedm 7C 116
Beckminster Rd. WV3: Wolv 2M 51
Becks, The B48: A'chu 2A 190
Beck's Cl. CV47: S'ton 1M 225
Becks La. CV47: S'ton 1M 225
CV7: Mer 4A 128
Beconsfield Cl. B93: Dorr 7F 168
Becton Gro. B42: Gt Barr 2K 79
Bedale Av. LE10: Hinc 7M 69
Bedcote Pl. DY8: Stourb 4B 116
Beddoe Cl. DY4: Tip 4D 76
Beddow Av. WV14: Cose 2J 75
Beddows Rd. WS3: Wals 4L 39
Bede Arc. CV12: Bed 6H 111
Bede Rd. CV6: Cov 3B 152
CV10: Nun 6D 88
CV12: Bed 5G 111
Bede Village CV12: Bed 1C 130
Bedford Cl. LE10: Hinc 6L 69
Bedford Dr. B75: S Cold 3L 59
Bedford Ho. B36: Cas B 3H 105
WV1: Wolv 5C 36
Bedford Pl. CV32: Lea S 1M 223
WS12: Hed 5H 9
Bedford Rd.
B11: S'brk 8A 102 (8M 5)
B71: W Brom 2H 77
B75: S Cold 3L 59
Bedford St. CV1: Cov 7A 152
CV32: Lea S 1M 223
DY4: Tip 4B 76
WV1: Wolv 2H 53
Bedford Ter. B19: Loz 1K 101
Bedlam La. CV6: Longf 7E 130
BEDLAM'S END 3B 196
Bedlam Wood Rd.
B31: Longb 8J 141
BEDWORTH 6H 111
Bedworth By-Pass
CV10: Nun 1H 111
Bedworth Cl. CV12: Bulk 7B 112
Bedworth Cft. DY4: Tip 5B 76
Bedworth Gro. B9: Bord G 7H 103
BEDWORTH HEATH 7E 110
Bedworth La. CV12: Bed 5C 110
Bedworth Leisure Cen. 8H 111
Bedworth Rd. CV6: Longf 4G 131
CV12: Bulk 7L 111
Bedworth Slough Local
Nature Reserve 6F 110
Bedworth Station (Rail) 7J 111
BEDWORTH WOODLANDS 6E 110
Beebee Rd. WS10: W'bry 3F 54
Beecham Bus. Pk.
WS9: A'rdge 1G 41
Beecham Cl. WS9: A'rdge 1G 41
Beech Av. B12: Bal H 4A 122
B32: Quin 2K 119
B37: Chel W 8H 105
B62: B'hth 1C 118
B77: Glas 6E 32
Beech Cliffe CV34: Warw 1F 222
Beech Cl. B75: Four O 5G 43
B78: K'bry 2C 62
B79: Tam 1A 32
CV9: Hurl 4J 63
CV10: Harts 1A 88
CV35: Row 8A 196
CV47: Sou 6G 225
DY3: Sed 8E 52
DY7: Kinv 5B 114
WV10: Oxl 1B 36
Beechcote Av. DY11: W'ley 7K 135
Beech Ct. B8: Salt 4E 102
B30: K Nor 5E 142
B43: Gt Barr 8D 56
B45: Redn 2K 163
B66: Smeth 1J 99
B73: Bold 1F 80
B91: Sol 4D 146
CV22: Hillm 1F 206
CV34: H'cte 7L 223
DY8: Stourb 5B 116
WS1: Wals 1A 56
WS6: Gt Wyr 5G 15
WS12: Hed 2H 9
Beech Cres. DY4: Tip 1C 76
WS7: Chase 3F 16
WS10: W'bry 4F 54
Beech Cft. CV12: Bed 8F 110
Beechcroft B15: Edg 2G 121
Beechcroft Av. B28: Hall G 3G 145
Beechcroft Ct. B74: Four O 8G 43
WS11: Cann 7E 8
Beechcroft Cres. B74: S'tly 8K 41
Beechcroft Dr. B61: B'gve 5B 188
Beechcroft Est. B63: Crad 3J 117
Beechcroft Pl. WV10: Oxl 2C 36
Beechcroft Rd. B36: Cas B 1B 104
B64: Old H 8L 97
DY11: Kidd 1G 157
Beechdale B68: O'bry 2H 119
Beechdale Av. B44: Gt Barr 7L 57
Beech Dene Gro. B23: Erd 4E 80
Beech Dr. CV8: Ken 4H 199
CV22: Bil 8J 179
CV23: Thurl 6F 204
Beechen Gro. WS7: C Ter 1F 16
Beecher Pl. B63: Crad 4K 117
Beecher Rd. B63: Crad 4K 117
Beecher Rd. E. B63: Crad 4K 117
Beecher's Keep CV8: Bran 4F 176
Beecher St. B63: Crad 4J 117
Beeches, The B15: Edg 1J 121
B70: W Brom 7L 77
B74: Four O 5D 42
B78: Pole 1A 48
CV12: Bed 7E 110
CV23: Clift D 4F 180
LE9: Earl S 1F 70
WV1: Wolv 6A 36
Beeches Av. B27: A Grn 5J 123
Beeches Cl. B45: Rubery 2D 162
DY6: K'wfrd 4K 95
Beeches Ct. B45: Redn 2H 163
Beeches Dr. B24: Erd 4J 81
Beeches Farm Dr.
B31: Longb 2A 164
Beeches M. DY9: Hag 5M 137
Beeches Pl. WS3: Blox 2K 39
Beeches Rd. B42: Gt Barr 2H 79
B65: B'hth 8B 98
B68: O'bry 6J 99
B70: W Brom 6L 77
(not continuous)
DY11: Kidd 8J 135
WS3: Blox 3K 39
Beeches Vw. Av. B63: Crad 5J 117
Beeches Wlk. B73: W Grn 6H 59
Beeches Way B31: Longb 2A 164
Beechey Cl. B43: Gt Barr 4K 57
Beech Farm Cft. B31: N'fld 6A 142
Beechfield Av. B11: S'brk 3B 122
Beechfield Cl. B62: B'hth 1C 118
Beechfield Dr. DY11: Kidd 8J 135
Beechfield Gro. WV14: Cose 2H 75
Beechfield Ri. WS13: Lich 1K 19
Beechfield Rd. B11: S'brk 3B 122
B67: Smeth 5M 99
Beech Gdns. WS14: Lich 3J 19
WV8: Cod 7F 20
Beech Ga. B74: Lit A 4B 42
Beechglade B20: Hand 5F 78
Beech Grn. DY1: Dud 4G 75
Beech Gro. B14: K Hth 4A 144
CV7: Old A 7E 86
CV34: Warw 8H 217
WS12: Hunt 1D 8
Beech Hill Rd. B72: W Grn 2J 81
Beech Ho. B31: N'fld 6B 142
(off Church Rd.)
B91: Sol 7M 145
Beechhouse La. WV5: Seis 1A 72
Beech Hurst B38: K Nor 1E 164
Beech Hurst Gdns. WV5: Seis . . .7A 50
BEECH LANES 2M 119
Beechlawn Dr. DY7: Stourt 2E 114
Beech M. B64: Old H 7L 97
Beechmore Rd. B26: Sheld 4M 123
Beechmount Dr. B23: Erd 3G 81
Beechnut Cl. B91: Sol 4D 146
CV4: Tile H 7D 150
Beechnut La. B91: Sol 5E 146
(not continuous)
Beech Pk. Dr. B45: B Grn 1J 189
Beech Pine Cl. WS12: Hed 1G 9
Beech Rd. B23: Erd 2F 80
B30: B'vlle 2E 142
B47: H'wd 3B 166
B61: B'gve 5M 187
B69: Tiv 1A 98
B79: Tam 1A 32
CV6: Cov 4B 152
DY1: Dud 5J 75
DY6: K'wfrd 4L 95
DY8: Stourb 6L 115
WS10: W'bry 4F 54
WV10: Oxl 1B 36
WV13: W'hall 7L 37
Beech St. WV14: Cose 1J 75
Beech Tree Av. CV4: Tile H 7H 151
WV11: Wed 1J 37
Beech Tree Cl. B97: Redd 5B 212
DY6: K'wfrd 1L 95
Beech Tree La. WS11: Cann 1D 14
Beechtree La.
DY10: Cookl, Ism 3D 136
Beechtree Rd. WS9: Wals W 6F 26
Beech Wlk. B38: K Nor 1F 164
Beech Way B66: Smeth 4B 100
BEECHWOOD 3A 172
Beechwood B20: Hand 6E 78
Beechwood Av. CV5: Cov 8L 151
LE10: Burb 6K 91
WV11: Wed 1H 37
Beechwood Bus. Pk.
WS11: Hth H 6H 9
Beechwood Cl. B90: Ches G 5L 167
WS3: Blox 6H 25
Beechwood Ct. B30: K Nor 6J 143
CV5: Cov 1M 173
CV21: Rugby 5M 179
WV6: Tett 6J 35
Beechwood Cres. B77: Amin 5F 32
Beechwood Cft. B74: Lit A 4D 42
CV8: Ken 7F 198
Beechwood Dr. WV6: Tett 7G 35
BEECHWOOD GARDENS 1L 173
Beechwood Pk. Rd. B91: Sol 3L 145
Beechwood Rd. B14: K Hth 4M 143
B43: Gt Barr 8F 56
B67: Smeth 1L 119
B70: W Brom 6H 77
CV10: Nun 3D 88
CV12: Bed 5J 111
DY2: Dud 8L 75
Beecroft Av. WS13: Lich 8H 13
Beecroft Rd. WS11: Cann 8E 8
Beehive Cl. B61: Cats 8A 162
Beehive Hill CV8: Ken 2D 198
Beehive La. B76: Curd 3J 83
Beehive Wlk. DY4: Tip 4L 75
Beekes Cft. B78: Faz 1A 46
Bee La. WV10: F'hses 6D 22
Beeston Cl. B6: Aston 2A 102
CV3: Bin 1M 175
DY5: Brie H 1D 116
Beeston Rd. DY10: Cookl 4A 136
Beeton Rd. B18: Win G 3E 100
Beet St. B65: B'hth 8C 98
Beever Rd. DY4: Tip 2D 76
Beggars Bush La. WV5: Wom . . .4H 73
Begonia Cl. LE10: Burb 4L 91
Begonia Dr. LE10: Burb 4L 91
Beighton Cl. B74: Four O 3F 42
Beilby Rd. B30: Stir 3H 143
BELBROUGHTON 2E 160
Belbroughton Cl. B98: Redd . . .7F 212
Belbroughton Rd. B63: Hale . . .7M 117
DY8: Stourb 6L 115
DY9: Brme 8J 137
DY9: Clent 8E 138
DY10: Blak 8J 137
Belcher's La. B9: Bord G 7G 103
Beldray Pk. WV14: Bils 3L 53
Beldray Rd. WV14: Bils 3L 53
Belfont Trad. Est. B62: Hale . . .5C 118
Belfry, The WV6: Pert 5D 34
Belfry Cl. LE10: Burb 5K 91
WS3: Blox 6G 25
Belfry Dr. DY8: Woll 3L 115
Belfry Golf Course, The 5J 61
BELFRY JUNC. 7J 61

Belgrade Rd.—Biddings La.

Belgrade Rd. WV10: Oxl ... 8B 22
Belgrade Theatre ... 6C 152 (4B 6)
BELGRAVE ... 8D 32
Belgrave Ct. DY6: K'wfrd ... 5M 95
Belgrave Dr. CV21: Brow ... 3D 180
Belgrave Interchange
B5: Birm ... 2K 121
Belgrave Middleway
B5: Birm ... 2L 121
B12: Birm ... 2L 121
Belgrave Recreation Cen.
B77: Wiln ... 8E 32
Belgrave Rd. B62: B'hth ... 1D 118
B77: Wiln ... 1E 46
CV2: Cov ... 5L 153
Belgrave Sq. CV2: Cov ... 5L 153
Belgrave Ter. B21: Hand ... 2G 101
Belgrave Wlk. WS2: Wals ... 6H 39
Belgravia Cl. B5: Bal H ... 2L 121
Belgravia Cl. Walkway
B5: Bal H ... 2L 121
Belgravia Ct. B37: K'hrst ... 4G 105
Belgrove Cl. B15: Edg ... 3E 120
Belinda Cl. WV13: W'hall ... 6M 37
Bellairs Av. CV12: Bed ... 8E 110
Bellamy Cl. B90: Shir ... 8K 145
Bellamy Farm Rd. B90: Shir ... 8K 145
Bellamy La. WV11: Wed ... 2J 37
Bell Av. WV13: W'hall ... 7A 38
Bell Barn Rd.
B15: Birm ... 1J 121 (8C 4)
Bell Barn Shop. Cen.
B15: Birm ... 8J 101 (8D 4)
Bellbrooke Cl. CV6: Cov ... 8H 131
Bell Cl. B9: Bord G ... 7E 102
B36: Cas B ... 3H 105
WS10: Darl ... 2D 54
WS13: Lich ... 8F 12
Bell Ct. CV32: Lea S ... 7M 217
Bellcroft B16: Birm ... 7H 101 (6A 4)
Bell Dr. B8: Salt ... 6F 102
CV7: Ash G ... 2E 130
WS5: Wals ... 4A 56
WS12: Hed ... 2J 9
Bellefield Av. B18: Win G ... 5E 100
Bellefield Rd. B18: Win G ... 5E 100
Belle Isle DY5: Brie H ... 6C 96
Bellemere Rd. B92: H Ard ... 4B 148
Bellencroft Gdns. WV3: Wolv ... 2J 51
BELL END ... 2H 161
Bell End B65: Row R ... 6C 98
Belle Orchard DY11: Kidd ... 4H 157
Bellevale B63: Hale ... 4L 117
Belle Vue CV10: Nun ... 6E 88
DY8: Word ... 7J 95
Bellevue B5: Bal H ... 2K 121
Bellevue Av. B16: Edg ... 5D 100
Bellevue Cl. B61: Marl ... 8C 162
Belle Vue Dr. B62: Hale ... 3D 118
Belle Vue Gdns. B65: Row R ... 6C 98
Belle Vue Rd. B65: Row R ... 7C 98
DY5: Quar B ... 8G 97
LE9: Earl S ... 1C 70
Bellevue Rd. B26: Sheld ... 2B 124
WV14: Bils ... 7A 54
Bellevue St. WV14: Cose ... 7F 52
Belle Vue Ter. B92: H Ard ... 3A 148
Belle Wlk. B13: Mose ... 7B 122
Bellfield B31: N'fld ... 5M 141
B94: Tan A ... 7C 193
Bellfield Ho. *B14: K Hth ... 8K 143*
(off Thornham Way)
Bellflower Cl. WV10: F'stne ... 2G 23
Bell Flwer Dr. WS5: Wals ... 6M 55
Bell Fold B68: O'bry ... 3J 99
BELL GREEN
Birmingham ... 3H 165
Coventry ... 1H 153
Bell Grn. La. B38: Head H ... 4H 165
Bell Grn. Rd. CV6: Cov ... 1G 153
BELL HEATH ... 1L 161
Bell Heather Rd. WS8: Clay ... 3D 26
Bell Heath Way B32: Bart G ... 7G 119
Bell Hill B31: N'fld ... 4A 142
Bell Holloway B31: N'fld ... 4M 141
Bellingham B77: Wiln ... 8K 33
Bellington Cft. B90: M'path ... 3A 168
Bell Inn Shop. Cen., The
B31: N'fld ... 5A 142
Bellis St. B16: Edg ... 8F 100
Bell La. B31: N'fld ... 5A 142
B33: Kitts G ... 8E 104
B80: Stud ... 5L 221
WS3: Blox ... 7G 25
WS5: Wals ... 5M 55
Bellman Cl. WS10: Darl ... 2D 54
Bell Mead B80: Stud ... 5L 221
Bell Mdw. DY9: Pedm ... 1B 138
Bell Mdw. Way B14: K Hth ... 7L 143
(not continuous)
Bell Pl. WV2: Wolv ... 1C 52 (8J 7)
Bell Rd. DY2: Neth ... 4J 97
WS5: Wals ... 3D 56
WV5: Try ... 8C 50
Bell Row *DY13: Stour S ... 6G 183*
(off Lion Hill)
Bells Farm Cl. B14: K Hth ... 7J 143
Bellsize Cl. WS11: Nort C ... 4M 15
Bells La. B14: K Hth ... 7H 143
DY8: Word ... 8K 95
WS7: C Ter ... 8F 10
Bells Moor Rd. B70: W Brom ... 3G 77
Bell St. B70: W Brom ... 7K 77
DY4: Tip ... 4L 75
DY5: Brie H ... 7D 96
DY5: P'ntt ... 3D 96
(Belmont Rd.)
DY5: P'ntt ... 2D 96
(Hartland St.)
DY8: Stourb ... 4M 115
WS10: Darl ... 2D 54
WV1: Wolv ... 8C 36 (5J 7)
WV14: Bils ... 3J 53
WV14: Cose ... 7J 53
Bell St. Sth. DY5: Brie H ... 7D 96
Bell Tower M. CV32: Lea S ... 6M 217
Bellview Way CV6: Cov ... 8H 131
Bell Wlk. B37: F'bri ... 8F 104
CV21: Hillm ... 1H 207
Bell Wharf Pl. WS5: Wals ... 3C 56
Bellwood Rd. B31: N'fld ... 5M 141
Belmont Av. WS11: Cann ... 7C 8
Belmont Cl. B97: Redd ... 8B 212
DY4: Tip ... 3M 75
WS9: A'rdge ... 3G 41
WS11: Cann ... 5G 15
Belmont Ct. CV32: Lill ... 5A 218
Belmont Covert B31: N'fld ... 4B 142
Belmont Cres. B31: N'fld ... 3B 142
Belmont Dr. CV32: Lill ... 5A 218
Belmont Gdns. WV14: Bils ... 5A 54
Belmont M. CV8: Ken ... 5F 198
CV32: Lill ... 5A 218
Belmont Pas.
B9: Birm ... 7A 102 (5M 5)
Belmont Rd. B21: Hand ... 1C 100
B45: Rubery ... 3G 163
B66: Smeth ... 7A 100
B77: Wiln ... 3E 46
CV6: Cov ... 2F 152
(not continuous)
CV22: Rugby ... 1A 206
DY5: P'ntt ... 3D 96
DY9: W'cte ... 4E 116
WV4: Penn ... 4A 52
Belmont Rd. E. B21: Hand ... 1C 100
Belmont Row
B4: Birm ... 6A 102 (3K 5)
Belmont St. WV14: Bils ... 5A 54
Belper, The DY1: Dud ... 8H 75
Belper Ent. Pk. B70: W Brom ... 5F 76
Belper Rd. B70: W Brom ... 6F 76
WS3: Blox ... 6J 25
Belper Row DY2: Neth ... 5L 97
Belsize B77: Glas ... 7E 32
Belstone Cl. B14: K Hth ... 3K 143
Belton Av. WV11: Wed ... 8H 23
Belton Cl. B94: H'ley H ... 4C 194
Belton Gro. B45: Redn ... 1J 163
Belt Rd. WS12: Hed ... 3F 8
Belvedere Av. WV4: Penn ... 4B 52
Belvedere Cl. B79: Tam ... 2C 32
DY6: K'wfrd ... 5M 95
DY10: Kidd ... 4A 158
WS7: Chase ... 4F 16
Belvedere Cres. DY12: Bew ... 4C 156
Belvedere Dr. B61: B'gve ... 5A 188
Belvedere Gdns.
WV6: Tett ... 2L 35
Belvedere Rd. B24: Erd ... 7G 81
CV5: Cov ... 1A 174
Belvide Gdns. WV8: Cod ... 5F 20
Belvide Gro. B29: W Cas ... 1B 142
Belvidere Gdns. B11: S'hll ... 5C 122
Belvidere Rd. WS1: Wals ... 1M 55
Belvoir B77: Two G ... 2C 46
Belvoir Cl. DY1: Dud ... 7E 74
Belvoir Rd. B60: B'gve ... 8C 188
Belwell Dr. B74: Four O ... 7G 43
Belwell La. B74: Four O ... 7G 43
Bembridge Cl. WV12: W'hall ... 1B 38
Bembridge Rd. B33: Yard ... 6A 104
Benacre Dr. B5: Birm ... 7M 101 (5K 5)
Benbeck Gro. DY4: Tip ... 4J 75
Benbow Cl. LE10: Hinc ... 5K 69
Benches Cl. WS7: C Ter ... 3D 16
Benches Furlong
CV23: Brow ... 1D 180
Bencroft WV8: Bilb ... 5H 21
Bendall Rd. B44: K'sdng ... 7B 58
Benedictine Ct. *CV1: Cov ... 4D 6*
(off Priory Pl.)
Benedictine Rd. CV3: Cov ... 2C 174
Benedict Sq. CV2: Cov ... 1J 153
Benedon Rd. B26: Sheld ... 2A 124
Bengrove Cl. B98: Redd ... 2G 221
Benion Rd. WS11: Cann ... 5F 8
Benmore Av. B5: Bal H ... 3K 121
Bennet Cl. CV13: Stoke G ... 2D 68
Bennett Av. DY1: Dud ... 3H 75
Bennett Ct. CV8: Wols ... 6F 176
Bennett Dr. CV34: Warw ... 2H 223
Bennett Rd. B74: Four O ... 6D 42
Bennett's Fold
WV3: Wolv ... 8C 36 (5H 7)
Bennett's Hill
B2: Birm ... 7K 101 (5F 4)
DY2: Dud ... 1L 97
Bennett's La. WV6: Tres ... 1A 50
Bennett's Rd. B8: Salt ... 3D 102
CV7: Ker E ... 3M 129
Bennett's Rd. Nth. CV7: Cor ... 1K 129
Bennett's Rd. Sth. CV6: Cov ... 6M 129
CV7: Ker E ... 6M 129
Bennett St. B19: Loz ... 1K 101
CV21: Rugby ... 6M 179
DY11: Kidd ... 3J 157
Ben Nevis Way DY8: Amb ... 3A 116
Bennfield Rd. CV21: Rugby ... 6A 180
Bennick Trad. Est.
WS11: Cann ... 3E 14
Bennitt Cl. B70: W Brom ... 8J 77
Benn Rd. CV12: Bulk ... 7B 112
Benn St. CV22: Rugby ... 7C 180
Benson Av. WV4: Penn ... 4C 52
Benson Cl. WS13: Lich ... 8K 13
WV6: Pert ... 4E 34
Benson Ind. Est. B18: Hock ... 3F 100
Benson Rd. B14: K Hth ... 8B 144
B18: Hock ... 3F 100
CV6: Cov ... 8A 130
Benson Vw. B79: Tam ... 1C 32
Bent Av. B32: Quin ... 3K 119
Benthall Rd. CV6: Cov ... 7F 130
Bentham Ct. B31: N'fld ... 4M 141
BENTLEY ... 6F 38
Bentley Bridge Leisure Pk. ... 5H 37
Bentley Bri. Way WV11: Wed ... 5H 37
Bentley Brook La. WS12: Haz ... 3A 10
Bentley Cl. B97: Redd ... 6D 212
CV32: Lill ... 6B 218
Bentley Ct. B76: Walm ... 1M 81
CV6: Cov ... 5C 130
Bentley Dr. WS2: Wals ... 7H 39
WV8: Cod ... 5F 20
Bentley Farm Cl. B93: Ben H ... 5E 168
Bentley Gro. B29: W Cas ... 1M 141
BENTLEY HEATH ... 4F 168
Bentley Heath Cotts.
B93: Know ... 4F 168
Bentley La. B46: Max ... 7J 107
B97: Up Ben ... 8H 211
WS2: Wals ... 5G 39
WV12: W'hall ... 4D 38
Bentley La. Ind. Pk.
WS2: Wals ... 6G 39
Bentley Mill Cl. WS2: Wals ... 8F 38
Bentley Mill La. WS2: Wals ... 8F 38
Bentley Mill Way WS2: Wals ... 8F 38
Bentley New Dr. WS2: Wals ... 6H 39
Bentley Pl. WS2: Wals ... 7H 39
Bentley Rd. B36: Cas B ... 2D 104
CV7: Exh ... 8G 111
CV11: Nun ... 5G 89
WV10: Bush ... 7E 22
Bentley Rd. Nth. WS2: Wals ... 8E 38
Bentley Rd. Sth. WS10: Darl ... 1D 54
Bentley Way B79: Tam ... 2M 31
Bentmead Gro. B38: K Nor ... 8G 143
Benton Av. B11: S'hll ... 3C 122
Benton Cl. WV12: W'hall ... 5D 38
Benton Cres. WS3: Blox ... 7K 25
BENTON GREEN ... 6M 149
Benton Grn. La. CV7: Berk ... 6M 149
Benton Rd. B11: S'brk ... 3C 122
Bentons Ct. DY11: Kidd ... 3J 157
Bentons La. WS6: Gt Wyr ... 8G 15
Bentons Mill Cft. B7: Nech ... 1C 102
Bentree, The CV3: Cov ... 1H 175
Bent St. DY5: Brie H ... 5D 96
Ben Willetts Wlk. B65: B'hth ... 8C 98
Benyon Cen., The WS2: Wals ... 2G 39
BEOLEY ... 2K 213
Beoley Cl. B72: W Grn ... 8J 59
Beoley Gro. B45: Rubery ... 2F 162
Beoley La. B98: Beo ... 1L 213
Beoley Rd. E. B98: Redd ... 5G 213
Beoley Rd. W. B98: Redd ... 6F 212
Berberry Cl. B30: B'vlle ... 3D 142
Berenska Dr. CV32: Lea S ... 7A 218
Beresford Av. CV6: Cov ... 8D 130
Beresford Cres.
B70: W Brom ... 6H 77
Beresford Dr. B73: Bold ... 8G 59
Beresford Rd. B69: O'bry ... 2J 99
WS3: Blox ... 1L 39
Berets, The B75: S Cold ... 3M 59
Bericote Cft. B27: A Grn ... 6K 123
Bericote Rd. CV32: B'dwn ... 1K 217
Berkeley Cl. B60: B'gve ... 1B 210
B98: Redd ... 6A 214
CV11: Nun ... 6H 89
WV6: Pert ... 6F 34
Berkeley Cres.
DY13: Stour S ... 8G 183
Berkeley Dr. DY6: K'wfrd ... 2J 95
Berkeley M. B25: Yard ... 2G 123
Berkeley Pct. B14: K Hth ... 7M 143
Berkeley Rd. B25: Yard ... 2G 123
B90: Shir ... 6F 144
CV8: Ken ... 3E 198
Berkeley Rd. E. B25: Yard ... 2H 123
Berkeley Rd. Nth. CV5: Cov ... 8A 152
Berkeley Rd. Sth. CV5: Cov ... 1A 174
Berkeley St. WS2: Wals ... 2H 55
Berkeswell Cl. B98: Redd ... 2H 213
Berkett Rd. CV6: Cov ... 6B 130
Berkley Cl. WS2: Wals ... 6F 38
Berkley Ct. B1: Birm ... 8J 101 (7C 4)
Berkley Cres. B13: Mose ... 8C 122
Berkley Ho. B23: Erd ... 3F 80
Berkley St. B1: Birm ... 7J 101 (6C 4)
Berkshire, The WS3: Blox ... 6G 25
Berkshire Cl. B71: W Brom ... 2H 77
CV10: Nun ... 6E 88
Berkshire Cres. WS10: W'bry ... 5J 55
BERKSWELL ... 6K 149
Berkswell Cl. B74: Four O ... 5E 42
B91: Sol ... 1B 146
DY1: Dud ... 6E 74
Berkswell Hall CV7: Berk ... 6J 149
Berkswell Rd. B24: Erd ... 5H 81
CV6: Cov ... 7G 131
CV7: Mer ... 3J 149
Berkswell Station (Rail) ... 1J 171
Berkswell Towermill ... 5K 171
BERMUDA ... 8G 89
Bermuda Bus. Pk.
CV10: Griff ... 2F 110
Bermuda Cl. DY1: Dud ... 3H 75
Bermuda Ind. Est.
CV10: Nun ... 1H 111
Bermuda Innovation Cen. ... 3G 111
Bermuda Rd. CV10: Nun ... 7G 89
Bernard Pl. B18: Hock ... 4F 100
Bernard Rd. B17: Edg ... 7B 100
B68: O'bry ... 7J 99
DY4: Tip ... 2B 76
Bernard St. B71: W Brom ... 5J 77
WS1: Wals ... 1A 56
Berners Cl. CV4: Tile H ... 7E 150
Berners St. B19: Loz ... 2K 101
Bernhard Dr. B21: Hand ... 1E 100
Bernie Crossland Wlk.
DY10: Kidd ... 6M 157
Bernwall Cl. DY8: Stourb ... 5M 115
Berrandale Rd.
B36: Hodg H ... 1M 103
Berrington Cl. B98: Redd ... 7J 213
Berrington Dr. WV14: Cose ... 1H 75
Berrington Rd. CV10: Nun ... 2C 88
CV31: Lea S ... 3B 224
Berrington Wlk. B5: Birm ... 2L 121
Berrow Cott. Homes
B93: Know ... 3J 169
Berrow Dr. B15: Edg ... 2E 120
Berrow Hill Rd. DY11: Kidd ... 8H 135
Berrowside Rd. B34: S End ... 3E 104
Berrow Vw. B61: B'gve ... 2K 209
Berry Av. WS10: Darl ... 4B 54
Berrybush Gdns. DY3: Sed ... 2E 74
Berry Cl. B19: Hock ... 3K 101
Berry Cres. WS5: Wals ... 5C 56
Berry Dr. B45: B Grn ... 8G 163
B66: Smeth ... 3A 100
WS9: A'rdge ... 4E 40
Berryfield Rd. B26: Sheld ... 3D 124
Berry Flds. CV7: Fill ... 5E 108
Berryfields WS9: A'rdge ... 4E 40
WS9: Ston ... 4L 27
Berryfields Rd. B76: Walm ... 6M 59
Berry Hall La.
B91: Cath B, Sol ... 5G 147
Berryhill WS12: Hed ... 5J 9
Berry La. B61: U War ... 7C 186
(Purshull Grn. La.)
B61: U War ... 3E 208
(Swan La.)
Berrymound Vw. B47: H'wd ... 2C 166
Berry Rd. B8: Salt ... 4E 102
DY1: Dud ... 4J 75
Berry St. B18: Hock ... 3F 100
CV1: Cov ... 5E 152
WV1: Wolv ... 7D 36 (4K 7)
Bertha Rd. B11: S'brk ... 4D 122
Bertie Ct. CV8: Ken ... 5G 199
Bertie Rd. CV8: Ken ... 5F 198
Bertie Ter. CV32: Lea S ... 8L 217
Bertram Cl. DY4: Tip ... 8C 54
Bertram Rd. B9: Small H ... 8D 102
B67: Smeth ... 3L 99
Berwick Cl. CV5: E Grn ... 5H 151
CV34: Warw ... 7E 216
Berwick Dr. WS11: Cann ... 1B 14
Berwick Gro. B31: N'fld ... 6K 141
B43: Gt Barr ... 5H 57
Berwicks La. B37: Chel W ... 8H 105
(not continuous)
Berwood Farm Rd.
B72: W Grn ... 3J 81
Berwood Gdns. B24: Erd ... 4J 81
Berwood Gro. B92: Olton ... 8B 124
Berwood La. B24: Erd ... 6L 81
Berwood Pk. B35: Cas V ... 7A 82
Berwood Rd. B72: W Grn ... 3K 81
Berwyn Av. CV6: Cov ... 8A 130
Berwyn Gro. WS6: C Hay ... 6F 14
Berwyn Way CV10: Nun ... 5B 88
Beryl Av. LE10: Hinc ... 7G 69
Besant Gro. B27: A Grn ... 8G 123
Besbury Cl. B93: Dorr ... 7E 168
BESCOT ... 3J 55
Bescot Cres. WS1: Wals ... 3K 55
Bescot Cft. B42: Gt Barr ... 3H 79
Bescot Dr. WS2: Wals ... 3H 55
Bescot Ind. Est. WS10: W'bry ... 5D 54
Bescot Rd. WS2: Wals ... 3H 55
Bescot Stadium Station (Rail)
... 4K 55
Bescot St. WS1: Wals ... 2K 55
Besford Gro. B31: N'fld ... 6K 141
B90: M'path ... 3B 168
Besom Way WS6: C Hay ... 7C 14
Bessborough Rd. B25: Yard ... 1K 123
Best Av. CV8: Ken ... 3J 199
Best Rd. WV14: Bils ... 2K 53
Best St. B64: Old H ... 7M 97
Beswick Gdns. CV22: Bil ... 2K 205
Beswick Gro. B33: Kitts G ... 5A 104
Beta Gro. B14: Yard W ... 5C 144
Betjeman Ct. DY10: Kidd ... 4B 158
Betjeman Pl. WV10: Bush ... 8G 23
Betley Gro. B33: Stech ... 4A 104
Betony Cl. WS5: Wals ... 6A 56
Betsham Cl. B44: K'sdng ... 8B 58
Bettany Glade WV10: Bush ... 5E 22
Betteridge Dr. B76: Walm ... 5L 59
Bettina Cl. CV10: Nun ... 4B 88
Bettman Cl. CV3: Cov ... 3E 174
Betton Rd. B14: K Hth ... 4L 143
Bett Rd. B20: Hand ... 6F 78
Betty's La. WS11: Nort C ... 5M 15
Beulah Ct. B63: Hale ... 5A 118
Bevan Av. WV4: E'shll ... 5E 52
Bevan Cl. WS4: S'fld ... 8C 26
WV14: Bils ... 3M 53
Bevan Ind. Est. DY5: Brie H ... 7A 96
Bevan Lee Rd. WS11: Cann ... 6D 8
Bevan Rd. DY4: Tip ... 5B 76
DY5: Brie H ... 7A 96
Bevan Way B66: Smeth ... 1M 99
Beverley Av. CV10: Nun ... 5B 88
Beverley Cl. B72: W Grn ... 2J 81
B96: A'wd B ... 7E 220
CV7: Bal C ... 2J 171
DY11: Kidd ... 3F 156
Beverley Ct. Rd. B32: Quin ... 3J 119
Beverley Cres. WV4: E'shll ... 5F 52
Beverley Cft. B23: Erd ... 8D 80
Beverley Dr. DY6: K'wfrd ... 2J 95
Beverley Gro. B26: Sheld ... 4B 124
Beverley Hill WS12: Hed ... 2K 9
Beverley Rd. B45: Rubery ... 2G 163
B71: W Brom ... 8K 55
CV32: Lea S ... 8K 217
Beverly Dr. CV4: Canly ... 7K 173
Beverston Rd. DY4: Tip ... 7B 54
WV6: Pert ... 5G 35
Bevington Cres. CV6: Cov ... 4L 151
Bevington Rd. B6: Aston ... 8M 79
Bevin Rd. WS2: Wals ... 6E 38
Bevis Gro. B44: Gt Barr ... 6M 57
BEWDLEY ... 6A 156
Bewdley Av. B12: Bal H ... 3A 122
Bewdley By-Pass
DY12: Bew, Ribb ... 3A 156
Bewdley Dr. WV1: Wolv ... 7H 37
Bewdley Grange DY11: Kidd ... 4G 157
Bewdley Hill DY11: Kidd ... 4G 157
Bewdley Ho. B26: Yard ... 7A 104
Bewdley Leisure Cen. ... 7C 156
Bewdley Mus. ... 6B 156
Bewdley Rd. B30: Stir ... 1H 143
DY11: Kidd ... 4J 157
DY13: Stour S ... 4F 182
Bewdley Rd. Nth.
DY13: Stour S ... 2D 182
Bewdley Station
Severn Valley Railway ... 6C 156
Bewdley Vs. *B18: Win G ... 5D 100*
(off Cape St.)
Bewell Ct. B61: B'gve ... 5M 187
Bewell Gdns. B61: B'gve ... 5M 187
BEWELL HEAD ... 4L 187
Bewell Head B61: B'gve ... 5M 187
Bewlay Cl. DY5: Brie H ... 2B 116
Bewley Rd. WV12: W'hall ... 5D 38
Bewlys Av. B20: Hand ... 5E 78
Bexfield Cl. CV5: Alle ... 3G 151
Bexley Gro. B71: W Brom ... 2L 77
Bexley Rd. B44: K'sdng ... 1B 80
Bexmore Dr. WS13: S'hay ... 8M 13
Beyer Cl. B77: Glas ... 7G 33
Bhylls Cres. WV3: Wolv ... 2J 51
Bhylls La. WV3: Wolv ... 1H 51
Biart Pl. CV21: Rugby ... 5D 180
Bibbey's Grn. WV10: Bush ... 5F 22
Bibsworth Av. B13: Mose ... 1D 144
Bibury Rd. B28: Hall G ... 2E 144
BICC & Symphony Hall
... 7J 101 (5C 4)
Bicester Sq. B35: Cas V ... 5B 82
BICKENHILL ... 8K 125
Bickenhill Grn. Ct. B92: Bick ... 8K 125
Bickenhill La. B37: Mars G ... 3J 125
(not continuous)
B92: Cath B ... 3J 147
Bickenhill Pk. Rd.
B92: Olton ... 8K 123
Bickenhill Parkway
B40: Nat E C ... 3K 125
Bickenhill Rd. B37: Mars G ... 2G 125
Bickenhill Trad. Est.
B40: Mars G ... 4K 125
Bickford Rd. B6: Witt ... 8A 80
WV10: Wolv ... 4F 36
Bickington Rd. B32: Bart G ... 8K 119
Bickley Av. B11: S'brk ... 3C 122
B74: Four O ... 4E 42
Bickley Gro. B26: Sheld ... 4B 124
Bickley Rd. WS4: Rus ... 2C 40
WV14: Bils ... 2A 54
Bicknell Cft. B14: K Hth ... 7L 143
Bickton Cl. B24: Erd ... 3J 81
Biddings La. WV14: Cose ... 7H 53

Biddles Hill—Black Lake

Biddles Hill B94: Earls 3C 192
Biddlestone Gro. WS5: Wals 5C 56
Biddlestone Pl. WS10: Darl 2B 54
Biddulph Ct. B73: S Cold 7G 59
Biddulph Mobile Homes Pk.
WS7: C Ter 8D 10
Bideford Dr. B29: S Oak 8C 120
Bideford Rd. B66: Smeth 4B 100
CV2: Cov 2J 153
Bideford Way WS11: Cann 1B 14
Bidford Cl. B90: Shir 7K 145
Bidford Rd. B31: N'fld 6L 141
Bierton Rd. B25: Yard 1J 123
Bigbury Cl. CV3: Cov 4E 174
Bigbury La. DY13: Stour S 3K 183
Biggin Cl. B35: Cas V 6A 82
WV6: Pert 4E 34
Biggin Hall Cres. CV3: Cov 7H 153
Biggin Hall La. CV23: Thurl 7E 204
Big Peg, The
B18: Birm 5J 101 (2C 4)
Bigwood Dr. B32: Bart G 8K 119
B75: S Cold 3A 60
Bilberry Bank WS11: Cann 3E 8
Bilberry Cl. DY13: Stour S 4E 182
Bilberry Cres. B76: Walm 6L 59
WS12: Hunt 4C 8
Bilberry Dr. B45: Rubery 3G 163
Bilberry Rd. B14: K Hth 3J 143
CV2: Cov 7K 131
Bilboe Rd. WV14: Bils 6M 53
BILBROOK 5H 21
Bilbrook Ct. WV8: Bilb 6H 21
Bilbrook Gro. B29: W Cas 7M 119
WV8: Bilb 6H 21
Bilbrook Ho. WV8: Bilb 6H 21
Bilbrook Rd. WV8: Bilb, Cod 5G 21
(not continuous)
Bilbrook Station (Rail) 7H 21
Bilbury Cl. B97: Redd 3C 220
Bilhay La. B70: W Brom 4G 77
Bilhay St. B70: W Brom 4G 77
Billau Rd. WV14: Cose 7K 53
Billesden Cl. CV3: Bin 1L 175
BILLESLEY 3C 144
Billesley Indoor Tennis Cen.
. . . . .2B 144
Billesley La. B13: Mose 1M 143
B48: A'chu 3K 191
Billingham Cl. B91: Sol 1B 168
Billing Rd. CV5: Cov 6K 151
Billingsley Rd. B26: Yard 1A 124
Billington Cl. CV2: Cov 7L 153
Billington Rd. E. LE9: Elme 4D 70
Billington Rd. W. LE9: Elme 4D 70
Bills La. B90: Shir 8F 144
Billsmore Grn. B92: Sol 2C 146
Bills St. WS10: Darl 2E 54
Billy Buns La. WV5: Wom 1G 73
Billy La. B45: B Grn 2G 189
B60: B'wll 2G 189
Billy Wright Cl. WV4: Penn 3L 51
Bilport La. WS10: W'bry 1F 76
BILSTON 4M 53
Bilston Central Ind. Est.
WV14: Bils 4L 53
Bilston Central (MM) 4K 53
Bilston Craft Gallery & Mus. . . .3L 53
Bilston Ind. Est. WV14: Bils 4A 54
Bilston Key Ind. Est.
WV14: Bils 4M 53
Bilston Leisure Cen. 3K 53
Bilston Rd. DY4: Tip 7B 54
WS10: W'bry 6D 54
WV2: Wolv 8E 36 (5L 7)
WV13: W'hall 2A 54
Bilston St. DY3: Sed 1D 74
WS10: Darl 3D 54
(not continuous)
WV1: Wolv 8D 36 (5K 7)
WV13: W'hall 8A 38
Bilston St. Island
WV1: Wolv 8D 36 (5L 7)
BILTON 1J 205
Bilton Grange Rd. B26: Yard . . .2M 123
Bilton Ind. Est. B38: K Nor 1E 164
CV3: Cov 8F 152
Bilton La. CV22: Bil 7H 179
CV22: Dunc 5K 205
CV23: Long L 6H 179
Bilton Rd. CV22: Bil, Rugby 1K 205
Binbrook Rd. WV12: W'hall 5D 38
Bincomb Av. B26: Sheld 3B 124
Binfield St. DY4: Tip 5A 76
Bingley Av. B8: W End 5H 103
Bingley Ent. Cen. *WV3: Wolv 1A 52*
(off Norfolk Rd.)
Bingley St. WV3: Wolv 1A 52
BINLEY 1L 175
Binley Av. CV3: Bin 2M 175
Binley Bus. Pk. CV3: Bin 8A 154
(Harry Weston Rd., not continuous)
CV3: Bin 1A 176
(Herald Way, not continuous)
Binley Cl. B25: Yard 3K 123
B90: Shir 1G 167
Binley Gro. CV3: Bin 2M 175
Binley Rd. CV3: Bin, Cov 6F 152
(not continuous)
CV3: Cov 7G 153
BINLEY WOODS 2C 176
Binns Cl. CV4: Tile H 1E 172
Binstead Rd. B44: K'sdng 7A 58
Binswood Av. CV32: Lea S 7M 217
Binswood Cl. CV2: Cov 7K 131
Binswood Cres.
CV32: Lea S 7M 217
Binswood Mans.
CV32: Lea S 7M 217
Binswood Rd. B62: Quin 2G 119
Binswood St. CV32: Lea S 8L 217
Binton Cl. B98: Redd 8M 213
Binton Cft. B13: Mose 1M 143
Binton Rd. B90: Shir 8F 144
CV2: Cov 8K 131
Birbeck Ho. B36: Cas B 3H 105
Birbeck Pl. DY5: P'ntt 3B 96
BIRCH ACRE 2K 191
Birchall St.
B12: Birm 8M 101 (8J 5)
Birch Av. B31: Longb 8J 141
DY5: Quar B 7G 97
WS7: Chase 3F 16
WS8: Bwnhls 1E 26
WS11: Cann 1C 14
Birch Bank DY12: Shat 3D 134
Birchbrook Ind. Pk.
WS14: Shens 3E 28
Birchbrook La. WS14: Shens 3E 28
Birch Bus. Pk. WS11: Cann 3F 14
Birch Cl. B17: Harb 4D 120
B30: B'vlle 3D 142
B76: Walm 7M 59
B78: K'bry 2D 62
CV5: Alle 3F 150
CV12: Bed 5K 111
LE9: Earl S 3D 70
WS11: Nort C 4A 16
Birch Coppice DY5: Quar B 8G 97
(not continuous)
WV5: Wom 3E 72
Birchcoppice Gdns.
WV12: W'hall 5E 38
Birch Cft. B30: K Nor 5E 142
B66: Smeth 1K 99
CV34: H'cte 7L 223
WS4: Wals 5A 40
(off Lichfield Rd.)
WV1: Wolv 5C 36 (1J 7)
Birch Cres. B69: Tiv 8A 76
Birch Cft. B24: Erd 4K 81
B37: Chel W 8J 105
WS9: A'rdge 1J 41
Birchcroft B66: Smeth 4C 100
Birch Cft. Rd. B75: S Cold 2K 59
Birchdale WV14: Bils 2K 53
Birchdale Av. B23: Erd 5E 80
Birchdale Rd. B23: Erd 4D 80
Birch Dr. B62: B'hth 8E 98
B74: Lit A 4D 42
B75: S Cold 2M 59
CV22: Bil 7H 179
DY8: Stourb 3L 115
BIRCHEN COPPICE 8G 157
Birch End CV34: Warw 1H 223
Birchensale Rd. B97: Redd 4C 212
Birches, The CV12: Bulk 5B 112
DY11: Hartl 7B 184
DY13: Stour S 6H 183
LE9: Barw 3A 70
Birches Av. WV8: Bilb 8J 21
Birches Barn Av. WV3: Wolv . . .2M 51
Birches Barn Rd. WV3: Wolv . . .1M 51
Birches Cl. B13: Mose 8M 121
BIRCHES GREEN 7G 81
Birches Grn. Rd. B24: Erd 7H 81
Birches La. B48: A'chu 3M 189
CV8: Ken 6G 199
Birches Pk. Rd. WV8: Cod 7G 21
Birches Ri. WV13: W'hall 8A 38
Birches Rd. WV8: Bilb 7G 21
BIRCHFIELD 7J 79
Birchfield Av. WV6: Tett 3H 35
Birchfield Cl. B63: Hale 7L 117
CV9: Wood E 8J 47
Birchfield Ct. B97: Redd 7B 212
Birchfield Cres. DY9: W'cte 6F 116
Birchfield Dr. DY13: Stour S . . .4E 182
Birchfield Gdns. B6: Aston 1K 101
WS5: Wals 5C 56
Birchfield La. B69: O'bry 5E 98
(not continuous)
Birchfield Rd. B19: Loz 1K 101
B20: Hand 8K 79
B97: Redd 5L 211
CV6: Cov 2M 151
DY9: W'cte 6F 116
DY11: Kidd 4H 157
Birchfields Dr. WS12: Hth H 8K 9
Birchfields Rd. WV12: W'hall . . .4A 38
Birchfield Twr. B20: Hand 8K 79
Birchfield Way WS5: Wals 5B 56
Birch Ga. DY9: W'cte 5F 116
Birchglade WV3: Wolv 8K 35
Birchgrave Cl. CV6: Cov 2G 153
Birch Gro. B68: O'bry 2K 119
B78: B'moor 2K 47
CV7: Bal C 1H 171
WS13: Lich 1K 19
Birch Hill Av. WV5: Wom 4F 72
Birch Hollow B15: Edg 3F 120
B68: O'bry 2K 119
Birchill Pl. WV5: Wom 4F 72
Birchills Canal Mus. 5J 39
Birchills Ho. Ind. Est.
WS2: Wals 5K 39
Birchills St. WS2: Wals 6J 39
Birch La. B68: O'bry 2K 119
WS4: S'fld 8C 26
WS9: A'rdge 8K 27
BIRCHLEY HEATH 7F 64
Birchley Heath Rd.
CV10: Ridge L 1F 86
Birchley Ho. B69: O'bry 3D 98
B97: Redd 8B 212
Birchley Ind. Est.
B69: O'bry 4E 98
Birchley Pk. Av. B69: O'bry 3E 98
Birchley Ri. B92: Olton 4M 123
Birch Mdw. Cl. CV34: Warw . . .2D 222
BIRCHMOOR 2L 47
Birchmoor Cl. B28: Hall G 2H 145
Birchmoor Rd. B78: B'moor 1L 47
Birchover Rd. WS2: Wals 5G 39
Birch Rd. B6: Witt 7A 80
B45: Rubery 3E 162
B68: O'bry 1K 119
DY3: Sed 8F 52
WV11: Wed 8M 23
Birch Rd. E. B6: Witt 7B 80
Birch St. B68: O'bry 3J 99
DY4: Tip 4M 75
WS2: Wals 6K 39
WV1: Wolv 7C 36 (3H 7)
Birch Ter. DY2: Neth 5J 97
WS7: C Ter 8G 11
Birch Tree Gdns. WS9: A'rdge . . .4H 41
Birchtree Gdns. DY5: Quar B . . .8G 97
Birch Tree Gro. B91: Sol 5L 145
Birchtree Hollow
WV12: W'hall 4D 38
Birch Tree Rd. CV10: Nun 3C 88
DY12: Bew 3B 156
Birchtrees B24: Erd 5K 81
Birchtrees Cft. B26: Yard 4K 123
Birchtrees Dr. B33: Kitts G 7D 104
Birch Wlk. B68: O'bry 2K 119
Birchway Cl. CV32: Lea S 8J 217
Birchwood Av. B78: Dord 2M 47
Birchwood Cl. DY11: Kidd 2G 157
WV11: Ess 6A 24
Birchwood Cres. B12: Bal H . . .5B 122
Birchwood Rd. B12: Bal H 5A 122
CV3: Bin W 2C 176
WS14: Lich 2M 19
WV4: Penn 4A 52
Birchwoods B32: Bart G 7H 119
Birchwood Wlk. DY6: K'wfrd 1L 95
Birchy Cl. B90: Dic H 3F 166
BIRCHY CROSS 5H 193
Birchy Leasowes La.
B90: Dic H 4E 166
Birdbrook Rd. B44: Gt Barr 8L 57
Birdcage Wlk. B38: K Nor 7F 142
DY2: Dud 8K 75
Bird End B71: W Brom 1M 77
Bird Gro. Ct.
CV1: Cov 4D 152 (1D 6)
Birdhope B77: Wiln 8J 33
Birdie Cl. B38: K Nor 8D 142
Birdingbury La. CV23: F'ton . . .8K 203
Birdingbury Rd.
CV23: Bour D 8M 203
Birdlip Gro. B32: Quin 3J 119
Bird Rd. CV34: H'cte 5J 223
Birds Bush Rd. B77: Wiln 1E 46
Birds Mdw. DY5: P'ntt 2B 96
Bird St. CV1: Cov 5D 152 (3D 6)
DY3: Lwr G 6C 74
WS13: Lich 1G 19
(not continuous)
Birdwell Cft. B13: Mose 3M 143
Birkdale Av. B29: S Oak 8F 120
B60: B'wll 4G 189
Birkdale Cl. CV6: Cov 5B 130
CV11: Nun 8A 90
DY8: Stourb 8M 115
WV1: Wolv 7G 37
Birkdale Dr. B69: Tiv 2A 98
Birkdale Gro. B29: S Oak 1G 143
Birkdale Rd. WS3: Blox 6G 25
Birkenshaw Rd. B44: Gt Barr 1L 79
Birley Gro. B63: Hale 1J 139
Birlingham Ho. *B60: B'gve 6B 188*
(off Burcot La.)
BIRMINGHAM 7K 101 (6F 4)
Birmingham Alexander
Sports Stadium 3J 79
Birmingham Botanical Gdns.
. . . . .2F 120
Birmingham Bus. Est.
B37: Mars G 1L 125
Birmingham City FC 8C 102
Birmingham Crematorium
B42: P Barr 4J 79
Birmingham Hippodrome Theatre
. . . . .8L 101 (8F 4)
BIRMINGHAM INTERNATIONAL
AIRPORT 5G 125
Birmingham International
Station (Rail) 5K 125
Birmingham Mus. & Art Gallery
. . . . .7K 101 (4E 4)
Birmingham Mus. of Transport, The
. . . . .6L 165
Birmingham Nature Cen. 5J 121
Birmingham New Rd.
DY1: Dud 4J 75
DY4: Tip 4J 75
WV4: E'shll 4E 52
WV14: Cose 4E 52
Birmingham One Bus. Pk.
B1: Birm 6H 101 (4B 4)
Birmingham Railway Mus. 4F 122
Birmingham Repertory Theatre
. . . . .7J 101 (5D 4)
Birmingham Rd. B31: Hopw . . .3B 164
B36: Cas B 1A 104
B37: K'hrst 4H 105
B43: Gt Barr 5E 56
B45: Rubery 5C 162
B46: Col 4J 105
B46: Neth W 2A 84
B46: Wat O 7F 82
B48: A'chu 1A 190
B48: Hopw 3B 164
B61: B'gve 6A 188
(not continuous)
B61: L Ash, Rubery 5C 162
B61: L End, Marl 4B 188
B63: Hale 6B 118
B65: Row R 7C 98
B69: O'bry 2H 99
B70: W Brom 8L 77
B71: W Brom 8A 78
B72: W Grn 2H 81
B76: Lea M 2A 84
B80: Map G, Stud 4L 221
B93: Chad E 3B 196
B97: Redd 8D 190
(not continuous)
CV5: Alle 1D 150
(Oak La.)
CV5: Alle 3G 151
(Rye Hill)
CV7: Mer 1L 149
(Church La.)
CV7: Mer 6D 126
(Kenilworth Rd.)
CV8: Ken 8M 171
CV8: S'lgh 2B 200
CV10: Ansl 3G 87
CV34: Warw 1B 222
CV35: Bud, Hase, Hatt, Wrox
. . . . .8A 216
DY1: Dud 7L 75
DY9: Hag 3C 138
DY10: Blak, Kidd 2M 157
WS1: Wals 8M 39
WS5: Wals 2B 56
(not continuous)
WS9: A'rdge 4G 41
WS13: Lich 3H 19
WS14: Shens, Shen W 2G 43
WV2: Wolv 8D 36 (6K 7)
Birmingham Sports Cen. 3M 121
Birmingham Squash Rackets Cen.
. . . . .7D 100
Birmingham St. B63: Hale 6B 118
B69: O'bry 2G 99
DY2: Dud 8K 75
DY8: Stourb 4A 116
DY9: Stourb 4A 116
WS1: Wals 8M 39
WS10: Darl 3E 54
WV13: W'hall 7B 38
Birmingham Wheel Adventure Pk.
. . . . .7C 102
Birnham Cl. DY4: Tip 4K 75
Birstall Dr. CV21: Brow 3D 180
Birstall Way B38: K Nor 1C 164
Birvell Ct. CV12: Bed 6J 111
Bisell Way DY5: Brie H 2D 116
Biset Av. DY10: Kidd 4B 158
Bishbury Cl. B15: Edg 1E 120
Bishop Asbury Cottage Mus. . . .1C 78
Bishop Asbury Cres.
B43: Gt Barr 1C 78
Bishop Cl. B45: Fran 8E 140
DY2: Dud 1L 97
WS11: Cann 7D 8
Bishopgate Bus. Pk.
CV1: Cov 4C 152
Bishop Hall Cres. B60: B'gve . . .2L 209
Bishop Rd. WS10: W'bry 7J 55
Bishop Ryder Ho. B4: Birm 3J 5
Bishops Cl. CV33: Bis T 8E 224
B66: Smeth 5C 100
Bishop's Ct. B31: N'fld 6B 142
B37: Mars G 1L 125
Bishops Ga. B31: N'fld 7A 142
BISHOPSGATE GREEN
. . . . .4D 152 (1C 6)
Bishopsgate Ind. Est.
CV1: Cov 4D 152
Bishopsgate St.
B15: Birm 8H 101 (7B 4)
Bishops Mdw. B75: R'ley 6L 43
Bishops Rd. B73: S Cold 6H 59
BISHOP'S TACHBROOK 8E 224
Bishopstone Cl. B98: Redd . . .7M 213
Bishop St. B5: Birm 1L 121 (8H 5)
CV1: Cov 6C 152 (3C 6)
DY13: Stour S 4G 183
Bishops Wlk.
CV5: Cov 1B 174 (8A 6)
B64: Crad H 3A 118
Bishops Way B74: Four O 4F 42
Bishopton Cl. B90: Shir 8J 145
CV5: E Grn 6H 151
Bishopton Rd. B67: Smeth 8M 99
Bishton Gro. DY2: Neth 5K 97
Bisley Gro. B24: Erd 7G 81
Bismillah Bldg.
B19: Birm 5K 101 (2E 4)
Bissell Cl. B28: Hall G 3F 144
Bissell Dr. WS10: W'bry 6H 55
Bissell St. B5: Birm 1L 121
B32: Quin 3G 119
WV14: Bils 4M 53
Bisset Cres. CV31: Lea S 3C 224
Bi-Tec Ind. Pk. WV1: Wolv 8G 37
Biton Cl. B17: Harb 4B 120
Bittell Cl. B31: Longb 2M 163
WV10: Bush 5E 22
Bittell Ct. B31: Longb 2M 163
Bittell Farm Rd. B45: B Grn . . .8M 163
B48: Hopw 8M 163
Bittell La. B45: B Grn 1L 189
Bittell Rd. B45: B Grn 1K 189
B48: A'chu 1K 189
Bitterne Dr. WV6: Wolv 5A 36
Bittern Wlk. CV2: Cov 7K 131
DY5: Brie H 3C 116
Bittern Wood Rd.
DY10: Kidd 6B 158
Bitterscote Dr. B78: Tam 6A 32
Bitterscote La. B78: Tam 7A 32
(not continuous)
BITTERSOTE 7A 32
Bixhill La. B46: Shu 7F 84
Blackacre Rd. DY2: Dud 1K 97
Black-a-Tree Ct. CV10: Nun 4F 88
Black-a-Tree Rd. CV10: Nun 5E 88
Blackbades Blvd.
CV34: Warw 6B 222
BLACK BANK 8H 111
Black Bank CV7: Exh 8H 111
Blackberry Av. B9: Bord G 6G 103
B94: H'ley H 3B 194
Blackberry Cl. CV23: Brow 1D 180
DY1: Dud 1E 96
Blackberry La. B63: Hale 7A 118
B65: Row R 4M 97
B74: Four O 4E 42
CV2: Cov 3H 153
CV7: Ash G 4B 130
WS9: Wals W 5H 27
Blackbird Cft. B36: Cas B 2G 105
Blackbrook Cl. DY2: Neth 6G 97
Blackbrook Rd.
DY2: Dud, Neth 4G 97
Blackbrook Valley Ind. Est.
DY2: Dud 4G 97
Blackbrook Way WV10: Bush . . .5E 22
Blackburn Av. WV6: Tett 2L 35
Blackburne Rd. B28: Hall G 3F 144
Blackburn Rd. CV6: Longf 6F 130
LE9: Barw 3A 70
Blackbushe Cl. B17: Harb 2M 119
Blackcat Cl. B37: F'bri 6G 105
Black Country Ho. B69: O'bry . . .2F 98
Black Country Mus. 5K 75
Black Country New Rd.
B70: W Brom 3E 76
DY4: Tip 3D 76
WS10: Darl, W'bry 5B 54
WS10: Tip, W'bry 6D 54
WV14: Bils 3A 54
Black Country Route
WS2: Wals 2B 54
WV13: W'hall 2B 54
WV14: Cose, Bils 6H 53
BLACKDOWN 4L 217
Blackdown B77: Wiln 8J 33
Blackdown Cl. B45: Fran 7G 141
Blackdown Rd. B93: Know 3H 169
Blackett Ct. B73: S Cold 7G 59
Blackfirs La. B37: Mars G 2J 125
Blackford Cl. B63: Hale 7K 117
DY11: Kidd 8G 157
Blackford Rd. B11: S'hll 5C 122
B90: Shir 2J 167
BLACKFORDS 7E 8
Blackford St. B18: Win G 4E 100
Blackfriars Cl. B79: Tam 4L 31
Blackgreaves La. B76: Lea M . . .8M 61
Black Hall La. CV7: Fill 5C 108
Blackhalve La.
WV11: Wed, Ess 1H 37
Blackham Dr. B73: Bold 2G 81
Blackham Rd. WV11: Wed 1M 37
Black Haynes Rd.
B29: W Cas 3A 142
BLACKHEATH 8C 98
Blackheath Mkt. B65: B'hth 8D 98
Blackheath Trad. Est.
B65: Row R 7E 98
Black Horse La. DY11: Kidd . . .3K 157
Blackhorse La. DY5: Brie H 8E 96
Black Horse Rd. CV6: Longf . . .4H 131
CV7: Exh 3G 131
Black Horse Yd. LE10: Hinc 8K 69
BLACK LAKE 3H 77
Black Lake B70: W Brom 3G 77

Black Lake Ind. Est.—Botteville Rd.

Black Lake Ind. Est.
B70: W Brom 3H 77
Black Lake La. B60: Lwr B 7F 210
B97: Up Ben 7F 210
Black Lake Stop (MM) 3G 77
Black La. CV32: Lea S 7B 218
Blacklea Cl. B25: Yard 8K 103
Blacklow Rd. CV34: Warw 8G 217
Blackman Way
CV21: Rugby 5M 179
Black Mill DY1: Dud 5K 75
Blackmoor Cft. B33: Kitts G 7D 104
Blackmore La. B60: B'gve 6A 188
Black Pad CV6: Cov 1C 152
Blackpit La. WV4: Lwr P 6E 58
Black Prince Av. CV3: Cov 2D 174
Blackrock Rd. B23: Erd 3B 80
Blackroot Cl. WS7: Hamm 5K 17
Blackroot Ho. *B73: New O 7C 58*
(off Welshmans Hill)
Blackroot Rd. B74: S Cold 2G 59
Blackshaw Dr.
CV2: W'grve S 3M 153
Blacksmith Dr. B75: R'ley 6L 43
Blacksmiths La.
B94: H'ley H 3C 194
Blacksmiths Yd.
CV13: Stoke G 2D 68
Blacksmith Way B70: W Brom 7J 77
Black Soils Rd. B98: Redd 4M 213
Blackstitch La. B97: Redd 8A 212
BLACKSTONE 8D 156
Blackstone DY12: Bew 2C 182
Blackstone Country Pk. 1C 182
Blackthorn Cl. B30: B'vlle 3C 142
CV4: Canly 4K 173
Blackthorn Ct. B98: Redd 8L 213
Blackthorn Cres. WS12: Haz 3A 10
Blackthorne Av. WS7: Chase 5F 16
Blackthorne Cl. B91: Sol 5L 145
DY1: Dud 5F 74
Blackthorne Rd. B67: Smeth 5K 99
DY1: Dud 5F 74
WS5: Wals 4M 55
WS14: Lich 2K 19
Blackthorn Gro. CV11: Nun 7M 89
Blackthorn Rd. B30: B'vlle 3C 142
B36: Cas B 1C 104
CV8: Ken 6G 199
DY8: Word 8M 95
Blackwatch Rd. CV6: Cov 1C 152
Blackwater Cl. DY5: P'ntt 3A 96
BLACKWELL 4G 189
Blackwell La. B97: Redd 4B 212
Blackwell Rd. B45: B Grn 4H 189
B60: B'wll 5F 188
B72: W Grn 8K 59
CV6: Cov 1E 152
Blackwell St. DY10: Kidd 3L 157
Blackwood Av. CV22: Bil 8J 179
WV11: Wed 1H 37
Blackwood Dr. B74: S'tly 1L 57
Blackwood Rd. B60: B'gve 7B 188
B74: S'tly 8L 41
B77: Two G 2C 46
Blades Ho. B71: W Brom 1A 78
Blades Rd. B70: W Brom 5D 76
Bladon Cl. CV11: Nun 1M 89
Bladon Wlk. CV31: Lea S 3C 224
Blaenwern Dr. B63: Crad 2H 117
Blagdon Rd. B63: Hale 3A 118
Blair Dr. CV12: Bed 8D 110
Blair Gro. B37: Chel W 8K 105
BLAKEBROOK 3J 157
Blakebrook DY11: Kidd 3J 157
Blakebrook Cl. DY11: Kidd 3J 157
Blakebrook Gdns.
DY11: Kidd 3J 157
Blake Cl. CV10: Gall C 4A 88
CV22: Bil 8J 179
LE10: Hinc 5K 69
WS11: Cann 4G 9
Blakedon Rd. WS10: W'bry 6E 54
BLAKEDOWN 7H 137
Blakedown Rd. B63: Hale 8L 117
Blakedown Station (Rail) 7J 137
Blakedown Way B69: O'bry 5E 98
Blake Hall Cl. DY5: Brie H 2C 116
Blake Ho. *WS2: Wals 1J 55*
(off St Johns Rd.)
Blakeland Rd. B44: K'sdng 3L 79
Blakelands Av. CV31: Lea S 3B 224
Blakeland St. B9: Bord G 7F 102
Blake La. B9: Bord G 7F 102
BLAKELEY 4G 73
Blakeley Av. WV6: Tett 2M 35
Blakeley Hall Gdns.
B69: O'bry 2H 99
Blakeley Hall Rd. B69: O'bry 2H 99
Blakeley Heath Dr.
WV5: Wom 4G 73
Blakeley Ri. WV6: Tett 2M 35
Blakeley Wlk. DY2: Neth 5J 97
Blakeley Wood Rd. DY4: Tip 1C 76
Blakemere Av. B25: Yard 1L 123
Blakemere Cl. B98: Redd 6M 213
Blakemere Ho. B16: Birm 6A 4
Blakemore Cl. B32: Bart G 6M 119
Blakemore Dr. B75: S Cold 3M 59
Blakemore Rd. B70: W Brom 7G 77
WS9: Wals W 6G 27
Blakenall Cl. WS3: Blox 1K 39
BLAKENALL HEATH 1K 39
Blakenall Heath WS3: Blox 1K 39
Blakenall La. WS3: Blox 2J 39
Blakenall Row WS3: Blox 1K 39
Blakeney Av. B17: Harb 2A 120
DY8: Woll 3K 115
Blakeney Cl. DY3: Sed 1C 74
Blakenhale Rd. B33: Sheld 8B 104
BLAKENHALL 2C 52 (8H 7)
Blakenhall Gdns. WV2: Wolv 2C 52
Blakenhall Ind. Est.
WV2: Wolv 2B 52
Blake Pl. B9: Bord G 7F 102
Blake Rd. B61: Cats 1B 188
Blakes Fld. Dr. B45: B Grn 8G 163
BLAKESHALL 2L 135
Blakeshall La. DY11: W'ley 3K 135
Blakesley Cl. B76: Walm 4M 81
Blakesley Gro. B25: Yard 8K 103
Blakesley Hall Mus. 8L 103
Blakesley M. B25: Yard 1K 123
Blakesley Rd. B25: Yard 8J 103
Blakesley Way B33: Stech 7K 103
Blake St. B74: Four O 3E 42
Blake Street Station (Rail) 3F 42
Blakewood Cl. B34: S End 4C 104
Blandford Av. B36: Cas B 8E 82
Blandford Dr. CV2: W'grve S 4M 153
DY8: Word 6L 95
Blandford Gdns. WS7: Burn 3J 17
Blandford Rd. B32: Quin 4L 119
CV32: Lea S 3J 217
Blandford Way CV35: H Mag 2A 222
Blanefield WV8: Pend 7L 21
Blanning Ct. B93: Dorr 5E 168
Blay Av. WS2: Wals 7H 39
Blaydon Av. B75: R'ley 7L 43
Blaydon Ct. *B17: Harb 5D 120*
(off Metchley La.)
Blaydon Rd. WV9: Pend 7A 22
Blaythorn Av. B92: Olton 6A 124
Blaze Hill Rd. DY6: W Hth 1G 95
Blaze La. B96: A'wd B, Redd 7A 220
B97: Redd 7A 220
Blaze Pk. DY6: W Hth 1H 95
Bleaberry CV21: Brow 2C 180
Bleachfield La. B98: Beo 1M 213
Bleak Hill Rd. B23: Erd 5C 80
Bleak Ho. Dr. WS7: C Ter 1D 16
Bleakhouse Rd. B68: O'bry 8J 99
Bleak St. B67: Smeth 3M 99
Blenheim Av. CV6: Cov 7C 130
Blenheim Cl. B77: Tam 5C 32
CV11: Nun 7M 89
LE10: Hinc 5M 69
WS4: Rus 2D 40
Blenheim Ct. B44: Gt Barr 1M 79
B91: Sol 5C 146
Blenheim Cres. B60: B'gve 1A 210
CV31: Lea S 4C 224
Blenheim Dr. B43: Gt Barr 1D 78
Blenheim Rd. B13: Mose 8M 121
B90: Shir 7K 145
DY6: K'wfrd 3M 95
WS7: C Ter 1G 17
WS11: Nort C 5B 16
WV12: W'hall 3B 38
Blenheim Wlk. CV6: Cov 5B 130
Blenheim Way B35: Cas V 7B 82
B44: Gt Barr 1M 79
DY1: Dud 7E 74
Bletchley Dr. B77: Two G 1C 46
CV5: Cov 5H 151
Bletchley Rd. B24: Erd 5L 81
Blewitt Cl. B36: Cas B 7D 82
Blewitt St. DY5: P'ntt 3C 96
WS12: Hed 3H 9
Blews St. B6: Birm 4L 101 (1H 5)
Blick Rd. CV34: H'cte 5J 223
Blind La. B94: Tan A 7C 192
CV7: Berk 5K 149
CV8: Ken 8F 172
Blindpit La. B76: Wis 1G 83
Bliss Cl. CV4: Tile H 6E 150
Blithe Cl. DY8: Amb 1A 116
Blithfield Dr. DY5: Brie H 2B 116
Blithfield Gro. B24: Erd 4J 81
Blithfield Pl. WS11: Hth H 8H 9
Blithfield Rd. WS8: Bwnhls 7B 16
Blockall WS10: Darl 2D 54
Blockall Cl. WS10: Darl 3C 54
Blockley Cl. B97: Redd 7L 211
Blockley Rd. CV12: Bed 5J 111
Blockleys Yd. LE10: Hinc 1J 91
Blondvil St. CV3: Cov 2C 174
BLOOMFIELD 2L 75
Bloomfield Cl. WV5: Wom 3D 72
Bloomfield Cres. WS13: Lich 7G 13
Bloomfield Dr. WV12: W'hall 8D 24
Bloomfield Pk. DY4: Tip 3K 75
Bloomfield Pk. Trad. Est.
DY4: Tip 3K 75
Bloomfield Rd. B13: Mose 6B 122
DY4: Tip 3L 75
Bloomfield St. Nth.
B63: Hale 4M 117
Bloomfield St. W. B63: Hale 5M 117
Bloomfield Ter. DY4: Tip 3K 75
Bloomfield Way B79: Tam 2M 31
Bloomsbury Gro. B14: K Hth 2J 143
Bloomsbury St.
WV2: Wolv 1C 52 (6H 7)
Bloomsbury Wlk. B7: Nech 4B 102
(not continuous)
Bloomsbury Way WS14: Lich 2L 19
Blossom Av. B29: S Oak 7F 120
Blossom Dr. B61: B'gve 4A 188
BLOSSOM FIELD 7M 145
Blossomfield Cl. B38: K Nor 1D 164
DY6: K'wfrd 1L 95
Blossomfield Club 1A 168
Blossomfield Ct. B38: K Nor 1D 164
Blossomfield Gdns. B91: Sol 5A 146
Blossomfield Rd. B91: Sol 8L 145
Blossom Gro. B36: Hodg H 1L 103
B64: Old H 8M 97
(off Cherry Dr.)
Blossom Hill B24: Erd 5G 81
Blossom Rd. B24: Erd 5J 81
Blossom's Fold
WV1: Wolv 7C 36 (4J 7)
Blossomville Way
B27: A Grn 5H 123
Blount Ho. DY11: Kidd 1H 157
Blounts Rd. B23: Erd 4C 80
Blount Ter. DY11: Kidd 6K 157
BLOWER'S GREEN 2H 97
Blowers Grn. Cres. DY2: Dud 2H 97
Blowers Grn. Pl. DY2: Dud 2H 97
Blower's Grn. Rd. DY2: Dud 2H 97
Bloxam Gdns. CV22: Rugby 7M 179
Bloxcidge St. B68: O'bry 5H 99
Bloxham Pl. CV21: Rugby 6A 180
BLOXWICH 8H 25
Bloxwich Bus. Pk. WS2: Wals 2G 39
Bloxwich La. WS2: Wals 5G 39
Bloxwich Library Theatre 8H 25
Bloxwich North Station (Rail) 6F 24
Bloxwich Rd. WS2: Wals 2J 39
WS3: Blox 2J 39
Bloxwich Rd. Nth.
WV12: W'hall 3D 38
Bloxwich Rd. Sth.
WV13: W'hall 6A 38
Bloxwich Station (Rail) 8G 25
Bloxwich Swimming Baths & Leisure Cen. 1J 39
Blucher St. B1: Birm 8K 101 (7E 4)
Blue Ball La. B63: Crad 3J 117
Blue Bell Cl. DY8: Word 7J 95
Bluebell Cl. CV23: Brow 1D 180
WS12: Hed 3H 9
Bluebell Cres. WV11: Wed 4K 37
Bluebell Cft. B23: Erd 2C 80
B31: N'fld 5M 141
Bluebell Dr. CV12: Bed 7E 110
Bluebell La. WS6: Gt Wyr 8G 15
Bluebell Rd. B64: Old H 6L 97
DY1: Dud 6H 75
WS9: Wals W 6H 27
Bluebell Wlk. CV4: Tile H 8F 150
Bluebellwood Cl. B76: Walm 6A 60
Bluebird Cl. WS14: Lich 1K 19
Blue Bird Pk. B62: Hunn 1A 140
Bluebird Trad. Est.
WV10: Wolv 4E 36
Blue Boar Yd. LE10: Hinc 1J 91
Blue Cedars DY8: Woll 3J 115
Blue Lake Rd. B93: Dorr 7H 169
Blue La. E. WS2: Wals 6K 39
Blue La. W. WS2: Wals 7K 39
Blue Rock Pl. B69: Tiv 2C 98
Blue Stone Wlk. B65: Row R 3C 98
Blundell Rd. B11: S'hll 4D 122
Blundells CV8: Ken 4G 199
Blundells, The CV8: Ken 4F 198
BLUNTINGTON 8M 159
BLUNT'S GREEN 4L 215
Blyth Cl. CV12: Bed 8C 110
Blyth Ct. B92: Olton 2M 145
CV11: Nun 6J 89
Blythe Av. CV7: Bal C 4J 171
Blythe Cl. B97: Redd 2D 220
WS7: Burn 3K 17
Blythe Ct. B46: Col 2A 106
B73: S Cold 4H 59
BLYTHE END 7C 84
Blythefield Av. B43: Gt Barr 7C 56
Blythe Gdns. WV8: Cod 5F 20
Blythe Gro. B44: Gt Barr 6M 57
Blythe Rd. B46: Col 2A 106
CV1: Cov 5E 152
Blythe St. B77: Tam 6C 32
Blythesway B48: A'chu 3A 190
Blythe Valley Innovation Cen.
B90: Bly P 7M 167
BLYTHE VALLEY PARK 6M 167
Blythe Valley Parkway
B90: Bly P 5M 167
Blythe Way B91: Sol 6E 146
Blythewood Cl. B91: Sol 8F 146
Blythsford Rd. B28: Hall G 5F 144
Blythswood Rd. B11: Tys 5G 123
Blyton Cl. B16: Birm 6F 100
Boar Cft. CV4: Tile H 7F 150
Board School Gdns.
DY3: Up Gor 3E 74
Boar Hound Cl.
B18: Hock 5G 101 (2A 4)
Boat La. WS14: Muck C 8M 17
Boatmans La. WS9: Wals W 7E 26
Bobbington Way DY2: Neth 4K 97
Bob's Coppice Wlk.
DY5: Quar B 2F 116
Bockendon Rd.
CV4: W'wd H 5D 172
Boddington Cl. CV32: Cubb 4E 218
Boddis Ind. Pk. B64: Old H 7M 97
Bodenham Cl. B98: Redd 6K 213
Bodenham Rd. B31: N'fld 7L 141
B68: O'bry 1H 119
Boden Rd. B28: Hall G 2F 144
Bodens La. WS9: A'rdge 2G 57
Bodiam Ct. WV6: Pert 6G 35
Bodicote Gro. B75: R'ley 7L 43
Bodington Cl. WS7: Burn 2L 17
Bodington Rd. B75: Four O 6H 43
Bodmin Cl. LE10: Hinc 5L 69
WS5: Wals 2D 56
Bodmin Ct. DY5: Brie H 7D 96
Bodmin Gro. B7: Birm 4B 102
Bodmin Ri. WS5: Wals 2D 56
Bodmin Rd. CV2: Cov 4M 153
DY2: Neth 7K 97
Bodnant Way CV8: Ken 3J 199
BODNETTS, THE 5H 31
BODYMOOR HEATH 5A 62
Bodymoor Heath Rd.
B76: Bod H, Mars 3K 61
B78: Midd 3K 61
Bodymoor Heath Vis. Cen. 5A 62
Bognop Rd. WV11: Ess 5J 23
Bohun St. CV4: Tile H 8F 150
BOLDMERE 1F 80
Boldmere Cl. B73: Bold 2G 81
Boldmere Ct. *B43: Gt Barr 2E 78*
(off South Vw.)
Boldmere Dr. B73: Bold 1G 81
Boldmere Gdns. B73: Bold 1F 80
Boldmere Rd. B73: Bold 7F 58
Boldmere Ter. B29: S Oak 8E 120
Bolebridge M. B79: Tam 4B 32
Bolebridge St. B79: Tam 5B 32
BOLEHALL 5C 32
Boley Cl. WS14: Lich 2J 19
Boley Cott. La. WS14: Lich 2K 19
Boley La. WS14: Lich 2K 19
Boleyn Cl. CV34: Warw 3J 223
WS6: C Hay 7D 14
Boleyn Rd. B45: Fran 8D 140
BOLEY PARK 2L 19
Boley Pk. Shop. Cen.
WS14: Lich 2L 19
Bolingbroke Dr. CV34: H'cte 6L 223
Bolingbroke Rd. CV3: Cov 8G 153
Bolney Rd. B32: Quin 4L 119
Bolton Cl. CV3: Cov 4E 174
Bolton Ct. DY4: Tip 1C 76
Bolton Ind. Cen. B19: Hock 3H 101
Bolton Rd. B10: Small H 1B 122
WV11: Wed 4J 37
Bolton St. B9: Birm 7B 102 (6M 5)
Bolton Way WS3: Blox 6F 24
Bolus La. B46: Max 5H 107
Bolyfant Cres. CV31: W'nsh 7A 224
Bomers Fld. B45: Redn 2J 163
Bond, The B5: Birm 7A 102 (6L 5)
Bond Dr. B35: Cas V 6A 82
Bondfield Rd. B13: Mose 3B 144
Bond Ga. CV11: Nun 5J 89
Bonds Ct. CV1: Cov 6C 152 (4B 6)
Bond Sq. B18: Hock 5G 101 (2A 4)
Bond St. B19: Birm 5K 101 (2E 4)
B30: Stir 2G 143
B65: Row R 6E 98
B70: W Brom 7J 77
B78: Midd 3L 61
CV1: Cov 6C 152 (4B 6)
CV11: Nun 4J 89
CV21: Rugby 6M 179
WV2: Wolv 8C 36 (6J 7)
WV14: Cose 1G 75
Bondway WS12: Hed 1F 8
BONEHILL 7L 31
Bonehill Ind. Est. B78: Faz 8A 32
Bonehill Rd. B78: M Oak, Tam 7K 31
(not continuous)
BONEY HAY 1F 16
Boney Hay Rd. WS7: Burn 1H 17
Bonfire Hill DY9: Belb 3L 161
Bonham Gro. B25: Yard 8K 103
Boningale Way B93: Dorr 6D 168
Bonner Dr. B76: Walm 4M 81
Bonner Gro. WS9: A'rdge 4F 40
Bonneville Cl. CV5: Alle 1B 150
Bonniksen Cl. CV31: Lea S 4M 223
Bonnington Cl. CV21: Hillm 8H 181
Bonnington Dr. CV12: Bed 5G 111
Bonnington Way B43: Gt Barr 5K 57
Bonny Stile La. WV11: Wed 3H 37
Bonsall Rd. B23: Erd 3G 81
Bonville Gdns. WV10: Bush 5E 22
Booth Cl. DY6: K'wfrd 3A 96
WS3: Blox 1K 39
WS13: Lich 7G 13
Booth Ct. DY5: Brie H 7D 96
Booth Ho. WS4: Wals 6M 39
Boot Hill CV9: Gren 7C 48
Booth Rd. WS10: W'bry 7J 55
Booth's Farm Rd.
B42: Gt Barr 2G 79
Booths Flds. CV6: Cov 7E 130
Booth's La. B42: Gt Barr 8H 57
(not continuous)
Booth St. B21: Hand 2C 100
B66: Hand, Smeth 2C 100
WS3: Blox 1J 39
WS10: Darl 1D 54
WS12: Hed 3H 9
Booton Ct. DY10: Kidd 8A 136
Boot Piece La. B97: Redd 4B 212
Bordeaux Cl. DY1: Dud 6E 74
Borden Cl. WV8: Pend 1M 35
BORDESLEY
Birmingham 7B 102 (6M 5)
Bromsgrove 8D 190
Bordesley Abbey 3F 212
Bordesley Abbey Vis. Cen. 3F 212
Bordesley Cir. B10: Small H 8B 102
Bordesley Cl. B9: Bord G 7G 103
Bordesley Ct. CV32: Lill 6A 218
BORDESLEY GREEN 7E 102
Bordesley Grn. B9: Bord G 7D 102
Bordesley Grn. E.
B9: Bord G 7H 103
B33: Stech 7H 103
Bordesley Grn. Rd. B8: Salt 7D 102
B9: Bord G 7D 102
Bordesley Grn. Trad. Est.
B9: Bord G 7E 102
Bordesley La. B97: Redd 3E 212
Bordesley Middleway
B11: S'brk 1A 122 (8M 5)
Bordesley Station (Rail)
....8A 102 (8M 5)
Bordesley St.
B5: Birm 7M 101 (5J 5)
Bordesley Trad. Est. B8: Salt 6D 102
Bore St. WS13: Lich 2H 19
Borman B79: Tam 4M 31
Borneo St. WS4: Wals 5M 39
Borough, The LE10: Hinc 1K 91
Borough Cres. B69: O'bry 4E 98
DY8: Stourb 4L 115
Borough La. WS15: Longd 2K 11
BOROUGH PARK 1C 32
Borough Rd. B79: Tam 2B 32
Borrington Gdns. DY10: Kidd 5B 158
Borrington Rd. DY10: Kidd 5B 158
Borrowcop La. WS14: Lich 3J 19
Borrowdale CV21: Brow 1C 180
Borrowdale Cl. CV6: Cov 1A 152
DY5: Brie H 2B 116
LE9: Earl S 2F 70
Borrowdale Dr. CV32: Lea S 7K 217
Borrowdale Gro. B31: N'fld 6K 141
Borrowdale Rd. B31: N'fld 6J 141
Borrowell La. CV8: Ken 5E 198
Borrowell Ter. CV8: Ken 5E 198
Borrow St. WV13: W'hall 6A 38
Borwick Av. B70: W Brom 6G 77
Bosbury Ter. B30: Stir 2H 143
Boscastle Cl. CV8: Ken 5H 199
Boscastle Ho. CV12: Bed 8C 110
Boscobel Av. DY4: Tip 5M 75
Boscobel Cl. DY1: Dud 6F 74
Boscobel Cres.
WV1: Wolv 5C 36 (1J 7)
Boscobel Rd. B43: Gt Barr 7D 56
B90: Ches G 4K 167
WS1: Wals 1B 56
Boscombe Av. B11: S'brk 3C 122
Boscombe Rd. B11: Tys 5E 122
Bosmere Ct. B31: N'fld 6M 141
Bosgate Cl. WV5: Wom 5G 73
Bostock Cl. LE9: Elme 5F 70
Bostock Cres. CV33: W Weth 2J 219
Boston Cl. WS12: Hth H 8L 9
Boston Gro. B44: K'sdng 1B 80
Boston Pl. CV6: Cov 1D 152
Boston Way LE9: Barw 3M 69
Bosty La. WS9: A'rdge 4C 40
Boswell Cl. WS10: Darl 4D 54
WS10: W'bry 8C 54
Boswell Dr. CV2: W'grve S 3A 154
Boswell Gro. CV34: Warw 8D 216
Boswell Rd. B44: K'sdng 3M 79
B74: S Cold 3J 59
CV22: Rugby 2L 205
WS11: Cann 5D 8
WV14: Bils 2M 53
Bosworth Cl. CV8: Bag 6E 174
DY3: Sed 3F 74
LE10: Hinc 8G 69
Bosworth Ct. B26: Sheld 4A 124
Bosworth Dr.
B37: Chel W, F'bri 7F 104
B37: F'bri 7F 104
Bosworth Grn. LE9: Earl S 1H 71
Bosworth Ho. *LE10: Hinc 8L 69*
(off Priory Wlk.)
Bosworth Rd. B26: Yard 5L 123
Botany Dr. DY3: Up Gor 4D 74
Botany Rd. WS5: Wals 4M 55
Botany Wlk.
B16: Birm 7G 101 (6A 4)
Botha Rd. B9: Bord G 6E 102
Botoner Rd. CV1: Cov 7F 152
Botteley Rd. B70: W Brom 3G 77
Botterham La. DY3: Swind 6E 72
Bottetourt Rd. B29: W Cas 6A 120
(not continuous)
Botteville Rd. B27: A Grn 7J 123

Bott La.—Brennand Rd.

Bott La. DY9: Lye 3D 116
WS1: Wals 8M 39
Bottrill St. CV11: Nun 4H 89
Bott Rd. CV5: Cov 1K 173
BOTTS GREEN 4J 85
Botts Grn. La. B46: Over W 4H 85
BOUCHALL 3B 116
Boughton La. Ind. Est.
CV21: Rugby 3B 180
Boughton Rd. B25: Yard 2J 123
CV21: Rugby 2B 180
Boulevard, The B73: W Grn 1H 81
DY5: Brie H 7E 96
Boultbee Rd. B72: W Grn 2J 81
Boulters La. CV9: Wood E 8J 47
Boulton Cl. WS7: Burn 1J 17
Boulton Ho. B70: W Brom 8K 77
Boulton Ind. Cen. B18: Hock 4H 101
Boulton Middleway
B18: Birm 4H 101
Boulton Retreat B21: Hand 2E 100
Boulton Rd. B21: Hand 2E 100
B66: Smeth 3D 100
B70: W Brom 8K 77
B91: Sol 2C 146
Boultons La. B97: Redd 3D 220
Boulton Sq. B70: W Brom 8K 77
Boulton Wlk. B23: Erd 5B 80
Boundary Av. B65: Row R 7E 98
Boundary Cl. WV13: W'hall 8J 37
Boundary Ct. B37: F'bri 7E 104
Boundary Cres. DY3: Lwr G 6C 74
Boundary Dr. B13: Mose 7K 121
Boundary Hill DY3: Lwr G 6C 74
Boundary Ho. B5: Edg 4J 121
B47: Wyt 6L 165
Boundary Ind. Est.
WV10: F'hses 4C 22
Boundary La. DY7: Stourt 8E 94
Boundary Pl. B21: Hand 8C 78
Boundary Rd. B74: S'tly 2M 57
CV21: Rugby 7D 180
WS9: Wals W 6F 26
Boundary Way WV4: Penn 4J 51
WV6: Tett 7F 34
Bourlay Cl. B45: Fran 7E 140
BOURNBROOK 7F 120
Bournbrook Ct. B5: S Oak 6G 121
Bournbrook Rd. B29: S Oak 6G 121
Bourne Av. B61: Cats 8M 161
B62: Quin 5F 118
B78: Faz 8L 31
DY4: Tip 2C 76
Bourne Brook Cl. CV7: Fill 6D 108
Bournebrook Cl. DY2: Neth 4J 97
Bournebrook Cres.
B62: Quin 5G 119
Bournebrook Vw. CV7: Old A 8E 86
Bourne Cl. B13: Mose 3D 144
B91: Sol 3E 146
CV9: Ath 7L 49
WS12: Hth H 7K 9
Bourne End CV47: Sou 6G 225
Bourne Grn. B32: Quin 3L 119
Bourne Hill Cl. DY2: Neth 6L 97
Bourne Rd. B6: Aston 2B 102
CV3: Cov 8J 153
Bournes Cl. B63: Hale 6M 117
Bournes Cres. B63: Hale 5L 117
BOURNES GREEN 7C 160
Bournes Hill B63: Hale 5L 117
Bourne St. DY2: Dud 8K 75
DY3: Sed 2G 75
WV14: Cose 2G 75
Bourne Va. WS9: A'rdge 6K 41
Bourne Wlk. B65: Row R 4M 97
Bourne Way Gdns.
B29: S Oak 1G 143
BOURNHEATH 8K 161
Bournheath Rd. B61: F'fld 7K 161
Bourn Mill Dr. B6: Aston 3L 101
BOURNVILLE 2E 142
Bournville La. B30: B'vlle 2D 142
Bournville Station (Rail) 2G 143
Bourton Cl. WS5: Wals 6A 56
Bourton Cft. B92: Olton 1M 145
Bourton Dr. CV31: Lea S 4B 224
BOURTON ON DUNSMORE 7L 203
Bourton Rd. B92: Olton 1M 145
CV23: F'ton 8K 203
Bovey Cft. B76: Walm 2A 82
Bovingdon Rd. B35: Cas V 6A 82
Bowater Av. B33: Stech 8K 103
Bowater Ct. CV3: Cov 3F 174
Bowater Ho. *B19: Birm 4K 101*
(off Aldgate Gro.)
B70: W Brom 7J 77
Bowater St. B70: W Brom 6J 77
Bowbrook Av. B90: M'path 4A 168
Bow Ct. CV5: Cov 1K 173
Bowcroft Gro. B24: Erd 3J 81
Bowden Rd. B67: Smeth 3L 99
Bowden Way CV3: Bin 8M 153
Bowdler Rd.
WV2: Wolv 1D 52 (8L 7)
Bowen Av. WV4: E'shll 6G 53
Bowen-Cooke Av. WV6: Pert 3E 34
Bowen Ct. B13: Mose 6B 122
Bowen Rd. CV22: Hillm 1D 206
Bowen St. WV4: E'shll 4E 52
Bower Bank DY13: Stour S 7E 182
Bower Cl. WS13: Lich 7K 13
Bowercourt Cl. B91: Sol 8B 146
Bower Hill Dr.
DY13: Stour S 7E 182
Bower La. DY5: Quar B 1F 116
Bowers Cft. CV32: Lill 5A 218
Bowes Dr. WS11: Cann 5F 8
Bowes Rd. B45: Rubery 2E 162
Bow Fell CV21: Brow 2D 180
Bowfell Cl. CV5: E Grn 5G 151
Bowker St. WV13: W'hall 8J 37
Bow La. CV7: Withy 4M 133
Bowlas Av. B74: Four O 1H 59
BOWLING GREEN 6K 97
Bowling Grn. Av. B77: Wiln 2E 46
Bowling Grn. Cl. B23: Erd 2E 80
WS10: Darl 2D 54
Bowling Grn. La. B20: Hand 1G 101
CV12: Bed 2E 130
Bowling Grn. Rd. DY2: Neth 6K 97
DY8: Stourb 4L 115
LE10: Hinc 8L 69
Bowling Grn. St.
CV34: Warw 3D 222
Bowlplex
Birmingham 8G 101
Dudley 6L 75
Bowls Ct. CV5: Cov 6M 151
Bowman Grn. LE10: Burb 3M 91
Bowman Rd. B42: Gt Barr 8H 57
Bowmans Ri. WV1: Wolv 6G 37
Bowmore Rd. B60: B'gve 8B 188
Bowness Cl. CV6: Cov 1A 152
Bowness Gro. WV12: W'hall 8B 24
Bowood Cres. B31: N'fld 7B 142
Bowood Dr. WV6: Tett 3K 35
Bowood End B76: Walm 6L 59
Bowpatch Cl. DY13: Stour S 7A 182
Bowpatch Rd. DY13: Stour S 8D 182
Bowshot Cl. B36: Cas B 8D 82
Bowstoke Rd. B43: Gt Barr 1C 78
Bow St. B1: Birm 8K 101 (8F 4)
WV13: W'hall 8B 38
WV14: Bils 3L 53
Bowyer Rd. B8: Salt 5E 102
Bowyer St.
B10: Small H 8A 102 (8M 5)
Box Cl. CV31: W'nsh 6B 224
Boxhill, The CV3: Cov 8H 153
Boxhill Cl. B6: Aston 3M 101
Boxnott Cl. B97: Redd 7A 212
Box Rd. B37: Chel W 1J 125
Box St. WS1: Wals 8M 39
BOX TREES 8B 168
Box Trees Rd. B93: Dorr 8C 168
B94: H'ley H 8C 168
Boxwood Dr. CV23: Kils 6M 207
Boyce Way CV23: Long L 4H 179
Boyd Cl. CV2: W'grve S 1M 153
Boyd Gro. B27: A Grn 7H 123
Boydon Cl. WS11: Cann 8B 8
WV2: E'shll 3G 53
Boyleston Rd. B28: Hall G 3G 145
Boyne Rd. B26: Sheld 2A 124
Boyslade Rd. LE10: Burb 4M 91
Boyslade Rd. E. LE10: Burb 4M 91
Boyton Gro. B44: Gt Barr 6M 57
Brabazon Gro. B35: Cas V 6M 81
Brabham Cl. DY11: Kidd 8K 135
Brabham Cres. B74: S'tly 3M 57
Bracadale Av. B24: Erd 5G 81
Bracadale Cl. CV3: Bin 6A 154
Bracebridge Cl. CV7: Bal C 3H 171
Bracebridge Ct. B17: Harb 4D 120
Bracebridge Rd. B24: Erd 8F 80
B74: Four O 1F 58
B78: K'bry 3C 62
CV9: Ath 2J 65
Bracebridge St. B6: Aston 3L 101
CV11: Nun 5H 89
Braceby Av. B13: Mose 2C 144
Braces La. B60: Marl 8B 162
Brace St. WS1: Wals 1L 55
(not continuous)
Brackenbury Rd. B44: K'sdng 1B 80
Bracken Cl. CV22: Bil 8L 179
WS7: Burn 2J 17
WS12: Hed 1K 9
WS14: Lich 3L 19
WV8: Pend 8L 21
Bracken Cft. B37: Chel W 6J 105
Brackendale Dr. CV10: Nun 7F 88
CV23: Barby 8J 207
WS5: Wals 6B 56
Brackendale Shop. Cen.
WV12: W'hall 5D 38
Brackendale Way
DY9: W'cte 5D 116
Bracken Dr. B75: S Cold 4A 60
CV22: Bil 8L 179
LE10: Wlvy 5K 113
Brackenfield Rd. B44: Gt Barr 7J 57
B63: Hale 6L 117
Brackenfield Vw. DY1: Dud 1D 96
Bracken Gro. B61: Cats 8A 162
Brackenhill Rd. WS7: C Ter 1G 17
Brackenhurst Rd. CV6: Cov 2M 151
Bracken Pk. Gdns.
DY8: Word 7M 95
Bracken Rd. B24: Erd 7J 81
WS12: Hunt 4C 8
Bracken Way B38: K Nor 2D 164
B74: S'tly 1M 57
Brackenwood WS5: Wals 4D 56
Brackenwood Dr. WV11: Wed 4M 37
Bracklesham Way B77: Amin 3G 33
Brackley Av. B20: Hand 8J 79
Brackley Cl. CV6: Cov 2M 151
Brackleys Way B92: Olton 7M 123
Bracknell Wlk.
CV2: W'grve S 2A 154
Bradbeer Ho. B16: Edg 8G 101
Bradburne Way B7: Birm 4A 102
Bradburn Rd. WV11: Wed 1H 37
Bradbury Cl. WS8: Bwnhls 4F 26
Bradbury Ct. WS12: Hed 2H 9
Bradbury La. WS12: Hed 1G 9
Bradbury Rd. B92: Olton 8M 123
Braddock Cl. CV3: Bin 8A 154
Brade Dr. CV2: W'grve S 2A 154
Braden Rd. WV4: Penn 6K 51
Brades Cl. B63: Crad 2H 117
Brades Ri. B69: O'bry 1D 98
Brades Rd. B69: O'bry 8E 76
Bradestone Rd. CV11: Nun 8K 89
BRADES VILLAGE 1D 98
Bradewell Rd. B36: Cas B 8D 82
Bradfield Cl. CV5: Cov 4J 151
Bradfield Ho. B26: Sheld 3E 124
Bradfield Rd. B42: Gt Barr 2K 79
Bradford Cl. B43: Gt Barr 2F 78
CV33: Bis T 8D 224
Bradford Ct.
B12: Birm 1A 122 (8L 5)
Bradford La. DY9: Belb 4D 160
WS1: Wals 8L 39
Bradford Mall WS1: Wals 8L 39
Bradford Pl. B11: S'brk 3A 122
B70: W Brom 1L 99
WS1: Wals 8L 39
Bradford Rd. B36: Cas B 1A 104
DY2: Dud 3F 96
WS8: Bwnhls 1E 26
Bradford St. B5: Birm 8M 101 (7J 5)
B79: Tam 4M 31
WS1: Wals 8L 39
WS11: Cann 4G 9
Bradgate Cl. WV12: W'hall 3C 38
Bradgate Dr. B74: Four O 4E 42
Bradgate Pl. B12: Bal H 4A 122
Bradgate Rd. LE9: Barw 1B 70
LE10: Hinc 7M 69
Brading Rd. CV10: Nun 3K 89
BRADLEY 6L 53
Bradley Cft. CV7: Bal C 3H 171
BRADLEY GREEN 4F 48
Bradley La. WV14: Bils 6M 53
Bradleymore Rd. DY5: Brie H 6D 96
Bradley Rd. B34: S End 3D 104
DY8: Stourb 3M 115
Bradleys Cl. B64: Crad H 2L 117
Bradley's La. DY4: Tip 1K 75
WV14: Cose 1K 75
Bradley St. DY4: Tip 7M 75
DY5: P'ntt 2B 96
WV14: Bils 5M 53
Bradley Thursfield Ct.
DY11: Kidd 2J 157
BRADMORE 1L 51
Bradmore Cl. B91: Sol 1A 168
Bradmore Gro. B29: W Cas 1A 142
Bradmore Rd. WV3: Wolv 1M 51
Bradney Grn. CV4: Tile H 2E 172
Bradnick Pl. CV4: Tile H 8F 150
Bradnock Cl. B13: Mose 2C 144
BRADNOCK'S MARSH 6E 148
Bradnocks Marsh Bus. Cen.
B92: H Ard 6E 148
Bradnocks Marsh La.
B92: H Ard 8D 148
Bradshaw Av. B38: K Nor 8D 142
WS10: Darl 4B 54
Bradshaw Cl. DY4: Tip 6A 76
Bradshawe Cl. B28: Hall G 6D 144
Bradshaw St.
WV1: Wolv 7E 36 (4M 7)
Bradstock Rd. B30: K Nor 5J 143
Bradwell Cft. B75: R'ley 6L 43
Bradwell La. WS15: Cann W 4F 10
Braeburn Cl. WS13: Lich 8K 13
Braemar Av. DY8: Word 8J 95
Braemar Cl. CV2: Cov 2L 153
DY3: Sed 8C 52
WV12: W'hall 3B 38
Braemar Dr. B23: Erd 4B 80
Braemar Gdns. WS12: Hed 2F 8
Braemar Rd. B73: S Cold 7F 58
B92: Olton 8L 123
CV32: Lill 5B 218
WS11: Nort C 5A 16
Braemar Way CV10: Nun 7G 89
Braeside Cft. B37: Chel W 7K 105
Braeside Way WS3: Pels 6M 25
Brafield Leys CV22: Rugby 3A 206
Bragg Rd. B20: Hand 7K 79
Braggs Farm La.
B90: Dic H, Shir 5F 166
Braham B79: Tam 3J 31
Braid Cl. B38: K Nor 8D 142
Braids Cl. CV21: Rugby 5D 180
Brailes Cl. B92: Sol 2E 146
Brailes Dr. B76: Walm 6M 59
Brailes Gro. B9: Bord G 8H 103
Brailsford Cl. WV11: Wed 1L 37
Brailsford Dr. B66: Smeth 4A 100
Brain St. B77: Glas 7G 33
Braithwaite Dr. DY6: K'wfrd 3K 95
Braithwaite Rd. B11: S'brk 2A 122
Brake, The DY8: Hag 3M 137
Brake La. DY8: Hag 3L 137
Brakesmead CV31: Lea S 4M 223
Bramah Way DY4: Tip 3C 76
Bramber B77: Wiln 8D 32
Bramber Dr. WV5: Wom 3F 72
Bramber Ho. B31: Longb 1M 163
Bramber Way DY8: Stourb 7M 115
Bramble Cl. B6: Aston 2L 101
B31: N'fld 3M 141
B46: Col 2M 105
B64: Old H 5M 97
CV11: Nun 7M 89
WS8: Clay 4E 26
WV12: W'hall 2C 38
Bramble Dell B9: Bord G 6G 103
Bramble Dr. B26: Sheld 3A 124
WS12: Hed 2J 9
Bramble Grn. DY1: Dud 4F 74
Bramble La. WS7: Burn 1H 17
Brambles B97: Redd 8B 212
Brambles, The B61: Cats 1A 188
B76: Walm 1A 82
DY9: W'cte 6D 116
WS11: Nort C 4A 16
WS14: Lich 3K 19
Brambleside DY8: Word 8M 95
Bramble St. CV1: Cov 7E 152
Bramblewood WV5: Wom 2G 73
Bramblewood Dr. WV3: Wolv 1L 51
Bramblewoods B34: S End 4C 104
Brambling B77: Wiln 2G 47
Brambling Cl. CV23: Brow 1C 180
Brambling Ri. DY10: Kidd 8B 158
Brambling Wlk. B15: Edg 2J 121
DY5: Brie H 3C 116
BRAMCOTE 3F 112
Bramcote Cl. CV12: Bulk 7D 112
LE10: Hinc 6M 69
Bramcote Dr. B91: Sol 2C 146
BRAMCOTE MAINS 6E 112
Bramcote Ri. B75: S Cold 2J 59
Bramcote Rd. B32: Quin 4J 119
(not continuous)
Bramdean Wlk. WV4: Penn 3J 51
Bramdene Av. CV10: Nun 1J 89
Brame Rd. LE10: Hinc 7J 69
Bramerton Cl. WV11: Wed 3G 37
Bramford Dr. DY1: Dud 3H 75
Bramley Cl. B43: Gt Barr 6K 57
WS5: Wals 1L 57
Bramley Ct. B90: Shir 7J 145
Bramley Dr. B20: Hand 6H 79
B47: H'wd 3B 166
Bramley M. Ct. B27: A Grn 4J 123
Bramley Rd. B27: A Grn 4J 123
WS5: Wals 5B 56
Bramley Way DY12: Bew 2A 156
Brampton Av. B28: Hall G 3G 145
Brampton Cl. DY10: Cookl 5B 136
Brampton Cres. B90: Shir 3H 145
Brampton Dr. WS12: Hth H 7L 9
Brampton Way CV12: Bulk 6B 112
Bramshall Dr. B93: Dorr 6E 168
Bramshaw Cl. B14: K Hth 7M 143
Bramshill Ct. B15: Edg 1H 121
Bramstead Av. WV6: Tett 7H 35
Bramston Cres. CV4: Tile H 8F 150
Bramwell Dr. WS6: C Hay 8D 14
Bramwell Gdns. CV6: Longf 4E 130
Brancaster Cl. B77: Amin 3G 33
Branchal Rd. WS9: A'rdge 8J 27
Branches Cl. DY12: Bew 3B 156
Branch Rd. B38: K Nor 1E 164
Branden Rd. B48: A'chu 3A 190
Brandfield Rd. CV6: Cov 1M 151
BRANDHALL 1H 119
Brandhall Ct. B68: O'bry 7G 99
Brandhall La. B68: O'bry 8H 99
Brandhall Rd. B68: O'bry 7H 99
BRANDON 4F 176
Brandon Cl. B70: W Brom 7G 77
DY3: Sed 2E 74
WS9: A'rdge 6M 41
Brandon Ct. B31: N'fld 8B 142
CV3: Bin 2A 176
Brandon Gro. B31: Longb 2M 163
Brandon La. CV3: W'hall 5K 175
CV8: Bran 5K 175
Brandon Marsh Nature Reserve 5A 176
Brandon Marsh Nature Reserve
Vis. Cen. 5B 176
Brandon Pde. CV32: Lea S 1A 224
Brandon Pk. WV3: Wolv 2L 51
Brandon Pas. B16: Birm 6E 100
Brandon Pl. B34: S End 2D 104
Brandon Rd. B28: Hall G 7E 122
B62: B'hth 8E 98
B91: Sol 2C 146
CV3: Bin 8M 153
CV23: Bret 3J 177
LE10: Hinc 2H 91
Brandon Thomas Ct.
B6: Aston 1B 102
Brandon Way B70: W Brom 6G 77
DY5: Quar B 1E 116
Brandon Way Ind. Est.
B70: W Brom 6F 76
BRANDWOOD END 5K 143
Brandwood Gro. B14: K Hth 4K 143
Brandwood Ho. B14: K Hth 2K 143
Brandwood Pk. Rd.
B14: K Hth 4H 143
Brandwood Rd. B14: K Hth 5K 143
Branfield Cl. WV14: Cose 8G 53
Branksome Av. B21: Hand 1F 100
Branksome Rd. CV6: Cov 3L 151
Branscombe Cl. B14: K Hth 4K 143
Bransdale Av. CV6: Cov 6D 130
Bransdale Cl. WV6: Wolv 4A 36
Bransdale Rd. WS8: Clay 2E 26
Bransford Av. CV4: Canly 4K 173
Bransford Ri. B91: Cath B 4H 147
Bransford Twr. B12: Birm 1M 121
BRANSON'S CROSS 8B 192
Branston Ct.
B18: Birm 4J 101 (1C 4)
Branston St.
B18: Birm 4J 101 (1C 4)
Branstree Dr. CV6: Cov 7D 130
Brantford Rd. B25: Yard 1J 123
Branthill Cft. B91: Sol 8B 146
Brantley Av. WV3: Wolv 8J 35
Brantley Rd. B6: Witt 7A 80
Branton Hill La. WS9: A'rdge 4J 41
Brantwood Av. WS7: Chase 4G 17
Brascote Rd. LE10: Hinc 1F 90
Brasshouse La. B66: Smeth 3M 99
Brassie Cl. B38: K Nor 8D 142
Brassington Av. B73: S Cold 5H 59
BRATCH, THE 2E 72
Bratch Cl. DY2: Neth 6J 97
Bratch Comn. Rd. WV5: Wom 2E 72
Bratch Hollow WV5: Wom 1G 73
Bratch La. WV5: Wom 1F 72
Bratch Pk. WV5: Wom 1F 72
Brathay Cl. CV3: Cov 3D 174
Bratt St. B70: W Brom 5J 77
Braunston Cl. B76: Walm 7A 60
Braunston Pl. CV22: Hillm 1D 206
Brawnes Hurst B26: Yard 8A 104
Bray Bank B46: Over W 6K 85
Brayford Av. CV3: Cov 3C 174
DY5: Brie H 2B 116
Bray Ho. WV11: Wed 4J 37
Braymoor Rd. B33: Kitts G 8E 104
Brays Cl. CV23: Brin 6L 155
Bray's La. CV2: Cov 6G 153
Brays Rd. B26: Sheld 3A 124
Bray St. WV13: W'hall 7B 38
Braytoft Cl. CV6: Cov 7C 130
Brazil St. CV4: Tile H 7E 150
Breaches La. B98: Redd 1K 221
Breach La. LE9: Earl S 2E 70
Breach Oak La. CV7: Cor 6J 109
Breadmarket St. WS13: Lich 1H 19
Break Bk. Rd. B61: B'gve 1K 209
Bream B77: Two G 2D 46
Bream Cl. B37: Chel W 7J 105
WV10: Wolv 5H 37
Breamore Cres. DY1: Dud 6F 74
Brean Av. B26: Yard 4M 123
Brearley Cl. B19: Birm 4L 101
Brearley St. B19: Birm 4K 101
B21: Hand 1D 100
Breaside Wlk. B37: Chel W 6J 105
Brechin Cl. LE10: Hinc 1G 91
Brecknell Ri. DY10: Kidd 1M 157
Brecknock Rd. B71: W Brom 3G 77
Brecon Av. B61: B'gve 4A 188
Brecon Dr. DY8: Amb 3B 116
Brecon Rd. B20: Hand 1H 101
Brecot Stadium 3K 55
Bredon Av. CV3: Bin 2M 175
DY9: Lye 4C 116
DY11: Kidd 8G 157
Bredon Ct. B63: Hale 6A 118
Bredon Cft. B18: Hock 4G 101
Bredon Ho. B98: Redd 2H 221
Bredon Rd. B61: B'gve 2K 209
B69: O'bry 4D 98
DY8: Amb 3A 116
Bredon Vw. B97: Redd 1D 220
Bredon Way DY13: Stour S 8D 182
Breech Cl. B74: S'tly 2L 57
Bree Cl. CV5: Alle 2G 151
Breeden Dr. B76: Curd 3H 83
Breedon Kingsley Gdns.
B98: Redd 6G 213
Breedon Rd. B30: K Nor 4G 143
Breedon Ter. *B18: Hock 4G 101*
(off Brookfield Rd.)
Breedon Way WS4: S'fld 8C 26
Breener Ind. Est. DY5: Brie H 8B 96
Breen Rydding Dr.
WV14: Cose 8H 53
Brees La. CV8: Fen E 8G 171
Breeze Av. WS11: Nort C 4B 16
Brelades Cl. DY1: Dud 7E 74
Brendan Cl. B46: Col 4A 106
Brendon B77: Wiln 8H 33
Brendon Way CV10: Nun 6A 88
Brenfield Dr. LE10: Hinc 1G 91
Brennand Cl. B68: O'bry 1H 119
Brennand Rd. B68: O'bry 8H 99

Brent—Bromfield Cl.

Brent B77: Wiln 2E 46
Brentford Rd. B14: K Hth 4A 144
B91: Sol 6L 145
Brentmill Cl. WV10: Bush 5F 22
Brentnall Dr. B75: Four O 6H 43
Brenton Rd. WV4: Penn 6M 51
Brent Rd. B30: Stir 1K 143
Brentwood Av. CV3: Finh 6C 174
Brentwood Cl. B91: Sol 6L 145
Brentwood Gro. B44: Gt Barr 1L 79
Brenwood Cl. DY6: K'wfrd 2H 95
Brereton Cl. DY2: Dud 1L 97
Brereton Rd. WV12: W'hall 2C 38
Brescot Stadium 3K 55
Brese Av. CV34: Warw 8F 216
Bretby Gro. B23: Erd 3G 81
BRETFORD 2K 177
Bretford Rd. CV2: Cov 8J 131
CV8: Bran 3G 177
CV23: Brin 8L 155
Bretshall Cl. B90: M'path 4M 167
Brett Dr. B32: Bart G 1J 141
Brettell La. DY5: Brie H 8A 96
DY8: Amb 1M 115
Brettell St. DY2: Dud 1H 97
Bretton Gdns. WV10: Wolv 3F 36
Bretton Rd. B27: A Grn 7K 123
Bretts Cl. CV1: Cov 5E 152 (1F 6)
Bretts Hall Est. CV10: Ans C . . .2M 87
Brett St. B71: W Brom 4H 77
Brett Young Cl. DY10: Kidd 4B 158
Brevitt Rd. WV2: Wolv 3D 52
Brewer Rd. CV12: Bulk 8D 112
Brewers Cl. CV3: Bin 8A 154
Brewer's Dr. WS3: Pels 8A 26
Brewers Ter. WS3: Pels 7A 26
Brewer St. WS2: Wals 5L 39
Brewery St. B6: Birm . . .4L 101 (1H 5)
B21: Hand 1D 100
B67: Smeth 3M 99
DY2: Dud 8L 75
DY4: Tip 5M 75
Brewhouse Ct. WS13: Lich 8F 12
(off Wheel La.)
Brewins Way DY5: Brie H 5G 97
Brewood Rd. WV10: C Grn 1C 22
Brewster Cl. B78: M Oak 8L 31
CV2: Cov 7L 153
Brewster St. DY2: Neth 4J 97
Breydon Gro. WV13: W'hall 1M 53
Brian Rd. B67: Smeth 3L 99
Brians Way CV6: Cov 6E 130
Briar B77: Amin 6G 33
Briar Av. B74: S'tly 8A 42
Briarbeck WS4: S'fld 1C 40
Briar Cl. B24: Erd 5G 81
B60: L End 3C 188
CV32: Lill 7B 218
LE10: Burb 3M 91
WS12: Hed 1G 9
Briar Coppice B90: Ches G 5K 167
Briar Ct. DY5: Brie H 7D 96
(off Hill St.)
Briardene Av. CV12: Bed 7H 111
Briarfield Rd. B11: Tys 6G 123
Briar Hill DY10: Chad C 8L 159
Briarley B71: W Brom 8M 55
Briarmead LE10: Burb 5L 91
Briar Rd. DY1: Dud 4F 74
Briars, The B23: Erd 3D 80
DY9: Hag 5M 137
Briars Cl. CV2: Cov 7J 153
CV11: Nun 4L 89
CV23: Long L 5H 179
DY5: Brie H 5C 96
Briars Way WS12: Haz 5D 10
Briar Way DY13: Stour S 5E 182
Briarwood Cl. B90: Ches G 5K 167
WV2: E'shll 2G 53
Brickbridge La. WV5: Wom 4E 72
Brickfield Rd. B25: Yard 3H 123
Brickheath Rd. WV1: Wolv 6G 37
Brickhill Dr. B37: F'bri 7G 105
Brick Hill La. CV5: Alle 1D 150
Brickhouse La. B60: S Prior . . .6J 209
B70: W Brom 3E 76
Brickhouse La. Sth. DY4: Tip . . .3D 76
Brickhouse Rd. B65: Row R 5A 98
Brickiln St. WS8: Bwnhls 2F 26
Brick Kiln La. B44: Gt Barr 3L 79
B47: Wyt 6L 165
B78: Midd 3J 61
B91: Sol 1M 167
DY3: Gorn 6A 74
Brickkiln La. CV9: Hurl 5H 63
Brick Kiln St. DY4: Tip 3L 75
DY5: Brie H 4E 96
DY5: Quar B 1G 117
LE10: Hinc 1J 91
Brickkiln St. WV13: W'hall 8M 37
Bricklin Ct. DY5: Brie H 7D 96
Brick St. DY3: Sed 1D 74
Brickyard La. B80: Stud 4J 221
Brickyard Rd. WS9: A'rdge 8F 26
Bridal Rd. B61: D'frd 3J 187
Briddsland Rd. B33: Kitts G 7E 104
Brides Wlk. B38: K Nor 2E 164
Bridge, The WS1: Wals 8L 39
Bridgeacre Gdns. CV3: Bin 6M 153
Bridge Av. DY4: Tip 2C 76
WS6: C Hay 4E 14
Bridgeburn Rd. B31: N'fld 1L 141
Bridge Cl. B11: S'hll 6B 122
WS8: Clay 3E 26
Bridgecote CV3: W'hall 3L 175
Bridge Ct. B64: Old H 1M 117
(off Edgewood Cl.)
CV47: Sou 6H 225
WS12: Hed 4H 9
Bridge Cft. B12: Bal H 3L 121
Bri. Cross Rd. WS7: C Ter 2F 16
BRIDGE END 3F 222
Bridge End CV34: Warw 3F 222
CV47: Sou 5H 225
Bridgefield Wlk. B65: Row R . . .4M 97
Bridgefoot Wlk. WV8: Pend 8M 21
Bridgeford Rd. B34: S End 3B 104
Bridgehead Wlk. B76: Walm 2M 81
Bridge Ind. Est. B91: Sol 2C 146
Bridgelands Way
B20: Hand 8K 79
Bridge La. CV9: With 2B 66
Bridge Mdw. Dr. B93: Know 4F 168
Bridgeman Cft. B36: Cas B 1C 104
Bridgeman Rd.
CV6: Cov 4B 152 (1A 6)
Bridgeman St. WS2: Wals 8K 39
Bridgemary Cl. WV10: Bush 5F 22
Bridgemeadow Ho.
B36: Hodg H 1L 103
Bridgend Cft. DY5: P'ntt 3B 96
Bridgenorth Ho. B33: Yard 8B 104
Bridge Piece B31: N'fld 7B 142
Bridge Rd. B8: Salt 5E 102
DY4: Tip 3C 76
DY10: Cookl 3A 136
LE10: Burb 2K 91
WS4: S'fld 8B 26
Bridges Cres. WS11: Nort C 4M 15
Bridgeside Trad. Est.
B77: Tam 6C 32
Bridges Rd. WS11: Nort C 4M 15
Bridge St. B1: Birm 7J 101 (6D 4)
B63: Crad 2J 117
B69: O'bry 2G 99
B70: W Brom 5H 77
B77: Amin 4E 32
B78: Pole 3K 49
B97: Redd 5D 212
CV6: Cov 2F 152
CV8: Ken 4F 198
CV9: Hurl 5J 63
CV11: Nun 5J 89
(Church St.)
CV11: Nun 7J 89
(Henry St.)
CV21: Rugby 6C 180
CV34: Warw 1H 223
DY8: Word 8L 95
DY10: Kidd 4L 157
DY13: Stour S 7F 182
WS1: Wals 7L 39
WS8: Clay 3E 26
WS10: W'bry 8F 54
WS11: Cann 4E 14
WV10: Wolv 4E 36
WV13: W'hall 8M 37
WV14: Bils 4L 53
WV14: Cose 1J 75
Bridge St. Ind. Est.
WS10: W'bry 8F 54
Bridge St. Nth. B66: Smeth 3B 100
Bridge St. Sth. B66: Smeth 3B 100
Bridge St. W. B19: Hock 4K 101
Bridge Trad. Cen., The
B64: Crad H 1K 117
Bridge Trad. Est., The
B66: Smeth 3B 100
Bridget St. CV21: Rugby 6M 179
Bridge Wlk. B27: A Grn 6K 123
Bridgewater Av. B69: O'bry 5G 99
Bridgewater Ct. B29: S Oak 8D 120
Bridgewater Cres. DY2: Dud 8L 75
Bridgewater Dr. WV5: Wom 2F 72
WV14: Cose 7J 53
Bridgewater St. B77: Tam 4D 32
Bridge Way WS8: Clay 3E 26
Bridge Works Ind. Est.
CV8: Ken 5G 199
Bridgnorth Av. WV5: Wom 5F 72
Bridgnorth Gro. WV12: W'hall . . .3B 38
Bridgnorth Rd. DY3: Himl 6H 73
DY3: Swind 4A 72
DY7: Stourt 2A 114
(not continuous)
DY8: Woll 3L 115
DY11: Kidd 4E 134
DY12: Arl, Shat 1A 134
WV5: Wom 4E 72
WV6: Pert, Tett, Tres 3A 50
BRIDGTOWN 3E 14
Bridgtown Bus. Cen.
WS11: Cann 3E 14
Bridgwater Cl. WS9: Wals W 6F 26
Bridle Brook La. CV5: Alle 5F 128
Bridle Gro. B71: W Brom 1M 77
Bridle La. B74: S'tly 2L 57
WS9: A'rdge 3J 57
Bridle Mead B38: K Nor 1D 164
Bridle Path, The B90: Shir 4H 145
CV5: Alle 3H 151
Bridle Path Rd. LE9: Elme 5D 70
Bridle Rd. CV21: Rugby 5L 179
DY8: Woll 3K 115
Bridlewood B74: S'tly 1M 57
Bridley Moor Rd. B97: Redd . . .5C 212
Bridport Cl. CV2: W'grve S 4A 154
Bridport Ho. B31: N'fld 2L 141
BRIERLEY HILL 7D 96
Brierley Hill Baths 7D 96
Brierley Hill Rd. DY5: Brie H 7L 95
DY8: Word 7L 95
Brierley La. WV14: Bils, Cose . . .7L 53
Brierley Rd. B60: B'gve 8C 188
CV2: Cov 1J 153
Brierley Trad. Est., The
DY5: Brie H 6C 96
Brier Mill Rd. B63: Hale 6C 118
Brierley Hill La. WS15: Gent . . .5H 11
Briery Cl. B64: Crad H 2M 117
Briery Rd. B63: Hale 6L 117
Briffen Ho. B16: Birm . . .7H 101 (5B 4)
Brigadoon Gdns. DY9: Pedm . . .7C 116
Brigfield Cres. B13: Mose 4B 144
Brigfield Rd. B13: Mose 4B 144
Bright Cres. B77: Wiln 7C 32
Brightmere Rd.
CV6: Cov 5B 152 (1A 6)
Brighton Cl. WS2: Wals 6K 39
Brighton Pl. WV3: Wolv 7A 36
Brighton Rd. B12: Bal H 4M 121
Bright Rd. B68: O'bry 4H 99
Brightstone Cl. WV10: Bush 5F 22
Brightstone Rd. B45: Fran 7H 141
Bright St. CV6: Cov 3E 152
DY8: Woll 4K 115
WS10: Darl 4D 54
WV1: Wolv 6B 36 (1G 7)
Bright Walton Rd. CV3: Cov . . .2D 174
Brightwell Cres. B93: Dorr 6E 168
Brill Cl. CV4: Canly 4J 173
Brimfield Pl. WV6: Wolv 5M 35
(off Newbridge St.)
Brimstone La. B61: D'frd 2J 187
Brindle Av. CV3: Cov 8J 153
Brindle Cl. B26: Yard 4L 123
Brindle Ct. B23: Erd 6B 80
Brindlefields Way DY4: Tip 7A 76
Brindle Rd. WS5: Wals 5C 56
Brindley Av. WV11: Wed 8A 24
Brindley Brae DY7: Kinv 5C 114
Brindley Bus. Pk. WS11: Hed 6H 9
Brindley Cl. CV9: Ath 8J 49
DY8: Word 8L 95
WS2: Wals 4F 38
WV5: Wom 3D 72
Brindley Ct. B68: O'bry 2H 119
DY4: Tip 4L 75
Brindley Cres. WS12: Hed 2J 9
Brindley Dr. B1: Birm . . .7J 101 (5C 4)
B77: Amin 3F 32
Brindley Heath Rd. WS12: Hed . . .2J 9
Brindley Paddocks
CV1: Cov 5C 152 (1C 6)
Brindley Pl. B1: Birm . . .7H 101 (6B 4)
Brindley Point
B16: Birm 7H 101 (5A 4)
Brindley Rd. B71: W Brom 1G 77
CV7: Exh 2H 131
CV21: Hillm 8G 181
LE10: Hinc 1E 90
Brindley St. DY13: Stour S 4F 182
Brindley Way B66: Smeth 4C 100
Brine Pits La. WR9: Wych 8C 208
Brineton Gro. B29: W Cas 8A 120
Brineton Ind. Est. WS2: Wals 8J 39
Brineton St. WS2: Wals 8J 39
Bringewood Gro.
B32: Bart G 1H 141
BRINKLOW 6L 155
Brinklow Cl. B98: Redd 1K 221
Brinklow Cft. B34: S End 2D 104
Brinklow Rd. B29: W Cas 7M 119
CV3: Bin 7M 153
CV7: Ansty 5E 132
CV23: Brin 6M 155
Brinklow Twr. B12: Birm 2M 121
Brinley Way DY6: K'wfrd 3J 95
BRINSFORD 2D 22
Brinsford La. WV10: Cov H 2D 22
Brinsford Rd. WV10: F'hses 6C 22
Brinsley Cl. B91: Sol 7B 146
Brinsley Rd. B26: Sheld 1B 124
Brinton Cl. DY11: Kidd 6J 157
Brinton Cres. DY11: Kidd 6J 157
Brisbane Cl. CV3: Cov 3E 174
Brisbane Ct. CV12: Bed 7G 111
Brisbane Rd. B67: Smeth 4L 99
Brisbane Way WS12: Wim 7L 9
Briscoe Rd. CV6: Cov 5C 130
Briseley Cl. DY5: Brie H 1C 116
Bristam Cl. B69: O'bry 3E 98
BRISTNALL FIELDS 7H 99
Bristnall Hall Cres.
B68: O'bry 6J 99
Bristnall Hall La. B68: O'bry 6J 99
Bristnall Hall Rd. B68: O'bry . . .7H 99
Bristnall Ho. B67: Smeth 5K 99
Bristol Cl. WS11: Hth H 8H 9
Bristol Ct. B29: W Cas 2C 142
Bristol Rd. B5: S Oak 6F 120
B23: Erd 6E 80
B29: S Oak 2D 142
Bristol Rd. CV5: Cov 7M 151
DY2: Neth 7K 97
Bristol Rd. Sth. B31: Longb 1K 163
B45: Redn 1G 163
Bristol St. B5: Birm 1K 121 (8F 4)
Briston Cl. DY5: Brie H 1C 116
Britannia Cl. B98: Redd 6F 212
Britannia Gdns. B65: Row R 6C 98
DY13: Stour S 7H 183
Britannia Grn. DY3: Up Gor 4E 74
Britannia Pk. WS10: W'bry 6D 54
Britannia Rd. B65: Row R 7C 98
LE10: Burb 4A 92
WS1: Wals 4K 55
WV14: Bils 6M 53
Britannia Shop. Cen.
LE10: Hinc 8K 69
Britannia St. B69: Tiv 7C 76
CV2: Cov 6F 152
Britannia Way WS14: Lich 1L 19
Britannic Gdns. B13: Mose 7K 121
Britannic Pk. B13: Mose 7K 121
Britford Cl. B14: K Hth 6M 143
Briton Rd. CV2: Cov 5G 153
Brittan Cl. B34: S End 3E 104
Britten Cl. CV11: Nun 2A 112
Britten St. B97: Redd 5D 212
Britton Dr. B72: W Grn 1J 81
Britwell Rd. B73: W Grn 7G 59
Brixfield Way B90: Dic H 4G 167
Brixham Cl. CV11: Nun 4M 89
Brixham Dr. CV2: Cov 3J 153
Brixham Rd. B16: Edg 5D 100
Brixworth Cl. CV3: Bin 1L 175
Broach Rd. DY13: Stour S 8H 183
Broadacres B31: N'fld 3L 141
Broadbent Cl. WS13: Lich 3F 18
Broadcott Ind. Est.
B64: Old H 8A 98
Broad Cft. DY4: Tip 3C 76
Broadfern Rd. B93: Know 1H 169
Broadfield Cl. B71: W Brom 8M 55
DY6: K'wfrd 4K 95
Broadfield House Glass Mus. 4J 95
Broadfields DY9: Hag 3A 138
Broadfields Rd. B23: Erd 2H 81
Broadfield Wlk.
B16: Birm 8H 101 (7B 4)
Broadgate CV1: Cov 7C 152 (5C 6)
BROAD GREEN 8G 189
Broad Ground Rd.
B98: Redd 7H 213
Broadhaven Cl. CV31: Lea S . . .2C 224
Broad Heath Cl. B97: Redd 4B 212
Broadheath Dr. WS4: S'fld 1D 40
Broadhidley Dr. B32: Bart G . . .8H 119
Broadhursr Cl. WS12: Hed 1F 8
Broadlands WV10: F'hses 4D 22
Broadlands Cl. CV5: Cov 7J 151
Broadlands Dr. DY5: Brie H 4E 96
Broadlands Ri. WS14: Lich 2K 19
Broad La. B14: K Hth 5K 143
B94: Tan A 7C 192
B98: Beo 8B 192
CV5: E Grn 5D 150
CV7: Berk 5A 150
CV7: Fill 5A 108
WS3: Blox 6F 24
WS4: S'fld 8C 26
WS13: Pip 5A 18
WS14: Lich 2K 19
WV3: Wolv 1L 51
WV11: Ess 3C 24
Broad La. Gdns. WS3: Blox 7G 25
Broad La. Nth. WV12: W'hall 3B 38
Broad Lanes WV14: Bils 6J 53
Broad La. Sth. WV11: Wed 4M 37
Broad La. Trad. Est.
CV4: Tile H 5C 150
Broadlee B77: Wiln 8J 33
Broadmead Ct. CV5: Cov 7J 151
Broadmeadow DY6: K'wfrd 1L 95
WS9: A'rdge 1H 41
Broadmeadow Cl.
B30: K Nor 6H 143
Broad Mdw. Grn. WV14: Bils 2J 53
Broadmeadow Ho.
B32: Bart G 1K 141
Broad Mdw. La. B30: K Nor 6H 143
Broadmeadow La.
WS6: Gt Wyr 7G 15
Broadmeadows Cl.
WV12: W'hall 1E 38
Broadmeadows Rd.
WV12: W'hall 1E 38
Broadmere Ri. CV5: E Grn 7G 151
Broadmoor Av. B67: Smeth 7K 99
B68: O'bry 7K 99
Broadmoor Cl. WV14: Bils 5J 53
Broadmoor Rd. WV14: Bils 5J 53
Broad Oak Ct. CV32: Lea S 7A 218
Broadoaks B76: Walm 1A 82
Broadoaks Cl. WS11: Nort C 3M 15
Broad Oaks Rd. B91: Sol 3M 145
Broad Pk. Rd. CV2: Cov 2K 153
Broad Rd. B27: A Grn 6H 123
Broadsmeath B77: Wiln 7C 32
Broadstone Av. B63: Crad 5H 117
WS3: Blox 3K 39
Broadstone Cl. WV4: Penn 4D 52
Broadstone Rd. B26: Yard 7M 103
Broad St. B1: Birm 8H 101
B15: Birm 8H 101 (8A 4)
B61: B'gve 6L 187
B69: O'bry 4G 99
CV6: Cov 2E 152
CV23: Brin 6L 155
CV34: Warw 2F 222
DY5: P'ntt 3C 96
DY6: K'wfrd 4K 95
DY10: Kidd 2L 157
WS11: Cann 3E 14
WV1: Wolv 7D 36 (3K 7)
WV14: Bils 3J 53
WV14: Cose 1J 75
Broad St. Jetty CV6: Cov 2E 152
Broad St. Junc.
WV1: Wolv 7D 36 (3L 7)
Broadsword Way LE10: Burb 5K 91
Broadwalk B1: Birm 8J 101 (7C 4)
Broadwalk Retail Pk.
WS1: Wals 3K 55
Broadwas Cl. B98: Redd 4J 213
Broadwater CV5: Cov 1A 174
BROADWATERS 8A 136
Broadwaters Av. WS10: Darl 5C 54
Broadwaters Dr. DY9: Hag 5B 138
DY10: Kidd 1A 158
Broadwaters Rd. WS10: Darl . . .5C 54
Broad Way WS4: S'fld 7C 26
Broadway B68: O'bry 8J 99
B90: Shir 5G 145
CV5: Cov 8A 152
CV32: Cubb 4E 218
WS1: Wals 3M 55
WS12: Hed 3F 8
WV3: Wolv 8J 35
WV8: Cod 6E 20
WV10: Bush 7E 22
Broadway, The B20: Hand 7K 79
B71: W Brom 2G 77
DY1: Dud 6G 75
DY8: Stourb 6K 115
WV5: Wom 4G 73
Broadway Av. B9: Bord G 7G 103
B63: Hale 7A 118
Broadway Community Leisure Cen.
. . . . .7L 79
Broadway Cft. B26: Sheld 3A 124
B68: O'bry 8J 99
Broadway Gdns. WV10: Bush 7E 22
Broadway Mans. CV5: Cov 8A 152
Broadway Nth. WS1: Wals 7M 39
Broadway Plaza 8G 101 (8A 4)
Broadway W. WS1: Wals 3J 55
Broadwell Ind. Pk. B69: O'bry . . .8F 76
Broadwell Rd. B69: O'bry 1G 99
B92: Olton 7A 124
Broadwells Ct. CV4: W'wd H . . .3F 172
Broadwells Cres.
CV4: W'wd H 4F 172
Broadwyn Trad. Est.
B64: Old H 8A 98
Broadyates Gro. B25: Yard 3J 123
Broadyates Rd. B25: Yard 3J 123
Brobury Cft. B91: Shir 5K 145
Broches, The WS11: Nort C 5B 16
BROCKENCOTE 1K 185
Brockenhurst Way
CV6: Longf 3H 131
Brockeridge Cl. WV12: W'hall . . .8C 24
Brocket Cl. DY13: Stour S 3E 182
Brockey Cl. LE9: Barw 2B 70
Brockfield Ho. WV10: Wolv 5F 36
Brockhall Gro. B37: K'hrst 4F 104
Brockhill Dr. B97: Redd 5M 211
Brockhill La. B48: A'chu 6H 165
B60: Tard 8H 189
B97: Redd 8H 189
B98: Beo 6M 191
Brockhurst Av. LE10: Burb 5K 91
Brockhurst Cres. WS5: Wals 4L 55
Brockhurst Dr. B28: Hall G 4G 145
CV4: Tile H 7D 150
WV6: Wolv 5A 36
Brockhurst Ho. WS2: Wals 6K 39
Brockhurst La. B75: Can 3A 44
Brockhurst Pl. WS5: Wals 4M 55
Brockhurst Rd. B36: Hodg H 3L 103
B75: R'ley 8K 43
Brockhurst St. WS1: Wals 3L 55
Brockley Cl. DY5: Brie H 6D 96
Brockley Gro. B13: Mose 8J 121
Brockley Pl. B7: Nech 2C 102
Brockleys Wlk. DY7: Kinv 6B 114
BROCKMOOR 5C 96
Brockmoor Cl. DY9: Pedm 7C 116
Brock Rd. DY4: Tip 5C 76
Brockton Pl. DY13: Stour S 8E 182
Brockton Rd. B29: W Cas 8A 120
Brockwell Gro. B44: Gt Barr 5L 57
Brockwell Rd. B44: Gt Barr 5L 57
Brockworth Rd. B14: K Hth 7J 143
Brocton Cl. WS3: Blox 1G 39
WV14: Cose 6H 53
Brodick Cl. LE10: Hinc 1G 91
Brodick Rd. LE10: Hinc 1F 90
Brodick Way CV10: Nun 6F 88
Brogden Cl. B71: W Brom 7M 55
Bromage Av. B78: K'bry 3C 62
Brome Hall La. B94: Lapw 7J 195
Bromfield Cl. B6: Aston 2L 101

Bromfield Ct.—Buckingham Gdns.

Bromfield Ct. WV6: Tett 7H 35
Bromfield Cres. WS10: W'bry 5J 55
Bromfield Rd. B97: Redd 7D 212
WS10: W'bry 6J 55
BROMFORD 7K 81
Bromford Cl. B20: Hand 8G 79
B23: Erd 4E 80
Bromford Ct. B31: N'fld 8B 142
Bromford Cres. B24: Erd 7G 81
Bromford Dale WV1: Wolv 6A 36
WV6: Wolv 6A 36
Bromford Dell B31: N'fld 5C 142
Bromford Dr. B36: Hodg H 1H 103
Bromford Gdns. B15: Edg 1C 120
Bromford Ga. B24: Erd 1G 103
Bromford Hill B20: Hand 6J 79
Bromford Ho. B73: Bold 7F 58
Bromford La. B8: W End 3H 103
B24: Erd 7G 81
B70: W Brom 8G 77
Bromford Mere B92: Olton 1L 145
Bromford Mills Ind. Est.
B24: Erd 8G 81
Bromford Pk. B69: O'bry 1G 99
Bromford Pk. Ho.
B13: Mose 7B 122
(off Wake Grn. Pk.)
Bromford Pk. Ind. Est.
B70: W Brom 8G 77
Bromford Ri.
WV3: Wolv 1B 52 (8G 7)
Bromford Rd. B36: Hodg H 2H 103
B69: O'bry 1G 99
B70: W Brom 8G 77
DY2: Dud 3G 97
Bromford Rd. Ind. Est.
B69: O'bry 8G 77
Bromford Wlk. B43: Gt Barr 8F 56
Bromhurst Way CV34: Warw 5B 222
Bromleigh Dr. CV2: Cov 7J 153
Bromleigh Vs. CV8: Bag 7F 174
BROMLEY 4B 96
Bromley DY5: P'ntt 4B 96
Bromley Cl. CV8: Ken 3E 198
WS12: Hed 2J 9
Bromley Gdns. WV8: Cod 5G 21
Bromley La. DY6: K'wfrd 5L 95
Bromley Pl. WV4: Penn 4A 52
Bromley St. B9: Birm 8A 102 (7L 5)
DY9: Lye 3F 116
WV2: Wolv 2C 52
Brompton Dr. DY5: Brie H 2B 116
Brompton Lawns WV6: Tett 6G 35
Brompton Pool Rd.
B28: Hall G 6E 144
Brompton Rd. B44: Gt Barr 5L 57
BROMSGROVE 7M 187
Bromsgrove Cricket Hockey & Tennis Club 3B 210
Bromsgrove Eastern By-Pass
B60: B'gve 5B 188
Bromsgrove Highway
B60: B'gve, Fins, Tutn 7C 188
B97: Redd 7C 188
Bromsgrove Indoor Bowls Cen. 2M 209
Bromsgrove Mus. 6A 188
Bromsgrove Rd. B61: D'frd 3K 187
B62: Hunn, Roms 5A 140
B63: Hale 6C 118
B80: Stud 6J 221
B97: Redd 6A 212
DY9: Clent, Hag 3C 138
DY10: Mus G, Stone 7E 158
Bromsgrove Station (Rail) 2B 210
Bromsgrove St.
B5: Birm 8L 101 (8F 4)
B63: Hale 5C 118
DY10: Kidd 3L 157
Bromwall Rd. B13: Mose 3B 144
Bromwich Cl. CV3: Bin 1M 175
Bromwich Ct. B46: Col 7L 83
Bromwich Dr. B75: S Cold 2J 59
Bromwich La. DY9: Pedm 2B 138
Bromwich Rd. CV21: Hillm 8F 180
Bromwich Wlk. B9: Bord G 6G 103
Bromwynd Cl. WV2: Wolv 3B 52
Bromyard Av. B76: Walm 1A 82
Bromyard Rd. B11: S'hll 6E 122
Bronte Cl. B90: Shir 8K 145
CV10: Gall C 4M 87
CV21: Rugby 6C 180
Bronte Ct. B79: Tam 3A 32
B90: Shir 8K 145
Bronte Dr. DY10: Kidd 3B 158
WS11: Hth H 7J 9
Bronte Farm Rd. B90: Shir 8K 145
Bronte Rd. WV2: E'shll 3F 52
Bronte Wlk. CV2: Cov 6K 153
Bronwen Ingham Ct.
DY10: Kidd 2L 157
Bronwen Rd. WV14: Cose 2J 75
Bronze Cl. CV11: Nun 1L 111
Brook Av. B77: Wiln 2G 47
Brookbank Av. B34: S End 3D 104
Brookbank Gdns. DY3: Gorn 7B 74
Brookbank Rd. DY3: Gorn 7B 74
Brook Cl. B33: Stech 5L 103
B78: K'bry 4D 62
B90: Shir 8F 144
CV1: Cov 6E 152
Brook Cl. WS9: Wals W 6G 27
WS13: Lich 8G 13
Brook Cott. Cl. B46: Over W 5K 85
Brook Ct. B60: B'gve 6B 188
Brook Cres. DY6: W Hth 2J 95
DY9: Hag 4B 138
DY9: W'cte 6F 116
Brook Cft. B26: Sheld 2B 124
B37: Mars G 2H 125
Brookdale DY3: Lwr G 6C 74
DY10: Kidd 1M 157
LE10: Hinc 1H 91
Brookdale Cl. B45: Redn 8G 141
Brookdale Dr. WV4: Penn 3L 51
Brookdale Rd. CV10: Nun 2K 89
Brook Dr. B32: Bart G 8K 119
Brooke Cl. CV34: Warw 4F 222
Brooke Ct. *CV21: Rugby 6M 179*
(off Lit. Pennington St.)
Brooke Farm Ind. Est.
B94: Earls 7H 167
Brooke M. CV34: Warw 3F 222
BROOK END 7K 63
Brook End B78: Faz 1A 46
WS7: Chase 5G 17
WS15: Longd 1M 11
Brookend Dr. B45: Rubery 1F 162
Brooke Rd. CV8: Ken 5H 199
WS12: Hed 3F 8
Brookes Cl. B69: Tiv 1B 98
Brookes Ho. *WS1: Wals 8M 39*
(off Paddock La.)
Brookes's Yard *LE10: Hinc 8K 69*
(off King St.)
Brooke St. DY2: Dud 1J 97
Brook Farm Wlk.
B37: Chel W 6K 105
Brookfield LE10: Sharn 4J 93
Brookfield Cl. B97: Redd 5D 220
WS9: A'rdge 8G 27
Brookfield Dr. LE10: Wlvy 5K 113
WS11: Cann 2E 14
Brookfield Rd. B18: Hock 4G 101
CV32: Cubb 4E 218
LE10: Burb 3J 91
WS9: A'rdge 8G 27
WV8: Bilb 6H 21
BROOKFIELDS 5H 101 (1B 4)
Brookfields Cl. B60: Marl 8C 162
Brookfields Rd. B68: O'bry 5J 99
Brookfield Ter. B18: Hock 4G 101
Brookfield Way B92: Olton 2K 145
DY4: Tip 3A 76
Brookford Av. CV6: Cov 6A 130
Brook Grn. La. B92: Bars 8A 148
Brook Gro. WV8: Bilb 6H 21
Brookhampton Cl. B97: Redd 5E 220
Brookhill Cl. WV12: W'hall 8C 24
Brook Hill Rd. B8: W End 5G 103
Brookhill Way WV12: W'hall 8D 24
Brook Holloway DY9: W'cte 5F 116
Brookhouse Cl. WV10: F'stne 2H 23
Brook Ho. La. WV10: F'stne 3E 22
Brookhouse Rd. B45: B Grn 2E 188
B60: B'wll 2E 188
WS5: Wals 2B 56
Brookhurst Ct. CV32: Lea S 8K 217
Brookhurst La. B90: Dic H 3H 167
Brookhus Farm Rd.
B76: Walm 1A 82
Brooking Cl. B43: Gt Barr 5K 57
Brookland Gro. WS9: Wals W 7F 26
Brookland Rd. DY9: Hag 5A 138
WS9: Wals W 6F 26
Brooklands B98: Redd 4M 213
DY3: Swind 8E 72
DY8: Word 8M 95
WS5: Wals 6B 56
Brooklands Av. WS6: Gt Wyr 5F 14
Brooklands Cl. B28: Hall G 8F 122
Brooklands Dr. B14: K Hth 4L 143
DY11: Kidd 8K 135
Brooklands La. B98: Redd 4H 213
Brooklands Pde. WV1: Wolv 8G 37
Brooklands Rd. B28: Hall G 8F 122
WS11: Cann 5G 9
Brooklands Way
B37: Mars G 1H 125
Brook La. B13: Mose 1A 144
B32: Harb 4M 119
B64: Old H 7L 97
B92: Olton 1K 145
CV10: Nun 3J 89
WS6: Gt Wyr 6G 15
WS9: Wals W 6F 26
Brooklea CV12: Bed 7F 110
Brooklea Gro. B38: K Nor 8G 143
Brooklime Dr. CV23: Brow 1E 180
Brooklime Gdns.
WV10: F'stne 2H 23
Brooklyn Av. B6: Aston 2M 101
Brooklyn Gro. DY6: W Hth 1H 95
WV14: Cose 1K 75
Brooklyn Rd. CV1: Cov 3D 152
WS7: Chase 5G 17
WS12: Hth H 8K 9
Brookmans Av. B32: Quin 5K 119
Brook Mdw. Ct. B28: Hall G 3D 144
Brook Mdw. Rd. B34: S End 3A 104
WS4: S'fld 1D 40
Brook Mdws. WV8: Bilb 5H 21
Brookmoor Ind. Est.
DY5: Brie H 6A 96
Brookpiece Ho. *B14: K Hth 7L 143*
(off Milston Cl.)
Brook Piece Wlk. B35: Cas V 6B 82
Brook Rd. B15: Edg 2E 120
B45: Rubery 2E 162
B61: B'gve 8L 187
B61: F'fld 8J 161
B68: O'bry 7G 99
DY8: Stourb 6B 116
WS6: C Hay 4E 14
WV5: Wom 3F 72
WV13: W'hall 8L 37
Brooksbank Dr. B64: Old H 5M 97
Brooksby Gro. B93: Dorr 7G 169
Brooks Cft. B35: Cas V 7A 82
Brookshaw Way
CV2: W'grve S 1M 153
Brookside B31: N'fld 4M 141
B43: Gt Barr 2D 78
B90: Ches G 6K 167
CV23: Stret D 3F 202
DY3: Gorn 7D 74
LE10: Burb 3K 91
WS10: W'bry 6H 55
Brookside Av. B13: Mose 2B 144
CV5: Cov 6J 151
CV8: Ken 5E 198
Brookside Cl. B23: Erd 2C 80
B48: A'chu 3B 190
B63: Hale 6K 117
CV22: Rugby 8A 180
WV5: Wom 3E 72
Brookside Dr. B61: Cats 1M 187
Brookside Ind. Est.
WS10: W'bry 6H 55
Brookside Rd. B78: M Oak 8K 31
Brookside Way B77: Wiln 3F 46
DY6: W Hth 2H 95
DY10: Blak 7H 137
Brooks Rd. B72: W Grn 1J 81
Brookstray Flats CV5: E Grn 6H 151
Brook St. B3: Birm 6J 101 (3D 4)
B66: Smeth 3B 100
B70: W Brom 6H 77
B98: Redd 5G 213
CV8: Wols 6G 177
CV12: Bed 4H 111
CV34: Warw 3E 222
DY3: Gorn 6C 74
DY3: Sed 2G 75
DY4: Tip 3L 75
DY5: Quar B 1G 117
DY6: W Hth 8H 73
DY8: Stourb 4L 115
DY8: Word 8M 95
DY9: Lye 4F 116
DY11: Kidd 3J 157
WS2: Wals 8K 39
WV14: Bils 4L 53
Brook St. Bus. Cen. DY4: Tip 3L 75
Brook Ter. WV14: Bils 4L 53
Brookthorpe Dr. WV12: W'hall 6C 38
Brook Va. DY12: Bew 6C 156
WS11: Cann 1F 14
Brookvale Av. CV3: Bin 8L 153
Brookvale Cl. B61: B'gve 5B 188
Brookvale Gro. B92: Olton 8K 123
Brookvale M. B29: S Oak 7H 121
Brookvale Pk. Rd. B23: Erd 4B 80
Brookvale Rd. B6: Witt 7A 80
B92: Olton 8K 123
Brookvale Trad. Est. B6: Witt 6M 79
Brook Vw. CV22: Dunc 6J 205
Brookview B67: Smeth 4M 99
Brook Vw. Cl. B19: Hock 3J 101
Brook Wlk. B32: Bart G 7K 119
CV9: Man 3M 65
Brookweed B77: Amin 6G 33
Brookwillow Rd. B63: Hale 8K 117
Brookwood Av. B28: Hall G 4D 144
Brookwood Dr. B45: B Grn 1J 189
Broom Cl. B60: B'gve 7B 188
CV22: Bil 8L 179
Broom Covert Rd. WS14: S'fen 1L 29
Broom Cres. DY10: Kidd 3A 158
Broomcroft Rd. B37: K'hrst 4F 104
Broomdene Av. B34: S End 2A 104
Broom Dr. B14: K Hth 5L 143
BROOME 7A 138
Broome Av. B43: Gt Barr 2C 78
Broome Cl. B63: Hale 6A 118
Broome Ct. B36: Cas B 1C 104
Broome Cft. CV6: Cov 6B 130
Broome Gdns. B75: S Cold 4J 59
Broomehill Cl. DY5: Brie H 2C 116
Broome La.
DY9: Brme, Clent 7M 137
DY10: Blak 6L 137
Broome Rd. WV10: Bush 2E 36
Broomfield B67: Smeth 4M 99
Broomfield Av. B78: Faz 1A 46
Broomfield Cl. DY11: Kidd 2H 157
Broomfield Grn. DY11: Kidd 2J 157
Broomfield Pl. CV5: Cov 7A 152
(not continuous)
Broomfield Ri. CV10: Nun 7F 88
Broomfield Rd. B23: Erd 7D 80
CV5: Cov 8M 151
DY11: Kidd 2H 157
Broomfields Av. B91: Sol 4D 146
Broomfields Cl. B91: Sol 4D 146
Broomfields Farm Rd.
B91: Sol 4D 146
Broomhall Av. WV11: Wed 3K 37
Broom Hall Cres.
B27: A Grn 2H 145
Broom Hall Gro. B27: A Grn 1J 145
BROOM HILL 6D 160
BROOMHILL 5E 8
Broomhill Bank WS11: Cann 6E 8
Broomhill Cl. B43: Gt Barr 1D 78
WS11: Cann 5E 8
Broomhill La. B43: Gt Barr 1D 78
Broomhill Rd. B23: Erd 2B 80
(not continuous)
Broom Ho. B71: W Brom 8M 55
Broomhurst B15: Edg 1E 120
Broomie Cl. B75: S Cold 4K 59
Broom La. B90: Dic H 3G 167
Broomlea Cl. B74: S'tly 1L 57
Broom Rd. DY1: Dud 4G 75
WS5: Wals 6B 56
Broom St. B12: Birm 1A 122 (8L 5)
Broomybank CV8: Ken 3H 199
Broomy Cl. B34: Stech 4A 104
DY13: Stour S 4D 182
Brosdale Dr. LE10: Hinc 8G 69
Broseley Av. B31: Longb 1B 164
Broseley Brook Cl.
B9: Bord G 8C 102
Brosil Av. B20: Hand 6E 78
Brotherton Av. B97: Redd 7M 211
Brougham St. B19: Loz 2H 101
(not continuous)
Brough Cl. B7: Nech 3B 102
WV4: E'shll 6F 52
Broughton Ct. WV6: Pert 6G 35
Broughton Cres. B31: Longb 1K 163
Broughton Rd. B20: Hand 1G 101
DY9: W'cte 6D 116
LE9: S Stan 7L 71
WV3: Wolv 8J 35
Browett Rd. CV6: Cov 4A 152
Brown Av. B77: Two G 1C 46
Brownfield Rd. B34: S End 3C 104
BROWNHILLS 2F 26
Brownhills Bus. Pk.
WS8: Bwnhls 4F 26
BROWNHILLS COMMON 1E 26
Brownhills Rd. WS8: Wals W 4F 26
WS11: Nort C 3M 15
BROWNHILLS WEST 7C 16
Brownhills West Station 6C 16
Browning Av. CV34: Warw 4C 222
Browning Cl. B79: Tam 1M 31
CV10: Gall C 4A 88
DY10: Kidd 3B 158
WV12: W'hall 2E 38
Browning Cres.
WV10: F'hses 7C 22
Browning Dr. LE10: Hinc 8J 69
Browning Gro. WV6: Pert 5E 34
Browning Rd. CV2: Cov 6J 153
CV21: Hillm 1H 207
DY3: Lwr G 5A 74
WS7: Burn 2J 17
Browning St.
B16: Birm 7H 101 (6A 4)
Browning Twr. B31: N'fld 6C 142
Brownley Rd. B90: Shir 2K 167
Brown Lion St. DY4: Tip 2L 75
Brownlow St. CV32: Lea S 7A 218
Brown Rd. WS10: Darl 2C 54
Brown's Bri. Rd. CV47: Sou 6H 225
Brown's Cl. LE9: Sap 1L 93
Brown's Coppice Av.
B91: Sol 4K 145
Browns Ct. B13: Mose 7B 122
Brown's Dr. B73: Bold 1F 80
Brownsea Cl. B45: Fran 8E 140
Brownsea Dr.
B1: Birm 8K 101 (7E 4)
Brownsfield Rd. WS13: Lich 8J 13
(not continuous)
BROWN'S GREEN
Birmingham 6F 78
Solihull 5L 193
Browns Grn. B20: Hand 6F 78
Brownshill Ct. CV6: Cov 1M 151
BROWNSHILL GREEN 8K 129
Brownshill Grn. Rd.
CV5: Alle 8K 129
CV6: Cov 8K 129
Brownshore La. WV11: Ess 5A 24
Browns La. B78: Dord 4M 47
CV5: Alle 1G 151
B79: Tam 1C 32
B93: Know 3E 168
BROWNSOVER 2D 180
Brownsover Cl. B36: Cas B 8B 82
Brownsover La. CV21: Brow 2B 180
Brownsover Rd.
CV21: N'bld A, Rugby 2L 179
Brown St. WV2: Wolv 2D 52 (8K 7)
Brownswall Est. DY3: Sed 2B 74
Brownswall Rd. DY3: Sed 2B 74
Brown Westhead Pk.
DY10: W'ley 6M 135
Browsholme B79: Tam 3K 31
Broxell Cl. CV34: Warw 1C 222
Broxell Cl. Ind. Est.
CV34: Warw 8C 216
Broxwood Pk. WV6: Tett 6H 35
Bruce Rd. CV6: Cov 1A 152
CV7: Exh 2F 130
DY10: Kidd 2B 158
Bruce Williams Way
CV22: Rugby 7B 180
Brudenell Cl. CV22: Caw 1G 205
Brueton Av. B60: B'gve 1A 210
B91: Sol 6D 146
Brueton Dr. B24: Erd 6G 81
B98: Redd 6G 213
Brueton Rd. WV14: Bils 2A 54
Bruford Rd. WV3: Wolv 1A 52
Brunel Cl. B12: Bal H 4A 122
B79: Tam 3B 32
CV2: Cov 6F 152
CV31: W'nsh 6B 224
DY13: Stour S 4G 183
WS7: Burn 1H 17
Brunel Ct. WS10: Darl 3F 54
WV5: Wom 2G 73
WV14: Cose 1L 75
Brunel Dr. DY4: Tip 8L 53
Brunel Gro. WV6: Pert 3E 34
Brunel Rd. B69: O'bry 3D 98
LE10: Hinc 1J 91
Brunel St. B2: Birm 7K 101 (6E 4)
Brunel Wlk. B78: Pole 1K 49
WS10: Darl 3F 54
Brunel Way WV2: E'shll 2G 53
Brunes Ct. CV21: Brow 2D 180
Brunslow Cl. WV10: Oxl 8C 22
WV13: W'hall 8C 38
Brunswick Arc. B1: Birm 6B 4
Brunswick Cl. CV21: Rugby 3C 180
Brunswick Ct. CV31: Lea S 4A 224
WS10: W'bry 6J 55
Brunswick Gdns. B21: Hand 8F 78
WS10: W'bry 5H 55
Brunswick Ga. DY8: Stourb 8A 116
Brunswick Ho. B34: S End 2A 104
B37: Mars G 1F 124
Brunswick Pk. Rd.
WS10: W'bry 6G 55
Brunswick Rd. B12: Bal H 4A 122
B21: Hand 8F 78
CV1: Cov 7A 152
WS11: Cann 7E 8
Brunswick Sq.
B1: Birm 7H 101 (6B 4)
Brunswick St.
B1: Birm 7H 101 (6B 4)
CV31: Lea S 3A 224
WS2: Wals 2J 55
Brunswick Ter. WS10: W'bry 6F 54
Bruntingthorpe Way
CV3: Bin 1L 175
Brunton Cl. CV3: Bin 8B 154
Brunton Rd. B10: Small H 2F 122
Brushfield Rd. B42: Gt Barr 1K 79
Brutus Dr. B46: Col 8L 83
Bryan Av. WV4: Penn 5K 51
Bryan Rd. WS2: Wals 3J 55
Bryanston Cl. CV2: W'grve S 5A 154
Bryanston Ct. B91: Sol 2M 145
Bryanston Rd. B91: Sol 2M 145
Bryans Way WS12: Hed 5M 9
Bryant Rd. CV7: Exh 2G 131
Bryant St. B18: Win G 4E 100
Bryce Rd. DY5: P'ntt 4A 96
(not continuous)
Bryher Wlk. B45: Fran 8E 140
Brylan Cft. B44: K'sdng 3M 79
Brymill Ind. Est. DY4: Tip 2L 75
Brympton Rd. CV3: Cov 7J 153
Bryn Arden Rd. B26: Yard 4L 123
Bryndale Av. B14: K Hth 4J 143
Bryn Jones Cl. CV3: Bin 1M 175
Brynmawr Rd. WV14: Cose 6G 53
Bryn Rd. CV6: Cov 2F 152
Brynside Cl. B14: K Hth 7K 143
Bryony Cl. CV12: Bed 8E 110
Bryony Cft. B23: Erd 2B 80
Bryony Gdns. WS10: Darl 2D 54
Bryony Rd. B29: W Cas 2B 142
BSA Bus. Pk. B11: Small H 3D 122
Bubbenhall Rd.
CV8: Bag, Bubb 8F 174
BUBENHALL 4J 201
Buccleuch Cl. CV22: Dunc 5J 205
Buchanan Av. WS4: Wals 6A 40
Buchanan Cl. WS4: Wals 6A 40
Buchanan Rd. CV22: Bil 8L 179
WS4: Wals 6A 40
Buchan Cl. CV10: Gall C 5M 87
Buckbury Cl. DY9: Pedm 8D 116
Buckbury Cft. B90: M'path 3B 168
Buckden B77: Wiln 8J 33
Buckden Cl. CV34: Warw 8F 216
Buckfast Cl. B61: B'gve 8K 187
CV3: Cov 4E 174
Buckhold Dr. CV5: Cov 4H 151
Buckingham Cl. CV10: Nun 8H 89
LE10: Hinc 5L 69
WS10: W'bry 5J 55
Buckingham Ct. B29: S Oak 8E 120
Buckingham Dr. WV12: W'hall 2B 38
Buckingham Gdns.
WS14: Lich 3H 19

Buckingham Gro.—Caesar Way

Buckingham Gro. DY6: K'wfrd . . .2J **95**
Buckingham Ho.
B31: Longb 1M **163**
Buckingham M. B73: W Grn 6G **59**
Buckingham Pl. WS12: Hth H 8J **9**
Buckingham Ri. CV5: Cov 5H **151**
DY1: Dud 7E **74**
Buckingham Rd. B36: Cas B 2F **104**
B65: Row R 5D **98**
B79: Tam 3K **31**
WV4: Penn 5A **52**
Buckingham St.
B19: Birm 5K **101** (1D **4**)
Buckinghams Way
LE10: Sharn 5H **93**
Buckland Cl. WS12: Hth H 8K **9**
BUCKLAND END 2M **103**
Buckland End B34: S End 3A **104**
Buckland Ho. *B15: Edg 2J 121*
(off Summer Rd.)
Buckland Rd. CV6: Cov 7B **130**
Bucklands End La.
B34: Hodg H 3M **103**
Buckle Cl. WS1: Wals 1M **55**
Buckley Ct. B13: K Hth 1M **143**
Buckley Rd. CV32: Lill 7B **218**
WV4: Penn 4K **51**
Buckleys, The B48: A'chu 3A **190**
Buckleys Grn. B48: A'chu 3A **190**
Bucklow Wlk. B33: Stech 5L **103**
Buckminster Dr. B93: Dorr 5E **168**
Bucknall Ct. B13: Mose 7B **122**
Bucknall Cres. B32: Bart G 1G **141**
Bucknall Rd. WV11: Wed 8B **24**
Bucknell Cl. B91: Sol 4C **146**
Bucknill Cres. CV21: Hillm 1H **207**
BUCKPOOL 7M **95**
Buckridge Cl. B38: K Nor 2D **164**
Buckridge La. B90: Dic H 4G **167**
(not continuous)
Bucks Hill CV10: Nun 2B **88**
Buckthorn Cl. WS12: Hed 1F **8**
Buckton Cl. B75: R'ley 7L **43**
Buckwell La. CV23: Clift D 4G **181**
Buckwell Rd. LE9: Sap 1K **93**
BUDBROOKE 2A **222**
Budbrooke Cl. CV2: Cov 7K **131**
Budbrooke Gro. B34: S End 3E **104**
Budbrooke Ind. Est.
CV34: Warw 2C **222**
Budbrooke Rd. CV34: Warw . . .2B **222**
Budden Rd. WV14: Cose 2K **75**
Bude Rd. WS5: Wals 2D **56**
Buds Rd. WS15: Cann W 4F **10**
Buffery Rd. DY2: Dud 2K **97**
Bufferys Cl. B91: Sol 1B **168**
Buildwas Cl. WS3: Blox 7F **24**
Bulford Cl. B14: K Hth 7M **143**
Bulger Rd. WV14: Bils 2J **53**
BULKINGTON
Bedworth 7C **112**
Kenilworth 7F **198**
Bulkington La. CV11: Nun 1A **112**
Bulkington Rd. CV7: Shil 2E **132**
CV12: Bed 7J **111**
LE10: Wlvy 5J **113**
Bullace Cft. B15: Edg 6D **120**
Bulldog La. WS13: Lich 8H **13**
Buller St. WV4: E'shll 4E **52**
Bullfield Av. CV4: Tile H 8E **150**
Bullfields Cl. B65: Row R 4M **97**
Bullfinch Cl. DY1: Dud 1E **96**
Bullfurlong La. LE10: Burb 4M **91**
Bullimore Gro. CV8: Ken 7G **199**
Bullivents Cl. B93: Ben H 4F **168**
Bull La. B70: W Brom 6G **77**
WS10: Mox 6B **54**
WV5: Wom 1G **73**
WV14: Bils 6B **54**
Bull Mdw. La. WV5: Wom 1G **73**
Bullmoor La. WS14: C'fld, Hilt . . .1A **28**
Bullock's Row WS1: Wals 8M **39**
Bullock St. B7: Birm . . .4A **102** (1L **5**)
B70: W Brom 1K **99**
Bullows Rd. WS8: Bwnhls 3C **26**
Bull Ring B63: Hale 6B **118**
CV10: Nun 7H **89**
DY3: Sed 1D **74**
DY10: Kidd 3L **157**
WV13: W'hall 6A **38**
Bullring Shop. Cen.
B5: Birm 7L **101** (6H **5**)
Bull Ring Trad. Est.
B12: Birm 8M **101** (7K **5**)
Bull's Head La. CV3: Cov 7H **153**
Bull's La. B76: Walm 6B **60**
(not continuous)
Bull St. B4: Birm 6L **101** (4G **5**)
B17: Harb 3D **120**
B70: W Brom 6K **77**
CV11: Nun 7K **89**
CV47: Sou 5H **225**
DY1: Dud 1G **97**
DY3: Gorn 7C **74**
DY5: Brie H 8B **96**
(Goldencross Way)
DY5: Brie H 7A **96**
(Hawbush Rd.)
WS10: Darl 3E **54**
Bull St. Trad. Est. DY5: Brie H . . .7B **96**
Bullus Rd. DY13: Stour S 4G **183**
Bull Yd. CV1: Cov 7C **152** (5B **6**)
Bull Yd., The CV47: Sou 5H **225**
Bulrush Cl. WS8: Bwnhls 2E **26**
Bulwell Cl. B6: Aston 2A **102**
Bulwer Rd. CV6: Cov 2A **152**
Bulwer St.
WV10: Wolv 6D **36** (1L **7**)
Bulwick Cl. CV3: Bin 8B **154**
Bumble Bee Gdns.
LE10: Sharn 5J **93**
Bumble Bee La. LE10: Sharn . . .8G **93**
BUMBLE HOLE 4L **97**
Bumble Hole La. B61: B'hth . . .2L **187**
B61: D'frd 4L **187**
Bumblehole Mdws.
WV5: Wom 2F **72**
Bumble Hole Nature Reserve . . .4L **97**
Bunbury Gdns. B30: K Nor 5C **142**
Bunbury Rd. B31: N'fld 5B **142**
Bundle Hill B63: Hale 6A **118**
Bungalows, The B70: W Brom . . .3F **76**
Bungay Lake La. B61: U War . . .5F **186**
BUNKER'S HILL 2L **53**
Bunkers Hill La.
CV23: Bret, Chu L 4K **177**
WV14: Bils 1L **53**
Bunn's La. DY2: Dud 8M **75**
Buntsford Dr. B60: Stoke H 3L **209**
Buntsford Hill
B60: Stoke H, Stoke P . . .3L **209**
Buntsford Pk. Rd.
B60: B'gve 3M **209**
Bunyan Pl. WS11: Cann 5E **8**
BURBAGE 4A **92**
Burbage Cl. WV10: Wolv 3F **36**
Burbage Common Country Pk.
. . . . .6B **70**
Burbage Common Country Pk.
Vis. Cen. 6B **70**
Burbage Comn. Rd.
LE9: Elme 6B **70**
Burbage Rd. LE10: Burb 1M **91**
Burbages La. CV6: Longf 4D **130**
Burbage Wood Country Pk. 8B **70**
Burberry Ct. DY4: Tip 1A **76**
Burberry Gro. CV7: Bal C 3G **171**
Burbidge Rd. B9: Bord G 6D **102**
Burbury Cl. CV12: Bed 5J **111**
CV32: Lill 7C **218**
Burbury Ct. CV34: Warw 1H **223**
Burbury St. B19: Loz 2J **101**
Burbury St. Sth. B19: Hock 3J **101**
Burcher Grn. DY10: Kidd 4B **158**
Burcombe Twr. B23: Erd 3H **81**
BURCOT 5E **188**
Burcot Av. B60: B'gve 5B **188**
WV1: Wolv 7G **37**
Burcot Ct. B74: Four O 7F **42**
Burcote Rd. B24: Erd 6K **81**
Burcot Ho. *B60: B'gve 6B 188*
(off Burcot La.)
Burcot La. B60: B'gve, Burc 6B **188**
(not continuous)
Burcot Wlk. WV1: Wolv 7G **37**
Burdock Cl. WS5: Wals 6A **56**
WS11: Hth H 6H **9**
Burdock Ho. B38: K Nor 8F **142**
Burdock Rd. B29: W Cas 3A **142**
Burdons Cl. B34: Stech 4A **104**
Bure Gro. WV13: W'hall 7D **38**
Burford Cl. B92: Olton 6A **124**
WS5: Wals 6A **56**
Burford Ct. B13: Mose 7B **122**
Burford M. CV31: Lea S 3C **224**
Burford Pk. Rd. B38: K Nor 1E **164**
Burford Rd. B44: K'sdng 2M **79**
B47: H'wd 3M **165**
Burgage Pl. CV11: Nun 5J **89**
Burgage Wlk. CV11: Nun 4H **89**
(Friary St.)
CV11: Nun 5J **89**
(Powell Way)
Burges, The CV1: Cov . . .6C **152** (3C **6**)
Burges Gro. CV34: Warw 8F **216**
Burgess Cft. B92: Sol 2F **146**
Burgesses, The DY7: Kinv 6B **114**
BURGESS GREEN 3J **185**
Burghley Cl. CV11: Nun 7M **89**
Burghley Dr. B71: W Brom 7M **55**
DY11: Kidd 4H **157**
Burghley Wlk. DY5: Brie H 1B **116**
Burgh Way WS2: Wals 4G **39**
Burgoyne St. WS11: Cann 4G **9**
Burhill Way B37: F'bri 4H **105**
Burke Av. B13: Mose 8D **122**
Burkitt Dr. DY4: Tip 1C **76**
Burland Av. WV6: Tett 2L **35**
Burleigh Cl. CV7: Bal C 2H **171**
WS12: Hed 1G **9**
WV12: W'hall 3B **38**
Burleigh Cft. WS7: Chase 5G **17**
Burleigh Rd. LE10: Hinc 7J **69**
WV3: Wolv 2A **52**
Burleigh St. WS1: Wals 8A **40**
Burleton Rd. B33: Kitts G 7E **104**
Burley Cl. B90: Shir 7F **144**
Burley Way B38: K Nor 1C **164**
Burlington Arc. B2: Birm 5F **4**
Burlington Av. B70: W Brom 8L **77**
Burlington Cl. DY10: Kidd 5A **158**
Burlington Ct. B78: Faz 8B **32**
Burlington Pas. B2: Birm 5F **4**
Burlington Rd. B10: Small H . . .8E **102**
B70: W Brom 8L **77**
CV2: Cov 5F **152**
(not continuous)
CV10: Nun 2H **111**
Burlington St. B6: Aston 3L **101**
Burlish Av. B92: Olton 8M **123**
Burlish Cl. DY13: Stour S 3E **182**
Burlish Crossing
DY13: Stour S 3E **182**
BURLISH PARK 3E **182**
Burltons Ter. DY12: Bew 6B **156**
Burman Cl. B90: Shir 7G **145**
Burman Dr. B46: Col 4M **105**
Burman Rd. B90: Shir 7F **144**
Burmarsh Wlk. WV8: Pend 1M **35**
Burmese Way B65: Row R 3M **97**
Burnaby Cl. CV10: Nun 4B **88**
Burnaby Rd. CV6: Cov 8B **130**
Burnaston Cres. B90: M'path . . .3C **168**
Burnaston Rd. B28: Hall G 8E **122**
Burnbank Gro. B24: Erd 5H **81**
Burn Cl. B66: Smeth 5A **100**
Burncross Way WV10: Wolv 3F **36**
Burnell Gdns. WV3: Wolv 1L **51**
Burnel Rd. B29: W Cas 7A **120**
Burnet Gro. WV10: F'stne 1H **23**
Burnett Ho. B69: O'bry 4D **98**
Burnett Rd. B74: Lit A 7B **42**
Burney La. B8: W End 4J **103**
Burnfields Way WS9: A'rdge 2G **41**
Burnham Av. B25: Yard 3J **123**
WV10: Oxl 1B **36**
Burnham Cl. DY6: K'wfrd 5M **95**
Burnham Ct. B23: Erd 7C **80**
DY5: Brie H 7D 96
(off Hill St.)
Burnham Grn. WS11: Cann 1B **14**
Burnham Mdw. B28: Hall G 3G **145**
Burnham Ri. CV11: Nun 3A **90**
Burnham Rd. B44: Gt Barr 2L **79**
CV3: Cov 3G **175**
Burnhill Gro. B29: W Cas 1A **142**
Burnlea Gro. B31: N'fld 8C **142**
Burnsall Cl. B37: F'bri 7F **104**
WV9: Pend 6A **22**
Burnsall Gro. CV5: Cov 1K **173**
Burnsall Rd. CV5: Cov 1J **173**
Burns Av. CV34: Warw 4C **222**
DY4: Tip 1A **76**
WV10: F'hses 7D **22**
Burns Cl. B97: Redd 1C **220**
DY8: Amb 1A **116**
DY10: Kidd 3B **158**
WS14: Lich 3H **19**
Burns Dr. WS7: Burn 2J **17**
Burns Gro. DY3: Lwr G 5A **74**
Burnside CV3: Bin 7A **154**
CV22: Rugby 7L **179**
Burnside Ct. B73: W Grn 8G **59**
Burnside Gdns. WS5: Wals 3D **56**
Burnside Way B31: Longb 2M **163**
Burns Pl. WS10: Mox 4A **54**
Burns Rd. B79: Tam 3A **32**
CV2: Cov 6J **153**
CV32: Lill 5B **218**
WS10: Mox 4A **54**
Burns St. WS11: Cann 5F **8**
Burns Wlk. CV12: Bed 8J **111**
Burnsway LE10: Hinc 8J **69**
Burnthorne La. DY13: Dunl 8C **182**
Burnthurst Cres.
B90: M'path 2A **168**
Burnthurst La. CV23: Prin 7A **202**
Burnt Mdw. Rd. B98: Redd 3L **213**
Burnt Oak Dr. DY8: Stourb 4B **116**
BURNT TREE 7M **75**
Burnt Tree DY4: Tip 7M **75**
BURNTWOOD 3J **17**
BURNTWOOD GREEN 3L **17**
BURNTWOOD JUNC. 6F **16**
Burntwood Leisure Cen. 3F **16**
Burntwood Rd. WS7: Hamm 5K **17**
WS11: Nort C 3A **16**
Burntwood Town Shop. Cen.
WS7: C Ter 2E **16**
Burrelton Way B43: Gt Barr 1D **78**
Burrington Rd. B32: Bart G 1G **141**
Burrowes St. WS2: Wals 6K **39**
Burrow Hill Cl. B36: Cas B 1C **104**
Burrow Hill La. CV7: Cor 2J **129**
Burrows Cl. CV31: W'nsh 6B **224**
Burrows Ho. *WS2: Wals 6K 39*
(off Burrowes St.)
Burrows Rd. DY6: K'wfrd 5M **95**
Bursledon Wlk. WV1: Wolv 1J **53**
Burslem Cl. WS3: Blox 5G **25**
Burstnips Rd. WV11: Ess 7B **24**
Burton Av. WS4: Rus 1B **40**
Burton Cl. B79: Tam 2C **32**
CV5: Alle 7J **129**
Burton Cres.
WV10: Wolv 6E **36** (1M **7**)
Burton Farm Rd. WS4: Wals 6B **40**
BURTON GREEN 5C **172**
Burton Gro. B64: Old H 1L **117**
BURTON HASTINGS 1G **113**
Burton La. B98: Redd 6F **212**
CV11: Burt H 3F **112**
Burton Old Rd. WS13: S'hay . . .8M **13**
WS14: Lich 1M **19**
(not continuous)
Burton Old Rd. E. WS14: Lich . . .1L **19**
Burton Old Rd. W. WS13: Lich . . .1J **19**
Burton Rd. DY1: Dud 5F **74**
WS13: S'hay 8M **13**
WV10: Wolv 6E **36** (1M **7**)
Burton Rd. E. DY1: Dud 5F **74**
Burton Wood Dr. B20: Hand 7K **79**
Buryfield Rd. B91: Sol 3A **146**
Bury Hill Rd. B69: O'bry 2D **98**
Bury Mound Ct. B90: Shir 7C **144**
Bury Rd. CV31: Lea S 2L **223**
Busby Cl. CV3: Bin 2M **175**
Bush Av. B66: Smeth 4C **100**
Bushbery Av. CV4: Tile H 8F **150**
BUSHBURY 8E **22**
Bushbury Ct. WV10: Bush 7E **22**
Bushbury Crematorium
WV10: Bush 6F **22**
Bushbury Cft. B37: Chel W 6J **105**
Bushbury La.
WV10: Oxl, Bush 3C **36**
Bushbury Rd. B33: Stech 4A **104**
WV10: Wolv 3G **37**
Bushbury Swimming Pool 8E **22**
Bush Cl. CV4: Tile H 6F **150**
Bushell Dr. B91: Sol 5D **146**
Bushelton Cl.
CV1: Cov 8D **152** (8E **6**)
Bushey Cl. B74: S'tly 7M **41**
Bushey Flds. Rd. DY1: Dud 1E **96**
Bush Gro. B21: Hand 8C **78**
Bushley Cl. B98: Redd 2G **221**
Bushley Cft. B91: Sol 1B **168**
Bushman Way B34: S End 4E **104**
Bushmore Rd. B28: Hall G 3G **145**
Bush Rd. DY2: Neth 7J **97**
DY4: Tip 5L **75**
Bush St. WS10: Darl 2D **54**
Bushway Cl. DY5: Brie H 7A **96**
Bushwood Ct. B15: Edg 1J **121**
B29: S Oak 8C **120**
Bushwood Dr. B93: Dorr 6G **169**
Bushwood Rd. B29: S Oak 8B **120**
(not continuous)
Bushy End CV34: H'cte 5L **223**
Business Cen., The B11: Tys 3F **122**
Bustleholme Av.
B71: W Brom 8M **55**
Bustleholme Cres.
B71: W Brom 8L **55**
Bustleholme La.
B71: W Brom 8L **55**
(not continuous)
Butcher's Cl. CV23: Brin 6M **155**
Butchers La. B63: Crad 2J **117**
CV5: Alle 3J **151**
Butchers Rd. B92: H Ard 3A **148**
BUTCROFT 3E **54**
Butcroft Gdns. WS10: Darl 3E **54**
Bute Cl. B45: Fran 8E **140**
LE10: Hinc 8J **69**
WV12: W'hall 3B **38**
Butler Cl. CV8: Ken 2J **199**
Butler Lane Station (Rail) 6G **43**
Butler Rd. B92: Olton 6M **123**
Butlers Cl. B20: Hand 6G **79**
B23: Erd 8D **58**
Butler's Cres. CV7: Exh 8G **111**
Butlers End CV35: Beau 7H **197**
Butler's Hill La. B97: Redd 4B **212**
Butlers La. B74: Four O 6F **42**
CV9: Gren 7C **48**
Butlers Leap CV21: Rugby 4C **180**
Butlers Pct. WS1: Wals 7L **39**
Butler's Rd. B20: Hand 6G **79**
Butler St. B70: W Brom 5G **77**
B19: A'wd B 8E 220
Butlin Rd. CV6: Cov 5C **130**
CV21: Rugby 6D **180**
Butlin St. B7: Nech 2C **102**
Buttercup Cl. DY11: Kidd 1K **157**
WS5: Wals 6A **56**
Buttercup Dr. B60: L End 3C **188**
Buttercup Way CV12: Bed 7D **110**
Butterfield Cl. WV6: Pert 6D **34**
Butterfield Ct. DY1: Dud 7G **75**
Butterfield Rd. DY5: P'ntt 2B **96**
Butterfly Way B64: Old H 8M **97**
Buttermere B77: Wiln 2H **47**
CV21: Brow 2D **180**
Buttermere Av. CV11: Nun 3A **90**
Buttermere Cl. CV3: Bin 2M **175**
DY5: Brie H 2B **116**
WS11: Cann 6G **9**
WV6: Tett 1K **35**
Buttermere Ct. WV6: Pert 5F **34**
Buttermere Dr. B32: Bart G . . .6M **119**
WV11: Ess 7A **24**
Buttermere Gro.
WV12: W'hall 8B **24**
Buttermere Rd.
DY13: Stour S 3F **182**
Butter Wlk. B38: K Nor 1C **164**
Butterworth Cl. WV14: Cose 8G **53**
Butterworth Dr.
CV4: W'wd H 3G **173**
Buttery Rd. B67: Smeth 3L **99**
Butt La. CV5: Alle 2G **151**
LE10: Hinc 8L **69**
Butt La. Cl. LE10: Hinc 8L **69**
Buttons Farm Rd. WV4: Penn . . .6K **51**
Buttress Way B66: Smeth 3A **100**
Butts CV1: Cov 7B **152** (6A **6**)
Butts, The CV34: Warw 2E **222**
WS4: Wals 6M **39**
WS14: Wall 7D **18**
Butts Cl. WS11: Nort C 5L **15**
Butts La. B94: Tan A 7G **193**
DY10: Shens, Stone 7D **158**
WS11: Nort C 5L **15**
Butts Rd. CV1: Cov 7A **152** (6A **6**)
WS4: Wals 6M **39**
WV4: Penn 5M **51**
Butts Stadium 7A **152**
Butts St. WS4: Wals 6M **39**
Butts Way WS11: Nort C 5L **15**
Buxton Av. B78: Faz 1B **46**
Buxton Cl. WS3: Blox 6J **25**
Buxton Rd. B23: Erd 3B **80**
B73: W Grn 8G **59**
DY2: Dud 3F **96**
WS3: Blox 6J **25**
Byeways WS3: Blox 6J **25**
Byfield Cl. B33: Kitts G 1E **124**
Byfield Pas. B9: Bord G 7E **102**
Byfield Pl. CV7: Bal C 4K **171**
Byfield Rd. CV6: Cov 4L **151**
Byfield Vw. DY3: Sed 2E **74**
Byfleet Cl. WV14: Cose 6G **53**
Byford Cl. B98: Redd 7E **212**
Byford Ct. CV10: Nun 5F **88**
Byford St. CV10: Nun 5F **88**
Byford Way B37: Mars G 1H **125**
Byland B77: Glas 6D **32**
Byland Cl. B61: B'gve 8L **187**
Byland Way WS3: Blox 7F **24**
By-Pass Link B91: Sol 6E **146**
Byrchen Moor Gdns.
DY5: P'ntt 2B **96**
Byrne Rd. WV2: Wolv 2D **52**
Byron Av. B23: Erd 6B **80**
CV12: Bed 7K **111**
CV34: Warw 5C **222**
WS14: Lich 4H **19**
Byron Cl. B10: Small H 2D **122**
DY10: Kidd 4B **158**
WS7: C Ter 8F **10**
Byron Ct. B74: Four O 4G **43**
B93: Know 3G **169**
Byron Cres. DY1: Dud 4H **75**
Byron Cft. B74: Four O 3F **42**
DY3: Lwr G 4A **74**
Byron Gdns. B71: W Brom 4H **77**
Byron Ho. B63: Crad 4H **117**
Byron Pl. WS11: Cann 4E **8**
Byron Rd. B10: Small H 2D **122**
B79: Tam 2A **32**
B97: Redd 1D **220**
WV10: Bush 1G **37**
WV12: W'hall 2E **38**
Byron St. B71: W Brom 3H **77**
CV1: Cov 5D **152** (2D **6**)
DY5: P'ntt 2D **96**
LE9: Barw 1B **70**
LE9: Earl S 2E **70**
Byron Way B61: Cats 1A **188**
Bywater Cl. CV3: Cov 5B **174**
Bywater Ho. *WS1: Wals 8M 39*
(off Paddock La.)

C

Caban Cl. B31: N'fld 4L **141**
Cable Dr. WS2: Wals 4J **39**
Cabot Gro. WV6: Pert 5E **34**
Cadbury Dr. B35: Cas V 8A **82**
Cadbury Ho. *B19: Birm 4K 101*
(off Gt. Hampton Row)
Cadbury Rd. B13: Mose 5B **122**
Cadbury Station 2F **142**
Cadbury Way B17: Harb 4B **120**
Cadden Dr. CV4: Tile H 7H **151**
Caddick Cres. B71: W Brom 2K **77**
Caddick Rd. B42: Gt Barr 8H **57**
Caddick St. WV14: Cose 1G **75**
(not continuous)
Cadeby Cl. LE10: Hinc 7H **69**
Cadet Dr. B90: Shir 6G **145**
Cadgwith Gdns. WV14: Bils 7A **54**
Cadine Gdns. B13: Mose 8J **121**
Cadleigh Gdns. B17: Harb 6C **120**
Cadle Rd. WV10: Bush 2E **36**
Cadles Cl. LE9: S Stan 5K **71**
Cadman Cl. CV12: Bed 6J **111**
Cadman Cres. WV10: Wolv 3G **37**
Cadman's La. WS3: Blox 3K **25**
WS6: Gt Wyr 1J **25**
(not continuous)
Cadnam Cl. B17: Harb 6C **120**
WV13: W'hall 1B **54**
Cadogan Rd. B77: Dost 4D **46**
Caen Cl. CV35: H Mag 2A **222**
Caernarvon Cl. WV12: W'hall 2C **38**
Caernarvon Dr. CV11: Nun 6K **89**
Caernarvon Way DY1: Dud 7E **74**
Caesar Rd. CV8: Ken 6E **198**
Caesar Way B46: Col 8M **83**

Cahill Av.—Carshalton Rd.

Cahill Av. WV10: Wolv ... 5G 37
Cairndhu Dr. DY10: Kidd ... 2A 158
Cairn Dr. WS2: Wals ... 7F 38
Cairns St. WS2: Wals ... 6J 39
Caister B77: Amin ... 3G 33
Caister Dr. WV13: W'hall ... 1M 53
Caistor Cl. B78: M Oak ... 1H 45
Caithness Cl. CV5: E Grn ... 5G 151
CAKEBOLE ... 4H 185
Cakebole La. DY10: Chad C ... 6J 185
WR9: Rush ... 6J 185
Cakemore La. B68: O'bry ... 7F 98
Cakemore Rd. B65: Row R ... 7E 98
Cala Dr. B15: Edg ... 2H 121
Calcot Dr. WV6: Tett ... 2L 35
Calcott Ho. CV3: Cov ... 3H 175
Calcutt Mdw. CV47: Sou ... 5K 225
Calcutt Way B90: Dic H ... 3G 167
(not continuous)
CALDECOTE ... 7G 67
Caldecote Cl. CV10: Nun ... 2J 89
Caldecote Gro. B9: Bord G ... 7J 103
Caldecote Hall Dr. CV10: Cald ... 8F 66
Caldecote La. CV10: Cald ... 8F 66
Caldecote Rd. CV6: Cov ... 4C 152
Caldecott Ct. CV21: Rugby ... 5B 180
Caldecott Pl. CV21: Rugby ... 7C 180
Caldecott St. CV21: Rugby ... 7C 180
Caldeford Av. B90: M'path ... 2A 168
Calder B77: Wiln ... 7H 33
Calder Av. WS1: Wals ... 7A 40
Calder Cl. CV3: Cov ... 2E 174
CV12: Bulk ... 7B 112
Calder Dr. B76: Walm ... 1M 81
Calderfields Cl. WS4: Wals ... 6A 40
Calder Gro. B20: Hand ... 7F 78
Calder Ri. DY3: Sed ... 3F 74
Calder Rd. DY13: Stour S ... 2E 182
Calder Twr. B20: Hand ... 8K 79
Calder Wlk. CV31: Lea S ... 3C 224
CALDMORE ... 1L 55
Caldmore Grn. WS1: Wals ... 1L 55
Caldmore Rd. WS1: Wals ... 8L 39
Caldon Cl. LE10: Hinc ... 1H 91
Caldwall Cres. DY11: Kidd ... 4K 157
Caldwell Cvn. Pk.
CV11: Nun ... 1K 111
Caldwell Ct. B91: Sol ... 4C 146
CV11: Nun ... 8K 89
Caldwell Gro. B91: Sol ... 4C 146
Caldwell Ho. B70: W Brom ... 7J 77
Caldwell Rd. B9: Bord G ... 6H 103
CV11: Nun ... 7J 89
Caldwell St. B71: W Brom ... 1K 77
Caldy Wlk. B45: Fran ... 8F 140
DY13: Stour S ... 3E 182
Cale Cl. B77: Wiln ... 7C 32
Caledonia DY5: Quar B ... 2D 116
Caledonian B77: Glas ... 7F 32
Caledonian Cl. WS5: Wals ... 6C 56
Caledonia Rd.
WV2: Wolv ... 1D 52 (8L 7)
(not continuous)
Caledonia St. WV14: Bils ... 3L 53
Caledon Pl. WS2: Wals ... 2J 55
Caledon St. WS2: Wals ... 2J 55
(not continuous)
Calewood Rd. DY5: Quar B ... 2D 116
Caliban M. CV34: H'cte ... 6L 223
CALIFORNIA ... 6M 119
California Ho. *B32: Bart G ... 7L 119*
(off Millmead Rd.)
Californian Gro. WS7: C Ter ... 1F 16
California Rd. B69: Tiv ... 1B 98
California Way B32: Bart G ... 6M 119
Callaghan Gro. WS11: Hth H ... 7J 9
Callcott Dr. DY5: Quar B ... 2D 116
Callear Rd. WS10: W'bry ... 8D 54
Callendar Cl. CV11: Nun ... 2A 90
Calley Cl. DY4: Tip ... 6M 75
Callier Cl. CV22: Caw ... 1H 205
Callis Wlk. B77: Wiln ... 3F 46
Callow Bri. Rd. B45: Rubery ... 2F 162
Callowbrook La.
B45: Rubery ... 1F 162
Callow Cl. DY13: Stour S ... 8D 182
CALLOW HILL ... 3A 220
Callow Hill La. B97: Redd ... 3A 220
Callow Hill Rd. B48: A'chu ... 2M 189
Callows La. DY10: Kidd ... 3L 157
Calmere Cl. CV2: W'grve S ... 1M 153
Calpurnia Av. CV34: H'cte ... 7L 223
Calshot Rd. B42: Gt Barr ... 8F 56
Calstock Rd. WV12: W'hall ... 5D 38
Calthorpe Cl. WS5: Wals ... 3E 56
Calthorpe Mans.
B15: Edg ... 8H 101 (8A 4)
Calthorpe Rd.
B15: Edg ... 1G 121 (8A 4)
B20: Hand ... 7J 79
WS5: Wals ... 3D 56
Caludon Castle ... 4L 153
Caludon Pk. Av. CV2: Cov ... 4L 153
Caludon Rd. CV2: Cov ... 5G 153
Calver Cres. LE9: Sap ... 2L 93
WV11: Wed ... 4M 37
Calver Gro. B44: Gt Barr ... 6K 57
Calverley Rd. B38: K Nor ... 8D 142
Calverston Rd. CV22: Caw ... 2G 205
Calvert Cl. CV3: Cov ... 3D 174
CV21: Brow ... 2E 180
Calverton Gro. B43: Gt Barr ... 1E 78
Calverton Wlk. WV6: Wolv ... 4B 36
Calves Cft. WV13: W'hall ... 6A 38
Calvin Cl. WV5: Wom ... 4F 72
WV10: F'hses ... 6D 22
Calving Hill WS11: Cann ... 7E 8
Camberley B71: W Brom ... 8M 55
Camberley Cres. WV4: E'shll ... 7E 52
Camberley Dr. WV4: Penn ... 5A 52
Camberley Gro. B23: Erd ... 3E 80
Camberley Rd. DY6: K'wfrd ... 6M 95
Camberwell Ter.
CV31: Lea S ... 2A 224
Camborne Cl. B6: Aston ... 2L 101
Camborne Ct. WS5: Wals ... 2D 56
Camborne Dr. CV11: Nun ... 4M 89
Camborne Rd. WS5: Wals ... 2D 56
Cambourne Rd. B65: Row R ... 6C 98
LE10: Burb ... 3A 92
Cambrai Dr. B28: Hall G ... 1E 144
Cambria Cl. B90: Maj G ... 2E 166
Cambrian B77: Glas ... 7G 33
Cambria St. WS11: Cann ... 5D 8
Cambridge Av. B73: W Grn ... 1H 81
B91: Sol ... 6L 145
Cambridge Cl. WS9: A'rdge ... 1G 41
Cambridge Cres. B15: Edg ... 2J 121
Cambridge Dr. B37: Mars G ... 1F 124
CV10: Nun ... 6E 88
Cambridge Gdns.
CV32: Lea S ... 8A 218
Cambridge Rd. B13: Mose ... 8M 121
B66: Smeth ... 2A 100
DY2: Dud ... 2G 97
Cambridge St.
B1: Birm ... 7J 101 (5C 4)
B70: W Brom ... 7H 77
CV1: Cov ... 4E 152 (1F 6)
CV21: Rugby ... 6C 180
WS1: Wals ... 2L 55
WV10: Wolv ... 5D 36 (1L 7)
Cambridge Twr.
B1: Birm ... 6J 101 (5C 4)
Cambridge Way B27: A Grn ... 5K 123
Camden Cl. B36: Cas B ... 1A 104
WS5: Wals ... 6B 56
Camden Dr. B1: Birm ... 6H 101 (3B 4)
B77: Glas ... 6E 32
Camden St. B1: Birm ... 5G 101
B18: Hock ... 5G 101 (2A 4)
CV2: Cov ... 5G 153
WS1: Wals ... 1K 55
WS9: Wals W ... 5E 26
Camden Way DY6: K'wfrd ... 8K 73
Camelia Rd. CV2: Cov ... 7H 131
Camellia Gdns. DY8: Word ... 7L 95
WV9: Pend ... 6M 21
Camelot Cl. WS11: Cann ... 5F 8
Camelot Gro. CV8: Ken ... 4J 199
Camelot M. LE10: Hinc ... 7H 69
Camelot Way B10: Small H ... 1C 122
Cameo Dr. DY8: Amb ... 1M 115
Cameron Cl. CV5: Alle ... 2G 151
CV32: Lill ... 5A 218
Cameronian Cft.
B36: Hodg H ... 1J 103
Cameron Rd. WS4: Wals ... 6A 40
Camford Gro. B14: K Hth ... 6M 143
Cam Gdns. DY5: P'ntt ... 3B 96
Camhouses B77: Wiln ... 8H 33
Camino Rd. B32: Bart G ... 6M 119
Camomile Cl. WS5: Wals ... 6A 56
Campbell Cl. B79: Tam ... 1M 31
CV10: Gall C ... 5A 88
WS4: Wals ... 6A 40
Campbells Grn. B26: Sheld ... 5B 124
Campbell St. CV21: Rugby ... 6L 179
DY5: Brie H ... 5C 96
Campden Cl. B97: Redd ... 3D 220
Campden Grn. B92: Olton ... 6A 124
CAMP HILL ... 3D 88
Camp Hill B12: Birm ... 1A 122 (8M 5)
DY8: Word ... 8L 95
Camp Hill Cir. B11: S'brk ... 1A 122
Camp Hill Dr. CV10: Nun ... 2D 88
Camp Hill Ind. Est.
B12: Birm ... 2A 122
Camphill La. WS10: W'bry ... 7F 54
Camphill Pct. WS10: W'bry ... 7F 54
Camp Hill Rd. CV10: Nun ... 2B 88
Campians Av. WS6: C Hay ... 7D 14
Campion Cl. B38: K Nor ... 1F 164
CV3: Cov ... 3D 174
WS5: Wals ... 6A 56
WV5: Wom ... 3E 72
Campion Ct. CV32: Lea S ... 7A 218
DY4: Tip ... 4K 75
Campion Dr. B77: Tam ... 6C 32
WV10: F'stne ... 2G 23
Campion Grn. CV32: Lea S ... 7A 218
Campion Gro. B63: Hale ... 6K 117
Campion Ho. B38: K Nor ... 1E 164
WV10: Wolv ... 5F 36
Campion Rd. CV32: Lea S ... 7A 218
Campion Ter. CV32: Lea S ... 8A 218
Campion Way B90: Dic H ... 4G 167
CV23: Brow ... 1D 180
DY12: Bew ... 4D 156
Camp La. B21: Hand ... 8B 78
B38: K Nor ... 6F 142
Camplea Cft. B37: F'bri ... 7G 105
Camplin Cres. B20: Hand ... 4E 78
Campling Cl. CV12: Bulk ... 7B 112
Campriano Dr. CV34: Warw ... 1G 223
Camp Rd. B75: R'ley ... 2H 43
WS14: Lit H ... 2H 43
Camp St. B9: Bord G ... 8C 102
WS10: W'bry ... 7F 54
WV1: Wolv ... 6C 36 (1J 7)
Campton Cl. LE10: Burb ... 2L 91
Campville Cres. B71: W Brom ... 8L 55
Campville Gro. B37: K'hrst ... 4F 104
Campwood Cl. B30: B'vlle ... 1E 142
Camrose Cft. B12: Bal H ... 4M 121
B34: S End ... 3B 104
Camrose Gdns. WV9: Pend ... 6A 22
Camsey La. WS7: Burn ... 1L 17
Camville CV3: Bin ... 7A 154
Canal Cotts. DY2: Neth ... 6H 97
Canal Ho. CV1: Cov ... 5C 152 (2C 6)
Canal La. B24: Erd ... 8G 81
Canal Rd. CV6: Cov ... 1F 152
Canal Side B30: K Nor ... 6G 143
B48: Hopw ... 7B 164
B69: O'bry ... 2F 98
DY2: Neth ... 5L 97
Canalside CV6: Longf ... 3H 131
DY13: Stour S ... 5H 183
Canalside Cl. WS3: Blox ... 8M 25
WS10: W'bry ... 7L 55
Canalside Ind. Est.
DY5: Brie H ... 8C 96
Canal St. B69: O'bry ... 2F 98
DY4: Tip ... 5K 75
DY5: Brie H ... 4E 96
DY8: Amb ... 3M 115
WS2: Wals ... 7K 39
WV14: Cose ... 1J 75
Canal Vw. Ind. Est.
DY5: Brie H ... 8B 96
Canal Way LE10: Hinc ... 2F 90
Canary Gro. B19: Loz ... 1J 101
Canberra Ct. CV12: Bed ... 7G 111
Canberra Rd. CV2: Ald G ... 5J 131
WS5: Wals ... 4C 56
Canberra Way B12: Birm ... 1A 122
LE10: Burb ... 5L 91
Candle La. LE9: Earl S ... 1F 70
Canford Cl. B12: Birm ... 2M 121
CV3: Finh ... 6C 174
Canford Cres. WV8: Cod ... 6E 20
Canford Pl. WS11: Cann ... 8F 8
CANLEY ... 3J 173
Canley Ford CV5: Cov ... 2L 173
(not continuous)
Canley Gdn. Cemetery & Crematorium
CV4: Canly ... 3K 173
Canley Rd. CV5: Cov ... 8K 151
(Pilkington Rd.)
CV5: Cov ... 2K 173
(Riddings, The)
Canley Station (Rail) ... 8K 151
Cannas Ct. CV4: Canly ... 3K 173
Cannel Rd. WS7: C Ter ... 3D 16
Canning Cl. WS5: Wals ... 3D 56
Canning Gdns. B18: Win G ... 5E 100
Canning Rd. B77: Amin ... 5E 32
WS5: Wals ... 3D 56
Canning St. LE10: Hinc ... 8J 69
CANNOCK ... 8E 8
Cannock Chase Ent. Cen.
WS12: Hed ... 1K 9
Cannock Ind. Cen.
WS11: Cann ... 4D 14
Cannock Motor Village
WS11: Hth H ... 6H 9
Cannock Rd. WS7: Burn ... 2H 17
WS7: C Ter ... 1C 16
WS11: Cann ... 7F 8
WS12: Hed, Cann ... 6F 8
WS12: Hth H ... 1J 15
WV10: Bush, F'stne, Share
... 4H 23 (1K 7)
WV10: Wolv ... 5D 36 (1K 7)
WV12: W'hall ... 2C 38
Cannocks Cl. CV4: Canly ... 3K 173
Cannock Shop. Cen.
WS11: Cann ... 8E 8
Cannock Sports Stadium ... 4F 8
Cannock Station (Rail) ... 1F 14
CANNOCK WOOD ... 4F 10
Cannock Wood Ind. Est.
WS12: Haz ... 3C 10
Cannock Wood Rd.
WS12: Haz ... 4B 10
Cannock Wood St. WS12: Haz ... 3A 10
Cannon Bus. Pk. WV14: Cose ... 2J 75
Cannon Cl. CV4: Cov ... 3L 173
Cannon Dr. WV14: Cose ... 7J 53
Cannon Hill Gro. B12: Bal H ... 4L 121
Cannon Hill Pl. B12: Bal H ... 4L 121
Cannon Hill Rd. B12: Bal H ... 4K 121
CV4: Canly ... 4K 173
Cannon Pk. District Cen.
CV4: Canly ... 3J 173
Cannon Pk. Rd. CV4: Canly ... 4L 173
Cannon Raceway ... 8J 53
Cannon Rd. WV5: Wom ... 3G 73
Cannon St. B2: Birm ... 7L 101 (5F 4)
WS2: Wals ... 5L 39
WV13: W'hall ... 7B 38
Cannon St. Nth. WS2: Wals ... 5L 39
Canon Dr. CV7: Ash G ... 3D 130
Canon Hudson Cl.
CV3: W'hall ... 3J 175
Canons Health Club ... 6K 223
Canon Young Rd.
CV31: W'nsh ... 5B 224
Canterbury Av. WV13: W'hall ... 7D 38
Canterbury Cl. B23: Erd ... 7D 80
B65: Row R ... 5E 98
B71: W Brom ... 1L 77
B77: Tam ... 6D 32
B80: Stud ... 5J 221
CV8: Ken ... 6J 199
WS3: Pels ... 5A 26
WS13: Lich ... 7J 13
Canterbury Dr. B37: Mars G ... 2G 125
WS7: Burn ... 3K 17
WV6: Pert ... 5D 34
Canterbury Rd. B20: Hand ... 8K 79
B71: W Brom ... 1K 77
DY11: Kidd ... 2F 156
WV4: Penn ... 4L 51
Canterbury St.
CV1: Cov ... 5E 152 (2F 6)
Canterbury Twr. B1: Birm ... 3A 4
Canterbury Way CV11: Nun ... 1A 90
WS12: Hth H ... 8H 9
Cantlow Cl. CV5: E Grn ... 6G 151
Cantlow Ho. B12: Birm ... 2M 121
Cantlow Rd. B13: Mose ... 3A 144
Canton La. B46: Col ... 4A 84
Canute Cl. WS1: Wals ... 2M 55
Canvey Cl. B45: Fran ... 8E 140
CANWELL ... 4A 44
Canwell Av. B37: K'hrst ... 4F 104
Canwell Dr. B75: Can ... 4A 44
Canwell Gdns. WV14: Bils ... 5J 53
Canwell Ga. B75: R'ley ... 5L 43
Capcroft Rd. B13: Mose ... 3B 144
CAPE, THE ... 1D 222
Cape Cl. WS8: Bwnhls ... 3G 27
Cape Hill B66: Smeth ... 5B 100
Cape Hill Retail Cen.
B66: Smeth ... 5B 100
Cape Ind. Est. CV34: Warw ... 2E 222
Capel Pits La. WR9: Wych ... 7D 208
Capener Rd. B43: Gt Barr ... 7G 57
Capern Gro. B32: Harb ... 4M 119
Cape Rd. CV34: Warw ... 1D 222
Cape St. B18: Win G ... 5D 100
B70: W Brom ... 5E 76
Capethorn Rd. B66: Smeth ... 6A 100
Capilano Rd. B23: Erd ... 2C 80
Capmartin Rd. CV6: Cov ... 2B 152
Capper's La. WS13: Lich ... 1L 19
WS14: Lich ... 2M 19
Capponfield Cl. WV14: Cose ... 6H 53
Capstone Av. B18: Hock ... 5G 101
WV10: Oxl ... 1B 36
Captain's Cl. WV3: Wolv ... 7K 35
Captain's Pool Rd.
DY10: Kidd ... 7A 158
Capulet Cl. CV3: W'hall ... 3J 175
CV22: Bil ... 3L 205
Capulet Dr. CV34: H'cte ... 6L 223
Caradoc B77: Glas ... 7G 33
Caradoc Cl. CV2: Cov ... 2K 153
Carcroft Rd. B25: Yard ... 1K 123
Cardale Cft. CV3: Bin ... 8M 153
Cardale St. B65: B'hth ... 7D 98
Carden Cl. B70: W Brom ... 5F 76
Carder Cres. WV14: Bils ... 5K 53
Carder Dr. DY5: Brie H ... 7C 96
Cardiff Cl. CV3: W'hall ... 4K 175
Cardigan Cl. B71: W Brom ... 2J 77
Cardigan Dr. WV12: W'hall ... 3B 38
Cardigan Ho. WS12: Hed ... 4J 9
Cardigan Pl. WS12: Hed ... 4J 9
Cardigan Rd. CV12: Bed ... 8B 110
Cardigan St.
B4: Birm ... 6M 101 (3K 5)
Cardinal Cres. B61: B'gve ... 8K 187
Cardinal Dr. DY10: Kidd ... 6B 158
Cardinal Way WS11: Cann ... 7D 8
Carding Cl. CV5: E Grn ... 5F 150
Cardington Av. B42: Gt Barr ... 8H 57
Cardington Cl. B98: Redd ... 6M 213
Cardoness Pl. DY1: Dud ... 7F 74
Cardy Cl. B97: Redd ... 5A 212
Careless Grn.
DY9: Lye, W'cte ... 5F 116
Carew Wlk. CV22: Bil ... 8J 179
Carey B77: Hock ... 4G 47
Carey Hill Rd. LE9: S Stan ... 7K 71
Careynon Ct. WS3: Blox ... 1H 39
Carey St. CV6: Cov ... 8H 131
Carfax WS11: Cann ... 1E 14
Cargill Cl. CV6: Longf ... 4F 130
Carhampton Rd. B75: S Cold ... 3A 60
Carillon Gdns. B65: Row R ... 6C 98
Carisbrooke B77: Glas ... 7G 33
Carisbrooke Av. B37: Chel W ... 7J 105
Carisbrooke Cl. WS10: W'bry ... 7L 55
Carisbrooke Cres.
WS10: W'bry ... 6L 55
Carisbrooke Dr. B62: Hale ... 5D 118
Carisbrooke Gdns.
WV10: Bush ... 6E 22
Carisbrooke Ho. B31: Longb ... 1M 163
Carisbrooke Rd. B17: Edg ... 8B 100
WS10: W'bry ... 7K 55
Carisbrooke Rd. WV6: Pert ... 6G 35
WV10: Bush ... 6E 22
Carisbrook Rd. CV10: Nun ... 3K 89
Carlcroft B77: Wiln ... 7H 33
Carless Av. B17: Harb ... 2B 120
Carless St. WS1: Wals ... 1L 55
Carlisle Rd. WS11: Cann ... 2B 14
Carlisle St. B18: Win G ... 4E 100
Carlson Pk. B17: Harb ... 4B 120
Carl St. WS2: Wals ... 4K 39
Carlton Av. B21: Hand ... 8E 78
B74: S'tly ... 7M 41
DY9: W'cte ... 6E 116
WV11: Wed ... 2G 37
WV14: Bils ... 2M 53
Carlton Cl. B75: S Cold ... 2K 59
B97: Redd ... 8B 212
CV12: Bulk ... 6B 112
DY1: Dud ... 3J 75
DY11: Kidd ... 1G 157
WS12: Hth H ... 8K 9
Carlton Ct. CV5: Cov ... 6M 151
Carlton Cres. B79: Tam ... 1M 31
WS7: C Ter ... 1G 17
Carlton Cft. B74: S'tly ... 7A 42
Carlton Gdns. CV5: Cov ... 1A 174
Carlton Ho. CV32: Lea S ... 1M 223
Carlton M. B36: Cas B ... 1D 104
Carlton M. Flats B36: Cas B ... 1D 104
Carlton Rd. B9: Small H ... 8D 102
B66: Smeth ... 1A 100
CV6: Cov ... 8F 130
CV22: Bil ... 8K 179
WV3: Wolv ... 2A 52
Carlyle Av. DY10: Kidd ... 3B 158
Carlyle Bus. Pk.
B70: W Brom ... 4F 76
Carlyle Cl. CV10: Gall C ... 4M 87
Carlyle Gro. WV10: Bush ... 1G 37
Carlyle Rd. B16: Edg ... 8E 100
B19: Loz ... 1J 101
B60: B'gve ... 1B 210
B65: Row R ... 7C 98
WV10: Bush ... 1G 37
Carlyon Rd. CV9: Ath ... 8L 49
Carlyon Rd. Ind. Est.
CV9: Ath ... 8M 49
(not continuous)
Carmel Cl. WS12: Hed ... 4J 9
Carmel Gro. B32: Bart G ... 8H 119
Carmelite Rd. CV1: Cov ... 7E 152
Carmichael Cl. WS14: Lich ... 2K 19
Carmodale Av. B42: P Barr ... 3H 79
Carnbroe Av. CV3: Bin ... 2M 175
Carnegie Av. DY4: Tip ... 5A 76
Carnegie Cl. CV3: W'hall ... 4H 175
Carnegie Dr. WS10: W'bry ... 6G 55
Carnegie Rd. B65: Row R ... 7B 98
Carnford Rd. B26: Sheld ... 3B 124
Carnforth Cl. DY6: K'wfrd ... 2H 95
Carnforth Rd. B60: B'gve ... 8B 188
Carnoustie B77: Amin ... 4H 33
Carnoustie Cl. B61: B'gve ... 1K 209
B75: S Cold ... 1J 59
CV11: Nun ... 1C 112
WS3: Blox ... 6G 25
Carnwath Rd. B73: New O ... 7E 58
Carol Av. B61: B'gve ... 6K 187
Carol Cres. B63: Hale ... 4M 117
WV11: Wed ... 3L 37
Carol Gdns. DY8: Amb ... 1M 115
CAROL GREEN ... 1M 171
Caroline Cl. CV11: Nun ... 2M 111
Caroline Pl. B13: Mose ... 6M 121
Caroline Rd. B13: Mose ... 5M 121
Caroline St. B3: Birm ... 5J 101 (2D 4)
B70: W Brom ... 7H 77
DY2: Dud ... 8L 75
Carolyn La. Ct.
CV21: Rugby ... 5M 179
(off Blackman Way)
Carousel Pk. LE9: Barw ... 1M 69
Carpathian, The B18: Birm ... 1C 4
Carpathian Ct.
B18: Birm ... 5J 101 (1C 4)
Carpenter Glade B63: Crad ... 4K 117
Carpenter Pl. B12: Bal H ... 3A 122
Carpenter Rd. B15: Edg ... 2G 121
Carpenters Cl. LE10: Burb ... 4M 91
Carpenters Ct. *B12: Birm ... 1M 121*
(off Vaughton St.)
CARPENTER'S HILL ... 8L 191
Carpenter's Rd. B19: Loz ... 2J 101
Carpet Trades Way
DY11: Kidd ... 2K 157
Carrick Cl. WS3: Pels ... 4A 26
Carriers Cl. WS2: Wals ... 8F 38
Carriers Fold WV5: Wom ... 2H 73
Carrington Rd. WS10: W'bry ... 7K 55
Carroll Wlk. DY10: Kidd ... 3B 158
CARROWAY HEAD ... 5C 44
Carroway Head Hill
B75: Bass P, Can ... 6B 44
Carr's Dr. LE9: Earl S ... 1F 70
Carrs Hill LE9: Barw ... 3C 70
Carrs La. B4: Birm ... 7L 101 (5H 5)
Carr's Rd. LE9: Earl S ... 1F 70
Carsal Cl. CV7: Ash G ... 4D 130
Carshalton Gro.
WV2: Wolv ... 2E 52 (8M 7)
Carshalton Rd. B44: K'sdng ... 7A 58

Cartbridge Cres.—Chalfont Ct.

Cartbridge Cres. WS3: Wals 3M 39
(not continuous)
Cartbridge La. WS4: Wals 4A 40
Cartbridge La. Sth.
WS4: Wals 5A 40
Cartbridge Wlk. WS3: Wals 3A 40
Carter Av. DY11: Kidd 5H 157
WV8: Bilb 6H 21
Carter Ct. DY11: Kidd 5J 157
Carter Rd. B43: Gt Barr 7F 56
CV3: Cov 1G 175
WV6: Wolv 4B 36
Carters Cl. B37: Mars G 2G 125
B61: B'gve 2K 209
B76: Walm 6M 59
Cartersfield La. WS9: Ston 3K 27
Carters Grn. B70: W Brom 5H 77
Carter's Hurst B33: Sheld 8B 104
Carter's La. B62: Quin 4F 118
Carthorse La. B97: Redd 4B 212
Carthusian Rd. CV3: Cov 1C 174
Cartland Rd. B11: S'brk 2C 122
B14: K Hth 1H 143
B30: Stir 1H 143
Cartmel Cl. CV5: E Grn 5G 151
Cartmel Ct. B23: Erd 5B 80
Cart's La. CV9: Gren 7C 48
Cartway, The WV6: Pert 5D 34
Cartwright Gdns. B69: Tiv 7C 76
Cartwright Ho. WS3: Blox 8H 25
Cartwright Rd. B60: S Prior 7K 209
B75: R'ley 6J 43
Cartwright St.
WV2: Wolv 1D 52 (8K 7)
Carvell Cl. CV5: Alle 8H 129
Carver Cl. CV2: Cov 7L 153
Carver Ct. B24: Erd 3J 81
DY4: Tip 8A 54
Carver Gdns. DY8: Stourb 7L 115
Carver St. B1: Birm 5H 101 (2A 4)
Cascade Cl. CV3: Cov 3E 174
Case La. CV35: Hatt 8D 196
Casern Vw. B75: S Cold 3A 60
Casewell Rd. DY6: W Hth 1J 95
Casey Av. B23: Erd 1D 80
Cash-Joynson Av. WS10: Darl 1C 54
Cashmore Av. CV31: Lea S 4M 223
Cashmore Rd. CV8: Ken 5J 199
CV12: Bed 8E 110
Cash's Bus. Cen. CV1: Cov 4D 152
Cash's La. CV1: Cov 3D 152
Casita Gro. CV8: Ken 5J 199
Caslon Cres. DY8: Stourb 5K 115
Caslon Rd. B63: Crad 3J 117
Caslow Flats B63: Crad 5J 117
Caspian Way CV2: W'grve S 1A 154
Cassandra Cl. CV4: Canly 6K 173
DY5: P'ntt 8C 74
Cassandra Gro. CV34: H'cte 5K 223
Cassowary Rd. B20: Hand 6F 78
Castello Dr. B36: Cas B 8D 82
Castillo Ct. B14: K Hth 4A 144
Castings, The WV14: Cose 7K 53
Castle, The DY8: Stourb 6B 116
Castle Barns DY10: Cookl 6B 136
Castlebridge Gdns.
WV11: Wed 2M 37
Castlebridge Rd. WV11: Wed 3M 37
CASTLE BROMWICH 1B 104
Castle Bromwich Bus. Pk.
B35: Cas V 8M 81
Castle Bromwich Hall
B36: Cas B 1A 104
Castle Cl. B64: Old H 8B 98
B77: Amin 5E 32
B92: Olton 8B 124
CV3: Cov 3D 174
CV7: Fill 7E 108
CV34: Warw 3E 222
LE9: Earl S 1F 70
LE9: Sap 2K 93
WS8: Bwnhls 7F 16
Castle Ct. B34: S End 2E 104
CV8: Ken 3G 199
CV34: Warw 3E 222
LE10: Burb 3K 91
Castle Cres. B36: Cas B 1C 104
CASTLECROFT 8G 35
Castle Cft. B68: O'bry 1K 119
Castlecroft WS11: Nort C 4L 15
Castlecroft Av. WV3: Wolv 1G 51
Castlecroft Gdns. WV3: Wolv 1J 51
Castlecroft La. WV3: Wolv 1F 50
Castle Cft. Rd. WV14: Bils 2L 53
Castlecroft Rd. WV3: Wolv 1F 50
Castleditch La. B98: Redd 2E 220
Castle Dr. B46: Col 4M 105
CV10: Asty 2L 109
WV12: W'hall 4B 38
Castle Dyke WS13: Lich 2H 19
CASTLE END 6G 199
Castle Farm DY10: Cookl 6B 136
Castle Farm Recreation Cen.
5E 198
Castleford Gro. B11: S'hll 5C 122
Castleford Rd. B11: S'hll 5C 122
Castlefort Rd. WS9: Wals W 6G 27
Castlegate Dr. DY1: Dud 7L 75
Castlegate Island DY1: Dud 7L 75
Castle Ga. M. CV34: Warw 2F 222
Castlegate Way DY1: Dud 7L 75
CASTLE GREEN 4D 198
Castle Grn. CV8: Ken 4D 198
Castle Gro. CV8: Ken 5E 198
DY8: Stourb 6B 116
Castlehall B77: Glas 7G 33
Castle Hgts. *B64: Old H 1B 118*
(off Granville Rd.)
Castle Hill CV8: Ken 4E 198
CV34: Warw 3E 222
DY1: Dud 7K 75
Castlehill Rd. WS9: Wals W 6H 27
Castlehills Dr. B36: Cas B 1A 104
Castle Ho. B33: Yard 8B 104
Castle La. B46: Max, Shu 7E 84
B92: Olton 8M 123
CV34: Warw 3E 222
DY12: Bew 6C 156
Castlemaine Dr. LE10: Hinc 6L 69
Castle M. CV21: Rugby 6B 180
Castlemill DY4: Tip 7M 75
Castle Mill Rd. DY1: Dud 5J 75
Castle Mound CV23: Barby 7J 207
Castle Pl. Ind. Est.
CV1: Cov 5D 152 (1E 6)
Castle Rd. B29: W Cas 7A 120
B30: K Nor 5F 142
B77: Hock 4F 46
B80: Stud 5L 221
CV8: Ken 4E 198
CV10: Harts 7B 66
CV10: Nun 2J 89
DY4: Tip 5K 75
DY10: Cookl 4A 136
DY11: Kidd 4K 157
WS9: Wals W 7G 27
Castle Rd. E. B68: O'bry 1K 119
Castle Rd. W. B68: O'bry 1J 119
Castle Sq. B29: W Cas 8A 120
Castle St. B70: W Brom 1G 77
B96: A'wd B 7E 220
CV1: Cov 5E 152 (2F 6)
CV21: Rugby 6B 180
CV34: Warw 3E 222
DY1: Dud 8K 75
DY3: Sed 1D 74
DY4: Tip 4L 75
DY7: Kinv 5A 114
LE10: Hinc 1K 91
WS8: Bwnhls 7F 16
WS10: Darl 1D 54
(not continuous)
WV1: Wolv 7D 36 (4K 7)
WV14: Cose 1J 75
Castleton Rd. B42: Gt Barr 2K 79
WS3: Blox 6J 25
Castleton St. DY2: Neth 4J 97
CASTLE VALE 5B 82
Castle Vale Baths 7A 82
Castle Va. Ind. Est. B76: Min 4A 82
Castle Va. Shop. Cen.
B35: Cas V 6M 81
Castle Vw. B77: Tam 6C 32
DY1: Dud 7H 75
Castle Vw. Cl. WS10: Mox 5A 54
Castle Vw. Enterprise Pk.
B35: Cas V 6C 82
Castle Vw. Ind. Est. DY4: Tip 6M 75
Castle Vw. Pk. Mobile Homes
CV10: Harts 8B 66
Castle Vw. Rd. WV14: Bils 5A 54
Castle Vw. Ter. WV14: Cose 1H 75
Castle Yd. CV1: Cov 5D 6
WV1: Wolv 7D 36 (4K 7)
Caswell Rd. CV31: Lea S 3B 224
DY3: Sed 1C 74
Cat & Kittens La.
WV10: F'stne 2E 22
CATCHEMS CORNER 4L 171
CATCHEMS END 4D 156
Caterbanck Way WS13: Lich 3F 18
Cater Dr. B76: Walm 7M 59
Caterham Dr. DY6: K'wfrd 6M 95
Catesby Dr. DY6: K'wfrd 1K 95
Catesby Ho. B37: K'hrst 4F 104
Catesby La. B94: Lapw 7H 195
Catesby Pk. B38: K Nor 6E 142
Catesby Rd. B90: Shir 8H 145
CV6: Cov 1B 152
CV22: Rugby 8D 180
Cateswell Rd. B11: Tys 5F 122
B28: Hall G 8F 122
Cathcart Rd. DY8: Stourb 4L 115
Cathedral Av. DY11: Kidd 3G 157
Cathedral Cl. DY4: Tip 4L 75
Cathedral Lanes Shop. Cen.
CV1: Cov 6C 152 (4C 6)
Cathedral Ri. WS13: Lich 1G 19
Cathel Dr. B42: Gt Barr 2G 79
Catherine Cl. B60: B'gve 1M 209
Catherine Ct. B24: Erd 5J 81
CATHERINE-DE-BARNES 4H 147
Catherine de Barnes La.
B92: Bick, Cath B 3J 147
Catherine Dr. B73: S Cold 3G 59
Catherine Rd. WV14: Cose 8G 53
Catherines Cl. B91: Cath B 5H 147
Catherine St. B6: Aston 2A 102
CV2: Cov 6F 152
Catherton Cl. DY4: Tip 7C 54
Cathiron La. CV23: Brin 6M 155
CV23: Harb M, Lit L 1G 179
Catholic La. DY3: Sed 3C 74
Catisfield Cres. WV8: Pend 8M 21
Cat La. B34: S End 2B 104
Catmeadow La. WS15: Longd 1K 11
Caton Gro. B28: Hall G 2G 145
Cato St. B7: Birm 5B 102
Cato St. Nth. B7: Nech 4C 102
CATSHILL
Bromsgrove 1M 187
Walsall 2G 27
Catshill Rd. WS8: Bwnhls 2G 27
Cattell Dr. B75: S Cold 4B 60
Cattell Rd. B9: Bord G 8C 102
CV34: Warw 2E 222
Cattells Gro. B7: Nech 3C 102
Cattermole Gro. B43: Gt Barr 6J 57
CATTHORPE 1L 181
Cattock Hurst Dr.
B72: W Grn 2K 81
CAUNSALL 3B 136
Caunsall Rd. DY11: Cau 3B 136
Causeway B65: Row R 7C 98
Causeway, The B25: Yard 2K 123
CAUSEWAY GREEN 6F 98
Causeway Grn. Rd.
B68: O'bry 6F 98
Causeway Rd. WV14: Cose 1K 75
Causey Farm Rd. B63: Hale 1J 139
Cavalier Cir. WV10: Bush 5E 22
Cavalier Cl. CV11: Nun 7L 89
Cavalier Dr. B63: Hale 6A 118
Cavandale Av. B44: Gt Barr 8L 57
Cavans Cl. CV3: Bin 1A 176
WS11: Cann 5E 8
Cavans Way CV3: Bin 1A 176
Cavans Wood Pk. Homes
WS12: Hunt 4D 8
Cave Cl. CV22: Caw 1G 205
Cavell Cl. WS2: Wals 7K 39
Cavell Ct. CV21: Rugby 6D 180
Cavell Rd. DY2: Dud 8M 75
WS7: Burn 1L 17
Cavendish B79: Tam 2L 31
Cavendish Cl. B38: K Nor 8H 143
B60: Marl 8C 162
CV22: Caw 8G 179
DY6: K'wfrd 5K 95
Cavendish Ct. B17: Harb 1B 120
B93: Dorr 6G 169
Cavendish Dr. DY9: Hag 5M 137
DY10: Kidd 2B 158
Cavendish Gdns. WS2: Wals 5G 39
WV1: Wolv 8J 37
Cavendish Rd. B16: Edg 6D 100
B62: Hale 5F 118
CV4: Tile H 7E 150
WS2: Wals 4G 39
WV1: Wolv 8H 37
Cavendish Way WS9: A'rdge 4H 41
Caversham Cl. CV11: Nun 2M 89
Caversham Pl. B73: S Cold 5H 59
Caversham Rd. B44: K'sdng 7A 58
Cawdon Gro. B93: Dorr 7F 168
Cawdor Cres. B16: Edg 8F 100
Cawney Hill DY2: Dud 1L 97
Cawnpore Rd. CV6: Cov 7B 130
CAWSTON 1G 205
Cawston Grange Dr.
CV22: Caw 1G 205
Cawston La.
CV22: Caw, Dunc 2G 205
Cawston Way CV22: Bil 1J 205
Cawthorne Cl. CV1: Cov 5E 152
Caxton Ct. WS11: Cann 1E 14
Caxton Ga. B2: Birm 5G 5
Caxton Gate Shop. Cen.
B2: Birm 7L 101
Caxton Gro. B44: K'sdng 8C 58
Caxton St. WS11: Cann 1E 14
Caynham Cl. B98: Redd 5K 213
Caynham Rd. B32: Bart G 1H 141
Cayton Gro. B23: Erd 3F 80
Cearl Ct. B27: A Grn 7J 123
Cecil Ct. CV31: Lea S 1A 224
Cecil Dr. B69: Tiv 7D 76
Cecil Leonard Knox Cres.
CV11: Nun 3F 112
Cecil Rd. B24: Erd 6F 80
B29: S Oak 8J 121
Cecil St. B19: Birm 5L 101 (1G 5)
DY8: Stourb 4M 115
WS4: Wals 6M 39
WS11: Cann 5F 8
Cecily Rd. CV3: Cov 2D 174
Cedar Av. B36: Cas B 1C 104
CV8: Rytn D 8B 176
WS8: Bwnhls 1G 27
WV14: Cose 2H 75
Cedar Bri. Cft. B74: Four O 1H 59
Cedar Cl. B30: B'vlle 3E 142
B68: O'bry 1J 119
CV32: Lill 5A 218
DY8: Stourb 7K 115
DY13: Stour S 7F 182
WS5: Wals 5B 56
WS7: Chase 3G 17
WS12: Hed 1G 9
WS14: Lich 2M 19
Cedar Ct. B77: Wiln 3E 46
CV5: Alle 3G 151
LE10: Burb 3A 92
Cedar Cres. B78: K'bry 3D 62
DY11: Kidd 3J 157
Cedar Dr. B24: Erd 4J 81
B31: Longb 2B 164
B60: B'gve 8A 188
B74: S'tly 8L 41
B79: Tam 1A 32
DY11: Kidd 2J 157
Cedar Gdns. DY7: Kinv 3A 114
Cedar Gro. CV34: Warw 8G 217
WS6: Gt Wyr 5H 15
WV3: Wolv 2M 51
WV8: Bilb 6H 21
WV14: Bils 2M 53
Cedargrove DY9: Hag 3A 138
Cedarhill Dr. WS11: Cann 7F 8
Cedar Ho. B36: Hodg H 1M 103
B91: Sol 8M 145
Cedarhurst B32: Harb 4A 120
B91: Sol 6C 146
Cedar Pk. Rd. B97: Redd 5D 212
WV12: W'hall 8C 24
Cedar Ri. DY13: Stour S 5E 182
Cedar Rd. B30: B'vlle 3E 142
B97: Redd 5C 212
CV10: Nun 3D 88
DY1: Dud 6H 75
(not continuous)
DY4: Tip 4K 75
LE9: Earl S 2D 70
WS7: Chase 2G 17
WS10: W'bry 7G 55
WV13: W'hall 7L 37
Cedars, The B25: Yard 8L 103
B93: Know 5G 169
CV7: Exh 1G 131
CV32: Lea S 1K 223
WV6: Tett 4K 35
WV6: Wolv 6M 35
Cedars Av. B27: A Grn 5J 123
CV6: Cov 4L 151
DY6: K'wfrd 5K 95
WV5: Wom 4G 73
Cedars Bus. Cen., The
WS11: Cann 2C 14
Cedars Rd. CV7: Exh 8H 111
Cedar Ter. B60: B'gve 8A 188
Cedar Tree B23: Erd 7E 80
Cedar Vw. B97: Redd 5C 212
Cedar Wlk. *B37: Chel W 7H 105*
(off Chelmsley Wood Shop. Cen.)
Cedar Way B31: Longb 8M 141
WV11: Wed 2J 37
Cedarwood B74: Four O 1H 59
Cedarwood Cft. B42: Gt Barr 1F 78
Cedarwood Dr. CV7: Bal C 3H 171
Cedarwood Rd.
DY3: Up Gor 4D 74
Cedric Cl. CV3: W'hall 4J 175
Celandine B77: Tam 6C 32
CV23: Brow 1E 180
Celandine Cl. DY6: K'wfrd 5J 95
Celandine Rd. CV2: Cov 7K 131
DY1: Dud 5G 75
Celandines, The WV5: Wom 3E 72
Celandine Way CV12: Bed 7E 110
Celbury Way B43: Gt Barr 1D 78
Celeste Rd. B60: B'gve 8C 188
Celtic Rd. WS11: Cann 6E 8
Celts Cl. B65: Row R 5C 98
Cemetery La. B18: Birm 4H 101
B97: Redd 6D 212
CV10: Harts 8B 66
Cemetery Rd. B66: Smeth 3J 99
B67: Smeth 5M 99
B68: O'bry 3J 99
B75: S Cold 3K 59
DY9: Lye 4D 116
WS10: Darl 1F 54
WS11: Cann 5D 8
WV13: W'hall 6A 38
Cemetery St. WS6: C Hay 7C 14
WV14: Bils 3J 53
Cemetery Way WS3: Blox 8H 25
Centaur Rd. CV5: Cov 7M 151
Centenary Bus. Pk.
CV11: Nun 6L 89
Centenary Cl. B31: N'fld 8A 142
Centenary Dr. B21: Hand 8E 78
Centenary Plaza
B1: Birm 7J 101 (6D 4)
Centenary Rd. CV4: Canly 2K 173
Centenary Sq.
B1: Birm 7J 101 (5D 4)
Centenary Way *B1: Birm 8K 101*
(off Blucher St.)
B1: Birm 5D 4
(off Queensway)
Central Arc.
WV1: Wolv 7C 36 (4J 7)
Central Av. B31: Longb 1L 163
B64: Crad H 2J 117
B65: Row R 7C 98
CV2: Cov 7G 153
CV11: Nun 4H 89
CV31: Lea S 3M 223
DY4: Tip 2M 75
DY9: W'cte 6E 116
WS11: Cann 4F 8
WV14: Bils 2L 53
Central Baths 7B 36 (3G 7)
Central Blvd. B90: Bly P 7M 167
CV7: Ash G, Ker E 3M 129
Central Bldgs.
CV3: Cov 8C 152 (7B 6)
Central Bus. Pk.
B33: Kitts G 8D 104
Central City Ind. Est.
CV6: Cov 4F 152
Central Cl. WS3: Blox 8G 25
Central Dr. DY3: Gorn 7C 74
WS3: Blox 1F 38
WV14: Cose 2J 75
Central Gro. B27: A Grn 7J 123
Central Links Ind. Est.
B7: Nech 3B 102
Central Pk. Dr. B18: Win G 4F 100
Central Pk. Ind. Est.
DY2: Neth 6L 97
Central Rd. B60: B'gve 8A 188
Central Six Retail Pk.
CV3: Cov 8B 152 (7A 6)
Central Sq. B1: Birm 7H 101 (6B 4)
B23: Erd 5G 81
Central Trad. Est.
DY6: K'wfrd 8M 73
Central Way DY5: Brie H 6E 96
Centre City B5: Birm 7F 4
Centre La. B63: Hale 6B 118
Centreway, The B14: Yard W 5D 144
Centrovell Ind. Est.
CV11: Nun 7J 89
Centurion Cl. B46: Col 8M 83
Centurion Pk. B77: Wiln 3H 47
Centurion Way B77: Wiln 3H 47
Century Ho. B69: O'bry 3D 98
Century Ind. Est. B44: Gt Barr 6L 57
Century Pk. B9: Bord G 7C 102
B37: Mars G 3J 125
Century Rd. B69: O'bry 1G 99
Century Twr. B5: Edg 4J 121
Ceolmund Cres.
B37: Chel W 7H 105
Chace Av. CV3: W'hall 4H 175
Chaceley Cl. CV2: W'grve S 1A 154
Chaceley Ct. B97: Redd 1D 220
Chaceley Gro. B23: Erd 2D 80
Chadbrook Crest B15: Edg 2E 120
Chadbury Cft. B91: Sol 1B 168
Chadbury Rd. B63: Hale 6C 118
Chadcote Way B61: Cats 8M 161
Chaddersley Cl. B45: Rubery 8F 140
Chaddesley Cl. B69: O'bry 4D 98
B98: Redd 8F 212
CHADDESLEY CORBETT 1L 185
Chaddesley Ct. DY1: Dud 8H 75
Chaddesley Dr. DY9: Pedm 8B 116
Chaddesley Gdns.
DY10: Kidd 4A 158
Chaddesley Rd. B31: N'fld 7D 142
B63: Hale 7M 117
DY10: Kidd 4A 158
Chaddesley Wood Nature Reserve
2B 186
Chadley Cl. B91: Sol 3A 146
Chad Rd. B15: Edg 1F 120
WV14: Cose 2G 75
Chadshunt Cl. B36: Cas B 7D 82
CHADSMOOR 5G 9
Chad Sq. B15: Edg 2E 120
Chadstone Cl. B90: M'path 4B 168
Chadswell Hgts. WS13: Lich 7K 13
CHAD VALLEY 2E 120
Chad Valley Cl. B17: Harb 3D 120
Chadwell Dr. B90: Shir 3H 145
Chadwell Gdns. WV8: Cod 5F 20
Chadwich La. B61: C'wich 3L 161
DY9: Belb 3L 161
Chadwick Av. B45: Redn 3H 163
Chadwick Bank Ind. Est.
DY13: C'wick 8K 183
Chadwick Cl. CV5: E Grn 6H 151
WV4: Penn 3J 51
Chadwick Ct. B43: Gt Barr 1E 78
CHADWICK END 2B 196
Chadwick Ho. B45: Rubery 2E 162
Chadwick La.
B93: Chad E, Know 6A 170
DY11: Hartl 7L 183
DY13: C'wick 8K 183
Chadwick Manor B93: Know 8A 170
Chadwick M. B93: Chad E 3B 196
B98: Redd 2G 221
Chadwick Rd. B75: S Cold 4M 59
Chadworth Av. B93: Dorr 5E 168
Chaffcombe Rd. B26: Sheld 3C 124
Chaffinch Cl. DY3: Sed 7C 52
WS12: Hed 5H 9
Chaffinch Dr. B36: Cas B 2H 105
DY10: Kidd 7M 157
Chaffinch Rd. DY9: W'cte 6D 116
Chainmakers Cl. WV14: Cose 7K 53
Chain Wlk. B19: Loz 1K 101
Chalcot Dr. WS12: Hed 2F 8
Chalcot Gro. B20: Hand 4E 78
Chaldon Cl. WV9: Pend 8A 22
Chale Gro. B14: K Hth 6A 144
Chalfield B79: Tam 3K 31
Chalfont Av. WS11: Cann 1C 14
Chalfont Cl. CV5: Cov 5H 151
CV12: Bed 5G 111
Chalfont Ct. WS11: Cann 2C 14

Chalfont Pl.—Chenies Cl.

Chalfont Pl. DY9: W'cte ... 7E **116**
Chalfont Rd. B20: Hand ... 7H **79**
Chalford Rd. B23: Erd ... 1C **80**
Chalford Way B90: Shir ... 8J **145**
Chalgrove Av. B38: K Nor ... 8D **142**
Chalgrove Cres. B91: Sol ... 8B **146**
Challenge Bus. Pk.
CV1: Cov ... 4D **152** (1D **6**)
Challenge Cl.
CV1: Cov ... 5D **152** (1D **6**)
Challenge Way WV10: Wolv ... 4E **36**
Challenor Av. WV13: W'hall ... 7K **37**
Chalybeate Cl. B45: Fran ... 8F **140**
Chamberlain Clock ... 5H **101** (2B **4**)
Chamberlain Cl. B69: Tiv ... 7D **76**
CV32: Cubb ... 4D **218**
Chamberlain Ct. B14: K Hth ... 8L **121**
B18: Birm ... 5J **101** (1C **4**)
Chamberlain Cres. B90: Shir ... 7G **145**
Chamberlaine St. CV12: Bed ... 5H **111**
Chamberlain Hall B15: Edg ... 3G **121**
Chamberlain Ho. *B16: Edg ... 8G 101*
(off Skipton Rd.)
Chamberlain Rd. B13: Mose ... 3M **143**
CV21: Hillm ... 1H **207**
Chamberlains Grn.
CV6: Cov ... 2M **151**
Chamberlains La. WV4: Penn ... 6L **51**
Chamberlain Sq.
B3: Birm ... 7K **101** (5E **4**)
(not continuous)
Chamberlain Wlk.
B66: Smeth ... 4B **100**
Chance Cft. B68: O'bry ... 1H **119**
Chance Flds. CV31: Rad S ... 3F **224**
Chancel Ind. Est. DY6: K'wfrd ... 1L **95**
WS10: Darl ... 4D **54**
WV1: Wolv ... 8G **37**
WV13: W'hall ... 7B **38**
Chancellors Cl. B15: Edg ... 1E **120**
CV4: Canly ... 5K **173**
Chancel Way B6: Witt ... 4M **79**
B62: Hale ... 3C **118**
Chancery Ct. CV10: Harts ... 2A **88**
Chancery Dr. WS12: Hed ... 2J **9**
Chancery La. CV10: Harts ... 2B **88**
Chancery M. B60: B'gve ... 8M **187**
Chancery Way DY5: Quar B ... 7F **96**
Chanders Rd. CV34: Warw ... 8D **216**
Chandler Av. DY7: Kinv ... 4A **114**
Chandler Ct.
CV5: Cov ... 1B **174** (8A **6**)
Chandler Dr. WV4: Penn ... 6K **51**
Chandler Ho. B69: O'bry ... 5D **98**
Chandlers Cl. B18: Win G ... 4F **100**
B97: Redd ... 3D **220**
WV9: Pend ... 8A **22**
Chandlers Dr. B77: Amin ... 4H **33**
Chandlers Keep WS8: Bwnhls ... 2F **16**
Chandlers Rd. CV31: W'nsh ... 6A **224**
Chandos Av. B13: Mose ... 6M **121**
Chandos Rd. B12: Birm ... 1A **122**
Chandos St. CV2: Cov ... 6G **153**
CV11: Nun ... 5G **89**
CV32: Lea S ... 8M **217**
Change Brook Cl. CV11: Nun ... 1M **89**
Channon Dr. DY5: Brie H ... 1D **116**
Chanston Av. B14: K Hth ... 5L **143**
Chanterelle Gdns. WV4: Penn ... 5A **52**
Chantrey Cres. B43: Gt Barr ... 5K **57**
WV14: Bils ... 2M **53**
Chantries, The CV1: Cov ... 4E **152**
Chantry, The CV34: Warw ... 8G **217**
Chantry Av. WS3: Blox ... 1J **39**
Chantry Cl. B47: H'wd ... 2A **166**
Chantry Dr. B62: Quin ... 3G **119**
Chantry Heath Cres.
B93: Know ... 1J **169**
Chantry Heath La.
CV8: S'lgh ... 3E **200**
Chantry Rd. B13: Mose ... 5L **121**
B21: Hand ... 1F **100**
DY7: Stourt ... 2J **115**
Chapel Ash WV3: Wolv ... 7B **36** (4G **7**)
Chapel Ash Island
WV1: Wolv ... 7B **36** (4G **7**)
Chapel Av. WS8: Bwnhls ... 7E **16**
Chapel Cl. B64: Old H ... 1B **118**
WV5: Wom ... 4F **72**
Chapel Ct. B96: A'wd B ... 8E **220**
CV32: Lea S ... 1M 223
(off Windsor St.)
CV32: Lea S ... 1A **224**
(Wood St.)
DY5: Brie H ... 7D 96
(off Promenade, The)
DY5: P'ntt ... 2C 96
(off Chapel St.)
DY10: Kidd ... 8A **136**
Chapel Dr. B47: Wyt ... 6M **165**
B78: M Oak ... 8J **31**
CV7: Bal C ... 1H **171**
WS8: Bwnhls ... 7E **16**
CHAPEL END ... 2B **88**
Chapel Farm Cl. CV3: W'hall ... 3J **175**
Chapelfield M. B45: Rubery ... 3F **162**
DY8: Stourb ... 5A **116**
Chapelfield Rd. B45: Redn ... 2G **163**
CHAPEL FIELDS ... 7M **151**
Chapel Flds. Rd. B92: Olton ... 7M **123**
CHAPEL GREEN ... 2C **128**
Chapel Grn. WV13: W'hall ... 7B **38**
Chapel Hill DY10: Kidd ... 8A **136**
Chapel Ho. La. B63: Crad ... 3J **117**
Chapelhouse Rd. B37: F'bri ... 7F **104**
Chapel Ho. St.
B12: Birm ... 8M **101** (7K **5**)
Chapel La. B29: S Oak ... 7E **120**
B43: Gt Barr ... 6E **56**
B47: Wyt ... 7L **165**
B48: Row G ... 5F **190**
B62: Roms ... 3J **139**
B94: Lapw ... 2K **195**
B95: Ullen ... 5K **215**
B98: Beo ... 1M **213**
CV7: Barn ... 3B **132**
CV8: Rytn D ... 7A **176**
CV9: With ... 1B **66**
DY3: Swind ... 5C **72**
DY9: Belb ... 2K **161**
DY13: Stour S ... 7B **182**
LE10: Sharn ... 5J **93**
WS14: Lich ... 3H **19**
WS15: Cann W ... 4E **10**
WS15: Gent ... 5G **11**
WV8: Cod ... 6E **20**
Chapel M. WR9: Wych ... 8E **208**
(not continuous)
Chapelon B77: Glas ... 8G **33**
Chapel Pas. B69: O'bry ... 5G **99**
Chapel Pl. DY11: Kidd ... 3K **157**
Chapel Rd. B96: A'wd B ... 8E **220**
Chapel Row CV34: Warw ... 2E **222**
Chapel Sq. WS6: C Hay ... 6D **14**
Chapel St. B21: Hand ... 2D **100**
B60: B'gve ... 7A **188**
B63: Hale ... 6A **118**
B69: O'bry ... 2E **98**
B70: W Brom ... 4H **77**
B96: A'wd B ... 8E **220**
B97: Redd ... 8D **212**
CV1: Cov ... 6C **152** (3B **6**)
CV11: Nun ... 5J **89**
CV12: Bed ... 6H **111**
(not continuous)
CV21: Rugby ... 6A **180**
CV23: Kils ... 7M **207**
CV23: Long L ... 5G **179**
CV31: Lea S ... 2A **224**
CV34: Warw ... 2E **222**
DY2: Neth ... 5K **97**
DY4: Tip ... 4L **75**
(not continuous)
DY5: P'ntt ... 2C **96**
DY5: Quar B ... 1F **116**
DY6: W Hth ... 1H **95**
DY8: Stourb ... 5A **116**
DY8: Word ... 6K **95**
DY9: Hag ... 4A **138**
DY9: Lye ... 4E **116**
DY11: Kidd ... 3K **157**
LE9: Barw ... 3A **70**
LE9: Earl S ... 1G **71**
LE10: Sharn ... 5J **93**
WS3: Blox ... 1K **39**
WS3: Pels ... 6M **25**
WS7: C Ter ... 1E **16**
WS8: Bwnhls ... 7E **16**
WS11: Nort C ... 4L **15**
WS12: Hth H ... 8L **9**
WV2: Wolv ... 2D **52**
WV5: Wom ... 4F **72**
(not continuous)
WV14: Bils ... 4M **53**
Chapel St. Pct. B60: B'gve ... 7A **188**
Chapel Vw. B67: Smeth ... 5M **99**
Chapel Wlk. B30: K Nor ... 6G **143**
B60: B'gve ... 7A **188**
DY3: Gorn ... 7C **74**
Chapelwood Gro. B42: P Barr ... 4K **79**
Chapel Yd. LE10: Hinc ... 1K **91**
Chaplain Rd. WS12: Hth H ... 7L **9**
Chapman Cl. CV31: Rad S ... 4E **224**
Chapman Ct. CV34: Warw ... 1J **223**
Chapman Rd. B10: Small H ... 1C **122**
CHAPMAN'S HILL ... 8B **140**
Chapman's Hill B62: Roms ... 8B **140**
Chapmans Pas.
B1: Birm ... 8K **101** (7E **4**)
Chapman St. B70: W Brom ... 6H **77**
Chapter Ho. B70: W Brom ... 4G **77**
Chard Rd. CV3: Bin ... 1K **175**
Charfield Cl. B30: B'vlle ... 2D **142**
CHARFORD ... 1M **209**
Charford Rd. B60: B'gve ... 1L **209**
Charingworth Rd. B92: Sol ... 7C **124**
Chariot Way CV21: Rugby ... 2A **180**
Charity Brick Way
B70: W Brom ... 7J **77**
Charity Rd. CV7: Ker E ... 2A **130**
Charlbury Av. B37: F'bri ... 7F **104**
Charlbury Cres. B26: Yard ... 1M **123**
Charlbury M. CV31: Lea S ... 3C **224**
Charlbury Twr. *B5: Birm ... 1L 121*
(off Southacre Av.)
Charlecote Cl. B98: Redd ... 7K **213**
Charlecote Cft. B90: Shir ... 1J **167**
Charlecote Dr. B23: Erd ... 2E **80**
DY1: Dud ... 6E **74**
Charlecote Gdns. B73: Bold ... 1G **81**
CV31: Lea S ... 4D **224**
Charlecote Ri. WV13: W'hall ... 1M **53**
Charlecote Rd. CV6: Cov ... 7A **130**
Charlecote Wlk. CV11: Nun ... 1M **111**
Charlecott Cl. B13: Mose ... 2D **144**
CHARLEMONT ... 1L **77**
Charlemont Av. B71: W Brom ... 1L **77**
Charlemont Cl. WS5: Wals ... 3C **56**
Charlemont Cres.
B71: W Brom ... 1L **77**
Charlemonte Cl. WS12: Hed ... 6K **9**
Charlemont Gdns. WS5: Wals ... 3C **56**
Charlemont Rd. B71: W Brom ... 1L **77**
WS5: Wals ... 3B **56**
Charles Av. B65: Row R ... 5C **98**
DY10: Kidd ... 8A **136**
WV4: Penn ... 4B **52**
WV11: Ess ... 5M **23**
Charles Cl. B8: Salt ... 5D **102**
WS6: C Hay ... 8D **14**
Charles Ct. B13: Mose ... 7B **122**
B76: Walm ... 6M 59
(off Berryfields Rd.)
CV34: Warw ... 1H **223**
Charles Cres. WS3: Pels ... 4A **26**
Charlesdale Dr. WS9: A'rdge ... 5H **41**
Charles Eaton Rd. CV12: Bed ... 6F **110**
Charles Edward Rd.
B26: Yard ... 3K **123**
Charlesfield Rd.
CV22: Rugby ... 1A **206**
Charles Foster St. WS10: Darl ... 3C **54**
Charles Gardner Rd.
CV31: Lea S ... 3M **223**
Charles Henry St.
B12: Birm ... 1M **121** (8J **5**)
Charles Holland St.
WV13: W'hall ... 7B **38**
Charles Lakin Cl. CV7: Shil ... 4C **132**
Charles Lanes Trust Ho's.
B28: Hall G ... 1G **145**
Charles Pearson Ct.
B66: Smeth ... 4B 100
(off Mill Dr.)
Charles Rd. B6: Aston ... 8A **80**
B9: Small H ... 7E **102**
B20: Hand ... 8J **79**
B63: Hale ... 5M **117**
B91: Sol ... 7L **145**
CV9: Man ... 2M **65**
DY4: Tip ... 2A **76**
DY5: Quar B ... 8G **97**
DY8: Stourb ... 5L **115**
Charles St. B66: Smeth ... 2C **100**
B70: W Brom ... 4E **76**
B97: Redd ... 8C **212**
CV1: Cov ... 5E **152** (2F **6**)
CV7: New A ... 1G **109**
CV9: Hurl ... 4J **63**
CV11: Nun ... 4G **89**
CV21: Rugby ... 6M **179**
CV34: Warw ... 1G **223**
DY10: Kidd ... 3M **157**
LE10: Hinc ... 8L **69**
WS2: Wals ... 7K **39**
WV13: W'hall ... 6C **38**
Charles St. Ind. Est.
B70: W Brom ... 4E **76**
Charleston Cres. LE9: Barw ... 3A **70**
Charles Wlk. B65: Row R ... 4C **98**
Charles Warren Cl.
CV21: Rugby ... 6B **180**
Charles Watson Ct.
CV32: Lill ... 7A **218**
Charles Wesley Ct.
WV3: Wolv ... 2A 52
(off Claremont Rd.)
Charlesworth Av.
B90: M'path ... 3B **168**
Charleville Rd. B19: Hock ... 2H **101**
Charlewood Rd. CV6: Cov ... 7B **130**
Charlock Gro. WS11: Hth H ... 6J **9**
Charlotte Cl. B69: Tiv ... 7A **76**
Charlotte Gdns. B66: Smeth ... 4B **100**
Charlotte Rd. B15: Edg ... 2J **121**
B30: Stir ... 3G **143**
WS10: W'bry ... 8C **54**
Charlotte St. B3: Birm ... 6J **101** (4D **4**)
CV21: Rugby ... 6B **180**
CV31: Lea S ... 3M **223**
DY1: Dud ... 1H **97**
WS1: Wals ... 7A **40**
CHARLTON ... 6L **183**
Charlton Dr. B64: Crad H ... 2K **117**
Charlton La.
DY11: Hartl, Tort ... 6L **183**
Charlton Pl. B8: Salt ... 4D **102**
Charlton Rd. B44: K'sdng ... 2A **80**
Charlton St. DY1: Dud ... 8H **75**
DY5: Brie H ... 6A **96**
Charminster Av. B25: Yard ... 1K **123**
Charminster Dr. CV3: Cov ... 5D **174**
Charnley Dr. B75: R'ley ... 7L **43**
Charnwood Av. CV10: Nun ... 7D **88**
DY3: Sed ... 7D **52**
Charnwood Bus. Pk.
WV14: Bils ... 4J **53**
Charnwood Cl. B45: Fran ... 6H **141**
DY5: Brie H ... 2B **116**
LE10: Hinc ... 7L **69**
WS12: Hed ... 6J **9**
WS13: Lich ... 8J **13**
WV14: Bils ... 6B **54**
Charnwood Ct. DY9: W'cte ... 7E **116**
Charnwood Dr. CV10: Harts ... 7A **66**
Charnwood Ho. WS13: Lich ... 7H **13**
Charnwood Rd. B42: Gt Barr ... 2F **78**
LE9: Barw ... 1B **70**
LE10: Hinc ... 7K **69**
WS5: Wals ... 5A **56**
Charnwood Way CV32: Lill ... 6C **218**
Charter App. CV34: Warw ... 4D **222**
Charter Av. CV4: Canly ... 2H **173**
CV4: Tile H ... 2D **172**
Charter Cl. WS11: Nort C ... 5L **15**
Charter Cres. B64: Old H ... 1B **118**
Charterfield Dr. DY6: K'wfrd ... 1K **95**
WS12: Hth H ... 8J **9**
Charterfield Shop. Cen.
DY6: K'wfrd ... 1L **95**
Charterhouse Dr. B91: Sol ... 8B **146**
Charterhouse Rd. CV1: Cov ... 7E **152**
Charter Rd. CV22: Hillm ... 1E **206**
DY4: Tip ... 8C **54**
Charters, The WS13: Lich ... 8H **13**
Charters Av. WV8: Bilb ... 8H **21**
Charters Cl DY4: Tip ... 4L **75**
Charter St. DY5: Brie H ... 4E **96**
Chartist Rd. B8: Salt ... 3D **102**
Chartley Cl. B93: Dorr ... 6E **168**
WV6: Pert ... 5F **34**
Chartley Rd. B23: Erd ... 8D **80**
B71: W Brom ... 3K **77**
Chartway, The WS3: Pels ... 5A **26**
Chartwell B79: Tam ... 2K **31**
Chartwell Cl. CV11: Nun ... 3M **89**
DY1: Dud ... 3H **75**
Chartwell Dr. B74: Four O ... 5D **42**
B90: Ches G ... 4K **167**
WV5: Wom ... 4F **72**
WV10: Bush ... 8E **22**
Charwelton Dr. CV21: Brow ... 3E **180**
Chase, The B76: Walm ... 2K **81**
WV6: Wolv ... 3B **36**
Chase Academy & Leisure Cen.
... 1E 14
(off Convent Cl.)
Chase Av. WS6: C Hay ... 6F **14**
Chase Cl. CV11: Nun ... 3K **89**
Chase Gro. B24: Erd ... 3K **81**
Chaselands WS7: C Ter ... 2D **16**
Chase La. CV8: Ken ... 3L **197**
Chase Leisure Cen. ... 7D **8**
Chaseley Av. WS11: Cann ... 7C **8**
Chaseley Cft. WS11: Cann ... 7C **8**
Chaseley Gdns. WS7: Burn ... 2J **17**
Chase Link, The
WS8: Bwnhls ... 8G **17**
Chase Pk. Ind. Est.
WS7: C Ter ... 2D **16**
Chasepool Rd. DY3: Swind ... 2C **94**
Chase Rd. DY3: Gorn ... 8B **74**
DY5: P'ntt ... 8B **74**
WS3: Blox ... 1G **39**
WS7: Chase ... 4G **17**
WS8: Bwnhls ... 8G **17**
Chase Sailing Club, The ... 5D **16**
Chaseside Dr. WS11: Hed ... 6H **9**
Chaseside Ind. Est.
WS11: Hed ... 6H **9**
CHASE TERRACE ... 1E **16**
CHASETOWN ... 3E **16**
Chasetown Ind. Est.
WS7: C Ter ... 2E **16**
Chasetown Station ... 4D **16**
Chase Va. WS7: Chase ... 3E **16**
Chase Vw. WV4: E'shll ... 7E **52**
Chase Wlk. WS12: Hunt ... 5C **8**
Chasewater Ct. Bus. Pk.
WS7: C Ter ... 2D **16**
Chasewater Heaths Station
Chasewater Railway ... 3D **16**
Chasewater Ind. Est.
WS7: Chase ... 3E **16**
Chasewater Railway Mus. ... 6D **16**
Chasewater Sports Cen. ... 6C **16**
Chasewater Way
WS11: Nort C ... 4M **15**
Chasewood Pk. Bus. Cen.
WS12: Hth H ... 8L **9**
Chassieur Wlk. B46: Col ... 1M **105**
Chater Dr. B76: Walm ... 8A **60**
Chatham Cl. CV3: Cov ... 8J **153**
Chatham Rd. B31: N'fld ... 6A **142**
Chatham Way B77: Wiln ... 4F **46**
Chatillon Cl. CV34: H'cte ... 6L **223**
Chatsworth B79: Tam ... 2J **31**
Chatsworth Av. B43: Gt Barr ... 8C **56**
Chatsworth Cl. B72: W Grn ... 2K **81**
B90: Ches G ... 4K **167**
LE10: Burb ... 3M **91**
WV12: W'hall ... 4B **38**
Chatsworth Cres. WS4: Rus ... 2D **40**
Chatsworth Dr. CV11: Nun ... 7M **89**
WS11: Cann ... 5G **9**
Chatsworth Gdns.
CV31: Lea S ... 3D **224**
WV6: Tett ... 2G **35**
Chatsworth Gro. CV8: Ken ... 4J **199**
Chatsworth M. DY8: Word ... 7H **95**
Chatsworth Ri. CV3: Cov ... 4E **174**
Chatsworth Rd. B62: Hale ... 2A **118**
Chattaway Dr. CV7: Bal C ... 3H **171**
Chattaway St. B7: Nech ... 2C **102**
Chatterton Av. WS13: Lich ... 3E **18**
Chatterton Wlk. DY10: Kidd ... 3B **158**
CHATTLE HILL ... 7L **83**
Chattle Hill B46: Col ... 7L **83**
Chattock Av. B91: Sol ... 5E **146**
Chattock Cl. B36: Hodg H ... 2L **103**
Chatwell Gro. B29: S Oak ... 7B **120**
Chatwin Pl. WV14: Bils ... 6L **53**
Chatwin St. B66: Smeth ... 2M **99**
Chatwins Wharf DY4: Tip ... 4M **75**
Chaucer Av. DY3: Lwr G ... 4A **74**
DY4: Tip ... 1B **76**
WV12: W'hall ... 1E **38**
Chaucer Cl. B23: Erd ... 6B **80**
B79: Tam ... 3A **32**
DY8: Amb ... 1A **116**
WS14: Lich ... 3H **19**
WV14: Cose ... 1K **75**
Chaucer Cres. DY10: Kidd ... 3C **158**
Chaucer Dr. CV10: Gall C ... 4A **88**
WS7: C Ter ... 8G **11**
Chaucer Gro. B27: A Grn ... 7H **123**
Chaucer Ho. B63: Crad ... 4H **117**
Chaucer Rd. B60: B'gve ... 1B **210**
CV22: Rugby ... 3M **205**
WS3: Blox ... 1L **39**
Chauntry Pl.
CV1: Cov ... 6D **152** (3D **6**)
Chauson Gro. B91: Sol ... 1A **168**
Chavasse Rd. B72: S Cold ... 6J **59**
Chawner Cl. WS7: C Ter ... 8E **10**
CHAWN HILL ... 6C **116**
Chawn Hill DY9: Pedm ... 6C **116**
Chawn Hill Cl. DY9: Pedm ... 6C **116**
Chawn Pk. Dr. DY9: Pedm ... 6C **116**
Chaynes Gro. B33: Kitts G ... 6D **104**
Chaytor Dr. CV10: Nun ... 2A **88**
Chaytor Rd. B78: Pole ... 1A **48**
Cheadle Cl. CV2: Ald G ... 5G **131**
Cheadle Dr. B23: Erd ... 1D **80**
Cheam Cl. CV6: Cov ... 8G **131**
Cheam Gdns. WV6: Tett ... 1L **35**
Cheapside B5: Birm ... 8M **101** (8J **5**)
B12: Birm ... 8M **101** (8J **5**)
DY13: Stour S ... 7G **183**
WV1: Wolv ... 7C **36** (4J **7**)
WV13: W'hall ... 8A **38**
Cheapside Ind. Est.
B12: Birm ... 8M **101** (8K **5**)
Cheatham St. B7: Nech ... 3C **102**
Cheatle Ct. B77: Dost ... 4D **46**
Checketts St. WS2: Wals ... 7J **39**
Checkley Cl. B90: Shir ... 5G **145**
Checkley Cft. B76: Walm ... 1M **81**
Cheddar Rd. B12: Bal H ... 3L **121**
Chedworth Cl. B29: W Cas ... 2B **142**
B98: Redd ... 4J **213**
Chedworth Ct. B29: S Oak ... 1E **142**
Cheedon Cl. B93: Dorr ... 7E **168**
Chelford Cres. DY6: K'wfrd ... 6A **96**
Chells Gro. B13: Mose ... 4B **144**
Chelmar Cl. B36: Cas B ... 1F **104**
Chelmar Dr. DY5: P'ntt ... 3A **96**
Chelmarsh CV6: Cov ... 3C **152**
Chelmarsh Av. WV3: Wolv ... 8G **35**
Chelmarsh Cl. B98: Redd ... 2J **213**
Chelmorton Rd. B42: Gt Barr ... 2K **79**
Chelmscote Rd. B92: Olton ... 8M **123**
Chelmsley Av. B46: Col ... 3M **105**
Chelmsley Circ.
B37: Chel W ... 7H **105**
Chelmsley Gro. B33: Kitts G ... 6E **104**
Chelmsley La. B37: Mars G ... 1F **124**
(not continuous)
Chelmsley Rd.
B37: Chel W, F'bri ... 6F **104**
CHELMSLEY WOOD ... 7H **105**
Chelmsley Wood Ind. Est.
B37: F'bri ... 5H **105**
Chelmsley Wood Shop. Cen.
B37: Chel W ... 7H **105**
Chelney Wlk. CV3: Bin ... 8A **154**
Chelsea *B37: K'hrst ... 4F 104*
(off Chilvers Gro.)
Chelsea Cl. B32: Quin ... 5M **119**
CV11: Nun ... 2M **89**
Chelsea Ct. B29: W Cas ... 2B **142**
Chelsea Dr. B74: Four O ... 5F **42**
Chelsea Way DY6: K'wfrd ... 3K **95**
Chelsey Rd. CV2: Cov ... 1L **153**
Chelston Dr. WV6: Wolv ... 5L **35**
Chelston Rd. B31: N'fld ... 7L **141**
Cheltenham Av. B61: Cats ... 8B **162**
Cheltenham Cl. CV12: Bed ... 5H **111**
WV6: Wolv ... 3B **36**
Cheltenham Cft.
CV2: W'grve S ... 2M **153**
Cheltenham Dr.
B36: Hodg H ... 1K **103**
DY6: K'wfrd ... 3H **95**
Chelthorn Way B91: Sol ... 7C **146**
Cheltondale Rd. B91: Sol ... 3M **145**
Chelveston Cres. B91: Sol ... 8B **146**
Chelveston Rd. CV6: Cov ... 4L **151**
Chelwood Gdns. WV14: Bils ... 4H **53**
Chelwood Gro.
CV2: W'grve S ... 8M **131**
Chelworth Rd. B38: K Nor ... 7H **143**
Chem Rd. WV14: Bils ... 4J **53**
Chenet Way WS11: Cann ... 7E **8**
Chenies Cl. CV5: Cov ... 6H **151**

Churchill Dr.—Cleves Cres.

Churchill Dr. B65: Row R 7B **98**
DY8: Amb 2A **116**
Churchill Gdns. DY3: Sed 2C **74**
Churchill La.
DY10: Blak, C'hll 8H **137**
Churchill Pde. B75: S Cold 4A **60**
Churchill Pl. B33: Sheld 8B **104**
Churchill Rd. B9: Bord G 6F **102**
B61: Cats 8A **162**
B63: Hale 7M **117**
B73: New O 6D **58**
B75: S Cold 4A **60**
CV22: Rugby 8A **180**
WS2: Wals 7D **38**
WS14: Shens 4G **29**
Churchill Shop. Pct., The
DY2: Dud 8K **75**
Churchill Wlk. DY4: Tip 1A **76**
Church La. B6: Aston 1A **102**
B20: Hand 7F **78**
B33: Stech 6M **103**
B46: Max 7G **107**
B60: Tard 2H **211**
B61: B'gve 7M **187**
B63: Hale 5B **118**
B71: W Brom 3H **77**
B76: Curd 3H **83**
B76: Lea M 2A **84**
B76: Wis 8F **60**
B78: K'bry 4D **62**
B78: Midd 8H **45**
B79: Shut 2L **33**
B79: Tam 4B **32**
B92: Bick 8K **125**
B94: Lapw 7D **194**
(not continuous)
CV2: Cov 6H **153**
CV5: E Grn 4C **150**
CV7: Ash G 2E **130**
CV7: Berk 6J **149**
CV7: Cor 2F **128**
CV7: Fill 6E **108**
CV7: Mer 1K **149**
CV7: Old A 7E **86**
CV8: S'lgh 3C **200**
CV10: Ansl 4F **86**
CV10: Nun 2J **89**
CV13: Fen D 3F **66**
CV23: Thurl 7F **204**
CV31: Rad S 3E **224**
CV31: W'nsh 5B **224**
CV32: Cubb 3E **218**
CV32: Lill 6A **218**
CV35: Leek W 3F **216**
LE9: Barw 3A **70**
LE10: Wig P 8F **92**
WR9: Wych 8E **208**
WS7: Hamm 6K **17**
WS9: Ston 5L **27**
WS11: Hton 8A **8**
WV2: Wolv 8C **36** (6H **7**)
WV5: Seis, Try 7A **50**
(not continuous)
WV8: Cod 5F **20**
Church La. Ind. Est.
B71: W Brom 3J **77**
CHURCH LAWFORD 4C **178**
Church Lawford Bus. Cen.
CV23: Chu L 4A **178**
Church Lees CV33: Bis T 8E **224**
Church M. DY4: Tip 2M **75**
Chu. Moat Way WS3: Blox 1H **39**
Churchover Cl. B76: Walm 3K **81**
Church Pk. Cl. CV6: Cov 8M **129**
Church Pl. WS3: Blox 1K **39**
Church Rd. B6: Aston 2B **102**
B13: Mose 6A **122**
B15: Edg 2G **121**
B24: Erd 5F **80**
B25: Yard 2K **123**
B26: Sheld 4B **124**
B31: N'fld 5A **142**
B33: Yard 1L **123**
B42: P Barr 4K **79**
B46: Shu 7F **84**
B61: B'gve 6M **187**
B61: Cats 1M **187**
B61: D'frd 2F **186**
B63: Crad 2J **117**
B65: Row R 6C **98**
B67: Smeth 5M **99**
B73: Bold 1F **80**
B73: S Cold 6H **59**
B77: Dost 5C **46**
B78: Dord 4A **48**
B90: Shir 7H **145**
B95: Ullen 7H **215**
B96: A'wd B 7E **220**
B97: Redd 5D **212**
(Adelaide St.)
B97: Redd 7L **211**
(Foxlydiate La.)
CV7: Shil 4E **132**
CV8: Bag 7E **174**
CV8: Bubb 3J **201**
CV8: Rytn D 7B **176**
CV9: With 1B **66**
CV10: Harts 1B **88**
CV10: Nun 6C **88**
CV23: Chu L 4C **178**
DY2: Neth 4H **97**
Church Rd. DY3: Swind 6D **72**
DY8: Stourb 6B **116**
DY8: Word 7K **95**
DY9: Belb 3D **160**
DY9: Lye 4E **116**
WS3: Pels 6A **26**
WS7: Burn 2K **17**
WS8: Bwnhls 2F **26**
(not continuous)
WS9: Ston 6L **27**
WS11: Hton 8A **8**
WS11: Nort C 5L **15**
WS14: Shens 4F **28**
WV3: Wolv 2L **51**
WV5: Wom 2H **73**
WV6: Pert 5E **34**
WV6: Tett 4L **35**
(Rock, The)
WV6: Tett 6H **35**
(School Rd.)
WV8: Cod 5F **20**
(not continuous)
WV10: Oxl 8C **22**
WV10: Share 1K **23**
WV12: W'hall 3D **38**
WV14: Cose 8K **53**
Churchside Arc.
CV21: Rugby 6A 180
(off Lit. Church St.)
Churchside Way WS9: A'rdge . . .7H **27**
Church Sq. B69: O'bry 2G **99**
Churchstone Cl. B61: Cats 1M **187**
Church St. B3: Birm 6K **101** (4F **4**)
B19: Loz 2J **101**
B61: B'gve 7M **187**
B62: B'hth 8D **98**
B64: Old H 8L **97**
B69: O'bry 1G **99**
B70: W Brom 5J **77**
B79: Tam 4B **32**
B80: Stud 6L **221**
CV1: Cov 5D **152** (1E **6**)
CV9: Ath 1K **65**
CV11: Nun 5J **89**
CV12: Bulk 7C **112**
CV21: Rugby 6A **180**
CV23: Clift D 4G **181**
CV31: Lea S 2A **224**
CV34: Warw 3E **222**
CV47: S'ton 1M **225**
DY2: Dud 1J **97**
DY3: Lwr G 6D **74**
DY4: Tip 7A **76**
DY5: Brie H 8C **96**
DY5: P'ntt 2D **96**
DY5: Quar B 8F **96**
DY8: Stourb 4A **116**
DY9: Hag 4A **138**
DY10: Kidd 3L **157**
LE9: Earl S 1F **70**
LE9: S Stan 7L **71**
LE9: Sap 2K **93**
LE10: Burb 3A **92**
WS1: Wals 8M **39**
WS3: Blox 1H **39**
WS7: Chase 4E **16**
WS8: Clay 3E **26**
WS10: Darl 2D **54**
(Bell St.)
WS10: Darl 5B **54**
(Black Country New Rd.)
WS11: Cann 5G **9**
(Cannock Rd.)
WS11: Cann 3D **14**
(New St.)
WS11: Cann 8E **8**
(Queens Sq., not continuous)
WS13: Lich 1J **19**
WV2: Wolv 8C **36** (6H **7**)
WV10: Wolv 5G **37**
WV11: Wed 4J **37**
WV13: W'hall 7B **38**
(not continuous)
WV14: Bils 4K **53**
Church Ter. B33: Yard 8L **103**
B75: Four O 6H **43**
CV31: Lea S 2A **224**
CV32: Cubb 4E **218**
Church Va. B20: Hand 8H **79**
B71: W Brom 3K **77**
WS11: Nort C 5L **15**
Church Va. M. B71: W Brom 4K **77**
Church Vw. B11: S'brk 3D **122**
B77: Wiln 2F **46**
CV8: Rytn D 7A **176**
DY12: Bew 6A **156**
WS9: A'rdge 4H **41**
WS9: Wals W 6F **26**
Church Vw. Cl. WS3: Blox 1J **39**
Church Vw. Dr. B64: Old H 8M **97**
Church Vw. Gdns. DY7: Kinv . . .5A **114**
Church Wlk. B8: W End 3G **103**
B46: Col 2A **106**
B65: Row R 5C **98**
CV5: Alle 3J **151**
CV9: Ath, Man 1L **65**
CV11: Nun 7L **89**
CV12: Bed 7H **111**
CV21: Rugby 6A **180**
CV22: Bil 1K **205**
CV23: Barby 8J **207**
Church Wlk. CV23: Thurl 6F **204**
CV31: Lea S 2M **223**
DY11: Kidd 3J **157**
(not continuous)
DY13: Stour S 7E **182**
LE9: Sap 2K **93**
LE10: Hinc 1K **91**
WV3: Wolv 2M **51**
WV6: Tett 4L **35**
WV13: W'hall 8B **38**
Church Walks CV13: Stoke G . . .2D **68**
Churchward Cl. DY8: Amb 3B **116**
Churchward Gro. WV5: Wom 2G **73**
Church Way CV12: Bed 6H **111**
WS4: S'fld 7B **26**
Churchwell Ct. B63: Hale 6B **118**
Churchwell Gdns.
B71: W Brom 3K **77**
Churchyard Rd. DY4: Tip 4B **76**
Churnet Gro. WV6: Pert 5F **34**
Churn Hill Rd. WS9: A'rdge 5G **41**
Churns Hill La. DY3: Himl 6H **73**
Churston Cl. WS3: Blox 6G **25**
Churton House
(Crystal Glass Cen., The)
. . . . .1L **115**
Churwell Ct. WV5: Wom 3G **73**
Chylds Ct. CV5: Cov 4G **151**
Cicero App. CV34: H'cte 7L **223**
Cicey La. CV11: Burt H 1G **113**
Cider Av. DY5: Quar B 1E **116**
(not continuous)
Cinder Bank DY2: Neth 2H **97**
Cinder Bank Island
DY2: Dud 2H **97**
CINDER HILL 8F **52**
Cinder Rd. DY3: Gorn 8B **74**
WS7: C Ter 2E **16**
Cinder Way WS10: W'bry 6E **54**
Cineworld
Rugby 3B **180**
Solihull 6C **146**
Wednesfield 5H **37**
Cinquefoil Leasow DY4: Tip 3C **76**
Circle, The B17: Harb 2C **120**
CV10: Nun 5E **88**
Circuit Cl. WV13: W'hall 6B **38**
Circular Rd. B27: A Grn 7J **123**
Circus Av. B37: Chel W 7J **105**
Cirencester Cl. B60: B'gve 8B **188**
City, The DY4: Tip 6A **76**
City Arc. *B2: Birm 5G 5*
(off Corporation St.)
CV1: Cov 7C **152** (5B **6**)
WS13: Lich 2H **19**
City Est. B64: Crad H 1K **117**
City Hgts. B4: Birm 2F **4**
City Plaza B2: Birm 5G **5**
City Rd. B16: Edg 8B **100**
B17: Edg 8B **100**
B69: Tiv 2B **98**
City Trad. Est. B16: Birm 6G **101**
City Vw. B8: Salt 5D **102**
City Wlk. B5: Birm 8L **101** (7G **5**)
Civic Cl. B1: Birm 7J **101** (5C **4**)
Cladsworth Ho. *B97: Redd 5A 212*
(off Lock Cl.)
Claerwen Av. DY13: Stour S . . .2E **182**
Claerwen Gro. B31: N'fld 4L **141**
Claines Cres. DY10: Kidd 4B **158**
Claines Rd. B31: N'fld 5C **142**
B63: Crad 4K **117**
Claire Ct. B26: Sheld 2C **124**
Clairvaux Gdns. B92: Olton 4K **145**
Clanbrook Rd. DY7: Kinv 2A **114**
Clandon Cl. B14: K Hth 7J **143**
Clanfield Av. WV11: Wed 1M **37**
Clapgate Gdns. WV14: Cose 6G **53**
Clap Ga. Gro. WV5: Wom 3E **72**
Clapgate La. B32: Bart G 7G **119**
Clapgate Rd. WV5: Wom 2E **72**
Clapham Sq. CV31: Lea S 2B **224**
Clapham St. CV31: Lea S 3B **224**
Clapham Ter. CV31: Lea S 2B **224**
Clapton Gro. B44: K'sdng 8B **58**
Clara St. CV2: Cov 7G **153**
Clare Av. WV11: Wed 8M **23**
Clare Cl. CV32: Lill 7C **218**
Clare Ct. B90: Shir 7D **144**
CV21: Rugby 6M **179**
Clare Cres. WV14: Cose 7F **52**
Clare Dr. B15: Edg 1F **120**
Clare Ho. B36: Cas B 2G **105**
Clarel Av. B8: Salt 6C **102**
Claremont Cl. CV12: Bulk 5B **112**
Claremont Ct. B64: Old H 8L **97**
Claremont M. WV3: Wolv 2A **52**
Claremont Pl. B18: Win G 4F **100**
Claremont Rd. B11: S'brk 2B **122**
B18: Hock 3H **101**
B66: Smeth 5B **100**
B79: Tam 1M **31**
CV21: Rugby 6C **180**
CV31: Lea S 3M **223**
DY3: Sed 1E **74**
WV3: Wolv 2A **52**
Claremont St. B64: Old H 8L **97**
WV14: Bils 3J **53**
Claremont Wlk. CV5: Alle 3J **151**
Claremont Way B63: Hale 6B **118**
Clarence Av. B21: Hand 1C **100**
Clarence Ct. B68: O'bry 7J **99**
LE10: Hinc 1L **91**
Clarence Gdns. B74: Four O 7F **42**
Clarence Mans.
CV32: Lea S 8M 217
(off Clarence Ter.)
Clarence M. B17: Harb 3D **120**
Clarence Rd. B11: S'hll 5C **122**
B13: K Hth 8A **122**
B17: Harb 3D **120**
B21: Hand 1C **100**
B23: Erd 6D **80**
B74: Four O 4E **42**
CV21: Rugby 6L **179**
DY2: Dud 3K **97**
LE10: Hinc 1L **91**
WV1: Wolv 7C **36** (3H **7**)
WV14: Bils 2L **53**
Clarence St. CV1: Cov 5E **152**
CV11: Nun 5G **89**
CV31: Lea S 3A **224**
DY3: Up Gor 3E **74**
DY10: Kidd 3M **157**
WV1: Wolv 7C **36** (4H **7**)
Clarence Ter. CV32: Lea S 8M **217**
Clarence Way DY12: Bew 5B **156**
Clarenden Pl. B17: Harb 4C **120**
Clarendon Av. CV32: Lea S 8M **217**
Clarendon Cl. B97: Redd 4B **212**
Clarendon Cres.
CV32: Lea S 8L **217**
Clarendon Dr. DY4: Tip 8D **54**
Clarendon Pl. B62: Quin 2F **118**
CV32: Lea S 8L **217**
WS3: Pels 5M **25**
Clarendon Rd. B16: Edg 8E **100**
B67: Smeth 5M **99**
B75: R'ley 6J **43**
CV8: Ken 6G **199**
LE10: Hinc 2J **91**
WS4: S'fld 7C **26**
Clarendon Sq. CV32: Lea S 8L **217**
(not continuous)
Clarendon St. CV5: Cov 8M **151**
CV32: Lea S 8A **218**
WS3: Blox 8H **25**
WV3: Wolv 7A **36**
Clarendon Way B91: Sol 6C **146**
Clare Rd. WS3: Wals 3A **40**
WV10: Bush 2E **36**
Clare's Ct. DY11: Kidd 3J **157**
Clarewell Av. B91: Sol 1B **168**
Clare Witnell Cl.
DY11: Kidd 1H **157**
Clarion Way WS11: Cann 4E **8**
Clarke Ho. WS3: Blox 8H **25**
Clarke's Av. CV8: Ken 6G **199**
WS12: Hed 1G **9**
Clarkes Gro. DY4: Tip 3C **76**
Clarke's La. B71: W Brom 2J **77**
WV13: W'hall 6C **38**
Clarke St. B97: Redd 5D **212**
Clarkes Yd. LE10: Hinc 8K **69**
Clark Rd. WV3: Wolv 7M **35**
Clarkson Dr. CV31: W'nsh 5A **224**
Clarkson Pl. DY5: Quar B 3E **116**
Clarkson Rd. WS10: W'bry 5G **55**
Clark St. B16: Birm 7F **100**
CV6: Cov 8G **131**
DY8: Stourb 4L **115**
Clarry Dr. B74: Four O 1F **58**
Clary Gro. WS5: Wals 6A **56**
Clatterbach La. DY9: Clent 5G **139**
CLATTERBATCH 4B **116**
Clattercut La. DY10: Chad C . . .5M **185**
WR9: Rush 8L **185**
Claughton Ct. DY11: Kidd 4J **157**
Claughton Rd. DY2: Dud 8K **75**
Claughton Rd. Nth.
DY2: Dud 8K **75**
Claughton St. DY11: Kidd 4J **157**
Clausen Cl. B43: Gt Barr 5L **57**
Clavedon Cl. B31: N'fld 2L **141**
Claverdon Cl. B91: Sol 6L **145**
B97: Redd 5D **220**
WS8: Bwnhls 1G **27**
Claverdon Dr. B43: Gt Barr 1D **78**
B74: Lit A 5B **42**
Claverdon Gdns. B27: A Grn . . .4H **123**
Claverdon Ho. B13: Mose 2A **144**
Claverdon Rd. CV5: E Grn 6H **151**
Claverley Ct. DY1: Dud 8H **75**
Claverley Dr. WV4: Penn 4K **51**
Clay Av. CV11: Nun 2L **89**
Claybrook Dr. B98: Redd 2L **221**
Claybrook St.
B5: Birm 8L **101** (8G **5**)
Claycroft Pl. DY9: Lye 4E **116**
Claycroft Ter. DY1: Dud 3H **75**
Claydon Gro. B14: K Hth 6A **144**
Claydon Rd. DY6: W Hth 8J **73**
Clay Dr. B32: Quin 4G **119**
Claygate Rd. WS12: Wim 6L **9**
CLAYHANGER 3E **26**
Clayhanger La.
WS8: Bwnhls, Clay 2D **26**
Clayhanger Rd. WS8: Bwnhls . . .3F **26**
Clayhill La.
CV23: Lit L, Long L 3F **178**
Clay La. B26: Yard 4L **123**
B69: O'bry 5G **99**
Clay La. CV2: Cov 5G **153**
CV5: Alle 5E **128**
Claymore B77: Wiln 2D **46**
Claypit Cl. B70: W Brom 6G **77**
Clay Pit La. B90: Dic H 4G **167**
(not continuous)
Claypit La. B61: B'hth 8L **161**
B70: W Brom 6G **77**
WS14: Lich, Wall 6E **18**
Clayton Cl. WV2: Wolv . . .2C **52** (8H **7**)
Clayton Dr. B36: Cas B 1C **104**
B60: B'gve 2B **210**
Clayton Gdns. B45: Lick 7G **163**
Clayton Ho. B16: Edg 8F **100**
Clayton Rd. B8: Salt 4D **102**
CV6: Cov 4L **151**
WV14: Cose 2H **75**
Clayton Wlk. B35: Cas V 7A **82**
Clear Vw. DY6: K'wfrd 3H **95**
Clearwell Gdns. DY1: Dud 6E **74**
Clearwell Rd. B98: Redd 6J **213**
Cleasby B77: Wiln 8J **33**
Cleaver Gdns. CV10: Nun 3J **89**
Clee Av. DY11: Kidd 7J **157**
Clee Hill Dr. WV3: Wolv 8G **35**
Clee Hill Rd. DY3: Lwr G 5C **74**
Clee Rd. B31: Longb 1A **164**
B68: O'bry 5J **99**
DY2: Dud 2G **97**
DY8: Amb 3A **116**
DY10: Cookl 4B **136**
Cleeton St. WS12: Hth H 8K **9**
Cleeve B77: Glas 6D **32**
Cleeve Cl. B98: Redd 4K **213**
DY13: Stour S 7A **182**
Cleeve Dr. B74: Four O 3F **42**
Cleeve Ho. B24: Erd 7G **81**
Cleeve Rd. B14: Yard W 5C **144**
WS3: Blox 6F **24**
Cleeves Av. CV34: Warw 3J **223**
Cleeve Way WS3: Blox 7F **24**
Clee Vw. Mdw. DY3: Sed 7D **52**
Clee Vw. Rd. WV5: Wom 4E **72**
Clegg Rd. WS7: Burn 2L **17**
Clematis B77: Amin 6F **32**
Clematis Dr. WV9: Pend 6M **21**
Clem Attlee Ct. WV14: Wolv 1J **53**
Clemens St. CV31: Lea S 2A **224**
Clement Pl. WV14: Bils 2K **53**
Clement Rd. B62: B'hth 8D **98**
WV14: Bils 2K **53**
Clements Cl. B69: O'bry 5F **98**
CV8: Ken 4G **199**
Clements Rd. B25: Yard 1K **123**
Clements St. CV2: Cov 6G **153**
Clement St. B1: Birm . . .6H **101** (4B **4**)
CV11: Nun 6H **89**
WS2: Wals 8K **39**
Clement Way CV22: Caw 1G **205**
Clemson St. WV13: W'hall 7A **38**
Clennon Ri. CV2: Cov 1K **153**
Clensmore St. DY10: Kidd 2K **157**
CLENT 6F **138**
Clent Av. B97: Redd 2D **220**
DY11: Kidd 8H **157**
Clent Ct. DY1: Dud 8H **75**
Clent Dr. CV10: Nun 6B **88**
DY9: Hag 3D **138**
Clent Hill Dr. B65: Row R 4A **98**
Clent Hills Country Pk. 4F **138**
Clent Ho. *B60: B'gve 6B 188*
(off Burcot La.)
B63: Hale 7A **118**
Clent Rd. B21: Hand 8D **78**
B45: Rubery 1E **162**
B68: O'bry 1J **119**
DY8: Amb 3A **116**
Clent Vw. B66: Smeth 6B **100**
Clent Vw. Rd. B32: Bart G 8G **119**
B63: Crad 5J **117**
DY8: Stourb 6J **115**
(not continuous)
Clent Vs. B12: Bal H 5B **122**
Clent Way B32: Bart G 1G **141**
Cleobury Cl. B97: Redd 3B **212**
Cleobury La. B90: Tid G 4F **166**
B94: Earls 4F **166**
Cleobury Rd. DY12: Bew 3A **156**
Cleopatra Gro. CV34: H'cte 5L **223**
Cleton St. DY4: Tip 6B **76**
Cleton St. Bus. Pk. DY4: Tip . . .6B **76**
Clevedon Av. B36: Cas B 1E **104**
Clevedon Rd. B12: Bal H 3L **121**
Cleveland Cl. WV11: Wed 8M **23**
WV13: W'hall 8K **37**
Cleveland Ct. B13: Mose 7B **122**
CV32: Lea S 7M **217**
Cleveland Dr. B45: Lick 7G **163**
WS11: Cann 5H **9**
Cleveland Pas.
WV1: Wolv 8C **36** (5J **7**)
Cleveland Rd. CV2: Cov 5G **153**
CV12: Bulk 6B **112**
LE10: Hinc 1J **91**
WV2: Wolv 8D **36** (6L **7**)
Cleveland St. DY1: Dud 8H **75**
DY8: Stourb 5L **115**
WV1: Wolv 8C **36** (5J **7**)
Cleveland Twr. B1: Birm 7F **4**
Cleveley Dr. CV10: Nun 2D **88**
Cleves Cres. WS6: C Hay 8D **14**

Cleves Dr.—Colwall Rd.

Cleves Dr. B45: Rubery . . . 2E 162
Cleves Rd. B45: Rubery . . . 1E 162
Clewley Dr. WV9: Pend . . . 6A 22
Clewley Gro. B32: Quin . . . 4H 119
Clews Cl. WS1: Wals . . . 2L 55
Clewshaw La. B38: Head H . . . 5H 165
Clews Rd. B98: Redd . . . 2F 220
Cley Cl. B5: Edg . . . 3K 121
Client Hill Camping & Caravaning Site
B62: Roms . . . 6L 139
Clifden Gro. CV8: Ken . . . 3J 199
CLIFF . . . 8C 46
Cliff, The DY7: Kinv . . . 6A 114
DY8: Stourb . . . 3A 116
Cliffe Ct. CV32: Lea S . . . 8K 217
Cliffe Dr. B33: Kitts G . . . 6C 104
Cliffe Rd. CV32: Lea S . . . 8K 217
Cliffe Way CV34: Warw . . . 1F 222
Cliff Hall La. B78: Cliff . . . 8B 46
Clifford Bri. Rd.
CV2: W'grve S . . . 4M 153
CV3: Bin . . . 7M 153
Clifford Cl. B77: Glas . . . 6F 32
Clifford Rd. B67: Smeth . . . 8M 99
B70: W Brom . . . 7G 77
B93: Ben H . . . 5F 168
Clifford St. B19: Loz . . . 2K 101
B77: Glas . . . 6E 32
DY1: Dud . . . 1H 97
WV6: Wolv . . . 6A 36
Clifford Wlk. B19: Loz . . . 2K 101
(not continuous)
Cliff Pool Nature Reserve . . . 1A 62
Cliff Rock Rd. B45: Redn . . . 2H 163
Clift Cl. WV12: W'hall . . . 3C 38
Clifton Av. B79: Tam . . . 2M 31
WS8: Bwnhls . . . 2D 26
WS9: A'rdge . . . 1J 41
WS11: Cann . . . 2C 14
Clifton Cl. B6: Aston . . . 2M 101
B69: O'bry . . . 5G 99
B98: Redd . . . 8K 213
Clifton Ct. LE10: Hinc . . . 8H 69
Clifton Cres. B91: Sol . . . 8L 145
Clifton Dr. B73: S Cold . . . 3H 59
Clifton Gdns. WV8: Bilb . . . 6J 21
Clifton Grn. B28: Hall G . . . 4G 145
Clifton Ho. B12: Bal H . . . 4A 122
Clifton La. B71: W Brom . . . 1L 77
Clifton Rd. B6: Aston . . . 2M 101
B12: Bal H . . . 4M 121
B36: Cas B . . . 1E 104
B62: B'hth . . . 1D 118
B67: Smeth . . . 5M 99
B73: S Cold . . . 5G 59
CV10: Nun . . . 5F 88
CV21: Rugby . . . 6B 180
DY10: W'ley . . . 6C 136
DY11: Kidd . . . 8G 157
WV6: Tett . . . 4K 35
Clifton Rd. Ind. Est.
B12: Bal H . . . 4M 121
(off Clifton Rd.)
Clifton St. B64: Old H . . . 8M 97
CV1: Cov . . . 5E 152 (1F 6)
DY8: Stourb . . . 5L 115
WV14: Cose . . . 8F 52
Clifton Ter. B23: Erd . . . 5F 80
CV8: Ken . . . 3G 199
CLIFTON UPON DUNSMORE
. . . 4G 181
Clifton Way LE10: Hinc . . . 7G 69
Clinic Dr. CV11: Nun . . . 6J 89
DY9: Lye . . . 4E 116
Clint Hill Dr. LE9: S Stan . . . 6L 71
Clinton Av. CV8: Ken . . . 3D 198
CV35: H Mag . . . 2A 222
Clinton Cres. WS7: C Ter . . . 1H 17
Clinton Gro. B90: Shir . . . 8L 145
Clinton La. CV8: Ken . . . 2D 198
Clinton Rd. B46: Col . . . 3M 105
B90: Shir . . . 1K 167
CV6: Cov . . . 7F 130
WV14: Bils . . . 2A 54
Clinton St. B18: Win G . . . 4E 100
CV31: Lea S . . . 2A 224
Clipper Vw. B16: Edg . . . 8E 100
Clipstone Rd. CV6: Cov . . . 3L 151
Clipston Rd. B8: Salt . . . 5F 102
Clissold Cl. B12: Birm . . . 2L 121
Clissold Pas. B18: Hock . . . 5G 101
Clissold St. B18: Hock . . . 5G 101
Clive Cl. B75: R'ley . . . 7K 43
Cliveden Av. B42: P Barr . . . 5J 79
WS9: A'rdge . . . 8H 27
Cliveden Coppice
B74: Four O . . . 8F 42
Cliveden Wlk. CV11: Nun . . . 1L 111
Clivedon Way B62: Hale . . . 2A 118
Cliveland St.
B19: Birm . . . 5L 101 (1G 5)
Clive Pl. B19: Birm . . . 5K 101 (2F 4)
Clive Rd. B32: Quin . . . 2K 119
B60: B'gve . . . 1B 210
B97: Redd . . . 5D 212
CV6: Bal C . . . 4J 171
WS7: C Ter . . . 2G 17
Clive St. B71: W Brom . . . 4J 77
Clives Way LE10: Hinc . . . 7J 69
Clockfields Dr. DY5: Brie H . . . 8A 96
Clock Ho., The B61: B'hth . . . 2L 187
Clock La. B92: Bick . . . 7K 125
Clockmill Av. WS3: Pels . . . 6L 25
Clockmill Pl. WS3: Pels . . . 6M 25
Clockmill Rd. WS3: Pels . . . 6L 25
Clock Towers Shop. Cen.
CV21: Rugby . . . 6A 180
Clodeshall Rd. B8: Salt . . . 5E 102
Cloister Cft. CV2: W'grve S . . . 3M 153
Cloister Crofts CV32: Lea S . . . 6M 217
Cloister Dr. B62: Hale . . . 6D 118
Cloisters, The B80: Stud . . . 5K 221
CV32: Lea S . . . 6M 217
CV47: Sou . . . 5J 225
LE9: Earl S . . . 1E 70
WS4: Wals . . . 6M 39
Cloister Way CV32: Lea S . . . 6M 217
Clonmel Rd. B30: Stir . . . 3G 143
Clopton Cres. B37: F'bri . . . 5H 105
Clopton Rd. B33: Sheld . . . 1C 124
Close, The B17: Harb . . . 2M 119
B29: S Oak . . . 1D 142
B47: H'wd . . . 4A 166
B62: Hunn . . . 2A 140
B63: Crad . . . 3K 117
B92: Olton . . . 1M 145
CV8: Bran . . . 4F 176
CV8: Ken . . . 3G 199
CV31: Lea S . . . 3A 224
DY3: Lwr G . . . 5C 74
DY3: Swind . . . 7E 72
LE9: Barw . . . 2B 70
LE10: Sharn . . . 5H 93
WS10: W'bry . . . 6E 54
WS13: Lich . . . 1G 19
Closers Bus. Cen. CV11: Nun . . . 7K 89
Clothier Gdns. WV13: W'hall . . . 6A 38
Clothier St. WV13: W'hall . . . 6A 38
Cloudbridge Dr. B92: Sol . . . 2F 146
Cloud Grn. CV4: Canly . . . 4K 173
Cloudsley Bush La.
LE10: Wlvy . . . 3M 113
Cloudsley Gro. B92: Olton . . . 6M 123
Clovelly Gdns. CV2: Cov . . . 4J 153
Clovelly Rd. CV2: Cov . . . 4H 153
Clovelly Way CV11: Nun . . . 4L 89
Clover Av. B37: Chel W . . . 7K 105
Clover Cl. CV23: Brow . . . 1D 180
Clover Ct. B38: K Nor . . . 7D 142
Cloverdale B60: S Prior . . . 6J 209
WV6: Pert . . . 5D 34
Cloverdale Cl. CV6: Cov . . . 5B 130
Clover Dr. B32: Bart G . . . 7J 119
Clover Fld. LE10: Hinc . . . 6J 69
Clover Hill WS5: Wals . . . 1E 56
Clover La. DY6: W Hth . . . 2G 95
Clover Lea Sq. B8: W End . . . 3G 103
Clover Ley WV10: Wolv . . . 6F 36
Clover Mdws. WS12: Hth H . . . 8J 9
Clover Pk. Trad. Est.
LE10: Hinc . . . 6H 69
Clover Piece DY4: Tip . . . 3C 76
Clover Ridge WS6: C Hay . . . 6C 14
Clover Rd. B29: W Cas . . . 2A 142
Cloweswood La. B94: Earls . . . 1F 192
Club La. WV10: Cov H . . . 3C 22
Club Row DY3: Up Gor . . . 4E 74
Club Vw. B38: K Nor . . . 7D 142
Clunbury Cft. B34: S End . . . 4B 104
Clunbury Rd. B31: Longb . . . 1A 164
Clun Cl. B69: Tiv . . . 8M 75
Clunes Av. CV11: Nun . . . 3L 89
Clun Rd. B31: N'fld . . . 3M 141
Clyde Av. B62: B'hth . . . 1E 118
Clyde Ct. B73: S Cold . . . 4H 59
Clyde M. DY5: P'ntt . . . 3B 96
Clyde Rd. B93: Dorr . . . 7G 169
CV12: Bulk . . . 6A 112
Clydesdale B26: Sheld . . . 4A 124
Clydesdale Rd. B32: Quin . . . 3H 119
DY2: Neth . . . 6J 97
WS8: Clay . . . 3E 26
Clydesdale Twr. B1: Birm . . . 8F 4
Clyde St. B12: Birm . . . 8A 102 (8L 5)
B64: Old H . . . 8L 97
Clyde Twr. B19: Loz . . . 1K 101
C M T Ind. Est. B69: O'bry . . . 1G 99
Coach Cotts. B45: B Grn . . . 1K 189
Coach Ho. M. CV34: Warw . . . 2F 222
Coach Ho. Ri. B77: Wiln . . . 2F 46
Coalash La. B60: Hnbry . . . 8C 210
COALBOURNBROOK . . . 1M 115
Coalbourn La. DY8: Amb . . . 2M 115
Coalbourn Way DY5: Brie H . . . 6A 96
Coal Haulage La.
WS11: Cann . . . 3F 14
Coal Haulage Rd.
WS11: Hth H . . . 1M 15
WS12: Hth H . . . 1M 15
Coalheath La. WS4: S'fld . . . 1C 40
Coalmeadow Cl. WS3: Blox . . . 6F 24
COALPIT FIELD . . . 7K 111
Coalpit Flds. Rd. CV12: Bed . . . 7J 111
Coal Pit La. LE10: Wlvy . . . 8J 113
Coalpit La. CV8: Wols . . . 5J 177
CV23: Law H . . . 5J 177
COAL POOL . . . 3M 39
Coalpool La. WS3: Wals . . . 3M 39
Coalpool Pl. WS3: Wals . . . 3M 39
Coalport Rd. WV1: Wolv . . . 8G 37
Coalway Av. B26: Sheld . . . 5C 124
WV3: Penn . . . 3A 52
Coalway Gdns. WV3: Wolv . . . 3K 51
Coalway Rd. WS3: Blox . . . 1G 39
WV3: Penn . . . 3K 51
Coates Rd. DY10: Kidd . . . 2B 158
Coat of Arms Bri. Rd.
CV3: Cov . . . 3M 173
Coatsgate Wlk. WV8: Pend . . . 8M 21
Cobbett Rd. WS7: C Ter . . . 2C 16
Cobbles, The B72: W Grn . . . 2J 81
Cobble Wlk. B18: Hock . . . 4G 101
Cobbs Rd. CV8: Ken . . . 3D 198
Cobbs Wlk. B65: Row R . . . 4M 97
Cobden Av. CV31: Lea S . . . 4C 224
Cobden Cl. DY4: Tip . . . 1M 75
WS10: Darl . . . 3F 54
WS12: Hed . . . 2J 9
Cobden Gdns. B12: Bal H . . . 3L 121
Cobden St. CV6: Cov . . . 4E 152
DY8: Woll . . . 3K 115
DY11: Kidd . . . 3J 157
WS1: Wals . . . 2K 55
WS10: Darl . . . 3F 54
Cobham Bus. Cen.
B9: Bord G . . . 7D 102
Cobham Cl. B35: Cas V . . . 6M 81
B60: B'gve . . . 2M 209
Cobham Ct. M. DY9: Hag . . . 3D 138
Cobham Cres. DY12: Bew . . . 6A 156
Cobham Grn. CV31: W'nsh . . . 5A 224
Cobham Rd. B9: Bord G . . . 7D 102
B63: Hale . . . 5B 118
DY8: Stourb . . . 7A 116
DY10: Kidd . . . 5L 157
WS10: W'bry . . . 7L 55
Cobia B77: Two G . . . 2D 46
Cob La. B30: B'vlle . . . 2C 142
COBLEY HILL . . . 5L 189
Cobley Hill B48: A'chu . . . 5L 189
Cobnall Rd. B61: Cats . . . 7A 162
Cobs Fld. B30: B'vlle . . . 3C 142
Coburg Cft. DY4: Tip . . . 3C 76
Coburn Dr. B75: R'ley . . . 7K 43
Cochrane Cl. DY4: Tip . . . 3C 76
DY9: Pedm . . . 1C 138
Cochrane Rd. DY2: Dud . . . 3E 96
Cock All. WS13: Lich . . . 2H 19
Cockerills Mdw. CV21: Hillm . . . 1G 207
Cockermouth Cl.
CV32: Lea S . . . 7K 217
COCK GREEN . . . 5B 98
Cock Hill La. B45: Rubery . . . 8F 140
Cockley Wharf Ind. Est.
DY5: Brie H . . . 5B 96
Cock Robin Wood Nature Reserve
. . . 3L 205
Cockshed La. B62: B'hth . . . 1C 118
Cockshut Hill B26: Yard . . . 1A 124
Cockshutt La. B61: D'frd . . . 3K 187
WV2: Wolv . . . 2D 52
Cocksmead Cft. B14: K Hth . . . 4K 143
Cocksmoor Ho. B14: K Hth . . . 2K 143
Cocks Moor Woods Leisure Cen.
B14: K Hth . . . 5M 143
Cocksparrow La. WS12: Hunt . . . 5A 8
Cocksparrow St.
CV34: Warw . . . 3D 222
Cockspur St. B78: B'moor . . . 2L 47
Cockthorpe Cl. B17: Harb . . . 2M 119
Cocton Cl. WV6: Pert . . . 4E 34
CODSALL . . . 5F 20
Codsall Coppice Nature Reserve
. . . 1L 117
Codsall Gdns. WV8: Cod . . . 5E 20
Codsall Ho. WV8: Cod . . . 5E 20
Codsall Leisure Cen. . . . 5G 21
Codsall Rd. B64: Crad H . . . 1L 117
WV6: Tett . . . 2L 35
WV8: Tett . . . 8J 21
Codsall Station (Rail) . . . 6E 20
CODSALL WOOD . . . 2B 20
Codsall Wood Rd.
WV8: Cod, Cod W . . . 2B 20
Cofa Ct. CV1: Cov . . . 6C 6
Cofield Rd. B73: Bold . . . 8F 58
Cofton Chu. La. B45: Coft H . . . 7J 163
Cofton Cl. B97: Redd . . . 4B 212
COFTON COMMON . . . 2B 164
Cofton Ct. B45: Redn . . . 2K 163
Cofton Gro. B31: Longb . . . 3L 163
COFTON HACKETT . . . 6J 163
Cofton Lake Rd. B45: Coft H . . . 6J 163
Cofton Rd. B31: Longb . . . 2A 164
Cokeland Pl. B64: Crad H . . . 1K 117
Colaton Cl. WV10: Wolv . . . 5E 36
Colbek Ct. CV10: Gall C . . . 5L 87
Colbourne Ct. B33: Stech . . . 6K 103
Colbourne Gro. CV32: Lea S . . . 7K 217
Colbourne Rd. B78: Tam . . . 7A 32
DY4: Tip . . . 5A 76
Colbrook B77: Wiln . . . 8D 32
Colchester St.
CV1: Cov . . . 6E 152 (3F 6)
Coldbath Rd. B13: Mose . . . 1B 144
Coldfield Dr. B98: Redd . . . 1D 220
Coldridge Cl. WV8: Pend . . . 8M 21
Coldstream Cl. LE10: Hinc . . . 8G 69
Coldstream Dr. DY8: Word . . . 6L 95
Coldstream Rd. B76: Walm . . . 1L 81
Coldstream Way B6: Witt . . . 7L 79
(not continuous)
COLDWELL . . . 5H 11
Coldwells Ct. *CV22: Rugby . . . 7A 180*
(off Union St.)
Cole Bank Rd. B13: Mose . . . 1D 144
B28: Hall G . . . 1D 144
Colebourne Rd. B13: Mose . . . 2C 144
Colebridge Cres. B46: Col . . . 1M 105
Colebrook Cl. CV3: Bin . . . 7M 153
Colebrook Cft. B90: Shir . . . 7F 144
Colebrook Rd. B11: S'hll . . . 4D 122
B90: Shir . . . 7E 144
Coleby Cl. CV4: W'wd H . . . 2D 172
Cole Ct. B37: Chel W . . . 7K 105
COLE END . . . 1M 105
Coleford Cl. B97: Redd . . . 7A 212
DY8: Word . . . 7J 95
Coleford Dr. B37: F'bri . . . 7G 105
Cole Grn. B90: Shir . . . 8E 144
COLEHALL . . . 4C 104
Cole Hall La. B34: S End . . . 3A 104
(not continuous)
Colehill B79: Tam . . . 4B 32
Cole Holloway B31: N'fld . . . 1L 141
Colehurst Cft. B90: M'path . . . 3M 167
Coleman Rd. WS10: W'bry . . . 4G 55
Coleman St. CV4: Tile H . . . 6F 150
WV6: Wolv . . . 5M 35
Colemeadow Rd. B13: Mose . . . 4B 144
B46: Col . . . 2M 105
B98: Redd . . . 3L 213
Colenso Rd. B16: Edg . . . 5D 100
Coleraine Rd. B42: Gt Barr . . . 3G 79
Coleridge Cl. B79: Tam . . . 3A 32
B97: Redd . . . 1C 220
WS3: Pels . . . 4A 26
WV12: W'hall . . . 2E 38
Coleridge Dr. WV6: Pert . . . 5E 34
Coleridge Pas.
B4: Birm . . . 6L 101 (3H 5)
Coleridge Ri. DY3: Lwr G . . . 5A 74
Coleridge Rd. B43: Gt Barr . . . 2E 78
CV2: Cov . . . 6J 153
Colesbourne Av. B14: K Hth . . . 7J 143
Colesbourne Rd. B92: Olton . . . 6A 124
Coles Cres. B71: W Brom . . . 2H 77
Colesden Wlk. WV4: Penn . . . 3J 51
Coleshaven B46: Col . . . 3A 106
COLESHILL . . . 2M 105
Coleshill Cl. B97: Redd . . . 4C 220
COLESHILL HEATH . . . 1J 125
Coleshill Heath Rd.
B37: Mars G . . . 2J 125
B46: Col . . . 8L 105
Coleshill Ind. Est. B46: Col . . . 7A 84
(Gorsey La.)
B46: Col . . . 7L 83
(Roman Way)
Coleshill Leisure Cen. . . . 3M 105
Coleshill Rd. B36: Hodg H . . . 3K 103
B37: Mars G . . . 2G 125
B46: Max . . . 4D 106
B46: Over W, Shu . . . 7J 85
B46: Shu . . . 7D 84
B46: Wat O . . . 6H 83
B75: S Cold . . . 4J 59
B76: Curd . . . 3H 83
(not continuous)
B78: Faz . . . 3M 45
CV9: Ath, Bntly . . . 6D 64
CV10: Ans C . . . 2J 87
CV10: Harts . . . 2A 88
Coleshill St.
B4: Birm . . . 6M 101 (3J 5)
B72: S Cold . . . 4J 59
B78: Faz . . . 1A 46
CV9: Ath . . . 1K 65
Coleshill Trad. Est. B46: Col . . . 8M 83
Coleside Av. B13: Mose . . . 2D 144
Coles La. B71: W Brom . . . 2G 77
B72: S Cold . . . 5J 59
Colesleys, The B46: Col . . . 3A 106
Cole St. DY2: Neth . . . 6L 97
Cole Valley Rd. B28: Hall G . . . 3D 144
Coleview Cres. B33: Kitts G . . . 6E 104
Coleville Rd. B76: Walm . . . 3B 82
Coley Cl. LE10: Hinc . . . 2K 91
Coley Pits La. WR9: Wych . . . 4D 208
Coley's La. B31: N'fld . . . 7A 142
Colgreave Av. B11: Mose . . . 7D 122
Colina Cl. CV3: W'hall . . . 4J 175
Colindale Rd. B44: K'sdng . . . 6A 58
Colinwood Cl. WS6: Gt Wyr . . . 8F 14
Collector Rd. B36: Cas B . . . 8B 82
B37: F'bri . . . 4J 105
Colledge Cl. CV23: Brin . . . 6L 155
Colledge Rd. CV6: Cov . . . 8D 130
Colleen Av. B30: K Nor . . . 6H 143
College Cl. WS10: W'bry . . . 7G 55
College Ct. WV6: Tett . . . 5K 35
College Dr. B20: Hand . . . 7F 78
CV32: Lea S . . . 7M 217
Coll. Farm Dr. B23: Erd . . . 1D 80
College Ga. B8: Salt . . . 5E 102
College Gro. B20: Hand . . . 2H 101
College High Community
Leisure Cen., The . . . 3B 80
College Hill B73: S Cold . . . 5H 59
College La. B79: Tam . . . 4B 32
CV8: Fen E . . . 8E 170
LE10: Hinc . . . 8L 69
College Rd. B8: Salt . . . 6E 102
B13: Mose . . . 7C 122
College Rd. B20: Hand . . . 7E 78
B32: Quin . . . 3G 119
B44: P Barr, K'sdng . . . 4L 79
B60: B'gve . . . 7A 188
B73: New O . . . 3A 80
DY8: Stourb . . . 5A 116
DY10: Kidd . . . 5L 157
WV6: Tett . . . 5K 35
College St. B18: Hock . . . 5G 101
CV10: Nun . . . 7H 89
College Vw. WV6: Tett . . . 6K 35
College Wlk. B29: S Oak . . . 1D 142
B60: B'gve . . . 7A 188
(not continuous)
DY10: Kidd . . . 5L 157
Collets Brook B75: Bass P . . . 7B 44
Collett B77: Glas . . . 8G 33
Collett Cl. DY8: Amb . . . 3A 116
Collett Rd. WV6: Pert . . . 4E 34
Colletts Gro. B37: K'hrst . . . 4F 104
Collett Wlk. CV1: Cov . . . 6B 152
CV8: Ken . . . 5F 198
Colley Av. WV10: Bush . . . 1F 36
Colley Ga. B63: Crad . . . 3J 117
Colley La. B63: Crad . . . 2J 117
Colley Orchard B63: Crad . . . 3J 117
Colley St. B70: W Brom . . . 5K 77
Collier Cl. WS6: C Hay . . . 7D 14
WS8: Bwnhls . . . 2C 26
Collier's Cl. WV12: W'hall . . . 3B 38
Colliers Fold DY5: P'ntt . . . 4B 96
Colliers Way CV7: Gun H . . . 1E 108
Colliery Dr. WS3: Blox . . . 6F 24
Colliery La. CV7: Exh . . . 8H 111
Colliery La. Nth. CV7: Exh . . . 8H 111
Colliery Rd. B71: W Brom . . . 8A 78
WV1: Wolv . . . 7F 36
Collindale Ct. DY6: K'wfrd . . . 8K 73
Collingbourne Av.
B36: Hodg H . . . 2K 103
Collingdon Av. B26: Sheld . . . 3C 124
Collings Ho. B16: Edg . . . 8G 101
Colling Wlk. B37: K'hrst . . . 3G 105
Collingwood Av. CV22: Bil . . . 8K 179
Collingwood Cen., The
B43: Gt Barr . . . 6K 57
Collingwood Dr. B43: Gt Barr . . . 5J 57
Collingwood Rd. CV5: Cov . . . 7A 152
WV10: Bush . . . 7E 22
Collins Cl. B32: Quin . . . 4G 119
Collins Gro. CV4: Canly . . . 4K 173
Collins Hill WS13: Lich . . . 7G 13
Collinson Cl. B98: Redd . . . 8G 213
Collins Rd. CV34: H'cte . . . 4K 223
WS8: Bwnhls . . . 4G 27
WS10: W'bry . . . 6J 55
Collins St. B70: W Brom . . . 6E 76
WS1: Wals . . . 2L 55
Collis Cl. B60: B'gve . . . 2L 209
Collis St. DY8: Amb . . . 1M 115
Collister Cl. B90: Shir . . . 5H 145
COLLYCROFT . . . 5H 111
Colly Cft. B37: K'hrst . . . 4F 104
Collycroft Pl. B27: A Grn . . . 4H 123
Colman Av. WV11: Wed . . . 3M 37
Colman Cres. B68: O'bry . . . 7J 99
Colman Hill B63: Crad . . . 4K 117
Colman Hill Av. B63: Crad . . . 3K 117
Colmers Farm Leisure Cen. . . . 1H 163
Colmers Wlk. B31: Longb . . . 8K 141
Colmore Av. B14: K Hth . . . 2K 143
Colmore Cir. Queensway
B4: Birm . . . 6L 101 (4G 5)
Colmore Cres. B13: Mose . . . 8B 122
Colmore Dr. B75: S Cold . . . 4A 60
Colmore Flats
B19: Birm . . . 5K 101 (1F 4)
Colmore Ga. B3: Birm . . . 4G 5
Colmore Rd. B14: K Hth . . . 2K 143
Colmore Row
B3: Birm . . . 7K 101 (5E 4)
Colmore Sq.
B4: Birm . . . 6L 101 (3G 5)
Coln Cl. B31: N'fld . . . 3M 141
Colonial Ind. Pk.
B64: Crad H . . . 2K 117
Colonial Rd. B9: Bord G . . . 6F 102
Colshaw Rd. DY8: Stourb . . . 5L 115
Colston Rd. B24: Erd . . . 2H 81
Colt Cl. B74: S'tly . . . 2L 57
Coltham Rd. WV12: W'hall . . . 3C 38
Coltishall Cl. B35: Cas V . . . 7M 81
Colton Cl. WS14: Lich . . . 2K 19
COLTON HILLS . . . 5A 52
Colton Hills Sports Cen. . . . 5B 52
Colts Cl. LE10: Burb . . . 5K 91
Coltsfoot Cl. WV11: Wed . . . 4L 37
Coltsfoot Vw. WS6: C Hay . . . 7E 14
Colts La. B98: Redd . . . 6K 213
Columbia Cl. B5: Bal H . . . 3K 121
Columbia Gdns. CV12: Bed . . . 7K 111
Columbian Cres. WS7: C Ter . . . 1F 16
Columbian Dr. WS11: Cann . . . 6F 8
Columbian Way WS11: Cann . . . 6F 8
Columbine Cl. WS5: Wals . . . 6A 56
Columbine Way CV12: Bed . . . 8E 110
Columbus Av. DY5: Brie H . . . 6F 96
Colville Cl. DY4: Tip . . . 1D 76
Colville Rd. B12: Bal H . . . 4B 122
Colville Wlk. B12: Bal H . . . 4B 122
Colwall Rd. DY3: Lwr G . . . 5D 74

Colwall Wlk.—Cornwall Av.

Colwall Wlk. B27: A Grn 5K 123
Colworth Rd. B31: N'fld 5L 141
Colyere Cl. CV7: Ker E 3A 130
Colyns Gro. B33: Stech 4M 103
Combe Flds. Rd.
CV2: W'grve S 6F 154
CV3: Bin 6F 154
CV7: Ansty 6F 154
COMBER 5A 114
Comber Cft. B13: Mose 1D 144
Comber Dr. DY5: P'ntt 3B 96
Comberford Ct. WS10: W'bry 7G 55
Comberford Dr. WS10: W'bry 4K 55
Comberford Rd. B79: Tam 1A 32
Comber Gro. DY7: Kinv 6A 114
Comber Rd. DY7: Kinv 7A 114
COMBERTON 4B 158
Comberton Av. DY10: Kidd 4B 158
Comberton Ct. DY10: Kidd 5A 158
Comberton Gdns.
DY10: Kidd 4B 158
Comberton Hill DY10: Kidd 4M 157
Comberton Mans.
DY10: Kidd 4A 158
Comberton Pk. Rd.
DY10: Kidd 5B 158
Comberton Pl. DY10: Kidd 4M 157
Comberton Rd. B26: Sheld 2B 124
DY10: Kidd 4M 157
Comberton Ter. DY10: Kidd 4M 157
Combine Cl. B75: R'ley 5K 43
Combrook Grn. B34: S End 3D 104
Comet Rd. B26: Birm A 5J 125
Commainge Cl. CV34: Warw 2D 222
Commander Cl. CV33: Bis T 8E 224
Commercial Rd. WS2: Wals 2G 39
WV1: Wolv 8E 36 (5M 7)
Commercial St.
B1: Birm 8J 101 (7D 4)
Commissary Rd.
B26: Birm A 6G 125
COMMON, THE 2J 199
Common, The
B94: Earls, Tan A 4G 193
CV9: Bad E, Gren, Bax 8C 48
LE9: Barw 3B 70
Comn. Barn La.
DY10: Cookl 4D 136
Commonfield Cft. B8: Salt 4D 102
Common La. B8: Salt 3F 102
B26: Sheld 4A 124
B78: Dord, Pole 1A 48
B79: Tam 5B 32
B80: Map G 6B 214
CV7: Cor 3E 128
CV8: Ken 2H 199
WS11: Cann 6G 9
Common La. Ind. Est.
CV8: Ken 2J 199
Common Rd. WV5: Wom 5F 72
COMMON SIDE 7A 16
Commonside DY5: P'ntt 3C 96
WS3: Pels 7A 26
WS8: Bwnhls 3G 27
WS15: Gent 5G 11
Common Vw. WS7: C Ter 8G 11
WS12: Hed 2H 9
Common Wlk. WS12: Hunt 4C 8
Common Way CV2: Cov 3G 153
Communication Row
B15: Birm 8J 101 (8C 4)
Compa, The DY7: Kinv 5A 114
Compass Ct.
CV1: Cov 6B 152 (4A 6)
COMPTON 7J 35
Compton Cl. B91: Sol 5K 145
B98: Redd 7E 212
CV32: Lill 7C 218
DY7: Kinv 5A 114
Compton Ct. B74: Four O 6F 42
CV22: Dunc 3H 205
DY2: Neth 3J 97
WV3: Wolv 7M 35
Compton Cft. B37: Chel W 8K 105
Compton Dr. B74: S'tly 2L 57
DY2: Dud 1M 97
DY6: K'wfrd 4K 95
Compton Gdns. DY7: Kinv 5A 114
Compton Grange
B64: Crad H 1J 117
Compton Gro. B63: Crad 5J 117
DY6: K'wfrd 4K 95
Compton Hill Dr. WV3: Wolv 7K 35
Compton Ho. B33: Yard 8B 104
Compton Pk. WV3: Wolv 7L 35
Compton Pk. Recreation Cen.
6L 35
Compton Rd. B24: Erd 8E 80
B62: Quin 4F 118
B64: Crad H 8J 97
B79: Tam 2M 31
CV6: Cov 7D 130
DY7: Kinv 5A 114
DY9: Pedm 8D 116
WV3: Wolv 7L 35
Compton Rd. W. WV3: Wolv 7J 35
Comrie Cl. CV2: Cov 3M 153
Comsey Rd. B43: Gt Barr 6H 57
Comwall Cl. WS3: Blox 3J 39
(not continuous)
Comyn St. CV32: Lea S 8B 218
Conchar Cl. B72: W Grn 7J 59
Conchar Rd. B72: W Grn 7J 59
Concorde Dr. B35: Cas V 7M 81
Concorde Rd. B26: Birm A 5J 125
Condor Gro. WS12: Hth H 8J 9
Condover Cl. WS2: Wals 6D 38
Condover Rd. B31: Longb 1B 164
Conduit Rd. WS11: Nort C 5A 16
Conduit St. WS13: Lich 1H 19
Coneybury Wlk. B76: Min 4D 82
Coneyford Rd. B34: S End 3C 104
(not continuous)
Coneygree Ind. Est. DY4: Tip 6M 75
Coney Grn. DY8: Stourb 4B 116
Coney Grn. Dr. B31: Longb 1M 163
Coney Grn. Ho. B31: Longb 1M 163
Coneygree Rd. DY4: Tip 7M 75
Congleton Cl. B97: Redd 4B 212
CV6: Cov 7E 130
Congreve Cl. CV34: Warw 7F 216
Congreve Pas.
B3: Birm 7K 101 (5E 4)
Congreve Wlk. CV12: Bed 7H 111
Conifer Cl. CV12: Bed 5J 111
DY5: Brie H 1C 116
WS12: Hed 1G 9
Conifer Ct. B13: Mose 7L 121
CV12: Bed 5J 111
Conifer Dr. B21: Hand 2E 100
B31: N'fld 6B 142
Conifer Gro. B61: B'gve 6M 187
CV31: Lea S 4A 224
Conifer Paddock B62: B'hth 1E 118
CV3: Bin 8L 153
Conifer Rd. B74: S'tly 1L 57
Conifers, The CV8: Ken 6H 199
Coningsby Cl. CV31: Lea S 3C 224
Coningsby Dr. DY11: Kidd 2G 157
Conington Gro. B17: Harb 4A 120
Coniston B77: Wiln 2H 47
Coniston Av. B92: Olton 5M 123
Coniston Cl. B28: Hall G 2F 144
B60: B'gve 8B 188
CV12: Bulk 6C 112
CV21: Brow 3D 180
LE9: Earl S 1F 70
Coniston Ct. CV11: Nun 2M 89
LE9: Earl S 1F 70
Coniston Cres. B43: Gt Barr 2F 78
DY13: Stour S 3F 182
Coniston Dr. CV5: E Grn 5D 150
DY6: K'wfrd 2H 95
Coniston Grange CV8: Ken 4G 199
Coniston Ho. B17: Harb 4D 120
B69: O'bry 4D 98
DY10: Kidd 2L 157
Coniston Rd. B23: Erd 4D 80
B74: S'tly 6M 41
CV5: Cov 8M 151
CV32: Lea S 8K 217
WV6: Tett 1K 35
Coniston Way CV11: Nun 2M 89
DY12: Bew 2A 156
WS11: Cann 8E 8
Conker La. B93: Dorr 5E 168
Connaught Av. DY11: Kidd 6J 157
WS10: W'bry 6J 55
Connaught Cl. WS5: Wals 2C 56
Connaught Dr. WV5: Wom 8G 51
Connaught Gdns. B5: Bal H 3L 121
Connaught Ho. WV1: Wolv 7A 36
Connaught Rd. B60: B'gve 8C 188
WV1: Wolv 7A 36
WV14: Bils 2M 53
Connops Way DY9: Lye 4E 116
Connor Rd. B71: W Brom 1L 77
Conolly Dr. B45: Redn 8H 141
Conrad Cl. B11: S'brk 2A 122
CV22: Rugby 3M 205
Conrad Rd. CV6: Cov 2A 152
Consort Cres. DY5: P'ntt 3C 96
Consort Dr. WS10: Darl 1D 54
Consort Pl. B79: Tam 4C 32
Consort Rd. B30: K Nor 6G 143
Constable Cl. B43: Gt Barr 6K 57
CV12: Bed 4G 111
Constable Rd. CV21: Hillm 8H 181
Constables, The B68: O'bry 7H 99
Constance Av. B70: W Brom 8K 77
Constance Cl. CV12: Bed 1F 130
Constance Rd. B5: Edg 4K 121
Constantine La. B46: Col 8M 83
Constantine Way WV14: Bils 7A 54
Constitution Hill
B19: Birm 5K 101 (1D 4)
DY2: Dud 1J 97
Constitution Hill E. DY2: Dud 1K 97
Consul Rd. CV21: Rugby 2M 179
Containerbase B44: P Barr 4L 79
Convent Cl. CV8: Ken 2G 199
CV9: Ath 2M 65
WS11: Cann 1D 14
WV2: Wolv 8D 36 (6K 7)
Convent La. CV9: Ath 2L 65
Conway Av. B32: Quin 3H 119
B68: O'bry 7H 99
B71: W Brom 8H 55
CV4: Tile H 1D 172
Conway Cl. B90: Shir 8K 145
DY1: Dud 3J 75
DY6: K'wfrd 5M 95
Conway Cres. WV12: W'hall 2C 38
Conway Gro. B43: Gt Barr 2D 78
Conway Ho. WS3: Blox 3K 39
Conway Rd. B11: S'brk 3C 122
B37: F'bri 6H 105
B60: B'gve 8M 187
B90: Shir 8K 145
CV32: Lea S 1K 223
WS11: Cann 1B 14
WV6: Pert 6F 34
Conwy Cl. CV11: Nun 6K 89
WS2: Wals 5G 39
Conybere St. B12: Birm 2L 121
Conyworth Cl. B27: A Grn 5K 123
Cook Av. DY2: Dud 2K 97
Cook Cl. B93: Know 3J 169
CV21: Brow 2C 180
WV6: Pert 5E 34
WV10: Oxl 8C 22
Cooke Cl. CV6: Longf 5G 131
CV34: Warw 8F 216
Cookes Cft. B31: N'fld 7B 142
Cookesley Cl. B43: Gt Barr 5K 57
COOKLEY 4A 136
Cookley Cl. B63: Hale 7M 117
Cookley La. DY7: Kinv 8B 114
Cookley Way B69: O'bry 4E 98
Cooknell Dr. DY8: Word 7L 95
Cook Rd. WS3: Blox 7K 25
Cooks Cl. CV9: Ath 1K 65
COOKSEY CORNER 4D 208
COOKSEY GREEN 1B 208
Cooksey Grn. La.
B61: U War 3A 208
WR9: Elmb 3A 208
Cooksey La. B43: Gt Barr 5L 57
B44: Gt Barr 5L 57
Cooksey Rd. B10: Small H 1B 122
(not continuous)
Cooks La. B37: K'hrst 6F 104
CV9: Bad E 7C 48
CV23: F'ton 8J 203
LE9: Sap 2K 93
Cookspiece Wlk.
B33: Stech 6M 103
Cook St. B7: Nech 2C 102
CV1: Cov 6C 152 (3C 6)
WS10: Darl 3F 54
WV2: Wolv 2C 52 (8J 7)
Coombe Abbey 5E 154
Coombe Abbey Country Pk. 6C 154
Coombe Abbey Vis. Cen. 5E 154
Coombe Av. CV3: Bin 2M 175
Coombe Ct. CV3: Bin 7A 154
Coombe Cft. WV9: Pend 6A 22
Coombe Dr. CV3: Bin W 2E 176
CV10: Nun 5B 88
Coombe Hill B64: Old H 1B 118
Coombe Pk. B74: Four O 2F 58
Coombe Pk. Rd. CV3: Bin 7M 153
Coombe Rd. B20: Hand 8L 79
B90: Shir 7J 145
Coombes La. B31: Longb 3M 163
Coombe St. CV3: Cov 7H 153
COOMBESWOOD 1D 118
Coombeswood Bus. Pk.
B62: B'hth 1B 118
Coombs Rd. B62: Hale 3B 118
Coombswood Way
B62: B'hth 2B 118
Co-operative St. CV2: Ald G 6H 131
Cooper Av. DY5: Brie H 7A 96
Cooper Cl. B60: B'gve 3L 209
B70: W Brom 7L 77
COOPER'S BANK 8C 74
Cooper's Bank Rd.
DY3: Gorn 8C 74
DY5: P'ntt 8C 74
Coopers Hill B48: A'chu 3K 189
Coopers La. B67: Smeth 4M 99
DY13: Stour S 6F 182
Coopers Rd. B20: Hand 6G 79
Cooper St. B70: W Brom 6K 77
CV11: Nun 5K 89
WV2: Wolv 1F 52
Coopers Wlk. CV8: Bubb 3J 201
Cope Arnolds Cl. CV6: Longf 5F 130
Copeland CV21: Brow 2C 180
Copelands, The DY7: Kinv 5A 114
Copeley Hill B23: Erd 8C 80
Copes Cres. WV10: Wolv 3G 37
Copes Dr. B79: Tam 2A 32
Copeshill Ct. B75: S Cold 5L 59
Cope St. B18: Hock 6G 101
CV1: Cov 6D 152 (4E 6)
WS3: Blox 3J 39
WS10: Darl 3E 54
Cophall St. DY4: Tip 4D 76
Cophams Cl. B92: Sol 7C 124
Copland Pl. CV4: Tile H 8E 150
Coplow Cl. CV7: Bal C 3G 171
Coplow Cotts. B16: Birm 6F 100
Coplow St. B16: Birm 6F 100
Coplow Ter. *B16: Birm 6F 100*
(off Coplow St.)
Copnor Gro. B26: Yard 3L 123
Coppenhall Gro.
B33: Kitts G 6A 104
Copperas St. CV2: Cov 7H 131
Copper Beech Cl. CV6: Cov 8E 130
Copperbeech Cl. B32: Harb 4M 119
Copper Beech Dr.
DY6: K'wfrd 8K 73
WV5: Wom 3H 73
Copperbeech Dr. B12: Bal H 4A 122
Copperbeech Gdns.
B20: Hand 7F 78
Copperfield Rd. CV2: Cov 6H 153
Copperfields WS14: Lich 2K 19
Copperkins Rd. WS12: Hed 5K 9
Coppermill Cl. WS12: Hed 2F 8
Coppice, The B20: Hand 7G 79
B31: Longb 7J 141
B42: P Barr 6L 79
CV3: Cov 1H 175
CV9: Man 3A 66
CV10: Nun 2J 89
DY4: Tip 8C 54
DY8: Hag 4M 137
LE10: Burb 1A 92
WS12: Hth H 8L 9
WV12: W'hall 3C 38
Coppice Ash Cft. B19: Loz 1K 101
Coppice Av. DY9: W'cte 6F 116
Coppice Cl. B24: Erd 6F 80
B45: Rubery 2F 162
B90: Ches G 5J 167
B91: Sol 2A 146
B97: Redd 6C 212
DY3: Sed 2B 74
DY5: Quar B 8F 96
LE10: Hinc 6M 69
WS6: C Hay 5D 14
WS7: C Ter 1F 16
WV11: Wed 8A 24
Coppice Ct. WS11: Cann 2B 14
Coppice Cres. WS8: Bwnhls 2D 26
Coppice Dr. B27: A Grn 7H 123
B78: Dord 2M 47
Coppice Farm Way
WV12: W'hall 8B 24
Coppice Gro. WS14: Lich 2M 19
Coppice Hgts. DY11: Kidd 8H 157
Coppice Hollow B32: Bart G 8H 119
Coppice Ho. B27: A Grn 7G 123
Coppice Ind. Est.
DY11: Kidd 1H 183
Coppice La. B78: Midd 7C 44
DY5: Quar B 8F 96
WS6: C Hay 5D 14
WS7: Hamm 6M 17
WS8: Bwnhls 1C 26
WS9: A'rdge 8F 26
WV6: Tett 3H 35
WV12: W'hall 3C 38
Coppice Oak B13: Mose 6A 122
Coppice Ri. DY5: Quar B 7G 97
Coppice Rd. B13: Mose 6A 122
B64: Crad H 2L 117
B92: Sol 2E 146
CV31: W'nsh 6B 224
WS9: Wals W 5F 26
WV3: Wolv 1K 51
WV14: Cose 1G 75
Coppice Side WS8: Bwnhls 1D 26
Coppice Side Ind. Est.
WS8: Bwnhls 2C 26
Coppice St. B70: W Brom 5G 77
DY4: Tip 5K 75
(Canal St.)
DY4: Tip 3L 75
(Furnace Pde.)
Coppice Vw. Rd. B73: S'tly 5A 58
Coppice Wlk. B90: Ches G 5J 167
LE10: Hinc 6M 69
Coppice Way *B37: Chel W 7H 105*
(off Chelmsley Wood Shop. Cen.)
Copplestone Cl. B34: S End 3B 104
Copps Rd. CV32: Lea S 1K 223
Coppy Hall Gro. WS9: A'rdge 8H 27
Coppy Nook La. WS7: Hamm 4H 17
Copse, The B74: Four O 8F 42
CV7: Exh 1G 131
Copse Cl. B31: N'fld 7A 142
Copse Cres. WS3: Pels 5A 26
Copse Dr. CV5: Alle 1B 150
Copse Rd. DY2: Neth 6H 97
Copsewood Av. CV11: Nun 2A 112
Copsewood Ter. CV3: Cov 7J 153
Copstone Dr. B93: Dorr 6F 168
Copston Gro. B29: W Cas 1B 142
Copthall Rd. B21: Hand 7C 78
Copthall Ter.
CV1: Cov 8C 152 (7C 6)
COPT HEATH 8G 147
Copt Heath Cft. B93: Know 1H 169
Copt Heath Dr. B93: Know 2G 169
Copt Heath Golf Course 1G 169
Copt Heath Wharf B91: Sol 7H 147
Copthorne Av. WS7: Chase 5F 16
Copthorne Rd. B44: Gt Barr 6L 57
CV6: Cov 1M 151
WV3: Wolv 2A 52
Copt Oak Cl. CV4: W'wd H 3C 172
COPYHOLT 5B 210
Copyholt La. B60: Lwr B 6E 210
B60: Stoke P, S Prior 5A 210
B97: Bks G 6E 210
Coral Cl. CV5: Cov 7J 151
LE10: Burb 5M 91
Coralin Cl. B37: Chel W 7H 105
Corbet Rd. CV6: Cov 2C 152
Corbett Cl. B60: B'gve 1B 210
Corbett Cres. DY8: Amb 2A 116
Corbett Dr. B60: S Prior 8J 209
Corbett Rd. B47: H'wd 2A 166
DY5: Brie H 8D 96
DY11: Kidd 1G 157
Corbetts Cl. B92: H Ard 2B 148
Corbett St. B66: Smeth 5B 100
CV21: Rugby 5C 180
Corbin Rd. B78: Dord 3M 47
Corbison Cl. CV34: Warw 8D 216
Corbizum Av. B80: Stud 5K 221
Corbridge Av. B44: Gt Barr 8M 57
Corbridge Rd. B73: S Cold 7F 58
Corbyn Rd. B9: Bord G 6H 103
DY1: Dud 1F 96
Corbyn's Cl. DY5: P'ntt 2B 96
Corbyn's Hall La. DY5: P'ntt 2B 96
Corbyn's Hall Rd. DY5: P'ntt 3B 96
Cordelia Grn. CV34: H'cte 5L 223
Cordelia Way CV22: Bil 3L 205
Cordle Marsh Rd. DY12: Bew 4C 156
Cordley St. B70: W Brom 5H 77
Corfe Cl. B32: Harb 4M 119
CV2: W'grve S 4M 153
WV6: Pert 6F 34
Corfe Dr. B69: Tiv 1A 98
Corfe Rd. WV14: Cose 1G 75
Corfe Way CV11: Nun 6H 89
Corfton Dr. WV6: Tett 5J 35
Coriander Cl. B45: Fran 8H 141
B60: S Prior 8J 209
Corinne Cl. B45: Redn 3G 163
Corinne Cft. B37: K'hrst 5G 105
Corinthian Pl. CV2: Cov 3K 153
Coriolanus Sq. CV34: H'cte 6M 223
Corisande Rd. B29: S Oak 7C 120
CORLEY 2J 129
CORLEY ASH 1G 129
Corley Av. B31: N'fld 6B 142
Corley Cl. B90: Shir 8E 144
CORLEY MOOR 3E 128
Corley Vw. CV7: Ash G 2C 130
Cormorant Gro. DY10: Kidd 6B 158
Cornbow Cen. B63: Hale 6B 118
Cornbrook Rd. B29: W Cas 2M 141
Cornbury Gro. B91: Shir 5K 145
Corncrake Cl. B72: S Cold 7K 59
Corncrake Dr. B36: Cas B 1G 105
Corncrake Rd. DY3: Lwr G 6E 74
Corndon Cl. DY11: Kidd 7H 157
Cornel B77: Amin 6F 32
Cornel Cl. B37: Chel W 1J 125
Cornelius St. CV3: Cov 1D 174
Corner Ho., The
CV32: Lea S 8M 217
(off Windsor St.)
Corner La. B97: Redd 7L 211
Cornerstone B13: Mose 6M 121
Cornerstone Country Club
B31: N'fld 4B 142
Cornerstone Ho. CV1: Cov 1E 6
Cornerway B38: K Nor 2F 164
CORNETS END 3H 149
Cornets End La. CV7: Mer 1E 148
Cornfield LE10: Hinc 5J 69
WV8: Pend 8L 21
Cornfield, The CV3: Cov 8J 153
Cornfield Av. B60: Stoke H 3K 209
Cornfield Cl. DY6: W Hth 1G 95
Cornfield Cft. B37: Chel W 6K 105
B76: Walm 6M 59
Cornfield Dr. WS14: Lich 1L 19
Cornfield Pl. *B65: Row R 5M 97*
(off Allsops Cl.)
Cornfield Rd. B31: N'fld 5B 142
B65: Row R 5M 97
B76: Walm 8M 59
Cornflower Cl. WV10: F'stne 2G 23
Cornflower Cres. DY2: Dud 1M 97
Corn Flower Dr. CV23: Brow 1D 180
Cornflower Rd. WS8: Clay 3D 26
Corngreaves, The
B34: S End 3C 104
Corngreaves Rd. B64: Crad H 8K 97
Corngreaves Trad. Est.
B64: Crad H 2K 117
Corngreaves Wlk.
B64: Crad H 2L 117
Cornhampton Cl. B97: Redd 4B 212
Corn Hill WS5: Wals 1E 56
WV10: Wolv 7D 36 (4L 7)
Cornhill WS11: Hunt 4E 8
Cornhill Gro. B30: Stir 3J 143
CV8: Ken 4J 199
Cornish Cl. CV10: Ans C 1M 87
Cornish Cres. CV10: Nun 7G 89
Corn Mdws. CV12: Bed 7J 111
Corn Mill Cl. B32: Bart G 8L 119
B76: Walm 8M 59
WS1: Wals 2K 55
Cornmill Gdns. B60: B'wll 4G 189
Cornmill Gro. WV6: Pert 6D 34
Cornovian Cl. WV6: Pert 4E 34
Corns Gro. WV5: Wom 4F 72
Corns Ho. *WS10: Darl 3E 54*
(off Birmingham St.)
Corns St. WS10: Darl 4E 54
Cornwall Av. B68: O'bry 1H 119
B78: Tam 8A 32
DY11: Kidd 8J 135

Cornwall Cl.—Cranmore Rd.

Cornwall Cl. CV34: Warw 8F 216
DY6: K'wfrd 1L 95
WS9: A'rdge 8G 27
WS10: W'bry 6K 55
Cornwall Ga. WV12: W'hall 4B 38
Cornwall Ho. B90: Bly P 6M 167
CV32: Lea S 8K 217
Cornwallis Rd. B70: W Brom ...8G 77
CV22: Bil 8H 179
Cornwall Pl. CV32: Lea S 8K 217
WS2: Wals 6E 38
Cornwall Rd. B20: Hand 7F 78
B45: Fran 8E 140
B66: Smeth 2B 100
CV1: Cov 8E 152 (7F 6)
DY8: Woll 1K 115
WS5: Wals 2B 56
WS12: Hed 4H 9
WV6: Tett 5J 35
Cornwall Rd. Ind. Est.
B66: Smeth 2B 100
Cornwall St. B3: Birm ...6K 101 (4E 4)
Cornwall Twr. B18: Hock 4H 101
Cornwall Way LE10: Hinc 5L 69
Cornwell Cl. B98: Redd 4H 221
DY4: Tip 4A 76
Cornyx La. B91: Sol 3D 146
Coronation Av. B78: M Oak 8K 31
B78: Pole 2L 49
WV13: W'hall 7D 38
Coronation Ct. CV11: Nun 5H 89
Coronation Cres. B79: Shut 2M 33
Coronation Rd. B8: Salt 3F 102
B29: S Oak 7F 120
B43: Gt Barr 5E 56
CV1: Cov 5F 152
CV9: Hurl 5J 63
CV23: Chu L 5B 178
DY4: Tip 1A 76
LE9: Earl S 3D 70
WS4: S'fld 7B 26
WS9: Wals W 6G 27
WS10: W'bry 6J 55
WV10: Wolv 4G 37
WV14: Bils 4J 53
Coronation St. B79: Tam 4A 32
Coronation Ter. B60: B'gve 2B 210
Coronation Wlk. CV10: Nun 3J 89
Coronation Way DY10: Kidd ...4B 158
Coronel Av. CV6: Longf 5E 130
Corporation Rd. DY2: Dud 7L 75
Corporation Sq.
B4: Birm 6L 101 (4H 5)
Corporation St.
B2: Birm 7L 101 (5G 5)
(not continuous)
B4: Birm 5L 101
B79: Tam 4B 32
CV1: Cov 7C 152 (5B 6)
(not continuous)
CV11: Nun 4H 89
(not continuous)
CV21: Rugby 6A 180
DY10: Kidd 4L 157
WS1: Wals 1L 55
WS10: W'bry 7G 55
WV1: Wolv 7C 36 (4H 7)
Corporation St. W.
WS1: Wals 1K 55
Correen B77: Wiln 7J 33
Corrie Cft. B26: Sheld 2B 124
B32: Bart G 1H 141
Corrie Ho. CV1: Cov 5A 6
Corrin Gro. DY6: W Hth 1J 95
Corron Hill *B63: Hale 5B 118*
(off Cobham Rd.)
Corsers Ct. WV6: Pert 5E 34
Corser St. DY1: Dud 7F 74
DY8: Stourb 6A 116
WV1: Wolv 8F 36
Corsican Cl. WS7: C Ter 1G 17
WV12: W'hall 2E 38
Corsican Dr. WS12: Hed 1G 9
Corston M. CV31: Lea S 3C 224
Cort Dr. WS7: Burn 1H 17
Corunna Rd. CV34: Warw 2C 222
Corvedale Rd. B29: W Cas 3A 142
Corve Gdns. WV6: Tett 4L 35
Corve Vw. DY3: Sed 8C 52
Corville Gdns. B26: Sheld 5C 124
Corville Rd. B62: Quin 3F 118
Corwen Cft. B31: N'fld 3L 141
Cory Cft. DY4: Tip 4A 76
COSELEY 1J 75
Coseley Baths 8K 53
Coseley Hall WV14: Cose 1J 75
Coseley Leisure Cen. 8H 53
Coseley Rd. WV14: Bils 4J 53
Coseley Station (Rail) 8J 53
Cosford Cl. B98: Redd 8M 213
CV32: Lill 6B 218
Cosford Ct. WV6: Pert 4E 34
Cosford Cres. B35: Cas V 6A 82
Cosford Dr. DY2: Neth 5L 97
Cosford La. CV21: Rugby 1A 180
Cosgrove Wlk. WV8: Pend 8M 21
Cossington Rd. B23: Erd 2D 80
Costard Av. CV34: H'cte 6L 223
Costers La. B98: Redd 6M 213
Costock Cl. B37: Mars G 1H 125
Cote La. DY7: Stourt 1A 114
Coten End CV34: Warw 2F 222
Cotes Rd. LE10: Burb 4M 91
Cotford Rd. B14: K Hth 7A 144
Cotheridge Cl. B90: M'path 3C 168
Cot La. DY6: K'wfrd 3J 95
DY8: Word 4J 95
Cotleigh Gro. B43: Gt Barr 6L 57
Cotman Cl. B43: Gt Barr 6J 57
CV12: Bed 5G 111
Cotman Dr. LE10: Hinc 6G 69
COTON 2K 31
Coton Grn. Pct. B79: Tam 2M 31
Coton Gro. B90: Shir 7E 144
Coton La. B23: Erd 5F 80
B79: Tam 2K 31
COTON LAWN 7E 88
Coton Rd. B46: Neth W 8D 62
B76: Lea M, Mars 6B 62
CV11: Nun 5J 89
CV21: Hillm 1G 207
WV4: Penn 4B 52
Cotsdale Rd. WV4: Penn 6L 51
Cotsford B91: Sol 6A 146
Cotswold Av. DY13: Stour S ...8D 182
WS6: Gt Wyr 6F 14
Cotswold Cl. B45: Fran 7H 141
B69: O'bry 4E 98
DY11: Kidd 7J 157
WS9: A'rdge 8J 27
Cotswold Cres. CV10: Nun 6B 88
Cotswold Cft. B63: Hale 8J 117
Cotswold Dr. CV3: Finh 6C 174
Cotswold Gro. WV12: W'hall 8B 24
Cotswold Rd. DY8: Amb 3B 116
WS12: Hed 1G 9
WV2: E'shll 2F 52
Cotswold Way B61: B'gve 4A 188
Cotsworld Cl. WS12: Hed 1G 9
Cotsworld Ct. *WV2: Wolv 3B 52*
(off Goldthorn Hill)
Cottage Cl. CV31: Lea S 3C 224
WS7: Chase 4F 16
WS12: Hed 4K 9
WV11: Wed 3J 37
(not continuous)
Cottage Ct. WS7: Chase 4F 16
Cottage Dr. B60: Marl 8D 162
Cottage Farm La. B60: Marl ...7C 162
Cottage Farm Lodge
CV6: Cov 8A 130
Cottage Farm Rd.
B77: Two G 2D 46
CV6: Cov 8A 130
Cottage Gdns. B45: Rubery 4F 162
LE9: Earl S 1F 70
Cottage La. B46: Neth W 3D 84
B60: Marl 7C 162
B76: Min 3D 82
WS7: Chase 4F 16
WV10: F'hses 6D 22
Cottage Leap CV21: Rugby 5D 180
Cottage M. WS9: A'rdge 5L 41
Cottage Sq. CV31: Lea S 3C 224
Cottage St. DY5: Brie H 6D 96
DY6: K'wfrd 2K 95
Cottage Vw. WV8: Bilb 5H 21
Cottage Wlk. B70: W Brom 7K 77
B77: Wiln 3F 46
Cotterell Rd. CV21: N'bld A ...3M 179
COTTERIDGE 5E 142
Cotteridge Rd. B30: K Nor 5G 143
Cotterills Av. B8: W End 5J 103
Cotterills Cl. CV31: W'nsh 6B 224
Cotterills La. B8: W End 5G 103
Cotterills Rd. DY4: Tip 2B 76
Cottesbrook Cl. CV3: Bin 8L 153
Cottesbrook Rd. B27: A Grn 5K 123
Cottesfield Cl. B8: W End 5H 103
Cottesmore Cl. B71: W Brom ...1M 77
Cottesmore Ho. B20: Hand 7F 78
Cottle Cl. WS2: Wals 6F 38
Cotton Ct. LE9: Earl S 1F 70
Cotton Dr. CV8: Ken 3J 199
Cotton Gro. WS12: Hed 1G 9
Cotton La. B13: Mose 7M 121
Cotton M. LE9: Earl S 2F 70
Cotton Mill Spinney
CV32: Cubb 3E 218
Cotton Pk. Dr. CV23: Brow 1C 180
Cotton Pool Rd. B61: B'gve 7L 187
Cotton Way WS7: C Ter 8F 10
Cottrells Cl. B14: Yard W 5C 144
Cottrells M. B46: Wat O 7H 83
Cottrell St. B71: W Brom 5K 77
Cottsmeadow Dr. B8: W End 5J 103
COTWALL END 2C 74
Cotwall End Countryside Cen.
.......................3C 74
Cotwall End Rd.
DY3: Lwr G, Sed 5B 74
Cotysmore Rd. B75: S Cold 3K 59
Couchman Rd. B8: Salt 5E 102
Coughton Cl. CV11: Nun 2M 111
Coughton Dr. CV31: Lea S 4D 224
Coulson Cl. WS7: C Ter 8D 10
Coulter Gro. WV6: Pert 5D 34
Coulter La. WS7: Burn 1L 17
(not continuous)
Council Cres. WV12: W'hall 5C 38
Council Rd. LE10: Hinc 8K 69
COUNDON 3M 151
Coundon Grn. CV6: Cov 2L 151
Coundon Rd. CV1: Cov 5B 152
Coundon St.
CV1: Cov 5B 152 (3A 6)
Coundon Wedge Dr.
CV5: Alle 8K 129
Counterfield Dr. B65: Row R ...4M 97
Countess Cft., The CV3: Cov ...2D 174
Countess Dr. WS4: Rus 2D 40
Countess Rd. CV11: Nun 5G 89
Countess St. WS1: Wals 2K 55
Counting Ho. Way
B60: Stoke H 3L 209
COUNTY BRIDGE 7D 38
County Cl. B30: Stir 3H 143
B32: Bart G 6J 119
County Dr. B78: Tam 7A 32
County La. DY8: I'ley 1K 137
WV7: Alb 4A 20
WV8: Cod W 4A 20
County Pk. Av. B62: Hale 6C 118
Court, The B93: Know 4B 170
Courtaulds Ind. Est.
CV6: Cov 3D 152
Courtaulds Way CV6: Cov 3D 152
Court Cl. CV33: Bis T 8D 224
DY11: Kidd 8H 135
Court Cres. DY6: K'wfrd 4H 95
Court Dr. DY13: Stour S 5F 182
WS14: Shens 4F 28
Courtenay Gdns. B43: Gt Barr ..7E 56
Courtenay Rd. B44: Gt Barr 2L 79
Court Farm Rd. B23: Erd 3E 80
Court Farm Way B29: W Cas ...2M 141
Courthouse Cft. CV8: Ken 5J 199
COURT HOUSE GREEN 1G 153
Courtland Av. CV6: Cov 4M 151
Courtland Rd. DY6: K'wfrd 1L 95
Courtlands, The WV6: Wolv 5L 35
Courtlands Cl. B5: Edg 3J 121
Court La. B23: Erd 1E 80
Court Leet CV3: Bin W 2D 176
Court Leet Rd. CV3: Cov 2E 174
Courtney Cl. CV11: Nun 2M 89
Court Oak Gro. B32: Harb 3M 119
Court Oak Rd. B32: Harb 3L 119
Court Pde. WS9: A'rdge 3H 41
Court Pas. DY1: Dud 8J 75
Court Rd. B11: S'hll 5C 122
B12: Bal H 3L 121
WV4: E'shll 6G 53
WV6: Wolv 5M 35
Court St. B64: Old H 8M 97
CV31: Lea S 2A 224
DY8: Stourb 4A 116
Court Way WS2: Wals 7L 39
Courtway Av. B14: K Hth 8B 144
Courtway Ho. B29: S Oak 8C 120
Court Yd., The *B70: W Brom ...6G 77*
(off Hambletts Rd.)
Courtyard, The B46: Col 7M 83
B91: Sol 5C 146
CV8: Ken 5J 199
CV34: Warw 3F 222
Coveley Gro. B18: Hock 4G 101
Coven Cl. WS3: Pels 4A 26
Coven Gro. B29: S Oak 7B 120
COVEN HEATH 3D 22
Coven La. WV9: Coven 4M 21
COVEN LAWN 1B 22
COVENTRY 7C 152 (5C 6)
Coventry Airpark
CV3: W'hall 8H 175
Coventry Airport 7G 175
Coventry Bus. Pk. CV5: Cov ...8K 151
(Elliott Ct.)
CV5: Cov 8J 151
(Renown Av.)
Coventry Canal Basin
CV1: Cov 2C 6
Coventry Cathedral 6D 152 (4D 6)
Coventry City Farm 5E 152 (2F 6)
Coventry City FC 6F 152
Coventry Eastern By-Pass
CV2: W'grve S 4B 154
CV3: Bin 6A 154
CV3: Bin W 5K 175
CV3: W'hall 5K 175
Coventry Golf Course 7D 174
Coventry Highway
B98: Redd 5F 212
Coventry Point
CV1: Cov 7C 152 (5B 6)
Coventry Rd.
B10: Small H 8A 102 (8M 5)
B25: Yard 2G 123
B26: Yard, Sheld 3L 123
B46: Col 6A 106
B46: Neth W 5D 62
B78: K'bry 5D 62
B92: Bick 6G 125
CV7: Ald G 2M 131
CV7: Berk 6K 149
CV7: Exh 2G 131
CV7: Fill 6E 108
CV8: Bag 6E 174
CV8: Ken 3F 198
CV8: S'lgh 3C 200
CV8: Stare 3C 200
CV10: Griff, Nun 4H 111
CV11: Nun 2J 111
Coventry Rd. CV12: Bed 8H 111
CV22: Caw 4C 204
CV22: Dunc 5F 204
CV23: Brin 6H 155
CV23: Chu L 3L 177
CV23: Dunc, Thurl 4C 204
(not continuous)
CV23: Long L 5C 178
CV32: Cubb 3E 218
CV34: Guys C, Warw 2F 222
CV47: Sou 3H 225
LE9: Sap 4L 93
LE10: Burb 5L 91
LE10: Hinc 2E 90
LE10: Sharn 4L 93
LE10: Wig P 8E 92
LE10: Wlvy 6K 113
Coventry RUFC 7A 152
Coventry Skydome 7B 152 (5A 6)
Coventry Sports Cen. ...6D 152 (4E 6)
Coventry Stadium 2F 176
Coventry Station (Rail)
...............8C 152 (8B 6)
Coventry St.
B5: Birm 7M 101 (6J 5)
CV2: Cov 5G 153
CV11: Nun 5J 89
DY8: Stourb 4A 116
DY10: Kidd 3L 157
WV14: Shens 7G 37
Coventry Toy Mus., The
...............7D 152 (6E 6)
Coventry Trad. Est.
CV3: W'hall 6J 175
Coventry Transport Mus.
...............6C 152 (3C 6)
Coventry University
Caradoc Hall 2K 153
Lanchester Gallery
...............7D 152 (5E 6)
Library 7E 152 (5F 6)
Performing Arts 5L 173
Priory St. 6D 152 (4D 6)
Sports Cen. 6E 152 (4F 6)
Coventry University Technology Pk.
CV1: Cov 8D 152 (7D 6)
(Puma Way)
CV1: Cov 8D 152 (8D 6)
(Quinton Rd.)
Cove Pl. CV2: Cov 2J 153
Cover Cft. B76: Walm 8A 60
Coverdale Rd. B92: Olton 5A 124
Coverley Pl. CV22: Rugby 6L 179
Covers, The B80: Stud 3L 221
Covers La. DY7: Stourt 8E 94
Covert, The WV8: Pend 8L 21
Covert La. DY8: Stourb 8K 115
WS15: Cann W 5F 10
Covey Cl. WS13: Lich 8K 13
Cowan Cl. CV22: Bil 8J 179
Cowdray Cl. CV31: Lea S 2C 224
Cow La. B78: What 6F 46
Cowles Cft. B25: Yard 8L 103
Cowley B77: Glas 7E 32
Cowley Cl. B36: Cas B 8F 82
Cowley Dr. B27: A Grn 5K 123
DY1: Dud 7F 74
Cowley Grn. WS12: Hed 1F 8
Cowley Gro. B11: Tys 4E 122
Cowley Rd. B11: Tys 4E 122
CV2: Cov 5K 153
Cowley Way CV23: Kils 7M 207
Cowper Cl. CV34: Warw 8F 216
WV12: W'hall 2E 38
Cowper Rd. LE10: Burb 3K 91
Cowper Wlk. DY10: Kidd 3C 158
Cowslip Cl. B29: W Cas 2A 142
B38: K Nor 1F 164
Cowslip Wlk. DY5: Brie H 3C 116
Cox Cres. CV22: Dunc 5J 205
Coxcroft Av. DY5: Quar B 1F 116
Coxmoor Cl. WS3: Blox 6F 24
Cox Rd. WV14: Cose 8L 53
Coxs Cl. CV10: Nun 6H 89
Cox's La. B64: Old H 7M 97
Cox's Orchard CV31: W'nsh 5A 224
Cox St. B3: Birm 5K 101 (2E 4)
CV1: Cov 7D 152 (5E 6)
(Gosford St.)
CV1: Cov 6D 152 (3E 6)
(White St.)
Coxwell Av. WV10: Wolv 3C 36
Coxwell Gdns. B16: Birm 7F 100
Coyne Cl. DY4: Tip 4K 75
Coyne Rd. B70: W Brom 7H 77
Cozens Cl. CV12: Bed 5G 111
Crabbe St. DY9: Lye 4F 116
CRABBS CROSS 3D 220
Crabbs Cross La. B97: Redd ...4D 220
Crab La. DY6: K'wfrd 5A 96
WS11: Cann 6G 9
WV12: W'hall 8D 24
Crabmill Cl. B38: K Nor 2E 164
B93: Know 2J 169
Crabmill La. B38: Head H 2J 165
CV6: Cov 2F 152
Crabourne Rd. DY2: Neth 7H 97
Crabtree Cl. B31: N'fld 7C 142
B71: W Brom 1M 77
B98: Redd 7G 213
DY9: Hag 3B 138
Crabtree Ct. B61: B'gve 6L 187
Crabtree Dr. B37: F'bri 7F 104
B61: B'gve 6M 187
Crabtree Gro. CV31: Lea S 3C 224
Crab Tree Ho. B33: Stech 6L 103
Crabtree La. B61: B'gve 5L 187
Crabtree Rd. B18: Hock 4G 101
LE9: Barw 4M 69
WS1: Wals 7A 40
CRACKLEY 2H 199
Crackley Cotts. CV8: Ken 1H 199
Crackley Cres. CV8: Ken 1H 199
Crackley Hill CV8: Ken 2H 199
Crackley La. CV8: Ken 5E 172
Crackley Way DY2: Dud 3G 97
Crackthorne Dr. CV23: Brow ...1D 180
Craddock Ct. CV10: Nun 2C 88
Craddock Dr. CV10: Nun 2C 88
Craddock Rd. B67: Smeth 3L 99
Craddock St. WV6: Wolv 5A 36
CRADLEY 2J 117
Cradley Cl. B98: Redd 8M 213
Cradley Cft. B21: Hand 6C 78
Cradley Flds. B63: Crad 4J 117
Cradley Forge DY5: Quar B 1G 117
CRADLEY HEATH 8L 97
Cradley Heath Factory Cen.
B64: Crad H 1J 117
Cradley Heath Station (Rail)
.......................1H 117
Cradley Leisure Cen. 2H 117
Cradley Mill DY5: Quar B 2F 116
Cradley Pk. Rd. DY2: Neth 7J 97
Cradley Rd. B64: Crad H 1J 117
DY2: Neth 5K 97
Cradock Rd. B8: Salt 4E 102
Craig Cl. CV31: Lea S 3B 224
Craig Cft. B37: Chel W 7K 105
Craigends Av. CV3: Bin 3M 175
Crail Gro. B43: Gt Barr 5H 57
Crakston Cl. CV2: Cov 7L 153
Cramlington Rd. B42: Gt Barr ..1G 79
Crammond Cl. LE10: Hinc 1H 91
Crampers Fld. CV6: Cov 4A 152
Cramp Hill WS10: Darl 3D 54
Cranberry Dr. DY13: Stour S ...5E 182
Cranborne Chase
CV2: W'grve S 4M 153
Cranbourne Av. WV4: E'shll 6E 52
Cranbourne Cl. B45: Fran 7G 141
Cranbourne Gro. B44: K'sdng ...1A 80
Cranbourne Pl. B71: W Brom ...5K 77
Cranbourne Rd. B44: K'sdng 1A 80
DY8: Stourb 5A 116
Cranbrook Ct. *WV13: W'hall 7C 38*
(off Mill St.)
Cranbrook Gro. WV6: Pert 6F 34
Cranbrook Rd. B21: Hand 8C 78
Cranby St. B8: Salt 4C 102
Craneberry Rd. B37: F'bri 7E 104
Cranebrook Hill B78: Hints 4E 44
Cranebrook La.
WS14: Hilt, Lynn 8A 18
Crane Cl. CV34: Warw 8D 216
Crane Ct. WS1: Wals 6A 40
Crane Dr. WS7: Chase 5G 17
Crane Flds. WS13: Lich 8G 13
Crane Hollow WS5: Wom 4E 72
Cranehouse Rd. B44: K'sdng 7B 58
Cranemoor Cl. B7: Nech 3C 102
Crane Rd. WV14: Bils 6M 53
Craner's Rd. CV1: Cov 5F 152
Cranesbill Cl. WV10: F'stne 2J 23
Cranesbill Rd. B29: W Cas 3A 142
Cranes Pk. Rd. B26: Sheld 4C 124
Crane St. DY11: Kidd 3J 157
Crane Ter. WV6: Tett 4L 35
Cranfield Gro. B26: Yard 1M 123
Cranfield Pl. WS5: Wals 5M 55
Cranfield Rd. WS7: C Ter 2G 17
Cranford Gro. B91: Sol 8B 146
Cranford Rd. CV5: Cov 5K 151
WV3: Wolv 1J 51
Cranford St. B66: Smeth 4C 100
Cranford Way B66: Smeth 4C 100
Cranham Cl. B97: Redd 1B 220
Cranham Dr. DY6: K'wfrd 4L 95
Cranhill Cl. B92: Olton 8B 124
Crankhall La. B71: W Brom 6H 55
WS10: W'bry 6H 55
Cranleigh Cl. WS9: A'rdge 4H 41
WV12: W'hall 8C 24
Cranleigh Ho. B23: Erd 3F 80
Cranleigh Pl. B44: P Barr 4L 79
Cranleigh Way WS14: Lich 2L 19
Cranley Dr. WV8: Cod 5F 20
Cranmer Av. WV12: W'hall 2D 38
Cranmer Cl. WS6: C Hay 8D 14
Cranmere Av. WV6: Tett 3G 35
Cranmere Ct. WV6: Tett 3G 35
Cranmer Gro. B74: Four O 3F 42
CV34: H'cte 6K 223
Cranmoor Cres. B63: Hale 4A 118
Cranmore Av. B21: Hand 2D 100
B90: Shir 1L 167
Cranmore Blvd. B90: Shir 1K 167
Cranmore Cl. DY4: Tip 1A 76
Cranmore Dr. B90: Shir 8L 145
Cranmore Rd. B36: Cas B 8D 82
B90: Shir 1K 167
WV3: Wolv 6M 35

Cransley Gro.—Curtis Cl.

Cransley Gro. B91: Sol . . . 8A **146**
Crantock Cl. WV11: Ess . . . 8C **24**
Crantock Rd. B42: P Barr . . . 5J **79**
Crantock Way CV11: Nun . . . 5M **89**
Cranwell Grn. WV5: Wom . . . 4F **72**
Cranwell Gro. B24: Erd . . . 6K **81**
Cranwell Ri. B78: M Oak . . . 8J **31**
Cranwell Way B35: Cas V . . . 6A **82**
Crathie Cl. CV2: Cov . . . 3M **153**
Crathorne Av. WV10: Oxl . . . 8C **22**
Crauford Ct. DY8: Stourb . . . 6A **116**
Crauford St. DY8: Stourb . . . 6A **116**
Craven B77: Wiln . . . 8G **33**
Craven Av. CV3: Bin W . . . 2C **176**
Craven Ct. *CV47: Sou . . . 5H 225*
(off Craven La.)
Craven Hgts. B92: H Ard . . . 2A **148**
Craven La. CV47: Sou . . . 5H **225**
Craven Rd. CV21: Rugby . . . 5B **180**
Craven St. CV5: Cov . . . 7M **151**
WV2: E'shll . . . 3F **52**
Crawford Av. B67: Smeth . . . 4M **99**
WS10: Darl . . . 2C **54**
WV4: E'shll . . . 6F **52**
Crawford Cl. CV32: Lill . . . 4B **218**
Crawford Rd. B76: Walm . . . 1M **81**
WV3: Wolv . . . 7A **36**
Crawford St. B8: Salt . . . 5C **102**
Crawley Wlk. B64: Crad H . . . 8K **97**
Crawshaws Rd. B36: Cas B . . . 8C **82**
Crayford Rd. B44: K'sdng . . . 8A **58**
Craythorne Av. B20: Hand . . . 4E **78**
Crecy Cl. B76: Walm . . . 5L **59**
Crecy Rd. CV3: Cov . . . 2E **174**
Credenda Rd. B70: W Brom . . . 8G **77**
Crediton Cl. CV11: Nun . . . 4M **89**
Credon Gro. B15: Edg . . . 5F **120**
Cregoe St. B15: Birm . . . 8J **101** (8D **4**)
Cremore Av. B8: Salt . . . 4E **102**
Cremorne Rd. B75: Four O . . . 7H **43**
Cremorne Wlk. B75: Four O . . . 7H **43**
Crendon Cl. B80: Stud . . . 4L **221**
Crendon Rd. B65: Row R . . . 3A **98**
Crescent, The B18: Hock . . . 3H **101**
B37: Mars G . . . 1L **125**
B43: Gt Barr . . . 8G **57**
(Handsworth Dr.)
B43: Gt Barr . . . 6K **57**
(King's Rd.)
B46: Wat O . . . 6H **83**
B60: B'gve . . . 8M **187**
B64: Crad H . . . 2A **118**
B65: Row R . . . 7B **98**
B90: Shir . . . 5G **145**
B91: Sol . . . 5B **146**
B92: H Ard . . . 2B **148**
CV7: Ker E . . . 3M **129**
CV9: Bad E . . . 6C **48**
CV23: Brin . . . 5M **155**
CV23: Law H . . . 3C **204**
DY1: Dud . . . 5L **75**
DY8: Hag . . . 4M **137**
DY9: Lye . . . 5C **116**
DY10: Cookl . . . 5B **136**
DY11: Kidd . . . 1M **183**
LE9: Elme . . . 4D **70**
WS1: Wals . . . 1A **56**
WS6: Gt Wyr . . . 7G **15**
WS7: C Ter . . . 8F **10**
WS10: W'bry . . . 5G **55**
WV6: Tett . . . 6H **35**
WV13: W'hall . . . 8C **38**
WV14: Bils . . . 4M **53**
Crescent Arc. *B91: Sol . . . 6C 146*
(off Touchwood Shop. Cen.)
Crescent Av. CV3: Cov . . . 7J **153**
DY5: Brie H . . . 7C **96**
Crescent Ho. *B97: Redd . . . 7D 212*
(off Mt. Pleasant)
Crescent Ind. Pk. DY2: Dud . . . 2H **97**
Crescent, The (MM) . . . 3K **53**
Crescent Rd. DY2: Neth . . . 4H **97**
DY11: Kidd . . . 3J **157**
WS10: Darl . . . 3D **54**
WV13: W'hall . . . 7C **38**
Crescent Studios B18: Hock . . . 3G **101**
Crescent Theatre . . . 7H **101** (6B **4**)
Crescent Twr. B1: Birm . . . 5C **4**
Cressage Av. B31: N'fld . . . 8A **142**
Cressage Rd. CV2: W'grve S . . . 3A **154**
Cressett Av. DY5: Brie H . . . 5B **96**
Cressett La. DY5: Brie H . . . 5C **96**
Cressida Cl. CV34: H'cte . . . 6M **223**
Cressington Dr. B74: Four O . . . 8G **43**
Cresswell Cl. CV10: Nun . . . 1J **89**
Cresswell Ct. WV9: Pend . . . 6A **22**
Cresswell Cres. WS3: Blox . . . 7F **24**
Cresswell Gro. B24: Erd . . . 5K **81**
Crest, The B31: Longb . . . 2B **164**
CV32: Lill . . . 6C **218**
Crest Vw. B14: K Hth . . . 5B **144**
B74: S'tly . . . 1M **57**
Crestwood B77: Amin . . . 4G **33**
Crestwood Av. DY11: Kidd . . . 4G **157**
Crestwood Dr. B44: Gt Barr . . . 2L **79**
Crestwood Glen WV6: Tett . . . 2L **35**
CRESWELL GREEN . . . 8L **11**
Creswell Rd. B28: Hall G . . . 2H **145**
Creswick Gro. B45: Redn . . . 2J **163**
Crew La. CV8: Ken . . . 3J **199**
Crew Rd. WS10: W'bry . . . 5G **55**
Creynolds Cl. B90: Ches G . . . 6K **167**
Creynolds La. B90: Ches G . . . 6K **167**
Cricket Cl. CV5: Cov . . . 6M **151**
WS5: Wals . . . 2B **56**
Cricketers Mdw.
B64: Crad H . . . 2L **117**
Cricket La. WS14: Lich . . . 5J **19**
Cricket Mdw. DY3: Up Gor . . . 4E **74**
WV10: F'hses . . . 5D **22**
Cricket St. B70: W Brom . . . 2F **76**
Crick La. B20: Hand . . . 1G **101**
Cricklewood Dr. B62: Hale . . . 6D **118**
Crick Rd. CV21: Hillm . . . 1H **207**
CV23: Kils . . . 1H **207**
Crigdon B77: Wiln . . . 7J **33**
Crimmond Ri. B63: Hale . . . 4L **117**
Crimscote Cl. B90: M'path . . . 3M **167**
Cringlebrook B77: Wiln . . . 8D **32**
Cripps Rd. WS2: Wals . . . 6E **38**
Critchley Dr. CV22: Dunc . . . 6K **205**
Criterion Works
WV13: W'hall . . . 1B **54**
Crocketts Av. B21: Hand . . . 2D **100**
Crockett's La. B66: Smeth . . . 4A **100**
Crocketts Rd. B21: Hand . . . 2C **100**
Crockett St. DY1: Dud . . . 7G **75**
Crockford Dr. B75: Four O . . . 6H **43**
Crockford Rd. B71: W Brom . . . 8J **55**
Crockington La.
WV5: Seis, Try . . . 7A **50**
Crocus Cres. WV9: Pend . . . 6A **22**
Croft, The B31: N'fld . . . 6B **142**
CV6: Longf . . . 5F **130**
CV7: Mer . . . 8J **127**
CV12: Bulk . . . 7B **112**
DY2: Dud . . . 3F **96**
DY3: Sed . . . 8E **52**
DY10: Blak . . . 7J **137**
DY11: Kidd . . . 5G **157**
WS5: Wals . . . 1E **56**
WS6: C Hay . . . 7E **14**
WV5: Wom . . . 4D **72**
WV12: W'hall . . . 3D **38**
Croft Apartments
WV13: W'hall . . . 7A 38
(off Croft St.)
Croft Av. B79: Tam . . . 3B **32**
WS12: Hed . . . 1G **9**
Croft Cl. B25: Yard . . . 1L **123**
B98: Redd . . . 6K **213**
CV23: Stret D . . . 3F **202**
CV33: Bis T . . . 8E **224**
CV34: Warw . . . 2J **223**
LE9: Barw . . . 3B **70**
LE10: Wlvy . . . 5L **113**
Croft Ct. B36: Cas B . . . 1B **104**
Croft Cres. WS8: Bwnhls . . . 2D **26**
Cft. Down Rd. B92: Sol . . . 5D **124**
Croftdown Rd. B17: Harb . . . 3M **119**
Crofters Cl. DY8: Stourb . . . 5B **116**
Crofters Ct. B15: Edg . . . 3E **120**
Crofters La. B75: R'ley . . . 6L **43**
Crofters Wlk. WV8: Pend . . . 8L **21**
Croft Flds. CV12: Bed . . . 7H **111**
Croft Gdns. WS7: C Ter . . . 1G **17**
Croft Ho. *WS1: Wals . . . 8M 39*
(off Paddock La.)
Croft Ind. Est. B37: Chel W . . . 7K **105**
WV13: W'hall . . . 7A **38**
Croft La. WV10: Bush . . . 2G **37**
(not continuous)
Croftleigh Gdns. B91: Sol . . . 7L **145**
Croft Mead CV10: Ansl . . . 6J **87**
Croft Pde. WS9: A'rdge . . . 3K **41**
Croft Pool CV12: Bed . . . 7F **110**
Croft Rd. B26: Yard . . . 1L **123**
CV1: Cov . . . 7B **152** (5A **6**)
CV9: Ath . . . 8K **49**
CV10: Nun . . . 7E **88**
CV12: Bed . . . 7F **110**
CV35: Leek W . . . 2G **217**
LE9: Thurl . . . 1M **71**
Crofts, The B76: Walm . . . 2A **82**
Crofts La. B96: A'wd B . . . 7A **220**
Croft St. B79: Tam . . . 3B **32**
WS2: Wals . . . 6K **39**
WV13: W'hall . . . 7A **38**
(not continuous)
Croftway, The B20: Hand . . . 3E **78**
Croftwood Rd. DY9: W'cte . . . 5D **116**
Cromane Sq. B43: Gt Barr . . . 2E **78**
Cromarty Cl. CV5: E Grn . . . 5G **151**
Cromarty Dr. LE10: Hinc . . . 8F **68**
Cromdale B77: Wiln . . . 8J **33**
Cromdale Cl. CV10: Nun . . . 6A **88**
Cromdale Dr. B63: Hale . . . 6K **117**
Cromer Gdns. WV6: Wolv . . . 4M **35**
Crome Rd. B43: Gt Barr . . . 6K **57**
Cromer Rd. B12: Bal H . . . 4M **121**
CV32: Lill . . . 7B **218**
Cromes Wood CV4: Tile H . . . 8D **150**
Crompton Av. B20: Hand . . . 8J **79**
Crompton Cl. WS2: Wals . . . 4G **39**
Crompton Ct. WV8: Bilb . . . 5H **21**
Crompton Rd. B7: Nech . . . 1C **102**
B20: Hand . . . 8J **79**
B45: Fran . . . 8D **140**
DY4: Tip . . . 5A **76**
Crompton St. CV34: Warw . . . 3D **222**
Cromwell Cl. B65: Row R . . . 4M **97**
WS2: Wals . . . 5E **38**
Cromwell Ct. WS6: Gt Wyr . . . 8G **15**
Cromwell Dr. DY2: Dud . . . 1M **97**
Cromwell La. B31: N'fld . . . 1K **141**
CV4: Tile H, W'wd H . . . 3C **172**
CV8: Burt G . . . 5B **172**
Cromwell Rd. B79: Tam . . . 1L **31**
CV22: Rugby . . . 8C **180**
WS12: Hth H . . . 8L **9**
WV10: Bush . . . 6E **22**
Cromwells Mdw. WS14: Lich . . . 4J **19**
Cromwell St. B7: Nech . . . 4B **102**
B71: W Brom . . . 5J **77**
CV6: Cov . . . 3F **152**
DY2: Dud . . . 1L **97**
Crondal Pl. B15: Edg . . . 2H **121**
Crondal Rd. CV7: Exh . . . 1H **131**
CRONEHILLS, THE . . . 6J **77**
Cronehills Linkway
B70: W Brom . . . 5K **77**
Cronehills St. B70: W Brom . . . 6K **77**
Crooked Ho. La.
DY3: Gorn, Himl . . . 7M **73**
Crookham Cl. B17: Harb . . . 2M **119**
Crookhay La. B71: W Brom . . . 1G **77**
Crook Ho. Yd. CV23: Brin . . . 5M **155**
Crook La. WS9: A'rdge . . . 2G **57**
Crooks La. B80: Stud . . . 5K **221**
Crooks La. Bus. Pk.
B80: Stud . . . 5K **221**
Croome Cl. B11: S'hll . . . 6B **122**
B98: Redd . . . 8M **213**
CV6: Cov . . . 5M **151**
Cropredy Rd. B31: Longb . . . 1A **164**
Cropthorne Cl. B98: Redd . . . 2G **221**
Cropthorne Dr. B47: H'wd . . . 2B **166**
Cropthorne Ho. *B60: B'gve . . . 6B 188*
(off Burcot La.)
Cropthorne Rd. B90: Shir . . . 6J **145**
Crosbie Rd. B17: Harb . . . 3B **120**
Crosbie Rd. CV5: Cov . . . 6L **151**
Crosby Cl. B1: Birm . . . 6H **101** (4A **4**)
WV6: Wolv . . . 4M **35**
Cross, The DY6: K'wfrd . . . 3K **95**
Cross Cheaping
CV1: Cov . . . 6C **152** (4C **6**)
(not continuous)
Cross Cl. B64: Old H . . . 7M **97**
Cross Farm Ct. LE9: S Stan . . . 7L **71**
Cross Farm Mnr. *B17: Harb . . . 5D 120*
(off Cross Farm Rd.)
Cross Farm Rd. B17: Harb . . . 5C **120**
Cross Farms La.
B45: Rubery . . . 8F **140**
Crossfell B77: Wiln . . . 8H **33**
Crossfield Ind. Est.
WS13: Lich . . . 1L **19**
Crossfield Rd. B33: Kitts G . . . 5B **104**
WS13: Lich . . . 1L **19**
Crossfields Rd. CV34: Warw . . . 1F **222**
Crossgate Rd. B98: Redd . . . 1J **221**
DY2: Dud . . . 3F **96**
CROSS GREEN . . . 1D **22**
Cross Ho. *WV2: Wolv . . . 2C 52*
(off Blakenhall Gdns.)
Crossings, The WS14: Lich . . . 1L **19**
Crossings Ind. Est., The
WS3: Blox . . . 1H 39
(off Fryer's Rd.)
Cross in Hand La.
WS13: Fare, Lich . . . 5A **12**
(not continuous)
Crosskey Cl. B33: Kitts G . . . 7E **104**
Cross Keys WS13: Lich . . . 1H **19**
Cross Keys M. DY9: Hag . . . 5M **137**
Crosskirk Rd. LE10: Hinc . . . 8F **68**
Crossland Cres. WV6: Tett . . . 3M **35**
Crossland Row LE10: Burb . . . 3A **92**
Cross La. B43: Gt Barr . . . 8E **56**
CV32: Cubb . . . 5E **218**
DY3: Sed . . . 1D **74**
WS14: Foot . . . 8E **28**
WS14: Lich . . . 3K **19**
Crossley Ct. CV6: Cov . . . 2F **152**
Crossley Retail Pk.
DY11: Kidd . . . 2K **157**
Crossley Rd. B60: S Prior . . . 7L **209**
Crossley St. DY2: Neth . . . 5K **97**
Crossley Wlk. B60: B'gve . . . 2L **209**
Cross Pl. DY3: Sed . . . 8E **52**
Cross Point Bus. Pk.
CV2: W'grve S . . . 1B **154**
(Ashcroft Way)
CV2: W'grve S . . . 1B **154**
(Olivier Way)
Cross Quays Ind. Est.
B69: Tiv . . . 7B 76
(off Hallbridge Way)
Cross Rd. CV6: Cov . . . 1E **152**
CV7: Ker E . . . 3M **129**
CV32: Lea S . . . 1K **223**
Cross Rd. Ind. Est.
CV6: Cov . . . 2F **152**
Cross Row WS11: Cann . . . 5F **8**
Cross St. B21: Hand . . . 1C **100**
B63: Hale . . . 6A **118**
B65: B'hth . . . 8C **98**
B66: Smeth . . . 3A **100**
B68: O'bry . . . 5G **99**
B77: Tam . . . 6C **32**
B79: Tam . . . 4B **32**
CV1: Cov . . . 5D **152** (2E **6**)
CV10: Nun . . . 6D **88**
Cross St. CV21: Rugby . . . 5C **180**
CV23: Long L . . . 4G **179**
CV32: Lea S . . . 8A **218**
CV34: Warw . . . 2F **222**
DY1: Dud . . . 8H **75**
DY6: K'wfrd . . . 3K **95**
DY6: W Hth . . . 1H **95**
DY8: Stourb . . . 4L **115**
DY8: Word . . . 6K **95**
WS3: Pels . . . 8A **26**
WS6: C Hay . . . 7D **14**
WS7: C Ter . . . 1E **16**
WS10: Darl . . . 2D **54**
WS10: W'bry . . . 6E **54**
WS11: Cann . . . 4E **14**
WS12: Hth H . . . 8L **9**
WV1: Wolv . . . 8F **36**
WV13: W'hall . . . 8A **38**
WV14: Bils . . . 7L **53**
(not continuous)
Cross St. Nth.
WV1: Wolv . . . 5D **36** (1K **7**)
Cross St. Sth. WV2: Wolv . . . 2C **52**
Cross Wlk. B69: Tiv . . . 1C **98**
B78: Dord . . . 3A **48**
Cross Walks Rd. DY9: Lye . . . 4E **116**
Crossway La. B44: K'sdng . . . 3M **79**
Crossway Rd. CV3: Finh . . . 5B **174**
Crossways LE10: Burb . . . 4M **91**
Crossways Cotts. CV7: Fill . . . 5G **109**
Crossways Ct. B44: K'sdng . . . 2B **80**
Crossways Grn. B44: K'sdng . . . 2B **80**
Crossways Shop. Cen.
WV10: Wolv . . . 6G **37**
Crosswells Rd. B68: O'bry . . . 4H **99**
Crosswell Way WV14: Bils . . . 4L **53**
Crowberry Cl. WS8: Clay . . . 3D **26**
Crowberry La. B78: Midd . . . 8J **45**
Crowden Rd. B77: Wiln . . . 8G **33**
Crowesbridge M.
WV14: Cose . . . 1H **75**
Crowhill Rd. CV11: Nun . . . 7M **89**
Crowhurst Rd. B31: Longb . . . 2L **163**
Crowland Av. WV6: Pert . . . 5E **34**
Crowle Dr. DY9: Lye . . . 4C **116**
Crowley's Cl. B95: Ullen . . . 6J **215**
Crowmere Rd.
CV2: W'grve S . . . 2M **153**
Crown & Anchor Yd.
LE10: Hinc . . . 8K **69**
Crown Av. B20: Hand . . . 7K **79**
Crown Cen., The
DY8: Stourb . . . 4A **116**
Crown Cl. B61: B'gve . . . 7M **187**
B65: Row R . . . 5D **98**
DY3: Sed . . . 8D **52**
Crown Ct. B74: Four O . . . 6E **42**
LE10: Hinc . . . 8K **69**
WS10: Darl . . . 1C **54**
Crown Grn. CV6: Cov . . . 7E **130**
Crownhill Mdw. B61: Cats . . . 1M **187**
Crown Hill Rd. LE10: Burb . . . 5K **91**
Crown La. B74: Four O . . . 6E **42**
DY8: I'ley . . . 2J **137**
DY8: Stourb . . . 4M **115**
DY11: Kidd . . . 3L **157**
WR9: Elmb, Wych . . . 5A **208**
WR9: Wych . . . 8E **208**
Crown Mdw. B48: A'chu . . . 3A **190**
Crownmeadow Dr. DY4: Tip . . . 2D **76**
Crown Rd. B9: Bord G . . . 7D **102**
B30: K Nor . . . 5G **143**
Crown St. WV1: Wolv . . . 5D **36**
Crown Ter. CV31: Lea S . . . 2M **223**
Crown Wlk. DY4: Tip . . . 7A **76**
Crown Way CV32: Lill . . . 6B **218**
Crown Wharf Shop. Pk.
WS2: Wals . . . 7K **39**
Crows Furlong CV23: Brow . . . 1D **180**
Crows Nest Cl. B76: Walm . . . 6M **59**
Crowther Gdns. B63: Crad . . . 2J **117**
Crowther Gro. WV6: Wolv . . . 5M **35**
Crowther Rd. B23: Erd . . . 4C **80**
WV6: Wolv . . . 5L **35**
Crowther St. DY11: Kidd . . . 3J **157**
WV10: Wolv . . . 5E **36**
Crowthorns CV21: Brow . . . 2C **180**
Croxall Dr. B46: Shu . . . 7G **85**
Croxall Way B66: Smeth . . . 4B **100**
Croxdene Av. WS3: Blox . . . 8F **24**
(not continuous)
Croxhall St. CV12: Bed . . . 7J **111**
Croxley Dr. WS12: Hed . . . 6J **9**
Croxley Gdns. WV13: W'hall . . . 1M **53**
Croxstalls Av. WS3: Blox . . . 1G **39**
Croxstalls Cl. WS3: Blox . . . 8G **25**
Croxstalls Pl. WS3: Blox . . . 1G **39**
Croxstalls Rd. WS3: Blox . . . 8G **25**
Croxton Gro. B33: Stech . . . 5A **104**
Croyde Av. B42: Gt Barr . . . 4G **79**
Croydon Cl. CV3: Cov . . . 3E **174**
Croydon Ct. *B29: W Cas . . . 2C 142*
(off Abdon Av.)
Croydon Rd. B24: Erd . . . 8G **80**
B29: S Oak . . . 6F **120**
Croy Dr. B35: Cas V . . . 5B **82**
Crucible, The WV14: Cose . . . 7J **53**
Crummock Cl. CV6: Cov . . . 6D **130**
Crumpfields La. B97: Redd . . . 8L **211**
Crundalls La. DY12: Bew . . . 4B **156**
Crusader Cl. B69: O'bry . . . 4E **98**
Crutch La. B61: U War . . . 5B **208**
WR9: Elmb . . . 8A **208**
(not continuous)
Crutchley Av. B78: Tam . . . 7A **32**
Crutchley Way CV31: W'nsh . . . 7A **224**
Crychan Cl. B45: Fran . . . 7H **141**
Cryersoak Cl. B90: M'path . . . 2B **168**
Cryfield Grange Rd.
CV4: Canly . . . 7J **173**
Cryfield Halls CV4: Canly . . . 5H **173**
Cryfield Hgts. CV4: Canly . . . 7J **173**
Cryfield Hurst Flats
CV4: Canly . . . 5H **173**
Cryfield Redfern Flats
CV4: Canly . . . 6H **173**
Crystal Av. DY8: Word . . . 8M **95**
Crystal Dr. B66: Smeth . . . 1J **99**
Crystal Gdns. DY7: Kinv . . . 6A **114**
Crystal Ho. B66: Smeth . . . 3B **100**
Crystal Leisure Cen. . . . 4M **115**
CUBBINGTON . . . 4E **218**
Cubbington Rd. CV6: Cov . . . 7G **131**
CV32: Lill . . . 6A **218**
Cubley Rd. B28: Hall G . . . 8E **122**
Cuckoo Cl. WS11: Hth H . . . 6J **9**
Cuckoo La. CV1: Cov . . . 6D **152** (4D **6**)
Cuckoo Rd. B7: Aston, Nech . . . 1C **102**
Cuin Rd. B66: Smeth . . . 4C **100**
Cuin Wlk. *B66: Smeth . . . 4C 100*
(off Cuin Rd.)
Culey Gro. B33: Kitts G . . . 7D **104**
Culey Wlk. B37: Chel W . . . 7K **105**
Culford Dr. B32: Bart G . . . 1J **141**
Culham Cl. B27: A Grn . . . 7K **123**
Cullwick St. WV1: Wolv . . . 2G **53**
Culmington Rd. B31: Longb . . . 1M **163**
Culmore Cl. WV12: W'hall . . . 5D **38**
Culmore Rd. B62: B'hth . . . 8E **98**
Culpepper Cl. CV10: Nun . . . 5E **88**
Culverhouse Dr. DY5: Brie H . . . 8A **96**
Culverley Cres. B93: Know . . . 3F **168**
Culvert Way B66: Smeth . . . 2K **99**
Culwell Ind. Est.
WV10: Wolv . . . 6E **36** (2M **7**)
Culwell St.
WV10: Wolv . . . 6D **36** (2L **7**)
Culwell Trad. Est.
WV10: Wolv . . . 5F **36**
Culworth Cl. CV21: Brow . . . 2E **180**
CV31: Lea S . . . 4M **223**
Culworth Ct. CV6: Cov . . . 2E **152**
CV31: Lea S . . . 4A **224**
Culworth Row CV6: Cov . . . 1E **152**
Cumberford Av. B33: Kitts G . . . 8E **104**
Cumberland Av. B5: Birm . . . 2L **121**
Cumberland Cl. DY6: K'wfrd . . . 5L **95**
Cumberland Cres. CV32: Lill . . . 6D **218**
WS7: C Ter . . . 1G **17**
Cumberland Dr. B78: Tam . . . 8A **32**
CV10: Nun . . . 6E **88**
Cumberland Ho. WV1: Wolv . . . 5C **36**
Cumberland Rd. B68: O'bry . . . 2H **119**
B71: W Brom . . . 3K **77**
WS11: Cann . . . 5G **9**
WV13: W'hall . . . 7D **38**
WV14: Bils . . . 2K **53**
Cumberland St.
B1: Birm . . . 7J **101** (6B **4**)
Cumberland Wlk. B75: S Cold . . . 4B **60**
Cumberland Way LE9: Barw . . . 2A **70**
Cumberledge Hill
WS15: Cann W . . . 4D **10**
Cumbernauld Wlk.
CV2: W'grve S . . . 3A **154**
Cumbrae Dr. LE10: Hinc . . . 8H **69**
Cumbria Cl. CV1: Cov . . . 6A **152**
Cumbrian Cft. B63: Hale . . . 7K **117**
Cumbria Way B8: Salt . . . 3D **102**
Cumming St. CV31: Lea S . . . 2A **224**
Cundall Cl. CV31: Lea S . . . 3B **224**
Cunnery, The CV8: S'lgh P . . . 6A **200**
Cunningham Rd. WS2: Wals . . . 7E **38**
WV6: Pert . . . 5E **34**
Cunningham Way CV22: Bil . . . 7J **179**
Cupfields Av. DY4: Tip . . . 1B **76**
Cupfields Cres. DY4: Tip . . . 2C **76**
Curbar Rd. B42: Gt Barr . . . 3J **79**
CURBOROUGH . . . 4K **13**
Curborough Rd. WS13: Lich . . . 6H **13**
Curdale Rd. B32: Bart G . . . 1H **141**
CURDWORTH . . . 3H **83**
Curdworth La. B76: Wis . . . 8F **60**
Curie Cl. CV21: Rugby . . . 6D **180**
Curlew B77: Wiln . . . 2G **47**
Curlew Cl. DY10: Kidd . . . 7B **158**
WS14: Lich . . . 2L **19**
Curlew Hill WS11: Cann . . . 6G **9**
Curlews Cl. B23: Erd . . . 1C **80**
Curlieu Cl. CV35: H Mag . . . 2A **222**
Curral Rd. B65: Row R . . . 6B **98**
Curran Cl. CV31: W'nsh . . . 6B **224**
Curriers Cl. CV4: Tile H . . . 2D **172**
Curriers Cl. Ind. Est.
CV4: Tile H . . . 2D **172**
Curr La. B97: Bks G, Redd . . . 6H **211**
Cursley La.
DY10: Hartl, Mus G, Shens
. . . 1F **184**
Curtin Dr. WS10: Mox . . . 5B **54**
Curtis Cl. B60: Tard . . . 1F **210**
B66: Smeth . . . 5C **100**

Dormington Rd.—Dunslade Cres.

Dormington Rd. B44: Gt Barr 6L 57
Dormston Cl. B91: Sol 2C 168
B98: Redd 8F 212
Dormston Dr. B29: W Cas 7M 119
DY3: Sed 1E 74
Dormston Sports & Art Cen. 1E 74
Dormston Trad. Est.
DY1: Dud 5E 74
Dormy Dr. B31: Longb 2A 164
Dorncliffe Av. B33: Sheld 2D 124
Dorney Cl. CV5: Cov 1L 173
Dornie Dr. B38: K Nor 8F 142
Dornton Rd. B30: Stir 1J 143
Dorothy Adams Cl.
B64: Old H 1L 117
Dorothy Gdns. B20: Hand 7G 79
Dorothy Powell Way
CV2: W'grve S 8M 131
Dorothy Rd. B11: Tys 4H 123
B67: Smeth 6A 100
Dorothy St. WS1: Wals 2K 55
DORRIDGE 6F 168
Dorridge Cl. B97: Redd 8B 212
Dorridge Cft. B93: Dorr 7F 168
Dorridge Rd. B93: Dorr 7G 169
Dorridge Station (Rail) 7F 168
Dorrington Grn. B42: P Barr 4G 79
Dorrington Rd. B42: P Barr 3G 79
Dorset Cl. B45: Fran 7F 140
B78: Tam 8A 32
CV10: Nun 6F 88
CV22: Caw 8H 179
Dorset Cotts. B30: Stir 3G 143
Dorset Ct. B29: W Cas 2B 142
(off Abdon Av.)
Dorset Dr. WS9: A'rdge 8G 27
Dorset Rd. B17: Edg 6B 100
CV1: Cov 4C 152
DY8: Woll 2K 115
WS12: Hth H 8L 9
Dorset Twr.
B18: Hock 5H 101 (2A 4)
Dorsett Pl. WS3: Blox 2J 39
Dorsett Rd. DY13: Stour S 4F 182
WS10: Darl 3C 54
WS10: W'bry 7K 55
Dorsett Rd. Ter. WS10: Darl 3C 54
Dorsheath Gdns. B23: Erd 5F 80
Dorsington Rd. B27: A Grn 8K 123
Dorstone Covert B14: K Hth 7J 143
Dorville Cl. B38: K Nor 1D 164
DOSTHILL 5C 46
Dosthill Rd. B77: Two G 2D 46
Dotterel Pl. DY10: Kidd 8A 158
Douay Rd. B24: Erd 3H 81
Double Row DY2: Neth 5L 97
Doudney Cl. LE9: S Stan 8K 71
Doughty St. DY4: Tip 4C 76
Douglas Av. B36: Hodg H 3K 103
B68: O'bry 4K 99
Douglas Davies Cl.
WV12: W'hall 5C 38
Douglas Ho. CV1: Cov 2E 6
Douglas Pl. WV10: Oxl 3C 36
Douglas Rd. B21: Hand 1E 100
B27: A Grn 5H 123
B47: H'wd 2A 166
B62: B'hth 8E 98
B68: O'bry 5K 99
B72: S Cold 6J 59
CV21: Rugby 3C 180
DY2: Dud 1K 97
WV14: Cose 1K 75
Doulton Cl. B32: Quin 6M 119
CV2: W'grve S 8L 131
Doulton Dr. B66: Smeth 3A 100
Doulton Rd. B64: Old H 6M 97
B65: Row R 6M 97
Doulton Trad. Est.
B65: Row R 5M 97
Dovebridge Cl. B76: Walm 5M 59
Dove Cl. B25: Yard 1L 123
CV12: Bed 5E 110
DY10: Kidd 7B 158
LE10: Hinc 1G 91
WS1: Wals 8A 40
WS7: Burn 3K 17
WS10: W'bry 5G 55
Dovecote 6L 121
Dovecote Cl. B91: Sol 1B 146
CV6: Cov 4K 151
DY4: Tip 4C 76
LE9: Sap 2K 93
WV6: Tett 5J 35
Dovecote Rd. B61: B'gve 8L 187
Dovecotes, The B75: Four O 6H 43
CV5: Cov 4H 151
Dovecote Way LE9: Barw 3B 70
Dovedale WS11: Cann 4G 9
Dovedale Av. B90: Shir 8H 145
CV6: Cov 7F 130
WS3: Pels 4A 26
WV12: W'hall 4A 38
Dovedale Cl. CV21: Brow 2C 180
Dovedale Ct. B29: W Cas 2C 142
B46: Wat O 6G 83
WV4: E'shll 7F 52
Dovedale Dr. B28: Hall G 3F 144
Dovedale Rd. B23: Erd 1C 80
DY6: K'wfrd 1L 95
WV4: E'shll 6E 52
Dove Dr. DY8: Amb 1A 116
Dove Gdns. B38: K Nor 7H 143
Dove Hollow WS6: Gt Wyr 8F 14
WS12: Hed 5L 9
Dove Ho. Ct. B91: Sol 2M 145
Dovehouse Flds.
WS14: Lich 3H 19
Dovehouse La. B91: Sol 2M 145
Dovehouse Pool Rd.
B6: Aston 1L 101
Dover Cl. B32: Bart G 2G 141
Dover Ct. B29: W Cas 2C 142
(off Abdon Av.)
Dovercourt Rd. B26: Sheld 4C 124
Doverdale Av. DY10: Kidd 4B 158
Doverdale Cl. B63: Crad 4K 117
B98: Redd 2H 221
Dover Farm Cl. B77: Wiln 1H 47
Dover Ho. WS3: Blox 2J 39
(off Providence Cl.)
Dove Ridge DY8: Amb 2A 116
Doveridge Cl. B91: Sol 2L 145
Doveridge Pl. WS1: Wals 1M 55
Doveridge Rd. B28: Hall G 4E 144
Doversley Rd. B14: K Hth 4J 143
Dover St. B18: Hock 3G 101
CV1: Cov 6B 152 (4A 6)
WV14: Bils 3K 53
Dovestone B77: Wiln 8K 33
Dove Way B36: Cas B 1F 104
Dovey Dr. B76: Walm 2A 82
Dovey Rd. B13: Mose 7D 122
B69: Tiv 1D 98
Dovey Twr. B7: Birm 5A 102 (2M 5)
Dowar Rd. B45: Redn 2J 163
Dowells Cl. B13: Mose 7M 121
Dowells Gdns. DY8: Word 6K 95
Doweries, The B45: Rubery 1F 162
Dower Rd. B75: Four O 8H 43
Dowlers Hill Cres.
B98: Redd 1G 221
Dowles DY12: Bew 1A 156
Dowles Cl. B29: W Cas 3B 142
Dowles Rd. DY11: Kidd 7H 157
DY12: Bew 1B 156
Dowley Cft. CV3: Bin 8B 154
Downcroft Av. B38: K Nor 7E 142
Downderry Way CV6: Cov 3G 153
Downend Cl. WV10: Bush 5F 22
Downes Ct. DY4: Tip 4L 75
Downesway WS11: Cann 7C 8
(not continuous)
Downey Cl. B11: S'brk 2B 122
Downfield Cl. WS3: Blox 5G 25
Downfield Dr. DY3: Sed 3E 74
Downham Cl. WS5: Wals 8E 40
Downham Pl. WV3: Wolv 1M 51
Downham Wood WS5: Wals 1E 56
Downie Rd. WV8: Bilb 6J 21
Downing Cl. B65: B'hth 8C 98
B93: Know 5G 169
WV11: Wed 2A 38
Downing Ct. B68: O'bry 2H 119
Downing Cres. CV12: Bed 5J 111
Downing Dr. B79: Tam 4L 31
Downing Ho. B37: Chel W 8H 105
Downing St. B63: Hale 4A 118
B66: Smeth 2B 100
Downing St. Ind. Est.
B66: Smeth 2C 100
Downland Cl. B38: K Nor 8F 142
Downs, The WS9: A'rdge 7L 41
WV10: Oxl 3C 36
Downsell Ho. B97: Redd 7M 211
Downsell Rd. B97: Redd 7A 212
Downsfield Rd. B26: Sheld 2B 124
Downside Rd. B24: Erd 8E 80
Downs Rd. WV13: W'hall 1C 54
Downton Cl. CV2: W'grve S 1A 154
Downton Cres. B33: Kitts G 6E 104
Dowry Ho. B45: Rubery 1F 162
(off Rubery La. Sth.)
Dowty Av. CV12: Bed 8D 110
Dowty Way WV9: Pend 6A 22
Doyle Dr. CV6: Longf 6F 130
Dragons Health Club 7L 179
Dragoon Flds. B60: B'gve 1B 210
Drainage Board Cotts.
B24: Erd 8F 80
(off Saltley Cotts.)
Drake Cl. WS3: Blox 8H 25
Drake Cres. DY11: Kidd 2F 156
Drake Cft. WS13: Lich 1J 19
DRAKELOW 3H 135
Drakelow La. DY11: W'ley 3H 135
Drake Rd. B23: Erd 6B 80
B66: Smeth 2L 99
WS3: Blox 8H 25
Drakes Cl. B97: Redd 3C 220
Drakes Cross Pde.
B47: H'wd 4A 166
Drakes Grn. WV14: Bils 6M 53
Drakes Hill Cl. DY8: Stourb 5J 115
Drake St. B71: W Brom 4J 77
CV6: Cov 2D 152
Drake Way LE10: Hinc 5K 69
Drancy Av. WV12: W'hall 3D 38
(not continuous)
Draper Cl. CV8: Ken 5J 199
Drapers Ct. CV1: Cov 5C 152 (2C 6)
DRAPER'S FIELD 5C 152 (2C 6)
Drapers Flds.
CV1: Cov 5C 152 (2C 6)
Drawbridge Rd. B90: Maj G 1E 166
DRAYCOTE 8B 204
Draycote Cl. B92: Sol 2D 146
Draycott Av. B23: Erd 5D 80
Draycott Cl. B97: Redd 4B 212
WV4: Penn 4J 51
Draycott Cres. B77: Wiln 8C 32
Draycott Dr. B31: N'fld 2L 141
Draycott Rd. B66: Smeth 2L 99
CV2: Cov 2H 153
Drayman Cl. WS1: Wals 1M 55
DRAYTON 4A 160
DRAYTON BASSETT 4L 45
Drayton Cl. B75: Four O 6H 43
B98: Redd 1K 221
CV10: Harts 1A 88
CV13: Fen D 3F 66
Drayton Ct. B60: B'gve 1B 210
CV10: Nun 3C 88
CV34: Warw 7F 216
Drayton Cres. CV5: E Grn 4D 150
Drayton Gro. DY9: Belb 5A 160
Drayton La. B78: Dray B 3F 44
CV13: Fen D 3D 66
Drayton Leys CV22: Rugby 2A 206
Drayton Mnr. Dr.
B78: Dray B 2M 45
B78: Faz 1M 45
Drayton Manor Theme Park 1L 45
Drayton Rd. B14: K Hth 1L 143
B66: Smeth 8A 100
B90: Shir 1L 167
CV12: Bed 7K 111
DY9: Belb 4B 160
DY10: Chad C 7M 159
Drayton St. WS2: Wals 7H 39
WV2: Wolv 1C 52 (8J 7)
Drayton St. E. WS2: Wals 7J 39
Drayton Way CV10: Nun 2C 88
Dreadnought Rd. DY5: P'ntt 2B 96
Dreamwell Ind. Est.
B11: Tys 3G 123
Dreel, The B15: Edg 2E 120
Dreghorn Rd. B36: Hodg H 1L 103
Drem Cft. B35: Cas V 7A 82
Dresden Cl. WV4: E'shll 5G 53
Drew Cres. CV8: Ken 5G 199
DY9: W'cte 7D 116
Drew Rd. DY9: W'cte 6D 116
Drew's Holloway B63: Crad 4K 117
Drew's Holloway Sth.
B63: Crad 4K 117
Drews Ho. B14: K Hth 8K 143
(off Netheravon Cl.)
Drews La. B8: W End 3G 103
Drews Mdw. Cl. B14: K Hth 7J 143
Dreyer Cl. CV22: Bil 7J 179
Driffield Cl. B98: Redd 7K 213
DRIFFOLD 5G 59
Driffold B73: S Cold 5H 59
Driffold Vs. B73: S Cold 6H 59
Driftwood Cl. B38: K Nor 2D 164
Drinkwater Ho. CV1: Cov 7B 152
(off Meadow St.)
Drive Flds. WV4: Lwr P 3H 51
Drive, The B20: Hand 7G 79
B23: Erd 7E 80
B46: Col 3A 106
B48: Hopw 6B 164
B63: Crad 4K 117
B63: Hale 6A 118
B97: Redd 3J 211
B98: Redd 6E 212
CV2: Cov 6K 153
CV22: Dunc 5K 205
DY5: Brie H 4C 96
LE9: Barw 1B 70
WS3: Blox 7L 25
WS4: S'fld 8C 26
WS14: S'fen 8L 19
WV6: Tett 4J 35
WV8: Cod 6F 20
Droicon Trad. Est.
B65: Row R 4C 98
Droitwich Rd. DY10: Hartl 5E 184
DY10: Tort 2A 184
WR9: Rush 6F 184
Dronfield Rd. CV2: Cov 6H 153
Drovers Way B60: B'gve 3L 209
CV47: Sou 5J 225
Droveway, The WV8: Pend 7L 21
WV9: Pend 7L 21
Droxford Wlk. WV8: Pend 8L 21
Droylesdon Pk. Rd.
CV3: Finh 6B 174
Druid Pk. Rd. WV12: W'hall 8C 24
Druid Rd. CV2: Cov 6H 153
Druids Av. B65: Row R 5D 98
WS9: A'rdge 8J 27
DRUID'S HEATH 8H 27
Druids La. B14: K Hth 7J 143
Druids Pl. LE10: Hinc 8K 69
Druid St. LE10: Hinc 8K 69
Druids Wlk. WS9: Wals W 6G 27
Drumart Ho. DY10: Cookl 4A 136
Drum La. CV35: Hase K 6G 197
Drummond Cl. CV6: Cov 2M 151
WV11: Wed 7A 24
Drummond Gro. B43: Gt Barr 6J 57
Drummond Rd. B9: Bord G 7F 102
B60: B'gve 1B 210
DY9: W'cte 4F 116
Drummond St.
WV1: Wolv 6C 36 (2H 7)
Drummond Way
B37: Chel W 7J 105
Drury La. B91: Sol 6C 146
(not continuous)
CV21: Rugby 6A 180
DY8: Stourb 4A 116
WV8: Cod 5F 20
Drybrook Cl. B38: K Nor 1E 164
Drybrooks Cl. CV7: Bal C 3H 171
Dryden Cl. CV8: Ken 6F 198
CV10: Gall C 4M 87
DY4: Tip 2A 76
WV12: W'hall 1E 38
Dryden Gro. B27: A Grn 7H 123
Dryden Pl. CV22: Rugby 6L 179
WS3: Blox 2L 39
Dryden Rd. B79: Tam 2A 32
WS3: Blox 2L 39
WV10: Bush 8F 22
Dryden Wlk. CV22: Rugby 6L 179
Drylea Gro. B36: Hodg H 2M 103
Dry Mill La. DY12: Bew 1A 156
Dual Way WS12: Hunt 1C 8
Dubarry Av. DY6: K'wfrd 2J 95
Duchess Pde. B70: W Brom 6K 77
Duchess Pl. B16: Edg 8G 101
Duchess Rd. B16: Edg 8G 101
WS1: Wals 4K 55
Duckhouse Rd. WV11: Wed 2K 37
Duck La. WV8: Bilb 7H 21
WV14: Bils 4L 53
Duddeston Dr. B8: Salt 5D 102
Duddeston Mnr. Rd.
B7: Birm 5A 102 (1M 5)
Duddeston Mill Rd. B7: Birm 5B 102
B8: Birm, Salt 5B 102
Duddeston Mill Trad. Est.
B8: Salt 5C 102
Duddeston Station (Rail) 5B 102
Dudding Rd. WV4: Penn 4D 52
Dudhill Rd. B65: Row R 6A 98
Dudhill Wlk. B65: Row R 6M 97
DUDLEY 8J 75
Dudley Castle 7K 75
Dudley Central Trad. Est.
DY2: Dud 1J 97
Dudley Cl. B65: Row R 3A 98
Dudley Cres. WV11: Wed 3L 37
DUDLEY FIELDS 5C 96
Dudley Grn. CV32: Lill 7B 218
Dudley Gro. B18: Win G 5E 100
Dudley Leisure Cen. 8H 75
Dudley Mus. & Art Gallery 8J 75
Dudley Pk. Rd. B27: A Grn 6J 123
DUDLEY PORT 5B 76
Dudley Port DY4: Tip 6A 76
Dudley Port Station (Rail) 5B 76
Dudley Ri. LE10: Burb 3K 91
Dudley Rd. B18: Win G 5D 100
B63: Hale 3B 118
B65: Row R 3M 97
B69: O'bry 8E 76
CV8: Ken 7E 198
DY3: Himl 6J 73
DY3: Sed 2E 74
DY4: Tip 4K 75
DY5: Brie H 6D 96
DY6: K'wfrd 2M 95
DY6: W Hth 1J 95
DY9: Lye 3E 116
WV2: Wolv 1D 52 (8K 7)
Dudley Rd. E. B69: O'bry, Tiv 7C 76
Dudley Rd. W. B69: Tiv 7A 76
DY4: Tip 7A 76
Dudley Row DY2: Dud 8K 75
DUDLEY'S FIELDS 1G 39
Dudley Southern By-Pass
DY2: Dud 2G 97
Dudley St. B5: Birm 7L 101 (6G 5)
B70: W Brom 4F 76
CV6: Cov 8G 131
CV9: Ath 2K 65
DY3: Sed 1D 74
DY10: Kidd 2L 157
WS1: Wals 8L 39
WS10: W'bry 7E 54
WV1: Wolv 7C 36 (4J 7)
WV14: Bils 4K 53
Dudley Ter. CV8: S'lgh 3B 200
Dudley Wlk. WV4: Penn 4C 52
Dudley Wood Av. DY2: Neth 7J 97
Dudley Wood Rd. DY2: Neth 8J 97
Dudley Zoo 7K 75
Dudmaston Way DY1: Dud 6E 74
Dudnill Gro. B32: Bart G 1G 141
Duffield Cl. WV8: Pend 8M 21
Duffy Pl. CV21: Hillm 1G 207
Dufton Rd. B32: Quin 4L 119
Dugdale Cl. WS12: Wim 6L 9
Dugdale Ct. CV31: Lea S 3A 224
Dugdale Cres. B75: Four O 6J 43
Dugdale Ho. B71: W Brom 1A 78
Dugdale Rd. CV6: Cov 3B 152
Dugdale St. B18: Win G 5D 100
CV11: Nun 5J 89
(not continuous)
Duggins La. CV4: Tile H 1C 172
CV7: Berk 1A 172
Duke Bus. Pk. CV2: Cov 4G 153
DUKE END 5D 106
Duke Rd. WS7: C Ter 8E 10
Dukes Jetty CV21: Rugby 6A 180
Dukes Rd. B30: K Nor 5G 143
B78: Dord 3M 47
Duke St. B65: Row R 7B 98
B70: W Brom 5H 77
B72: S Cold 5H 59
CV5: Cov 7M 151
CV11: Nun 5G 89
CV21: Rugby 5A 180
CV32: Lea S 8A 218
DY3: Up Gor 4D 74
DY8: Stourb 3A 116
WV1: Wolv 8E 36 (5M 7)
WV3: Wolv 2A 52
WV11: Wed 4K 37
Dulais Cl. B98: Redd 8E 212
Dulvern Gro. B14: K Hth 4K 143
Dulverton Av. CV5: Cov 4K 151
Dulverton Ct. CV5: Cov 5K 151
Dulverton Rd. B6: Witt 8A 80
Dulwich Gro. B44: K'sdng 1B 80
Dulwich Rd. B44: K'sdng 1A 80
Dumbleberry Av. DY3: Sed 2C 74
Dumblederry La. WS9: A'rdge 1E 40
(not continuous)
Dumble Pit La. B48: A'chu 2L 191
Dumolos La. B77: Glas 6F 32
Dumphouse La. B48: A'chu 6J 191
Dunard Rd. B90: Shir 6F 144
Dunbar Cl. B32: Bart G 8K 119
DY10: Kidd 3C 158
Dunbar Gro. B43: Gt Barr 5H 57
Dunblane Dr. CV32: Cubb 4C 218
Dunblane Way LE10: Hinc 7G 69
Duncalfe Dr. B75: Four O 6H 43
Duncan Dr. CV22: Bil 3K 205
Duncan Edwards Cl.
DY1: Dud 1G 97
Duncan Ho. B73: W Grn 8H 59
DUNCHURCH 6J 205
Dunchurch Cl. B98: Redd 8M 213
CV7: Bal C 2H 171
Dunchurch Cres. B73: New O 6C 58
Dunchurch Dr. B31: N'fld 2L 141
Dunchurch Hall CV22: Dunc 6J 205
Dunchurch Highway
CV5: Alle, Cov 3G 151
Dunchurch Ho. B5: Birm 1L 121
Dunchurch Rd. CV22: Rugby 3L 205
Dunchurch Trad. Est.
CV23: Dunc 4D 204
Dunclent DY10: Stone 6E 158
Dunclent Cres. DY10: Kidd 4B 158
Dunclent La. DY10: Stone 6D 158
Duncombe Grn. B46: Col 2M 105
Duncombe Gro. B17: Harb 2M 119
Duncombe St. DY8: Woll 3K 115
Dun Cow Cl. CV23: Brin 6L 155
Duncroft Av. CV6: Cov 2M 151
Duncroft Rd. B26: Yard 1M 123
Duncroft Wlk. DY1: Dud 3H 75
Duncumb Rd. B75: S Cold 4A 60
Dundalk La. WS6: C Hay 7D 14
Dundas Av. DY2: Dud 1M 97
Dunedin B77: Glas 8G 33
Dunedin Dr. B45: B Grn 8G 163
Dunedin Ho. B32: Quin 5M 119
Dunedin Rd. B44: Gt Barr 6L 57
Dunham Cft. B93: Dorr 6D 168
Dunhampton Dr. DY10: Kidd 8B 136
Dunhill Av. CV4: Tile H 6E 150
Dunkirk Av. B70: W Brom 5D 76
Dunkirk Pl. CV3: Bin 2M 175
Dunkley St.
WV1: Wolv 6C 36 (2H 7)
Dunley Ct. B23: Erd 7C 80
(off Dunlin Cl.)
Dunley Cft. B90: M'path 3M 167
Dunley Gdns. DY13: Stour S 7E 182
Dunley Rd.
DY13: Dunl, Stour S 8C 182
Dunlin Cl. B23: Erd 7C 80
DY6: K'wfrd 3A 96
Dunlin Dr. DY10: Kidd 7M 157
WV10: F'stne 2G 23
Dunlop Rd. B97: Redd 4C 220
Dunlop Way B35: Cas V 8L 81
Dunmore Rd. DY12: Bew 4C 156
Dunnerdale CV21: Brow 2D 180
Dunnerdale Rd. WS8: Clay 3D 26
Dunnigan Rd. B32: Bart G 6M 119
Dunnington Av. DY10: Kidd 8A 136
Dunnose Cl. CV6: Cov 1E 152
DUNN'S BANK 2F 116
Dunn's Bank DY5: Quar B 2F 116
(Lynval Rd.)
DY5: Quar B 2G 117
(Saltbrook Rd.)
Dunn's La. B78: Dord 3B 48
Dunrose Cl. CV2: Cov 7L 153
Dunsfold Cl. WV14: Cose 6G 53
Dunsfold Cft. B6: Aston 3M 101
Dunsford Cl. DY5: Brie H 2B 116
Dunsford Rd. B66: Smeth 7A 100
Dunsink Rd. B6: Aston 8M 79
Dunslade Cres. DY5: Quar B 1F 116

Dunslade Rd.—Edward Rd.

Dunslade Rd. B23: Erd . . . 2D 80
DUNSLEY . . . 5B 114
Dunsley Dr. DY7: Kinv . . . 5C 114
DY8: Word . . . 6L 95
Dunsley Gro. WV4: Penn . . . 5A 52
Dunsley Rd. DY7: Kinv . . . 6B 114
DY8: Woll . . . 5J 115
Dunsmore Av. CV3: W'hall . . . 3J 175
CV22: Hillm . . . 1E 206
Dunsmore Dr. DY5: Quar B . . . 1F 116
Dunsmore Gro. B91: Sol . . . 2M 145
Dunsmore Heath
CV22: Dunc . . . 6J 205
Dunsmore Rd. B28: Hall G . . . 7E 122
Dunstall Av. WV6: Wolv . . . 4C 36
Dunstall Cl. B97: Redd . . . 7A 212
Dunstall Cres. CV33: Bis T . . . 8D 224
Dunstall Gro. B29: W Cas . . . 1M 141
DUNSTALL HILL . . . 4B 36
Dunstall Hill WV6: Wolv . . . 4C 36
Dunstall Hill Trad. Est.
WV6: Wolv . . . 4C 36
Dunstall La. B78: Hop . . . 3J 31
WV6: Wolv . . . 4A 36
Dunstall Pk. . . . 3A 36
Dunstall Pk. WV6: Wolv . . . 3B 36
Dunstall Rd. B63: Hale . . . 6K 117
WV6: Wolv . . . 5B 36
Dunstan Cft. B90: Shir . . . 1J 167
Dunster B77: Two G . . . 2C 46
Dunster Cl. B30: K Nor . . . 5H 143
Dunster Gro. WV6: Pert . . . 6F 34
Dunster Pl. CV6: Cov . . . 6D 130
Dunster Rd. B37: Chel W . . . 6J 105
Dunston Cl. DY6: K'wfrd . . . 2K 95
WS6: Gt Wyr . . . 1E 24
Dunston Dr. WS7: C Ter . . . 1G 17
Dunsville Dr. CV2: W'grve S . . . 1M 153
Dunton Cl. B75: Four O . . . 5G 43
Dunton Hall Rd. B90: Shir . . . 1G 167
DUNTON INTERCHANGE . . . 2K 83
Dunton La. B76: Wis . . . 8H 61
Dunton Rd. B37: K'hrst . . . 5F 104
Dunton Trad. Est. B7: Nech . . . 2D 102
Dunvegan Cl. CV3: Bin . . . 7A 154
CV8: Ken . . . 5J 199
Dunvegan Rd. B24: Erd . . . 5G 81
Duport Rd. LE10: Burb . . . 2M 91
Durant Cl. B45: Fran . . . 7D 140
Durban Rd. B66: Smeth . . . 5C 100
Durbar Av. CV6: Cov . . . 1D 152
Durbar Av. Ind. Est.
CV6: Cov . . . 1D 152
D'Urberville Cl. *WV2: E'shll . . . 3F 52*
(off D'urberville Rd.)
D'Urberville Rd. WV2: E'shll . . . 2F 52
(not continuous)
Durberville Rd. Ind. Est.
WV2: E'shll . . . 2F 52
D'Urberville Wlk. WS11: Cann . . . 7B 8
Durham Av. WV13: W'hall . . . 6C 38
Durham Cl. B61: B'gve . . . 5L 187
B78: Tam . . . 7A 32
CV7: Ker E . . . 5M 129
Durham Ct. *B29: W Cas . . . 2C 142*
(off Abdon Av.)
Durham Cres. CV5: Alle . . . 2G 151
Durham Cft. B37: Chel W . . . 7H 105
Durham Dr. B71: W Brom . . . 2K 77
Durham Ho.
WV1: Wolv . . . 5C 36 (1J 7)
Durham Pl. WS2: Wals . . . 8H 39
Durham Rd. B11: S'hll . . . 5B 122
B65: Row R . . . 5E 98
DY2: Neth . . . 7K 97
DY8: Woll . . . 1K 115
WS2: Wals . . . 1H 55
WS10: W'bry . . . 5K 55
Durham Twr.
B1: Birm . . . 6H 101 (4A 4)
Durley Dean Rd. B29: S Oak . . . 7C 120
Durley Dr. B73: New O . . . 6C 58
Durley Rd. B25: Yard . . . 3J 123
Durlston Cl. B77: Amin . . . 4G 33
Durlston Gro. B28: Hall G . . . 1G 145
Durnford Cft. B14: K Hth . . . 8L 143
Durrell Dr. CV22: Caw . . . 1G 205
Dursley Cl. B92: Olton . . . 1B 146
WV12: W'hall . . . 5D 38
Dursley Dr. WS11: Cann . . . 7B 8
Dursley La. B98: Redd . . . 6A 214
Dursley Rd. WS7: C Ter . . . 2G 17
Dusthouse La.
B60: Fins, Tard . . . 3C 210
Dutton Rd. CV2: Ald G . . . 6K 131
Dutton's La. B75: R'ley . . . 5L 43
Duxford Cl. B97: Redd . . . 1B 220
Duxford Rd. B42: Gt Barr . . . 1H 79
Dwarris Wlk. CV34: Warw . . . 7E 216
Dwellings La. B32: Quin . . . 4H 119
Dyas Av. B42: Gt Barr . . . 2F 78
Dyas Rd. B44: Gt Barr . . . 8K 57
B47: H'wd . . . 2A 166
Dyce Cl. B35: Cas V . . . 5A 82
Dyers La. CV8: Wols . . . 6G 177
B94: H'ley H . . . 1K 193
Dyers Rd. CV11: Bram . . . 3F 112
Dymoke St. B12: Birm . . . 1M 121
Dymond Rd. CV6: Cov . . . 6C 130
Dynes Wlk. B67: Smeth . . . 4A 100
Dyott Cl. WS13: S'hay . . . 8M 13
Dyott Rd. B13: Mose . . . 8A 122
Dysart Cl. CV1: Cov . . . 5E 152 (2F 6)
Dyson Cl. CV21: Hillm . . . 8F 180
WS2: Wals . . . 6F 38
Dyson Gdns. B8: Salt . . . 4E 102
Dyson St. CV4: Tile H . . . 6E 150

E

Eachelhurst Rd. B24: Erd . . . 5L 81
B76: Walm . . . 5L 81
Eachus Rd. WV14: Cose . . . 1K 75
EACHWAY . . . 3F 162
Eachway B45: Rubery . . . 3F 162
Eachway Farm Cl.
B45: Redn . . . 3G 163
Eachway La. B45: Redn . . . 3G 163
Eacott Cl. CV6: Cov . . . 6A 130
Eadgar Ct. B43: Gt Barr . . . 2D 78
Eadie M. B97: Redd . . . 8D 212
Eadie St. CV10: Nun . . . 5D 88
Eagle Cl. B65: Row R . . . 5M 97
CV11: Nun . . . 1B 112
DY1: Dud . . . 1F 96
WS6: C Hay . . . 7D 14
Eagle Ct. *CV34: Warw . . . 2D 222*
(off Saltisford)
WV3: Wolv . . . 3A 52
Eagle Ct. Bus. Pk.
B26: Sheld . . . 5E 124
Eagle Cft. B14: K Hth . . . 7L 143
Eagle Dr. B77: Amin . . . 5H 33
Eagle Gdns. B24: Erd . . . 7G 81
Eagle Gro. B36: Cas B . . . 1G 105
WS12: Hth H . . . 8J 9
Eagle Ind. Est. DY4: Tip . . . 2E 76
Eagle La. CV8: Ken . . . 6F 198
DY4: Tip . . . 3D 76
Eagle Rd. B98: Redd . . . 4L 213
Eagle St. CV1: Cov . . . 4D 152 (1D 6)
CV31: Lea S . . . 3A 224
DY4: Tip . . . 3C 76
WV2: Wolv . . . 1E 52 (7M 7)
WV3: Wolv . . . 2A 52
Eagle St. E. CV1: Cov . . . 4D 152 (1E 6)
Eagle Trad. Est. B63: Hale . . . 5A 118
Eales Yd. LE10: Hinc . . . 1K 91
Ealing Gro. B44: K'sdng . . . 8A 58
Ealingham B77: Wiln . . . 7H 33
Eanwulf Ct. B15: Edg . . . 1J 121
Eardisley Cl. B98: Redd . . . 8M 213
Earl Dr. WS7: C Ter . . . 8E 10
Earles Cl. CV47: S'ton . . . 1M 225
Earleswood Trad. Est.
B94: Earls . . . 3C 192
Earl Pl. Bus. Pk.
CV4: Tile H . . . 8H 151
Earl Rivers Av. CV34: H'cte . . . 6K 223
Earlsbury Gdns. B20: Hand . . . 8K 79
Earls Cl. B97: Redd . . . 7M 211
Earls Ct. Rd. B17: Harb . . . 3A 120
Earl's Cft., The CV3: Cov . . . 2C 174
EARLSDON . . . 1M 173
Earlsdon Av. Nth. CV5: Cov . . . 7M 151
Earlsdon Av. Sth. CV5: Cov . . . 8A 152
Earlsdon Bus. Cen.
CV5: Cov . . . 1M 173
Earlsdon St. CV5: Cov . . . 1M 173
Earls Ferry Gdns.
B32: Bart G . . . 2H 141
EARL SHILTON . . . 1E 70
Earl Shilton Rd. LE9: Thurl . . . 1J 71
Earlsmead Rd. B21: Hand . . . 1C 100
Earlsmere B94: Earls . . . 8H 167
Earls Rd. CV11: Nun . . . 4G 89
WS4: Rus . . . 2C 40
Earlston Way B43: Gt Barr . . . 1D 78
Earl St. B70: W Brom . . . 5H 77
CV1: Cov . . . 7D 152 (5D 6)
CV12: Bed . . . 7J 111
CV21: Rugby . . . 6B 180
CV32: Lea S . . . 8A 218
DY6: K'wfrd . . . 5K 95
LE9: Earl S . . . 1G 71
WS1: Wals . . . 2K 55
WV14: Bils . . . 4K 53
WV14: Cose . . . 1K 75
Earls Wlk. CV3: Bin W . . . 2D 176
Earls Way B63: Hale . . . 5B 118
EARLSWOOD . . . 8H 167
Earlswood Ct. B20: Hand . . . 7G 79
Earlswood Cres. WV9: Pend . . . 6A 22
Earlswood Dr. B74: S Cold . . . 2J 59
Earlswood Ho. *B5: Birm . . . 2L 121*
(off Barrow Wlk.)
Earlswood Lakes Craft Cen. . . . 8G 167
Earlswood Rd. B93: Dorr . . . 7D 168
DY6: K'wfrd . . . 2L 95
Early River Pl. DY12: Bew . . . 2B 156
Easby Way B8: Salt . . . 4E 102
WS3: Blox . . . 7F 24
Easedale Cl. CV3: Cov . . . 3B 174
CV11: Nun . . . 3A 90
Easemore Rd. B98: Redd . . . 5E 212
Easenhall Cl. B93: Know . . . 5G 169
Easenhall La. B98: Redd . . . 8L 213
Easmore Cl. B14: K Hth . . . 7K 143
Eastacre WV13: W'hall . . . 8A 38
East Av. B69: Tiv . . . 2C 98
CV2: Cov . . . 6G 153
East Av. CV12: Bed . . . 7K 111
WV11: Wed . . . 3J 37
Eastboro Flds. CV11: Nun . . . 5M 89
Eastborough Ct. CV11: Nun . . . 7L 89
Eastboro' Way CV11: Nun . . . 7L 89
Eastbourne Av. B34: Hodg H . . . 3K 103
Eastbourne Cl. CV6: Cov . . . 3L 151
Eastbourne St. WS4: Wals . . . 6M 39
Eastbrook Cl. B76: Walm . . . 5K 59
Eastburn B77: Wiln . . . 8H 33
Eastbury Dri B92: Olton . . . 6A 124
Eastbury Dr. B92: Olton . . . 6A 124
E. Cannock Ind. Est.
WS12: Hth H . . . 6H 9
E. Cannock Rd. WS12: Hed . . . 6H 9
E. Car Pk. Rd. B40: Nat E C . . . 5M 125
East Cl. LE10: Burb . . . 2K 91
WR9: Wych . . . 8E 208
EASTCOTE . . . 6M 147
Eastcote Cl. B90: Shir . . . 6K 145
Eastcote Cres. WS7: Chase . . . 4G 17
Eastcote La. B92: H Ard . . . 6M 147
Eastcote Rd. B27: A Grn . . . 8G 123
WV10: Wolv . . . 4F 36
Eastcotes CV4: Tile H . . . 8H 151
E. Croft Rd. WV4: Penn . . . 5J 51
Eastdean Cl. B23: Erd . . . 3D 80
East Dene CV32: Lill . . . 7B 218
East Dr. B5: Edg . . . 5J 121
Eastern Av. DY5: Brie H . . . 7B 96
WS13: Lich . . . 7E 12
Eastern Cl. WS10: Mox . . . 6C 54
Eastern Grn. Rd. CV5: E Grn . . . 6F 150
EASTERN HILL . . . 7F 220
Eastern Hill B96: A'wd B . . . 7E 220
Eastern Rd. B29: S Oak . . . 6H 121
B73: W Grn . . . 8H 59
Eastern Way WS11: Cann . . . 8G 9
Easterton Cft. B14: K Hth . . . 7L 143
E. Farm Cft. B10: Small H . . . 1D 122
Eastfield Cl. WS9: A'rdge . . . 3G 41
Eastfield Dr. B92: Sol . . . 1E 146
Eastfield Gro. WV1: Wolv . . . 7F 36
Eastfield Pl. CV21: Rugby . . . 6A 180
Eastfield Retreat WV1: Wolv . . . 7F 36
Eastfield Rd. B8: W End . . . 5J 103
B9: Bord G . . . 5J 103
CV10: Nun . . . 3K 89
CV32: Lea S . . . 1A 224
DY4: Tip . . . 1A 76
WV1: Wolv . . . 7F 36
East Ga. B16: Edg . . . 6E 100
Eastgate WS12: Haz . . . 4A 10
Eastgate M. CV34: Warw . . . 3E 222
Eastgate St. WS7: C Ter . . . 1E 16
East Grn. LE9: Barw . . . 3A 70
WV4: Penn . . . 3K 51
East Gro. CV31: Lea S . . . 3A 224
Eastham Rd. B13: Mose . . . 3C 144
East Holme B9: Bord G . . . 7C 102
Easthope Cl. DY13: Stour S . . . 7K 187
Easthope Rd. B33: Stech . . . 5A 104
E. House Dr. CV9: Hurl . . . 5K 63
Eastlake Cl. B43: Gt Barr . . . 6K 57
Eastlands Ct. CV21: Rugby . . . 6C 180
Eastlands Gro. CV5: Cov . . . 5L 151
Eastlands Pl. CV21: Rugby . . . 6C 180
Eastlands Rd. B13: Mose . . . 8A 122
CV21: Rugby . . . 6D 180
Eastlang Rd. CV7: Fill . . . 6E 108
Eastleigh DY3: Sed . . . 1C 74
Eastleigh Av. CV5: Cov . . . 2M 173
Eastleigh Cft. B76: Walm . . . 2A 82
Eastleigh Dr. B62: Roms . . . 5A 140
Eastleigh Gro. B25: Yard . . . 1K 123
Eastley Cres. CV34: Warw . . . 1B 222
E. Meadway B33: Kitts G . . . 7D 104
East M. B44: Gt Barr . . . 7K 57
E. Moons Ho. B98: Redd . . . 5L 213
E. Moons Moat Ind. Area
B98: Redd . . . 4L 213
E. Moor Cl. B74: S'tly . . . 7B 42
Eastney Cres. WV8: Pend . . . 1L 35
Eastnor Cl. B98: Redd . . . 8E 212
DY10: Kidd . . . 8L 157
Eastnor Gro. CV31: Lea S . . . 2B 224
Easton Gdns. WV11: Wed . . . 4M 37
Easton Gro. B27: A Grn . . . 8J 123
B47: H'wd . . . 2B 166
E. Park Trad. Est. WV1: Wolv . . . 1F 52
East Pk. Way WV1: Wolv . . . 8H 37
East Pathway B17: Harb . . . 3C 120
Eastridge Cft. WS14: Shens . . . 4G 29
East Ri. B75: S Cold . . . 3K 59
East Rd. B24: Erd . . . 7K 81
B60: B'gve . . . 8A 188
DY4: Tip . . . 1B 76
DY13: Stour S . . . 4G 183
WV10: B'frd, F'stne . . . 1F 22
East St. B77: Dost . . . 4D 46
CV1: Cov . . . 6E 152
CV21: Rugby . . . 5D 180
DY2: Dud . . . 1L 97
DY3: Gorn . . . 6D 74
DY5: Quar B . . . 1G 117
DY10: Kidd . . . 3M 157
WS1: Wals . . . 2M 55
WS11: Cann . . . 3E 14
WV1: Wolv . . . 8E 36 (5M 7)
E. Union St. CV22: Rugby . . . 7A 180
East Vw. B77: Glas . . . 6E 32
E. View Rd. B72: S Cold . . . 6K 59
Eastville B31: N'fld . . . 6B 142
Eastward Glen WV8: Bilb . . . 8J 21
East Way B17: Harb . . . 3C 120
Eastway B40: Nat E C . . . 6M 125
B92: Bick . . . 6M 125
Eastwood Av. WS7: C Ter . . . 1G 17
Eastwood Bus. Village
CV3: Bin . . . 8M 153
Eastwood Cl. CV31: Lea S . . . 3D 224
Eastwood Ct. B96: A'wd B . . . 8E 220
Eastwood Dr. DY10: Kidd . . . 5B 158
Eastwood Gro. CV21: Hillm . . . 1J 207
Eastwood Rd. B12: Bal H . . . 4K 121
B43: Gt Barr . . . 1E 78
DY2: Dud . . . 3L 97
Eastwoods Rd. LE10: Hinc . . . 7M 69
Easy La. CV21: Rugby . . . 6M 179
Eatesbrook Rd. B33: Kitts G . . . 6C 104
Eathorpe Cl. B34: S End . . . 3D 104
B98: Redd . . . 1L 221
CV2: Cov . . . 8J 131
Eaton Av. B70: W Brom . . . 5G 77
Eaton Cl. CV32: Lea S . . . 7K 217
Eaton Ct. B74: S Cold . . . 2H 59
Eaton Cres. DY3: Gorn . . . 6B 74
Eaton Pl. DY6: K'wfrd . . . 4L 95
Eaton Ri. WV12: W'hall . . . 3B 38
Eaton Rd. CV1: Cov . . . 8C 152 (7B 6)
Eaton Wood B24: Erd . . . 6K 81
Eaton Wood Dr. B26: Yard . . . 4K 123
Eaves Ct. Dr. DY3: Sed . . . 8C 52
EAVES GREEN . . . 7M 127
Eaves Grn. Gdns.
B27: A Grn . . . 4H 123
Eaves Grn. La. CV7: Mer . . . 8L 127
Eaves Grn. Pk. CV7: Mer . . . 7M 127
Ebbw Va. Ter. CV3: Cov . . . 2D 174
Ebenezer St. B70: W Brom . . . 3F 76
WS12: Hed . . . 2G 9
WV14: Cose . . . 1H 75
Ebley Rd. B20: Hand . . . 5G 79
Ebmore Dr. B14: K Hth . . . 7K 143
Eborall Cl. CV34: Warw . . . 7E 216
Eborne Cft. CV7: Bal C . . . 1J 171
Ebourne Cl. CV8: Ken . . . 5G 199
Ebrington Av. B92: Sol . . . 6B 124
Ebrington Cl. B14: K Hth . . . 5K 143
Ebrington Rd. B71: W Brom . . . 3K 77
Ebro Cres. CV3: Bin . . . 8M 153
Ebrook Rd. B72: S Cold . . . 5J 59
EBSTREE . . . 5C 50
Ebstree Mdw. WV5: Seis . . . 7A 50
Ebstree Rd. WV5: Seis, Try . . . 7A 50
Eburne Rd. CV2: Ald G . . . 6H 131
Ebury Rd. B30: K Nor . . . 5H 143
Eccles Cl. CV2: Cov . . . 1J 153
Eccleshall Av. WV10: Oxl . . . 1B 36
Eccleston Cl. B75: S Cold . . . 4M 59
Ecclestone Rd. WV11: Wed . . . 1A 38
Echells Cl. B61: B'gve . . . 7K 187
Echo Way WV4: E'shll . . . 5G 53
Eckersall Rd. B38: K Nor . . . 6E 142
Eckington Cl. B98: Redd . . . 1H 221
Eckington Wlk. B38: K Nor . . . 2E 164
Eclipse Ind. Est. DY4: Tip . . . 4L 75
Ecton Leys CV22: Rugby . . . 2A 206
Edale B77: Wiln . . . 8H 33
Edale Cl. DY6: K'wfrd . . . 2H 95
WV4: E'shll . . . 6E 52
Edale Grn. LE10: Burb . . . 3M 91
Edale Rd. B42: Gt Barr . . . 2J 79
Edale Way CV6: Cov . . . 2G 153
Eddens Wood Cl. B78: Dray B . . . 4L 45
Eddie Miller Ct. CV12: Bed . . . 7G 111
Eddish Rd. B33: Kitts G . . . 6B 104
Eddison Rd. B46: Col . . . 5L 83
Eddy Rd. DY10: Kidd . . . 2L 157
Edelweiss Cl. WS5: Wals . . . 6B 56
Edenbridge Rd. B28: Hall G . . . 1G 145
Edenbridge Vw. DY1: Dud . . . 6E 74
Eden Cl. B31: Longb . . . 1L 163
B69: Tiv . . . 7D 76
B80: Stud . . . 6K 221
WS12: Hth H . . . 7L 9
Eden Ct. CV10: Nun . . . 2C 88
CV32: Lill . . . 6D 218
Eden Cft. CV8: Ken . . . 5H 199
Edencroft B15: Edg . . . 1J 121
Edendale Dr. LE10: Hinc . . . 6L 69
Edendale Rd. B26: Sheld . . . 3B 124
Edenfield Cl. B97: Redd . . . 4A 212
Edenfield Pl. B77: Wiln . . . 8H 33
Eden Gdns. DY3: Sed . . . 1E 74
Eden Gro. B37: Chel W . . . 8K 105
B71: W Brom . . . 4K 77
Edenhall Rd. B32: Quin . . . 3H 119
Eden Ho. DY8: Stourb . . . 4A 116
Edenhurst Rd. B31: Longb . . . 3M 163
Eden Pl. B3: Birm . . . 7K 101 (5E 4)
Eden Rd. B92: Sol . . . 6D 124
CV2: W'grve S . . . 8A 132
CV21: Hillm . . . 8F 180
Edensor Cl.
WV10: Wolv . . . 5E 36 (1M 7)
Eden St. CV6: Cov . . . 2F 152
Edgar Cl. B79: Tam . . . 2M 31
EDGBASTON . . . 4G 121
Edgbaston . . . 4K 121
Edgbaston Archery &
Lawn Tennis Society . . . 2F 120
Edgbaston Pk. Rd. B15: Edg . . . 4G 121
Edgbaston Priory Club . . . 3J 121
Edgbaston Rd. B5: Edg . . . 4K 121
B12: Bal H . . . 4K 121
B66: Smeth . . . 5A 100
Edgbaston Rd. E.
B12: Bal H . . . 4M 121
Edgbaston Shop. Cen.
B16: Edg . . . 1G 121 (8A 4)
Edgbaston St.
B5: Birm . . . 8L 101 (7G 5)
Edgcombe Rd. B28: Hall G . . . 8F 122
Edgecote Cl. CV21: Hillm . . . 8F 180
Edgefield Rd. CV2: W'grve S . . . 1A 154
EDGE HILL . . . 8J 47
Edge Hill CV9: Wood E . . . 7G 47
DY7: Kinv . . . 5A 114
Edge Hill Av. WV10: Bush . . . 7G 23
Edge Hill Dr. DY3: Sed . . . 7C 52
WV6: Pert . . . 6E 34
Edgehill Pl. CV4: Tile H . . . 8C 150
Edge Hill Rd. B74: Four O . . . 5D 42
Edgehill Rd. B31: Longb . . . 1A 164
Edgemond Av. B24: Erd . . . 5M 81
Edgemoor Mdw. WS12: Hth H . . . 8J 9
Edge St. WV14: Cose . . . 1K 75
Edgewood Cl. B64: Old H . . . 1M 117
Edgewood Dr. B45: B Grn . . . 8H 163
(not continuous)
Edgewood Rd. B38: K Nor . . . 2E 164
B45: Redn . . . 2H 163
Edgeworth Cl. B98: Redd . . . 4J 213
WV12: W'hall . . . 5C 38
Edgeworth Ho. WS13: Lich . . . 7G 13
Edgmond Cl. B98: Redd . . . 5K 213
Edgware Rd. B23: Erd . . . 4D 80
EDGWICK . . . 1E 152
Edgwick Pk. Ind. Est.
CV6: Cov . . . 1F 152
Edgwick Rd. CV6: Cov . . . 2F 152
EDIAL . . . 3M 17
Edinburgh Av. WS2: Wals . . . 6E 38
Edinburgh Cl. DY10: Kidd . . . 2L 157
Edinburgh Ct. B24: Erd . . . 5K 81
Edinburgh Cres.
CV31: Lea S . . . 3M 223
DY8: Word . . . 8J 95
Edinburgh Dr. WS4: Rus . . . 2D 40
WV12: W'hall . . . 3B 38
Edinburgh La. WS2: Wals . . . 5G 39
Edinburgh Rd. B68: O'bry . . . 1H 119
CV9: Hurl . . . 4J 63
CV10: Nun . . . 3C 88
DY2: Dud . . . 3K 97
LE9: Earl S . . . 2D 70
WS5: Wals . . . 1B 56
WV14: Bils . . . 6M 53
Edinburgh Vs. CV8: Bag . . . 6F 174
Edinburgh Way
CV23: Long L . . . 4H 179
Edingale Rd. CV2: W'grve S . . . 8M 131
Edison Cl. WS12: Hed . . . 2J 9
Edison Ct. *WV12: W'hall . . . 2D 38*
(off Huntington Rd.)
Edison Gro. B32: Quin . . . 4K 119
Edison Rd. WS2: Wals . . . 4G 39
Edison Wlk. WS2: Wals . . . 4H 39
Edith Pope Ho. B42: Gt Barr . . . 1K 79
Edith Rd. B66: Smeth . . . 6B 100
Edith St. B70: W Brom . . . 6H 77
Edmondes Cl. CV34: Warw . . . 8F 216
Edmonds Cl. B33: Kitts G . . . 7B 104
Edmondscote Rd.
CV32: Lea S . . . 1J 223
Edmonds Ct. B10: Small H . . . 2D 122
B26: Yard . . . 2M 123
Edmondson Cl. CV22: Dunc . . . 5K 205
Edmonds Rd. B68: O'bry . . . 7J 99
Edmonton Av. B44: K'sdng . . . 8B 58
Edmonton Cl. WS11: Hth H . . . 7H 9
Edmonton Ho. B5: Bal H . . . 2K 121
Edmoor Cl. WV12: W'hall . . . 3C 38
Edmund Rd. B8: Salt . . . 5D 102
CV1: Cov . . . 4D 152
DY3: Up Gor . . . 3E 74
Edmund St. B3: Birm . . . 6K 101 (4E 4)
Ednall La. B60: B'gve . . . 8M 187
Ednam Cl. B71: W Brom . . . 1M 77
Ednam Gro. WV5: Wom . . . 8G 51
Ednam Rd. DY1: Dud . . . 8J 75
WV4: Penn . . . 3C 52
Edsome Way B36: Hodg H . . . 1M 103
Edstone Cl. B93: Dorr . . . 5F 168
Edstone M. B36: Hodg H . . . 1M 103
Edward Av. WS9: A'rdge . . . 2G 41
Edward Bailey Cl. CV3: Bin . . . 2L 175
Edward Cl. WV14: Bils . . . 6L 53
Edward Ct. B16: Edg . . . 8C 100
B76: Walm . . . 6M 59
B77: Amin . . . 5E 32
CV21: Rugby . . . 6B 180
(off Pinders La.)
WS1: Wals . . . 1A 56
Edward Fisher Dr. DY4: Tip . . . 4A 76
Edward Rd. B5: Edg . . . 3K 121
B12: Bal H . . . 3K 121
B14: K Hth . . . 8M 143
B46: Wat O . . . 6J 83
B63: Hale . . . 5M 117
B67: Smeth . . . 5M 99
B68: O'bry . . . 1J 119

Edward Rd.—Ensor Dr.

Edward Rd. CV6: Cov 6A 130
CV12: Bed 6J 111
DY4: Tip 2A 76
WV6: Pert 4E 34
Edwards Cen. *LE10: Hinc* 1K 91
(off Horsefair, The)
Edwards Gro. CV8: Ken 4J 199
Edwards Rd. WS7: Chase 4F 16
B24: Erd 4G 81
B75: R'ley 6K 43
DY2: Neth 5J 97
Edward St. B1: Birm 7H 101 (5B 4)
B68: O'bry 5G 99
B70: W Brom 6J 77
B79: Tam 4A 32
B97: Redd 5D 212
CV6: Cov 4E 152
CV11: Nun 5H 89
CV21: Rugby 5M 179
CV32: Lea S 8J 217
CV34: Warw 2D 222
DY1: Dud 8H 75
LE10: Hinc 7J 69
WS2: Wals 6H 39
WS10: Darl 3E 54
WS11: Cann 5E 8
WV4: E'shll 3F 52
Edward Tyler Rd. CV7: Exh 8G 111
Edwin Av. DY11: Kidd 8L 157
Edwin Cl. CV22: Caw 2G 205
Edwin Ct. B60: B'gve 1M 209
Edwin Cres. B60: B'gve 1M 209
Edwin Phillips Dr.
B71: W Brom 1H 77
Edwin Rd. B30: Stir 2H 143
Edyth Rd. CV2: Cov 5L 153
Edyvean Cl. CV22: Bil 3L 205
Edyvean Walker Ct.
CV11: Nun 4H 89
Eel St. B69: O'bry 2F 98
Effingham Rd. B13: Mose 3C 144
Egbert Cl. B6: Aston 1B 102
Egelwin Cl. WV6: Pert 4E 34
Egerton Cl. CV21: N'bld A 3M 179
Egerton Rd. B24: Erd 6K 81
B74: S'tly 8M 41
WV10: Bush 6E 22
EGG HILL 6H 141
Egghill La. B31: N'fld 5G 141
B32: Fran 5G 141
B45: Fran 5G 141
Eggington Rd. DY8: Woll 2K 115
Egginton Rd. B28: Hall G 4E 144
Egg La. DY9: Belb 1L 159
DY9: Brme 1L 159
DY10: Hillp 1L 159
Eglamour Way CV34: H'cte 6M 223
Egmont Gdns. WV11: Wed 3M 37
Egret Ct. DY10: Kidd 8A 158
Egret Wlk. CV2: Ald G 6H 131
Eider Cl. DY10: Kidd 8B 158
Eights Cft. WS7: C Ter 1D 16
Eileen Gdns. B37: K'hrst 5F 104
Eileen Rd. B11: S'hll 6B 122
Elan Av. DY13: Stour S 2E 182
Elan Cl. CV32: Lill 6C 218
DY3: Lwr G 6D 74
DY10: Cookl 5B 136
DY12: Bew 2B 156
Elan Rd. B31: Longb 7J 141
DY3: Sed 1C 74
Elborow St. CV21: Rugby 6A 180
Elbow St. B64: Old H 7M 97
Elbury Cft. B93: Know 4F 168
Elcock Dr. B42: P Barr 4K 79
Eldalade Way WS10: W'bry 7K 55
Elderberry Cl. DY8: Stourb 6J 115
DY13: Stour S 5E 182
WS5: Wals 6M 55
Elderberry Way CV2: Cov 3H 153
Elder Cl. B78: K'bry 2D 62
CV22: Bil 8H 179
WS11: Hth H 7J 9
Elderfield B33: Sheld 1B 124
Elderfield Rd. B30: K Nor 6H 143
Elder Gro. WV5: Wom 3F 72
Elder La. WS7: Burn 2J 17
Eldersfield Cl. B98: Redd 2L 213
Eldersfield Gro. B91: Sol 2B 168
Elderside Cl. WS8: Bwnhls 1F 26
Elder Way B23: Erd 7E 80
Eldon Ct. *WS1: Wals* 8M 39
(off Eldon St.)
Eldon Dr. B76: Walm 2L 81
Eldon Rd. B16: Edg 8F 100
B62: Quin 6G 119
Eldon St. WS1: Wals 8M 39
WS10: Darl 2D 54
Eldorado Cl. B80: Stud 5K 221
Eldridge Cl. WV9: Pend 7M 21
Eld Rd. CV6: Cov 2E 152
Eleanor Harrison Dr.
DY10: Cookl 4B 136
Eleanor Rd. WV14: Bils 3K 53
Electra Pk. B6: Witt 8B 80
Electric Av. B6: Witt 8B 80
Elford Cl. B14: K Hth 4L 143
Elford Gro. B37: Mars G 8H 105
WV14: Bils 5J 53
Elford Rd. B17: Harb 6B 120
B71: W Brom 8L 55
Elgar Cl. B97: Redd 1C 220
CV11: Nun 2A 112
WS11: Cann 4E 8
WS13: Lich 7H 13
Elgar Ct. B15: Edg 2G 121
Elgar Cres. DY5: P'ntt 2D 96
Elgar Ho. B16: Birm 7H 101 (6B 4)
Elgar M. B60: B'gve 7M 187
Elgar Rd. CV6: Cov 1H 153
Elgin Cl. DY3: Sed 8E 52
DY8: Amb 2A 116
Elgin Ct. WV6: Pert 5E 34
Elgin Rd. WS3: Blox 5G 25
Elias Cl. WS14: Lich 3L 19
Eligin Gro. B25: Yard 2J 123
Eliot Cl. B79: Tam 2A 32
CV34: Warw 7E 216
Eliot Ct. CV22: Rugby 6L 179
Eliot Cft. WV14: Cose 7K 53
Eliot St. B7: Nech 1C 102
Eliot Wlk. DY10: Kidd 3C 158
Eliot Way CV10: Nun 7H 89
Elisha Cl. LE9: S Stan 7L 71
Elizabeth Av. B78: Pole 2K 49
WS10: W'bry 6J 55
WV4: Penn 4B 52
WV14: Bils 6M 53
Elizabeth Ct. *B17: Harb* 5D 120
(off Metchley La.)
CV34: Warw 3H 223
Elizabeth Cres. B68: O'bry 7K 99
Elizabeth Dr. B79: Tam 3A 32
Elizabeth Gro. B90: Shir 7J 145
DY2: Dud 2M 97
Elizabeth Ho. B76: Walm 6M 59
DY9: Lye 4D 116
WS5: Wals 2D 56
Elizabeth M. B69: Tiv 7A 76
Elizabeth Prout Gdns.
B65: B'hth 8B 98
Elizabeth Rd. B13: Mose 7J 121
B33: Stech 6J 103
B63: Hale 6M 117
B70: W Brom 5D 76
B73: New O 7C 58
CV31: Lea S 3L 223
LE10: Hinc 6K 69
WS5: Wals 2B 56
WS11: Cann 3E 8
Elizabeth Sports Cen. 6J 111
Elizabeth Wlk. DY4: Tip 8A 54
Elizabeth Way B97: Redd 4D 212
CV8: Ken 4E 198
CV23: Long L 4H 179
Elkington Cft. B90: M'path 4A 168
Elkington La. CV23: Barby 8H 207
Elkington St. B6: Aston 4L 101
CV6: Cov 1F 152
Elkstone Cl. B92: Olton 6B 124
Elkstone Covert B14: K Hth 7J 143
Ellacombe Rd. CV2: Cov 1K 153
Elland Gro. B27: A Grn 7J 123
Ellards Dr. WV11: Wed 4M 37
Ellenbrook Cl. B97: Redd 4B 212
Ellen St. B18: Hock 5G 101 (2A 4)
(not continuous)
Ellenvale Cl. WV14: Cose 1G 75
Ellerbeck B77: Wiln 8H 33
(not continuous)
Ellerby Gro. B24: Erd 5L 81
Ellerdene Cl. B98: Redd 1D 220
Ellerman Gdns. CV6: Longf 6F 130
Ellerside Gro. B31: N'fld 7M 141
Ellerslie Cl. DY5: Quar B 1D 116
Ellerslie Rd. B13: Mose 2C 144
Ellerton Rd. B44: K'sdng 8B 58
Ellerton Wlk. WV10: Wolv 4F 36
Ellesborough Rd. B17: Harb 1B 120
Ellesmere Dr. DY12: Bew 2B 156
Ellesmere Rd. B8: Salt 5D 102
CV12: Bed 7G 111
WS11: Cann 1B 14
Ellice Dr. B36: Cas B 2H 105
Elliots Fld. Retail Pk.
CV21: Rugby 2B 180
Elliott Cl. WS11: Cann 4F 8
Elliott Ct. CV5: Cov 8K 151
Elliott Gdns. B45: Redn 4J 163
Elliott Rd. B29: S Oak 8E 120
Elliotts La. WV8: Cod 6G 21
Elliotts Rd. DY4: Tip 4L 75
Elliott Way B6: Witt 5L 79
Elliot Way B6: Witt 6M 79
Ellis Av. DY5: Brie H 7A 96
Ellison Cl. LE9: S Stan 6K 71
Ellison St. B70: W Brom 8J 77
Ellis Pk. Dr. CV3: Bin 8B 154
Ellis St. B1: Birm 8K 101 (7E 4)
Elliston Av. B44: Gt Barr 1L 79
Elliston Gro. CV31: Lea S 3C 224
Ellis Wlk. WS11: Cann 1F 14
Ell La. CV23: Brin 5M 155
Ellowes Rd. DY3: Lwr G 5C 74
Ellys Rd. CV1: Cov 4C 152 (1B 6)
Elm Av. B12: Bal H 4A 122
WS10: W'bry 5F 54
WV11: Wed 1H 37
WV14: Bils 3K 53
Elmay Rd. B26: Sheld 2A 124
Elm Bank B13: Mose 6A 122
Elmbank CV47: Sou 6H 225
Elm Bank Cl. CV32: Lill 5A 218
Elmbank Gro. B20: Hand 4E 78
Elmbank Rd. CV8: Ken 3E 198
WS5: Wals 5C 56
ELMBRIDGE 5A 208
Elmbridge Cl. B63: Crad 4K 117
Elmbridge Dr. B90: M'path 3B 168
Elmbridge La. WR9: Elmb 3A 208
Elmbridge Rd. B44: K'sdng 3L 79
Elmbridge Way B31: N'fld 7D 142
DY3: Sed 3E 74
Elm Cl. CV3: Bin W 2C 176
CV47: Sou 6H 225
DY3: Gorn 7B 74
DY8: Stourb 7K 115
DY10: Cookl 5B 136
Elm Ct. B13: Mose 5M 121
B66: Smeth 1J 99
B97: Redd 5D 212
CV5: Alle 1C 150
WS1: Wals 1A 56
Elm Cres. DY4: Tip 3M 75
Elm Cft. B68: O'bry 2J 119
Elmcroft Av. B32: Bart G 8G 119
Elmcroft Ct. WS11: Cann 8E 8
Elmcroft Gdns. WV10: Bush 6E 22
Elmcroft Rd. B26: Yard 2M 123
Elmdale B62: Quin 2G 119
Elmdale Cres. B31: N'fld 4L 141
Elmdale Dr. DY10: Kidd 4C 158
WS9: A'rdge 1J 41
Elmdale Gro. B31: N'fld 5L 141
Elmdale Rd. LE9: Earl S 3D 70
WV4: Penn 4A 52
WV14: Cose 2G 75
Elmdene Cl. CV8: Wols 5G 177
Elmdene Rd. CV8: Ken 5H 199
ELMDON 7F 124
Elmdon Cl. B92: Sol 7D 124
WV10: Oxl 8A 22
Elmdon Coppice B92: Sol 2F 146
Elmdon Ct. *B29: W Cas* 2C 142
(off Abdon Av.)
B37: Mars G 2G 125
ELMDON HEATH 3E 146
Elmdon La. B26: Birm A 6G 125
B37: Mars G 2F 124
Elmdon Pk. 7E 124
Elmdon Pk. Rd. B92: Sol 7D 124
Elmdon Rd. B27: A Grn 5K 123
B29: S Oak 7G 121
B37: Mars G 2G 125
WV10: Oxl 8A 22
Elmdon Trad. Est.
B37: Mars G 4J 125
Elm Dr. B31: Longb 8J 141
B43: Gt Barr 8D 56
B62: B'hth 8E 98
DY10: Blak 7H 137
ELMESTHORPE 4E 70
Elmesthorpe Est. LE9: Elme 4E 70
Elmesthorpe La.
LE9: Earl S, Elme 2C 70
Elm Farm Av. B37: Mars G 2F 124
Elm Farm Rd.
WV2: Wolv 2D 52 (8K 7)
Elmfield Av. B24: Erd 5M 81
Elmfield Cres. B13: Mose 7M 121
Elmfield Rd. B36: Cas B 2E 104
CV10: Nun 2J 89
DY11: Hartl 8A 184
Elmfield Vw. DY1: Dud 6G 75
Elmfield Wlk. DY13: Stour S 5D 182
Elm Gdns. WS14: Lich 2J 19
Elm Grn. DY1: Dud 4G 75
Elm Gro. B37: K'hrst 3F 104
B61: B'gve 5A 188
CV7: Bal C 3J 171
CV7: Old A 7E 86
CV9: Hurl 5J 63
DY7: Kinv 6C 114
DY13: Stour S 7A 182
WS12: Hunt 1D 8
WV8: Bilb 6G 21
ELMHURST 4G 13
Elmhurst Av. B65: Row R 6C 98
Elmhurst Cl. B97: Redd 5D 220
Elmhurst Dr. B78: Tam 6A 32
DY6: K'wfrd 5M 95
WS7: Chase 5G 17
Elmhurst Rd. B21: Hand 8E 78
CV6: Longf 5G 131
Elmley Cl. DY11: Kidd 6H 157
WV14: Cose 2H 75
Elmley Gro. B30: K Nor 7H 143
WV6: Pert 6F 34
Elmley Ho. *B97: Redd* 5A 212
(off Cardy Cl.)
ELMLEY LOVETT 8F 184
Elm Lodge B92: H Ard 2A 148
Elmore Cl. B37: F'bri 5G 105
CV3: Bin 1K 175
Elmore Grn. Cl. WS3: Blox 1H 39
Elmore Grn. Rd. WS3: Blox 8G 25
Elmore Rd. B33: Kitts G 6A 104
CV22: Bil 8M 179
Elmore Row WS3: Blox 8H 25
Elm Pl. DY10: Cookl 5B 136
Elm Rd. B30: B'vlle 1F 142
B76: Walm 7M 59
Elm Rd. B97: Redd 5D 212
CV32: Lill 6B 218
DY1: Dud 5J 75
DY6: K'wfrd 3L 95
DY10: Kidd 3A 158
WS3: Blox 3K 39
WS11: Nort C 4B 16
Elm Row CV47: S'ton 1M 225
Elms, The B16: Birm 6F 100
CV12: Bed 7E 110
CV35: Leek W 3F 216
Elms Cl. B38: K Nor 1C 164
B91: Sol 4D 146
Elmsdale WV6: Tett 7G 35
Elmsdale Av. CV6: Cov 7E 130
Elmsdale Ct. WS1: Wals 1M 55
Elms Dr. CV22: Hillm 1F 206
WS11: Cann 8C 8
Elms La. WV10: Share 1K 23
Elms Paddock, The
CV23: Clift D 4F 180
Elms Rd. B15: Edg 5F 120
B72: S Cold 6J 59
Elmstead Av. B33: Sheld 2D 124
Elmstead Cl. WS5: Wals 8E 40
Elmstead Twr. *B5: Birm* 2L 121
(off Berrington Wlk.)
Elmstead Wood WS5: Wals 8E 40
Elmstone Cl. B97: Redd 4C 220
Elm St. WV3: Wolv 8A 36
WV13: W'hall 7C 38
Elm Ter. B69: Tiv 8A 76
Elm Tree Av. CV4: Tile H 7G 151
Elm Tree Cl. B78: K'bry 3D 62
WV5: Wom 4F 72
Elm Tree Dr. LE10: Burb 1M 91
Elm Tree Gro. B63: Crad 3K 117
Elm Tree Ri. B92: H Ard 3A 148
Elm Tree Rd. B17: Harb 3A 120
B30: Stir 3G 143
CV12: Bulk 7D 112
Elmtree Rd. B74: S'tly 8K 41
Elm Tree Wlk. B79: Tam 2M 31
Elm Tree Way B64: Old H 8M 97
Elm Way CV10: Harts 1A 88
Elmwood Av. CV6: Cov 4M 151
WV11: Ess 6A 24
Elmwood Cl. B5: Edg 3K 121
CV7: Bal C 3J 171
WS11: Cann 6G 9
Elmwood Ct. B73: S'tly 4A 58
CV1: Cov 5C 152 (1B 6)
Elmwood Gdns. B20: Hand 7H 79
Elmwood Gro. B47: H'wd 3A 166
Elmwood Ri. DY3: Sed 8B 52
Elmwood Rd. B24: Erd 7J 81
B74: S'tly 4A 58
DY8: Word 6J 95
Elmwoods B32: Bart G 7H 119
Elphin Cl. CV6: Cov 6A 130
Elphinstone End B24: Erd 3J 81
Elsee Rd. CV21: Rugby 6B 180
Elsma Rd. B68: O'bry 1J 119
Elsmore Mdw. WS13: Lich 3G 19
Elston Hall La. WV10: Bush 8D 22
Elstop Av. CV23: Brow 1D 180
Elstree Rd. B23: Erd 4D 80
Elswick Gro. B44: K'sdng 1B 80
Elswick Rd. B44: K'sdng 8B 58
Elsworth Gro. B25: Yard 3J 123
Elsworth Rd. B31: N'fld 7D 142
Elter Cl. CV21: Brow 2D 180
Eltham Gro. B44: K'sdng 8B 58
Eltham Rd. CV3: Cov 2E 174
Elton Cl. CV32: Lill 7C 218
WV10: Bush 5E 22
Elton Cft. B93: Dorr 5F 168
Elton Gro. B27: A Grn 7G 123
Eltonia Cft. B26: Sheld 3B 124
Elton Rd. DY12: Bew 2B 156
Elunda Gro. WS7: Chase 3E 16
Elva Cft. B36: Cas B 8F 82
Elvers Grn. La. B93: Know 3L 169
Elvetham Rd. Nth.
B15: Birm 1J 121 (8C 4)
Elviron Dr. WV6: Tett 4H 35
Elwell Av. LE9: Barw 1B 70
Elwell Cres. DY1: Dud 3F 74
Elwells Cl. WV14: Cose 6G 53
Elwell St. B70: W Brom 4E 76
WS10: W'bry 6H 55
Elwy Circ. CV7: Ash G 2B 130
Elwyn Rd. B73: S Cold 6G 59
Ely Cl. B37: Chel W 7H 105
B65: Row R 5E 98
CV2: W'grve S 3A 154
DY11: Kidd 3G 157
WS11: Hth H 8H 9
Ely Cres. B71: W Brom 2H 77
Ely Gro. B32: Quin 5M 119
Ely Pl. WS2: Wals 8H 39
Ely Rd. WS2: Wals 8H 39
Emay Cl. B70: W Brom 1F 76
Embankment, The
DY5: Brie H 6E 96
Embassy Dr.
B15: Edg 1G 121 (8A 4)
B69: O'bry 1E 98
Embassy Rd. B69: O'bry 1E 98
Embassy Wlk. CV2: Cov 1K 153
Emberton Way B77: Amin 4F 32
Embleton Cl. LE10: Hinc 8H 69
Embleton Gro. B34: Hodg H 3A 104
Emerald Ct. B8: W End 4J 103
B92: Olton 8M 123
Emerald Way CV31: Lea S 4M 223
Emerson Cl. DY3: Lwr G 5A 74
Emerson Gro. WV10: Bush 1F 36
Emerson Rd. B17: Harb 3C 120
CV2: Cov 6J 153
WV10: Bush 8F 22
Emery Cl. B23: Erd 8D 80
CV2: Cov 2L 153
WS1: Wals 1M 55
Emery Ct. DY10: Kidd 2L 157
Emery Ho. B23: Erd 3C 80
Emery St. WS1: Wals 1M 55
Emily Gdns. B16: Birm 6F 100
Emily Rd. B26: Yard 3K 123
Emily Smith Ho. *CV2: Cov* 8H 131
(off Roseberry Av.)
Emily St. B12: Birm 1M 121
B70: W Brom 7H 77
Emmanuel Rd. B73: W Grn 2H 81
WS7: Burn 2H 17
Emmeline St. B9: Birm 8B 102
Emmott Dr. CV31: Lea S 3B 224
Emperor Pl. *DY11: Kidd* 1L 157
(off Oxbow Way)
Emperor Way CV21: Rugby 2M 179
Empire Cl. WS9: A'rdge 1F 40
Empire Ct. B97: Redd 4E 212
Empire Ind. Pk. WS9: A'rdge 1F 40
Empire Rd. CV4: Tile H 7E 150
Empress Arc. CV3: Cov 7H 153
Empress Way WS10: Darl 1D 54
EMSCOTE 1F 222
Emscote Dr. B73: W Grn 2H 81
Emscote Grn. B91: Sol 7L 145
Emscote Rd. B6: Aston 8M 79
CV3: Cov 7J 153
CV34: Warw 2G 223
Emsworth Cres. WV9: Pend 7A 22
Emsworth Gro. B14: K Hth 3K 143
Ena Rd. CV1: Cov 4D 152
Endeavour Pl.
DY13: Stour S 7G 183
Endemere Rd. CV6: Cov 1D 152
Enderby Cl. B93: Ben H 5F 168
Enderby Dr. WV4: Penn 5M 51
Enderley Cl. WS3: Blox 6H 25
Enderley Dr. WS3: Blox 6H 25
End Hall Rd. WV6: Tett 6G 35
Endhill Rd. B44: K'sdng 5A 58
Endicott Rd. B6: Aston 8M 79
Endmoor Gro. B23: Erd 3D 80
Endsleigh Gdns.
CV31: Lea S 3B 224
Endsleigh Gro. B28: Hall G 1G 145
Endwood Ct. B20: Hand 7G 79
Endwood Ct. Rd. B20: Hand 7G 79
Endwood Dr. B74: Lit A 5C 42
B91: Sol 7M 145
Energy Way B10: Small H 3F 122
(not continuous)
ENFIELD 4C 212
Enfield Cl. B23: Erd 3F 80
Enfield Ct. *B29: W Cas* 2C 142
(off Abdon Av.)
Enfield Ind. Est. B97: Redd 4D 212
Enfield Rd. B15: Edg 1H 121 (8B 4)
B65: Row R 6D 98
B97: Redd 4D 220
(not continuous)
CV2: Cov 6H 153
Enford Cl. B34: S End 3D 104
Engadine Rd. B60: B'gve 8C 188
Engine La. B77: Glas 7G 33
DY9: Lye 3D 116
DY13: Stour S 6F 182
WS8: Bwnhls 1B 26
WS10: Mox 5A 54
Engine St. B66: Smeth 3B 100
B69: O'bry 3G 99
England Cres. CV31: Lea S 2L 223
Englestede Cl. B20: Hand 6F 78
Engleton Rd. CV6: Cov 3A 152
Englewood Dr. B28: Hall G 1G 145
Ennerdale CV21: Brow 2C 180
Ennerdale Cl. CV32: Lea S 7K 217
WS8: Clay 2E 26
Ennerdale Cres. CV11: Nun 3M 89
Ennerdale Dr. B63: Hale 7K 117
WV6: Pert 5F 34
Ennerdale La. CV2: Cov 5M 153
Ennerdale Rd. B43: Gt Barr 3F 78
DY13: Stour S 3F 182
WV6: Tett 1K 35
Ennersdale Bungs. B46: Col 8M 83
Ennersdale Cl. B46: Col 8M 83
Ennersdale Rd. B46: Col 8M 83
Enright Cl. CV32: Lea S 7L 217
Ensall Dr. DY8: Word 8L 95
Ensbury Cl. WV12: W'hall 5D 38
Ensdale Row WV13: W'hall 8A 38
Ensdon Gro. B44: K'sdng 8B 58
Ensford Cl. B74: Four O 4E 42
Ensign Bus. Cen.
CV4: W'wd H 3F 172
Ensign Cl. CV4: Tile H 8D 150
Ensor Cl. CV11: Nun 4A 90
Ensor Dr. B78: Pole 8M 33

Enstone Rd.—Far High Dr.

Enstone Rd. B23: Erd 2G **81**
DY1: Dud 1F **96**
Enterprise Dr. B74: S'tly 2L **57**
DY9: Lye 3G **117**
Enterprise Gro. WS3: Pels 4B **26**
Enterprise Ind. Pk.
WS14: Lich 1M **19**
Enterprise Trad. Est.
DY5: Brie H 6F **96**
Enterprise Way
B7: Birm 5M **101** (1J **5**)
Enville Cl. B37: Mars G 8H **105**
WS3: Blox 6G **25**
Enville Comn. Rd. DY7: Env 5A **94**
Enville Gro. B11: S'brk 4D **122**
Enville Pl. *DY8: Stourb 4M **115***
(off Short St.)
Enville Rd. DY3: Lwr G 5D **74**
DY6: W Hth 1G **95**
DY7: Kinv 3A **114**
WV4: Penn 5J **51**
Enville St. DY8: Stourb 4M **115**
Enville Twr. Mill DY7: Env 5B **94**
Epperston Ct. CV31: Lea S 2M **223**
Epping Cl. B45: Fran 7H **141**
WS3: Wals 3M **39**
Epping Gro. B44: K'sdng 2A **80**
Epping Way CV32: Lill 5C **218**
Epsom Cl. B77: Dost 5C **46**
B97: Redd 1C **220**
CV12: Bed 5H **111**
WS14: Lich 2K **19**
WV6: Pert 5F **34**
Epsom Ct. B29: W Cas 2C **142**
Epsom Dr. CV3: W'hall 3J **175**
Epsom Gro. B44: K'sdng 1B **80**
Epsom Rd. B61: Cats 8A **162**
CV22: Bil 8K **179**
CV32: Lill 5C **218**
Epwell Gro. B44: K'sdng 3M **79**
Epwell Rd. B44: K'sdng 3M **79**
Epworth Ct. DY5: P'ntt 4B **96**
Equipoint B25: Yard 2K **123**
Equity Rd. LE9: Earl S 2E **70**
Equity Rd. E. LE9: Earl S 1E **70**
Erasmus Rd. B11: S'brk 2A **122**
Erasmus Way WS13: Lich 1G **19**
Ercall Cl. B23: Erd 3A **80**
ERDINGTON **5F 80**
Erdington Hall Rd. B24: Erd 7E **80**
Erdington Ind. Pk. B24: Erd 5M **81**
Erdington Rd. CV9: Ath 2K **65**
WS9: A'rdge 5H **41**
Erdington Sports Club **1F 80**
Erdington Station (Rail) **4F 80**
Erdington Swimming Pool &
Turkish Suite **5G 81**
Erica Av. CV12: Bed 7F **110**
Erica Cl. B29: W Cas 1A **142**
DY11: Kidd 8K **135**
Erica Dr. CV31: W'nsh 7B **224**
Erica Rd. WS5: Wals 6B **56**
Eric Grey Cl. CV2: Cov 4G **153**
Eric Inott Ho. CV3: Cov 3E **174**
Eringden B77: Wiln 8H **33**
Erithway Rd. CV3: Finh 5B **174**
Ermington Cres.
B36: Hodg H 1L **103**
Ermington Rd. WV4: Penn 4D **52**
Erneley Cl. DY13: Stour S 8F **182**
Ernest Clarke Cl.
WV12: W'hall 5C **38**
Ernest Richards Rd.
CV12: Bed 5H **111**
Ernest Rd. B12: Bal H 5B **122**
B67: Smeth 3L **99**
DY2: Dud 8M **75**
Ernest St. B1: Birm 8K **101** (8E **4**)
Ernsford Av. CV3: Cov 8H **153**
Ernsford Cl. B93: Dorr 7F **168**
Erskine Cl. LE10: Hinc 7G **69**
Erskine St. B7: Birm . . .5B **102** (2M **5**)
Erwood Cl. B97: Redd 7B **212**
Esher Dr. CV3: Cov 2E **174**
Esher Rd. B44: Gt Barr 5M **57**
B71: W Brom 3K **77**
Eskdale CV21: Brow 1C **180**
Eskdale Cl. WV1: Wolv 7G **37**
Eskdale Rd. LE10: Hinc 1G **91**
Eskdale Wlk. CV3: W'hall 2K **175**
DY5: Brie H 1B **116**
Eskrett St. WS12: Hed 4H **9**
Esme Rd. B11: S'hll 5B **122**
Esmond Cl. B30: B'vlle 4D **142**
Esporta Health & Fitness
Birmingham **8G 101** (**8A 4**)
Broadlands **4D 22**
Rugby **3B 180**
Shenstone **8G 19**
Whitley **2F 174**
Essendon Gro. B8: W End 5H **103**
Essendon Rd. B8: W End 5H **103**
Essendon Wlk. B8: W End 5H **103**
Essen La. CV23: Kils 6M **207**
Essex Av. B71: W Brom 2J **77**
DY6: K'wfrd 4H **95**
WS10: W'bry 5J **55**
Essex Cl. CV5: E Grn 6H **151**
CV8: Ken 7E **198**
Essex Ct. B29: W Cas 2C **142**
CV34: Warw 1E **222**
Essex Dr. WS12: Hed 5H **9**
Essex Gdns. DY8: Woll 2K **115**
Essex Ho. WV1: Wolv 5C **36** (1J **7**)
Essex Rd. B75: R'ley 8K **43**
DY2: Dud 3G **97**
Essex St. B5: Birm 8K **101** (8F **4**)
CV21: Rugby 5A **180**
WS2: Wals 4L **39**
ESSINGTON **6A 24**
Essington Cl. DY8: Word 8L **95**
WS14: Lich 4G **19**
WS14: Shens 3F **28**
Essington Ho. B8: W End 4G **103**
Essington Ind. Est.
WV11: Ess 5M **23**
Essington Rd. WV12: W'hall 7B **24**
Essington St.
B16: Birm 8H **101** (7B **4**)
Essington Way WV1: Wolv 8H **37**
Este Rd. B26: Yard 1A **124**
Esterton Cl. CV6: Cov 7C **130**
Estone Wlk. B6: Aston 2M **101**
Estria Rd. B15: Edg 2H **121**
Estridge La. WS6: Gt Wyr 7G **15**
Etchell Rd. B78: Tam 6M **31**
Ethelfield Rd. CV2: Cov 6H **153**
Ethelfleda Rd. B77: Hock 4F **46**
Ethelfleda Ter. WS10: W'bry 6F **54**
Ethelred Cl. B74: Four O 6G **43**
Ethel Rd. B17: Harb 4D **120**
Ethel St. B2: Birm 7K **101** (5F **4**)
B67: Smeth 7M **99**
B68: O'bry 5G **99**
Etheridge Rd. WV14: Bils 2J **53**
Eton Cl. DY3: Sed 2F **74**
Eton Ct. *B74: Four O 7F **42***
(off Vesey Cl.)
WS14: Lich 3H **19**
Eton Dr. DY8: Stourb 6A **116**
Etone Ct. CV11: Nun 4H **89**
Etone Sports Cen. **4K 89**
Eton Rd. B12: Bal H 5B **122**
Eton Wlk. DY9: Hag 3A **138**
Etruria Way WV14: Bils 2L **53**
Etta Gro. B44: Gt Barr 5M **57**
Ettingley Cl. B98: Redd 4H **221**
ETTINGSHALL **4G 53**
ETTINGSHALL PARK **5E 52**
Ettingshall Pk. Farm La.
WV4: E'shll 5E **52**
Ettingshall Rd. WV2: E'shll 2G **53**
WV14: Cose 7G **53**
Ettington Cl. B93: Dorr 7D **168**
Ettington Rd. B6: Aston 1L **101**
CV5: E Grn 6G **151**
Ettymore Cl. DY3: Sed 1D **74**
Ettymore Rd. DY3: Sed 1D **74**
Ettymore Rd. W. DY3: Sed 1C **74**
Etwall Rd. B28: Hall G 4E **144**
Euan Cl. B17: Harb 1C **120**
Eunal Ct. *B97: Redd 4E **220***
(off Well Cl.)
Euro Bus. Pk. B69: O'bry 8D **76**
Euro Ct. B13: Mose 7B **122**
Europa Av. B70: W Brom 7M **77**
(not continuous)
Europa Way CV34: Warw 8H **223**
WS14: Lich 1M **19**
European Bus. Pk. B69: O'bry . . .2E **98**
Euroway Pk. B69: O'bry 1J **99**
Eustace Rd. CV12: Bulk 8D **112**
Euston Cres. CV3: W'hall 2J **175**
Euston Pl. CV32: Lea S 1M **223**
Euston Sq. CV32: Lea S 1M **223**
Evans Cl. CV12: Bed 6J **111**
DY4: Tip 4J **75**
DY11: W'ley 6J **135**
Evans Cft. B78: Faz 8A **32**
Evans Gdns. B29: S Oak 8D **120**
Evans Gro. CV31: W'nsh 7A **224**
Evans Pl. WV14: Bils 2L **53**
Evans Rd. CV22: Bil 7J **179**
Evans St. WV6: Wolv 5A **36**
WV13: W'hall 8K **37**
WV14: Cose 8F **52**
Eva Rd. B18: Win G 3D **100**
B68: O'bry 6J **99**
Evason Ct. B6: Aston 8L **79**
EVE HILL **7H 75**
Eve La. DY1: Dud 4F **74**
Evelyn Av. CV6: Cov 7E **130**
Evelyn Cft. B73: Bold 1G **81**
Evelyn Rd. B11: S'hll 5C **122**
Evenlode Cl. B92: Olton 6B **124**
B98: Redd 8F **212**
Evenlode Cres. CV6: Cov 4M **151**
Evenlode Gro. WV13: W'hall 8D **38**
Evenlode Rd. B92: Olton 6A **124**
Everard Cl. CV23: Clift D 4G **181**
Everard Ct. CV11: Nun 7L **89**
Everdon Cl. CV22: Hillm 1D **206**
Everdon Rd. CV6: Cov 7B **130**
(not continuous)
Evered Bardon Ho. *B69: O'bry . . .2E **98***
(off Round's Grn. Rd.)
Everest Rd. B20: Hand 6G **79**
CV22: Rugby 1L **205**
WS2: Wals 6F **38**
Everglade Rd. CV9: Wood E 7H **47**
Evergreen Cl. WV14: Cose 1H **75**
Evergreen Hgts. WS12: Hed 1G **9**
Everitt Dr. B93: Know 3G **169**
Eversleigh Rd. CV6: Cov 2L **151**
Eversley Dale B24: Erd 7G **81**
Eversley Gro. DY3: Sed 7C **52**
WV11: Wed 3J **37**
Eversley Rd. B9: Small H 8D **102**
(not continuous)
Evers St. DY5: Quar B 1G **117**
Everton Rd. B8: W End 5J **103**
Eves Cft. B32: Bart G 8J **119**
Evesham Cres. WS3: Blox 6F **24**
Evesham Ho. *B60: B'gve 6B **188***
(off Burcot La.)
Evesham M. B97: Redd 6E **212**
Evesham Ri. DY2: Neth 6K **97**
Evesham Rd. B96: A'wd B 6E **220**
B97: Redd 8D **212**
Evesham Sq. B97: Redd 6E **212**
Evesham St. B97: Redd 6E **212**
Evesham Wlk. B97: Redd 5E **212**
(not continuous)
CV4: Canly 4K **173**
Eveson Rd. DY8: Stourb 7K **115**
Evreux Way CV21: Rugby 6A **180**
Ewart Rd. WS2: Wals 6E **38**
Ewell Rd. B24: Erd 5H **81**
Ewhurst Av. B29: S Oak 8F **120**
(Heeley Rd.)
B29: S Oak 1G **143**
(Umberslade Rd.)
Ewhurst Cl. WV13: W'hall 1M **53**
Ewloe Cl. DY10: Kidd 8L **157**
Exbury Cl. WV9: Pend 7M **21**
Exbury Way CV11: Nun 1L **111**
Excel Cl. B11: S'brk 2B **122**
Excelsior Gro. WS3: Pels 4B **26**
Exchange, The WS3: Blox 8H **25**
Exchange Ind. Est., The
WS11: Cann 3E **14**
Exchange St. DY5: Brie H 5D **96**
DY10: Kidd 4L **157**
WV1: Wolv 7C **36** (4J **7**)
Exe Cft. B31: Longb 1B **164**
Exeter Cl. CV3: Bin 1K **175**
DY11: Kidd 3G **157**
Exeter Dr. B37: Mars G 1F **124**
B79: Tam 3L **31**
Exeter Pas. B1: Birm 8K **101** (8F **4**)
Exeter Pl. WS2: Wals 8H **39**
Exeter Rd. B29: S Oak 7F **120**
B66: Smeth 4B **100**
DY2: Neth 7K **97**
WS11: Cann 1B **14**
Exeter St. B1: Birm 8K **101** (8F **4**)
Exford Cl. DY5: Brie H 2B **116**
EXHALL **2G 131**
Exhall CV7: Exh 8G **111**
Exhall Basin CV6: Longf 4H **131**
Exhall Cl. B91: Sol 7L **145**
B98: Redd 4K **213**
Exhall Ct. B23: Erd 7C **80**
Exhall Grn. CV7: Exh 2F **130**
EXHALL HALL GREEN **2F 130**
Exhall Mobile Homes
CV7: Ash G 2B **130**
Exhall Rd. CV7: Ker E 3M **129**
Exham Cl. CV34: Warw 8E **216**
Exhibition Way B40: Nat E C . . .5K **125**
Exis Ct. CV11: Nun 7L **89**
Exley B77: Wiln 8D **32**
Exminster Rd. CV3: Cov 4E **174**
Exmoor Ct. B61: B'gve 5A **188**
Exmoor Dr. B61: B'gve 5A **188**
CV32: Lill 5C **218**
Exmoor Grn. WV11: Wed 2J **37**
Exmouth Cl. CV2: Cov 2J **153**
Exonbury Wlk. WS11: Cann 7F **8**
Exon Ct. DY4: Tip 3M **75**
Expressway, The
B70: W Brom 5H **77**
Exton Cl. CV7: Ash G 2C **130**
WV11: Wed 1M **37**
Exton Gdns. *B66: Smeth 3D **100***
(off Foundry La.)
Exton Way B8: Salt 4D **102**
Eydon Cl. CV21: Brow 3E **180**
Eyffler Cl. CV34: Warw 2D **222**
Eyland Gro. WS1: Wals 7M **39**
Eymore Cl. B29: W Cas 3B **142**
Eyre St. B18: Hock 6G **101**
Eyston Av. DY4: Tip 1D **76**
Eyton Cl. B98: Redd 6K **213**
Eyton Cft. B12: Birm 2M **121**
Ezekiel La. WV12: W'hall 3C **38**

F

Fabian Cl. B45: Fran 7F **140**
CV3: W'hall 2K **175**
Fabian Cres. B90: Shir 8H **145**
Fabius Cl. LE10: Hinc 2J **91**
Facet Rd. B38: K Nor 7G **143**
Factory Est. B44: P Barr 3L **79**
Factory La. B61: B'gve 8L **187**
Factory Rd. B18: Hock 3F **100**
DY4: Tip 3L **75**
LE10: Hinc 8K **69**
Factory St. WS10: Darl 3C **54**
Fair Acre Rd. LE9: Barw 3A **70**
Fairbanks Cl. CV2: W'grve S . . .2A **154**
Fairbourne Av. B44: Gt Barr 7L **57**
B65: Row R 5E **98**
Fairbourne Gdns. B97: Redd . . .1C **220**
Fairbourne Way CV6: Cov 1L **151**
Fairbourn Twr. B23: Erd 3G **81**
Fairburn Cres. WS3: Pels 4B **26**
Fair Cl. CV23: F'ton 8J **203**
Faircroft CV8: Ken 6F **198**
Faircroft Av. B76: Walm 3M **81**
Faircroft Rd. B36: Cas B 8D **82**
Fairdene Way B43: Gt Barr 1D **78**
Fairey Ind. Est. B77: Wiln 1D **46**
Fairfax Ct. CV34: Warw 2F **222**
Fairfax Rd. B31: Longb 1A **164**
B75: S Cold 4M **59**
WV10: Bush 7D **22**
Fairfax St. CV1: Cov 6D **152** (4D **6**)
FAIRFIELD
Bromsgrove **6K 161**
Kidderminster **6J 135**
Fairfield CV7: Exh 8G **111**
Fairfield Cl. WS12: Hth H 8K **9**
Fairfield Ct. CV3: Cov 2G **175**
Fairfield Dr. B62: B'hth 8E **98**
DY7: Kinv 6A **114**
WS3: Pels 5B **26**
WV8: Cod 5E **20**
Fairfield Gro. B62: B'hth 8E **98**
Fairfield Ho. *B60: B'gve 6B **188***
(off Burcot La.)
Fairfield La. DY11: Kidd 6H **135**
Fairfield Mt. WS1: Wals 1M **55**
Fairfield Pk. Ind. Est.
B62: B'hth 8E **98**
Fairfield Pk. Rd. B62: B'hth 8E **98**
Fairfield Ri. CV7: Mer 8J **127**
DY8: Woll 4J **115**
Fairfield Rd. B14: K Hth 1L **143**
B61: B'hth 8K **161**
B62: B'hth 8E **98**
B63: Hale 7A **118**
DY2: Dud 2K **97**
DY8: Word 7M **95**
Fairfields Hill B78: Pole 1M **47**
Fairford Cl. B91: Shir 4K **145**
B98: Redd 2L **213**
Fairford Gdns. DY8: Word 6L **95**
WS7: Burn 3J **17**
Fairford Rd. B44: K'sdng 3M **79**
Fairgreen Gdns. DY5: P'ntt 4B **96**
Fairgreen Way B29: S Oak 8F **120**
B74: S'tly 8A **42**
Fair Ground Way WS1: Wals 1K **55**
Fairhaven Cft. B62: B'hth 8E **98**
Fairhills DY3: Sed 1D **74**
Fairhill Way B11: S'brk 2B **122**
Fairholme Rd. B36: Hodg H . . .2H **103**
Fairhurst Dr. CV32: Lea S 6L **217**
Fair Isle Dr. CV10: Nun 6F **88**
Fair Lady Dr. WS7: C Ter 8D **10**
Fairlands Pk. CV4: Canly 4L **173**
Fairlawn B15: Edg 2G **121**
Fairlawn Cl. CV32: Lea S 8K **217**
WV12: W'hall 8C **24**
Fairlawn Dr. DY6: K'wfrd 5K **95**
Fairlawns B26: Yard 8A **104**
B76: Walm 1A **82**
Fairlawn Way WV12: W'hall 8C **24**
Fairlie Cres. B38: K Nor 8D **142**
Fairlight Dr. B45: B Grn 8G **163**
Fairmead Ri. B38: K Nor 8E **142**
Fairmile Cl. CV3: Bin 1J **175**
Fairmile Rd. B63: Hale 3M **117**
Fairmont Rd. B60: B'gve 1B **210**
Fairmount Dr. WS11: Cann 1E **14**
Fairoak Dr. B60: B'gve 3L **209**
WV6: Tett 6H **35**
Fair Oaks Dr. WS6: Gt Wyr 1G **15**
Fairview Av. B42: Gt Barr 3H **79**
Fairview Cl. B77: Amin 4F **32**
WS6: C Hay 7D **14**
WV11: Wed 3H **37**
Fairview Cotts. *B48: A'chu 3M **189***
(off Birches La.)
Fairview Ct. WS2: Wals 7D **38**
Fairview Cres. DY6: K'wfrd 4M **95**
WV11: Wed 2H **37**
Fairview Gro. WV11: Wed 2H **37**
Fairview Ind. Est. B76: Curd 2H **83**
Fairview Rd. DY1: Dud 6G **75**
WV4: Penn 5J **51**
WV11: Wed 2H **37**
Fairview Wlk. CV6: Longf 7E **130**
Fairway B31: N'fld 7L **141**
B77: Hock 4E **46**
CV11: Nun 8B **90**
WS4: S'fld 8D **26**
WS11: Cann 3D **14**
Fairway, The B38: K Nor 7D **142**
LE10: Burb 2M **91**
Fairway Av. B69: Tiv 1A **98**
Fairway Ct. B77: Amin 6J **33**
CV21: Rugby 5D **180**
Fairway Dr. B45: Rubery 3F **162**
Fairway Grn. WV14: Bils 2K **53**
Fairway Ri. CV8: Ken 3J **199**
Fairway Rd. B68: O'bry 7F **98**
Fairways, The CV32: Lea S 7K **217**
Fairways Av. DY8: Stourb 7L **115**
Fairways Cl. CV5: Alle 3G **151**
DY8: Stourb 7L **115**
Fairways Ct. DY10: Kidd 5A **158**
LE10: Hinc 6A **70**
Fairways Dr. B60: B'wll 4G **189**
Fairyfield Av. B43: Gt Barr 8D **56**
Fairyfield Ct. B43: Gt Barr 8D **56**
Fakenham Cft. B17: Harb 2M **119**
Falcon B77: Wiln 3G **47**
Falcon Av. CV3: Bin 1M **175**
Falcon Cl. CV11: Nun 1B **112**
DY10: Kidd 6L **157**
WS6: C Hay 7C **14**
WS11: Cann 7C **8**
Falcon Ct. *CV47: Sou 5H **225***
(off Bull St.)
Falcon Cres. WV14: Cose 7F **52**
Falcondale Rd. WV12: W'hall . . .8C **24**
Falconers Grn. LE10: Burb 3M **91**
Falconhurst Rd. B29: S Oak 7C **120**
FALCON LODGE **4B 60**
Falcon Lodge Cres.
B75: S Cold 4M **59**
Falcon Pk. B77: Wiln 2E **46**
Falcon Pl. B69: Tiv 2C **98**
Falcon Ri. DY8: Woll 3J **115**
Falcon Rd. B68: O'bry 7F **98**
Falconry Cen., The **6M 137**
Falcons, The B75: S Cold 4B **60**
Falcon Vw. B30: K Nor 5G **143**
Falcon Way DY1: Dud 8F **74**
Falfield Cl. B65: Row R 3D **98**
Falfield Gro. B31: Longb 2L **163**
Falkener Ho. CV6: Cov 2E **152**
Falkland Cl. CV4: Tile H 2D **172**
Falkland Cft. B30: Stir 3H **143**
Falklands Cl. DY3: Swind 7E **72**
Falkland Way B36: Cas B 4H **105**
Falkwood Gro. B93: Know 3F **168**
Fallindale Rd. B26: Sheld 3B **124**
FALLINGS HEATH **3F 54**
Fallings Heath Cl. WS10: Darl . . .2F **54**
FALLINGS PARK **4F 36**
Fallings Pk. Ind. Est.
WV10: Wolv 4F **36**
Fallow Fld. B74: Lit A 6B **42**
WS11: Cann 6E **8**
WS13: Lich 6J **13**
Fallowfield B15: Edg 1E **120**
WV6: Pert 5D **34**
WV8: Pend 7L **21**
Fallowfield Av. B28: Hall G 4F **144**
Fallowfield Rd. B63: Hale 6K **117**
B65: Row R 6A **98**
B92: Sol 7C **124**
WS5: Wals 1E **56**
Fallowfields Cl. B61: B'gve 6L **187**
Fallowfields Cres. CV6: Cov . . .5B **130**
Fallow Hill CV31: Lea S 3C **224**
Fallow Rd. B78: Faz 8M **31**
Fallows Ho. B19: Hock 4L **101**
Fallows Rd. B11: S'brk 3C **122**
Fallow Wlk. B32: Bart G 7G **119**
Falmouth Cl. CV11: Nun 4A **90**
Falmouth Dr. B77: Amin 4F **32**
LE10: Hinc 5L **69**
Falmouth Rd. B34: Hodg H 4L **103**
WS5: Wals 2D **56**
Falna Cres. B79: Tam 2M **31**
Falstaff Av. B47: H'wd 3A **166**
Falstaff Cl. B76: Walm 2B **82**
CV11: Nun 8A **90**
(not continuous)
Falstaff Ct. B75: S Cold 4C **60**
Falstaff Dr. CV22: Bil 4K **205**
Falstaff Gro. CV34: H'cte 6L **223**
Falstaff Rd. B90: Shir 7H **145**
CV4: Tile H 2E **150**
Falstone Rd. B73: New O 7D **58**
Fancott Dr. CV8: Ken 3F **198**
Fancott Rd. B31: N'fld 4A **142**
Fancourt Av. WV4: Penn 5K **51**
Fane Rd. WV11: Wed 8A **24**
Fanshawe Rd. B27: A Grn 8J **123**
Fanum Ho. B63: Hale 6B **118**
Faraday Av. B32: Quin 4K **119**
B46: Col 4M **83**
B76: Curd 4L **83**
Faraday Ct. B32: Quin 4K **119**
Faraday Ho. B15: Birm 1J **121**
Faraday Rd. CV22: Rugby 8C **180**
LE10: Hinc 2E **90**
WS2: Wals 3H **39**
Faraday Wharf
B7: Birm 5M **101** (1K **5**)
Farber Rd. CV2: W'grve S 3A **154**
Farbrook Way WV12: W'hall 3B **38**
Farclose Ho. B15: Edg 3J **121**
Farcroft Av. B21: Hand 1D **100**
CV5: E Grn 5D **150**
Farcroft Gro. B21: Hand 8D **78**
Farcroft Rd. B21: Hand 8D **78**
Fareham Av. CV22: Hillm 1E **206**
Fareham Cres. WV4: Penn 3J **51**
FAREWELL **5A 12**
Farewell Hall M. WS13: Fare . . .5A **12**
Farewell La. WS7: Burn 3L **17**
Farfield B60: S Prior 5M **209**
DY10: Kidd 4M **157**
Farfield Cl. B31: N'fld 7B **142**
Far Gosford St.
CV1: Cov 7E **152** (5F **6**)
Far High Dr. DY4: Tip 4B **76**

Far Highfield—Fircroft Ho.

Far Highfield B76: Walm 5K 59
Farhill Cl. B71: W Brom 1M 77
Faringdon B77: Glas 8F 32
Farlands Dr. DY8: Stourb 6A 116
Farlands Gro. B43: Gt Barr 2F 78
Farlands Rd. DY8: Stourb 6A 116
Far Lash LE10: Burb 2M 91
Far Lash Extension
LE10: Burb 3M 91
Farleigh Dr. WV3: Wolv 1G 51
Farleigh Rd. WV6: Pert 6G 35
Farley Cen. B70: W Brom 7K 77
Farley La. B62: Roms 1L 161
DY9: Belb 1L 161
Farley Rd. B23: Erd 5B 80
Farley St. CV31: Lea S 2B 224
DY4: Tip 4D 76
Farlow Cl. B98: Redd 6K 213
CV6: Cov 3G 153
Farlow Cft. B37: Mars G 1F 124
Farlow Rd. B31: N'fld 6C 142
Farlows End B38: K Nor 2D 164
Farmacre B9: Birm 7B 102
Farman Rd. CV5: Cov 7M 151
Farm Av. B68: O'bry 6G 99
Farmbridge Cl. WS2: Wals 6D 38
Farmbridge Rd. WS2: Wals 6D 38
Farmbridge Way WS2: Wals 6D 38
Farmbrook Av. WV10: F'hses 6D 22
Farm Cl. B79: Tam 2C 32
B92: Sol 7C 124
CV6: Cov 6B 130
DY3: Sed 2B 74
DY11: Kidd 7H 157
WS12: Hed 6J 9
WV8: Bilb 7H 21
Farmcote Cl. B97: Redd 5D 220
Farmcote Lodge *CV2: Ald G 5H 131*
(off Farmcote Rd.)
Farmcote Rd. B33: Stech 5A 104
CV2: Ald G 5H 131
Farm Cft. B19: Hock 3J 101
Farmcroft Rd. DY9: W'cte 6E 116
Farmdale Gro. B45: Redn 3G 163
Farmer Rd. B10: Small H 2G 123
Farmers Cl. B76: Walm 5L 59
Farmers Ct. B63: Hale 5M 117
Farmers Fold
WV1: Wolv 7C 36 (4J 7)
Farmers Rd. B60: B'gve 3L 209
Farmers Wlk. B21: Hand 2D 100
Farmer Ward Rd. CV8: Ken 5G 199
Farmer Way DY4: Tip 8B 54
Farm Gro. CV22: Rugby 8C 180
Farm Ho. La. B75: R'ley 6L 43
Farmhouse Rd. WV12: W'hall 4D 38
Farm Ho. Way B43: Gt Barr 5E 56
Farmhouse Way
B90: M'path 2B 168
WV12: W'hall 4E 38
Farm La. CV9: Gren 2F 48
Farmoor Gro. B34: S End 3E 104
Far Moor La. B98: Redd 4M 213
Farmoor Way WV10: Bush 5E 22
Farm Pl. CV3: Cov 1J 175
Farm Rd. B11: S'brk 2B 122
B65: Row R 5A 98
B67: Smeth 6L 99
B68: O'bry 6G 99
B98: Redd 6G 213
CV8: Ken 7E 198
CV32: Lill 6B 218
DY2: Neth 6G 97
DY4: Tip 2C 76
DY5: Quar B 8E 96
DY13: Stour S 4H 183
LE9: Barw 1C 70
LE10: Burb 3L 91
WV3: Wolv 1J 51
Farmside CV3: W'hall 4K 175
Farmside Cl. DY9: W'cte 6F 116
Farmside Grn. WV9: Pend 7M 21
Farmstead, The CV3: Cov 1J 175
Farmstead Cl. B75: R'ley 6K 43
WS1: Wals 4L 55
Farmstead Rd. B92: Sol 7C 124
Farm St. B19: Hock 3H 101
B70: W Brom 8J 77
WS2: Wals 5L 39
Farm Wlk. CV33: Bis T 7E 224
Farnborough Cl. B98: Redd 8M 213
Farnborough Ct. B75: Four O 7H 43
Farnborough Dr.
B90: M'path 3M 167
Farnborough Rd. B35: Cas V 7A 82
Farnbury Cft. B38: K Nor 7H 143
Farn Cl. B33: Stech 6M 103
Farncote Dr. B74: Four O 6F 42
Farndale Av. CV6: Cov 6D 130
WV6: Wolv 4M 35
Farndale Cl. DY5: Brie H 3B 116
Farndon Av. B37: Mars G 2H 125
Farndon Cl. CV12: Bulk 6B 112
Farndon Dr. LE9: S Stan 7J 71
Farndon Rd. B8: Salt 5F 102
Farndon Way B23: Erd 1D 80
Farneway LE10: Hinc 8H 69
Farnham Cl. B43: Gt Barr 1F 78
Farnham Rd. B21: Hand 7D 78
Farnhurst Rd. B36: Hodg H 2H 103
Farnol Rd. B26: Yard 1M 123
Farnworth Gro. B36: Cas B 8E 82
Farquhar Rd. B13: Mose 6M 121
B15: Edg 3F 120
Farquhar Rd. E. B15: Edg 3F 120
Farran Way B43: Gt Barr 2E 78
Farr Dr. CV4: Tile H 7H 151
Farren Rd. B31: Longb 8K 141
CV2: Cov 5K 153
Farrier Cl. B60: B'gve 3L 209
B76: Walm 1M 81
Farrier Rd. B43: Gt Barr 6K 57
Farriers, The B26: Sheld 4B 124
Farriers Ga. CV13: Fen D 3G 67
Farriers Mill WS3: Pels 5L 25
Farriers Way CV11: Nun 7M 89
LE10: Burb 4M 91
Farrier Way DY6: W Hth 2G 95
Farringdon Ho. *WS2: Wals 6K 39*
(off Green La.)
Farringdon St. WS2: Wals 7K 39
Farrington Rd. B23: Erd 4B 80
WV4: E'shll 6D 52
Farrow Rd. B44: Gt Barr 6L 57
Farthing Ct. B1: Birm 6J 101 (3C 4)
Farthing La. B72: S Cold 5H 59
B76: Curd 3J 83
B97: Redd 4B 212
Farthing Pools Cl.
B72: S Cold 5J 59
Farthings, The B17: Harb 3D 120
Farthings La. DY2: Dud 2G 97
Farthing Wlk. CV4: W'wd H 3D 172
Farvale Rd. B76: Min 3C 82
Far Vw. WS9: A'rdge 7H 27
Farway Gdns. WV8: Cod 7F 20
Far Wood Rd. B31: N'fld 1L 141
Farzens Av. CV34: Warw 6B 222
Faseman Av. CV4: Tile H 6F 150
Fashoda Rd. B29: S Oak 8H 121
Fasson Cl. B77: Two G 1C 46
Fastlea Rd. B32: Bart G 8K 119
Fastmoor Oval B33: Kitts G 8E 104
Fast Pits Rd. B25: Yard 1H 123
Fatherless Barn Cres.
B63: Crad 5J 117
Faulconbridge Av.
CV5: E Grn 5E 150
Faulconbridge Way
CV34: H'cte 6L 223
Faulkland Cres.
WV1: Wolv 6D 36 (2K 7)
Faulkner Cl. DY8: Stourb 5M 115
Faulkner Rd. B92: Olton 8B 124
Faulkners Farm Dr. B23: Erd 3B 80
Faulknor Dr. DY5: P'ntt 2B 96
Faultlands Cl. CV11: Nun 1M 111
(not continuous)
Faversham Cl. WS2: Wals 6D 38
WV8: Pend 1L 35
Fawdry Cl. B73: S Cold 4H 59
Fawdry St. B9: Birm 7A 102 (5M 5)
B66: Smeth 4C 100
WV1: Wolv 6B 36 (1G 7)
Fawley Cl. CV3: W'hall 3K 175
WV13: W'hall 1M 53
Fawley Gro. B14: K Hth 4H 143
Fawn Cl. WS12: Hunt 3C 8
Fawsley Leys CV22: Rugby 2A 206
Faygate Cl. CV3: Bin 6A 154
FAZELEY 8M 31
Fazeley Rd. B78: Tam 5A 32
Fazeley St. B5: Birm 7M 101 (5J 5)
Fazeley St. Ind. Est.
B5: Birm 7A 102 (5K 5)
Fearnings Cotts. B97: Redd 4D 220
Fearon Pl. B66: Smeth 4A 100
Featherbed La. B97: Redd 4B 220
CV4: W'wd H 4G 173
CV7: Withy 3M 133
CV21: Hillm 1G 207
WS13: Lich 6E 12
Featherston Dr. LE10: Burb 2K 91
FEATHERSTONE 2H 23
Featherstone Cl. B90: Shir 7K 145
CV10: Nun 7J 89
Featherstone Cres.
B90: Shir 7K 145
Featherstone La.
WV10: F'stne 1H 23
Featherstone Rd. B14: K Hth 3L 143
Featherston Rd. B74: S'tly 7A 42
Feckenham Ho. *B60: B'gve 6B 188*
(off Burcot La.)
Feckenham Rd. B96: A'wd B 7E 220
B97: Redd 5B 220
(Blaze La.)
B97: Redd 1C 220
(Headless Cross)
Fecknam Way WS13: Lich 7J 13
FEIASHILL 2B 72
Feiashill Cl. WV5: Try 2B 72
Feiashill Rd. WV5: Try 1B 72
Fein Bank CV4: Tile H 7C 150
Felbrigg Cl. DY5: Brie H 1C 116
Feldings, The B24: Erd 5J 81
Feldon La. B62: B'hth 2E 118
Felgate Cl. B90: M'path 3A 168
Fellbrook Cl. B33: Stech 5M 103
Fell Gro. B21: Hand 7C 78
CV32: Lill 6C 218
Fellmeadow Rd. B33: Yard 7A 104
Fellmeadow Way DY3: Sed 3E 74
Fellmore Gro. CV31: Lea S 2C 224
Fellows Av. DY6: W Hth 1J 95
Fellows La. B17: Harb 3A 120
Fellows Pk. Gdns.
WS2: Wals 3H 55
Fellows Rd. WV14: Bils 2K 53
Fellows St. WV2: Wolv 1C 52 (8H 7)
Fellows Way CV21: Hillm 2F 206
Felspar Rd. B77: Amin 6G 33
Felstead Cl. B77: Dost 5C 46
Felsted Way
B7: Birm 5A 102 (2M 5)
Felstone Rd. B44: Gt Barr 8L 57
Feltham Cl. B33: Kitts G 8E 104
Felton Cl. B98: Redd 8L 213
CV2: W'grve S 8L 131
Felton Cft. B33: Kitts G 6A 104
Felton Gro. B91: Sol 8B 146
Fenbourne Cl. WS4: S'fld 1C 40
Fenchurch Cl. WS2: Wals 5K 39
Fen Cl. DY11: Kidd 1L 157
Fencote Av. B37: F'bri 5G 105
FEN END 6F 170
Fen End Rd. CV8: Fen E 6F 170
Fen End Rd. W. B93: Know 4B 170
CV8: Fen E 4B 170
Fenmere Cl. WV4: Penn 4D 52
Fennel Cl. WS6: C Hay 6D 14
Fennel Cft. B34: S End 2B 104
Fennell Ho. *CV1: Cov 7B 152*
(off Meadow St.)
Fennel Rd. DY5: Brie H 2C 116
Fennis Cl. B93: Dorr 6F 168
Fenn Lanes
CV13: Fen D, Stoke G, Upton
2G 67
Fenn Ri. DY8: Word 6K 95
WV12: W'hall 3B 38
Fenn St. B77: Wiln 8E 32
FENNY DRAYTON 3G 67
Fens Cres. DY5: Brie H 4C 96
Fenside Av. CV3: Cov 5D 174
Fens Pool Av. DY5: Brie H 4D 96
Fensway, The B34: Stech 4A 104
Fenter Cl. B13: Mose 4M 121
Fentham Cl. B92: H Ard 3B 148
Fentham Ct. B92: Olton 1M 145
Fentham Grn. B92: H Ard 2A 148
Fentham Rd. B6: Aston 1K 101
B23: Erd 6D 80
B92: H Ard 3A 148
Fenton Rd. B27: A Grn 4H 123
B47: H'wd 2A 166
Fenton St. B66: Smeth 2L 99
DY5: Brie H 6D 96
Fenton Way B27: A Grn 5H 123
Fenwick Cl. B97: Redd 8B 212
Fenwick Dr. CV21: Hillm 1G 207
Fereday Rd. WS9: Wals W 6H 27
Fereday's Cft. DY3: Sed 2D 74
Fereday St. DY4: Tip 1M 75
Ferguson Dr. DY4: Tip 3B 76
DY11: Kidd 8G 157
Ferguson Rd. B68: O'bry 4K 99
Ferguson St. WV11: Wed 8A 24
Fern Av. DY4: Tip 2M 75
Fern Bank Cl. B63: Hale 7K 117
Fernbank Cres. WS5: Wals 5C 56
Fernbank Rd. B8: W End 5G 103
Ferncliffe Rd. B17: Harb 5B 120
Fern Cl. CV2: Cov 7J 131
CV23: Brow 1D 180
WS4: S'fld 8C 26
WV14: Cose 1H 75
Fern Cft. WS13: Lich 8F 12
Ferndale Av. B43: Gt Barr 2F 78
Ferndale Cl. B61: Cats 8A 162
CV11: Nun 4L 89
DY9: Hag 4A 138
DY13: Stour S 6J 183
WS7: Burn 3H 17
WS13: Lich 8F 12
Ferndale Ct. *B17: Harb 5D 120*
(off Metchley La.)
B46: Col 4A 106
Ferndale Cres. B12: Birm 1A 122
DY11: Kidd 1G 157
Ferndale Dr. CV8: Ken 7G 199
Ferndale Gro. LE10: Hinc 2G 91
Ferndale Housing Est.
DY11: Kidd 1G 157
Ferndale M. B46: Col 4A 106
Ferndale Pk. DY9: Pedm 1B 138
Ferndale Rd. B28: Hall G 1F 144
B46: Col 4A 106
B68: O'bry 8F 98
B74: S'tly 1M 57
CV3: Bin W 2D 176
CV7: Bal C 3F 170
WS13: Lich 7F 12
WV11: Ess 6B 24
Ferndell Cl. WS11: Cann 7C 8
Ferndene Rd. B11: Tys 6F 122
Ferndown Av. DY3: Sed 2C 74
Ferndown Cl. B26: Yard 8A 104
CV4: Tile H 6F 150
WS3: Blox 5H 25
Ferndown Ct. CV22: Bil 8L 179
Ferndown Gdns.
WV11: Wed 4M 37
Ferndown Rd. B91: Sol 3B 146
CV22: Bil 8L 179
Ferndown Ter. CV22: Bil 8L 179
Fern Dr. WS6: Gt Wyr 5G 15
Ferneley Av. LE10: Hinc 6G 69
Ferness Cl. LE10: Hinc 7H 69
Ferness Rd. LE10: Hinc 7H 69
Ferney Hill Av. B97: Redd 6C 212
Fernfail Ct. B23: Erd 4E 80
Fern Gro. CV12: Bed 7E 110
Fernhill Cl. CV8: Ken 3E 198
Fernhill Ct. B23: Erd 7C 80
Fernhill Dr. CV32: Lea S 8B 218
Fernhill Gro. B44: Gt Barr 6H 57
Fernhill La. CV7: Bal C 5F 170
CV8: Fen E 5E 170
Fernhill Rd. B92: Olton 7L 123
Fern Hill Way LE10: Wlvy 5K 113
Fernhurst Dr. DY5: P'ntt 2B 96
Fernhurst Rd. B8: Salt 6G 103
Fernleigh *B60: B'gve 8A 188*
(off New Rd.)
Fernleigh Av. WS7: C Ter 1G 17
Fernleigh Ct. B91: Sol 4C 146
Fernleigh Gdns. DY8: Word 6J 95
Fernleigh Rd. WS4: Wals 6B 40
Fernley Av. B29: S Oak 7H 121
Fernley Rd. B11: S'hll 5C 122
Fern Leys WV3: Wolv 8K 35
Fern Rd. B24: Erd 5G 81
DY1: Dud 5J 75
WS12: Hunt 4D 8
WV3: Wolv 1B 52 (7G 7)
Fernside Gdns. B13: Mose 6B 122
Fernside Rd. WV13: W'hall 6K 37
Fernwood Cl. B73: Bold 8E 58
B98: Redd 4H 221
Fernwood Cft. B14: K Hth 3L 143
DY4: Tip 5M 75
Fernwood Rd. B73: Bold 1E 80
Fernwoods B32: Bart G 7H 119
Ferrers Cl. B75: R'ley 7K 43
CV4: Tile H 7F 150
Ferrers Rd. B77: Tam 5D 32
Ferrie Gro. WS8: Bwnhls 2E 26
Ferrieres Cl. CV22: Dunc 6J 205
Ferris Gro. B27: A Grn 8G 123
Festival Av. WS10: Darl 5C 54
Festival Ct. DY2: Neth 4J 97
WS11: Cann 4E 8
Festival M. WS12: Cann 3F 8
Festival Way WV6: Wolv 4B 36
Fetherston Ct. CV31: Lea S 3M 223
Fetherston Cres.
CV8: Rytn D 8B 176
Fibbersley WV11: Wed 5M 37
WV13: W'hall 5M 37
Fibbersley Bank
WV13: W'hall 5M 37
Fiddlers Grn. B92: H Ard 2A 148
Field Av. B31: N'fld 4M 141
Fld. Barn Rd. CV35: H Mag 2A 222
Field Cl. B26: Sheld 3A 124
B60: Stoke H 3L 209
CV8: Ken 4H 199
CV34: Warw 2H 223
DY8: Word 7A 96
LE10: Hinc 6M 69
WS3: Blox 1J 39
WS4: S'fld 7B 26
Field Cott. Dr. DY8: Stourb 6B 116
Field Ct. CV2: Cov 2J 153
WS4: S'fld 7B 26
Field End DY13: Stour S 5E 182
Fieldfare WS7: Hamm 4K 17
Fieldfare Cl. B64: Old H 5M 97
CV23: Brow 1C 180
Fieldfare Ct. DY10: Kidd 8A 158
Fieldfare Cft. B36: Cas B 1G 105
Fieldfare Rd. DY9: W'cte 5D 116
Fld. Farm Rd. B77: Wiln 7D 32
B98: Redd 7K 213
Fieldgate La. CV8: Ken 3E 198
CV31: W'nsh 7B 224
Fieldgate Lawn CV8: Ken 3F 198
Fieldgate Trad. Est.
WS1: Wals 8M 39
Fieldhead La. CV34: Warw 3H 223
Fld. Head Pl. WV6: Tett 5H 35
Fieldhead Rd. B11: Tys 6G 123
Fieldhouse La. B62: Roms 5K 139
Fieldhouse Rd. B25: Yard 1J 123
WS7: C Ter 2G 17
WS12: Hed 2F 8
WV4: E'shll 5E 52
Fielding Cl. CV2: W'grve S 3A 154
CV9: Ath 7K 49
Fielding Way CV10: Gall C 4A 88
Field La. B32: Bart G 1G 141
B91: Sol 3G 147
DY8: Stourb 6A 116
DY9: Clent 5C 138
WS4: S'fld 7B 26
WS6: Gt Wyr 2F 14
Field March CV3: W'hall 4L 175
Field M. DY2: Neth 6L 97
Fieldon Cl. B90: Shir 6J 145
Field Rd. DY2: Dud 8L 75
DY4: Tip 1M 75
WS3: Blox 1J 39
WS13: Lich 6H 13
Field Rd. Ind. Est. WS3: Blox 1J 39
Fields, The WV8: Bilb 5H 21
Fields Ct. CV34: Warw 1F 222
Fieldside La. CV3: Bin 6M 153
Fieldside Wlk. WV14: Bils 1K 53
Fieldstone Vw. DY3: Lwr G 5D 74
Field St. WS11: Cann 6F 8
WV10: Wolv 6E 36 (1M 7
WV13: W'hall 7A 38
WV14: Bils 6L 53
Field Vw. CV22: Caw 1H 205
Field Vw. Cl. CV7: Exh 1G 131
Fieldview Cl. WV14: Cose 7L 53
Field Vw. Dr. B65: Row R 6F 98
Field Wlk. WS9: A'rdge 2H 41
Field Way LE9: Earl S 1D 70
Fieldway B94: H'ley H 3C 194
Fieldways Cl. B47: H'wd 2A 166
Fiery Hill Dr. B45: B Grn 2J 189
Fiery Hill Rd. B45: B Grn 1H 189
Fife Rd. CV5: Cov 7M 151
Fife St. CV11: Nun 5G 89
Fifield Cl. CV11: Nun 7K 89
Fifield Gro. B33: Yard 6M 103
Fifth Av. B9: Bord G 7F 102
DY5: Brie H 6F 96
WV10: Bush 2D 36
Filey B77: Amin 3F 32
Filey Cl. WS11: Cann 1C 14
Filey Rd. WV10: Oxl 7B 22
Fillingham Cl. B37: Chel W 8K 105
FILLONGLEY 6E 108
Fillongley Rd. B46: Max 4H 107
CV7: Fill 4H 107
CV7: Mer 8J 127
Filton Av. WS7: C Ter 1G 17
Filton Cft. B35: Cas V 5A 82
Fimbrell Cl. DY5: Brie H 1A 116
Finbury Cl. B92: Olton 8M 123
Finchall Cft. B92: Sol 2E 146
Fincham Cl. WV9: Pend 6A 22
Finch Cl. B65: Row R 5M 97
CV6: Cov 7C 13
Finch Cft. CV7: Bal C 2H 17
Finchdene Gro. WV3: Wolv 8K 35
Finch Dr. B74: S'tly 4A 58
Finches End B34: S End 4C 104
Finchfield Cl. DY8: Stourb 5J 115
Finchfield Gdns. WV3: Wolv 8L 35
Finchfield Hill WV3: Wolv 7J 35
(not continuous
Finchfield La. WV3: Wolv 1J 5
Finchfield Rd. WV3: Wolv 8L 35
Finchfield Rd. W. WV3: Wolv 8K 35
Finchley Av. B19: Loz 1J 10
Finchley Cl. DY3: Lwr G 7D 74
Finchley Rd. B44: K'sdng 7B 5
Finchmead Rd. B33: Kitts G 8E 10
Finchpath Rd. B70: W Brom 3G 7
Finch Rd. B19: Loz 1J 10
Findlay Rd. B14: K Hth 8L 12
Findley Cl. CV9: Man 3M 6
Findon Cl. B97: Redd 4A 21
CV12: Bulk 6C 11
Findon Rd. B8: W End 3H 10
Findon St. DY10: Kidd 3M 15
Fineacre La. CV8: Rytn D 4C 20
CV23: Stret D 4C 20
Finford Cft. CV7: Bal C 3H 17
Fingal Cl. CV3: W'hall 3J 17
Fingerpost Dr. WS3: Pels 4A 2
Fingest Cl. CV5: Cov 5H 15
FINHAM 6C 17
Finham Cres. CV8: Ken 3H 19
Finham Flats CV8: Ken 3H 19
Finham Grn. Rd. CV3: Finh 6B 17
Finham Gro. CV3: Finh 6C 17
Finham Pk. CV3: Finh 7C 17
Finham Rd. CV8: Ken 3H 19
Finings Ct. CV32: Lea S 7M 21
Finlarigg Dr. B15: Edg 3F 12
Finlay Ct. CV1: Cov 8D 152 (7C 6
Finmere CV21: Brow 3D 18
Finmere Rd. B28: Hall G 1F 14
Finmere Way B90: Shir 6K 14
Finnemore Cl. CV3: Cov 4B 17
Finnemore Rd. B9: Bord G 7G 10
Finneywell Cl. WV14: Cose 6H 5
Finsbury Dr. DY5: Brie H 2C 11
Finsbury Gro. B23: Erd 3D 8
FINSTALL 8E 18
Finstall Cl. B7: Birm 5A 102 (2M 5
B72: W Grn 8J 5
Finstall Rd. B60: B'gve, Fins 1B 21
Finwood Cl. B92: Sol 1E 14
Finwood Rd. CV35: Row 8L 19
Fir Av. B12: Bal H 4A 12
Firbank Cl. B30: B'vlle 2E 14
Firbank Way WS3: Pels 7M 2
Firbarn Cl. B76: Walm 6K 5
Firbeck Gro. B44: K'sdng 8A 5
Firbeck Rd. B44: K'sdng 8A 5
Fir Cl. WS12: Hunt 1D
Fir Cft. DY5: Brie H 1C 11
Fircroft B31: N'fld 1M 14
B78: K'bry 2C 6
B91: Sol 3M 14
WV14: Bils 6A 5
Fircroft Cl. B60: Stoke H 3K 20
WS11: Cann 6G
Fircroft Ho. B37: Chel W 7G 10

Fountain Cl.—Gainsborough Av.

Fountain Cl. B31: Longb 3L 163
Fountain Ct. B4: Birm 3G 5
Fountain Ho. B63: Hale 6B 118
Fountain La. B69: O'bry 8F 76
DY4: Tip 1K 75
WV14: Cose 1K 75
Fountain Rd. B17: Edg 8B 100
Fountains Rd. WS3: Blox 7E 24
Fountains Way WS3: Blox 7E 24
Four Acres B32: Quin 5J 119
Four Ashes Rd.
B93: Ben H, Dorr 6D 168
Four Crosses Rd. WS4: S'fld 8C 26
Four Dwellings Leisure Cen.
. . . . .5H 119
Fourfields Way CV7: Gun H 2F 108
Fourlands Av. B72: W Grn 2K 81
Fourlands Rd. B31: N'fld 3L 141
FOUR LANES END 8D 110
FOUR OAKS
Coventry 3K 149
Sutton Coldfield 6G 43
Four Oaks Cl. B98: Redd 1D 220
Four Oaks Comn. Rd.
B74: Four O 6E 42
Four Oaks Ct. B74: Four O 8H 43
FOUR OAKS PARK 1F 58
Four Oaks Rd. B74: Four O 7G 43
Four Oaks Station (Rail) 1H 59
Four Pounds Av. CV5: Cov 6M 151
Four Stones Cl. B91: Sol 8A 146
Four Stones Gro. B5: Bal H 3L 121
Fourth Av. B9: Bord G 7F 102
B29: S Oak 6J 121
WS8: Bwnhls 8G 17
(not continuous)
WV10: Bush 3D 36
Fourways B64: Crad H 8K 97
Fourways Rd. CV9: Ath 1M 65
Four Winds Rd. DY2: Dud 3L 97
Fowey Cl. B76: Walm 2A 82
Fowey Rd. B34: Hodg H 3M 103
Fowgay Dr. B91: Sol 8M 145
Fowler Cl. B66: Smeth 1A 100
WV6: Pert 3E 34
Fowler Pl. DY13: Stour S 4G 183
Fowler Rd. B75: S Cold 4A 60
CV6: Cov 4B 152
Fowler St. B7: Nech 4B 102
WV2: Wolv 3C 52
Fowlmere Rd. B42: Gt Barr 1H 79
Fownhope Cl. B98: Redd 6L 213
Fow Oak CV4: Tile H 7C 150
Fox & Goose Shop. Cen.
B8: W End 4J 103
Fox Av. CV10: Nun 1J 89
Foxbank Ind. Est. LE9: S Stan . . .6K 71
Foxbury Dr. B93: Dorr 6G 169
Fox Cl. B75: S Cold 2M 59
B77: Two G 1C 46
CV21: Hillm 8H 181
FOXCOTE 6G 117
Foxcote Av. B21: Hand 2E 100
Foxcote Cl. B90: Shir 1K 167
B98: Redd 5L 213
Foxcote Dr. B90: Shir 1K 167
Foxcote La. B63: Crad 6H 117
Fox Covert DY8: Stourb 4M 115
Fox Covert La.
CV13: Stoke G 2A 68
Fox Cres. B11: S'hll 5D 122
Foxcroft Cl. WS7: Burn 4G 17
Foxdale Dr. DY5: Brie H 6B 96
Foxdale Gro. B33: Kitts G 7C 104
Foxdale Wlk. CV31: Lea S 3C 224
Foxes Cl. B60: B'wll 4H 189
Foxes Mdw. B30: K Nor 5F 142
B76: Walm 1A 82
Foxes Rake WS11: Cann 6E 8
Foxes Ridge B64: Crad H 1L 117
Foxes Way CV7: Bal C 3H 171
CV34: Warw 5D 222
Foxfield B31: N'fld 5M 141
Foxfield Dr. DY8: Stourb 6A 116
Foxfields Way WS12: Hunt 2C 8
Fox Foot Dr. DY5: Brie H 5C 96
Foxford Cl. B36: Cas B 8D 82
B72: W Grn 2K 81
Foxford Cres. CV2: Ald G 5H 131
Foxglove B77: Amin 5G 33
Foxglove Cl. B27: A Grn 8H 123
CV6: Cov 7C 130
CV12: Bed 8E 110
CV23: Brow 1E 180
WS3: Pels 4A 26
WS14: Lich 4H 19
WV10: F'stne 2H 23
WV11: Wed 4L 37
Foxglove Cres. B37: K'hrst 6E 104
Foxglove Rd. DY1: Dud 5F 74
Foxglove Wlk. WS12: Hed 2J 9
Foxglove Way B21: Hand 2D 100
B23: Erd 2B 80
B60: L End 3C 188
Fox Grn. Cres. B27: A Grn 8G 123
Fox Gro. B27: A Grn 7G 123
Fox Hill B29: S Oak 1C 142
Foxhill Barns B48: A'chu 4L 189
Fox Hill Cl. B29: S Oak 1C 142
Foxhill Cl. WS12: Hth H 7K 9
Foxhill La. B48: A'chu 3K 189
Fox Hill Rd. B75: R'ley 7L 43
(not continuous)
Foxhills Cl. WS7: Burn 4G 17
CV11: Nun 8C 90
Foxhills Pk. DY2: Neth 5J 97
Foxhills Rd. DY8: Word 8K 95
WV4: Penn 6J 51
Foxholes, The DY10: Kidd 1M 157
Foxholes La. B97: Redd 3A 220
Fox Hollies LE10: Sharn 5H 93
Foxhollies Dr. B63: Hale 5L 117
Fox Hollies Leisure Cen. 8G 123
Fox Hollies Rd. B28: Hall G 2F 144
B76: Walm 1M 81
(not continuous)
Fox Hollow WV6: Tett 7J 35
Foxhollow B61: B'gve 1K 209
Fox Hollow Cl. B45: Redn 2J 163
Foxhope Cl. B38: K Nor 7J 143
Foxhunt Rd. B63: Hale 7L 117
Foxland Av. B45: Redn 2J 163
WS6: Gt Wyr 6G 15
Foxland Cl. B37: Chel W 7K 105
B90: Ches G 5K 167
Foxlands Av. WV4: Penn 6K 51
Foxlands Cres. WV4: Penn 6J 51
Foxlands Dr. B72: W Grn 2K 81
DY3: Up Gor 4D 74
WV4: Penn 6J 51
Fox La. B61: B'gve 1M 209
DY10: Chad C 3K 185
WS13: Elmh 5G 13
Foxlea Rd. B63: Hale 8K 117
Foxley Dr. B91: Cath B 4H 147
FOXLYDIATE 6L 211
Foxlydiate Cl. B97: Redd 6A 212
Foxlydiate Cres. B97: Redd . . .5M 211
Foxlydiate La. B97: Redd 7L 211
Foxmeadow Cl. DY3: Sed 2E 74
Fox Mill Est. B11: S'hll 6D 122
Foxoak Ent. Cen. B64: Crad H . . .8K 97
(off Foxoak St.)
Foxoak St. B64: Crad H 8J 97
Foxon's Barn Rd.
CV21: Brow 3C 180
Fox's Covert CV13: Fen D 3F 66
Fox's La. WV1: Wolv 5C 36
Fox St. B5: Birm 6M 101 (4J 5)
DY7: Stour 3J 75
Foxtail Way WS12: Hed 5L 9
Foxton Rd. B8: Salt 4F 102
CV3: Bin 8L 153
Fox Wlk. WS9: Wals W 6H 27
Foxwalks Av. B61: B'gve 1K 209
Foxwell Gro. B9: Bord G 6J 103
Foxwell Rd. B9: Bord G 6H 103
Foxwood Av. B43: Gt Barr 7H 57
Foxwood Dr. CV3: Bin W 2D 176
Foxwood Gro. B37: K'hrst 4F 104
Foxwood Rd. B78: B'moor 1M 47
Foxyards Rd. DY4: Tip 4K 75
Foyle Rd. B38: K Nor 8E 142
Fozdar Cres. WV14: Cose 8H 53
Fradley Cl. B30: K Nor 5D 142
Fradley Distribution Pk.
WS13: Frad 2M 13
Framefield Dr. B91: Sol 3E 146
Framlingham Gro. CV8: Ken . . .3J 199
WV6: Pert 6G 35
Frampton Cl. B30: B'vlle 2D 142
B37: Chel W 6K 105
Frampton Wlk.
CV2: W'grve S 5M 153
Frampton Way B43: Gt Barr 5K 57
Frances Av. CV34: Warw 2G 223
Frances Cres. CV12: Bed 6G 111
Frances Dr. WS3: Blox 7H 25
Frances Gibbs Gdns.
CV31: W'nsh 5A 224
Frances Havergal Cl.
CV31: Lea S 3M 223
Frances Rd. B19: Loz 1J 101
B23: Erd 6D 80
B30: K Nor 4G 143
FRANCHE 1H 157
Franche Ct. DY11: Kidd 8H 135
Franche Ct. Dr. DY11: Kidd 8H 135
Franche Rd. DY11: Kidd 1H 157
DY11: W'ley 7J 135
Franchise Gdns. WS10: W'bry . . .4F 54
Franchise St. B42: P Barr 7L 79
DY11: Kidd 4J 157
WS10: W'bry 4E 54
Franciscan Rd. CV3: Cov 1C 174
Francis Cl. B74: S'tly 1M 57
B78: Pole 2K 49
DY6: K'wfrd 1K 95
Francis Dr. CV22: Caw 1G 205
Francis Rd. B16: Edg 8G 101
B25: Yard 3G 123
B27: A Grn 4K 123
B33: Stech 7K 103
B60: B'gve 2M 209
B67: Smeth 4K 99
CV8: Bag 6E 174
DY8: Woll 4J 115
DY13: Stour S 3E 182
WS13: Lich 7G 13
Francis Sharp Ho. WS3: Blox . . .7G 25
Francis St. B7: Birm . . .5A 102 (2M 5)
B70: W Brom 8K 77
Francis St. CV6: Cov 2E 152
WV1: Wolv 5C 36 (1H 7)
Francis Wlk. B31: Longb 2A 164
Francis Ward Cl.
B71: W Brom 1G 77
Frank Booton Cl. LE9: Earl S 1H 71
Frankburn Rd. B74: S'tly 1L 57
Frankel Gdns. CV34: Warw 8F 216
Frankfort St. B19: Hock 3K 101
Frank Freeman Ct.
DY10: Kidd 1M 157
Frankholmes Dr.
B90: M'path 3M 167
Frankland Rd. CV6: Cov 8G 131
FRANKLEY 4H 141
Frankley Av. B62: Quin 4F 118
FRANKLEY BEECHES 5G 141
Frankley Beeches Rd.
B31: Longb, N'fld 7J 141
Frankley Community Leisure Cen.
. . . . .8F 140
FRANKLEY GREEN 4G 141
Frankley Grn. B32: Fran 4D 140
Frankley Grn. La. B32: Fran 4E 140
FRANKLEY HILL 6F 140
Frankley Hill La. B32: Fran 6F 140
Frankley Hill Rd. B45: Fran 6F 140
Frankley Ind. Pk. B45: Fran . . .7H 141
Frankley La. B31: N'fld 3K 141
B32: Bart G, N'fld 3J 141
Frankley Lodge Rd.
B31: Fran 5K 141
Frankley Rd. B68: O'bry 1H 119
Frankley Ter. B17: Harb 4B 120
Franklin Ct. CV11: Nun 8K 89
Franklin Dr. WS7: Burn 3H 17
Franklin Gro. CV4: Tile H 8E 150
Franklin Rd. B30: B'vlle 4E 142
CV11: Nun 8K 89
CV31: W'nsh 6A 224
Franklins Gdns. CV3: Bin 8B 154
Franklin St. B18: Win G 4E 100
Franklin Way B30: B'vlle 3F 142
Franklyn Cl. WV6: Pert 4E 34
Frankpledge Rd. CV3: Cov 2E 174
Frank Rd. B67: Smeth 3J 99
Frank St. B12: Birm 2M 121
CV11: Nun 6H 89
Franks Way B33: Stech 7L 103
Frank Tommey Cl. B65: B'hth . . .8C 98
FRANKTON 8K 203
Frankton Av. CV3: Cov 4C 174
Frankton Cl. B92: Sol 7B 124
B98: Redd 1L 221
Frankton Gro. B9: Bord G 7H 103
Frankton La. CV23: Stret D 4G 203
Frankton Rd. CV23: Bour D 6L 203
Frank Walsh Ho.
CV1: Cov 5D 152 (1E 6)
Frankwell Dr. CV2: W'grve S . . .8L 131
Fraser Cl. CV10: Nun 3B 88
Fraser Rd. B11: S'brk 4D 122
CV6: Cov 8A 130
Fraser St. WV14: Bils 4L 53
(not continuous)
Frayne Av. DY6: K'wfrd 2J 95
FREASLEY 5J 47
Freasley Cl. B90: Shir 7K 145
Freasley La. B77: Wiln 3G 47
Freasley Rd. B34: S End 4D 104
Freda Eddy Ct. DY10: Kidd 3L 157
Freda Ri. B69: Tiv 1D 98
Freda Rd. B70: W Brom 8K 77
Freda's Gro. B17: Harb 4A 120
Frederick Av. LE10: Hinc 7G 69
Frederick Ct. B77: Glas 6E 32
Frederick Neal Av.
CV5: E Grn 5D 150
Frederick Press Way
CV21: Rugby 6M 179
Frederick Rd. B6: Aston 1L 101
B11: S'hll 5C 122
B15: Edg 1H 121 (8A 4)
B23: Erd 7D 80
B29: S Oak 7D 120
B33: Stech 6K 103
B68: O'bry 2K 119
B73: W Grn 7G 59
CV7: New A 1F 108
DY11: Kidd 8L 157
WV11: Wed 4J 37
Fredericks Cl. DY8: Stourb 5L 115
Frederick St.
B1: Birm 5J 101 (2C 4)
B70: W Brom 5J 77
CV21: Rugby 6M 179
WS2: Wals 7K 39
WV2: Wolv 1C 52 (7J 7)
Frederick William St.
WV13: W'hall 7B 38
Fred Lee Gro. CV3: Cov 5D 174
Fred Smith Cl. WS10: W'bry 4H 55
Freeboard La. CV8: Rytn D 2E 202
Freeburn C'way. CV4: Canly . . .2J 173
Freeford Gdns. WS14: Lich 3L 19
Freehold St. CV1: Cov 4F 152
Freeland Gro. DY6: K'wfrd 5M 95
Freeman Cl. CV10: Nun 5D 88
Freeman Ct. DY11: Kidd 6H 157
Freeman Dr. B76: Walm 5M 59
Freeman Pl. WV14: Bils 1L 53
Freeman Rd. B7: Nech 3B 102
WS10: W'bry 6J 55
Freemans Cl. CV32: Lea S 8L 217
Freemans La. LE10: Burb 4A 92
Freeman St. B5: Birm . . .7L 101 (5H 5)
CV6: Cov 3F 152
WV10: Wolv 7F 36
Freeman's Way
CV1: Cov 7C 152 (6B 6)
Freemantle Rd. CV22: Bil 7J 179
Freemount Sq. B43: Gt Barr 2E 78
Free Port B26: Birm A 6F 124
Freer Dr. WS7: Burn 2L 17
Freer Rd. B6: Aston 1K 101
Freers M. CV34: Warw 5B 222
Freer St. CV11: Nun 7L 89
WS1: Wals 7L 39
Freesland Ri. CV10: Nun 3B 88
Freeth Rd. WS8: Bwnhls 8G 17
Freeth St. B16: Birm 7F 100
B69: O'bry 1F 98
Freezeland St. WV14: Bils 3H 53
Fremantle Dr. WS12: Wim 7L 9
Fremont Dr. DY1: Dud 6E 74
French Av. B78: M Oak 8J 31
Frenchmans Wlk.
WS14: Lich 2J 19
French Rd. DY2: Dud 8L 75
French Walls B66: Smeth 4C 100
Frensham Cl. B37: Chel W 7J 105
WS6: C Hay 5E 14
Frensham Dr. CV10: Nun 4B 88
Frensham Way B17: Harb 3C 120
Frenshaw Gro. B44: Gt Barr . . .1M 79
Freshfield Cl. CV5: Alle 8J 129
Freshwater Dr. DY5: Brie H 1B 116
Freshwater Gro.
CV31: Lea S 3C 224
Freswick Cl. LE10: Hinc 8F 68
Fretton Cl. CV6: Cov 2F 152
Freville Cl. B79: Tam 3A 32
Frevill Rd. CV6: Cov 1H 153
Frewen Dr. LE9: Sap 1K 93
Friardale Cl. WS10: W'bry 6K 55
FRIAR PARK 7J 55
Friar Pk. Farm WS10: W'bry 5K 55
Friar Pk. Rd. WS10: W'bry 6J 55
Friars All. WS13: Lich 2H 19
Friars Cl. CV3: Bin W 2E 176
DY8: Word 6J 95
Friar's Cl. CV9: Ath 1K 65
Friars Gorse DY7: Stourt 2J 115
Friars Rd. CV1: Cov 7C 152 (7C 6)
Friars St. CV34: Warw 3D 222
Friar St. WS10: W'bry 6H 55
Friars Wlk. B37: Chel W 7K 105
B77: Tam 6C 32
Friary, The WS13: Lich 2G 19
Friary Av. B90: M'path 3A 168
WS13: Lich 2G 19
Friary Cl. B20: Hand 6F 78
LE10: Hinc 8L 69
Friary Cres. WS4: Rus 3C 40
Friary Dr. B74: Four O 6F 42
Friary Gdns. B21: Hand 7D 78
WS13: Lich 2G 19
Friary Grange Leisure Cen. 7E 12
Friary Ho WS13: Lich 8L 13
Friary Rd. B20: Hand 7E 78
CV9: Ath 8K 49
WS13: Lich 2G 19
Friary St. CV11: Nun 4H 89
Friary Vw. WS13: Lich 2H 19
Friday Acre WS13: Lich 8G 13
Friday La.
B92: Cath B, H Ard 4J 147
Friday Wharf B1: Birm 7C 4
Friends Cl. CV8: Bag 6D 174
Friesland Dr. WV1: Wolv 6H 37
Friezeland Rd. WS2: Wals 7H 39
Friezland La. WS8: Bwnhls 4F 26
Friezland Way WS8: Bwnhls 4G 27
Frilsham Way CV5: Cov 5H 151
Fringe Grn. B60: B'gve 2A 210
Fringe Grn. Cl. B60: B'gve 2A 210
Fringe Mdw. Rd. B98: Redd 3M 213
Frinton Gro. B21: Hand 2C 100
Frisby Ct. CV11: Nun 7L 89
Frisby Rd. CV4: Tile H 7E 150
LE9: Barw 2B 70
Friston Av. B16: Birm . . .8H 101 (7A 4)
Friswell Dr. CV6: Cov 1F 152
Friswell Ho. CV2: Cov 1K 153
Friswell La. LE9: Barw 2A 70
Frith Way LE10: Hinc 6G 69
Frobisher Cl. LE10: Hinc 5K 69
WS6: Gt Wyr 8F 14
Frobisher Rd. CV3: Cov 4C 174
CV22: Bil 8J 179
Frobisher Way B66: Smeth 2K 99
Frodesley Rd. B26: Sheld 1B 124
Froggatt Rd. WV14: Bils 2K 53
Froggatts Ride B76: Walm 6M 59
Frog Hall Cotts. DY7: I'ley 6J 115
Frog La. CV7: Bal C 4G 171
WS13: Lich 2H 19
Frogmere Cl. CV5: Alle 3H 151
Frogmill Rd. B45: Fran 8H 141
Frogmoor Ho. B25: Yard 2L 123
Frogmore La. CV8: Fen E 7F 170
Frolesworth Rd. LE10: Sharn . . .4K 93
Frome Cl. DY3: Lwr G 7D 74
Frome Dr. WV11: Wed 4J 37
Frome Way B14: K Hth 3J 143
Front Cotts. B48: A'chu 3M 189
Frost St. WV2: E'shll 3G 53
Froxmere Cl. B91: Sol 1B 168
Froyle Cl. WV6: Tett 4J 35
Froysell St. WV13: W'hall 7B 38
Fryer Av. CV32: Lea S 7L 217
Fryer Rd. B31: Longb 2B 164
Fryer's Cl. WS3: Blox 2H 39
Fryer's Rd. WS2: Wals 3G 39
WS3: Blox 3G 39
Fryer St. WV1: Wolv 7D 36 (3K 7)
Frythe Cl. CV8: Ken 3J 199
Fuchsia Cl. CV2: Cov 7H 131
Fuchsia Dr. WV9: Pend 6M 21
Fugelmere Cl. B17: Harb 2M 119
Fulbrook Gro. B29: W Cas 1M 141
Fulbrook La.
CV35: Lwr F, Sher 8A 222
Fulbrook Rd. CV2: Cov 8J 131
DY1: Dud 8G 75
Fulford Dr. B76: Min 4B 82
Fulford Gro. B26: Sheld 3C 124
Fulford Hall Rd. B90: Tid G 6D 166
Fulford Hall Rd. B94: Earls 6D 166
FULFORD HEATH 7D 166
Fulham Rd. B11: S'hll 4B 122
FULLBROOK 3M 55
Fullbrook Cl. B90: M'path 4A 168
Fullbrook Rd. WS5: Wals 4L 55
Fullelove Rd. WS8: Bwnhls 2G 27
Fuller M. B24: Erd 6F 80
Fullers Cl. CV6: Cov 2M 151
Fullerton Cl. WV8: Pend 8L 21
Fullwood Cl. CV2: Ald G 7L 131
Fullwood Cres. DY2: Dud 3E 96
Fullwoods End WV14: Cose 8J 53
Fulmar Cres. DY10: Kidd 7B 158
Fulton Cl. B60: B'gve 8B 188
Fulwell Gro. B44: K'sdng 2A 80
Fulwell M. B37: Mars G 1H 125
Fulwood Av. B62: B'hth 1F 118
Furber Pl. DY6: K'wfrd 3M 95
Furlong, The WS10: W'bry 4E 54
Furlong La. B63: Crad 3J 117
Furlong Mdw. B31: N'fld 7C 142
Furlong Rd. CV1: Cov . . .8D 152 (8E 6)
Furlongs, The DY8: Stourb 6B 116
WV11: Wed 4H 37
Furlongs Rd. DY3: Sed 3D 74
Furlong Wlk. DY3: Lwr G 5D 74
Furnace Cl. CV12: Bed 5K 111
WV5: Wom 4E 72
FURNACE END 6K 85
Furnace Hill B63: Hale 3B 118
Furnace La. B63: Hale 4B 118
Furnace Pde. DY4: Tip 3L 75
Furnace Rd. CV12: Bed 5K 111
DY2: Dud 1J 97
Furness B77: Glas 6D 32
Furness Cl. CV21: Brow 2D 180
WS3: Blox 6F 24
Furnivall Cres. WS13: Lich 8K 13
Furr Marsh, The
CV34: Warw 5B 222
Furrow Cl. CV21: Rugby 5D 180
Furrows, The B60: Stoke H 3K 209
CV47: Sou 4J 225
Furst St. WS8: Bwnhls 1G 27
Furzebank Way WV12: W'hall . . .5E 38
Furze La. B98: Redd 5A 214
Furze Way WS5: Wals 1E 56
Fylde Ho. CV2: Cov 5K 153
Fynford Rd. CV6: Cov 4B 152

G

Gable Cl. CV22: Bil 1K 205
Gable Cft. WS14: Lich 3L 19
Gables, The B24: Erd 5K 81
B78: Pole 2K 49
DY6: W Hth 1H 95
Gabor Cl. CV21: Rugby 3C 180
Gaddesby Rd. B14: K Hth 1M 143
Gadds Dr. B65: Row R 5D 98
Gadsby Av. WV11: Wed 2A 38
Gadsby Ct. CV11: Nun 6L 89
Gadsby St. CV11: Nun 6K 89
Gads Grn. DY2: Neth 4L 97
Gads Grn. Cres. DY2: Dud 3L 97
Gadshill CV34: H'cte 5L 223
Gads La. B70: W Brom 7G 77
DY1: Dud 8J 75
Gadwall Cft. B23: Erd 6B 80
Gaelic Rd. WS11: Cann 5D 8
Gagarin B79: Tam 4M 31
Gaiafields Rd. WS13: Lich 8H 13
Gaialands Cres. WS13: Lich 8H 13
Gaia La. WS13: Lich 1G 19
Gaia Stowe WS13: Lich 8H 13
Gail Cl. WS9: Wals W 5H 27
Gailey Cft. B44: Gt Barr 6L 57
Gail Pk. WV3: Wolv 2K 51
Gainford Cl. WV8: Pend 8M 21
Gainford Ri. CV3: Bin 6M 153
Gainford Rd. B44: K'sdng 8C 58
Gainsborough Av. LE10: Hinc 6G 69

Gainsborough Cres.—Gladys Ter.

Gainsborough Cres.
B43: Gt Barr .5K 57
B93: Know .3G 169
CV21: Hillm .8H 181
Gainsborough Dr.
B78: M Oak .1H 45
CV12: Bed .5G 111
CV31: Lea S .3C 224
WV6: Pert .5F 34
Gainsborough Hill
DY8: Stourb .6M 115
Gainsborough M.
DY11: Kidd .4H 157
Gainsborough Pl. DY1: Dud .7E 74
Gainsborough Rd.
B42: Gt Barr .3H 79
Gainsborough Trad. Est.
CV47: Sou .6G 225
DY9: Lye .5C 116
Gainsbrook Cres.
WS11: Nort C .4M 15
Gainsford Dr. B62: Hale .3B 118
Gains La. WS3: Lit W .7J 15
WS11: Lit W .7J 15
Gairloch Rd. WV12: W'hall .8B 24
Gaitskell Ter. B69: Tiv .7D 76
Gaitskell Way B66: Smeth .2M 99
Gala Bingo
Aldridge .3H 41
Bushbury .1D 36
Coventry .6D 152 (4E 6)
Darlaston .2F 54
Dudley .7K 75
Great Park .8H 141
Harborne .4C 120
Kings Heath .8L 121
Radford .3B 152
Rugby .6A 180
Stockland Green .4D 80
Tamworth .4B 32
Tower Hill .3H 79
Tyburn .6L 81
Walsall .8K 39
Walsgrave on Sowe .2B 154
Wednesfield .2M 37
Yardley .3K 123
(off Swan Shop. Cen., The)
Gala Casino .7K 101 (6F 4)
Galahad Way DY13: Stour S .5F 182
WS10: W'bry .7G 55
Gala Leisure Cen. .6J 77
Galbraith Cl. WV14: Cose .1K 75
Galena Cl. B77: Amin .7H 33
Galena Way B6: Aston .3L 101
Gale Wlk. B65: Row R .4M 97
Galey's Rd. CV3: Cov .1D 174
Gallagher Bus. Pk.
CV6: Longf .4E 130
Gallagher Ct. B13: Mose .7B 122
(off Wake Grn. Pk.)
Gallagher Retail Pk.
CV6: Cov .1F 152
Gallagher Rd. CV12: Bed .7G 111
Gallagher Way CV6: Cov .2F 152
CV34: H'cte .6K 223
Gallery, The
WV1: Wolv .8C 36 (5J 7)
Gallery Sq. WS2: Wals .7K 39
GALLEY COMMON .4M 87
Galliards, The CV4: Canly .5K 173
Galliers Cl. B77: Hock .4F 46
Galloway Av. B34: Hodg H .3M 103
Galloway Cl. LE9: Barw .3M 69
Gallows Hill CV34: Warw .4G 223
DY7: Kinv .3A 114
Gallus Dr. LE10: Hinc .8G 69
Galmington Dr. CV3: Cov .3B 174
Galton Cl. B24: Erd .5M 81
DY4: Tip .3C 76
Galton Dr. DY2: Dud .3H 97
Galton Rd. B67: Smeth .7M 99
Galtons La. DY9: Belb .2G 161
Galton Twr. B1: Birm .7J 101 (5C 4)
Galway Rd. WS7: C Ter .2G 17
Gamecock Barracks
CV11: Bram .4F 112
Gamesfield Grn. WV3: Wolv .8M 35
Gammage St. DY2: Dud .1H 97
Gamson Cl. DY10: Kidd .5L 157
Ganborough Cl. B98: Redd .8L 213
Gandy Rd. WV12: W'hall .3A 38
Gannah's Farm Cl.
B76: Walm .6M 59
GANNOW GREEN .8C 140
Gannow Grn. La.
B45: Roms .8C 140
Gannow Mnr. Cres.
B45: Fran .7E 140
Gannow Mnr. Gdns.
B45: Fran .8F 140
Gannow Rd. B45: Rubery .2E 162
Gannow Shop. Cen.
B45: Fran .8E 140
Gannow Wlk. B45: Rubery .2E 162
Ganton Rd. WS3: Blox .5G 25
Ganton Wlk. WV8: Pend .1M 35
Garage Cl. B77: Tam .4D 32
Garden Cl. B8: W End .4G 103
B45: Fran .7G 141
B93: Know .3F 168
LE10: Burb .3J 91
Garden Ct. CV34: Warw .1J 223
(Bridge St.)
CV34: Warw .2E 222
(Priory Rd.)
Garden Cres. WS3: Pels .6M 25
Garden Cft. WS9: A'rdge .2H 41
Gardeners Cl. DY11: Kidd .1J 157
Gardeners Wlk. B91: Sol .6C 146
Gardeners Way WV5: Wom .5F 72
Garden Flds. DY7: Kinv .5A 114
Garden Flats CV5: E Grn .4D 150
Garden Gro. B20: Hand .3E 78
CV12: Bed .1F 130
Gardenia Dr. CV5: Alle .3G 151
Garden Rd. LE10: Hinc .8K 69
Gardens, The B23: Erd .6E 80
B72: W Grn .1H 81
CV8: Ken .6G 199
CV23: Thurl .6F 204
CV31: Rad S .4E 224
Garden St. WS2: Wals .6L 39
Garden Wlk. DY2: Dud .8J 75
DY3: Gorn .7C 74
(not continuous)
WV14: Bils .3M 53
Gardner Ho. CV1: Cov .7B 152
(off Vincent St.)
Gardners Mdw. DY12: Bew .6B 156
Gardner Way CV8: Ken .7G 199
Garfield Rd. B26: Sheld .1B 124
Garganey Ct. DY10: Kidd .8M 157
Garibaldi Ter. B60: B'gve .8A 188
Garland Cres. B62: B'hth .1E 118
Garland Rd. DY13: Stour S .3D 182
Garlands, The WV11: Wed .2J 37
Garlands Cft. CV7: Ker E .3A 130
Garland St. B9: Birm .6C 102
Garland Way B31: N'fld .4B 142
(not continuous)
Garlick Dr. CV8: Ken .3J 199
Garman Cl. B43: Gt Barr .7E 56
Garner Cl. WV14: Cose .6K 53
Garnet Av. B43: Gt Barr .5H 57
Garnet Cl. WS9: Ston .5L 27
Garnet Ct. B92: Olton .8M 123
Garnett Dr. B75: S Cold .3L 59
Garnette Cl. CV10: Nun .4B 88
Garrard Gdns. B73: S Cold .4H 59
Garratt Cl. B68: O'bry .5J 99
CV23: Long L .4H 179
Garratt's La. B64: Old H .7M 97
Garratt St. B71: W Brom .4H 77
DY5: Brie H .4E 96
Garret Cl. DY6: K'wfrd .1K 95
GARRETT'S GREEN .1C 124
Garrett's Grn. Ind. Est.
B33: Sheld .8C 104
Garretts Grn. La.
B26: Sheld .2M 123
Garrett St. CV11: Nun .7L 89
Garretts Wlk. B14: K Hth .7L 143
Garrick Cl. CV5: E Grn .5C 150
DY1: Dud .6F 74
WS13: Lich .7F 12
Garrick Ct. WS13: Lich .7F 12
Garrick Ri. WS7: Burn .2H 17
Garrick Rd. B60: B'gve .8C 188
WS11: Cann .5D 8
WS13: Lich .7F 12
Garrick St. WV1: Wolv .8D 36 (5K 7)
Garrigill B77: Wiln .8G 33
Garrington St. WS10: Darl .2C 54
Garrison Cir.
B9: Birm .7A 102 (5M 5)
Garrison Ct. B9: Birm .7B 102
(off Barwell Rd.)
Garrison La.
B9: Birm .7B 102 (5M 5)
Garrison St.
B9: Birm .7B 102 (5M 5)
Garston Way B43: Gt Barr .1D 78
Garth, The B14: Yard W .5D 144
WS13: Lich .7H 13
Garth Cres. CV3: Bin .1K 175
Garth Ho. CV3: Bin .2K 175
Gartree Cres. LE9: Earl S .1D 70
Garway Cl. B98: Redd .8L 213
CV32: Lill .5A 218
Garway Gro. B25: Yard .3H 123
Garwood Rd. B26: Yard .7M 103
Garyth Williams Cl.
CV22: Bil .1L 205
Gas Sq. B61: B'gve .8L 187
Gas St. B1: Birm .7J 101 (6C 4)
CV21: Rugby .6B 180
CV31: Lea S .2M 223
Gatacre St. DY3: Gorn .6D 74
Gatcombe Cl. WV10: Bush .5F 22
Gatcombe Pl. B79: Tam .2B 32
Gatcombe Rd. DY1: Dud .7E 74
Gatehouse, The
CV31: Lea S .2K 223
Gatehouse Cl. CV21: Hillm .1G 207
Gatehouse Fold DY2: Dud .8K 75
(off Birmingham St.)
Gate Ho. La. CV7: Bal C .5J 171
Gatehouse La. CV12: Bed .7G 111
Gatehouse Trad. Est.
WS8: Bwnhls .8H 17
Gate La. B46: Neth W .3F 84
B73: Bold .7F 58
Gate La. B93: Dorr .5B 168
B94: H'ley H .5B 168
Gateley Cl. B98: Redd .5A 214
Gateley Rd. B68: O'bry .2L 119
Gateside Rd. CV6: Cov .7E 130
Gate St. B8: Salt .4D 102
DY3: Sed .2E 74
DY4: Tip .7A 76
Gatis St. WV6: Wolv .5A 36
Gatwick Rd. B35: Cas V .5C 82
Gauden Rd. DY9: W'cte .8D 116
Gaulby Wlk. CV3: Bin .8A 154
Gaunts, The B48: A'chu .3B 190
Gaveston Cl. CV34: Warw .1F 222
Gaveston Rd. CV6: Cov .3L 151
CV32: Lea S .8L 217
Gavin Way B6: Witt .5M 79
Gawsworth B79: Tam .2K 31
Gaydon Cl. B98: Redd .8F 212
CV6: Cov .1G 153
WV6: Pert .4E 34
Gaydon Gro. B29: S Oak .7A 120
Gaydon Pl. B73: S Cold .5H 59
Gaydon Rd. B92: Sol .6D 124
WS9: A'rdge .5G 41
Gayer St. CV6: Cov .8G 131
Gayfield Av. DY5: Brie H .8D 96
GAY HILL .2H 165
Gayhill La. B38: Head H .8H 143
Gayhurst Cl. CV3: Bin .1L 175
Gayhurst Dr. B25: Yard .1L 123
Gayle B77: Wiln .8G 33
Gayle Gro. B27: A Grn .1J 145
Gaymore Rd. DY10: Cookl .4B 136
Gayton Rd. B71: W Brom .3K 77
Gaza Cl. CV4: Tile H .8G 151
Gazelle Cl. CV1: Cov .6E 152 (3F 6)
Geach Twr. B19: Birm .4K 101
(off Uxbridge St.)
Gedney Cl. B90: Shir .6C 144
Geeson Cl. B35: Cas V .5B 82
Gee St. B19: Hock .3K 101
Gem Ho. B4: Birm .3J 5
Gemini Dr. WS11: Cann .3F 14
Geneva Rd. DY4: Tip .4K 75
Genge Av. WV4: E'shll .5E 52
Genners App. B31: N'fld .1K 141
Genners La. B31: N'fld .2K 141
B32: Bart G .1J 141
Genthorn Cl. WV4: E'shll .5F 52
Gentian B74: Four O .5F 42
Gentian Cl. B31: N'fld .3M 141
Gentian Way CV23: Brow .1E 180
Gentlemans La. B95: Ullen .4H 215
GENTLESHAW .5G 11
Geoffrey Cl. B76: Walm .2B 82
CV2: Cov .4H 153
Geoffrey Pl. B11: S'hll .6C 122
Geoffrey Rd. B11: S'hll .6C 122
B90: Shir .6F 144
George Arthur Rd. B8: Salt .5D 102
George Av. B65: Row R .7D 98
B78: M Oak .8J 31
George Birch Cl. CV23: Brin .6L 155
George Bird Cl. B66: Smeth .3A 100
George Cl. DY2: Dud .1L 97
George Dance Cl.
DY10: Kidd .3C 158
George Eliot Av. CV12: Bed .7K 111
George Eliot Bldgs.
CV11: Nun .5J 89
(off Mill St.)
George Eliot Rd. CV1: Cov .4D 152
George Eliot St. CV11: Nun .7J 89
George Foster Cl. LE9: Earl S .1G 71
George Fox La. CV13: Fen D .3G 67
George Frederick Rd.
B73: S'tly .5A 58
George Geary Cl. LE9: Barw .2C 70
George Henry Rd. DY4: Tip .2E 76
George Hill Cl. LE9: S Stan .6K 71
George Hodgkinson Cl.
CV4: Tile H .6F 150
George La. WS13: Lich .1J 19
George Marriott Cl.
LE9: S Stan .8J 71
George Marston Rd.
CV3: Bin .8L 153
George Pk. Cl. CV2: Cov .8J 131
George Poole Ho. CV1: Cov .7B 152
(off Windsor St.)
George Rd. B15: Edg .1H 121 (8B 4)
B23: Erd .5B 80
B25: Yard .3G 123
B29: S Oak .6E 120
B43: Gt Barr .7F 56
B46: Wat O .6J 83
B48: A'chu .3A 190
B63: Hale .5M 117
B68: O'bry .7H 99
B73: New O .8D 58
B91: Sol .6C 146
CV34: Warw .1G 223
DY4: Tip .3K 75
WV14: Cose .8K 53
George Robertson Cl.
CV3: Bin .2L 175
George Rose Gdns.
WS10: Darl .3C 54
George Ryan Cen.
B78: M Oak .8K 31
George St. B3: Birm .6J 101 (4C 4)
B12: Bal H .4L 121
B19: Loz .2H 101
B21: Hand .1C 100
B61: B'gve .7M 187
B70: W Brom .7K 77
B79: Tam .5B 32
CV1: Cov .4D 152 (1E 6)
(not continuous)
CV7: New A .1G 109
CV11: Nun .7L 89
CV12: Bed .6H 111
CV21: Rugby .6M 179
CV31: Lea S .2A 224
CV47: S'ton .1M 225
DY1: Dud .3H 75
DY8: Word .8M 95
DY10: Kidd .3M 157
LE9: Barw .3B 70
LE10: Hinc .1K 91
WS1: Wals .8L 39
WS12: Hed .5J 9
WV2: E'shll .2G 53
WV2: Wolv .8D 36 (6K 7)
WV13: W'hall .5A 38
George St. Ringway
CV12: Bed .6H 111
George St. W.
B18: Hock .5G 101 (2A 4)
George Wlk. B97: Redd .6E 212
George Ward Ct. LE9: Barw .2B 70
Georgian Gdns. WS10: W'bry .6F 54
Georgian Pl. WS11: Cann .7E 8
Georgina Av. WV14: Cose .6K 53
Geraldine Rd. B25: Yard .2H 123
Gerald Rd. DY8: Woll .2L 115
Geranium Gro. B9: Bord G .6F 102
Geranium Rd. DY2: Dud .1M 97
Gerard B79: Tam .2L 31
Gerard Av. CV4: Canly .1H 173
Gerard Cl. CV22: Caw .1G 205
Gerard Pl. CV22: Caw .1G 205
Gerard Rd. CV22: Caw .1G 205
Gerardsfield Rd.
B33: Kitts G .6D 104
Germander Dr. WS5: Wals .6B 56
Gerrard Cl. B19: Loz .2J 101
Gerrard Rd. WV13: W'hall .8L 37
Gerrard St. B19: Loz .2J 101
CV34: Warw .3E 222
Gertrude Pl. B18: Hock .4G 101
Gervase Dr. DY1: Dud .6J 75
Geston Rd. DY1: Dud .1F 96
Gettings Cl. WS7: Burn .2L 17
Gheluvelt Av. DY10: Kidd .2M 157
Gheluvelt Ct. DY13: Stour S .5F 182
GIBBET HILL .7K 173
Gibbet Hill Rd. CV4: Canly .4H 173
Gibbet La. DY7: Kinv .4E 114
(not continuous)
Gibbins Rd. B29: S Oak .8C 120
Gibb La. B61: Cats .1A 188
Gibbons Cl. CV4: Tile H .7F 150
Gibbons Cres. DY13: Stour S .5F 182
Gibbons Gro. WV6: Wolv .5M 35
Gibbons Hill Rd. DY3: Sed .7D 52
Gibbons Ind. Est. DY6: K'wfrd .2A 96
Gibbon's La. DY5: P'ntt .2A 96
Gibbons Rd. B75: Four O .6H 43
WV6: Wolv .5M 35
Gibbs Cl. CV2: W'grve S .3B 154
Gibbs Hill Rd. B31: Longb .2B 164
Gibb Sq. B9: Birm .8A 102 (7L 5)
Gibbs Rd. B98: Redd .4G 213
DY9: Lye .4G 117
Gibbs St. WV6: Wolv .5A 36
Gibb St. B9: Birm .8M 101 (7K 5)
GIB HEATH .3F 100
Gibraltar DY7: Kinv .5B 114
Gibson Cres. CV12: Bed .8G 111
Gibson Dr. B20: Hand .1H 101
B66: Smeth .3A 100
CV21: Hillm .8G 181
Gibson Rd. B20: Hand .1H 101
WV6: Pert .6E 34
Giddywell La. WS15: Longd .1M 11
Gideon Cl. B25: Yard .3K 123
Gideons Cl. DY3: Up Gor .4D 74
Gielgud Way CV2: W'grve S .1B 154
Giffard Rd. WV1: Wolv .2H 53
WV10: Bush .6E 22
Giffard Way CV34: Warw .8E 216
Gifford Ct. DY5: Brie H .7D 96
(off Hill St.)
Giffords Cft. WS13: Lich .8G 13
Giggetty La. WV5: Wom .3E 72
Gigg La. B76: Wis .6H 61
Gigmill Way DY8: Stourb .5L 115
Gilbanks Rd. DY8: Woll .2K 115
Gilberry Cl. B93: Know .4G 169
Gilbert Av. B69: Tiv .2B 98
CV22: Bil .7K 179
Gilbert Cl. CV1: Cov .6E 152
WV11: Wed .2A 38
Gilbert Ct. WS4: Wals .5A 40
(off Lichfield Rd.)
Gilbert Ent. Pk. WV12: W'hall .5B 38
Gilbert La. WV5: Wom .2H 73
Gilbert Rd. B60: B'gve .2L 209
B66: Smeth .5B 100
WS13: Lich .7J 13
Gilbert Scott Way
DY10: Kidd .2M 157
GILBERT'S GREEN .6E 192
GILBERTSTONE .2L 123
Gilbertstone Av. B26: Yard .4L 123
Gilbertstone Cl. B98: Redd .8E 212
Gilbert St. DY4: Tip .7M 75
Gilbert Wlk. WS13: Lich .7J 13
(off Gilbert Rd.)
Gilbeys Cl. DY8: Word .8L 95
Gilby Rd. B16: Birm .7G 101 (7A 4)
Gilchrist Dr. B15: Edg .1E 120
Gildas Av. B38: K Nor .8G 143
Giles Cl. B33: Stech .6L 103
B92: Sol .2F 146
CV6: Cov .7C 130
Giles Cl. Ho. B33: Stech .6L 103
Giles Hill DY8: Stourb .3A 116
Giles Rd. B68: O'bry .4H 99
WS13: Lich .6G 13
Gilfil Rd. CV10: Nun .8H 89
Gilgal DY13: Stour S .5G 183
Gilldown Pl. B15: Edg .2H 121
Gillespie Cft. B6: Aston .2M 101
Gillett Cl. CV11: Nun .6H 89
Gillhurst Rd. B17: Harb .2B 120
Gillian's Wlk. CV2: W'grve S .1A 154
Gillies Ct. B33: Stech .6K 103
Gilling Gro. B34: Hodg H .3A 104
Gillingham Cl. WS10: W'bry .4K 55
Gillity Av. WS5: Wals .1B 56
Gillity Cl. WS5: Wals .1B 56
Gillity Ct. WS5: Wals .2D 56
Gilliver Rd. B90: Shir .7H 145
Gillman Cl. B26: Sheld .5D 124
Gillott Cl. B91: Sol .6E 146
Gillott Rd. B16: Edg .8C 100
Gillows Cft. B90: M'path .2A 168
Gillquart Way
CV1: Cov .8D 152 (8E 6)
Gillscroft Rd. B33: Kitts G .5A 104
Gill St. B70: W Brom .8J 77
DY2: Neth .5L 97
GILLWAY .2A 32
Gillway La. B79: Tam .1A 32
Gilmorton Cl. B17: Harb .2B 120
B91: Sol .8C 146
Gilpin Cl. B8: W End .2J 103
Gilpin Cres. WS3: Pels .5A 26
Gilpins Cft. WS6: C Hay .8D 14
GILSON .8K 83
Gilson Dr. B46: Col .2K 105
Gilson Rd. B46: Col .8K 83
Gilson St. DY4: Tip .1C 76
Gilson Way B37: K'hrst .4G 105
Gilt Edge Leisure Cen. .1H 183
Gilwell Rd. B34: S End .3E 104
WS15: Cann W .3F 10
Gimble Wlk. B17: Harb .1A 120
(not continuous)
Gin Cridden DY9: Lye .3E 116
Gingles Ct. CV21: Hillm .1G 207
Ginkgo Wlk. CV31: Lea S .4M 223
Gipsy Cl. CV7: Bal C .4H 171
Gipsy La. B23: Erd .4A 80
CV7: Bal C .4J 171
CV10: Nun .3J 111
CV11: Nun .3J 111
DY11: W'ley .1M 135
LE10: Wlvy .1L 113
WV13: W'hall .8B 38
Girdlers Cl. CV3: Cov .4B 174
Girtin Cl. CV12: Bed .5G 111
Girton Ho. B36: Cas B .1F 104
Girton Rd. WS11: Cann .1E 14
Girvan Gro. CV32: Cubb .4C 218
Gisborn Cl. B10: Small H .1B 122
Gisburn Cl. B97: Redd .4B 212
CV34: Warw .8F 216
Givens Ho. CV1: Cov .5A 6
GK Davies Trad. Est.
B63: Crad .3G 117
Glade, The B26: Sheld .5D 124
B74: S'tly .8L 41
CV5: E Grn .6F 150
DY9: Lye .4E 116
WS11: Cann .7C 8
WV8: Pend .8L 21
Glades, The WS9: A'rdge .2H 41
Gladeside Cl. WS4: S'fld .1D 40
Gladiator Way CV21: Rugby .2M 179
Gladstone Cl. LE10: Hinc .6L 69
Gladstone Ct. CV32: Lea S .8M 217
Gladstone Dr. B69: Tiv .7C 76
DY8: Woll .4K 115
Gladstone Gro. DY6: K'wfrd .1K 95
Gladstone Rd. B11: S'brk .3B 122
B23: Erd .6D 80
B26: Yard .3K 123
B93: Dorr .7G 169
DY8: Woll .3K 115
WS12: Hth H .8K 9
Gladstone St. B6: Aston .1A 102
B71: W Brom .3J 77
CV21: Rugby .5M 179
WS2: Wals .5K 39
WS10: Darl .3E 54
Gladstone Ter. LE10: Hinc .1L 91
Gladys Rd. B25: Yard .2H 123
B67: Smeth .7M 99
Gladys Ter. B67: Smeth .7M 99

Glaisdale Av.—Granby Bus. Pk.

Glaisdale Av. CV6: Cov 6E 130
Glaisdale Gdns. WV6: Wolv 4A 36
Glaisdale Rd. B28: Hall G 1G 145
Glaisedale Gro. WV13: W'hall ...7C 38
Glaisher Dr. WV10: Wolv 3C 36
Glamis Rd. WV12: W'hall 2B 38
Glamorgan Cl. CV3: W'hall 4K 175
Glanville Dr. B75: Four O 5G 43
Glaramara Cl. CV21: Brow 2D 180
Glasbury Cft. B38: K Nor 2E 164
GLASCOTE 7F 32
Glascote Cl. B90: Shir 5G 145
Glascote Ct. B77: Amin 5E 32
Glascote Gro. B34: S End 2C 104
Glascote La. B77: Wiln 2F 46
(not continuous)
Glascote Rd.
B77: Glas, Tam, Wiln 5C 32
Glasscroft Cotts. WS7: Burn ...2M 17
Glassford Dr. WV6: Tett 3L 35
Glasshouse Hill DY8: Stourb ..6B 116
Glasshouse La. B94: H'ley H ...4E 194
CV8: Ken 4J 199
Glastonbury Cl. DY11: Kidd ...3G 157
Glastonbury Cres. WS3: Blox ...7E 24
Glastonbury Rd.
B14: Yard W 5C 144
B71: W Brom 8K 55
Glastonbury Way WS3: Blox 8E 24
Glaston Dr. B91: Sol 8A 146
Gleads Cft. B62: Quin 6G 119
Gleaston Wlk. WV1: Wolv 1J 53
Gleave Rd. B29: S Oak 8E 120
CV31: W'nsh 6A 224
Glebe, The B98: Beo 2M 213
CV7: Cor 2H 129
DY9: Belb 3E 160
Glebe Av. CV12: Bed 8E 110
Glebe Cl. B98: Redd 7K 213
CV4: Tile H 2G 173
CV47: S'ton 1M 225
Glebe Cres. CV8: Ken 6G 199
CV21: Rugby 6L 179
Glebe Dr. B73: Bold 1F 80
Glebe Farm Gro. CV3: Bin 6M 153
Glebe Farm Ind. Est.
CV21: Rugby 2M 179
Glebe Farm Rd. B33: Stech ...4A 104
CV21: Rugby 2M 179
Glebe Flds. B76: Curd 3H 83
Glebefields Rd. DY4: Tip 1A 76
Glebeland Cl.
B16: Birm 8H 101 (7A 4)
Glebe La. CV11: Nun 3M 89
(not continuous)
DY8: Stourb 5L 115
Glebe Pl. CV31: Lea S 2B 224
WS10: Darl 3B 54
Glebe Rd. B48: A'chu 2A 190
B91: Sol 4D 146
CV11: Nun 5K 89
CV47: Sou 4G 225
LE10: Hinc 1M 91
WV13: W'hall 1M 53
Glebe St. WS1: Wals 1L 55
Glebe Way CV7: Bal C 2G 171
Gledhill Pk. WS14: Lich 4J 19
Gleeson Dr. CV34: Warw 8E 216
Glen, The B60: B'wll 3G 189
Glenavon Rd. B14: K Hth 6M 143
Glen Bank LE10: Hinc 8L 69
Glenbarr Cl. LE10: Hinc 1G 91
Glenbarr Dr. LE10: Hinc 1G 91
Glen Cl. WS4: Wals 6A 40
WS11: Cann 4E 8
Glencoe Dr. WS11: Cann 5G 9
Glencoe Rd. B16: Edg 5C 100
CV3: Cov 7H 153
Glen Ct. WV3: Wolv 7L 35
WV8: Cod 5G 21
Glencroft Rd. B92: Sol 5D 124
Glendale Av. CV8: Ken 3G 199
Glendale Cl. B63: Hale 5B 118
WV3: Wolv 1J 51
Glendale Ct. B77: Wiln 3H 47
Glendale Dr. B33: Stech 6M 103
WV5: Wom 3G 73
Glendale Gdns. WS11: Cann 5F 8
Glendale Twr. B23: Erd 3H 81
Glendale Way CV4: Tile H 7C 150
Glendawn Cl. WS11: Cann 6G 9
Glendene Cres. B38: K Nor 2C 164
Glendene Dr. B43: Gt Barr 1D 78
Glendene Rd. WS12: Hed 3K 9
Glendevon Cl. B45: Fran 7G 141
Glendon Gdns. CV12: Bulk 6C 112
Glendon Rd. B23: Erd 3D 80
Glendon Way B93: Dorr 6D 168
Glendower App. CV34: H'cte ...6L 223
Glendower Av. CV5: Cov 7K 151
Glendower Rd. B42: P Barr 5J 79
WS9: A'rdge 8H 27
Gleneagles Av. B77: Amin 4H 33
Gleneagles Cl. CV11: Nun 8C 90
LE10: Burb 5K 91
Gleneagles Dr. B43: Gt Barr 6E 56
B60: B'wll 4G 189
B69: Tiv 2A 98
B75: S Cold 2J 59
Gleneagles Rd. B26: Yard 1A 124
CV2: Cov 3L 153
Gleneagles Rd. WS3: Blox 6F 24
WV6: Pert 4D 34
Glenelg Dr. DY8: Stourb 7B 116
Glenelg M. WS5: Wals 4D 56
Glenfern Gdns. CV8: Rytn D ...7L 175
Glenfern Rd. WV14: Cose 1G 75
Glenfield B77: Wiln 8C 32
WV8: Pend 7L 21
Glenfield Av. CV10: Nun 2J 89
Glenfield Cl. B76: Walm 6L 59
B91: Sol 1C 168
B97: Redd 3D 220
Glenfield Gro. B29: S Oak 8G 121
Glengarry Cl. B32: Bart G 2H 141
Glengarry Gdns. WV3: Wolv 8B 34
Glenhill Dr. B38: K Nor 1G 165
Glenhurst Cl. WS2: Wals 6D 38
Glenmead Rd. B44: Gt Barr 1K 79
Glenmore Av. WS7: Burn 3G 17
Glenmore Cl. WV3: Wolv 2L 51
Glenmore Dr. B38: K Nor 7D 142
CV6: Longf 4F 130
Glenmount Av. CV6: Longf 4F 130
Glenn St. CV6: Cov 6D 130
Glen Pk. Rd. DY3: Gorn 7D 74
Glenpark Rd. B8: Salt 4E 102
Glenridding Cl. CV6: Longf 4F 130
Glen Ri. B13: Mose 3C 144
Glen Rd. DY3: Up Gor 3E 74
DY8: Stourb 6M 115
Glenrosa Wlk. CV4: Tile H 2G 173
Glenroy Cl. CV2: Cov 3L 153
Glenroyde B38: K Nor 2E 164
Glen Side B32: Bart G 7K 119
Glenside Av. B92: Sol 6C 124
Glenthorne Dr. WS6: C Hay 6E 14
Glenthorne Rd. B24: Erd 7G 81
Glenthorne Way B24: Erd 7G 81
Glentworth B76: Walm 7A 60
Glentworth Av. CV6: Cov 7A 130
Glentworth Gdns. WV6: Wolv ...4B 36
Glenville Av. CV9: Wood E 8J 47
Glenville Dr. B23: Erd 2F 81
Glenwood Cl. DY5: Quar B 1D 116
Glenwood Dr. B90: Ches G 5K 167
Glenwood Gdns. B77: Wiln 3H 47
CV12: Bed 5G 111
Glenwood Ri. WS9: Ston 6K 27
Glenwood Rd. B38: K Nor 1D 164
Globe St. WS10: W'bry 8F 54
Gloster Dr. CV8: Ken 3F 198
Gloucester Cl. CV11: Nun 2A 90
WS13: Lich 6J 19
Gloucester Flats B65: Row R 5E 98
Gloucester Ho.
WV1: Wolv 5C 36 (1J 7)
Gloucester Pl. WV13: W'hall 7D 38
Gloucester Rd. DY2: Neth 7K 97
WS5: Wals 1B 56
WS10: W'bry 6J 55
Gloucester St.
B5: Birm 8L 101 (7G 5)
CV1: Cov 6B 152 (4A 6)
CV31: Lea S 2A 224
WV6: Wolv 5B 36
Gloucester Way
B37: Mars G 8G 105
DY12: Bew 5B 156
WS11: Hth H 8H 9
Glover Cl. B28: Hall G 3F 144
CV34: Warw 5B 222
Glover Rd. B75: S Cold 4M 59
Glovers Cl. CV7: Mer 8J 127
CV9: Man 2M 65
WS12: Haz 4A 10
Glovers Cft. B37: F'bri 6F 104
Glovers Fld. Dr. B7: Nech 2C 102
Glover's Rd. B10: Small H 1C 122
Glover St. B9: Birm 7A 102 (6N 5)
B70: W Brom 8K 77
B98: Redd 6E 212
CV3: Cov 1D 174
WS12: Wim 6M 9
Glovers Trust Homes
B73: Bold 1F 80
Glyme Dr. WV6: Tett 4L 35
Glyn Av. WV14: Bils 6B 54
Glyn Cl. LE9: Barw 2A 70
Glyndebourne B79: Tam 2K 31
Glyn Dr. WV14: Bils 6B 54
Glyne Ct. B73: S Cold 4H 59
Glyn Farm Rd. B32: Quin 4J 119
Glynn Cres. B63: Crad 2H 117
Glynne Av. DY6: K'wfrd 5K 95
Glyn Rd. B32: Quin 3K 119
Glynside Av. B32: Quin 3K 119
Godfrey Cl. CV31: Rad S 4E 224
Godiva Pl. CV1: Cov 6E 152 (4F 6)
Godiva Trading Est.
CV6: Cov 1F 152
Godolphin B79: Tam 3K 31
Godrich Ho. B13: Mose 6A 122
Godson Cres. DY11: Kidd 6H 157
Godson Pl. DY11: Kidd 6J 157
Goffs Cl. B32: Bart G 6M 119
Gofton B77: Wiln 8G 33
Goldacre Cl. CV31: W'nsh 5M 223
Gold Av. CV22: Caw 1H 205
Goldborough Cl. WV14: Cose 6K 53
Gold Cl. CV11: Nun 1L 111
Goldcrest B77: Wiln 4G 47
Gold Crest Cl. DY2: Neth 7K 97
Goldcrest Cft. B36: Cas B 1G 105
Goldcrest Dr. DY10: Kidd 7B 158
Golden Acres La. CV3: Bin 2M 175
Goldencrest Dr. B69: O'bry 1E 98
Golden Cft. B20: Hand 8F 78
Golden Cross La. B61: Cats ...8A 162
Goldencross Way DY5: Brie H ...8B 96
GOLDEN END 3K 169
Golden End Dr. B93: Know 3K 169
Golden Hillock Rd.
B10: Small H 4D 122
B11: S'brk 4D 122
DY2: Neth 6J 97
Golden Hind Dr.
DY13: Stour S 7G 183
Goldfinch Cl. B30: B'vlle 1D 142
Goldfinch Rd. DY9: W'cte 6C 116
Goldicroft Rd. WS10: W'bry 5G 55
Goldieslie Cl. B73: W Grn 7H 59
Goldieslie Rd. B73: W Grn 7H 59
Golding St. DY2: Neth 3J 97
Goldsborough B77: Wiln 8G 33
GOLDS GREEN 2E 76
Golds Hill Gdns. B21: Hand 2F 100
Golds Hill Rd. B21: Hand 1F 100
Golds Hill Way DY4: Tip 2D 76
Goldsmith Av. CV22: Rugby ...2M 205
CV34: Warw 4C 222
Goldsmith Pl. B79: Tam 2A 32
Goldsmith Rd. B14: K Hth 1M 143
WS3: Blox 2L 39
Goldsmith Wlk. DY10: Kidd 4C 158
Goldstar Way B33: Kitts G 7C 104
Goldthorn Av. WS11: Cann 7F 8
WV4: Penn 3B 52
Goldthorn Cl. CV5: E Grn 5D 150
Goldthorn Cres. WV4: Penn 3A 52
Goldthorne Av. B26: Sheld 5C 124
Goldthorne Cl. B97: Redd 8C 212
GOLDTHORN HILL 4B 52
Goldthorn Hill WV2: Penn 3A 52
Goldthorn Hill Rd.
WV2: Penn 3B 52
GOLDTHORN PARK 5C 52
Goldthorn Pl. DY11: Kidd 7J 157
Goldthorn Rd. DY11: Kidd 6H 157
WV2: Wolv 3B 52
Goldthorn Ter. WV2: Wolv 2B 52
Goldthorn Wlk. DY5: Brie H ...1D 116
Golf Club Dr. WS1: Wals 3A 56
Golf Dr. CV11: Nun 1A 112
Golf La. CV31: W'nsh 6B 224
WV14: Bils 2K 53
Golson Cl. B75: S Cold 3M 59
Gomeldon Av. B14: K Hth 6M 143
Gomer St. WV13: W'hall 7A 38
Gomer St. W. WV13: W'hall 7A 38
Gonville Ho. B36: Cas B 1F 104
Gooch Cl. DY8: Amb 3A 116
Gooch St. B5: Birm 1L 121
Gooch St. Nth.
B5: Birm 8L 101 (8G 5)
Gooch's Way CV31: W'nsh 5A 224
Goodacre Cl. CV23: Clift D 4G 181
Goodall Gro. B43: Gt Barr 4L 57
Goodall St. WS1: Wals 8M 39
Goodby Rd. B13: Mose 6K 121
Goode Av. B18: Hock 4G 101
Goode Cl. B68: O'bry 5J 99
CV34: Warw 2C 222
Goode Cft. CV4: Tile H 7F 150
Goodere Av. B78: Pole 1A 48
Goodere Dr. B78: Pole 2K 49
Goodeve Wlk. B75: S Cold 4B 60
Goodfellow St. CV32: Lea S 8J 217
Goodison Gdns. B24: Erd 4H 81
Goodleigh Av. B31: Longb 3L 163
Goodman Cl. B28: Hall G 3F 144
Goodman St.
B1: Birm 6H 101 (4A 4)
Goodman Way CV4: Tile H 8C 150
Goodrest Av. B62: Quin 4F 118
Goodrest Cft. B14: Yard W 5C 144
Goodrest La. B38: Head H 3F 164
(not continuous)
Goodrich Av. WV6: Pert 6G 35
Goodrich Cl. B98: Redd 7M 213
Goodrich Covert B14: K Hth 7J 143
Goodrick Way B7: Nech 3B 102
GOOD'S GREEN 3A 134
Goodway Ho. B4: Birm 2G 5
(off Shadwell St.)
CV32: Lea S 1K 223
Goodway Rd. B44: Gt Barr 1L 79
B92: Sol 6E 124
Goodwin Cl. DY11: Kidd 2J 157
Goodwood Cl. B36: Hodg H 1K 103
CV3: W'hall 3J 175
WS12: Haz 3A 10
WS14: Lich 2K 19
Goodwood Dr. B74: S'tly 2M 57
Goodwood Rd. B61: Cats 8B 162
Goodwyn Av. B68: O'bry 2K 119
Goodyear Av. WV10: Bush 1E 36
Goodyear Rd. B67: Smeth 7K 99
GOODYERS END 1C 130
Goodyers End La.
CV12: Bed 1C 130
Goosehill Cl. B98: Redd 8L 213
Goosehills Rd. LE10: Burb 4L 91
Goose La. LE9: Barw 4A 70
GOOSEMOOR GREEN 5J 11
Goosemoor La. B23: Erd 2E 80
Goostry Cl. B77: Tam 5D 32
Goostry Rd. B77: Tam 4D 32
Gopsall Rd. LE10: Hinc 7K 69
Gopsal St. B4: Birm 6A 102 (3L 5)
GORCOTT HILL 3C 214
Gorcott Hill B98: Beo 5B 214
Gorcott La. B90: Dic H 4G 167
Gordon Anstis Ho.
B98: Redd 3K 213
Gordon Av. B19: Loz 2K 101
B71: W Brom 1J 77
WV4: E'shll 6F 52
Gordon Cl. B69: Tiv 7D 76
CV12: Bed 5H 111
Gordon Ct. B33: Stech 6K 103
Gordon Cres. DY5: Brie H 4E 96
Gordon Dr. DY4: Tip 3C 76
Gordon Pas. CV31: Lea S 2A 224
Gordon Pl. WV14: Bils 4J 53
Gordon Rd. B17: Harb 3D 120
B19: Loz 1J 101
Gordon St. *B9: Birm* *7B 102*
(off Garrison La.)
CV1: Cov 8A 152
CV31: Lea S 2A 224
WS10: Darl 3D 54
WV2: Wolv 1D 52 (7L 7)
Gorey Cl. WV12: W'hall 1B 38
Gorge Rd. DY3: Sed 1E 74
WV14: Cose 1E 74
Goring Rd. CV2: Cov 5G 153
Gorleston Gro. B14: K Hth 7B 144
Gorleston Rd. B14: K Hth 7B 144
GORNALWOOD 6C 74
Gornal Wood Crematorium
DY3: Gorn 7C 74
Gorsebrook Rd. WV6: Wolv 4B 36
WV10: Wolv 4C 36
Gorse Cl. B29: W Cas 1A 142
B37: F'bri 7F 104
CV22: Bil 8L 179
Gorse Dr. WS12: Hunt 4D 8
Gorse Farm Rd. B43: Gt Barr ...1E 78
CV11: Nun 1B 112
Gorse Farm Wood Nature Reserve
........................1F 78
Gorsefield Rd. B34: S End 4C 104
Gorse Grn. La. DY9: Belb 1G 161
Gorse La. WS13: Frad 3M 13
WS14: Lich 3K 19
WV5: Try 3A 72
Gorse Lea CV47: Sou 4G 225
Gorsemeadow Dr.
B45: B Grn 1H 189
Gorsemoor Rd. WS12: Hth H 8J 9
Gorsemoor Way WV11: Ess 6B 24
Gorse Rd. DY1: Dud 5G 75
WV11: Wed 1A 38
Gorse Way WS12: Hed 1J 9
Gorseway CV5: Cov 6J 151
WS7: Burn 4H 17
Gorsey Cl. B96: A'wd B 8E 220
Gorsey La. B46: Col 7L 83
B47: Wyt 5A 166
WS3: Lit W 7K 15
WS6: Gt Wyr 8F 14
WS11: Cann 8B 8
Gorsey Way B46: Col 7L 83
WS9: A'rdge 4E 40
Gorsly Piece B32: Quin 5J 119
Gorstey Lea WS7: Burn 2J 17
GORSTEY LEY 1J 17
Gorstie Cft. B43: Gt Barr 1E 78
Gorsty Av. DY5: Brie H 6C 96
Gorsty Bank WS14: Lich 1L 19
Gorsty Cl. B71: W Brom 1M 77
Gorsty Hayes WV8: Cod 6F 20
Gorsty Hill Rd. B65: B'hth 1B 118
Gorsy Bank Rd. B77: Hock 4F 46
Gorsymead Gro. B31: Longb 7J 141
Gorsy Rd. B32: Quin 5K 119
Gorsy Way CV10: Nun 4D 88
Gorton Cft. CV7: Bal C 2H 171
Gorway Cl. WS1: Wals 2M 55
Gorway Gdns. WS1: Wals 2A 56
Gorway Rd. WS1: Wals 2M 55
GOSCOTE 7L 25
Goscote Cl. B97: Redd 3A 212
WS3: Wals 2M 39
Goscote Ind. Est. WS3: Blox 8L 25
Goscote La. WS3: Blox, Wals ...8L 25
Goscote Lodge Cres.
WS3: Wals 2A 40
Goscote Pl. WS3: Wals 2A 40
Goscote Rd. WS3: Pels 8M 25
Gosford Dr. LE10: Hinc 8G 69
GOSFORD GREEN 7F 152
Gosford Ind. Est. CV1: Cov 7F 152
Gosford St. B12: Bal H 3M 121
CV1: Cov 7D 152 (5E 6)
Gosford Wlk. B92: Olton 8B 124
Gosmoor Ho. B26: Yard 2L 123
Gospel End Rd. DY3: Sed 1A 74
Gospel End St. DY3: Sed 2D 74
GOSPEL END VILLAGE 1A 74
Gospel Farm Rd.
B27: A Grn 1H 145
Gospel La. B27: A Grn 2J 145
Gospel Oak Rd. CV6: Cov 5B 130
DY4: Tip 8B 54
Gosport Cl. WV1: Wolv 2H 53
Gosport Rd. CV6: Cov 1E 152
Goss, The DY5: Brie H 8D 96
Goss Cft. B29: S Oak 8D 120
Gossett La. CV3: Bin W 2E 176
Gossey La. B33: Kitts G 7C 104
Gosta Grn. B4: Birm 5M 101 (2J 5
Gotham Rd. B26: Yard 3L 123
GOTHERSLEY 6E 94
Gothersley La. DY7: Stourt 7C 94
Goths Cl. B65: Row R 5C 98
Gough Av. WV11: Wed 1H 37
Gough Rd. B11: S'brk 4D 122
B15: Edg 2J 121
WV14: Cose 8J 53
Gough St. B1: Birm 8K 101 (7E 4
WV1: Wolv 7E 36 (4M 7
WV13: W'hall 6C 38
Gould Av. E. DY11: Kidd 7G 157
Gould Av. W. DY11: Kidd 8G 157
Gould Firm La. WS9: A'rdge 3L 41
Gould Rd. CV35: H Mag 2A 222
Governor's Ct. CV34: Warw 1D 222
Gowan Rd. B8: Salt 5E 102
Gower Av. DY6: K'wfrd 5M 95
Gower Ho. *B62: Quin* *3F 118*
(off Lockington Cft.
Gower Rd. B62: Quin 3E 118
DY3: Sed 1B 74
Gower St. B19: Loz 2K 101
WS2: Wals 2H 55
WV2: Wolv 1E 52 (7M 7
(not continuous)
WV13: W'hall 7A 38
Gowland Dr. WS11: Cann 8B 8
Gowrie Cl. LE10: Hinc 7H 69
Goya Cl. WS11: Hth H 7J 9
Gozzard St. WV14: Bils 4L 53
Gracechurch Cen.
B72: S Cold 4H 59
Gracemere Cres. B28: Hall G ..6E 144
Grace Moore Ct. WS11: Cann 5F 8
Grace Rd. B11: S'brk 2C 122
B69: Tiv 1C 98
CV5: Alle 1A 150
DY4: Tip 2A 76
LE9: Sap 1L 93
Gracewell Homes B13: Mose ...8D 122
Gracewell Rd. B13: Mose 8D 122
Grafton Cl. B98: Redd 2H 221
Grafton Ct. WV6: Wolv 5M 35
Grafton Cres. B60: B'gve 2L 209
Grafton Dr. WV13: W'hall 1K 53
Grafton Gdns. DY3: Lwr G 6B 74
Grafton Gro. B19: Loz 2J 101
Grafton Ho. *B60: B'gve* *6B 188*
(off Burcot La.
Grafton La. B61: U War 2H 209
Grafton Pl. WV14: Bils 2L 53
Grafton Rd. B11: S'brk 2B 122
B21: Hand 8D 78
B68: O'bry 8F 98
B71: W Brom 5K 77
B90: Shir 7C 144
Grafton St. CV1: Cov 7E 152
Graham Cl. CV6: Cov 8H 131
DY4: Tip 8B 54
Graham Cres. B45: Rubery 2G 163
Graham Rd. B8: Salt 6F 102
B25: Yard 3J 123
B62: B'hth 1C 118
B71: W Brom 5K 77
CV21: Rugby 5C 180
DY8: Word 5K 95
Graham St. B1: Birm ...6J 101 (3C 4
B19: Loz 2J 101
CV11: Nun 4J 89
Grainger Cl. DY4: Tip 3D 76
Grainger Ct. WS11: Cann 7D 8
Graingers La. B64: Crad H 1J 117
Grainger St. DY2: Dud 2K 97
Graiseley Ct.
WV3: Wolv 8C 36 (6H 7)
Graiseley Hill
WV2: Wolv 1C 52 (8G 7)
Graiseley La. WV11: Wed 4H 37
Graiseley Recreation Cen.
..................1C 52 (8H 7)
Graiseley Row
WV2: Wolv 1C 52 (8H 7)
Graiseley St.
WV3: Wolv 8B 36 (6G 7)
Graith Cl. B28: Hall G 6E 144
Gramer Ct. CV9: Man 3M 65
Grammar School La.
B63: Hale 5A 118
Grampian Rd. DY8: Amb 3A 116
Granada Ind. Est. B69: O'bry 2F 98
Granary, The WS9: A'rdge 2H 41
Granary Cl. DY6: W Hth 1G 95
WS12: Hed 4H 9
Granary La. B76: Walm 6M 59
Granary Rd. B60: Stoke H 3L 209
WV8: Pend 8L 21
Granborough Cl. CV3: Bin 1M 175
Granborough Ct. CV32: Lill 6A 218
Granbourne Rd. WS2: Wals 5D 38
Granby Av. B33: Sheld 8C 104
Granby Bus. Pk. B33: Sheld ...8D 104

Hadley Ct.—Hardwick Ct.

Hadley Ct. B16: Edg 8D 100
Hadley Cft. B66: Smeth 2A 100
Hadley Pl. WV14: Bils 2J 53
Hadley Rd. WS2: Wals 3F 38
WV14: Bils 2J 53
Hadleys Cl. DY2: Neth 5L 97
Hadleys Cft. B78: K'bry 4D 62
Hadley Stadium 6A 100
Hadley St. B68: O'bry 5G 99
Hadley Way WS2: Wals 3F 38
Hadlow Cft. B33: Sheld 2D 124
Hadrian Cl. CV32: Lill 5B 218
LE10: Hinc 8F 68
Hadrian Dr. B46: Col 8M 83
Hadrians Cl. B77: Two G 1D 46
Hadrians Way CV21: Rugby ..2M 179
Hadyn Gro. B26: Sheld 3B 124
Hadzor Ho. B97: Redd 5A 212
Hadzor Rd. B68: O'bry 1K 119
Hafren Cl. B45: Fran 7H 141
Hafren Ct. DY12: Bew 6B 156
Hafren Way DY13: Stour S 5F 182
Hafton Gro. B9: Small H 8D 102
Haggar St. WV2: Wolv 3C 52
HAGLEY 3C 138
Hagley C'way. DY9: Hag 2F 138
Hagley Cl. DY9: Hag 3C 138
Hagley Hall 3E 138
Hagley Hall Gdns. DY9: Hag ...3D 138
Hagley Hill DY9: Hag 2E 138
Hagley Ho. B60: B'gve 6B 188
(off Burcot La.)
Hagley Mall B63: Hale 6B 118
Hagley M. DY9: Hag 3D 138
Hagley Pk. Dr. B45: Redn 3G 163
Hagley Rd. B16: Edg ...8A 100 (8A 4)
B63: Hale 1J 139
DY8: Pedm, Stourb 5A 116
DY9: Pedm 8C 116
Hagley Rd. W. B17: Harb 2L 119
B32: Quin 3G 119
B62: Quin 3G 119
B68: O'bry 3G 119
Hagley Station (Rail) 4A 138
Hagley St. B63: Hale 6B 118
Hagley Vw. Rd. DY2: Dud 1J 97
Hagley Vs. B12: Bal H 5B 122
(off Taunton Rd.)
B12: S'hll 4B 122
(off Taunton Rd.)
Hagley Wood La. B62: Roms ...1H 139
DY9: Hag 1H 139
Haig Cl. B75: S Cold 2J 59
WS11: Cann 4G 9
Haig Ct. CV22: Bil 8L 179
Haig Pl. B13: Mose 2A 144
Haig Rd. DY2: Dud 8M 75
Haig St. B71: W Brom 4J 77
Hailes Pk. Cl. WV4: Wolv 3E 52
Hailsham Rd. B23: Erd 4F 80
Hailstone Cl. B65: Row R 4A 98
Haines Cl. DY4: Tip 5B 76
Haines St. B70: W Brom 7K 77
Hainfield Dr. B91: Sol 4E 146
Hainge Rd. B69: Tiv 7C 76
Hainult Cl. DY8: Word 5K 95
Halas Ind. Est. B62: Hale 4B 118
Halberd Cl. LE10: Burb 5K 91
Halberton St. B66: Smeth 5D 100
Haldane Ct. B33: Yard 7B 104
Haldon Gro. B31: Longb 2L 163
Halecroft Av. WV11: Wed 4K 37
Hale Gro. B24: Erd 5K 81
Halesbury Ct. B63: Hale 7M 117
(off Ombersley Rd.)
Hales Cres. B67: Smeth 6L 99
Halescroft Sq. B31: N'fld 3L 141
Hales Gdns. B23: Erd 1C 80
Hales Ind. Pk. CV6: Longf 5E 130
Hales La. B67: Smeth 5L 99
Halesmere Way B63: Hale 6C 118
HALESOWEN 6B 118
Halesowen By-Pass
B62: Hale 6D 118
B62: Roms, Hale 8M 117
Halesowen Ind. Pk.
B62: Hale 3B 118
(Coombs Rd.)
B62: Hale 3C 118
(Hereward Ri.)
Halesowen Leisure Cen. 6B 118
Halesowen Rd. B61: L Ash ...7C 162
B62: Quin 3E 118
B64: Crad H 1M 117
B64: Old H 7L 97
B65: B'hth 1C 118
DY2: Neth 4J 97
(Baptist End Rd.)
DY2: Neth 5K 97
(Cradley Rd.)
Halesowen St. B69: O'bry 2F 98
HALES PARK 2B 156
Hales Pk. DY12: Bew 2B 156
Hales Rd. B63: Hale 6A 118
(Highfield La.)
B63: Hale 5A 118
(Islington)
WS10: W'bry 5G 55
Hales St. CV1: Cov 6C 152 (3C 6)
(not continuous)
Hales Way B69: O'bry 2F 98
Halesworth Rd. WV9: Pend 8M 21
Hale Trad. Est. DY4: Tip 3B 76
Halewood Gro. B28: Hall G 2G 145
Haley St. WV12: W'hall 4C 38
HALFCOT 2F 114
Halfcot Av. DY9: Pedm 6C 116
Halford Cres. WS3: Wals 4M 39
Halford Gro. B24: Erd 5L 81
Halford La. B79: Tam 4A 32
CV6: Cov 8A 130
Halford Lodge CV6: Cov 7A 130
Halford Rd. B91: Sol 3L 145
Halford's La. B66: Smeth 2A 100
B71: W Brom 2A 100
Halford's La. Ind. Est.
B66: Smeth 1A 100
Halfords Pk. B66: Smeth 1A 100
Halford St. B79: Tam 4A 32
Halfpenny Fld. Wlk.
B35: Cas V 7A 82
Halfs Hire La. DY10: Blak 8H 137
Halfway Cl. B44: Gt Barr 3L 79
Halfway La. CV22: Dunc 6H 205
Halifax Cl. CV5: Alle 2G 151
Halifax Ct. DY11: Kidd 1G 157
Halifax Ho. B5: Bal H 2K 121
Halifax Rd. B90: Shir 6H 145
Haliscombe Gro. B6: Aston 1L 101
Halkett Glade B33: Stech 6K 103
Halladale B38: K Nor 8F 142
Hallam Cl. B71: W Brom 4L 77
LE9: Earl S 1G 71
Hallam Ct. B71: W Brom 4K 77
Hallam Cres. WV10: Wolv 3E 36
Hallam Dr. B71: W Brom 4L 77
Hallam Rd. CV6: Cov 6B 130
Hallam's Cl. CV8: Bran 4F 176
Hallam St. B12: Bal H 4L 121
B71: W Brom 5K 77
Hallbridge Cl. WS3: Pels 7M 25
Hallbridge Way B69: Tiv 7B 76
Hallbrook Rd. CV6: Cov 6A 130
Hallchurch Rd. DY2: Dud 2F 96
Hall Cl. CV8: S'lgh 3B 200
Hall Cl., The CV22: Dunc 7J 205
Hall Ct. B78: Pole 3K 49
Hallcourt Cl. WS11: Cann 1E 14
Hallcourt Cres. WS11: Cann 1E 14
Hallcourt La. WS11: Cann 1E 14
Hall Cres. B71: W Brom 3J 77
Hallcroft Cl. B72: W Grn 2J 81
Hallcroft Way B93: Know 3G 169
WS9: A'rdge 4J 41
Hall Dale Cl. B28: Hall G 4F 144
Hall Dr. B37: Mars G 2G 125
CV8: Bag 6E 174
CV13: Stoke G 2E 68
DY9: Hag 3D 138
HALL END
Tamworth 4L 47
West Bromwich 3K 77
HALLEND 6M 215
Hall End CV11: Nun 7K 89
WS10: W'bry 6F 54
Hall End Pl. CV11: Nun 7K 89
Hallens Dr. WS10: W'bry 6D 54
Hallett Dr. WV3: Wolv ..8B 36 (6G 7)
Hallewell Rd. B16: Edg 6D 100
Hallfields CV31: Rad S 4E 224
HALL FLAT 2C 188
HALL GREEN
Bilston 7L 53
Birmingham 1F 144
Coventry 7H 131
West Bromwich 8J 55
Hall Green Little Theatre 7G 123
Hall Grn. Rd. B71: W Brom 3J 77
CV6: Cov 7H 131
Hall Green Stadium 8F 122
Hall Green Station (Rail) 8F 122
Hall Grn. St. WV14: Bils 6L 53
Hall Gro. CV23: Brin 5L 155
WV14: Cose 1J 75
Hall Hays Rd. B34: S End 2E 104
Hall La. CV2: W'grve S 3M 153
CV9: With 1B 66
DY2: Neth 6G 97
DY4: Tip 1B 76
DY9: Hag 3C 138
LE10: Wlvy 5K 113
WS3: Pels 6M 25
WS6: Gt Wyr 5F 14
WS7: Hamm 5K 17
WS9: Wals W 5E 26
WS14: Muck C 7M 17
WV14: Cose 8F 52
Hall Mdw. DY9: Hag 2D 138
WS11: Cann 3B 14
Hallmeadow Rd. CV7: Bal C ...8H 149
Hallmoor Rd. B33: Kitts G 6B 104
Hall of Memory, The 7J 101 (5D 4)
Hallot Cl. B23: Erd 1D 80
Halloughton Rd. B74: S Cold ...2G 59
Hall Pk. St. WV2: E'shll 3H 53
Hall Rd. B8: Salt 5D 102
B20: Hand 1G 101
B36: Cas B 1A 104
B67: Smeth 5L 99
CV32: Lea S 8M 217
LE10: Burb 3K 91
LE10: Wlvy 5K 113
Hall Rd. Av. B20: Hand 1G 101
Hall's Cl. CV31: W'nsh 6B 224
Halls Ct. LE9: S Stan 7L 71
Halls Cres. LE10: Sharn 4J 93
(not continuous)
Halls Farm La. DY12: Trim 8B 134
Hallstead Rd. B13: Mose 4B 144
Hall St. B18: Birm 5J 101 (1D 4)
B64: Old H 7M 97
B68: O'bry 4H 99
B70: W Brom 7J 77
DY2: Dud 8K 75
DY3: Sed 1D 74
DY4: Tip 4L 75
DY8: Stourb 6A 116
WS2: Wals 6K 39
WS10: Darl 2B 54
WV11: Wed 4J 37
WV13: W'hall 8B 38
WV14: Bils 4L 53
Hall St. E. WS10: Darl 2C 54
Hall St. Sth. B70: W Brom 1K 99
Hallswelle Gro. B43: Gt Barr ...5L 57
Hall Wlk. B46: Col 4L 105
(not continuous)
Hallway Dr. CV7: Shil 3E 132
Halow Cl. B31: N'fld 7D 142
Halsbury Gro. B44: K'sdng 1B 80
Halstead Gro. B91: Sol 1A 168
Halston Rd. WS7: C Ter 1H 17
Haltonlea B77: Wiln 1G 47
Halton Rd. B73: New O 6D 58
Halton St. DY2: Neth 4J 97
Hamar Way B37: Mars G 8H 105
Hamberley Ct. B18: Win G 5D 100
Hamble B77: Wiln 7D 32
Hamble Cl. DY5: P'ntt 3A 96
Hamble Ct. B73: S Cold 4H 59
Hambledon Cl. WV9: Pend 7A 22
Hamble Gro. WV6: Pert 6E 34
Hamble Rd. B42: Gt Barr 8F 56
WV4: Penn 3J 51
Hambleton Rd. B63: Hale 7K 117
Hambletts Rd. B70: W Brom 6G 77
Hambrook Cl. WV6: Wolv 4A 36
Hambury Dr. B14: K Hth 2K 143
Hamelin St. WS11: Cann 6E 8
Hamilton Av. B17: Harb 1A 120
B62: Hale 6C 118
DY8: Woll 3K 115
Hamilton Cl. B60: L End 3C 188
CV10: Nun 5D 88
CV12: Bed 8C 110
DY3: Sed 2C 74
DY8: Word 7J 95
LE10: Hinc 7G 69
WS12: Hed 5M 9
Hamilton Ct. B13: Mose 5M 121
B30: K Nor 5E 142
CV10: Nun 5D 88
Hamilton Dr. B29: S Oak 1D 142
B69: Tiv 7C 76
B80: Stud 6K 221
DY8: Word 7J 95
Hamilton Gdns. WV10: Bush 6E 22
Hamilton Ho. B66: Smeth 4C 100
WS3: Blox 8J 25
Hamilton Lea WS11: Nort C 3A 16
Hamilton Rd. B21: Hand 1D 100
B67: Smeth 7L 99
B97: Redd 1C 220
CV2: Cov 6G 153
CV31: Rad S 4E 224
DY4: Tip 3C 76
DY11: Kidd 6H 157
Hamilton St. WS3: Blox 8J 25
Hamilton Ter. CV32: Lea S 1M 223
Ham La. DY6: K'wfrd 8L 73
DY9: Pedm 8C 116
Hamlet, The CV35: Leek W 2G 217
WS11: Nort C 4L 15
Hamlet Cl. CV11: Nun 8A 90
CV22: Bil 3K 205
Hamlet Gdns. B28: Hall G 1F 144
Hamlet Rd. B28: Hall G 1F 144
Hammer Bank DY5: Quar B 1G 117
Hammersley Cl. B63: Crad 2H 117
Hammersley St. CV12: Bed 8E 110
HAMMERWICH 5K 17
Hammerwich Link
WS7: Hamm 6M 17
Hammerwich Rd. WS7: Burn ...3K 17
Hammond Av. WV10: Bush 1E 36
Hammond Bus. Pk.
CV11: Nun 6L 89
Hammond Cl. CV11: Nun 6L 89
Hammond Dr. B23: Erd 4F 80
Hammond Rd. CV2: Cov 5F 152
Hammonds Ter. CV8: Ken 4D 198
Hammond Way DY8: Amb 2A 116
Hampden Cl. DY5: Quar B 1G 117
Hampden Retreat B12: Bal H ...3L 121
Hampden Way CV22: Bil 2J 205
Hamps Cl. WS7: Burn 2K 17
Hampshire Cl. B78: Tam 7A 32
CV3: Bin 1M 175
Hampshire Ct. B29: W Cas 2B 142
Hampshire Dr. B15: Edg 1E 120
Hampshire Rd. B71: W Brom 1G 77
Hampson Cl. B11: S'brk 3B 122
Hampstead Glade B63: Hale ...7C 118
Hampton Av. B60: B'gve 1A 210
CV10: Nun 5B 88
Hampton Cl. B73: New O 7C 58
B79: Tam 2C 32
B98: Redd 2H 221
CV6: Cov 3F 152
Hampton Ct. B15: Edg 8B 4
B71: W Brom 1J 55
B92: H Ard 3B 148
WV10: Bush 7H 23
Hampton Ct. Rd. B17: Harb ...3M 119
Hampton Dr. B74: Four O 1H 59
Hampton Gdns. DY9: Pedm 6C 116
Hampton Grange CV7: Mer 8H 127
Hampton Grn. WS11: Cann 2E 14
Hampton Gro. CV32: Lea S 8B 218
DY7: Kinv 5C 114
WS3: Pels 5M 25
HAMPTON IN ARDEN 3A 148
Hampton in Arden Station (Rail)
....................2B 148
Hampton La.
B91: Cath B, Sol 5D 146
(not continuous)
CV7: Mer 1E 148
HAMPTON MAGNA 3A 222
Hampton Pl. WS10: Darl 1C 54
Hampton Rd. B6: Aston 8K 79
B23: Erd 5D 80
B93: Know 2J 169
CV6: Cov 3F 152
CV34: Warw 4A 222
CV35: H Hill 4A 222
WV10: Oxl 8B 22
Hamptons, The B93: Know 3J 169
Hampton St.
B19: Birm 5K 101 (1E 4)
CV34: Warw 3D 222
DY2: Neth 4J 97
WS11: Cann 2D 14
WV14: Cose 1H 75
Hampton Vw. WV10: Wolv 5F 36
Hampton Wlk.
WV1: Wolv 7C 36 (4J 7)
HAMS HALL 5B 84
Hams Hall Distribution Pk.
B46: Col 5B 84
(Faraday Av.)
B46: Col 4M 83
(Hams La.)
Hams La. B76: Lea M 4L 83
Hams Rd. B8: Salt 5D 102
HAMSTEAD 2F 78
Hamstead Cl. WV11: Wed 3K 37
Hamstead Hall Av. B20: Hand ...4E 78
Hamstead Hall Rd.
B20: Hand 5E 78
Hamstead Hill B20: Hand 6F 78
Hamstead Ho. B43: Gt Barr 2F 78
Hamstead Ind. Est.
B42: P Barr 4G 79
Hamstead Rd. B20: Hand 8H 79
B43: Gt Barr 1C 78
Hamstead Station (Rail) 3F 78
Hamstead Ter. WS10: W'bry 7G 55
Hams Way LE10: Sharn 5H 93
Hanam Cl. B75: S Cold 3M 59
Hanbury Cl. B60: B'gve 1A 210
B63: Hale 7M 117
Hanbury Ct. DY8: Stourb 5A 116
(off College Rd.)
Hanbury Cres. WV4: Penn 3L 51
Hanbury Cft. B27: A Grn 6L 123
Hanbury Dr. B69: O'bry 5E 98
Hanbury Hill DY8: Stourb 5A 116
Hanbury Ho. B97: Redd 5B 212
(off Cardy Cl.)
Hanbury Pas. DY8: Stourb 4A 116
Hanbury Pl. CV6: Cov 7G 131
Hanbury Rd.
B60: Stoke H, S Prior 3K 209
B70: W Brom 6G 77
B77: Amin 5F 32
B93: Dorr 5F 168
CV12: Bed 5J 111
WS8: Bwnhls 7E 16
WS11: Nort C 4M 15
HANCH 1E 12
Hanch Pl. WS1: Wals 1M 55
Hancock Grn. CV4: Tile H 1F 172
Hancock Rd. B8: Salt 5F 102
Hancox Cl. CV33: W Weth 2K 219
Hancox St. B68: O'bry 7H 99
Handcross Gro. CV3: Finh 4A 174
Handel Ct. WS11: Hth H 7J 9
Handel Wlk. WS13: Lich 7J 13
Handley Gro. B31: Longb 7J 141
CV34: Warw 8D 216
Handleys Cl. CV8: Rytn D 8A 176
Handley St. WS10: W'bry 5G 55
HANDSWORTH 8E 78
Handsworth Booth
Street Station (Rail) 2C 100
Handsworth Cl. B21: Hand 2D 100
Handsworth Cres. CV5: E Grn ...5E 150
Handsworth Dr. B43: Gt Barr ...6G 57
Handsworth Horticultural Institute
....................7E 78
(off Oxhill Rd.)
Handsworth Leisure Cen.
B20: Hand 8F 78
Handsworth New Rd.
B18: Win G 3E 100
HANDSWORTH WOOD 7G 79
Handsworth Wood Rd.
B20: Hand 6F 78
Hanford Cl. CV6: Cov 3E 152
Hanford Cl. Ind. Est.
CV6: Cov 3E 152
Hangar Rd. B26: Birm A 6G 125
Hanging La. B31: N'fld 7L 141
Hangleton Dr. B11: S'brk 3D 122
Hangmans La. LE10: Hinc 6L 69
Hanley Cl. B63: Hale 5L 117
Hanley St. B19: Birm ...5K 101 (1F 4)
Hanlith B77: Wiln 1G 47
Hannaford Way WS11: Cann 7F 8
Hannafore Rd. B16: Edg 6D 100
Hannah Rd. WV14: Bils 6A 54
Hanney Hay Rd.
WS7: Chase, Hamm 5G 17
Hannon Rd. B14: K Hth 4L 143
Hanover Cl. B6: Aston 2L 101
Hanover Ct. B79: Tam 2L 31
B97: Redd 1D 220
LE10: Burb 3L 91
WS2: Wals 8E 38
WV6: Tett 5J 35
Hanover Dr. B24: Erd 1F 102
Hanover Gdns. CV21: Rugby ...5B 180
CV32: Lea S 8A 218
Hanover Glebe CV11: Nun 7J 89
Hanover Pl. B61: B'gve 8M 187
WS11: Cann 7E 8
Hanover Rd. B65: Row R 5C 98
Hanover St. B61: B'gve 7M 187
Hans Cl. CV2: Cov 5F 152
Hansell Dr. B93: Dorr 7E 168
Hansom Ct. LE10: Hinc 1K 91
Hansom Rd. B32: Quin 4J 119
LE10: Hinc 7M 69
Hanson Gro. B92: Olton 4M 123
Hansons Bri. Rd. B24: Erd 4M 81
Hanson Way CV6: Longf 5G 131
Hanstone Rd. DY13: Stour S ...8F 182
Hanwell Cl. B76: Walm 2B 82
Hanwood Cl. B12: Birm 1M 121
CV5: E Grn 5C 150
Hanworth Cl. CV32: Lill 6C 218
Hanworth Rd. CV34: Warw 1D 222
Harald Cl. WV6: Pert 4E 34
Harbeck Av. B44: Gt Barr 1M 79
Harberrow Cl. DY9: Hag 3A 138
Harbet Dr. B40: Nat E C 5L 125
Harbinger Rd. B38: K Nor 7H 143
HARBORNE 3B 120
Harborne Ct. B17: Harb 5C 120
Harborne Ho. B17: Harb 5A 120
Harborne La.
B17: Harb, S Oak 6D 120
B29: S Oak 7E 120
Harborne Pk. Rd. B17: Harb ...4C 120
Harborne Pool & Fitness Cen.
....................4B 120
Harborne Rd.
B15: Edg 3E 120 (8A 4)
B68: O'bry 8K 99
Harborough Cotts.
B94: Lapw 6J 195
Harborough Ct. B74: Four O 7G 43
Harborough Dr. B36: Cas B 8D 82
WS9: A'rdge 4G 41
Harborough Rd. CV6: Cov 7B 130
CV23: Harb M 1J 179
Harborough Wlk. DY9: Pedm ...7C 116
Harbours Cl. B61: B'gve 2K 209
HARBOURS HILL 8M 209
Harbours Hill B61: Wild 3L 161
DY9: Belb 3L 161
Harbour Ter. WV3: Wolv 8A 36
Harbury Cl. B76: Walm 3B 82
B98: Redd 8K 213
Harbury La.
CV33: Bis T, Ches 7M 223
CV34: H'cte 5J 223
Harbury Rd. B12: Bal H 4K 121
Harby Cl. B37: Mars G 1H 125
Harcourt CV3: W'hall 4L 175
Harcourt Dr. B74: Four O 5F 42
DY3: Gorn 7D 74
Harcourt Gdns. CV11: Nun 6J 89
Harcourt Ho. B79: Tam 5A 32
Harcourt Rd. B23: Erd 3E 80
B64: Crad H 1M 117
WS10: W'bry 5F 54
HARDEN 2L 39
Harden Cl. WS3: Blox 2L 39
Harden Ct. B31: N'fld 8L 141
Harden Gro. WS3: Blox 2L 39
Harden Keep B66: Smeth 5A 100
Harden Mnr. Ct. B63: Hale 6C 118
Harden Rd. WS3: Blox, Wals 2K 39
Harden Va. B63: Hale 4L 117
Hardie Grn. WS11: Cann 6F 8
Harding St. WV14: Cose 7K 53
Hardingwood La. CV7: Fill 7L 107
Hardon Rd. WV4: E'shll 4F 52
Hardware St. B70: W Brom 5K 77
HARDWICK 8L 41
Hardwick Cl. CV5: E Grn 5G 151
Hardwick Ct. B74: S'tly 7M 41
B79: Tam 4C 32

Hardwick Dr.—Hawthorne Rd.

Hardwick Dr. B62: Hale 2A 118
Hardwicke Wlk. B14: K Hth 7K 143
Hardwicke Way DY9: Lye 4D 116
Hardwick La. B80: Out 8E 214
B80: Stud 4M 221
Hardwick Rd. B26: Yard 5L 123
B74: S'tly 7M 41
B92: Olton 5L 123
Hardwyn Cl. CV3: Bin 8B 154
Hardy Av. DY10: Kidd 3A 158
Hardy Cl. CV10: Gall C 5A 88
CV22: Bil 7J 179
LE10: Hinc 5K 69
Hardy Ct. B13: Mose 5M 121
Hardy Rd. CV6: Cov 2A 152
WS3: Blox 1L 39
WS10: W'bry 6G 55
Hardy Sq. WV2: E'shll 3F 52
Hare & Hounds La.
CV10: Nun 7G 89
Harebell B77: Amin 5G 33
Harebell Cl. WS5: Wals 6A 56
WS12: Hth H 7K 9
WV10: F'stne 2G 23
Harebell Cres. DY1: Dud 5G 75
Harebell Gdns. B38: K Nor 1F 164
Harebell Wlk. B37: Chel W 7K 105
Harebell Way CV23: Brow 1D 180
Harecroft Cres. LE9: Sap 1L 93
Harefield Ho. CV2: Cov 6H 153
Harefield La.
CV10: Arb, Nun 1E 110
Harefield Rd. CV2: Cov 6H 153
CV11: Nun 5J 89
Hare Gro. B31: N'fld 6K 141
Haresfield B90: Dic H 4G 167
Haresfield Cl. B97: Redd 7D 212
Hare St. WV14: Bils 4M 53
(not continuous)
Harewell Dr. B75: R'ley 8J 43
Harewood Av. B43: Gt Barr 7C 56
WS10: W'bry 6J 55
Harewood Cl. B28: Hall G 4E 144
Harewood Rd. CV5: Cov 6J 151
Harford St. B19: Birm ...5J 101 (1D 4)
Hargate La. B70: W Brom 5J 77
B71: W Brom 5J 77
Harger Ct. CV8: Ken 5F 198
Harger M. CV8: Ken 5F 198
Hargrave Cl. B46: Wat O 6H 83
CV3: Bin 8A 154
Hargrave Rd. B90: Shir 7C 144
Hargreave Cl. B76: Walm 2M 81
Hargreaves Ct. DY11: Kidd 6H 157
Hargreaves St. WV1: Wolv 2G 53
Harland Cl. B61: B'gve 6K 187
Harland Rd. B74: Four O 6G 43
Harlech Cl. B32: Bart G 2G 141
B69: Tiv 8A 76
CV8: Ken 4J 199
Harlech Ho. *WS3: Blox 3J 39*
(off Providence Cl.)
Harlech Rd. WV12: W'hall 3C 38
Harlech Twr. B23: Erd 3G 81
Harlech Way DY1: Dud 7F 74
DY10: Kidd 7L 157
Harleston Rd. B44: Gt Barr 1M 79
Harley Cl. WS8: Bwnhls 3G 27
Harley Dr. WV14: Bils 4J 53
Harley St. CV2: Cov 6G 153
Harlow Gro. B28: Hall G 3G 145
Harlow Wlk. CV2: W'grve S 2A 154
Harlstones Cl. DY8: Amb 1A 116
Harlyn Cl. WV14: Bils 7A 54
Harman Dr. WS13: Lich 3F 18
Harman Rd. B72: W Grn 2H 81
Harmar Cl. CV34: Warw 8D 216
Harmer Cl. CV2: W'grve S 2A 154
Harmon Rd. DY8: Woll 4J 115
Harmony Ct. CV10: Nun 7H 89
Harmony Ho. B10: Small H 8C 102
Harnall Cl. B90: Shir 2L 167
Harnall La. CV1: Cov 5D 152 (1D 6)
Harnall La. E.
CV1: Cov 5D 152 (1E 6)
Harnall La. Ind. Est.
CV1: Cov 5D 152 (1E 6)
Harnall La. W.
CV1: Cov 5D 152 (1C 6)
Harnall Row *CV1: Cov 7E 152*
(off Far Gosford St.)
CV1: Cov 6E 152
(West St.)
Harness Cl. WS5: Wals 5M 55
Harold Cox Pl. CV22: Bil 3L 205
Harold Davies Dr.
DY13: Stour S 7F 182
Harold Evers Way
DY10: Kidd 2M 157
Harold Rd. B16: Edg 8F 100
B67: Smeth 6L 99
CV2: Cov 7K 153
Harold St. CV11: Nun 6J 89
Harpenden Dr. CV5: Alle 4G 151
Harper Av. WV11: Wed 2J 37
Harper Rd. CV1: Cov 7E 152 (6F 6)
WV14: Bils 3K 53
Harper's La. CV9: Man 3A 66
Harpers Rd. B14: K Hth 8A 144
B31: N'fld 8A 142
Harper St. WV13: W'hall 7A 38
Harport Rd. B98: Redd 8G 213
Harpur Cl. WS4: Wals 5A 40
Harpur Rd. WS4: Wals 5A 40
Harrier Rd. B27: A Grn 7K 123
Harriers Grn. DY10: Kidd 1B 158
Harriers Ind. Est.
DY10: Kidd 4M 157
Harrier Way B42: P Barr 6K 79
Harriet Cl. DY5: P'ntt 4B 96
Harringay Dr. DY8: Stourb 6L 115
Harringay Rd. B44: K'sdng 7M 57
Harrington Cft. B71: W Brom ...2M 77
Harrington Rd. CV6: Cov 4A 152
Harrington Wlk. WS13: Lich 8F 12
Harrington Way CV10: Griff 2G 111
Harringworth Ct. WS4: S'fld 1C 40
Harriots Hayes Rd.
WV8: Cod W 2A 20
Harriott Dr. CV34: H'cte 5K 223
Harris Bus. Pk. B60: S Prior ...7K 209
Harris Cl. B98: Redd 1F 220
Harris Ct. B18: Hock 3G 101
Harris Dr. B42: Gt Barr 1G 79
B66: Smeth 6B 100
CV22: Rugby 1M 205
Harris Ind. Pk. B60: S Prior 7L 209
Harrison Cl. CV21: Hillm 1H 207
LE9: Earl S 1F 70
WS3: Blox 8J 25
WS6: C Hay 8D 14
Harrison Ct. DY8: Amb 8A 96
Harrison Cres. CV12: Bed 7G 111
Harrison Ho. B14: K Hth 6M 143
Harrison Rd. B24: Erd 5F 80
B74: Four O 4E 42
B97: Redd 1C 220
DY8: Word 8A 96
WS4: S'fld 7C 26
WS11: Cann 2E 14
Harrison's Fold DY2: Neth 4J 97
Harrisons Grn. B15: Edg 3E 120
Harrisons Pleck B13: Mose 6M 121
Harrison's Rd. B15: Edg 3E 120
Harrison St. WS3: Blox 8H 25
Harrison Way CV31: Lea S 4M 223
Harris Rd. CV3: Cov 7H 153
CV34: Warw 1C 222
Harrold Av. B65: Row R 6E 98
Harrold Rd. B65: Row R 6E 98
Harrold St. DY4: Tip 2C 76
Harrop Way DY8: Amb 1L 115
Harrowbrook Ind. Est.
LE10: Hinc 2E 90
Harrowbrook Rd. LE10: Hinc 2E 90
Harrowby Dr. DY4: Tip 5A 76
Harrowby Pl. WV13: W'hall 8D 38
WV14: Bils 5A 54
Harrowby Rd. WV10: F'hses 6B 22
WV14: Bils 5A 54
Harrow Cl. B60: Stoke H 3L 209
CV6: Longf 5G 131
DY9: Hag 3A 138
Harrowfield Rd. B33: Stech 5L 103
Harrow Rd. B29: S Oak 6F 120
CV31: W'nsh 6B 224
DY6: K'wfrd 8K 73
Harrow St. WV1: Wolv ...5B 36 (1G 7)
Harry Caplan Ho. CV5: Alle 3H 151
Harry Edwards Ho. CV2: Cov ...1K 153
Harry Mitchell Leisure Cen. 4M 99
Harry Perks St. WV13: W'hall ...6A 38
Harry Price Ho. B69: O'bry 4D 98
Harry Rose Rd. CV2: Cov 6L 153
Harry Salt Ho. CV1: Cov 3F 6
Harry Stanley Ho. CV6: Cov 1G 153
Harry Taylor Ho. B98: Redd 6G 213
Harry Truslove Cl. CV6: Cov ...2A 152
Harry Weston Rd. CV3: Bin 8M 153
Hart Cl. CV21: Hillm 7D 180
Hart Dr. B73: Bold 1G 81
Hartfield Cres. B27: A Grn 7G 123
Hartfields Way B65: Row R 4M 97
Hartford Cl. B17: Harb 2A 120
Hartford Rd. B60: B'gve 1B 210
Hartill Rd. WV4: Penn 6K 51
Hartill St. WV13: W'hall 1B 54
Hartington Cl. B93: Dorr 6E 168
Hartington Cres. CV5: Cov 8L 151
Hartington Grn. LE10: Burb 3L 91
Hartington Rd. B19: Loz 1K 101
Hartland Av. CV2: Cov 3H 153
WV14: Cose 1G 75
Hartland Rd. B31: Longb 3L 163
B71: W Brom 1M 77
DY4: Tip 4K 75
Hartland St. DY5: P'ntt 2D 96
HARTLE 3F 160
HARTLEBURY 7B 184
Hartlebury Castle 6M 183
Hartlebury Cl. B93: Dorr 6F 168
B98: Redd 2K 213
WS11: Hth H 6J 9
Hartlebury Common Nature Reserve
.......................7J 183
Hartlebury Rd. B63: Hale 7M 117
B69: O'bry 4D 98
DY13: Stour S 6H 183
Hartlebury Station (Rail) 7B 184
Hartlebury Trad. Est.
DY10: Hartl 8D 184
Hartledon Rd. B17: Harb 4B 120
Hartle La. DY9: Belb 2E 160
Hartlepool Rd.
CV1: Cov 5E 152 (1F 6)
Hartleyburn B77: Wiln 1G 47
Hartley Dr. WS9: A'rdge 5H 41
Hartley Gdns. CV47: Sou 6G 225
Hartley Gro. B44: K'sdng 6B 58
Hartley Pl. B15: Edg 1F 120
Hartley Rd. B44: K'sdng 6B 58
Hartley St. WV3: Wolv 7A 36
Harton Way B14: K Hth 4J 143
Hartopp Rd. B8: Salt 5E 102
B74: Four O 8F 42
Hartridge Wlk. CV5: Cov 5H 151
Hart Rd. B24: Erd 4G 81
WV11: Wed 5K 37
Hartsbourne Dr. B62: Hale 5D 118
Harts Cl. B17: Harb 3D 120
HARTS GREEN 4A 120
Harts Grn. Rd. B17: Harb 4A 120
HART'S HILL 4E 96
HARTSHILL 1A 88
Hartshill Cl. B34: S End 3A 104
Hartshill Hayes Country Pk. ...8A 66
Hartshill Hayes Country Pk. Vis. Cen.
.........................8M 65
Hartshill Rd. B27: A Grn 7K 123
B34: S End 3A 104
Hartshorn St. WV14: Bils 4K 53
Hartside Cl. B63: Hale 7K 117
Hartslade WS14: Lich 3L 19
Harts Rd. B8: Salt 4E 102
Hart St. WS1: Wals 1L 55
Hartswell Dr. B13: Mose 3M 143
Hartwell Cl. B91: Sol 8B 146
Hartwell La. WS6: Gt Wyr 6G 15
Hartwell Rd. B24: Erd 7H 81
Hartwood Cres. WV4: Penn 4M 51
Harvard Cl. DY1: Dud 5F 74
Harvard Rd. B92: Olton 5B 124
Harvest Cl. B30: Stir 3H 143
B60: Stoke H 3K 209
DY3: Up Gor 4E 74
Harvest Ct. B65: Row R 5A 98
Harvesters Cl. CV3: Bin 7A 154
WS9: A'rdge 7L 41
Harvesters Rd. WV12: W'hall ...4D 38
Harvesters Wlk. WV8: Pend 8L 21
Harvesters Way
WV12: W'hall 4D 38
Harvester Way DY6: W Hth 1G 95
Harvest Flds. Way B75: R'ley ...5K 43
Harvest Gdns. B68: O'bry 5G 99
Harvest Hill Cl. CV31: Lea S ...3C 224
Harvest Hill La. CV5: Alle 5C 128
CV7: Mer 5A 128
Harvest Rd. B65: Row R 5A 98
B67: Smeth 6K 99
Harvest Wlk. B65: Row R 5A 98
Harvey Cl. CV5: Alle 2G 151
Harvey Ct. B33: Kitts G 6D 104
Harvey Dr. B75: R'ley 7J 43
Harvey M. B30: B'vlle 2E 142
Harvey Rd. B26: Yard 2K 123
WS2: Wals 4H 39
Harveys Cl. LE9: Sap 2K 93
Harvey's Ter. DY2: Neth 5K 97
HARVILLS HAWTHORN 2F 76
Harvills Hawthorn
B70: W Brom 2F 76
Harvine Wlk. DY8: Stourb 6L 115
HARVINGTON 7G 159
Harvington Cl. B97: Redd 4B 212
DY11: Kidd 1G 157
Harvington Dr. B90: M'path 3B 168
Harvington Hall 8H 159
Harvington Hall La.
DY10: Chad C, Harv 7H 159
Harvington Rd. B29: W Cas 1A 142
B60: B'gve 1A 210
B63: Hale 7M 117
B68: O'bry 2G 119
WV14: Cose 1H 75
Harvington Wlk. B65: Row R 6C 98
Harvington Way B76: Walm 1A 82
Harwell Cl. B79: Tam 2C 32
Harwin Cl. WV6: Tett 2M 35
Harwood Dr. B77: Dost 5D 46
LE10: Hinc 5M 69
Harwood Gro. B90: Shir 1J 167
Harwood Rd. WS13: Lich 6H 13
Harwood St. B70: W Brom 6H 77
HASBURY 7L 117
Hasbury Cl. B63: Hale 7L 117
Hasbury Rd. B32: Bart G 1G 141
Haselbech Rd. CV3: Bin 8M 153
Haselbury Cnr. CV10: Nun 8F 88
Haseley Cl. B98: Redd 8L 213
CV31: Lea S 4B 224
Haseley Grange CV35: Hase 8F 196
HASELEY KNOB 6G 197
Haseley Rd. B21: Hand 2E 100
B91: Sol 3L 145
CV2: Cov 8J 131
Haselor Rd. B73: New O 8E 58
Haselour Rd. B37: K'hrst 4F 104
Hasilwood Sq. CV3: Cov 7H 153
Haskell St. WS1: Wals 2M 55
Haslemere Gro. WS11: Cann 1B 14
Haslucks Cft. B90: Shir 6G 145
HASLUCKS GREEN 8E 144
Haslucks Grn. Rd.
B90: Maj G 2E 166
Hassall Cl. CV33: Bis T 8E 224
Hassop Rd. B42: Gt Barr 2K 79
Hastang Flds. CV31: Lea S 4C 224
Hastings Cl. B77: Wiln 3F 46
Hastings Ct. DY1: Dud 7E 74
Hastings Dr. LE9: Barw 2B 70
Hastings Rd. B23: Erd 2B 80
(not continuous)
B60: B'gve 2L 209
CV2: Cov 5G 153
Hastingwood Ind. Pk.
B24: Erd 8H 81
Haswell Cl. CV22: Rugby 7C 180
Haswell Rd. B63: Hale 6K 117
Hatcham Rd. B44: K'sdng 7C 58
Hatchett St. B19: Birm 4L 101
Hatchford Av. B92: Sol 6C 124
Hatchford Brook Rd.
B92: Sol 6C 124
Hatchford Ct. B92: Sol 6C 124
Hatchford Wlk. B37: Chel W ...8H 105
Hatchford Way B26: Sheld 5E 124
Hatch Heath Cl. WV5: Wom 2F 72
Hateley Dr. WV4: E'shll 5E 52
HATELEY HEATH 2J 77
Hatfield Cl. B23: Erd 2D 80
B98: Redd 8L 213
Hatfield Rd. B19: Loz 1K 101
DY9: Lye 5C 116
Hathaway Cl. CV7: Bal C 2H 171
WV13: W'hall 1M 53
Hathaway Dr. CV11: Nun 8A 90
CV34: Warw 7D 216
Hathaway M. DY8: Word 6H 95
Hathaway Rd. B75: Four O 5G 43
B90: Shir 8H 145
CV4: Tile H 8D 150
Hatherden Dr. B76: Walm 7A 60
Hatherell Rd. CV31: Rad S 4E 224
Hathersage Rd. B42: Gt Barr 2K 79
HATHERTON 8A 8
Hatherton Cft. WS11: Cann 8C 8
Hatherton Gdns. WV10: Bush 7E 22
Hatherton Gro. B29: W Cas 8M 119
Hatherton Hollow WS11: Cann ...8C 8
Hatherton Pl. WS9: A'rdge 2G 41
Hatherton Rd. WS1: Wals 7L 39
WS11: Cann 8B 8
WV14: Bils 3M 53
Hatherton St. WS1: Wals 7L 39
WS6: C Hay 7C 14
Hatters Ct. CV12: Bed 7J 111
Hatters Dr. CV9: Ath 7K 49
Hattersley Gro. B11: Tys 6G 123
Hatton Cres. WV10: Wolv 2G 37
Hatton Gdns. B42: Gt Barr 2H 79
Hatton Rd. WS11: Cann 8A 8
WV6: Wolv 6M 35
Hattons Gro. WV8: Bilb 7H 21
Hatton St. WV14: Bils 5L 53
Haughton Rd. B20: Hand 8J 79
Hauley Gro. CV31: W'nsh 5A 224
Haunch La. B13: Mose 3M 143
B76: Lea M 1A 84
Haunchwood Dr. B76: Walm 2M 81
Haunchwood Pk. Dr.
CV10: Gall C 5L 87
Haunchwood Pk. Ind. Est.
CV10: Gall C 5L 87
Haunchwood Rd. CV10: Nun 5D 88
Havacre La. WV14: Cose 7J 53
Havefield Av. WS14: Lich 2K 19
Havelock Cl. WV3: Wolv 1L 51
Havelock Rd. B8: Salt 4D 102
B11: Tys 5E 122
B20: Hand 8J 79
Haven, The B14: Yard W 5D 144
B45: B Grn 1G 189
DY8: Word 7K 95
WV2: Wolv 1C 52 (8J 7)
Haven Cvn. Pk. B92: Bick 7J 125
Haven Cft. B43: Gt Barr 1D 78
Havendale Cl. CV6: Cov 4B 152
Haven Dr. B27: A Grn 6H 123
Haverford Dr. B45: Redn 3H 163
Havergal Wlk. B63: Crad 5H 117
Haverhill Cl. WS3: Blox 6G 25
Hawbridge Cl. B90: M'path 3B 168
HAWBUSH 7A 96
Hawbush Gdns. DY5: Brie H 8A 96
Hawbush Rd. DY5: Brie H 7A 96
WS3: Blox 3K 39
Hawbush Urban Farm Vis. Cen.
.........................7B 96
Hawcroft Gro. B34: S End 3C 104
Hawes Cl. WS1: Wals 3M 55
Hawes La. B65: Row R 5B 98
Hawes Rd. WS1: Wals 3M 55
Haweswater Dr. DY6: K'wfrd 3K 95
Hawfield Cl. B69: Tiv 2C 98
Hawfield Gro. B72: W Grn 2J 81
Hawfield Rd. B69: Tiv 2C 98
Hawfinch B77: Wiln 3G 47
Hawfinch Ri. DY10: Kidd 7A 158
Hawford Av. DY10: Kidd 4A 158
Hawk Cl. CV11: Nun 1B 112
Hawker Dr. B35: Cas V 7M 81
HAWKESBURY 3H 131
Hawkesbury La. CV2: Ald G 4K 131
Hawkesbury Rd. B90: Shir 8F 144
Hawkes Cl. B30: Stir 1G 143
Hawkes Dr. CV34: H'cte 5K 223
HAWKES END 7H 129
Hawkesford Cl. B36: Cas B 1A 104
B74: Four O 8H 43
Hawkesford Rd. B33: Kitts G ..6D 104
Hawkeshaw Path B90: Bly P ...5A 168
(not continuous)
Hawkeshead CV21: Brow 2D 180
Hawkes La. B70: W Brom 2G 77
HAWKESLEY 2E 164
Hawkesley Cres.
B31: Longb 8M 141
Hawkesley Dr. B31: Longb 1M 163
Hawkesley End B38: K Nor 2E 164
Hawkesley Mill La.
B31: N'fld 7M 141
Hawkesley Rd. DY1: Dud 1F 96
Hawkesley Sq. B38: K Nor 2E 164
Hawkes Mill La. CV5: Alle 7G 129
Hawkesmoor Dr. WS14: Lich 2K 19
Hawkes St. B10: Small H 1D 122
Hawkestone Cres.
B70: W Brom 3F 76
Hawkestone Rd. B29: W Cas ..2A 142
Hawkesville Dr. WS11: Cann 7F 8
Hawkeswell Cl. B92: Olton 8L 123
Hawkeswell La. B46: Col 6A 106
Hawkesworth Dr. CV8: Ken 3G 199
Hawkesyard Rd. B24: Erd 8E 80
Hawkhurst Rd. B14: K Hth 7M 143
Hawkinge Dr. B35: Cas V 6A 82
Hawkins Cl. B5: Bal H 3L 121
CV22: Bil 8L 179
LE10: Hinc 5K 69
WS13: Lich 7H 13
Hawkins Cft. DY4: Tip 6A 76
Hawkins Dr. WS11: Cann 5C 14
Hawkins Pl. WV14: Bils 6M 53
Hawkins Rd. CV5: Cov 7A 152
Hawkins St. B70: W Brom 1G 77
Hawkley Cl. WV1: Wolv 7H 37
Hawkley Rd. WV1: Wolv 7H 37
Hawkmoor Gdns.
B38: K Nor 1G 165
Hawksbury Cl. B98: Redd 4K 213
Hawks Cl. WS6: C Hay 7D 14
Hawksford Cres. WV10: Bush ...2D 36
HAWK'S GREEN 8H 9
Hawks Grn. District Cen.
WS12: Hth H 7J 9
Hawks Grn. La.
WS11: Cann, Hth H 7G 9
(not continuous)
Hawkshead Dr. B93: Know 3F 168
Hawkside B77: Wiln 1H 47
Hawksmill Ind. Est.
B9: Small H 8C 102
Hawksmoor Dr. WV6: Pert 6D 34
Hawkstone Cl. DY11: Kidd 1K 157
Hawkstone Ct. WV6: Pert 4D 34
Hawkswell Av. WV5: Wom 4G 73
Hawkswell Dr. DY6: K'wfrd 1K 95
WV13: W'hall 8M 37
Hawkswood Dr. CV7: Bal C 2H 171
WS10: Mox 6B 54
Hawkswood Gro. B14: K Hth 6B 144
Hawksworth B77: Glas 7F 32
Hawksworth Dr. CV1: Cov 6A 152
Hawkyard Ct. WS11: Cann 5G 9
Hawlands CV21: Brow 3C 180
Hawley Cl. WS4: Wals 5M 39
Hawley Ct. B43: Gt Barr 8E 56
Hawley Rd. LE10: Hinc 2J 91
Hawnby Gro. B76: Walm 7A 60
HAWNE 3L 117
Hawne Cl. B63: Hale 3L 117
Hawnelands, The B63: Hale ...4M 117
Hawne La. B63: Hale 3L 117
Hawthorn Av. CV9: Hurl 4J 63
WS6: Gt Wyr 8G 15
Hawthorn Brook Way
B23: Erd 1E 80
Hawthorn Cl. B23: Erd 2F 80
WS13: Lich 1K 19
Hawthorn Coppice
B30: K Nor 5E 142
DY9: Hag 3A 138
Hawthorn Ct. CV4: Tile H 7E 150
Hawthorn Cres. DY12: Bew 3A 156
LE10: Burb 4L 91
Hawthorn Cft. B68: O'bry 2K 119
Hawthornden Ct. B76: Walm 2K 81
Hawthorn Dr. B47: H'wd 3B 166
CV7: Bal C 1H 171
Hawthorne Av. B79: Tam 1A 32
CV7: New A 1H 109
Hawthorne Cl. CV8: Wols 5G 177
Hawthorne Cres. WS7: Chase 3G 17
Hawthorne Cft. B30: K Nor 4D 142
Hawthorne Gro. DY3: Gorn 7D 74
Hawthorne Ho. WV10: Wolv 6F 36
Hawthorne La. WV8: Cod 7F 20
Hawthorne Rd. B15: Edg 2E 120
B30: K Nor 5D 142
B36: Cas B 2E 104
B63: Hale 7L 117
DY1: Dud 5J 75
WS5: Wals 4M 55
WS6: C Hay 5E 14

Hawthorne Rd.—Hemlingford Cft.

Hawthorne Rd. WS12: Hunt 1D 8
WS12: Wim 6M 9
WV2: Wolv 3D 52
WV11: Ess 5A 24
WV11: Wed 4M 37
WV12: W'hall 2D 38
Hawthorne Ter. CV10: Nun 4E 88
Hawthorne Way DY7: Kinv 6C 114
LE9: Barw 3B 70
Hawthorn Gro. B19: Loz 1J 101
DY11: Kidd 3G 157
Hawthorn La. CV4: Tile H 6E 150
(Delius St.)
CV4: Tile H 7E 150
(Roosevelt Dr.)
Hawthorn Pk. B20: Hand 6E 78
Hawthorn Pk. Dr. B20: Hand 6F 78
Hawthorn Pl. WS2: Wals 6E 38
Hawthorn Rd. B44: K'sdng 1M 79
B61: B'gve 4A 188
B72: W Grn 8J 59
B74: S'tly 8A 42
B97: Redd 5A 212
CV31: Lea S 3M 223
DY4: Tip 1A 76
DY5: Quar B 1E 116
WS4: S'fld 8B 26
WS10: W'bry 5F 54
WV1: Wolv 1H 53
Hawthorns, The 8B 78
Hawthorns, The B13: Mose 6M 121
B68: O'bry 2K 119
B78: K'bry 2C 62
DY9: Hag 5M 137
(off Cavendish Dr.)
DY10: Kidd 4A 158
Hawthorns Bus. Cen.
B66: Smeth 1A 100
Hawthorns Ind. Est.
B21: Hand 8B 78
Hawthorns Station, The (Rail & MM)
.....1B 100
Hawthorn Ter. WS10: W'bry 5F 54
Hawthorn Way CV10: Harts 1A 88
CV22: Bil 8H 179
Haxby Av. B34: Hodg H 3A 104
Haybarn, The B76: Walm 1A 82
Haybridge Av. DY8: Hag 4M 137
Haybrook Dr. B11: Tys 5F 122
Hay Cl. DY11: Kidd 2J 157
Haycock Pl. WS10: Darl 2C 54
Haycroft Av. B8: Salt 4E 102
Haycroft Dr. B74: Four O 5G 43
Haydn Sanders Sq.
WS1: Wals 1L 55
Haydock Cl. B36: Hodg H 1J 103
B77: Dost 5D 46
CV6: Ald G 5H 131
WV6: Wolv 3B 36
Haydock Rd. B61: Cats 8B 162
Haydon Cl. B80: Stud 5L 221
B93: Dorr 7F 168
Haydon Cft. B33: Kitts G 6A 104
Haydon Way B49: Cou 8M 221
Hayehouse Gro. B36: Hodg H 2L 103
Haye La. B80: Map G 8A 214
HAYES, THE 3G 117
Hayes, The B31: Longb 2C 164
DY9: Lye 4F 116
WV12: W'hall 3B 38
Hayes Bus. Pk. DY9: Lye 3F 116
Hayes Cl. CV21: Brow 2D 180
Hayes Cres. B68: O'bry 4K 99
Hayes Cft. B38: K Nor 2E 164
Hayes Dr. B24: Erd 4K 81
Hayes Grn. Rd. CV12: Bed 8F 110
Hayes Gro. B24: Erd 3K 81
Hayes La. CV7: Exh 1F 130
DY9: Lye 3G 117
Hayes Mdw. B72: W Grn 2K 81
Hayes Rd. B68: O'bry 4K 99
CV10: Harts 1A 88
DY11: W'ley 6H 135
Hayes St. B70: W Brom 5G 77
Hayes Trad. Est., The
DY9: Lye 3G 117
Hayes Vw. WS13: Lich 8F 12
Hayes Vw. Dr. WS6: C Hay 5E 14
Hayes Way WS12: Hth H 8G 9
Hayfield Ct. B13: Mose 7B 122
Hayfield Gdns. B13: Mose 7C 122
Hayfield Hill WS15: Cann W 6F 10
Hayfield Rd. B13: Mose 7B 122
Hayford Cl. B98: Redd 4G 213
HAY GREEN 4D 116
Hay Grn. DY9: Lye 4D 116
Hay Grn. Cl. B30: B'vlle 3D 142
Hay Grn. La. B30: B'vlle 4C 142
Hay Gro. WS8: Bwnhls 1F 26
Hay Hall Rd. B11: Tys 4F 122
Hay Head Wood (Nature Reserve)
.....6E 40
Hay Hill WS5: Wals 1E 56
Hayland Rd. B23: Erd 3E 80
Hay La. B90: M'path 3M 167
CV1: Cov 7D 152 (5D 6)
WS15: Longd 2A 12
Hayle B77: Wiln 8D 32
Hayle Av. CV34: Warw 8F 216
Hayle Cl. B38: K Nor 7H 143
CV11: Nun 4A 90
Hayley Ct. B24: Erd 3J 81
HAYLEY GREEN 8K 117
Hayley Grn. Rd. B32: Bart G 1H 141
Hayley Pk. Rd. B63: Hale 1J 139
Hayling Cl. B45: Fran 8F 140
Hayling Gro. WV2: Wolv 3B 52
Hayloft Cl. B60: Stoke H 3L 209
Haylofts, The B63: Hale 8J 117
Haymaker Way WS12: Wim 5M 9
Haymarket, The WV8: Pend 8L 21
HAY MILLS 3H 123
Haymoor WS14: Lich 2L 19
Haynes Cl. B61: Cats 1B 188
Haynes Ho. *B98: Redd 7D 212*
(off Mt. Pleasant)
Haynes La. WS5: Wals 5B 56
Haynestone Rd. CV6: Cov 3L 151
Haynes Way CV21: Rugby 1M 179
Hay Pk. B5: Bal H 3K 121
Haypits Cl. B71: W Brom 2L 77
Hayrick Dr. DY6: W Hth 2G 95
Hay Rd. B25: Yard 2G 123
Hayseech B64: Crad H 2M 117
Hayseech Rd. B63: Hale 3M 117
Hays Kent Moat, The
B26: Yard 8A 104
Hays La. LE10: Hinc 2H 91
Hayton Grn. CV4: Tile H 1F 172
(not continuous)
Haytor Av. B14: K Hth 4K 143
Haytor Ri. CV2: Cov 2J 153
Haywain Cl. WV9: Pend 7A 22
Hayward Ind. Pk.
WS9: A'rdge 2G 41
Hayward Rd. B75: S Cold 1J 59
Haywards Cl. B23: Erd 4E 80
WS3: Pels 6M 25
Haywards Grn. CV6: Cov 2A 152
Haywards Ind. Est.
B35: Cas V 8B 82
Hayward St. WV14: Cose 1H 75
Hayway, The WS2: Wals 6G 39
Haywharf Rd. DY5: P'ntt 4B 96
Haywood Dr. B62: B'hth 1C 118
WV6: Tett 5J 35
Haywood La. B93: Bad C 4A 196
CV35: Row 4A 196
Haywood Rd. B33: Kitts G 7E 104
Haywood's Farm
B71: W Brom 7M 55
Hayworth Cl. B79: Tam 1M 31
Hayworth Rd. WS13: Lich 7J 13
Hazel Av. B73: New O 8C 58
WS10: W'bry 5G 55
Hazelbank B38: K Nor 7E 142
Hazelbeach Rd. B8: Salt 4F 102
Hazelbeech Rd.
B70: W Brom 7H 77
Hazel Cl. CV10: Harts 2A 88
CV32: Lea S 7A 218
Hazel Cft. B31: N'fld 6A 142
B37: Chel W 8H 105
Hazelcroft B78: K'bry 2C 62
Hazeldene DY13: Stour S 6J 183
Hazeldene Gro. B6: Aston 1L 101
Hazeldene Rd. B33: Sheld 2D 124
B63: Hale 7L 117
Hazel Dr. B47: H'wd 4B 166
WS12: Haz 3A 10
Hazeley Cl. B17: Harb 2M 119
Hazel Gdns. B27: A Grn 5J 123
WV8: Cod 5G 21
Hazelgarth B77: Wiln 1G 47
Hazelglen Gro. *B18: Win G 5E 100*
(off Heath Grn. Rd.)
Hazel Gro. B70: W Brom 8J 77
B94: H'ley H 3C 194
CV12: Bed 6K 111
DY8: Stourb 6J 115
WS14: Lich 2J 19
WV5: Wom 2G 73
WV11: Wed 2J 37
WV14: Bils 2L 53
Hazelhurst Rd. B14: K Hth 3L 143
B36: Cas B 2E 104
Hazel La. WS6: Gt Wyr 7H 15
Hazell Way CV10: Nun 8G 89
Hazell Way Ind. Est.
CV10: Nun 8G 89
Hazelmead Ct. B73: Bold 2G 81
Hazelmere Cl. CV5: Cov 5H 151
Hazelmere Dr. WS7: Chase 5F 16
WV3: Wolv 8G 35
Hazelmere Rd. B28: Hall G 8F 122
Hazeloak Rd. B90: Shir 8G 145
Hazel Rd. B45: Rubery 3F 162
B97: Redd 4C 212
CV6: Cov 8H 131
CV10: Nun 4D 88
DY1: Dud 7J 75
DY4: Tip 8C 54
DY6: K'wfrd 4L 95
WV3: Wolv 2L 51
Hazels, The *DY9: Hag 4M 137*
(off Greenway, The)
HAZELSLADE 3A 10
Hazelton Cl. B61: Marl 1C 188
B91: Sol 8B 146
Hazelton Rd. B61: Marl 1B 188
Hazeltree Cft. B27: A Grn 7H 123
Hazeltree Gro. B93: Dorr 6E 168
Hazelville Gro. B28: Hall G 3G 145
Hazelville Rd. B28: Hall G 3G 145
Hazel Way LE9: Barw 2A 70
Hazelwell Cres. B30: Stir 3H 143
Hazelwell Dr. B14: K Hth 3K 143
Hazelwell Fordrough
B30: Stir 2H 143
Hazelwell La. B30: Stir 2G 143
Hazelwell Rd. B30: Stir 3G 143
Hazelwell St. B30: Stir 2G 143
Hazelwood Cl. CV22: Dunc 6H 205
DY11: Kidd 5G 157
WS6: C Hay 7D 14
Hazelwood Dr. WV11: Wed 4G 37
Hazelwood Gro. WS11: Cann 1C 14
WV12: W'hall 4D 38
Hazelwood Rd. B27: A Grn 7H 123
B74: S'tly 8K 41
DY1: Dud 4F 74
Hazlemere Dr. B74: Four O 1G 59
Hazlitt Gro. B30: K Nor 5D 142
HDA Sports & Social Club 5B 212
Headborough Rd. CV2: Cov 4G 153
Headborough Wlk.
WS9: A'rdge 8H 27
Headingley Dr. DY7: Stourt 8F 94
Headingley Rd. B21: Hand 7E 78
Headington Av. CV6: Cov 7A 130
Headland Dr. B8: Salt 4D 102
Headland Rd. WV3: Wolv 8F 34
Headlands, The B74: Lit A 6C 42
CV5: Cov 5K 151
HEADLESS CROSS 1D 220
Headless Cross Dr.
B97: Redd 8D 212
Headley Ct. B97: Redd 1D 220
Headley Cft. B38: K Nor 1D 164
HEADLEY HEATH 3J 165
Headley Heath La.
B38: Head H 2H 165
Headley Ri. B90: Shir 7K 145
Headway Rd. WV10: F'hses 6C 22
Heale Cl. B63: Crad 2G 117
Healey B77: Glas 7E 32
Healey Cl. CV21: Brow 2C 180
Healey Ct. CV34: Warw 2F 222
Health Cen. Rd. CV4: Canly 5J 173
Heanley La. CV9: Hurl 2K 63
Heanor Cft. B6: Aston 1B 102
Heantum Cft. WV10: Wolv 4G 37
Heantun Ho.
WV3: Wolv 8C 36 (5H 7)
Heantun Mill Ct.
WS10: W'bry 8D 54
Heantun Ri.
WV1: Wolv 5C 36 (1H 7)
Hearsall Comn. CV5: Cov 7L 151
Hearsall Ct. CV4: Cov 7K 151
Hearsall La. CV5: Cov 7M 151
Heartland M. B65: Row R 7B 98
Heartlands High Community
Leisure Cen. 5A 102 (1M 5)
Heartlands Parkway
B7: Nech 4C 102
Heartlands Pl. B8: Salt 5E 102
Heart of England Crematorium
CV11: Nun 6M 89
Heart of England Way
CV11: Nun 6M 89
HEATH
Rugby 5J 205
Stourbridge 5M 115
HEATH, THE 4E 156
Heath, The CV22: Dunc 6J 205
Heath Acres WS10: Darl 5C 54
Heath Av. CV12: Bed 8E 110
Heathbank Dr. WS12: Hunt 3C 8
Heath Bri. Cl. WS4: Rus 1A 40
Heathbrook Av. DY6: W Hth 2H 95
Heath Bus. Pk. CV8: Wols 8K 177
Heathcliff Rd. B11: Tys 5F 122
DY2: Dud 2M 97
Heath Cl. B30: B'vlle 4D 142
B60: Stoke H 3L 209
B75: S Cold 3M 59
DY4: Tip 4B 76
WS9: Ston 4L 27
HEATHCOTE 6L 223
Heathcote Av. B91: Sol 6L 145
Heathcote Cl. B77: Wiln 2G 47
Heathcote Ho. *B17: Harb 4C 120*
(off Vivian Cl.)
Heathcote Ind. Est.
CV34: H'cte 5J 223
Heathcote La. CV34: H'cte 5J 223
Heathcote Pk. CV34: H'cte 7L 223
Heathcote Rd. B30: K Nor 4G 143
CV31: W'nsh 6M 223
Heathcote St. CV6: Cov 3A 152
Heathcote Way CV34: H'cte 5K 223
Heath Ct. LE9: Earl S 2D 70
Heath Cres. CV2: Cov 3G 153
Heath Cft. B31: Longb 2A 164
Heath Cft. Rd. B75: R'ley 8J 43
Heath Dr. DY10: Kidd 8B 136
HEATH END
Nuneaton 7F 88
Walsall 7A 26
Heath End Rd. CV10: Nun 7E 88
DY9: Belb 2J 161
Heather Av. WS5: Wals 5B 56
Heather Cl. B36: Cas B 1G 105
CV10: Nun 6F 88
CV22: Bil 8L 179
CV47: Sou 4H 225
WS3: Blox 1G 39
WS13: Lich 8K 13
WV11: Wed 4L 37
Heather Ct. CV9: Ath 8K 49
Heather Ct. Gdns.
B74: Four O 1H 59
Heather Cft. B44: Gt Barr 8M 57
Heather Dale B13: Mose 7J 121
Heather Dr. B45: Rubery 3F 162
CV12: Bed 7E 110
DY7: Kinv 5A 114
WS12: Hunt 4D 8
Heather Gro. B91: Sol 3E 146
WV12: W'hall 5E 38
Heather Ho. B38: K Nor 8F 142
Heatherleigh Rd. B36: Cas B 1F 104
Heather M. WS12: Hed 1G 9
Heather Rd. B10: Small H 2F 122
B43: Gt Barr 1C 78
B67: Smeth 3L 99
CV2: Cov 7J 131
CV3: Bin W 2C 176
DY1: Dud 5J 75
WS3: Blox 1G 39
WS12: Hed 1G 9
Heather Valley WS12: Hed 3K 9
Heath Farm Rd. DY8: Stourb 7K 115
WV8: Bilb 7H 21
Heathfield Av. B20: Hand 1H 101
Heathfield Cl. B64: Old H 7M 97
B93: Know 4G 169
Heathfield Ct. B19: Loz 2H 101
Heathfield Cres. DY11: Kidd 5H 157
Heathfield Dr. B74: Four O 6F 42
WS3: Blox 7H 25
Heathfield Gdns.
DY8: Stourb 5M 115
Heathfield La. WS10: Darl 3C 54
Heathfield La. W. WS10: Darl 4B 54
Heathfield Rd. B14: K Hth 1L 143
B19: Hand 1H 101
B63: Hale 6L 117
B97: Redd 8M 211
CV5: Cov 7J 151
DY12: Bew 5C 156
DY13: Stour S 8H 183
Heathfields WV8: Cod 8E 20
Heath Gap Rd. WS11: Cann 6F 8
Heath Gdns. B91: Sol 3D 146
HEATH GREEN 6M 191
Heath Grn. DY1: Dud 4F 74
Heathgreen Cl. B37: Chel W 6K 105
Heath Grn. Gro. *B18: Win G 5E 100*
(off Heath Grn. Rd.)
Heath Grn. Rd. B18: Win G 5E 100
Heath Grn. Way
CV4: W'wd H 3F 172
Heath Gro. WV8: Bilb 6H 21
HEATH HAYES 8L 9
Heath Hill Rd. WV6: Tett 8E 34
Heath Ho. B14: K Hth 7M 143
Heath Ho. Dr. WV5: Wom 4D 72
Heath Ho. La. WV8: Cod 1E 34
Heathland Av. B34: S End 2A 104
Heathland Cl. WS12: Hth H 7K 9
Heathlands DY13: Stour S 6H 183
Heathlands, The B65: B'hth 8C 98
DY8: Stourb 5B 116
WS2: Wals 6G 39
WV5: Wom 4D 72
Heathlands Cl. DY6: K'wfrd 1L 95
Heathlands Cres. B73: Bold 8F 58
Heathlands Gro. B31: N'fld 8A 142
Heathlands Rd. B73: Bold 7F 58
Heath La. B71: W Brom 2K 77
CV23: Brin 1J 177
DY8: Stourb 5A 116
DY10: Stone 8C 158
LE9: Barw 1C 70
Heath La. Sth. LE9: Earl S 1D 70
Heathleigh Rd. B38: K Nor 1C 164
Heathley La. B78: Dray B 3K 45
Heathmere Av. B25: Yard 1K 123
Heathmere Dr. B37: F'bri 7F 104
Heath Mill Cl. WV5: Wom 5D 72
Heath Mill La.
B9: Birm 8A 102 (7L 5)
Heath Mill Rd. WV5: Wom 5D 72
Heath Pk. WV10: Cov H 3C 22
Heath Ri. B14: K Hth 8A 144
Heath Rd. B30: B'vlle 4C 142
B47: H'wd 2A 166
B91: Sol 3D 146
CV2: Cov 5F 152
CV12: Bed 8F 110
DY2: Neth 7H 97
WS10: Darl 1E 54
WV12: W'hall 1C 38
Heath Rd. Sth. B31: N'fld 5A 142
Heathside Dr. B38: K Nor 8H 143
WS3: Pels 5A 26
Heath St. B18: Win G 4D 100
B65: B'hth 8C 98
B66: Smeth 4D 100
B79: Tam 4C 32
DY8: Stourb 4M 115
WS12: Hed 1G 9
Heath St. Ind. Est.
B66: Smeth 4D 100
Heath St. Sth. B18: Win G 5F 100
Heath Ter. CV32: Lea S 8L 217
CV35: Beau 7J 197
HEATH TOWN 5H 37
Heath Town Leisure Cen. 5G 37
Heath Trad. Pk. B66: Smeth 4D 100
Heath Vw. WS2: Wals 6F 38
WS7: C Ter 8G 11
WS12: Hth H 8L 9
Heath Way
B34: Hodg H, S End 2M 103
CV22: Hillm 1D 206
WS11: Hth H 7H 9
WS12: Hth H 8J 9
Heathway Cl. B34: S End 3A 104
Heathy Farm Cl. B32: Bart G 8H 119
Heathy Ri. B32: Bart G 7G 119
Heaton Cl. WV10: Bush 4E 22
Heaton Dr. B15: Edg 1E 120
B74: Four O 1F 58
Heaton Rd. B91: Sol 3M 145
Heaton St. B18: Hock 4H 101
Hebden B77: Wiln 1H 47
Hebden Av. CV34: Warw 8E 216
Hebden Gro. B28: Hall G 6E 144
WV12: W'hall 8B 24
Hebden Way CV11: Nun 7A 90
Heckley Rd. CV7: Exh 2G 131
Heddle Gro. CV6: Cov 1H 153
Heddon Pl. B7: Birm 6A 102 (3M 5)
Hedera Cl. WS5: Wals 6B 56
Hedera Rd. B98: Redd 3M 213
Hedgefield Gro. B63: Crad 5J 117
Hedgefield Way CV4: Tile H 1F 172
Hedgerow Cl. WS12: Hed 2F 8
Hedgerow Dr. DY6: K'wfrd 8K 73
Hedgerows, The B62: Roms 5M 139
B77: Wiln 1F 46
CV10: Nun 3F 88
Hedgerow Wlk. CV6: Cov 5B 130
WV8: Pend 8L 21
Hedges, The WV5: Wom 3E 72
Hedges Way B60: B'gve 8B 188
Hedgetree Cft. B37: Chel W 7J 105
Hedge Way CV10: Nun 2C 88
Hedging La. B77: Dost 4D 46
Hedging La. Ind. Est.
B77: Wiln 4E 46
Hedgings, The *B34: S End 3B 104*
(off Meadow Rd.)
Hedgley Gro. B33: Stech 5A 104
Hedingham Gro.
B37: Chel W 7K 105
Hedley Cft. B35: Cas V 5B 82
HEDNESFORD 4H 9
Hednesford Hills Raceway 4M 9
Hednesford Rd. WS8: Bwnhls 6C 16
WS11: Cann 8E 8
WS11: Nort C 2M 15
WS12: Hth H 7K 9
Hednesford Station (Rail) 4H 9
Hednesford St. WS11: Cann 8E 8
Heeley Rd. B29: S Oak 7E 120
Heemstede La. CV32: Lea S 7A 218
Heenan Gro. WS13: Lich 7F 12
Heera Cl. CV6: Cov 2D 152
Hefford Dr. B66: Smeth 3A 100
Heightington Pl.
DY13: Stour S 8E 182
Heightington Rd.
DY12: H'ton, Ribb 1A 182
Helena Cl. CV10: Nun 6F 88
Helena Pl. B66: Smeth 2J 99
Helena St. B1: Birm 6J 101 (4C 4)
Helenny Cl. WV11: Wed 4G 37
Helen St. CV6: Cov 3F 152
Hele Rd. CV3: Cov 3D 174
Helford Cl. DY4: Tip 4K 75
Heligan Pl. WS12: Hth H 7K 9
Hellaby Cl. B72: S Cold 5H 59
Hellaby Ct. B73: Bold 2G 81
Hellaby Ho. B74: Four O 6F 42
Hellidon Cl. CV32: Lill 7A 218
Hellier Av. DY4: Tip 5B 76
Hellier Dr. WV5: Wom 2E 72
Hellier Rd. WV10: Bush 7E 22
Hellier St. DY2: Dud 1J 97
Helmdon Cl. CV21: Brow 3D 180
Helming Dr. WV1: Wolv 6H 37
Helmingham B79: Tam 2K 31
Helmsdale Rd. CV32: Lill 5B 218
Helmsdale Way DY3: Sed 2G 75
Helmsley Cl. DY5: Brie H 1C 116
Helmsley Rd. WV11: Wed 1J 37
Helmswood Dr. B37: Chel W 1J 125
Helston Cl. B79: Tam 1C 32
CV11: Nun 4A 90
DY8: Word 7J 95
WS5: Wals 2D 56
Helstone Gro. B11: Tys 6G 123
Helston Rd. WS5: Wals 2D 56
Helvellyn Way CV21: Brow 2D 180
Hembs Cres. B43: Gt Barr 1C 78
Hemdale CV11: Nun 5A 90
Hemingford Rd.
CV2: W'grve S 1M 153
Heming Rd. B98: Redd 2L 221
Hemlingford Cft.
B37: Mars G 2G 125

Hemlingford Rd.—High St.

Hemlingford Rd. B37: K'hrst ... 3E 104
B76: Walm ... 2A 82
B78: K'bry ... 5D 62
Hemlock Bus. Cen.
WS11: Hth H ... 7H 9
Hemlock Pk. WS11: Hth H ... 7H 9
Hemlock Way WS11: Hth H ... 7H 9
Hemmings Cl. CV31: Rad S ... 4E 224
DY8: Stourb ... 4M 115
Hemmings Entry B97: Redd ... 5E 212
Hemmings St. WS10: Darl ... 1C 54
Hemming St. DY11: Kidd ... 5J 157
Hemming Way
DY10: Chad C ... 1L 185
Hempit La. B76: Wis ... 2F 82
Hemplands Rd.
DY8: Stourb ... 4M 115
Hempole La. DY4: Tip ... 2D 76
Hemsby Cl. CV4: Canly ... 2G 173
Hemsworth Dr. CV12: Bulk ... 7B 112
Hemyock Rd. B29: W Cas ... 1B 142
HENBROOK ... 7F 208
Henbury Rd. B27: A Grn ... 6K 123
Henderson Cl CV5: Alle ... 2J 151
Henderson Cl. WS14: Lich ... 2K 19
Henderson Ct. B68: O'bry ... 1H 119
Henderson Wlk. DY4: Tip ... 1B 76
Henderson Way B65: B'hth ... 8C 98
Hendon Cl. DY3: Lwr G ... 7D 74
WV10: Bush ... 1E 36
Hendon Rd. B11: S'hll ... 4B 122
Hendre Cl. CV5: Cov ... 7J 151
Heneage Pl.
B7: Birm ... 5A 102 (2M 5)
Heneage St. B7: Birm ... 5A 102 (1L 5)
Heneage St. W.
B7: Birm ... 5M 101 (2K 5)
(not continuous)
Henfield Cl. WV11: Wed ... 2K 37
Hengham Rd. B26: Yard ... 8A 104
Hen La. CV6: Cov ... 6C 130
Henley Cl. B73: W Grn ... 1H 81
B79: Tam ... 3C 32
CV11: Nun ... 1M 89
DY4: Tip ... 4D 76
WS3: Blox ... 8L 25
WS7: Burn ... 4H 17
Henley Ct. CV2: Cov ... 2K 153
WS14: Lich ... 3H 19
Henley Cres. B91: Sol ... 2B 146
Henley Dr. B75: Four O ... 6G 43
HENLEY GREEN ... 1K 153
Henley Ind. Pk. CV2: Cov ... 2L 153
Henley Mill La. CV2: Cov ... 2H 153
Henley Rd. B80: Map G, Out ... 7B 214
B95: Hen A, Ullen ... 8L 215
B95: Ullen ... 6J 215
CV2: Cov, W'grve S ... 8H 131
CV31: Lea S ... 4B 224
WV10: Oxl ... 8B 22
Henley St. B11: S'brk ... 2A 122
Henley Vs. *B12: Bal H ... 4B 122*
(off Chesterton Rd.)
Henley Wlk. CV2: Cov ... 1K 153
Henlow Cl. DY4: Tip ... 4K 75
Henlow Rd. B14: K Hth ... 7M 143
Hennalls, The B36: Hodg H ... 2M 103
Hennals Av. B97: Redd ... 7M 211
Henn Dr. DY4: Tip ... 1L 75
Henne Dr. WV14: Cose ... 8J 53
Henn St. DY4: Tip ... 1A 76
Henrietta St.
B19: Birm ... 5K 101 (2E 4)
CV6: Cov ... 4E 152
Henry Boteler Rd.
CV4: Canly ... 2H 173
Henry Rd. B25: Yard ... 2J 123
Henry St. CV1: Cov ... 6C 152 (3C 6)
CV8: Ken ... 4G 199
CV11: Nun ... 7J 89
CV21: Rugby ... 6A 180
LE10: Hinc ... 7G 69
WS2: Wals ... 8K 39
Henry's Way *CV31: W'nsh ... 5A 224*
(off Dobson La.)
Henry Tanday Ct.
CV32: Lea S ... 8L 217
Henry Wlk. B60: B'gve ... 2L 209
Hensborough B90: Dic H ... 4G 167
Hensel Dr. WV3: Wolv ... 1J 51
Henshaw Gro. B25: Yard ... 2J 123
Henshaw Rd. B10: Small H ... 1D 122
Henson Rd. CV12: Bed ... 8E 110
Henson Way LE10: Sharn ... 4H 93
Henstead St.
B5: Birm ... 1K 121 (8F 4)
Hentland Cl. B98: Redd ... 5K 213
Henwood Cl. WV6: Tett ... 6J 35
Henwood La. B91: Cath B ... 4H 147
Henwood Rd. WV6: Tett ... 7J 35
Hepburn Cl. WS9: A'rdge ... 5G 41
Hepburn Edge B24: Erd ... 5H 81
Hepworth Cl. WV6: Pert ... 5F 34
Hepworth Rd. CV3: Bin ... 7B 154
Herald Av. CV5: Cov ... 8J 151
Herald Bus. Pk. CV3: Bin ... 2M 175
Herald Ct. DY1: Dud ... 8J 75
Herald Rd. B26: Birm A ... 5J 125
Heralds Ct. CV34: Warw ... 1H 223
Herald Way CV3: Bin ... 2A 176
LE10: Burb ... 4K 91
Herbert Art Gallery, The & Mus.
... 7D 152 (5D 6)
Herbert Austin Dr. B60: Marl ... 8E 162
Herbert Rd. B10: Small H ... 8C 102
B21: Hand ... 8F 78
B67: Smeth ... 8A 100
B91: Sol ... 6B 146
WS9: A'rdge ... 8G 27
Herberts La. CV8: Ken ... 4G 199
Herberts Pk. Rd. WS10: Darl ... 3B 54
Herbert St. B70: W Brom ... 6K 77
B98: Redd ... 5E 212
CV10: Nun ... 6E 88
WV1: Wolv ... 6D 36 (2K 7)
WV14: Bils ... 3H 53
Herbhill Cl. WV4: Penn ... 5D 52
Herdwycke Cl. CV47: Sou ... 5K 225
Hereford Av. B12: Bal H ... 3A 122
Hereford Cl. B45: Fran ... 7G 141
CV10: Nun ... 5E 88
DY11: Kidd ... 4G 157
LE9: Barw ... 2M 69
WS9: A'rdge ... 1G 41
Hereford Ho.
WV1: Wolv ... 6C 36 (1H 7)
Hereford Pl. B71: W Brom ... 2H 77
Hereford Rd. B68: O'bry ... 2H 119
CV11: Bram ... 3F 112
DY2: Neth ... 6L 97
WS12: Hed ... 5H 9
Hereford St. WS2: Wals ... 5L 39
Hereford Wlk. B37: Mars G ... 8F 104
Hereford Way B78: Tam ... 7A 32
Hereward Ri. B62: Hale ... 4B 118
Herford Way LE10: Burb ... 3M 91
Heritage, The *WS1: Wals ... 1L 55*
(off Sister Dora Gdns.)
Heritage Cl. B68: O'bry ... 5J 99
Heritage Ct. B18: Birm ... 2C 4
CV4: Canly ... 6K 173
WS14: Lich ... 3K 19
Heritage Dr. CV6: Longf ... 3J 131
Heritage Way B33: Kitts G ... 6D 104
DY4: Tip ... 4B 76
Hermes Cl. CV34: Warw ... 4L 223
Hermes Ct. B74: Four O ... 6F 42
Hermes Cres. CV2: Cov ... 2K 153
Hermes Rd. B26: Birm A ... 5J 125
WS13: Lich ... 8K 13
Hermione Cl. CV34: H'cte ... 6M 223
Hermitage, The B91: Sol ... 3C 146
Hermitage Cl. B78: Pole ... 8M 33
Hermitage Dr. B76: Walm ... 6M 59
Hermitage La. B78: B'moor ... 8L 33
Hermitage Rd. B15: Edg ... 8C 100
B23: Erd ... 6D 80
B91: Sol ... 4C 146
CV2: Cov ... 5J 153
Hermitage Way CV8: Ken ... 6G 199
DY13: Stour S ... 8E 182
Hermit's Cft.
CV3: Cov ... 1D 174 (8E 6)
Hermit St. DY3: Up Gor ... 4D 74
Hermon Row B11: S'brk ... 4D 122
Hernall Cft. B26: Sheld ... 2A 124
Hernefield Rd. B34: S End ... 2A 104
Hernehurst B32: Quin ... 4H 119
Herne's Nest DY12: Bew ... 7A 156
Hern Rd. DY5: Brie H ... 3C 116
Heronbank CV4: Tile H ... 7C 150
Heron Cl. B48: A'chu ... 2A 190
B90: Ches G ... 5K 167
B95: Bwnhls ... 2E 26
Heron Ct. *B73: W Grn ... 2H 81*
(off Florence Av.)
Herondale Cres. DY8: Stourb ... 5J 115
Herondale Rd. B26: Sheld ... 3M 123
WS12: Hed ... 5H 9
Heronfield Cl. B98: Redd ... 3J 213
Heronfield Dr. B31: Longb ... 3M 163
Heronfield Way B91: Sol ... 4E 146
Heron Ho. CV2: Cov ... 6H 153
Heron Mill WS3: Pels ... 6L 25
Heron Rd. B68: O'bry ... 7G 99
Heronry, The WV6: Tett ... 7F 34
Herons Ct. LE10: Hinc ... 2F 90
Heronsdale Rd. DY8: Stourb ... 6J 115
Herons Way B29: S Oak ... 6C 120
Heronswood Dr. DY5: Brie H ... 8D 96
Heronswood Rd. B45: Redn ... 3H 163
DY10: Kidd ... 7M 157
Heronville Dr. B70: W Brom ... 2G 77
Heronville Ho. DY4: Tip ... 6B 76
Heronville Rd. B70: W Brom ... 3F 76
Heron Way B45: Rubery ... 2F 162
Herrick Rd. B8: Salt ... 4E 102
CV2: Cov ... 6K 153
Herrick St. WV3: Wolv ... 8B 36 (5G 7)
Herring Rd. CV9: Ath ... 2L 65
Herringshaw Cft. B76: Walm ... 6L 59
Hertford Pl. CV1: Cov ... 7B 152 (6A 6)
Hertford St. B12: Bal H ... 4A 122
CV1: Cov ... 7C 152 (5C 6)
Hertford Way B93: Know ... 5H 169
Hervey Gro. B24: Erd ... 3K 81
Hesketh Cres. B23: Erd ... 4C 80
Heskett Av. B68: O'bry ... 8J 99
Hesleden B77: Wiln ... 1H 47
Heslop Cl. CV3: Bin ... 1M 175
Hessian Cl. WV14: Cose ... 7H 53
Hestia Dr. B29: S Oak ... 1E 142
Heston Av. B42: Gt Barr ... 1G 79
Hetton Cl. CV34: Warw ... 8F 216
Hever Av. B44: K'sdng ... 8A 58
Hever Cl. DY1: Dud ... 6E 74
Hewell Av. B60: B'gve ... 2M 209
Hewell Cl. B31: Longb ... 2M 163
B97: Redd ... 3J 211
DY6: K'wfrd ... 8K 73
Hewell La. B45: B Grn ... 1J 189
B60: Tard ... 6F 188
B97: Redd ... 6F 188
HEWELL PARK ... 2K 211
Hewell Pl. *B45: B Grn ... 1K 189*
(off Hewell Rd.)
Hewell Rd. B45: B Grn ... 1K 189
B97: Redd ... 4C 212
Hewell Road Swimming Pool
... 4C 212
Hewitson Gdns. B67: Smeth ... 7M 99
Hewitt Av. CV6: Cov ... 4B 152 (1A 6)
Hewitt Cl. WS13: Lich ... 7G 13
Hewitt St. WS10: Darl ... 3C 54
Hewston Cft. WS12: Hed ... 5K 9
Hexby Cl. CV2: W'grve S ... 3A 154
Hexham Cft. B36: Hodg H ... 1J 103
Hexham Way DY1: Dud ... 7F 74
Hexton Cl. B90: Shir ... 7D 144
Hexworthy Av. CV3: Cov ... 4B 174
Heybarnes Cir. B10: Small H ... 2F 122
Heybarnes Rd. B10: Small H ... 2F 122
Heybrook Cl. CV2: Cov ... 2J 153
Heycott Gro. B38: K Nor ... 7J 143
Heycroft CV4: Canly ... 5K 173
Heydon Rd. B60: Fins ... 8D 188
DY5: P'ntt ... 4B 96
Heyford Cl. CV2: Ald G ... 6K 131
Heyford Gro. B91: Sol ... 1C 168
Heyford Leys CV22: Rugby ... 3M 205
Heyford Way B35: Cas V ... 4B 82
Heygate Way WS9: A'rdge ... 7H 27
Heynesfield Rd. B33: Kitts G ... 6C 104
Heythrop Gro. B13: Mose ... 1D 144
Heyville Cft. CV8: Ken ... 6J 199
Heywood Cl. CV6: Cov ... 2G 153
Hibberd Ct. CV8: Ken ... 5F 198
Hibbert Cl. CV22: Rugby ... 8M 179
Hickman Av. WV1: Wolv ... 8G 37
Hickman Gdns. B16: Edg ... 8F 100
Hickman Pl. WV14: Bils ... 3J 53
Hickman Rd. B11: S'brk ... 3B 122
CV10: Gall C ... 5L 87
DY4: Tip ... 1M 75
DY5: Brie H ... 5C 96
WV14: Bils ... 4J 53
Hickman's Av. B64: Old H ... 7L 97
Hickmans Cl. B62: Quin ... 3G 119
Hickman St. DY9: Lye ... 3C 116
Hickmerelands La. DY3: Sed ... 1D 74
Hickory Ct. WS11: Hth H ... 7J 9
Hickory Dr. B17: Edg ... 7A 100
Hicks Cl. CV34: Warw ... 7F 216
Hidcote Av. B76: Walm ... 1A 82
Hidcote Cl. CV11: Nun ... 1M 111
CV31: Lea S ... 4C 224
Hidcote Gro. B33: Sheld ... 1C 124
B37: Mars G ... 2G 125
Hidcote Rd. CV8: Ken ... 3J 199
Hidson Rd. B23: Erd ... 4C 80
Higgins Av. WV14: Cose ... 7K 53
Higgins La. B32: Quin ... 4J 119
Higgins Wlk. B66: Smeth ... 3B 100
Higgs Fld. Cres. B64: Old H ... 8A 98
Higgs Rd. WV11: Wed ... 4E 36
Higham La. CV11: Nun ... 4L 89
CV13: Stoke G ... 3C 68
LE10: Wykin ... 6E 68
HIGHAM ON THE HILL ... 6A 68
Highams Cl. B65: Row R ... 6B 98
Higham Way LE10: Burb ... 2L 91
WV10: Wolv ... 3E 36
Higham Way Ho. LE10: Burb ... 2L 91
High Arcal Dr. DY3: Sed ... 2F 74
High Arcal Rd. DY3: Lwr G ... 6M 73
High Ash Cl. CV7: Exh ... 2F 130
High Av. B64: Crad H ... 1M 117
High Bank WS11: Cann ... 1E 14
High Beech CV5: Alle ... 3G 151
High Beeches B43: Gt Barr ... 8D 56
HIGHBRIDGE ... 4A 26
Highbridge Rd. B73: Bold ... 8F 58
DY2: Neth ... 6G 97
High Brink Rd. B46: Col ... 2M 105
Highbrook Cl. WV9: Pend ... 7A 22
High Broom Ct. B78: Tam ... 6A 32
High Brow B17: Harb ... 2B 120
High Bullen WS10: W'bry ... 6F 54
Highbury Av. B21: Hand ... 1F 100
B65: Row R ... 6D 98
Highbury Cl. B65: Row R ... 6D 98
Highbury Ct. B13: Mose ... 2L 143
Highbury Grn. CV10: Nun ... 2C 88
Highbury Little Theatre ... 2G 81
Highbury Rd. B14: K Hth ... 1K 143
B66: Smeth ... 2K 99
B68: O'bry ... 4H 99
B74: Four O ... 6C 42
High Clere B64: Crad H ... 2A 118
Highclere DY12: Bew ... 7A 156
Highclere Dr. DY12: Bew ... 7A 156
Highcliffe Rd. B77: Two G ... 8D 32
Highcrest Cl. B31: Longb ... 2A 164
High Cft. B43: Gt Barr ... 8C 56
WS3: Pels ... 4B 26
Highcroft WS9: A'rdge ... 7H 27
Highcroft Av. DY8: Word ... 6J 95
Highcroft Cl. B92: Sol ... 7C 124
Highcroft Cres. CV32: Lea S ... 8J 217
WS14: Lich ... 3J 19
Highcroft Dr. B74: Four O ... 6E 42
Highcroft Rd. B23: Erd ... 6E 80
Highdown Cres. B90: M'path ... 3A 168
Highdown Rd. CV31: Lea S ... 3B 224
High Elms La. B60: Lwr B ... 8E 210
HIGH ERCAL ... 7C 96
High Ercal Av. DY5: Brie H ... 7C 96
High Farm Rd. B62: B'hth ... 1F 118
B63: Hale ... 6L 117
Highfield CV7: Mer ... 8J 127
Highfield Av. B77: Amin ... 4G 33
B97: Redd ... 1D 220
WS4: S'fld ... 1C 40
WS7: Burn ... 2H 17
WV10: Bush ... 7G 23
Highfield Cl. B28: Hall G ... 4D 144
CV8: Ken ... 5E 198
WS7: Burn ... 2H 17
Highfield Ct. B73: W Grn ... 8H 59
LE9: Earl S ... 2E 70
WS11: Cann ... 4H 9
Highfield Cres. B63: Crad ... 3K 117
B65: B'hth ... 1B 118
WV11: Wed ... 3H 37
Highfield Dr. B73: Bold ... 2F 80
Highfield Gdns. WS14: Lich ... 3L 19
Highfield La. B32: Quin ... 3H 119
B63: Hale ... 6M 117
CV7: Cor ... 8H 109
DY9: Clent ... 7F 138
Highfield M. B63: Crad ... 3K 117
Highfield Pas. WS1: Wals ... 1L 55
Highfield Pl. B14: Yard W ... 4D 144
Highfield Road ... 6F 152
Highfield Rd. B8: Salt ... 5E 102
B13: Mose ... 6B 122
B14: Yard W ... 4D 144
B15: Edg ... 1G 121
B28: Hall G ... 4D 144
B43: Gt Barr ... 2C 78
B61: B'gve ... 1L 209
B63: Crad ... 4K 117
B65: B'hth ... 8B 98
B67: Smeth ... 4M 99
B80: Stud ... 5K 221
B97: Redd ... 1D 220
CV2: Cov ... 5F 152
CV11: Nun ... 7K 89
DY2: Dud ... 8L 75
DY3: Sed ... 8D 52
DY4: Tip ... 2A 76
DY8: Word ... 7A 96
DY10: Cookl ... 4A 136
DY10: Kidd ... 1A 158
WS3: Pels ... 5A 26
WS7: Burn ... 2H 17
WS12: Hth H ... 8L 9
Highfield Rd. Nth. WS3: Pels ... 4M 25
HIGHFIELDS ... 4F 16
Highfields B23: Erd ... 5C 80
B61: B'gve ... 8L 187
WS7: Burn ... 2H 17
Highfields, The WV6: Tett ... 7G 35
Highfields Av. WV14: Bils ... 5L 53
Highfields Ct. WV4: Penn ... 3J 51
Highfields Dr. WV5: Wom ... 4G 73
WV14: Cose ... 6K 53
Highfields Farm Ent. Cen.
LE9: S Stan ... 5K 71
Highfields Grange
WS6: C Hay ... 8D 14
Highfields Pk. WS6: C Hay ... 8D 14
Highfields Rd. LE10: Hinc ... 8L 69
WS7: Chase ... 5F 16
WV14: Bils, Cose ... 6J 53
Highfields St. LE9: S Stan ... 6K 71
Highfield St. LE9: Earl S ... 2D 70
Highfield Ter. B18: Hock ... 4G 101
CV32: Lea S ... 8K 217
Highfield Way WS9: A'rdge ... 7H 27
HIGHGATE ... 1M 121
Highgate B74: S'tly ... 8A 42
DY3: Up Gor ... 4E 74
Highgate Av. WS1: Wals ... 1M 55
WV4: Penn ... 3K 51
Highgate Bus. Cen.
B12: Bal H ... 3B 122
Highgate Cl. B12: Birm ... 2M 121
DY11: Kidd ... 5G 157
WS1: Wals ... 2M 55
Highgate Common Country Pk.
... 1A 94
Highgate Comn. E.
DY3: Swind ... 2A 94
DY7: Env ... 2A 94
Highgate Dr. WS1: Wals ... 2M 55
Highgate Ho. B5: Birm ... 8G 5
Highgate Middleway
B12: Birm ... 2M 121
Highgate Pl. B12: Birm ... 2A 122
Highgate Rd. B12: Bal H ... 3A 122
DY2: Dud ... 3F 96
WS1: Wals ... 1M 55
Highgate Sq. B12: Birm ... 2M 121
Highgate St. B12: Birm ... 2M 121
B64: Old H ... 7M 97
(not continuous)
Highgate Trad. Est.
B12: Birm ... 2A 122
High Grange WS11: Cann ... 4G 9
WS13: Lich ... 8F 12
High Grn. WS11: Cann ... 8D 8
High Grn. Ct. WS11: Cann ... 8D 8
Highgrove CV4: W'wd H ... 4F 172
CV22: Bil ... 2K 205
WV6: Tett ... 6J 35
Highgrove Cl. WV12: W'hall ... 2B 38
Highgrove Ct. DY10: Kidd ... 8A 136
Highgrove Pl. *B79: Tam ... 2B 32*
(off Wiggington Rd.)
DY1: Dud ... 7F 74
HIGH HABBERLEY ... 2F 156
High Haden Cres.
B64: Crad H, Old H ... 1A 118
High Haden Rd.
B64: Crad H, Old H ... 1A 118
HIGH HEATH
Sutton Coldfield ... 1B 60
Walsall ... 7C 26
High Heath Cl. B30: B'vlle ... 4D 142
High Hill WV11: Ess ... 7A 24
High Holborn DY3: Sed ... 2D 74
High Ho. Dr. B45: Lick ... 6F 162
High Ho. La. B60: Tard ... 3G 211
Highland Ho. B62: B'hth ... 1C 118
Highland M. WV14: Cose ... 8K 53
Highland Ridge B62: Quin ... 4E 118
Highland Rd. B23: Erd ... 4F 80
B43: Gt Barr ... 6E 56
B64: Old H ... 7L 97
CV5: Cov ... 8M 151
CV8: Ken ... 2H 199
CV32: Lill ... 5B 218
DY1: Dud ... 6G 75
WS9: Wals W ... 6H 27
WS12: Hunt ... 5C 8
Highlands Cl. CV34: Warw ... 1F 222
DY11: Kidd ... 4G 157
Highlands Ct. B90: Shir ... 1L 167
Highlands Ind. Est., The
B90: Shir ... 1L 167
Highlands Rd. B90: Shir ... 1L 167
WV3: Wolv ... 1K 51
Highland Way B98: Redd ... 1G 221
High Leasowes B63: Hale ... 5A 118
High Lees LE10: Sharn ... 5H 93
Highley Cl. B98: Redd ... 5L 213
DY11: Kidd ... 7H 157
Highley Dr. CV6: Cov ... 2C 152
Highlow Av. DY11: Kidd ... 8J 135
High Mdw. WS15: Cann W ... 4F 10
High Mdw. Rd. B38: K Nor ... 7G 143
High Mdws. B60: Stoke H ... 3K 209
WV5: Wom ... 3G 73
WV6: Tett ... 7J 35
Highmoor Cl. WV12: W'hall ... 2B 38
WV14: Cose ... 6K 53
Highmoor Rd. B65: Row R ... 6B 98
Highmore Dr. B32: Bart G ... 1J 141
High Mt. St. WS12: Hed ... 3H 9
High Oak DY5: P'ntt ... 2C 96
Highover Dr. B75: Four O ... 5G 43
Highpark Av. DY8: Woll ... 4K 115
High Pk. Cl. B66: Smeth ... 4B 100
CV5: E Grn ... 6F 150
DY3: Sed ... 8D 52
High Pk. Cres. DY3: Sed ... 8D 52
HIGH PARK ESTATE ... 4J 115
High Pk. Rd. B63: Crad ... 4J 117
High Pk. St. B7: Nech ... 3B 102
High Point B15: Edg ... 3E 120
High Ridge WS9: A'rdge ... 4F 40
High Ridge Cl. WS9: A'rdge ... 4E 40
WS10: Mox ... 5A 54
High Rd. WV12: W'hall ... 4C 38
High St B61: B'gve ... 7M 187
High St. B4: Birm ... 7L 101 (5G 5)
B6: Aston ... 2L 101
B8: Salt ... 4C 102
B14: K Hth ... 1L 143
B17: Harb ... 4C 120
B23: Erd ... 5F 80
B32: Quin ... 3G 119
B46: Col ... 1M 105
B63: Hale ... 5B 118
B64: Crad H ... 1J 117
B65: B'hth ... 8B 98
B66: Smeth ... 3M 99
B70: W Brom ... 5H 77
(not continuous)
B72: S Cold ... 3J 59
B77: Dost ... 5C 46
B78: Pole ... 2K 49
B80: Stud ... 5L 221
B90: Shir ... 7C 144
B91: Sol ... 5C 146
B92: H Ard ... 3A 148
B93: Know ... 3J 169
B96: A'wd B ... 8E 220
CV1: Cov ... 7C 152 (5C 6)
CV6: Cov ... 8M 129
CV8: Ken ... 4E 198
CV8: Rytn D ... 8B 176
CV9: Hurl ... 4J 63
CV11: Nun ... 5H 89

High St.—Hockley Hill Ind. Est.

High St. CV12: Bed .7H **111**
CV13: Stoke G .2D **68**
CV21: Hillm .1F **206**
CV21: Rugby .6A **180**
CV31: Lea S .2M **223**
CV32: Cubb .4E **218**
CV34: Warw .3E **222**
CV47: S'ton .1M **225**
CV47: Sou .5H **225**
DY1: Dud .1J **97**
DY3: Sed .8D **52**
DY3: Swind .7E **72**
DY4: Tip .1L **75**
(Princes End)
DY4: Tip .4L **75**
(Tipton)
DY5: Brie H .7D **96**
(Brierley Hill)
DY5: Brie H .5B **96**
(Brockmoor)
DY5: P'ntt .2A **96**
DY5: Quar B .8F **96**
DY6: K'wfrd .3K **95**
DY6: W Hth .1H **95**
DY7: Kinv .5A **114**
DY8: Stourb .4A **116**
DY8: Woll .3L **115**
DY8: Word .6L **95**
DY9: Belb .2D **160**
DY9: Lye .4E **116**
DY10: Kidd .3L **157**
DY12: Bew .6B **156**
DY13: Stour S .6G **183**
LE9: Barw .4A **70**
LE9: Earl S .1F **70**
WS1: Wals .8L **39**
WS3: Blox .1H **39**
WS3: Pels .5A **26**
WS6: C Hay .7D **14**
WS7: C Ter .1E **16**
WS7: Chase .4F **16**
(not continuous)
WS8: Bwnhls .2F **26**
WS8: Clay .3E **26**
WS9: A'rdge .3H **41**
(not continuous)
WS9: Wals W .6F **26**
WS10: Mox .5A **54**
WS11: Nort C .4B **16**
WV5: Wom .3H **73**
WV6: Tett .5K **35**
WV11: Wed .4J **37**
WV14: Bils .4K **53**
High St. Amblecote
DY8: Amb .1M **115**
High St. Bordesley
B12: Birm .8A **102** (7L **5**)
High St. Deritend
B12: Birm .8M **101** (7K **5**)
Highters Cl. B14: K Hth .7B **144**
HIGHTER'S HEATH .7A **144**
Highter's Heath La.
B14: K Hth .8A **144**
Highters Rd. B14: K Hth .6A **144**
High Timbers B45: Fran .8F **140**
High Tor E. LE9: Earl S .1E **70**
High Tor W. LE9: Earl S .1E **70**
HIGH TOWN .4G **9**
High Town B63: Crad .3J **117**
CV23: Prin .7E **202**
Hightree Cl. B32: Bart G .8H **119**
High Trees B20: Hand .6F **78**
High Trees Cl. B98: Redd .2E **220**
High Trees Rd. B93: Know .2G **169**
High Vw. WV14: Cose .8F **52**
Highview CV9: Hurl .5J **63**
WS1: Wals .1M 55
(off Highgate Rd.)
High Vw. Dr. CV7: Ash G .2C **130**
Highview Dr. DY6: K'wfrd .5M **95**
High Vw. Rd. CV32: Cubb .4C **218**
Highview St. DY2: Dud .8L **75**
Highwayman's Cft.
CV4: Canly .4K **173**
Highwood Av. B92: Olton .8A **124**
High Wood Cl. DY6: K'wfrd .3J **95**
Highwood Cft. B38: K Nor .8D **142**
Hiker Gro. B37: Chel W .7K **105**
Hilary Bevins Cl.
CV13: High H .5M **67**
Hilary Cres. DY1: Dud .3H **75**
Hilary Dr. B76: Walm .6A **60**
WS9: A'rdge .4G **41**
WV3: Wolv .2K **51**
Hilary Gro. B31: N'fld .5M **141**
Hilary Rd. CV4: Canly .3K **173**
CV10: Nun .4F **88**
Hilden Rd. B7: Birm .5A **102** (2M **5**)
Hilderic Cres. DY1: Dud .2F **96**
Hilderstone Rd. B25: Yard .3J **123**
Hildicks Cres. WS3: Wals .2M **39**
Hildicks Pl. WS3: Wals .2M **39**
HILL .5G **43**
Hill, The B32: Bart G .7L **119**
CV47: S'ton .1M **225**
Hillaire Cl. B38: K Nor .7J **143**
Hillaries Rd. B23: Erd .7D **80**
Hillary Av. WS10: W'bry .6J **55**
Hillary Crest DY3: Up Gor .4E **74**
Hillary Rd. CV22: Rugby .1L **205**
DY13: Stour S .2K **183**
Hillary St. WS2: Wals .2J **55**
Hill Av. WV4: E'shll .6F **52**
Hill Bank DY9: Lye .4F **116**
Hillbank B69: Tiv .8D **76**
Hill Bank Dr. B33: Stech .5K **103**
Hill Bank Rd. B38: K Nor .7G **143**
B63: Crad .3K **117**
Hillboro Ri. DY7: Kinv .4A **114**
Hillborough Rd. B27: A Grn .7L **123**
Hillbrook Gro. B33: Stech .6M **103**
Hillbrow Cres. B62: B'hth .1F **118**
Hillbury Dr. WV12: W'hall .1B **38**
Hill Cl. B31: N'fld .8B **142**
CV32: Lill .6A **218**
DY3: Sed .8E **52**
Hill Cres. CV23: Stret D .3F **202**
Hillcrest B77: Wiln .2F **46**
CV32: Cubb .4E **218**
DY3: Lwr G .5C **74**
Hillcrest Av. B43: Gt Barr .7E **56**
B63: Crad .2H **117**
DY5: Brie H .8C **96**
WV10: Bush .8E **22**
Hillcrest Bus. Pk.
DY2: Neth .2J **97**
Hillcrest Cl. B79: Tam .3B **32**
DY2: Neth .4J **97**
Hillcrest Community Leisure Cen.
.4H **97**
Hill Crest Dr. WS13: Lich .8G **13**
Hillcrest Gdns. WV12: W'hall .4D **38**
Hillcrest Gro. B44: K'sdng .2A **80**
Hillcrest Ind. Est.
B64: Crad H .1K **117**
Hillcrest Pk. B47: Wyt .1M **191**
Hillcrest Ri. WS7: Burn .5H **17**
Hill Crest Rd. B13: Mose .7L **121**
Hillcrest Rd. B43: Gt Barr .7E **56**
B62: Roms .5A **140**
B72: W Grn .1J **81**
B78: Dord .2A **48**
CV10: Nun .3D **88**
DY2: Dud .8L **75**
Hillcroft Cvn. Pk. DY12: Bew .2A **156**
Hillcroft Ho. B14: K Hth .7M **143**
Hill Cft. Rd. B14: K Hth .3J **143**
Hillcroft Rd. DY6: K'wfrd .2L **95**
Hillcross Wlk. B36: Hodg H .1M **103**
Hilldene Rd. DY6: K'wfrd .5J **95**
Hillditch La. DY11: Hartl .7L **183**
Hilldrop Gro. B17: Harb .6D **120**
Hilleys Cft. B37: F'bri .6F **104**
Hill Farm Av. CV11: Nun .8B **90**
HILLFIELD .8B **146**
Hillfield M. B91: Sol .1B **168**
Hillfield Rd. B11: S'hll .6D **122**
B91: Sol .1B **168**
(not continuous)
CV22: Bil .8J **179**
HILLFIELDS .5E **152** (2F **6**)
Hillfields B67: Smeth .6K **99**
Hillfields Ho.
CV1: Cov .6E **152** (3F **6**)
Hillfields Rd. DY5: Brie H .2B **116**
Hillfield Wlk. B65: Row R .4M **97**
Hillfray Dr. CV3: Cov .4G **175**
Hill Gro. B20: Hand .7J **79**
Hill Gro. Cres. DY10: Kidd .4A **158**
Hillgrove Gdns. DY10: Kidd .5A **158**
HILL HOOK .4E **42**
Hill Hook Nature Reserve .4F **42**
Hill Hook Rd. B74: Four O .4E **42**
Hill Ho. La. B33: Stech .6M **103**
(not continuous)
Hillhurst Gro. B36: Cas B .8D **82**
Hillhurst Rd. B73: New O .6B **58**
Hilliard Cl. CV12: Bed .5G **111**
Hilliards Cft. B42: Gt Barr .1G **79**
Hillingford Av. B43: Gt Barr .6J **57**
Hill La. B43: Gt Barr .7E **56**
B47: Wyt .8J **165**
B48: A'chu .8J **165**
B60: B'gve .8M **187**
B60: Lwr B .8G **211**
B75: Bass P .7B **44**
DY9: Clent .5E **138**
WS7: C Ter .8E **10**
Hillman B77: Glas .7E **32**
Hillman Dr. DY2: Dud .2L **97**
Hillman Gro. B36: Cas B .8E **82**
Hillmeads Dr. DY2: Dud .2L **97**
Hillmeads Rd. B38: K Nor .8G **143**
HILLMORTON .1G **207**
Hillmorton B74: Four O .6F **42**
Hillmorton Cl. B98: Redd .3L **213**
Hillmorton La. CV23: Clift D .7G **181**
CV23: Lilb .4M **181**
Hill Morton Rd. B74: Four O .5F **42**
Hillmorton Rd. B93: Know .4G **169**
CV2: Cov .7J **131**
CV22: Rugby .7A **180**
Hillmount Cl. B28: Hall G .7E **122**
Hill Pk. WS9: Wals W .5G **27**
Hill Pas. B64: Old H .7L **97**
Hill Pl. WV11: Wed .8A **24**
HILLPOOL .4L **159**
Hillrise LE10: Burb .1M **91**
Hill Ri. Vw. B60: L End .3C **188**
Hill Rd. B69: Tiv .7A **76**
CV7: Ker E .3M **129**
WV13: W'hall .1K **53**
Hill Side B78: K'bry .5D **62**
Hillside B98: Redd .7D **212**
CV2: Cov .3G **153**
CV10: Harts .1A **88**
DY3: Lwr G .5C **74**
WS8: Bwnhls .3G **27**
WS14: Lich .3K **19**
WV5: Wom .2E **72**
Hillside Av. B63: Crad .3K **117**
B65: B'hth .1B **118**
DY5: Quar B .1G **117**
Hillside Cl. B32: Bart G .1G **141**
DY13: Stour S .7B **182**
WS7: Chase .4E **16**
WS8: Bwnhls .3G **27**
WS12: Hed .2G **9**
Hillside Ct. B43: Gt Barr .7D **56**
Hillside Cres. WS3: Pels .7M **25**
Hillside Cft. B92: Sol .5E **124**
Hillside Dr. B37: K'hrst .5F **104**
B42: Gt Barr .3G **79**
B61: L End .3B **188**
B74: S'tly .2M **57**
CV10: Nun .2C **88**
DY11: Kidd .2G **157**
Hillside Gdns. B37: K'hrst .5F **104**
WV1: Wolv .6G **37**
Hillside Gro. DY10: Cookl .6C **136**
Hillside Ho. B45: Rubery .1F **162**
Hillside Nth. CV2: Cov .3G **153**
Hillside Rd. B23: Erd .7D **80**
B43: Gt Barr .7D **56**
B74: Four O .5G **43**
DY1: Dud .4G **75**
LE10: Burb .3K **91**
Hillside Wlk. WV1: Wolv .6G **37**
Hills Pl. B61: B'gve .2K **209**
Hillstone Gdns. WV10: Bush .1F **36**
Hillstone Rd. B34: S End .4D **104**
Hill St. B2: Birm .7K **101** (5E **4**)
B5: Birm .7K **101** (5E **4**)
B63: Hale .6A **118**
B66: Smeth .3A **100**
CV1: Cov .6B **152** (4A **6**)
CV10: Nun .5D **88**
CV12: Bed .4H **111**
CV21: Rugby .5M **179**
CV32: Lea S .8A **218**
CV34: Warw .1H **223**
DY2: Neth .4H **97**
DY3: Up Gor .4D **74**
DY4: Tip .5M **75**
DY5: Brie H .7D **96**
DY5: Quar B .1G **117**
DY8: Amb .1M **115**
DY8: Stourb .5M **115**
DY9: Lye .4F **116**
DY11: Kidd .3K **157**
LE9: Barw .3B **70**
LE10: Hinc .1K **91**
WS1: Wals .8M **39**
WS6: C Hay .7C **14**
WS7: Chase .4E **16**
WS10: Darl .3E **54**
WS11: Nort C .3M **15**
WS12: Hed, Hth H .5J **9**
WV11: Ess .6M **23**
WV14: Bils .6L **53**
HILL TOP
Bromsgrove .8K **187**
Cannock .5J **9**
Coventry .8H **87**
West Bromwich .2G **77**
Hill Top B70: W Brom .1G **77**
B97: Redd .8M **211**
CV1: Cov .6D **152** (4D **6**)
CV9: Bad E .7B **48**
LE9: Earl S .1F **70**
Hilltop DY9: W'cte .6E **116**
Hill Top Av. B62: B'hth .2E **118**
B79: Tam .1B **32**
Hilltop Av. DY12: Bew .5D **156**
Hill Top Cl. B44: Gt Barr .3L **79**
Hilltop Cl. CV8: Fen E .1E **196**
CV47: Sou .4G **225**
Hill Top Dr. B36: Hodg H .2K **103**
Hill Top Ind. Est. B70: W Brom .1F **76**
(Bilport La.)
B70: W Brom .1E **76**
(Pikehelve St.)
Hilltop Pk. CV23: Prin .7F **202**
Hill Top Rd. B31: N'fld .6M **141**
B68: O'bry .7J **99**
Hilltop Rd. DY2: Dud .1L **97**
Hill Top Wlk. WS9: A'rdge .8J **27**
Hillview WS9: A'rdge .7H **27**
Hillview Cl. B60: L End .3C **188**
B63: Hale .3L **117**
Hillview Rd. B45: Rubery .1E **162**
B60: L End .3C **188**
Hill Village Rd. B75: Four O .4G **43**
Hillville Gdns. DY8: Stourb .6B **116**
HILL WOOD .5J **43**
Hillwood WS3: Pels .7M **25**
Hillwood Av. B90: M'path .3A **168**
Hillwood Cl. DY6: K'wfrd .5J **95**
Hillwood Comn. Rd.
B75: Four O .5H **43**
Hillwood Rd. B31: N'fld .2L **141**
B62: B'hth .2C **118**
B75: Four O, R'ley .5H **43**
Hill Wooton Rd.
CV32: B'dwn .3H **217**
HILL WOOTTON .3J **217**
Hill Wootton Rd.
CV35: Hill W, Leek W .3G **217**
Hillyard Rd. CV47: Sou .4G **225**
Hillyfields Rd. B23: Erd .5C **80**
Hilly Rd. WV14: Bils .7L **53**
Hilmore Way B77: Wiln .1E **46**
Hilsea Cl. WV8: Pend .8M **21**
Hilston Av. B63: Hale .5M **117**
WV4: Penn .5J **51**
HILTON .1A **28**
Hilton Av. B28: Hall G .5E **144**
CV10: Nun .3B **88**
Hilton Cl. WS3: Blox .7F **24**
Hilton Ct. CV5: Cov .7M **151**
Hilton Cross WV10: F'stne .4H **23**
Hilton Cross Bus. Pk.
WV10: F'stne .4H **23**
Hilton Dr. B72: W Grn .1J **81**
Hilton La. WS6: Gt Wyr .7F **14**
WV10: Share .1K **23**
WV11: Ess .1K **23**
Hilton Main Ind. Est.
WV10: F'stne .4J **23**
Hilton Pk. WV11: Ess .2L **23**
Hilton Pl. WV14: Bils .4M **53**
Hilton Rd. B69: Tiv .1C **98**
WS7: C Ter .1C **16**
WV4: E'shll .4F **52**
WV10: F'stne .2H **23**
WV12: W'hall .1C **38**
Hilton St. B70: W Brom .6G **77**
WV10: Wolv .6E **36** (1M **7**)
Hilton Trad. Est. WV4: E'shll .4F **52**
Hilton Way WV12: W'hall .1C **38**
Himbleton Cl. B98: Redd .8F **212**
Himbleton Cft. B90: M'path .2A **168**
HIMLEY .6H **73**
Himley Av. DY1: Dud .7F **74**
Himley By-Pass DY3: Himl .6G **73**
Himley Cl. B43: Gt Barr .7C **56**
WV12: W'hall .4B **38**
Himley Ct. *DY3: Lwr G .6E 74*
(off Peak Dr.)
Himley Cres. WV4: Penn .4B **52**
Himley Gdns. DY3: Lwr G .5M **73**
Himley Gro. B45: Redn .3H **163**
Himley House & Model Village
.6J **73**
Himley La. DY3: Himl, Swind .7E **72**
(not continuous)
Himley Ri. B90: Ches G .5L **167**
Himley Rd. CV12: Bed .7D **110**
DY1: Dud .7C **74**
DY3: Gorn .6M **73**
Himley St. DY1: Dud .8G **75**
Himley Wood Nature Reserve
.6G **73**
Hinbrook Rd. DY1: Dud .8E **74**
Hinchliffe Av. WV14: Cose .7H **53**
Hinckes Rd. WV6: Tett .4H **35**
HINCKLEY .1K **91**
Hinckley Bus. Pk.
LE10: Hinc .1E **90**
Hinckley Ct. B68: O'bry .2H **119**
Hinckley Greyhound Stadium .3F **90**
Hinckley La. CV13: High H .6B **68**
Hinckley Leisure Cen. .1J **91**
Hinckley Rd. CV2: W'grve S .2A **154**
CV7: Ansty .7C **132**
CV11: Burt H .1G **113**
CV11: Nun .4K **89**
CV13: Dad .1F **68**
CV13: Stoke G .2D **68**
LE9: Barw .3L **69**
LE9: Earl S .2C **70**
LE9: S Stan .8J **71**
LE9: Sap .1C **92**
LE9: Stap .1M **69**
LE10: Aston F .2C **92**
LE10: Burb .2A **92**
(Sapcote Rd.)
LE10: Burb, Wlvy .3L **113**
(Temple Hill)
Hinckley Station (Rail) .2K **91**
Hinckley St. B5: Birm .8K **101** (7F **4**)
Hincks St. WV2: E'shll .2G **53**
Hind Cl. CV34: Warw .7F **216**
Hinde Cl. CV21: Brow .2C **180**
Hindhead Rd. B14: Yard W .5C **144**
Hindlip Cl. B63: Hale .7M **117**
B98: Redd .5A **214**
Hindlow Cl. B7: Birm .5B **102** (2M **5**)
Hindon Gro. B27: A Grn .2J **145**
Hindon Sq. B15: Edg .1F **120**
Hindon Wlk. B32: Bart G .7J **119**
Hingeston St.
B18: Hock .5H **101** (1A **4**)
Hingley Cft. WS9: A'rdge .6M **41**
Hingley Ind. Pk. B64: Crad H .8J **97**
Hingley Rd. B63: Crad .3G **117**
Hingley St. B64: Crad H .8K **97**
Hinkley Concordia Theatre, The
.8K **69**
Hinkley United FC .6J **69**
HINKSFORD .1F **94**
Hinksford Gdns. DY3: Swind .7E **72**
Hinksford La. DY3: Swind .7E **72**
DY6: K'wfrd .7E **72**
Hinksford Pk. Res. Mobile Homes
DY6: K'wfrd .1E **94**
Hinsford Cl. DY6: K'wfrd .1L **95**
Hinstock Cl. WV4: Penn .5A **52**
Hinstock Rd. B20: Hand .8F **78**
Hintlesham Av. B15: Edg .4D **120**
Hinton Av. B48: A'chu .3A **190**
Hinton Flds. B61: B'hth .2L **187**
Hinton Gro. WV11: Wed .4M **37**
Hintons Coppice B93: Know .3E **168**
HINTS .7D **30**
Hints Ct. B78: Hints .7D **30**
HINTS HILL .6F **30**
Hints La. B78: Hints, Hop .6E **30**
(not continuous)
Hints Rd. B78: Hop .2H **31**
B78: M Oak .7F **30**
(not continuous)
Hipkins St. DY4: Tip .2L **75**
Hiplands Rd. B62: Hale .5F **118**
Hipsley Cl. B36: Cas B .8C **82**
Hipsley La. CV9: Bax, Hurl .4L **63**
Hipsmoor Cl. B37: K'hrst .6F **104**
Hipswell Highway CV2: Cov .5K **153**
Hirdemonsway B90: Dic H .4G **167**
Hiron, The CV3: Cov .1C **174**
Hiron Cft. CV3: Cov .1C **174**
Hiron Way CV34: Warw .2B **222**
Hirsel Gdns. CV32: Lea S .7M **217**
Hirst Cl. CV23: Long L .4G **179**
Histons Dr. WV8: Cod .7F **20**
Histons Hill WV8: Cod .7F **20**
Hitchcock Cl. B67: Smeth .4K **99**
Hitches La. B15: Edg .2H **121**
Hitchman Ct. CV31: Lea S .4A **224**
Hitchman M. CV31: Lea S .4A **224**
Hitchman Rd. CV31: Lea S .3A **224**
Hither Grn. La. B98: Redd .2F **212**
Hitherside B90: Dic H .4H **167**
Hive Development Cen.
B18: Hock .2G **101**
HMP Birmingham
B18: Win G .4E **100**
HMP Brockhill B97: Redd .1K **211**
HMP Brokenhurst B97: Redd .1K **211**
HMP Featherstone
WV10: F'stne .2F **22**
HMP Hewell Grange
B97: Redd .3K **211**
HMP Rye Hill CV23: W'hby .8D **206**
HM Young Offenders Institution
Brimsford WV10: B'frd .1E **22**
Onley CV23: W'hby .8C **206**
Hoarestone Av. CV11: Nun .2A **112**
Hoarstone DY8: Hag .4M **137**
Hoarstone Cl. DY12: Bew .4C **156**
Hoarstone La.
DY12: Bew, Trim .2C **156**
Hobacre Cl. B45: Rubery .1G **163**
Hobart Ct. B74: Four O .6G **43**
Hobart Cft. B7: Birm .5A **102** (1M **5**)
Hobart Dr. WS5: Wals .3C **56**
Hobart Rd. DY4: Tip .8L **53**
WS12: Hth H .7L **9**
Hobbis Ho. B38: K Nor .2C **164**
HOBBLE END .2G **25**
Hobble End La. WS6: Gt Wyr .3G **25**
Hobgate Cl. WV10: Wolv .5F **36**
Hobgate Rd. WV10: Wolv .5F **36**
Hobgoblin La. CV7: Fill .7F **108**
Hob Grn. Rd. DY9: W'cte .7E **116**
Hobhouse Cl. B42: Gt Barr .2F **78**
Hob La. B92: Bars .3A **170**
CV7: Bal C .4K **171**
CV8: Burt G .4K **171**
Hobley Cl. CV22: Bil .2K **205**
Hobley St. WV13: W'hall .7C **38**
Hobmoor Cft. B25: Yard .2K **123**
Hob Moor Rd. B10: Small H .8F **102**
B25: Yard .1J **123**
Hobnock Rd. WV11: Ess .5A **24**
HOBRO .3G **135**
Hobs Hole La. WS9: A'rdge .2H **41**
Hob's Mdw. B92: Olton .7A **124**
Hobs Moat Rd.
B92: Olton, Sol .7B **124**
Hobson Cl. B18: Hock .4G **101**
Hobson Rd. B29: S Oak .8H **121**
Hobs Rd. WS10: W'bry .5G **55**
WS13: Lich .8L **13**
HOBSTONE HILL .8A **12**
Hobstone Hill La. WS13: Lich .8L **11**
Hockett St. CV3: Cov .1D **174** (8E **6**)
Hocking Rd. CV2: Cov .4K **153**
HOCKLEY
Birmingham .4H **101**
Coventry .5C **150**
Tamworth .4F **46**
Hockley Brook La. DY9: Belb .5E **160**
Hockley Brook Trad. Est.
B18: Hock .3G **101**
Hockley Cen. *B18: Birm .1C 4*
(off Big Pen, The)
Hockley Cir. B19: Hock .3H **101**
Hockley Cl. B19: Hock .3K **101**
Hockley Ct. B94: H'ley H .2C **194**
Hockley Flyover B19: Hock .3H **101**
HOCKLEY HEATH .3C **194**
Hockley Hill B18: Birm .4H **101**
Hockley Hill Ind. Est.
B18: Hock .4H **101** (1A **4**)

Hood Gro.—Ilmington Dr.

Hood Gro. B30: K Nor 5D **142**
Hood La. CV10: Ansl 5F **86**
Hood St. CV1: Cov 6E **152** (4F **6**)
Hood's Way CV22: Bil 7K **179**
Hoo Farm Ind. Est.
DY11: Kidd 8M **157**
Hook Dr. B74: Four O 5F **42**
Hooke La. WS14: Foot 6C **28**
Hoopers La. B96: A'wd B 8E **220**
Hooper St. B18: Win G 5F **100**
Hoo Rd. DY10: Kidd 5L **157**
Hoosen Cl. B62: Quin 3G **119**
Hope Aldridge Bus. Cen.
CV10: Nun 3J **89**
Hope Cl. CV7: Ker E 2A **130**
Hopedale Cl. CV2: Cov 6L **153**
Hopedale Rd. B32: Quin 4J **119**
Hope Dr. WS11: Nort C 4B **16**
Hope Pl. B29: S Oak 7F **120**
Hope Rd. DY4: Tip 3C **76**
Hope St. B5: Birm 1K **121**
B62: B'hth 1D **118**
B70: W Brom 7L **77**
CV1: Cov 7B **152**
DY2: Dud 1J **97**
DY8: Word 6K **95**
WS1: Wals 1L **55**
Hope Ter. DY2: Neth 4J **97**
WS10: Darl 5D **54**
Hopgardens Av. B60: B'gve 7B **188**
Hopkins Ct. WS10: W'bry 6G **55**
Hopkins Dr. B71: W Brom 2L **77**
Hopkins Rd. CV6: Cov 5A **152**
Hopkins St. DY4: Tip 7A **76**
Hopley's Cl. B77: Amin 5E **32**
Hop Pole La. DY12: Bew 2A **156**
HOPSFORD 4J **133**
Hopstone Gdns. WV4: Penn 4M **51**
Hopstone Rd. B29: W Cas 8A **120**
Hopton Cl. CV5: E Grn 5G **151**
DY4: Tip 7C **54**
WV6: Pert 6F **34**
Hopton Cres. WV11: Wed 3L **37**
Hopton Crofts CV32: Lea S 7J **217**
Hopton Dr. DY10: Kidd 8L **157**
Hopton Gdns. DY1: Dud 6G **75**
Hopton Gro. B13: Mose 4C **144**
Hopton Mdw. WS12: Hth H 8J **9**
HOPWAS 2H **31**
Hopwas Gro. B37: K'hrst 4F **104**
Hopwas Hill B78: Hop 3G **31**
HOPWOOD 6C **164**
Hopwood Cl. B63: Hale 7A **118**
Hopwood Gro. B31: Longb 3L **163**
Hopyard Cl. DY3: Gorn 6B **74**
Hopyard Gdns. WV14: Cose 6H **53**
Hopyard La. B98: Redd 6K **213**
DY3: Gorn 7B **74**
Hopyard Rd. WS2: Wals 7E **38**
Horace Partridge Rd.
WS10: Mox 4A **54**
Horace St. WV14: Cose 1G **75**
Horatio Dr. B13: Mose 5M **121**
Hordern Cl. WV6: Wolv 4M **35**
Hordern Cres. DY5: Quar B 1D **116**
Hordern Gro. WV6: Wolv 4M **35**
Hordern Pk. WV10: Cov H 3C **22**
Hordern Rd. WV6: Wolv 4M **35**
HORESTON GRANGE 4L **89**
Horeston Grange Shop. Cen.
CV11: Nun 4A **90**
Hornbeam B77: Amin 5G **33**
Hornbeam Cl. B29: W Cas 2B **142**
DY12: Bew 2A **156**
Hornbeam Cres. WS12: Haz 3A **10**
Hornbeam Dr. CV4: Tile H 8D **150**
Hornbeam Gro. CV31: Lea S 3C **224**
Hornbeam Ho. DY12: Bew 2A **156**
Hornbeam Wlk. WV3: Wolv 8A **36**
Hornbrook Gro. B92: Olton 2J **145**
Hornby Gro. B14: Yard W 5C **144**
Hornby Rd. WV4: Penn 5C **52**
Hornchurch Cl.
CV1: Cov 8C **152** (8C **6**)
Hornchurch Cl. Ind. Est.
CV1: Cov 8C **152** (8C **6**)
Horndean Cl. CV6: Cov 1E **152**
Horne Cl. CV21: Hillm 1H **207**
Horner Way B65: B'hth 8C **98**
Horne Way B34: S End 4E **104**
HORNGROVE 1A **184**
Horning Dr. WV14: Bils 6J **53**
Horninghold Cl. CV3: Bin 1L **175**
Hornsey Cl. CV2: Cov 2L **153**
Hornsey Gro. B44: K'sdng 7A **58**
Hornsey Rd. B44: K'sdng 7A **58**
Hornton Cl. B74: Lit A 4D **42**
Horobins Yd. CV12: Bed 4H **111**
Horrell Rd. B26: Sheld 2A **124**
B90: Shir 7F **144**
Horse Bri. La. DY7: Kinv 7C **114**
Horsecroft Dr. *B71: W Brom* *1A 78*
(off Tompstone Rd.)
Horse Fair B5: Birm 8K **101** (7F **4**)
DY10: Kidd 2L **157**
Horsefair, The LE10: Hinc 1K **91**
Horsehills Dr. WV3: Wolv 7L **35**
Horselea Cft. B8: W End 5J **103**
Horseley Flds.
WV1: Wolv 7D **36** (4L **7**)
HORSELEY HEATH 3C **76**
Horseley Heath DY4: Tip 5B **76**
Horseley Hill DY11: W'ley 4F **134**
Horseley Rd. DY4: Tip 3C **76**
Horsepool LE10: Burb 4A **92**
Horsepool Hollow
CV31: Lea S 4C **224**
Horseshoe, The B68: O'bry 7J **99**
Horseshoe Cl. *WS2: Wals* *2H 55*
(off Wellington St.)
Horseshoe Dr. WS12: Wim 5M **9**
Horse Shoe Rd. CV6: Longf . . .5G **131**
Horse Shoes La. B26: Sheld 4B **124**
Horseshoe Wlk. *DY4: Tip* *4L 75*
(off New Cross St.)
Horsewell CV47: Sou 5H **225**
Horsey La. WS15: Longd 1J **11**
Horsfall Rd. B75: S Cold 4A **60**
Horsford Rd. CV3: Cov 3D **174**
Horsham Av. DY8: Word 6J **95**
Horsley La. WS14: C'fld 1D **28**
Horsley Rd. B43: Gt Barr 5K **57**
B74: Lit A 7B **42**
Horton Cl. CV7: Exh 2F **130**
DY3: Sed 1C **74**
WS10: Darl 2D **54**
WS11: Cann 5F **8**
Horton Cres. CV22: Rugby 7A **180**
Horton Gro. B90: M'path 4A **168**
Horton Pl. WS10: Darl 2D **54**
Horton Rd. DY7: Kinv 4A **114**
Horton Sq. B12: Birm 2L **121**
Horton St. B70: W Brom 7J **77**
DY4: Tip 4D **76**
WS10: Darl 2D **54**
Hosiery St. CV12: Bed 7J **111**
Hoskyn Cl. CV21: Hillm 1F **206**
Hospital Dr. B15: Edg 5E **120**
Hospital La. B69: Tiv 7B **76**
CV12: Bed 7B **110**
WS6: C Hay 6B **14**
WV14: Cose 2H **75**
Hospital Rd. WS7: Burn 5G **17**
Hospital St.
B19: Birm, Hock . . .4K **101** (1F **4**)
(not continuous)
B79: Tam 4B **32**
WS2: Wals 5K **39**
WV2: Wolv 8D **36** (6L **7**)
Hossil La.
DY9: Belb, Brme, Clent . . .2B **160**
Hotchkiss Way CV3: Bin 2A **176**
Hothersall Dr. B73: Bold 1F **80**
Hothorpe Cl. CV3: Bin 8M **153**
Hotspur Rd. B44: K'sdng 8M **57**
Hough Pl. WS2: Wals 2H **55**
Hough Rd. B14: K Hth 3K **143**
WS2: Wals 2G **55**
Houghton Ct. B28: Hall G 5D **144**
Houghton St. B69: O'bry 3F **98**
B70: W Brom 1K **99**
Houlbrooke Ho. WS13: Lich 1J **19**
Houldey Rd. B31: N'fld 8B **142**
Houldsworth Cres. CV6: Cov . . .5C **130**
Houliston Cl. WS10: W'bry 4H **55**
Houndsfield Cl. B47: H'wd 3C **166**
Houndsfield Ct. B47: Wyt 4A **166**
Houndsfield Gro. B47: Wyt 4A **166**
(not continuous)
Houndsfield La. B47: H'wd 3C **166**
B47: Wyt 4A **166**
B90: Dic H 3C **166**
Houndsfield M. B47: Wyt 4B **166**
Housman Cl. B60: B'gve 1L **209**
Housman Ct. *B60: B'gve* *7A 188*
(off Housman Pk.)
Housman Pk. B60: B'gve 7A **188**
Housman Wlk. DY10: Kidd 3C **158**
Houston Rd. CV21: Rugby 3C **180**
Houting B77: Dost 4D **46**
Houx, The DY8: Amb 1L **115**
Hove Av. CV5: E Grn 5E **150**
Hovelands Cl. CV2: Cov 1J **153**
Hove Rd. B27: A Grn 8J **123**
Hoveton Cl. B98: Redd 8H **213**
Howard Av. B61: B'gve 6L **187**
Howard Cl. CV5: E Grn 5E **150**
CV22: Dunc 5K **205**
LE9: Barw 2A **70**
Howard Cres. WS12: Hed 2J **9**
Howard Ho. B92: H Ard 3B **148**
Howard Rd. B14: K Hth 2K **143**
B20: Hand 7H **79**
B25: Yard 2J **123**
B43: Gt Barr 1C **78**
B92: Olton 6L **123**
B98: Redd 1H **221**
CV10: Nun 6G **89**
WV11: Wed 1M **37**
WV14: Bils 6M **53**
Howard Rd. E. B13: Mose 2M **143**
Howard St. B19: Birm . . .5K **101** (1E **4**)
B70: W Brom 2F **76**
CV1: Cov 5D **152** (1D **6**)
DY4: Tip 4B **76**
WV2: Wolv 1D **52** (7K **7**)
Howard St. Ind. Est.
B70: W Brom 2F **76**
Howard Wlk. CV34: Warw 3K **223**
Howarth Way B6: Aston 2A **102**
Howat Rd. CV7: Ker E 2M **129**
Howcotte Grn. CV4: Tile H 2E **172**
Howden Pl. B33: Stech 4A **104**
Howdle's La. WS8: Bwnhls 7F **16**
Howe Cl. LE9: S Stan 8J **71**
Howe Cres. WV12: W'hall 3C **38**
HOWE GREEN 4K **109**
Howe Grn. La. CV7: Cor 5K **109**
CV10: Asty 5K **109**
Howell Rd. WV2: Wolv 2E **52**
Howells Cl. CV12: Bed 8D **110**
Howes Cft. B35: Cas V 7A **82**
Howes La. CV3: Finh 7C **174**
Howe St. B4: Birm 6M **101** (3K **5**)
Howford Gro. B7: Birm 5B **102**
Howkins Rd. CV21: Rugby 3C **180**
Howland Cl. WV9: Pend 7M **21**
Howlette Rd. CV4: Tile H 7E **150**
Howley Av. B44: Gt Barr 8L **57**
Howley Grange Rd.
B62: Quin 4F **118**
Howl Pl. DY4: Tip 4M **75**
Hoylake B77: Amin 5H **33**
Hoylake Cl. CV11: Nun 8B **90**
WS3: Blox 6H **25**
Hoylake Dr. B69: Tiv 2A **98**
Hoylake Rd. WV6: Pert 4D **34**
Hoyland Way B30: B'vlle 1E **142**
HRS Ind. Pk. B33: Sheld 8C **104**
Huband Cl. B98: Redd 4G **213**
Hubert Cft. B29: S Oak 7F **120**
Hubert Rd. B29: S Oak 7F **120**
Hubert St. B6: Aston 4M **101**
Hucker Cl. WS2: Wals 2G **55**
Hucker Rd. WS2: Wals 2G **55**
Huddesford Dr. CV7: Bal C 1J **171**
Huddisdon Cl. CV34: Warw 8F **216**
Huddlestone Cl. WV10: F'stne . . .3H **23**
Huddleston Way B29: S Oak . . .8C **120**
Huddocks Vw. WS3: Pels 4M **25**
Hudson Av. B46: Col 3M **105**
Hudson Cl. WS11: Hth H 7H **9**
Hudson Dr. WS7: Burn 3J **17**
Hudson Gro. WV6: Pert 4E **34**
Hudson Rd. B20: Hand 5F **78**
CV22: Bil 8L **179**
DY4: Tip 5C **76**
Hudson's Dr. B30: K Nor 5G **143**
Hudswell Dr. DY5: Brie H 1D **116**
Huggins Cl. CV7: Bal C 2J **171**
Hughes, The CV34: Warw 3E **222**
Hughes Av. WV3: Wolv 1M **51**
Hughes Cl. CV31: W'nsh 7A **224**
CV34: Warw 7D **216**
Hughes Pl. WV14: Bils 2K **53**
Hughes Rd. WS10: Mox 4A **54**
WV14: Bils 2K **53**
Hugh Gaitskell Ct.
WV14: Wolv 1J **53**
Hugh Porter Way WV6: Tett 2M **35**
Hugh Rd. B10: Small H 8E **102**
B67: Smeth 4K **99**
CV3: Cov 7G **153**
Hugh Vs. B10: Small H 8E **102**
Huins Cl. B98: Redd 5G **213**
Hulbert Dr. DY2: Dud 3H **97**
Hulland Pl. DY5: Brie H 6C **96**
Hullbrook Rd. B13: Mose 4C **144**
Hulme Cl. CV3: Bin 8B **154**
Humber Av. B76: Walm 2A **82**
CV1: Cov 8E **152**
CV3: Cov 8F **152**
Humber Gdns. B63: Crad 4J **117**
Humber Gro. B36: Cas B 8F **82**
Humber Rd. CV3: Cov 8F **152**
WV3: Wolv 8A **36**
Humberstone Rd. B24: Erd 5L **81**
CV6: Cov 4A **152**
Humber Twr.
B7: Birm 5A **102** (1M **5**)
Hume St. B66: Smeth 5B **100**
(not continuous)
DY11: Kidd 4J **157**
Humpage Rd. B9: Bord G 7E **102**
Humphrey Av. B60: B'gve 2L **209**
Humphrey Burton's Rd.
CV3: Cov 1C **174**
Humphrey-Davy Rd.
CV12: Bed 1D **130**
Humphrey Middlemore Dr.
B17: Harb 5D **120**
Humphrey's Rd. WV10: Bush . . .2D **36**
Humphrey St. DY3: Lwr G 6D **74**
Humphries Cres. WV14: Bils 8M **53**
Humphries Dr. DY10: Kidd 7M **157**
Humphries Ho. WS8: Bwnhls 2F **26**
Humphris St. CV34: Warw 1H **223**
Huncote Rd. LE9: S Stan 6K **71**
Hundred Acre Rd. B74: S'tly . . .2M **57**
Hungary Cl. DY9: Lye 4C **116**
Hungary Hill DY9: Lye 4C **116**
Hungerfield Rd. B36: Cas B 8C **82**
Hungerford Rd. DY8: Stourb . . .7L **115**
Hunger Hill B95: Hen A 8M **215**
Hungry La. WS14: W'frd 5M **29**
HUNNINGHAM 4L **219**
Hunningham Gro. B91: Sol 1B **168**
Hunningham Rd.
CV33: H'ham, W Weth . . .2K **219**
CV33: Off 8J **219**
HUNNINGTON 2B **140**
Hunnington Cl. B32: Bart G 8G **119**
Hunnington Cres. B63: Hale . . .7B **118**
Hunscote Cl. B90: Shir 8F **144**
Hunslet Cl. B32: Quin 5M **119**
Hunslet Rd. B32: Quin 5M **119**
WS7: Burn 1H **17**
Hunstanton Av. B17: Harb 2M **119**
Hunstanton Cl. DY5: Brie H 2C **116**
HUNT END 4C **220**
Hunt End Ind. Est.
B97: Redd 4C **220**
Hunt End La. B97: Redd 4C **220**
Hunter Av. WS7: Burn 2H **17**
Hunter Cl. WS14: Lich 3K **19**
Hunter Ct. B5: Edg 4K **121**
Hunter Cres. WS3: Blox 3M **39**
Hunter Rd. WS11: Cann 1E **14**
Hunters Cl. CV3: Bin 7A **154**
WV14: Bils 2A **54**
Hunters Ct. *B98: Redd* *7G 213*
(off Shakespeare Av.)
Hunters La. CV13: Fen D 3G **67**
CV21: Rugby 4A **180**
Hunters La. Ind. Est.
CV21: Rugby 4A **180**
Hunters Pk. CV9: Bad E 8C **48**
Hunters Ride DY7: Stourt 7H **95**
Hunters Ri. B63: Hale 8K **117**
Hunter's Rd. B19: Hock 2H **101**
Hunter St. CV21: Rugby 5C **180**
WV6: Wolv 5A **36**
Hunters Wlk. B23: Erd 1C **80**
CV9: With 2B **66**
Hunter Ter. CV5: Cov 1K **173**
Huntingdon Cl. B78: Tam 7M **31**
Huntingdon Ho. B23: Erd 3B **80**
Huntingdon Rd. B71: W Brom . . .3H **77**
CV5: Cov 8A **152**
Huntingdon Way CV10: Nun 6E **88**
HUNTINGTON 2C **8**
Huntington Belt WS12: Hunt 3D **8**
Huntington Cl. B98: Redd 7L **213**
Huntington Rd. WV12: W'hall . . .2D **38**
Huntington Ter. Rd.
WS11: Cann 5F **8**
Huntingtree Rd. B63: Hale 5L **117**
Huntlands Rd. B63: Hale 7L **117**
Hunt La. CV9: With 2B **66**
Huntley Dr. B91: Sol 7B **146**
Huntly Rd. B16: Edg 8G **101**
Hunton Ct. *B23: Erd* *7E 80*
(off Gravelly Hill N.)
Hunton Hill B23: Erd 6D **80**
Hunton Rd. B23: Erd 6E **80**
Hunt Paddocks CV8: Ken 8E **198**
HUNTS GREEN 2J **61**
Hunt's La. WV12: W'hall 3D **38**
Huntsman Cl. WV14: Cose 7K **53**
Huntsmans Dr. DY7: Kinv 3A **114**
Huntsmans Ga. WS7: Burn 1H **17**
Huntsmans Ri. WS12: Hunt 1C **8**
Huntsmans Wlk. DY7: Kinv 3A **114**
Hunts Mill Dr. DY5: P'ntt 8C **74**
Hunts Ri. DY12: Bew 6C **156**
Hunt's Rd. B30: Stir 2G **143**
Hunt Ter. CV4: Canly 2H **173**
HURCOTT 1C **158**
Hurcott Ct. DY10: Kidd 2M **157**
Hurcott La. DY10: Hurc 1C **158**
Hurcott Rd. DY10: Kidd 2L **157**
Hurcott Village DY10: Hurc 1C **158**
Hurdis Rd. B90: Shir 6G **145**
Hurdlow Av. B18: Hock 4H **101**
Hurlbutt Rd. CV34: H'cte 5J **223**
HURLEY 5J **63**
Hurley Cl. B72: W Grn 7J **59**
CV32: Lea S 7A **218**
WS5: Wals 3D **56**
HURLEY COMMON 2J **63**
Hurley Comn. CV9: Hurl 4H **63**
Hurley Gro. B37: K'hrst 4F **104**
Hurley La. B46: Over W 3K **85**
CV9: Hurl 7E **62**
Hurley's Fold DY2: Neth 4H **97**
Hurlingham Rd. B44: K'sdng 7A **58**
Hurn Way CV6: Ald G 5H **131**
Huron Cl. WS11: Hth H 7H **9**
Hurricane Pk. B24: Erd 1G **103**
Hurricane Way B35: Cas V 7A **82**
Hursey Dr. DY4: Tip 4A **76**
Hurst, The B13: Mose 2C **144**
B47: H'wd 3A **166**
Hurstbourne Cres.
WV1: Wolv 8H **37**
Hurst Cl. B36: Cas B 2E **104**
Hurstcroft Rd. B33: Kitts G 6B **104**
Hurst Grn. Rd. B62: B'hth 8E **98**
B76: Min 3D **82**
B93: Ben H 5F **168**
Hurst Grn. Shop. Cen.
B62: B'hth 1F **118**
HURST HILL 1G **75**
Hurst Hill Ct. *WV14: Cose* *1G 75*
(off Caddick St.)
WV14: Cose 1G **75**
(Hartland Av.)
Hurst La. B34: S End 3D **104**
DY4: Tip 4K **75**
DY5: Brie H 6F **96**
Hurst La. Nth. B36: Cas B 2E **104**
Hurst Rd. B67: Smeth 6K **99**
CV6: Longf 5G **131**
(not continuous)
Hurst Rd. CV12: Bed 6H **111**
CV47: Sou 6G **225**
LE9: Earl S 2E **70**
LE10: Hinc 1K **91**
WV14: Cose 8G **53**
Hurst St. B5: Birm 8L **101** (7G **5**)
(not continuous)
Hurst Wlk. CV6: Longf 5G **131**
Hurstway, The B23: Erd 1C **80**
Hurstwood Rd. B23: Erd 1C **80**
Huskison Cl. B69: Tiv 8B **76**
Husphins La.
WV8: Cod, Cod W 4A **20**
Hussey Rd. WS8: Bwnhls 1E **26**
WS11: Nort C 4M **15**
Husum Way DY10: Kidd 2C **158**
Hutchings La. B90: Dic H 4H **167**
Hut Hill La. WS6: Gt Wyr 5G **15**
Hutton Av. B8: Salt 4D **102**
Hutton Rd. B8: Salt 4D **102**
B20: Hand 8H **79**
Huxbey Dr. B92: Sol 1F **146**
Huxley Cl. WV9: Pend 6A **22**
Hyacinth Cl. WS5: Wals 6M **55**
Hyacinth Way LE10: Burb 4K **91**
Hyatt Sq. DY5: Brie H 2C **116**
Hyatts Wlk. B65: Row R 4M **97**
Hyde, The DY9: W'cte 7D **116**
Hyde Cl. B60: B'gve 7B **188**
DY7: Kinv 4A **114**
Hyde La. DY7: Kinv 4A **114**
Hyde Pl. CV32: Lea S 1L **223**
Hyde Rd. CV2: Cov 5L **153**
CV8: Ken 4F **198**
WV11: Wed 3K **37**
Hydes La. LE10: Hinc 5E **90**
Hydes Rd. B71: W Brom 8J **55**
WS10: W'bry 6G **55**
Hyett Way WV14: Bils 7B **54**
Hylda Rd. B20: Hand 8H **79**
Hylstone Cres. WV11: Wed 3K **37**
Hylton St. B18: Birm 4J **101** (1B **4**)
Hypericum Gdns. CV2: Cov 5J **153**
Hyperion Dr. WV4: Penn 6A **52**
Hyperion Rd. B36: Hodg H 8L **81**
DY7: Stourt 2J **115**
Hyron Hall Rd. B27: A Grn 7J **123**
Hyssop Cl. B7: Birm 4A **102**
WS11: Hth H 7H **9**
Hytall Rd. B90: Shir 7C **144**
Hythe Gro. B25: Yard 1K **123**

I

Iago Way CV34: H'cte 6K **223**
Ibberton Rd. B14: K Hth 6B **144**
Ibex Cl. CV3: Bin 8M **153**
Ibis Cl. DY10: Kidd 6B **158**
Ibis Gdns. DY6: K'wfrd 3A **96**
Ibstock Cl. B98: Redd 5L **213**
Ibstock Dr. DY8: Stourb 5A **116**
Ibstock Ho. B98: Redd 5L **213**
Ibstock Rd. CV6: Longf 4G **131**
Icknield Cl. B74: S'tly 8A **42**
Icknield Port Rd. B16: Birm 5E **100**
Icknield St B98: Beo 2J **213**
Icknield Sq. B16: Birm 6G **101**
Icknield St.
B18: Birm 5H **101** (3A **4**)
(not continuous)
B38: Forh 6G **165**
B38: Head H, K Nor 1G **165**
B48: A'chu 1H **191**
B98: Beo 6H **191**
B98: Redd 7K **213**
Icknield St. Dr. B98: Redd 7K **213**
Ida Rd. B70: W Brom 8K **77**
WS2: Wals 8H **39**
Idbury Rd. B44: K'sdng 2A **80**
Ideal Bldgs. DY11: Kidd 3K **157**
Ideal Works DY9: Lye 3G **117**
Iden Rd. CV1: Cov 5E **152**
Idmiston Cft. B14: K Hth 7M **143**
Idonia Rd. WV6: Pert 4E **34**
Ikon Gallery 7J **101** (6C **4**)
Ikon Trad. Est. DY10: Hartl 3D **184**
Ilam Pk. CV8: Ken 4J **199**
Ilex Ct. CV34: Warw 2G **223**
Ilford Cl. CV12: Bed 6G **111**
Ilford Ct. CV3: Bin W 2D **176**
Ilford Dr. CV3: Cov 3B **174**
Ilford Rd. B23: Erd 3D **80**
Ilfracombe Gro. CV3: Finh 4A **174**
Iliffe Way B17: Harb 5D **120**
Ilkley Gro. B37: F'bri 7F **104**
ILLEY 1E **140**
Illeybrook Sq. B32: Bart G 7K **119**
Illey Cl. B31: Longb 8H **141**
Illey La. B32: Fran 1E **140**
B62: Hunn 8C **118**
Illshaw WV9: Pend 6B **22**
Illshaw Cl. B98: Redd 5A **214**
ILLSHAW HEATH 8L **167**
Illshaw Heath Rd.
B94: H'ley H 6K **167**
Illshaw Path B90: Bly P 6M **167**
Ilmer Cl. CV21: Brow 2E **180**
Ilmington Cl. B98: Redd 8K **213**
CV3: Cov 4B **174**
Ilmington Dr. B73: New O 6C **58**

Ilmington Rd.—Johnson Av.

Ilmington Rd. B29: W Cas 8M 119
Ilminster Cl. LE10: Burb 2B 92
Ilsham Gro. B31: Longb 3L 163
Ilsley Rd. B23: Erd 5E 80
Imax Theatre 6M 101 (3K 5)
Imber Rd. DY10: Kidd 8A 158
Imex Bus. Cen. B98: Redd 5L 213
I-MEX Bus. Pk. B11: Tys 3F 122
Imex Bus. Pk. B9: Bord G 7D 102
B33: Stech 5L 103
DY4: Tip 6A 76
WV2: Wolv 2C 52
Imogen Gdns. CV34: H'cte 6L 223
Imperial Av. DY10: Kidd 1M 157
Imperial Gro. DY10: Kidd 1M 157
Imperial Ri. B46: Col 7L 83
Imperial Rd. B9: Bord G 7E 102
Impey Rd. B31: N'fld 8M 141
Impney Cl. B98: Redd 3K 213
Impsley Cl. B36: Cas B 1B 104
Inca Cl. CV3: Bin 1M 175
Ince Rd. WS10: Darl 2C 54
Inchbrook Rd. CV8: Ken 2J 199
Inchcape Av. B20: Hand 6G 79
Inchcape Cl. CV22: Caw 1H 205
Inchford Av. CV34: Warw 7E 216
Inchford Cl. CV11: Nun 8M 89
Inchford Rd. B92: Sol 2E 146
Inchlaggan Rd. WV10: Wolv 3F 36
Independent St. CV23: Kils 6M 207
Infantry Pl. B75: S Cold 3A 60
Ingatestone Dr. DY8: Word 6J 95
Ingestre Cl. WS3: Blox 6F 24
WS11: Hth H 8H 9
Ingestre Dr. B43: Gt Barr 8D 56
Inge St. B5: Birm 8L 101 (8F 4)
Ingestre Rd. B28: Hall G 2F 144
WV10: Oxl 8C 22
Ingeva Dr. B45: B Grn 8G 163
Ingham Way B17: Harb 1A 120
Ingleby Gdns. WV6: Wolv 4M 35
Ingle Ct. CV31: Lea S 2L 223
Ingledew Cl. WS2: Wals 6D 38
Inglefield Rd. B33: Stech 6M 103
Inglemere Gro. B29: W Cas . . .2M 141
Inglenook Dr. B20: Hand 7H 79
Ingleside Vs. B11: S'hll 4C 122
(off Warwick Rd.)
Ingleton Cl. CV11: Nun 7A 90
Ingleton Rd. B8: W End 2G 103
Inglewood Av. WV3: Wolv 1M 51
Inglewood Cl. CV32: Lill 6A 218
DY6: K'wfrd 4K 95
Inglewood Gro. B74: S'tly 7M 41
Inglewood Rd. B11: S'hll 4C 122
Ingoldsby Ct. B13: Mose 7B 122
Ingoldsby Rd. B31: N'fld 5C 142
Ingot Cl. WS2: Wals 3H 39
Ingram Cres. DY12: Bew 5A 156
Ingram Gro. B27: A Grn 7G 123
Ingram Pit La. B77: Amin 4G 33
Ingram Pl. WS3: Blox 8K 25
Ingram Rd. CV5: Cov 1K 173
WS3: Blox 8J 25
Inhedge, The DY1: Dud 8J 75
Inhedge St. DY3: Up Gor 4E 74
Inkberrow Cl. B69: O'bry 5E 98
Inkberrow Rd. B63: Hale 7M 117
Inkerman Gro. WV10: Wolv 7F 36
Inkerman Ho. B19: Hock 3L 101
(off Newtown Shop. Cen.)
Inkerman St. WV10: Wolv 6F 36
INKFORD 8M 165
Inland Rd. B24: Erd 7H 81
Innage, The B47: H'wd 4A 166
Innage Cl. CV31: Lea S 1A 224
Innage Pk. CV9: Ath 8J 49
Innage Rd. B31: N'fld 5B 142
Innage Ter. CV9: Ath 1K 65
Innisfree Cl. B47: Wyt 5C 166
Innis Rd. CV5: Cov 1L 173
Inn La. DY11: Hartl 7A 184
Innsworth Dr. B35: Cas V 5A 82
Insetton Cl. B98: Redd 5K 213
Inshaw Cl. B33: Stech 6L 103
Institute Rd. B14: K Hth 1M 143
Instone Rd. B63: Hale 6M 117
CV6: Cov 8A 130
Instow Cl. WV12: W'hall 1B 38
Insull Av. B14: K Hth 8B 144
Intended St. B63: Crad 2J 117
International Ho.
B37: Mars G 4K 125
CV4: Canly 5H 173
International Sq.
B37: Mars G 3J 125
Intown WS1: Wals 7M 39
Intown Row WS1: Wals 7M 39
Inverary Cl. CV8: Ken 5J 199
Inverclyde Rd. B20: Hand 6G 79
Inverness Cl. CV5: E Grn 5G 151
Inverness Ho.
WV1: Wolv 6C 36 (1H 7)
Inverness Rd. B31: N'fld 6L 141
Invicta Rd. CV3: Bin 1M 175
Inworth WV9: Pend 6B 22
IO Cen., The B98: Redd 8J 213
IPSLEY 7K 213
Ipsley Alders Marsh Nature Reserve
. . . . .5M 213
Ipsley Chu. La. B98: Redd 7J 213
Ipsley Gro. B23: Erd 4A 80
Ipsley La. B98: Redd 7K 213
Ipsley St. B98: Redd 6E 212
Ipstones Av. B33: Stech 5M 103
Ipswich Cres. B42: Gt Barr 2H 79
Ipswich Wlk. B37: Chel W 7H 105
Ireland Grn. Rd.
B70: W Brom 7H 77
Ireton Cl. CV4: Tile H 8C 150
Ireton Rd. B20: Hand 5G 79
WV10: Bush 6E 22
Iris Cl. B29: W Cas 1B 142
B79: Tam 3C 32
DY2: Dud 8M 75
LE10: Burb 4L 91
Iris Dr. B14: K Hth 5K 143
Irnham Rd. B74: Four O 7G 43
Iron Bri. Wlk. DY9: Pedm 1B 138
Ironbridge Way CV6: Longf 3H 131
Iron La. B33: Stech 5K 103
Ironmonger Row
CV1: Cov 6C 152 (4C 6)
Ironside Cl. DY12: Bew 2B 156
Ironstone Rd. WS7: C Ter 8D 10
WS12: Haz 6C 10
(not continuous)
Irvan Av. B70: W Brom 4F 76
Irvine Cl. WS3: Blox 2H 39
Irvine Rd. WS3: Blox 1H 39
Irving Cl. DY3: Lwr G 5A 74
WS13: Lich 7E 12
Irving Rd. B92: Sol 5E 124
CV1: Cov 7E 152
WV14: Bils 8A 54
Irving St. B1: Birm 8K 101 (8E 4)
Irwell B77: Wiln 8E 32
Irwin Av. B45: Redn 3J 163
Isaac Walton Pl. B70: W Brom . . .2E 76
Isambard Dr. CV6: Longf 4F 130
Isbourne Way B9: Birm 7B 102
Isis Gro. B36: Cas B 1F 104
WV13: W'hall 7C 38
Island, The B78: M Oak 8J 31
Island Cl. LE10: Hinc 7L 69
Island Dr. DY10: Kidd 5L 157
ISLANDPOOL 4C 136
Island Rd. B21: Hand 8C 78
Islington B63: Hale 5A 118
Islington Row Middleway
B15: Birm 8H 101 (8A 4)
Ismere Rd. B24: Erd 7H 81
Ismere Way DY10: Kidd 8M 135
ISMRERE 5F 136
Itchen Gro. WV6: Pert 6E 34
Ithon Gro. B38: K Nor 1E 164
Ivanhoe Av. CV11: Nun 8L 89
Ivanhoe Rd. B43: Gt Barr 6H 57
WS14: Lich 3H 19
WV2: E'shll 3G 53
Ivanhoe St. DY2: Dud 2G 97
Ivatt B77: Glas 7F 32
Ivatt Cl. WS4: Rus 2B 40
IVERLEY 1K 137
Iverley La. DY8: I'ley 5J 137
Iverley Rd. B63: Hale 5C 118
Iverley Wlk. DY9: Pedm 7C 116
Ivor Rd. B11: S'hll 5B 122
B97: Redd 7D 212
CV6: Cov 7F 130
CV9: Ath 2M 65
Ivy Av. B12: Bal H 4A 122
(Clifton Rd.)
B12: Bal H 4A 122
(Runcorn Rd.)
Ivybridge Gro. B42: P Barr 6J 79
Ivybridge Rd. CV3: Cov 3D 174
Ivy Cl. CV13: Stoke G 2D 68
WS8: Wals W 5G 27
WS11: Cann 1D 14
Ivy Cft. WV9: Pend 6M 21
Ivydale Av. B26: Sheld 4C 124
Ivydene Cl. LE9: Earl S 1F 70
Ivy Farm La. CV4: Canly 3K 173
Ivyfield Rd. B23: Erd 4B 80
Ivy Gdns. WS11: Nort C 4A 16
Ivy Gro. B18: Win G 5E 100
(off Heath Grn. Rd.)
CV10: Nun 3D 88
Ivyhouse La. WV14: Cose 1H 75
Ivy Ho. Rd. B69: O'bry 3D 98
Ivyhouse Rd. B38: K Nor 1C 164
Ivyhouse Wlk. B77: Wiln 3F 46
Ivy La. B62: Roms 4K 139
WS15: Cann W 4F 10
Ivy Lodge Cl. B37: Mars G 2G 125
Ivy Pl. B29: S Oak 7F 120
Ivy Rd. B21: Hand 2G 101
B30: Stir 3G 143
B73: Bold 7F 58
DY1: Dud 5G 75
DY4: Tip 2G 77
Ivy Way B90: Dic H 3G 167
Izons Ind. Est. B70: W Brom 8F 76
Izons La. B70: W Brom 8F 76
Izons Rd. B70: W Brom 6J 77

J

Jacey Rd. B16: Edg 7D 100
B90: Shir 5H 145
Jack Ball Ho.
CV2: W'grve S 8M 131
Jack David Ho. DY4: Tip 4D 76
Jackdaw Cl. DY3: Sed 7C 52
Jackdaw Dr. B36: Cas B 1G 105
Jacker's Rd. CV2: Ald G 5H 131
Jackfield Cl. B98: Redd 8L 213
Jack Hayward Way
WV1: Wolv 6C 36 (1H 7)
Jack Holden Av. WV14: Cose . . .7G 53
Jacklin Dr. CV3: Finh 5C 174
Jacknell Cl. LE10: Hinc 1D 90
Jacknell Rd. LE10: Hinc 1D 90
Jack Newell Ct. WV14: Cose 1J 75
(off Castle St.)
Jack O'Watton Ind. Est.
B46: Wat O 6K 83
Jackson Av. B8: Salt 5F 102
Jackson Cl. B11: S'brk 2B 122
B68: O'bry 4H 99
CV7: Ker E 2A 130
DY4: Tip 8B 54
WS11: Nort C 5L 15
WV10: F'stne 3G 23
Jackson Ct. DY5: Quar B 8F 96
Jackson Cres.
DY13: Stour S 8E 182
Jackson Dr. B67: Smeth 4K 99
Jackson Gro. CV8: Ken 5J 199
Jackson Ho. B69: O'bry 2G 99
Jackson Rd. B8: Salt 5F 102
CV6: Cov 8D 130
CV21: Hillm 8G 181
WS13: Lich 6H 13
Jackson St. B68: O'bry 5H 99
DY9: Lye 4E 116
WV6: Wolv 5B 36
Jackson Wlk. B35: Cas V 7A 82
Jackson Way B32: Quin 4G 119
Jackwood Grn. CV12: Bed 1C 130
Jacmar Cres. B67: Smeth 3L 99
Jacob Dr. CV4: Canly 3K 173
Jacobean La. B91: Sol 8G 147
B93: Know 8G 147
Jacob's Hall La.
WS6: Gt Wyr 8G 15
Jacob's Ladder
DY11: Low H 8D 134
Jacoby Pl. B5: Edg 4J 121
Jacox Cres. CV8: Ken 4J 199
Jacquard Cl. CV3: Cov 5D 174
Jacquard Ho. CV1: Cov 5E 152
Jade Cl. CV1: Cov 5D 152 (1E 6)
Jade Gro. WS11: Hth H 7J 9
Jaffray Cres. B24: Erd 6F 80
Jaffray Rd. B24: Erd 6F 80
Jaguar B77: Glas 7E 32
Jaguar Arena, The 5E 130
Jake Cade Way CV34: H'cte . . .5L 223
Jakeman Rd. B12: Bal H 4L 121
Jakemans Cl. B98: Redd 5L 213
Jamaica Row
B5: Birm 8L 101 (7H 5)
James Bri. Cl. WS2: Wals 2H 55
James Brindley Wlk.
B1: Birm 7J 101 (5C 4)
James Clift Ho. B69: O'bry 4D 98
James Cl. B67: Smeth 4A 100
WS10: Darl 3F 54
James Ct. B13: Mose 7B 122
B38: K Nor 7F 142
CV21: Rugby 6B 180
(off James Wlk.)
CV34: Warw 2F 222
Jamescroft CV3: W'hall 3L 175
James Dawson Dr.
CV5: Alle 1B 150
James Dee Cl. DY5: Quar B 8G 97
James Diskin Ct. CV11: Nun 7L 89
James Eaton Cl.
B71: W Brom 4J 77
James Galloway Cl.
CV3: Bin 2L 175
James Gilbert Rugby
Football Mus., The 6A 180
James Grn. Rd. CV4: Tile H 7F 150
James Greenway WS13: Lich . . .7G 13
James Ho. B17: Harb 4B 120
(off Cadbury Way)
B19: Hock 3J 101
(off Newtown Dr.)
CV2: Cov 1J 153
James Lloyd Trust Flats
B30: B'vlle 4C 142
James Memorial Homes
B7: Nech 2C 102
(off Stuart St.)
Jameson Rd. B6: Aston 1C 102
Jameson St. WV6: Wolv 5B 36
James Rd. B11: Tys 3F 122
B43: Gt Barr 2E 78
B46: Col 1M 105
DY10: Kidd 1A 158
James Row B69: O'bry 1D 98
James Samuel Pl.
B12: Birm 2M 121
James Scott Rd. B63: Crad 3G 117
James St. B3: Birm 6J 101 (3D 4)
CV7: New A 1G 109
CV11: Nun 4G 89
CV21: Rugby 6B 180
James St. DY7: Kinv 5A 114
LE9: Earl S 2E 70
LE9: S Stan 6K 71
WS11: Cann 4F 8
WV13: W'hall 6A 38
WV14: Bils 3L 53
James Turner St.
B18: Win G 3E 100
James Wlk. CV21: Rugby 6B 180
James Watt Dr. B19: Hand 1H 101
James Watt Ho. B66: Smeth . . .4B 100
James Watt Ind. Pk.
B66: Smeth 3C 100
James Watt Queensway
B4: Birm 6L 101 (3H 5)
James Watt St. B4: Birm 4H 5
(off Dalton St.)
B71: W Brom 1H 77
(not continuous)
Jane La. Cl. WS2: Wals 5F 38
Janice Gro. B14: Yard W 5C 144
Janine Av. WV11: Wed 2L 37
Jaques Cl. B46: Wat O 7H 83
Jardine Cres. CV4: Tile H 7F 150
Jardine Rd. B6: Aston 8M 79
Jardine Shop. Cen.
CV4: Tile H 7F 150
Jarratt Hall B29: S Oak 6E 120
Jarvis Cl. LE10: Hinc 5K 69
Jarvis Cres. B69: O'bry 5F 98
Jarvis Rd. B23: Erd 3F 80
Jarvis Way B24: Erd 1E 102
J A S Ind. Pk. B65: Row R 5E 98
Jasmin Cft. B14: K Hth 5L 143
Jasmine Cl. WV9: Pend 6M 21
Jasmine Gro. B61: B'gve 5M 187
CV3: Cov 1J 175
CV32: Lea S 7A 218
WV8: Bilb 6H 21
Jasmine Rd. B77: Amin 5G 33
DY2: Dud 8M 75
Jasmine Way WS10: Darl 2D 54
Jason Cl. B77: Tam 4D 32
Jason Rd. DY9: W'cte 5F 116
Javelin Av. B35: Cas V 6B 82
Jayne Cl. B71: W Brom 8L 55
WV11: Wed 2K 37
Jay Pk. Cres. DY10: Kidd 7A 158
Jay Rd. DY6: K'wfrd 1K 95
Jay's Av. DY4: Tip 5B 76
Jays Cl. B98: Redd 6A 214
Jays Cres. B48: A'chu 8B 164
Jayshaw Av. B43: Gt Barr 8E 56
Jeal Cl. B47: Wyt 7L 165
Jean Dr. DY4: Tip 3D 76
Jean St. CV9: Bad E 8C 48
Jeavons Pl. WV14: Bils 4J 53
Jedburgh Av. WV6: Pert 5E 34
Jedburgh Gro. CV3: Finh 5A 174
Jeddo St. WV2: Wolv 1C 52 (7H 7)
Jeffcock Rd. WV3: Wolv 1M 51
Jefferson Cl. B71: W Brom 1H 77
Jeffrey Av. WV4: E'shll 4F 52
Jeffrey Cl. CV12: Bed 1D 130
Jeffrey Rd. B65: Row R 6E 98
Jeffries Cl. LE10: Hinc 7L 69
Jeffries Ho. B69: O'bry 2G 99
Jeffs Av. WV2: Wolv 1D 52 (8L 7)
Jeliff St. CV4: Tile H 7F 150
Jelleyman Cl. DY11: Kidd 3H 157
Jellicoe Way LE10: Hinc 5K 69
Jenkins Av. CV5: E Grn 5F 150
Jenkins Cl. WV14: Bils 4J 53
Jenkinson Rd. WS10: W'bry 8D 54
Jenkins Rd. CV21: Hillm 8G 181
Jenkins St. B10: Small H 1C 122
Jenkinstown Rd. WS12: Haz 3A 10
Jenks Av. DY7: Kinv 4A 114
WV10: Bush 1E 36
Jenks Rd. WV5: Wom 4F 72
Jennens Rd.
B4: Birm 6M 101 (4J 5)
B7: Birm 6M 101 (2K 5)
Jenner Cl. WS2: Wals 3G 39
Jenner Ho. WS2: Wals 3F 38
Jenner Rd. WS2: Wals 3F 38
Jenner St. CV1: Cov 5D 152 (1E 6)
WV2: Wolv 8E 36 (6M 7)
Jennifer Wlk. B25: Yard 1L 123
Jennings St. B64: Old H 7M 97
Jennings Wood La.
DY12: H'ton 6A 182
DY13: Dunl 6A 182
Jenny Cl. WV14: Bils 8L 53
Jennyns Ct. WS10: W'bry 6F 54
Jenny Walkers La. WV6: Pert . . .1D 50
Jensen B77: Glas 7E 32
Jenton Rd. CV31: Lea S 3B 224
Jephcott Gro. B8: Salt 5G 103
Jephcott Ho. CV1: Cov 3F 6
Jephcott Rd. B8: Salt 5G 103
Jephson Ct. CV2: Ald G 5J 131
Jephson Dr. B26: Yard 2M 123
Jephson Pl. CV31: Lea S 2B 224
Jeremy Gro. B92: Sol 5B 124
Jeremy Rd. WV4: Penn 4C 52
Jerome Cl. WS11: Nort C 4A 16
Jerome Ct. B74: S'tly 8M 41
Jerome Dr. WS11: Nort C 4A 16
Jerome K Jerome Birthplace 8L 39
Jerome Retail Pk. WS1: Wals . . .8K 39
Jerome Rd. B72: S Cold 5K 59
WS2: Wals 8H 39
WS11: Nort C 4M 15
Jerome Way WS7: Burn 2H 17
Jerrard Ct. B75: S Cold 4J 59
Jerrard Dr. B75: S Cold 4J 59
Jerry's La. B23: Erd 2D 80
WS14: S'fen 2B 30
Jersey Cl. B98: Redd 2K 213
Jersey Cft. B36: Cas B 3H 105
Jersey Rd. B8: Salt 5D 102
Jersey Way LE9: Barw 3A 70
Jerusalem Wlk. DY10: Kidd . . .2L 157
(not continuous)
Jervis Cl. DY5: P'ntt 2C 96
Jervis Ct. WS1: Wals 7M 39
(off Dog Kennel La.)
Jervis Cres. B74: Four O 6D 42
Jervis Pk. B74: Lit A 5C 42
Jervis Rd. B77: Hock 4F 46
Jervis Ter. B21: Hand 1D 100
Jervoise Dr. B31: N'fld 4B 142
Jervoise La. B71: W Brom 8L 55
Jervoise Rd. B29: W Cas 8M 119
Jervoise St. B70: W Brom 5G 77
Jesmond Cl. WS12: Haz 3A 10
Jesmond Gro. B24: Erd 5L 81
Jesmond Rd. CV1: Cov 5F 152
Jessel Rd. WS2: Wals 7J 39
Jessie Rd. WS9: A'rdge 8G 27
Jesson Cl. WS1: Wals 2A 56
Jesson Ct. WS1: Wals 1A 56
Jesson Rd. B75: S Cold 4A 60
DY3: Sed 3G 75
WS1: Wals 1M 55
Jesson St. B70: W Brom 7L 77
Jessop Dr. B77: Tam 4D 32
Jevons Dr. DY4: Tip 4B 76
Jevons Rd. B73: New O 6C 58
Jevon St. WV14: Cose 1H 75
(not continuous)
JEWELLERY QUARTER
. . . . .5H 101 (2B 4)
Jewellery Quarter Station (Rail)
. . . . .5H 101 (1B 4)
Jew's La. DY3: Up Gor 5E 74
Jiggin's La. B32: Bart G 1J 141
Jill Av. B43: Gt Barr 1C 78
Jillcot Rd. B92: Sol 6B 124
Jill La. B80: Stud 8F 220
B96: Sam 8F 220
Jim Forrest Cl. CV3: Bin 1M 175
Jinnah Cl. B12: Birm 1M 121
Jinnah Rd. B98: Redd 7E 212
Jitty, The CV34: Warw 3D 222
JM Halls CV4: Canly 5J 173
Joanna Dr. CV3: Finh 6C 174
Joan of Arc Ho. CV3: Cov 3E 174
Joans Cl. CV31: Lea S 3C 224
Joan St. WV2: E'shll 3E 52
Joan Ward St.
CV3: Cov 1D 174 (8D 6)
Job's La. CV4: Tile H 6G 151
Jockey Fld. DY3: Up Gor 3E 74
Jockey La. WS10: W'bry 5G 55
Jockey Rd. B73: New O 7D 58
Jodrell St. CV11: Nun 4H 89
Joe Jones Ct. DY3: Sed 8E 52
Joe O'Brien Cl. CV3: W'hall 3J 175
Joe Williams Cl. CV3: Bin 1M 175
Joey's La. WV8: Bilb 5J 21
John Bold Av. LE9: S Stan 6L 71
John Bright Cl. DY4: Tip 1M 75
John Bright St.
B1: Birm 7K 101 (6F 4)
Johndory B77: Dost 4D 46
John F Kennedy Wlk.
DY4: Tip 1A 76
John Fletcher Cl.
WS10: W'bry 5H 55
John Grace St. CV3: Cov 1D 174
John Harper St.
WV13: W'hall 7B 38
John Howell Dr. DY4: Tip 4A 76
John Kempe Way
B12: Birm 2A 122
John Knight Rd. CV12: Bed 5H 111
John McGuire Cres.
CV3: Bin 2L 175
John Nash Sq. CV8: Ken 6F 198
John Nichols St. LE10: Hinc 2H 91
John of Gaunt Ho. CV3: Cov . . .2E 174
John O'Gaunt Rd. CV8: Ken 6E 198
John Riley Dr.
WV12: W'hall 1C 38
John Rd. B62: Hale 6F 118
John Rous Av. CV4: Canly 2H 173
John's Cl. B80: Stud 5J 221
LE10: Burb 4K 91
Johns Gro. B43: Gt Barr 1C 78
John Shelton Dr. CV6: Cov 5C 130
John Simpson Cl.
CV8: Wols 6G 177
John Sinclair Ho. CV1: Cov 2C 6
Johns La. B69: Tiv 6C 76
DY4: Tip 5B 76
WS6: Gt Wyr 6F 14
John Smyth Ho.
B1: Birm 6J 101 (4C 4)
Johnson Av. CV22: Rugby 7K 179
WV11: Wed 2M 37

Johnson Cl.—Keppel Cl.

Johnson Cl. B8: W End 3J 103
B11: S'hll 4C 122
B98: Redd 4G 213
WS10: Darl 4D 54
WS13: Lich 8J 13
Johnson Dr. B35: Cas V 6M 81
Johnson Pl. WV14: Bils 2M 53
Johnson Ri. LE9: S Stan 8L 71
Johnson Rd. B23: Erd 4F 80
CV6: Cov 1G 153
CV12: Bed 6J 111
WS7: C Ter 1F 16
WS10: Darl 4D 54
WS10: W'bry 7J 55
WS11: Cann 5D 8
WV12: W'hall 2D 38
Johnson Row WV14: Cose 8F 52
Johnsons Bri. Rd.
B71: W Brom 3J 77
Johnsons Gro. B68: O'bry 1J 119
Johnson St. B7: Nech 3C 102
CV9: Wood E 8J 47
WV2: Wolv 2D 52 (8K 7)
WV14: Cose 8F 52
Johnstone St. B19: Loz 1K 101
Johnston St. B70: W Brom 8K 77
John St. B19: Loz 2H 101
B65: B'hth 8C 98
B69: O'bry 2G 99
B70: W Brom 5H 77
(Guns La.)
B70: W Brom 4F 76
(Phoenix St.)
B77: Amin 6E 32
CV10: Nun 6E 88
CV11: Nun 7J 89
CV12: Bed 7G 111
CV32: Lea S 1M 223
DY5: Brie H 5D 96
DY8: Word 8M 95
LE10: Hinc 8L 69
WS2: Wals 6L 39
WS11: Cann 4F 8
WV2: E'shll 3G 53
WV13: W'hall 8B 38
John St. Nth. B71: W Brom 4H 77
John Thwaites Cl.
CV22: Rugby 7A 180
John Tofts Ho.
CV1: Cov 5C 152 (2C 6)
John Wilmott Community
Leisure Cen. 5M 59
John Wooton Ho. *WS10: Darl 3D 54*
(off Lawrence Way)
Joiners Cft. B92: Sol 1E 146
Joinings Bank B68: O'bry 5H 99
Jolly Sailor Island
B78: Tam 5A 32
Jolly Sailor Retail Pk.
B78: Tam 6M 31
Jonathan Rd.
CV2: W'grve S 1M 153
Jon Baker Ct. LE10: Hinc 1L 91
Jones Fld. Cres. WV1: Wolv 7G 37
Jones Ho. WS2: Wals 6K 39
Jones' La. WS7: Burn 2M 17
Jones Rd. CV7: Exh 8G 111
WV10: Oxl 3C 36
WV12: W'hall 8D 24
Jones's La. WS6: Gt Wyr 8G 15
Jones Wood Cl. B76: Walm 2M 81
Jonfield Gdns. B43: Gt Barr 8F 56
Jonkel Av. B77: Hock 4F 46
Jordan Cl. B66: Smeth 4B 100
B75: Four O 8H 43
CV8: Ken 7H 199
WS13: Lich 6J 19
Jordan Ho. B36: Hodg H 1K 103
Jordan Leys DY4: Tip 4B 76
Jordan Pl. WV14: Bils 6L 53
Jordan Rd. B75: Four O 8H 43
Jordans, The CV5: Cov 5J 151
Jordans Cl. B97: Redd 3D 220
Jordan Way WS9: A'rdge 8H 27
Jordan Well
CV1: Cov 7D 152 (5D 6)
Jorden's Wlk. DY12: Bew 5D 156
Jordon Cl. DY11: Kidd 3G 157
Joseph Creighton Cl.
CV3: Bin 2L 175
Joseph Dewsbury Cl.
WS7: C Ter 1F 16
Joseph Halpin Ho. CV1: Cov 2E 6
Joseph Latham Ho.
CV2: Cov 8H 131
Joseph Luckman Rd.
CV12: Bed 5G 111
Joseph St. B69: O'bry 3F 98
Josiah Mason Mall
DY10: Kidd 3L 157
Josiah Rd. B31: N'fld 7K 141
Jourdain Pk. CV34: H'cte 6L 223
Jovian Dr. LE10: Hinc 8G 69
Jowett B77: Glas 7D 32
Jowett's La. B71: W Brom 1H 77
Joyberry Dr. DY8: Stourb 6M 115
Joyce Pool CV34: Warw 2E 222
Joyce Way CV22: Caw 1G 205
Joynson St. WS10: Darl 4E 54
Jubilee Av. B71: W Brom 2H 77
B97: Redd 2D 220
Jubilee Cl. WS3: Wals 3L 39
WS6: Gt Wyr 7F 14
Jubilee Ct. B27: A Grn 7J 123
B31: N'fld 8B 142
B78: K'bry 4D 62
(not continuous)
Jubilee Cres. CV6: Cov 1B 152
Jubilee Dr. LE9: Earl S 2E 70
Jubilee Dr. Nth. DY11: Kidd 7H 157
Jubilee Dr. Sth. DY11: Kidd 7H 157
Jubilee Gdns. B23: Erd 2B 80
Jubilee Rd. B45: Fran 7E 140
DY4: Tip 2A 76
WV14: Bils 5A 54
Jubilee Sports Cen. 6G 89
Jubilee St. B71: W Brom 2K 77
CV21: Rugby 6L 179
Jubilee Ter. B60: S Prior 8J 209
CV12: Bed 5H 111
Jubilee Trad. Cen.
B5: Birm 8L 101 (8H 5)
Judd Cl. CV12: Bed 6F 110
Judd's La. CV6: Longf 5E 130
Jude Wlk. WS13: Lich 7F 12
Judge Cl. B69: O'bry 2G 99
CV23: Long L 4G 179
Judge Rd. DY5: Quar B 2F 116
Judith Way CV22: Caw 1G 205
Juggins La. B94: Earls 2B 192
Julia Av. B24: Erd 5M 81
Julia Gdns. B71: W Brom 1M 77
Julian Cl. B61: Cats 1A 188
CV2: W'grve S 1M 153
WS6: Gt Wyr 6G 15
WV1: Wolv 7H 37
Julian Rd. WV1: Wolv 7H 37
Julie Cft. WV14: Bils 8L 53
Juliet Cl. CV11: Nun 8A 90
Juliet Dr. CV22: Bil 3K 205
CV34: H'cte 6M 223
Juliet Rd. B62: Hale 6F 118
Julius Dr. B46: Col 8M 83
Junction, The DY8: Word 1L 115
Junction 6 Ind. Pk. B6: Witt 8B 80
Junction Ind. Est.
B66: Smeth 1M 99
Junction One CV21: Rugby 3B 180
Junction Rd. B21: Hand 1C 100
B61: B'gve 6L 187
DY8: Stourb 5B 116
DY8: Word 1L 115
DY9: Stourb 5B 116
WV2: E'shll 2H 53
Junction St. B69: O'bry 8E 76
CV1: Cov 7B 152 (6A 6)
DY2: Dud 1H 97
WS1: Wals 1K 55
Junction St. Sth. B69: O'bry 4G 99
Junc. Two Ind. Est.
B69: O'bry 4F 98
(off Demuth Way)
June Cres. B77: Amin 4E 32
June Cft. B26: Sheld 4D 124
Junewood Cl. CV21: Brow 2D 180
Juniper B77: Amin 5G 33
Juniper Cl. B27: A Grn 4H 123
B76: Walm 6M 59
CV12: Bed 7E 110
WS12: Haz 3A 10
Juniper Ct. DY10: Kidd 5A 158
Juniper Dr. B76: Walm 2A 82
CV5: Alle 4F 150
WS5: Wals 5B 56
Juniper Ho. B20: Hand 6F 78
B36: Hodg H 2M 103
Juniper Ri. B63: Crad 4J 117
Juno Dr. CV31: Lea S 4M 223
Jupiter B16: Birm 7H 101 (6A 4)
(not continuous)
Jury Rd. DY5: Quar B 2F 116
Jury St. CV34: Warw 3E 222
Justice Cl. CV31: W'nsh 5A 224
Jutland Rd. B13: Mose 2B 144

K

Kalfs Dr. CV22: Caw 1H 205
Kanzan Rd. CV2: Ald G 5H 131
Kareen Gro. CV3: Bin W 2C 176
Karen Cl. CV10: Nun 2E 88
Karen Way DY5: Brie H 1D 116
Karlingford Cl. CV5: Cov 1K 173
KATE'S HILL 8M 75
Kateshill DY12: Bew 7B 156
Kateshill Ho. DY12: Bew 7B 156
Katherine Ho. *B17: Harb 4B 120*
(off Cadbury Way)
Katherine Rd. B67: Smeth 7M 99
Kathleen Av. CV12: Bed 8E 110
Kathleen Fld. Ct.
B61: B'gve 6M 187
Kathleen Rd. B25: Yard 2J 123
B72: S Cold 5J 59
Katie Rd. B29: S Oak 8E 120
Katmandu Rd. B60: B'gve 8C 188
Katrine Cl. CV10: Nun 4C 88
Katrine Rd. DY13: Stour S 2E 182
Kay Cl. CV21: Brow 2C 180
Kayne Cl. DY6: K'wfrd 3J 95
Kaysbrook Dr. CV23: Stret D 3G 203
Kean Cl. WS13: Lich 7E 12
Keanscott Dr. B68: O'bry 5J 99
Keasdon Gro. WV13: W'hall 6C 38
Keating Gdns. B75: Four O 5G 43
Keatley Av. B33: Kitts G 7E 104
Keats Av. B10: Small H 2D 122
WS11: Cann 4E 8
Keats Cl. B74: Four O 3F 42
B79: Tam 1M 31
CV10: Gall C 4A 88
DY3: Lwr G 4A 74
DY8: Amb 1A 116
LE9: Earl S 1F 70
Keats Dr. WV14: Cose 7K 53
Keats Gro. B27: A Grn 8H 123
WV10: Bush 1G 37
Keats Ho. B68: O'bry 5J 99
B97: Redd 1C 220
Keats La. LE9: Earl S 1E 70
Keats Pl. DY10: Kidd 3B 158
Keats Rd. CV2: Cov 7K 153
WS3: Blox 2L 39
WV10: Bush 7G 23
WV12: W'hall 2E 38
Keble Cl. WS7: Burn 2J 17
WS11: Cann 1E 14
Keble Gro. B26: Sheld 3B 124
WS1: Wals 2A 56
Keble Ho. B37: F'bri 7G 105
Keble Wlk. B79: Tam 3A 32
(not continuous)
Kebull Grn. CV4: Tile H 1E 172
Kedleston Cl. WS3: Blox 6G 25
Kedleston Ct. B28: Hall G 5F 144
Kedleston Rd. B28: Hall G 3F 144
Keegan Wlk. WS2: Wals 5F 38
Keel Dr. B13: Mose 8D 122
Keele Cl. B98: Redd 3L 213
Keele Ho. B37: F'bri 5H 105
Keeley St. B9: Birm 7B 102
Keeling Dr. WS11: Cann 8B 8
Keelinge St. DY4: Tip 4B 76
Keeling Rd. CV8: Ken 4H 199
Keenan Dr. CV12: Bed 8D 110
Keen St. B66: Smeth 5D 100
Keepers Cl. WS7: Burn 3G 17
B18: Win G 4F 100
B46: Col 5M 105
DY6: W Hth 1H 95
WS9: Wals W 6F 26
WS14: Lich 2L 19
Keepers Ga. Cl. B74: S Cold 2J 59
Keepers Ho. *B73: New O 7C 58*
(off Welshmans Hill)
Keepers La. WV6: Tett 7G 21
WV8: Cod 7G 21
Keepers Rd. B74: Lit A 4C 42
Keepers Wlk. CV12: Bed 8D 110
Keer Ct. B9: Birm 7B 102
Kegworth Cl. CV6: Longf 5G 131
Kegworth Rd. B23: Erd 7C 80
Keir Cl. CV32: Lea S 7A 218
Keir Hardie Wlk. B69: Tiv 7D 76
Keir Pl. DY8: Amb 1L 115
Keir Rd. WS10: W'bry 7J 55
Keith Rd. CV32: Lill 5B 218
Keith Winter Cl. B61: B'gve 3M 187
Kelby Cl. B31: N'fld 5L 141
Kelby Rd. B31: N'fld 5M 141
Keldy Cl. WV6: Wolv 4M 35
Kele Rd. CV4: Tile H 2F 172
Kelfield Av. B17: Harb 5B 120
Kelham Pl. B92: Olton 8B 124
Kelia Dr. B67: Smeth 3M 99
Kellett Rd. B7: Birm 5A 102 (1L 5)
Kelling Cl. DY5: Brie H 1C 116
Kellington Cl. B8: W End 5F 102
Kelmarsh Dr. B91: Sol 8B 146
Kelmscote Rd. CV6: Cov 1M 151
Kelmscott Rd. B17: Harb 2B 120
Kelsall Cl. WV1: Wolv 7H 37
Kelsall Cft. B1: Birm 6H 101 (4A 4)
Kelsey Cl. B7: Birm 5B 102 (1M 5)
CV11: Nun 6L 89
Kelsey La. CV7: Bal C 4J 171
Kelsey's Cl. CV8: Wols 6F 176
Kelso Gdns. WV6: Pert 5D 34
Kelsull Cft. B37: F'bri 7G 105
Kelton Ct. B15: Edg 2G 121
Kelvedon Gro. B91: Sol 5C 146
Kelverdale Gro. B14: K Hth 5J 143
Kelverley Gro. B71: W Brom 8A 56
Kelverstone Ho. WS11: Cann 8D 8
Kelvin Av. CV2: Cov 4K 153
Kelvin Cl. DY11: Kidd 1G 157
Kelvin Dr. WS11: Cann 6G 9
Kelvin Ho. DY1: Dud 7K 75
Kelvin Pl. WS2: Wals 3H 39
Kelvin Rd. B31: N'fld 8A 142
CV32: Lill 4B 218
WS2: Wals 3G 39
Kelvin Way B70: W Brom 8H 77
Kelvin Way Ind. Est.
B70: W Brom 8H 77
Kelway CV3: Bin 7A 154
Kelway Av. B43: Gt Barr 6H 57
Kelwood Dr. B63: Hale 4A 118
Kelynmead Rd. B33: Yard 7A 104
Kemberton Cl. WV3: Wolv 8J 35
Kemberton Rd. B29: S Oak 7A 120
WV3: Wolv 8J 35
Kemble Cl. WV12: W'hall 6D 38
Kemble Cft. B5: Bal H 2L 121
Kemble Dr. B35: Cas V 6A 82
Kemelstowe Cres. B63: Hale 1J 139
Kemerton Ho. B97: Redd 5B 212
Kemerton Way B90: M'path 4M 167
Kemp Cl. CV34: Warw 2G 223
Kempe Rd. B33: Kitts G 5A 104
Kempley Av. CV2: Cov 6J 153
Kempsey Cl. B63: Hale 5L 117
B69: O'bry 5E 98
B92: Olton 6A 124
B98: Redd 2H 221
Kempsey Covert B38: K Nor 2E 164
Kempsey Ho. B32: Bart G 1G 141
Kempsford Cl. B98: Redd 3F 220
KEMPS GREEN 8A 194
Kemps Grn. Rd.
B94: H'ley H 8M 193
CV7: Bal C 3H 171
Kempson Av. B71: W Brom 4H 77
B72: W Grn 8J 59
Kempson Rd. B36: Hodg H 1L 103
Kempsons Gro. WV14: Cose 6H 53
Kempthorne Av. WV10: Bush 8E 22
Kempthorne Gdns. WS3: Blox 7G 25
Kempthorne Rd. WV14: Bils 3M 53
Kempton Cl. WS12: Haz 3A 10
Kempton Ct. B61: Cats 8A 162
Kempton Cres. CV32: Lill 5C 218
Kempton Dr. B77: Dost 5D 46
WS6: Gt Wyr 7F 14
Kempton Pk. Rd.
B36: Hodg H 1K 103
Kempton Way DY8: Stourb 6L 115
Kemsey Dr. WV14: Bils 6M 53
Kemshead Av. B31: Longb 1L 163
Kemsley Rd. B14: K Hth 7M 143
Kem St. CV11: Nun 7K 89
Kenchester Cl. B98: Redd 7L 213
Kendal Av. B45: Redn 2H 163
B46: Col 2M 105
CV32: Lea S 7J 217
Kendal Cl. B60: B'gve 8B 188
B98: Redd 6A 214
CV11: Nun 3A 90
WV6: Tett 3M 35
Kendal Ct. B23: Erd 6B 80
B29: W Cas 2C 142
WS9: Wals W 5F 26
WS11: Cann 1B 14
Kendal Dr. B45: Coft H 8K 163
KENDAL END 7K 163
Kendal End Rd.
B45: B Grn, Coft H 7K 163
Kendal Gro. B92: Sol 1F 146
Kendal Ho. B69: O'bry 5D 98
Kendall Ri. DY6: K'wfrd 4M 95
Kendal Ri. B68: O'bry 6H 99
CV5: Cov 5J 151
WV6: Tett 3M 35
Kendal Ri. Rd. B45: Redn 2H 163
Kendal Rd. B11: S'brk 2B 122
Kendal Twr. B17: Harb 4D 120
Kendlewood Rd. DY10: Kidd 8B 136
Kendon Av. CV6: Cov 3L 151
Kendrick Av. B34: S End 4E 104
Kendrick Cl. B92: Sol 3F 146
CV6: Longf 5G 131
Kendrick Pl. WV14: Bils 5A 54
Kendrick Rd. B76: Walm 4M 81
WV10: Bush 3E 36
WV14: Bils 5A 54
Kendricks Rd. WS10: Darl 2F 54
Kendrick St. WS10: W'bry 6G 55
Keneggy M. B29: S Oak 7F 120
Kenelm Ct. CV3: W'hall 4J 175
Kenelm Rd. B10: Small H 1E 122
B68: O'bry 6G 99
B73: S Cold 5H 59
WV14: Cose 8J 53
Kenelm's Ct. B62: Roms 5A 140
Kenilcourt CV8: Ken 3D 198
KENILWORTH 5F 198
Kenilworth By-Pass
CV3: Finh 1A 200
CV8: Ken 7J 199
CV35: Ken, Leek W 4G 217
Kenilworth Castle 4D 198
Kenilworth Cl. B74: Four O 1G 59
B97: Redd 3D 220
CV7: Bal C 3G 171
DY4: Tip 5K 75
DY8: Word 7K 95
Kenilworth Ct. B16: Edg 1F 120
B24: Erd 7E 80
CV3: Cov 1C 174
DY1: Dud 1F 96
WS11: Cann 8E 8
Kenilworth Cres. WS2: Wals 5G 39
WV4: E'shll 5E 52
Kenilworth Dr. CV11: Nun 6H 89
DY10: Kidd 7L 157
WS11: Cann 5D 8
Kenilworth Ho. B13: Mose 3A 144
WS3: Blox 3J 39
(off Providence La.)
Kenilworth M. CV8: Ken 4F 198
Kenilworth Rd. B20: Hand 8L 79
B46: Col 8A 106
B68: O'bry 1K 119
Kenilworth Rd. B77: Amin 5E 32
B92: H Ard 3D 148
B93: Know 3K 169
CV3: Cov 3M 173
CV4: Canly 6K 173
CV7: Bal C 7G 149
CV7: Mer 7C 126
CV8: Ken 4J 171
(Kelsey La.)
CV8: Ken 1H 199
(Redthorne Gro.)
CV32: B'dwn, Lea S 1J 217
CV32: Cubb 3C 218
WS14: Lich 3H 19
WV6: Pert 5F 34
Kenilworth St. CV32: Lea S 8M 217
Kenley Gro. B30: K Nor 6H 143
Kenley Way B91: Shir 5K 145
Kenmare Way WV11: Wed 5J 37
Ken Marriot Leisure Cen. 8B 180
Kenmore Av. WS12: Hed 2F 8
Kenmore Dr. LE10: Hinc 7H 69
Kenmure Rd. B33: Sheld 2C 124
Kennan Av. CV31: Lea S 2M 223
Kennedy Cl. B72: S Cold 5J 59
B77: Two G 8C 32
DY10: Kidd 6M 157
Kennedy Ct. DY8: Stourb 4M 115
Kennedy Cres. DY3: Lwr G 5D 74
WS10: Darl 2C 54
Kennedy Cft. B26: Sheld 2A 124
Kennedy Dr. CV22: Bil 7J 179
Kennedy Gro. B30: Stir 3H 143
Kennedy Ho. B68: O'bry 1H 119
Kennedy Rd.
WV10: Wolv 6D 36 (2L 7)
Kennedy Sq. CV32: Lea S 8A 218
Kennedy Twr. B4: Birm 3G 5
Kennel La. CV9: With 2B 66
Kennerley Rd. B25: Yard 3K 123
Kennet B77: Wiln 8D 32
Kennet Cl. CV2: Cov 1J 153
WS8: Bwnhls 7C 16
Kennet Gro. B36: Cas B 1F 104
Kenneth Gro. B23: Erd 4A 80
Kenneth Vincent Cl.
B97: Redd 5E 220
Kennford Cl. B65: Row R 3C 98
Kennington Rd. WV10: Wolv 4F 36
Kenpas Highway CV3: Cov 3M 173
Kenrick Cft. B35: Cas V 7A 82
Kenrick Ho. B70: W Brom 8L 77
Kenrick Park Stop (MM) 8L 77
Kenrick Way B70: W Brom 1K 99
B71: W Brom 8M 77
Kenrose Mill DY7: Kinv 6B 114
Kensington Av. B12: Bal H 5A 122
Kensington Ct. CV5: Cov 8A 152
CV10: Nun 3C 88
Kensington Dr. B74: Four O 4F 42
B79: Tam 2B 32
Kensington Gdns. DY8: Word 8J 95
WS11: Cann 7C 8
Kensington Pl. WS12: Hth H 8J 9
Kensington Rd. B29: S Oak 7G 121
CV5: Cov 8M 151
WV12: W'hall 2B 38
Kensington St. B19: Hock 3K 101
Kenswick Dr. B63: Hale 7A 118
Kent, The CV21: Hillm 7G 181
Kent Av. B78: Tam 7M 31
WS2: Wals 6H 39
Kent Cl. B71: W Brom 2H 77
CV3: Cov 3E 174
DY10: Kidd 6L 157
WS2: Wals 4L 39
WS9: A'rdge 8H 27
Kent Dr. LE10: Hinc 5L 69
Kenthurst Cl. CV5: E Grn 5C 150
Kentish Rd. B21: Hand 1C 100
Kentmere Cl. CV2: W'grve S 7L 131
Kentmere Rd. B60: B'gve 8B 188
Kentmere Twr. B23: Erd 3H 81
Kent M. WS11: Cann 1F 14
Kenton Av. WV6: Wolv 5M 35
Kenton Wlk. B29: S Oak 7F 120
Kent Pl. DY2: Dud 3G 97
WS12: Hth H 8L 9
Kent Rd. B45: Fran 8F 140
B62: Quin 3E 118
DY8: Woll 2K 115
WS2: Wals 6F 38
WS10: W'bry 5J 55
WV2: Wolv 2E 52
Kents Cl. B92: Olton 6M 123
Kents Ho. B33: Yard 7B 104
Kent St. B5: Birm 1L 121 (8G 5)
DY3: Up Gor 4E 74
WS2: Wals 4L 39
Kent St. Nth. B18: Hock 4F 100
Kentwell B79: Tam 2K 31
Kenward Cft. B17: Harb 2M 119
Kenway B47: H'wd 2A 166
Kenwick Rd. B17: Harb 5B 120
Kenwood Rd. B9: Bord G 6H 103
Kenwyn Grn. CV7: Exh 1H 131
Kenyon Cl. B60: B'gve 8A 188
DY8: Amb 2A 116
Kenyon St. B18: Birm 5J 101 (2D 4)
Kepler B79: Tam 2L 31
Keppel Cl. CV22: Bil 8J 179

Keppel St.—Kinman Way

Keppel St. CV1: Cov 4E 152
Kerby Rd. B23: Erd 5C 80
Kererwin Cl. B64: Old H 8A 98
KERESLEY 8M 129
Keresley Brook Rd.
CV6: Cov 7M 129
Keresley Cl. B91: Sol 4C 146
CV6: Cov 7M 129
Keresley Grn. Rd. CV6: Cov 8M 129
Keresley Gro. B29: W Cas 7M 119
KERESLEY NEWLAND 3M 129
Keresley Rd. CV6: Cov 1M 151
Kernthorpe Rd. B14: K Hth 5K 143
Kerr Dr. DY4: Tip 1L 75
Kerria Cen. B77: Amin 5G 33
Kerria Ct. B15: Birm 1K 121 (8E 4)
Kerria Rd. B77: Amin 5H 33
Kerridge Cl. WV9: Pend 7A 22
Kerrison Ride B73: Bold 8F 58
Kerris Way CV3: Bin 8A 154
Kerry Cl. B31: N'fld 3M 141
DY5: Brie H 5C 96
LE9: Barw 2M 69
Kerry Ct. WS1: Wals 1A 56
Kerry Cft. Cl. B97: Redd 4E 220
Kerry Hill B60: Stoke H 3L 209
Kerrys Ho. CV1: Cov 7B 152
(off Windsor St.)
Kersley Gdns. WV11: Wed 3M 37
Kerswell Cl. B97: Redd 4B 212
Kerswell Dr. B90: M'path 4M 167
Kesterton Rd. B74: Four O 4E 42
Kesteven Cl. B15: Edg 3H 121
Kesteven Rd. B71: W Brom 2J 77
Keston Rd. B44: Gt Barr 5M 57
Kestral Ct. WS7: Burn 1M 17
Kestrel B77: Wiln 3G 47
Kestrel Av. B25: Yard 1H 123
Kestrel Cl. B23: Erd 3D 80
B35: Cas V 6B 82
DY10: Kidd 6L 157
LE10: Burb 3M 91
Kestrel Cft. CV3: Bin 1M 175
Kestrel Dr. B74: Four O 4F 42
Kestrel Gro. B30: B'vlle 1D 142
WS12: Hth H 8J 9
WV12: W'hall 1C 38
Kestrel Ri. WV6: Tett 2M 35
Kestrel Rd. B63: Crad 2H 117
B68: O'bry 7F 98
DY1: Dud 1F 96
Kestrel Vw. B60: L End 1C 188
Kestrel Way WS6: C Hay 7C 14
Keswick Cl. CV11: Nun 3A 90
Keswick Dr. CV21: Brow 1C 180
DY6: K'wfrd 3K 95
Keswick Grn. CV32: Lea S 8K 217
Keswick Gro. B74: S'tly 7M 41
Keswick Ho. B69: O'bry 5D 98
Keswick Rd. B92: Olton 5M 123
Keswick Wlk. CV2: Cov 5M 153
Ketley Cft. B12: Birm 2M 121
Ketley Flds. DY6: K'wfrd 4A 96
Ketley Hill Rd. DY1: Dud 1F 96
Ketley Rd. DY6: K'wfrd 3M 95
(not continuous)
KETTLEBROOK 6C 32
Kettlebrook Rd. B77: Tam 5C 32
B90: M'path 3B 168
Kettlehouse Rd. B44: Gt Barr 6M 57
Kettles Bank Rd. DY3: Gorn 7C 74
(not continuous)
Kettles Wood Dr.
B32: Bart G 7H 119
Kettlewell Cl. CV34: Warw 8E 216
Kettlewell Way B37: F'bri 7F 104
Ketton Gro. B33: Sheld 2D 124
Keviliok St. CV3: Cov 3D 174
Kew Cl. B37: K'hrst 6F 104
CV8: Ken 4J 199
Kew Dr. DY1: Dud 7G 75
Kew Gdns. B33: Stech 8K 103
Kew Rd. CV21: Rugby 5A 180
Kewstoke Cl. WV12: W'hall 8B 24
Kewstoke Cft. B31: N'fld 3L 141
Kewstoke Rd. WV12: W'hall 8B 24
Key Bus. Pk. B24: Erd 6L 81
Key Cl. WS12: Hed 6J 9
Keyes Dr. CV22: Bil 7J 179
DY6: K'wfrd 8K 73
Key Hill B18: Birm 4H 101
Key Hill Cir. B18: Birm 4H 101
Key Hill Dr. B18: Birm 4H 101
Key Ind. Pk. WV13: W'hall 6K 37
Keynell Covert B30: K Nor 6J 143
Keynes Dr. WV14: Bils 3L 53
Keys Cres. B71: W Brom 3J 77
Keyse Rd. B75: S Cold 2M 59
Keys Hill CV9: Bad E 8C 48
Keys Pk. Rd. WS12: Hed, Wim 6J 9
Keyte Cl. DY4: Tip 4A 76
Keyway, The WV13: W'hall 8M 37
Keyway Retail Pk.
WV13: W'hall 1B 54
Keyworth Cl. DY4: Tip 4A 76
Khalsa Ind. Est.
B66: Smeth 5D 100
Khyber Cl. WS10: Darl 2C 54
Kidd Cft. DY4: Tip 7C 54
KIDDERMINSTER 4M 157
Kidderminster Harriers FC 5M 157
Kidderminster Railway Mus. 4M 157
Kidderminster Rd.
B61: B'gve, D'frd 4C 186
DY6: K'wfrd, W Hth 1F 114
DY7: I'ley 3H 137
DY7: Stourt 1F 114
DY9: Hag 4A 138
DY10: I'ley 3H 137
DY12: Bew 6B 156
Kidderminster Rd. Sth.
DY9: Hag 6L 137
Kidderminster Station (Rail) 4M 157
Kidderminster Town Station 4M 157
Kielder Cl. WS5: Wals 6C 56
WS12: Hth H 7L 9
Kielder Dr. CV10: Nun 7E 88
Kielder Gdns. DY9: Pedm 8B 116
Kier's Bri. Cl. DY4: Tip 6A 76
Kilberry Cl. LE10: Hinc 8G 69
Kilburn Dr. CV5: Cov 6M 151
DY6: K'wfrd 8L 73
Kilburn Gro. B44: Gt Barr 6M 57
Kilburn Pl. DY2: Dud 3K 97
Kilburn Rd. B44: Gt Barr 6M 57
Kilby Av. B16: Birm 7G 101 (5A 4)
(not continuous)
Kilbye Cl. B77: Hock 4F 46
Kilby Grn. LE10: Burb 3M 91
Kilby Gro. CV31: Lea S 4C 224
Kilbys Gro. B20: Hand 7F 78
Kilcote Rd. B90: Shir 7C 144
Kildale Cl. CV1: Cov 6E 152 (3F 6)
Kilderkin Ct.
CV1: Cov 8D 152 (8E 6)
Kildwick Way CV34: Warw 8E 216
Kilmarie Cl. LE10: Hinc 8G 69
Kilmet Wlk. B67: Smeth 4A 100
Kilmore Cft. B36: Hodg H 8L 81
Kilmorie Rd. B27: A Grn 4J 123
WS11: Cann 7C 8
Kiln Cl. B80: Stud 5J 221
CV10: Nun 6E 88
CV32: Lea S 7A 218
Kiln Cl. B48: A'chu 4A 190
Kiln Cft. B65: Row R 5A 98
Kiln La. B25: Yard 3H 123
B90: Dic H 4G 167
CV23: Stret D 3H 203
Kilnsey Gro. CV34: Warw 8E 216
Kiln Way B78: Pole 8M 33
Kilpeck Cl. B98: Redd 7M 213
KILSBY 6M 207
Kilsby Gro. B91: Sol 1C 168
Kilsby La. CV21: Hillm 2J 207
Kilsby Rd. CV23: Barby 8J 207
Kilvert Rd. WS10: W'bry 7H 55
Kilworth Ho. CV32: Lea S 8M 217
(off Windsor St.)
Kilworth Rd. CV21: Hillm 2H 207
Kimbells Wlk. B93: Know 3J 169
Kimberlee Av. DY10: Cookl 5B 136
Kimberley B77: Wiln 2F 46
Kimberley Av. B8: Salt 4E 102
Kimberley Cl. B74: S'tly 6A 42
B98: Redd 2H 213
CV5: E Grn 5F 150
Kimberley Pl. WV14: Cose 2H 75
Kimberley Rd. B66: Smeth 2A 100
B92: Olton 7A 124
CV8: Bag 7E 174
CV12: Bed 5J 111
CV21: Rugby 5B 180
Kimberley St. WV3: Wolv 8A 36
Kimberley Wlk. B76: Min 3D 82
Kimble Cl. CV5: Cov 5H 151
Kimble Gro. B24: Erd 6K 81
Kimbley Ri. B71: W Brom 2G 77
Kimbolton Dr. B60: B'wll 4G 189
Kimpton Cl. B14: K Hth 7L 143
Kimsan Cft. B74: S'tly 2A 58
Kinchford Cl. B91: Sol 1C 168
Kineton Cl. B98: Redd 8K 213
Kineton Cft. B32: Bart G 1K 141
Kineton Grn. Rd.
B92: Olton 1K 145
Kineton Ho. B13: Mose 3A 144
Kineton La. B94: H'ley H 8M 167
Kineton Ri. DY3: Sed 7C 52
Kineton Rd. B45: Rubery 2E 162
B73: New O 8E 58
CV2: Cov 3J 153
CV8: Ken 5J 199
CV47: Sou 6G 225
Kineton Rd. Ind. Est.
CV47: Sou 6G 225
Kinfare Dr. WV6: Tett 5H 35
Kinfare Ri. DY3: Up Gor 5E 74
King Charles Av. WS2: Wals 7E 38
King Charles Cl. DY11: Kidd 3J 157
King Charles Ct. B44: K'sdng 7B 58
King Charles Rd. B62: Quin 5F 118
King Charles Sq. DY10: Kidd 3L 157
King Edmund St. DY1: Dud 7H 75
(not continuous)
King Edward VI Ho.
B4: Birm 6M 101
(off Aston St.)
King Edward VI Leisure Cen. 3J 19
King Edward Av. B61: B'gve 5M 187
King Edward Ct. B63: Hale 5A 118
King Edward Rd. B13: Mose 6M 121
B61: B'gve 4M 187
CV1: Cov 5E 152
CV11: Nun 5K 89
CV21: Rugby 5B 180
King Edwards Cl. B20: Hand 1H 101
King Edwards Dr.
B16: Birm 7H 101 (6A 4)
King Edwards Gdns.
B20: Hand 2H 101
King Edwards Rd.
B1: Birm 6G 101 (3A 4)
(Ladywood Middleway)
B1: Birm 7H 101 (5B 4)
(Summer Hill St.)
King Edward's Row
WV2: Wolv 1C 52 (8J 7)
King Edwards Sq. B73: S Cold 3J 59
King Edward St. WS10: Darl 3D 54
King Edwards Wharf
B16: Birm 7H 101 (6A 4)
Kingfield Ind. Est. CV1: Cov 3C 152
Kingfield Rd. B90: Shir 7C 144
CV1: Cov 3C 152
CV6: Cov 3D 152
Kingfisher B77: Wiln 3G 47
Kingfisher Av. CV10: Nun 4C 88
Kingfisher Bus. Pk.
B98: Redd 6G 213
Kingfisher Cl. B26: Sheld 3A 124
DY3: Sed 7C 52
WS8: Bwnhls 2E 26
Kingfisher Ct. B48: A'chu 2A 190
WS7: Burn 1M 17
Kingfisher Dr. B36: Cas B 1G 105
DY8: Stourb 6J 115
WS12: Hed 5J 9
Kingfisher Gro. DY10: Kidd 6B 158
WV12: W'hall 1B 38
Kingfisher Ind. Est.
B70: W Brom 5F 76
Kingfisher Rd. B23: Erd 2C 80
Kingfisher Shop. Cen.
B97: Redd 5E 212
Kingfisher Sq. B97: Redd 5D 212
Kingfisher Vw. B34: Stech 4A 104
Kingfisher Wlk. B97: Redd 5D 212
Kingfisher Way B30: B'vlle 1D 142
King George VI Av.
WS1: Wals 1C 56
King George Av. B61: B'gve 5M 187
King George Cl. B61: B'gve 5L 187
King George Cres. WS4: Rus 3B 40
King George Pl. WS4: Rus 3B 40
King George's Av. CV6: Cov 7E 130
CV12: Bed 4H 111
King George's Ct.
CV23: Long L 4G 179
King George's Way
LE10: Hinc 2H 91
Kingham Cl. B98: Redd 5M 213
DY3: Gorn 7C 74
Kingham Covert B14: K Hth 7K 143
Kingland Dr. CV32: Lea S 8J 217
King Richard Rd. LE10: Hinc 7J 69
King Richards Hill
LE9: Earl S 1H 71
King Richard St. CV2: Cov 6F 152
Kings Arms La.
DY13: Stour S 7B 182
Kings Av. B69: Tiv 7B 76
CV9: Ath 1L 65
WS12: Hed 5J 9
Kingsbridge Ho. B23: Erd 3B 80
Kingsbridge Rd. B32: Bart G 8K 119
CV10: Nun 3K 89
Kingsbridge Wlk.
B66: Smeth 4B 100
Kingsbrook Dr. B91: Sol 1B 168
KINGSBURY 4D 62
Kingsbury Av. B24: Erd 6K 81
Kingsbury Bus. Pk. B76: Min 3E 82
Kingsbury Cl. B76: Min 4D 82
WS4: Wals 5B 40
Kingsbury Leisure Cen. 7F 80
Kingsbury Link B78: Picc 8G 47
Kingsbury Pl. B24: Erd 5H 81
Kingsbury Rd. B24: Erd 7E 80
B35: Cas V 7K 81
B76: Curd, Mars 1K 83
B76: K'bry, Mars 6B 62
B76: Min, Curd 4C 82
CV6: Cov 3K 151
DY4: Tip 1A 76
Kingsbury Water Camping &
Caravaning Site
B76: Bod H 3A 62
Kingsbury Water Pk. 2A 62
(not continuous)
Kings Bus. Pk. B44: Gt Barr 6L 57
Kings Cinema 6K 77
Kingsclere Wlk. WV4: Penn 3J 51
Kingscliff Rd.
B10: Small H 1G 123
King's Cl. B14: K Hth 3J 143
Kingscote Cl. B98: Redd 2K 213
Kingscote Gro. CV3: Finh 5M 173
Kingscote Rd. B15: Edg 3D 120
B93: Dorr 7E 168
Kings Ct. B37: Mars G 8L 105
B1: Birm 8J 101 (7D 4)
B3: Birm 8J 101 (2E 4)
B75: Four O 6H 43
DY4: Tip 5A 76
WS10: W'bry 6E 54
Kings Cft. B26: Sheld 4A 124
B36: Cas B 2F 104
Kingscroft Ho. WS12: Wim 5L 9
Kingscroft Cl. B74: S'tly 2A 58
Kingscroft Rd. B74: S'tly 1A 58
Kingsdene Av. DY6: K'wfrd 5J 95
Kingsdown Av. B42: Gt Barr 3F 78
Kingsdown Rd. B31: N'fld 8M 119
WS7: C Ter 8D 10
Kingsfield Rd. B14: K Hth 1L 143
LE9: Barw 2B 70
KINGSFORD 1J 135
Kingsford Cvn. Pk.
DY11: W'ley 2H 135
Kingsford Cl. B36: Cas B 8D 82
Kingsford Country Pk. 1K 135
Kingsford Ct. B92: Olton 6B 124
Kingsford La. DY11: W'ley 3H 135
Kingsford Nouveau
DY6: K'wfrd 4A 96
Kingsford Rd. CV6: Cov 3C 152
Kings Gdns. B30: K Nor 5E 142
CV12: Bed 7J 111
Kingsgate Ho. B37: Chel W 7G 105
Kings Grn. Av. B38: K Nor 7F 142
Kings Gro. CV2: Cov 6H 153
Kingshayes Rd. WS9: A'rdge 7H 27
KING'S HEATH 1L 143
KING'S HILL 4D 54
Kings Hill Bus. Pk.
WS10: W'bry 5E 54
Kings Hill Cl. WS10: Darl 4E 54
Kingshill Dr. B38: K Nor 7F 142
Kings Hill Fld. WS10: Darl 4E 54
King's Hill La. CV3: Finh 8M 173
Kings Hill M. WS10: Darl 4D 54
King's Hill Rd. WS14: Lich 3J 19
Kingsholm Cl. CV3: Bin 8B 154
KINGSHURST 4F 104
Kingshurst CV31: Rad S 3E 224
Kingshurst Ho. B37: K'hrst 4F 104
Kingshurst Rd. B31: N'fld 6A 142
B90: Shir 8F 144
Kingshurst Way B37: K'hrst 5F 104
Kingsland Av. CV5: Cov 7M 151
Kingsland Dr. B93: Dorr 6E 168
Kingsland Rd. B44: Gt Barr 5L 57
Kingslea Rd. B91: Sol 7L 145
Kingsleigh Cft. B75: Four O 7H 43
Kingsleigh Dr. B36: Cas B 1A 104
Kingsleigh Rd. B20: Hand 7H 79
Kingsley Av. CV21: Hillm 8E 180
WS12: Hed 2J 9
WV6: Tett 5H 35
Kingsley Bank Way
B26: Sheld 2B 124
Kingsley Cl. B79: Tam 3A 32
Kingsley Ct. B25: Yard 1L 123
CV3: Bin W 3D 176
Kingsley Cres. CV12: Bulk 6B 112
Kingsley Gdns. WV8: Cod 6E 20
Kingsley Gro. DY3: Lwr G 4A 74
Kingsley Orchard
CV21: Hillm 8E 180
Kingsley Rd. B12: Bal H 3A 122
B30: K Nor 5D 142
CV33: Bis T 8D 224
DY6: K'wfrd 4H 95
Kingsley Sports Cen. 3J 221
Kingsley St. DY2: Neth 4J 97
WS2: Wals 2H 55
Kingsley Ter. CV2: Cov 1L 153
Kingsley Wlk.
CV2: W'grve S 1M 153
Kingslow Av. WV4: Penn 3K 51
Kingsmead M. CV3: W'hall 3K 175
Kings Mdw. DY9: Clent 7E 138
CV10: Nun 6A 88
Kingsmere Cl. B24: Erd 7E 80
KING'S NEWNHAM 2C 178
Kings Newnham La.
CV23: Bret, K New 2L 177
Kings Newnham Rd.
CV23: Chu L, K New 2B 178
KINGS NORTON 7D 142
King's Norton Bus. Cen.
B30: K Nor 5G 143
Kings Norton Community Leisure Cen. 1F 164
King's Norton Golf Course 8J 165
Kings Norton Station (Rail) 5F 142
Kingsoak Gdns. DY2: Dud 2L 97
Kings Pde. B4: Birm 5H 5
Kings Pk. Dr. CV3: Bin 8B 154
Kingspiece Ho. B36: Hodg H 1L 103
Kings Rd. B14: K Hth 3J 143
B44: Gt Barr, K'sdng 6L 57
B73: New O 7A 58
DY3: Sed 1E 74
DY11: Kidd 3J 157
B11: Tys 4G 123
B23: Erd 5C 80
WS4: Rus 2C 40
Kings Rd. Ind. Est. B11: Tys 3G 123
King's Row LE9: Earl S 1E 70
Kings Sq. B70: W Brom 6K 77
WV14: Cose 1G 75
King's Standing Ancient Monument 5M 57
KINGSTANDING 8B 58
Kingstanding Cen., The
B44: Gt Barr 6M 57
Kingstanding Leisure Cen. 1A 80
Kingstanding Rd.
B44: K'sdng 3M 79
King's Ter. B14: K Hth 3K 143
Kingsthorpe Rd. B14: K Hth 6A 144
Kingston Cl. B79: Tam 2C 32
Kingston Ct. B29: W Cas 2B 142
B74: S Cold 2H 59
WS11: Cann 8E 8
Kingston Dr. LE10: Hinc 5L 69
Kingston Ind. Est. B9: Birm 7M 5
Kingston M. CV31: Lea S 3C 224
Kingston Rd. B9: Birm 8B 102
B75: S Cold 3M 59
CV5: Cov 7M 151
Kingston Row
B1: Birm 7J 101 (5C 4)
Kingston Way DY6: K'wfrd 2J 95
King St. B11: S'brk 2A 122
B63: Hale 5A 118
B64: Old H 8M 97
B66: Smeth 2B 100
B79: Tam 4B 32
CV12: Bed 7H 111
(not continuous)
CV21: Rugby 5A 180
CV32: Lea S 8A 218
DY2: Dud 1J 97
DY5: Quar B 1G 117
DY8: Woll 3L 115
DY9: Lye 5F 116
LE9: Barw 3B 70
LE10: Hinc 8K 69
WS1: Wals 2K 55
WS7: Chase 4F 16
WS9: Wals W 7F 26
WS10: W'bry 6E 54
WV1: Wolv 7C 36 (4J 7)
WV13: W'hall 7B 38
WV14: Bils 6L 53
WV14: Cose 1G 75
King St. Pas. DY2: Dud 8J 75
DY5: Quar B 1G 117
King St. Pct. WS10: Darl 3D 54
King's Wlk. LE9: Earl S 1E 70
Kingsway B68: O'bry 2G 119
B78: K'bry 3C 62
CV2: Cov 6G 153
CV11: Nun 5H 89
CV22: Rugby 8A 180
CV31: Lea S 3L 223
DY8: Woll 1K 115
DY13: Stour S 2E 182
WS11: Cann 5G 9
WV10: Wolv 3G 37
WV11: Ess 5A 24
Kingsway Av. DY4: Tip 1A 76
Kingsway Dr. B38: K Nor 7F 142
Kingsway Nth. WS9: A'rdge 3E 40
Kingsway Rd. WV10: Wolv 3G 37
Kingsway Sth. WS9: A'rdge 3E 40
Kingswear Av. WV6: Pert 6F 34
KINGSWINFORD 3K 95
Kingswinford Rd. DY1: Dud 2E 96
KING'S WOOD 1L 165
KINGSWOOD
Solihull 6K 195
Wolverhampton 7A 20
Kingswood Av. CV7: Cor 2H 129
WS11: Cann 2C 14
KINGSWOOD BROOK 7L 195
Kingswood Cl. B90: Shir 8K 145
B94: Lapw 4L 195
CV6: Cov 8D 130
Kingswood Ct. B94: H'ley H 2C 194
CV10: Nun 5B 88
Kingswood Cft. B7: Nech 2C 102
Kingswood Dr. B30: K Nor 6J 143
B74: S'tly 5M 57
WS6: Gt Wyr 5G 15
WS11: Nort C 4M 15
Kingswood Gdns. CV10: Nun 5B 88
WV4: Penn 3M 51
Kingswood Ho. B14: K Hth 7L 143
Kingswood Rd. B13: Mose 5A 122
B31: Longb 3M 163
CV10: Nun 5A 88
DY6: K'wfrd 5J 95
Kingswood Wlk.
B31: Longb 2M 163
Kington Cl. WV12: W'hall 1B 38
Kington Gdns. B37: F'bri 8F 104
Kington Way B33: Stech 7K 103
King William St.
CV1: Cov 5E 152 (2F 6)
DY8: Amb 1M 115
Kiniths Cres. B71: W Brom 4L 77
Kiniths Way B62: B'hth 8E 98
B71: W Brom 5L 77
Kinlet Cl. B98: Redd 6L 213
WV3: Wolv 1G 51
Kinlet Gro. B31: N'fld 7C 142
Kinloch Dr. DY1: Dud 6F 74
Kinman Way CV21: Rugby 3C 180

Kinmond Ct.—Langdon Wlk.

Kinmond Ct. CV32: Lea S 8M 217
Kinnerley St. WS1: Wals 8A 40
Kinnersley Cl. B98: Redd 6L 213
Kinnersley Cres. B69: O'bry 4D 98
Kinnerton Cres. B29: W Cas . . .7M 119
Kinross Av. WS12: Hed 2F 8
Kinross Cl. CV10: Nun 7F 88
Kinross Cres. B43: Gt Barr 5H 57
Kinross Rd. CV32: Lill 5B 218
Kinross Way LE10: Hinc 8F 68
Kinsall Grn. B77: Wiln 3J 47
Kinsey Gro. B14: K Hth 5M 143
Kinsham Dr. B91: Sol 1B 168
Kintore Cft. B32: Bart G 2H 141
Kintyre, The CV2: W'grve S . . .2B 154
Kintyre Cl. B45: Fran 8E 140
LE10: Hinc 8H 69
KINVER 4A 114
Kinver Av. DY11: Kidd 1G 183
WV12: W'hall 4B 38
Kinver Cl. CV2: W'grve S 8L 131
Kinver Cres. WS9: A'rdge 8J 27
Kinver Cft. B12: Bal H 2L 121
B76: Walm 1A 82
Kinverdale DY11: W'ley 3H 135
Kinver Dr. DY9: Hag 2C 138
WV4: Penn 4J 51
Kinver La. DY11: Cau 3A 136
Kinver Leisure Cen. 4A 114
Kinver M. B37: Mars G 1G 125
Kinver Mt. DY7: Kinv 6A 114
Kinver Rd. B31: N'fld 7D 142
Kinver St. DY8: Word 8K 95
KINWALSEY 2M 127
Kinwalsey La. CV7: Mer 4H 127
Kinwarton Cl. B25: Yard 3K 123
Kipling Av. CV34: Warw 5C 222
WS7: C Ter 8G 11
WV14: Cose 8H 53
Kipling Cl. CV10: Gall C 4A 88
DY4: Tip 1A 76
Kipling Ri. B79: Tam 1M 31
Kipling Rd. B30: K Nor 5C 142
CV6: Cov 1A 152
DY3: Lwr G 4A 74
WV10: F'hses 7D 22
WV12: W'hall 2E 38
Kipling Wlk. DY10: Kidd 3B 158
Kirby Av. CV34: Warw 8F 216
Kirby Cl. CV1: Cov 3D 152
CV8: Bran 4F 176
LE9: Sap 1K 93
WV14: Bils 6L 53
KIRBY CORNER 4H 173
Kirby Cnr. CV4: Canly 3J 173
Kirby Cnr. Rd. CV4: Canly 4H 173
Kirby Dr. DY1: Dud 6E 74
Kirby La. CV7: Withy 4M 133
Kirby Rd. B18: Win G 3E 100
CV5: Cov 7M 151
Kirfield Dr. LE10: Hinc 6M 69
Kirkby Cl. CV21: Brow 3E 180
Kirkby Grn. B73: S Cold 6H 59
Kirkby Rd. CV21: Hillm 8F 180
LE9: Barw 3A 70
Kirkdale Av. CV6: Cov 6D 130
Kirkham Gdns. DY5: P'ntt 3C 96
Kirkham Gro. B33: Stech 5M 103
Kirkham Way DY4: Tip 4A 76
Kirkland Way B78: M Oak 1H 45
Kirkside Gro. WS8: Bwnhls 2F 26
Kirkside M. WS8: Bwnhls 2F 26
Kirkstall Cl. WS3: Blox 7F 24
Kirkstall Cres. WS3: Blox 7F 24
Kirkstone CV21: Brow 2D 180
Kirkstone Ct. DY5: Brie H 2B 116
Kirkstone Cres. B43: Gt Barr 3F 78
WV5: Wom 3F 72
Kirkstone Rd. CV12: Bed 7G 111
Kirkstone Wlk. CV11: Nun 3A 90
Kirkstone Way DY5: Brie H 2B 116
Kirkwall CV47: Sou 5H 225
Kirkwall Rd. B32: Bart G 8K 119
Kirkwood Av. B23: Erd 2F 80
Kirmond Wlk. WV6: Wolv 4B 36
Kirstead Gdns. WV6: Tett 6H 35
Kirtley B77: Glas 7F 32
Kirton Cl. CV6: Cov 8M 129
CV31: W'nsh 6B 224
Kirton Gro. B33: Stech 5A 104
B91: Sol 8A 146
WV6: Tett 4J 35
Kitchener Rd. B29: S Oak 8H 121
CV6: Cov 1E 152
DY2: Dud 8M 75
Kitchener St. B66: Smeth 3D 100
Kitchen La. WV11: Wed 8L 23
Kitebrook Cl. B90: M'path 2A 168
B98: Redd 5L 213
Kite La. B97: Redd 4A 212
Kites Cl. CV34: Warw 7E 216
Kites Nest La. CV35: Beau 8J 197
Kitsland Rd. B34: S End 3E 104
Kitswell Gdns. B32: Bart G 1G 141
Kittermaster Rd. CV7: Mer 8J 127
Kittiwake Dr. DY5: Brie H 2C 116
DY10: Kidd 6B 158
Kittoe Rd. B74: Four O 6F 42
KITT'S GREEN 6C 104
Kitts Grn. B33: Kitts G 6B 104
Kitts Grn. Rd. B33: Kitts G 5A 104
Kitwell La. B32: Bart G 1G 141
Kitwood Av. B78: Dord 3M 47
Kitwood Dr. B92: Sol 2D 146
Kixley La. B93: Know 3J 169
Klaxon Ind. Est. B11: Tys 5F 122
Klevedon Cl. CV11: Nun 8A 90
Knapton Cl. LE10: Hinc 6G 69
Knarsdale Cl. DY5: Brie H 1C 116
Knaves Castle Av.
WS8: Bwnhls 7F 16
Knebley Cres. CV10: Nun 8J 89
Knebworth Cl. B44: Gt Barr 1L 79
Knibbs Shop. Cen., The
CV34: Warw 2E 222
(off Smith St.)
Knight Av. CV1: Cov 8E 152
Knightcote Dr. B91: Sol 1B 168
CV32: Lea S 1L 223
Knight Ct. B75: S Cold 4C 60
Knightley Cl. CV32: Cubb 4E 218
Knightley Rd. B91: Sol 7M 145
Knightlow Av. CV3: W'hall 3J 175
Knightlow Cl. CV8: Ken 6J 199
KNIGHTLOW HILL 1F 202
Knightlow Lodge CV3: W'hall . . .3J 175
Knightlow Rd. B17: Harb 1A 120
Knighton Cl. B74: Four O 6F 42
Knighton Dr. B74: Four O 7F 42
Knighton Rd. B31: N'fld 5C 142
B74: Four O 4D 42
DY2: Neth 5K 97
WS12: Wim 6L 9
Knight Rd. DY11: W'ley 6J 135
WS7: C Ter 8E 10
Knights Av. WV6: Tett 3K 35
Knightsbridge Av. CV12: Bed . . .4J 111
Knightsbridge Cl. B74: Four O . . .5F 42
Knightsbridge Ho.
B37: K'hrst 4F 104
Knightsbridge La.
WV12: W'hall 3C 38
Knightsbridge Rd.
B92: Olton 8M 123
Knights Cl. B23: Erd 7E 80
LE9: S Stan 6K 71
LE10: Burb 5K 91
Knights Ct. CV34: Warw 3D 222
LE10: Hinc 1E 90
WS11: Nort C 5A 16
Knights Cres. WV6: Tett 2L 35
Knightsfield Cl. B73: New O 6C 58
Knightsford Cl. B97: Redd 7M 211
Knights Hill WS9: A'rdge 6H 41
Knights Link LE9: Earl S 1H 71
Knight's Rd. B11: Tys 5G 123
Knights Templar Way
CV4: Tile H 8G 151
Knightstowe Av.
B18: Hock 5G 101 (1A 4)
Knightswood Cl. B75: S Cold . . .2K 59
Knightwick Cres. B23: Erd 4C 80
Knipersley Rd. B73: Bold 3G 81
Knob Hill CV23: Stret D 3F 202
Knoll, The B32: Bart G 8J 119
DY6: K'wfrd 4L 95
Knoll Cl. WS7: Chase 4G 17
Knoll Cft. B90: Ches G 5K 167
CV3: Cov 3C 174
WS9: A'rdge 8J 27
Knollcroft B16: Birm 7G 101
Knoll Dr. CV3: Cov 3C 174
CV34: Warw 8E 216
Knott Ct. DY5: Brie H 7D 96
Knottesford Cl. B80: Stud 6J 221
Knottsall La. B68: O'bry 6H 99
Knotts Farm Rd. DY6: K'wfrd 5A 96
Knowesley Cl. B60: B'gve 7B 188
Knowlands Rd. B90: M'path . . .2A 168
KNOWLE 3J 169
Knowlebury Cross
B94: Tan A 7G 193
Knowle Cl. B45: Redn 2K 163
B98: Redd 3J 213
KNOWLE GROVE 6G 169
Knowle Hill CV8: Ken 3J 199
CV9: Hurl 5H 63
Knowle Hill Rd. DY2: Neth 5H 97
Knowle La. WS14: Lich 7G 19
Knowle Rd. B11: S'hll 6D 122
B65: Row R 5M 97
B92: H Ard 8L 147
Knowles Av. CV10: Nun 5C 88
Knowles Dr. B74: Four O 2G 59
Knowles Rd. WV1: Wolv 8F 36
Knowles St. WS10: W'bry 6G 55
Knowle Wood Rd. B93: Dorr 6H 169
Knox Cres. CV11: Nun 1M 89
Knox Rd. WV2: Wolv 3D 52
Knox's Grave La. B78: Hop 2C 30
WS14: Hop, S'fen 2B 30
Knoyle Ct. *DY8: Stourb 3M 115*
(off Scott's Rd.)
Knutsford St. B12: Bal H 3M 121
Knutswood Cl. B13: Mose 2D 144
Kohima Dr. DY8: Stourb 4L 115
Koi Water Gdns. 2E 134
Kossuth Rd. WV14: Cose 8G 53
Kurtus B77: Dost 3D 46
Kyle Cl. WV10: Oxl 8B 22
Kylemilne Way
DY13: Stour S 6J 183
Kyles Way B32: Bart G 2H 141
Kynaston Cres. WV8: Cod 7H 21
Kyngsford Rd. B33: Kitts G 6D 104
Kynner Way CV3: Bin 1A 176
Kyotts Lake Rd. B11: S'brk 2A 122
Kyrwicks La. B11: S'brk 3A 122
Kyter La. B36: Cas B 1B 104

L

Laburnum Av. B37: K'hrst 3F 104
B67: Smeth 5L 99
B79: Tam 1B 32
CV6: Cov 4M 151
CV8: Ken 5G 199
WS11: Cann 2D 14
Laburnum Cl. B37: K'hrst 3F 104
B47: H'wd 4A 166
B78: K'bry 3D 62
B98: Redd 7E 212
CV12: Bed 7E 110
DY7: Kinv 4A 114
DY8: Woll 2L 115
WS3: Pels 7A 26
WS11: Cann 2E 14
Laburnum Cotts. B21: Hand 1E 100
Laburnum Ct. WS14: Lich 4J 19
Laburnum Cft. B69: Tiv 7B 76
Laburnum Dr. B76: Walm 6A 60
CV31: W'nsh 6B 224
LE9: Earl S 2D 70
Laburnum Gro. B13: Mose 6M 121
B61: B'gve 5M 187
CV10: Nun 3D 88
CV22: Bil 1K 205
CV34: Warw 8H 217
DY11: Kidd 1H 157
WS2: Wals 6F 38
WS7: Chase 3F 16
Laburnum Ho. B30: B'vlle 2F 142
Laburnum Rd. B30: B'vlle 1F 142
DY1: Dud 5H 75
DY4: Tip 2M 75
DY6: K'wfrd 3L 95
WS5: Wals 5C 56
WS9: Wals W 6G 27
WS10: W'bry 5H 55
WV1: Wolv 1H 53
WV4: E'shll 6E 52
Laburnum St. DY8: Woll 2L 115
WV3: Wolv 8A 36
Laburnum Trees *B47: H'wd 3A 166*
(off May Farm Cl.)
Laburnum Vs. B11: S'hll 4C 122
Laburnum Way B31: Longb 8A 142
Laceby Gro. B13: Mose 8D 122
Lacell Cl. CV34: Warw 8D 216
Ladbroke Dr. B76: Walm 7M 59
Ladbroke Gro. B27: A Grn 1J 145
Ladbroke Pk. CV34: Warw 8E 216
Ladbrook Cl. B98: Redd 2E 220
Ladbrook Gro. DY3: Lwr G 6A 74
Ladbrook Rd. B91: Sol 6C 146
CV5: E Grn 5G 151
Ladbury Gro. WS5: Wals 5M 55
Ladbury Rd. WS5: Wals 5A 56
Ladeler Gro. B33: Kitts G 7E 104
Ladies Holloway
DY10: Stone 5F 158
Ladies Wlk. DY3: Sed 1D 74
Lady Bank B32: Bart G 2H 141
B79: Tam 5B 32
Lady Bracknell M.
B31: N'fld 5C 142
Lady Byron La. B93: Know 2F 168
Ladycroft B16: Birm 7G 101 (6A 4)
CV32: Cubb 5E 218
Ladyfields Way CV6: Cov 5B 130
Lady Godiva's Statue 5C 6
Lady Grey Av. CV34: H'cte 6L 223
Lady Grey's Wlk.
DY8: Stourb 5K 115
Ladygrove Cl. B98: Redd 1G 221
Lady Harriet's La.
B98: Redd 5F 212
Lady Herbert's Homes
CV1: Cov 6D 152 (3D 6)
Lady La. B90: Shir 8G 167
B94: Earls 8G 167
CV6: Longf 5F 130
CV8: Ken 5F 198
Lady Lane Mobile Home Pk.
CV6: Longf 5F 130
Ladymead Dr. CV6: Cov 7B 130
Lady Meadow Cl. B78: Tam 6A 32
Ladymoor Rd. WV14: Bils 6J 53
Ladypool Av. B11: S'brk 3B 122
Ladypool Cl. B62: Hale 5C 118
WS4: Wals 4A 40
Ladypool Rd. B12: Bal H 5A 122
Ladysmith Rd. B63: Crad 3J 117
Ladysmock CV23: Brow 1D 180
Ladywalk Bird Sanctuary 5C 84
Lady Warwick Av. CV12: Bed . . .7J 111
Ladywell Cl. WV5: Wom 1G 73
Ladywell Wlk.
B5: Birm 8L 101 (7G 5)
LADYWOOD 7H 101 (5A 4)
Ladywood Arts & Leisure Cen.
. . . . .7F 100
Ladywood Cir. B16: Birm 7G 101
Ladywood Cl. DY5: Quar B 8F 96
Ladywood Middleway
B1: Birm 6G 101
B16: Birm 6G 101 (3A 4)
Ladywood Rd. B16: Edg 8F 100
B74: Four O 2G 59
Laertes Gro. CV34: H'cte 7M 223
LA Fitness 2G 81
Laggan Cl. CV10: Nun 4C 88
Lagonda B77: Glas 6E 32
Lagrange B79: Tam 3L 31
Laing Ho. B69: O'bry 4D 98
Lair, The B78: B'moor 1M 47
Lake Av. WS5: Wals 2B 56
Lake Cl. WS5: Wals 2C 56
Lakedown Cl. B14: K Hth 8L 143
Lakefield B31: N'fld 5M 141
Lakefield Cl. B28: Hall G 2H 145
Lakefield Rd. WV11: Wed 4L 37
Lakehouse Ct. B23: Erd 1E 80
Lakehouse Gro. B38: K Nor 6D 142
Lakehouse Rd. B73: Bold 1E 80
Lakeland Dr. B77: Wiln 2G 47
Lakeland Ho. CV34: Warw 2G 223
Lakenheath Rd. B79: Tam 2C 32
Laker Cl. DY8: Amb 2A 116
LAKES, THE 1B 156
Lake's Cl. DY11: Kidd 2J 157
Lakes Ct. DY12: Bew 2B 156
LAKESIDE 6G 213
Lakeside B74: Lit A 4B 42
B97: Redd 2K 211
CV12: Bed 7G 111
Lakeside Cen., The 6G 143
Lakeside Cl. WV13: W'hall 6L 37
Lakeside Club 5F 104
Lakeside Ct. B61: U War 6H 209
DY5: Brie H 1B 116
Lakeside Dr. B90: M'path 2M 167
WS11: Nort C 3A 16
Lakeside Ind. Est.
B98: Redd 6G 213
Lakeside Ind. Pk. B78: Faz 8M 31
Lakeside Residences
B4: Birm 6M 101 (3H 5)
CV4: Canly 5G 173
Lakeside Rd. B70: W Brom 3G 77
Lakeside Superbowl 3G 111
Lakeside Trad. Cen.
B98: Redd 5G 213
Lakeside Wlk. B23: Erd 5B 80
Lakes Rd. B23: Erd 4A 80
Lakes Rd., The DY12: Bew 2B 156
Lakes Station, The (Rail) 1F 192
Lake St. DY3: Lwr G 6D 74
Lake Vw. Rd. CV5: Cov 5L 151
Lakewood Dr. B45: Redn 8H 141
Lakey La. B28: Hall G 1G 145
Lakin Ct. CV34: Warw 1F 222
Lakin Rd. CV34: Warw 1F 222
Lambah Cl. WV14: Bils 2M 53
Lamb Cl. B34: S End 4E 104
Lamb Cres. WV5: Wom 3F 72
(not continuous)
Lambert Cl. B23: Erd 3D 80
Lambert Ct. DY6: K'wfrd 1K 95
Lambert Dr. WS7: C Ter 2G 17
Lambert End B70: W Brom 6H 77
Lambert Fold DY2: Dud 1L 97
Lambert Rd. WV10: Wolv 3F 36
LAMBERT'S END 6H 77
Lambert St. B70: W Brom 6H 77
Lambeth Cl. B37: F'bri 5H 105
CV2: Cov 2L 153
Lambeth Rd. B44: Gt Barr 6L 57
WV14: Bils 2H 53
Lambourn Cl. WS3: Blox 7J 25
Lambourn Cres.
CV31: Lea S 3C 224
Lambourne Cl. CV5: E Grn 5G 151
WS6: Gt Wyr 6F 14
WS14: Lich 1L 19
Lambourne Dr. DY12: Bew 1B 156
Lambourne Way DY5: Brie H . . .1B 116
WS11: Nort C 4A 16
Lambourn Rd. B23: Erd 5D 80
WV13: W'hall 8D 38
Lambscote Cl. B90: Shir 7C 144
Lambsie La. DY10: Shens 1E 184
Lamb St. CV1: Cov 6C 152 (3B 6)
Lamford Cl. LE10: Hinc 8H 69
Lamgley Rd. WV3: Penn 4E 50
Lamintone Dr. CV32: Lea S 6K 217
Lammas Cl. B92: Sol 8C 124
Lammas Ct. CV8: Wols 6G 177
CV34: Warw 3D 222
Lammas Cft. CV31: W'nsh 6A 224
Lammas Ho. CV6: Cov 5A 152
Lammas Rd. CV6: Cov 5M 151
DY8: Word 6J 95
Lammas Wlk. CV34: Warw 2D 222
Lammermoor Av.
B43: Gt Barr 7F 56
Lammerton Cl. CV2: Cov 3J 153
Lamont Av. B32: Bart G 6M 119
Lamorna Cl. CV11: Nun 5M 89
WV3: Wolv 1H 51
Lamp La. CV7: Gun H 2F 108
Lamprey B77: Dost 3D 46
Lanark Cl. DY6: K'wfrd 4M 95
Lanark Cft. B35: Cas V 6M 81
Lancaster Av. B45: Rubery 1G 163
WS9: A'rdge 1H 41
WS10: W'bry 6J 55
Lancaster Cir. Queensway
B4: Birm 5L 101 (2H 5)
Lancaster Cl. B30: B'vlle 3G 143
CV9: Ath 8L 49
Lancaster Dr. B35: Cas V 7B 82
Lancaster Gdns. WV4: Penn 4L 51
Lancaster Ho. B65: Row R 5E 98
WS12: Hth H 8K 9
Lancaster Pl. CV8: Ken 7E 198
WS3: Blox 7J 25
Lancaster Rd. CV21: Rugby . . .5A 180
DY5: Brie H 7C 96
DY12: Bew 2B 156
LE10: Hinc 1K 91
Lancaster St.
B4: Birm 5L 101 (1H 5)
Lance Cl. LE10: Burb 4K 91
Lance Dr. WS7: C Ter 8E 10
Lancelot Cl. B8: Salt 6E 102
Lancelot Ho. DY10: Hurc 1C 158
Lancelot Pl. DY4: Tip 5E 76
Lanchester Cl. B79: Tam 2L 31
Lanchester Rd. B38: K Nor 8G 143
CV6: Cov 3B 152
Lanchester Way B36: Cas B 8E 82
Lancia Cl. CV6: Ald G 5H 131
Lancing Rd. CV12: Bulk 6C 112
Lander Cl. B45: Rubery 3G 163
Landgate Rd. B21: Hand 7C 78
Land La. B37: Mars G 2G 125
Land Oak Dr. DY10: Kidd 1B 158
Landor Ho. CV31: W'nsh 7A 224
Landor Rd. B93: Know 3G 169
B98: Redd 8G 213
CV31: W'nsh 6A 224
CV34: Warw 1D 222
Landor St.
B8: Birm, Salt 6B 102 (4M 5)
Landport Rd. WV2: Wolv 1F 52
Landrail Wlk. B36: Cas B 1G 105
(not continuous)
Landrake Rd. DY6: K'wfrd 4M 95
Landsberg B79: Tam 4L 31
Landseer Cl. CV21: Hillm 8H 181
Landseer Dr. LE10: Hinc 6H 69
Landseer Gro. B43: Gt Barr 5K 57
Landsgate DY8: Stourb 8A 116
Land Society La. LE9: Earl S 1E 70
Landswood Cl. B44: K'sdng 8A 58
Landswood Rd. B68: O'bry 5J 99
LANDYWOOD 7G 15
Landywood Ent. Pk.
WS6: Gt Wyr 1F 24
Landywood Grn. WS6: C Hay . . .7E 14
Landywood La.
WS6: C Hay, Gt Wyr 7D 14
Landywood Station (Rail) 7F 14
Lane Av. WS2: Wals 6H 39
Lane Cl. WS2: Wals 6H 39
Lane Ct. WV1: Wolv 5C 36 (1J 7)
Lane Cft. B76: Walm 1A 82
Lane End Wlk.
DY13: Stour S 8F 182
LANE GREEN 6H 21
Lane Grn. Av. WV8: Bilb 8J 21
Lane Grn. Ct. WV8: Bilb 6H 21
Lane Grn. Rd. WV8: Bilb 6H 21
Lane Grn. Shop. Pde
WV8: Bilb 6H 21
LANE HEAD 3C 38
Lane Rd. WV4: E'shll 6G 53
Lanes Cl. WV5: Wom 4E 72
LANESFIELD 5F 52
Lanesfield Dr. WV4: E'shll 5G 53
Lanesfield Ind. Est.
WV4: E'shll 5G 53
Lanes Hill Gro. LE9: S Stan 8L 71
Laneside CV3: W'hall 3L 175
Laneside Av. B74: S'tly 2M 57
Laneside Dr. LE10: Hinc 6M 69
Laneside Gdns. DY12: Bew 2B 156
WS2: Wals 7H 39
Lanes Shop. Cen., The
B72: W Grn 2H 81
Lane St. WV14: Bils, Cose 6K 53
LANEY GREEN 7A 14
Langbank Av. CV3: Bin 1J 175
Langbay Ct. CV2: W'grve S . . .3M 153
Langcliffe Av. CV34: Warw 8F 216
Langcomb Rd. B90: Shir 1G 167
Langdale Av. CV6: Cov 6D 130
Langdale Cl. CV21: Brow 2C 180
CV32: Lill 6D 218
WS8: Clay 3E 26
Langdale Ct. B77: Amin 3G 33
Langdale Cft. B21: Hand 2E 100
Langdale Dr. CV11: Nun 3A 90
WS11: Cann 2B 14
WV14: Bils 2K 53
Langdale Grn. WS11: Cann 2C 14
Langdale Rd. B43: Gt Barr 2F 78
DY13: Stour S 8D 182
LE10: Hinc 1F 90
Langdale Way DY9: W'cte 5D 116
Langdon St.
B9: Birm 7B 102 (5M 5)
Langdon Wlk. B26: Yard 5L 123

Langfield Rd.—Leeming Cl.

Langfield Rd. B93: Know 2G 169
Langford Av. B43: Gt Barr 1E 78
Langford Cl. WS1: Wals 8A 40
Langford Cft. B91: Sol 7C 146
Langford Gro. B17: Harb 6C 120
Langham Cl. B26: Sheld 2A 124
Langham Grn. B74: S'tly 8M 41
Langholm Dr. WS12: Hth H 7K 9
Langholme Dr. B44: K'sdng 8D 58
Langland Dr. DY3: Sed 1C 74
Langlands Pl. CV23: Brow 1E 180
LANGLEY 4G 99
Langley Av. WV14: Cose 1J 75
Langley Cl. B98: Redd 8K 213
WS9: Wals W 5G 27
Langley Ct. B69: O'bry 4G 99
WV4: Penn 3K 51
Langley Cres. B68: O'bry 5H 99
Langley Cft. CV4: Tile H 7G 151
Langley Dr. B35: Cas V 8A 82
Langley Gdns. B68: O'bry 5H 99
WV3: Wolv 2K 51
LANGLEY GREEN 5H 99
Langley Grn. Rd. B69: O'bry ...5G 99
Langley Green Station (Rail) ...4H 99
Langley Gro. B10: Small H 1D 122
Langley Hall Dr. B75: S Cold ...4B 60
Langley Hall Rd. B75: S Cold ...4B 60
B92: Olton 2J 145
Langley Heath Dr.
B76: Walm 6M 59
Langley High St. B69: O'bry 4G 99
Langley Mill Junc.
Falcon Lodge 3D 60
Littleworth End 8C 44
Langley Pk. Way B75: S Cold ...3M 59
Langley Ri. B92: Sol 6E 124
Langley Rd. B10: Small H 1D 122
B68: O'bry 5H 99
CV31: W'nsh 5A 224
WV4: Lwr P 4E 50
Langleys Rd. B29: S Oak 8E 120
Langley Swimming Cen. 5H 99
Langlodge Rd. CV6: Cov 7B 130
Langmead Cl. WS2: Wals 6D 38
Langnor Rd. CV2: Cov 3J 153
Langstone Rd. B14: K Hth 7B 144
DY1: Dud 8E 74
Langton Cl. B36: Cas B 3H 105
CV3: Bin 1L 175
Langton Ct. WS13: Lich 8G 13
Langton Pl. WV14: Bils 3A 54
Langton Rd. B8: Salt 5E 102
CV21: Hillm 8E 180
Langtree Av. B91: Sol 8B 146
Langtree Cl. WS12: Hth H 8K 9
Langwood Cl. CV4: Canly 2H 173
Langwood Ct. B36: Cas B 1B 104
Langworth Av. B27: A Grn 4J 123
Lannacombe Rd.
B31: Longb 3L 163
Lansbury Av. WS10: Darl 5C 54
Lansbury Cl. CV2: Cov 2L 153
Lansbury Dr. WS11: Cann 5E 8
Lansbury Grn. B64: Old H 1B 118
Lansbury Rd. B64: Old H 1B 118
Lansbury Wlk. DY4: Tip 1A 76
Lansdale Av. B92: Sol 1F 146
Lansdowne Av. WV8: Cod 7E 20
Lansdowne Cir. CV32: Lea S ...8A 218
Lansdowne Cl. CV12: Bed 6G 111
WV14: Cose 2G 75
Lansdowne Ct. DY9: Pedm 8B 116
Lansdowne Cres. B77: Two G ...8D 32
B80: Stud 6K 221
CV32: Lea S 8A 218
Lansdowne Ho.
B15: Birm 1K 121 (8E 4)
Lansdowne Pl. CV21: Rugby ...7D 180
Lansdowne Rd. B21: Hand 2G 101
B24: Erd 6F 80
B62: B'hth 1F 118
B63: Hale 7K 117
B80: Stud 6K 221
CV32: Lea S 8A 218
DY2: Dud 3M 97
WV1: Wolv 6B 36 (2G 7)
WV14: Bils 2L 53
Lansdowne St. B18: Win G 5F 100
(not continuous)
CV2: Cov 6F 152
CV32: Lea S 8A 218
Lansdown Grn. DY11: Kidd 4H 157
Lansdown Pl. B18: Win G 4F 100
Lant Cl. CV4: Tile H 1B 172
Lantern Rd. DY2: Neth 7J 97
LAPAL 6F 118
Lapal La. B62: Bart G 7F 118
Lapal La. Nth. B62: Hale 6E 118
Lapal La. Sth. B62: Hale 6E 118
Lapley Cl. WV1: Wolv 7H 37
Lappath Ho. B32: Bart G 1K 141
Lapper Av. WV4: E'shll 6F 52
Lapwing B77: Wiln 3G 47
Lapwing Cl. DY10: Kidd 8B 158
WS6: C Hay 8C 14
Lapwing Cft. B23: Erd 2C 80
Lapwing Dr. B92: H Ard 2B 148
Lapwood Av. DY6: K'wfrd 3M 95
LAPWORTH 6E 194
Lapworth Cl. B98: Redd 2F 220
Lapworth Dr. B73: New O 6C 58
Lapworth Gro. B12: Bal H 3M 121
Lapworth Ho. B5: Birm 2L 121
Lapworth Mus. 6F 120
Lapworth Oaks B94: Lapw 6K 195
Lapworth Rd. CV2: Cov 7J 131
Lapworth Station (Rail) 5K 195
Lapworth St. B94: Lapw 7H 195
Lara Cl. B17: Harb 1B 120
Lara Gro. DY4: Tip 7A 76
Larch Av. B21: Hand 7D 78
Larch Cl. CV22: Bil 7H 179
DY7: Kinv 6C 114
WS14: Lich 2L 19
Larch Cft. B37: Chel W 7H 105
B69: Tiv 7B 76
Larch Dr. B31: Longb 8J 141
Larches, The B78: K'bry 2D 62
CV7: Exh 1G 131
Larches Cott. Gdns.
DY11: Kidd 6J 157
Larches La. WV3: Wolv 7A 36
Larches Rd. DY11: Kidd 6K 157
Larches St. B11: S'brk 3A 122
Larchfield Cl. B20: Hand 6H 79
Larchfields CV8: Wols 5G 177
Larch Gro. CV34: Warw 8G 217
DY3: Sed 2E 74
Larch Ho. B20: Hand 6F 78
B36: Hodg H 1M 103
Larchmere Dr. B28: Hall G 1F 144
B61: B'gve 6L 187
WV11: Ess 6B 24
Larch Rd. DY6: K'wfrd 3L 95
Larch Tree Av. CV4: Tile H 6G 151
Larch Wlk. B25: Yard 1H 123
Larchwood Cres. B74: S'tly 1L 57
Larchwood Dr. WS11: Cann 5G 9
Larchwood Grn. WS5: Wals 5B 56
Larchwood Rd. CV7: Exh 1H 131
WS5: Wals 5A 56
Larcombe Dr. WV4: Penn 4D 52
Larford Wlk. DY13: Stour S 8F 182
Large Av. WS10: Darl 5C 54
Lark Cl. B14: K Hth 7A 144
Larkfield Av. B36: Cas B 1B 104
Larkfield Rd. B98: Redd 8G 213
Larkfield Way CV5: Alle 3G 151
LARKHILL 1L 157
Larkhill DY10: Kidd 2L 157
Larkhill Rd. DY8: Stourb 5J 115
Larkhill Wlk. B14: K Hth 8K 143
Larkin Cl. CV12: Bulk 6B 112
WV10: Bush 8G 23
Larkin Gro. CV2: W'grve S 3M 153
Lark Mdw. Dr. B37: K'hrst 6E 104
Larksfield *B66: Smeth* *5B 100*
(off Windmill La.)
Larksfield M. DY5: Brie H 2C 116
Larks Mill WS3: Pels 5L 25
Larkspur B77: Dost 5D 46
CV23: Brow 1D 180
Larkspur Av. WS7: Burn 4G 17
Larkspur Ct. CV12: Bed 1C 130
Larkspur Cft. B36: Hodg H 1K 103
Larkspur Dr. WV10: F'stne 2H 23
Larkspur Rd. DY2: Dud 1M 97
Larkspur Way WS8: Clay 3D 26
Larkswood Dr. DY3: Sed 2D 74
WV4: Penn 6J 51
Larne Rd. B26: Sheld 2A 124
Lashbrooke Ho. B45: Rubery ...2F 162
LASH HILL 1M 91
Lash Hill Path LE10: Burb 1L 91
Lassington Cl. B98: Redd 5L 213
Latches Cl. WS10: Darl 3E 54
Latchford Cl. B98: Redd 3L 213
Latelow Rd. B33: Yard 7A 104
Latham Av. B43: Gt Barr 2E 78
Latham Cres. DY4: Tip 6A 76
Latham Rd. CV5: Cov 7A 152
Lath La. B66: Smeth 1K 99
Lathom Gro. B33: Stech 4M 103
Latimer Cl. CV8: Ken 7F 198
Latimer Gdns. B15: Edg 2K 121
Latimer Pl. B18: Win G 3E 100
Latimer Rd. B48: A'chu 4A 190
Latimer St. WV13: W'hall 6B 38
Latymer Cl. B76: Walm 2A 82
Lauder Cl. DY3: Sed 8C 52
WV13: W'hall 8K 37
Lauderdale Av. CV6: Cov 6D 130
Lauderdale Cl.
CV23: Long L 5H 179
WS8: Clay 3E 26
Lauderdale Gdns.
WV10: Bush 6E 22
Laughton Cl. B31: Longb 2B 164
Launce Gro. CV34: H'cte 7M 223
Launceston Cl. B77: Wiln 7D 32
WS5: Wals 2D 56
Launceston Dr. CV11: Nun 5M 89
Launceston Rd. WS5: Wals 2D 56
Launde, The B28: Hall G 6E 144
Laundry Rd. B66: Smeth 6C 100
Laureates Wlk.
B74: Four O 8G 43
Laurel Av. B12: Bal H 4A 122
B78: Pole 1A 48
Laurel Bank B79: Tam 3B 32
Laurel Bank M. B60: B'wll 5F 188
Laurel Cl. B98: Redd 7E 212
CV2: W'grve S 7L 131
DY1: Dud 6G 75
WS13: Lich 1K 19
Laurel Ct. B13: Mose 7M 121
Laurel Dr. B66: Smeth 1A 100
B74: S'tly 1L 57
CV10: Harts 1A 88
CV22: Bil 8H 179
CV47: S'ton 1L 225
WS7: Burn 2J 17
WS12: Hed 5L 9
Laurel Gdns. B21: Hand 8E 78
B27: A Grn 4J 123
B45: B Grn 1L 189
CV22: Rugby 1M 205
Laurel Gro. B30: B'vlle 3E 142
B61: B'gve 5M 187
WV3: Wolv 3L 51
WV14: Bils 5A 54
Laurel La. B63: Hale 6B 118
Laurel Rd. B21: Hand 8E 78
B30: K Nor 5G 143
DY1: Dud 5F 74
DY4: Tip 2M 75
WS5: Wals 5B 56
Laurels, The *B16: Birm* *6F 100*
(off Marroway St.)
B26: Sheld 4C 124
B47: Wyt *1M 191*
(off Hillcrest Pk.)
B78: K'bry 2D 62
CV12: Bed 7E 110
Laurels Cres. CV7: Bal C 3J 171
Laurel Ter. B6: Aston 8M 79
Laurence Ct. B31: N'fld 4B 142
Laurence Gro. WV6: Tett 2L 35
Lauriston Cl. DY1: Dud 6F 74
Lavender Av. CV6: Cov 4L 151
Lavender Cl. CV12: Bed 8E 110
CV23: Brow 1E 180
WS5: Wals 6M 55
WV9: Pend 6M 21
Lavender Ct. *B71: W Brom* *2J 77*
(off Sussex Av.)
Lavender Gdns. B23: Erd 2B 80
Lavender Gro. WS3: Wals 4L 39
WV14: Bils 3M 53
Lavender Hall La.
CV7: Bal C 1H 171
Lavender Ho. B38: K Nor 1F 164
Lavender La. DY8: Stourb 6K 115
Lavender Rd. B77: Amin 5F 32
DY1: Dud 6H 75
Lavendon Rd. B42: P Barr 4H 79
Lavenham Cl. CV11: Nun 1C 112
Lavinia Rd. B62: Hale 6E 118
Law Cliff Rd. B42: Gt Barr 3H 79
Law Cl. B69: Tiv 7D 76
Lawden Rd.
B10: Small H 1B 122 (8M 5)
Lawford Av. WS14: Lich 2L 19
Lawford Cl. B7: Birm ...6A 102 (3M 5)
CV3: Bin 8L 153
Lawford Gro. B5: Birm 1L 121
B90: Shir 7D 144
LAWFORD HEATH 2D 204
Lawford Heath Ind. Est.
CV23: Law H 2C 204
Lawford Heath La.
CV23: Law H, Long L 3B 204
Lawford La. CV22: Bil 8H 179
Lawford Rd. CV21: Rugby 5J 179
CV31: Lea S 4B 224
Lawfred Av. WV11: Wed 4K 37
Lawley, The B63: Hale 8K 117
Lawley Cl. CV4: Tile H 7G 151
WS4: S'fld 8B 26
Lawley Middleway B4:
Birm 5A 102 (2L 5)
Lawley Rd. WV14: Bils 3H 53
Lawley St. B70: W Brom 6F 76
DY1: Dud 8G 75
Lawn Av. DY8: Stourb 5L 115
Lawn La. WV9: Coven 4M 21
Lawn Oaks Cl. WS8: Bwnhls 7D 16
Lawn Rd. WV2: E'shll 3F 52
Lawns, The B47: Wyt 2M 191
CV12: Bed 7D 110
CV23: Kils 7M 207
LE10: Hinc 1L 91
Lawnsdale Cl. B46: Col 2M 105
Lawnsdown Rd.
DY5: Quar B 2F 116
Lawnsfield Gro. B23: Erd 3D 80
Lawnside Grn. WV14: Bils 1K 53
Lawn St. DY8: Stourb 5L 115
LAWNS WOOD 7G 95
Lawns Wood LE10: Hinc 1G 91
Lawnswood B76: Walm 1A 82
DY7: Stourt 5G 95
Lawnswood Av. B90: Shir 6K 145
DY8: Word 5J 95
WS7: Chase 4F 16
WV4: E'shll 5E 52
WV6: Tett 1L 35
Lawnswood Cl. WS12: Hth H 8K 9
Lawnswood Dr. DY7: Stourt 7G 95
WS9: Wals W 6G 27
Lawnswood Gro. B21: Hand 8C 78
Lawnswood Ri. WV6: Tett 1M 35
Lawnswood Rd. DY3: Up Gor ...4D 74
DY8: Word 6J 95
Lawnwood Rd. DY2: Neth 7H 97
Lawrence Av. WV10: Wolv 5G 37
WV11: Wed 3M 37
Lawrence Ct. B68: O'bry 1H 119
B79: Tam 3A 32
Lawrence Dr. B76: Min 3D 82
Lawrence Gdns. CV8: Ken 3F 198
Lawrence La. B64: Old H 8L 97
Lawrence Rd. CV7: Exh 1G 131
CV21: Rugby 6D 180
Lawrence Saunders Rd.
CV6: Cov 4A 152
Lawrence Sheriff St.
CV22: Rugby 6A 180
Lawrence St. DY9: Lye 3C 116
WV13: W'hall 6A 38
Lawrence Twr. B4: Birm 3J 5
Lawrence Wlk. B43: Gt Barr 5K 57
Lawson Cl. WS9: A'rdge 5H 41
Lawson St. B4: Birm 5L 101 (2H 5)
Law St. B71: W Brom 4J 77
Lawton Av. B29: S Oak 7H 121
Lawton Cl. B65: Row R 3D 98
LE10: Hinc 1F 90
Lawyers Wlk. WS1: Wals 8M 39
Laxey Rd. B16: Edg 6D 100
Laxford Cl. B12: Bal H 3L 121
LE10: Hinc 8F 68
Lax Lane DY12: Bew 6B 156
Laxton Cl. DY6: K'wfrd 4A 96
Laxton Dr. DY12: Bew 2B 156
Laxton Gro. B25: Yard 8K 103
Layamon Wlk.
DY13: Stour S 8F 182
Lay Gdns. CV31: Rad S 4E 224
Lazy Hill B38: K Nor 7H 143
WS9: A'rdge 7J 27
Lazy Hill Rd. WS9: A'rdge 1H 41
WS9: Ston 6K 27
Lea, The B33: Yard 7A 104
DY11: Kidd 4G 157
Lea Av. WS10: W'bry 8D 54
Lea Bank WV3: Wolv 7J 35
Lea Bank Av. DY11: Kidd 4G 157
Lea Bank Rd. DY2: Neth 6H 97
Leabon Gro. B17: Harb 5C 120
Leabrook B26: Yard 1M 123
Leabrook Rd. DY4: Tip 8C 54
WS10: W'bry 8C 54
Leabrook Rd. Nth.
WS10: W'bry 8D 54
Lea Castle Cl. DY10: Kidd ...8M 135
Lea Castle Dr. DY10: Cookl ...5C 136
DY10: W'ley 7B 136
Lea Causeway, The
DY11: Kidd 5G 157
Leach Grn. La. B45: Redn 2G 163
Leach Heath La.
B45: Rubery 2F 162
Leacliffe Way WS9: A'rdge 6M 41
Leacote Dr. WV6: Tett 5J 35
Lea Cres. CV21: N'bld A 3K 179
Leacrest Rd. CV6: Cov 7A 130
LEACROFT 3E 14
Leacroft WV12: W'hall 2C 38
Leacroft Av. WV10: Bush 1E 36
Leacroft Cl. WS9: A'rdge 8H 27
Leacroft Gro. B71: W Brom 1H 77
Leacroft La. WS11: Cann 1G 15
(Lichfield Rd.)
WS11: Cann 4F 14
(Walsall Rd.)
Lea Cft. Rd. B97: Redd 4D 220
Leacroft Rd. DY6: K'wfrd 1L 95
Leadbeater Ho. *WS3: Blox* *1H 39*
(off Somerfield Rd.)
Leadbetter Dr. B61: B'gve 7K 187
Lea Dr. B26: Sheld 3A 124
LEA END 6F 164
Lea End La. B38: Forh 6F 164
B48: Hopw 5C 164
Leaf Ct. CV3: Cov 5D 174
Leafdown Cl. WS12: Hed 5K 9
Leafenden Av. WS7: Burn 3G 17
Leafield Cl. CV2: W'grve S ...8M 131
Leafield Cres. B33: Stech 4A 104
Leafield Gdns. B62: B'hth 1D 118
Leafield Rd. B92: Sol 8B 124
Leaf La. CV3: Cov 5E 174
Lea Ford Rd. B33: Kitts G 5C 104
Leaford Way DY6: K'wfrd 4M 95
Leafy Glade B74: S'tly 6A 42
Leafy La. B94: Earls 1H 193
Leafy Ri. DY3: Lwr G 5D 74
Lea Gdns. WV3: Wolv 1B 52 (8G 7)
Leagh Cl. CV8: Ken 2H 199
Lea Grn. Av. DY4: Tip 4J 75
Lea Grn. Dr. B47: Wyt 5C 166
Lea Grn. La. B47: Wyt 3C 166
Lea Hall Dr. WS7: C Ter 8D 10
Lea Hall Rd. B33: Yard 6A 104
Lea Hall Station (Rail) 6B 104
Leahill Cft. B37: F'bri 7F 104
Lea Hill Rd. B20: Hand 7J 79
Leaholme Ct. CV5: Cov 1M 173
Leaholme Gdns. DY9: Pedm ...7B 116
Leahouse Gdns. B68: O'bry 6G 99
Lea Ho. Rd. B30: Stir 2G 143
Leahouse Rd. B68: O'bry 6G 99
Leahurst Cres. B17: Harb 5C 120
Lea La. DY10: Cookl 6L 135
WS6: Gt Wyr 6G 15
Lea Mnr. Dr. WV4: Penn 6L 51
LEA MARSTON 2A 84
Lea Marston Leisure Cen. 8A 62
Leam Cl. CV11: Nun 8M 89
Leam Cres. B92: Sol 8B 124
Leam Dr. WS7: Burn 2K 17
Leam Grn. CV4: Canly 4K 173
Leamington Cl. WS11: Cann 1C 14
Leamington Rd. B12: Bal H 4A 122
CV3: Cov 2C 174
CV8: Ken 7G 199
CV8: Rytn D 1A 202
CV23: Prin 8A 202
Leamington Spa Station (Rail)
.....................2M 223
LEAMONSLEY 3F 18
LEAMORE 4H 39
Leamore Cl. WS2: Wals 2G 39
Leamore Ent. Pk. WS2: Wals ...3G 39
(Fryer's Rd.)
WS2: Wals 2G 39
(Willenhall La., not continuous)
Leamore Ind. Est.
WS2: Wals 3H 39
Leamore La. WS2: Wals 2G 39
WS3: Blox 3H 39
Leamount Dr. B44: K'sdng 7C 58
Leam Rd. CV31: Lea S 2K 223
Leam St. CV31: Lea S 2B 224
Leam Ter. CV31: Lea S 2A 224
Leander Cl. WS6: Gt Wyr 8F 14
WS7: C Ter 8D 10
Leander Gdns. B14: K Hth 4M 143
Leander Rd. DY9: W'cte 5F 116
Leandor Dr. B74: S'tly 2A 58
Lea Pk. Ri. B61: B'gve 4M 187
Leapgate La. DY11: Tort 4K 183
DY13: Stour S 4K 183
Lear Gro. CV34: H'cte 5L 223
Lea Rd. B11: S'hll 5D 122
WV3: Wolv 2A 52 (7G 7)
Lear Rd. WV5: Wom 1H 73
Leas, The WV10: F'stne 2J 23
Leas Cl. CV12: Bed 6G 111
Leason La. WV10: Bush 1G 37
Leasow, The WS9: A'rdge 4E 40
Leasow Dr. B15: Edg 6D 120
Leasowe, The WS13: Lich 8G 13
Leasowe Dr. WV6: Pert 5D 34
Leasowe Rd. B45: Rubery 1F 162
DY4: Tip 5L 75
Leasowes Av. CV3: Finh 5M 173
Leasowes Country Pk., The ...5D 118
Leasowes Ct. B63: Hale 7A 118
Leasowes Dr. WV4: Penn 3K 51
Leasowes La. B62: Hale 4D 118
Leasowes Rd. B14: K Hth 8M 121
Leasowes Sports Cen. 3E 118
Lea St. DY10: Kidd 4M 157
Leatherhead Cl. B6: Aston 3M 101
Leathermill La. CV10: Harts 6C 66
Leather Mus., The 6L 39
Lea Va. Rd. DY8: Stourb 7M 115
Leavesden Gro. B26: Sheld 1B 124
Lea Vw. WS9: A'rdge 4E 40
WV12: W'hall 4A 38
Lea Wlk. B45: Rubery 1F 162
CV8: Rytn D 8B 176
Leaward Cl. CV10: Nun 7E 88
Leawood Gro. DY11: Kidd 4G 157
Lea Yield Cl. B30: Stir 2G 143
Lebanon Gro. WS7: C Ter 1F 16
Lechlade Cl. B98: Redd 2H 213
(not continuous)
Lechlade Rd. B43: Gt Barr 1E 78
Leckie Rd. WS2: Wals 5L 39
Ledbrook Rd. CV32: Cubb 4D 218
Ledbury Cl. B16: Birm 7G 101
B98: Redd 7M 213
WS9: A'rdge 8J 27
Ledbury Ct. *B29: W Cas* *2C 142*
(off Ruthall Cl.)
WV12: W'hall 5B 38
Ledbury Dr. WV1: Wolv 8H 37
Ledbury Ho. B33: Kitts G 7E 104
B97: Redd 5B 212
Ledbury Rd. CV31: Lea S 3C 224
Ledbury Way B76: Walm 1A 82
Ledsam Gro. B32: Harb 3M 119
Ledsam St. B16: Birm 7G 101
Ledwell B90: Dic H 3G 167
Lee, The CV5: Cov 5J 151
LEE BANK 1J 121 (8D 4)
Lee Bank Middleway
B15: Birm 1J 121 (8C 4)
Leebank Rd. B63: Hale 7L 117
Leech St. DY4: Tip 4C 76
Lee Cl. CV34: Warw 7E 216
LE9: S Stan 6L 71
Lee Ct. WS9: Wals W 6F 26
Lee Cres. B15: Edg 1J 121
Leecrofts, The LE9: Earl S 1F 70
Leeder Cl. CV6: Cov 7C 130
Leedham Av. B77: Tam 4D 32
Lee Gdns. B67: Smeth 4L 99
LEEK WOOTTON 2F 216
Lee Medowe CV34: Warw 5B 222
Leeming Cl. CV4: Canly 3J 173

Long Acre Ind. Est.—Lychgate Cl.

Long Acre Ind. Est.
B7: Nech .2B 102
(not continuous)
Longacre Ind. Est. B7: Nech . . .1C 102
Longacres B74: Lit A .5C 42
WS12: Hed .4M 9
Long Acre St. WS2: Wals .6K 39
Longbank Rd. B69: Tiv .1C 98
Longboat La. DY8: Word .1L 115
DY13: Stour S .5G 183
Longboat Quay DY2: Neth .5K 97
Longborough Cl. B97: Redd . . .3B 220
Longbow Rd. B29: W Cas .2M 141
LONGBRIDGE
B31 .1M 163
CV34 .7B 222
Longbridge La. B31: Longb . . .1L 163
Long Bri. Rd. WS14: Lich .4J 19
Longbridge Station (Rail) 1L 163
Longbrook La. CV7: Bal C .3E 170
CV8: Fen E .3E 170
Long Cl. DY9: Hag .5M 137
Long Cl. Av. CV5: Alle .3H 151
Long Cl. Wlk. B35: Cas V .6B 82
Long Compton Dr. DY9: Hag . . .3A 138
Long Cft. WS12: Hunt .5C 8
Longcroft, The B63: Hale .6L 117
WS4: Rus .2C 40
Longcroft Av. WS10: W'bry .6G 55
Longcroft Cl. B35: Cas V .7M 81
Longdales Rd. B38: K Nor .2D 164
LONGDON .1M 11
Longdon Av. WV4: Penn .4D 52
Longdon Cl. B98: Redd .2H 221
Longdon Cft. B93: Know .1G 169
Longdon Dr. B74: Four O .5E 42
LONGDON GREEN .1B 12
Longdon Rd. B93: Know .3G 169
LONG EYE .4D 188
Longfellow Av. CV34: Warw . . .5C 222
Longfellow Cl. B97: Redd .2C 220
Longfellow Ct. CV2: Cov .6J 153
Longfellow Grn. DY10: Kidd . . .3B 158
Longfellow Pl. WS11: Cann .5E 8
Longfellow Rd. B30: K Nor .5D 142
CV2: Cov .6J 153
DY3: Lwr G .4A 74
WS7: C Ter .8F 10
Longfellow Wlk. B79: Tam .1M 31
Longfield Cl. B28: Hall G .3F 144
B77: Amin .5E 32
Longfield Dr. B74: Lit A .5D 42
Longfield Ho. CV6: Cov .1G 153
WV10: Wolv .6F 36
Longfield Rd. B31: N'fld .1L 141
CV31: Lea S .3B 224
DY9: Lye .4D 116
LONGFORD
CV6 .5G 131
WS11 .2B 14
Longford Cl. B32: Bart G .2G 141
B93: Dorr .6H 169
WV5: Wom .4D 72
Longford Ct. WS11: Cann .1B 14
Longford Grn. WS11: Cann .2C 14
Longford Gro. B44: K'sdng .6A 58
Longford Ind. Est.
WS11: Cann .3D 14
Longford Rd. B44: K'sdng .6A 58
CV6: Longf .6F 130
CV7: Exh .3G 131
WS11: Cann .8B 8
WV10: Wolv .5F 36
Longford Sq. CV6: Longf .5F 130
Long Furlong CV22: Rugby . . .2M 205
Long Furrow WV8: Pend .8L 21
Longham Cft. B32: Harb .5M 119
Longhope Cl. B98: Redd .5A 214
Longhurst Cft. B31: Longb . . .2B 164
Long Hyde Rd. B67: Smeth .8M 99
Long Innage B63: Crad .3H 117
Long Itchington Rd.
CV33: H'ham .4M 219
Long Knowle La. WV11: Wed . . .1H 37
Longlake Av. WV6: Tett .6G 35
Longlands, The B45: B Grn . . .2K 189
WV5: Wom .3G 73
Longlands Cl. B38: K Nor .1C 164
(off Nearhill Rd.)
Longlands Dr. B77: Amin .5F 32
Longlands Rd. B62: Hale .6E 118
Long La. B62: B'hth .8D 98
B65: B'hth .8D 98
CV5: Alle .7K 129
CV7: Ker E .7L 129
WS6: Ess, Gt Wyr .4D 24
WS11: Nort C .1L 15
Long La. Trad. Est.
B62: B'hth .1D 118
LONG LAWFORD .4G 179
Long Leasow B29: W Cas .2A 142
Longleat B43: Gt Barr .7D 56
B79: Tam .2K 31
Longleat Dr. B90: Ches G .4L 167
DY1: Dud .7E 74
Longleat Gro. CV31: Lea S . . .3C 224
Longleat Rd. WS9: A'rdge .8G 27
Long Ley WV10: Wolv .6F 36
Longley Av. B76: Min .4D 82
Longley Cres. B26: Yard .5L 123
Long Leys Ct. B46: Wat O .6H 83
Longleys Cft. B46: Wat O .7H 83
Longley Wlk. B37: Chel W .7J 105
Long Mdw. B65: Row R .6C 98
Longmeadow Cl. B75: S Cold . . .4M 59
Longmeadow Cres.
B34: S End .3E 104
Long Mdw. Dr. DY3: Sed .7B 52
Longmeadow Gro.
B31: Longb .3A 164
Long Mdw. Rd. B60: L End . . .3C 188
Longmeadow Rd. WS5: Wals . . .1E 56
Long Mill Av. WV11: Wed .2H 37
Long Mill Nth. WV11: Wed .2H 37
Long Mill Sth. WV11: Wed .2H 37
Longmoor Cl. B97: Redd .3B 212
WV11: Wed .4M 37
Longmoor Rd. B63: Hale .6L 117
B73: S'tly .6B 58
Longmore Av. WS2: Wals .8F 38
Longmore Cl. B73: S'tly .4A 58
Longmore Rd. B90: Shir .7J 145
Longmore St. B12: Bal H .2L 121
WS10: W'bry .6F 54
Long Mynd B63: Hale .8K 117
Long Mynd Cl. WV12: W'hall . . .8B 24
Long Mynd Rd. B31: N'fld .3L 141
Longmynd Way
DY13: Stour S .8D 182
Long Nuke Rd. B31: N'fld .2L 141
Longrood Rd. CV22: Bil .3K 205
Long Saw Dr. B31: Longb .8K 141
Longshaw Gro. B34: S End . . .3D 104
Long Shoot, The CV11: Nun . . .4A 90
Longstaff Av. WS12: Haz .5C 10
Longstaff Cft. WS13: Lich .7F 12
Longstone Cl. B90: M'path . . .3B 168
Longstone Rd. B42: Gt Barr . . .2J 79
Longstork Rd. CV23: Brow . . .1D 180
Long St. B11: S'brk .3A 122
B78: Dord .4A 48
CV9: Ath .1K 65
CV12: Bulk .7D 112
LE9: S Stan .6L 71
WS2: Wals .8K 39
WV1: Wolv .7D 36 (3K 7)
Long Wood B30: B'vlle .4E 142
Longwood Cl. CV4: W'wd H . . .3F 172
Longwood La. WS4: Wals .7E 40
WS5: Wals .7E 40
Longwood Path B78: M Oak . . .8K 31
Longwood Pathway
B34: S End .4C 104
Longwood Ri. WV12: W'hall . . .4D 38
Longwood Rd. B45: Redn .2G 163
WS9: A'rdge .6H 41
Lonicera Cl. WS5: Wals .6B 56
Lonscale Dr. CV3: Cov .4B 174
Lonsdale Cl. B33: Stech .7K 103
WV12: W'hall .4B 38
Lonsdale Ct. B17: Harb .3C 120
Lonsdale Rd. B17: Harb .3B 120
B66: Smeth .2K 99
CV32: Lill .5B 218
WS5: Wals .3C 56
WV3: Wolv .2B 52 (8G 7)
WV14: Bils .3M 53
Lord Austin Dr. B60: Marl . . .8E 162
Lord Cromwell Ct.
WS11: Cann .4G 9
Lord Lytton Av. CV2: Cov .7K 153
Lords B17: Harb .3B 120
Lords Dr. WS2: Wals .6L 39
Lords La. B80: Stud .6L 221
DY7: Stourt .8E 94
Lordsmore Cl. WV14: Cose . . .8L 53
Lord St. B7: Birm .5M 101 (1K 5)
CV5: Cov .7M 151
WS1: Wals .2K 55
(not continuous)
WV3: Wolv .7B 36
(not continuous)
WV14: Bils .6L 53
Lord St. W. WV14: Bils .6L 53
Lordswood Cl. B97: Redd .7M 211
Lordswood Rd. B17: Harb .1A 120
Lordswood Sq. B17: Harb .2B 120
Lorenzo Cl. CV3: W'hall .3K 175
Lorimer Way B43: Gt Barr .4K 57
Lorne Gro. DY10: Kidd .3A 158
Lorne St. DY4: Tip .1M 75
DY10: Kidd .4A 158
DY13: Stour S .4G 183
WS7: C Ter .1E 16
Lorrainer Av. DY5: Brie H . . .1A 116
Lorton B79: Tam .2K 31
Lossiemouth Rd. LE10: Hinc . . .8F 68
Lothersdale B77: Wiln .1H 47
(not continuous)
Lothians Rd. WS3: Pels .4A 26
WV6: Tett .3L 35
Lottie Rd. B29: S Oak .8E 120
Lotus B77: Glas .6E 32
Lotus Ct. B16: Edg .8E 100
Lotus Cft. B67: Smeth .5M 99
Lotus Dr. B64: Old H .7M 97
WS11: Cann .4E 8
Lotus Wlk. B36: Cas B .8F 82
Lotus Way B65: Row R .5A 98
Loudon Av. CV6: Cov .4A 152
Loudon Ga. CV11: Nun .8M 89
Loughshaw B77: Wiln .8J 33
Loughton Gro. B63: Hale .5M 117
Louisa Pl. B18: Hock .4G 101
Louisa St. B1: Birm .6J 101 (4C 4)
Louis Ct. B67: Smeth .4M 99
Louise Ct. B27: A Grn .6J 123
B91: Sol .8L 145
Louise Cft. B14: K Hth .7L 143
Louise Lorne Rd.
B13: Mose .5M 121
Louise Rd. B21: Hand .2F 100
Louise St. DY3: Gorn .6B 74
Lound Rd. LE9: Sap .1K 93
Lount Wlk. B19: Hock .4L 101
Lovage Rd. B98: Redd .3M 213
Lovatt Cl. DY4: Tip .8C 54
Lovatt Pl. WS11: Cann .4E 8
Lovatt St. WV1: Wolv .7B 36 (4G 7)
Loveday Cl. CV9: Ath .7K 49
Loveday Dr. CV32: Lea S .7L 217
Loveday Ho. B70: W Brom .6K 77
Loveday St. B4: Birm . . .5L 101 (2G 5)
(not continuous)
Lovelace Av. B91: Sol .1D 168
Lovelace Cres. LE9: Elme .4F 70
Love La. B7: Birm .5M 101 (1J 5)
B47: H'wd .2L 165
B69: Tiv .8A 76
CV8: Ken .3F 198
DY8: Stourb .6A 116
DY9: Lye .4E 116
LE10: Burb .3A 92
WS1: Wals .2L 55
WS6: Gt Wyr .6G 15
WV6: Tett .3K 35
Lovell B79: Tam .3M 31
Lovell Cl. B29: W Cas .3B 142
CV7: Exh .1G 131
Lovell Rd. CV12: Bed .6G 111
Love Lyne B97: Redd .3A 220
Loveridge Cl. WV8: Cod .6F 20
Loverock Cres. CV21: Hillm . . .7E 180
Lovers Wlk. B6: Aston .1B 102
B78: Tam .5A 32
WS10: W'bry .6F 54
Lovett Av. B69: O'bry .4D 98
Lovetts Cl. LE10: Hinc .1F 90
Lowans Hill Vw. B97: Redd . . .5C 212
Low Av. B43: Gt Barr .7F 56
Lowbridge Cl. WV12: W'hall . . .4C 38
Lowbrook La. B90: Tid G .5D 166
Lowcroft Gdns. WV10: Bush . . .1E 36
Lowden Cft. B26: Yard .5L 123
Lowdham B77: Wiln .8J 33
Lowe Av. WS10: Darl .2B 54
Lowe Dr. B73: New O .6D 58
DY6: K'wfrd .5L 95
Lowe La. DY11: Kidd .7H 135
Lower Av. CV31: Lea S .2M 223
Lwr. Beeches Rd.
B31: Longb .7J 141
LOWER BENTLEY .8D 210
Lwr. Bentley La. B60: Lwr B . . .8D 210
Lwr. Bond St. LE10: Hinc .8K 69
LOWER BRADLEY .6A 54
Lwr. Cape CV34: Warw .8D 216
Lwr. Chapel St. B69: Tiv .7C 76
Lwr. Church La. DY4: Tip .4B 76
Lwr. City Rd. B69: Tiv .8C 76
LOWER CLENT .5D 138
Lwr. Common La.
B97: Redd .7B 212
Lowercroft Way B74: Four O . . .4E 42
Lwr. Dartmouth St.
B9: Birm .7B 102 (5M 5)
Lwr. Derry St. DY5: Brie H 7D 96
LOWER EASTERN GREEN . . .5F 150
Lwr. Eastern Grn. La.
CV5: E Grn .5F 150
Lower End CV8: Bubb .3J 201
Lwr. Essex St.
B5: Birm .8L 101 (8G 5)
Lwr. Ford St. CV1: Cov .7E 152
(Far Gosford St.)
CV1: Cov .6D 152 (3E 6)
(Ford St.)
Lwr. Forster St. WS1: Wals . . .7M 39
Lwr. Friars CV34: Warw .4D 222
Lwr. Gambolds La.
B60: Fins .3B 210
LOWER GORNAL .6D 74
Lower Grn. DY4: Tip .4L 75
WS10: Darl .1D 54
WV6: Tett .4L 35
Lwr. Grinsty La. B97: Redd . . .2A 220
Lwr. Ground Cl. B6: Aston .8M 79
(off Emscote Rd.)
Lwr. Gungate B79: Tam .4B 32
Lwr. Hall La. WS1: Wals .8L 39
Lwr. Hall St. WV13: W'hall .8B 38
(off Walsall St.)
LOWER HEATH .8H 183
Lwr. High St. B64: Crad H 1J 117
DY8: Stourb .3M 115
WS10: W'bry .7F 54
Lwr. Higley Cl. B32: Quin .5K 119
Lwr. Hillmorton Rd.
CV21: Hillm, Rugby .6B 180
Lwr. Holyhead Rd.
CV1: Cov .6B 152 (4A 6)
Lwr. House La. CV9: Bad E . . .8L 47
Lwr. Keys Bus. Pk. WS12: Hed . .6K 9
LOWER LADYES HILLS .4G 199
Lwr. Ladyes Hills CV8: Ken . . .3G 199
Lower La. WS13: Chor .7J 11
Lwr. Leam St. CV31: Lea S 1B 224
Lwr. Lichfield St.
WV13: W'hall .7A 38
Lwr. Lickhill Rd.
DY13: Stour S .4D 182
Lwr. Loveday St.
B19: Birm .5K 101 (1F 4)
Lower Mall CV32: Lea S .1M 223
(in Royal Priors Shop. Cen.)
Lwr. Mall & Up. Mall
B5: Birm .7L 101 (6H 5)
LOWER MARLBROOK .8C 162
Lwr. Mill St. DY11: Kidd .3K 157
Lower Moor B30: B'vlle .1E 142
Lwr. North St. WS4: Wals .6M 39
Lowe Rd. CV6: Cov .7M 129
Lower Pde., The B72: S Cold . .4J 59
Lower Pk. DY12: Bew .6B 156
Lowerpark B77: Wiln .8C 32
Lwr. Parklands DY11: Kidd . . .4J 157
LOWER PENN .4G 51
Lower Pct. CV1: Cov . . .6C 152 (4B 6)
Lwr. Prestwood Rd.
WV11: Wed .2J 37
Lwr. Queen St. B72: S Cold 5J 59
Lwr. Reddicroft B73: S Cold . . .4J 59
Lower Rd. CV7: Barn .3B 132
WS12: Hed .6H 9
LOWER ROWNEY GREEN .5F 190
Lwr. Rushall St. WS1: Wals . . .7M 39
Lwr. Sandford St. WS13: Lich . .2G 19
Lwr. Severn St.
B1: Birm .7K 101 (6F 4)
Lwr. Shepley La.
B60: L End .3D 188
Lowerstack Cft. B37: F'bri .6F 104
LOWER STOKE .7G 153
LOWER STONNALL .5A 28
Lower St. CV21: Hillm .8H 181
WV6: Tett .4L 35
Lwr. Temple St.
B2: Birm .7K 101 (5F 4)
Lwr. Tower St.
B19: Birm .4L 101 (1F 4)
Lwr. Trinity St.
B9: Birm .8A 102 (7L 5)
B70: W Brom .8K 77
(off Glover St.)
Lwr. Valley Rd. DY5: Brie H . . .7A 96
Lwr. Vauxhall WV1: Wolv .7A 36
Lwr. Villiers St. CV32: Lea S . . .8A 218
WV2: Wolv .2C 52 (8J 7)
Lwr. White Rd. B32: Quin .4K 119
Lowes Av. CV34: Warw .8E 216
Lowes Ct. B61: B'gve .4A 188
LOWES HILL .4A 188
Lowesmoor Rd. B26: Sheld . . .2C 124
Lowe St. WV6: Wolv .5A 36
Loweswater Cl. CV11: Nun .3A 90
Loweswater Dr. DY3: Lwr G . . .6D 74
Loweswater Ho. B38: K Nor . . .8G 143
Loweswater Rd. CV3: Bin .8L 153
DY13: Stour S .2E 182
Lowfield Cl. B62: Quin .6G 119
Low Fld. La. B97: Redd .4B 212
Low Force B77: Wiln .1J 47
LOW HABBERLEY .1F 156
LOW HILL
Bushbury .2E 36
Torton .2A 184
Low Hill Cres. WV10: Bush 1E 36
Lowhill La. B45: Redn .3J 163
Lowland Cl. B64: Old H .8M 97
Lowland Rd. WS12: Hunt .4C 8
(not continuous)
Lowlands Av. B74: S'tly .1K 57
WV6: Tett .3L 35
Lowlands Ct. WV6: Tett .3L 35
Lowlands La. B98: Redd .6K 213
Lowndes Rd. DY8: Woll .3L 115
Lowry Cl. B67: Smeth .3M 99
CV12: Bed .5G 111
WV6: Pert .5F 34
WV13: W'hall .7L 37
Low St. WS6: C Hay .6D 14
Low Thatch B38: K Nor .2E 164
Lowther Ct. DY5: Brie H .7D 96
Lowther St. CV2: Cov .5F 152
Low Town B69: O'bry .2G 99
Low Wood Rd. B23: Erd .4D 80
LOXDALE .5M 53
Loxdale Ind. Est. WV14: Bils . . .5L 53
Loxdale Sidings WV14: Bils . . .5M 53
Loxdale St. WS10: W'bry .7F 54
WV14: Bils .5M 53
Loxley Av. B14: Yard W .6C 144
B90: Shir .8F 144
Loxley Cl. B31: N'fld .1L 141
B98: Redd .3K 213
CV2: Cov .7K 131
Loxley Ct. CV2: Cov .7K 131
Loxley Rd. B67: Smeth .8M 99
B75: R'ley .5K 43
Loxley Sq. B92: Olton .1K 145
Loxley Way CV32: Lill .7A 218
Loxton Cl. B74: Lit A .4D 42
Loxton Ct. B7: Birm .4B 102
Loynells Rd. B45: Redn .2H 163
Loyns Cl. B37: F'bri .6F 104
LOZELLS .2H 101
Lozells Rd. B19: Loz .2H 101
Lozells St. B19: Loz .2J 101
Lozells Wood Cl. B19: Loz 2H 101
Luanne Cl. B64: Old H .8A 98
Lucas Cir. B19: Birm .4J 101
Lucas Ct. CV21: Rugby .5B 180
CV32: Lea S .1K 223
Lucas Rd. LE10: Burb .3K 91
Lucas Way B90: Shir .2J 167
LE9: Earl S .2E 70
Luce Cl. B35: Cas V .5B 82
Lucerne Cl. CV2: Ald G .6J 131
Lucerne Ct. B23: Erd .3D 80
Luce Rd. WV10: Bush .3E 36
Lucian Cl. CV2: W'grve S .2B 154
Lucknow Rd. WV12: W'hall 5B 38
Lucton Ho. B30: B'vlle .4E 142
Lucy Edwards Ct.
DY11: Kidd .4J 157
Luddington Rd. B92: Sol .1E 146
Ludford Cl. B75: S Cold .2L 59
CV10: Ansl .5H 87
Ludford Rd. B32: Bart G .8G 119
CV10: Nun .3C 88
Ludgate B79: Tam .4A 32
Ludgate Av. DY11: Kidd .4G 157
Ludgate Cl. B46: Wat O .6G 83
B69: Tiv .1B 98
Ludgate Ct. WS5: Wals .2D 56
Ludgate Hill B3: Birm . . .6K 101 (3E 4)
Ludgate Ho. B13: Mose .5M 121
Ludgate Loft Apartments
B3: Birm .3E 4
Ludgate St. DY1: Dud .8H 75
Lud La. B79: Tam .4A 32
Ludlow Cl. B37: Chel W .7J 105
WS11: Hth H .7J 9
WV12: W'hall .3B 38
Ludlow Ct. B11: S'brk .3B 122
Ludlow Ho. B13: Mose .3A 144
WS3: Blox .3J 39
(off Providence La.)
Ludlow La. WS2: Wals .5G 39
Ludlow Rd. B8: Salt .6F 102
B97: Redd .6D 212
CV5: Cov .7A 152
DY10: Kidd .7L 157
Ludlow Way DY1: Dud .7E 74
Ludmer Way B20: Hand .7J 79
Ludstone Av. WV4: Penn .4K 51
Ludstone Rd. B29: W Cas .8M 119
Ludworth Av. B37: Mars G . . .8H 105
Luff Cl. CV3: Cov .1H 175
Lugtrout La.
B91: Cath B, Sol .3E 146
Lukes, The DY2: Neth .8J 97
Lukes Wlk. WS13: Lich .7G 13
Lulworth Cl. B63: Crad .3J 117
Lulworth Pk. CV8: Ken .3J 199
Lulworth Rd. B28: Hall G .1G 145
WS7: C Ter .2G 17
Lulworth Wlk. WV4: Penn .3J 51
Lumley Gro. B37: Chel W .7K 105
Lumley Rd. WS1: Wals .8A 40
Lumsden Cl.
CV2: W'grve S .1M 153
Lunar Cl. CV4: Canly .4K 173
Lundy Cl. LE10: Hinc .8H 69
Lundy Vw. B36: Cas B .4H 105
Lunn Av. CV8: Ken .6E 198
Lunnon La. WR9: Rush .7J 185
Lunn's Cft. WS13: Lich .1J 19
LUNT, THE .2A 54
Lunt Gro. B32: Quin .4K 119
Lunt Pl. WV14: Bils .3A 54
Lunt Rd. WV14: Bils .3M 53
Lunt Roman Fort Mus. .6E 174
Lupin Cl. LE10: Burb .3K 91
Lupin Gro. B9: Bord G .6F 102
WS5: Wals .5B 56
Lupin Rd. DY2: Dud .8M 75
Lupton Av. CV3: Cov .2C 174
Lupton Ct. B60: B'gve .8A 188
Lusbridge Cl. B63: Crad .5H 117
Luscombe Rd. CV2: Cov .1L 153
Luther Way CV5: E Grn .5F 150
LUTLEY .6J 117
Lutley Av. B63: Hale .5K 117
Lutley Cl. WV3: Wolv .2L 51
Lutley Dr. DY9: Pedm .6C 116
Lutley Gro. B32: Bart G .8H 119
Lutley La. B63: Hale, Lutley . .6H 117
(not continuous)
Lutley Mill Rd. B63: Hale .5L 117
Luton Rd. B29: S Oak .6F 120
Lutterworth Rd. CV2: Cov .4J 153
CV11: Bram, Burt H .3F 112
CV11: Nun .7L 89
CV23: Brin .5M 155
LE10: Burb .4A 92
LE10: Wlvy .3F 112
Lutterworth Rd. Trad. Est.
LE10: Burb .4A 92
Luttrell Rd. B74: Four O .1F 58
Luxor La. CV5: Alle .1B 150
Lyall Gdns. B45: Fran .8E 140
Lyall Gro. B27: A Grn .7G 123
Lychgate Av. DY9: Pedm .8C 116
Lychgate Cl. LE10: Burb .4A 92

Lychgate La.—Manor Ho., The

Lychgate La.
LE10: Aston F, Burb 4A 92
Lydate Rd. B62: Quin 5F 118
Lydbrook Covert B38: K Nor . . .1E 164
Lydbury Gro. B33: Kitts G 5A 104
Lyd Cl. WV11: Wed 4H 37
Lydd Cft. B35: Cas V 5B 82
Lyddington Dr. B62: Hale 2B 118
Lyde Grn. B63: Crad 2H 117
Lydford Cl. CV2: Cov 2J 153
Lydford Gro. B24: Erd 7G 81
Lydford Rd. WS3: Blox 7H 25
Lydgate Ct. CV11: Nun 6J 89
CV12: Bed 5G 111
Lydgate Rd. CV6: Cov 4B 152
DY6: K'wfrd 3M 95
Lydget Gro. B23: Erd 2D 80
Lydham Cl. B44: K'sdng 3A 80
B98: Redd 4E 212
WV14: Bils 5H 53
Lydia Cft. B74: Four O 3E 42
Lydiat Av. B31: Longb 8K 141
LYDIATE ASH 6C 162
Lydiate Ash Rd. B61: L Ash 6B 162
(not continuous)
Lydiates Cl. DY3: Sed 2B 74
Lydney Cl. B98: Redd 2K 213
WV12: W'hall 6D 38
Lydney Gro. B31: N'fld 6M 141
Lydstep Gro. CV31: Lea S 2C 224
LYE 4E 116
Lye Av. B32: Bart G 7G 119
Lye Bus. Cen. DY9: Lye 3F 116
Lye By-Pass DY9: Lye 3E 116
Lye Cl. La. B32: Bart G 7F 118
B62: Hale 7F 118
Lyecroft Av. B37: Chel W 7K 105
Lye Cross Rd. B69: Tiv 2B 98
Lye Station (Rail) 3E 116
Lye Valley Ind. Est.
DY9: Lye 3F 116
Lygon Cl. B98: Redd 4G 213
Lygon Ct. B62: Hale 3B 118
Lygon Gro. B32: Quin 5L 119
Lymedene Rd. B42: P Barr 4H 79
Lyme Grn. Rd. B33: Stech 5M 103
Lymer Rd. WV10: Oxl 8C 22
Lymesy St. CV3: Cov 3D 174
Lymington Cl. CV6: Cov 1D 152
Lymington Dr. CV6: Longf 3H 131
Lymington Rd. WS7: C Ter 8F 10
WV13: W'hall 7D 38
Lymore Cft. CV2: W'grve S 1A 154
Lymsey Cft. DY8: Word 6J 95
Lyn Av. WS13: Lich 8F 12
Lynbrook Cl. B47: H'wd 2A 166
DY2: Neth 3K 97
Lynbrook Rd. CV5: Cov 1K 173
Lynch, The B78: Pole 8M 33
CV11: Nun 7K 89
Lynchgate Ct. CV4: Canly 3J 173
Lynchgate Rd. CV4: Canly 3J 173
Lyncourt Gro. B32: Quin 3H 119
Lyncroft Rd. B11: Tys 7F 122
Lyndale B77: Wiln 3F 46
Lyndale Cl. CV5: Cov 6J 151
(Harewood Rd.)
CV5: Cov 6J 151
(Overdale Rd.)
Lyndale Dr. WV11: Wed 3L 37
Lyndale Rd. CV5: Cov 6J 151
DY2: Dud 3L 97
DY3: Sed 7B 52
Lynden Cl. B61: B'gve 6L 187
Lyndene Cl. LE9: Earl S 2F 70
Lyndenwood B97: Redd 7A 212
Lyndholm Rd. DY10: Kidd 3A 158
Lyndhurst Cl. CV6: Longf 4H 131
LE10: Burb 3A 92
Lyndhurst Cft. CV5: E Grn 5C 150
Lyndhurst Dr. DY8: Word 8M 95
DY10: Kidd 1L 157
Lyndhurst Rd. B24: Erd 7F 80
B71: W Brom 2L 77
CV21: Hillm 1F 206
WS12: Hth H 8K 9
WV3: Wolv 2A 52
LYNDON 4K 77
Lyndon B71: W Brom 4K 77
Lyndon Cl. B20: Hand 7J 79
B36: Cas B 1C 104
B63: Hale 5L 117
DY3: Sed 8E 52
Lyndon Ct. B26: Sheld 5C 124
CV32: Lea S 1L 223
Lyndon Cft. B37: Mars G 2H 125
B92: Olton 7A 124
LYNDON GREEN 2A 124
Lyndon Gro. B71: W Brom 5K 77
DY6: W Hth 1H 95
Lyndon Ho. B31: N'fld 6B 142
Lyndon Rd. B33: Stech 6L 103
B45: Rubery 2E 162
B73: S Cold 4H 59
B92: Olton 7M 123
Lyndworth Rd. B30: Stir 2J 143
Lyneham Cl. B79: Tam 1B 32
LE10: Hinc 8G 69
Lyneham Gdns. B76: Walm 3A 82
Lyneham Way B35: Cas V 6M 81
Lyne Ho. CV2: Cov 8K 131
Lynfield Cl. B38: K Nor 2F 164
Lynfield Rd. WS13: Lich 8F 12
Lyng Cl. CV5: E Grn 6G 151
Lyng La. B70: W Brom 6J 77
(not continuous)
Lynmouth Cl. CV11: Nun 4L 89
WS9: A'rdge 4G 41
Lynmouth Rd. CV2: Cov 1L 153
LYNN .4M 27
Lynn Gro. B29: S Oak 6C 120
Lynn La. WS14: Lynn, Shens . . .4M 27
Lynnon Fld. CV34: Warw 5B 222
Lynton Av. B66: Smeth 3A 100
B71: W Brom 2J 77
WV6: Tett 2L 35
Lynton Cl. CV34: Warw 8D 216
Lynton Ho. B23: Erd 3B 80
Lynton Rd. B6: Aston 2A 102
CV6: Cov 8F 130
Lynval Rd. DY5: Quar B 2F 116
Lynwood Av. DY6: W Hth 2H 95
Lynwood Cl. WV12: W'hall 1E 38
Lynwood Dr. DY10: Blak 7H 137
Lynwood Wlk. B17: Harb 5D 120
CV31: Lea S 3C 224
Lynwood Way B45: Lick 7G 163
Lyon Ct. *B72: S Cold* *4J 59*
(off Midland Dr.)
Lyons Gro. B11: S'hll 6C 122
Lysander Cl. LE10: Burb 5L 91
Lysander Rd. B45: Fran 7G 141
Lysander Way B35: Cas V 7B 82
WS11: Cann 6E 8
Lyster Cl. CV34: Warw 1B 222
Lysways La. WS13: Hanch 1B 12
WS15: Longd 1B 12
Lysways St. WS1: Wals 1M 55
Lythall Cl. CV31: Rad S 4F 224
Lythalls La. CV6: Cov 7D 130
Lythalls La. Ind. Est.
CV6: Cov 8E 130
Lytham B77: Amin 4J 33
Lytham Cl. B76: Walm 3B 82
DY8: Stourb 7A 116
Lytham Cft.
B15: Birm 1K 121 (8E 4)
Lytham Gro. WS3: Blox 5G 25
Lytham Rd. CV22: Bil 8K 179
WV6: Pert 5D 34
Lythwood Dr. DY5: Brie H 1C 116
Lyttelton Pl. DY9: Hag 3C 138
Lyttelton Rd. B16: Edg 8D 100
B33: Stech 7K 103
CV34: Warw 1E 222
DY8: Stourb 4K 115
Lyttleton Av. B60: B'gve 2L 209
B62: B'hth 2E 118
Lyttleton Cl. CV3: Bin 8A 154
DY2: Neth 5J 97
Lyttleton Ho. B63: Hale 7A 118
Lyttleton Rd. DY12: Bew 5A 156
Lyttleton St. B70: W Brom 7J 77
Lytton Av. WV4: Penn 5K 51
Lytton Gro. B27: A Grn 8H 123
Lytton La. B32: Bart G 6M 119

M

Maas Rd. B31: N'fld 6A 142
Mabey Av. B98: Redd 4F 212
Macadam Cl. WS7: Burn 1H 17
Macarthur Rd. B64: Crad H 1J 117
Macaulay Ho. B70: W Brom 8K 77
Macaulay Rd. CV2: Cov 5K 153
CV22: Rugby 2L 205
McBean Rd. WV6: Wolv 5M 35
Macbeth App. CV34: H'cte 5K 223
Macbeth Cl. CV22: Bil 3L 205
McConnell Cl. B60: B'gve 2B 210
Macdonald Cl. B69: Tiv 7D 76
Macdonald Rd. CV2: Cov 6K 153
McDonnell Dr. CV7: Exh 3F 130
McDougall Rd. WS10: W'bry 6J 55
Macefield Cl. CV2: Ald G 6K 131
Mace St. B64: Old H 8L 97
McGeough Wlk. WS11: Cann 4H 9
McGhie St. WS12: Hed 3H 9
McGregor Cl. B6: Aston 8M 79
MacGregor Cres. B77: Amin 5F 32
MacGregor Tithe B79: Tam 4B 32
Machin Rd. B23: Erd 5F 80
Mackadown La.
B33: Kitts G, Sheld 7D 104
Mackay Rd. WS3: Blox 7K 25
McKean Rd. B69: O'bry 8G 77
McKen Ct. B70: W Brom 8J 77
Mackenzie Cl. CV5: Alle 2G 151
Mackenzie Ct. B31: N'fld 1L 141
Mackenzie Rd. B11: S'hll 7C 122
McKinnell Cres. CV21: Hillm . . .7E 180
Mackmillan Rd. B65: Row R 7B 98
McLean Rd. WV10: Oxl 7C 22
McMahon Rd. CV12: Bed 1E 130
Macmillan Cl. B69: Tiv 7C 76
Macrome Rd. WV6: Tett 1L 35
Madams Hill Rd. B90: Shir 2K 167
Madden Pl. CV22: Bil 7J 179
Maddocks Hill B72: W Grn 7J 59
Madehurst Rd. B23: Erd 3E 80
Madeira Av. WV8: Cod 7G 21
Madeira Cft. CV5: Cov 7L 151
Madeleine Ho. B33: Stech 6L 103
MADELEY HEATH 2L 161
Madeley Rd. B11: S'brk 4C 122
B98: Redd 4M 213
DY6: K'wfrd 5M 95
DY9: Belb 4K 161
Madin Rd. DY4: Tip 5L 75
Madison Av. B36: Hodg H 3K 103
DY5: Brie H 6F 96
WS2: Wals 7H 39
Madley Cl. B45: Rubery 1E 162
Madox Cl. B79: Tam 2L 31
Madresfield Dr. B63: Hale 7B 118
Madrona B77: Amin 5H 33
Maer Cl. B65: Row R 5C 98
Mafeking Rd. B66: Smeth 2A 100
Maffey Ct. CV22: Rugby 7A 180
Magdala St. B18: Win G 4E 100
Magdalen Cl. DY1: Dud 7G 75
Magdalen Ct. *B16: Edg* *8E 100*
(off Vernon Ct.)
Magdalene Rd. WS1: Wals 2A 56
Magee Cl. LE10: Hinc 7J 69
Magna Cl. WS6: C Hay 6E 14
Magness Cres. WV12: W'hall . . .4C 38
Magnet La. CV22: Bil 1J 205
Magneto Rd. CV3: Cov 8J 153
Magnet Wlk. B23: Erd 6C 80
Magnolia B77: Amin 5G 33
Magnolia Cl. B29: W Cas 2A 142
CV3: Cov 4B 174
Magnolia Dr. WS5: Wals 5M 55
Magnolia Gro. WV8: Bilb 6G 21
WV12: W'hall 5B 38
Magnolia Way DY8: Word 1M 115
Magnum Cl. B74: S'tly 2M 57
Magnus B77: Wiln 3E 46
Magpie Cl. DY2: Neth 6L 97
Magpie Ho. CV5: E Grn 4D 150
Magpie La. CV7: Bal C 2E 170
Magpie Way DY10: Kidd 7B 158
Magreal Ind. Est. B16: Birm . . .6F 100
Maguire Ind. Est.
CV4: Tile H 1F 172
Magyar Cres. CV11: Nun 2M 111
Maidavale Cres. CV3: Cov 4C 174
Maidendale Rd. DY6: K'wfrd . . .2H 95
Maidenhair Dr. CV23: Brow 1D 180
Maidensbridge Dr.
DY6: W Hth 1J 95
Maidensbridge Gdns.
DY6: W Hth 8H 73
Maidensbridge Rd.
DY6: W Hth 8H 73
Maidstone Dr. DY8: Word 6L 95
WS7: Burn 3K 17
Maidstone Rd. B20: Hand 8L 79
Maidwell Dr. B90: Shir 1L 167
Mailbox, The
B1: Birm 7K 101 (7E 4)
Mailbox Sq. B1: Birm . . .7K 101 (6E 4)
Maine Cl. CV6: Cov 1D 152
Main Rd. B26: Birm A 6F 124
B79: Shut 2L 33
B79: Tam 1B 32
CV7: Ansty 6D 132
CV7: Mer 8J 127
CV9: Bax 2M 63
CV23: Kils 6M 207
Mainstone Cl. B98: Redd 6L 213
Mainstream 47 Ind. Pk.
B7: Birm 4C 102
Mainstream Way B7: Birm 5C 102
Main St. B11: S'brk 2A 122
CV8: Wols 5F 176
CV13: Dad 1E 68
CV13: High H 6M 67
CV13: Stoke G 2D 68
CV21: N'bld A 2K 179
CV22: Bil 1J 205
CV23: Bour D 7L 203
CV23: Clift D 4F 180
CV23: F'ton 8K 203
CV23: Long L 5G 179
CV23: Newt 1G 181
CV23: Thurl 7F 204
CV33: H'ham 3L 219
LE10: Aston F 4E 92
LE10: Withy, Wlvy 8J 113
LE17: Frol 7M 93
WS9: Ston 6K 27
WS14: Shens 3F 28
Main Ter. B11: S'brk 2A 122
Mainwaring Dr. B75: R'ley 7L 43
Maisemore Cl. B98: Redd 2K 213
Maitland B77: Glas 7F 32
Maitland Ho. B36: Cas B 8D 82
Maitland Rd. B8: Salt 5F 102
DY1: Dud 8E 74
Maizefield LE10: Hinc 5J 69
Majestic Way B65: Row R 5C 98
Major Ct. B13: Mose 7B 122
MAJOR'S GREEN 1D 166
Majuba Rd. B16: Edg 5C 100
Makepeace Av. CV34: Warw 8F 216
Malam Cl. CV4: Tile H 8G 151
Malcolm Av. B24: Erd 4J 81
B61: B'gve 6L 187
Malcolm Ct. B26: Sheld 4A 124
WV1: Wolv 6A 36
Malcolm Gro. B45: Redn 2G 163
Malcolm Rd. B90: Shir 8H 145
Malcolmson Cl. B15: Edg 1F 120
Maldale B77: Wiln 8J 33
Malfield Av. B97: Redd 6M 211
Malfield Dr. B27: A Grn 6L 123
Malham Cl. CV11: Nun 7A 90
Malham Rd. B77: Wiln 1H 47
CV34: Warw 8F 216
DY13: Stour S 2E 182
Mali Jenkins Ho.
WS1: Wals 8B 40
Malins, The CV34: Warw 3H 223
Malins Rd. B17: Harb 4D 120
WV4: E'shll 4E 52
Malkit Cl. WS2: Wals 5F 38
Mallaby Cl. B90: Shir 1G 167
Mallard Av. CV10: Nun 4C 88
DY10: Kidd 6B 158
Mallard Cl. B27: A Grn 6J 123
B98: Redd 4F 212
DY5: Brie H 2C 116
WS3: Pels 3A 26
Mallard Cft. WS13: Lich 1J 19
Mallard Dr. B23: Erd 6B 80
B69: O'bry 5F 98
LE10: Hinc 2G 91
Mallard Rd. B80: Stud 5M 221
Mallards Reach
B92: Olton 1L 145
Mallender Dr. B93: Know 3F 168
Mallen Dr. B69: Tiv 8B 76
Mallerin Cft. CV10: Nun 4B 88
Mallicot Cl. WS13: Lich 8K 13
Mallin Gdns. DY1: Dud 1E 96
Mallin St. B66: Smeth 2K 99
Mallory Cres. WS3: Blox 7K 25
Mallory Dr. CV34: Warw 2D 222
DY11: Kidd 8K 135
Mallory Ri. B13: Mose 8C 122
Mallory Rd. WV6: Pert 6E 34
Mallory St. LE9: Earl S 1C 70
Mallory Way CV6: Longf 5E 130
Mallow Cl. WS5: Wals 6A 56
Mallow Ct. WV6: Wolv 4B 36
Mallow Cres. DY10: Kidd 5M 157
Mallow Cft. CV12: Bed 7E 110
Mallow Dr. B61: B'gve 4M 187
Mallow Ri. B23: Erd 2B 80
Mallows Cl. WS10: Darl 3D 54
Mallow Way CV23: Brow 1C 180
Malmesbury Pk. B15: Edg 2E 120
Malmesbury Rd.
B10: Small H 3E 122
CV6: Cov 7A 130
Malpas Dr. B32: Bart G 1J 141
Malpass Gdns. WV8: Cod 5E 20
Malpass Rd. DY5: Quar B 2F 116
Malpas Wlk. WV10: Wolv 4G 37
Malt Cl. B17: Harb 3D 120
Malthouse B66: Smeth 2L 99
Malthouse Cl. CV10: Ansl 5H 87
Malthouse Cft. B6: Aston 1L 101
Malthouse Dr. DY1: Dud 7G 75
Malthouse Gdns. B19: Loz 2K 101
Malthouse Gro. B25: Yard 8L 103
Malt Ho. La. B94: Earls 3E 192
WV13: W'hall 7A 38
Malthouse La. B8: Salt 3E 102
B42: Gt Barr 1K 79
B61: C'wich 4B 162
(not continuous)
CV8: Ken 2E 198
WV6: Tett 3L 35
Malt Ho. Rd. WS15: Gent 4G 11
Malthouse Rd. DY4: Tip 4L 75
Malt Ho. Row B37: Mars G 1G 125
Maltings, The
B1: Birm 8J 101 (8D 4)
B80: Stud 5K 221
CV11: Nun 4L 89
CV32: Lea S 7M 217
(not continuous)
WS9: A'rdge 3J 41
WV1: Wolv 6D 36 (1K 7)
WV5: Wom 3G 73
Malt Mill Bank LE9: Barw 3A 70
Malt Mill La. B62: B'hth 1C 118
Malton Av. B69: O'bry 3D 98
Malton Gro. B13: Mose 2B 144
Malvern Av. CV10: Nun 6B 88
CV22: Rugby 8D 180
DY9: Lye 4C 116
Malvern Ct. B15: Edg 1C 120
B71: W Brom 4K 77
DY13: Stour S 7A 182
WV12: W'hall 5B 38
Malvern Ct. B27: A Grn 5J 123
WV10: Bush 1D 36
Malvern Cres. DY2: Dud 3F 96
Malvern Dr. B76: Walm 1A 82
DY10: Kidd 6L 157
WS9: A'rdge 8J 27
WV1: Wolv 8H 37
Malvern Edge Ct.
DY13: Stour S 8B 182
Malvern Hill Rd. B7: Nech 2C 102
Malvern Ho. *B63: Hale* *6A 118*
(off Pickersleigh Cl.)
B97: Redd 8C 212
Malvern Pk. Rd. B91: Sol 6D 146
Malvern Rd. B21: Hand 8C 78
B27: A Grn 5J 123
B45: Lick 7G 163
B61: B'gve 2K 209
B68: O'bry 1H 119
B97: Redd 1D 220
CV5: Cov 5M 151
CV7: Bal C 3J 171
Malvern St. B12: Bal H 4A 122
Malvern Vw. DY10: Chad C 8L 159
DY11: Kidd 8H 157
Malvern Vw. Rd. DY3: Lwr G 5D 74
Mamble Rd. DY8: Stourb 4L 115
Mammouth Dr. WV10: Wolv 4D 36
Manby Cl. WV6: Wolv 5B 36
Manby Rd. B35: Cas V 5A 82
Manby St. DY4: Tip 1M 75
MANCETTER 3A 66
Mancetter Rd. B90: Shir 6J 145
CV9: Man 2M 65
(not continuous)
CV10: Nun 2D 88
Manchester St.
B6: Birm 4L 101 (1H 5)
B69: O'bry 2H 99
Mancroft Cl. DY6: K'wfrd 2H 95
Mancroft Gdns. WV6: Tett 4J 35
Mancroft Rd. WV6: Tett 4J 35
Mandale Rd. WV10: Wolv 3F 36
Mandarin Av. DY10: Kidd 6B 158
Mandarin Cl. LE10: Hinc 3G 91
Mander Cen.
WV1: Wolv 7C 36 (4J 7)
Mander Gro. CV34: Warw 5B 222
Manderley Cl. CV5: E Grn 4C 150
DY3: Sed 7C 52
Manders Ind. Est. WV1: Wolv . . .6F 36
Mander Sq. WV1: Wolv . . .8C 36 (5J 7)
Manderston Cl. DY1: Dud 6E 74
Mander St. WV3: Wolv . . .1B 52 (7G 7)
Manderville Gdns.
DY6: K'wfrd 3J 95
Manderville Ho.
B31: Longb 1M 163
Mandeville Gdns. WS1: Wals . . .1M 55
Mandeville Way B61: B'gve 4A 188
Mandrake Cl. CV6: Cov 5D 130
MANEY 5J 59
Maney Cnr. B72: S Cold 5H 59
Maney Hill Rd. B72: W Grn 6H 59
Manfield Av. CV2: W'grve S . . .2A 154
Manfield Rd. WV13: W'hall 6J 37
Manifold Cl. WS7: Burn 3K 17
Manifoldia Grange
B70: W Brom 7H 77
Manilla Rd. B29: S Oak 8H 121
Manitoba Cft. B38: K Nor 1F 164
Manley Cl. B70: W Brom 6H 77
Manley Rd. WS13: Lich 8K 13
Manlove St. WV3: Wolv 1A 52
Manningford Ct. B14: K Hth . . .7M 143
Manningford Rd. B14: K Hth . . .7L 143
Manning Wlk. *CV21: Rugby* . . .*6A 180*
(in Clock Towers Shop. Cen.)
Mann's Cl. CV8: Rytn D 1B 202
Mnr. Abbey Rd. B62: Hale 6E 118
Manor Av. DY11: Kidd 2G 157
WS6: Gt Wyr 5G 15
WS11: Cann 8D 8
Manor Av. Sth. DY11: Kidd 2G 157
Mnr. Brook Cl. LE9: S Stan 6L 71
Manor Cl. CV9: Bad E 7B 48
DY11: Kidd 3G 157
DY13: Stour S 4H 183
LE10: Burb 4J 91
WV4: Penn 5M 51
WV8: Bilb 5H 21
WV13: W'hall 6A 38
Manor Ct. B27: A Grn 7K 123
B30: K Nor 7G 143
B62: Quin *2G 119*
(off Binswood Rd.)
B78: M Oak 8K 31
B93: Dorr 7F 168
CV8: Ken 3G 199
CV31: Lea S 2M 223
DY2: Neth 5J 97
WS2: Wals 7J 39
Manor Ct. Av. CV11: Nun 4H 89
Manor Ct. Rd. B60: B'gve 1L 209
CV11: Nun 5G 89
Manor Dr. B73: S Cold 5H 59
CV23: Stret D 3F 202
DY3: Gorn 6B 74
DY3: Swind 7E 72
Manor Est. CV8: Wols 6F 176
Manor Farm Cl. CV23: Barby . . .7J 207
Manor Farm Dr.
WV12: W'hall 4D 38
Manor Farm Rd. B11: Tys 5E 122
Manor Fold WV8: Oaken 7D 20
Manorford Av. B71: W Brom 8A 56
Manor Gdns. B33: Stech 7K 103
WS10: W'bry 5F 54
WV5: Wom 2H 73
Mnr. Hall M. CV3: W'hall 3K 175
Manor Hill B73: S Cold 5H 59
Manor Ho. B31: N'fld 2B 142
CV2: W'grve S 2M 153
Manor Ho., The *B44: Gt Barr* *7L 57*
(off Amblecote Av.)

Manor Ho. Cl.—Mary Ann St.

Manor Ho. Cl. B29: W Cas 8M 119
CV21: N'bld A 2K 179
LE10: Aston F 3E 92
Manor Ho. Dr. B31: N'fld 2B 142
CV1: Cov 7C 152 (7B 6)
Manor Ho. La. B26: Yard 3M 123
B46: Wat O 6H 83
B96: A'wd B 6E 220
Manor Ho. Pk. WV8: Bilb 5H 21
Manor Ho. Rd. WS10: W'bry 6F 54
Manorial Rd. B75: R'ley 6L 43
Manor Ind. Est. WS2: Wals 8J 39
Manor La.
B61: C'wich, L Ash 4C 162
B62: Hale 6E 118
CV23: Clift D 3G 181
(not continuous)
CV35: Wrox 6F 196
DY8: Stourb 6K 115
DY11: Ware 8A 184
Manor M. B80: Stud 5L 221
Manor Pk. DY6: K'wfrd 3K 95
Manor Pk. Cl. B13: Mose 7A 122
Manor Pk. Gro. B31: Longb 8J 141
Manor Pk. Rd. B36: Cas B 2D 104
CV11: Nun 4G 89
Manor Pl. LE10: Hinc 8K 69
Manor Ri. WS7: Burn 4G 17
WS14: Lich 3J 19
Manor Rd. B6: Aston 8M 79
B16: Edg 8D 100
B33: Stech 6L 103
B47: Wyt 6A 166
B67: Smeth 4K 99
B73: S Cold 4H 59
B74: S'tly 1A 58
B77: Tam 5C 32
B78: M Oak 8K 31
B80: Stud 5L 221
B91: Sol 4B 146
B93: Dorr 6E 168
B97: Up Ben 8G 211
CV1: Cov 8C 152 (7B 6)
CV8: Ken 3F 198
CV9: Man 2L 65
CV21: Rugby 5B 180
CV23: Kils 6M 207
CV32: Lill 6B 218
CV47: S'ton 1M 225
DY4: Tip 5M 75
DY8: Word 7L 95
DY13: Stour S 4G 183
LE9: Sap 1K 93
WS2: Wals 7J 39
WS10: W'bry 7K 55
WV4: E'shll 4G 53
WV4: Penn 5M 51
WV10: Oxl 2C 36
Manor Rd. Ind. Est.
CV9: Man 2L 65
Manor Rd. Nth. B16: Edg 8D 100
Manor Rd. Pct. WS2: Wals 7J 39
Manor Side Ind. Est.
B98: Redd 3L 213
Manor Sq. B91: Sol 6C 146
Manor Stables B93: Know 8A 170
Manor St. LE10: Hinc 8J 69
WV6: Tett 4J 35
Manor Ter. CV1: Cov 7C 152 (6C 6)
Manor Wlk. B91: Sol 6C 146
Manor Way B62: Hale 8L 117
B73: S Cold 5H 59
LE10: Burb 4K 91
Manor Yd. CV1: Cov 7C 152 (6C 6)
Mansard Cl. WV3: Wolv 1M 51
WV11: Bush 1H 37
Mansard Ct. B46: Col 2A 106
Manse Cl. CV7: Exh 8G 111
Manse Gdns. B80: Stud 5L 221
Mansell Cl. B63: Crad 2H 117
Mansell Rd. B97: Redd 2D 220
DY4: Tip 1A 76
Mansel Rd. B10: Small H 2E 122
Mansel St. CV6: Cov 1E 152
Mansfield Cl. B79: Tam 3L 31
Mansfield Ho. B37: Chel W 6J 105
Mansfield Rd. B6: Aston 1K 101
B25: Yard 4J 123
Mansion Cl. DY1: Dud 6G 75
Mansion Ct. *WV5: Wom* . . . . *.4D 72*
(off Heath Ho. Dr.)
Mansion Cres. B67: Smeth 5L 99
Mansion Dr. DY4: Tip 4C 76
WS7: Hamm 5K 17
Mansion St. LE10: Hinc 8K 69
Manson Dr. B64: Old H 8A 98
Manston Dr. WV6: Pert 4E 34
Manston Rd. B26: Sheld 2B 124
Manston Vw. B79: Tam 1C 32
Mansty La. ST19: Penk 1A 8
WS12: Penk 4A 8
Manta Rd. B77: Dost 3D 46
Mantilla Dr. CV3: Cov 4A 174
Manton Cft. B93: Dorr 6E 168
Manton Ho. B19: Loz 2L 101
Manway Cl. B20: Hand 4F 78
Manwoods Cl. B20: Hand 7H 79
Maple Av. CV7: Exh 8H 111
WS10: W'bry 5J 55
Maple Bank B15: Edg 2G 121
Maplebeck Ct. B91: Sol 4C 146
Maple Bus. Pk. B7: Nech 3B 102
Maple Cen., The WS10: Mox . . .6B 54
Maple Cl. B21: Hand 8E 78
DY7: Kinv 4A 114
DY8: Stourb 7K 115
DY11: Kidd 1H 157
DY13: Stour S 5E 182
LE10: Burb 4L 91
WS7: Chase 2F 16
WV14: Cose 2G 75
Maple Ct. *B24: Erd* . . . . *.6F 80*
(off Coppice Cl.)
B66: Smeth 1K 99
WS14: Lich 4J 19
Maple Cres. WS11: Cann 8C 8
Maple Cft. B13: Mose 3M 143
Mapledene B13: Mose 7B 122
Mapledene Rd. B26: Sheld 3D 124
Maple Dr. B44: K'sdng 1B 80
B78: K'bry 2D 62
DY3: Gorn 7B 74
WS4: S'fld 1B 40
WS5: Wals 5B 56
WS10: Mox 5B 54
WS12: Hunt 1D 8
Maple Grn. DY1: Dud 4G 75
Maple Gro. B19: Loz 1J 101
B37: K'hrst 3F 104
CV21: Rugby 5A 180
CV34: Warw 8G 217
DY6: K'wfrd 3L 95
WS14: Lich 2M 19
WV3: Wolv 7J 35
WV14: Bils 5M 53
Maple Leaf Dr. B37: Mars G . . .1H 125
Maple Leaf Ind. Est.
WS2: Wals 6G 39
Maple Leaf Rd. WS10: W'bry . . .8C 54
Maple Ri. B68: O'bry 7J 99
B77: Amin 5G 33
Maple Rd. B30: B'vlle 1E 142
B45: Rubery 3F 162
B62: B'hth 1D 118
B72: S Cold 6J 59
CV10: Nun 4E 88
CV31: Lea S 3M 223
DY1: Dud 6J 75
WS3: Pels 7M 25
WV3: Wolv 2L 51
Maple Row DY5: Brie H 7D 96
Maples, The CV12: Bed 7E 110
Maple St. WS3: Blox 7K 25
Mapleton Gro. B28: Hall G 2H 145
Mapleton Rd. B28: Hall G 2H 145
CV6: Cov 1M 151
Maple Tree La. B63: Crad 3J 117
Maple Wlk. *B37: Chel W* . . . . . . *.7H 105*
(off Chelmsley Wood Shop. Cen.)
Maple Way B31: Longb 8M 141
LE9: Earl S 3D 70
Maplewood B76: Walm 1A 82
Mapperley Cl.
CV2: W'grve S 1A 154
Mapperley Gdns. B13: Mose . . .6J 121
Mappleborough Cl.
B97: Redd 4B 212
MAPPLEBOROUGH GREEN . . .1M 221
Mappleborough Rd.
B90: Shir 8E 144
Marans Cft. B38: K Nor 2D 164
Marble All. B80: Stud 5L 221
Marbury Cl. B38: K Nor 7D 142
Marbury M. DY5: Brie H 8D 96
Marchant Rd. LE10: Hinc 1J 91
WV3: Wolv 7M 35
WV14: Bils 2J 53
March Cl. WS6: C Hay 8D 14
March Ct. CV22: Rugby 8A 180
MARCH END 4L 37
March End Rd. WV11: Wed 4K 37
(not continuous)
Marchfont Cl. CV11: Nun 7A 90
March Gro. DY12: Bew 5B 156
Marchmont Rd. B9: Bord G 7G 103
Marchmount Rd. B72: W Grn . . .1J 81
March Way CV3: Bin 2K 175
WS9: A'rdge 8J 27
Marchwood Cl. B97: Redd 4A 212
Marcliff Cres. B90: Shir 7C 144
Marconi Pl. WS12: Hed 2J 9
Marcos Dr. B36: Cas B 8F 82
Marcot Rd. B92: Olton 4M 123
Marcroft Pl. CV31: Lea S 3D 224
Marden Cl. WV13: W'hall 8M 37
Marden Gro. B31: Longb 2A 164
Marden Wlk. B23: Erd 6B 80
Mardol Cl. CV2: Cov 2K 153
Mardon Rd. B26: Sheld 4B 124
Maree Gro. WV12: W'hall 8B 24
Marfield Cl. B76: Walm 3A 82
Margam Cres. WS3: Blox 7F 24
Margam Ter. WS3: Blox 7F 24
Margam Way WS3: Blox 7F 24
Margaret Av. B63: Hale 5M 117
CV12: Bed 6G 111
Margaret Cl. DY5: Quar B 1E 116
Margaret Dr. DY8: Stourb 5B 116
WS11: Cann 3E 8
Margaret Gdns. B67: Smeth 4L 99
Margaret Gro. B17: Harb 2C 120
Margaret Ho. B17: Harb 4B 120
Margaret Rd. B17: Harb 4C 120
B73: New O 8D 58
CV9: Ath 2L 65
WS2: Wals 6E 38
WS10: Darl 5C 54
Margarets Ho. B76: Walm 6M 59
Margaret St.
B3: Birm 6K 101 (4E 4)
B70: W Brom 7H 77
Margaret Va. DY4: Tip 8C 54
Margaret Vine Ct. B62: B'hth 8F 98
Margeson Cl. CV2: Cov 7L 153
Margesson Dr. B45: B Grn 8K 163
Margetts Cl. CV8: Ken 5F 198
Marholm Cl. WV9: Pend 7M 21
Marian Cft. B26: Sheld 4D 124
Maria St. B70: W Brom 1L 99
Marie Brock Cl. CV4: Tile H 8H 151
Marie Cl. CV9: Man 2A 66
Marie Dr. B27: A Grn 1H 145
Marigold Cl. WS11: Hth H 6J 9
Marigold Cres. DY1: Dud 5G 75
Marigold Dr. LE10: Burb 4L 91
Marina Cl. CV4: Tile H 2E 172
Marina Cres. WS12: Hed 4G 9
Marine Cres. DY8: Word 8L 95
Marine Dr. B44: K'sdng 3L 79
Marine Gdns. DY8: Word 8L 95
Mariner B79: Tam 2L 31
Mariner Av. B16: Edg 8E 100
Marion Cl. DY5: Quar B 7F 96
Marion Rd. B67: Smeth 3K 99
CV6: Cov 2D 152
Marion Way B28: Hall G 2E 144
Marita Cl. DY2: Neth 6L 97
Marjoram Cl. B38: K Nor 1F 164
Marjorie Av. B30: K Nor 6H 143
Mark Antony Dr. CV34: H'cte . . .5K 223
Mark Av. WS10: W'bry 6E 54
Markby Rd. B18: Win G 3E 100
Mark Cl. B98: Redd 7E 212
Mark Ct. WS1: Wals 6A 40
Market Cnr. CV31: Lea S 3M 223
MARKET END 7D 110
Mkt. End Cl. CV12: Bed 8D 110
Mkt. Hall Pct. WS11: Cann 8E 8
Mkt. Hall St. WS11: Cann 8E 8
Market Hill CV47: Sou 5H 225
Market La. WS14: Wall 7D 18
WV4: Lwr P 3F 50
Market Mall *CV21: Rugby* . . . . . *.6A 180*
(in Clock Towers Shop. Cen.)
Market Pl. B61: B'gve 7M 187
B65: B'hth 8C 98
B69: O'bry . . . . *.1G 99*
(off Market St.)
B98: Redd 5E 212
CV9: Ath . . . . *.1K 65*
(off Market St.)
CV11: Nun 5J 89
CV21: Rugby 6A 180
CV34: Warw 3E 222
CV47: Sou 5H 225
DY2: Dud 8J 75
DY2: Neth 4J 97
DY4: Tip 4D 76
LE10: Hinc 1K 91
WS3: Blox 8H 25
WS10: W'bry 7F 54
WS11: Cann 8D 8
(not continuous)
WV13: W'hall 8A 38
Market Sq. B64: Crad H 1J 117
Market St. B61: B'gve 7M 187
B69: O'bry 1G 99
B78: Pole 3K 49
B79: Tam 4B 32
CV9: Ath 1K 65
CV21: Rugby 5B 180
CV34: Warw 3D 222
DY6: K'wfrd 3K 95
DY8: Stourb 4A 116
DY10: Kidd 4L 157
WS12: Hed 3H 9
WS13: Lich 2H 19
(not continuous)
WV1: Wolv 7D 36 (4K 7)
Market Wlk. B97: Redd 5E 212
Market Way
CV1: Cov 7C 152 (5B 6)
DY9: Hag 3C 138
WV14: Bils 4K 53
Markfield Rd. B26: Sheld 1B 124
Markford Wlk. B19: Hock 3K 101
Markham Cres. B92: Sol 8F 124
Markham Cft. WV9: Pend 7A 22
Markham Dr. CV31: W'nsh 6B 224
DY6: K'wfrd 5L 95
Markham Rd. B73: New O 6C 58
Mark Ho. B13: Mose 7A 122
Marklew Cl. WS8: Bwnhls 4G 27
Marklin Av. WV10: Oxl 8D 22
Mark Rd. WS10: W'bry 6E 54
Marksbury Cl. WV6: Wolv 4A 36
Marks M. CV34: Warw 3E 222
Marks Wlk. WS13: Lich 7G 13
Marlbank Rd. DY8: Word 8A 96
Marlborough Av. B60: B'gve 2A 210
Marlborough Cl.
B74: Four O 3E 42
LE10: Burb 2B 92
Marlborough Ct.
B60: B'gve 1B 210
B74: Four O . . . . *.7F 42*
(off Vesey Cl.)
WS13: Lich 2H 19
Marlborough Dr.
CV31: Lea S 3D 224
DY8: Stourb 6A 116
DY13: Stour S 7B 182
Marlborough Gdns.
DY8: Word 7J 95
WV6: Wolv 5L 35
Marlborough Gro. B25: Yard . . .8K 103
Marlborough M. B80: Stud 5L 221
Marlborough Rd.
B10: Small H 8E 102
B36: Cas B 1C 104
B66: Smeth 6A 100
CV2: Cov 7G 153
CV11: Nun 5H 89
CV22: Bil 8L 179
DY3: Sed 2F 74
Marlborough St. DY10: Kidd 4L 157
WS3: Blox 8H 25
Marlborough Way B77: Wiln 8D 32
Marlbrook Cl. B92: Sol 5C 124
Marlbrook Dr. WV4: Penn 3B 52
Marlbrook Gdns. B61: Cats 8B 162
Marlbrook La. B60: Marl 8D 162
Marlburn Way WV5: Wom 3E 72
Marlcliff Gro. B13: Mose 3A 144
Marlcroft CV3: W'hall 3L 175
Marldon Rd. B14: K Hth 3L 143
Marlene Cft. B37: Chel W 8J 105
Marler Rd. CV4: Tile H 2F 172
Marley Rd. DY6: K'wfrd 5A 96
Marlfield B98: Redd 4J 213
Marlfield La. B98: Redd 5H 213
(not continuous)
Marlin B77: Dost 3D 46
Marling Cft. B92: Sol 2E 146
Marlissa Dr. CV6: Cov 7E 130
Marloes Wlk. CV31: Lea S 3C 224
Marlow Cl. CV5: Cov 5H 151
DY2: Neth 6L 97
Marlowe Cl. CV10: Gall C 4M 87
DY10: Kidd 3B 158
Marlowe Dr. WV12: W'hall 2A 38
Marlow Rd. B23: Erd 4D 80
B77: Tam 4D 32
CV9: Hurl 4J 63
Marlow St. B65: B'hth 8B 98
WS2: Wals 5L 39
Marlpit La. B75: R'ley 7K 43
B97: Redd 8B 212
(not continuous)
Marlpit Ri. B75: R'ley 6L 43
Marlpool Cl. DY11: Kidd 8H 135
Marlpool Dr. B97: Redd 6C 212
WS3: Pels 8A 26
Marlpool La. DY11: Kidd 8J 135
Marlpool Pl. DY11: Kidd 1H 157
Marl Rd. DY2: Neth 5H 97
Marlston Wlk. CV5: Cov 5H 151
Marl Top B38: K Nor 7F 142
Marlwood Cl. CV6: Longf 5F 130
Marmion Dr. B43: Gt Barr 7F 56
Marmion Gro. DY1: Dud 1G 97
Marmion Pk. B79: Tam 3B 32
Marmion St. B79: Tam 4B 32
Marmion Way B70: W Brom 3F 76
Marne Cl. CV34: Warw 1G 223
Marnel Dr. WV3: Wolv 1K 51
Marner Cres. CV6: Cov 3B 152
Marner Rd. CV10: Nun 8H 89
CV12: Bed 6G 111
Marnhull Cl. CV2: W'grve S 5M 153
Marpool Ct. DY11: Kidd 1J 157
Marquis Dr. B62: Hale 2A 118
Marrick B77: Wiln 1J 47
Marriner's La. CV5: Cov 4H 151
Marriott Forest of Arden Golf Course
. . . . .2F 126
Marriott Rd. B66: Smeth 2K 99
CV6: Cov 5A 152
CV12: Bed 7D 110
DY2: Neth 5J 97
Marroway St. B16: Birm 6F 100
Marrowfat La. B21: Hand 2F 100
Mars Cl. WV14: Cose 8G 53
Marsdale Dr. CV10: Nun 6E 88
Marsden Cl. B92: Olton 8L 123
Marsden Rd. B98: Redd 6E 212
Marsett B77: Wiln 2J 47
Marsh, The WS10: W'bry 6E 54
Marshall Cl. WS9: A'rdge 5H 41
Marshall Gro. B44: Gt Barr 2M 79
Marshall Ho. *WS2: Wals* . . . . *.1J 55*
(off St Quentin St.)
Marshall Lake Rd. B90: Shir . . .1K 167
Marshall Rd. B68: O'bry 8J 99
CV7: Exh 1F 130
WV13: W'hall 8J 37
Marshalls Ind. Est.
WV2: Wolv 2C 52 (8J 7)
Marshall St. B1: Birm . . .8K 101 (7E 4)
B67: Smeth 2K 99
B77: Tam 4E 32
Marsham Cl. CV34: Warw 1H 223
Marsham Ct. Rd. B91: Sol 2M 145
Marsham Rd. B14: K Hth 6M 143
Marshbrook Cl. B24: Erd 5L 81
CV2: Ald G 7K 131
Marsh Cl. B23: Erd 4F 80
Marsh Cres. DY8: Word 6J 95
Marshdale Av. CV6: Cov 6E 130
Marsh End B38: K Nor 1G 165
Marshfield B90: Dic H 4H 167
Marshfield Cl. B98: Redd 2H 213
Marshfield Dr. CV4: Canly 7K 173
Marshfield Gdns. B24: Erd 7E 80
Marsh Gro. DY3: Swind 7E 72
DY11: Kidd 1L 157
Marsh Hill B23: Erd 5B 80
Marsh Ho. CV2: W'grve S 2A 154
Marsh Ho. Farm La.
B92: H Ard 6D 148
Marshland Way WS2: Wals 8E 38
Marsh La. B23: Erd 4D 80
B46: Wat O 6H 83
B71: W Brom 2J 77
B76: Curd 4J 83
B91: Sol 5E 146
B92: H Ard 3A 148
(not continuous)
WS2: Wals 7K 39
WS14: Lich 4H 19
WV10: F'hses 6B 22
Marsh La. Pde. WV10: Oxl 7C 22
Marshmont Way B23: Erd 1D 80
Marsh St. WS2: Wals 7K 39
Marsh Way B61: Cats 8M 161
Marshwood Cl. WS11: Cann 7G 9
Marshwood Cft. B62: Quin 6G 119
Marsland Cl. B17: Edg 8C 100
Marsland Rd. B92: Olton 2L 145
MARSTON
B76 . . . . .7B 62
CV8 . . . . .4J 177
Marston Av. WS10: Darl 3C 54
Marston Cl. CV32: Lill 7B 218
DY8: Stourb 5K 115
LE9: S Stan 5L 71
Marston Cft. B37: Mars G 2F 124
Marston Dr. B37: K'hrst 4G 105
MARSTON GREEN 1F 124
Marston Green Station (Rail)
. . . . .2F 124
Marston Gro. B43: Gt Barr 1C 78
MARSTON JABBETT 4M 111
Marston La. B76: Curd 8L 61
CV11: Nun 7L 89
CV12: Bed, Bulk 5H 111
Marston Pk. B78: Tam 5M 31
Marston Rd. B29: W Cas 1M 141
B73: Bold 2G 81
DY1: Dud 1D 96
WS12: Hed 3F 8
WV2: Wolv 2B 52 (8G 7)
Marston Rd. Ind. Est.
WV2: Wolv 2C 52 (8G 7)
Marston St. WV13: W'hall 7C 38
Marten Cl. CV35: H Mag 2A 222
Martham Dr. WV6: Tett 7H 35
Martin Cl. B25: Yard 3K 123
B61: B'gve 8L 187
CV5: E Grn 5E 150
LE9: S Stan 8K 71
WV14: Cose 2K 75
Martin Cft. WS13: Lich 8G 13
Martindale WS11: Cann 7G 9
Martindale Rd. CV7: Exh 1J 131
Martindale Trad. Est.
WS11: Cann 7G 9
Martindale Wlk. DY5: Brie H 3B 116
Martin Dr. WV12: W'hall 4C 38
Martineau Pl.
B2: Birm 7L 101 (5G 5)
Martineau Twr. *B19: Birm* . . . . . *.4K 101*
(off Uxbridge St.)
Martineau Way *B2: Birm* . . . . *.5G 5*
(off Union St.)
Martingale Cl. B60: B'gve 3L 209
WS5: Wals 5M 55
Martin Hill St. DY2: Dud 1J 97
Martinique Sq. CV34: Warw . . .3D 222
Martin La. CV22: Bil 2K 205
Martin Ri. B37: Mars G 1F 124
Martin Rd. DY4: Tip 4A 76
WS5: Wals 1C 56
WV14: Bils 6M 53
Martins Dr. CV9: Ath 7K 49
Martins Rd. CV12: Bed 8E 110
Martin St. WV4: E'shll 4F 52
Martins Way DY13: Stour S 6F 182
Mart La. DY13: Stour S 6G 183
Martlesham Sq. B35: Cas V 5A 82
Martley Cl. B98: Redd 2H 221
Martley Cft. B32: Quin 5L 119
B91: Sol 1B 168
Martley Dr. DY9: Lye 5C 116
Martley Rd. B69: O'bry 3D 98
DY13: Stour S 7A 182
WS4: S'fld 8C 26
Marton Av. WS7: C Ter 1G 17
Marton Ct. CV22: Dunc 2H 205
Martyrs Cl., The CV3: Cov 1D 174
Marwood Cl. CV11: Nun 2L 111
Marwood Cft. B74: S'tly 7A 42
Mary Ann St.
B3: Birm 5K 101 (2E 4)
WV1: Wolv 8E 36 (5M 7)

Mary Herbert St.—Melvina Rd.

Mary Herbert St. CV3: Cov 2D 174
Maryland Av. B34: Hodg H 4L 103
Maryland Cl. LE9: Barw 3M 69
Maryland Dr. B31: N'fld 4B 142
Maryland Rd. DY5: Quar B 2F 116
Marylebone Cl. DY8: Amb 2A 116
Mary Macarthur Dr.
B64: Crad H 8J 97
Mary Rd. B21: Hand 2E 100
B33: Stech 6K 103
B69: Tiv 1C 98
B70: W Brom 8K 77
Mary Slessor St. CV3: W'hall 3J 175
Marystow Cl. CV5: Alle 1H 151
Mary St. B3: Birm 5J 101 (2D 4)
B12: Bal H 4L 121
LE9: Earl S 1F 70
WS2: Wals 6K 39
WS12: Hed 2H 9
Maryvale Ct. WS1: Wals 8L 39
WS14: Lich 2K 19
Mary Va. Rd. B30: B'vlle 3E 142
Marywell Cl. B32: Bart G 2H 141
LE10: Hinc 8F 68
Masefield Av. CV34: Warw 5C 222
DY1: Dud 2J 75
Masefield Cl. LE9: Barw 1B 70
WS7: C Ter 8G 11
WS14: Lich 3H 19
WV14: Bils 7M 53
Masefield Dr. B79: Tam 2A 32
Masefield Gdns. DY10: Kidd 3B 158
Masefield Gro. WS11: Cann 5E 8
Masefield M. WV10: Bush 8G 23
Masefield Ri. B62: Hale 6D 118
Masefield Rd. DY3: Lwr G 5A 74
WS3: Blox 2L 39
WV10: Bush 8G 23
Masefield Sq. B31: N'fld 5C 142
Masham Cl. B33: Stech 7L 103
Mashie Gdns. B38: K Nor 8D 142
Maslen Pl. B63: Hale 6B 118
Maslin Dr. WV14: Cose 8G 53
Mason Av. CV32: Lill 6C 218
Mason Cl. B97: Redd 2D 220
Mason Ct. B27: A Grn 7L 123
LE10: Hinc 1H 91
Mason Cres. WV4: Penn 4L 51
Mason Hall B15: Edg 3G 121
Mason Ho. B90: Shir 8E 144
Mason La. B94: Earls 8F 166
Masonleys Rd. B31: N'fld 6K 141
Mason Rd. B24: Erd 5G 81
B97: Redd 2D 220
CV6: Cov 8F 130
DY11: Kidd 3J 157
WS2: Wals 4H 39
Mason's Cl. B63: Crad 3J 117
Masons Cotts. B24: Erd 4H 81
Mason St. B70: W Brom 5M 77
WV2: Wolv 2C 52 (8J 7)
WV14: Cose 2H 75
Mason's Way B92: Olton 7L 123
Massbrook Gro. WV10: Wolv 3F 36
Massbrook Rd. WV10: Wolv 3F 36
Masser Rd. CV6: Cov 5C 130
Masshouse La. B38: K Nor 8F 142
Masters La. B62: B'hth 8E 98
Masters Rd. CV31: W'nsh 4A 224
MATCHBOROUGH 8L 213
Matchborough Cen.
B98: Redd 8L 213
Matchborough Way
B98: Redd 2L 221
Matchlock Cl. B74: S'tly 2L 57
Matfen Av. B73: S Cold 7F 58
Mathecroft CV31: Lea S 4C 224
Math Mdw. B32: Harb 4M 119
Matlock Cl. CV21: Brow 2C 180
DY2: Neth 6K 97
WS3: Blox 6J 25
Matlock Dr. WS11: Cann 5G 9
Matlock Rd. B11: Tys 6F 122
CV1: Cov 3D 152
WS3: Blox 6J 25
Matlock Vs. *B12: Bal H 4B 122*
(off Chesterton Rd.)
Matterson Rd. CV6: Cov 4A 152
Matthew La. DY11: Kidd 8M 157
Matthews Cl. B65: B'hth 8B 98
Matthews Wlk. WS13: Lich 7G 13
Mattox Rd. WV11: Wed 3K 37
Matty Rd. B68: O'bry 5H 99
Maud Rd. B46: Wat O 6K 83
B70: W Brom 8J 77
Maudslay Rd. CV5: Cov 7L 151
Maughan St. DY1: Dud 8G 75
DY5: Quar B 1F 116
LE9: Earl S 1F 70
Maund Cl. B60: B'gve 2L 209
Maureen Cl. CV4: Tile H 8C 150
Maurice Gro. WV10: Wolv 3G 37
Maurice Mead Ct.
CV31: Lea S 3A 224
Maurice Rd. B14: K Hth 4L 143
B67: Smeth 7L 99
Mavis Gdns. B68: O'bry 1H 119
Mavis Rd. B31: N'fld 8L 141
WS12: Hed 2H 9
Mavor Av. WS7: C Ter 8D 10
Mavor Dr. CV12: Bed 8D 110
Mawgan Dr. WS14: Lich 3K 19
Mawnan Cl. CV7: Exh 1H 131
Maw St. WS1: Wals 3M 55
Maxholm Rd. B74: S'tly 1L 57
Max Rd. B32: Quin 4K 119
MAXSTOKE 7H 107
Maxstoke Castle 2E 106
Maxstoke Cl. B32: Bart G 2G 141
B73: New O 7E 58
B77: Dost 5C 46
B98: Redd 8K 213
CV7: Mer 8H 127
WS3: Blox 6G 25
Maxstoke Ct. B46: Col 5A 106
Maxstoke Cft. B90: Shir 1J 167
Maxstoke Gdns.
CV31: Lea S 3M 223
Maxstoke La. B46: Col 3A 106
CV7: Mer 1H 127
(not continuous)
Maxstoke Rd. B73: New O 7E 58
Maxstoke St. B9: Birm 7B 102
Maxted Rd. B23: Erd 1C 80
Maxtock Av. WS13: Lich 3G 19
Maxwell Av. B20: Hand 8H 79
Maxwell Cl. WS13: Lich 2J 19
Maxwell Rd.
WV2: Wolv 1D 52 (7L 7)
Mayall Dr. B75: R'ley 5J 43
Mayama Rd. B78: Faz 1M 45
May Av. B12: Bal H 4A 122
Maybank B9: Bord G 6F 102
Maybank Cl. WS14: Lich 1L 19
Maybank Pl. B44: P Barr 3L 79
Maybank Rd. DY2: Neth 6J 97
Mayberry Cl. B14: K Hth 7B 144
DY13: Stour S 5E 182
Maybridge Dr. B91: Sol 1B 168
Maybrook Ho. B63: Hale 5A 118
Maybrook Ind. Est.
WS8: Bwnhls 4F 26
(not continuous)
Maybrook Rd. B76: Min 4A 82
WS8: Bwnhls 5F 26
Maybury Cl. WV8: Cod 5E 20
Maybush Gdns. WV10: Oxl 8C 22
May Cl. WS7: C Ter 8F 10
Maycock Rd. CV6: Cov 2D 152
Maycroft Cl. WS12: Hed 2F 8
Maydene Cft. B12: Bal H 3M 121
MAYERS GREEN 5L 77
Mayfair *B37: K'hrst 4F 104*
(off Haselour Rd.)
DY9: W'cte 7D 116
Mayfair Cl. B44: K'sdng 2B 80
DY1: Dud 7G 75
Mayfair Dr. B78: Faz 2A 46
CV10: Gall C 5M 87
DY6: K'wfrd 2J 95
Mayfair Gdns. DY4: Tip 5A 76
WV3: Wolv 7K 35
Mayfair Pde. B44: K'sdng 2B 80
May Farm Cl. B47: H'wd 3A 166
Mayfield B77: Wiln 1J 47
CV12: Bed 6H 111
Mayfield Av. B29: S Oak 7H 121
Mayfield Cl. B61: Cats 8M 161
B91: Sol 8C 146
CV12: Bed 6H 111
CV31: Lea S 3C 224
DY11: Kidd 1G 157
Mayfield Ct. B13: Mose 7A 122
Mayfield Cres. B65: Row R 6A 98
Mayfield Dr. CV8: Ken 5J 199
Mayfield Rd. B11: Tys 5G 123
B13: Mose 7A 122
B19: Hand 1J 101
B27: A Grn 6G 123
B30: Stir 3G 143
B62: B'hth 8F 98
B63: Hale 7K 117
B73: W Grn 7G 59
B74: S'tly 1M 57
CV5: Cov 1A 174
CV11: Nun 7L 89
CV47: Sou 4H 225
DY1: Dud 4H 75
WV1: Wolv 8H 37
Mayfields B98: Redd 7D 212
Mayfields Dr. WS8: Bwnhls 7B 16
Mayfield Way LE9: Barw 2C 70
Mayflower Cl. B19: Loz 3K 101
DY13: Stour S 7G 183
Mayflower Dr. CV2: Cov 7K 153
DY5: P'ntt 2A 96
Mayford Gro. B13: Mose 3B 144
Maygrove Rd. DY6: K'wfrd 2J 95
Mayhurst Cl. B47: H'wd 2C 166
DY4: Tip 1A 76
Mayhurst Rd. B47: H'wd 2B 166
Mayland Dr. B74: S'tly 4M 57
Mayland Rd. B16: Edg 7C 100
May La. B14: K Hth 4M 143
B47: H'wd 2A 166
CV22: Bil 8K 179
Maynard Av. CV12: Bed 1D 130
CV34: Warw 2G 223
DY8: Stourb 6K 115
Mayo Dr. CV8: Ken 5G 199
Mayor's Cft. CV4: Canly 2H 173
Mayou Ct. WS3: Pels 5A 26
Maypole Cl. B64: Crad H 1H 117
DY12: Bew 6C 156
Maypole Ct. WV5: Wom 3G 73
Maypole Dr. DY8: Stourb 4L 115
Maypole Flds. B63: Crad 2G 117
Maypole Gro. B14: K Hth 7B 144
Maypole Hill B63: Crad 1G 117
Maypole La. B14: K Hth 7M 143
CV9: Gren 8C 48
Maypole Rd. B68: O'bry 8H 99
Maypole St. WV5: Wom 2H 73
Mays Farm Dr. LE9: S Stan 6K 71
Mays Farm Rd. LE9: S Stan 5K 71
May St. CV6: Cov 1E 152
WS3: Blox 3J 39
Mayswood Dr. WV6: Tett 8F 34
Mayswood Gro. B32: Quin 5K 119
Mayswood Rd. B92: Sol 7C 124
Maythorn Av. B76: Walm 3A 82
Maythorn Gdns. WV6: Tett 6J 35
WV8: Bilb 5G 21
Maythorn Gro. B91: Sol 1B 168
Maytree Cl. B37: F'bri 7G 105
May Tree Gro. B20: Hand 6F 78
May Trees B47: H'wd 3M 165
Maywell Dr. B92: Sol 1F 146
Maywood Cl. DY6: K'wfrd 3J 95
Meaburn Cl. B29: W Cas 2A 142
Mead, The DY3: Sed 1B 74
Mead Cl. WS9: A'rdge 3H 41
Mead Cres. B9: Bord G 6H 103
Meadfoot Av. B14: K Hth 6M 143
Meadfoot Dr. DY6: K'wfrd 2H 95
Meadfoot Rd. CV3: W'hall 3K 175
Meadlands, The WV5: Wom 3E 72
Meadow Av. B71: W Brom 8B 56
Meadow Bank CV7: Berk 6K 149
Meadowbank B78: Tam 8B 32
Meadowbank Grange
WS6: Gt Wyr 5E 14
Meadowbank Rd. WS13: Lich 6H 13
Meadowbrook Gdns.
WV8: Bilb 5H 21
Mdw. Brook Rd. B31: N'fld 4M 141
Meadowbrook Rd. B63: Hale 6K 117
WS13: Lich 6H 13
Meadow Cl. B17: Harb 1B 120
B74: S'tly 7M 41
B76: Walm 8M 59
B78: K'bry 4D 62
B90: Shir 1K 167
B94: H'ley H 3C 194
CV7: Ansty 6D 132
CV23: Stret D 3G 203
CV32: Lill 5C 218
LE9: S Stan 6K 71
LE10: Wlvy 5K 113
WS4: S'fld 1C 40
WV12: W'hall 1C 38
Meadow Ct. B17: Edg 8B 100
B20: Hand 6E 78
CV11: Nun 4H 89
Meadowcourt Rd. LE9: Earl S 2E 70
Meadow Cft. B47: Wyt 6A 166
CV7: Old A 8E 86
DY9: Hag 5M 137
WS12: Hunt 5C 8
WS13: S'hay 8M 13
WV6: Pert 6D 34
Meadowcroft Cl. CV4: Tile H 1F 172
Meadow Dr. B92: H Ard 3B 148
LE10: Burb 2A 92
Meadowfield Rd.
B45: Rubery 2G 163
Meadowfields Cl. DY8: Word 7L 95
Meadow Furlong
CV23: Brow 1D 180
Meadow Gdns. CV9: Bad E 1C 64
Mdw. Grange Dr.
WV12: W'hall 2C 38
Meadow Gro. B92: Olton 8K 123
WS6: Gt Wyr 7G 15
Mdw. Hill Cl. DY11: Kidd 4G 157
Meadowhill Cres. B98: Redd 4F 212
Meadow Hill Dr. DY8: Word 7L 95
WS11: Cann 7G 9
Meadow Hill Rd. B38: K Nor 7E 142
Meadowhill Rd. B98: Redd 4F 212
Meadow Ho. CV1: Cov 6B 152
Meadowlands Dr. WS4: S'fld 1D 40
Meadow La. B48: A'chu 3B 190
B94: Lapw 6K 195
WV5: Wom 1G 73
WV10: Cov H 3C 22
WV12: W'hall 4A 38
WV14: Cose 7H 53
(not continuous)
Meadowlark Cl. WS12: Hed 5H 9
Mdw. Mills Ind. Est.
DY10: Kidd 4L 157
Meadow Pk. B79: Tam 4M 31
Meadow Pk. Rd. DY8: Woll 1K 115
Mdw. Pleck La. B90: Dic H 3G 167
Meadow Ri. B30: B'vlle 2D 142
B95: Ullen 6J 215
CV7: Bal C 2J 171
DY12: Bew 5C 156
Meadow Rd. B17: Harb 8B 100
B32: Quin 3G 119
B47: Wyt 6A 166
Meadow Rd. B61: Cats 1M 187
B62: B'hth 1C 118
B67: Smeth 5A 100
B68: O'bry 7H 99
B78: Tam 6L 31
CV6: Cov 5B 130
CV8: Wols 5G 177
CV9: Hurl 4J 63
CV10: Harts 1A 88
CV21: N'bld A 3K 179
CV34: Warw 2G 223
CV47: Sou 4H 225
DY1: Dud 5G 75
LE9: Barw 2C 70
WS9: A'rdge 5G 41
WV3: Wolv 1J 51
Meadows, The
CV35: Leek W 2G 217
DY9: Pedm 1B 138
LE10: Burb 2A 92
WS9: A'rdge 4E 40
Meadowside CV11: Nun 8B 90
Meadowside Cl. B43: Gt Barr 8E 56
Meadowside Rd. B74: Four O 5F 42
Meadow St. B64: Old H 1M 117
B77: Tam 6C 32
CV1: Cov 7B 152 (5A 6)
CV9: Ath 2K 65
CV11: Nun 4H 89
WS1: Wals 1K 55
Meadowsweet CV23: Brow 1C 180
Meadowsweet Av.
B38: K Nor 1F 164
Meadowsweet Pl.
DY11: Kidd 1K 157
(off Alder Av.)
Meadowsweet Way
DY6: K'wfrd 3A 96
WS12: Hed 5L 9
Meadow Va. WV8: Bilb 7H 21
Meadowvale Rd. B60: L End 3C 188
Meadow Vw. B13: Mose 1C 144
DY3: Sed 8C 52
DY13: Stour S 7B 182
WS7: Burn 3K 17
WV6: Tett 5L 35
Meadow Vw. Mobile Home Pk.
WV10: Cov H 3C 22
Meadow Vw. Ter. WV6: Tett 5L 35
(not continuous)
Meadow Vw. Wharf WV6: Tett 5L 35
Meadow Wlk. B14: K Hth 8L 143
B64: Crad H 1K 117
Meadow Way DY8: Word 7J 95
WS12: Hth H 8J 9
WV8: Cod 7E 20
Mdw. Wyrthe B79: Tam 2B 32
Mead Ri. B15: Edg 3F 120
Meadthorpe Rd. B44: Gt Barr 1K 79
Meadvale Rd. B45: Redn 3H 163
Meadway B33: Yard 7M 103
CV2: Cov 3H 153
Meadway, The B97: Redd 8C 212
LE10: Burb 2M 91
WV6: Tett 4G 35
Meadway Cl. WS12: Hed 6J 9
Meadway Nth. CV2: Cov 3H 153
Meadway St. WS7: Chase 4G 17
Meadwood Ind. Est.
WV14: Bils 4L 53
Meakins Cl. CV34: Warw 5B 222
Mears Cl. B23: Erd 1D 80
Mears Coppice DY5: Quar B 3E 116
DY9: Lye 3E 116
Mears Dr. B33: Stech 5K 103
Mearse La. B45: B Grn 1F 188
DY9: Belb 3F 160
Mease Av. WS7: Burn 3K 17
Mease Cft. B9: Birm 7B 102
Measham Gro. B26: Yard 4L 123
Measham Way WV11: Wed 2L 37
Meaton Gro. B32: Bart G 1H 141
Mecca Bingo
Acocks Green 5H 123
Bilston 5J 53
Brierley Hill 7D 96
Great Barr 6M 57
Oldbury 2F 98
Wednesbury 7E 54
Wolverhampton 8C 36 (5H 7)
Medcroft Av. B20: Hand 5E 78
Meddins Cl. DY7: Kinv 5A 114
Meddins La. DY7: Kinv 5A 114
Meddins Ri. DY7: Kinv 5A 114
Medhurst Cl. CV22: Dunc 6H 205
Medici Rd. B60: B'gve 7C 188
Medina B77: Wiln 8E 32
Medina Cl. WV10: Bush 5F 22
Medina Rd. B11: Tys 5E 122
CV6: Cov 8E 130
Medina Way DY6: K'wfrd 3J 95
Medland Av. CV3: Finh 4M 173
Medley Gdns. DY4: Tip 5D 76
Medley Gro. CV31: W'nsh 6M 223
Medley Rd. B11: S'brk 4D 122
Medlicott Rd. B11: S'brk 3C 122
Medway B77: Wiln 8D 32
Medway Cl. DY5: P'ntt 3A 96
Medway Ct. B73: S Cold 4H 59
Medway Cft. B36: Cas B 2F 104
Medway Gro. B38: K Nor 1E 164
Medway Rd. WS8: Bwnhls 7C 16
Medway Twr. B7: Nech 4B 102
Medway Wlk. WS8: Bwnhls 7C 16
Medwin Gro. B23: Erd 2D 80
Meerash La. WS7: Hamm 6H 17
MEER END 8J 171
Meer End B38: K Nor 2D 164
Meer End Rd. CV8: Hon 1H 197
Meerhill Av. B90: M'path 3A 168
Meeting Ho. La. CV7: Bal C 2J 171
Meetinghouse La. B31: N'fld 5A 142
Meeting La. DY5: Brie H 8B 96
(not continuous)
Meeting La. Ind. Est.
DY5: Brie H 8B 96
Meeting St. DY2: Neth 4J 97
DY4: Tip 3D 76
WS10: W'bry 6E 54
Megabowl
Birmingham 8L 101 (7H 5)
Brierley Hill 7D 96
Nechells 1D 102
(in Star City)
Royal Leamington Spa 3L 223
Walsgrave on Sowe 1B 154
Meg La. WS7: Burn 8G 11
Meir Rd. B98: Redd 1J 221
Melbourne Av. B19: Hock 3J 101
B61: B'gve 5L 187
B66: Smeth 2B 100
Melbourne Cl. B61: B'gve 6L 187
B70: W Brom 2G 77
CV11: Nun 1L 111
DY6: K'wfrd 5L 95
Melbourne Ct. CV12: Bed 7G 111
Melbourne Cres. WS12: Hth H 7M 9
Melbourne Gdns. WS5: Wals 3B 56
Melbourne Rd. B61: B'gve 5L 187
B63: Hale 4B 118
B66: Smeth 2A 100
CV5: Cov 7A 152
WS12: Hth H 7L 9
Melbourne St.
WV2: Wolv 8D 36 (6K 7)
Melbury Cl. WV3: Wolv 8A 36
Melbury Gro. B14: K Hth 4L 143
Melbury Way WS11: Cann 7F 8
Melchester Wlk. WS11: Cann 7F 8
Melchett Rd. B30: K Nor 6F 142
Melcote Gro. B44: Gt Barr 1L 79
Meldon Dr. WV14: Bils 7A 54
Meldrum Rd. CV10: Nun 6D 88
Melen St. B97: Redd 5D 212
Melford B79: Tam 3L 31
Melford Cl. DY3: Sed 7C 52
Melford Grange WS7: C Ter 8E 10
Melford Hall Rd. B91: Sol 2M 145
Melford Ri. WS7: C Ter 8F 10
Melfort Cl. CV3: Bin 7M 153
CV10: Nun 4C 88
Melfort Gro. B14: K Hth 6A 144
Melksham Sq. B35: Cas V 6A 82
Mellis Gro. B23: Erd 4A 80
Mellish Ct. CV22: Bil 8L 179
WS4: Wals 6A 40
(off Mellish Rd.)
Mellish Dr. WS4: Wals 6B 40
Mellish Rd. CV22: Bil 8L 179
WS4: Wals 6A 40
Mellor Dr. B74: Four O 6E 42
Mellor Rd. CV21: Hillm 1H 207
Mellors Cl. B17: Harb 6B 120
Mellowdew Rd. CV2: Cov 5J 153
DY8: Word 6J 95
Mellowship Rd. CV5: E Grn 4C 150
Mell Sq. B91: Sol 5C 146
Mellwaters B77: Wiln 1J 47
Melmerby B77: Wiln 1J 47
Melplash Av. B91: Sol 5A 146
Melrose Av. *B11: S'hll 3C 122*
(off Walford Rd.)
B12: Bal H 3A 122
B71: W Brom 1K 77
B73: S Cold 7E 58
CV12: Bed 1D 130
DY8: Stourb 7M 115
Melrose Cl. B38: K Nor 8F 142
LE10: Hinc 1H 91
Melrose Cotts.
WS14: Muck C 8M 17
Melrose Dr. WS12: Hed 2F 8
WV6: Pert 5D 34
Melrose Gro. B19: Loz 2H 101
Melrose Pl. B66: Smeth 1K 99
Melrose Rd. B20: Hand 8L 79
Melstock Cl. DY4: Tip 4K 75
Melstock Rd. B14: K Hth 5G 143
Melton Av. B92: Olton 5A 124
Melton Dr. B15: Edg 2J 121
Melton Gro. B33: Kitts G 6E 104
Melton Rd. B14: K Hth 1M 143
CV32: Lill 5B 218
Melton St. LE9: Earl S 1E 70
Melverley Gro. B44: K'sdng 1M 79
Melverton Av. WV10: Bush 1D 36
Melville Cl. CV7: Exh 1G 131
CV22: Bil 8L 179
Melville Hall B16: Edg 8C 100
Melville Rd. B16: Edg 8C 100
CV1: Cov 6A 152
Melvina Rd. B7: Birm 5B 102

Membury Rd.—Mill Gdns.

Membury Rd. B8: Salt ... 3D 102
Memorial Cl. WV13: W'hall ... 7A 38
Memory La. WS10: Darl ... 1D 54
WV11: Wed ... 4H 37
Menai Cl. WV12: W'hall ... 3C 38
Menai Wlk. B37: F'bri ... 5H 105
Mendip Av. B8: Salt ... 4E 102
Mendip Cl. B61: B'gve ... 4A 188
B63: Hale ... 8K 117
DY3: Lwr G ... 6D 74
WV2: E'shll ... 3F 52
Mendip Dr. CV10: Nun ... 6B 88
Mendip Ho. B98: Redd ... 3K 213
Mendip Rd. B8: Salt ... 5E 102
B63: Hale ... 8K 117
DY8: Amb ... 3B 116
WS12: Hed ... 1G 9
Mendip Way B77: Wiln ... 8J 33
Menin Cres. B13: Mose ... 2B 144
Menin Pas. B13: Mose ... 1B 144
Menin Rd. B13: Mose ... 1B 144
DY4: Tip ... 4K 75
Menteith Cl. DY13: Stour S ... 2E 182
Mentone Ct. B20: Hand ... 6E 78
Meon Gro. B33: Sheld ... 1B 124
WV6: Pert ... 5F 34
Meon Ri. DY9: Pedm ... 6C 116
Meon Way WV11: Wed ... 2M 37
Meranti Cl. WV12: W'hall ... 1C 38
Mercer Av. B46: Wat O ... 6G 83
CV2: Cov ... 4G 153
Mercer Ct. CV22: Hillm ... 1F 206
Mercer Gro. WV11: Wed ... 2L 37
Mercers Mdw. CV7: Ker E ... 3A 130
Merchants Way WS9: A'rdge ... 2G 41
Mercia Av. CV8: Ken ... 5E 198
Mercia Bus. Village
CV4: W'wd H ... 3F 172
Mercia Cl. B60: B'gve ... 2M 209
B79: Tam ... 2L 31
Mercia Dr. B14: K Hth ... 3K 143
WV6: Pert ... 4E 34
Mercia Ho. CV1: Cov ... 6C 152 (4B 6)
Mercian Ct. WS13: Lich ... 2J 19
Mercian Pk. B77: Amin ... 6G 33
Mercian Way B77: Amin ... 4G 33
Mercia Way CV34: Warw ... 2H 223
Mercot Cl. B98: Redd ... 3G 221
Mercote Hall La. CV7: Mer ... 4G 149
Mercury Ct. B77: Amin ... 6J 33
Mercury Rd. WS11: Cann ... 4G 9
Mere Av. B35: Cas V ... 6A 82
Mere Cl. WV12: W'hall ... 4A 38
Merecote Rd. B92: Olton ... 2K 145
Mere Cft. WS11: Nort C ... 4M 15
Meredith Grn. DY11: Kidd ... 8G 157
Meredith Rd. CV2: Cov ... 6K 153
DY3: Lwr G ... 4A 74
WV11: Wed ... 1J 37
Merediths Pool Cl.
B18: Hock ... 3F 100
Meredith St. B64: Crad H ... 8K 97
MERE GREEN ... 6J 43
Mere Grn. Cl. B75: Four O ... 7J 43
Mere Grn. Rd. B75: Four O ... 7H 43
Mere Oak Rd. WV6: Pert ... 4E 34
Mere Pool Rd. B75: R'ley ... 7K 43
Mere Rd. B23: Erd ... 6C 80
DY8: Stourb ... 6L 115
Mereside Way B92: Olton ... 1L 145
Meres Rd. B63: Crad ... 4J 117
Merestone Cl. CV47: Sou ... 3H 225
Merevale Av. CV11: Nun ... 5G 89
LE10: Hinc ... 2J 91
Merevale Cl. B98: Redd ... 1K 221
LE10: Hinc ... 2J 91
Merevale Ct. CV11: Nun ... 5G 89
Merevale La. CV9: Ath ... 2E 64
Merevale Rd. B92: Sol ... 7B 124
CV9: Ath ... 8J 49
Merevale Vw. CV9: Ath ... 2J 65
Mere Vw. WS4: S'fld ... 1C 40
Merganser B77: Wiln ... 3G 47
Merganser Way DY10: Kidd ... 7B 158
MERIDEN ... 8J 127
Meriden Av. DY8: Woll ... 3K 115
Meriden Cl. B25: Yard ... 2H 123
B98: Redd ... 6A 214
DY8: Woll ... 3K 115
WS11: Cann ... 1B 14
Meriden Dr. B37: K'hrst ... 3G 105
Meriden Pk. Homes
CV7: Mer ... 1J 149
Meriden Ri. B92: Sol ... 6D 124
Meriden Rd. B92: H Ard ... 2B 148
CV7: Berk ... 4J 149
CV7: Fill ... 2A 128
CV7: Mer ... 2B 148
WV10: Oxl ... 1A 36
Meriden St. B5: Birm ... 7M 101 (7J 5)
CV1: Cov ... 6B 152 (3A 6)
Meridian Pl. B60: B'gve ... 7A 188
Meridian Point CV1: Cov ... 6C 6
Merino Av. B31: Longb ... 1A 164
Merlin Av. CV10: Nun ... 3B 88
Merlin Cl. B35: Cas V ... 6A 82
B77: Wiln ... 3G 47
CV23: Brow ... 1C 180
DY1: Dud ... 1F 96
WS11: Cann ... 7C 8
Merlin Ct. WS7: Burn ... 1M 17
Merlin Dr. DY10: Kidd ... 6B 158
Merlin Gro. B26: Sheld ... 4B 124
Merrick Cl. B63: Hale ... 7K 117
Merrick Ct. LE10: Burb ... 4M 91
Merrick Rd. WV11: Wed ... 3A 38
Merricks Cl. DY12: Bew ... 2B 156
Merricks La. DY12: Bew ... 2B 156
MERRIDALE ... 8M 35
Merridale Av. WV3: Wolv ... 8M 35
Merridale Ct. WV3: Wolv ... 8M 35
Merridale Cres. WV3: Wolv ... 7A 36
Merridale Gdns. WV3: Wolv ... 8A 36
Merridale Gro. WV3: Wolv ... 8L 35
(not continuous)
Merridale La. WV3: Wolv ... 7A 36
Merridale Rd. WV3: Wolv ... 8M 35
Merridale St.
WV3: Wolv ... 8B 36 (6G 7)
Merridale St. W. WV3: Wolv ... 1A 52
Merriemont Dr. B45: B Grn ... 8G 163
Merrifield Gdns. LE10: Burb ... 4L 91
Merrill Cl. WS6: C Hay ... 7E 14
Merrill Gdns. B60: Marl ... 8D 162
Merrill's Hall La. WV11: Wed ... 5L 37
Merrington Cl. B91: Sol ... 1C 168
Merrions Cl. B43: Gt Barr ... 5E 56
Merrishaw Rd. B31: Longb ... 1A 164
Merritts Brook Cl.
B29: W Cas ... 4A 142
Merritt's Brook La.
B31: N'fld ... 5L 141
Merritt's Hill B31: N'fld ... 3K 141
Merrivale Rd. B62: B'hth ... 1F 118
B66: Smeth ... 7A 100
CV5: Cov ... 6L 151
Merryfield Cl. B92: Sol ... 2D 146
Merryfield Gro. B17: Harb ... 5C 120
Merryfield Rd. DY1: Dud ... 1D 96
Merryfields Way
CV2: W'grve S ... 8M 131
MERRY HILL
Brierley Hill ... 6E 96
Wolverhampton ... 2K 51
Merry Hill
DY5: Brie H, Quar B ... 8F 96
Merry Hill Cen. DY5: Brie H ... 6F 96
Merry Hill Ct. B66: Smeth ... 3D 100
Merryhill Dr. B18: Hock ... 3F 100
Merryhills Ent. Pk.
WV10: Wolv ... 4F 36
Merry Hurst Way LE10: Hinc ... 2F 90
Merse Rd. B98: Redd ... 3L 213
Mersey Gro. B38: K Nor ... 1E 164
Mersey Pl. WS3: Blox ... 8L 25
Mersey Rd. CV12: Bulk ... 7A 112
WS3: Blox ... 8L 25
Merstal Dr. B92: Sol ... 2F 146
Merstone Cl. WV14: Bils ... 3J 53
Merstowe Cl. B27: A Grn ... 6H 123
Merton Cl. B68: O'bry ... 7H 99
DY10: Kidd ... 2A 158
DY12: Bew ... 1B 156
Merton Ho. B37: F'bri ... 7F 104
Merton Rd. B13: Mose ... 6B 122
Merttens Dr. CV22: Rugby ... 7M 179
Mervyn Pl. WV14: Bils ... 6M 53
Mervyn Rd. B21: Hand ... 8E 78
WV14: Bils ... 6M 53
Meryhurst Rd. WS10: W'bry ... 4G 55
Meryton Av. CV4: Canly ... 3L 173
Meschede Way
CV1: Cov ... 7D 152 (5D 6)
Meschines St. CV3: Cov ... 3D 174
Mesnes Grn. WS14: Lich ... 2J 19
Messenger La. B70: W Brom ... 6K 77
Messenger Rd. B66: Smeth ... 3B 100
MESTY CROFT ... 6H 55
Metcalf Cl. LE9: S Stan ... 7K 71
WS7: Burn ... 1J 17
Metcalfe Cl. WS12: Hed ... 3J 9
Metcalfe St. LE9: Earl S ... 2E 70
Metchley Abbey B17: Harb ... 4D 120
Metchley Ct. B17: Harb ... 5D 120
Metchley Cft. B90: M'path ... 3M 167
Metchley Dr. B17: Harb ... 4C 120
Metchley Gro. *B18: Win G ... 5E 100*
(off Heath Grn. Rd.)
Metchley Ho. B17: Harb ... 4D 120
Metchley La. B17: Harb ... 5D 120
Metchley Pk. Rd. B15: Edg ... 5D 120
Metfield Cl. B79: Tam ... 1C 32
Metfield Cft. B17: Harb ... 5D 120
DY6: K'wfrd ... 3M 95
Metric Wlk. B67: Smeth ... 4A 100
Metropolitan Ho. B16: Birm ... 8A 4
Metropolitan Lofts *DY1: Dud ... 8J 75*
(off Parson's St.)
Metro Triangle B7: Nech ... 2D 102
Metro Way B66: Smeth ... 2C 100
Mews, The B27: A Grn ... 6H 123
B44: K'sdng ... 2B 80
B65: Row R ... 7B 98
CV8: Ken ... 6E 198
CV9: Ath ... 1L 65
CV12: Bed ... 7H 111
CV21: Hillm ... 8G 181
Mews Rd. CV32: Lea S ... 1K 223
Meynell Ho. B20: Hand ... 6F 78
Meyrick Rd. B70: W Brom ... 3G 77
Meyrick Wlk. B16: Edg ... 8F 100
Miall Pk. Rd. B91: Sol ... 4L 145
Miall Rd. B28: Hall G ... 1G 145
Mica Cl. B77: Amin ... 7H 33
Michael Blanning Gdns.
B93: Dorr ... 6E 168
Michael Blanning Ho.
B13: Mose ... 7B 122
(off Wake Grn. Pk.)
Michael Blanning Pl.
CV7: Bal C ... 2H 171
Michael Ct. B5: Edg ... 3K 121
Michael Dr. B15: Edg ... 2J 121
Michaelmas Rd.
CV3: Cov ... 8C 152 (8B 6)
Michael Rd. B67: Smeth ... 3L 99
WS10: Darl ... 2B 54
Michaelwood Cl. B97: Redd ... 7M 211
Michel Ho. CV1: Cov ... 5D 152 (1E 6)
Michell Cl. CV3: Cov ... 1H 175
Michelle Cl. B13: Mose ... 4A 144
Michigan Cl. WS11: Hth H ... 7H 9
Micklehill Dr. B90: Shir ... 1H 167
Mickle Mdw. B46: Wat O ... 6H 83
Mickleover Rd. B8: W End ... 4J 103
Mickleton B77: Wiln ... 1J 47
Mickleton Av. B33: Sheld ... 1C 124
Mickleton Cl. B98: Redd ... 2E 220
Mickleton Rd. B92: Olton ... 1K 145
CV5: Cov ... 8A 152
Mickley Av. WV10: Wolv ... 4E 36
Midacre WV13: W'hall ... 8A 38
Middelburg Cl. CV11: Nun ... 8A 90
Middle Acre Rd. B32: Bart G ... 7L 119
Middle Av. WV13: W'hall ... 1L 53
Middle Bickenhill La.
B92: Bick ... 4A 126
Middleborough Rd.
CV1: Cov ... 6B 152 (3A 6)
Middlecotes CV4: Tile H ... 8H 151
Middle Cres. WS3: Wals ... 2A 40
Middle Cross
WV1: Wolv ... 8D 36 (4M 7)
Middle Dr. B45: Coft H ... 5K 163
Middle Entry B79: Tam ... 4B 32
MIDDLEFIELD ... 6J 69
Middlefield WV8: Pend ... 7L 21
Middlefield Av. B62: B'hth ... 1F 118
B93: Know ... 5H 169
Middlefield Cl. B62: B'hth ... 8F 98
LE10: Hinc ... 7K 69
Middlefield Ct. LE10: Hinc ... 7K 69
Middlefield Dr. CV3: Bin ... 8A 154
Middlefield Gdns.
B62: B'hth ... 1F 118
(off Hurst Grn. Rd.)
Middlefield Ho. *B14: K Hth ... 6M 143*
(off Britford Cl.)
Middlefield La. DY9: Hag ... 3B 138
LE10: Hinc ... 6K 69
(Middlefield Pl.)
LE10: Hinc ... 5J 69
(Normandy Way)
Middlefield Pl. LE10: Hinc ... 6K 69
Middle Fld. Rd. B31: N'fld ... 7C 142
Middlefield Rd. B60: B'gve ... 2B 210
B69: Tiv ... 1A 98
Middle Gdns. WV13: W'hall ... 7B 38
MIDDLE HILL JUNC. ... 5A 14
Middlehill Ri. B32: Bart G ... 7K 119
Middle Ho. Dr. B60: Marl ... 8D 162
Middlehouse La. B97: Redd ... 3E 212
Middle La. B38: Head H ... 3J 165
B46: Neth W ... 3E 84
B47: Wyt ... 5L 165
WV8: Oaken ... 7C 20
WV9: Coven ... 5M 21
Middle Leaford B34: Stech ... 4A 104
Middle Leasowe B32: Quin ... 5J 119
Middlemarch Bus. Pk.
CV3: W'hall ... 5K 175
(London Rd.)
CV3: W'hall ... 8J 175
(Siskin Parkway E.)
Middlemarch Rd. CV6: Cov ... 3B 152
CV10: Nun ... 8H 89
Middle Mdw. DY4: Tip ... 4B 76
Middle Mdw. Av. B32: Quin ... 4J 119
Middlemist Gro. B43: Gt Barr ... 3F 78
Middlemore Bus. Pk.
WS9: A'rdge ... 4D 40
Middlemore Cl. B80: Stud ... 6K 221
Middlemore Ind. Est.
B21: Hand ... 1B 100
Middlemore La. WS9: A'rdge ... 3F 40
Middlemore La. W.
WS9: A'rdge ... 3D 40
Middlemore Rd. B21: Hand ... 2B 100
B31: N'fld ... 7B 142
B66: Hand, Smeth ... 2B 100
B71: W Brom ... 2B 100
Middle Pk. Cl. B29: W Cas ... 1B 142
Middle Pk. Dr. B31: N'fld ... 3B 142
Middle Pk. Rd. B29: W Cas ... 1B 142
Middlepark Rd. DY1: Dud ... 1E 96
Middle Piece Dr. B97: Redd ... 7A 212
Middle Ride CV3: W'hall ... 3K 175
Middle Rd. B60: Lwr B ... 7G 211
B61: Wild ... 5M 161
Middlesmoor B77: Wiln ... 1J 47
MIDDLE STOKE ... 6G 153
Middle St. CV23: Kils ... 6M 207
MIDDLETON ... 8H 45
Middleton Cl. B98: Redd ... 7M 213
LE9: S Stan ... 7L 71
WS5: Wals ... 4M 55
(not continuous)
Middleton Gdns. B30: K Nor ... 5D 142
Middleton Grange B31: N'fld ... 5C 142
Middleton Hall ... 8L 45
Middleton Hall Rd.
B30: K Nor ... 5D 142
Middleton La. B78: Midd ... 3F 60
Middleton M. B98: Redd ... 7M 213
Middleton Rd. B14: K Hth ... 2L 143
B61: B'gve ... 5M 187
B74: S'tly ... 8A 42
B90: Shir ... 7G 145
DY11: Kidd ... 8J 135
WS8: Bwnhls ... 8G 17
Middleton Trad. Est.
WV13: W'hall ... 7L 37
MIDDLETOWN ... 8K 221
Middletown B80: Stud ... 8K 221
Middletown La. B80: Stud ... 8J 221
B96: Sam ... 8J 221
Middletree Rd. B63: Crad ... 2J 117
Middle Vauxhall WV1: Wolv ... 7A 36
Middleway B15: Birm ... 1H 121
WS12: Haz ... 3A 10
Middleway Av. DY8: Word ... 6J 95
Middleway Grn. WV14: Bils ... 1J 53
Middleway Ind. Est.
B12: Birm ... 2M 121
(off Moseley Rd.)
Middleway Rd. WV14: Bils ... 1J 53
Middleway Vw.
B18: Hock ... 6G 101 (3A 4)
Midgley Dr. B74: Four O ... 7G 43
Midhill Dr. B65: Row R ... 3C 98
Midhurst Dr. WS12: Hed ... 2J 9
Midhurst Gro. WV6: Tett ... 4J 35
Midhurst Rd. B30: K Nor ... 6H 143
Midland Air Mus. ... 6H 175
Midland Cl. B21: Hand ... 2G 101
Midland Ct. *B3: Birm ... 5J 101*
(off Cox St.)
Midland Cft. B33: Kitts G ... 7D 104
Midland Dr. B72: S Cold ... 4J 59
Midland Karting ... 5K 39
Midland Oak Trad. Est.
CV6: Cov ... 7E 130
Midland Rd. B30: K Nor ... 4F 142
B74: S Cold ... 2G 59
CV6: Cov ... 4E 152
CV11: Nun ... 4G 89
WS1: Wals ... 8K 39
WS10: Darl ... 1C 54
WS12: Hunt ... 5D 8
Midland Sailing Club ... 6E 100
Midlands Art Cen. ... 5K 121
Midlands Hydroplane Club, The
... 5B 62
Midland Sports Cen. ... 2C 172
Midland St. B8: Birm ... 6C 102
Midland Trad. Est.
CV21: Rugby ... 3A 180
Midpoint Blvd. B76: Min ... 4C 82
Midpoint Pk. B76: Min ... 5C 82
Midvale Dr. B14: K Hth ... 7K 143
Mikado Rd. B60: B'gve ... 8D 188
Milburn B77: Wiln ... 1J 47
Milburn Rd. B44: K'sdng ... 6A 58
Milby Ct. CV11: Nun ... 7J 89
Milby Dr. CV11: Nun ... 1M 89
Milcote Cl. B98: Redd ... 2F 220
Milcote Dr. B73: New O ... 6C 58
WV13: W'hall ... 8K 37
Milcote Rd. B29: W Cas ... 1A 142
B67: Smeth ... 7M 99
B91: Sol ... 5B 146
Milcote Way DY6: K'wfrd ... 2H 95
Mildenhall B79: Tam ... 1C 32
Mildenhall Rd. B42: Gt Barr ... 8G 57
Mildred Rd. B64: Old H ... 7L 97
Mildred Way B65: Row R ... 3C 98
Milebrook Gro. B32: Bart G ... 1H 141
Mile End B94: Tan A ... 7G 193
Mile Flat DY6: K'wfrd ... 5G 73
Mile La. CV1: Cov ... 8D 152 (7D 6)
CV3: Cov ... 8D 152 (7D 6)
MILE OAK ... 8J 31
Mile Oak Ct. B66: Smeth ... 3B 100
Milesbush Av. B36: Cas B ... 8D 82
Miles Gro. DY2: Dud ... 2M 97
Miles Mdw. CV6: Cov ... 8H 131
Miles Mdw. Cl. WV12: W'hall ... 1C 38
Milestone Ct. WV6: Tett ... 6G 35
Milestone Dr. CV22: Rugby ... 1M 205
DY9: Hag ... 5M 137
Milestone Ho. *CV1: Cov ... 7B 152*
(off Windsor St.)
Milestone La. B21: Hand ... 1D 100
Milestone Way WS7: Chase ... 3E 16
WV12: W'hall ... 1B 38
Mile Tree La. CV2: Ald G ... 3L 131
Milfoil Cl. LE10: Hinc ... 2F 90
Milford Av. B12: Bal H ... 3A 122
DY13: Stour S ... 3E 182
WV12: W'hall ... 4A 38
Milford Cl. B97: Redd ... 2B 220
CV5: Alle ... 3H 151
DY8: Word ... 6L 95
Milford Copse B17: Harb ... 4B 120
Milford Cft.
B19: Birm ... 4K 101 (1E 4)
B65: Row R ... 3M 97
Milford Gro. B90: M'path ... 2C 168
Milford Pl. B14: K Hth ... 1L 143
Milford Rd. B17: Harb ... 4B 120
WV2: Wolv ... 2C 52 (8H 7)
Milford St. CV10: Nun ... 7H 89
Milhill Rd. B98: Redd ... 8L 213
Milholme Grn. B92: Sol ... 1D 146
MILKING BANK ... 7E 74
Milking Bank DY1: Dud ... 7D 74
Milk St. B5: Birm ... 8M 101 (7K 5)
Millais Cl. CV12: Bed ... 5G 111
Millais Rd. LE10: Hinc ... 6G 69
Millard Ind. Est.
B70: W Brom ... 8G 77
Millard Rd. WV14: Cose ... 8H 53
Mill Bank B46: Over W ... 6K 85
DY3: Sed ... 1D 74
Millbank CV34: Warw ... 8G 217
Millbank Gro. B23: Erd ... 3B 80
(not continuous)
Millbank M. CV8: Ken ... 3H 199
Millbank St. WV11: Wed ... 8M 23
Millbeck CV21: Brow ... 2D 180
Millbrook Cl. WS11: Cann ... 7F 8
Mill Brook Dr. B31: Longb ... 1L 163
Millbrook Dr. WS14: Shens ... 3F 28
Millbrook Rd. B14: K Hth ... 3J 143
Millbrook Way DY5: Brie H ... 1B 116
Millburn Hill Rd. CV4: Canly ... 3H 173
Mill Burn Way B9: Birm ... 7B 102
Mill Cl. B47: H'wd ... 2A 166
B60: B'gve ... 3M 209
CV2: Ald G ... 6H 131
CV8: Wols ... 6F 176
CV11: Nun ... 8M 89
CV47: Sou ... 4G 225
DY10: Blak ... 7H 137
DY13: Stour S ... 6H 183
LE9: Sap ... 1L 93
Mill Cotts. CV21: Rugby ... 3D 180
Mill Ct. WS14: Shens ... 3G 29
Mill Cres. B78: K'bry ... 4D 62
CV47: Sou ... 4G 225
WS11: Hth H ... 7H 9
Mill Cft. WV14: Bils ... 3L 53
Millcroft Cl. B32: Bart G ... 7L 119
Millcroft Rd. B74: S'tly ... 1A 58
Milldale Cl. DY10: Kidd ... 1L 157
Milldale Cres. WV10: F'hses ... 5D 22
Milldale Rd. WV10: F'hses ... 5D 22
Mill Dr. B66: Smeth ... 4B 100
MILL END ... 3H 199
Mill End CV8: Ken ... 3G 199
Millenium Gdns. B64: Old H ... 7M 97
Millennium Apartments
B3: Birm ... 3E 4
Millennium Cl. WS3: Pels ... 6A 26
Millennium Pk. B70: W Brom ... 4G 77
Millennium Point ... 6M 101 (4K 5)
Millennium Way CV8: Wols ... 6F 176
WV8: Bilb ... 5H 21
Miller Cl. B60: B'gve ... 3L 209
Miller Ct. B33: Stech ... 6L 103
Miller Cres. WV14: Cose ... 8G 53
Millers Cl. CV22: Dunc ... 5G 205
WS2: Wals ... 8F 38
Millers Ct. *B66: Smeth ... 4B 100*
(off Corbett St.)
B90: Shir ... 7F 144
Millers Dale Cl. CV21: Brow ... 2C 180
Millersdale Dr. B71: W Brom ... 7M 55
Millers Grn. LE10: Burb ... 3M 91
Millers Grn. Dr. DY6: W Hth ... 1G 95
Millers Rd. CV34: Warw ... 1D 222
Miller St. B6: Aston ... 4L 101
Millers Va. WS12: Hth H ... 8K 9
WV5: Wom ... 4D 72
Millers Wlk. WS3: Pels ... 6L 25
Millers Wharf B78: Pole ... 8M 33
Mill Farm Cvn. Pk.
CV12: Bulk ... 3B 112
Mill Farm Cl. CV22: Dunc ... 6J 205
Mill Farm Rd. B17: Harb ... 6C 120
Millfield B31: N'fld ... 5A 142
CV31: Lea S ... 1A 224
Millfield Av. WS3: Blox ... 7K 25
WS4: S'fld ... 8B 26
Millfield Ct. *DY1: Dud ... 7G 75*
(off Pelham Dr.)
Millfield Gdns. DY11: Kidd ... 3K 157
Millfield Rd. B20: Hand ... 4E 78
B61: B'gve ... 8K 187
WS8: Bwnhls ... 2G 27
Mill Flds. DY7: Kinv ... 6B 114
Millfields B33: Kitts G ... 6D 104
(not continuous)
Millfields Av. CV21: Hillm ... 1F 206
Millfields Cl. B71: W Brom ... 8H 55
Millfields Rd. B71: W Brom ... 8H 55
WV4: E'shll ... 4G 53
WV14: Bils ... 4G 53
Millfields Way WV5: Wom ... 3E 72
Millfield Vw. B63: Hale ... 5L 117
Millford Cl. B28: Hall G ... 4G 145
Mill Furlong CV23: Brow ... 1D 180
Mill Gdns. B14: Yard W ... 4D 144
B67: Smeth ... 6M 99
CV10: Nun ... 7H 89

West Midlands Atlas 281

Mill Gdns.—Moor Farm Cl.

Mill Gdns. CV13: High H 6M 67
MILL GREEN
Aldridge 2A 42
Cannock 1F 14
Mill Grn. WV10: F'hses 5D 22
Mill Green Nature Pk. 8G 9
Mill Gro. WV8: Bilb 6J 21
Millhaven Av. B30: Stir 3H 143
Mill Hill B67: Smeth 6M 99
CV8: Bag 5D 174
Mill Hill Rd. LE10: Hinc 8J 69
Millholme Cl. CV47: Sou 5J 225
Mill Ho. B8: W End 5K 103
Mill Ho. Cl. CV32: Lea S 1J 223
Mill Ho. Ct. CV6: Cov 2F 152
Mill Ho. Dr. CV32: Lea S 1J 223
Mill Ho. La. B75: Can 1M 43
Millhouse Rd. B25: Yard 1H 123
Mill Ho. Ter. CV32: Lea S 1J 223
Millicent Cl. WS12: Hed 3H 9
Millicent Pl. B12: Bal H 3A 122
Millichip Rd. WV13: W'hall 8L 37
Milliners Ct. CV9: Ath 1K 65
Millington Rd. B36: Hodg H 1L 103
DY4: Tip 8M 53
WV10: Bush 3E 36
Millison Gro. B90: M'path 2A 168
Mill La. B5: Birm 8M 101 (7J 5)
B31: N'fld 8M 141
B32: Bart G 7K 119
B47: Wyt 8B 166
B61: B'gve 7M 187
B61: Wild 6L 161
B63: Hale 5C 118
B69: O'bry 5G 99
B78: Faz 1A 46
B79: Tam 4C 32
B91: Sol 6C 146
B93: Dorr 5E 168
B94: Earls 8B 166
B94: Lapw 6J 195
CV3: Bin 7M 153
CV7: Fill 4C 108
CV9: Man 3A 66
CV9: With 1A 66
CV11: Burt H 1F 112
CV12: Bulk 6A 112
CV23: Clift D 3E 180
CV32: Cubb 4F 218
CV35: Row 8M 195
DY3: Swind 6D 72
DY7: Env, Stourt 6A 94
DY10: Blak 7H 137
DY10: Kidd 7M 157
DY11: Kidd 3K 157
DY11: W'ley 6K 135
DY13: Stour S 5H 183
LE9: Earl S, Thurl 1G 71
LE10: Sharn 4J 93
LE10: Wlvy 4M 113
WR9: Wych 8E 208
WS3: Wals 5M 39
WS4: Wals 5M 39
WS7: Hamm 6K 17
WS9: A'rdge 2M 41
WS9: Ston 4A 28
WS14: Shens 3G 29
WV5: Wom 2H 73
WV6: Tett 6G 35
WV8: Cod 3E 20
WV11: Wed 2G 37
WV12: W'hall 4C 38
Mill La. Arc. B91: Sol 6C 146
(off Touchwood Shop. Cen.)
Millmead Lodge B13: Mose 1D 144
Mill Mdw. DY8: Amb 3A 116
Millmead Rd. B32: Bart G 7L 119
Mill Pk. WS11: Cann 7G 9
Mill Pk. Ind. Est. WS11: Cann 7G 9
Mill Pl. WS3: Wals 5L 39
Mill Pleck B80: Stud 6L 221
Millpond, The WS13: Lich 7J 13
Millpool, The WV5: Seis 7A 50
Mill Pool Cl. WV5: Wom 4D 72
Millpool Cl. DY9: Hag 5A 138
Millpool Gdns. B14: K Hth 6M 143
Millpool Hill B14: K Hth 5M 143
Mill Pool La.
B93: Dorr, Know 8F 168
Millpool Rd. WS12: Hed 3H 9
Millpool Way B66: Smeth 5A 100
Mill Race La. CV6: Cov 6G 131
DY8: Amb 3A 116
Millrace Rd. B98: Redd 3E 212
Mill Race Vw. CV9: Ath 7K 49
Millridge Way DY11: Hartl 8M 183
Mill Rd. B64: Crad H 2L 117
CV21: Rugby 4C 180
CV31: Lea S 1A 224
CV47: Sou 4G 225
DY13: Stour S 5H 183
WS4: S'fld 8B 26
WS8: Bwnhls 2G 27
Mill Row LE10: Wlvy 4M 113
Mills Av. B76: Walm 5L 59
Millsborough Rd. B98: Redd 6E 212
(not continuous)
Mills Cl. WV11: Wed 1H 37
Mills Cres. WV2: Wolv 1E 52 (8M 7)
Millside B28: Hall G 6E 144
WV5: Wom 4E 72
Millside Ct. DY12: Bew 6B 156
Mills Rd. WV2: Wolv 1E 52 (8M 7)
Millstone Cl. B76: Walm 8M 59
Mill Stream Cl. WV8: Bilb 5H 21
Mill St. B6: Birm 4M 101 (1J 5)
B63: Crad 2J 117
B70: W Brom 5J 77
B72: S Cold 4J 59
B97: Redd 5D 212
CV1: Cov 6B 152 (2A 6)
CV11: Nun 5J 89
CV12: Bed 6H 111
CV31: Lea S 2A 224
CV34: Warw 3F 222
DY4: Tip 4D 76
DY5: Brie H 7D 96
DY8: Word 7L 95
DY11: Kidd 2J 157
LE9: Barw 4M 69
WS2: Wals 6L 39
WS10: Darl 3C 54
WS11: Cann 8E 8
WV13: W'hall 7C 38
WV14: Bils 4J 53
Mill St. Chambers WS11: Cann 8E 8
(off Mill St.)
Mill St. Ind. Est. LE9: Barw 3A 70
Millsum Ho. WS1: Wals 8M 39
(off Paddock La.)
Mills Wlk. DY4: Tip 2M 75
Mill Ter. CV12: Bed 4H 111
Millthorpe Cl. B8: W End 4F 102
Mill Vw. B33: Kitts G 5C 104
LE10: Hinc 8L 69
Mill Wlk. CV11: Nun 5J 89
Mill Wlk., The B31: N'fld 8M 141
Millwalk Dr. WV9: Pend 6A 22
Millward St. B9: Small H 8C 102
B70: W Brom 6G 77
Millway Dr. CV33: Bis T 7E 224
Millwright Cl. DY4: Tip 4B 76
Milner Cl. CV12: Bulk 7D 112
Milner Cres. CV2: W'grve S 8L 131
Milner Dr. B79: Shut 2L 33
Milner Rd. B29: S Oak 8G 121
Milner Way B13: Mose 1D 144
Milnes Walker Ct.
B44: Gt Barr 8L 57
Milo Cres. B78: Tam 7A 32
Milrose Way CV4: Tile H 1F 172
Milsom Gro. B34: S End 3D 104
Milstead Rd. B26: Yard 8A 104
Milston Cl. B14: K Hth 8L 143
Milton Av. B12: Bal H 3A 122
B79: Tam 2A 32
CV34: Warw 4C 222
Milton Cl. B93: Ben H 5F 168
B97: Redd 1C 220
CV12: Bed 8K 111
DY8: Amb 2A 116
DY11: Kidd 3G 157
LE10: Hinc 8J 69
WS1: Wals 3K 55
WV12: W'hall 2E 38
Milton Ct. B66: Smeth 8A 100
WV6: Pert 5E 34
Milton Cres. B25: Yard 2K 123
DY3: Lwr G 4A 74
Milton Dr. DY9: Hag 2D 138
Milton Gro. B29: S Oak 6F 120
Milton Pl. WS1: Wals 3K 55
Milton Rd. B61: Cats 1A 188
B67: Smeth 4K 99
B93: Ben H 5F 168
WS11: Cann 5E 8
WV10: Wolv 4G 37
WV14: Cose 1K 75
Milton St. B71: W Brom 4H 77
CV2: Cov 4G 153
DY5: P'ntt 3D 96
WS1: Wals 1K 55
MILVERTON 8J 217
Milverton Cl. B63: Hale 3A 118
B76: Walm 2M 81
Milverton Ct. B62: Quin 2G 119
(off Binswood Rd.)
CV32: Lea S 1L 223
Milverton Cres. CV32: Lea S 8L 217
Milverton Cres. W.
CV32: Lea S 8L 217
Milverton Hill CV32: Lea S 1L 223
Milverton Lodge
CV32: Lea S 8L 217
(off Milverton Cres. W.)
Milverton Rd. B23: Erd 5E 80
B93: Know 4J 169
CV2: Cov 7J 131
Milverton Ter. CV32: Lea S 1L 223
Milward Sq. B97: Redd 6E 212
Mimosa Cl. B29: W Cas 1B 142
Mimosa Wlk. DY6: K'wfrd 1L 95
Mincing La. B65: Row R 6D 98
Mindelsohn Way B15: Edg 5D 120
Minden Gro. B29: S Oak 8B 120
Minehead Rd. DY1: Dud 1D 96
WV10: Oxl 7B 22
Miner St. WS2: Wals 6J 39
Miners Wlk. B78: Pole 8M 33
Minerva Cl. B77: Tam 4D 32
WV12: W'hall 5E 38
Minewood Cl. WS3: Blox 6F 24
Minions Cl. CV9: Ath 1K 65
Minith Rd. WV14: Cose 1K 75
Miniva Dr. B76: Walm 8A 60
Minivet Dr. B12: Bal H 3L 121
Minley Av. B17: Harb 2M 119
Minories B4: Birm 6L 101 (4G 5)
Minories, The DY2: Dud 8J 75
Minors Hill WS14: Lich 3K 19
Minstead Rd. B24: Erd 8D 80
Minster, The WV3: Wolv 2M 51
Minster Cl. B65: Row R 6E 98
B93: Know 1H 169
Minster Ct. B13: Mose 5A 122
B29: W Cas 2C 142
(off Abdon Av.)
Minster Dr. B10: Small H 2D 122
Minsterley Cl. WV3: Wolv 1L 51
Minsterpool Wlk. WS13: Lich 1H 19
Minster Rd. CV1: Cov 6B 152
DY13: Stour S 5G 183
Minster Wlk. B61: Cats 1M 187
Mintern Rd. B25: Yard 1J 123
Minto Ho. B12: Bal H 4L 121
Minton Cl. WV1: Wolv 8G 37
Minton M. B60: B'gve 1B 210
Minton Rd. B32: Quin 5M 119
CV2: W'grve S 1L 153
MINWORTH 4D 82
Minworth Cl. B97: Redd 7B 212
Minworth Ind. Est. B76: Min 3A 82
Minworth Ind. Pk. B76: Min 3C 82
Minworth Rd. B46: Wat O 6G 83
Mira Dr. CV10: Fen D 6J 67
Miranda Cl. B45: Fran 6G 141
CV3: W'hall 2K 175
Miranda Dr. CV34: H'cte 7L 223
Miras Bus. Est. WS12: Hed 6K 9
Mirfield Cl. WV9: Pend 6A 22
Mirfield Rd. B33: Kitts G 7B 104
B91: Sol 3A 146
Mission Cl. B64: Old H 8A 98
Mission Dr. DY4: Tip 6A 76
Mistletoe Dr. WS5: Wals 6B 56
Mistral Cl. LE10: Hinc 1M 91
Mitcham Cl. WS12: Hed 2F 8
Mitcham Ct. B29: W Cas 2C 142
(off Abdon Av.)
Mitcham Gro. B44: K'sdng 8B 58
Mitcheldean Cl. B98: Redd 2E 220
Mitcheldean Covert
B14: K Hth 7K 143
Mitchell Av. CV4: Canly 2G 173
WV14: Cose 8H 53
Mitchell Rd. CV12: Bed 7J 111
Mitchells Art & Craft Cen. 7L 43
Mitchells Ct. B79: Tam 4B 32
(off Lwr. Gungate)
Mitchel Rd. DY6: K'wfrd 5M 95
Mitchison Cl. CV23: Barby 8J 207
Mitford Dr. B92: Sol 2D 146
Mitre Cl. WV11: Ess 6A 24
WV12: W'hall 2D 38
Mitre Ct. B61: B'gve 6A 188
(off Strand, The)
B74: S Cold 3J 59
Mitre Fold WV1: Wolv 7C 36 (3H 7)
Mitre Rd. DY9: Lye 4E 116
WS6: C Hay 7C 14
Mitten Av. B45: Fran 8F 140
Mitton Cl. DY13: Stour S 5G 183
Mitton Gdns. DY13: Stour S 6G 183
Mitton Mill Ind. Est.
DY13: Stour S 5J 183
Mitton Rd. B20: Hand 7E 78
Mitton St. DY13: Stour S 6G 183
Mitton Wlk. DY13: Stour S 6G 183
Moat Av. CV3: Finh 5M 173
MOAT BANK 7B 18
Moatbrook Av. WV8: Cod 5E 20
Moatbrook La. WV8: Cod 4C 20
Moat Cl. CV8: Bubb 3J 201
CV23: Thurl 7F 204
Moat Coppice B32: Bart G 8H 119
Moat Cft. B37: F'bri 7G 105
B76: Walm 2B 82
Moat Dr. B62: B'hth 8E 98
B78: Dray B 4L 45
Moat Farm Dr. B32: Bart G 8G 119
CV12: Bed 1C 130
CV21: Hillm 2G 207
Moat Farm La. B95: Ullen 4K 215
Moat Farm Way WS3: Pels 4A 26
Moatfield Ter. WS10: W'bry 6G 55
Moat Gdns. LE9: Sap 2K 93
Moat Grn. CV35: Sher 8A 222
Moat Grn. Av. WV11: Wed 2L 37
Moat Ho. B31: Longb 1M 163
Moat Ho. Ct. B80: Map G 1M 221
Moat Ho. La. B46: Shu 8F 84
CV4: Canly 2J 173
Moat Ho. La. E. WV11: Wed 2K 37
Moat Ho. La. W. WV11: Wed 2K 37
Moat Ho. Rd. B8: W End 5G 103
Moat La. B5: Birm 7L 101 (7H 5)
B26: Yard 2L 123
B91: Sol 3C 146
LE10: Wlvy 3L 113
WS6: Gt Wyr 7G 15
Moat Mdws. B32: Quin 5L 119
Moatmead Wlk.
B36: Hodg H 1L 103
Moat Mill La. B61: B'gve 8M 187
Moat Rd. B68: O'bry 7H 99
DY4: Tip 2A 76
WS2: Wals 7H 39
Moatside Cl. WS3: Pels 4A 26
Moat St. WV13: W'hall 7A 38
Moat Way LE9: Barw 3M 69
Moatway, The B38: K Nor 2E 164
Mobberley Rd. WV14: Cose 8G 53
Mob La. WS4: S'fld 7C 26
Mockleywood Rd.
B93: Know 2H 169
Modbury Av. B32: Bart G 8K 119
Modbury Cl. CV3: Cov 4D 174
MODEL VILLAGE 1G 225
Model Village, The
CV47: Long I 1G 225
Moden Cl. DY3: Up Gor 4D 74
Moden Hill DY3: Sed 3C 74
Moffit Way DY13: Stour S 5E 182
Mogul La. B63: Crad 2G 117
Moilliett Ct. B66: Smeth 3C 100
Moilliett St. B18: Win G 5D 100
Moira Cres. B14: Yard W 5C 144
Moises Hall Rd. WV5: Wom 2H 73
Moland St. B4: Birm 5L 101 (1H 5)
Mole St. B11: S'brk 3B 122
Molesworth Av. CV3: Cov 8G 153
Molineux 6C 36 (2H 7)
Molineux All.
WV1: Wolv 6C 36 (1H 7)
(not continuous)
Molineux Fold
WV1: Wolv 6C 36 (2J 7)
Molineux St.
WV1: Wolv 6C 36 (2J 7)
Mollington Cres. B90: Shir 6J 145
Mollington Rd. CV31: W'nsh 6A 224
Molyneux Rd. DY2: Neth 7L 97
Momus Blvd. CV2: Cov 7J 153
Monaco Ho. B5: Birm 1K 121 (8F 4)
Monarch Dr. DY4: Tip 3C 76
Monarch Ind. Est. B11: Tys 3G 123
Monarchs Ga. B91: Sol 4E 146
Monarch Way DY2: Neth 5J 97
Mona Rd. B23: Erd 4F 80
Monastery Dr. B91: Sol 3K 145
Mona St. LE9: Earl S 2E 70
Monckton Rd. B68: O'bry 2G 119
Moncrieff Dr. CV31: Lea S 4C 224
Moncrieffe Cl. DY2: Dud 1L 97
Moncrieffe St. WS1: Wals 8A 40
Mondrain Rd. B60: B'gve 8C 188
Money La. B61: C'wich 4A 162
Monica Rd. B10: Small H 2F 122
Monins Av. DY4: Tip 6A 76
Monk Cl. DY4: Tip 6B 76
Monk Rd. B8: W End 4H 103
Monks Cl. CV22: Caw 1G 205
WV5: Wom 3E 72
Monks Cft., The CV3: Cov 2C 174
Monks Dr. B80: Stud 5K 221
Monkseaton Rd. B72: W Grn 7H 59
Monksfield Av. B43: Gt Barr 8D 56
Monk's Fld. Cl. CV4: Tile H 8G 151
Monkshood M. B23: Erd 2B 80
Monkshood Retreat
B38: K Nor 1F 164
Monks Kirby Rd. B76: Walm 6M 59
MONKSPATH 3A 168
Monks Path B97: Redd 5M 211
Monkspath B76: Walm 1M 81
Monkspath Bus. Pk.
B90: Shir 1M 167
Monkspath Cl. B90: Shir 2K 167
Monkspath Hall Rd.
B90: M'path 3M 167
B91: Sol 1B 168
Monkspath Leisure Pk. 3L 167
Monks Rd. CV1: Cov 7F 152
CV3: Bin W 2C 176
Monks Way B77: Amin 4F 32
CV34: Warw 3D 222
Monksway B38: K Nor 8H 143
Monkswell Cl. B10: Small H 2D 122
DY5: Brie H 8D 96
Monkswood Cres. CV2: Cov 1K 153
Monkswood Rd. B31: N'fld 7C 142
Monkton Rd. B29: W Cas 6A 120
Monmar Ct. WV12: W'hall 4B 38
Monmer Cl. WV13: W'hall 6B 38
Monmer Cl. Ind. Est.
WV13: W'hall 6C 38
Monmer La. WV12: W'hall 5B 38
WV13: W'hall 5B 38
Monmore Bus. Pk.
WV2: Wolv 2F 52
MONMORE GREEN 1E 52 (8M 7)
Monmore Green Stadium 1G 53
Monmore Pk. Ind. Est.
WV2: E'shll 2F 52
Monmore Rd. WV1: Wolv 1G 53
Monmouth Cl. CV5: E Grn 6H 151
CV8: Ken 3F 198
Monmouth Dr. B71: W Brom 2H 77
B73: New O, S Cold 6C 58
Monmouth Gdns. CV10: Nun 6E 88
Monmouth Ho. B33: Kitts G 7E 104
Monmouth Rd. B32: Bart G 1K 141
B67: Smeth 1L 119
WS2: Wals 6E 38
Monsal Av.
WV10: Wolv 5E 36 (1M 7)
Monsaldale Cl. WS8: Clay 3D 26
Monsal Rd. B42: Gt Barr 2J 79
Monsieurs Hall La.
B61: D'frd 7H 187
Mons Rd. DY2: Dud 8L 75
Montague Rd. B16: Edg 8E 100
B21: Hand 1F 100
B24: Erd 8G 81
B66: Smeth 6B 100
CV22: Bil 4K 205
CV34: Warw 8G 217
Montague St. B6: Aston 1B 102
B9: Birm 7A 102 (6M 5)
Montalt Rd. CV3: Cov 2D 174
Montana Av. B42: P Barr 4G 79
Montana Wlk. CV10: Nun 6E 88
Monteagle Dr. DY6: K'wfrd 8K 73
Montford Gro. DY3: Sed 2D 74
Montfort Rd. B46: Col 4M 105
WS2: Wals 3H 55
Montfort Wlk. B32: Bart G 7G 119
Montgomery Cl. B61: Cats 8A 162
CV3: W'hall 5J 175
Montgomery Ct.
CV34: Warw 2F 222
Montgomery Cres.
DY5: Quar B 2F 116
Montgomery Cft. B11: S'brk 2C 122
Montgomery Dr. CV22: Bil 8J 179
Montgomery Rd.
CV31: W'nsh 5M 223
LE9: Earl S 1G 71
(not continuous)
WS2: Wals 7E 38
Montgomery St. B11: S'brk 2B 122
Montgomery St. Bus. Cen.
B11: S'brk 2C 122
Montgomery Wlk.
B71: W Brom 5K 77
Montgomery Way B8: Salt 5G 103
Montjoy Cl. CV3: W'hall 2K 175
Montley B77: Wiln 1J 47
Montpelier Ho. CV8: Ken 4F 198
(off Southbank Rd.)
Montpelier Rd. B24: Erd 8G 81
Montpellier Cl. CV3: Cov 3C 174
Montpellier Gdns. DY1: Dud 7E 74
Montpellier St. B12: Birm 3A 122
Montreal Ho. B5: Bal H 2K 121
Montrose Av. CV32: Lill 5A 218
Montrose Cl. WS11: Cann 4F 8
Montrose Dr. B35: Cas V 6A 82
CV10: Nun 6F 88
DY1: Dud 1G 97
Montrose Rd. CV22: Rugby 8A 180
Montsford Cl. B93: Know 3F 168
Monument Av. DY9: W'cte 5E 116
Monument Dr. WV10: F'stne 1J 23
Monument La. B45: Lick 5F 162
DY3: Sed 8E 52
DY9: Hag 2D 138
Monument Rd. B16: Edg 8F 100
(not continuous)
Monument Vw. B78: Pole 1A 48
Monway Ind. Est.
WS10: W'bry 6E 54
Monway Ter. WS10: W'bry 6E 54
MONWODE LEA 5B 86
Monwode Lea La.
B46: Over W 5A 86
Monwood Gro. B91: Sol 7M 145
Monyhull Hall Rd.
B30: K Nor 7H 143
Moodyscroft Rd.
B33: Kitts G 6C 104
Moons La. WS6: C Hay 7D 14
MOONS MOAT 4K 213
Moons Moat Dr. B98: Redd 4K 213
Moons Pk. B98: Redd 3L 213
Moor, The B76: Walm 1A 82
Moorbrooke CV10: Harts 2A 88
Moor Burgess Activity Cen. 8G 33
Moor Cen., The DY5: Brie H 6D 96
Moor Cl. WS7: Burn 2H 17
Moorcroft WV14: Bils 6A 54
Moorcroft Cl. B97: Redd 3B 220
CV11: Nun 8B 90
Moorcroft Dr. WS10: W'bry 7C 54
Moorcroft Gdns. B97: Redd 3B 220
Moorcroft Pl.
B7: Birm 5A 102 (2M 5)
Moorcroft Rd. B13: Mose 6L 121
Moordown Av. B92: Olton 7A 124
Moore Cl. B74: Four O 3F 42
CV6: Longf 5G 131
CV34: Warw 7E 216
WV6: Pert 5F 34
Moore Cres. B68: O'bry 6J 99
Moorend Av.
B37: Chel W, Mars G 1F 124
Moor End La. B24: Erd 5G 81
Moore Rd. LE9: Barw 1B 70
WV12: W'hall 1D 38
Moore's Row
B5: Birm 8M 101 (7K 5)
Moore St. WS12: Hed 2J 9
WV1: Wolv 8F 36
Moore Wlk. CV34: Warw 2J 223
Moor Farm Cl. CV23: Stret D 3F 202

Nally Dr.—New Rd.

Nally Dr. WV14: Cose 7G **53**
Nanaimo Way DY6: K'wfrd 5A **96**
Nansen Rd. B8: Salt 4E **102**
B11: S'hll 6C **122**
Nantmel Gro. B32: Bart G 1J **141**
Naomi Way WS9: Wals W 5H **27**
Napier B77: Glas 6E **32**
Napier Dr. DY4: Tip 3C **76**
Napier Rd. WS2: Wals 4G **39**
WV2: Wolv 2D **52**
Napier St. CV1: Cov 6E **152**
Napier St. Ind. Est.
CV1: Cov 6E 152
(off Napier St.)
Napton Cl. B98: Redd 8K **213**
Napton Ct. CV22: Dunc 3H **205**
Napton Dr. CV32: Lill 7A **218**
Napton Grn. CV5: E Grn 6G **151**
Napton Gro. B29: W Cas 7M **119**
Napton Ri. CV47: Sou 5K **225**
Napton Rd. CV47: S'ton 1L **225**
Narberth Way
CV2: W'grve S 2M **153**
Narborough Ct. CV32: Lea S . . .1K **223**
Nares Cl. CV22: Bil 8L **179**
Narraway Gro. DY4: Tip 1D **76**
Narrowboat Cl. CV6: Longf 3H **131**
Narrowboat Way DY2: Dud 5G **97**
DY5: Brie H 5G **97**
Narrow Hall Mdw.
CV34: Warw 5B **222**
Narrow La. B62: B'hth 1E **118**
WS2: Wals 2H **55**
WS8: Bwnhls 1F **26**
Narrows, The LE10: Hinc 1L **91**
Naseby Cl. B98: Redd 3K **213**
CV3: Bin 1M **175**
Naseby Dr. B63: Hale 7K **117**
Naseby Rd. B8: Salt 4F **102**
B91: Sol 3B **146**
CV22: Rugby 8C **180**
WV6: Pert 6F **34**
Nash Av. WV6: Pert 6E **34**
Nash Cl. B65: B'hth 8C **98**
DY10: Kidd 4C **158**
Nash Cft. B37: Mars G 1H **125**
Nash La. DY9: Belb 2D **160**
WS13: Elmh 4G **13**
Nash Rd. B98: Redd 1H **221**
Nash Sq. B42: P Barr 5K **79**
Nash Wlk. *B66: Smeth 4C 100*
(off Poplar St.)
Nason Gro. CV8: Ken 4H **199**
Nately Gro. B29: S Oak 7C **120**
Nathan Cl. B75: S Cold 1H **59**
National Agricultural Cen.
CV8: S'lgh P 5A **200**
National Diving Cen. 8L **71**
National Exhibition Cen. 4K **125**
National Indoor Arena
. . . . .7H **101** (5B **4**)
National Motorcycle Mus. 7A **126**
National Sea Life Cen.
. . . . .7H **101** (5B **4**)
Naul's Mill Ho.
CV1: Cov 5B **152** (2A **6**)
Naunton Cl. B29: W Cas 2A **142**
Naunton Rd. WS2: Wals 6G **39**
Navenby Cl. B90: Shir 6C **144**
Navigation Dr. DY5: Brie H 5G **97**
Navigation La. WS10: W'bry . . .7M **55**
Navigation Rdbt. DY4: Tip 3E **76**
Navigation St.
B2: Birm 7K **101** (6E **4**)
WS2: Wals 7K **39**
WV1: Wolv 8E **36** (6M **7**)
Navigation Way B18: Win G . . .4F **100**
B70: W Brom 7F **76**
CV6: Cov 1G **153**
WS11: Cann 7G **9**
Nayland Cft. B28: Hall G 4G **145**
Nayler Cl. CV21: Rugby 3C **180**
Naylor Cl. DY11: Kidd 6H **157**
Naylors Gro. DY3: Up Gor 5E **74**
NEACHELL 7K **37**
Neachells La. WV11: Wed 4K **37**
WV13: W'hall 7K **37**
Neachells La. Ind. Est.
WV11: Wed 5K **37**
Neachless Av. WV5: Wom 4G **73**
Neachley Gro. B33: Stech 5M **103**
Neal Ct. CV2: W'grve S 1A **154**
Neale Av. CV5: Alle 3G **151**
Neale Cl. CV12: Bulk 8C **112**
Neale Ho. B70: W Brom 8K **77**
WV2: Wolv 2C 52
(off Blakenhall Gdns.)
Neales Ct. LE10: Hinc 8K **69**
Neale St. WS2: Wals 7J **39**
NEAL'S GREEN 3D **130**
Neander B79: Tam 3M **31**
Nearhill Rd. B38: K Nor 1C **164**
Near Lands Cl. B32: Quin 5H **119**
Nearmoor Rd. B34: S End 3D **104**
Near Oak Ho. B32: Bart G 1K **141**
Neasden Gro. B44: K'sdng 1B **80**
Neath Rd. WS3: Blox 7F **24**
Neath Way DY3: Sed 3G **75**
WS3: Blox 7F **24**
Nebsworth Cl. B90: Shir 4K **145**
NECHELLS 2D **102**
Nechells Community Sports Cen.
. . . . .4A **102**
NECHELLS GREEN 4B **102** (1M **5**)
Nechells Pk. Rd. B7: Nech 3B **102**
Nechell's Parkway
B7: Birm 5A **102** (2L **5**)
Nechells Pl. B7: Nech 3B **102**
NEC House B40: Nat E C 4K **125**
Needham St. B7: Nech 2C **102**
Needhill Cl. B93: Know 3F **168**
Needle Cl. B80: Stud 5L **221**
Needle Mill La. B98: Redd 3E **212**
NEEDLERS END 2H **171**
Needlers End La. CV7: Bal C . . .3F **170**
Needlers End Rd. CV7: Bal C . . .2F **170**
Needles Ho. B80: Stud 4L **221**
Needless All.
B2: Birm 7K **101** (5F **4**)
Needwood Cl. WV2: Wolv 3B **52**
Needwood Dr. WV4: E'shll 5F **52**
Needwood Gro. B71: W Brom . . .8L **55**
Needwood Hill WS13: Lich 7G **13**
Needwood Ho. B27: A Grn 6K **123**
Neighbrook Cl. B97: Redd 7M **211**
Neilston St. CV31: Lea S 2A **224**
Nelson Av. CV34: Warw 1G **223**
WV14: Bils 2J **53**
Nelson Ct. B13: Mose 5M **121**
Nelson Dr. LE10: Hinc 5K **69**
WS12: Hed 5L **9**
Nelson Ho. DY4: Tip 2A **76**
Nelson La. CV34: Warw 1F **222**
Nelson Rd. B6: Aston 8M **79**
DY1: Dud 8H **75**
DY13: Stour S 8H **183**
Nelson St. B1: Birm 6H **101** (4B **4**)
B69: O'bry 3H **99**
B71: W Brom 4J **77**
CV1: Cov 5E **152**
WV2: Wolv 1C **52** (7J **7**)
WV13: W'hall 6B **38**
Nelson Way CV22: Bil 8J **179**
Nemesia B77: Amin 5H **33**
Nene Cl. CV3: Bin 2K **175**
DY8: Stourb 5A **116**
Nene Ct. CV23: Long L 5J **179**
Nene Way B36: Cas B 1F **104**
Neptune Ind. Est.
WV13: W'hall 1B **54**
Neptune St. DY4: Tip 4L **75**
Nesbit Gro. B9: Bord G 6H **103**
Nesfield Cl. B38: K Nor 8C **142**
Nesfield Gro. B92: H Ard 2B **148**
Nesscliffe Gro. B23: Erd 2D **80**
Nest Comn. WS3: Pels 4M **25**
(not continuous)
Neston Gro. B33: Stech 7J **103**
Netheravon Cl. B14: K Hth 7K **143**
Nether Beacon WS13: Lich 8G **13**
Netherbridge Av. WS14: Lich 1L **19**
Netherby Rd. DY3: Sed 1C **74**
Nethercote Gdns. B90: Shir 6E **144**
Netherdale Cl. B72: W Grn 2J **81**
Netherdale Rd. B14: K Hth 8A **144**
NETHEREND 2G **117**
Netherend Cl. B63: Crad 2G **117**
Netherend La. B63: Crad 2H **117**
Netherend Sq. B63: Crad 2G **117**
Netherfield B98: Redd 1G **221**
Netherfield Gdns.
B27: A Grn 6H **123**
Nethergate DY3: Up Gor 4F **74**
Nether La. WS7: Burn 1J **17**
Netherley Cl. LE10: Hinc 6K **69**
Netherley Rd. LE10: Hinc 6K **69**
Nethermill Rd. CV6: Cov 4A **152**
Nethersole St. B78: Pole 2K **49**
Netherstone Gro. B74: Four O . . .4F **42**
NETHER STOWE 7H **13**
Netherstowe WS13: Lich 8J **13**
Netherstowe La. WS13: Lich 7K **13**
Netherton Bus. Pk. DY2: Neth . . .5K **97**
(not continuous)
Netherton Gro. B33: Kitts G 6D **104**
Netherton Hill DY2: Neth 4J **97**
Netherton La. DY12: Bew 7C **156**
Netherton Lodge DY2: Neth 4J **97**
NETHER WHITACRE 3G **85**
Netherwood Cl. B91: Sol 3L **145**
Netherwood Ind. Est.
CV9: Ath 8M **49**
Netherwood La.
B93: Chad E 2M **195**
Nethy Dr. WV6: Tett 4H **35**
Netley Gro. B11: Tys 6F **122**
Netley Ho. B32: Harb 4M **119**
Netley Rd. WS3: Blox 7E **24**
Netley Way WS3: Blox 7E **24**
Network Pk. B8: Salt 5C **102**
Nevada Way B37: Chel W 8J **105**
Neve Av. WV10: Bush 8J **22**
Neve's Opening WV1: Wolv 7F **36**
Nevill Cl. CV31: Lea S 3M **223**
Neville Av. DY11: Kidd 6K **157**
WV4: Penn 4D **52**
Neville Cl. B98: Redd 4F **212**
Neville Ct. CV34: Warw 3E **222**
DY11: Kidd 6K **157**
Neville Gro. CV34: Warw 8F **216**
Neville Rd. B23: Erd 6C **80**
B36: Cas B 8E **82**
B90: Shir 8F **144**
Neville Smith Cl. LE9: Sap 2K **93**
Neville St. B77: Glas 6E **32**
Neville Wlk. B35: Cas V 7A **82**
Nevill St. B79: Tam 4A **32**
Nevin Gro. B42: P Barr 4J **79**
Nevis Ct. WV3: Wolv 7L **35**
Nevis Gro. WV12: W'hall 8B **24**
Nevison Gro. B43: Gt Barr 5H **57**
Newall Cl. CV23: Clift D 4E **180**
Newark Cft. B26: Sheld 3B **124**
Newark Rd. DY2: Neth 7K **97**
WV12: W'hall 2C **38**
NEW ARLEY 1G **109**
New Art Gallery Walsall, The
. . . . .7L **39**
New Ash Dr. CV5: Alle 4F **150**
New Bank Gro. B9: Bord G 6G **103**
New Barns La. WS14: Foot 5B **28**
New Bartholomew St.
B5: Birm 7M **101** (5J **5**)
NEW BILTON 6L **179**
New Birmingham Rd.
B69: Tiv 7M **75**
DY2: Dud 7M **75**
Newbold Cl. B93: Ben H 4F **168**
CV3: Bin 8M **153**
WS13: Lich 4G **19**
Newbold Comyn Leisure Cen.
. . . . .1C **224**
Newbold Ct. B63: Hale 6B **118**
Newbold Footpath
CV21: Rugby 5L **179**
(Edward St.)
CV21: Rugby 6M **179**
(Oliver St.)
NEWBOLD ON AVON 3L **179**
Newbold Pl. CV32: Lea S 1M **223**
Newbold Rd.
CV21: N'bld A, Rugby 2L **179**
NEWBOLDS 3G **37**
Newbolds Rd. WV10: Wolv 3G **37**
Newbold St. CV32: Lea S 1A **224**
Newbold Ter. CV32: Lea S 1M **223**
Newbold Ter. E. CV32: Lea S . . .1A **224**
Newbolt Rd. WV14: Bils 3L **53**
Newbolt St. WS5: Wals 4L **55**
New Bond St.
B9: Birm 8B **102** (7M **5**)
DY2: Dud 1K **97**
Newborough Gro.
B28: Hall G 5F **144**
Newborough Rd. B28: Hall G . . .5F **144**
B90: Shir 5F **144**
Newbourne Hill B48: Row G . . .5E **190**
NEWBRIDGE 6L **35**
Newbridge Av. WV6: Wolv 6L **35**
Newbridge Cres. WV6: Wolv 5L **35**
Newbridge Dr. WV6: Wolv 5L **35**
Newbridge Gdns. WV6: Wolv 5L **35**
Newbridge M. WV6: Wolv 5M **35**
Newbridge Rd. B9: Bord G 1H **123**
DY6: W Hth 1J **95**
Newbridge St. WV6: Wolv 5M **35**
New Brook St. CV32: Lea S 1L **223**
New Bldgs. CV1: Cov . . .6D **152** (4C **6**)
DY11: Kidd 3K **157**
LE10: Hinc 8K **69**
Newburgh Cres.
CV34: Warw 1E **222**
Newburn Cft. B32: Quin 4H **119**
Newbury Cl. B61: Cats 8B **162**
B62: Hale 6D **118**
CV31: Lea S 3D **224**
WS6: Gt Wyr 6F **14**
Newbury Ho. B69: O'bry 4D **98**
Newbury La. B69: O'bry 3C **98**
Newbury Rd. B19: Hock 2L **101**
DY8: Word 7J **95**
WS11: Nort C 4A **16**
WV10: F'hses 7C **22**
Newbury Wlk. B65: Row R 3C **98**
Newby Cl. CV3: Cov 3E **174**
Newby Gro. B37: F'bri 4H **105**
New Canal St.
B5: Birm 7M **101** (6J **5**)
New Cannon Pas.
B2: Birm 7L **101** (5G **5**)
Newcastle Cft. B35: Cas V 6C **82**
New Century Pk. CV3: Cov 8K **153**
New Century Way CV11: Nun . . .5H **89**
Newchurch Gdns. B24: Erd 7E **80**
New Church Rd. B73: Bold 1G **81**
New Cole Hall La.
B34: Stech 4B **104**
New Coll. Cl. WS1: Wals 2A **56**
Newcombe Cl. CV22: Dunc 6J **205**
Newcombe Rd. B21: Hand 7D **78**
CV5: Cov 8M **151**
Newcome Cl. B24: Erd 5K **81**
Newcomen Cl. CV12: Bed 1D **130**
WS7: Burn 1J **17**
Newcomen Ct. WS4: Rus 2B **40**
Newcomen Dr. DY4: Tip 6M **75**
Newcomen Rd. CV12: Bed 8D **110**
New Cotts. CV10: Nun 6F **88**
Newcott Cl. WV9: Pend 7M **21**
New Ct. *DY5: Brie H 7D 96*
(off Promenade, The)
New Coventry Rd.
B26: Sheld 4M **123**
New Cft. B19: Loz 2L **101**
Newcroft Gro. B26: Yard 2L **123**
NEW CROSS 4G **37**
New Cross Av. WV10: Wolv 5H **37**
WV11: Wed 5H **37**
New Cross Ind. Est.
WV1: Wolv 6G **37**
New Cross St. DY4: Tip 4L **75**
WS10: Darl 4D **54**
Newdegate Pl. CV11: Nun 5J **89**
Newdegate St. CV11: Nun 5J **89**
Newdigate CV31: Lea S 4C **224**
Newdigate Cl. CV12: Bed 6G **111**
Newdigate Rd. B75: S Cold 4A **60**
CV6: Cov 4F **152**
CV12: Bed 5G **111**
New Dudley Rd. DY6: W Hth 1J **95**
Newells Dr. DY4: Tip 2D **76**
Newells Rd. B26: Yard 1A **124**
New End Rd. B46: Max 5G **107**
New England B62: B'hth 2E **118**
New England Cl. B69: O'bry 8E **76**
Newent Cl. B98: Redd 6A **214**
WV12: W'hall 6D **38**
New Ent. Cen. WV1: Wolv 1G **53**
New Enterprise Workshops
B18: Hock 4G **101**
Newent Rd. B31: N'fld 5C **142**
Newey Av. CV12: Bed 1D **130**
Newey Bus. Pk. DY4: Tip 3K **75**
Newey Cl. B45: Redn 3G **163**
Newey Dr. CV8: Ken 7G **199**
Newey Rd. B28: Hall G 3F **144**
CV2: Cov 5K **153**
WV11: Wed 1A **38**
Newey St. DY1: Dud 7G **75**
New Farm Rd. DY9: Lye 5C **116**
Newfield Av. CV8: Ken 6H **199**
Newfield Cl. B91: Sol 3D **146**
WS2: Wals 3J **39**
Newfield Cres. B63: Hale 4A **118**
Newfield Dr. DY6: K'wfrd 5L **95**
Newfield Gdns. DY9: Hag 5A **138**
Newfield La. B63: Hale 4A **118**
Newfield Pl. DY9: Hag 5A **138**
Newfield Rd. B69: O'bry 1F **98**
CV1: Cov 4C **152**
DY9: Hag 5A **138**
New Forest Rd. WS3: Wals 4L **39**
Newgale Wlk. CV31: Lea S 2C **224**
New Gas St. B70: W Brom 4G **77**
Newgate Ct.
CV1: Cov 7D **152** (6E **6**)
Newgate St. WS7: Chase 4G **17**
New Grn. Pk. Cvn. Site
CV2: Cov 2K **153**
Newhall Ct. B3: Birm 6J **101** (3C **4**)
Newhall Cres. WS11: Hth H 6H **9**
New Hall Dr. B76: Walm 5K **59**
(not continuous)
Newhall Farm Cl. B76: Walm 5K **59**
Newhall Gdns. WS11: Cann 7F **8**
NEWHALL GREEN 8A **108**
Newhall Hill B1: Birm . . .6J **101** (3C **4**)
Newhall Ho. *WS1: Wals 1L 55*
(off Newhall St.)
New Hall Pl. WS10: W'bry 6G **55**
Newhall Pl. B3: Birm 3C **4**
Newhall Rd. B65: Row R 6C **98**
CV2: Cov 2K **153**
New Hall St. WV13: W'hall 7A **38**
Newhall St. B3: Birm . . .6J **101** (3D **4**)
B70: W Brom 7J **77**
DY4: Tip 1L **75**
WS1: Wals 1L **55**
WS11: Cann 1D **14**
Newhall Wlk. B72: S Cold 5J **59**
Newham Grn. CV10: Nun 2C **88**
Newhampton Ho.
WV1: Wolv 6B **36** (2H **7**)
New Hampton Lofts
B18: Birm 4J **101** (1C **4**)
New Hampton Rd. E.
WV1: Wolv 6B **36** (1G **7**)
New Hampton Rd. W.
WV6: Wolv 5M **35**
Newhaven Cl.
B7: Birm 4A **102** (1L **5**)
CV6: Cov 4L **151**
Newhay Cft. B19: Loz 2J **101**
New Hayes Rd. WS12: Haz 5C **10**
New Heath Cl. WV11: Wed 4H **37**
New Henry St. B68: O'bry 5G **99**
New High Dr. DY4: Tip 4B **76**
Newhope Cl. B15: Birm 1K **121**
New Hope Rd. B66: Smeth 5C **100**
New Horse Rd. WS6: C Hay 6E **14**
Newhouse Cres. CV7: Bal C 3H **171**
Newhouse Farm Cl.
B76: Walm 6M **59**
New Ho. Farm Dr. B31: N'fld . . .3B **142**
Newhouse La. B61: U War 1D **208**
Newick Av. B74: Lit A 6B **42**
Newick Gro. B14: K Hth 5J **143**
Newick St. DY2: Neth 5J **97**
Newington Cl. CV6: Cov 3K **151**
Newington Rd. B37: Mars G 1H **125**
New Inn Rd. B19: Loz 8K **79**
New Inns Cl. B21: Hand 1D **100**
New Inns La. B45: Fran 8E **140**
NEW INVENTION 2D **38**
New John St. B6: Birm 4L **101**
B62: B'hth 8C **98**
New John St. W. B19: Hock 3J **101**
New King St. DY2: Dud 8J **75**
Newland Cl. B98: Redd 2H **221**
WS4: S'fld 7C **26**
Newland Ct. B23: Erd 6B **80**
Newland Gdns. B64: Crad H . . .2L **117**
Newland Gro. DY2: Dud 2F **96**
Newland La. CV7: Ash G 2B **130**
Newland Rd. B9: Small H 8F **102**
CV1: Cov 4D **152** (1E **6**)
CV32: Lill 6C **218**
Newlands, The B34: S End 2C **104**
B80: Stud 6K **221**
Newlands Cl. DY11: Kidd 2J **157**
WV13: W'hall 8A **38**
Newlands Ct. WS12: Hth H 1L **15**
Newlands Dr. B62: B'hth 2E **118**
Newlands Grn. B66: Smeth 5A **100**
Newlands La. B37: Mars G 3G **125**
WS12: Hth H 1H **15**
(not continuous)
Newlands Rd. B30: Stir 2H **143**
B93: Ben H 5F **168**
CV9: Bad E 1C **64**
LE9: Barw 2B **70**
Newland St. CV22: Rugby 6L **179**
Newlands Wlk. *B68: O'bry 5H 99*
(off Jackson St.)
New Landywood La.
WV11: Ess 3E **24**
New Leasow B76: Walm 2A **82**
Newlyn Cl. CV11: Nun 5M **89**
WS14: Lich 2K **19**
Newlyn Rd. B31: N'fld 6M **141**
B64: Crad H 1K **117**
Newman Av. WV4: E'shll 5F **52**
Newman Cl. CV12: Bed 5H **111**
Newman Coll. Cl.
B32: Bart G 1J **141**
Newman Ct. B21: Hand 8E **78**
Newman Pl. WV14: Bils 2M **53**
Newman Rd. B24: Erd 5F **80**
DY4: Tip 8C **54**
WV10: Bush 8G **23**
Newmans Cl. B66: Smeth 5C **100**
Newman Way B45: Redn 2G **163**
Newmarket Cl. CV6: Ald G 5H **131**
WV6: Wolv 4A **36**
Newmarket Rd. WS11: Nort C . . .5A **16**
New Mkt. St.
B3: Birm 6K **101** (4E **4**)
Newmarket Way
B36: Hodg H 1H **103**
Newmarsh Rd. B76: Walm 3A **82**
New Mdw. Cl. B31: N'fld 7B **142**
New Mdw. Rd. B98: Redd 6H **213**
New Meeting St.
B4: Birm 7L **101** (5H **5**)
B69: O'bry 1G **99**
New Mill La. B78: Faz 2A **46**
New Mills St. WS1: Wals 2K **55**
New Mill St. DY2: Dud 8J **75**
Newmore Gdns. WS5: Wals 4C **56**
New Moseley Rd. B12: Birm . . .1A **122**
Newnham Gro. B23: Erd 3E **80**
Newnham Ho. B36: Cas B 4H **105**
Newnham La.
CV23: Brin, K New 7M **155**
Newnham Ri. B90: Shir 6K **145**
Newnham Rd. B16: Edg 7C **100**
CV1: Cov 4F **152**
CV32: Lill 6B **218**
NEW OSCOTT 8C **58**
New Penkridge Rd.
WS11: Cann, Hton 5A **8**
New Pool Rd. B64: Crad H 1H **117**
Newport B77: Amin 4F **32**
Newport Cl. B97: Redd 3B **220**
Newport Rd. B12: Bal H 5A **122**
B36: Hodg H 1M **103**
CV6: Cov 8D **130**
Newport St. WS1: Wals 8L **39**
WV10: Wolv 5E **36**
Newquay Cl. CV11: Nun 4M **89**
LE10: Hinc 5L **69**
WS5: Wals 2E **56**
Newquay Rd. WS5: Wals 2D **56**
New Railway St.
WV13: W'hall 7B **38**
New River Wlk. CV31: Lea S . . .1K **223**
New Rd. B18: Win G 3E **100**
B45: Rubery 2F **162**
B46: Wat O 6H **83**
B47: H'wd 1M **165**
B60: B'gve 7M **187**
B61: B'gve 6L **187**
B61: F'fld 7L **161**
B63: Hale 5B **118**
B77: Wiln 2F **46**
B79: Shut 1L **33**
B80: Stud 5L **221**
B91: Sol 6C **146**
B96: A'wd B 8E **220**
CV6: Cov 8M **129**
CV7: Ash G 3C **130**
CV9: Ath 2K **65**
CV12: Bed 5M **109**
(not continuous)
DY2: Dud, Neth 3J **97**

New Rd.—Norwich Cft.

New Rd. DY3: Swind 6A **72**
DY4: Tip 3D **76**
DY8: Stourb 4A **116**
DY10: Kidd 5L **157**
DY10: W'ley 6C **136**
DY11: Cau 2B **136**
DY12: Bew 4D **156**
LE9: S Stan 7K **71**
LE10: Burb 3A **92**
WS7: Burn 3H **17**
WS8: Bwnhls 2F **26**
WS9: A'rdge 4G **41**
WS10: Darl 3D **54**
WS14: Shens 3F **28**
WV6: Wolv 5L **35**
WV10: Bush 1H **37**
WV10: C Grn, S Hth 1D **22**
WV13: W'hall 8A **38**
New Row B78: Dray B 4L **45**
New Rowley Rd. DY2: Dud 2L **97**
New Royal Briery Experience, The
..................6K 75
New Shipton Cl. B76: Walm ...8M **59**
Newsholme Cl. CV34: Warw ...8F **216**
(not continuous)
New Spring St.
B18: Hock 5G **101** (1A **4**)
New Spring St. Nth.
B18: Hock 4G **101**
New Sreet Station (Rail)
..............7K 101 (6F 4)
Newstead B79: Tam 3K **31**
Newstead Av. LE10: Burb 5K **91**
Newstead Cl. CV11: Nun 7M **89**
Newstead Dr. CV47: Sou 6G **225**
Newstead Rd. B44: K'sdng 6A **58**
Newstead Way CV3: Bin 8B **154**
New St. B2: Birm 7K **101** (5F **4**)
B23: Erd 4F **80**
B36: Cas B 1B **104**
B45: Fran 7F **140**
B66: Smeth 3A **100**
B70: W Brom 2G **77**
(Norbury Rd.)
B70: W Brom 6K **77**
(St Michael St.)
B77: Amin 5E **32**
B77: Two G 8C **32**
B78: B'moor 2L **47**
B78: Dord 4A **48**
B78: Faz 1B **46**
B79: Tam 5A **32**
CV8: Ken 3F **198**
CV9: Bad E 8C **48**
CV12: Bed 7J **111**
CV12: Bulk 7C **112**
CV22: Rugby 6L **179**
CV31: Lea S 2A **224**
CV32: Cubb 4E **218**
CV34: Warw 3E **222**
DY1: Dud 8J **75**
DY3: Gorn 6C **74**
DY4: Tip 4M **75**
DY5: Quar B 1G **117**
DY6: K'wfrd 5K **95**
DY6: W Hth 1J **95**
DY8: Stourb 4M **115**
DY8: Word 7K **95**
DY13: Stour S 6F **182**
LE9: Earl S 2E **70**
LE9: S Stan 6K **71**
LE10: Hinc 8K **69**
WS1: Wals 8M **39**
WS3: Blox 8H **25**
WS4: Rus 2B **40**
WS4: S'fld 8D **26**
WS6: Gt Wyr 7G **15**
WS7: C Ter 2E **16**
WS7: Chase 4E **16**
WS10: Darl 3D **54**
WS10: W'bry 8F **54**
WS11: Cann 1E **14**
(Mill St.)
WS11: Cann 3D **14**
(Watling St.)
WS12: Hed 5J **9**
WV2: E'shll 3G **53**
WV3: Wolv 2K **51**
WV4: E'shll 4E **52**
WV11: Ess 6A **24**
WV13: W'hall 8L **37**
New St. Nth. B71: W Brom 6K **77**
New Summer St.
B19: Birm 5K **101** (1F **4**)
New Swan La. B70: W Brom 4G **77**
(not continuous)
New Swinford Hall DY9: Lye ...5C **116**
NEWTON
B43 ....1C 78
CV23 ....1G 181
DY9 ....1J 161
Newton Av. B74: S Cold 2H **59**
Newton Bldgs. CV12: Bed 7H **111**
Newton Chambers *B2: Birm 5F 4*
(off Cannon St.)
Newton Cl. B43: Gt Barr 8C **56**
B98: Redd 3G **221**
CV2: W'grve S 2M **153**
CV10: Harts 7B **66**
DY12: Bew 1B **156**
Newton Ct. WV9: Pend 6M **21**
Newton Gdns. B43: Gt Barr 1C **78**
Newton Gro. B29: S Oak 7F **120**
Newton Ho. WV13: W'hall 8B **38**
Newton Ind. Est. B9: Bord G ...7D **102**
Newton La. CV23: Newt 1F **180**
Newton Mnr. Cl. B43: Gt Barr ...1D **78**
Newton Mnr. La.
CV23: Brow, Newt 1C **180**
Newton Pl. B18: Hock 2F **100**
WS2: Wals 3H **39**
Newton Rd. B11: S'hll 4B **122**
B43: Gt Barr 2A **78**
B60: B'gve 2A **210**
B71: W Brom 3L **77**
B93: Know 2H **169**
CV23: Clift D, Newt 1G **181**
LE10: Hinc 2E **90**
WS2: Wals 4H **39**
WS13: Lich 7F **12**
Newtons Coll. WS13: Lich 1G **19**
Newton Sq. B43: Gt Barr 8E **56**
Newton St. B4: Birm 6L **101** (3H **5**)
B71: W Brom 2L **77**
NEW TOWN
Brownhills 8H 17
West bromwich 5E 76
NEWTOWN
Great Wyrley 4G 25
Hockley 3K 101
Netherton 7J 97
New Town DY5: Brie H 5C **96**
(not continuous)
Newtown DY2: Neth 8J **97**
Newtown Dr. B19: Hock 3J **101**
Newtown La. B46: Shu 2M **107**
B62: Roms 8C **140**
B64: Crad H 8K **97**
CV7: Fill 2M **107**
DY9: Belb 1K **161**
Newtown Middleway
B6: Birm 4L **101**
Newtown Rd. CV11: Nun 4J **89**
CV12: Bed 7F **110**
(not continuous)
NEW TOWN ROW 3L 101
New Town Row
B6: Aston 3L **101** (1G **5**)
Newtown Shop. Cen.
B19: Hock 3L **101**
Newtown St. B64: Crad H 7K **97**
New Union St.
CV1: Cov 7C **152** (6C **6**)
New Village DY2: Neth 8J **97**
New Villas WV11: Wed 4G **37**
New Wlk. B97: Redd 5E **212**
LE9: Sap 2K **93**
New Wharf B60: Tard 2H **211**
New Wharf Cotts. B60: Tard ...2G **211**
New Wood Cl. DY7: Stourt 1J **115**
New Wood Dr. B31: Longb 8K **141**
New Wood Gro.
WS9: Wals W 6G **27**
New Wood La. DY10: Blak 1G **159**
Next Generation Health Club ..5D 96
Ney Ct. DY4: Tip 7M **75**
Niall Cl. B15: Edg 1E **120**
Nibletts Hill B61: D'frd 2H **187**
Nicholas Rd. B74: S'tly 1L **57**
Nicholds Cl. WV14: Cose 8H **53**
Nicholls Fold WV11: Wed 4K **37**
Nicholls Rd. DY4: Tip 8L **53**
Nicholls St. B70: W Brom 7L **77**
CV2: Cov 6F **152**
Nicholls Way WS12: Hth H 8M **9**
Nichols Cl. B92: Sol 2F **146**
Nicholson Cl. CV34: Warw 8F **216**
Nickson Rd. CV4: Tile H 1E **172**
Nicolas Everton Cl.
CV8: Bran 4G **177**
Nigel Av. B31: N'fld 4A **142**
Nigel Ct. B16: Edg 8E **100**
Nigel Rd. B8: Salt 3E **102**
DY1: Dud 7G **75**
Nightingale B77: Wiln 3G **47**
Nightingale Av. B36: Cas B 1G **105**
Nightingale Cl. B23: Erd 2C **80**
CV9: Ath 8L **49**
WS12: Hunt 2C **8**
Nightingale Ct. B91: Sol 5C **146**
CV31: Lea S 1B **224**
WS7: Burn 1M **17**
Nightingale Cres.
DY5: Brie H 2D **116**
WV12: W'hall 1B **38**
Nightingale Dr. DY4: Tip 4C **76**
DY10: Kidd 7B **158**
Nightingale La. CV5: Cov 1K **173**
(not continuous)
Nightingale Pl. WV14: Bils 3K **53**
Nightingale Wlk. B15: Edg 2J **121**
WS7: Burn 2L **17**
Nightingdale Gdns.
CV23: Brow 1C **180**
Nightjar Gro. B23: Erd 3C **80**
Nighwood Dr. B74: S'tly 2M **57**
Nijon Cl. B21: Hand 8C **78**
Nimbus B77: Dost 5D **46**
Nimmings Cl. B31: Longb 3M **163**
Nimmings Rd. B62: B'hth 1D **118**
Nimmings Vis. Cen. 3H 139
Nina Cl. DY13: Stour S 6H **183**
Nineacres Dr. B37: F'bri 7G **105**
Nine Days La. B98: Redd 3H **221**
Nine Elms La. WV10: Wolv 4E **36**
Ninefoot La. B77: Wiln 1E **46**
(not continuous)
Nine Leasowes B66: Smeth 2L **99**
Nine Locks Ridge
DY5: Brie H 7D **96**
Nine Pails Wlk. B70: W Brom ...8K **77**
Ninestiles Community Leisure Cen.
..................8H 123
Nineveh Av. B21: Hand 2F **100**
Nineveh Rd. B21: Hand 2E **100**
Ninfield Rd. B27: A Grn 6G **123**
Ninian Pk. B77: Wiln 3D **46**
Ninian Way B77: Wiln 4E **46**
Nirvana Cl. WS11: Cann 7C **8**
Nith Pl. DY1: Dud 7H **75**
Niton Rd. CV10: Nun 3K **89**
Niven Cl. CV5: Alle 3G **151**
Noakes Ct. WS10: Darl 2F **54**
Nobel Dr. CV22: Caw 1G **205**
Noble Cl. CV34: Warw 4D **222**
Nocke Rd. WV11: Wed 8M **23**
Nock St. DY4: Tip 2C **76**
Nock Verges LE9: S Stan 7K **71**
Noddy Pk. WS9: A'rdge 2H **41**
Noddy Pk. Rd. WS9: A'rdge 2H **41**
Node Hill B80: Stud 6K **221**
Node Hill Cl. B80: Stud 6K **221**
Nod Ri. CV5: E Grn 5G **151**
Noel Av. B12: Bal H 3A **122**
Noel Ct. B97: Redd 1C **220**
Noel Rd. B16: Edg 8F **100**
Nolan Cl. CV6: Longf 5D **130**
Nolton Cl. B43: Gt Barr 1D **78**
No Name Rd. WS7: C Ter 2E **16**
Nook, The CV11: Nun 7L **89**
DY5: P'ntt 4B **96**
WS6: C Hay 8C **14**
Nooklands Cft. B33: Yard 7A **104**
Noonam Cl. B97: Redd 7B **212**
Noose Cres. WV13: W'hall 7L **37**
Noose La. WV13: W'hall 7L **37**
Nora Rd. B11: S'hll 6C **122**
Norbiton Rd. B44: K'sdng 1A **80**
Norbreck Cl. B43: Gt Barr 8D **56**
Norbury Av. WS3: Pels 6M **25**
Norbury Cl. B98: Redd 2H **213**
Norbury Cres. WV4: E'shll 5F **52**
Norbury Dr. DY5: Brie H 8D **96**
Norbury Gro. B92: Olton 6A **124**
Norbury Rd. B44: Gt Barr 6M **57**
B70: W Brom 2G **77**
WV10: Wolv 3F **36**
WV14: Bils 3M **53**
Norcombe Gro. B90: M'path ...4A **168**
Nordic Drift CV2: W'grve S 3A **154**
Nordley Rd. WV11: Wed 4J **37**
Nordley Wlk. WV11: Wed 3J **37**
Norfolk Av. B71: W Brom 2K **77**
Norfolk Cl. B30: Stir 3H **143**
LE10: Burb 5K **91**
Norfolk Ct. B16: Edg 8D **100**
B29: W Cas 2B **142**
Norfolk Cres. CV10: Nun 6E **88**
WS9: A'rdge 1H **41**
Norfolk Dr. B78: Tam 8A **32**
WS10: W'bry 5K **55**
Norfolk Gdns. B75: S Cold 1H **59**
Norfolk Gro. WS6: Gt Wyr 8F **14**
Norfolk Ho. B23: Erd 4F **80**
B30: K Nor 6G **143**
Norfolk New Rd. WS2: Wals 5G **39**
Norfolk Pl. WS2: Wals 4K **39**
Norfolk Rd. B15: Edg 2D **120**
B23: Erd 4F **80**
B45: Fran 7F **140**
B68: O'bry 2H **119**
B75: S Cold 2H **59**
DY2: Dud 2G **97**
DY8: Woll 1K **115**
WV3: Wolv 1A **52**
Norfolk St. CV1: Cov 6B **152** (4A **6**)
CV32: Lea S 8A **218**
Norfolk Twr. B18: Hock 4H **101**
Norgrave Rd. B92: Sol 7C **124**
Norlan Dr. B14: K Hth 6M **143**
Norland Rd. B27: A Grn 8J **123**
Norley Gro. B13: Mose 2C **144**
Norley Trad. Est. B33: Sheld ...8C **104**
Norman Ashman Coppice
CV3: Bin W 2C **176**
Norman Av. B32: Harb 2L **119**
CV2: W'grve S 8M **131**
CV11: Nun 5H **89**
Normanby Mdws.
CV31: W'nsh 7A **224**
Norman Cl. B79: Tam 2L **31**
Norman Dagley Cl.
LE9: Earl S 2E **70**
Normandy Cl. CV35: H Mag ...2A **222**
Normandy Rd. B20: Hand 8K **79**
Normandy Way LE9: Barw 5L **69**
LE10: Hinc 8F **68**
Norman Green Athletics Cen. ..6A 146
Norman Pl. Rd. CV6: Cov 2L **151**
Norman Rd. B31: N'fld 6B **142**
B67: Smeth 8K **99**
CV21: N'bld A 3M **179**
WS5: Wals 1C **56**
Normansell Twr. B6: Aston 1B **102**
Norman St. B18: Win G 4E **100**
DY2: Dud 1K **97**
Norman Ter. B65: Row R 5C **98**
Normanton Av. B26: Sheld 4D **124**
Normanton Twr. B23: Erd 3G **81**
Normid Ct. *B31: N'fld 5C 142*
(off Bunbury Rd.)
Norrington Gro. B31: N'fld 6J **141**
Norrington Rd. B31: N'fld 6J **141**
Norris Dr. B33: Stech 6M **103**
Norris Rd. B6: Aston 8M **79**
Norris Way B75: S Cold 4K **59**
Northampton La.
CV22: Dunc 5H **205**
CV23: Dunc 5D **204**
Northampton St.
B18: Birm 5J **101** (1C **4**)
Northam Wlk. WV6: Wolv 5B **36**
Northanger Rd. B27: A Grn 7H **123**
North Av. B40: Nat E C 4L **125**
CV2: Cov 6G **153**
CV12: Bed 7K **111**
WV11: Wed 3J **37**
Northbourne Dr. CV11: Nun 2L **111**
Northbrook Ct. B90: Shir 4J **145**
Northbrook Rd. B90: Shir 4J **145**
CV6: Cov 1K **151**
Northbrook St. B16: Birm 5F **100**
Northcliffe Hgts. DY11: Kidd ...2J **157**
North Cl. CV32: Cubb 4E **218**
LE10: Burb 3L **91**
Northcote Rd. B33: Stech 5K **103**
CV22: Rugby 7M **179**
Northcote St. CV31: Lea S 2B **224**
WS2: Wals 5K **39**
Northcote Wlk. CV9: Ath 7K **49**
Northcott Rd. DY2: Neth 5K **97**
WV14: Bils 5L **53**
North Cres. WV10: F'stne 2H **23**
North Dale WV6: Tett 5H **35**
Northdown Rd. B91: Sol 8M **145**
North Dr. B5: Edg 4J **121**
B20: Hand 1H **101**
B75: S Cold 3J **59**
Northey Rd. CV6: Cov 1D **152**
NORTHFIELD 6A 142
Northfield Cl. B98: Redd 3K **213**
Northfield Gro. WV3: Wolv 2J **51**
Northfield Pool & Fitness Cen.
..................6A 142
Northfield Rd. B17: Harb 6A **120**
B30: K Nor 5D **142**
CV1: Cov 7E **152**
CV47: Sou 6G **225**
DY2: Neth 4K **97**
LE10: Hinc 2H **91**
Northfield Station (Rail) 7A 142
Northfields Way WS8: Clay 3D **26**
Northfolk Ter. CV4: Canly 2J **173**
North Ga. B17: Harb 2C **120**
Northgate B64: Crad H 1K **117**
CV34: Warw 2E **222**
WS9: A'rdge 7G **27**
Northgate Cl. DY11: Kidd 5G **157**
Northgate St. CV34: Warw 2E **222**
Northgate Way WS9: A'rdge 1G **41**
North Grn. WV4: Penn 3K **51**
North Holme B9: Bord G 7C **102**
Northicote Recreation & Community
Cen. 6E 22
Northland Rd. B90: Shir 8L **145**
Northlands Rd. B13: Mose 8A **122**
Northleach Av. B14: K Hth 7K **143**
Northleach Cl. B98: Redd 4H **213**
Northleigh Rd. B8: W End 3G **103**
Northleigh Way LE9: Earl S 2F **70**
Northmead B33: Yard 7A **104**
Nth. Moons Moat Ind. Area
B98: Redd 4L **213**
Northolt Dr. B35: Cas V 6A **82**
Northolt Gro. B42: Gt Barr 8F **56**
North One M. DY3: Sed 8C **52**
North Oval DY3: Up Gor 4E **74**
Northover Cl. WV9: Pend 7A **22**
North Pk. Rd. B23: Erd 5B **80**
North Pathway B17: Harb 2B **120**
North Rd. B17: Harb 3D **120**
B20: Hand 7L **79**
B29: S Oak 6F **120**
B60: B'gve 7A **188**
CV23: Clift D 4F **180**
DY4: Tip 1B **76**
DY13: Stour S 4G **183**
WV1: Wolv 5C **36** (1J **7**)
North Roundhay B33: Kitts G ...5A **104**
Northside Bus. Cen.
B18: Win G 4E **100**
Northside Cl. B98: Redd 2E **220**
Northside Dr. B74: S'tly 1M **57**
North Solihull Sports Cen. 6G 105
Nth. Springfield DY3: Sed 8E **52**
North St. B67: Smeth 4M **99**
CV2: Cov 4G **153**
CV9: Ath 1K **65**
CV10: Nun 6F **88**
CV21: Rugby 6A **180**
CV23: Kils 6M **207**
DY2: Dud 8K **75**
DY5: Brie H 7C **96**
WS2: Wals 5L **39**
North St. WS7: C Ter 8F **10**
WS10: W'bry 5F **54**
WS11: Cann 3E **14**
WV1: Wolv 7C **36** (3J **7**)
(not continuous)
North St. Ind. Est.
DY5: Brie H 7C **96**
Northumberland Av.
CV10: Nun 5E **88**
DY11: Kidd 6J **157**
Northumberland Cl. B78: Tam ...8A **32**
Northumberland Lodge
CV32: Lea S 6M 217
(off Kenilworth Rd.)
Northumberland M.
CV32: B'dwn 6L **217**
Northumberland Rd.
CV1: Cov 6A **152**
CV32: Lea S 6L **217**
Northumberland St.
B7: Birm 6A **102** (3M **5**)
Northvale Cl. CV8: Ken 3H **199**
North Vw. CV2: W'grve S 8A **132**
North Vw. Dr. DY5: Brie H 4D **96**
Nth. Villiers St. CV32: Lea S ...8A **218**
North Wlk. B31: N'fld 8C **142**
Nth. Warwick St.
B9: Small H 8D **102**
Northway B40: Nat E C 3M **125**
CV21: Rugby 6A 180
(in Clock Towers Shop. Cen.)
CV31: Lea S 3A **224**
DY3: Sed 6C **52**
(Alderdale Av.)
DY3: Sed 8B **52**
(Sunningdale Rd.)
Nth. Western Arc.
B2: Birm 6L **101** (4G **5**)
Nth. Western Rd.
B66: Smeth 3M **99**
Nth. Western Ter. B18: Hock ...2F **100**
Northwick Cres. B91: Sol 8B **146**
Nth. Wodloes CV35: Leek W ...5G **217**
Northwood Ct. DY5: Brie H 7D **96**
Northwood La. DY12: Bew 4A **156**
Northwood Pk. Cl.
WV10: Bush 6D **22**
Northwood Pk. Rd.
WV10: Bush 6E **22**
Northwood St.
B3: Birm 5J **101** (3D **4**)
Northwood Way DY5: Brie H ...1B **116**
North Yd. B9: Birm 7K **5**
Northycote Farm Country Pk. ...6G 23
Northycote La. WV10: Bush 5F **22**
Nortoft La. CV23: Kils 4L **207**
NORTON 7L 115
NORTON CANES 4A 16
Norton Cl. B31: N'fld 6A **142**
B66: Smeth 4C **100**
B79: Tam 2C **32**
B98: Redd 7M **213**
WV4: Penn 6J **51**
Norton Cres. B9: Bord G 6H **103**
DY2: Neth 6L **97**
WV14: Cose 8K **53**
Norton Dr. B47: Wyt 5C **166**
CV34: Warw 7E **216**
NORTON EAST 2C 16
Norton E. Rd. WS11: Nort C 4A **16**
Norton Ga. B38: K Nor 8E **142**
Norton Grange CV5: Alle 3J **151**
WS11: Nort C 5M **15**
Norton Grange Cres.
WS11: Nort C 5M **15**
NORTON GREEN
Knowle 7H 169
Norton Canes 6M 15
Norton Grn. La. B93: Know 7H **169**
WS11: Nort C 5L **15**
Norton Hall La. WS11: Nort C ...5K **15**
Norton Hill Dr. CV2: Cov 3L **153**
Norton Lakeside Station 3C 16
Norton La. B47: Tid G, Wyt 5C **166**
B94: Earls 5C **166**
WS6: Gt Wyr 5G **15**
WS7: Burn 4J **17**
WS11: Cann, Nort C 2J **15**
Norton Leys CV22: Rugby 2M **205**
Norton Rd. B46: Col 8M **83**
DY8: Stourb 8K **115**
DY10: Kidd 3B **158**
LE9: Earl S 2C **70**
WS3: Pels 3A **26**
WS12: Hth H 1M **15**
Norton Springs WS11: Nort C ...4M **15**
Norton St. B18: Hock 4G **101**
CV1: Cov 3D **6**
Norton Ter. *B30: Stir 3H 143*
(off Warren Rd.)
WS11: Nort C 3M **15**
Norton Twr. B1: Birm 5C **4**
Norton Vw. B14: K Hth 2K **143**
Norton Wlk. B23: Erd 6C **80**
Norton Wildlife Reserve 3B 16
Nortune Cl. B38: K Nor 7D **142**
Norwich Av. DY11: Kidd 3F **156**
Norwich Cl. CV11: Nun 1A **90**
WS13: Lich 6J **13**
Norwich Cft.
B37: Mars G 8F **104**

Norwich Dr.—Old Chapel Wlk.

Norwich Dr. B17: Harb 1M 119
CV3: Cov 4B 174
Norwich Rd. DY2: Neth 7K 97
WS2: Wals 8H 39
Norwood Av. B64: Crad H 2L 117
Norwood Cl. LE10: Hinc 6L 69
Norwood Gro. B19: Hock 2H 101
CV2: W'grve S 7L 131
Norwood Rd. B9: Bord G 7E 102
DY5: Brie H 5C 96
Notley Mnr. Dr. LE9: Barw 1C 70
Nottingham Dr. WV12: W'hall 2C 38
Nottingham New Rd.
WS2: Wals 4G 39
Nottingham Way DY5: Quar B 7F 96
Nova Ct. B43: Gt Barr 8H 57
Nova Cft. CV5: E Grn 5C 150
Nova Scotia St.
B4: Birm 6M 101 (4J 5)
Nowell St. WS10: Darl 4E 54
Nuffield Ho. B36: Cas B 1G 105
Nuffield Rd. CV6: Cov 1G 153
LE10: Hinc 2E 90
Nugent Cl. B6: Aston 2L 101
Nugent Gro. B90: Ches G 6K 167
Number 9 The Gallery 6B 4
NUNEATON 5J 89
Nuneaton Arts Cen. 5H 89
Nuneaton Borough F.C. 5F 88
Nuneaton La. CV13: High H 7M 67
Nuneaton Mus. & Art Gallery 5J 89
Nuneaton R.F.C. 5M 89
Nuneaton Rd. B46: Over W 6L 85
CV7: Fill 6E 108
CV9: Man 3A 66
CV10: Ansl 3E 86
CV10: Harts 7B 66
(Grange Rd.)
CV10: Harts 6C 66
(Woodford La.)
CV12: Bed 4H 111
CV12: Bulk 3B 112
Nuneaton Station CV10: Nun 4J 89
Nunts La. CV6: Cov 6B 130
Nunts Pk. Av. CV6: Cov 5B 130
Nunwood La. CV23: Prin 5M 201
Nursery Av. B12: Bal H 4M 121
WS9: A'rdge 4H 41
Nursery Cl. B30: K Nor 4F 142
DY9: Hag 5A 138
DY11: Kidd 1H 157
Nursery Cft. WS13: Lich 8F 12
Nursery Dr. B30: K Nor 4F 142
WV5: Wom 5F 72
Nursery Gdns. B90: Maj G 1E 166
DY8: Word 8M 95
LE9: Earl S 2D 70
WV8: Cod 5F 20
Nursery Gro. DY11: Kidd 1H 157
Nursery La. B74: Four O 7G 43
B78: Hop 3H 31
CV31: Lea S 4A 224
(not continuous)
Nursery Rd. B15: Edg 3D 120
B19: Loz 3H 101
CV9: Ath 2M 65
CV10: Ans C 1L 87
DY12: Bew 5B 156
WS3: Blox 1H 39
Nursery St. WV1: Wolv 6C 36 (2J 7)
Nursery Vw. Cl. WS9: A'rdge 7L 41
Nursery Wlk. WV6: Tett 5K 35
NURTON 6A 34
Nurton Bank WV6: Nur 6A 34
Nutbrook Av. CV4: Tile H 7E 150
Nutbush Dr. B31: N'fld 3K 141
Nutfield Wlk. B32: Harb 4M 119
Nutgrove Cl. B14: K Hth 2M 143
Nuthatch Dr. DY5: Brie H 2C 116
NUTHURST 5C 194
Nuthurst B75: S Cold 5B 60
Nuthurst Cres. CV10: Ansl 6J 87
Nuthurst Dr. WS11: Cann 5F 14
Nuthurst Grange La.
B94: H'ley H 5C 194
Nuthurst Gro. B14: K Hth 7M 143
B93: Ben H 5G 169
Nuthurst La. CV10: Asty 7J 87
Nuthurst Rd. B31: Longb 3M 163
B94: H'ley H 7A 194
Nutley Dr. DY4: Tip 1D 76
Nutmeg Gro. WS1: Wals 7A 40
Nuttall Gro. B21: Hand 2C 100
Nutt's La. LE10: Hinc 3F 90
Nymet B77: Wiln 1E 46

O

Oakalls Av. B60: B'gve 7B 188
Oak Apple Cl. DY13: Stour S 8B 182
Oak Apple Ct. B61: Cats 1B 188
Oak Apple Rd. B61: Cats 1B 188
Oak Av. B12: Bal H 4A 122
B70: W Brom 6H 77
CV7: Old A 7E 86
WS2: Wals 6E 38
WS6: Gt Wyr 8G 15
WS12: Hunt 1D 8
Oak Bank B18: Hock 3G 101
Oak Barn Rd. B62: B'hth 1E 118
Oak Cl. B17: Harb 3A 120
CV8: Bag 7F 174
CV12: Bed 5J 111
DY4: Tip 8A 54
DY7: Kinv 6C 114
LE10: Burb 4L 91
Oak Ct. B45: Redn 2J 163
B63: Hale 7M 117
B66: Smeth 1J 99
CV34: H'cte 7L 223
DY8: Stourb 5A 116
WS5: Wals 5A 56
Oak Cres. B69: Tiv 8B 76
WS3: Blox 3K 39
Oak Cft. B37: F'bri 6F 104
Oakcroft Rd. B13: Mose 2B 144
Oakdale Cl. B68: O'bry 7G 99
DY5: P'ntt 2B 96
Oakdale Rd. B36: Hodg H 1L 103
B68: O'bry 7G 99
CV3: Bin W 2C 176
LE9: Earl S 2D 70
Oakdale Trad. Est.
DY6: K'wfrd 8K 73
Oakdene DY13: Stour S 6H 183
Oakdene Cl. WS6: C Hay 7D 14
Oakdene Cres. CV10: Nun 2J 89
Oakdene Dr. B45: B Grn 1J 189
Oakdene Rd. WS7: Chase 3G 17
Oakden Pl. DY11: Kidd 2J 157
Oak Dr. B23: Erd 2C 80
CV10: Harts 1A 88
WV5: Seis 7A 50
OAKEN 7D 20
Oaken Covert WV8: Cod 7E 20
Oaken Dr. B91: Sol 4M 145
WV8: Cod, Oaken 7D 20
WV12: W'hall 2E 38
Oakenfield WS13: Lich 7G 13
Oaken Gdns. WS7: C Ter 1G 17
Oaken Grange WS6: Gt Wyr 8F 14
Oaken Gro. WV8: Cod 7E 20
Oakenhayes Cres. B76: Min 4C 82
WS8: Bwnhls 8F 16
Oakenhayes Dr. WS8: Bwnhls 8F 16
Oaken La. WV8: Oaken 6C 20
Oaken Lanes WV8: Cod 6E 20
Oaken Pk. WV8: Cod 7G 21
OAKENSHAW 3E 220
Oakenshaw Rd. B90: Shir 8K 145
B98: Redd 1F 220
Oakeswell St. WS10: W'bry 6G 55
Oakey Cl. CV6: Longf 5F 130
Oakeywell St. DY2: Dud 8K 75
OAKFARM 8L 73
Oak Farm Cl. B76: Walm 2A 82
Oak Farm Rd. B30: B'vlle 4D 142
Oakfield Av. B11: S'brk 3C 122
B12: Bal H 3A 122
B21: Hand 2D 100
DY1: Dud 2H 75
DY6: K'wfrd 4L 95
Oakfield Cl. B66: Smeth 3C 100
DY8: Word 8M 95
Oakfield Ct. *DY5: Brie H 7D 96*
(off Promenade, The)
Oakfield Dr. B45: Coft H 5K 163
WS3: Pels 4B 26
Oakfield Gdns. CV9: Ath 2L 65
Oakfield Ho. CV32: Lea S 7M 217
Oakfield Pk. *CV22: Rugby 7M 179*
(off Bilton Rd.)
Oakfield Rd. B12: Bal H 4L 121
B24: Erd 6F 80
B29: S Oak 6G 121
B66: Smeth 3C 100
CV22: Rugby 7M 179
DY8: Word 8A 96
DY9: W'cte 7F 116
DY11: Kidd 4H 157
WV8: Bilb 7H 21
Oakfields Way B91: Cath B 4H 147
Oakford Dr. CV5: Alle 3F 150
Oak Grn. DY1: Dud 4G 75
WV6: Tett 6H 35
Oak Grn. Way B68: O'bry 5G 99
Oak Gro. B31: Longb 8L 141
DY10: Kidd 4A 158
WV11: Wed 2H 37
Oakhall Dr. B93: Dorr 5F 168
OAKHAM 2B 98
Oakham Av. DY2: Dud 2L 97
Oakham Cl. B98: Redd 4G 221
Oakham Ct. DY2: Dud 1L 97
Oakham Cres. CV12: Bulk 7D 112
DY2: Dud 2L 97
Oakham Dr. DY2: Dud 1M 97
Oakhampton Rd.
DY13: Stour S 7B 182
Oakham Rd. B17: Harb 2B 120
B69: Tiv 1L 97
DY2: Dud 1L 97
Oakham Way B92: Olton 8A 124
Oak Hill WV3: Wolv 1J 51
Oakhill Av. DY10: Kidd 5L 157
Oakhill Cl. B17: Harb 1B 120
Oakhill Cres. B27: A Grn 1H 145
Oak Hill Dr. B15: Edg 2E 120
Oakhill Dr. DY5: Brie H 2B 116
Oakhill Rd. WS11: Cann 7F 8
Oak Ho. WS6: Gt Wyr 8G 15
Oak House Mus. 7H 77
Oakhurst WS14: Lich 2J 19
Oakhurst Dr. B60: B'gve 6A 188
Oakhurst Rd. B27: A Grn 8H 123
B72: W Grn 1H 81
Oak Ind. Pk. DY6: K'wfrd 8L 73
Oakington Ho. B35: Cas V 6A 82
Oakland Cl. B91: Sol 5E 146
Oakland Dr. DY3: Gorn 7B 74
Oakland Gro. B61: B'gve 5B 188
Oakland Rd. B13: Mose 6A 122
B21: Hand 1E 100
(not continuous)
WS3: Blox 2L 39
Oaklands B31: N'fld 5M 141
B62: Quin 5G 119
B76: Curd 3H 83
Oaklands, The B37: Mars G 2G 125
CV4: Tile H 7G 151
DY10: Kidd 2A 158
WV3: Wolv 1B 52
Oaklands Av. B17: Harb 4B 120
Oaklands Cl. WS12: Hunt 3C 8
Oaklands Ct. B79: Tam 4A 32
CV8: Ken 7G 199
Oaklands Cft. B76: Walm 2B 82
Oaklands Dr. B20: Hand 7F 78
B74: S'tly 8M 41
Oaklands Grn. WV14: Bils 1K 53
Oaklands Ind. Est. WS12: Hed 6H 9
Oaklands Rd. B74: Four O 1H 59
WV3: Wolv 1B 52 (8G 7)
Oaklands Sports & Social Cen.
1D 100
Oaklands Way B31: Longb 8H 141
WS3: Pels 6B 26
Oak La. B70: W Brom 6H 77
B92: Bars 8B 148
CV5: Alle 1C 150
DY6: K'wfrd 8L 73
WS7: C Ter 8F 10
Oak La. Pk. Homes
CV5: Alle 8D 128
Oaklea Dr. B64: Old H 7M 97
Oakleaf Cl. B32: Bart G 7K 119
Oak Leaf Dr. B13: Mose 6A 122
Oak Leasow B32: Quin 5H 119
Oakleigh B31: N'fld 7C 142
Oakleigh Dr. DY3: Sed 2C 74
WV8: Bilb 6G 21
Oakleigh Rd. DY8: Stourb 7A 116
Oakleighs DY8: Word 8J 95
Oakleigh Wlk. DY6: K'wfrd 1L 95
Oakley CV8: Fen E 8F 170
Oakley Av. DY4: Tip 3A 76
WS9: A'rdge 4G 41
Oakley Cl. WS13: Lich 7H 13
WV4: Penn 4K 51
Oakley Ct. B15: Edg 4E 120
CV12: Bed 8D 110
(off Newcomen Rd.)
Oakley Gro. WV4: Penn 4K 51
Oakley Ho. B60: B'gve 7A 188
Oakley Rd. B10: Small H 2C 122
(not continuous)
B30: Stir 4H 143
WV4: Penn 4K 51
Oak Leys WV3: Wolv 8J 35
Oakley Wood Dr. B91: Sol 5E 146
Oakley Wood Rd.
CV33: Bis T 8E 224
(not continuous)
Oakly Rd. B97: Redd 6D 212
Oakmeadow Av. B24: Erd 6K 81
Oakmeadow Cl. B26: Yard 4K 123
B33: Kitts G 7D 104
Oakmeadow Way B24: Erd 6K 81
Oakmoor Rd. CV6: Longf 6G 131
Oakmount Cl. WS3: Pels 6M 25
Oak Mt. Rd. B74: S'tly 2A 58
Oak Pk. Ct. *B74: Four O 6E 42*
(off Walsall Rd.)
Oak Pk. Ind. Est.
WR9: Elm L 6E 184
Oak Pk. Leisure Cen. 5F 26
Oak Pk. Rd. DY8: Word 8M 95
Oakridge Cl. B98: Redd 2J 213
WV12: W'hall 5C 38
Oakridge Dr. WS6: C Hay 7F 14
WV12: W'hall 5C 38
Oakridge Rd. B31: N'fld 7D 142
CV32: Lill 5C 218
Oak Ri. B46: Col 4M 105
Oak Rd. B61: Cats 1B 188
B68: O'bry 2H 119
B70: W Brom 7H 77
DY1: Dud 6J 75
DY4: Tip 2L 75
WS3: Pels 4M 25
WS4: S'fld 8C 26
WS9: Wals W 6G 27
WV13: W'hall 7L 37
Oakroyd Cres. CV10: Nun 2D 88
Oaks, The B17: Harb 1B 120
B34: S End 2B 104
B38: K Nor 2F 164
B47: Wyt 1M 191
B67: Smeth 4M 99
B72: W Grn 2H 81
B76: Walm 6A 60
CV4: W'wd H 3G 173
Oaks, The CV12: Bed 7F 110
CV32: Lea S 1K 223
WS3: Blox 8G 25
WV3: Wolv 7A 36
Oaks Cres. WV3: Wolv 8A 36
Oaks Dr. WS11: Cann 8C 8
WV3: Wolv 7A 36
WV5: Wom 4G 73
WV10: B'frd 1F 22
Oaks Ind. Est. LE9: Earl S 1E 70
Oakslade Dr. B92: Sol 1E 146
Oak's Pl. CV6: Longf 6G 131
Oaks Pct. CV8: Ken 6E 198
Oaks Rd. CV8: Ken 7E 198
Oak St. B64: Crad H 8K 97
CV22: Rugby 7A 180
DY2: Neth 5L 97
DY5: Quar B 8F 96
DY6: K'wfrd 4J 95
WV3: Wolv 8A 36
WV14: Cose 2H 75
Oak Street Ind. Est.
B64: Crad H 8K 97
(off Oak St.)
Oak St. Trad. Est.
DY5: Quar B 8F 96
Oaks Way LE9: Earl S 1E 70
Oakthorpe Dr. B37: K'hrst 4F 104
Oakthorpe Gdns. B69: Tiv 7A 76
Oak Tree Av. B97: Redd 5B 212
CV3: Cov 3A 174
Oak Tree Cl. B48: A'chu 2A 190
B93: Ben H 5E 168
CV32: Lea S 7A 218
Oaktree Cl. B78: K'bry 3D 62
Oak Tree Ct. B28: Hall G 4G 145
B70: W Brom 6H 77
CV32: Lea S 7A 218
Oaktree Cres. B62: Quin 3F 118
Oak Tree Dr. B8: Salt 3D 102
Oak Tree Gdns. B28: Hall G 6E 144
DY8: Word 8A 96
Oak Tree La. B29: S Oak 8E 120
B47: H'wd 3B 166
B96: Sam 7H 221
Oak Tree Mobile Home Pk.
B94: Earls 2B 192
Oak Tree Pk. B98: Redd 3M 213
Oaktree Pk. WV10: F'stne 1F 22
Oaktree Ri. WV8: Cod 5E 20
Oak Tree Rd. CV3: Bin 2A 176
Oaktree Rd. WS10: W'bry 6H 55
Oak Trees B47: H'wd 3M 165
Oak Tree Wlk. B79: Tam 2L 31
Oak Vw. WS2: Wals 6E 38
Oak Wlk., The B31: Longb 8A 142
Oak Way B76: Walm 7M 59
CV4: Tile H 7D 150
Oakwood Cl. CV9: Gren 8C 48
WS9: Wals W 5E 26
WS14: Shens 3G 29
WV11: Ess 6B 24
Oakwood Cres. DY2: Dud 3F 96
Oakwood Cft. B91: Sol 8C 146
Oakwood Dr. B14: K Hth 5K 143
B74: S'tly 1L 57
Oakwood Gro. CV34: Warw 8G 217
Oakwood Rd. B11: S'hll 6C 122
B47: H'wd 3A 166
B67: Smeth 5M 99
B73: Bold 7E 58
DY12: Bew 2B 156
WS3: Blox 2L 39
Oakwoods WS11: Cann 1D 14
Oakwood St. B70: W Brom 4H 77
Oakworth Cl. CV2: W'grve S 1M 153
Oasis, The DY9: Hag 4M 137
Oast Ho. B8: W End 5J 103
Oasthouse Cl. B60: Stoke H 3K 209
DY6: W Hth 2G 95
Oaston Rd. B36: Cas B 1D 104
CV11: Nun 5K 89
Oatfield Cl. WS7: Chase 5G 17
Oatlands Cl. CV6: Cov 5C 130
Oatlands Wlk. B14: K Hth 7J 143
Oatlands Way WV6: Pert 6D 34
Oat Mill Cl. WS10: Darl 4E 54
Oban Dr. CV10: Nun 7G 89
Oban Rd. B92: Olton 8M 123
CV6: Longf 4F 130
LE10: Hinc 2G 91
Oberon Cl. B45: Fran 7G 141
CV11: Nun 8A 90
CV22: Bil 3K 205
CV34: H'cte 5L 223
Oberon Dr. B90: Shir 8G 145
Occupation Rd. CV2: Cov 6J 153
LE9: S Stan 4K 71
WS8: Wals W 5G 27
Occupation St. DY1: Dud 7G 75
Ocean Dr. WS10: W'bry 8D 54
Ockam Cft. B31: N'fld 7C 142
OCKER HILL 1C 76
Ocker Hill Rd. DY4: Tip 8B 54
O'Connor Dr. DY4: Tip 8C 54
Oddicombe Cft. CV3: Cov 4D 174
Oddingley Ct. B23: Erd 6C 80
Oddingley Rd. B31: N'fld 7C 142
Odell Cres. WS3: Blox 2J 39
Odell Pl. B5: Edg 4J 121
Odell Rd. WS3: Blox 2H 39
Odell Way WS3: Blox 2H 39
Odensil Grn. B92: Sol 7B 124
Odeon Cinema
Birmingham 7L 101 (6G 5)
Coventry 7B 152 (4A 6)
Griff 3G 111
Odiham Cl. B79: Tam 1C 32
Odin Cl. WS11: Cann 4G 9
Odnall La. DY9: Clent 5E 138
Odstone Dr. LE10: Hinc 1F 90
Offa Dr. CV8: Ken 4G 199
Offadrive B79: Tam 4B 32
Offa Rd. CV31: Lea S 3B 224
Offa's Dr. WV6: Pert 4E 34
Offa St. B79: Tam 4B 32
OFFCHURCH 8H 219
Offchurch La. CV31: Rad S 3F 224
Offchurch Rd. CV32: Cubb 4D 218
CV33: H'ham, Off 6L 219
Offenham Cl. B98: Redd 3H 213
Offenham Covert B38: K Nor 1E 164
Offini Cl. B70: W Brom 7M 77
Offmoor Rd. B32: Bart G 1H 141
OFFMORE FARM 3A 158
Offmore Farm Cl.
DY10: Kidd 3C 158
Offmore La. DY10: Kidd 3A 158
Offmore Rd. DY10: Kidd 3M 157
Offwell Cl. B98: Redd 8K 213
Ofield La. CV23: Kils 6M 207
Ogbury Cl. B14: K Hth 7J 143
Oglay Hay Rd. WS7: Chase 7G 17
Ogley Cres. WS8: Bwnhls 2G 27
Ogley Dr. B75: S Cold 4M 59
Ogley Hay Rd. WS7: C Ter 7G 11
WS8: Bwnhls 7G 17
Ogley Rd. WS8: Bwnhls 2G 27
Ogley Va. WS7: Burn 1H 17
Ogmore Rd. CV31: Lea S 3B 224
O'Hare Ho. WS4: Wals 6M 39
O'Keeffe Cl. B11: S'brk 3B 122
Okeford Way CV10: Nun 8G 89
Okehampton Dr.
B71: W Brom 3J 77
Okehampton Rd. CV3: Cov 4E 174
Okement Dr. WV11: Wed 4H 37
Okement Gro. CV23: Long L 4H 179
Oken Ct. CV34: Warw 2D 222
Oken Rd. CV34: Warw 1D 222
Okens House and Doll Mus. 3E 222
Olaf Pl. CV2: W'grve S 2A 154
Old Abbey Gdns. B17: Harb 5D 120
Oldacre Cl. B76: Walm 3K 81
Old Acre Dr. B21: Hand 2E 100
Oldacre Rd. B68: O'bry 2G 119
Oldany Way CV10: Nun 7F 88
OLD ARLEY 7E 86
Old Bakery Ct. DY9: Hag 4A 138
Old Bank Pl. B72: S Cold 4J 59
Old Bank Top B31: N'fld 7B 142
Old Barn Rd. B30: B'vlle 3D 142
DY8: Word 8A 96
Old Beeches B23: Erd 1C 80
Old Bell Rd. B23: Erd 3H 81
OLDBERROW 8J 215
Oldberrow Cl. B90: M'path 3A 168
OLDBERROW HILL 4E 214
Old Berrow La.
B95: Hen A, Oldb 8J 215
Old Birchills WS2: Wals 6J 39
Old Birmingham Rd.
B45: Lick 8C 162
B48: A'chu 1A 190
B60: L End, Marl 2C 188
Old Bri. St. B19: Hock 3J 101
Old Bri. Wlk. B65: Row R 4M 97
Old Bromford La. B8: W End 2H 103
Old Brookside B33: Stech 7L 103
Old Budbrooke Rd.
CV35: H Mag 2A 222
OLDBURY
B69 1G 99
CV10 7L 65
Oldbury Bus. Cen. B68: O'bry 7G 99
Oldbury Cl. B98: Redd 3H 213
Oldbury Ct. B79: Tam 3B 32
Oldbury Grn. Retail Pk.
B69: O'bry 1F 98
Oldbury Leisure Cen. 3D 98
Oldbury Ringway B69: O'bry 1F 98
Oldbury Rd. B65: Row R 7D 98
B66: Smeth 2J 99
B70: W Brom 6E 76
CV10: Harts 8J 65
Oldbury Rd. Ind. Est.
B66: Smeth 2K 99
B70: W Brom 7F 76
Oldbury St. WS10: W'bry 6H 55
Oldbury Vw. CV10: Harts 8B 66
Old Bush St. DY5: Brie H 6E 96
Old Camp Hill
B11: S'brk 1A 122 (8M 5)
Old Canal Wlk. DY4: Tip 4B 76
Old Cannock Rd.
WV10: Share 1K 23
Old Castle Gro. WS8: Bwnhls 7F 16
Old Cathedral 4D 6
Old Chapel, The
B3: Birm 6K 101 (3E 4)
Old Chapel Rd. B67: Smeth 6M 99
Old Chapel Wlk. B68: O'bry 5G 99

Old Chester Rd. Sth.—Othello Av.

Old Chester Rd. Sth.
DY10: Kidd 7M 157
Old Chu. Av. B17: Harb 4C 120
Old Chu. Grn. B33: Stech 7L 103
Old Chu. Rd. B17: Harb 4B 120
B46: Wat O 6H 83
CV6: Cov 8F 130
Old Coton La. B79: Tam 3M 31
Old Ct. Cft. B9: Bord G 8C 102
Old Ct. Yd., The
CV33: W Weth 2K 219
Old Crest Av. B98: Redd 6E 212
Old Cft. La. B34: S End 1B 104
B36: Cas B 1B 104
Old Cross B4: Birm 3J 5
Old Cross St. DY4: Tip 4L 75
Old Crown Cl. B32: Bart G 8H 119
Old Crown M. CV2: Ald G 5K 131
Old Damson La. B92: Sol 7F 124
Old Dickens Heath Rd.
B90: Dic H 4G 167
Old Edwardians Sports Club 3J 145
Olde Hall Ct. WV10: F'stne 2J 23
Olde Hall La. WS6: Gt Wyr 5F 14
Olde Hall Rd. WV10: F'stne 2J 23
Old End La. WV14: Cose 2J 75
Old Fails Cl. WS6: C Hay 6D 14
OLD FALLINGS 1F 36
Old Fallings Cres.
WV10: Bush 2E 36
Old Fallings La. WV10: Bush 8F 22
OLDFALLOW 6D 8
Old Fallow Av. WS11: Cann 6E 8
Old Fallow Rd. WS11: Cann 6E 8
Old Farm Dr. WV8: Bilb 5G 21
Old Farm Gro. B14: Yard W 4D 144
Old Farm La. B46: Neth W 5F 84
Old Farm Mdw. WV3: Wolv 1J 51
Old Farm Rd. B33: Stech 5L 103
CV9: Man 3M 65
Oldfield Dr. DY8: Stourb 6A 116
Oldfield Rd. B12: Bal H 3A 122
CV5: Cov 6K 151
WV14: Cose 1G 75
Oldfields B64: Crad H 1K 117
DY9: Hag 3B 138
Oldfield Trad. Est.
B64: Crad H 1K 117
Old Fire Sta., The
B17: Harb 3D 120
Old Flour Mills B70: W Brom 7J 77
Old Ford Av. CV47: Sou 4G 225
Old Fordrove B76: Walm 6K 59
Old Ford Wlk.
DY13: Stour S 7B 182
Old Forest Way B34: S End 3B 104
Old Forge Cl. WS1: Wals 1M 55
Old Forge Dr. B98: Redd 7H 213
Old Forge Gdns. DY11: Hartl 7B 184
Old Forge Rd. CV13: Fen D 3G 67
Old Forge Trad. Est.
DY9: Lye 3E 116
Old Grange Rd. B11: S'hll 5C 122
Old Grn. La. B93: Know 7B 170
CV8: Fen E 7B 170
Old Gro. Gdns. DY9: W'cte 6D 116
Old Hall Cl. DY8: Amb 1A 116
Old Hall Ind. Est. WS3: Blox 1J 39
Old Hall La. WS9: A'rdge 4H 57
WS11: Cann 2H 15
Old Hall St.
WV1: Wolv 8D 36 (5K 7)
Oldham Av. CV2: Cov 5K 153
Old Ham La. DY9: Pedm 7C 116
Old Hampton La.
WV10: Bush 7H 23
Oldham Way CV23: Long L 5H 179
Old Hawne La. B63: Hale 4A 118
Old Heath Cres. WV1: Wolv 8G 37
Old Heath Rd. WV1: Wolv 8G 37
Old Hedging La. B77: Dost 4D 46
Old Hednesford Rd.
WS11: Cann, Hed 7F 8
Old High St. DY5: Quar B 8F 96
OLD HILL 1B 118
Old Hill WV6: Tett 4K 35
Old Hill By-Pass B64: Old H 7M 97
Old Hill Station (Rail) 1A 118
Old Hinckley Rd. CV10: Nun 4K 89
Old Hobicus La. B68: O'bry 4H 99
Old Holly La. CV9: Ath 7J 49
Old Horns Cres. B43: Gt Barr 7J 57
Oldhouse Farm Cl.
B28: Hall G 3F 144
Old Ho. La. B62: Roms 8B 140
CV7: Cor 2G 129
Oldington Gro. B91: Sol 1B 168
Oldington La. DY11: Kidd 1H 183
Oldington Trad. Est.
DY11: Kidd 8H 157
Old Kingsbury Rd. B76: Mars 7A 62
B76: Min 4C 82
Oldknow Rd.
B10: Small H 3E 122
Old Landywood La.
WV11: Ess 3C 24
Old La. B48: A'chu 5J 191
WS3: Blox 2J 39
WV6: Tett 7F 34
WV10: F'stne 2J 23
Old Langley Hall B75: S Cold 5B 60
Old Leicester Rd.
CV21: Rugby 2A 180
(not continuous)
Old Level Way DY2: Neth 5K 97
Old Lime Gdns. B38: K Nor 1E 164
Old Lindens Cl. B74: S'tly 2L 57
Old Lode La. B92: Sol 5B 124
Old London Rd. WS14: S'fen 1J 29
Old Mnr., The WV6: Tett 4K 35
Old Manor Cl. B78: Dray B 4L 45
Old Masters Cl. WS1: Wals 8A 40
Old Mdw. Rd. B31: Longb 2C 164
Old Meeting Rd. WV14: Cose 1J 75
Old Meeting St.
B70: W Brom 4H 77
(not continuous)
Old Meeting Yd. CV12: Bed 6H 111
Old Mill Av. CV4: Canly 4K 173
Old Mill Cl. B90: Shir 7D 144
Old Mill Ct. B46: Col 2M 105
Old Mill Gdns. B33: Stech 7L 103
WS4: S'fld 7C 26
Old Mill Gro. B20: Hand 7J 79
Old Mill House Cl. WS4: S'fld 8B 26
Old Mill Rd. B46: Col 2M 105
OLD MILVERTON 6J 217
Old Milverton La.
CV32: B'dwn 6J 217
Old Milverton Rd.
CV32: Lea S, Old M 6J 217
Old Moat Dr. B31: N'fld 6B 142
Old Moat Way B8: W End 3H 103
OLD MOXLEY 5A 54
Oldnall Cl. DY9: W'cte 5F 116
Oldnall Rd. B63: Crad 5F 116
DY9: W'cte 5F 116
DY10: Kidd 5M 157
Old Oak Cl. WS9: A'rdge 1H 41
Old Oak Rd. B38: K Nor 7G 143
OLD OSCOTT 8L 57
Old Oscott Hill B44: Gt Barr 8L 57
Old Oscott La. B44: Gt Barr 1L 79
Old Pk. B31: N'fld 4A 142
Old Pk. Cl. B6: Aston 2L 101
Old Pk. La. B69: O'bry 4G 99
Old Pk. Rd. DY1: Dud 5F 74
WS10: Darl, W'bry 3E 54
WS12: Haz 4A 10
Old Pk. Trad. Est.
WS10: W'bry 5E 54
Old Pk. Wlk. B6: Aston 2L 101
Old Penkridge M. WS11: Cann 8D 8
Old Penkridge Rd.
WS11: Cann 7C 8
Old Penns La. B46: Col 2M 105
Old Pl. WS3: Blox 1J 39
Old Pleck Rd. WS2: Wals 1H 55
Old Port Cl. DY4: Tip 7B 76
Old Portway B38: K Nor 2E 164
Old Postway B19: Loz 2K 101
Old Pound CV34: Warw 2E 222
Old Quarry Cl. B45: Rubery 1F 162
Old Quarry Dr. DY3: Up Gor 4D 74
Old Rectory Gdns.
WS9: A'rdge 3J 41
Old Rectory La. B48: A'chu 2B 190
Old Repertory Theatre, The
7K 101 (6F 4)
Old Rd. CV7: Mer 8L 127
CV47: Sou 6H 225
Old School Cl. WV13: W'hall 7A 38
Old School Dr. B65: Row R 6B 98
Old School M. CV32: Lill 6B 218
Old School Row *B78: Dray B* *4L 45*
(off Drayton La.)
Old School Wlk. B79: Tam 3B 32
Old Scott Cl. B33: Kitts G 7C 104
Old Snow Hill
B4: Birm 5K 101 (2F 4)
Old Sq. B4: Birm 6L 101 (4H 5)
CV34: Warw 3E 222
Old Sq. Shop. Pct.
WS1: Wals 8L 39
Old Stables Wlk. B7: Nech 2C 102
Old Stafford Rd.
WV10: C Grn, S Hth 1C 22
Old Sta. Rd. B33: Stech 5K 103
B60: B'gve 8M 187
(Ednall La.)
B60: B'gve 1A 210
(Stonehouse Rd.)
B92: H Ard 7M 125
Old Stone Cl. B45: Fran 8F 140
Old Stone Yd. CV32: Lea S 8L 217
Old Stow Heath La.
WV1: Wolv 8J 37
Old Stratford Rd. B60: B'gve 7C 188
OLD SWINFORD 7A 116
Old Tamworth Rd. B77: Amin 3G 33
Old Tannery Ct. *DY12: Bew* *6B 156*
(off Severn Side S.)
Old Tokengate B17: Harb 3D 120
Old Town Cl. B38: K Nor 7F 142
Old Town La. WS3: Pels 6M 25
Old Union Mill
B16: Birm 7H 101 (6B 4)
Old Vicarage Cl. WS3: Pels 7A 26
WV5: Wom 2H 73
Old Vicarage Gdns.
B80: Stud 5L 221
Old Walsall Rd. B42: P Barr 4F 78
Old Warstone La. WV11: Ess 1B 24
Old Warwick Ct. B92: Olton 8L 123
Old Warwick Rd. B92: Olton 8L 123
B94: Lapw 4C 194
CV31: Lea S 2L 223
CV35: Row 6K 195
Old Waste La. CV7: Bal C 4L 171
Old Watling St. *CV9: Ath* *1J 65*
(off Long St.)
Oldway Dr. B91: Sol 7E 146
Old Well Cl. WS4: Rus 2B 40
Old Wharf B60: Tard 8H 189
Old Wharf Rd. DY8: Amb 3M 115
OLDWICH LANE 8D 170
Oldwich La. E. CV8: Fen E 8D 170
Oldwich La. W. B93: Chad E 2B 196
CV8: Fen E 2B 196
Old Winnings Rd.
CV7: Ker E 3M 129
Old Woodyard, The
DY9: Hag 3D 138
Old Worcester Rd.
DY11: Ware, Hartl 8A 184
Olga Dr. DY4: Tip 8B 54
Olinthus Av. WV11: Wed 2L 37
Olive Av. CV2: Cov 4K 153
WV4: E'shll 4E 52
Olive Dr. B62: B'hth 1C 118
Olive Gro. DY13: Stour S 5F 182
Olive Hill Rd. B62: B'hth 1D 118
Olive La. B62: B'hth 1C 118
Olive Mt. B69: O'bry 1D 98
Olive Pl. B14: K Hth 2M 143
Oliver Cl. DY2: Dud 1L 97
Oliver Ct. B65: Row R 7B 98
Oliver Cres. WV14: Bils 7L 53
Oliver Rd. B16: Birm 7F 100
B23: Erd 3F 80
B66: Smeth 6C 100
Oliver St. B7: Birm 4A 102
CV6: Cov 3F 152
CV21: Rugby 6M 179
Olivier Way CV2: W'grve S 1B 154
Ollerton Rd. B26: Yard 2M 123
Ollison Dr. B74: S'tly 7M 41
Olliver Cl. B62: Quin 6G 119
Olorenshaw Rd. B26: Sheld 4D 124
OLTON 8L 123
Olton Av. CV5: E Grn 5F 150
Olton Blvd. E. B27: A Grn 7G 123
Olton Blvd. W. B11: Tys 6F 122
Olton Cl. CV11: Burt H 1G 113
Olton Cft. B27: A Grn 6K 123
Olton Mere B92: Olton 8L 123
Olton Pl. CV11: Nun 5F 88
Olton Rd. B90: Shir 5H 145
Olton Station (Rail) 8L 123
Olton Wharf B92: Olton 7L 123
Olympus Av. CV34: Warw 4K 223
Olympus Cl. CV5: Alle 1B 150
Olympus Dr. DY4: Tip 3D 76
Olympus Gdns.
DY13: Stour S 6J 183
Omar Rd. CV2: Cov 7K 153
Ombersley Cl. B69: O'bry 4D 98
B98: Redd 2H 221
Ombersley Rd. B12: Bal H 3A 122
B63: Hale 7M 117
Omega Pl. CV21: Rugby 5B 180
Omersley Way B31: N'fld 7D 142
One O'Clock Ride
CV3: Bin W 2E 176
One Stop Shop. Cen.
B42: P Barr 6K 79
Onibury Rd. B21: Hand 8D 78
ONLEY 8C 206
Onley La. CV22: Rugby 3C 206
CV23: Barby 7H 207
Onley Pk. CV23: W'hby 8C 206
Onley Ter. CV4: Canly 2J 173
On Line Bus. Cen.
WS11: Cann 3D 14
Onslow Cres. B92: Olton 8A 124
Onslow Cft. CV32: Lea S 7M 217
Onslow Rd. B11: Tys 5G 123
Ontario Cl. B38: K Nor 1G 165
Oozells Sq. B1: Birm 7J 101 (6C 4)
Oozells St. B1: Birm 7J 101 (6C 4)
Oozells St. Nth.
B1: Birm 7H 101 (6B 4)
Open Fld. Cl. B31: N'fld 7B 142
Openfield Cft. B46: Wat O 7J 83
Ophelia Dr. CV34: H'cte 6L 223
Oracle Bldg. B90: Bly P 6A 168
Orangery, The B98: Beo 8J 191
Oratory, The 8F 100
Oratory Dr. CV3: W'hall 3J 175
Orbital Retail Cen.
WS11: Cann 3F 14
Orbital Way WS11: Cann 3F 14
Orchard, The B37: Mars G 1F 124
B61: B'gve 5L 187
B68: O'bry 5J 99
CV9: Bax 2C 64
(not continuous)
CV34: Warw 4F 222
DY12: Bew 2A 156
LE9: S Stan 7L 71
WS3: Blox 7K 25
WS7: Chase 2E 16
WV6: Tett 3L 35
Orchard, The WV14: Bils 4L 53
Orchard Av. B91: Sol 4D 146
WS11: Cann 7C 8
Orchard Blythe B46: Col 3A 106
Orchard Bus. Pk.
CV21: Rugby 5A 180
Orchard Cl. B21: Hand 7F 78
B46: Col 2M 105
B63: Crad 3J 117
B65: Row R 6A 98
B73: Bold 1G 81
B76: Curd 3H 83
B77: Dost 4C 46
B78: Pole 1K 49
CV9: Hurl 5J 63
CV9: With 1B 66
CV10: Harts 2A 88
DY9: Hag 5B 138
DY13: Stour S 5H 183
LE10: Burb 4A 92
LE10: Wlvy 5K 113
WS4: Rus 4C 40
WS6: C Hay 6E 14
WS13: Lich 8F 12
WV3: Wolv 2H 51
WV13: W'hall 8B 38
Orchard Cotts. CV9: Ath 2L 65
Orchard Ct. B23: Erd 5B 80
(Marsh Hill)
B23: Erd 4G 81
(Sutton Rd.)
B65: Row R 6B 98
CV3: Bin 8A 154
CV9: Ath 2K 65
CV32: Lea S 7M 217
DY6: K'wfrd 3K 95
Orchard Cres. B60: S Prior 6J 209
CV3: Cov 1C 174 (8B 6)
WV3: Wolv 2H 51
Orchard Cft. B45: B Grn 1K 189
Orchard Dr. B31: Longb 2M 163
CV5: E Grn 5C 150
Orchard Gdns. WS11: Cann 3F 8
Orchard Gro. B74: Four O 6F 42
CV47: S'ton 1M 225
DY3: Lwr G 6B 74
DY7: Kinv 5B 114
DY11: Cau 3A 136
WS9: A'rdge 5H 41
WV4: Penn 5A 52
Orchard Ho. B24: Erd 4G 81
Orchard La. CV8: Ken 6J 199
WV8: Bilb 6H 21
Orchard Mdw. Wlk.
B35: Cas V 6B 82
Orchard Pl. B80: Map G 1M 221
Orchard Retail Pk.
CV3: W'hall 4K 175
Orchard Ri. B26: Yard 2M 123
CV9: Gren 7C 48
DY12: Bew 6A 156
Orchard Rd. B12: Bal H 3M 121
B24: Erd 4G 81
B61: B'gve 5M 187
B94: H'ley H 3C 194
DY2: Neth 7J 97
DY10: Cookl 5C 136
WS5: Wals 6B 56
WV11: Wed 2J 37
WV13: W'hall 8B 38
Orchards, The B47: H'wd 2A 166
B74: Four O 1G 59
B90: Ches G 5K 167
B96: A'wd B 8D 220
CV23: Newt 1F 180
DY11: Kidd 8H 135
Orchard St. B77: Tam 6C 32
B79: Tam 4B 32
B98: Redd 6E 212
CV11: Nun 5K 89
CV12: Bed 4H 111
DY4: Tip 7M 75
DY5: Brie H 5C 96
DY10: Kidd 3L 157
LE10: Hinc 1L 91
Orchards Way B12: Bal H 3L 121
Orchard Vs. B47: Wyt 8M 165
B61: F'fld 7K 161
Orchard Way B27: A Grn 5H 123
B43: Gt Barr 8F 56
B47: H'wd 1A 166
B64: Old H 8M 97
B80: Stud 7L 221
CV8: Bubb 4J 201
CV10: Nun 3C 88
CV22: Bil 1K 205
CV23: Stret D 3F 202
CV47: Sou 4H 225
Orcheston Wlk. B14: K Hth 8K 143
Orchid Cl. B66: Smeth 2K 99
CV12: Bed 7E 110
Orchid Way CV23: Brow 1D 180
Ordnance Rd. CV6: Cov 4E 152
Oregon Cl. DY6: K'wfrd 3M 95
Oregon Dr. WV12: W'hall 2E 38
Oregon Gdns. WS7: C Ter 1F 16
Orford Gro. B21: Hand 1C 100
Orford Ri. CV10: Gall C 5L 87
Oriel Cl. DY1: Dud 7E 74
WS11: Cann 1E 14
Oriel Dr. WV10: F'hses 6D 22
Oriel Ho. B37: F'bri 6G 105
Oriel Vs. *B11: S'hll* *4C 122*
(off Warwick Rd.)
Oriole Gro. DY10: Kidd 7B 158
Orion Cl. B8: W End 5H 103
WS6: Gt Wyr 8F 14
Orion Cres. CV2: W'grve S 7L 131
Orion Way WS11: Cann 4F 8
Orkney Av. B34: Hodg H 3M 103
Orkney Cl. CV10: Nun 7F 88
LE10: Hinc 8H 69
Orkney Cft. B36: Cas B 2H 105
Orkney Dr. B77: Wiln 2F 46
Orlando Cl. CV22: Bil 3K 205
WS1: Wals 1L 55
Orlando Ho. *WS1: Wals* *1M 55*
(off Barleyfield Row)
Orlescote Rd. CV4: Canly 3K 173
Orme Cl. DY5: Brie H 1A 116
Ormes La. WV6: Tett 6J 35
Ormond Cl. LE9: Barw 2A 70
Ormonde Cl. B63: Crad 2H 117
Ormond Pl. WV14: Bils 3M 53
Ormond Rd. B45: Fran 8E 140
Ormonds Cl. WS13: Lich 3E 18
Ormsby Ct. B15: Edg 2E 120
Ormsby Gro. B27: A Grn 2H 145
Ormscliffe Rd. B45: Redn 3H 163
Orphanage Rd. B24: Erd 4G 81
B72: W Grn 3J 81
Orpington Dr. CV6: Cov 5D 130
Orpington Rd. B44: Gt Barr 6L 57
Orpwood Rd. B33: Yard 7A 104
Orsino Cl. CV34: H'cte 7L 223
Orslow Wlk. WV10: Wolv 4G 37
Orson Leys CV22: Rugby 2M 205
ORTON 6F 50
Orton Av. B76: Walm 3M 81
Orton Cl. B46: Wat O 6G 83
Orton Gro. WV4: Penn 5K 51
Orton La. WV4: Lwr P 6F 50
WV5: Wom 6F 50
Orton Rd. B79: Wart 2M 49
CV6: Cov 6C 130
LE9: Earl S 1F 70
Orton Way B35: Cas V 8A 82
Orwell Cl. CV10: Gall C 4A 88
CV23: Clift D 4G 181
DY8: Stourb 5J 115
WV11: Wed 4M 37
Orwell Ct. CV1: Cov 5D 152 (2E 6)
Orwell Dr. B38: K Nor 1B 164
B71: W Brom 3K 77
Orwell Pas. B5: Birm 7L 101 (6H 5)
Orwell Rd. CV1: Cov 8F 152
WS1: Wals 1B 56
Osbaston Cl. CV5: E Grn 5E 150
LE10: Hinc 6M 69
Osberton Dr. DY1: Dud 7F 74
Osborn Ct. B73: W Grn 8H 59
Osborne B79: Tam 2K 31
Osborne Cl. DY10: Kidd 3B 158
Osborne Ct. CV31: W'nsh 5A 224
Osborne Dr. WS10: Darl 1D 54
Osborne Gro. B19: Loz 2J 101
Osborne Rd. B21: Hand 1F 100
B23: Erd 4F 80
B60: B'gve 8C 188
B70: W Brom 6J 77
CV5: Cov 1A 174
WV4: Penn 4M 51
Osborne Rd. Sth. B23: Erd 5F 80
Osborne Twr. B6: Aston 1A 102
Osborn Rd. B11: S'brk 3C 122
Osbourne Cl. B6: Aston 2A 102
DY5: Quar B 1F 116
Osbourne Cft. B90: Ches G 4K 167
Oscott Ct. B23: Erd 1E 80
Oscott Gdns. B42: P Barr 6L 79
Oscott Rd. B6: Witt 6L 79
B42: P Barr 6L 79
Oscott School La.
B44: Gt Barr 7L 57
Osier Gro. B23: Erd 3B 80
Osier Pl. WV1: Wolv 7F 36
Osier St. WV1: Wolv 7F 36
Osler St. B16: Birm 7F 100
Oslo Gdns. CV2: W'grve S 2A 154
Osmaston Rd. B17: Harb 6A 120
DY8: Stourb 7L 115
Osmington Gro. B63: Crad 3K 117
Osnor Ct. B60: B'gve 2B 210
Osprey B77: Wiln 3G 47
Osprey Cl. CV2: W'grve S 2B 154
CV11: Nun 1B 112
Osprey Ct. WS7: Burn 1M 17
Osprey Dr. DY1: Dud 8F 74
Osprey Gro. WS12: Hth H 8J 9
Osprey Pk. Dr. DY10: Kidd 6B 158
Osprey Rd. B23: Erd 3C 80
B27: A Grn 7K 123
Ostler Cl. DY6: W Hth 2G 95
Oswald Rd. CV32: Lea S 1K 223
Oswald St. B98: Redd 6E 212
Oswald Way CV22: Rugby 6K 179
Oswestry Cl. B97: Redd 2C 220
Oswestry Cft. B11: S'brk 3B 122
Oswin Gro. CV2: Cov 5J 153
Oswin Pl. WS3: Wals 4M 39
Oswin Rd. WS3: Wals 4M 39
Othello Av. CV34: H'cte 6M 223

Pemberton Cres.—Pine Tree Av.

Pemberton Cres.
DY10: Cookl 6C 136
WS10: W'bry 5J 55
Pemberton Rd.
B70: W Brom 3G 77
WV14: Cose 8K 53
Pemberton St.
B18: Birm 5H 101 (1B 4)
Pembridge Cl. B32: Bart G 2G 141
B98: Redd 6K 213
DY5: Quar B 8F 96
Pembridge Rd. B93: Dorr 6D 168
Pembroke Av. WV2: E'shll 2G 53
Pembroke Cl. *B71: W Brom 8H 55*
(off Pembroke Rd.)
B79: Tam 3L 31
CV12: Bed 8C 110
CV34: Warw 8F 216
WV12: W'hall 3C 38
Pembroke Cft. B28: Hall G 4G 145
Pembroke Gdns. DY8: Word 8J 95
Pembroke Ho. B36: Cas B 2G 105
WS3: Blox 3J 39
(off Cornwall Clo.)
Pembroke Rd. B12: Bal H 5A 122
B71: W Brom 1H 77
Pembroke Way B8: Salt 4C 102
B28: Hall G 4G 145
B71: W Brom 2H 77
CV11: Nun 6K 89
DY13: Stour S 3E 182
Pembrook Rd. CV6: Cov 7C 130
Pembury Av. CV6: Longf 6G 131
Pembury Cl. B74: S'tly 3M 57
Pembury Cft. B44: K'sdng 8A 58
Penarth Gro. CV3: Bin 2M 175
Pencombe Dr. WV4: Penn 4D 52
Pencraig Cl. CV8: Ken 4J 199
Pencroft Rd. B34: S End 2B 104
Penda Ct. B20: Hand 1G 101
Penda Gro. WV6: Pert 4F 34
Pendeen Rd. B14: Yard W 5B 144
PENDEFORD 6A 22
Pendeford Av. WV6: Tett 1L 35
Pendeford Bus. Pk.
WV9: Pend 6M 21
Pendeford Cl. WV6: Tett 1L 35
Pendeford Hall La.
WV9: Coven, Pend 4H 21
Pendeford Hall Mobile Home Pk.
WV9: Pend 5L 21
Pendeford La. WV9: Pend 5A 22
Pendeford Mill La. WV8: Bilb . . .6H 21
Pendene Ct. WV4: Penn 4A 52
Pendenis Cl. CV6: Cov 1G 153
Pendennis Cl. B30: B'vlle 4D 142
Pendennis Dr. B69: Tiv 1A 98
Penderell Cl. WV10: F'stne 3G 23
Penderel St. WS3: Blox 1J 39
Pendicke Ct. *CV47: Sou 5H 225*
(off Pendicke St.)
Pendicke St. CV47: Sou 5H 225
Pendigo Way B40: Nat E C 5L 125
(not continuous)
Pendinas Dr. WV8: Bilb 6H 21
Pendine Ct. CV32: Lea S 1K 223
Pendle Hill WS12: Hed 5J 9
Pendleton Gro. B27: A Grn 1H 145
Pendragon Rd. B42: P Barr 5J 79
Pendred Rd. CV22: Rugby 6L 179
Pendrel Cl. WS6: Gt Wyr 1F 24
Pendrell Cl. B37: F'bri 6G 105
WV8: Cod 6G 21
Pendrell Ct. WV8: Cod 6G 21
Pendrill Rd. WV10: Bush 6E 22
Penfields Rd. DY8: Amb 3A 116
Penfold Cl. CV33: Bis T 8E 224
LE9: Sap 1K 93
Penge Gro. B44: Gt Barr 6L 57
Penhallow Dr. WV4: E'shll 4E 52
Penk Dr. WS7: Burn 3K 17
Penkridge Cl. WS2: Wals 5K 39
Penkridge Gro. B33: Stech 5M 103
Penkridge St. WS2: Wals 6K 39
Penk Ri. WV6: Tett 5G 35
Penleigh Gdns. WV5: Wom 2F 72
Penley Gro. B8: W End 3H 103
Penmanor B60: Fins 8D 188
Penmark Cl. B35: Cas V 6B 82
Penmire Cl. CV9: Gren 6C 48
PENN .4L 51
Pennant Ct. B65: Row R 6B 98
Pennant Gro. B29: W Cas 7A 120
Pennant Rd. B64: Crad H 8K 97
B65: Row R 6B 98
LE10: Burb 4K 91
Pennard Gro. B32: Quin 5M 119
Penn Cl. WS3: Blox 1J 39
Penn Comn. Rd. WV4: Penn 8L 51
Penncricket La. B65: Row R 6E 98
B68: O'bry 6F 98
Penncroft La. WV4: Penn 8M 51
Penn Dale Cl. B24: Erd 3J 81
PENN FIELDS 3A 52
Penn Gro. B29: W Cas 7B 120
Penn Ho. CV4: Tile H 8F 150
Pennhouse Av. WV4: Penn 4M 51
Penn Ind. Est. B64: Crad H 8K 97
Pennine Dr. DY3: Lwr G 6D 74
WS11: Cann 7E 8
Pennine Rd. B61: B'gve 4A 188
Pennine Way B8: Salt 4C 102
B77: Wiln 8H 33
CV10: Nun 5B 88
DY8: Amb 3A 116
WV12: W'hall 4D 38
Pennington Cl.
B70: W Brom 7G 77
Pennington M.
CV21: Rugby 6M 179
Pennington St.
CV21: Rugby 6M 179
Pennington Way CV6: Cov 1E 152
Pennis Ct. B76: Walm 2M 81
Penn La. B48: Earls 5A 192
B94: Tan A 5A 192
Penn Rd. B65: Row R 6E 98
DY3: Sed 8M 51
WV2: Wolv 2B 52 (8G 7)
WV3: Wolv 2B 52
WV4: Penn 6K 51 (8G 7)
Penn Rd. Island
WV2: Wolv 8C 36 (6H 7)
Penn Rd. Retail Pk.
WV2: Wolv 1C 52 (8H 7)
Penns Cl. CV32: Cubb 4E 218
Penns Lake Rd. B76: Walm 1L 81
Penns La. B72: W Grn 2J 81
B76: Walm 2J 81
Penn St. B4: Birm 6A 102 (3L 5)
B64: Old H 1M 117
WV3: Wolv 1B 52 (7G 7)
Penns Wood Cl. DY3: Sed 7C 52
Penns Wood Dr. B76: Walm 2M 81
Pennwood Ct. WV4: Penn 3K 51
Pennwood La. WV4: Penn 6M 51
Pennyacre Rd. B14: K Hth 7K 143
Penny Ct. WS6: Gt Wyr 1F 24
Pennycress Gdns.
WV10: F'stne 2J 23
Pennycress Grn.
WS11: Nort C 5M 15
Pennycroft Ho. B33: Stech 6L 103
Pennyfield Cft. B33: Stech 6L 103
Pennyford Cl. B97: Redd 4A 212
Penny Hapenny Ct. CV9: Ath 1J 65
Pennyhill La. B71: W Brom 2L 77
Pennyland La. CV8: Ken 2H 199
Penny La. LE9: Barw 2A 70
Pennymoor Rd. B77: Wiln 1H 47
Penny Pk. La. CV6: Cov 6A 130
Penny Royal Cl. DY3: Lwr G 7D 74
Pennyroyal Cl. WS5: Wals 6B 56
Pennys Cft. WS13: Lich 8L 13
Pennystone Cl. CV31: Lea S . . .3D 224
Penrice Dr. B69: Tiv 8M 75
Penrith Cl. CV6: Cov 7C 130
CV32: Lea S 7J 217
DY5: Brie H 1B 116
Penrith Cft. B32: Bart G 1K 141
Penrith Gro. B37: Chel W 7J 105
Penrose Cl. CV4: Tile H 2G 173
Penryhn Cl. CV8: Ken 4J 199
Penryn Cl. CV11: Nun 5A 90
WS5: Wals 2D 56
Penryn Rd. WS5: Wals 2D 56
Pensby Cl. B13: Mose 1D 144
Pensford Rd. B31: N'fld 6C 142
Pensham Cft. B90: M'path 3A 168
Penshaw Cl. WV9: Pend 6A 22
Penshaw Gro. B13: Mose 8D 122
Penshurst Av. B20: Hand 8K 79
Penshurst Rd. B60: B'gve 8C 188
Penshurst Way CV11: Nun 1M 111
Pensilva Way CV1: Cov 5E 152
PENSNETT 3C 96
Pensnett Rd. DY1: Dud 2E 96
DY5: Brie H 4C 96
Pensnett Trad. Est.
DY6: P'ntt 1M 95
Penstock Ct. DY10: Hurc 1C 158
Penstock Dr. B69: O'bry 5G 99
Penstone La. WV4: Lwr P 5E 50
Pentire Cl. CV11: Nun 4M 89
Pentire Rd. WS14: Lich 2K 19
Pentland Cl. LE10: Hinc 8H 69
Pentland Cft. B12: Birm 2M 121
Pentland Gdns. WV3: Wolv 7L 35
Pentos Dr. B11: S'hll 5D 122
Pentridge Cl. B76: Walm 4M 81
Penwood Gdns. WV14: Cose 1J 75
Penzance Cl. LE10: Hinc 5L 69
Penzance Way CV11: Nun 4M 89
Penzer Dr. B45: B Grn 1K 189
Penzer St. DY6: K'wfrd 2K 95
Peolsford Rd. WS3: Pels 5A 26
Peony Wlk. B23: Erd 6B 80
Peplins Way B30: K Nor 6H 143
Peplow Rd. B33: Stech 5A 104
Pepperbox Dr. DY4: Tip 4A 76
Peppercorn Pl. B70: W Brom 5J 77
Pepper Hill DY8: Stourb 5A 116
Pepper La. CV1: Cov 7C 152 (5C 6)
Pepperwood Cl. B61: F'fld 6J 161
Pepper Wood Dr.
B31: Longb 8J 141
Pepper Wood Nature Reserve
. . . . .7H 161
Pepys Cnr. CV4: Tile H 6E 150
Pepys Ct. B43: Gt Barr 2E 78
Perch Av. B37: F'bri 6G 105
Perch Cl. WV10: Wolv 5H 37
Perchfoot Cl.
CV1: Cov 8D 152 (8E 6)
Perch Rd. WS2: Wals 5G 39
Percival Rd. B16: Edg 8C 100
CV22: Hillm 1D 206
Percy Bus. Pk. B69: O'bry 2F 98
Percy Cres. CV8: Ken 7E 198
Percy Rd. B11: S'hll 6D 122
CV8: Ken 7E 198
CV34: Warw 1E 222
Percy St. CV1: Cov 6B 152 (4A 6)
Percy Ter. CV32: Lea S 8K 217
Peregrine Cl. DY1: Dud 8F 74
Peregrine Dr. CV5: Alle 4G 151
Peregrine Gro. DY10: Kidd 7A 158
Pereira Rd. B17: Harb 2C 120
Pericles Cl. CV34: H'cte 6L 223
Perimeter Rd. B40: Nat E C 5K 125
(not continuous)
Perivale Gro. WV14: Cose 1K 75
Perivale Way DY8: Amb 1A 116
Periwinkle Cl. WS8: Clay 3D 26
Perkins Cl. DY1: Dud 3J 75
Perkins Gro. CV21: Hillm 8F 180
Perkins St. CV1: Cov . . .6D 152 (3E 6)
Perks Rd. WV11: Wed 8A 24
Permian Cl. CV21: Rugby 3C 180
Perott Dr. B75: R'ley 7K 43
Perrett Wlk. DY11: Kidd 3K 157
Perrin Av. DY11: Kidd 5H 157
Perrins Gro. B8: W End 3G 103
Perrin's La. DY9: W'cte 5F 116
Perrins Ri. DY9: W'cte 5F 116
Perrott Gdns. DY5: Brie H 8A 96
Perrott's Folly B16: Edg 8F 100
Perrott St. B18: Win G 3D 100
PERRY 3L 79
Perry Av. B42: P Barr 5J 79
WV10: Bush 1F 36
PERRY BARR 4G 79
Perry Barr Stadium (Greyhound)
. . . . .6K 79
Perry Barr Station (Rail) 7K 79
PERRY BEECHES 2H 79
Perry Beeches Swimming Pool
. . . . .2H 79
Perry Cl. B79: Tam 3B 32
DY2: Dud 1K 97
PERRY COMMON 1D 80
Perry Comn. Rd. B23: Erd 2B 80
Perry Ct. B68: O'bry 2H 119
PERRY CROFTS 2C 32
Perrycrofts Cres. B79: Tam 2C 32
PERRYFIELDS 5K 187
Perryfields Cl. B98: Redd 4F 220
Perryfields Cres.
B61: B'gve 4M 187
Perryfields Rd. B61: B'gve 6K 187
Perryford Dr. B91: Sol 1C 168
Perry Hall Dr. WV12: W'hall 4B 38
Perry Hall Rd. WV11: Wed 3M 37
Perry Hill Cres. B68: O'bry 2H 119
Perry Hill Ho. B68: O'bry 1J 119
Perry Hill La. B68: O'bry 2H 119
Perry Hill Rd. B68: O'bry 2H 119
Perry La. B61: B'gve 7M 187
DY10: Tort 4B 184
Perryman Dr. B78: Picc 1F 62
Perry Mill La. B95: Ullen 4J 215
Perrymill La. B96: Sam 8H 221
Perry Pk. Cres. B42: P Barr 3J 79
Perry Pk. Rd. B64: Old H 8B 98
B65: B'hth 8B 98
Perry St. B66: Smeth 2M 99
DY4: Tip 5A 76
WS10: Darl 1D 54
(not continuous)
WS10: W'bry 7F 54
WV14: Bils 6L 53
Perry Trad. Est. WV14: Bils 6L 53
Perry Villa Dr. B42: P Barr 4K 79
Perry Wlk. B23: Erd 3B 80
Perry Well Dr. B6: Witt 5M 79
Perry Well Rd. B6: Witt 4M 79
Perry Wood Rd. B42: Gt Barr 1G 79
Persehouse St. WS1: Wals 7M 39
Pershore Av. B29: S Oak 7H 121
Pershore Cl. WS3: Blox 7F 24
Pershore Pl. CV4: Canly 3L 173
Pershore Rd. B29: S Oak 8H 121
B30: K Nor 5G 143
B63: Hale 7A 118
DY11: Kidd 3G 157
WS3: Blox 7F 24
Pershore Rd. Sth.
B30: K Nor 5F 142
Pershore St.
B5: Birm 8L 101 (7G 5)
Pershore Way WS3: Blox 7F 24
Pertemps Bees RUFC 5M 145
Perth Ri. CV5: E Grn 5G 151
Perth Rd. WV12: W'hall 3B 38
PERTON 5E 34
Perton Brook Va. WV6: Tett 7F 34
Perton Gro. B29: W Cas 8A 120
WV6: Tett 7F 34
Perton Rd. WV6: Tett 7E 34
Pestilence La. B48: A'chu 8C 164
(not continuous)
Petard Cl. B77: Two G 1C 46
Petchells Cl. DY5: P'ntt 4B 96
Peter Av. WV14: Bils 7M 53
Peterborough Dr. WS12: Hth H . . .8J 9
Peterbrook Cl. B98: Redd 2F 220
Peterbrook Ri. B90: Shir 8D 144
Peterbrook Rd. B90: Maj G 2D 166
B90: Shir 7C 144
Peter Ct. CV21: Rugby 6C 180
Peterdale Dr. WV4: Penn 6M 51
Peter Hall La.
CV2: W'grve S 3F 154
Peterhead B77: Amin 4F 32
Peter Lee Wlk.
CV2: W'grve S 3A 154
Peters Av. B31: N'fld 7M 141
Petersbourne Ct. B28: Hall G . . .1E 144
Peter's Cl. LE9: S Stan 7J 71
Petersfield WS11: Cann 5F 8
Petersfield Ct. B28: Hall G 1F 144
Petersfield Dr. B65: Row R 6E 98
Petersfield Rd. B28: Hall G 2E 144
Peter's Finger B61: B'gve 8M 187
Petersham Pl. B15: Edg 3E 120
Petersham Rd. B44: K'sdng 8C 58
Peter's Hill Rd. DY5: Brie H 2C 116
Petershouse Dr. B74: Four O 4F 42
Peter's La. WS7: Burn 4A 18
Peters St. B70: W Brom 2G 77
Peters Wlk. CV6: Longf 5G 131
WS13: Lich 7G 13
Petford St. B64: Old H 8L 97
Petitor Cres. CV2: Cov 1J 153
Peto Gro. CV34: H'cte 7M 223
Pettitt Cl. B14: K Hth 7L 143
Pettiver Cres. CV21: Hillm 8F 180
Petton Cl. B98: Redd 6M 213
Pettyfield Cl. B26: Sheld 3B 124
Pettyfields Cl. B93: Know 4F 168
Petworth Cl. WV13: W'hall 1M 53
Petworth Gro. B26: Yard 3L 123
Pevensey Cl. B69: Tiv 1M 97
Pevensey Rd. B60: B'gve 8C 188
Peverell Dr. B28: Hall G 2F 144
Peveril Dr. CV3: Cov 4A 174
Peveril Gro. B76: Walm 5L 59
Peverill Rd. WV4: E'shll 6E 52
WV6: Pert 5F 34
Peveril Way B43: Gt Barr 7F 56
Pewterers All. DY12: Bew 5B 156
Peyto Cl. CV6: Cov 7C 130
Pheasant Cl. CV12: Bed 8D 110
DY10: Kidd 7A 158
Pheasant Cft. B36: Cas B 1G 105
Pheasant La. B98: Redd 3E 220
Pheasant Oak CV4: Tile H 7C 150
Pheasant Rd. B67: Smeth 7K 99
Pheasant St. DY5: Brie H 6C 96
PHEASEY 5K 57
Phebe Cl. CV34: H'cte 6L 223
Philip Ct. B76: Walm 6M 59
Philip Gro. WS11: Cann 3E 8
Philip Rd. B63: Hale 6M 117
DY4: Tip 4D 76
Philip Sidney Rd. B11: S'hll 6C 122
Philips Ter. B98: Redd 5F 212
Philip St. WV14: Cose 8K 53
Philip Victor Rd. B20: Hand 8F 78
Phillimore Rd. B8: Salt 4D 102
Phillip Docker Ct.
CV12: Bulk 7B 112
Phillippes Rd. CV34: Warw 8F 216
Phillip Rd. WS2: Wals 3J 55
Phillips Av. WV11: Wed 8M 23
Phillips St. B6: Aston 3L 101
Phillips St. Ind. Est.
B6: Aston 3M 101
Phipps Av. CV21: Hillm 8F 180
(not continuous)
Phipson Rd. B11: S'hll 5B 122
Phoenix, The B90: Bly P 6M 167
Phoenix Bus. Pk. LE10: Hinc 1E 90
Phoenix Cen. WS11: Cann 3E 14
Phoenix Ct. B35: Cas V 6M 81
Phoenix Dr. WS9: A'rdge 2G 41
Phoenix Grn. B15: Edg 2E 120
Phoenix Ho. CV1: Cov 2E 6
Phoenix Ind. Est. WV14: Bils . . .5M 53
Phoenix Intl. Ind. Est.
B70: W Brom 4F 76
Phoenix Pk. B7: Nech 3A 102
B65: Row R 7E 98
CV7: Exh 2H 131
Phoenix Pk. Trad. Est.
WS11: Cann 7G 9
Phoenix Pas. *DY2: Dud 8K 75*
(off Hall St.)
Phoenix Ri. B23: Erd 2B 80
WS10: Darl 5D 54
WV2: Wolv 3C 52
(off Blakenhall Gdns.)
Phoenix Rd. DY4: Tip 3M 75
WS11: Cann 7G 9
WV11: Wed 6K 37
Phoenix Rd. Ind. Est.
WV11: Wed 6K 37
Phoenix St. B70: W Brom 5F 76
WV2: Wolv 3D 52
Phoenix Vis. Cen. 4D 6
Phoenix Way
CV6: Cov, Longf 6E 130
CV7: Ash G 5E 130
Phoenix Works Ind. Est.
WS10: Darl 2E 54
Picasso Cl. WS11: Hth H 7K 9
PICCADILLY 8F 46
Piccadilly B78: Picc 8F 46
Piccadilly Arc. B2: Birm 5F 4
Piccadilly Cl. B37: Chel W 8J 105
Piccadilly Cres. B78: Picc 1F 62
Piccadilly Way B78: K'bry 5D 62
Pickard Cl. CV21: Brow 2E 180
Pickard St. CV34: Warw 2G 223
Pickenham Rd. B14: K Hth 8A 144
Pickering Cft. B32: Bart G 8J 119
Pickering Rd. WV11: Wed 4K 37
Pickersleigh Cl. B63: Hale 6A 118
PICKFORD 1D 150
Pickford Cl. CV11: Nun 8A 90
Pickford Grange La.
CV5: Alle 2C 150
PICKFORD GREEN 2C 150
Pickford Grn. La.
CV5: Alle, E Grn 4C 150
Pickford St. B5: Birm 7M 101 (6K 5)
Pickford Way CV5: Alle, Cov . . .3G 151
Pickrell Rd. WV14: Cose 8H 53
Pickwick Cl. B13: Mose 7B 122
Pickwick Gro. B13: Mose 7C 122
Pickwick Pl. WV14: Bils 5L 53
Picton Cft. B37: Chel W 7K 105
Picton Gro. B13: Mose 4B 144
Picturedrome Way
WS10: Darl 3D 54
Picture House, The 8E 8
Piddock Rd. B66: Smeth 4A 100
Pierce Av. B92: Olton 6L 123
Piercy St. B70: W Brom 6G 77
Piers Cl. CV34: Warw 1F 222
Piers Rd. B21: Hand 2G 101
(not continuous)
Pier St. WS8: Bwnhls 2F 26
Piggotts Cft. B37: F'bri 6F 104
Pike Cl. B20: Hand 8F 78
LE10: Burb 4K 91
Pike Dr. B37: Chel W 6J 105
Pikehelve St. B70: W Brom 2E 76
Pike Hill B60: B'wll 2G 189
(not continuous)
Pikehorne Cft. B36: Cas B 7D 82
Pike Rd. WS2: Wals 5G 39
Piker's La. CV7: Cor 6G 129
Pikes, The B45: Rubery 1F 162
Pikes Pool La.
B60: Burc, Fins 8D 188
Pikewater Rd. B9: Bord G 7E 102
Pilgrims Ga. LE10: Burb 4A 92
Pilgrims La. CV23: Newt 1F 180
Pilgrims Wlk. CV7: Ker E 4A 130
Pilkington Av. B72: W Grn 6H 59
Pilkington Rd. CV5: Cov 8K 151
Pillaton Dr. WS12: Hunt 3C 8
Pilling Cl. CV2: W'grve S 1M 153
Pilson Cl. B36: Hodg H 1M 103
Pimbury Rd. WV12: W'hall 2D 38
Pimlico Ct. DY3: Lwr G 6D 74
Pimpernel Dr. WS5: Wals 6A 56
Pinbury Cft. B37: Mars G 8H 105
Pinchers Cl. DY9: Belb 2E 160
Pinders Ct. CV21: Rugby 6B 180
Pinders La. CV21: Rugby 6B 180
(not continuous)
Pineapple Cl. B14: K Hth 3J 143
Pineapple Gro. B30: Stir 1J 143
Pineapple Rd. B30: Stir 2J 143
Pine Av. B66: Smeth 2L 99
WS10: W'bry 4F 54
Pine Cl. B79: Tam 1B 32
B91: Sol 7M 145
CV13: Stoke G 2E 68
DY6: K'wfrd 4K 95
DY7: Kinv 6C 114
WS6: Gt Wyr 5F 14
WV3: Wolv 8A 36
Pine Ct. CV32: Lill 6B 218
Pinedene DY13: Stour S 6H 183
Pine Grn. DY1: Dud 3G 75
Pine Gro. B14: K Hth 4A 144
B45: Lick 7F 162
CV21: Hillm 8G 181
WS7: Chase 4F 16
Pine Ho. B36: Hodg H 1M 103
Pinehurst CV32: Cubb 3E 218
Pinehurst Dr. B38: K Nor 6F 142
Pine Leigh B74: Four O 8H 43
Pineneedle Cft. WV12: W'hall . . .5E 38
Pineridge Dr. DY11: Kidd 4H 157
Pine Rd. B69: Tiv 1A 98
DY1: Dud 4J 75
Pines, The B45: Redn 8G 141
B90: Ches G 4K 167
CV4: Tile H 2D 172
CV12: Bed 7E 110
WS1: Wals 1M 55
WS14: Lich 2M 19
WV3: Wolv 8K 35
Pineside Av.
WS15: Cann W 3F 10
Pines Pk. Homes, The
WS12: Hunt 4D 8
Pine Sq. B37: Chel W 7H 105
Pine St. WS3: Blox 7K 25
Pine Tree Av. CV4: Tile H 7G 151

Pine Tree Cl.—Potters Cl.

Pine Tree Cl. B97: Redd 6M 211
WS12: Hed 1G 9
Pine Tree Ct. CV12: Bed 5J 111
Pine Tree Cres. CV47: Sou 4J 225
Pinetree Dr. B74: S'tly 8K 41
Pine Tree Rd. CV12: Bed 5J 111
Pinetree Rd. DY12: Bew 3B 156
Pineview B31: N'fld 7M 141
Pine Wlk. B31: N'fld 6B 142
DY9: W'cte 6D 116
DY13: Stour S 5E 182
WV8: Cod 7F 20
Pinewall Av. B38: K Nor 8G 143
Pineways B74: Four O 6C 42
DY8: Word 7J 95
Pineways, The B69: O'bry 4C 98
Pineways Dr. WV6: Wolv 5L 35
Pinewood Av. CV9: Wood E 8J 47
WS11: Cann 5D 8
Pinewood Cl. B44: Gt Barr 2L 79
B45: Rubery 1D 162
DY11: Kidd 8J 135
WS5: Wals 4A 56
WS8: Bwnhls 7E 16
WV3: Wolv 1G 51
WV5: Wom 3G 73
WV12: W'hall 3D 38
Pinewood Dr. B32: Bart G 8G 119
CV3: Bin W 2C 176
Pinewood Gro. B91: Sol 7M 145
CV5: Cov 1B 174
Pinewoods B31: N'fld 1M 141
B32: Bart G 7G 119
B62: Quin 2G 119
Pinewoods Av. DY9: Hag 5M 137
Pinewoods Cl. DY9: Hag 5M 137
Pinewoods Ct. DY9: Hag 5M 137
Pinewood Wlk. DY6: K'wfrd 1L 95
Pinfield Dr. B45: B Grn 8H 163
Pinfold, The WS3: Blox 1J 39
Pinfold Cl. LE10: Hinc 2F 90
Pinfold Ct. WS10: Darl 4C 54
Pinfold Cres. WV4: Penn 3K 51
Pinfold Gdns. WV11: Wed 4K 37
Pinfold Gro. WV4: Penn 3K 51
Pinfold Hill WS14: Shens 3F 28
Pinfold Ind. Est. WS3: Blox 1J 39
Pinfold La. WS9: A'rdge 4G 57
WS11: Nort C 5L 15
WV4: Penn 3K 51
Pinfold Rd. B91: Sol 4E 146
WS13: Lich 8F 12
Pinfold St. B2: Birm 7K 101 (5E 4)
B69: O'bry 1G 99
CV21: Rugby 6L 179
WS10: Darl 4C 54
(not continuous)
WV14: Bils 4K 53
Pinfold St. Extension
WS10: Darl 4C 54
Pinford La. WS6: C Hay 7C 14
Pingle Cl. B71: W Brom 8M 55
Pingle Ct. CV11: Nun 7K 89
Pingle La. LE9: Pot M 3L 71
WS7: Hamm 4K 17
Pingles Leisure Cen. 7K 89
Pingles Stadium, The 7J 89
PINKETT'S BOOTH 8C 128
Pinkfield La. B98: Beo 1C 214
PINK GREEN 1B 214
Pink Grn. La. B97: Redd 4C 212
B98: Beo 1B 214
Pinkney Pl. B68: O'bry 6J 99
Pink Pas. B66: Smeth 5B 100
PINLEY 2J 175
Pinley Flds. CV3: Cov 1H 175
Pinley Gro. B43: Gt Barr 6J 57
Pinley Way B91: Sol 1A 168
Pinnacle Ho. *B97: Redd 4E 220*
(off Evesham Rd.)
Pinner Ct. B17: Harb 3C 120
Pinner Gro. B32: Quin 5L 119
Pinner's Cft. CV2: Cov 4G 153
Pinnock Pl. CV4: Tile H 8F 150
Pinson Gdns. WV13: W'hall 7M 37
Pinson Rd. WV13: W'hall 7M 37
Pinta Dr. DY13: Stour S 6H 183
Pintail Dr. B23: Erd 7C 80
Pintail Gro. DY10: Kidd 6B 158
Pinto Cl. B16: Birm 7F 100
Pinvin Ho. B97: Redd 5A 212
PINWALL 4K 49
Pinwall La. CV9: Pin, Rat C 4K 49
Pinza Cft. B36: Hodg H 1K 103
Pioli Pl. WS2: Wals 4K 39
Pioneer Cl. B97: Redd 5D 212
Pioneer Ho. CV1: Cov 2F 6
CV1: Cov 1E 6
(off Leicester C'way.)
Pioneer Units CV11: Nun 6L 89
Pioneer Way B35: Cas V 7B 82
PIPEHILL 4C 18
Piper Cl. WV6: Pert 5F 34
Piper Pl. DY8: Amb 1M 115
Piper Rd. WV3: Wolv 1J 51
Pipers Cl. B61: B'gve 2K 209
Pipers Cft. WS13: Lich 7G 13
Piper's End LE10: Wlvy 5K 113
Pipers Grn. B28: Hall G 4F 144
Pipers La. CV8: Ken 4G 199
CV10: Ans C 1J 87
Pipers Rd. B98: Redd 3K 221
Piper's Row
WV1: Wolv 7D 36 (4L 7)
Pipes Mdw. WV14: Bils 4L 53
Pipewell Cl. CV22: Bil 8J 179
Pipit Ct. DY10: Kidd 7A 158
Pipit Wlk. CV23: Brow 1C 180
Pipkin Ct. CV1: Cov 8D 152 (8E 6)
Pippin Av. B63: Crad 2H 117
Pirbright Cl. WV14: Bils 6L 53
Pirrey Cl. WV14: Cose 8L 53
Pitcairn Cl. B30: Stir 3H 143
Pitcairn Dr. B62: Hale 4B 118
Pitcairn Rd. B67: Smeth 8K 99
Pitcheroak Cotts. B97: Redd 6A 212
Pitclose Rd. B31: N'fld 8B 142
Pitfield Rd. B33: Kitts G 8E 104
Pitfield Row DY1: Dud 8H 75
Pitfields Cl. B68: O'bry 1G 119
Pitfields Rd. B68: O'bry 1G 119
Pitfield St. DY1: Dud 8J 75
Pithall Rd. B34: S End 4D 104
Pit Hill CV8: Bubb 4J 201
Pit Leasow Cl. B30: Stir 1H 143
Pitman Rd. B32: Quin 4J 119
Pitmaston Ct. B13: Mose 6K 121
Pitmaston Rd. B28: Hall G 3G 145
Pitmeadow Ho. *B14: K Hth 7L 143*
(off Pound Rd.)
Pitsford St.
B18: Hock 4G 101 (1A 4)
Pitt La. B92: Bick 7K 125
Pittoms La. CV23: Barby 8J 207
Pitts Farm Rd. B24: Erd 4J 81
Pitts La. DY11: Kidd 3L 157
Pitt St. B4: Birm 6A 102 (3L 5)
DY10: Kidd 8A 136
WV3: Wolv 8C 36 (5H 7)
Pixall Dr. B15: Edg 2H 121
Pixhall Wlk. B35: Cas V 6B 82
(not continuous)
Plainview Cl. WS9: A'rdge 7L 41
Plaistow Av. B36: Hodg H 2J 103
Plane Gro. B37: Chel W 8H 105
Planetary Ind. Est.
WV13: W'hall 6J 37
Planetary Rd. WV13: W'hall 5H 37
Plane Tree Cl. DY10: Kidd 2M 157
Planetree Cl. B60: B'gve 7B 188
Plane Tree Rd. B74: S'tly 1K 57
WS5: Wals 5B 56
Planet Rd. DY5: Brie H 5D 96
Plank La. B46: Wat O 7G 83
Planks La. WV5: Wom 3F 72
Plantagenet Dr. CV22: Bil 3L 205
Plantagent Pk. CV34: H'cte 6L 223
Plantation, The DY5: P'ntt 2B 96
Plantation Dr. B75: S Cold 3M 59
Plantation La.
B78: Hop, M Oak 3G 31
(not continuous)
DY3: Himl 5H 73
Plantation Rd. WS5: Wals 5A 56
WS12: Hed 1H 9
Plant Ct. *DY5: Brie H 7D 96*
(off Hill St.)
Planter Cl. CV22: Caw 1G 205
Plant La. WS7: C Ter 2D 16
Plantsbrook Community Nature
Reserve 7K 59
Plants Brook Nature Reserve 4A 82
Plants Brook Rd. B76: Walm 3M 81
Plants Cl. B73: New O 8D 58
WS6: Gt Wyr 1G 25
Plants Gro. B24: Erd 4K 81
Plants Hill Cres. CV4: Tile H 1E 172
Plants Hollow DY5: Brie H 8E 96
Plant St. B64: Old H 8K 97
DY8: Word 7L 95
Plant Way WS3: Pels 5M 25
Plascom Rd. WV1: Wolv 8E 36
Plato Cl. CV34: Warw 4K 223
Platts Cres. DY8: Amb 1L 115
Platts Dr. DY8: Amb 1L 115
Platts Rd. DY8: Amb 1L 115
Platt St. WS10: Darl 4D 54
WS11: Cann 4G 9
Playbox Theatre 5C 222
Playdon Gro. B14: K Hth 6A 144
Pleasant Cl. DY6: K'wfrd 5J 95
Pleasant Harbour
DY12: Bew 5B 156
Pleasant St. B70: W Brom 7J 77
(Farm St.)
B70: W Brom 1G 77
(Lee St.)
DY10: Kidd 2L 157
Pleasant Vw. DY3: Gorn 7D 74
Pleasant Way CV32: Lea S 7A 218
PLECK 1H 55
Pleck Bus. Pk. WS2: Wals 8J 39
Pleck Ho. *B14: K Hth 8J 143*
(off Winterbourne Cft.)
Pleck Ind. Est. WS2: Wals 1J 55
Pleck Rd. WS2: Wals 1J 55
Pleck Wlk. B38: K Nor 8G 143
Plestowes Cl. B90: Shir 4H 145
Plexfield Rd. CV22: Bil 8J 179
Pleydell Cl. CV3: W'hall 4J 175
Plimsoll Gro. B32: Quin 4J 119
Plimsoll St. DY11: Kidd 4K 157
Plomer Cl. CV22: Bil 1J 205
Plott La. CV8: Rytn D 3E 202
CV23: Stret D 3E 202
Plough & Harrow Rd.
B16: Edg 8F 100
Plough Av. B32: Bart G 7J 119
Plough Hill Rd.
CV10: Gall C, Ash C 4M 87
Ploughmans Holt CV47: Sou 3H 225
Ploughmans Pl. B75: R'ley 5K 43
Ploughmans Wlk.
B60: Stoke H 3K 209
DY6: W Hth 2G 95
WS13: Lich 6J 13
WV8: Pend 8L 21
Plough M. DY7: Kinv 5A 114
Plover Cl. WV10: F'stne 2H 23
Plover Ct. B33: Stech 6L 103
Ploverdale Cres. DY6: K'wfrd 2A 96
Plover Gro. DY10: Kidd 8B 158
Plowden Rd. B33: Stech 5M 103
Plowman St. CV21: Rugby 6M 179
Plume St. B6: Aston 1C 102
Plummers Ho. B6: Aston 2L 101
Plumstead Cl. B97: Redd 3B 212
Plumstead Rd. B44: K'sdng 1A 80
Plym Cl. WV11: Wed 4J 37
Plymouth Cl. B31: Longb 2A 164
B97: Redd 7C 212
CV2: Cov 2J 153
Plymouth Ct. B97: Redd 8C 212
Plymouth Dr. B45: B Grn 1G 189
Plymouth Pl. CV31: Lea S 2A 224
Plymouth Rd. B30: Stir 2H 143
B45: B Grn 8G 163
B97: Redd 7D 212
Plympton M. B71: W Brom 3J 77
Pochard Cl. DY10: Kidd 8M 157
Pocklington Pl. B31: N'fld 3C 142
PODMOOR 5E 184
Poets Cnr. B10: Small H 2D 122
Point 3 B3: Birm 6J 101 (3D 4)
Pointon Cl. WV14: Cose 7G 53
Poitiers Rd. CV3: Cov 3D 174
Polars, The DY5: P'ntt 2B 96
Polden Cl. B63: Hale 8J 117
POLESWORTH 2K 49
Polesworth Cl. B98: Redd 8K 213
Polesworth Gro. B34: S End 3B 104
Polesworth Sports Cen. 1M 47
Polesworth Station (Rail) 1K 49
Pollard Rd. B27: A Grn 8J 123
Pollards, The B23: Erd 1E 80
Polly Brooks Yd. DY9: Lye 4E 116
Polo Flds. DY9: Pedm 8B 116
Polperro Dr. CV5: Alle 4G 151
Pomeroy Cl. CV4: Tile H 2D 172
Pomeroy Rd. B32: Bart G 8J 119
B43: Gt Barr 5K 57
Pommel Cl. WS5: Wals 5M 55
Pond Farm M. CV5: E Grn 4E 150
Pond La. WV2: Wolv 1D 52 (8L 7)
Pondthorpe CV3: W'hall 3L 175
Ponesfield Rd. WS13: Lich 7H 13
Ponesgreen WS13: Lich 7H 13
Pontypool Av. CV3: Bin 3M 175
Pool Av. WS11: Nort C 1D 22
Pool Bank B97: Redd 8D 212
B98: Redd 8D 212
Pool Bank St. CV11: Nun 5H 89
Pool Cl. CV22: Bil 1K 205
WV10: Share 1K 23
Pool Cotts. WS7: Chase 5E 16
Poole Cres. B17: Harb 6C 120
WS8: Bwnhls 7C 16
WV14: Cose 7K 53
Poole Ho. Rd. B43: Gt Barr 6E 56
Pool End Cl. B93: Know 3F 168
Poole Rd. CV6: Cov 3M 151
Pooles Ct. DY10: Kidd 2L 157
Pooles La. WV12: W'hall 1E 38
Poole St. DY8: Stourb 5L 115
Poole's Way WS7: Burn 2J 17
Pooley Fields Heritage Cen. 6M 33
Pooley La. B78: Pole 8M 33
Pooley Vw. B78: Pole 2K 49
Pool Farm Rd. B27: A Grn 8H 123
Pool Fld. Av. B31: N'fld 2L 141
Poolfield Dr. B91: Sol 6M 145
Poolfield Rd. WS13: Lich 3E 18
Pool Furlong DY9: Clent 8E 138
POOL GREEN 4F 40
Pool Grn. WS9: A'rdge 4G 41
Pool Grn. Ter. WS9: A'rdge 4G 41
Pool Hall Cres. WV3: Wolv 1F 50
Pool Hall Rd. WV3: Wolv 1F 50
Pool Hayes La.
WV12: W'hall 4A 38
Poolhead La.
B94: Earls, Tan A 1B 192
Pool Ho. Rd. WV5: Wom 4D 72
Pool La. B69: O'bry 5F 98
Pool Mdw. WS6: C Hay 8D 14
Poolmeadow B76: Walm 1A 82
Pool Mdw. Cl. B13: Mose 8C 122
B91: Sol 8F 146
Pool Pl. B98: Redd 6E 212
Pool Rd. B63: Hale 6B 118
B66: Smeth 4B 100
B80: Stud 5L 221
CV10: Nun 4F 88
Pool Rd. WS7: Chase 5E 16
(not continuous)
WS8: Bwnhls 7E 16
WV11: Wed 3A 38
Pool Rd. Bus. Cen.
CV10: Nun 4F 88
Pool Rd. Ind. Est. CV10: Nun 4F 88
Poolside Gdns. CV3: Finh 4A 174
Pool St. DY1: Dud 3G 75
WS1: Wals 8M 39
WV2: Wolv 1C 52 (7H 7)
(not continuous)
Pooltail Wlk. B31: Longb 8K 141
Pool Vw. WS4: Rus 2D 40
WS6: Gt Wyr 5G 15
Pool Way B33: Yard 8A 104
Poor's Piece Nature Reserve 2D 88
Pope Gro. WS12: Hed 3F 8
Pope Rd. WV10: Bush 1G 37
Popes La. B69: O'bry 3H 99
B30: K Nor 5D 142
B38: K Nor 5D 142
B96: A'wd B 7E 220
WV6: Tett 3G 35
Pope St. B1: Birm 6H 101 (2A 4)
B66: Smeth 2B 100
CV22: Rugby 6L 179
Poplar Arc. *B91: Sol 5C 146*
(off Gardeners Wlk.)
Poplar Av. B11: S'brk 3B 122
B12: Bal H 5A 122
B14: K Hth 1M 143
B17: Edg 8A 100
B19: Loz 1J 101
B23: Erd 5F 80
B37: Chel W 1J 125
B69: O'bry 5G 99
B69: Tiv 1B 98
B70: W Brom 7L 77
B75: S Cold 2M 59
CV12: Bed 7K 111
DY4: Tip 4K 75
WS2: Wals 6D 38
WS5: Wals 5A 56
WS7: Chase 3F 16
WS8: Bwnhls 1G 27
WS11: Cann 5F 8
WV11: Wed 2H 37
Poplar Cl. B61: Cats 1M 187
B69: Tiv 8C 76
WS2: Wals 5E 38
WV5: Wom 3H 73
Poplar Cres. DY1: Dud 6H 75
DY8: Stourb 6L 115
Poplar Dr. B6: Witt 4M 79
B8: Salt 3D 102
B45: B Grn 1K 189
Poplar Grn. DY1: Dud 3G 75
Poplar Gro. B19: Loz 1J 101
B66: Smeth 6B 100
B70: W Brom 8L 77
CV8: Rytn D 8B 176
CV21: Rugby 5A 180
Poplar Ho. CV12: Bed 7K 111
Poplar La. B62: Roms 5A 140
WS11: Hton, Cann 1A 14
Poplar Ri. B42: Gt Barr 2H 79
B69: Tiv 1C 98
B74: Lit A 4D 42
Poplar Rd. B11: S'hll 4B 122
B14: K Hth 1L 143
B66: Smeth 8A 100
B69: O'bry 1G 99
B91: Sol 5C 146
B93: Dorr 5F 168
B97: Redd 6A 212
CV5: Cov 8M 151
DY6: K'wfrd 4L 95
DY8: Stourb 6L 115
DY11: Kidd 5J 157
WS6: Gt Wyr 8F 14
WS8: Bwnhls 1G 27
WS10: W'bry 3G 55
WV3: Wolv 3A 52
WV14: Bils 2M 53
Poplar Row DY11: Kidd 5J 157
Poplars, The B11: S'brk 3C 122
B16: Birm 5F 100
CV10: Nun 6D 88
DY8: Word 7M 95
LE9: Earl S 1G 71
WS11: Cann 5E 8
Poplars Dr. B36: Cas B 1B 104
WV8: Cod 7F 20
Poplars Ind. Est., The
B6: Witt 4M 79
Poplars La. B96: A'wd B 8A 220
Poplars Trad. Est. B80: Stud 3C 221
Poplar St. B66: Smeth 4C 100
WS11: Nort C 3A 16
WV2: Wolv 3D 52
Poplar Trees *B47: H'wd 3A 166*
(off May Farm Cl.)
Poplar Way CV10: Harts 2A 88
Poplar Way Shop. Cen.
B91: Sol 5C 146
Poplarwoods B32: Bart G 7H 119
Poppy Ct. CV3: W'hall 3K 175
Poppy Dr. CV23: Brow 1E 180
WS5: Wals 6M 55
Poppyfield Ct. CV4: Canly 6K 173
Poppy Gro. B8: Salt 5F 102
Poppy La. B24: Erd 4J 81
Poppymead B23: Erd 1B 80
Porchester Cl. CV3: Bin 7A 154
WS9: Wals W 6G 27
Porchester Dr. B19: Hock 3K 101
Porchester St. B19: Hock 3K 101
Porlock Cl. CV3: Cov 4E 174
Porlock Cres. B31: N'fld 6K 141
Porlock Rd. DY8: Amb 3A 116
Portal Rd. WS2: Wals 7F 38
Portchester Dr. WV11: Wed 4K 37
Porter Cl. B72: W Grn 2H 81
CV4: Tile H 1E 172
Porters Cft. B17: Harb 1A 120
Porter's Fld. DY2: Dud 8K 75
Portersfield Ind. Est.
B64: Crad H 2K 117
Portersfield Rd. B64: Crad H 1J 117
Portershill Dr. B90: Shir 8J 145
Porter St. DY2: Dud 8K 75
Porter St. Sth. DY2: Dud 8K 75
Porters Way B9: Bord G 7E 102
Portfield Dr. DY4: Tip 6A 76
Portfield Gro. B23: Erd 3G 81
Porth Kerry Gro. DY3: Sed 2B 74
Port Hope Rd. B11: S'brk 2A 122
Porthouse Gro. WV14: Cose 6H 53
Portia Av. B90: Shir 7H 145
Portia Cl. CV11: Nun 8A 90
Portia Way CV34: H'cte 6L 223
Portland Av. B79: Tam 1M 31
WS9: A'rdge 4H 41
Portland Ct. CV32: Lea S 8M 217
WS9: A'rdge 4H 41
Portland Cres. DY9: Pedm 8B 116
Portland Dr. B69: Tiv 7D 76
CV10: Nun 5B 88
DY9: Pedm 8B 116
LE10: Hinc 6L 69
Portland M. CV32: Lea S 1M 223
Portland Pl. CV21: Rugby 7D 180
WS11: Cann 2C 14
WV14: Cose 2H 75
Portland Pl. E. CV32: Lea S 1M 223
Portland Pl. W. CV32: Lea S 1L 223
Portland Rd. B16: Edg 6B 100
B17: Edg 6B 100
CV21: Rugby 7D 180
WS9: A'rdge 3H 41
Portland Row CV32: Lea S 1L 223
Portland St. B6: Aston 2A 102
CV32: Lea S 1M 223
WS2: Wals 6L 39
Port La. WV9: Coven 3H 21
Portleys La. B78: Dray B 5J 45
Portman Rd. B13: Mose 2M 143
Port Manteau M.
B94: H'ley H 3C 194
PORTOBELLO 1L 53
Portobello Cl. WV13: W'hall 8K 37
Portobello Rd. B70: W Brom 1G 77
Portreath Dr. CV11: Nun 4A 90
Portree Av. CV3: Bin 7M 153
Portrush Av. B38: K Nor 8C 142
Portrush Rd. WV6: Pert 5D 34
Portsdown Cl. WV10: Bush 2F 36
Portsdown Rd. B63: Hale 8J 117
Portsea Cl. CV3: Cov 3D 174
Portsea St. WS3: Blox 3J 39
Port St. WS1: Wals 2K 55
Portswood Cl. WV9: Pend 8M 21
PORTWAY
Earlswood 3M 191
Rowley Regis 4C 98
Portway, The DY6: K'wfrd 4L 95
Portway Cl. B91: Sol 8L 145
CV4: Tile H 1E 172
CV31: Lea S 3D 224
DY6: K'wfrd 4L 95
Portway Hill B65: Row R 3B 98
Portway Pl. DY10: Cookl 4A 136
Portway Rd. B65: Row R 5B 98
B69: O'bry 2E 98
WS10: W'bry 6E 54
WV14: Bils 2L 53
Portway Rd. Ind. Est.
B69: O'bry 2E 98
Portway Wlk. B65: Row R 3C 98
Portwrinkle Av. CV6: Cov 3G 153
Poseidon Way CV34: Warw 5M 223
Posey Cl. B21: Hand 6D 78
Postbridge Rd. CV3: Cov 4D 174
Postle Cl. CV23: Kils 7M 207
Post Office La. CV9: With 2B 66
CV47: S'ton 1M 225
Post Office Rd. CV9: Bad E 8C 48
WV5: Seis 6A 50
Post Office Row CV10: Asty 2L 109
Post Office Wlk.
B96: A'wd B 8E 220
Post Office Yd. CV23: Brin 5M 155
Poston Cft. B14: K Hth 5K 143
Potland Ter. *B18: Hock 4G 101*
(off Crabtree Rd.)
Pottal Pool Rd. ST19: Penk 1A 8
Potter Cl. B23: Erd 1D 80
Potter Ct. *DY5: Brie H 7D 96*
(off Promenade, The)
Potters Brook DY4: Tip 4B 76
Potters Cl. CV23: Brin 6L 155

Potter's Cross—Quantock Cl.

POTTER'S CROSS 4A 114
POTTER'S GREEN 8L 131
Potter's Grn. Rd.
CV2: W'grve S 8L 131
Potters La. WS10: W'bry 7E 54
B6: Aston 3L 101
B78: Pole 1A 48
POTTERS MARSTON 4M 71
Potters Marston La.
LE9: Thurl 1L 71
Potters Rd. CV12: Bed 8E 110
Potterton Way B66: Smeth 1M 99
Potterton Works
CV34: Warw 1J 223
Pottery Rd. B66: Smeth 2A 100
B68: O'bry 8J 99
Potton Cl. CV3: W'hall 3L 175
Potts Cl. CV8: Ken 5J 199
Pougher Cl. LE9: Sap 2L 93
Pouk Hill Cl. WS2: Wals 6G 39
Pouk La. WS14: Hilt 1L 27
Poultney Rd. CV6: Cov 3A 152
Poultney St. B70: W Brom 2F 76
Poulton Cl. B13: Mose 7A 122
Pound Cl. B68: O'bry 6F 98
B94: Lapw 6H 195
CV7: Berk 6K 149
Pound Grn. B8: Salt 3F 102
Pound Ho. La. B94: H'ley H 5L 193
Pound La. B32: Fran 6F 140
B46: Col 5A 106
B46: Over W 5K 85
CV32: Lill 6A 218
Poundley Cl. B36: Cas B 1C 104
Pound Rd. B14: K Hth 8L 143
B68: O'bry 6F 98
(not continuous)
WS10: W'bry 6G 55
Pound Way CV47: Sou 5J 225
Pountney St.
WV2: Wolv 1C 52 (7H 7)
Poverty B96: A'wd B 7E 220
Powell Av. B32: Quin 3G 119
Powell Cl. CV33: Bis T 8E 224
Powell Pl. DY4: Tip 4C 76
WV14: Bils 6L 53
Powell Rd. CV2: Cov 5G 153
Powells Ho. B73: New O 7C 58
Powell St. B1: Birm 6H 101 (3B 4)
B63: Hale 6B 118
WV10: Wolv 5F 36
Powell Way CV11: Nun 5J 89
Powerleague Soccer Cen. 8C 80
Powers Ct. CV32: Lea S 8M 217
Powers Rd. LE9: Barw 4M 69
Power Sta. Rd.
DY13: Stour S 7G 183
Power Way DY4: Tip 1D 76
Powick Pl. B19: Loz 2J 101
Powick Rd. B23: Erd 8D 80
Powis Av. DY4: Tip 3A 76
Powis Gro. CV8: Ken 4J 199
Powke La. B64: Old H 6M 97
B65: Row R 7A 98
Powke La. Ind. Est.
B65: Row R 7A 98
Powlers Cl. DY9: W'cte 7E 116
Powlett St. WV2: Wolv . . .8D 36 (6L 7)
Poxon Rd. WS9: Wals W 5G 27
Poynings, The WV6: Tett 4J 35
Poyser Rd. CV10: Nun 1J 111
Praetor Ho. LE10: Hinc 8K 69
Pratts La. B80: Map G 2M 221
Precinct, The B79: Tam 4B 32
CV1: Cov 7C 152 (5B 6)
CV34: Warw 8G 217
WV12: W'hall 4B 38
Premier Bus. Pk. WS2: Wals 8K 39
Premier Ct. B30: K Nor 6J 143
Premier Pk. B73: New O 7D 58
Premier Partnership Ind. Est.
DY6: K'wfrd 6B 96
Premier St. B7: Nech 1D 102
Premier Trad. Est.
B7: Birm 4M 101 (1J 5)
Prentice Cl. CV23: Long L 4H 179
Prescelly Cl. CV10: Nun 6B 88
Prescot Rd. DY9: Lye 5C 116
Prescott St.
B18: Hock 5H 101 (1A 4)
Prestbury Cl. B98: Redd 6A 214
Prestbury Rd. B6: Aston 1L 101
Presthope Rd. B29: W Cas 2B 142
Preston Av. B76: Walm 6L 59
Preston Cl. B98: Redd 3H 213
CV4: Tile H 2F 172
Preston Ho. *WS1: Wals 8M 39*
(off Paddock La.)
Preston Rd. B18: Win G 3E 100
B26: Yard 3K 123
LE10: Hinc 7H 69
Prestons Row WV14: Cose 6G 53
Prestwick Cl. B75: S Cold 1J 59
Prestwick Rd. B35: Cas V 5B 82
DY6: K'wfrd 3J 95
PRESTWOOD 8E 94
Prestwood Av. WV11: Wed 2K 37
Prestwood Dr. DY7: Stourt 1F 114
Prestwood Rd. B29: W Cas 1B 142
DY7: Stourt 3E 114
WV11: Wed 4G 37
Prestwood Rd. W.
WV11: Wed 3G 37
Pretorian Way CV21: Rugby . . .2A 180
Pretoria Rd. B9: Bord G 6E 102
Priam Cir. CV34: H'cte 6M 223
Priam Gro. WS3: Pels 3B 26
Price Av. B78: M Oak 8K 31
Price Cl. E. CV34: Warw 5B 222
Price Cl. W. CV34: Warw 5B 222
Price Cres. WV14: Bils 2K 53
Price Rd. CV32: Cubb 5E 218
WS10: W'bry 6J 55
Prices Rd. DY3: Gorn 6C 74
Price St. B4: Birm 5L 101 (2G 5)
B66: Smeth 4B 100
B70: W Brom 6J 77
DY2: Dud 1L 97
WS11: Cann 8E 8
WV14: Bils 4M 53
Pridmore Rd. CV6: Cov 2D 152
PRIESTFIELD 3H 53
Priestfield WV2: E'shll 2G 53
Priestfield Cl. B44: Gt Barr 7J 57
Priestfield Rd. B97: Redd 4E 220
Priestfield St. WV14: Bils 3H 53
Priesthills Rd. LE10: Hinc 1K 91
Priestland Rd. B34: S End 2B 104
Priestley Cl. B20: Hand 8G 79
B63: Crad 3H 117
Priestley Rd. B11: S'brk 2A 122
WS2: Wals 4G 39
Priestly Wharf
B7: Birm 5M 101 (1K 5)
Priest Mdw. Cl. B96: A'wd B . . .8D 220
Priest St. B64: Old H 8M 97
Primary Wlk. CV22: Caw 1G 205
Primley Av. B36: Hodg H 2K 103
B77: Hock 4F 46
WS2: Wals 8H 39
Primley Cl. WS2: Wals 7H 39
Primrose Av. B11: S'hll 3C 122
DY4: Tip 1C 76
WV10: F'hses, Bush 6D 22
Primrose Bank B68: O'bry 5H 99
Primrose Cl. B60: L End 3C 188
B64: Crad H 1H 117
CV23: Brow 1E 180
WS3: Pels 4A 26
Primrose Cres. DY1: Dud 5J 75
Primrose Cft. B23: Erd 2C 80
B28: Hall G 4F 144
Primrose Dr. CV12: Bed 8E 110
LE10: Burb 4L 91
Primrose Gdns. B38: K Nor 1F 164
WV8: Cod 6G 21
WV10: F'stne 2H 23
PRIMROSE HILL 5K 97
Primrose Hill B38: K Nor 8F 142
(not continuous)
B67: Smeth 5K 99
CV34: Warw 8C 216
DY8: Word 8L 95
Primrose Hill St.
CV1: Cov 5D 152 (2E 6)
Primrose Hill Trad. Est.
DY2: Neth 5K 97
Primrose La. B28: Hall G 4F 144
B90: Dic H 4G 167
WV10: Bush 5E 22
(Cromwell Rd.)
WV10: Bush 1F 36
(Old Fallings La.)
Primrose Mdw. WS11: Hth H 7J 9
Primrose Pk. DY5: P'ntt 2C 96
Primrose Rd. DY2: Neth 5J 97
Primroses, The WS5: Wals 5B 56
Primrose Way DY10: Kidd 5M 157
Primrose Woods
B32: Bart G 7H 119
Primsland Cl. B90: M'path 2C 168
Prince Albert St.
B9: Small H 8D 102
(not continuous)
Prince Andrew Cres.
B45: Fran 7E 140
Prince Charles Cl. B45: Fran . . .7E 140
Prince Charles Rd.
WV14: Bils 6M 53
Prince Edward Dr. B45: Fran . . .7E 140
Prince George Rd.
WS10: W'bry 4G 55
Prince of Wales Cen.
WS11: Cann 8E 8
Prince of Wales La.
B14: K Hth, Yard W 7C 144
Prince of Wales Rd.
CV5: Cov 6L 151
Prince of Wales Way
B66: Smeth 4C 100
Princep Cl. B43: Gt Barr 5K 57
Prince Philip Cl. B45: Fran 7E 140
Prince Regent Ct.
CV31: Lea S 3M 223
Prince Rd. B30: K Nor 6F 142
Prince Rupert M. WS13: Lich . . .1G 19
Prince Rupert Rd.
DY13: Stour S 7E 182
Prince Rupert's Way
WS13: Lich 1G 19
Princes Av. CV11: Nun 6H 89
WS1: Wals 1A 56
Princes Cl. CV3: Cov 1H 175
Princes Dr. CV31: Lea S 2K 223
CV32: Lea S 1K 223
CV8: Ken 2H 199
WV8: Cod 6G 21
Princes Dr. Ind. Est.
CV8: Ken 1G 199
PRINCES END 1M 75
Princes End Ind. Est.
DY4: Tip 8L 53
Princes Gdns. WV8: Cod 6F 20
Princes Ga. B91: Sol 5B 146
Princes Rd. B78: Pole 2L 49
B69: Tiv 7A 76
CV9: Hurl 4J 63
DY8: Stourb 7K 115
Princess Alice Dr.
B73: New O 7D 58
Princess All.
WV1: Wolv 7D 36 (4K 7)
Princess Anne Dr. B45: Fran . . .7E 140
Princess Anne Rd. WS2: Wals . . .6F 38
WV14: Bils 6M 53
Princess Cl. WS7: C Ter 2E 16
Princess Ct. WV10: Wolv 3G 37
Princess Cres. B63: Hale 3L 117
Princess Diana Way
B45: Fran 7E 140
Princess Dr. CV6: Cov 8H 131
Princess Gro. B71: W Brom 1K 77
Princess Pde. B70: W Brom 6K 77
Princes Sq.
WV1: Wolv 7D 36 (3K 7)
Princess Rd. B5: Bal H 3L 121
B68: O'bry 7K 99
CV9: Ath 8L 49
LE10: Hinc 1L 91
Princess Sq. WV14: Bils 6M 53
Princess St. CV6: Cov 2F 152
WS7: C Ter 1E 16
WS11: Cann 4E 8
WV1: Wolv 7D 36 (4K 7)
Princes St. CV32: Lea S 8B 218
CV11: Nun 6H 89
CV21: Rugby 5A 180
Princess Way DY13: Stour S . . .8E 182
WS10: Darl 1C 54
Prince St. B64: Crad H 1K 117
DY2: Neth 3J 97
WS2: Wals 1J 55
WS9: Wals W 7F 26
WS11: Cann 3E 8
Prince's Way B91: Sol 5B 146
PRINCETHORPE 7E 202
Princethorpe Cl. B34: S End . . .2D 104
B90: Shir 7G 145
Prince Thorpe Ct. CV3: Bin 2L 175
Princethorpe Rd.
B29: W Cas 8A 120
Princethorpe Way CV3: Bin 2K 175
Princeton Gdns. WV9: Pend 7M 21
Prince William Cl. B23: Erd 7D 80
CV6: Cov 3L 151
Principal Ct. B67: Smeth 4A 100
Princip St. B4: Birm 5L 101 (2G 5)
Printing Ho. St.
B4: Birm 6L 101 (3G 5)
Prior Av. B60: S Prior 6J 209
Prior Cl. DY10: Kidd 4C 158
Prior Deram Wlk.
CV4: Canly 1H 173
Priors, The CV12: Bed 7J 111
Priors Cl. CV7: Bal C 3H 171
Priorsfield Rd. CV6: Cov 5A 152
CV8: Ken 2D 198
Priorsfield Rd. Nth.
CV6: Cov 5A 152
Priorsfield Rd. Sth.
CV6: Cov 5A 152
Priors Harnall
CV1: Cov 5E 152 (1F 6)
Priors Mdw. CV47: Sou 5J 225
Priors Mill DY3: Up Gor 4E 74
Priors Oak B97: Redd 5B 212
Priors Way B23: Erd 1C 80
Priory, The 6J 75
Priory, The DY3: Sed 1D 74
DY13: Stour S 4G 183
Priory Av. B29: S Oak 7H 121
Priory Chambers *DY1: Dud 8J 75*
(off Priory St.)
Priory Cl. B46: Col 4A 106
B66: Smeth 5C 100
B70: W Brom 7M 77
B79: Tam 2M 31
B94: Lapw 4K 195
DY1: Dud 7H 75
DY8: Stourb 6B 116
Priory Ct. B80: Stud 4L 221
B90: M'path 2B 168
CV11: Nun 5G 89
(not continuous)
DY1: Dud 8J 75
DY8: Stourb 6B 116
WS9: Wals W 5G 27
WV1: Wolv 6C 36 (2H 7)
Priory Cft. CV8: Ken 5F 198
Priory Dr. B68: O'bry 4J 99
Priory Fld. Cl. WV14: Cose 8F 52
Priory Fields Nature Reserve
. . . . .7D 144
Priory Gdns. B28: Hall G 5D 144
Priory Ga. Way B9: Bord G 7E 102
Priory Ho. B63: Hale 4M 117
Priory Ho. Ind. Est.
B18: Hock 4G 101 (1A 4)
Priory La. DY3: Sed 2D 74
Priory M. CV34: Warw 2E 222
Priory New Way Ind. Est.
B6: Aston 4L 101
Priory Pk. Karting Circuit 7J 33
Priory Pl. CV1: Cov 6D 152 (4D 6)
Priory Queensway, The
B4: Birm 6L 101 (4G 5)
Priory Rd. B5: Edg 4H 121
B6: Aston 1B 102
B14: K Hth 2J 143
B15: Edg 3H 121
B28: Hall G 4D 144
B61: D'frd 4G 187
B62: Hale 5E 118
CV8: Ken 4F 198
CV8: Wols 5H 177
CV34: Warw 2E 222
DY1: Dud 4J 75
DY8: Stourb 6B 116
WS12: Hed 5K 9
Priory Row CV1: Cov . . .6D 152 (4D 6)
Priory Sq. B80: Stud 4L 221
Priory Sq. Shop. Cen.
B4: Birm 4H 5
Priory St. CV1: Cov 6D 152 (5D 6)
CV10: Nun 6C 88
CV31: Lea S 3M 223
DY1: Dud 8J 75
Priory Ter. CV31: Lea S 2M 223
Priory Wlk. B4: Birm . . .6L 101 (4H 5)
B72: W Grn 2J 81
CV9: Man 3M 65
CV34: Warw 2F 222
LE10: Hinc 8L 69
Priory Woods Nature Reserve
. . . . .5A 78
Pritchard Av. WV11: Wed 3L 37
Pritchard Cl. B66: Smeth 4B 100
Pritchard Ct. DY12: Bew 6B 156
Pritchard St. DY5: Brie H 6B 96
WS10: W'bry 6G 55
Pritchatts Rd. B15: Edg 4E 120
Pritchett Av. WV4: E'shll 6F 52
Pritchett Rd. B31: Longb 2B 164
Pritchett St. B6: Birm . . .4L 101 (1J 5)
Pritchett Twr. B10: Small H 8C 102
Private Rd. B47: Wyt 7B 166
CV34: Warw 1B 222
(not continuous)
LE9: S Stan 6K 71
Private Way B45: Coft H 5J 163
Privet Cl. B44: Gt Barr 6L 57
Privet Rd. CV2: Cov 7H 131
Probert Rd. WV10: Oxl 1A 36
Proctors Barn La.
B98: Redd 5H 213
Proctor St. B7: Birm 4A 102 (1L 5)
Proffitt Av. CV6: Cov 8G 131
Proffitt Cl. WS2: Wals 5L 39
WS8: Bwnhls 4G 27
Proffitt St. WS2: Wals 5L 39
Progress Cl. CV3: Bin 2A 176
Progress Dr. WS11: Cann 2E 14
Progress Ind. Cen.
WS11: Cann 3E 14
Progress Way CV3: Bin 1A 176
Projects Dr. CV21: Rugby 3C 180
Prole St. WV10: Wolv 5E 36
Prologis Pk. CV7: Ker E 4A 130
(not continuous)
Promenade, The DY5: Brie H 7D 96
Prophet's Cl. B97: Redd 6D 212
Prospect Dr. WS14: Lich 1M 19
Prospect Gdns. DY8: Stourb . . .5A 116
Prospect Hill B97: Redd 4E 212
DY8: Stourb 5A 116
DY10: Kidd 3L 157
Prospect La. B91: Sol 4K 145
DY10: Kidd 3L 157
Prospect Mnr. Ct. WS12: Hed . . .6J 9
Prospect Pk. WS11: Cann 2D 14
Prospect Pl. B12: Bal H 4M 121
Prospect Rd. B13: Mose 8M 121
B62: Hale 4C 118
CV31: Lea S 4B 224
DY3: Gorn 7B 74
DY13: Stour S 5G 183
WS7: Burn 3H 17
Prospect Rd. Nth.
B98: Redd 5G 213
Prospect Rd. Sth.
B98: Redd 5G 213
Prospect Row DY2: Dud 2K 97
DY8: Stourb 6A 116
Prospect St. B79: Tam 4A 32
DY4: Tip 8C 54
WV14: Bils 3L 53
Prospect Ter. DY10: Kidd 3L 157
Prospect Trad. Est. B1: Birm 4C 4
PROSPECT VILLAGE 5C 10
Prospect Way CV21: Rugby 4C 180
LE9: Earl S 1E 70
Prosper Mdw. DY6: K'wfrd 2L 95
Prospero Cl. B45: Fran 7G 141
Prospero Dr. CV34: H'cte 6L 223
Prosser St. WV10: Wolv 4E 36
WV14: Bils 4K 53
Prossers Wlk. B46: Col 2M 105
Proud Cross Ringway
DY11: Kidd 3J 157
Prouds La. WV14: Bils 1K 53
Provence Cl. WV10: Wolv 5F 36
Providence Cl. WS3: Blox 2J 39
(not continuous)
Providence Dr. DY9: Lye 3E 116
Providence Ind. Est.
DY9: Lye 3E 116
Providence La. WS3: Blox 3J 39
Providence Rd. B61: B'gve 6M 187
Providence Row WV14: Cose 1H 75
Providence St. B64: Crad H 8K 97
CV5: Cov 1M 173
DY4: Tip 4C 76
DY9: Lye 3E 116
Pruden Av. WV4: E'shll 6F 52
Pryor Rd. B68: O'bry 6J 99
Ptarmigan Pl. CV11: Nun 6M 89
Puckerings La. CV34: Warw . . .3E 222
Pudding Bag La.
CV23: Thurl 7F 204
Pudsey Dr. B75: Four O 6J 43
Pugh Cres. WS2: Wals 7E 38
Pughe's Cl. LE10: Burb 4A 92
Pugh Rd. B6: Aston 2A 102
WV14: Bils 6L 53
WV14: Cose 7F 52
Pugin Cl. WV6: Pert 6D 34
Pugin Gdns. B23: Erd 1D 80
Pullman Cl. B77: Glas 7G 33
DY13: Stour S 5G 183
Pulman Cl. B97: Redd 5C 212
Puma Way CV1: Cov . . .8D 152 (7D 6)
Pumphouse Cl. CV6: Longf 3H 131
Pumphouse La. B45: B Grn 1F 188
B60: B'wll 1F 188
B97: Redd, Up Ben 8H 211
Pumphouse Way B69: O'bry 5F 98
Pump La. CV7: Fill 7B 108
Pump St. DY10: Kidd 5L 157
WV2: E'shll 2G 53
Puppy Grn. DY4: Tip 4A 76
Purbeck Cl. B63: Hale 8K 117
Purbeck Cft. B32: Harb 4M 119
Purbrook B77: Wiln 1E 46
Purbrook Rd. WV1: Wolv 1F 52
Purcell Av. CV11: Nun 2A 112
WS13: Lich 7H 13
Purcell Cl. CV32: Lea S 1A 224
Purcell Ho. DY11: Kidd 3F 156
Purcell Rd. CV6: Cov 1H 153
Purcel Rd. WV10: Bush 1D 36
Purdy Rd. WV14: Bils 7L 53
Purefoy Rd. B13: Mose 4C 144
CV3: Cov 1D 174
Purley Chase La. CV9: Man 7H 65
Purley Gro. B23: Erd 4A 80
Purley Vw. CV9: Man 3M 65
Purlieu La. CV8: Ken 4D 198
Purnells Way B93: Know 4G 169
Purser Dr. CV34: Warw 5B 222
Purshall Cl. B97: Redd 6C 212
PURSHULL GREEN 5A 186
Purshull Grn. La.
WR9: Elmb 7L 185
Purslet Rd. WV1: Wolv 8G 37
Purslow Gro. B31: N'fld 7A 142
Purton M. CV31: Lea S 3C 224
Putney Av. B20: Hand 8J 79
Putney La. B62: Roms 7A 140
Putney Rd. B20: Hand 8H 79
Putney Wlk. B37: F'bri 6H 105
Puxton Dr. DY11: Kidd 8K 135
Puxton La. DY11: Kidd 2J 157
PYE GREEN 1G 9
Pye Grn. Rd. WS11: Cann 7D 8
WS12: Hed 3E 8
PYEGREEN VALLEY 3G 9
Pyeharps Rd. LE10: Burb 4L 91
Pype Hayes Cl. B24: Erd 5K 81
Pype Hayes Rd. B24: Erd 5K 81
Pype Marshbrook Rd.
B24: Erd 5K 81
Pyree Sq. CV34: Warw 5B 222
Pytchley Ho. B20: Hand 6F 78
Pytchley Rd. CV22: Rugby 8C 180
Pytman Dr. B76: Walm 2A 82
Pyt Pk. CV5: Cov 5J 151

Q

Quadrangle, The
B30: B'vlle 3F 142
B90: Shir 1L 167
Quadrant, The
CV1: Cov 7C 152 (6B 6)
CV11: Nun 6L 89
DY3: Sed 8D 52
Quadrille Lawns WV9: Pend 7M 21
Quail Grn. WV6: Tett 7F 34
Quail Pk. Dr. DY10: Kidd 7A 158
Quaker Cl. CV13: Fen D 3G 67
Qualcast Rd. WV1: Wolv 7F 36
Quantock Cl. B45: Fran 7H 141
B63: Hale 7K 117
WS8: Wals W 5G 27

Quantock Dr.—Ravenstone

Quantock Dr. CV10: Nun 6B 88
DY10: Kidd 3A 158
Quantock Rd. DY8: Amb 3B 116
Quantry La. DY9: Belb 2L 161
Quarrington Gro. B14: K Hth ...6A 144
Quarry, The DY10: Kidd 1M 157
QUARRY BANK 8G 97
Quarry Bank DY11: Hartl 7A 184
Quarry Brow DY3: Up Gor 4E 74
Quarry Cl. CV21: N'bld A 2M 179
CV35: Leek W 2F 216
WS6: C Hay 6E 14
Quarryfield La.
CV1: Cov 8E 152 (7F 6)
Quarry Flds. CV35: Leek W ...2F 216
Quarry Hill B63: Hale 7M 117
B77: Wiln 2F 46
Quarry Hills La. WS14: Lich 4K 19
Quarry Ho. B45: Rubery 1F 162
Quarry Ho. Cl. B45: Fran 8F 140
Quarry La. B31: N'fld 6M 141
B61: B'gve 1K 209
B63: Hale 7M 117
CV9: Man 4L 65
CV11: Nun 8M 89
CV35: Row 8B 196
Quarry Pk. Rd. DY8: Stourb ...1A 138
Quarry Ri. B69: Tiv 1B 98
Quarry Rd. B29: W Cas 8M 119
CV8: Ken 3E 198
DY2: Neth 7H 97
Quarry St. CV32: Lea S 1J 223
Quarry Wlk. B45: Redn 2G 163
Quarrywood Gro. CV2: Cov 5G 153
Quarry Yd. CV10: Nun 5C 88
Quasar Cen. WS1: Wals 7L 39
Quatford Gdns. WV10: Wolv 4E 36
Quayle Gro. DY8: Word 6K 95
Quayside B18: Win G 4G 101
Quayside Cl. B69: O'bry 1E 98
Quayside Dr. WS2: Wals 1J 55
Qube 4C 4
Queen Eleanors Dr.
B93: Know 1H 169
Queen Elizabeth Av.
WS2: Wals 6F 38
Queen Elizabeth Ct.
B19: Hock 3H 101
Queen Elizabeth Rd.
B45: Fran 7E 140
CV10: Nun 3C 88
DY10: Kidd 3B 158
Queen Isabel's Av. CV3: Cov ...1D 174
Queen Margaret's Rd.
CV4: Canly 1H 173
Queen Mary's Rd. CV6: Cov 1D 152
CV12: Bed 4J 111
Queen Mary St. WS1: Wals 3K 55
Queen Mother Ct.
B30: B'vlle 1D 142
Queen Mother Gdns.
B17: Harb 3A 120
Queen Philippa St.
CV3: Cov 3D 174
Queens Arc.
WV1: Wolv 7C 36 (4J 7)
CV11: Nun 5J 89
Queens Av. B14: K Hth 1L 143
B90: Shir 8H 145
B18: Hock 3F 100
B69: Tiv 8B 76
Queensbridge Rd.
B13: Mose 7K 121
Queens Cl. CV8: Ken 6F 198
B24: Erd 7F 80
B67: Smeth 4A 100
Queen's Cotts. B97: Redd 5B 212
Queens Ct. B1: Birm 8J 101 (7D 4)
B3: Birm 5K 101 (2E 4)
B91: Sol 5D 146
CV11: Nun 5G 89
WV10: Wolv 3G 37
Queens Ct. Trad. Est.
B70: W Brom 6F 76
Queens Cres. DY8: Amb 2A 116
WV14: Cose 8G 53
Queen's Cross DY1: Dud 1H 97
Queens Dr. B65: Row R 5D 98
CV35: Row 8A 196
B5: Birm 7K 101 (6F 4)
B30: K Nor 5G 143
WS7: Chase 4F 16
Queens Dr., The B62: Hale 4C 118
Queensferry Cl. CV22: Bil 1J 205
Queens Gdns. B23: Erd 2B 80
DY2: Neth 5J 97
WS10: W'bry 6E 54
WV8: Cod 6F 20
WV14: Bils 2K 53
Queen's Head Rd.
B21: Hand 2E 100
Queens Hill DY9: Belb 2D 160
Queens Hospital Cl.
B15: Birm 8J 101 (8C 4)
Queensland Av. CV5: Cov 7M 151
Queens Lea WV12: W'hall 4C 38
Queens Pde. WS3: Blox 8H 25
Queen's Pk. CV31: Lea S 3L 223
Queen's Pk. Flats LE10: Hinc ...1L 91
(off Queen's Rd.)
Queen's Pk. Rd. B32: Harb 3M 119
Queens Pk. Ter. LE10: Hinc 1L 91
Queen Sq. WV1: Wolv 7C 36 (4J 7)
Queen's Ride B5: Edg 5J 121
Queens Rd. B23: Erd 6C 80
B67: Smeth 5K 99
CV8: Ken 6F 198
CV9: Ath 1L 65
DY8: Stourb 3M 115
DY13: Stour S 8F 182
WS5: Wals 3B 56
B6: Aston 1A 102
B26: Yard 8M 103
CV1: Cov 7B 152 (6A 6)
CV11: Nun 5G 89
CV23: Bret 2L 177
DY3: Sed 1E 74
DY4: Tip 4M 75
LE10: Hinc 1L 91
WS4: Rus 2C 40
Queens Sq. B70: W Brom 6K 77
CV34: Warw 3D 222
WS11: Cann 8E 8
Queen St. B12: Bal H 4B 122
B63: Hale 5A 118
B64: Crad H 8K 97
B69: O'bry 1G 99
B70: W Brom 6K 77
B72: S Cold 5J 59
B96: A'wd B 8E 220
B98: Redd 5E 212
CV1: Cov 5D 152 (2E 6)
CV12: Bed 7J 111
CV21: Rugby 6A 180
CV32: Cubb 4D 218
CV32: Lea S 8A 218
DY4: Tip 1M 75
DY5: P'ntt 3C 96
(not continuous)
DY5: Quar B 1G 117
(not continuous)
DY6: K'wfrd 2K 95
DY8: Stourb 4M 115
DY8: Word 6K 95
DY10: Kidd 2L 157
LE9: Barw 3B 70
WS2: Wals 8K 39
WS6: C Hay 6D 14
WS7: Chase 4F 16
WS9: Wals W 7E 26
WS10: Darl 1D 54
WS10: W'bry 6E 54
WS11: Cann 4G 9
(Bradford St.)
WS11: Cann 8D 8
(Newhall St.)
WS13: Lich 2G 19
WV1: Wolv 7D 36 (4K 7)
(not continuous)
WV14: Bils 4L 53
(Bridge St.)
WV14: Bils 5B 54
(Tudor Rd.)
Queen St. Ind. Est.
WS7: Chase 4F 16
Queen St. Pas. DY5: Quar B ...1G 117
Queens Way DY12: Bew 4C 156
B78: Dord 3M 47
Queensway B1: Birm 7J 101
B6: Witt 6M 79
B63: Hale 6A 118
B68: O'bry 8H 99
B74: S'tly 1A 58
B79: Tam 1A 32
CV9: Hurl 1C 64
CV10: Nun 3K 89
CV31: Lea S 3L 223
DY9: W'cte 7E 116
LE9: Barw 2B 70
Queensway Cl. B68: O'bry 8H 99
Queensway Mall B63: Hale 6B 118
(off Hagley Mall)
Queensway Trad. Est. B5: Birm ...4J 5
CV34: Warw 3L 223
Queenswood Ct. CV7: Ker E 5K 129
Queenswood Rd. B13: Mose 5A 122
B75: Four O 8H 43
Queen Victoria Rd.
CV1: Cov 7B 152 (6B 6)
(Ringway Queens)
CV1: Cov 6B 152 (4A 6)
(Spon St.)
Queen Victoria St.
CV21: Rugby 6C 180
Quenby Dr. DY1: Dud 6G 75
Quendale WV5: Wom 3E 72
Quentin Dr. DY1: Dud 1F 96
Queslade Cl. B43: Gt Barr 6E 56
QUESLETT 7K 57
Queslett Pk. Golf Cen. 1J 79
(off Booth's La.)
Queslett Rd. B43: Gt Barr 8F 56
(not continuous)
Queslett Rd. E. B74: S'tly 4L 57
Quibury Cl. B98: Redd 6M 213
Quicksand La. WS9: A'rdge 5F 40
Quillets Rd. DY8: Word 6J 95
Quilletts Cl. CV6: Cov 8G 131
Quilter Cl. WS2: Wals 6F 38
WV14: Cose 1G 75
Quilter Rd. B24: Erd 7H 81
Quince B77: Amin 6H 33
Quincey Dr. B24: Erd 6J 81
Quincy Ri. DY5: Brie H 2C 116
Quinn Cl. CV3: Cov 2G 175
Quinneys La. B98: Redd 3H 221
QUINTON 3J 119
Quinton Av. WS6: Gt Wyr 6F 14
Quinton Bus. Pk.
B32: Quin 4G 119
Quinton Cl. B92: Sol 6D 124
B98: Redd 8K 213
Quintondale B90: Shir 1J 167
Quinton Expressway
B32: Quin 5H 119
Quinton La. B32: Quin 3J 119
Quinton Lodge CV3: Cov 2D 174
Quinton Pde. CV3: Cov 2D 174
Quinton Pk. CV3: Cov 2D 174
Quinton Pl. WS11: Nort C 5A 16
Quinton Rd. B17: Harb 6A 120
CV1: Cov 8D 152 (8D 6)
CV3: Cov 8D 152
Quinton Rd. W. B32: Quin 4H 119
Quilsnam Ct. B13: Mose 7B 122
Quonian's La. WS13: Lich 1H 19
Quorn Cres. DY8: Word 6J 95
Quorn Gro. B24: Erd 7H 81
Quorn Ho. B20: Hand 6F 78
Quorn Way CV3: Bin 1L 175

R

Rabbit La. CV12: Bed 5C 110
WV10: F'stne 2G 23
Rabone La. B66: Smeth 3B 100
Raby Cl. B69: Tiv 1M 97
Raby St. WV2: Wolv 1D 52 (7L 7)
Racecourse La. DY8: Stourb ...7L 115
Racecourse Rd. WV6: Wolv 4A 36
Racecourse Rd. Ind. Est.
WV6: Wolv 4A 36
Racemeadow Cres.
DY2: Neth 8J 97
Racemeadow Rd. CV9: Ath 8L 49
Raceway, The 8M 77
Rachael Gdns. WS10: W'bry 5H 55
Rachel Cl. DY4: Tip 8C 54
Rachel Gdns. B29: S Oak 7D 120
Radbourn Dr. B74: S Cold 2J 59
Radbourne Cl. CV47: Sou 6J 225
Radbourne Dr. B63: Crad 2G 117
Radbourne Rd. B90: Shir 6K 145
Radbrook Way CV31: Lea S 3D 224
Radcliffe Dr. B62: Quin 3E 118
Radcliffe Gdns. CV31: Lea S ...3A 224
Radcliffe Ho. CV4: Canly 5H 173
Radcliffe Rd. CV5: Cov 1M 173
Radcliffe Twr. B12: Birm 1M 121
Raddens Rd. B62: Hale 6F 118
Raddington Dr. B92: Olton 1K 145
Raddlebarn Farm Dr.
B29: S Oak 8F 120
Raddlebarn Rd. B29: S Oak 8E 120
RADFORD 4B 152
Radford Av. DY10: Kidd 2L 157
Radford Circ. CV6: Cov 5B 152
Radford Cl. CV9: Ath 7L 49
WS5: Wals 6A 56
Radford Dr. WS4: S'fld 7C 26
Radford Hall CV31: Rad S 3E 224
Radford Ho. B97: Redd 5A 212
CV6: Cov 2A 152
Radford La. WV3: Wolv 3F 50
WV4: Lwr P 3F 50
Radford Ri. B91: Sol 4E 146
Radford Rd. B29: W Cas 3A 142
B48: A'chu 3B 190
CV1: Cov 2A 152 (1A 6)
CV6: Cov 2A 152 (1A 6)
CV31: Lea S 2A 224
RADFORD SEMELE 4E 224
Radley Ct. B26: Sheld 2C 124
Radley Dr. CV10: Nun 8G 89
Radley Gro. B29: W Cas 7A 120
Radley Rd. DY9: W'cte 5F 116
WS4: Rus 2C 40
Radleys, The
B33: Kitts G, Sheld 2C 124
Radley's Wlk. B33: Sheld 2C 124
Radlow Cres. B37: Mars G 1H 125
Radmore Cl. WS7: C Ter 1D 16
Radmore Rd. LE10: Hinc 6K 69
Radnell Ho. B69: O'bry 3D 98
Radnor Cl. B45: Fran 7H 141
Radnor Ct. WS9: Wals W 5F 26
Radnor Cft. WS5: Wals 6C 56
Radnor Dr. CV10: Nun 7D 88
Radnor Grn. B71: W Brom 2J 77
Radnor Ri. WS12: Hed 5H 9
Radnor Rd. B20: Hand 1H 101
B68: O'bry 2H 119
DY3: Sed 1C 74
Radnor St. B18: Hock 3G 101
Radnor Wlk. CV2: W'grve S ...1M 153
Radstock Av. B36: Hodg H 2J 103
Radstock Rd. WV12: W'hall 8C 24
Radway Cl. B98: Redd 3H 213
Radway Rd. B90: Shir 2L 167
Raeburn Rd. B43: Gt Barr 5J 57
Raford Rd. B23: Erd 3D 80
Ragees Rd. DY6: K'wfrd 5M 95
Raglan Av. B66: Smeth 5C 100
WV6: Pert 6F 34
Raglan Cl. CV11: Nun 6K 89
DY3: Sed 2B 74
WS9: A'rdge 6M 41
Raglan Ct. B60: B'gve 8A 188
CV1: Cov 6E 152
Raglan Gro. CV8: Ken 4H 199
Raglan Rd. B5: Edg 3K 121
B21: Hand 1C 100
B66: Smeth 5C 100
Raglan St. CV1: Cov 6E 152 (4F 6)
DY5: Brie H 5C 96
WV3: Wolv 7B 36 (4G 7)
Raglan Way B37: Chel W 7K 105
Ragley Cl. B93: Know 2H 169
WS3: Blox 8G 25
Ragley Cres. B60: B'gve 1A 210
Ragley Dr. B26: Sheld 3C 124
B43: Gt Barr 7D 56
WV13: W'hall 1M 53
Ragley Ho. B97: Redd 5A 212
Ragley Wlk. B65: Row R 6C 98
Ragley Way CV11: Nun 7M 89
Raglis Cl. B97: Redd 8A 212
Ragnall Av. B33: Sheld 2D 124
Raikes La.
WS14: C'fld, Shens 2C 28
Rail Bri. Est. B70: W Brom 8G 77
Railswood Dr. WS3: Pels 6A 26
Railway Cl. B80: Stud 5K 221
Railway Dr.
WV1: Wolv 7D 36 (3L 7)
WV14: Bils 4L 53
Railway La. WS7: C Ter 8E 10
WV13: W'hall 8A 38
Railway Rd. B20: Hand 7M 79
B73: S Cold 4H 59
Railwayside Cl. B66: Smeth 2L 99
(off Forest Cl.)
Railway St. B70: W Brom 5H 77
CV23: Long L 5G 179
DY4: Tip 4C 76
WS11: Cann 1E 14
WS11: Nort C 4A 16
WV1: Wolv 7D 36 (3L 7)
WV13: W'hall 8A 38
WV14: Bils 4L 53
Railway Ter. B7: Nech 3B 102
B42: Gt Barr 3F 78
CV12: Bed 7J 111
CV21: Rugby 6B 180
WS10: W'bry 7F 54
Railway Vw. B10: Small H 2C 122
Railway Wlk. WS11: Cann 1F 14
WS11: Nort C 5A 16
Railwharf Sidings DY2: Neth 5K 97
Rainbow St.
WV2: Wolv 1C 52 (8K 7)
WV14: Cose 6K 53
Rainford Way B38: K Nor 1C 164
(off Nearhill Rd.)
Rainham Cl. DY4: Tip 4K 75
RAINSBROOK 3C 206
Rainsbrook Av. CV22: Hillm 1E 206
Rainsbrook Cl. CV47: Sou 5K 225
Rainsbrook Dr. B90: M'path 3M 167
CV11: Nun 8M 89
Rainscar B77: Wiln 2H 47
Raison Av. CV11: Nun 1M 89
Rake Hill WS7: Burn 1H 17
Rake Way B15: Birm ...8H 101 (7B 4)
Raleigh Cl. B21: Hand 8B 78
LE10: Hinc 5K 69
Raleigh Cft. B43: Gt Barr 6E 56
Raleigh Ind. Est. B21: Hand 8B 78
Raleigh Rd. B9: Bord G 6D 102
CV2: Cov 6H 153
WV14: Bils 6M 53
Raleigh St. B71: W Brom 5J 77
WS2: Wals 7J 39
Ralph Barlow Gdns.
B44: K'sdng 1B 80
Ralph Cres. B78: K'bry 3C 62
Ralph Gdns. B44: K'sdng 1B 80
Ralph Rd. B8: Salt 5D 102
B90: Shir 5H 145
CV6: Cov 4M 151
Ralphs Mdw. B32: Bart G 7K 119
Ralston Cl. WS3: Blox 5G 25
Ramblers Way B75: R'ley 6L 43
Rambures Cl. CV34: H'cte 6M 223
Ramillies Cres. WS6: Gt Wyr 8F 14
Ramp Rd. B26: Birm A 4J 125
Ramsay Cres. CV5: Alle 2H 151
Ramsay Rd. B68: O'bry 8J 99
Ramsden Av. CV10: Nun 2C 88
Ramsden Cl. B29: W Cas 2B 142
Ramsden Rd. CV9: Man 2A 66
Ramsey Cl. B45: Fran 8E 140
B71: W Brom 1M 77
LE10: Hinc 8H 69
Ramsey Ho. WS2: Wals 2J 55
Ramsey Rd. B7: Nech 2C 102
CV31: Lea S 2B 224
DY4: Tip 2L 75
WS2: Wals 4G 39
Ramshill La. B94: Dan G 2K 215
B95: Ullen 2K 215
Ranby Rd. CV2: Cov 5F 152
Randall Av. B48: A'chu 3A 190
Randall Cl. DY6: K'wfrd 5M 95
Randall Lines Ho.
WV1: Wolv 6C 36 (1J 7)
Randall Rd. CV8: Ken 6F 198
Randle Dr. B75: R'ley 6J 43
Randle Rd. CV10: Nun 5D 88
DY9: Lye 5C 116
Randle St. CV6: Cov 4A 152 (1A 6)
Randolph Cl. CV31: Lea S 3C 224
Randwick Gro. B44: Gt Barr 8K 57
Ranelagh Ho. WV2: Wolv 2D 52
(off Blakenhall Gdns.)
Ranelagh Rd. WV2: Wolv 3C 52
Ranelagh St. CV31: Lea S 3A 224
Ranelagh Ter. CV31: Lea S 3M 223
Range Mdw. Cl. CV32: Lea S ...6J 217
Rangemoor CV3: W'hall 3K 175
Rangeview Cl. B74: S'tly 3M 57
Range Way B78: K'bry 4D 62
Rangeways Rd. DY6: K'wfrd 5M 95
DY11: Kidd 1G 157
Rangeworthy Cl. B97: Redd 2C 220
Rangifer Rd. B78: Faz 1M 45
Rangoon Rd. B92: Sol 5E 124
Rankine Cl. CV21: N'bld A 2K 179
Ranleigh Av. DY6: K'wfrd 5M 95
Rannoch Cl. DY5: Brie H 1B 116
DY13: Stour S 2E 182
LE10: Hinc 1H 91
Rannoch Dr. CV10: Nun 4C 88
Rannock Cl. CV3: Bin 7A 154
Ranscombe Dr. DY3: Gorn 7D 74
Ransome Rd. CV7: New A 1G 109
Ransom Rd. B23: Erd 5C 80
CV6: Cov 1E 152
Ranton Bus. Pk. WS11: Cann 7G 9
Ranulf Cft. CV3: Cov 2C 174
Ranulf St. CV3: Cov 2C 174
Ranworth Ri. WV4: Penn 5D 52
Raphael Cl. CV5: Cov 6J 151
Rashwood Cl. B94: H'ley H 3B 194
Ratcliffe Cl. DY3: Sed 2F 74
Ratcliffe Ct. CV10: Nun 5C 88
Ratcliffe La. CV9: S Mag 5M 49
Ratcliffe Rd. B91: Sol 2C 146
CV9: Ath 1L 65
LE10: Burb 3M 91
WV11: Wed 3A 38
Ratcliffe St. CV9: Ath 1K 65
Ratcliff Wlk. B69: O'bry 2G 99
Ratcliff Way DY4: Tip 3D 76
Rathbone Cl. B5: Bal H 2L 121
CV7: Ker E 3M 129
CV21: Hillm 1G 207
WV14: Bils 4K 53
Rathbone Rd. B67: Smeth 7M 99
Rathlin Cl. WV9: Pend 6A 22
Rathlin Cft. B36: Cas B 3H 105
Rathmore Cl. DY8: Stourb 7K 115
Rathwell Cl. WV9: Pend 7A 22
Ratliffe Rd. CV22: Rugby 2M 205
Rattle Cft. B33: Stech 6L 103
Raveloe Dr. CV11: Nun 8K 89
Ravenall Cl. B34: S End 2B 104
Raven Cl. WS6: C Hay 7D 14
WS12: Hed 5L 9
WS12: Hunt 2C 8
(Foxfields Way)
WS12: Hunt 5C 8
(Highland Rd.)
Raven Ct. DY5: Brie H 7D 96
(off Lit. Potter St.)
Raven Cragg Rd. CV5: Cov 1L 173
Raven Cres. WV11: Wed 1M 37
Ravenfield Cl. B8: W End 4F 102
Ravenglass CV21: Brow 2D 180
Ravenhayes La. B32: Fran 2G 141
Raven Hays Rd. B31: Longb 7J 141
Ravenhill Dr. WV8: Cod 6G 21
Ravenhurst Dr. B43: Gt Barr 6E 56
Ravenhurst M. B23: Erd 6E 80
Ravenhurst Rd. B17: Harb 2C 120
Raven Rd. WS5: Wals 3B 56
Ravensbank Bus. Pk.
B98: Redd 3M 213
Ravensbank Dr. B98: Redd 2J 213
Ravensbourne Gro.
WV13: W'hall 7C 38
Ravens Ct. WS8: Bwnhls 2F 26
Ravenscroft DY8: Woll 3J 115
Ravenscroft Rd. B92: Olton 1A 146
WV12: W'hall 4B 38
Ravensdale Av. CV32: Lea S 7J 217
Ravensdale Cl. WS5: Wals 2B 56
Ravensdale Gdns. WS5: Wals 3B 56
Ravensdale Rd.
B10: Small H 2F 122
CV2: Cov 6J 153
Ravenshaw B91: Sol 7H 147
Ravenshaw La. B91: Sol 5G 147
(not continuous)
Ravenshaw Rd. B16: Edg 7C 100
Ravenshaw Way B91: Sol 7G 147
Ravenshill Rd. B14: Yard W 5C 144
Ravensholme WV6: Tett 7F 34
Ravenside Retail Pk.
B24: Erd 6L 81
Ravensitch Wlk. DY5: Brie H 8E 96
Ravensmere Rd. B98: Redd 8H 213
Ravensthorpe Cl. CV3: Bin 1L 175
Ravenstone B77: Wiln 1H 47

Richardson Way—Romilly Av.

Richardson Way
CV2: W'grve S 1B 154
Richards Rd. DY4: Tip 8M 53
Richards St. WS10: Darl 1D 54
Richard St. B6: Aston 4M 101
B7: Birm 4M 101 (1K 5)
B70: W Brom 6H 77
Richard St. Sth. B70: W Brom . . . 7J 77
Richard St. W. B70: W Brom . . . 7H 77
Richard Williams Rd.
WS10: W'bry 7H 55
Richborough Dr. DY1: Dud 6E 74
Rich Cl. CV34: Warw 2G 223
Riches St. WV6: Wolv 6M 35
Richford Gro. B33: Kitts G 7D 104
Richmere Ct. WV6: Tett 6H 35
Richmond Ashton Dr.
DY4: Tip 4A 76
Richmond Av. B12: Bal H 4M 121
WV3: Wolv 8M 35
Richmond Cl. B20: Hand 6G 79
B47: H'wd 2B 166
B79: Tam 4A 32
WS11: Cann 4G 9
Richmond Ct. B15: Edg 8B 4
B29: W Cas 2C 142
B63: Hale 6L 117
B68: O'bry 4J 99
B72: W Grn 2H 81
DY9: Pedm 8B 116
(off Redlake Rd.)
Richmond Cft. B42: Gt Barr 3F 78
Richmond Dr. WS14: Lich 2K 19
WV3: Wolv 8L 35
WV6: Pert 5F 34
Richmond Gdns. DY8: Amb . . . 2M 115
WV5: Wom 4G 73
Richmond Gro. DY8: Woll 1L 115
Richmond Hill B68: O'bry 4J 99
Richmond Hill Gdns.
B15: Edg 2E 120
Richmond Hill Rd. B15: Edg . . . 3E 120
Richmond Ho. B37: Chel W 8J 105
Richmond Pk. DY6: W Hth 1J 95
Richmond Pl. B14: K Hth 1M 143
Richmond Rd. B18: Hock 3H 101
B33: Stech 7K 103
B45: Rubery 2E 162
B66: Smeth 7A 100
B73: S Cold 3H 59
B92: Olton 8L 123
CV9: Ath 2K 65
CV11: Nun 6G 89
CV21: Rugby 7C 180
DY2: Dud 1J 97
DY3: Sed 2E 74
DY12: Bew 1B 156
LE10: Hinc 6J 69
WV3: Wolv 7L 35
Richmond St. B63: Hale 5A 118
B70: W Brom 3F 76
CV2: Cov 6G 153
WS1: Wals 8M 39
Richmond St. Sth.
B70: W Brom 4E 76
Richmond Way B37: Chel W . . . 6J 105
Rickard Cl. B93: Know 4E 168
Ricketts Pl. DY12: Bew 6B 156
Rickman Dr.
B15: Birm 1K 121 (8F 4)
Rickyard Cl. B25: Yard 8K 103
B29: W Cas 3A 142
B78: Pole 2K 49
Rickyard La. B98: Redd 4K 213
Rickyard Piece B32: Quin 5L 119
Riddfield Rd. B36: Hodg H 1L 103
Ridding Gdns. B78: Pole 1A 48
Ridding La. WS10: W'bry 7F 54
Riddings, The B33: Stech 5L 103
B76: Walm 1B 82
B77: Amin 4E 32
CV5: Cov 2K 173
CV9: Gren 7C 48
DY9: W'cte 7D 116
WV10: Bush 2G 37
Riddings Cl. DY12: Bew 4C 156
Riddings Cres. WS3: Pels 5M 25
Riddings Hill CV7: Bal C 2J 171
Riddings La. CV9: Gren 6C 48
Riddon Dr. LE10: Hinc 1H 91
Rideswell Gro. CV31: W'nsh . . . 8A 224
RIDGACRE 3K 119
Ridgacre Ent. Pk.
B71: W Brom 3H 77
Ridgacre La. B32: Quin 3H 119
Ridgacre Rd. B32: Quin 3H 119
(not continuous)
B71: W Brom 3H 77
Ridgacre Rd. W. B32: Quin . . . 3G 119
Ridge Cl. B13: Mose 3C 144
WS2: Wals 6D 38
Ridge Ct. CV5: Alle 3G 151
Ridge Dr. CV21: Rugby 5D 180
Ridgefield Rd. B62: B'hth 1C 118
Ridge Gro. DY9: Lye 4C 116
Ridge Hill DY8: Word 6M 95
RIDGE LANE 7G 65
Ridge La. CV10: Ridge L 7G 65
WV11: Wed 2K 37
Ridgeley Cl. CV34: Warw 7E 216
Ridgemount Dr. B38: K Nor . . . 2D 164
Ridge Rd. DY6: K'wfrd 4H 95
Ridge St. DY8: Woll 3J 115
Ridgethorpe CV3: W'hall 4L 175
Ridgewater Cl. B45: Redn 3H 163
Ridge Way B32: Quin 5G 119
Ridgeway B17: Edg 7B 100
WS9: A'rdge 5H 41
Ridgeway, The B23: Erd 3A 80
CV23: Barby, Kils 8L 207
CV34: Warw 8G 217
DY3: Sed 3D 74
DY13: Stour S 4F 182
LE10: Burb 3K 91
WS7: Burn 4G 17
Ridgeway Av. B62: Quin 3G 119
CV3: Cov 3C 174
Ridgeway Cl. B80: Stud 7L 221
Ridgeway Ct. WS2: Wals 8F 38
Ridgeway Dr. WV4: Penn 6M 51
Ridgeway La.
CV33: H'ham 6M 219
Ridgeway Rd. DY4: Tip 1A 76
DY8: Word 7M 95
Ridgeway Trad. Est.
B96: A'wd B 7E 220
Ridgewood B34: S End 3B 104
Ridgewood Av. DY8: Woll 2J 115
Ridgewood Cl. CV32: Lea S . . . 8J 217
WS1: Wals 1M 55
Ridgewood Dr. B75: Four O 8H 43
Ridgewood Gdns.
B44: Gt Barr 2L 79
Ridgewood Ri. B77: Amin 4G 33
Ridgley Rd. CV4: Tile H 8E 150
Ridgmont Cft. B32: Quin 4L 119
Riding Cl. B71: W Brom 1M 77
Ridings, The WS11: Cann 1F 14
Ridings Brook Dr. WS11: Cann . . 7G 9
Ridings La. B98: Redd 2H 213
Riding Way WV12: W'hall 3D 38
Ridley La. B46: Neth W 4G 85
Ridley St. B1: Birm 8J 101 (8D 4)
Ridpool Rd. B33: Kitts G 6B 104
Ridware Ho. *WS13: Lich 8L 13*
(off Hobs Rd.)
Rifle Range Rd. DY11: Kidd . . . 6H 157
Rifle St. WV14: Cose 6G 75
Rigby Cl. CV34: H'cte 5K 223
Rigby Dr. WS11: Cann 5E 8
Rigby La. B60: B'gve 1B 210
Rigby St. WS10: W'bry 8F 54
Rigdale Cl. CV2: Cov 7L 153
Righton Ho. B77: Wiln 8D 32
Riland Av. B75: S Cold 4K 59
Riland Ct. B72: W Grn 2J 81
Riland Gro. B75: S Cold 4J 59
Riland Ind. Est. B75: S Cold . . . 4K 59
Riland Rd. B75: S Cold 4K 59
Riley B77: Glas 6E 32
Riley Cl. CV8: Ken 5J 199
LE9: S Stan 8K 71
Riley Ct. CV21: Rugby 6C 180
Riley Cres. WV3: Wolv 3M 51
Riley Dr. B36: Cas B 8G 83
Riley Ho. CV1: Cov 7C 152 (6C 6)
Riley Rd. B14: Yard W 6D 144
Riley Sq. CV2: Cov 8H 131
Riley St. WV13: W'hall 7B 38
Rills, The LE10: Hinc 7L 69
Rilstone Rd. B32: Harb 4M 119
Rindleford Av. WV4: Penn 3J 51
Ring, The B25: Yard 1J 123
Ringhills Rd. WV8: Bilb 7H 21
Ringinglow Rd. B44: Gt Barr . . . 7J 57
Ringmere Av. B36: Cas B 1B 104
Ring Rd. WS7: C Ter 2D 16
Ring Rd. Nth. B15: Edg 5F 120
Ring Rd. St Andrews
WV1: Wolv 7B 36 (4G 7)
Ring Rd. St Davids
WV1: Wolv 7D 36 (4L 7)
Ring Rd. St Georges
WV2: Wolv 8D 36 (6K 7)
Ring Rd. St Johns
WV2: Wolv 8C 36 (6H 7)
Ring Rd. St Marks
WV3: Wolv 8B 36 (5G 7)
Ring Rd. St Patricks
WV1: Wolv 6D 36 (2K 7)
Ring Rd. St Peters
WV1: Wolv 7C 36 (3H 7)
Ring Rd. Sth. B15: Edg 5F 120
Ringswood Rd. B92: Olton 5L 123
Ringway WS11: Cann 8E 8
Ringway, The DY10: Kidd 3L 157
Ringway Bus. Pk. B7: Birm . . . 4A 102
Ringway Hillcross
CV1: Cov 6B 152 (4A 6)
Ringway Ind. Est. WS13: Lich . . . 6J 13
Ringway Queens
CV1: Cov 7B 152 (6A 6)
Ringway Rudge
CV1: Cov 7B 152 (5A 6)
Ringway St Johns
CV1: Cov 7D 152 (6D 6)
Ringway St Nicholas
CV1: Cov 6C 152 (3B 6)
Ringway St Patrick's
CV1: Cov 8C 152 (7B 6)
Ringway Swanswell
CV1: Cov 6D 152 (3D 6)
Ringway Whitefriars
CV1: Cov 7D 152 (4E 6)
Ringwood Av. WS9: A'rdge 4H 41
Ringwood Dr. B45: Fran 8G 141
Ringwood Highway
CV2: W'grve S 7L 131
Ringwood Rd. WV10: Bush 8D 22
Rinill Gro. CV31: Lea S 3D 224
Ripley Cl. B69: Tiv 1M 97
Ripley Gro. B23: Erd 4B 80
Riplingham CV32: Lea S 7M 217
Ripon Cl. CV5: Alle 1G 151
Ripon Dr. B71: W Brom 8K 55
Ripon Rd. B14: Yard W 5C 144
WS2: Wals 7H 39
WV10: Oxl 2C 36
Rippingille Rd. B43: Gt Barr . . . 5J 57
Ripple Rd. B30: Stir 2H 143
Risborough Cl. CV5: Cov 6J 151
Risborough Ho. B31: Longb . . . 1M 163
Rischale Way WS4: Rus 1D 40
Risdale Cl. CV32: Lea S 7K 217
Rise, The B37: Mars G 2G 125
B42: Gt Barr 1G 79
B48: Hopw 5B 164
DY6: K'wfrd 4L 95
Rise Av. B45: Redn 2G 163
Riseley Cres. B5: Bal H 3K 121
Rising Brook WV6: Tett 5H 35
Rising La. B93: Bad C 4L 195
B94: Lapw 5H 195
Rissington Av. B29: S Oak . . . 1G 143
Ritchie Cl. B13: Mose 8A 122
Rivendell Ct. B28: Hall G 8E 122
Rivendell Gdns. WV6: Tett 4H 35
Riverbank Rd. WV13: W'hall . . . 7D 38
River Brook Dr. B30: Stir 1H 143
River Cl. CV12: Bed 8F 110
CV32: Lea S 1K 223
River Ct. CV1: Cov 6B 152
River Dr. B78: Tam 6A 32
CV9: Ath 7K 49
Riverdrive B77: Tam 6A 32
Riverfield Gro. B77: Tam 4D 32
Riverford Cft. CV4: Canly 5K 173
River Lee Rd. B11: Tys 4E 122
Rivermead CV11: Nun 5G 89
Rivermead Pk. B34: S End 4A 104
Riversdale CV32: Lea S 1L 223
Riversdale Rd. B14: Yard W . . . 6D 144
CV9: Ath 1M 65
RIVERSIDE 4F 212
Riverside B80: Stud 5L 221
CV9: With 2B 66
CV32: Lea S 1L 223
Riverside Cvn. Pk.
DY12: Bew 5A 156
Riverside Cl. B60: L End 3C 188
CV3: Cov 2F 174
Riverside Ct. B38: K Nor 6D 142
B46: Col 2A 106
(off Prossers Wlk.)
Riverside Cres. B28: Hall G . . . 5D 144
Riverside Dr. B29: S Oak 6J 121
B33: Stech 5K 103
B91: Sol 7E 146
Riverside Gdns. WV8: Bilb 5H 21
Riverside Ind. Est. B78: Faz . . . 1B 46
B98: Redd 1J 221
Riverside Nth. DY12: Bew 5B 156
Riverside Wlk. CV34: Warw . . . 3F 222
Riversleigh Dr. DY8: Word . . . 1L 115
Riversleigh Rd. CV32: Lea S . . 8J 217
Riversley Rd. CV11: Nun 6J 89
River St. B5: Birm 7A 102 (6L 5)
River Wlk. CV2: Cov 7J 131
Riverway WS10: W'bry 7H 55
Riverway Dr. DY12: Bew 5B 156
Rivington Cl. DY8: Stourb 5L 115
Rivington Cres. B44: K'sdng . . . 8C 58
Roach B77: Dost 3D 46
Roach Cl. B37: Chel W 6J 105
DY5: Brie H 4D 96
Roach Cres. WV11: Wed 1M 37
Roach Pool Cft. B16: Edg 7C 100
Road No. 1 DY10: Kidd 7L 157
DY11: Kidd 2J 183
Road No. 2 DY10: Kidd 7L 157
DY11: Kidd 2H 183
Road No. 3 DY10: Kidd 7L 157
Roadway Cl. CV12: Bed 7H 111
Roanne Ringway
CV11: Nun 5H 89
Robbins Ct. CV22: Hillm 1F 206
Robert Av. B23: Erd 3E 80
Robert Cl. B79: Tam 2M 31
CV3: W'hall 5J 175
Robert Ct. B13: Mose 7B 122
Robert Cramb Av.
CV4: Tile H 1F 172
Robert Hill Cl. CV21: Hillm . . . 8G 181
Robert Rd. B20: Hand 8H 79
CV7: Exh 1F 130
DY4: Tip 3M 75
Roberts Cl. CV23: Stret D 3F 202
WS9: Wals W 7F 26
WS10: Mox 5B 54
Roberts Ct. B24: Erd 3J 81
Roberts Grn. Rd.
DY3: Up Gor 5E 74
Roberts La. DY9: Pedm 1B 138
Robertson Cl. CV23: Clift D . . . 4G 181
LE9: S Stan 7K 71
Robertson Knoll
B36: Hodg H 2M 103
Robertsons Gdns. B7: Nech . . . 2C 102
Roberts Rd. B27: A Grn 6J 123
WS3: Wals 4M 39
WS10: W'bry 6L 55
Robert St. DY3: Lwr G 5D 74
Robert Wynd WV14: Cose 8F 52
Robeson Cl. DY4: Tip 4K 75
Robey's La.
B78: A'cte, B'moor 7K 33
Robin Cl. B36: Cas B 1G 105
B77: Two G 1C 46
DY6: K'wfrd 3A 96
WS12: Hunt 2C 8
Robin Ct. DY10: Kidd 7A 158
Robin Gro. WV11: Wed 2J 37
Robin Hood Crematorium
B90: Shir 4H 145
Robin Hood Cres.
B28: Hall G 2E 144
Robin Hood Cft. B28: Hall G . . . 3F 144
Robin Hood Island
B28: Hall G 4G 145
(off Stratford Rd.)
Robin Hood La. B28: Hall G . . . 2D 144
Robin Hood Rd. CV3: W'hall . . . 3J 175
DY5: Quar B 7F 96
Robinia B77: Amin 5G 33
Robinia Cl. CV32: Lill 8B 218
Robin Rd. B23: Erd 5E 80
Robins Bus. Pk.
DY4: W Brom 2E 76
Robins Cl. DY8: Stourb 6A 116
WS6: C Hay 8D 14
Robins Ct. B14: K Hth 8M 121
Robinsfield Dr. B31: Longb . . . 2A 164
Robins Gro. CV34: Warw 5B 222
Robins Hill Dr. B48: A'chu 4A 190
Robins La. B97: Redd 3C 212
Robinson Cl. B79: Tam 2L 31
Robinson Rd. CV12: Bed 1D 130
WS7: C Ter 8F 10
ROBINSON'S END 6A 88
Robinsons Way B76: Min 4D 82
Robinsons Way LE10: Burb 5M 91
Robins Rd. WS7: C Ter 3D 16
Robins Way CV10: Nun 6A 88
Robin Wlk. WS2: Wals 6F 38
Robotham Cl.
CV21: N'bld A 3M 179
Robottom Cl. WS2: Wals 3H 39
Robson Cl. WS8: Bwnhls 4G 27
Rocester Av. WV11: Wed 2L 37
Rochdale Wlk. B10: Small H . . . 2C 122
Roche, The WS13: Lich 8M 11
Rocheberie Way
CV22: Rugby 1M 205
Roche Rd. WS3: Blox 8F 24
Rochester Av. WS7: C Ter 2G 17
Rochester Cl. B97: Redd 1C 220
CV11: Nun 6H 89
Rochester Cft. WS2: Wals 5G 39
Rochester Rd. B31: N'fld 5A 142
CV5: Cov 1L 173
Rochester Wlk. DY10: Kidd . . . 4B 158
Rochester Way WS12: Hth H 8J 9
Roche Way WS3: Blox 8F 24
Rochford Cl. B45: Rubery 2E 162
B63: Hale 7M 117
B76: Walm 1A 82
WS2: Wals 2J 55
Rochford Ct. B90: M'path 3A 168
CV31: Lea S 2L 223
Rochford Gro. WV4: Penn 4K 51
Rock, The WV6: Tett 4K 35
Rock Av. B45: Redn 2J 163
Rock Cl. CV6: Cov 8H 131
CV10: Gall C 5M 87
Rocken End CV6: Cov 1D 152
Rocket Pool Dr. WV14: Bils 7M 53
Rockface, The 6M 101 (3K 5)
Rock Farm La. CV8: Bag 1F 200
Rockford Cl. B98: Redd 4F 220
Rockford Rd. B42: Gt Barr 2G 79
Rock Gro. B92: Olton 6L 123
ROCK HILL 2K 209
Rock Hill B61: B'gve 2K 209
Rockingham Cl. B93: Dorr 7D 168
DY3: Gorn 6B 74
WS3: Blox 8H 25
Rockingham Dr. CV11: Nun . . . 2M 111
WV6: Pert 6E 34
Rockingham Gdns.
B74: S Cold 3H 59
Rockingham Hall Gdns.
DY9: Hag 2D 138
Rockingham Rd. B25: Yard . . . 1K 123
Rockland Dr. B33: Stech 5L 103
Rockland Gdns.
WV13: W'hall 1M 53
Rocklands Cres. WS13: Lich . . . 8K 13
Rocklands Dr. B75: S Cold 1H 59
Rock La. CV7: Cor 2J 129
Rockley Gro. B45: Redn 2H 163
Rockley Rd. B65: Row R 3A 98
Rockmead Av. B44: Gt Barr 7M 57
Rock Mill La. CV32: Lea S 8J 217
Rockmoor Cl. B37: K'hrst 6E 104
Rock Rd. B92: Olton 6L 123
WV14: Cose 1F 74
Rockrose Gdns. WV10: F'stne . . 2G 23
Rocks, The DY9: Clent 6E 138
Rocks Hill DY5: Brie H 8D 96
Rock St. DY3: Up Gor 4E 74
Rockville Rd. B8: Salt 5G 103
Rockwell La. B48: Row G 5E 190
Rocky La. B6: Aston 3A 102
B7: Nech 3A 102
B42: Gt Barr 3G 79
B61: B'hth 1L 187
CV8: Ken 6J 199
(not continuous)
Rodborough Rd. B26: Sheld . . . 3B 124
B93: Dorr 7E 168
Rodbourne Rd. B17: Harb 6C 120
Roddis Cl. B23: Erd 1D 80
Roden Av. DY10: Kidd 2M 157
Roderick Dr. WV11: Wed 2K 37
Roderick Rd. B11: S'brk 4C 122
Rodhouse Cl. CV4: Tile H 8D 150
Rodlington Av. B44: Gt Barr . . . 8M 57
Rodman Cl. B15: Edg 1D 120
Rodney Cl. B16: Birm 7G 101
B92: Olton 8B 124
CV22: Bil 8J 179
LE10: Hinc 5K 69
Rodney Rd. B92: Olton 8B 124
Rodway Cl. B19: Loz 2L 101
DY5: Quar B 2D 116
WV4: E'shll 6D 52
Rodway Dr. CV5: E Grn 5D 150
Rodwell Gro. B44: K'sdng 1A 80
Rodyard Way
CV1: Cov 8D 152 (8E 6)
Roebuck Cl. B34: S End 4E 104
Roebuck Glade WV12: W'hall . . . 5E 38
Roebuck La. B66: Smeth 2L 99
B70: W Brom 8L 77
Roebuck Pl. WS3: Blox 3L 39
Roebuck Rd. WS3: Blox 3L 39
Roebuck St. B70: W Brom 8M 77
Roe Cl. CV34: Warw 1F 222
Roedean Cl. B44: K'sdng 2B 80
Roford Ct. DY3: Up Gor 3E 74
Rofs Cft. B78: Pole 2K 49
Rogerfield Rd. B23: Erd 3G 81
Rogers Cl. WV11: Wed 8A 24
Rogers Rd. B8: W End 4H 103
Rogers Way CV34: Warw 5B 222
Rogue's La. LE10: Hinc 4G 69
Rokeby Cl. B76: Walm 5L 59
Rokeby Ct. CV22: Rugby 2M 205
Rokeby Rd. B43: Gt Barr 7F 56
Rokeby St. CV21: Rugby 6D 180
Rokeby Wlk. B34: Hodg H 3M 103
Rokewood Cl. DY6: K'wfrd 8K 73
Rokholt Cres. WS11: Cann 8C 8
Roland Av. CV6: Cov 6B 130
Roland Gdns. B19: Loz 1J 101
Roland Gro. B19: Loz 1J 101
Roland Mt. CV6: Cov 6C 130
Rolan Dr. B90: Maj G 1E 166
Roland Rd. B19: Loz 1J 101
Roland Vernon Way DY4: Tip . . . 2C 76
Rolfe St. B66: Smeth 3A 100
Rollason Cl. CV6: Cov 1C 152
Rollason Rd. B24: Erd 6G 81
CV6: Cov 1B 152
DY2: Dud 1K 97
Rollasons Yd. CV6: Cov 6G 131
Rollesby Dr. WV13: W'hall 1M 53
Rollingmill Bus. Pk.
WS2: Wals 8J 39
Rolling Mill Cl. B5: Bal H 2L 121
Rollingmill St. WS2: Wals 8J 39
Rollswood Dr. B91: Sol 5M 145
Roman Cl. WS8: Bwnhls 7E 16
Roman Ct. B38: K Nor 1G 165
B77: Wiln 2E 46
WS11: Cann 4E 14
Romani Cl. CV34: Warw 2D 222
Roman La. B74: Lit A 5B 42
Roman Pk. B46: Col 8M 83
B74: Lit A 5B 42
Roman Pl. B74: Lit A 7B 42
Roman Rd. B74: Lit A 4C 42
CV2: Cov 6H 153
DY7: Stourt 7J 115
DY8: Stourb 5J 115
(not continuous)
Roman Vw. WS11: Cann 4F 14
Roman Wlk. WS14: Wall 7D 18
Roman Way B15: Edg 6D 120
B46: Col 7L 83
B61: B'gve 5B 188
B65: Row R 5C 98
B78: Dord 3A 48
B79: Tam 2L 31
CV3: Finh 6D 174
CV21: Rugby 2A 180
CV47: Sou 5J 225
WS14: Lich 2K 19
Romany Rd. B45: Fran 8D 140
Romany Way DY8: Stourb 6J 115
Roma Rd. B11: Tys 4E 122
Romeo Arbour CV34: H'cte 6L 223
Romford Cl. B26: Sheld 3B 124
Romford Rd. CV6: Cov 7B 130
Romilly Av. B20: Hand 7H 79

Romilly Cl.—Ruiton

Romilly Cl. B76: Walm ... 5A 60
DY8: Woll ... 3L 115
WS14: Lich ... 2L 19
Romney B77: Wiln ... 1F 46
Romney Cl. B28: Hall G ... 2F 144
LE10: Hinc ... 6G 69
Romney Ho. Ind. Est.
WS10: Darl ... 2B 54
(off Wolverhampton St.)
Romney Pl. CV22: Rugby ... 2M 205
Romney Way B43: Gt Barr ... 5K 57
Romsey Av. CV10: Nun ... 1K 89
Romsey Gro. WV10: F'hses ... 6C 22
Romsey Rd. WV10: F'hses ... 6C 22
Romsey Way WS3: Blox ... 6F 24
ROMSLEY ... 5A 140
Romsley Cl. B45: Rubery ... 1E 162
B63: Hale ... 7B 118
B98: Redd ... 6M 213
WS4: S'fld ... 7C 26
ROMSLEY HILL ... 7A 140
Romsley Hill Grange
B62: Roms ... 8L 139
Romsley La. DY12: Shat ... 1B 134
Romsley Rd. B32: Bart G ... 1H 141
B68: O'bry ... 7H 99
CV6: Cov ... 3C 152
DY9: Lye ... 4C 116
Romulus Cl. B20: Hand ... 6H 79
Ronald Gro. B36: Cas B ... 8D 82
Ronald Pl. B9: Bord G ... 7E 102
Ronald Rd. B9: Bord G ... 7D 102
Ronald Toon Rd. LE9: Earl S ... 1G 71
Ron Davis Cl. B66: Smeth ... 4B 100
Ro-Oak Rd. CV6: Cov ... 4M 151
ROOD END ... 3J 99
Rood End Rd. B68: O'bry ... 3J 99
B69: O'bry ... 2J 99
Rooker Av. WV2: E'shll ... 2E 52
Rooker Cres. WV2: E'shll ... 3F 52
Rookery, The B62: Quin ... 7G 119
CV10: Gall C ... 4L 87
CV10: Ridge L ... 7F 64
Rookery Av. DY5: Brie H ... 7A 96
WV4: E'shll ... 6G 53
Rookery Cl. B97: Redd ... 8D 212
CV13: Fen D ... 2G 67
Rookery Ct. WS13: Lich ... 2E 18
Rookery La. B75: Can, Hints ... 7C 30
B78: Hints ... 7C 30
CV6: Cov ... 5B 130
WS9: A'rdge ... 3H 41
WV3: Wolv ... 3A 52
Rookery Pde. WS9: A'rdge ... 3H 41
Rookery Pk. DY5: P'ntt ... 4B 96
Rookery Ri. WV5: Wom ... 3H 73
Rookery Rd. B21: Hand ... 1E 100
B29: S Oak ... 7F 120
WV4: E'shll ... 6G 53
WV5: Wom ... 3H 73
Rookery St. WV11: Wed ... 4J 37
Rooks Mdw. DY9: Hag ... 3B 138
Rooks Nest CV23: Brin ... 6L 155
Rookwood Dr. WV6: Tett ... 7F 34
Rookwood Rd. B27: A Grn ... 5H 123
Roosevelt Dr. CV4: Tile H ... 7E 150
Rootes Halls CV4: Canly ... 5J 173
Rooth St. WS10: W'bry ... 5H 55
Roper Cl. CV21: Hillm ... 1G 207
Roper Wlk. DY3: Sed ... 3F 74
Roper Way DY3: Sed ... 3F 74
Rope Wlk. DY12: Bew ... 5D 156
(off Heathfield Rd.)
WS1: Wals ... 8A 40
Rosafield Av. B62: Quin ... 3F 118
Rosalind Av. DY1: Dud ... 2H 75
Rosalind Gro. WV11: Wed ... 4A 38
Rosamond St. WS1: Wals ... 2K 55
Rosary Rd. B23: Erd ... 6D 80
Rosary Vs. B11: S'hll ... 4B 122
Rosaville Cres. CV5: Alle ... 3G 151
Rose Av. B48: A'chu ... 3A 190
B68: O'bry ... 2K 119
CV6: Cov ... 4M 151
DY6: K'wfrd ... 4M 95
Rose Bank B74: Lit A ... 4D 42
Rose Bank Dr. WS3: Wals ... 5L 39
Rosebay Av. B38: K Nor ... 1F 164
Rosebay Gro. WV5: Wom ... 3E 72
Rosebay Mdw. WS11: Hth H ... 7J 9
Roseberry Av. CV2: Cov ... 8H 131
Roseberry Gdns.
DY10: W'ley ... 6C 136
Rosebery Rd. B66: Smeth ... 5C 100
B77: Dost ... 5D 46
Rosebery St. B18: Hock ... 5G 101
Rosebriars B90: Maj G ... 2E 166
Rose Cl. B66: Smeth ... 4C 100
Rose Cott. Dr. DY8: Word ... 6K 95
(off Barnett La.)
Rose Cott. Flats CV5: E Grn ... 4D 150
Rose Cotts. B29: S Oak ... 7F 120
B30: Stir ... 3G 143
Rose Ct. CV7: Bal C ... 1H 171
Rose Cft. CV8: Ken ... 3E 198
Rosecroft Rd. B26: Sheld ... 3C 124
Rosedale Av. B23: Erd ... 6E 80
B66: Smeth ... 4C 100
Rosedale Cl. B97: Redd ... 5A 212
Rosedale Gro. B25: Yard ... 1J 123
Rosedale Pl. WV13: W'hall ... 1A 54
Rosedale Rd. B25: Yard ... 1J 123
Rosedale Wlk. DY6: K'wfrd ... 1L 95
Rose Dene DY13: Stour S ... 5E 182
Rosedene Dr. B20: Hand ... 7F 78
Rose Dr. WS8: Clay ... 3E 26
Rosefield Ct. B67: Smeth ... 5A 100
Rosefield Cft. B6: Aston ... 2M 101
Rosefield Pl. CV32: Lea S ... 1M 223
Rosefield Rd. B67: Smeth ... 5A 100
Rosefields B31: N'fld ... 4B 142
Rosefield St. CV32: Lea S ... 1M 223
Rosefield Wlk. CV32: Lea S ... 1M 223
(off Rosefield St.)
Rose Gdns., The B63: Hale ... 7L 117
Rosegreen Cl. CV3: Cov ... 3E 174
Rosehall Cl. B91: Sol ... 8M 145
B98: Redd ... 3E 220
Rose Hill B45: Coft H, Lick ... 6G 163
DY5: Quar B ... 8G 97
WV13: W'hall ... 1A 54
Rosehill CV9: Ath ... 2M 65
WS12: Hed ... 1F 8
Rose Hill Cl. B36: Cas B ... 1B 104
Rosehill Ct. DY1: Dud ... 8J 75
(off Wolverhampton St.)
Rose Hill Gdns. WV13: W'hall ... 8A 38
Rose Hill Rd. B21: Hand ... 2G 101
Rose Hill Shop. Cen.
WS12: Hed ... 1F 8
Rosehip Cl. WS5: Wals ... 6A 56
Rosehip Dr. CV2: Cov ... 3H 153
Roseland Av. DY2: Dud ... 8M 75
Roseland Rd. CV8: Ken ... 6F 198
Roselands Av. CV2: Cov ... 1K 153
Roseland Way
B15: Birm ... 8H 101 (8B 4)
Rose La. B61: D'frd ... 3G 187
B69: Tiv ... 7C 76
CV11: Nun ... 6J 89
WS7: Burn ... 2J 17
Roseleigh Rd. B45: Redn ... 3H 163
Rosemary Av. WS6: C Hay ... 6D 14
WV4: Penn ... 3C 52
WV14: Bils ... 3M 53
Rosemary Cl. CV4: Tile H ... 6E 150
WS8: Clay ... 3D 26
Rosemary Ct. WV11: Wed ... 2M 37
Rosemary Cres. DY1: Dud ... 3F 74
WV4: Penn ... 4C 52
Rosemary Cres. W.
WV4: Penn ... 4B 52
Rosemary Dr. B60: S Prior ... 8J 209
B74: Lit A ... 6C 42
Rosemary Hill CV8: Ken ... 4F 198
Rosemary Hill Rd.
B74: Four O ... 6C 42
Rosemary La. DY8: Stourb ... 6K 115
Rosemary M. CV8: Ken ... 4F 198
Rosemary Nook B74: Lit A ... 4D 42
Rosemary Rd. B33: Stech ... 7M 103
B63: Hale ... 7K 117
B77: Amin ... 5F 32
DY4: Tip ... 3A 76
DY10: Kidd ... 2B 158
WS6: C Hay ... 5D 14
(not continuous)
Rosemary Way LE10: Hinc ... 2H 91
Rosemoor Dr. DY5: Brie H ... 2B 116
Rosemount B32: Quin ... 5L 119
Rosemount Cl. CV2: Cov ... 2L 153
Rosemullion Cl. CV7: Exh ... 1H 131
Rosenhurst Dr. DY12: Bew ... 6A 156
Rose Pl. B18: Birm ... 5J 101 (2C 4)
Rose Rd. B17: Harb ... 3D 120
B46: Col ... 1M 105
Rose St. WV14: Bils ... 7M 53
Rose Ter. B45: B Grn ... 1K 189
Rosetti Cl. DY10: Kidd ... 3C 158
ROSEVILLE ... 2H 75
Roseville Ct. WV14: Cose ... 1J 75
(off Castle St.)
Roseville Gdns. WV8: Cod ... 5G 21
Roseville Pct. WV14: Cose ... 1J 75
(off Castle St.)
Roseway CV13: Stoke G ... 2D 68
Rosewood CV11: Nun ... 8M 89
Rosewood Av. CV22: Rugby ... 1A 206
Rose Wood Cl. LE10: Burb ... 3M 91
Rosewood Cl. B74: Lit A ... 4D 42
B77: Tam ... 5D 32
Rosewood Ct. B77: Tam ... 5D 32
Rosewood Cres. CV32: Lill ... 7B 218
Rosewood Dr. B23: Erd ... 7D 80
B45: B Grn ... 2J 189
WV12: W'hall ... 1B 38
Rosewood Gdns. WV11: Ess ... 6B 24
Rosewood Pk. WS6: C Hay ... 7D 14
Rosewood Rd. DY1: Dud ... 4H 75
Roshven Rd. B12: Bal H ... 5A 122
Roslin Cl. B60: B'gve ... 8B 188
Roslin Gro. B19: Hock ... 3J 101
Roslyn Cl. B66: Smeth ... 3A 100
Ross B65: Row R ... 7B 98
Ross Cl. CV5: E Grn ... 4G 151
WV3: Wolv ... 7L 35
Ross Ct. CV21: Rugby ... 6D 180
Ross Dr. DY6: K'wfrd ... 2J 95
Rosse Ct. B92: Sol ... 1F 146
Rossendale Cl. B63: Crad ... 3K 117
Rossendale Rd. LE9: Earl S ... 1D 70
Rossendale Way CV10: Nun ... 7D 88
Ross Hgts. B65: Row R ... 6B 98
Rosslyn Av. CV6: Cov ... 3L 151
Rosslyn Rd. B76: Walm ... 3M 81
Ross Rd. WS3: Wals ... 3M 39
Ross Way CV11: Nun ... 2B 112
Roston Dr. LE10: Hinc ... 8F 68
Rostrevor Rd. B10: Small H ... 8F 102
Rosy Cross B79: Tam ... 4C 32
Rotary Ho. DY1: Dud ... 8F 74
Rothay B77: Wiln ... 1F 46
Rothbury Grn. WS12: Hth H ... 7L 9
Rotherby Gro. B37: Mars G ... 2H 125
Rotherfield Cl. CV31: Lea S ... 2B 224
Rotherfield Rd. B26: Sheld ... 1B 124
Rotherham Rd. CV6: Cov ... 7B 130
Rotherhams Hill CV9: Bad E ... 1C 64
Rotherhams Oak La.
B94: H'ley H ... 3M 193
Rothesay Av. CV4: Tile H ... 7H 151
Rothesay Cl. CV10: Nun ... 7G 89
Rothesay Cft. B32: Bart G ... 2H 141
Rothesay Dr. DY8: Word ... 6J 95
Rothesay Way WV12: W'hall ... 3B 38
Rothley Dr. CV21: Brow ... 2E 180
Rothley Wlk. B38: K Nor ... 1C 164
Rothwell Dr. B91: Shir ... 4K 145
Rothwell Rd. CV34: Warw ... 8C 216
Rotten Row WS13: Lich ... 2J 19
Rotton Pk. Rd. B16: Edg ... 5D 100
(not continuous)
Rotton Pk. St. B16: Birm ... 6F 100
ROTTON ROW ... 5J 169
Rough, The B97: Redd ... 1D 220
Rough Coppice Wlk.
B35: Cas V ... 7A 82
ROUGH HAY ... 2C 54
Rough Hay Pl. WS10: Darl ... 2C 54
Rough Hay Rd. WS10: Darl ... 2C 54
Rough Hill Dr. B65: Row R ... 3M 97
B98: Redd ... 4E 220
Rough Hills Cl. WV2: E'shll ... 3F 52
Rough Hills Rd. WV2: E'shll ... 3F 52
Rough Hill Wood Nature Reserve
... 4G 221
Roughknowles Rd.
CV4: W'wd H ... 3D 172
Roughlea Av. B36: Hodg H ... 2M 103
ROUGHLEY ... 6J 43
Roughley Dr. B75: R'ley ... 7J 43
Roughley Farm Rd.
B75: R'ley ... 6L 43
Rough Rd. B44: K'sdng ... 6A 58
Rough Wood Country Pk. ... 3E 38
Rouncil Cl. B92: Sol ... 2D 146
Rouncil La. CV8: Ken ... 7M 197
Roundabout, The
B31: Longb ... 8K 141
Round Av. CV23: Long L ... 4G 179
Round Cft. WV13: W'hall ... 7A 38
Round Hill DY3: Sed ... 7D 52
Round Hill Av. DY9: Pedm ... 8C 116
Roundhill Cl. B76: Walm ... 6L 59
Round Hill Ct. DY11: Kidd ... 4K 157
Roundhill Ho. DY6: K'wfrd ... 8K 73
Roundhills, The LE9: Elme ... 4F 70
Roundhills Rd. B62: B'hth ... 1F 118
Roundhill Ter. B62: B'hth ... 8E 98
Roundhill Way WS8: Bwnhls ... 7F 16
Round Hill Wharf
DY11: Kidd ... 4K 157
Round Ho. Rd. CV3: Cov ... 1G 175
Roundhouse Rd. DY3: Up Gor ... 5E 74
Roundlea Cl. WV12: W'hall ... 1B 38
Roundlea Rd. B31: N'fld ... 1L 141
Round Moor Wlk.
B35: Cas V ... 6A 82
ROUND OAK ... 5D 96
Round Rd. B24: Erd ... 7H 81
Roundsaw Cft. B45: Rubery ... 1F 162
Rounds Gdns. CV21: Rugby ... 6M 179
ROUND'S GREEN ... 2E 98
Round's Grn. Rd. B69: O'bry ... 2E 98
Rounds Hill CV8: Ken ... 7E 198
Rounds Hill Rd.
WV14: Cose ... 1K 75
Rounds Rd. WV14: Cose ... 6K 53
Round St. CV21: Rugby ... 6M 179
DY2: Neth ... 3J 97
Roundway Down WV6: Pert ... 6E 34
Rounton Cl. B74: Four O ... 5D 42
Rousay Cl. B45: Fran ... 8F 140
Rousdon Gro. B43: Gt Barr ... 1D 78
Rover Dr. B27: A Grn ... 5K 123
B36: Cas B ... 8F 82
Rover Rd. CV1: Cov ... 7C 152 (5B 6)
Rovex Bus. Pk. B11: Tys ... 4F 122
Row, The CV7: Ansty ... 6D 132
CV8: Bag ... 7F 174
Rowallan Rd. B75: R'ley ... 8K 43
Rowanberry Cl.
DY13: Stour S ... 5E 182
Rowan Cen., The CV9: Ath ... 1L 65
Rowan Cl. B47: H'wd ... 4B 166
B61: B'gve ... 7L 187
B76: Walm ... 7M 59
B78: K'bry ... 3D 62
CV3: Bin W ... 2D 176
WS13: Lich ... 1K 19
Rowan Ct. B30: K Nor ... 7G 143
B66: Smeth ... 1K 99
WS11: Cann ... 8E 8
Rowan Cres. B97: Redd ... 5A 212
WV3: Wolv ... 2L 51
WV14: Cose ... 8H 53
Rowan Dr. B28: Hall G ... 4G 145
CV22: Bil ... 7H 179
CV34: Warw ... 1F 222
WV11: Ess ... 6B 24
Rowan Gdns. B78: Pole ... 1B 48
Rowan Grange B74: Lit A ... 4C 42
Rowan Gro. CV2: W'grve S ... 7L 131
WS7: Chase ... 2F 16
Rowan Ho. CV4: W'wd H ... 3F 172
DY11: Kidd ... 8H 135
Rowan Ri. DY6: K'wfrd ... 3L 95
Rowan Rd. B72: S Cold ... 7J 59
B97: Redd ... 5A 212
CV10: Nun ... 3C 88
DY3: Sed ... 8F 52
WS5: Wals ... 5M 55
WS11: Cann ... 7B 8
Rowans, The CV12: Bed ... 7E 110
Rowantrees B45: Redn ... 4H 163
Rowan Way B31: Longb ... 8M 141
B37: Chel W ... 8J 105
CV10: Harts ... 1M 87
Roway La. B69: O'bry ... 8E 76
Rowborough Cl.
B96: A'wd B ... 7E 220
Rowbrook Cl. B90: Maj G ... 1E 166
Rowchester Ct. B4: Birm ... 3G 5
Rowcroft Covert B14: K Hth ... 6J 143
Rowcroft Rd.
CV2: W'grve S ... 3A 154
Rowdale Rd. B42: Gt Barr ... 2J 79
Rowden Dr. B23: Erd ... 3G 81
B91: Sol ... 7L 145
Rowena Gdns. DY3: Sed ... 7C 52
Rowheath Ho. B30: B'vlle ... 3E 142
Rowheath Rd. B30: K Nor ... 5F 142
Rowington Av. B65: Row R ... 6D 98
Rowington Cl. CV6: Cov ... 4K 151
ROWINGTON GREEN ... 8A 196
Rowington Grn. CV35: Row ... 8M 195
Rowington Rd. B34: S End ... 3E 104
Rowland Av. B78: Pole ... 1K 49
B80: Stud ... 6L 221
Rowland Cl. CV7: Old A ... 8E 86
Rowland Gdns. WS2: Wals ... 6J 39
Rowland Hill Av.
DY11: Kidd ... 4H 157
Rowland Hill Cen.
DY10: Kidd ... 3L 157
(off Worcester St.)
Rowland Hill Dr. DY4: Tip ... 4C 76
Rowlands Av. WS2: Wals ... 6E 38
WV1: Wolv ... 7H 37
Rowlands Cl. WS2: Wals ... 5E 38
Rowlands Cres. B91: Sol ... 1B 146
Rowlands Rd. B26: Yard ... 2L 123
Rowland St. CV21: Rugby ... 6M 179
WS2: Wals ... 6J 39
Rowlands Way CV9: Ath ... 7J 49
Rowland Way DY11: Kidd ... 8L 157
Rowley Cl. WS12: Hed ... 1H 9
Rowley Dr. CV3: W'hall ... 5H 175
Rowley Gro. B33: Kitts G ... 6D 104
Rowley Hall Av. B65: Row R ... 5C 98
Rowley Hill Vw.
B64: Crad H ... 1M 117
Rowley La. CV3: W'hall ... 6K 175
Rowley Pl. WS4: Rus ... 2B 40
ROWLEY REGIS ... 6C 98
Rowley Regis Crematorium
B65: Row R ... 7A 98
Rowley Regis Station (Rail) ... 7E 98
Rowley Rd. CV3: W'hall ... 6F 174
CV8: Bag ... 6F 174
CV31: W'nsh ... 6A 224
ROWLEYS GREEN ... 5E 130
Rowley's Grn. CV6: Longf ... 5E 130
Rowleys Grn. Ind. Est.
CV6: Longf ... 5E 130
Rowley's Grn. La.
CV6: Longf ... 5E 130
Rowley St. WS1: Wals ... 7M 39
Rowley Vw. B70: W Brom ... 6H 77
WS10: Darl ... 5C 54
WV14: Bils ... 6A 54
Rowley Village B65: Row R ... 6C 98
Rowney Cft. B28: Hall G ... 4E 144
ROWNEY GREEN ... 5E 190
Rowney Grn. La.
B48: Row G ... 2E 190
Rowood Dr. B91: Sol ... 2C 146
B92: Sol ... 2D 146
Rowse Cl. CV21: Brow ... 2C 180
Rowthorn Cl. B74: S'tly ... 2A 58
Rowthorn Dr. B90: M'path ... 3A 168
Rowton Av. WV6: Pert ... 6E 34
Rowton Dr. B74: S'tly ... 4M 57
Roxall Cl. DY10: Blak ... 7J 137
Roxborough Ho. B97: Redd ... 7D 212
Roxburgh Cft. CV32: Cubb ... 4B 218
Roxburgh Gro. B43: Gt Barr ... 5J 57
Roxburgh Rd. B73: S Cold ... 6G 59
CV11: Nun ... 8L 89
Roxby Gdns. WV6: Wolv ... 4A 36
Royal Arch Apartments
B1: Birm ... 8J 101 (7D 4)
Royal Cl. B65: Row R ... 4C 98
DY5: Brie H ... 1C 116
Royal Ct. B72: W Grn ... 7H 59
CV21: Rugby ... 6M 179
LE10: Hinc ... 2K 91
Royal Cres. CV3: W'hall ... 4J 175
Royal Doulton Crystal ... 2M 115
Royal Gro. B23: Erd ... 2B 80
ROYAL LEAMINGTON SPA ... 2M 223
Royal Mdw. Dr. CV9: Ath ... 7L 49
Royal Oak La. CV7: Ash G ... 2C 130
CV12: Bed ... 2C 130
Royal Oak Rd. B62: Quin ... 5F 118
B65: Row R ... 4M 97
Royal Oak Yd. CV12: Bed ... 5H 111
Royal Priors Shop. Cen.
CV32: Lea S ... 1M 223
Royal Pump Rooms, The ... 1M 223
(off Parade)
Royal Rd. B72: S Cold ... 4J 59
Royal Scot Gro. WS1: Wals ... 4L 55
Royal Spa Cen., The ... 1A 224
Royal Sq. B97: Redd ... 6E 212
Royal Star Cl. B33: Kitts G ... 7C 104
Royal Stop, The (MM)
... 8E 36 (6M 7)
Royal Way DY4: Tip ... 7A 76
Royal Worcester Cres.
B60: B'gve ... 8C 188
Roydon Rd. B27: A Grn ... 1J 145
Roylesden Cres. B73: New O ... 7C 58
Royston Chase B74: Lit A ... 6B 42
Royston Cl. CV3: Bin ... 6A 154
Royston Ct. B13: Mose ... 7B 122
(off Wake Grn. Pk.)
Royston Cft. B12: Bal H ... 3M 121
Royston Way DY3: Sed ... 1C 74
Rozel Av. DY10: Kidd ... 8B 136
RSPB Sandwell Valley Nature
Reserve ... 3C 78
Rubens Cl. CV5: Cov ... 6J 151
DY3: Up Gor ... 4D 74
RUBERY ... 2F 162
Rubery By-Pass B45: Rubery ... 2E 162
Rubery Ct. WS10: Darl ... 2C 54
Rubery Farm Gro.
B45: Rubery ... 1F 162
Rubery Fld. Cl. B45: Redn ... 8G 141
Rubery La. B45: Fran ... 8F 140
Rubery La. Sth. B45: Rubery ... 1F 162
Rubery St. WS10: Darl ... 1D 54
Ruckley Av. B19: Loz ... 2J 101
Ruckley Rd. B29: W Cas ... 1A 142
Rudd Gdns. WV10: Wolv ... 5H 37
Ruddington Way B19: Hock ... 4L 101
Rudgard Rd. CV6: Longf ... 5G 131
Rudge Av. WV1: Wolv ... 6H 37
Rudge Cl. WV12: W'hall ... 5C 38
Rudge Cft. B33: Kitts G ... 5A 104
Rudge Rd. CV1: Cov ... 7B 152 (5A 6)
Rudge St. WV14: Cose ... 7L 53
Rudge Wlk. B18: Hock ... 6G 101
Rudgewick Cft. B6: Aston ... 3M 101
Rudyard Cl. WV10: Bush ... 5E 22
Rudyard Gro. B33: Kitts G ... 6B 104
Rudyngfield Dr. B33: Stech ... 6M 103
Rufford B79: Tam ... 3L 31
Rufford Cl. B23: Erd ... 1D 80
LE10: Burb ... 6K 91
Rufford Rd. DY9: Lye ... 5C 116
Rufford St. DY9: Lye ... 3D 116
Rufford Way WS9: A'rdge ... 2E 40
RUGBY ... 6A 180
Rugby La. CV23: Stret D ... 3G 203
Rugby Library, Mus. & Art Gallery
... 6A 180
(off Lit. Elborow St.)
Rugby Rd. CV3: Bin W ... 1B 176
CV7: Withy ... 5L 133
CV8: Bran ... 4G 177
CV8: Wols ... 5J 177
CV12: Bulk ... 7D 112
CV22: Dunc ... 6K 205
CV23: Barby ... 7J 207
CV23: Brin ... 6M 155
CV23: Chu L ... 4C 178
CV23: Clift D ... 4F 180
(Vicarage Hill)
CV23: Clift D, Lilb ... 3L 181
(Lilbourne Rd.)
CV23: Harb M ... 1J 179
CV23: Kils ... 3K 207
CV23: Long L ... 5H 179
CV23: Prin ... 7E 202
CV32: Cubb, W Weth ... 4C 218
CV32: Lea S ... 8K 217
CV33: Wapp, W Weth ... 1K 219
CV47: Sou, S'ton ... 3H 225
DY8: Woll ... 2K 115
LE10: Burb, Hinc ... 1J 91
Rugby School Mus. ... 6A 180
Rugby School Sports Cen. ... 7B 180
Rugby Station (Rail) ... 5C 180
Rugby St. WV1: Wolv ... 6B 36 (1G 7)
Rugeley Av. WV12: W'hall ... 1D 38
Rugeley Cl DY4: Tip ... 4L 75
Rugeley Rd. WS7: Burn ... 7J 11
WS7: C Ter ... 2F 16
WS12: Haz ... 3M 9
WS12: Hed ... 4J 9
WS15: Cann W ... 3A 10
Ruislip Cl. B35: Cas V ... 5A 82
RUITON ... 5D 74

Ruiton St.—St Ives Cl.

Ruiton St. DY3: Lwr G 5D 74
Rumbow B63: Hale 5B 118
Rumbow La. B62: Roms 5J 139
RUMBUSH 6E 166
Rumbush La.
B90: Dic H, Tid G 6E 166
(not continuous)
B94: Earls 8D 166
RUMER HILL 1E 14
Rumer Hill Bus. Est.
WS11: Cann 2E 14
Rumer Hill Ind. Est.
WS11: Cann 2F 14
Rumer Hill Rd. WS11: Cann . . . 1E 14
Runcorn Cl. B37: F'bri 5J 105
B98: Redd 1F 220
Runcorn Rd. B12: Bal H 4M 121
Runcorn Wlk. CV2: W'grve S . . 2A 154
Runnymede Dr. CV7: Bal C . . . 4J 171
Runnymede Gdns. CV10: Nun . . 6F 88
Runnymede Rd. B11: S'hll 6E 122
Rupert Brooke Rd.
CV22: Rugby 2L 205
Rupert Rd. CV6: Cov 1B 152
Rupert St. B7: Birm . . . 5A 102 (1L 5)
WV3: Wolv 7A 36
RUSHALL 2B 40
Rushall Cl. DY8: Word 1L 115
WS4: Wals 5B 40
Rushall Ct. B43: Gt Barr 2E 78
(off West Rd.)
Rushall Mnr. Cl. WS4: Wals . . . 5B 40
Rushall Mnr. Rd. WS4: Wals . . . 5B 40
Rushall Path CV4: Canly 2H 173
Rushall Rd. WV10: Bush 7E 22
RUSHBROOK 6D 192
Rushbrook Cl. B92: Olton 7L 123
WS8: Clay 3E 26
Rushbrooke Cl. B13: Mose . . . 5M 121
Rushbrooke Dr. B73: New O . . . 6C 58
Rushbrook Gro. B14: K Hth . . . 6J 143
Rushbrook La. B94: Tan A 5C 192
Rushbury Cl. B90: Shir 5K 145
WV14: Bils 4H 53
Rushden Cft. B44: K'sdng 8M 57
Rushes Mill WS3: Pels 6L 25
Rushey La. B11: Tys 4G 123
Rushford Av. WV5: Wom 3G 73
Rushford Cl. B90: M'path 2A 168
Rush Grn. B32: Bart G 7L 119
Rushlake Grn. B34: S End 4B 104
Rush La. B77: Dost 6D 46
B98: Redd 3H 213
Rushleigh Rd. B90: Maj G 1E 166
Rushmead Gro. B45: Redn 2G 163
Rushmere Rd. DY4: Tip 1A 76
Rushmoor Cl. B74: S Cold 3H 59
Rushmoor Dr. CV5: Cov 6M 151
Rushmore Ho. B45: Rubery . . . 1F 162
Rushmore Pl. CV31: Lea S . . . 2B 224
Rushmore St. CV31: Lea S . . . 2B 224
RUSHOCK 7J 185
Rushock Cl. B98: Redd 2J 221
Rushock Trad. Est.
WR9: Rush 7G 185
Rushton Cl. CV7: Bal C 2J 171
Rushwater Cl. WV5: Wom 3E 72
Rushwick Cft. B34: S End 3D 104
Rushwick Gro. B90: M'path . . . 3A 168
Rushwood Cl. WS4: Wals 6A 40
Rushy Piece B32: Bart G 6K 119
Rusina Ct. CV31: Lea S 3M 223
Ruskin Av. B65: Row R 7D 98
DY3: Lwr G 4A 74
DY10: Kidd 3C 158
WV4: E'shll 7F 52
Ruskin Cl. B6: Aston 2M 101
CV6: Cov 3K 151
CV10: Gall C 4A 88
CV22: Rugby 3M 205
Ruskin Ct. B66: Smeth 2K 99
B68: O'bry 1H 119
Ruskin Gro. B27: A Grn 7H 123
Ruskin Hall Gro. B6: Aston . . 2M 101
Ruskin Rd. WV10: Bush 1F 36
Ruskin St. B71: W Brom 4J 77
Russel Cft. B60: B'gve 2A 210
Russell Av. CV22: Dunc 5K 205
Russell Bank Rd. B74: Four O . . 5E 42
Russell Cl. B69: Tiv 7D 76
DY4: Tip 8C 54
WV11: Wed 8M 23
Russell Ct. B74: Four O 6D 42
WV3: Wolv 8B 36 (6G 7)
Russell Ho. WS10: W'bry 7F 54
WV8: Cod 5E 20
Russell Rd. B13: Mose 6K 121
B28: Hall G 7E 122
DY10: Kidd 5M 157
WV14: Bils 2M 53
Russells, The B13: Mose 6K 121
RUSSELL'S HALL 8F 74
Russells Hall Rd. DY1: Dud . . . 8E 74
Russell St. CV1: Cov . . 5D 152 (1D 6)
CV32: Lea S 8M 217
DY1: Dud 8H 75
WS10: W'bry 7F 54
WV3: Wolv 8B 36 (6G 7)
WV13: W'hall 7B 38
Russell St. Nth.
CV1: Cov 5D 152 (1D 6)
Russell Ter. CV31: Lea S 2A 224
Russelsheim Way
CV22: Rugby 7A 180
Russett Cl. WS5: Wals 1E 56
WS7: Burn 3G 17
Russett Way DY5: P'ntt 2B 96
DY12: Bew 1B 156
Russet Wlk. WV8: Pend 8L 21
Russet Way B31: N'fld 3L 141
Ruston St. B16: Birm . . 8H 101 (7A 4)
Ruthall Cl. B29: W Cas 2C 142
Ruth Chamberlain Ct.
DY11: Kidd 3K 157
(off Paternoster Row)
Ruth Cl. DY4: Tip 7C 54
Rutherford Glen CV11: Nun . . . 8M 89
Rutherford Rd. B23: Erd 2E 80
B60: B'gve 3B 210
WS2: Wals 3G 39
Rutherglen Av. CV3: Cov 3G 175
Rutland Av. CV10: Nun 5F 88
LE10: Hinc 2J 91
WV4: Penn 5K 51
Rutland Ct. B29: W Cas 2C 142
Rutland Cres. WS9: A'rdge 8H 27
WV14: Bils 2K 53
Rutland Cft. CV3: Bin 1M 175
Rutland Dr. B26: Yard 2L 123
B60: B'gve 1A 210
B78: Tam 8A 32
Rutland Pas. DY1: Dud 8J 75
Rutland Pl. DY8: Woll 1K 115
Rutland Rd. B66: Smeth 8A 100
B71: W Brom 2J 77
WS10: W'bry 5J 55
WS12: Hth H 8L 9
Rutland St. WS3: Wals 4L 39
Rutland Ter. B18: Hock 4G 101
(off Crabtree Rd.)
Rutley Gro. B32: Quin 5M 119
Rutters Mdw. B32: Quin 5H 119
Rutter St. WS1: Wals 2K 55
Ryan Av. WV11: Wed 1A 38
Ryan Pl. DY2: Neth 3J 97
(not continuous)
Rycroft Gro. B33: Kitts G 7C 104
Rydal B77: Wiln 2G 47
Rydal Av. CV11: Nun 3A 90
Rydal Cl. B74: S'tly 7M 41
CV5: Alle 1H 151
CV21: Brow 3D 180
DY13: Stour S 3F 182
LE10: Hinc 2F 90
WS12: Hed 1G 9
WV11: Wed 2J 37
Rydal Dr. WV6: Pert 5F 34
Rydal Ho. B69: O'bry 4D 98
Rydal Way B28: Hall G 2F 144
Rydding La. B71: W Brom 1H 77
Rydding Sq. B71: W Brom 1H 77
Ryde Av. CV10: Nun 3K 89
Ryde Gro. B27: A Grn 8G 123
Ryde Pk. Rd. B45: Redn 3J 163
Ryder Cl. CV35: H Mag 3A 222
Ryder Ho. B70: W Brom 6E 76
Ryder Row CV7: New A 1G 109
Ryders Grn. Rd. B70: W Brom . . 5E 76
Ryders Hayes La. WS3: Pels . . . 5A 26
Ryders Hill Cres. CV10: Nun . . . 2C 88
Ryder St. B4: Birm 6L 101 (3H 5)
B70: W Brom 4F 76
DY8: Word 7K 95
Ryebank Cl. B30: B'vlle 4C 142
Ryeclose Cft. B37: Chel W 6K 105
RYECROFT 5K 39
Rye Cft. B27: A Grn 4J 123
B47: H'wd 4A 166
DY9: W'cte 6E 116
Ryecroft Av. WV4: Penn 4B 52
Ryecroft Cl. DY3: Sed 1C 74
Ryecroft Dr. WS7: C Ter 1G 17
Ryecroft Pk. WS2: Wals 6L 39
Ryecroft Pl. WS3: Wals 3M 39
Ryecroft Shop. Cen.
WS7: C Ter 1G 17
Ryecroft St. WS2: Wals 6L 39
Ryefield WV8: Pend 7L 21
Ryefield Cl. B91: Sol 4L 145
DY9: Hag 5A 138
Ryefield La. B76: Wis 8H 61
Ryefields Rd. B60: S Prior 6J 209
Ryefield Way DY6: K'wfrd 3J 95
Rye Flds CV33: Bis T 8D 224
Rye Grass La. B97: Redd 3C 220
Rye Grass Wlk. B35: Cas V 6B 82
Rye Gro. B11: Tys 5F 122
Rye Hill CV5: Alle 3G 151
Rye Hill Office Pk. CV5: Alle . . . 2G 151
Ryelands, The CV23: Law H . . . 2C 204
Ryelands Bus. Cen.
WR9: Elm L 6F 184
Ryelands La. DY10: Hartl 7F 184
WR9: Elm L 7F 184
Ryemarket DY8: Stourb 4A 116
Rye Piece CV12: Bed 7J 111
Rye Piece Ringway
CV12: Bed 6H 111
Ryhope Cl. CV12: Bed 8C 110
Ryhope Wlk. WV9: Pend 6A 22
(not continuous)
Ryknild Cl. B74: Four O 3F 42
Ryknild St. WS14: Lich 3L 19
Ryland Cl. B63: Hale 7L 117
CV31: Lea S 3C 224
DY4: Tip 4B 76
Ryland Ho. B19: Birm 4K 101
(off Gt. Hampton Row)
Ryland Rd. B11: S'hll 5D 122
B15: Edg 2J 121
B24: Erd 8F 80
Rylands Dr. WV4: Penn 5M 51
Ryland St. B16: Birm . . . 8H 101 (7A 4)
Ryle St. WS3: Blox 7K 25
Ryley St. CV1: Cov 6C 152 (4A 6)
Rylston Av. CV6: Cov 8A 130
Rylstone Way CV34: Warw 8E 216
Rymond Rd. B34: Hodg H 3L 103
RYTON 7D 112
Ryton B77: Wiln 1F 46
Ryton Cl. B73: S Cold 4H 59
B98: Redd 8K 213
CV4: Canly 1H 173
WV10: Wolv 4G 37
Ryton End La. B92: Bars 8C 148
Ryton Gro. B34: S End 2D 104
RYTON-ON-DUNSMORE 8B 176
Ryton Organic Gdns. 8D 176
Ryton Rd. CV8: Bubb 5H 201
Ryvere Cl. DY13: Stour S 7F 182

S

Sabell Rd. B67: Smeth 3M 99
Sabin Dr. CV33: W Weth 2K 219
Sabrina Dr. DY12: Bew 5A 156
Sabrina Rd. WV6: Tett 8E 34
Sackville Ho. CV1: Cov 1F 6
Saddington Rd. CV3: Bin 1L 175
Saddlers Cen. WS1: Wals 8L 39
Saddlers Cl. B63: Crad 4H 117
LE10: Burb 3M 91
WS14: Lich 1L 19
Saddlers Ct. WS2: Wals 2H 55
Saddlers Ct. Ind. Est.
WS2: Wals 2G 39
Saddlers M. B91: Sol 8C 146
Saddleworth Rd. WS3: Blox 5G 25
Sadler Cres. B11: S'hll 5D 122
(off Lea Rd.)
Sadler Gdns. CV12: Bed 7J 111
Sadler Ho. B19: Hock 3J 101
(off Guest Gro.)
Sadler Rd. B75: S Cold 2M 59
CV6: Cov 8A 130
WS8: Bwnhls 2G 27
Sadlers Mdw. B46: Over W 7A 86
Sadlers Mill WS8: Bwnhls 2G 27
Sadlers Wlk. B16: Edg 8G 101
Sadlerswell La. B94: H'ley H . . . 3B 194
Saffron B77: Amin 5H 33
Saffron Cl. CV23: Brow 1E 180
LE9: Barw 1C 70
Saffron Ct. LE9: Barw 3A 70
Saffron Gdns. WV4: Penn 5A 52
Saffron Ho. B38: K Nor 1E 164
Sagebury Dr. B60: S Prior 8J 209
Sage Cft. B31: N'fld 4M 141
St Agatha's Rd. B8: W End 4H 103
CV2: Cov 6G 153
St Agnes Cl. B13: Mose 7B 122
B80: Stud 5J 221
St Agnes Rd. B13: Mose 7B 122
St Agnes Way CV11: Nun 5L 89
St Aidan's Rd. WS11: Cann 5E 8
St Aidans Wlk. B10: Small H . . . 1C 122
St Alban's Av. DY11: Kidd 2G 157
St Albans Cl. B67: Smeth 3L 99
CV32: Lea S 7J 217
WV11: Wed 1A 38
St Albans Ho. B32: Harb 4M 119
St Albans Rd. B67: Smeth 3L 99
B13: Mose 6A 122
St Alphege Cl. B91: Sol 6C 146
St Andrew Cl. WS12: Haz 4A 10
St Andrews B77: Amin 5H 33
St Andrew's Av. WS3: Pels 4A 26
St Andrews Cl. WV6: Wolv 5A 36
B32: Bart G 6A 120
DY3: Lwr G 6A 74
DY8: Stourb 7M 115
St Andrews Ct. CV21: Rugby . . . 5A 180
St Andrews Cres.
CV22: Rugby 1A 206
St Andrews Dr. B69: Tiv 2B 98
CV11: Nun 8B 90
WV6: Pert 4D 34
St Andrews Grn. DY10: Kidd . . . 5L 157
St Andrews Ind. Est.
B9: Bord G 7C 102
St Andrews Rd.
B9: Birm 7B 102 (5M 5)
CV5: Cov 1M 173
CV32: Lill 4B 218
B75: S Cold 2J 59
St Andrews Stadium 8C 102
St Andrews St. DY2: Neth 4J 97
B9: Birm 7B 102
St Andrews Way
B61: B'gve 1K 209
St Annes Cl. WS7: Chase 5E 16
B20: Hand 5F 78
St Annes Ct. WV13: W'hall 8B 38
B13: Mose 5L 121
B44: K'sdng 2A 80
B64: Crad H 8J 97
St Annes Gro. B93: Know 3G 169
St Annes Ind. Est.
WV13: W'hall 6B 38
St Annes Rd. B64: Crad H 8J 97
CV22: Bil 8L 179
WV10: Oxl 7C 22
WS13: Lich 6H 13
WV13: W'hall 6B 38
St Anne's Way B44: K'sdng 3A 80
St Ann's Cl. CV31: Lea S 2C 224
St Ann's Rd. CV2: Cov 6G 153
St Ann's Ter. WV13: W'hall 6B 38
St Anthony's Dr. WS3: Pels 4B 26
St Asaphs Av. B80: Stud 5K 221
St Athan Cft. B35: Cas V 6B 82
St Audries Ct. B91: Sol 7M 145
St Augustine's Rd. B16: Edg . . 8D 100
St Augustines Sports Cen. 4D 220
St Augustine's Wlk.
CV6: Cov 2A 152
St Augustus Cl.
B70: W Brom 7M 77
St Austell Cl. B79: Tam 3A 32
CV11: Nun 4A 90
St Austell Rd. CV2: Cov 6L 153
WS5: Wals 2E 56
St Bartholomews Cl.
CV3: Bin 7A 154
St Bartholomew's Rd.
DY13: Stour S 7E 182
St Bartholomew's Ter.
WS10: W'bry 6F 54
St Benedicts Cl. B70:
W Brom 7M 77
CV9: Ath 1K 65
St Benedicts Rd. WS7: Burn . . . 3H 17
B10: Small H 2F 122
WV5: Wom 3G 73
St Bernards Cl. WS12: Haz 5C 10
St Bernards Rd. B92: Olton . . . 4K 145
B72: W Grn 7J 59
St Bernards Wlk.
CV3: W'hall 3K 175
St Blaise Av. B46: Wat O 7H 83
St Blaise Rd. B75: R'ley 6K 43
St Brades Cl. B69: Tiv 2C 98
St Brides Cl. CV31: Lea S 3C 224
DY3: Sed 1C 74
WV5: Wom 3F 72
St Buryan Cl. CV11: Nun 4A 90
Saintbury Dr. B91: Sol 2C 168
St Caroline Cl. B70: W Brom . . . 7M 77
St Catharines Cl. WS1: Wals . . . 2A 56
St Catherines Cl. CV3: Cov . . . 1H 175
DY2: Dud 8A 76
LE10: Burb 2M 91
B60: B'wll 4G 189
B75: S Cold 2M 59
St Catherine's Ct. B91: Sol . . . 5B 146
St Catherine's Cres.
CV31: W'nsh 6M 223
WV4: Penn 5M 51
St Catherines Lodge
CV6: Cov 5A 152
St Catherines Rd. B60: B'wll . . . 3F 188
WS13: Lich 6H 13
St Cecilias Cl. DY10: Kidd 7L 157
St Chad Ct. B77: Glas 7F 32
St Chads WV14: Cose 2H 75
St Chads Cir. Queensway
B4: Birm 5K 101 (2F 4)
St Chads Cl. DY3: Lwr G 6B 74
WS13: Lich 8H 13
WS11: Cann 5G 9
St Chads Ct. WS13: Lich 1H 19
St Chads Ind. Est.
B19: Birm 4K 101 (1G 5)
St Chads M. B94: Lapw 6K 195
St Chad's Queensway
B4: Birm 5L 101 (3F 4)
St Chads RC Cathedral
. . . . 5L 101 (2F 4)
St Chads Rd. B45: Rubery 2F 162
WS13: Lich 8H 13
B75: S Cold 4L 59
B80: Stud 5J 221
CV33: Bis T 8D 224
WV10: Bush 1F 36
WV14: Bils 2M 53
St Christian's Cft.
CV3: Cov 1D 174 (8E 6)
St Christian's Rd. CV3: Cov . . . 1E 174
St Christopher Cl.
B70: W Brom 7M 77
WS12: Haz 4A 10
St Christophers B20: Hand 5F 78
St Christopher's Cl.
CV34: Warw 1D 222
St Christopher's Dr. B77: Tam . . 8C 32
St Clements Av. WS3: Blox 2K 39
St Clements Ct. B63: Hale 6A 118
CV2: Cov 1K 153
St Clements La.
B71: W Brom 5K 77
St Clements Rd. B7: Nech 3C 102
St Columbas Cl.
CV1: Cov 5C 152 (2B 6)
St Columbas Dr. B45: Redn 2J 163
St Cuthbert's Cl.
B70: W Brom 7M 77
St David Cl. WS12: Haz 3A 10
St Davids Cl. B70: W Brom 7M 77
DY11: Kidd 3F 156
DY13: Stour S 3E 182
WS3: Pels 4B 26
CV31: Lea S 2C 224
St Davids Ct. B69: O'bry 2G 99
St Davids Dr. B32: Quin 4H 119
St Davids Gro. B20: Hand 5B 78
St David's Ho. B97: Redd 5B 212
St Davids Orchard CV3: Bin . . 2M 175
St Davids Pl. WS3: Blox 7K 25
St Davids Way CV10: Griff 3G 111
St Denis Rd. B29: W Cas 3A 142
St Dennis Ho. B16: Edg 8D 100
(off Melville Rd.)
St Dominic's Rd. B24: Erd 8E 80
(not continuous)
St Edburgh's Rd. B25: Yard 8L 103
St Editha's Cl. B79: Tam 4B 32
St Editha's Ct. B79: Tam 2B 32
(off Kensington Dr.)
St Edithas Rd. B78: Pole 1A 48
St Ediths Grn. CV34: Warw . . . 1H 223
St Edmonds Rd. CV9: Hurl 4J 63
St Edmund's Cl.
B70: W Brom 7M 77
WV6: Wolv 6M 35
St Edwards Rd. B29: S Oak 7F 120
Sainte Foy Av. WS13: Lich 4F 18
St Eleanors Cl. B70: W Brom . . . 7M 77
St Elizabeth's Rd. CV6: Cov . . . 2E 152
St Francis Av. B91: Sol 3L 145
St Francis Cl. LE10: Hinc 6J 69
WS12: Haz 4A 10
WS3: Pels 4B 26
St Francis Factory Est.
B70: W Brom 7K 77
St Fremund Way
CV31: Lea S 4C 224
St George Dr. B66: Smeth 2A 100
WS12: Haz 4A 10
ST GEORGES
Redditch 5F 212
Wolverhampton . . . 8D 36 (5K 7)
St Georges Av. LE10: Hinc 8J 69
B23: Erd 4G 81
CV22: Rugby 8A 180
St Georges Cl. B75: S Cold 3M 59
WS10: Darl 2D 54
B15: Edg 2G 121
St Georges Ct. WS10: Darl 2D 54
(off St George's St.)
B30: B'vlle 2E 142
B74: Four O 4E 42
DY10: Kidd 3M 157
WS1: Wals 7M 39
(off Persehouse St.)
St Georges Gdns. B98: Redd . . 5F 212
St George's Pde.
WV2: Wolv 8D 36 (5K 7)
St Georges Pl. DY10: Kidd . . . 2L 157
B70: W Brom 6J 77
WS1: Wals 7M 39
St Georges Rd. CV1: Cov 7F 152
CV9: Ath 7K 49
DY2: Dud 3K 97
DY8: Stourb 7K 115
B90: Shir 1K 167
B98: Redd 5F 212
CV31: Lea S 3M 223
St George's St.
B19: Birm 5K 101 (1E 4)
WS10: Darl 2D 54
St George's Ter. DY10: Kidd . . . 3M 157
St Georges Way B77: Amin 5E 32
CV10: Nun 8H 89
St Gerards Ct. B91: Sol 7L 145
St Gerards Rd. B91: Sol 7L 145
St Giles Av. B65: Row R 5B 98
St Giles Cl. B65: Row R 5C 98
St Giles Ct. B65: Row R 6D 98
WV13: W'hall 8B 38
St Giles Cres. WV1: Wolv 7G 37
St Giles Rd. B33: Kitts G 7D 104
CV7: Ash G 3D 130
WS7: Burn 3H 17
WV1: Wolv 7G 37
WV13: W'hall 8B 38
St Giles Row DY8: Stourb 3A 116
(off Lwr. High St.)
St Giles St. DY2: Neth 4J 97
St Godwald's Cres.
B60: B'gve 1B 210
St Godwalds Rd. B60: B'gve . . . 2B 210
St Govans Cl. CV31: Lea S . . . 3C 224
ST HELENA 1A 48
St Helena Rd. B78: Pole 1B 48
St Helens Av. DY4: Tip 4C 76
St Helen's Cl. LE10: Sharn 4J 93
St Helens Pas.
B1: Birm 5J 101 (2C 4)
St Helens Rd. B91: Sol 3A 146
CV31: Lea S 4M 223
WS13: Lich 6H 13
St Helen's Way CV5: Alle 1H 151
St Heliers Rd. B31: N'fld 5L 141
St Ives Cl. B79: Tam 3B 32

St Ives Rd.—Sams La.

St Ives Rd. CV2: Cov 6K 153
WS5: Wals 2D 56
St Ives Way CV11: Nun 4M 89
St James Av. B65: Row R 5B 98
St James Cl. B70: W Brom 7M 77
WS15: Longd 1A 12
WS3: Pels 4B 26
St James Ct. B61: B'gve 6A 188
(off Strand, The)
CV3: W'hall 3L 175
CV47: Sou 5H 225
(off Market Hill)
St James Cres. CV47: Sou 4G 225
St James Gdns. CV12: Bulk 7C 112
WS8: Bwnhls 2F 26
St James La. CV3: W'hall 4J 175
St James Mdw. Rd.
CV32: Lea S 7J 217
St James Pk. WV10: S Hth 1F 22
St James Pl.
B7: Birm 6A 102 (3M 5)
B15: Edg 1H 121
B90: Bly P 7M 167
B90: Shir 7H 145
St James Rd. B69: O'bry 1D 98
B75: Four O 7J 43
CV47: Sou 4H 225
WS11: Cann 8C 8
WS11: Nort C 4B 16
B21: Hand 1D 100
St James's Cl. LE10: Burb 4K 91
St James's Rd. DY1: Dud 7H 75
St James's Ter. DY1: Dud 7G 75
St James St. WS10: W'bry 7E 54
WV1: Wolv 8E 36 (5M 7)
DY3: Lwr G 6D 74
St James Wlk. WS8: Bwnhls 2F 26
(off Short St.)
St John Bosco Cl.
B71: W Brom 2H 77
St John Cl. B75: R'ley 5K 43
St Johns CV34: Warw 2F 222
LE10: Hinc 8L 69
St John's Arc.
WV1: Wolv 7C 36 (4J 7)
St Johns Av. CV8: Ken 6F 198
DY11: Kidd 2G 157
B65: Row R 5B 98
CV22: Hillm 1E 206
St John's Cl. B70: W Brom 7M 77
B93: Know 3H 169
DY3: Swind 7D 72
DY11: Kidd 3J 157
WS9: Wals W 6F 26
WS11: Cann 1D 14
WS13: Lich 3H 19
St Johns Ct. B31: N'fld 8B 142
CV34: Warw 2F 222
B17: Harb 3B 120
DY5: Brie H 7D 96
(off Hill St.)
WS3: Blox 8H 25
WS10: W'bry 7F 54
WS12: Hth H 8L 9
St Johns Dr. WS14: Shens 4F 28
St Johns Flats CV8: Ken 6G 199
St Johns Gro. B37: K'hrst 6F 104
St Johns Hill WS14: Shens 4F 28
St John's Ho. B70: W Brom 7J 77
CV34: Warw 2F 222
St John's La. CV23: Long L 4G 179
St Johns Retail Pk.
WV2: Wolv 8C 36 (7J 7)
St Johns Rd. B11: S'hll 4C 122
B17: Harb 3D 120
B63: Hale 5L 117
B68: O'bry 4J 99
DY2: Dud 1L 97
DY8: Stourb 3A 116
DY13: Stour S 4G 183
WS2: Wals 1H 55
WS3: Pels 4B 26
WS11: Cann 1D 14
CV10: Ans C 1L 87
CV31: Lea S 3A 224
DY4: Tip 2M 75
WS8: Bwnhls 4G 27
WS10: Darl 4C 54
WV11: Ess 6A 24
St John's Sq.
WV2: Wolv 8C 36 (6J 7)
St Johns St.
CV1: Cov 7D 152 (6D 6)
CV8: Ken 6G 199
DY2: Neth 4J 97
DY11: Kidd 3J 157
WV1: Wolv 4J 7
B79: Tam 4B 32
St John St. B61: B'gve 7M 187
CV21: Rugby 5A 180
WS13: Lich 2H 19
St Johns Wlk. B42: P Barr 5K 79
St John's Way B93: Know 3J 169
St Johns Wood B45: Redn 4H 163
WS14: Shens 4G 29
St Joseph's Av. B31: N'fld 4B 142
St Josephs Cl. WS3: Pels 5A 26
St Joseph's Ct. WV4: Penn 3J 51
St Joseph's Rd. B8: W End 4J 103
St Joseph St. DY2: Dud 8K 75
St Judes Av. B80: Stud 5J 221
St Judes Cl. B14: K Hth 7M 143
B75: S Cold 3M 59
St Jude's Ct. WV6: Wolv 6M 35
St Jude's Cres. CV3: W'hall 2K 175
St Judes Pas.
B5: Birm 8K 101 (7F 4)
St Jude's Rd. WV6: Wolv 6M 35
St Jude's Rd. W. WV6: Wolv 6M 35
St Just's Rd. CV2: Cov 5M 153
St Katherines Rd. B68: O'bry 7H 99
St Kenelms Av. B63: Hale 8L 117
St Kenelm's Cl.
B70: W Brom 7M 77
St Kenelm's Pass
DY9: Clent 5G 139
St Kenelm's Rd. B62: Roms 3K 139
St Kilda's Rd. B8: Salt 5E 102
St Laurence Av.
CV34: Warw 4D 222
St Laurence Cl. B48: A'chu 3B 190
St Laurence M. B31: N'fld 6A 142
St Laurence Rd. B31: N'fld 4B 142
St Lawrence Cl. B93: Know 4H 169
St Lawrence Dr. WS11: Hth H 7H 9
St Lawrence Ho. B16: Edg 8D 100
(off Melville Rd.)
St Lawrence Rd. CV10: Ansl 5H 87
St Lawrence's Rd. CV6: Cov 8F 130
St Lawrence Way WS10: Darl 2D 54
St Leonards Cl.
B37: Mars G 2G 125
B78: Dord 3A 48
St Leonard's Priory (Remains of)
7E 196
St Leonards Sq. DY9: Clent 6F 138
St Leonards Vw.
B78: Dord, Pole 1M 47
St Leonard's Wlk.
CV8: Rytn D 8A 176
St Loye's Cl. B62: B'hth 1D 118
St Lukes Cl. WS11: Cann 1C 14
B65: Row R 5B 98
St Luke's Cotts. B97: Redd 8D 212
St Luke's Rd. B5: Birm 1K 121
(not continuous)
CV6: Cov 6D 130
WS7: Burn 3J 17
WS10: W'bry 6G 55
St Lukes St. B64: Crad H 8K 97
St Luke's Ter. DY1: Dud 1G 97
St Luke's Way CV10: Nun 5C 88
St Margaret Rd. CV1: Cov 7F 152
CV13: Stoke G 2E 68
St Margaret's B74: Four O 6C 42
St Margarets Av. B8: W End 3H 103
St Margaret's Ct. B92: Olton 8L 123
St Margarets Dr. B63: Hale 7M 117
St Margarets Ho.
CV31: W'nsh 5B 224
St Margarets Rd.
B8: W End 3G 103
B43: Gt Barr 7F 56
B79: Tam 2B 32
CV31: Lea S 4B 224
B92: Olton 8L 123
WS3: Pels 5A 26
WS13: Lich 7H 13
St Mark's Av. CV22: Bil 2J 205
St Marks Cl. B95: Ullen 5J 215
CV10: Nun 5C 88
WS6: Gt Wyr 5F 14
St Mark's Ct. CV22: Bil 1K 205
St Marks Cres.
B1: Birm 6G 101 (4A 4)
St Mark's Factory Cen.
DY9: Lye 4D 116
St Mark's La. CV32: Lea S 8L 217
St Mark's M. CV32: Lea S 8L 217
St Marks Rd. CV32: Lea S 8K 217
DY2: Dud 7M 75
DY4: Tip 1M 75
WS3: Pels 5A 26
WS7: Burn 3J 17
WV3: Wolv 8A 36 (5G 7)
(not continuous)
B67: Smeth 6K 99
DY9: Lye 4D 116
WS8: Bwnhls 4G 27
St Marks St.
WV3: Wolv 8B 36 (5G 7)
B1: Birm 6H 101 (3A 4)
St Martin's LE10: Burb 3K 91
St Martin's Av. B80: Stud 5K 221
St Martins Cl. B70: W Brom 7M 77
WV2: E'shll 3E 52
St Martins Dr. DY4: Tip 4A 76
St Martins Ind. Est.
B69: O'bry 3H 99
(Engine St.)
B69: O'bry 2H 99
(Parsonage St.)
St Martin's Queensway
B2: Birm 7L 101 (6G 5)
St Martin's Rd. B75: S Cold 4M 59
CV3: Finh 5C 174
(not continuous)
St Martin's St.
B15: Birm 8H 101 (8B 4)
St Martin's Ter. WV14: Bils 5L 53
St Mary's Abbey 4E 198
St Mary's Av. LE9: Barw 4M 69
St Marys Cl. B24: Erd 5K 81
B95: Ullen 6J 215
CV47: Sou 4J 225
B27: A Grn 6H 123
CV34: Warw 1D 222
DY3: Sed 1F 74
St Marys Ct. CV8: Ken 6F 198
CV11: Nun 4H 89
(off Abbey Grn.)
LE9: Barw 3A 70
WV13: W'hall 7A 38
(off Wolverhampton St.)
DY5: Brie H 7D 96
St Mary's Cres. CV31: Lea S 2B 224
St Mary's Hall
WV2: Wolv 8D 36 (6K 7)
St Mary's La. DY8: Stourb 6B 116
St Mary's Mobile Home Pk.
B47: Wyt 7L 165
St Mary's Ringway
DY10: Kidd 3K 157
St Marys Rd. B17: Harb 4C 120
B67: Smeth 8M 99
CV7: Fill 6E 108
CV9: Ath 1L 65
CV11: Nun 4H 89
CV31: Lea S 2B 224
LE10: Hinc 1K 91
WS10: W'bry 6F 54
WS13: Lich 6H 13
St Marys Row
B4: Birm 6L 101 (3G 5)
B13: Mose 6M 121
St Mary's St.
WV1: Wolv 7D 36 (3K 7)
St Mary's Ter. CV31: Lea S 2B 224
St Mary St. CV1: Cov 7D 152 (5D 6)
St Mary's Vw. B23: Erd 1D 80
St Marys Way B77: Amin 5E 32
WS9: A'rdge 4G 41
St Matthew Cl. WS12: Haz 4A 10
St Matthew's Av. WS7: Burn 2M 17
St Matthews Cl. CV10: Nun 5C 88
WS3: Pels 4B 26
WS1: Wals 8M 39
St Matthews Rd. WS7: Burn 2L 17
B66: Smeth 4C 100
B68: O'bry 7G 99
(not continuous)
St Matthews St.
CV22: Rugby 6A 180
WV1: Wolv 8F 36
St Mawes Rd. WV6: Pert 6F 34
St Mawgan Cl. B35: Cas V 5C 82
St Michael Rd. WS13: Lich 8J 13
St Michael's Av. CV1: Cov 4D 6
(off Bayley La.)
St Michaels Cl. CV7: Gun H 1F 108
CV33: W Weth 2J 219
DY13: Stour S 5G 183
CV9: Ath 8L 49
CV9: Wood E 8J 47
WS3: Pels 7A 26
St Michaels Ct. B70: W Brom 6J 77
LE9: S Stan 7K 71
WV6: Tett 4L 35
St Michaels Cres.
CV47: S'ton 1M 225
B69: O'bry 5F 98
St Michaels Dr. WS12: Haz 4A 10
St Michael's Gro. DY2: Dud 8A 76
St Michael's Hill B18: Hock 2G 101
St Michael's M. B69: Tiv 7A 76
St Michaels Rd. B18: Hock 2G 101
B73: Bold 1F 80
CV2: Cov 6G 153
DY3: Lwr G 4M 73
CV34: Warw 1C 222
St Michael St. B70: W Brom 6J 77
WS1: Wals 1L 55
St Michaels Way CV10: Nun 5C 88
DY4: Tip 6A 76
St Nicholas Av. CV8: Ken 6F 198
St Nicholas Chu. St.
CV34: Warw 3F 222
St Nicholas Cl.
CV1: Cov 4C 152 (1B 6)
WS3: Pels 5A 26
St Nicholas Ct. CV6: Cov 2F 152
(Crabmill La.)
CV6: Cov 3B 152
(Dugdale Rd.)
St Nicholas Est. CV9: Gren 7C 48
St Nicholas Gdns.
B38: K Nor 7F 142
St Nicholas Pk. CV34: Warw 3F 222
St Nicholas Pk. Leisure Cen.
2G 223
St Nicholas Rd. CV31: Rad S 4F 224
St Nicholas St.
CV1: Cov 4C 152 (1B 6)
St Nicholas Ter.
CV31: Rad S 5E 224
St Nicholas Wlk. B76: Curd 3H 83
ST NICOLAS PARK 2M 89
St Nicolas Pk. Dr. CV11: Nun 2L 89
St Nicolas Rd. CV11: Nun 4K 89
St Osburg's Rd. CV2: Cov 6G 153
St Oswalds Cl. DY10: Kidd 1M 157
St Oswald's Ct.
B10: Small H 1E 122
St Oswald's Rd.
B10: Small H 1E 122
St Patrick Cl. WS12: Haz 4A 10
St Patricks Cl. B14: K Hth 4L 143
St Patricks Ct. DY11: Kidd 8H 157
St Patricks Rd.
CV1: Cov 7C 152 (7C 6)
St Paul's Av. B12: Bal H 4A 122
DY11: Kidd 3G 157
St Paul's Cl. CV34: Warw 3D 222
WS1: Wals 7L 39
WS11: Hth H 8H 9
St Pauls Ct. B77: Dost 5C 46
B46: Wat O 6H 83
B65: B'hth 8D 98
St Paul's Cres. B46: Col 2M 105
B70: W Brom 2E 76
WS3: Pels 5B 26
St Pauls Dr. B62: B'hth 8D 98
DY4: Tip 5B 76
St Paul's Gdns. LE10: Hinc 8L 69
St Paul's Rd. B12: Bal H 3M 121
B66: Smeth 2K 99
CV6: Cov 3E 152
CV10: Nun 6C 88
DY2: Neth 4K 97
WS7: Burn 3J 17
WS10: W'bry 4H 55
WS12: Wim 6L 9
St Pauls Sq. B3: Birm 6J 101 (3D 4)
CV32: Lea S 8A 218
St Pauls Stop (MM) 5K 101 (2E 4)
St Paul's St. WS1: Wals 7L 39
St Pauls Ter. CV34: Warw 3D 222
B3: Birm 5J 101 (2D 4)
St Peter's Av. CV9: With 2B 66
St Peters Cl. B72: W Grn 6H 59
B77: Wiln 8D 32
B97: Redd 4E 220
CV9: With 2B 66
DY4: Tip 5D 76
WS9: Ston 5L 27
B28: Hall G 3D 144
B46: Wat O 7H 83
B61: B'gve 8L 187
WV1: Wolv 7C 36 (3J 7)
St Peters Ct. CV1: Cov 2F 6
(off Vine St.)
WS3: Blox 8H 25
St Peter's Dr. CV10: Gall C 5M 87
WS3: Pels 5A 26
St Peters La. B92: Bick 8K 125
St Peters Rd. B17: Harb 4B 120
B20: Hand 8J 79
CV21: Rugby 7C 180
CV32: Lea S 1M 223
WS7: Burn 3J 17
CV9: Man 2A 66
DY2: Dud, Neth 3K 97
DY9: Pedm 8C 116
WS12: Hed 5K 9
St Peter's Sq.
WV1: Wolv 7C 36 (3J 7)
St Peters Ter. WS2: Wals 5L 39
St Philips Av. WV3: Wolv 2M 51
St Philips Cathedral 6K 101 (4F 4)
St Philips Gro. WV3: Wolv 2M 51
St Philips Pl.
B3: Birm 6L 101 (4G 5)
St Phillips Ct. B46: Col 2A 106
St Quentin St. WS2: Wals 1J 55
St Richards Cl. WR9: Wych 8E 208
St Richards Rd. WR9: Wych 8E 208
St Saviours Cl. WV2: E'shll 3F 52
St Saviour's Ct. DY9: Hag 3B 138
St Saviour's Rd. B8: Salt 5D 102
St Silas' Sq. B19: Loz 2H 101
St Simons Cl. B75: S Cold 3M 59
St Stephens Av.
WV13: W'hall 7M 37
St Stephen's Cen.
B21: Hand 3E 100
St Stephens Ct.
WV13: W'hall 8M 37
WS12: Hed 5J 9
St Stephens Gdns.
B98: Redd 4F 212
WV13: W'hall 7A 38
St Stephens Rd. WS7: Burn 3J 17
B29: S Oak 1H 143
B71: W Brom 8B 78
St Stephen's St. B6: Aston 3L 101
Saints Way CV10: Nun 4K 89
St Thomas Cl. B75: S Cold 4M 59
WS3: Wals 3L 39
WS9: A'rdge 8H 27
St Thomas' Ct. CV1: Cov 7B 152
St Thomas Dr. WS12: Haz 4A 10
St Thomas Ho. CV1: Cov 7B 152
(off St Thomas' Ct.)
St Thomas Rd. CV6: Cov 6G 131
B23: Erd 6D 80
St Thomas's Cl. CV10: Nun 6C 88
St Thomas St. DY2: Neth 4J 97
DY8: Stourb 4M 115
St Valentines Cl.
B70: W Brom 7M 77
St Vincent Cres.
B70: W Brom 3F 76
St Vincent St.
B16: Birm 7H 101 (5A 4)
St Vincent St. W.
B16: Birm 7G 101 (6A 4)
St Wilfreds Cotts. CV7: Old A 7E 86
St Wulstan Ct. CV47: Sou 5J 225
St Wulstan Way CV47: Sou 4J 225
Saladin Av. B69: O'bry 4E 98
Salcombe Av. B26: Sheld 4C 124
Salcombe Cl. CV3: W'hall 3K 175
CV11: Nun 4M 89
WS11: Cann 2C 14
Salcombe Dr. DY5: Brie H 2C 116
Salcombe Gro. WV14: Cose 8K 53
Salcombe Rd. B66: Smeth 4B 100
Saldavian Ct. WS2: Wals 3H 55
Salemorton Ct. CV22: Dunc 3H 205
Salem Rd. LE10: Burb 4M 91
Salem St. DY4: Tip 4D 76
Salford Circ. B6: Aston 8D 80
Salford Cl. B98: Redd 3H 221
CV2: Cov 4G 153
Salford St. B6: Aston 1C 102
Salford Trad. Est. B6: Aston 1C 102
Salisbury Av. CV3: Cov 3C 174
CV10: Nun 2B 88
Salisbury Cl. B13: Mose 5L 121
CV8: Wols 6F 176
DY1: Dud 6F 74
WS13: Lich 6J 13
Salisbury Ct. B91: Sol 5C 146
Salisbury Dr. B46: Wat O 6J 83
CV10: Nun 2B 88
DY11: Kidd 3F 156
WS12: Hth H 8H 9
Salisbury Gro. B72: W Grn 2J 81
Salisbury Rd. B8: Salt 4E 102
B13: Mose 5L 121
B19: Loz 1K 101
B66: Smeth 5B 100
B70: W Brom 8L 77
LE10: Burb 2A 92
Salisbury St. WS10: Darl 2E 54
Salisbury Twr.
B18: Hock 6G 101 (3A 4)
Sallow Gro. WS8: Bwnhls 8F 16
Sally Ward Dr. WS9: Wals W 5G 27
Salop Cl. B71: W Brom 3H 77
Salop Dr. B68: O'bry 7J 99
WS11: Cann 1F 14
Salop Rd. B68: O'bry 6J 99
B97: Redd 7D 212
Salop St. B12: Birm 1M 121
B69: O'bry 8E 76
DY1: Dud 7H 75
WV3: Wolv 8C 36 (5H 7)
WV14: Bils 5L 53
Salstar Cl. B6: Aston 3L 101
Saltash Gro. B25: Yard 8J 103
Saltbrook Rd. B63: Crad 2G 117
DY9: Lye 2F 116
Saltbrook Trad. Est.
B63: Crad 2G 117
Salter Rd. DY4: Tip 2M 75
Salters La. B71: W Brom 5L 77
B97: Redd 5A 212
B79: Tam 3B 32
Salter's Rd. WS9: Wals W 5G 27
SALTER STREET 7J 167
Salter St. B94: Earls, H'ley H 7J 167
Salters Va. B70: W Brom 8L 77
Saltisford CV34: Warw 2D 222
Saltisford Gdns.
CV34: Warw 1D 222
Salt La. CV1: Cov 7C 152 (5C 6)
SALTLEY 5D 102
Saltley Bus. Pk. B8: Salt 3D 102
Saltley Cotts. B24: Erd 1F 102
Saltley Ind. Cen. B8: Salt 6C 102
Saltley Leisure Cen. 6G 103
Saltley Rd. B7: Birm 4B 102
Saltley Trad. Est. B8: Salt 3D 102
Saltley Viaduct B7: Birm 4C 102
B8: Salt 4C 102
Saltney Cl. B24: Erd 4K 81
Salts La. B78: Dray B 4L 45
Saltwells La. DY2: Neth 7G 97
DY5: Brie H, Quar B 7F 96
Saltwells Nature Reserve 6G 97
Saltwells Rd. DY2: Neth 7H 97
Salwarpe Gro. B29: W Cas 7M 119
Salwarpe Rd. B60: B'gve 1L 209
Sam Barber Ct. WS12: Hth H 8L 9
Sambar Rd. B78: Faz 8M 31
Sambourn Cl. B91: Sol 3E 146
SAMBOURNE 8J 221
Sambourne Dr. B34: S End 2D 104
Sambourne La.
B96: A'wd B 8E 220
B96: Sam 8F 220
Sambourne Pk. B96: Sam 8G 221
Sambrook Rd. WV10: Wolv 3G 37
Sam Gault Cl. CV3: Bin 2M 175
Sammons Way CV4: Tile H 8D 150
Sampson Cl. B21: Hand 8C 78
B69: Tiv 2C 98
CV2: Cov 8J 131
Sampson Rd. B11: S'brk 2B 122
Sampson Rd. Nth.
B11: S'brk 1B 122
Sampson St. WS10: W'bry 6H 55
Samsara Rd. B60: B'gve 8C 188
Sams La. B70: W Brom 7J 77

Sam Spencer Ct.—Seaton Cl.

Sam Spencer Ct.
DY10: Harv 8G 159
Samuel Cl. WS13: Lich 7J 13
Samuel Hayward Ho.
CV2: Cov 8H 131
(off Roseberry Av.)
Samuel Johnson Birthplace Mus.
....1H 19
Samuels Rd. B32: Quin 4G 119
Samuel St. WS3: Blox 8H 25
Samuel Va. Ho.
CV1: Cov 5C 152 (2B 6)
Sanda Cft. B36: Cas B 3H 105
Sandalls Cl. B31: Longb 8K 141
Sandal Ri. B91: Sol 6E 146
Sandals Ri. B62: Hale 6D 118
Sandalwood Cl. WV12: W'hall 1B 38
Sandbank WS3: Blox 8G 25
Sandbarn Cl. B90: M'path 3M 167
Sandbeds Rd. WV12: W'hall 5C 38
Sandbourne Dr. DY12: Bew 6C 156
Sandbourne Rd.
B8: W End 5G 103
Sandby Cl. CV12: Bed 5G 111
Sanderling Cl. WV10: F'stne 2H 23
Sanderling Ct. DY10: Kidd 8A 158
Sanderling Ri. DY6: K'wfrd 3A 96
WS7: Burn 1H 17
Sanders Cl. B97: Redd 5A 212
CV9: Ath 8L 49
DY2: Dud 2L 97
Sanders Ct. CV34: Warw 1J 223
Sanders Ind. Est. B61: B'gve 8L 187
Sanderson Ct. DY11: Kidd 4J 157
Sanders Rd. B61: B'gve 8L 187
CV6: Longf 3H 131
Sanders St. DY4: Tip 4B 76
Sandfield B66: Smeth 2L 99
Sandfield Bri. DY5: P'ntt 8B 74
Sandfield Cl. B90: Shir 1G 167
Sandfield Farm Home Pk.
WS8: Bwnhls 8H 17
Sandfield Gro. DY3: Gorn 7B 74
Sandfield Mdw. WS13: Lich 3G 19
Sandfield Rd. B71: W Brom 8L 55
DY8: Word 7M 95
SANDFIELDS 4G 19
Sandfields Av. B10: Small H 1B 122
Sandfields Rd. B68: O'bry 7J 99
Sandford Av. B65: Row R 6C 98
Sandford Cl. CV2: Ald G 6K 131
LE10: Hinc 8M 69
Sandford Ho. WS13: Lich 2G 19
Sandford Ri. WV6: Tett 3L 35
Sandford Rd. B13: Mose 5A 122
DY1: Dud 8E 74
Sandford St. WS13: Lich 2H 19
Sandford Wlk. B12: Bal H 4M 121
Sandford Way CV22: Dunc 6J 205
Sandgate Cres. CV2: Cov 7K 153
Sandgate Rd. B28: Hall G 5F 144
DY4: Tip 1A 76
Sandhill Farm Cl. B19: Loz 2K 101
Sandhills Cres. B91: Sol 1B 168
Sandhills Grn. B48: A'chu 1L 189
Sandhills La. B45: B Grn 2K 189
Sandhills Rd. B45: B Grn 1K 189
Sandhill St. WS3: Blox 8G 25
Sandhurst Av. B36: Hodg H 3K 103
DY9: W'cte 7D 116
Sandhurst Cl. B98: Redd 3J 213
Sandhurst Dr. WV4: Penn 5A 52
Sandhurst Gro. CV6: Cov 4B 152
DY8: Word 6L 95
Sandhurst Ho. B38: K Nor 8G 143
Sandhurst Rd. B13: Mose 7L 121
B74: Four O 4F 42
DY6: K'wfrd 5A 96
Sandicliffe Cl. DY11: Kidd 1J 157
Sandilands Cl. CV2: Cov 5L 153
Sandland Cl. WV14: Bils 3M 53
Sandland Rd. WV12: W'hall 1D 38
Sandmartin Cl. DY2: Neth 7J 97
Sand Martin Way
DY10: Kidd 7A 158
Sandmeadow Pl. DY6: K'wfrd 4J 95
Sandmere Gro. B14: Yard W 6D 144
Sandmere Ri. WV10: Bush 8E 22
Sandmere Rd. B14: Yard W 6D 144
Sandon Cl. B98: Redd 6G 213
Sandon Gro. B24: Erd 5H 81
Sandon Rd. B17: Edg 7A 100
B66: Smeth 7A 100
CV11: Nun 4H 89
DY9: W'cte 5F 116
WV10: F'hses 7B 22
Sandown B77: Amin 4F 32
Sandown Av. CV6: Cov 7F 130
WS6: C Hay 6E 14
Sandown Cl. CV32: Lill 5C 218
WS7: C Ter 8F 10
WS12: Haz 3A 10
Sandown Ct. B29: W Cas 2C 142
Sandown Dr. B61: Cats 8B 162
WV6: Pert 5F 34
Sandown Rd. B36: Hodg H 1K 103
CV21: Rugby 5C 180
Sandown Twr. B31: N'fld 8A 142
Sandpiper B77: Wiln 4G 47
Sandpiper Cl. CV23: Brow 1C 180
DY9: W'cte 4F 116
Sandpiper Cl. DY10: Kidd 7B 158
WS12: Hed 2J 9
Sandpiper Gdns. B38: K Nor 2F 164
Sandpiper Rd. CV2: Ald G 6H 131
Sandpiper Way B23: Erd 3C 80
Sandpit Cl. WS10: W'bry 7L 55
Sand Pits B1: Birm 6H 101 (4B 4)
Sandpits, The B30: B'vlle 1E 142
CV12: Bulk 7C 112
Sandpits Cl. B76: Curd 3H 83
Sandpits Ind. Est.
B1: Birm 6H 101 (4B 4)
Sandpits La. CV6: Cov 7L 129
CV7: Ker E 7L 129
Sandra Cl. WS9: A'rdge 4H 41
Sandringham Av. LE9: Earl S 2D 70
WV12: W'hall 2B 38
Sandringham Cl.
CV4: W'wd H 3F 172
WS7: C Ter 8E 10
Sandringham Ct. B43: Gt Barr 8F 56
B79: Tam 2B 32
(off Wigginton Rd.)
CV10: Nun 3F 88
Sandringham Dr. B65: Row R 5C 98
WS9: A'rdge 8H 27
Sandringham Pl. DY8: Word 8K 95
Sandringham Rd. B42: P Barr 3H 79
B62: Hale 2B 118
DY8: Word 8J 95
WV4: Penn 5A 52
WV5: Wom 3F 72
Sandringham Way
DY5: Brie H 1C 116
Sandstone Av. B45: Rubery 1G 163
Sandstone Cl. DY3: Lwr G 5D 74
Sandstone Ct. B77: Wiln 2G 47
Sandstone Rd. DY12: Bew 6C 156
Sand St. B70: W Brom 5E 76
Sandway Gdns. B8: Salt 3D 102
Sandway Gro. B13: Mose 2C 144
SANDWELL 1A 100
Sandwell & Dudley Station (Rail)
....8G 77
Sandwell Av. WS10: Darl 4B 54
Sandwell Bus. Development Cen.
B66: Smeth 2J 99
Sandwell Bus. Pk.
B66: Smeth 1J 99
Sandwell Cen. B70: W Brom 6K 77
Sandwell Ct. B21: Hand 1D 100
Sandwell Ind. Est.
B66: Smeth 1J 99
Sandwell Pk. Farm 6M 77
Sandwell Pl. B66: Smeth 1A 100
WV12: W'hall 2D 38
Sandwell Rd. B21: Hand 8D 78
B70: W Brom 5J 77
WV10: Oxl 8B 22
Sandwell Rd. Nth.
B71: W Brom 5K 77
Sandwell Rd. Pas.
B70: W Brom 5J 77
Sandwell St. WS1: Wals 1M 55
Sandwell Valley Country Pk.
Forge La. 3A 78
Salter's La. 5M 77
Tanhouse Av. 3C 78
Sandwell Wlk. WS1: Wals 1M 55
Sandwick Cl. CV3: Bin 1M 175
Sandwood Dr. B44: Gt Barr 1M 79
Sandy Acre Way
DY8: Stourb 4B 116
Sandy Bank DY12: Bew 6A 156
Sandy Cres. LE10: Hinc 8H 69
WV11: Wed 1A 38
Sandy Cft. B13: Mose 2C 144
Sandycroft B72: W Grn 6J 59
Sandyfields Rd.
DY3: Lwr G, Sed 4M 73
Sandygate Cl. B97: Redd 7M 211
Sandy Gro. WS8: Bwnhls 8F 16
Sandy Hill Ri. B90: Shir 5G 145
Sandy Hill Rd. B90: Shir 5G 145
Sandy Hollow WV6: Tett 7J 35
Sandy La. B6: Aston 2B 102
B42: Gt Barr 1J 79
B46: Over W 5L 85
B61: L Ash, Wild 4K 161
CV1: Cov 4C 152
CV6: Cov 4C 152 (1B 6)
CV7: Fill 6F 108
CV21: Rugby 6L 179
CV32: B'dwn 3L 217
DY7: Kinv 7A 114
DY8: Stourb 5K 115
DY10: Blak, Harv 1H 159
DY11: Kidd 8F 134
(not continuous)
DY13: Stour S 8H 183
WS10: W'bry 6M 55
WS11: Cann 8A 8
(not continuous)
WV6: Tett 3L 35
WV8: Cod 5F 20
WV10: Bush 8E 22
Sandy La. Bus. Pk.
CV1: Cov 4C 152 (1B 6)
Sandy La. Ind. Est.
DY13: Stour S 8H 183
Sandy Mt. WV5: Wom 2H 73
Sandymount Rd. WS1: Wals 1M 55
Sandy Rd. DY8: Stourb 8K 115
Sandys Gro. DY4: Tip 4L 75
Sandythorpe CV3: W'hall 3L 175
Sandy Wlk. LE10: Hinc 7G 69
Sandy Way B15: Birm 8H 101 (7B 4)
B77: Amin 6G 33
Sandy Way La. B78: Dord 2C 48
Sangwin Rd. WV14: Cose 2J 75
Sankey Rd. WS11: Cann 6F 8
Sansome Ri. B90: Shir 7F 144
Sansome Rd. B90: Shir 7F 144
Sanstone Cl. WS3: Blox 6J 25
Sanstone Rd. WS3: Blox 6H 25
Santa Maria Way
DY13: Stour S 6H 183
Santolina Dr. WS5: Wals 6A 56
Santos Cl. CV3: Bin 1M 175
Santridge Ct. *B61: B'gve 5A 188*
(off Bewell Head)
Santridge La. B61: B'gve 5A 188
Sant Rd. B31: Longb 2B 164
SAPCOTE 2K 93
Sapcote Bus. Pk.
B10: Small H 3E 122
Sapcote Gro. CV6: Ald G 5H 131
Sapcote Rd. LE9: S Stan 7L 71
LE10: Burb 2A 92
Sapcote Trad. Cen.
B64: Old H 6M 97
Saplings, The B76: Walm 1A 82
Sapphire Ct. B3: Birm 5J 101 (2D 4)
B92: Olton 8M 123
CV2: W'grve S 8B 132
Sapphire Dr. CV31: Lea S 4M 223
WS11: Hth H 7J 9
Sapphire Ga. CV2: Cov 7J 153
Sapphire Hgts.
B1: Birm 6H 101 (2B 4)
Sapphire Ho. (E.) B91: Sol 5A 146
Sapphire Ho. (W.) B91: Sol 5A 146
Sapphire Twr. *B6: Aston 3M 101*
(off Park La.)
Saracen Dr. B75: S Cold 3M 59
CV7: Bal C 3E 170
Sara Cl. B74: Four O 6G 43
Sarah Cl. WV14: Bils 8L 53
Sarah Ct. B73: New O 8D 58
Sarah Gdns. WS5: Wals 5M 55
Sarah Seager Cl.
DY13: Stour S 3E 182
Sarah Siddons Ho.
WS13: Lich 2H 19
(off Wade St.)
Sarah St. B9: Birm 7B 102
Sarawak Pl. CV22: Caw 1H 205
Saredon Cl. WS3: Pels 8A 26
Saredon Rd. WS6: C Hay 5B 14
WV10: Share 5A 14
(not continuous)
Sarehole Mill Mus. 1D 144
Sarehole Rd. B28: Hall G 2D 144
Sargeaunt St. CV31: Lea S 2M 223
Sargent Cl. B43: Gt Barr 5K 57
Sargent Ho.
B16: Birm 7H 101 (5B 4)
Sargent's Hill WS5: Wals 3C 56
Sargent Turner Trad. Est.
DY9: Lye 3F 116
Sark Dr. B36: Cas B 3H 105
Satchwell Ct. CV32: Lea S 1M 223
Satchwell Pl. CV31: Lea S 2A 224
Satchwell Wlk. *CV32: Lea S 1M 223*
(in Royal Priors Shop. Cen.)
Satellite Ind. Pk.
WV13: W'hall 5K 37
Saturday Bri. B1: Birm 7D 4
Saturn Rd. WS11: Cann 4F 8
Saumur Way CV34: Warw 3J 223
Saunders Av. CV12: Bed 7H 111
Saunders Cl. WS12: Haz 3M 9
Saunton Cl. CV5: Alle 8H 129
Saunton Rd. CV22: Bil 8M 179
WS3: Blox 6G 25
Saunton Way B29: S Oak 8C 120
Savages Cl. CV33: Bis T 8F 224
Saveker Dr. B76: Walm 5L 59
Savernake Cl. B45: Fran 7G 141
Saville Cl. B45: Redn 2H 163
LE10: Hinc 6L 69
Saville Gro. CV8: Ken 3J 199
Savoy Cl. B32: Harb 4M 119
Saw Mill Cl. WS4: Wals 6L 39
Sawpits La.
WS14: Lit H, W'frd 8K 29
Saxelby Cl. B14: K Hth 7L 143
(not continuous)
Saxelby Ho. B14: K Hth 7L 143
Saxifrage Pl. DY10: Kidd 5M 157
Saxon Bus. Pk. B60: S Prior 7L 209
Saxon Cl. B77: Wiln 3F 46
B78: Pole 8M 33
B80: Stud 4L 221
CV3: Bin W 2D 176
CV22: Caw 1G 205
WS6: Gt Wyr 7G 15
Saxon Ct. WS13: Lich 2E 18
WV6: Tett 4J 35
Saxondale Av. B26: Sheld 3M 123
Saxon Dr. B65: Row R 5C 98
B79: Tam 5C 32
Saxonfields WV6: Tett 4J 35
Saxon Mdws. CV32: Lea S 7J 217
Saxon Mill La. B79: Tam 4C 32
Saxon Rd. CV2: Cov 5H 153
Saxons Way B14: K Hth 7A 144
Saxon Wlk. WS13: Lich 2E 18
Saxon Way B37: K'hrst 6F 104
Saxon Wood Cl. B31: N'fld 5A 142
Saxon Wood Rd.
B90: Ches G 4K 167
Saxton Dr. B74: Four O 3F 42
Scafell CV21: Brow 2D 180
Scafell Cl. CV5: E Grn 5G 151
Scafell Dr. B23: Erd 4D 80
WV14: Bils 2M 53
Scafell Rd. DY8: Amb 3B 116
Scaife Rd. B60: B'gve 2B 210
Scammerton B77: Wiln 2H 47
Scampton Cl. WV6: Pert 4E 34
Scampton Way B79: Tam 1C 32
Scar Bank CV34: Warw 8E 216
Scarborough Cl. WS2: Wals 1H 55
Scarborough Rd. WS2: Wals 1H 55
Scarborough Way
CV4: Tile H 2F 172
Scarecrow La. B75: R'ley 5L 43
Scarfield Cotts. B48: A'chu 4A 190
Scarfield Hill B48: A'chu 4K 189
Scarman Ho. CV4: Canly 4G 173
Scarman Rd. CV4: Canly 5G 173
Scarsdale Rd. B42: Gt Barr 1K 79
Schofield Av. B71: W Brom 1H 77
Schofield Rd. B37: K'hrst 4G 105
Scholars Ct. DY10: Kidd 5L 157
Scholars Dr. CV22: Caw 1H 205
Scholars Ga. B33: Kitts G 7B 104
WS7: Burn 3K 17
Scholars Wlk. WS4: Rus 2B 40
Scholefield Twr. *B19: Birm 4K 101*
(off Uxbridge St.)
Scholfield Rd. CV7: Ker E 3A 130
Schoolacre Ri. B74: S'tly 8L 41
Schoolacre Rd. B34: S End 3B 104
School Av. WS3: Blox 1J 39
WS8: Bwnhls 1F 26
School Bell M. CV8: S'lgh 3B 200
School Cl. B35: Cas V 6B 82
B37: K'hrst 3G 105
B69: Tiv 2C 98
CV3: Cov 7F 152
LE10: Burb 3A 92
WS7: C Ter 1D 16
WS11: Nort C 3A 16
WV3: Wolv 2H 51
WV5: Try 1C 72
WV8: Cod 5G 21
School Ct. WS12: Hed 3J 9
School Cres. WS11: Nort C 3A 16
School Cft. CV35: Beau 7J 197
School Dr. B47: Wyt 6A 166
B60: B'gve 7A 188
B73: S Cold 5H 59
DY8: Amb 1M 115
WV14: Bils 7A 54
School Dr., The DY2: Dud 2K 97
Schoolfield Gro.
CV21: Rugby 6M 179
Schoolfields Rd.
WS14: Shens 4G 29
School Gdns. CV21: Hillm 8G 181
Schoolgate Cl. B8: W End 3G 103
WS4: S'fld 8D 26
School Grn. WV14: Bils 1J 53
School Hill CV10: Harts 2A 88
CV33: Off 8H 219
Schoolhouse Cl. B38: K Nor 7H 143
School Ho. La.
CV2: W'grve S 3A 154
School La. B33: Yard 8M 103
B34: S End 3B 104
B48: A'chu 4B 190
B60: L End 3B 188
B61: U War 6F 208
B63: Hale 7M 117
B76: Lea M 2A 84
B77: Dost 4D 46
B78: Hints 6D 30
B78: Hop 2H 31
B79: Shut 2M 33
B91: Sol 4D 146
CV7: Exh 2E 130
CV8: Ken 4F 198
CV10: Gall C 3L 87
CV23: Stret D 3F 202
CV31: Rad S 4E 224
CV33: H'ham 5L 219
CV35: Beau 7H 197
CV35: Wrox 3E 196
DY5: Brie H 5B 96
DY9: Hag 3D 138
LE10: Sharn 5J 93
LE10: Wlvy 5L 113
WS3: Lit W 7L 15
WS3: Pels 5M 25
WS7: C Ter 1D 16
WS15: Gent 4G 11
WV3: Wolv 8C 36 (5H 7)
WV10: Bush 7D 22
School Pas. DY5: Quar B 8G 97
School Rd. B13: Mose 8M 121
B14: Yard W 5B 144
School Rd. B28: Hall G 1F 144
B45: Rubery 3E 162
B90: Shir 7H 145
B94: H'ley H 1M 193
CV12: Bulk 7B 112
DY3: Himl 6H 73
DY5: Quar B 7G 97
WR9: Wych 8E 208
WS10: W'bry 7K 55
WS11: Nort C 3A 16
WV5: Try 1C 72
WV5: Wom 2H 73
WV6: Tett 5G 35
WV11: Wed 3H 37
School St. B64: Crad H 8K 97
B77: Amin 5E 32
CV8: Wols 6G 177
CV21: Hillm 8G 181
CV22: Dunc 6J 205
CV23: Chu L 4B 178
CV23: Long L 5G 179
CV47: S'ton 1M 225
CV47: Sou 5J 225
DY1: Dud 8H 75
(not continuous)
DY3: Sed 1E 74
DY5: P'ntt 2D 96
DY8: Stourb 3M 115
WS4: S'fld 8D 26
WS10: Darl 3C 54
(Alma St.)
WS10: Darl 4E 54
(Nowell St., not continuous)
WV3: Wolv 8C 36 (5H 7)
WV13: W'hall 7M 37
WV14: Cose 1J 75
School St. W. WV14: Cose 1J 75
School Ter. B29: S Oak 7F 120
School Wlk. B79: Tam 3B 32
CV11: Nun 6L 89
WS7: C Ter 1D 16
WV14: Bils 1J 53
Scimitar Cl. B79: Tam 2L 31
Scorers Cl. B90: Shir 3H 145
Scotchill, The CV6: Cov 8A 130
Scotchings, The
B36: Hodg H 1L 103
Scotch Orchard WS13: Lich 8K 13
Scotia Rd. WS11: Cann 6D 8
Scotland La. B32: Bart G 1H 141
Scotland Pas. B70: W Brom 6K 77
SCOTLANDS 1G 37
Scotland St. B1: Birm 6J 101 (4C 4)
Scots Cl. CV22: Bil 2J 205
Scots La. CV6: Cov 3M 151
Scott Arms Shop. Cen.
B42: Gt Barr 8F 56
Scott Av. CV10: Nun 1K 89
WS10: W'bry 7H 55
WV4: Penn 5L 51
Scott Cl. B71: W Brom 4K 77
WS14: Lich 3H 19
Scott Gro. B92: Olton 6L 123
Scott Ho. B43: Gt Barr 2F 78
Scott Rd. B43: Gt Barr 7F 56
B77: Amin 5E 32
B92: Olton 6L 123
B97: Redd 1C 220
CV8: Ken 7E 198
CV31: Lea S 3B 224
WS5: Wals 3D 56
SCOTT'S GREEN 1G 97
Scotts Grn. Cl. DY1: Dud 1F 96
Scotts Grn. Island DY1: Dud 2F 96
Scott's Rd. DY8: Stourb 3M 115
Scott St. DY4: Tip 4C 76
WS12: Wim 6L 9
Scott Way WS7: C Ter 8F 10
Scotwell Cl. B65: Row R 6B 98
Scout Cl. B33: Kitts G 7C 104
Scribbans Cl. B66: Smeth 5B 100
Scriber's La. B28: Hall G 5D 144
Scribers Mdw. B28: Hall G 5E 144
Scrimshaw Ho. *WS2: Wals 2J 55*
(off Pleck Rd.)
Sculthorpe Rd. DY10: Blak 7H 137
Seabroke Av. CV22: Rugby 6M 179
Seacole Ho. B97: Redd 7B 212
Seacroft Av. B25: Yard 8L 103
Seafield B77: Amin 4F 32
Seafield Cl. DY6: K'wfrd 5L 95
Seafield La. B48: A'chu 3L 191
B98: Beo 6M 191
Seaford Cl. CV6: Ald G 5H 131
Seaforth Dr. LE10: Hinc 8G 69
Seaforth Gro. WV12: W'hall 8B 24
Seagar St. B71: W Brom 5L 77
Seagers La. DY5: Brie H 7D 96
Seagrave Rd.
CV1: Cov 7E 152 (6F 6)
Seagull Bay Dr. WV14: Cose 8K 53
Sealand Dr. CV12: Bed 6G 111
Seal Cl. B76: Walm 5L 59
Seals Grn. B38: K Nor 2D 164
Seamless Dr. WV11: Wed 5K 37
Sear Hills Cl. CV7: Bal C 3H 171
Sear Retail Pk. B90: Shir 8K 145
Seathwaite CV21: Brow 2C 180
Seaton B77: Wiln 1F 46
Seaton Cl. CV11: Nun 4M 89
LE10: Burb 2A 92

Seaton Cl.—Shepherds Hill

Seaton Cl. WV11: Wed 4M 37
Seaton Gro. B13: Mose 8K 121
Seaton Pl. DY8: Word 7J 95
Seaton Rd. B66: Smeth 4B 100
Sebastian Cl. CV3: W'hall 4H 175
Sebastian Coe Health Club ...4D 156
Sebright Grn. DY11: W'ley 6J 135
Sebright Rd. DY11: W'ley 6H 135
Sebright Wlk. DY11: W'ley 6J 135
Seckham Rd. WS13: Lich 1G 19
Second Av. B6: Witt 6M 79
B9: Bord G 8E 102
B29: S Oak 6H 121
CV3: Cov 8J 153
DY6: P'ntt 2M 95
WS8: Bwnhls 8G 17
WV10: Bush 2E 36
Second Exhibition Av.
B40: Nat E C 5K 125
Securehold Bus. Cen.
B98: Redd 8H 213
Security Ho. WV1:
Wolv 8C 36 (5J 7)
Sedge Av. B38: K Nor 6F 142
Sedgeberrow Covert
B38: K Nor 1E 164
Sedgeberrow Rd. B63: Hale ...7A 118
Sedgebourne Way
B31: Longb 8J 141
Sedge Dr. B61: B'gve 3A 188
Sedgefield Cl. DY1: Dud 6E 74
Sedgefield Gro. WV6: Pert 5F 34
Sedgefield Wlk. B61: Cats 8B 162
Sedgefield Way
WS11: Nort C 5A 16
Sedgeford Cl. DY5: Brie H 1D 116
Sedgehill Av. B17: Harb 5B 120
Sedgemere Gro. CV7: Bal C 4J 171
WS4: S'fld 1C 40
Sedgemere Rd. B26: Yard 8M 103
Sedgemoor Av. WS7: Burn 4H 17
Sedgemoor Rd. CV3: W'hall ...4H 175
SEDGLEY 1D 74
Sedgley Cl. B98: Redd 5F 212
Sedgley Gro. B20: Hand 5E 78
Sedgley Hall Av. DY3: Sed 1C 74
Sedgley Hall Est. DY3: Sed 8C 52
Sedgley Rd. DY1: Dud 3H 75
WV4: Penn 6L 51
Sedgley Rd. E. DY4: Tip 5A 76
Sedgley Rd. W. DY4: Tip 3K 75
Sedlescombe Lodge
CV22: Rugby 1M 205
Sedlescombe Pk.
CV22: Rugby 1M 205
Seed Fld. Cft. CV3: Cov 2D 174
Seedgreen Cl.
DY13: Stour S 7B 182
Seedhouse Ct. B64: Old H 1A 118
Seeds La. WS8: Bwnhls 1F 26
Seedymill La. WS13: Hanch 2E 12
Seekings, The CV31: W'nsh 6B 224
Seekings Dr. CV8: Ken 5H 199
Seeleys Rd. B11: Tys 4D 122
Seeney La. B76: Mars 7B 62
Seeswood Cl. CV10: Nun 7C 88
Sefton Dr. B65: Row R 3M 97
Sefton Gro. DY4: Tip 7C 54
Sefton Rd. B16: Edg 7F 100
B77: Dost 5C 46
CV4: Canly 3L 173
Segbourne Rd. B45: Rubery 1E 162
Segundo Cl. WS5: Wals 5M 55
Segundo Rd. WS5: Wals 5M 55
SEISDON 7A 50
Seisdon Hollaway WV5: Seis ...6A 50
Seisdon Rd. WV5: Seis, Try 7A 50
Selba Dr. DY11: Kidd 3F 156
Selborne Cl. WS1: Wals 8A 40
Selborne Gro. B13: Mose 4C 144
Selborne Rd. B20: Hand 7G 79
CV22: Bil 1K 205
DY2: Dud 2K 97
Selborne St. WS1: Wals 8A 40
Selbourne Cres. WV1: Wolv 8H 37
Selby Cl. B26: Yard 8M 103
Selby Gro. B13: Mose 4B 144
Selby Ho. B69: O'bry 3D 98
Selby Way CV10: Nun 4B 88
WS3: Blox 7E 24
Selcombe Way B38: K Nor 2F 164
Selco Way B76: Min 4A 82
Selcroft Av. B32: Harb 4M 119
Selecta Av. B44: Gt Barr 7K 57
Selina Dix Ho. CV1: Cov 2E 6
Selker Dr. B77: Amin 4E 32
Selkirk Cl. B71: W Brom 3J 77
Selly Av. B29: S Oak 7G 121
Selly Cl. B29: S Oak 7H 121
Selly Hall Cft. B30: B'vlle 3G 143
Selly Hill Rd. B29: S Oak 7F 120
SELLY OAK 8E 120
Selly Oak Ind. Est.
B29: S Oak 8E 120
Selly Oak Rd. B30: B'vlle 2E 142
Selly Oak Station (Rail) 7E 120
SELLY PARK 7H 121
Selly Pk. Rd. B29: S Oak 6G 121
Selly Wharf B29: S Oak 7E 120
Selly Wick Dr. B29: S Oak 7H 121
Selly Wick Rd. B29: S Oak 7G 121
Sellywood Rd. B30: B'vlle 2D 142
Selma Gro. B14: Yard W 4D 144
Selman's Hill WS3: Blox 6J 25
Selman's Pde. WS3: Blox 7J 25
Selsdon Cl. B47: Wyt 4C 166
DY11: Kidd 4H 157
Selsdon Rd. WS3: Blox 6F 24
Selsey Av. B17: Edg 6B 100
Selsey Cl. CV3: W'hall 5J 175
Selsey Rd. B17: Edg 6B 100
Selside CV21: Brow 2D 180
Selston Rd. B6: Aston 2L 101
Selvey Av. B43: Gt Barr 6H 57
Selworthy Rd. B36: Cas B 2F 104
CV6: Cov 6D 130
Selwyn Cl. WV2: Wolv ...2C 52 (8J 7)
Selwyn Ho. B37: Chel W 6K 105
Selwyn Rd. B16: Edg 6D 100
WS7: Burn 2M 17
WV14: Bils 3M 53
Selwyn Wlk. B74: Lit A 5C 42
Semele Cl. CV31: Rad S 4E 224
Senate Ho. CV4: Canly 5H 173
Seneschal Rd. CV3: Cov 2E 174
Senior Cl. WV11: Ess 6A 24
Senneley's Pk. Rd.
B31: N'fld 1L 141
Sennen Cl. CV11: Nun 4A 90
WV13: W'hall 8M 37
Sensall Rd. DY9: W'cte 6F 116
Sentry Way B75: S Cold 3M 59
Sephton Dr. CV6: Longf 3J 131
Serin Cl. DY10: Kidd 8A 158
Serpentine, The DY11: Kidd ...5J 157
Serpentine Rd. B6: Aston 8A 80
B17: Harb 3C 120
B29: S Oak 6G 121
Servite Ct. B14: K Hth 7A 144
Servite Ho. B44: Gt Barr 7M 57
B92: Olton 2K 145
CV8: Ken 6F 198
Seth Somers Track 7C 118
Settle Av. B34: Hodg H 3A 104
Settle Cft. B37: F'bri 8F 104
Setton Dr. DY3: Sed 2E 74
Seven Acre Cl. CV33: Bis T 8D 224
Seven Acres WS9: A'rdge 4H 41
Sevenacres La. B98: Redd 4J 213
Seven Acres Rd. B31: N'fld 8C 142
B62: Quin 4G 119
Sevendwellings Vw.
DY5: Brie H 8C 96
Sevens Rd. WS12: Haz 5C 10
Seven Star Rd. B91: Sol 4A 146
Seven Stars Ind. Est.
CV3: Cov 2H 175
(Allard Way)
CV3: Cov 2G 175
(Wheler Rd.)
Seven Stars Rd. B69: O'bry 2G 99
Severn Av. LE10: Hinc 1G 91
Severn Bank Pk. DY12: Bew 2B 182
Severn Cl. B36: Cas B 2F 104
B61: Cats 1A 188
CV32: Lill 6C 218
DY4: Tip 4M 75
WV12: W'hall 2A 38
Severn Ct. B23: Erd 6B 80
B73: S Cold 4H 59
Severn Dr. DY5: P'ntt 2B 96
WS7: Burn 3K 17
WV6: Pert 5E 34
Severne Gro. B27: A Grn 8J 123
Severne Rd. B27: A Grn 1J 145
Severn Gro. B11: S'brk 3C 122
B19: Loz 2J 101
(not continuous)
DY11: Kidd 6H 157
Severnhills Dr.
DY13: Stour S 7A 182
Severn Manor Gdns.
DY13: Stour S 8E 182
Severn Quay DY12: Bew 6B 156
Severn Ri. DY13: Stour S 4E 182
Severn Rd. B63: Crad 4H 117
CV1: Cov 8F 152
CV12: Bulk 6A 112
DY8: Stourb 6M 115
DY13: Stour S 7G 183
WS3: Blox 8L 25
WS8: Bwnhls 7C 16
Severn Side DY13: Stour S 7G 183
Severnside Bus. Pk.
DY13: Stour S 7G 183
Severnside Cvn. Pk.
DY13: Stour S 8H 183
Severnside Mill DY12: Bew 6B 156
Severn Side Nth. DY12: Bew ...6B 156
Severn Side Sth. DY12: Bew ...6B 156
Severns Rd. WS15: Cann W 7E 10
Severn St. B1: Birm 8K 101 (7E 4)
Severn St. Pl. B1: Birm 7E 4
Severn Twr. B7: Nech 4B 102
Severn Valley Railway 7F 156
Severn Way B47: Wyt 7L 165
DY12: Bew 3B 156
Sevilla Cl. CV3: Bin 7A 154
Sevington Cl. B91: Sol 1C 168
Sewall Highway CV2: Cov 3H 153
CV6: Cov 1G 153
Seward Cl. WS14: Lich 3K 19
Seymour Cl. B29: S Oak 7G 121
CV3: W'hall 4J 175
WS6: C Hay 8D 14
Seymour Dr. B98: Redd 4G 213
Seymour Gdns. B74: Four O 6E 42
Seymour Gro. CV34: Warw 3K 223
Seymour Pl. CV8: Ken 3E 198
Seymour Rd. B69: O'bry 2J 99
CV11: Nun 6K 89
CV21: Rugby 3C 180
DY4: Tip 8C 54
DY9: W'cte 4F 116
DY11: Kidd 1H 157
Shackleton Dr. LE10: Burb 5L 91
WV6: Pert 4E 34
Shackleton Hall B15: Edg 3G 121
Shackleton Rd. WS3: Blox 7K 25
Shadowbrook La.
B92: H Ard 1K 147
Shadowbrook Rd. CV6: Cov 4A 152
Shadrack Cl. LE9: S Stan 8K 71
Shadwell Dr. DY3: Lwr G 6D 74
Shadwell St.
B4: Birm 5K 101 (2F 4)
Shady La. B44: Gt Barr 7K 57
Shadymoor Dr. DY5: Brie H 1C 116
Shaftesbury Av. B63: Crad 2H 117
CV7: Ker E 2A 130
DY9: Pedm 6C 116
Shaftesbury Cl. B60: B'gve 7B 188
Shaftesbury Dr. WS12: Hed 2J 9
Shaftesbury Rd. CV5: Cov 1M 173
WS10: W'bry 7H 55
Shaftesbury Sq. B71: W Brom ...4J 77
Shaftesbury St. B70: W Brom ...5J 77
B71: W Brom 5J 77
Shaft La. CV7: Mer 5M 127
Shaftmoor Ind. Est.
B28: Hall G 7F 122
Shaftmoor La. B27: A Grn 7E 122
B28: Hall G 7E 122
Shaftsbury Cl. WV14: Bils 2M 53
Shaftsbury Dr. WS7: Burn 2M 17
Shaftsbury Rd. B26: Sheld 4C 124
Shahjalal Rd. B8: Salt 4D 102
Shakels Cl. B97: Redd 5E 220
Shakespeare Av. B98: Redd 7G 213
CV12: Bed 7K 111
CV34: Warw 4C 222
WS14: Lich 3H 19
Shakespeare Cl. B79: Tam 3A 32
WV14: Cose 7K 53
Shakespeare Cres. WS3: Blox ...1L 39
(not continuous)
Shakespeare Dr. B90: Shir 8G 145
CV11: Nun 8A 90
DY10: Kidd 3A 158
LE10: Hinc 8J 69
Shakespeare Gdns.
CV22: Rugby 1L 205
Shakespeare Gro. WS11: Cann ...5D 8
Shakespeare Ho.
B31: Longb 1A 164
Shakespeare Pl. WS3: Blox 2L 39
Shakespeare Rd. B23: Erd 6B 80
B67: Smeth 5L 99
B90: Shir 8K 145
DY3: Lwr G 5A 74
DY4: Tip 1A 76
WS7: C Ter 1F 16
Shakespeare St. B11: S'hll 4C 122
CV2: Cov 4H 153
WV1: Wolv 8E 36 (5M 7)
Shakleton Rd. CV5: Cov 7A 152
Shaldon Wlk. B66: Smeth 4B 100
Shales, The WV5: Wom 4E 72
Shale St. WV14: Bils 4J 53
Shalford Rd. B92: Olton 5L 123
Shallcross La. DY3: Lwr G 6D 74
Shalnecote Gro. B14: K Hth 4J 143
Shambles, The WS10: W'bry 7F 54
Shandon Cl. B32: Bart G 6M 119
Shanklin Dr. CV10: Nun 3K 89
Shanklin Rd. CV3: W'hall 5H 175
Shanklyn Cl. WS6: Gt Wyr 6F 14
Shannon B77: Wiln 1F 46
Shannon Dr. WS8: Bwnhls 7C 16
Shannon Rd. B38: K Nor 2D 164
Shannons Mill B79: Tam 4A 32
Shannon Wlk. WS8: Bwnhls 7C 16
Shanti Niketan
WV2: Wolv 2D 52 (8K 7)
Shapfell CV21: Brow 2D 180
Shapinsay Dr. B45: Fran 8F 140
SHARD END 2C 104
Shard End Cres. B34: S End 3C 104
Shardlow Rd. WV11: Wed 1L 37
Shardway, The B34: S End 4C 104
(not continuous)
Sharesacre St. WV13: W'hall ...6B 38
SHARESHILL 1K 23
Sharington Cl. DY2: Dud 1L 97
Sharman Rd. WV10: Bush 3E 36
SHARMANS CROSS 5L 145
Sharmans Cross Rd.
B91: Sol 5L 145
Sharnbrook Gdns.
LE10: Sharn 5J 93
SHARNFORD 5J 93
Sharnford Rd. LE9: Sap 2L 93
LE10: Aston F 3E 92
Sharon Cl. WV4: E'shll 4E 52
Sharon Way WS12: Hed 6J 9
Sharp Cl. CV6: Cov 7C 130
Sharpe Cl. CV34: Warw 1E 222
Sharpe St. B77: Amin 4G 33
Sharpless Rd. LE10: Burb 2L 91
Sharpley Ct. CV2: W'grve S 1A 154
Sharps Cl. B45: Redn 2G 163
Sharrat Fld. B75: R'ley 7K 43
Sharratt Rd. CV12: Bed 7F 110
Sharrocks St.
WV2: Wolv 8E 36 (6M 7)
SHATTERFORD 3C 134
Shatterford La. DY11: W'ley 5G 135
SHAVER'S END 6H 75
Shaw Av. DY10: Kidd 3B 158
Shawbank Rd. B98: Redd 6H 213
Shawberry Av. B35: Cas V 6A 82
Shawberry Rd. B37: K'hrst 4F 104
SHAWBROOK 5M 165
Shawbrook Gro. B14: K Hth 6A 144
Shawbury Cl. B98: Redd 6L 213
Shawbury Gro. B12: Birm 1M 121
WV6: Pert 4E 34
Shawbury La. B46: Shu 7J 85
CV7: Fill 4A 108
Shawbury Rd. WV10: Wolv 4F 36
Shawbury Village B46: Shu 3L 107
Shaw Dr. B33: Yard 7L 103
WS7: C Ter 8G 11
Shawe Av. CV10: Nun 2J 89
Shawfield B47: H'wd 4A 166
Shaw Hall La. WV10: Cov H 3B 22
Shaw Hedge Rd. DY12: Bew 5C 156
Shawhellier Av. DY5: Brie H 7E 96
Shaw Hill Gro. B8: W End 5G 103
Shaw Hill Rd. B8: W End 5G 103
Shawhurst Cft. B47: H'wd 2A 166
Shawhurst Gdns. B47: H'wd 2B 166
Shawhurst La. B47: H'wd 4A 166
Shaw La. B60: S Prior 8J 209
WR9: Wych 8G 209
WS13: Hanch 1E 12
WS13: Lich 1G 19
WS15: Gent 5G 11
WV6: Tett 6H 35
Shaw La. Ind. Est.
B60: S Prior 7J 209
Shawley Cft. B27: A Grn 5L 123
Shaw Pk. Bus. Village
WV10: Bush 3D 36
Shaw Rd. DY2: Dud 2H 97
(not continuous)
DY4: Tip 5C 76
WV2: Wolv 3C 52
WV10: Bush 3C 36
(not continuous)
WV14: Cose 8H 53
Shaws Cl. B97: Redd 7M 211
Shawsdale Rd.
B36: Hodg H 2M 103
Shaws La. WS6: Gt Wyr 7G 15
Shaw's Pas.
B5: Birm 7M 101 (6J 5)
Shaw St. B70: W Brom 1E 76
WS2: Wals 7K 39
Sheaf La. B26: Sheld 4B 124
Sheapecote Ho.
B71: W Brom 7M 55
Shearers Pl. B75: R'ley 6L 43
Shearwater Cl. B45: Rubery 3F 162
DY10: Kidd 8B 158
Shearwater Dr. CV23: Brow 1C 180
DY5: Brie H 2C 116
Shearwater Wlk. B23: Erd 2B 80
Sheaves Cl. WV14: Cose 6H 53
Shedden St. DY2: Dud 1K 97
Sheddington Rd. B23: Erd 2D 80
Sheen Rd. B44: Gt Barr 5L 57
Sheepclose Dr. B37: F'bri 6G 105
Sheepcote Cl. CV32: Lea S 8A 218
Sheepcote Grange
B61: B'gve 4M 187
Sheepcote La. B77: Amin 6F 32
Sheepcote St.
B16: Birm 7H 101 (5A 4)
Sheepcroft Cl. B97: Redd 7M 211
Sheep Dip La. CV23: Prin 6E 202
Sheepfold Cl. B65: Row R 5A 98
Sheepmoor Cl. B17: Harb 1M 119
Sheep St. CV21: Rugby 6A 180
Sheepwash La. DY4: Tip 4D 76
DY11: W'ley 1J 135
Sheepwash Nature Reserve 5D 76
Sheepy Cl. LE10: Hinc 8M 69
Sheepy Rd. CV9: Ath 6K 49
CV9: Pin 4K 49
Sheffield Rd. B73: Bold 2G 81
Sheffield St. DY5: Quar B 8G 97
Shefford Rd. B6: Aston 4M 101
Sheila Av. WV11: Wed 2L 37
Shelah Rd. B63: Hale 3M 117
Shelbourne Cl. B69: Tiv 7D 76
SHELDON 4D 124
Sheldon Av. WS10: W'bry 5G 55
Sheldon Cl. WV14: Bils 6K 53
Sheldon Country Pk. 3C 124
Sheldon Dr. B31: Longb 7K 141
Sheldonfield Rd. B26: Sheld 4D 124
Sheldon Gro. B26: Sheld 4B 124
CV34: Warw 8F 216
Sheldon Hall Av.
B33: Kitts G 6D 104
(not continuous)
Sheldon Health Leisure Cen.
.......1C 124
Sheldon Heath Rd.
B26: Yard, Sheld 8A 104
Sheldon Rd. B71: W Brom 1L 77
B98: Redd 8G 213
WV10: Oxl 8A 22
Sheldon Wlk. B33: Sheld 8C 104
Sheldrake Cl. CV3: Bin 8A 154
Shelduck Gro. DY10: Kidd 6B 158
SHELFIELD 8C 26
Shelfield Cl. B94: H'ley H 3C 194
CV5: E Grn 6H 151
Shelfield Rd. B14: K Hth 6J 143
Shelley Av. CV34: Warw 5C 222
DY4: Tip 1A 76
DY10: Kidd 2L 157
Shelley Cl. B61: Cats 1A 188
B97: Redd 1C 220
CV12: Bed 8K 111
DY3: Lwr G 4A 74
DY8: Amb 1A 116
Shelley Ct. CV2: Cov 5J 153
Shelley Dr. B23: Erd 6B 80
B74: Four O 3F 42
Shelley Gdns. LE10: Hinc 6L 69
Shelley Rd. B79: Tam 2M 31
CV2: Cov 6J 153
WS7: C Ter 8G 11
WS11: Cann 4E 8
WV10: F'hses 7D 22
WV12: W'hall 2E 38
Shelley Twr. B31: N'fld 6C 142
Shellon Cl. CV3: Bin 1M 175
Shelly Cl. B37: F'bri 7F 104
Shelly Cres. B90: M'path 2B 168
Shelly Cft. B33: Kitts G 6A 104
Shelly Ho. B68: O'bry 5H 99
Shelly La. B90: M'path 3B 168
Shelly Manor Mus. 1F 142
Shelly Shop. Cen.
B90: M'path 2B 168
Shelsley Av. B69: O'bry 4D 98
Shelsley Dr. B13: Mose 8B 122
Shelsley Way B91: Sol 8B 146
Shelton Cl. WS10: W'bry 4J 55
Shelton La. B63: Crad 4L 117
Shelton Sq. CV1: Cov ...7C 152 (5B 6)
Shelton St. B77: Wiln 2F 46
Sheltwood Cl. B97: Redd 7A 212
Sheltwood La. B60: Tard 6G 211
Shelwick Gro. B93: Dorr 5E 168
Shenley Av. DY1: Dud 3H 75
Shenley Court Leisure Cen. ...2L 141
SHENLEY FIELDS 3L 141
Shenley Flds. Dr. B31: N'fld ...1L 141
Shenley Flds. Rd.
B29: W Cas 2M 141
Shenley Gdns. B29: W Cas 2A 142
Shenley Grn. B29: W Cas 3A 142
Shenley Hill B31: N'fld 3L 141
Shenley La. B29: W Cas 8M 119
Shenley Lane Community &
Sports Cen. 3A 142
SHENSTONE
DY10 ....2D 184
WS14 ....3F 28
Shenstone Av. B62: Hale 4E 118
CV22: Hillm 8E 180
DY8: Stourb 6K 115
Shenstone Bus. Pk.
WS14: Shens 3E 28
Shenstone Cl. B60: B'gve 6A 188
B74: Four O 3E 42
Shenstone Ct. B60: B'gve 6B 188
B90: Shir 7D 144
WV3: Wolv 3A 52
Shenstone Dr. CV7: Bal C 3G 171
WS9: A'rdge 1G 41
Shenstone Flats B62: Quin 4F 118
Shenstone Ho. *WS13: Lich* *8L 13*
(off Hobs Rd.)
SHENSTONE JUNC. 1G 29
Shenstone Rd. B14: K Hth 8A 144
B16: Edg 6C 100
B43: Gt Barr 1E 78
Shenstone Station (Rail) 3F 28
Shenstone Trad. Est.
B63: Hale 5C 118
Shenstone Valley Rd.
B62: Quin 3E 118
Shenstone Wlk. B62: Hale 4D 118
SHENSTONE WOODEND 8G 29
Shenton Cl. CV13: Stoke G 2E 68
Shenton La. CV13: Dad 1E 68
Shenton Rd. LE9: Barw 2B 70
Shenton Wlk. B37: K'hrst 4G 105
Shepheard Rd. B26: Sheld 4D 124
Shepherd Cl. CV4: Tile H 6F 150
WS13: Lich 6J 13
Shepherd Dr. WV12: W'hall 4C 38
Shepherds Brook Rd.
DY9: Lye 4D 116
Shepherds Fold B65: Row R 7B 98
Shepherds Gdns.
B15: Birm 8H 101 (8C 4)
Shepherds Grn. Rd. B24: Erd 7F 80
Shepherds Hill CV47: Sou 5J 225

Shepherds La.—Sketchley Mdws.

Shepherds La. CV7: Mer 6G 127
Shepherds Pool Rd.
B75: R'ley 7L 43
Shepherds Standing
B34: S End 3B 104
Shepherds Wlk. B60: B'gve . . .2L 209
WV8: Pend 7M 21
Shepherds Way B23: Erd 1C 80
Shepley Mdw. B45: B Grn 1H 189
Shepley Rd. B45: B Grn 2G 189
B45: Redn 3H 163
Shepperton Bus. Pk.
CV11: Nun 8J 89
Shepperton Ct. CV11: Nun 7J 89
Shepperton St. CV11: Nun 7J 89
Sheppey Dr. B36: Cas B 4H 105
Shepwell Gdns. WV10: F'stne . . .1J 23
SHEPWELL GREEN 7C 38
Shepwell Grn. WV13: W'hall . . .8C 38
Sherard Cft. B36: Cas B 3H 105
Sheraton Cl. WS9: A'rdge 3H 41
WS12: Hed 2F 8
Sheraton Dr. DY10: Kidd 3B 158
Sheraton Grange
DY8: Stourb 7M 115
Sheraton Rd. B60: B'gve 8C 188
Sherborne Cl. B46: Col 5A 106
WS3: Blox 2J 39
Sherborne Gdns. WV8: Cod 6G 21
Sherborne Gro.
B1: Birm 6G 101 (4A 4)
Sherborne Lofts
B16: Birm 7H 101 (6A 4)
Sherborne Rd. LE10: Burb 2B 92
WV10: Bush 8D 22
Sherborne St.
B16: Birm 7H 101 (6A 4)
Sherborne Wharf
B16: Birm 7H 101 (6A 4)
SHERBOURNE 8A 222
Sherbourne Arc.
CV1: Cov 7C 152 (5B 6)
Sherbourne Av. CV10: Nun 4B 88
WS12: Hed 5L 9
Sherbourne Cl. B98: Redd 7K 213
Sherbourne Ct. B27: A Grn 5J 123
CV1: Cov 8C 152 (7C 6)
CV35: Sher 8A 222
Sherbourne Cres. CV5: Cov 5L 151
Sherbourne Dr. B27: A Grn 5J 123
Sherbourne Pl. CV32: Lea S 8A 218
Sherbourne Rd. B12: Bal H 3M 121
(Arter St.)
B12: Bal H 2L 121
(Longmore St.)
B27: A Grn 5J 123
B64: Old H 1A 118
DY8: Stourb 5B 116
Sherbourne St. CV1: Cov 7A 152
Sherbourne Ter.
CV32: Lea S 7A 218
Sherbrooke Av. B77: Wiln 3E 46
Sherbrook Rd. WS11: Cann 8C 8
Sherdmore Cft. B90: M'path . . .3A 168
Sheridan Cl. CV22: Rugby 2M 205
WS2: Wals 2H 55
Sheridan Dr. CV10: Gall C 4M 87
Sheridan Gdns. DY3: Lwr G 4M 73
Sheridan St. B71: W Brom 5K 77
WS2: Wals 2H 55
Sheridan Wlk. B35: Cas V 6A 82
Sheriff Av. CV4: Canly 2H 173
Sheriff Dr. DY5: Quar B 7F 96
Sheriff Rd. CV21: Rugby 6D 180
Sheriffs Cl. WS14: Lich 3L 19
Sheriffs Orchard
CV1: Cov 7C 152 (6B 6)
Sherifoot La. B75: Four O 5H 43
Sheringham B15: Edg 1E 120
Sheringham Cl. CV11: Nun 7M 89
Sheringham Rd. B30: K Nor 6H 143
Sherington Av. CV5: Cov 5J 151
Sherington Dr. WV4: Penn 4D 52
Sherlock Cl. WV12: W'hall 4D 38
Sherlock Rd. CV5: Cov 6K 151
Sherlock St. B5: Birm . . .2L 121 (8H 5)
Sherrans Dell WV4: E'shll 6E 52
Sherratt Cl. B76: Walm 1M 81
Sherringham Dr. WV11: Ess 8C 24
Sherron Gdns. B12: Bal H 4M 121
Sherston Covert B30: K Nor . . .7J 143
Shervale Cl. WV4: Penn 3A 52
Sherwin Av. WV14: Cose 7G 53
Sherwood Av. DY4: Tip 5M 75
Sherwood Cl. B28: Hall G 4F 144
B92: Olton 2M 145
CV9: Wood E 8H 47
Sherwood Dr. DY5: Quar B 8F 96
WS11: Cann 6G 9
Sherwood Jones Cl.
CV6: Cov 3B 152
Sherwood M. B28: Hall G 3E 144
Sherwood Rd. B28: Hall G 2E 144
B60: B'gve 2A 210
B67: Smeth 8A 100
CV13: Stoke G 2D 68
DY8: Woll 2L 115
Sherwood St.
WV1: Wolv 6C 36 (1H 7)
Sherwood Wlk. B45: Fran 6H 141
CV32: Lill 5C 218
Sherwood Wlk. WS9: A'rdge 2E 40
Shetland Av. B77: Wiln 2F 46
Shetland Cl. B16: Birm 7F 100
CV5: E Grn 5G 151
WV6: Wolv 4B 36
Shetland Dr. B66: Smeth 2K 99
CV10: Nun 7F 88
Shetland Rd. CV3: W'hall 4H 175
Shetland Wlk. B36: Cas B 3H 105
Shevlock Way CV6: Cov 3G 153
Shidas La. B69: O'bry 2E 98
Shifnal Rd. WV7: Alb 8A 20
Shifnal Wlk. B31: Longb 1M 163
Shifrall Way B75: S Cold 2M 59
Shillcock Gro. B19: Birm 4L 101
Shillingstone Cl.
CV2: W'grve S 5A 154
Shillingstone Dr. CV10: Nun 8F 88
SHILTON 4E 132
Shilton Cl. B90: M'path 3M 167
Shilton Gro. B29: W Cas 1M 141
Shilton La. CV2: W'grve S 7L 131
CV7: Shil 6M 131
CV12: Bulk 8D 112
Shilton La. Ind. Est.
CV7: Shil 2E 132
Shilton Rd. CV7: Withy 5L 133
LE9: Barw 3B 70
Shinwell Cres. B69: Tiv 7D 76
Shipbourne Cl. B32: Harb 4M 119
Shipley Flds. B24: Erd 6G 81
Shipley Gro. B29: W Cas 1A 142
Shipston Cl. B97: Redd 5A 212
Shipston Rd. B31: N'fld 8B 142
CV2: Cov 3J 153
Shipton Cl. DY1: Dud 6E 74
Shipton Rd. B72: S Cold 6J 59
Shipway Rd. B25: Yard 2G 123
Shirebrook Cl. B6: Aston 1L 101
CV2: Cov 7K 131
Shire Brook Ct. B19: Loz 1K 101
Shire Cl. B16: Birm 7F 100
B68: O'bry 7H 99
CV6: Cov 8H 131
Shire Hall Pl. WS11: Hth H 7H 9
Shirehampton Cl.
B97: Redd 7M 211
Shireland Brook Gdns.
B18: Win G 5D 100
Shireland Cl. B20: Hand 6E 78
Shireland La. B97: Redd 5A 212
Shireland Rd. B66: Smeth 5B 100
Shire Lea WS8: Bwnhls 3H 27
Shirelea Cl. WS7: Burn 1H 17
SHIRE OAK 4F 26
Shire Oak Pk. (Nature Reserve)
. . . . .5H 27
Shire Ridge WS9: Wals W 5G 27
Shires Ga. Trad. Est.
CV31: Lea S 3L 223
Shires Ind. Est. WS14: Lich 3G 19
Shires Retail Pk., The
CV34: Warw 3K 223
Shirestone Rd. B33: Kitts G . . .7D 104
Shireview Gdns. WS3: Pels 5B 26
Shireview Rd. WS3: Pels 5A 26
Shirewood WS11: Cann 7B 8
Shirland Rd. B37: Mars G 8G 105
Shirlett Cl. CV2: Ald G 5H 131
SHIRLEY 6H 145
Shirleydale B90: Shir 8J 145
Shirley Dr. B72: S Cold 5J 59
SHIRLEY HEATH 1H 167
Shirley La. CV7: Mer 4A 150
Shirley Pk. Rd. B90: Shir 7H 145
Shirley Rd. B27: A Grn 3G 145
B28: Hall G 3G 145
B30: K Nor 4G 143
B68: O'bry 3J 99
CV2: W'grve S 2M 153
DY2: Dud 1L 97
Shirley Station (Rail) 8F 144
SHIRLEY STREET 7H 145
Shirley Trad. Est. B90: Shir . . .1M 167
Shirley Wlk. B79: Tam 2M 31
Shirrall Dr. B78: Dray B 5C 44
Shirrall Gro. B37: K'hrst 4F 104
Shoal Hill Cl. WS11: Cann 7B 8
Shoesmith Cl. LE9: Barw 3A 70
Sholing Cl. WV8: Pend 8M 21
Shooters Cl. B5: Bal H 3K 121
Shooters Hill B72: S Cold 7K 59
Shop La. WV6: Tres 2B 50
WV8: Oaken 8C 20
Shopping Cen., The
CV31: Lea S 4B 224
Shopton Rd. B34: S End 2A 104
Shoreham Cl. WV13: W'hall 8K 37
Shorncliffe Rd. CV6: Cov 3K 151
Short Acre St. WS2: Wals 6K 39
Shortbutts La. WS14: Lich 4H 19
SHORT CROSS 5M 117
Shorters Av. B14: K Hth 5B 144
Shortfield Cl. CV7: Bal C 2H 171
Short Fishers Wlk.
CV23: Brow 1D 180
SHORT HEATH
Erdington 3D 80
Willenhall 4D 38
Short Heath Ct. B23: Erd 4F 80
Short Heath Rd. B23: Erd 3D 80
Shortland Cl. B93: Know 2G 169
Shortlands CV7: Ash G 3D 130
Shortlands Cl. B30: K Nor 7G 143
Shortlands La. WS3: Pels 5M 25
Short La. WS6: C Hay 6E 14
Shortley Rd. CV3: Cov 1E 174
Short Rd. B67: Smeth 6K 99
WV10: Bush 8E 22
Shortstones Wlk.
CV23: Brow 1D 180
Short St. B63: Hale 5M 117
B65: B'hth, Row R 7C 98
(not continuous)
B90: Dic H 4G 167
CV1: Cov 7D 152 (6E 6)
CV10: Nun 5C 88
DY1: Dud 7G 75
DY4: Tip 1L 75
DY8: Stourb 4M 115
WS2: Wals 8K 39
WS8: Bwnhls 1F 26
WS10: Darl 2F 54
WS10: W'bry 6E 54
WS11: Cann 6F 8
WV1: Wolv 7D 36 (3K 7)
WV12: W'hall 4C 38
WV14: Bils 3K 53
Shortwheat Hill CV23: Brow . . .1D 180
Shortwood Ct.
CV2: W'grve S 8M 131
Shortwoods, The B78: Dord 4A 48
Shortyard, The DY11: W'ley . . .5L 135
Shorwell Pl. DY5: Brie H 1C 116
Shottery Cl. B76: Walm 8M 59
CV5: E Grn 6H 151
Shottery Gro. B76: Walm 8M 59
Shottery Rd. B90: Shir 8H 145
Shotteswell Rd. B90: Shir 2H 167
Showcase Cinema
Dudley 7L 75
Erdington 7K 81
Walsall 8G 39
Walsgrave on Sowe 8B 132
Showell Cir. WV10: Bush 2E 36
SHOWELL GREEN 5B 122
Showell Grn. La. B11: S'hll 6B 122
Showell Ho. B69: O'bry 2G 99
Showell La. CV7: Mer 7A 128
WV4: Lwr P 6G 51
Showell Rd. WV10: Bush 2D 36
Showell Rd. Ind. Est.
WV10: Wolv 3D 36
Showells Gdns. B7: Nech 2C 102
Shrawley Av. DY11: Kidd 6H 157
Shrawley Cl. B45: Rubery 2F 162
B63: Hale 7A 118
Shrawley Rd. B31: N'fld 7C 142
Shreres Dyche CV34: Warw . . .5B 222
Shrewley Cres. B33: Kitts G . . .8E 104
Shrewsbury Cl. LE9: Barw 2A 70
WS3: Blox 8F 24
Shrewsbury Rd. DY11: Kidd . . .4G 157
Shrewton Av. B14: K Hth 8K 143
Shrubberies, The CV4: Canly . . .5K 173
Shrubbery, The B16: Birm 6F 100
DY1: Dud 7H 75
DY4: Tip 3C 76
Shrubbery Av. DY4: Tip 4K 75
Shrubbery Cl. B76: Walm 3K 81
CV10: Cookl 4B 136
Shrubbery Ct. DY10: Kidd 2M 157
Shrubbery Hill DY10: Cookl 4A 136
Shrubbery Rd. B61: B'gve 8L 187
Shrubbery St. DY10: Kidd 2M 157
Shrublands Av. B68: O'bry 2H 119
Shrubland St. CV31: Lea S 3A 224
(not continuous)
Shrub La. B24: Erd 5H 81
Shuckburgh Cres.
CV22: Hillm 1D 206
CV23: Bour D 7L 203
Shuckburgh Gro. CV32: Lill 7B 218
Shugborough Cl. WS3: Blox 8H 25
Shugborough Dr. DY1: Dud 7E 74
Shugborough Way
WS11: Hth H 8H 9
Shulmans Wlk. CV2: Cov 2K 153
Shultern La. CV4: Canly 3J 173
Shuna Cft. CV2: W'grve S 2A 154
SHUSTOKE 7F 84
Shustoke La. WS5: Wals 5B 56
Shustoke Rd. B34: S End 3C 104
B91: Sol 4D 146
Shustoke Sailing Club 6F 84
Shute Hill WS13: Chor 6L 11
SHUT END 8A 74
Shutlock La. B13: Mose 8K 121
Shut Mill La. B62: Roms 1K 161
SHUTTINGTON 2M 33
Shuttington Rd. B79: A'cte 3H 33
Shuttle La. B94: Earls 8H 167
Shuttle St. CV6: Cov 1H 153
Shuttleworth Rd.
CV23: Clift D 4F 180
Shylock Gro. CV34: H'cte 7L 223
Shyltons Cft.
B16: Birm 7G 101 (6A 4)
Sibdon Gro. B31: Longb 1A 164
Sibree Rd. CV3: W'hall 5H 175
Sibton Cl. CV2: Cov 8H 131
Sidaway Cl. B65: Row R 3C 98
Sidaway St. B64: Old H 8L 97
Sidbury Gro. B93: Dorr 6E 168
Sidbury Rd. CV6: Cov 3C 152
Sidcup Cl. WV14: Cose 6H 53
Sidcup Rd. B44: K'sdng 8A 58
Siddaw Ho. *CV21: Brow 2C 180*
(off Millers Dale Cl.)
Siddeley Av. CV3: Cov 8G 153
CV8: Ken 6E 198
Siddeley Wlk. B36: Cas B 8F 82
Siddons Cl. WS13: Lich 7F 12
Siddons Factory Est.
B70: W Brom 1F 76
Siddons Rd. WV14: Cose 7K 53
Siddons Way B70: W Brom 2G 77
SIDEMOOR 5L 187
Sidenhill Cl. B90: Shir 1H 167
Sidford Gdns. B24: Erd 6J 81
Sidford Gro. B23: Erd 2E 80
Sidings, The B20: Hand 1J 101
B70: W Brom 7J 77
CV21: Rugby 5B 180
DY8: Hag 3A 138
WS12: Hed 2K 9
Sidlaw Cl. B63: Hale 7K 117
WV10: Oxl 3C 36
Sidmouth Cl. CV2: Cov 2J 153
CV11: Nun 4M 89
Sidney Rd. CV22: Hillm 1D 206
Sidney St. WV2: Wolv . . .1C 52 (7H 7)
Sidon Hill Way WS11: Hth H 6J 9
Sidwick Cres. WV2: E'shll 3H 53
Sigmund Cl. WV1: Wolv 6H 37
Signal Gro. WS3: Blox 8G 25
Signal Hayes Rd. B76: Walm . . .7M 59
(not continuous)
Signal Wlk. B77: Glas 7G 33
Silesbourne Cl. B36: Cas B 1C 104
Silhill Hall Rd. B91: Sol 3A 146
Silica Rd. B77: Amin 7H 33
Silken Ct. CV11: Nun 6H 89
Silksby St. CV3: Cov 1D 174
Sillins Av. B98: Redd 6G 213
Silva Av. DY6: K'wfrd 5M 95
Silver Birch Av. CV12: Bed 7E 110
Silver Birch Cl. B8: Salt 3D 102
CV3: Bin W 2D 176
Silverbirch Cl. CV10: Harts 2A 88
Silver Birch Coppice
B74: Four O 4D 42
Silver Birch Ct. *DY10: Kidd 5A 158*
(off Oldnall Rd.)
Silverbirch Ct. B24: Erd 3H 81
Silver Birch Dr. B47: H'wd 3B 166
DY7: Kinv 4A 114
DY10: Kidd 4C 158
Silver Birches Bus. Pk.
B60: B'gve 3A 210
Silver Birch Gro.
CV31: Lea S 4M 223
Silver Birch Rd. B24: Erd 3H 81
B37: K'hrst 3F 104
B74: S'tly 8M 41
WS11: Nort C 5B 16
WS12: Hunt 1D 8
WV2: Wolv 2D 52
Silverbirch Rd. B91: Sol 6E 146
Silver Ct. WS8: Bwnhls 2F 26
Silver Ct. Gdns. WS8: Bwnhls . . .2F 26
Silvercroft Av. B20: Hand 6C 78
Silverdale B61: B'gve 5M 187
Silverdale Cl. CV2: Ald G 5H 131
Silverdale Dr. WV10: Wolv 5E 36
Silverdale Gdns. DY8: Word 6J 95
Silverdale Rd. B24: Erd 4K 81
SILVER END 8B 96
Silver End Bus. Est.
DY5: Brie H 8C 96
Silver End Ind. Est.
DY5: Brie H 8B 96
Silverfield Cl. B14: K Hth 1L 143
Silver Fir Cl. WS12: Hed 1G 9
Silver Innage B63: Crad 2J 117
Silverlands Av. B68: O'bry 6H 99
Silverlands Cl. B28: Hall G 8F 122
Silver Link Rd. B77: Glas 7F 32
Silvermead Ct. B47: Wyt 4M 165
Silvermead Rd. B73: W Grn 8G 59
Silvermere Rd. B26: Sheld 3D 124
Silvers Cl. WS3: Pels 4M 25
Silverstone Av. DY11: Kidd 8K 135
Silverstone Cl. WS2: Wals 6E 38
Silverstone Dr. B74: S'tly 3M 57
CV6: Longf 4E 130
SILVER STREET 4L 165
Silver St. B14: K Hth 1L 143
B38: Head H 4K 165
B47: Wyt 4L 165
B79: Tam 5B 32
B97: Redd 6E 212
CV1: Cov 6C 152 (3C 6)
CV23: Newt 1G 181
DY5: Brie H 8C 96
DY10: Kidd 2L 157
WS8: Bwnhls 2E 26
Silverthorne Av. DY4: Tip 4K 75
Silverthorne La. B64: Crad H 8H 97
Silverton Cres. B13: Mose 8D 122
Silverton Hgts. B67: Smeth 3M 99
Silverton Rd. B67: Smeth 3L 99
CV6: Cov 2F 152
Silverton Way WV11: Wed 4M 37
Silver Trees Dr. CV12: Bulk 5B 112
Silvertrees Rd. DY4: Tip 4L 75
Silver Wlk. CV10: Nun 6F 88
Silvester Ct. B70: W Brom 6K 77
Silvester Rd. WV14: Bils 3L 53
Silvester Way DY5: Brie H 1B 116
Silvington Cl. B29: W Cas 2C 142
Simcox Gdns. B32: Bart G 7K 119
Simcox Rd. WS10: W'bry 4F 54
Simcox St. WS12: Hed 5K 9
Simeon Bissell Cl. DY4: Tip 4M 75
Simeon's Wlk. DY5: Quar B 2F 116
Simmonds Cl. WS3: Blox 6K 25
Simmonds Pl. WS3: Blox 6K 25
WS10: Darl 2E 54
Simmonds Rd. WS3: Blox 6K 25
Simmonds Way CV9: Ath 7K 49
WS8: Bwnhls 4G 27
Simmons Cl. B78: Midd 8H 45
Simmons Dr. B32: Quin 4J 119
Simmons Leasow
B32: Bart G 7K 119
Simmons Rd. WV11: Wed 8B 24
Simms La. B47: H'wd 4A 166
(not continuous)
DY2: Neth 4J 97
Simon Cl. B71: W Brom 8L 55
CV11: Nun 7K 89
Simon Ct. CV7: Exh 1G 131
Simon Rd. B47: H'wd 2A 166
Simon Stone St. CV6: Cov 1F 152
Simpkins Cl. CV33: W Weth . . .2K 219
WS9: Wals W 6G 27
Simpson Gro. CV3: W'hall 3J 175
WV10: Bush 3E 36
Simpson Rd. B72: W Grn 8J 59
WS2: Wals 4H 39
WS13: Lich 6H 13
WV10: Bush 3E 36
Simpson St. B69: O'bry 2G 99
Sinclair Ct. B13: Mose 5L 121
Sinclair Dr. CV6: Longf 3J 131
Singer Cl. CV6: Cov 1G 153
Singer Cft. B36: Cas B 8F 82
Singh Cl. B21: Hand 8E 78
Sion Av. DY10: Kidd 8M 135
Sion Cl. DY5: Brie H 6D 96
Sion Gdns. DY13: Stour S 6F 182
(not continuous)
Sion Hill DY10: Kidd, W'ley . . .7M 135
Sion Hill Ho. DY10: W'ley 7M 135
Sir Alfred's Way B76: Walm 6L 59
Sir Frank Whittle Bus. Cen.
CV21: Rugby 4D 180
Sir George's Mall
DY10: Kidd 3L 157
Sir Harrys Rd. B15: Edg 3H 121
Sir Henry Parkes Rd.
CV4: Canly 2J 173
CV5: Cov 2J 173
Sir Hilton's Rd. B31: Longb . . .2B 164
Sir Johns Rd. B29: S Oak 6J 121
Sir Richards Dr. B17: Harb 2M 119
Sir Thomas White's Rd.
CV5: Cov 7M 151
Sir Toby Belch Dr.
CV34: H'cte 6M 223
Sir Walters Mall DY10: Kidd . . .3L 157
Sir William Lyons Rd.
CV4: Canly 3J 173
Sir Winston Churchill Pl.
CV3: Bin W 2C 176
Sisefield Rd. B38: K Nor 8G 143
Siskin Cl. CV23: Brow 1C 180
WS7: Hamm 4K 17
Siskin Dr. B12: Bal H 3L 121
CV3: W'hall 5J 175
Siskin Parkway E.
CV3: W'hall 8J 175
Siskin Parkway W.
CV3: W'hall 8H 175
Siskin Rd. DY9: W'cte 6D 116
Siskin Way DY10: Kidd 8B 158
Sisley Way LE10: Hinc 6G 69
Sister Dora Av. WS7: Burn 2L 17
Sister Dora Bldgs. *WS1: Wals . . .8L 39*
(off Bridge, The)
Sister Dora Gdns. WS1: Wals . . .8L 39
Siviters Cl. B65: Row R 6C 98
Siviters La. B65: Row R 6B 98
Siviter St. B63: Hale 5B 118
Six Acres B32: Quin 5J 119
Sixes Sports Cen. 8L 73
Six Foot Rd. DY2: Neth 4J 97
Six Towers Rd. WS2: Wals 5J 39
Six Ways B23: Erd 5F 80
Skelcher Rd. B90: Shir 5G 145
Skelwith Ri. CV11: Nun 3A 90
Skemp Cl. WV14: Bils 6K 53
SKETCHLEY 4L 91
Sketchley Cl. B66: Smeth 4A 100
Sketchley Hall Gdns.
LE10: Burb 4J 91
SKETCHLEY HILL 3L 91
Sketchley La. LE10: Burb 4H 91
Sketchley La. Ind. Est.
LE10: Burb 4H 91
Sketchley Mnr. La.
LE10: Burb 4K 91
Sketchley Mdws. LE10: Burb 4J 91

Sketchley Mdws. Bus. Pk.—Sovereign Rd.

Sketchley Mdws. Bus. Pk.
LE10: Burb .4J 91
Sketchley Old Village
LE10: Burb .4J 91
Sketchley Rd. LE10: Burb .4L 91
Skey Dr. CV10: Nun .3B 88
Skiddaw CV21: Brow .2C 180
Skidmore Av. B77: Dost .4C 46
WV3: Wolv .1M 51
Skidmore Dr. B70: W Brom .6G 77
Skidmore Rd. WV14: Cose .7K 53
Skilts Av. B98: Redd .8F 212
Skinner La. B5: Birm .8L 101 (8H 5)
Skinner St. WV1: Wolv .7C 36 (4H 7)
Skip La. WS5: Wals .4D 56
Skipness B77: Amin .4E 32
Skipton Gdns. CV2: Cov .3H 153
Skipton Grn. WV6: Wolv .4A 36
Skipton Lodge CV2: Cov .3H 153
Skipton Pl. WS11: Cann .2B 14
Skipton Rd. B16: Edg .8G 101
Skipwith Cl. CV23: Brin .6K 155
Skipworth Rd. CV3: Bin .7A 154
Skomer Cl. B45: Fran .8E 140
Sky Blue Way
CV1: Cov .6E 152 (5F 6)
Skye Cl. B36: Cas B .3H 105
B77: Wiln .2F 46
CV10: Nun .7F 88
Skye Wlk. B64: Old H .8L 97
Sky Lark Cl. DY5: P'ntt .8C 74
Skylark Cl. B23: Erd .2C 80
WS12: Hunt .2C 8
Skylark Way DY10: Kidd .7A 158
Skywalk B40: Nat E C .5K 125
Slack La. B20: Hand .7E 78
Slack's Av. CV9: Ath .2K 65
Slacky La. WS3: Blox .8L 25
Slad, The DY13: Stour S .3K 183
SLADD, THE .4G 135
Sladd La. DY11: W'ley .4G 135
Slade Av. WS7: C Ter .1G 17
Slade Cl. B71: W Brom .7M 55
CV11: Nun .1C 112
Sladefield Rd. B8: W End .4G 103
Slade Gdns. WV8: Cod .5G 21
Slade Gro. B93: Know .3F 168
Slade Hill WV6: Wolv .6M 35
Slade La. B28: Hall G .6E 144
B75: R'ley .6A 44
B77: Dost .5C 46
Slade Lanker B34: Stech .4A 104
Slade Mdw. CV31: Rad S .4E 224
Sladepool Farm Rd.
B14: K Hth .6M 143
Slade Rd. B23: Erd .5D 80
B63: Crad .3J 117
B75: R'ley, Can .6L 43
CV21: Rugby .7C 180
WV10: F'hses .6C 22
Slade Vw. Ri. WS12: Haz .3A 10
Slaithwaite Rd. B71: W Brom .5L 77
Slaney Ct. WS2: Wals .2J 55
Slaney Rd. WS2: Wals .3H 55
Slang La. WS15: Cann W .4E 10
Slatch Ho. Rd. B67: Smeth .7L 99
Slate La. WV8: Cod .4D 20
Slateley Cres. B90: M'path .3A 168
Slater Cl. B64: Old H .8M 97
Slate Row WS3: Pels .6A 26
Slater Rd. B93: Ben H .5E 168
Slater's La. WS2: Wals .2H 55
Slater's Pl. WS2: Wals .2H 55
Slater St. DY4: Tip .5A 76
(Crompton Rd.)
DY4: Tip .4D 76
(Sheepwash La.)
WS10: Darl .2D 54
WV13: W'hall .6C 38
WV14: Bils .5L 53
Sleaford Gro. B28: Hall G .2G 145
Sleaford Rd. B28: Hall G .2H 145
Sleath's Yd. CV12: Bed .6H 111
Sledmere Cl. CV2: Ald G .6H 131
Sledmore Rd. DY2: Dud .2K 97
Sleets Yd. CV12: Bed .7H 111
SLIDESLOW .7C 188
Slideslow Av. B60: B'gve .7B 188
Slideslow Dr. B60: B'gve .6B 188
Slieve, The B20: Hand .6G 79
Slim Av. WV14: Bils .6L 53
Slimbridge Cl. B90: M'path .3A 168
B97: Redd .4E 220
Slim Rd. WS2: Wals .7E 38
Slims Ga. B63: Hale .5A 118
Sling, The DY2: Neth .3J 97
Slingfield Rd. B31: N'fld .7C 142
Slingsby B77: Two G .2C 46
Slingsby Cl. CV11: Nun .7L 89
Slitting Mill Cl. B21: Hand .1C 100
Sloane Ho. B1: Birm .3C 4
Sloane St. B1: Birm .6J 101 (4C 4)
Slough, The B80: Stud .4E 220
B97: Redd .4E 220
Slough La. B38: Head H .1L 165
B47: H'wd .1L 165
Slowley Hill CV7: Old A .8A 86
Smallbrook La. WV5: Wom .2H 73
Smallbrook Queensway
B5: Birm .8K 101 (7F 4)
Small Cl. B67: Smeth .4K 99
Smalldale Rd. B42: Gt Barr .2K 79
Smalley Cl. WS11: Cann .4G 9
Smalley Ct. WS7: Burn .4H 17
Smalley Pl. CV8: Ken .5F 198
SMALL HEATH .1D 122
Small Heath Bri.
B10: Small H .2B 122
B11: S'brk .2B 122
Small Heath Bus. Pk.
B10: Small H .2F 122
Small Heath Highway
B10: Small H .1B 122
Small Heath Leisure Cen. .1D 122
Small Heath Station (Rail) .2D 122
Small Heath Trad. Est.
B11: Small H .3D 122
Small La. B94: Earls .3D 192
Smallman Rd. CV10: Nun .2A 88
Smallridge WS13: Lich .7F 12
Smallshire Cl. WV11: Wed .4M 37
Smallshire Way DY8: Word .1K 115
Small St. B71: W Brom .3H 77
WS1: Wals .1L 55
SMALLWOOD .6F 212
Smallwood Almshouses
B98: Redd .6E 212
Smallwood Arch
B98: Redd .5E 212
(off Herbert St.)
Smallwood Cl. B24: Erd .6K 81
B76: Walm .6L 59
Smallwood Rd. WV8: Pend .7L 21
Smallwood St. B98: Redd .6E 212
Smarts Av. WS14: Shen W .2G 43
Smarts Est. CV23: Kils .6M 207
Smarts Rd. CV12: Bed .8F 110
Smeaton Gdns. B18: Win G .5E 100
Smeaton La. CV23: Stret F .3J 155
Smedley Crooke Pl.
B48: Hopw .7C 164
Smeed Gro. B24: Erd .6H 81
Smercote Cl. CV12: Bed .8D 110
SMESTOW .5C 72
Smestow Ga. DY3: Swind .4B 72
Smestow La. DY3: Swind .5C 72
Smestow St. WV10: Wolv .5D 36
Smestow Valley Local Nature
Reserve .3M 35
Smestow Wildlife Cen. .5D 72
SMETHWICK .4A 100
Smethwick Galton Bridge Station
(Rail) .2L 99
Smethwick New Ent. Cen.
B66: Smeth .3A 100
Smethwick Rolfe Street Station (Rail)
.3A 100
Smethwick Swimming Cen. .7M 99
Smillie Pl. WS11: Cann .6F 8
Smirrells Rd. B28: Hall G .4E 144
Smith Av. WS10: Darl .5D 54
Smith Cl. B67: Smeth .6K 99
WV14: Cose .8G 53
Smithfield Ri. WS13: Lich .1J 19
Smithfield Rd. WS3: Blox .8K 25
Smithfields DY8: Stourb .4A 116
Smithfield St.
B5: Birm .8L 101 (7J 5)
Smithford Way
CV1: Cov .6C 152 (4B 6)
Smithhill Pl. CV23: Brow .1D 180
Smith Ho. WS3: Blox .6J 25
Smithmoor Cres.
B71: W Brom .1M 77
Smith Pl. DY4: Tip .5B 76
Smith Rd. WS2: Wals .3J 55
WS10: W'bry .8E 54
Smiths Cl. WS7: C Ter .2D 16
B32: Bart G .7H 119
Smiths La. B93: Know .3E 168
Smiths Orchard
CV21: Rugby .6C 180
Smith St. B19: Birm .4J 101 (1D 4)
B98: Redd .5E 212
CV6: Cov .4F 152
CV9: Wood E .8J 47
CV12: Bed .8E 110
CV31: Lea S .2M 223
CV34: Warw .2E 222
DY2: Dud .2K 97
WV14: Bils .4K 53
Smiths Way B46: Wat O .6G 83
SMITH'S WOOD .2G 105
Smithy, The B26: Sheld .3C 124
Smithy Dr. WS3: Pels .5A 26
Smithy Farm Dr. LE9: S Stan .7J 71
Smithy La. B77: Wiln .2F 46
CV9: Bax .4C 64
CV23: Chu L .4B 178
DY5: P'ntt .8B 74
WS13: Lich .8G 13
WS15: Longd .1M 11
SMOCKINGTON .8C 92
Smockington La.
LE10: Wlvy .3M 113
Smorrall La. CV7: Cor .8K 109
CV12: Bed .8K 109
Smout Cres. WV14: Cose .7F 52
Smythe Gro. CV34: Warw .8E 216
Snake La. B48: A'chu .3A 190
DY11: W'ley .2L 135
Snakes Lake La. B61: D'frd .3K 187
Snake Ter. B48: A'chu .3A 190
Snapdragon Dr. WS5: Wals .6M 55
Snape Rd. CV2: Cov .4M 153
WV11: Wed .8A 24
Snapes Lodge WV12: W'hall .3C 38
Snape Way B60: S Prior .7L 209
Snellsdale Cl. CV23: Brow .1E 180
Sneyd Hall Cl. WS3: Blox .1G 39
Sneyd Hall Rd. WS3: Blox .8G 25
Sneyd La. WS3: Blox .8F 24
WV11: Ess .7B 24
Snipe Cl. WV10: F'stne .2H 23
Snowberry Cl.
DY13: Stour S .5E 182
Snowberry Dr. DY5: P'ntt .8C 74
Snowberry Gdns. B27: A Grn .4J 123
Snowdome & Peaks Leisure Cen.
.6B 32
Snowdon Cl. CV10: Nun .6B 88
DY11: Kidd .8J 135
Snowdon Gro. B63: Hale .8K 117
Snowdon Ri. DY3: Sed .3D 74
Snowdon Rd. DY8: Amb .3B 116
WS11: Cann .3E 8
Snowdon Way WV10: Oxl .3B 36
WV12: W'hall .8B 24
Snowdrop Cl. CV12: Bed .8E 110
WS8: Clay .3D 26
Snowford Cl. B90: Shir .8F 144
Snow Hill WV2: Wolv .8D 36 (5K 7)
Snow Hill Junc.
WV2: Wolv .8D 36 (6K 7)
Snow Hill Queensway
B4: Birm .6L 101 (3F 4)
Snow Hill Station (Rail)
.6K 101 (3F 4)
Snowshill Cl. B98: Redd .3H 213
CV11: Nun .1M 111
Snowshill Dr. B90: Ches G .4K 167
Snowshill Gdns. DY1: Dud .5F 74
Snuff Mill Wlk. DY12: Bew .7A 156
Soar Way LE10: Hinc .1G 91
Soberton Cl. WV11: Wed .2M 37
Soden Cl. CV3: W'hall .3K 175
Soden's Av. CV8: Rytn D .8A 176
SOHO .2C 100
Soho Av. B18: Hock .2G 101
Soho Benson Road Station (Rail)
.3F 100
Soho Cl. B66: Smeth .4C 100
Soho Hill B19: Hock .2G 101
Soho Ho. B66: Smeth .4C 100
Soho Pool Way B18: Hock .3G 101
Soho Rd. B21: Hand .1E 100
Soho St. B66: Smeth .3C 100
Soho Way B66: Smeth .3B 100
Solari Cl. DY4: Tip .1C 76
Solcum La. DY11: W'ley .3K 135
Solent Cl. WV9: Pend .7M 21
Solent Ct. B73: S Cold .4H 59
Solent Dr. CV2: W'grve S .8M 131
SOLIHULL .6C 146
Solihull By-Pass B91: Sol .4C 146
Solihull Ice Rink .6B 124
Solihull La. B28: Hall G .3G 145
SOLIHULL LODGE .7C 144
Solihull Parkway
B37: Mars G .2K 125
Solihull Retail Pk. B90: Shir .8K 145
Solihull Rd. B11: S'hll .6D 122
B90: Shir .6J 145
B92: H Ard .3J 147
Solihull Station (Rail) .5A 146
Soliway Cl. WS10: W'bry .5J 55
Solly Gro. DY4: Tip .2D 76
Solva Cl. WV1: Wolv .8H 37
Solway Cl. B79: Tam .2A 32
CV31: Lea S .3C 224
Somerby Dr. B91: Sol .1A 168
Somercotes Rd. B42: Gt Barr .1K 79
Somerdale Rd. B31: N'fld .5C 142
Somerfield Cl. WS4: S'fld .8C 26
Somerfield Rd. WS3: Blox .1H 39
Somerford Cl. WS6: Gt Wyr .8E 14
Somerford Gdns. WV10: Bush .7E 22
Somerford Pl. WV13: W'hall .8M 37
Somerford Rd. B29: W Cas .1M 141
Somerford Way WV14: Cose .1H 75
Somerland Rd. B26: Yard .8A 104
Somerleyton Av. DY10: Kidd .4A 158
Somerleyton Ct. DY10: Kidd .4A 158
Somerly Cl. CV3: Bin .1M 175
Somerset Cl. B78: Tam .8A 32
Somerset Cres. WS10: W'bry .5K 55
Somerset Dr. B31: Longb .2M 163
CV10: Nun .5E 88
DY8: Woll .2K 115
DY11: Kidd .8J 135
Somerset Pl. CV22: Caw .8H 179
WS11: Cann .6F 8
Somerset Rd. B15: Edg .3E 120
B20: Hand .7F 78
B23: Erd .3F 80
B71: W Brom .3K 77
CV1: Cov .4C 152
WS4: Wals .5A 40
WV13: W'hall .7D 38
Somers Pl. CV32: Lea S .1L 223
Somers Rd. B62: Hale .4C 118
CV7: Ker E .3M 129
CV7: Mer .8F 126
Somers Rd. CV22: Rugby .6K 179
WS2: Wals .2G 55
Somers Wood Cvn. & Camping Pk.
CV7: Mer .8F 126
Somerton Dr. B23: Erd .3G 81
B37: Mars G .2G 125
Somerville Ct. B73: S Cold .7G 59
B79: Tam .3K 31
Somerville Dr. B73: S Cold .5G 59
Somerville Ho. B37: Chel W .6K 105
Somerville Rd.
B10: Small H .1D 122
B73: S Cold .5G 59
Somery Rd. B29: W Cas .7A 120
DY1: Dud .6J 75
Sommerfield Rd.
B32: Bart G .7J 119
Sommerville Rd. CV2: Cov .5J 153
Sonata Rd. B60: B'gve .8C 188
Sonning Dr. WV9: Pend .7M 21
Sopwith Cft. B35: Cas V .7A 82
Sorbus B77: Amin .5H 33
Sordale Cft. CV3: Bin .8A 154
Sorrel B77: Amin .4H 33
Sorrel Cl. B69: Tiv .7B 76
CV4: Tile H .1E 172
WS13: Lich .3E 18
WV10: F'stne .2H 23
Sorrel Dr. B78: K'bry .2D 62
CV23: Brow .1D 180
WS5: Wals .6A 56
Sorrel Gro. B24: Erd .6K 81
Sorrel Ho. B24: Erd .6K 81
Sorrell Dr. B27: A Grn .7H 123
Sorrell Pl. CV10: Nun .1K 111
Sorrell Rd. CV10: Nun .8K 89
Sorrel Wlk. DY5: Brie H .3B 116
Sorrento Ct. B13: Mose .6A 122
Sot's Hole Nature Reserve .4L 77
Soudan B97: Redd .7D 212
Souters Ho. B32: Bart G .1K 141
Southacre Av. B5: Birm .1L 121
(not continuous)
Southall Cres. WV14: Cose .8J 53
Southall Dr. DY11: Hartl .8A 184
Southall Rd. WV11: Wed .1A 38
Southalls La. DY1: Dud .8H 75
SOUTHAM .5H 225
Southam Cl. B28: Hall G .1E 144
CV4: Tile H .2E 172
Southam Dr. B73: W Grn .8H 59
CV47: Sou .7G 225
Southam Ho. B13: Mose .2A 144
Southam Leisure Cen. .4G 225
Southampton St.
WV1: Wolv .6D 36 (2L 7)
Southam Rd. B28: Hall G .1E 144
CV22: Dunc .7H 205
CV23: Prin .7E 202
CV31: Rad S .3E 224
CV47: Long I, Sou .2H 225
South Av. CV2: Cov .7G 153
DY8: Stourb .5M 115
WV11: Wed .4J 37
Southbank Ct. CV8: Ken .5F 198
Southbank Rd. B64: Old H .8L 97
CV6: Cov .4L 151
CV8: Ken .4F 198
Southbank Vw. DY6: K'wfrd .5L 95
Southborough Ter.
CV31: Lea S .3A 224
Southbourne Av.
B34: Hodg H .3K 103
WS2: Wals .8H 39
Southbourne Cl. B29: S Oak .7G 121
Southbourne Pl. WS11: Cann .7D 8
Southbourne Rd.
WV10: F'hses .6C 22
Southbrook Rd.
CV22: Rugby .8A 180
Sth. Car Pk. Rd.
B40: Nat E C .6L 125
South Cl. WS11: Cann .1C 14
Southcote Gro. B38: K Nor .8D 142
Southcott Av. DY5: Brie H .1D 116
Southcott Way
CV2: W'grve S .8M 131
South Cres. B60: B'gve .8A 188
WV10: F'stne .3H 23
SOUTHCREST .8C 212
Southcrest Gdns. B97: Redd .8D 212
Southcrest Rd. B98: Redd .7F 212
South Dene B67: Smeth .4M 99
Southdown Av. B18: Hock .3G 101
South Dr. B5: Edg .5J 121
B46: Col .2K 105
B75: S Cold .3J 59
LE9: S Stan .8L 71
Southern Cl. DY6: K'wfrd .6M 95
Southern Cross WS13: Lich .2J 19
Southerndown Rd. DY3: Sed .2B 74
Southern Rd. B8: W End .4J 103
Southern Way WS10: Mox .6C 54
WS10: W'bry .6C 54
Southey Cl. B91: Sol .1B 168
WV12: W'hall .1E 38
Southey Rd. CV22: Rugby .2L 205
Southfield Av. B16: Edg .6D 100
B36: Cas B .1A 104
Southfield Cl. CV10: Nun .4K 89
WS9: A'rdge .3G 41
Southfield Dr. B28: Hall G .4G 145
CV8: Ken .3G 199
Southfield Gro. WV3: Wolv .2J 51
Southfield Rd. B16: Edg .6D 100
CV22: Rugby .8C 180
CV47: Sou .7G 225
LE10: Hinc .2K 91
WV11: Wed .4M 37
Southfields CV32: Lea S .6A 218
Southfields Cl. B46: Col .5A 106
Southfields Rd. B91: Sol .8M 145
Southfield Way WS6: Gt Wyr .7F 14
South Gdns. DY9: Hag .5A 138
South Ga. WS11: Cann .2B 14
Southgate B64: Crad H .1K 117
WV1: Wolv .7B 36 (3G 7)
Southgate Cl. DY11: Kidd .5G 157
Sth. Gate End WS11: Cann .2B 14
Southgate Rd. B44: Gt Barr .7L 57
South Grn. WV4: Penn .4K 51
South Gro. B6: Aston .1K 101
B19: Hand .1H 101
B23: Erd .4F 80
South Holme B9: Bord G .7C 102
Southlands CV9: Ath .2L 65
Southlands Rd. B13: Mose .8A 122
Southlea Av. CV31: Lea S .3L 223
Southlea Cl. CV31: Lea S .3L 223
Southleigh Av. CV5: Cov .2M 173
Southmead Cres. B98: Redd .6F 212
Southmead Dr. B60: L End .3B 188
Southmead Gdns. B80: Stud .6L 221
Southminster Dr. B14: K Hth .3L 143
Sth. Moons Moat Ind. Area
B98: Redd .5K 213
Southorn Ct. CV32: Lill .6D 218
South Oval DY3: Up Gor .4E 74
South Pde. B72: S Cold .4J 59
South Pk. M. DY5: Brie H .7C 96
Southport Cl. CV3: W'hall .4H 175
South Range B11: Bal H .3B 122
South Ridge CV5: Cov .5H 151
South Rd. B11: S'brk .2B 122
B14: K Hth .1L 143
B18: Hock .2G 101
B23: Erd .5F 80
B31: N'fld .7M 141
B60: B'gve .2B 210
B67: Smeth .4M 99
CV23: Clift D .4F 180
DY4: Tip .1B 76
DY8: Stourb .5K 115
DY9: Hag .5A 138
South Rd. Av. B18: Hock .3G 101
South Roundhay
B33: Kitts G .6A 104
Southside Bus. Cen.
B12: Bal H .4A 122
(off Ladypool Rd.)
Sth. Staffordshire Bus. Pk.
WS11: Cann .5C 14
South Staffordshire Golf Course
.3K 35
South St. B17: Harb .4D 120
B98: Redd .6E 212
CV1: Cov .6E 152
CV9: Ath .1K 65
CV21: Rugby .5D 180
DY5: Brie H .7C 96
WS1: Wals .1K 55
WV10: Oxl .3C 36
WV13: W'hall .8M 37
South St. Gdns. WS1: Wals .1K 55
South Ter. CV31: W'nsh .6A 224
South Vw. B43: Gt Barr .2E 78
B78: K'bry .5D 62
CV35: H Mag .3A 222
Sth. View Cl. WV8: Bilb .7H 21
WV10: F'stne .3H 23
Southview Ridge
DY5: Brie H .2D 116
South Vw. Rd. CV23: Long L .5F 178
CV32: Lill .4C 218
DY3: Sed .1C 74
Southville Bungalows
B14: K Hth .5B 144
South Wlk. B31: N'fld .8C 142
Southwark Cl. WS13: Lich .6J 13
Sth. Warwickshire Bus. Pk.
CV47: Sou .6G 225
South Way B40: Nat E C .6M 125
Southway CV31: Lea S .4A 224
Southway Ct. DY6: K'wfrd .5M 95
Southwick Pl. WV14: Bils .2K 53
Southwick Rd. B62: B'hth .1D 118
Southwold Av. B30: K Nor .6J 143
Southwood Av. B34: S End .2B 104
Southwood Cl. DY6: K'wfrd .4L 95
Southwood Covert
B14: K Hth .7K 143
SOUTH YARDLEY .3K 123
Sovereign Cl. CV8: Ken .8F 198
Sovereign Ct.
B1: Birm .6J 101 (3C 4)
CV4: Canly .3J 173
CV47: Sou .5H 225
Sovereign Dr. DY1: Dud .7E 74
Sovereign Hgts. B31: Longb .8J 141
Sovereign Rd. B30: K Nor .5F 142
CV5: Cov .7M 151
(not continuous)

Sovereign Row—Stanhope Ho.

Sovereign Row CV5: Cov 7A 152
Sovereign Wlk. WS1: Wals 7A 40
Sovereign Way B13: Mose 5M 121
SOWE COMMON 6M 131
Sowerby March B24: Erd 5K 81
Sowers Cl. WV12: W'hall 4D 38
Sowers Ct. B75: R'ley 5K 43
Sowers Gdns. WV12: W'hall 4D 38
Spa Cl. LE10: Hinc 8L 69
SPADE GREEN 1A 18
Spadesbourne Rd.
B60: L End 3C 188
Spa Dr. LE9: Sap 1K 93
Spa Gro. B30: Stir 1J 143
Spa La. LE10: Hinc 8L 69
SPARKBROOK 2B 122
Sparkbrook St. CV1: Cov 6F 152
Sparkbrook St. Ind. Est.
CV1: Cov 6F 152
SPARKHILL 5C 122
Sparkhill Pool & Fitness Cen.
5C 122
Spark St. B11: S'brk 2A 122
Sparrey Dr. B30: Stir 1G 143
Sparrow Cl. WS10: W'bry 4H 55
Sparrow Cock La.
B93: Chad E 8C 170
Sparta Cl. CV21: Rugby 3A 180
Spartan Cl. CV34: Warw 5L 223
Spartan Ind. Cen.
B70: W Brom 3E 76
Spa Vw. CV31: W'nsh 5B 224
Speakers Cl. B69: Tiv 2B 98
Spearhill WS14: Lich 2L 19
Speed Rd. DY4: Tip 3L 75
Speedway La. CV8: Bran 2F 176
Speedwell Cl. B25: Yard 3G 123
CV23: Brow 2E 180
WS9: A'rdge 4F 40
WV11: Wed 4L 37
Speedwell Dr. CV7: Bal C 3G 171
Speedwell Gdns.
DY5: Brie H 3B 116
WV10: F'stne 1H 23
Speedwell Ho. B38: K Nor 8G 143
Speedwell La. CV9: Bad E 8B 49
Speedwell Rd. B5: Bal H 3K 121
B25: Yard 3G 123
Speedwell Trad. Est.
B11: Tys 3G 123
Speedy Cl. WS11: Cann 4E 8
Spelter Works WS3: Blox 2G 39
Spencer Av. CV5: Cov 8A 152 (8A 6)
DY12: Bew 5C 156
WV14: Cose 1J 75
Spencer Cl. B24: Erd 5K 81
B69: Tiv 1B 98
B71: W Brom 1M 77
DY3: Lwr G 5A 74
Spencer Dr. WS7: C Ter 1E 16
Spencer Rd.
CV5: Cov 8B 152 (8A 6)
WS14: Lich 3H 19
Spencer's La. CV7: Berk 7K 149
Spencer St.
B18: Birm 4J 101 (1C 4)
(not continuous)
CV31: Lea S 2M 223
DY11: Kidd 5J 157
LE10: Hinc 8K 69
Spencer Yd. CV31: Lea S 2M 223
SPENNELLS 7A 158
Spennells Trad. Est.
DY10: Kidd 7M 157
Spennells Valley Rd.
DY10: Kidd 7M 157
Spenser Av. WV6: Pert 5F 34
Spenser Cl. B79: Tam 3A 32
Spenser Wlk. B61: Cats 1A 188
Spernal Ash B80: Stud 8M 221
Spernal La. B80: Stud 8M 221
Spernall Gro. B29: W Cas 8A 120
Spetchley Cl. B97: Redd 3C 220
Spey Cl. B5: Edg 3K 121
Sphinx Dr. CV3: Cov 8H 153
Spiceland Rd. B31: N'fld 3M 141
Spicer Pl. CV22: Bil 8K 179
Spiers Cl. B93: Know 3G 169
Spies Cl. B62: Quin 3F 118
Spies La. B62: Quin 4F 118
Spills Mdw. DY3: Up Gor 4E 74
Spilsbury Cl. CV32: Lea S 7L 217
Spilsbury Cft. B91: Sol 1A 168
Spindle Cl. DY11: Kidd 8K 135
Spindle La. B90: Dic H 3G 167
(not continuous)
Spindles, The LE10: Burb 4M 91
Spindle St. CV1: Cov 3D 152
Spindlewood Cl. WS12: Hth H 8K 9
Spinners End Dr. B64: Crad H 8K 97
Spinners End Ind. Est.
B64: Crad H 1K 117
Spinney, The B15: Edg 4E 120
B20: Hand 5E 78
B38: K Nor 8F 142
B47: Wyt 5B 166
B74: Lit A 4B 42
B91: Sol 1C 168
CV4: Canly 6K 173
CV9: Man 2A 66
CV23: Long L 4G 179
Spinney, The CV32: Lea S 8K 217
DY3: Gorn 7C 74
WV3: Wolv 8K 35
Spinney Cl. B31: N'fld 6A 142
B78: B'moor 1M 47
CV3: Bin W 2E 176
CV7: Gun H 1E 108
DY8: Word 6J 95
DY11: Kidd 2G 157
WS3: Pels 7A 26
WS7: C Ter 8G 11
WS11: Nort C 4M 15
Spinney Dr. B90: Ches G 5K 167
Spinney Farm Rd.
WS11: Cann 2B 14
Spinney Hill CV34: Warw 8G 217
Spinney La. CV10: Nun 5C 88
WS7: C Ter 8F 10
Spinney M. B97: Redd 8C 212
Spinney Path CV3: Finh 4M 173
Spinney Rd. LE10: Burb 3J 91
Spinney Wlk. B76: Walm 2M 81
B97: Redd 8C 212
Spinning School La.
B79: Tam 4B 32
Spiral Cl. B62: B'hth 1E 118
Spiral Ct. B24: Erd 7E 80
B76: Walm 6M 59
DY3: Lwr G 6D 74
(off Yorkdale Cl.)
DY8: Stourb 5A 116
WV11: Wed 2K 37
Spiral Grn. B24: Erd 5J 81
Spire Bank CV47: Sou 6H 225
Spirehouse La.
B60: B'wll, Burc 4D 188
Spires, The CV10: Nun 5C 88
WS14: Lich 3L 19
Spire Vw. B61: B'gve 6M 187
Spitalfields CV12: Bed 7J 111
Spitfire Pk. B24: Erd 7K 81
Spitfire Rd. B24: Erd 7J 81
Spitfire Way B35: Cas V 7A 82
Splash La. WS12: Hed 6J 9
Spode Pl. WS11: Hth H 7H 9
Spondon Gro. B34: S End 4C 104
Spondon Rd. WV11: Wed 1L 37
SPON END 6A 152
Spon End CV1: Cov 6A 152
Spon Ga. Ho. CV1: Cov 7A 152
Spon La. B70: W Brom 8K 77
CV9: Gren 6D 48
Spon La. Ind. Est.
B66: Smeth 1K 99
Spon La. Sth. B66: Smeth 1K 99
B70: Smeth, W Brom 1K 99
Spon La. Trad. Est.
B70: W Brom 7K 77
Spon St. CV1: Cov 6B 152 (4A 6)
Spoon Dr. B38: K Nor 7D 142
Spooner Cft. B5: Birm 1L 121
Spooners Cl. B92: Sol 2F 146
Spot La. WS8: Clay 3F 26
Spottiswood Cl. CV22: Caw 1G 205
Spouthouse La. B43: Gt Barr 2E 78
Spout La. WS1: Wals 2L 55
(not continuous)
Spreadbury Cl. B17: Harb 1M 119
Sprig Cft. B36: Hodg H 1J 103
SPRING, THE 2F 198
Spring Av. B65: Row R 7C 98
Spring Avon Cft. B17: Harb 3B 120
SPRING BANK 6B 38
Springbank B9: Bord G 6F 102
Spring Bank Ho.
WV13: W'hall 6A 38
Springbank Rd. B15: Edg 2J 121
Springbrook Cl. B36: Cas B 8D 82
Springbrook La. B94: Earls 2F 192
Spring Cl. B91: Sol 6M 145
CV1: Cov 6E 152
CV23: Kils 7M 207
DY7: Kinv 4A 114
DY9: Hag 5M 137
WS4: S'fld 7C 26
Spring Coppice Dr.
B93: Dorr 6G 169
Spring Ct. B66: Smeth 4C 100
B70: W Brom 7K 77
CV8: Bubb 4J 201
WS1: Wals 2A 56
Spring Cres. B64: Crad H 2M 117
Springcroft Rd. B11: Tys 7F 122
Springdale Ct. CV11: Nun 6K 89
Spring Dr. WS6: Gt Wyr 7G 15
Spring Dr. Ind. Est.
WV4: E'shll 5G 53
SPRINGFIELD
Bedworth 8H 111
Moseley 8D 122
Rowley Regis 3M 97
Wolverhampton 6E 36 (1M 7)
Springfield B23: Erd 6D 80
Springfield Av. B12: Bal H 3A 122
B60: B'gve 2A 210
B68: O'bry 5J 99
DY3: Sed 8E 52
DY9: W'cte 5E 116
Springfield Cl. B65: Row R 4A 98
Springfield Ct. B28: Hall G 1F 144
B75: S Cold 4C 60
Springfield Cres.
B70: W Brom 8L 77
B76: Walm 5A 60
B92: Sol 6C 124
CV12: Bed 7H 111
DY2: Dud 1M 97
Springfield Dr. B14: K Hth 8L 121
B62: B'hth 2D 118
Springfield Grn. DY3: Sed 8E 52
Springfield Gro. CV47: Sou 4H 225
DY3: Sed 8D 52
Springfield Ind. Est.
B69: O'bry 2H 99
Springfield La. B65: Row R 4M 97
DY10: Kidd 1M 157
WV10: F'hses 5D 22
Springfield Pk. LE10: Hinc 6G 69
Springfield Pl.
CV1: Cov 5D 152 (1D 6)
Springfield Ri. WS12: Hed 3J 9
Springfield Rd. B13: Mose 8D 122
B14: K Hth 1M 143
B36: Cas B 1D 104
B62: B'hth 2D 118
B68: O'bry 5J 99
B76: Walm 7M 59
B77: Two G 1D 46
CV1: Cov 5D 152 (1D 6)
CV11: Nun 7L 89
DY5: Brie H 7B 96
LE10: Hinc 2K 91
WV10: Wolv 5E 36 (1M 7)
WV14: Bils 2L 53
Springfields B46: Col 4A 106
WS4: Rus 2B 40
Springfield Ter. B65: Row R 4M 97
Spring Gdns. B21: Hand 2E 100
B66: Smeth 6B 100
DY2: Dud 1K 97
DY3: Gorn 7C 74
LE9: Sap 1L 93
Spring Gro. B19: Hock 3H 101
Spring Gro. Cres.
DY11: Kidd 6H 157
Spring Gro. Gdns.
B18: Hock 3F 100
Spring Gro. Rd. DY11: Kidd 6H 157
Spring Head WS10: W'bry 7F 54
SPRING HILL 5J 51
SPRINGHILL
Great Wyrley 4D 24
Lynn 2L 27
Spring Hill B1: Birm 6H 101 (3A 4)
B18: Hock 5G 101 (3A 4)
B24: Erd 6F 80
CV7: Gun H 1E 108
CV8: Bubb 4J 201
Springhill CV10: Harts 1A 88
Springhill Av. WV4: Penn 6J 51
Spring Hill Bus. Pk.
CV7: Gun H 1F 108
Springhill Cl. WS4: S'fld 8D 26
WV12: W'hall 2D 38
Springhill Ct. WS1: Wals 1A 56
Springhill Gdns. B97: Redd 7M 211
Springhill Gro. WV4: Penn 5J 51
Springhill Ho's.
CV22: Rugby 1C 206
Spring Hill Ind. Est.
B18: Hock 6G 101
Springhill La. WV4: Lwr P 4F 50
WV4: Penn 6J 51
Springhill Pk. WV4: Penn 6H 51
Springhill Ri. DY12: Bew 5C 156
Spring Hill Rd. CV10: Nun 3C 88
Springhill Rd. WS1: Wals 8M 39
WS7: Burn 3G 17
WS8: Bwnhls 2G 27
WV11: Wed 1L 37
Spring Hill Ter. WV4: Penn 3A 52
Spring Ho. B37: K'hrst 4H 105
Spring La. B24: Erd 6G 81
B62: Roms 5K 139
B94: H'ley H 5A 194
B94: Lapw 5D 194
CV8: Ken 4G 199
CV31: Rad S 4E 224
WS4: S'fld 7C 26
WV12: W'hall 5B 38
Springle Styche La.
WS7: Burn 8J 11
Spring Mdw. B63: Hale 7M 117
B64: Old H 8M 97
DY4: Tip 3C 76
WS6: C Hay 8D 14
Springmeadow Gro.
B19: Hock 3K 101
Springmeadow Rd.
DY2: Neth 7J 97
Spring Mdws. Cl. WV8: Bilb 5H 21
Spring Parklands DY1: Dud 1G 97
Spring Pool CV34: Warw 2E 222
Spring Rd. B11: Tys 6F 122
B15: Edg 2K 121
B66: Smeth 1K 99
CV6: Cov 1F 152
CV7: Barn 3B 132
DY2: Neth 3K 97
WS4: S'fld 8D 26
WS13: Lich 7K 13
WV4: E'shll 4G 53
Spring Rd. Ind. Est.
WV4: E'shll 5G 53
Spring Road Station (Rail) 7G 123
Springs, The B64: Old H 8A 98
Springs Av. B61: Cats 8M 161
Springs Cres. CV47: Sou 4H 225
Springside B98: Redd 1H 221
Springslade B32: Harb 4M 119
Springslade Dr. B24: Erd 6K 81
SPRINGS MIRE 1E 96
Spring St. B15: Birm 1K 121
B63: Crad 3J 117
CV1: Cov 6E 152
CV21: Rugby 6B 180
DY4: Tip 4A 76
(Alexandra Rd.)
DY4: Tip 1C 76
(Oaker Hill Rd.)
DY9: Lye 5E 116
WS11: Cann 1E 14
Spring Ter. WS7: Chase 4E 16
Springthorpe Grn. B24: Erd 5J 81
Springthorpe Rd. B24: Erd 6K 81
(Pype Hayes Rd.)
B24: Erd 5K 81
(Woodcote Rd.)
SPRING VALE 5H 53
Springvale Av. WS5: Wals 2C 56
WV14: Bils 5H 53
Springvale Bus. Cen.
WV14: Bils 5H 53
Spring Va. Cl. WV14: Cose 8G 53
Springvale Dr. B97: Redd 6M 211
Spring Va. Ind. Pk.
WV14: Bils 4J 53
Spring Va. Rd. B65: Row R 4A 98
Springvale Rd. B97: Redd 7M 211
Springvale St. WV13: W'hall 6B 38
Springvale Way WV14: Bils 5J 53
Spring Vs. B63: Hale 6A 118
Spring Wlk. B63: Hale 8K 117
B69: O'bry 4G 99
WS2: Wals 6H 39
Springwell Rd. CV31: Lea S 3D 224
Sproat Av. WS10: Darl 4C 54
Spruce B77: Amin 5H 33
Spruce Gro. B24: Erd 7H 81
CV31: Lea S 4M 223
Spruce Rd. CV2: Cov 7J 131
WS5: Wals 6B 56
WS12: Hed 1F 8
Spruces, The DY9: Hag 5M 137
Spruce Way WV3: Wolv 8K 35
Spur Tree Av. WV3: Wolv 8G 35
Squadron Cl. B35: Cas V 5C 82
Square, The
B15: Birm 8H 101 (7A 4)
B17: Harb 4C 120
(off High St.)
B17: Harb 3B 120
(Carless Av.)
B48: A'chu 3B 190
B91: Sol 6C 146
CV8: Ken 5F 198
CV11: Nun 7L 89
CV22: Dunc 6J 205
CV47: S'ton 1M 225
DY2: Dud 3F 96
DY4: Tip 2D 76
LE9: Earl S 1E 70
LE9: Sap 2K 93
LE10: Wlvy 5K 113
WS9: A'rdge 3H 41
WV2: Wolv 1D 52 (8L 7)
WV8: Cod 5F 20
WV12: W'hall 1D 38
Square Cl. B32: Bart G 6J 119
Square La. CV7: Cor 8G 109
Square St. CV32: Lea S 8M 217
Squires Ct. DY5: Brie H 1C 116
Squires Cft. B76: Walm 8A 60
CV2: W'grve S 8M 131
Squires Ga. WS7: Burn 1J 17
Squires Ga. Wlk. B35: Cas V 6A 82
Squires Grn. LE10: Burb 3M 91
Squires Rd. CV23: Stret D 3F 202
Squires Wlk. WS10: W'bry 6F 54
Squires Way CV4: Canly 3K 173
Squirhill Pl. CV31: Lea S 2B 224
Squirrel Cl. WS12: Hth H 7K 9
WS12: Hunt 3C 8
Squirrel Hollow B76: Walm 7A 60
Squirrels, The WS14: Lich 2J 19
Squirrels Hollow B68: O'bry 2K 119
WS7: C Ter 7G 11
Squirrel Wlk. B74: Lit A 4C 42
WV4: Penn 5A 52
Stable Ct. DY3: Sed 3E 74
Stable Cft. B71: W Brom 2M 77
Stableford Cl. B32: Bart G 6M 119
B97: Redd 2D 220
Stables, The B29: S Oak 7G 121
LE10: Burb 4K 91
Stable Wlk. CV11: Nun 7M 89
Stable Way B60: Stoke H 3L 209
Stablewood Gro. WS1: Wals 2A 56
Stacey Cl. B64: Old H 8L 97
Stacey Ct. CV22: Bil 3K 205
Stacey Dr. B13: Mose 4A 144
Stacey Grange Gdns.
B45: Redn 3G 163
Stackhouse Cl. WS9: Wals W 5G 27
Stackhouse Dr. WS3: Pels 5A 26
Staddlestones, The
WV6: Pert 5D 34
Stadium Cl. CV6: Cov 7D 130
DY10: Kidd 5M 157
WV13: W'hall 6B 38
Stadium Dr. DY2: Neth 8J 97
Stafford Cl. CV12: Bulk 7C 112
WS3: Blox 7H 25
Stafford Ct. *B43: Gt Barr 2E 78*
(off West Rd.)
WV10: F'hses 4C 22
Stafford Dr. B71: W Brom 3H 77
Stafford Ho. B33: Kitts G 7E 104
Stafford La. WS12: Hed 4H 9
WV8: Cod 8D 20
Stafford Rd. B21: Hand 1F 100
WS3: Blox 3G 25
WS6: Gt Wyr 3G 25
WS10: Darl 3C 54
WS11: Cann 4C 8
WS12: Hunt 1C 8
WS13: Lich, Longd 6E 12
(not continuous)
WV10: Cov H 1C 22
WV10: F'hses, Oxl, Wolv 1C 36
Staffordshire Pool Cl.
B6: Aston 8M 79
(off Emscote Rd.)
Stafford St. CV9: Ath 2K 65
DY1: Dud 8H 75
LE9: Barw 3A 70
WS2: Wals 6L 39
WS10: W'bry 7E 54
WS12: Hth H 8L 9
WV1: Wolv 5C 36 (1K 7)
WV13: W'hall 7A 38
(not continuous)
WV14: Bils 4K 53
Stafford St. Junc.
WV1: Wolv 6C 36 (2J 7)
Stafford Twr.
B4: Birm 6M 101 (3H 5)
Stafford University Lichfield Cen.
2H 19
Stafford Way B43: Gt Barr 2E 78
Staffs Moor Ind. Est.
B79: Tam 4M 31
Stagborough Way
DY13: Stour S 4E 182
WS12: Hed 5H 9
Stag Cres. WS3: Blox 3L 39
WS11: Nort C 3A 16
Stag Dr. WS12: Hunt 3C 8
Stag Hill Rd. WS3: Blox 2L 39
Stag Ind. Est. WV14: Bils 5M 53
Stag Wlk. B76: Walm 2K 81
Staines Cl. CV11: Nun 2M 89
Stainforth Cl. CV11: Nun 7M 89
Stainsby Av. B19: Birm 4J 101
Stainsby Cft. B90: M'path 4B 168
Staircase La. CV5: Alle 3J 151
(not continuous)
Staite Dr. DY10: Cookl 4A 136
(not continuous)
STAKENBRIDGE 5K 137
Stakenbridge La. DY9: Hag 5J 137
DY10: C'hll 5J 137
Staley Cft. WS12: Hunt 5C 8
Stallings La. DY6: K'wfrd 1K 95
Stambermill Cl. DY9: Lye 4D 116
Stambermill Ho. DY9: Lye 4E 116
Stambermill Ind. Est.
DY9: Lye 3C 116
Stamford Av. CV3: Cov 3C 174
Stamford Cres. WS7: C Ter 1G 17
Stamford Cft. B91: Sol 7B 146
Stamford Gdns. CV32: Lea S 8L 217
Stamford Gro. B20: Hand 8J 79
Stamford Rd. B20: Hand 8J 79
DY5: Brie H 2C 116
DY8: Amb 4B 116
Stamford St. DY8: Amb 2M 115
Stamford Way WS9: A'rdge 7H 27
Stanbrook Rd. B90: M'path 3A 168
Stanbury Av. WS10: Darl 3B 54
Stanbury Rd. B14: K Hth 5B 144
Stancroft Gro. B26: Yard 1A 124
Standard Av. CV4: Tile H 8G 151
Standard Way B24: Erd 1F 102
Standbridge Way DY4: Tip 4A 76
Standedge B77: Wiln 2G 47
Standhills Rd. DY6: K'wfrd 3L 95
Standish Cl. CV2: Cov 7L 153
Standlake Av. B36: Hodg H 2K 103
Standlake M. CV31: Lea S 3C 224
Standleys Twr. B23: Erd 3G 81
Stand St. CV34: Warw 3D 222
Stanfield Rd. B32: Quin 2K 119
B43: Gt Barr 4K 57
Stanford Av. B42: Gt Barr 2G 79
Stanford Cl. B97: Redd 3B 220
Stanford Dr. B65: Row R 5B 98
Stanford Gro. B63: Hale 8J 117
Stanford Rd.
WV2: Wolv 2C 52 (8H 7)
Stanford Way *B69: O'bry 5E 98*
(off Kempsey Cl.)
Stanhoe Cl. DY5: Brie H 1D 116
Stanhope Ho. B79: Tam 5A 32

Stanhope Rd.—Stone Pine Cl.

Stanhope Rd. B67: Smeth ... 6M 99
Stanhope St. B12: Birm ... 2M 121
DY2: Neth ... 5L 97
WV3: Wolv ... 8B 36 (5G 7)
Stanhope Way B43: Gt Barr ... 5K 57
Stanhurst Way B71: W Brom ... 7A 56
Stanier Av. CV1: Cov ... 6A 152
Stanier Cl. WS4: Rus ... 2B 40
Stanier Gro. B20: Hand ... 7H 79
Staniforth St.
B4: Birm ... 5L 101 (1H 5)
STANKLYN ... 7D 158
Stanklyn La.
DY10: Kidd, Stone ... 1A 184
Stanley Av. B32: Harb ... 2L 119
B75: S Cold ... 5M 59
B90: Shir ... 5H 145
Stanley Cl. B28: Hall G ... 4G 145
B98: Redd ... 4G 213
WV11: Wed ... 1M 37
Stanley Ct. *B13: Mose ... 7B 122*
(off Wake Grn. Pk.)
CV31: Lea S ... 2C 224
WV6: Pert ... 5E 34
Stanley Dr. DY3: Swind ... 7E 72
Stanley Gro. B11: S'brk ... 3B 122
Stanley Pl. B13: Mose ... 6M 121
WS4: Rus ... 3B 40
WV14: Bils ... 4H 53
Stanley Rd. B7: Nech ... 2C 102
B14: K Hth ... 2K 143
B68: O'bry ... 1J 119
B71: W Brom ... 2L 77
CV5: Cov ... 1M 173
CV9: Ath ... 2K 65
CV11: Nun ... 4G 89
CV21: Hillm ... 8E 180
DY8: Stourb ... 6M 115
LE10: Hinc ... 7J 69
WS4: Rus ... 3B 40
WS10: Darl ... 4D 54
WS12: Hed ... 4G 9
(not continuous)
WV10: Bush ... 8D 22
Stanley St. LE9: Barw ... 3A 70
WS3: Blox ... 1J 39
Stanmore Gro. B62: Quin ... 6G 119
Stanmore Rd. B16: Edg ... 8C 100
Stansbury Ho. *WS2: Wals ... 1J 55*
(off St Quentin St.)
Stansfield Gro. CV8: Ken ... 5J 199
Stanton Av. DY1: Dud ... 3F 74
Stanton Gro. B26: Yard ... 1M 123
B90: Shir ... 5G 145
DY4: Tip ... 4A 76
Stanton Ho. B71: W Brom ... 8M 55
Stanton La. LE9: Pot M ... 5M 71
LE9: Sap ... 1H 93
Stanton Rd. B43: Gt Barr ... 2D 78
B90: Shir ... 5G 145
CV31: Lea S ... 3C 224
LE9: Elme ... 5G 71
LE9: Sap ... 2K 93
WV1: Wolv ... 7F 36
Stanton Wlk. CV34: Warw ... 8D 216
Stanville Rd. B26: Sheld ... 3C 124
Stanway Gdns. B71: W Brom ... 3K 77
Stanway Gro. B44: Gt Barr ... 6M 57
Stanway Rd. B71: W Brom ... 3K 77
B90: Shir ... 6H 145
CV5: Cov ... 1A 174
Stanwell Gro. B23: Erd ... 3E 80
Stanwick Av. B33: Kitts G ... 6E 104
Stan Williams Ct. CV11: Nun ... 5K 89
Stapenhall Rd. B90: M'path ... 3A 168
Staple Flat B60: L End ... 2C 188
Stapleford Cft. B14: K Hth ... 7J 143
Stapleford Gdns. WS7: Burn ... 3K 17
Stapleford Gro. DY8: Word ... 6L 95
Staplehall Rd. B31: N'fld ... 7B 142
STAPLE HILL ... 1C 188
Staplehurst Rd. B28: Hall G ... 1F 144
Staple Lodge Rd. B31: N'fld ... 8B 142
Staples Cl. CV12: Bulk ... 6C 112
Stapleton Cl. B76: Walm ... 3B 82
B80: Stud ... 6K 221
B98: Redd ... 6K 213
Stapleton Dr. B37: F'bri ... 6H 105
Stapleton La. CV13: Dad ... 1F 68
LE9: Barw ... 1M 69
Stapleton Rd. B80: Stud ... 6K 221
WS9: A'rdge ... 4F 40
Stapylton Av. B17: Harb ... 4B 120
Stapylton Ct. *B17: Harb ... 4B 120*
(off Old Church Rd.)
Starbank Rd. B10: Small H ... 1G 123
Starbold Ct. B93: Know ... 3H 169
Starbold Cres. B93: Know ... 4G 169
Star City ... 1D 102
Star Cl. DY4: Tip ... 4C 76
WS2: Wals ... 5F 38
Star Cnr. CV23: Barby ... 8J 207
Starcrest Ind. Est.
DY5: Brie H ... 8E 96
Starcross Cl. CV2: Cov ... 2J 153
Starcross Rd. B27: A Grn ... 7J 123
Stare Grn. CV4: Canly ... 3K 173
STARETON ... 5D 200
Stareton Cl. CV4: Cov ... 3L 173
Star Hill B15: Edg ... 1H 121
Star Ind. Est. CV2: Cov ... 4M 153
Starkey Cft. B37: Chel W ... 7J 105
Starkie Dr. B68: O'bry ... 5J 99
Starley Ct. CV3: Bin ... 2A 176
Starley Pk. CV7: Exh ... 1H 131
Starley Rd. CV1: Cov ... 7B 152 (6A 6)
Starley Way B37: Mars G ... 3J 125
Star St. DY9: Lye ... 4F 116
WV3: Wolv ... 1L 51
Startin Cl. CV7: Exh ... 2F 130
Start Point Trad. Est.
B11: S'hll ... 5D 122
Statham Dr. B16: Edg ... 7C 100
Station App. B45: B Grn ... 1K 189
B73: S Cold ... 3H 59
B74: Four O ... 3F 42
B91: Sol ... 5A 146
B93: Dorr ... 7F 168
CV31: Lea S ... 2M 223
DY10: Kidd ... 4M 157
WS13: Lich ... 1L 19
Station Av. B16: Edg ... 8C 100
CV4: Tile H ... 1D 172
CV34: Warw ... 2F 222
Station Bldgs. *B46: Wat O ... 6H 83*
(off Minworth Rd.)
Station Cl. WS3: Blox ... 1H 39
WV8: Cod ... 6F 20
Station Cotts. B60: B'wll ... 5G 189
Station Dr. B28: Hall G ... 8F 122
B46: Wat O ... 6H 83
B74: Four O ... 1H 59
B92: Olton ... 8L 123
B94: Earls ... 8D 166
DY4: Tip ... 5B 76
DY5: Brie H ... 7E 96
(Brierley Hill)
DY5: Brie H ... 8B 96
(Silver End)
DY9: Hag ... 4A 138
DY10: Blak ... 7J 137
Stationfields B79: Tam ... 4C 32
Station Hill CV7: Old A ... 2C 108
Station La. B94: Lapw ... 6K 195
Station Link Rd.
B26: Birm A ... 5K 125
B40: Nat E C ... 5K 125
Station Pl. WS3: Blox ... 1H 39
Station Rd. B6: Aston ... 8M 79
B14: K Hth ... 1K 143
B17: Harb ... 3C 120
B21: Hand ... 1C 100
B23: Erd ... 4F 80
B27: A Grn ... 6J 123
B30: K Nor ... 4E 142
B31: N'fld ... 7A 142
B33: Stech ... 5K 103
B37: Mars G ... 1F 124
B38: K Nor ... 4E 142
B46: Col ... 1M 105
B46: Neth W ... 3G 33
B47: Wyt ... 6A 166
B48: A'chu ... 4A 190
B60: B'wll ... 4G 189
B64: Old H ... 8M 97
B65: Row R ... 7D 98
B69: O'bry ... 4G 99
B73: Bold, W Grn ... 8G 59
B78: Pole ... 2K 49
B79: Pole ... 2K 49
B80: Stud ... 5J 221
B91: Sol ... 5B 146
B92: H Ard ... 2B 148
B93: Dorr ... 6G 169
CV7: Bal C ... 3G 171
CV7: Old A ... 2D 108
CV8: Ken ... 5F 198
CV13: High H ... 5M 67
CV13: Stoke G ... 2C 68
CV23: Clift D ... 4F 180
CV23: Lilb ... 2M 181
CV34: Warw ... 2F 222
CV47: S'ton ... 1M 225
DY5: Brie H ... 5C 96
DY9: Hag ... 3M 137
DY9: Lye ... 3E 116
DY11: Hartl ... 7B 184
DY12: Bew ... 6C 156
LE9: Earl S ... 3E 70
LE9: Elme ... 4E 70
LE10: Hinc ... 1K 91
WS3: Pels ... 6A 26
WS4: Rus ... 3A 40
WS6: Gt Wyr ... 5F 14
WS7: Hamm ... 6L 17
WS9: A'rdge ... 4G 41
WS12: Hed ... 3H 9
WS13: Lich ... 2H 19
WS14: Shens ... 3F 28
WV5: Wom ... 1G 73
WV8: Cod ... 6E 20
WV14: Bils ... 4L 53
Station Rd. Ind. Est.
B65: Row R ... 7D 98
Station Sq. CV1: Cov ... 8C 152 (7B 6)
Station St. B5: Birm ... 8K 101 (7F 4)
B60: B'gve ... 7M 187
B64: Crad H ... 1J 117
B73: S Cold ... 4H 59
CV9: Ath ... 1K 65
DY4: Tip ... 4B 76
WS2: Wals ... 8K 39
Station St. WS3: Blox ... 1H 39
WS6: C Hay ... 6E 14
WS10: Darl ... 3E 54
Station St. E. CV6: Cov ... 2E 152
Station St. W. CV6: Cov ... 1D 152
Station St. W. Bus. Pk.
CV6: Cov ... 2D 152
Station Ter. WV14: Cose ... 8J 53
Station Twr. CV1: Cov ... 8C 152 (7B 6)
Station Way B37: Mars G ... 6K 125
B40: Nat E C ... 5K 125
B97: Redd ... 6D 212
Station Yd. LE10: Hinc ... 2K 91
Staulton Grn. B69: O'bry ... 5E 98
Staunton Rd. CV31: Lea S ... 4A 224
Staveley Rd. B14: K Hth ... 3K 143
WV1: Wolv ... 5C 36 (1H 7)
Staveley Way CV21: Brow ... 3D 180
Staverton Cl. CV5: E Grn ... 6F 150
Staverton Leys CV22: Rugby ... 2A 206
Stead Cl. DY4: Tip ... 8B 54
WS2: Wals ... 4J 39
Steadman Cft. DY4: Tip ... 1D 76
Steatite Way DY13: Stour S ... 4E 182
STECHFORD ... 7L 103
Stechford Cascades ... 6L 103
Stechford La. B8: W End ... 4J 103
Stechford Retail Pk.
B33: Stech ... 5L 103
Stechford Rd. B34: Hodg H ... 4K 103
Stechford Station (Rail) ... 6K 103
Stechford Trad. Est.
B33: Stech ... 6L 103
Steel Bright Rd. B66: Smeth ... 3C 100
Steel Dr. WV10: Bush ... 1D 36
Steele St. CV22: Rugby ... 6L 179
Steel Gro. B25: Yard ... 2J 123
Steelhouse La.
B4: Birm ... 6L 101 (3G 5)
WV2: Wolv ... 8E 36 (6H 7)
Steelmans Rd. WS10: Darl ... 2F 54
Steelpark Rd. B62: Hale ... 2B 118
Steelpark Way WV11: Wed ... 5K 37
Steel Rd. B31: N'fld ... 7M 141
Steel Rdbt. WS10: W'bry ... 7E 54
Steene Gro. B31: N'fld ... 6K 141
Steeping Rd. CV23: Long L ... 4H 179
Steeplefield Rd. CV6: Cov ... 4A 152
Steeples, The DY8: Stourb ... 6B 116
Steepwood Cft. B30: K Nor ... 5D 142
Steere Av. B79: Tam ... 2C 32
Stella Cft. B37: Chel W ... 7J 105
Stella Gro. B43: Gt Barr ... 1B 78
Stella Rd. DY4: Tip ... 3M 75
Stenbury Cl. WV10: Bush ... 5F 22
Stencills Dr. WS4: Wals ... 6B 40
Stencills Rd. WS4: Wals ... 5B 40
Stennels Cl. CV6: Cov ... 1M 151
Stennels Cres. B62: Hale ... 5E 118
Stephanie Gro. B77: Amin ... 3G 33
Stephens Cl. WV11: Wed ... 1M 37
Stephens Ind. Est. B11: Tys ... 5F 122
Stephenson Av. WS2: Wals ... 3G 39
Stephenson Cl. B77: Glas ... 7G 33
CV32: Lea S ... 8J 217
Stephenson Ct. CV23: Kils ... 7M 207
Stephenson Dr. B37: Chel W ... 6H 105
WV6: Pert ... 3E 34
Stephenson Pl.
B2: Birm ... 7L 101 (5G 5)
DY12: Bew ... 6C 156
Stephenson Rd. CV7: Exh ... 2J 131
LE10: Hinc ... 2E 90
Stephenson Sq. WS2: Wals ... 4H 39
Stephenson St.
B2: Birm ... 7K 101 (5F 4)
WV3: Wolv ... 8B 36 (5G 7)
Stephenson Twr. B5: Birm ... 6F 4
Stephenson Way WS12: Hed ... 4H 9
Stephens Rd. B76: Walm ... 5A 60
Stephen St. CV21: Rugby ... 6M 179
Stephens Wlk. WS13: Lich ... 7G 13
Stepney Rd. CV2: Cov ... 5G 153
Steppey La. CV9: Man ... 5K 65
Stepping Stone Cl.
WS2: Wals ... 5F 38
Stepping Stones
DY8: Stourb ... 4B 116
Stepping Stones Rd.
CV5: Cov ... 5M 151
Steppingstone St. DY1: Dud ... 8H 75
Sterling Pk. B77: Wiln ... 2D 46
DY5: Brie H ... 5F 96
Sterling Way CV11: Nun ... 1L 111
Sterndale Rd. B42: Gt Barr ... 3J 79
Sterrymere Gdns. DY7: Kinv ... 5B 114
Stevenage Wlk.
CV2: W'grve S ... 2A 154
Steven Dr. WV14: Bils ... 8L 53
Stevens Av. B32: Bart G ... 7K 119
Stevens Cl. LE9: S Stan ... 7L 71
Stevens Dr. WS12: Hed ... 3K 9
Stevens Ga.
WV2: Wolv ... 1C 52 (8J 7)
Stevens Ho.
CV1: Cov ... 5D 152 (2E 6)
Stevenson Av. B98: Redd ... 6F 212
Stevenson Rd. B79: Tam ... 3A 32
CV6: Cov ... 1A 152
Stevenson Wlk. WS14: Lich ... 3H 19
Stevens Rd. DY9: W'cte ... 7D 116
Steve Roberts Ct.
DY11: Kidd ... 3G 157
Steward St. B18: Hock ... 6G 101
Stewart Cl. CV4: Cov ... 7K 151
Stewart Ct. CV7: New A ... 1G 109
DY10: Kidd ... 5M 157
Stewart Rd. DY6: K'wfrd ... 5K 95
WS9: Wals W ... 6G 27
Stewarts Rd. B62: B'hth ... 2D 118
Stewart St. CV11: Nun ... 6H 89
WV2: Wolv ... 1C 52 (7J 7)
Stewkins DY8: Word ... 1L 115
STEWPONEY ... 3E 114
Stewponey, The DY7: Stourt ... 3E 114
Stewponey Lock DY7: Stourt ... 3E 114
Stewponey Wharf
DY7: Stourt ... 3E 114
Steyning Rd. B26: Yard ... 4L 123
Stickley La. DY3: Lwr G ... 5C 74
Stidfall Gro. CV31: Lea S ... 3D 224
Stilehouse Cres. B65: Row R ... 7C 98
Stilthouse Gro. B45: Redn ... 2G 163
Stiper's Hill B79: Wart ... 2L 49
STIRCHLEY ... 3H 143
Stirchley Indoor Bowling Cen.
... 2G 143
Stirchley Trad. Est.
B30: Stir ... 2H 143
Stirling Av. CV32: Cubb, Lill ... 4B 218
LE10: Hinc ... 8G 69
Stirling Cl. CV3: Bin ... 1M 175
Stirling Ct. B16: Edg ... 8F 100
Stirling Cres. WV12: W'hall ... 3B 38
Stirling Pl. WS11: Cann ... 1B 14
Stirling Rd. B16: Edg ... 8E 100
B73: New O ... 7D 58
B90: Shir ... 1L 167
DY2: Dud ... 3L 97
WV14: Bils ... 6M 53
Stirrup Cl. WS5: Wals ... 5M 55
STIVICHALL ... 3A 174
Stivichall & Cheylesmore By-Pass
CV3: Cov ... 5E 174
Stivichall Cft. CV3: Cov ... 3B 174
Stockbridge Cl. WV6: Tett ... 7F 34
Stockdale Pl. B15: Edg ... 1D 120
Stock Exchange Bldg. B3: Birm ... 4E 4
STOCKFIELD ... 4J 123
Stockfield Rd. B25: Yard ... 4J 123
B27: A Grn ... 5H 123
Stockhay La. WS7: Hamm ... 4K 17
Stockhill Dr. B45: Rubery ... 3F 162
STOCKINGFORD ... 6D 88
Stockings La. WS14: Lich ... 8G 19
Stocking St. DY9: Lye ... 4F 116
Stockland Ct. B74: S'tly ... 1A 58
STOCKLAND GREEN ... 5C 80
Stockland Green Community Leisure
Cen. ... 5C 80
Stockland Rd. B23: Erd ... 5D 80
Stockley Cres. B90: Shir ... 6K 145
Stockley Rd. CV6: Longf ... 3H 131
Stockmans Cl. B38: K Nor ... 1E 164
Stocks La. CV23: Thurl ... 6F 204
Stocks Wood B30: B'vlle ... 1F 142
STOCKTON ... 1M 225
Stockton Cl. B76: Min ... 4C 82
B93: Know ... 5H 169
WS2: Wals ... 5K 39
Stockton Ct. WV14: Cose ... 1H 75
Stockton Gro. B33: Kitts G ... 8D 104
CV32: Lea S ... 7A 218
Stockton Rd.
CV1: Cov ... 5E 152 (1F 6)
CV47: S'ton ... 1L 225
Stockwell Av. DY5: Quar B ... 1D 116
STOCKWELL END ... 4K 35
Stockwell End WV6: Tett ... 3K 35
Stockwell Head LE10: Hinc ... 8K 69
Stockwell Ri. B92: Sol ... 2D 146
Stockwell Rd. B21: Hand ... 7E 78
WV6: Tett ... 4K 35
STOKE ... 7K 153
STOKE ALDERMOOR ... 1H 175
STOKE CROSS ... 1E 210
STOKE END ... 2F 60
Stoke Floods Nature Reserve
... 6M 153
STOKE GOLDING ... 2D 68
Stoke Grn. CV3: Cov ... 7G 153
Stoke Grn. Cres. CV3: Cov ... 8H 153
STOKE HEATH
Coventry ... 3H 153
Stoke Prior ... 4K 209
Stoke La. B98: Redd ... 2H 213
CV13: Dad ... 1E 68
CV13: High H, Stoke G ... 5A 68
LE10: Wykin ... 5F 68
WR9: Wych ... 8F 208
Stoke Pk. M. CV2: Cov ... 6G 153
STOKE POUND ... 5A 210
Stoke Pound La.
B60: Stoke P, S Prior ... 6L 209
STOKE PRIOR ... 5K 209
Stoke Rd. B60: B'gve ... 2A 210
CV13: Stoke G ... 2F 68
CV13: Upton ... 1K 67
LE10: Hinc ... 4G 69
Stoke Row CV2: Cov ... 5G 153
Stokes Av. DY4: Tip ... 1A 76
WV13: W'hall ... 1M 53
Stokesay Av. WV6: Pert ... 6F 34
Stokesay Cl. B69: Tiv ... 1A 98
CV11: Nun ... 6G 89
DY10: Kidd ... 7L 157
Stokesay Gro. B31: Longb ... 1M 163
Stokesay Ho. B23: Erd ... 3F 80
Stokesay Ri. DY1: Dud ... 6E 74
Stokes La. WS11: Nort C ... 3L 15
Stokes St. WS3: Blox ... 1H 39
Stoke Turn Ct. B61: Stoke H ... 2K 209
Stoke Way B15: Birm ... 8J 101 (7C 4)
STOKE WHARF ... 6L 209
STOKE WORKS ... 8K 209
Stom Rd. WV14: Bils ... 4H 53
STONE ... 6D 158
Stoneacre Cl. WV3: Wolv ... 8G 35
STONEA LEA ... 7F 8
Stone Av. B75: S Cold ... 4A 60
Stonebow Av. B91: Sol ... 1B 168
STONEBRIDGE ... 7C 126
Stonebridge Cres.
B37: K'hrst ... 4F 104
Stonebridge Highway
CV3: Cov, W'hall ... 5C 174
Stonebridge Ind. Est.
CV3: W'hall ... 6H 175
Stonebridge Rd. B46: Col ... 2M 105
(not continuous)
Stonebridge Trad. Est.
CV3: W'hall ... 5H 175
Stonebrook Way
B29: W Cas ... 7M 119
CV6: Longf ... 6F 130
Stonebury B15: Edg ... 1D 120
Stonebury Av. CV5: E Grn ... 5D 150
Stonechat Cl. DY10: Kidd ... 7B 158
Stonechat Dr. B23: Erd ... 7C 80
Stonechat Rd. CV23: Brow ... 1D 180
Stone Cl. B38: K Nor ... 7F 142
Stonecroft Av. B45: Redn ... 2G 163
Stonecrop Cl. B38: K Nor ... 1F 164
WS8: Clay ... 3D 26
Stonecross B46: Wat O ... 6H 83
Stonedown Cl. WV14: Cose ... 6G 53
Stonefield Cl.
CV2: W'grve S ... 1A 154
Stonefield Dr. DY5: P'ntt ... 2B 96
Stonefield Rd. WV14: Bils ... 4K 53
Stonefield Wlk. *WV14: Bils ... 4K 53*
(off Stonefield Rd.)
Stoneford Rd. B90: Shir ... 5G 145
Stonehall Rd. CV22: Caw ... 1G 205
Stonehaven B77: Amin ... 4F 32
Stonehaven Dr. CV3: Finh ... 6C 174
Stonehaven Gro.
B28: Hall G ... 1H 145
Stonehenge Cft. B14: K Hth ... 8K 143
Stone Hill DY10: Stone ... 6D 158
Stone Hill Cft. B90: M'path ... 3M 167
Stonehills CV21: Brow ... 2C 180
Stonehill Wlk. B77: Wiln ... 3F 46
Stonehouse Av.
WV13: W'hall ... 5M 37
Stonehouse Cl. B97: Redd ... 8C 212
CV32: Cubb ... 4D 218
Stonehouse Cres.
WS10: W'bry ... 7H 55
Stonehouse Dr. B74: Lit A ... 5C 42
Stonehouse Gro.
B32: Bart G ... 7K 119
Stonehouse Hill B29: W Cas ... 6A 120
Stonehouse La. B32: Bart G ... 7K 119
B48: Hopw ... 7D 164
CV3: W'hall ... 5J 175
CV7: Cor ... 3F 128
CV7: Gun H ... 2D 108
Stone Ho. M. CV35: Leek W ... 3F 216
Stonehouse Rd. B60: B'gve ... 1A 210
B73: S Cold ... 6F 58
Stonehurst Rd. B43: Gt Barr ... 5J 57
Stone La. DY7: Kinv ... 5A 114
Stone Lea WS9: A'rdge ... 4H 41
Stonelea Cl. B71: W Brom ... 1L 77
STONELEIGH ... 3B 200
Stoneleigh Abbey ... 6M 199
Stoneleigh Av. CV5: Cov ... 2M 173
CV8: Ken ... 3G 199
Stoneleigh Cl. B74: Four O ... 1F 58
B98: Redd ... 3F 220
CV8: S'lgh ... 3B 200
CV10: Harts ... 7B 66
Stoneleigh Ct. CV11: Nun ... 6J 89
Stoneleigh Deer Pk.
CV8: Stare ... 5E 200
Stoneleigh Deer Pk. Bus. Village
CV8: Stare ... 5D 200
Stoneleigh Gdns. WV8: Cod ... 5F 20
Stoneleigh Ho. B32: Harb ... 4L 119
Stoneleigh Rd. B20: Hand ... 8L 79
B91: Sol ... 4K 145
CV4: Canly ... 7K 173
CV8: Bag ... 2E 200
CV8: Bubb ... 4F 200
CV8: Ken ... 3G 199
CV8: S'lgh ... 6C 200
CV8: S'lgh P ... 8A 200
CV32: B'dwn, Cubb ... 4M 217
Stoneleigh Way DY3: Up Gor ... 3D 74
Stoneley Rd. CV13: Stoke G ... 3D 68
Stone Mdw. CV7: Ker E ... 3A 130
Stone Pine Cl. WS12: Hed ... 1F 8

Stonepine Pl.—Sun St.

Stonepine Pl. DY3: Up Gor 3E 74
Stonepit B77: Wiln 8C 32
Stonepits La. B97: Redd 5D 220
Stone Rd. B15: Edg 2K 121
Stonerwood Av. B28: Hall G 1E 144
Stones Grn. B23: Erd 3F 80
Stone St. B69: O'bry 2G 99
DY1: Dud 8J 75
WV14: Bils 4L 53
Stoneton Cl. CV47: Sou 6J 225
Stoneton Cres. CV7: Bal C 3G 171
Stoneton Gro. B29: W Cas 1A 142
Stoneway Gro. CV31: Lea S ...3D 224
Stonewell Cres. CV11: Nun 1B 112
Stone Yd. B12: Birm ...8M 101 (7K 5)
B64: Crad H 1J 117
STONEYBRIDGE 4K 161
Stoneybrook Leys WV5: Wom ...4E 72
Stoney Cl. B92: Sol 2E 146
Stoney Ct. CV3: Bin 2A 176
Stoney Cft. WS11: Cann 8F 8
Stoneycroft Rd. LE9: Earl S 2D 70
Stoneycroft Twr.
B36: Hodg H 1L 103
STONEYDELPH 8H 33
Stoneydelph La. B77: Wiln 2G 47
Stoneyfields Cl. WS11: Cann 7F 8
Stoneyford Gro.
B14: Yard W 5B 144
STONEYGATE 7L 69
Stoneygate Dr. LE10: Hinc 6L 69
STONEY HILL 8A 188
Stoney Hill Cl. B60: B'gve 8A 188
Stoneyhurst Rd. B24: Erd 8F 80
Stoney La. B12: Bal H 4B 122
B25: Yard 1K 123
B32: Quin 3H 119
B48: A'chu 8G 189
B60: Tard 8G 189
B71: W Brom 5K 77
DY2: Neth 6J 97
DY10: Kidd 2L 157
WS3: Blox 6H 25
(not continuous)
WV4: Penn 4B 52
Stoney La. Ind. Est.
DY10: Kidd 2K 157
Stoney Lea Rd. WS11: Cann 7F 8
Stoneymoor Dr. B36: Cas B 8C 82
Stoney Rd. CV1: Cov ...8C 152 (8C 6)
CV3: Cov 8C 152 (8C 6)
CV10: Nun 3G 89
STONEY STANTON 7L 71
Stoney Stanton Rd.
CV1: Cov 5D 152 (2D 6)
CV6: Cov 5D 152
Stoneythorpe Cl. B91: Sol 8B 146
Stoneywood Rd.
CV2: W'grve S 1M 153
Stonnal Gro. B23: Erd 3G 81
STONNALL 5L 27
Stonnall Ga. WS9: A'rdge 1J 41
Stonnall Rd. WS9: A'rdge 1J 41
Stonor Pk. Rd. B91: Sol 4M 145
Stonor Rd. B28: Hall G 4G 145
Stonydelph La. B77: Wiln 2G 47
Stony La. B67: Smeth 4M 99
Stony St. B67: Smeth 3M 99
STONYWELL 4M 11
Stonywell La. WS15: Longd 3K 11
Stoop, The CV3: Bin 8B 154
Stornoway Rd. B35: Cas V 5B 82
Storrage La. B48: A'chu 6D 190
Storrs Cl. B9: Small H 8D 102
Storrs Pl. B10: Small H 8D 102
Storrs Way, The B32: Bart G ...2H 141
Stotfold Rd. B14: K Hth 7M 143
Stour B77: Hock 4G 47
STOURBRIDGE 4A 116
Stourbridge Crematorium
DY8: Stourb 5K 115
Stourbridge Ind. Est.
DY8: Amb 3A 116
Stourbridge Junction Station (Rail)
.....................6B 116
Stourbridge Lawn Tennis & Squash
Club 8J 115
Stourbridge RFC 3H 115
Stourbridge Rd.
B61: B'gve, Cats 2M 187
B61: Cats, F'fld 5K 161
B63: Hale 4L 117
DY1: Dud 4E 96
DY3: Himl 5J 73
DY5: Brie H 4E 96
DY9: Brme 4J 159
DY9: Clent, Hag 4C 138
DY9: Hag 2C 138
DY9: Lye 4C 116
DY10: Blak, Harv, Mus G
.....................8G 159
DY10: Hurc, Ism, I'ley, Kidd
.....................2L 157
WV4: Penn 8J 51
WV5: Wom 4J 73
Stourbridge Town Station (Rail)
.....................4A 116
Stour Cl. B63: Hale 3L 117
WS7: Burn 3K 17
Stourdale Rd. B64: Crad H 2J 117
Stourdell Rd. B63: Crad 3L 117
Stour Hill DY5: Quar B 2G 117
Stour La. DY13: Stour S 6G 183
Stourmore Cl. WV12: W'hall 3D 38
Stourport Cvn. Pk.
DY13: Stour S 8G 183
Stourport Marina
DY13: Stour S 8H 183
STOURPORT-ON-SEVERN 5G 183
Stourport Rd. DY11: Kidd 1H 183
DY12: Bew 6B 156
DY13: Titt, C'wick 8K 183
Stourport Sports Cen. 7F 182
Stour St. B18: Hock 6G 101
B70: W Brom 6E 76
STOURTON 3D 114
Stourton Castle 3D 114
Stourton Cl. B76: Walm 5M 59
B93: Know 2H 169
Stourton Cres. DY7: Stourt 3F 114
Stourton Dr. WV4: Penn 4J 51
Stourton Rd. B32: Quin 4H 119
Stour Va. Rd. DY9: Lye 3F 116
Stour Valley Cl.
DY5: Quar B 2D 116
Stourville Ind. Est. DY9: Lye ...3F 116
Stow Dr. DY5: Brie H 3B 116
STOWE 8J 13
Stowecroft WS13: Lich 7J 13
Stowe Dr. CV47: Sou 6H 225
Stowe Hill Gdns. WS13: Lich 8J 13
Stowell Rd. B44: K'sdng 2M 79
Stowe Pl. CV4: Tile H 8C 150
Stowe Rd. WS13: Lich 1H 19
Stowe St. WS3: Blox 2J 39
WS13: Lich 1J 19
(not continuous)
Stow Gro. B36: Hodg H 2L 103
STOW HEATH 2H 53
Stowheath La. WV1: Wolv 2H 53
Stow Heath Pl. WV1: Wolv 2H 53
STOW LAWN 1J 53
Stowmans Cl. WV14: Cose 6H 53
Strachey Av. CV32: Lea S 7L 217
Stradey Cl. CV3: Bin 8B 154
Straight Mile CV23: Bour D 6L 203
Straight Rd. WV12: W'hall 3D 38
STRAITS, THE 5A 74
Straits, The DY3: Lwr G 4M 73
Straits Est. DY3: Lwr G 5A 74
Straits Grn. DY3: Lwr G 5B 74
Straits Rd. DY3: Lwr G 6B 74
Strand, The B61: B'gve 6A 188
Stratford Av. CV9: Ath 2J 65
Stratford Cl. DY1: Dud 7E 74
Stratford Ct. B72: S Cold 6H 59
B90: Shir 1K 167
Stratford Dr. WS9: A'rdge 1J 41
Stratford Gdns. B60: B'gve 7A 188
Stratford Pl. B12: Birm 1A 122
Stratford Rd. B11: S'brk 2A 122
(not continuous)
B28: Hall G 4G 145
B60: B'gve 7C 188
(Verona Rd.)
B60: B'gve 7A 188
(Windsor St., not continuous)
B90: M'path, Shir 3L 167
B94: H'ley H, Lapw 6B 168
CV34: Warw 7B 222
CV35: Sher 8A 222
Stratford St. B11: S'hll 4C 122
(not continuous)
CV2: Cov 5G 153
CV11: Nun 5J 89
Stratford St. Nth. B11: S'brk ...1A 122
Stratford Wlk. B36: Hodg H 2J 103
Stratford Way WS11: Cann 4F 8
Strath Cl. CV21: Hillm 2G 207
Strathdene Gdns.
B29: S Oak 8C 120
Strathdene Rd. B29: S Oak 7C 120
Strathearn Rd. CV32: Lea S 8L 217
Strathern Dr. WV14: Cose 8G 53
Strathfield Wlk. WV4: Penn 3J 51
Strathmore Av.
CV1: Cov 7E 152 (6F 6)
Strathmore Cres.
WV5: Wom 8G 51
Strathmore Pl. WS11: Cann 7F 8
Strathmore Rd. DY4: Tip 1A 76
LE10: Hinc 2G 91
Stratton St. CV9: Ath 1L 65
WV10: Wolv 5E 36
Strawberry Cl. B69: Tiv 2C 98
Strawberry Flds. CV7: Mer 8H 127
Strawberry La. WS6: Gt Wyr 1E 24
WV13: W'hall 6J 37
Strawberry La. Ind. Est.
WV13: W'hall 7J 37
Strawberry Wlk. CV2: Cov 7K 131
Strawmoor La.
WV8: Oaken, Cod 7B 20
Stray, The DY5: P'ntt 3C 96
Stream Mdw. WS4: S'fld 8C 26
Stream Pk. DY6: K'wfrd 5L 95
Stream Rd. DY6: K'wfrd 4K 95
(Greenfields Rd.)
DY6: K'wfrd 5L 95
(Lesley Dr.)
DY8: Word 4K 95
Streamside Cl. CV5: Alle 1G 151
Streamside Way B92: Sol 5D 124
WS4: S'fld 1D 40
Streatham Gro. B44: K'sdng 7A 58
Streather Rd. B75: R'ley 8J 43
STREETHAY 8M 13
STREETLY 8M 41
Streetly Crematorium
WS9: A'rdge 7K 41
Streetly Cres. B74: Four O 6D 42
Streetly Dr. B74: Four O 6D 42
Streetly La. B74: Four O 7C 42
Streetly Rd. B23: Erd 4D 80
Streetly Wood B74: S'tly 7A 42
Streetsbrook Rd. B90: Shir 3H 145
B91: Sol 4L 145
Streets Cnr. Gdns.
WS9: Wals W 5G 27
Streets La. WS6: Gt Wyr 1E 24
Streetway Rd. WS14: Shens 2H 29
Strensham Ct. B13: Mose 5L 121
Strensham Hill B13: Mose 5L 121
Strensham Rd. B12: Bal H 5L 121
Stretton Av. CV3: W'hall 4J 175
Stretton Cl. LE10: Burb 3K 91
Stretton Ct. B24: Erd 7E 80
CV21: Brow 2D 180
Stretton Cres. CV31: Lea S 4B 224
Stretton Dr. B45: B Grn 7G 163
Stretton Gdns. WV8: Cod 5F 20
Stretton Gro. B8: W End 3J 103
B11: S'brk 3C 122
(off Sydenham Rd.)
B19: Loz 2J 101
Stretton Ho. B97: Redd 5A 212
Stretton Lodge CV3: W'hall 3J 175
STRETTON-ON-DUNSMORE ...3F 202
Stretton Pl. DY2: Neth 5K 97
WV14: Cose 8G 53
Stretton Rd. B90: Shir 1H 167
CV8: Wols 2G 203
CV10: Nun 6G 89
DY11: Kidd 5H 157
WV12: W'hall 1C 38
Stretton St. B77: Glas 6E 32
Stringer Cl. B75: Four O 5G 43
Stringers Hill WS12: Hed 2K 9
Stringes Cl. WV13: W'hall 6C 38
Stringes La. WV13: W'hall 7B 38
Strode Ho. B79: Tam 5A 32
Strode Rd. WV2: Wolv 3C 52
Stroma Way CV10: Nun 7F 88
Stronsay Cl. B45: Fran 8F 140
Stroud Av. WV12: W'hall 5C 38
Stroud Cl. WV12: W'hall 5C 38
Stroud Rd. B90: Shir 7F 144
Strutt Cl. B15: Edg 1D 120
Strutt Rd. LE10: Burb 4A 92
Strykers Pleasure Bowling Alley
......................5B 32
Stuart Cl. CV34: Warw 4D 222
Stuart Ct. CV6: Cov 1G 153
CV32: Lea S 8L 217
Stuart Cres. DY2: Dud 8L 75
Stuart Rd. B62: Quin 4F 118
B65: Row R 5C 98
Stuarts Ct. DY9: Hag 4A 138
Stuarts Dr. B33: Stech 8K 103
Stuarts Grn. DY9: Pedm 1B 138
Stuarts Rd. B33: Stech 7K 103
Stuart St. B7: Nech 2C 102
WS3: Blox 1H 39
Stuarts Way B32: Bart G 2G 141
STUBBERS GREEN 1E 40
Stubbers Grn. Rd.
WS9: A'rdge 8D 26
Stubbington Cl. WV13: W'hall 8K 37
Stubbs Cl. CV12: Bed 5G 111
Stubbs Gro. CV2: Cov 4H 153
Stubbs Rd. WV3: Wolv 2A 52
Stubby La. WV11: Wed 3M 37
Stubley Dr. WV10: Wolv 3E 36
Stud Farm Cotts. B78: M Oak 7L 31
Studland Av. CV21: Hillm 8F 180
Studland Grn.
CV2: W'grve S 5A 154
Studland Rd. B28: Hall G 1G 145
Stud La. B33: Stech 6M 103
STUDLEY 5L 221
Studley Cft. B92: Sol 5D 124
Studley Dr. DY5: Brie H 1C 116
Studley Ga. DY8: Stourb 5K 115
Studley Rd. B98: Redd 6G 213
WV3: Wolv 1J 51
Studley St. B12: Bal H 3B 122
Studley Swimming Pool 5L 221
Studley Twr. *B12: Birm 2M 121*
(off Canford Cl.)
Sturgeon's Hill WS14: Lich 2J 19
Sturley Cl. CV8: Ken 3H 199
Sturman Dr. B65: B'hth 8B 98
Sturminster Cl.
CV2: W'grve S 5A 154
Stychbrook Gdns. WS13: Lich 7H 13
Styles Cl. CV31: Lea S 2A 224
CV35: H Mag 2A 222
Styvechale Av. CV5: Cov 1M 173
SUCKLE GREEN 6C 48
Suckling Grn. La. WV8: Cod 7F 20
Sudbury Cl. CV32: Lill 7C 218
WV11: Wed 1L 37
Sudbury Gro. B44: K'sdng 7B 58
Sudeley B77: Two G 2C 46
Sudeley Cl. B36: Cas B 8B 82
Sudeley Gdns. DY1: Dud 7D 74
Sudeley Rd. CV10: Nun 1J 111
Suffield Gro. B23: Erd 4B 80
Suffolk Cl. B68: O'bry 5H 99
CV5: E Grn 6H 151
CV10: Nun 6E 88
CV12: Bed 6G 111
WV11: Wed 2J 37
Suffolk Dr. DY5: Brie H 2C 116
Suffolk Gro. WS9: A'rdge 1H 41
Suffolk Ho. B23: Erd 4F 80
Suffolk Pl. B1: Birm 8K 101 (7F 4)
WS2: Wals 4K 39
Suffolk Rd. DY2: Dud 2G 97
WS10: W'bry 6J 55
Suffolk St. CV32: Lea S 8A 218
Suffolk St. Queensway
B1: Birm 7K 101 (6E 4)
Suffolk Way B78: Tam 8A 32
Suffrage St. B66: Smeth 4B 100
Sugarbrook La.
B60: Stoke P 4M 209
Sugarbrook Rd. B60: B'gve 2A 210
Sugar Loaf La. DY7: I'ley 3G 137
DY10: I'ley 4G 137
Sulgrave Cl. CV2: Cov 2L 153
DY1: Dud 6F 74
Sullivan Ct. CV6: Cov 2H 153
Sullivan Rd. CV6: Cov 2H 153
Sullivan Wlk. WS13: Lich 7J 13
Sullivan Way WS13: Lich 7J 13
Sumburgh Cft. B35: Cas V 6A 82
Summercourt Dr. DY6: K'wfrd 3J 95
Summercourt Ho.
B29: S Oak 8B 120
Summercourt Sq. DY6: K'wfrd 4J 95
Summercroft DY13: Stour S 7B 182
Summer Dr. DY3: Lwr G 6C 74
SUMMERFIELD 2M 183
Summerfield Av.
B70: W Brom 5J 77
(not continuous)
DY6: W Hth 2J 95
Summerfield Cen.
B18: Win G 5E 100
Summerfield Cl. B77: Tam 5D 32
Summerfield Ct. B15: Edg 1C 120
Summerfield Cres. B16: Edg 6E 100
Summerfield Dr.
B29: W Cas 2A 142
Summerfield Gro.
B18: Win G 5E 100
Summerfield Ind. Est.
B18: Win G 5G 101
Summerfield La.
DY11: Kidd 2M 183
Summer Fld. Rd. DY9: Clent 7E 138
Summerfield Rd. B16: Edg 6E 100
B77: Tam 5D 32
B92: Olton 7A 124
DY2: Dud 2K 97
DY13: Stour S 5H 183
WS7: Chase 4G 17
Summerfields Av. B62: B'hth ...1F 118
Summergate DY3: Lwr G 6C 74
Summer Gro. WS13: Lich 7K 13
SUMMER HILL 1A 76
SUMMERHILL
Kidderminster 4G 157
Lynn 1L 27
Summer Hill B63: Hale 6B 118
DY6: K'wfrd 3J 95
Summerhill Av. DY11: Kidd 3G 157
Summer Hill Ind. Pk. *B1: Birm ...3A 4*
(off Anderton St.)
Summer Hill Rd.
B1: Birm 6H 101 (3A 4)
WV14: Cose 8K 53
Summerhill Rd. DY4: Tip 2M 75
Summer Hill St.
B1: Birm 6H 101 (4B 4)
Summer Hill Ter.
B1: Birm 6H 101 (3B 4)
Summerhouse Cl.
B97: Redd 3A 220
Summerhouse La.
WS13: Chor 6K 11
Summerhouse Rd.
WV14: Cose 8G 53
Summer La.
B19: Birm 5K 101 (2F 4)
B76: Min 3D 82
DY3: Lwr G 6C 74
WS4: S'fld 7C 26
Summerlee Rd. B24: Erd 7H 81
Summer Pl. DY11: Kidd 4J 157
Summer Rd. B15: Edg 2J 121
(not continuous)
B23: Erd 4F 80
B27: A Grn 7G 123
B65: Row R 6D 98
DY1: Dud 5G 75
DY11: Kidd 6J 157
Summer Row
B3: Birm 6J 101 (4D 4)
WV2: Wolv 8C 36 (5J 7)
Summerside Av. WS12: Haz 5C 10
Summer St. B71: W Brom 5K 77
B98: Redd 6E 212
Summer St. DY6: K'wfrd 3K 95
DY8: Stourb 4M 115
DY9: Lye 4E 116
WV13: W'hall 7M 37
Summerton Rd. B69: O'bry 8D 76
CV31: W'nsh 6A 224
Summervale Cl. DY9: Hag 4A 138
Summervale Rd. DY9: Hag 4M 137
Summerville Ter. B17: Harb 4C 120
Summerway La. DY11: Tort 3L 183
Summit, The DY9: W'cte 5D 116
Summit Cres. B66: Smeth 1L 99
Summit Gdns. B63: Hale 6M 117
Summit Pl. DY3: Gorn 7B 74
Sumner Cl. CV35: H Mag 3A 222
Sumner Rd. B46: Col 3A 106
Sunart Way CV10: Nun 4C 88
Sunbeam B77: Glas 6E 32
Sunbeam Cl. B36: Cas B 8F 82
CV21: Rugby 6C 180
Sunbeam Dr. WS6: Gt Wyr 6F 14
Sunbeam St. WV2: Wolv 2C 52
Sunbeam Way B33: Kitts G 7C 104
Sunbridge Ter. CV21: Rugby 6C 180
Sunbury Av. WS14: Lich 2L 19
Sunbury Cl. WV14: Cose 8L 53
Sunbury Cotts. B31: N'fld 5A 142
Sunbury Rd. B31: Longb 2L 163
B63: Hale 5M 117
CV3: W'hall 4J 175
Suncliffe Dr. CV8: Ken 7F 198
Suncroft B32: Quin 4J 119
Sundbury Ri. B31: N'fld 4B 142
Sunderland Dr. DY8: Amb 1A 116
Sunderton Rd. B14: K Hth 4L 143
Sundew Cft. B36: Hodg H 1K 103
Sundew St. CV2: Cov 7K 131
Sundial La. B43: Gt Barr 8F 56
Sundorne Cl. CV5: E Grn 5G 151
Sundour Cres. WV11: Wed 8H 23
Sundridge Rd. B44: Gt Barr 5L 57
Sundridge Wlk. WV4: Penn 3J 51
Sunfield Rd. WS11: Cann 8A 8
Sunfields Cl. B78: Pole 1B 48
Sunleigh Gro. B27: A Grn 5L 123
Sunley Dr. WS12: Hed 2K 9
Sunningdale *B60: B'gve 8A 188*
(off New Rd.)
B62: Hale 5E 118
B77: Amin 4J 33
Sunningdale Av. CV6: Cov 7D 130
CV8: Ken 5H 199
WV6: Pert 4D 34
Sunningdale Cl. B20: Hand 5E 78
B73: W Grn 7G 59
B98: Redd 4F 212
CV11: Nun 8A 90
DY8: Stourb 7M 115
Sunningdale Dr. B69: Tiv 2A 98
Sunningdale Rd. B11: Tys 6G 123
B61: B'gve 1K 209
DY3: Sed 1B 74
Sunningdale Way WS3: Blox 6G 25
Sunny Av. B12: Bal H 4A 122
Sunnybank Av. B44: K'sdng 2B 80
CV3: W'hall 4H 175
Sunnybank Cl. WS9: A'rdge 7L 41
Sunny Bank Ct. B68: O'bry 2J 119
Sunny Bank Rd. B68: O'bry 2J 119
Sunnybank Rd.
B73: Bold, W Grn 1G 81
DY3: Up Gor 4F 74
Sunnydale Cres. LE10: Hinc 2G 91
Sunnydale Rd. LE10: Hinc 2F 90
Sunnydale Wlk. B71: W Brom 5J 77
Sunnydene B8: W End 4G 103
Sunnyhill LE10: Burb 2M 91
Sunny Hill Cl. WV5: Wom 3H 73
Sunnyhill Sth. LE10: Burb 3M 91
Sunnymead B60: B'gve 8A 188
Sunnymead Rd. B26: Sheld 3M 123
WS7: C Ter 8F 10
Sunnymead Way B74: S'tly 2M 57
Sunnymede Rd. DY6: K'wfrd 5A 96
Sunnyside B69: Tiv 2B 98
LE10: Hinc 6L 69
WS9: Wals W 7G 27
Sunnyside Av. B23: Erd 6E 80
Sunnyside Cl. CV5: Cov 6M 151
CV7: Bal C 2J 171
Sunnyside Ct. CV10: Nun 6F 88
Sunnyside Gdns.
DY11: Kidd 8H 135
Sunnyside La. CV7: Bal C 2J 171
Sunnyside Pk. LE10: Hinc 5K 69
Sunnyside Pk. Ind. Est.
LE10: Hinc 5J 69
Sunnyside Ter. CV7: Bal C 2J 171
Sunridge Av. B19: Hock 3K 101
WV5: Wom 2G 73
Sunrise Hill WS12: Hed 3H 9
Sunrise Wlk. B68: O'bry 6J 99
Sunset Cl. B78: Pole 1A 48
B79: Tam 4A 32
WS6: Gt Wyr 6F 14
Sunset Pl. WV4: E'shll 6F 52
Sunshine Cl. CV8: Ken 7G 199
Sun St. CV21: Rugby 6C 180
DY5: Quar B 8F 96
WS1: Wals 2K 55
(not continuous)

Sun St.—Tanworth La.

Sun St. WV1: Wolv 7E 36 (3M 7)
WV10: Wolv 7E 36 (2M 7)
Sunway Gro. CV3: Cov 3B 174
Surfeit Hill Rd. B64: Crad H ...1K 117
Surrey Cl. CV10: Nun 6E 88
LE10: Burb 5L 91
WS11: Cann 1F 14
Surrey Ct. CV34: Warw 1E 222
Surrey Cres. B71: W Brom 1G 77
Surrey Dr. B78: Tam 8A 32
DY6: K'wfrd 5M 95
WV3: Wolv 8L 35
Surrey Rd. B44: Gt Barr 5L 57
DY2: Dud 2G 97
Surrey Wlk. WS9: A'rdge 8G 27
Sussex Av. B71: W Brom 3J 77
WS9: A'rdge 1G 41
WS10: W'bry 5K 55
Sussex Cl. CV10: Nun 6E 88
Sussex Ct. B29: W Cas 2C 142
CV34: Warw 1E 222
Sussex Dr. WS12: Hed 4H 9
WV3: Wolv 8L 35
Sussex Rd. CV5: Cov 5M 151
Sutherland Av. B90: Shir 6J 145
CV5: E Grn 5G 151
WV2: Wolv 1F 52
Sutherland Cl. B43: Gt Barr 5K 57
CV34: Warw 8E 216
Sutherland Dr. B13: Mose 5M 121
CV12: Bed 5G 111
WV5: Wom 1G 73
Sutherland Gro. WV6: Pert 5F 34
Sutherland Ho. WV1: Wolv 7A 36
Sutherland Pl.
WV2: Wolv 8D 36 (6L 7)
Sutherland Rd. B64: Old H 1L 117
WS6: C Hay 6E 14
WV4: Penn 4B 52
Sutherland St. B6: Aston 1B 102
Sutton App. B8: W End 5G 103
Sutton Arts Theatre 5J 59
Sutton Av. B78: Tam 7A 32
CV5: E Grn 4C 150
Sutton Cl. B98: Redd 7K 213
LE10: Hinc 6M 69
Sutton Coalfield Crematorium
B75: S Cold 7A 44
SUTTON COLDFIELD 4J 59
Sutton Coldfield By-Pass
B75: Bass P, S Cold 7B 44
B76: Min, Wis 3C 82
Sutton Coldfield Station (Rail)
.........................4H 59
Sutton Coldfield Tennis &
Squash Club 7H 59
Sutton Ct. B43: Gt Barr 2E 78
B75: S Cold 2J 59
(not continuous)
WV4: E'shll 7E 52
Sutton Cres. B70: W Brom 6G 77
SUTTON FARM 5J 157
Sutton Ho. CV22: Bil 8J 179
Sutton La. CV13: Dad 1E 68
Sutton Lodge B91: Sol 6A 146
Sutton New Rd. B23: Erd 5F 80
Sutton Oak Cnr. B73: S'tly 4A 58
Sutton Oak Rd. B73: S'tly 5A 58
Sutton Pk. 2E 58
Sutton Pk. CV10: Nun 2B 88
Sutton Pk. Ct. B72: W Grn 7H 59
Sutton Pk. Gro. DY11: Kidd 6J 157
Sutton Pk. Ri. DY11: Kidd 6G 157
Sutton Pk. Rd. DY11: Kidd 5G 157
Sutton Pk. Vis. Cen. 4G 59
Sutton Rd. B23: Erd 4G 81
B24: Erd 3H 81
B78: Dray B 3F 44
DY11: Kidd 4J 157
WS1: Wals 1M 55
WS5: Wals 1B 56
WS10: Mox 4A 54
Suttons Dr. B43: Gt Barr 5F 56
Sutton Sq. B76: Min 3E 82
Sutton Stop CV6: Longf 4H 131
Sutton St. B1: Birm 8K 101 (8E 4)
B6: Aston 3M 101
DY8: Word 8L 95
Suttton Rd. WS9: A'rdge 1B 56
Swadling St. CV31: Lea S 3M 223
Swain Crofts CV31: Lea S 3B 224
Swains Grn. LE10: Burb 3M 91
Swains Gro. B44: Gt Barr 5M 57
Swaledale CV4: Canly 3K 173
Swaledale Cl. B60: Stoke H ...3L 209
Swale Gro. B38: K Nor 8F 142
WV13: W'hall 7D 38
Swale Rd. B76: Walm 8A 60
Swallow Av. B36: Cas B 1G 105
Swallow Cl. B12: Bal H 4B 122
DY2: Neth 7K 97
WS10: W'bry 5H 55
WS12: Hunt 2C 8
Swallow Ct. CV12: Bed 1C 130
WV10: Bush 2D 36
Swallow Cft. WS13: Lich 8G 13
Swallowdale WS9: Wals W 5H 27
WV6: Tett 7F 34
Swallowdean Rd. CV6: Cov 1L 151
Swallow Dr. DY10: Kidd 7A 158
Swallowfall Av. DY8: Stourb ...5J 115
Swallowfield B79: Tam 3L 31
Swallowfields Dr. WS12: Hed 6H 9
Swallowfields Rd. DY3: Sed 7C 52
Swallowgate Bus. Pk.
CV6: Cov 8C 130
Swallow Rd. CV6: Cov 8B 130
Swallows Cl. WS3: Pels 4A 26
Swallows Mdw. B90: Shir 1K 167
(not continuous)
Swallows Reach WS13: Lich ...8G 13
Swallows Ri. Bus. Pk.
DY5: Brie H 6E 96
Swallow St. B2: Birm ...7K 101 (6E 4)
B70: W Brom 5G 77
Swanage Grn.
CV2: W'grve S 5A 154
Swanage Rd. B10: Small H 1D 122
Swan Av. B66: Smeth 2L 99
Swan Bank WV4: Penn 5M 51
Swan Cen. DY10: Kidd 3L 157
Swan Cl. DY10: Blak 8H 137
WS6: C Hay 7D 14
Swan Copse B25: Yard 4J 123
Swan Cnr. Shop. Cen.
WS7: Burn 3J 17
Swancote Dr. WV4: Penn 3J 51
Swancote Rd. B33: Stech 4M 103
DY1: Dud 8H 75
Swancote St. DY1: Dud 1G 97
Swan Courtyard B26: Yard 3K 123
Swan Cres. B69: O'bry 5F 98
Swan Cft. Rd. CV2: Cov 4F 152
Swancroft Rd. DY4: Tip 1M 75
Swan Dr. WS8: Bwnhls 2E 26
Swanfield Rd. DY8: Word 8M 95
Swanfields WS7: Burn 3J 17
Swan Gdns. B23: Erd 5F 80
Swanhurst Community Leisure Cen.
B13: Mose 2A 144
Swan Island B25: Yard 3K 123
WS7: Burn 3J 17
Swan La. B61: F'fld, Wild 5K 161
B61: U War 3E 208
B70: W Brom 4G 77
CV2: Cov 5F 152
DY8: Word 7M 95
Swan La. Ind. Est.
B70: W Brom 4G 77
Swanley Cl. B62: Quin 6G 119
Swanmore Cl. WV3: Wolv 1L 51
Swanmore Ri. B79: Tam 4M 31
Swann Rd. WV14: Cose 7G 53
Swann Wlk. DY4: Tip 1A 76
Swan Pas. DY13: Stour S 6G 183
Swan Pool Gro. WS4: S'fld 8D 26
Swan Rd. WS13: Lich 2G 19
Swan Rdbt. B70: W Brom 4F 76
Swansbrook Gdns.
B38: K Nor 7J 143
Swan Shop. Cen., The
B25: Yard 3K 123
Swanshurst La. B13: Mose 1C 144
Swans Length B48: A'chu 2A 190
Swan St. B48: A'chu 3B 190
CV32: Lea S 8A 218
CV34: Warw 3E 222
DY2: Neth 3J 97
DY5: P'ntt 2C 96
DY8: Stourb 4L 115
WV1: Wolv 7F 36
Swans Wlk. B48: A'chu 3A 190
Swanswell Rd. B92: Olton 1K 145
Swanswell St.
CV1: Cov 5D 152 (2E 6)
Swanswood Gro.
B37: Chel W 6J 105
SWAN VILLAGE
Coseley 2H 75
West Bromwich 4G 77
Swan Village B70: W Brom 4G 77
Swan Village Ind. Est.
B70: W Brom 4G 77
Swarthmore Rd. B29: W Cas ...2A 142
Sweetbriar La. WV12: W'hall ...4D 38
Sweetbriar Rd. WV2: E'shll 2G 53
Sweetbriar Way WS12: Hth H ...7K 9
Sweetbrier Dr. DY8: Word 8L 95
Sweetman Pl. WV6: Wolv 6A 36
Sweetman St. WV6: Wolv 5M 35
(not continuous)
Sweetmoor Cl. B36: Cas B 1C 104
Sweetpool La. DY8: Hag 4M 137
Swift B77: Glas 6E 32
Swift Cl. B36: Cas B 1G 105
B61: B'gve 1L 209
CV8: Ken 7G 199
Swift Pk. CV21: Rugby 2A 180
(not continuous)
Swift Pk. Gro. DY10: Kidd 7B 158
Swift Point CV21: Rugby 1M 179
Swift's Cnr. CV3: Cov 1E 174
Swift Valley Ind. Est.
CV21: Rugby 1M 179
Swillington Rd.
CV6: Cov 4B 152 (1A 6)
Swinbrook Gro. B44: Gt Barr 8L 57
Swinbrook Way B90: Shir 5K 145
Swinburne Av. CV2: Cov 7K 153
Swinburne Cl. CV10: Gall C 4A 88
Swinburne Rd. B97: Redd 2C 220
LE10: Hinc 8J 69
Swincross Rd. DY8: Stourb 5B 116
Swindale B77: Wiln 2H 47
Swindale Cft. CV3: Bin 1M 175
Swindell Rd. DY9: Pedm 8C 116
SWINDON 7E 72
Swindon Rd. B17: Edg 6B 100
DY6: K'wfrd 1F 94
SWINFEN 1L 29
Swinfen Broun Rd.
WS13: Lich 1G 19
Swinfen La. WS14: S'fen 1J 29
Swinford Gro. B93: Dorr 6E 168
Swinford Leys WV5: Wom 4D 72
Swinford Rd. B29: W Cas 6A 120
DY8: Stourb 7A 116
WV10: Wolv 4E 36
Swin Forge Way DY3: Swind 7E 72
Swiss Dr. DY8: Word 7M 95
Swiss Hgts. DY13: Stour S 8E 182
Swiss Lodge Dr. B78: Faz 1M 45
Sword Dr. LE10: Hinc 6H 69
Swynnerton Dr. WV11: Ess 5M 23
Sycamore B77: Wiln 3E 46
Sycamore Av. B12: Bal H 4A 122
B78: Pole 1A 48
B98: Redd 7E 212
Sycamore Cl. B24: Erd 6F 80
B76: Walm 7M 59
CV47: S'ton 1L 225
DY8: Stourb 7K 115
DY10: Kidd 2M 157
LE10: Burb 4L 91
WS4: S'fld 1B 40
Sycamore Ct. B23: Erd 2C 80
B30: K Nor 5E 142
CV5: Alle 2F 150
Sycamore Cres. B24: Erd 6F 80
B37: Mars G 1G 125
CV7: New A 1H 109
DY4: Tip 2M 75
Sycamore Dr. B47: H'wd 4A 166
WV3: Wolv 8K 35
Sycamore Grn. DY1: Dud 4F 74
WS11: Cann 3E 8
Sycamore Gro.
CV21: Rugby 5A 180
CV34: Warw 8G 217
CV47: Sou 3H 225
Sycamore Hill
WS15: Cann W 4F 10
Sycamore Ho. B13: Mose 6A 122
B31: N'fld 6B 142
(off Rectory Rd.)
Sycamore Ind. Est.
B21: Hand 2D 100
Sycamore Paddock
DY8: Word 8A 96
Sycamore Pl. B67: Smeth 5M 99
WV14: Bils 6A 54
Sycamore Rd. B6: Aston 1A 102
B21: Hand 2D 100
B23: Erd 2F 80
B30: B'vlle 2F 142
B43: Gt Barr 6E 56
B66: Smeth 6B 100
B69: O'bry 5G 99
B78: K'bry 2C 62
CV2: Cov 7H 131
CV10: Nun 3D 88
DY6: K'wfrd 3L 95
WS4: S'fld 1B 40
WS5: Wals 4M 55
WS7: Chase 2F 16
WS10: W'bry 7G 55
WS12: Wim 5M 9
Sycamores, The CV12: Bed 7E 110
DY9: Hag 4M 137
WS14: Lich 4H 19
WV10: Bush 1F 36
Sycamore Ter. B14: K Hth 3J 143
Sycamore Way B27: A Grn 5J 123
WS12: Hunt 1D 8
SYDENHAM 3C 224
Sydenham Dr. CV31: Lea S 3B 224
Sydenham Ind. Est.
CV31: Lea S 3B 224
(Longfield Rd.)
CV31: Lea S 3B 224
(St Mary's Rd.)
Sydenham Rd. B11: S'brk 3C 122
B66: Smeth 2A 100
WV1: Wolv 7H 37
Sydenham Sports Cen. 4C 224
Sydnall Cl. B97: Redd 7M 211
Sydnall Flds.
CV6: Longf 5F 130
Sydnall Rd. CV6: Longf 5F 130
Sydney Cl. B70: W Brom 2G 77
Sydney Ct. CV12: Bed 7G 111
Sydney Ho. B34: S End 3E 104
Sydney Rd. B9: Bord G 7C 102
B61: B'gve 6L 187
B64: Crad H 8J 97
B67: Smeth 7L 99
Sykesmoor B77: Wiln 2H 47
Sylvan Av. B31: N'fld 6M 141
Sylvan Dr. CV3: Cov 3M 173
Sylvan Grn. B62: Hale 4D 118
Sylvan Gro. B90: Shir 4H 145
Sylvia Av. B31: Longb 1B 164
Symphony Ct. B16: Birm 6B 4
Synkere Cl. CV7: Ker E 3A 130
Sytch La. WV5: Wom 4G 73
Sywell Leys CV22: Rugby 3M 205

T

Tabbs Gdns. DY10: Kidd 2A 158
Table Oak La. CV8: Fen E 7F 170
Tachbrook Cl. CV2: Cov 7J 131
Tachbrook Ct. CV31: Lea S 3M 223
TACHBROOK MALLORY 7F 224
Tachbrook Pk. Bus. Cen.
CV34: Warw 4L 223
Tachbrook Pk. Dr.
CV34: Warw 3K 223
Tachbrook Rd.
CV31: Lea S, W'nsh 6M 223
Tachbrook St. CV31: Lea S 3A 224
(not continuous)
Tack Farm Rd. DY8: Word 8K 95
Tackford Cl. B36: Cas B 8C 82
Tackford Rd. CV6: Cov 2G 153
Tackley Cl. B90: Shir 1H 167
Tadmore Cl. WV14: Bils 4J 53
Tadworth Cl. WV1: Wolv 7G 37
Tainters Hill CV8: Ken 3F 198
Tait Cft. B92: Sol 1F 146
Talaton Cl. WV9: Pend 7A 22
Talbot B77: Glas 6E 32
Talbot Av. B74: Lit A 6B 42
Talbot Cl. B23: Erd 1D 80
DY11: Hartl 8A 184
WS2: Wals 3J 39
Talbot Ct. CV32: Lea S 8A 218
Talbot Pas. *DY8: Stourb 4A 116*
(off Talbot St.)
Talbot Pl. WV14: Bils 3J 53
Talbot Rd. B60: B'gve 2L 209
B66: Smeth 6A 100
DY2: Neth 5H 97
WV2: Wolv 3C 52
Talbotshill La. DY10: Cookl 5C 136
Talbots La. DY5: Brie H 8E 96
Talbot St. B18: Hock 3F 100
B63: Crad 3J 117
DY5: Brie H 6D 96
(Adelaide St.)
DY5: Brie H 6D 96
(Albion St.)
DY8: Stourb 4A 116
DY9: Lye 4F 116
DY11: Kidd 5J 157
Talbot Way B10: Small H 2F 122
Talfourd St. B9: Small H 8D 102
Talgarth Covert B38: K Nor 2E 164
Talisman Cl. CV8: Ken 6F 198
Talisman Sq. CV8: Ken 5F 198
Talisman Theatre 6F 198
Talke Rd. WS5: Wals 4M 55
Talladale B32: Bart G 2H 141
Talland Av. B77: Amin 4E 32
CV6: Cov 3G 153
Tallants Cl. CV6: Cov 1G 153
Tallants Rd. CV6: Cov 1F 152
Tallington Rd. B33: Sheld 2C 124
Tall Trees Cl. B61: Cats 1M 187
B74: Four O 5D 42
WV12: W'hall 3D 38
Tall Trees Dr. DY9: Pedm 7D 116
Talton Cl. B90: M'path 4A 168
Tamar Cl. CV12: Bulk 6B 112
CV23: Long L 4H 179
WS8: Bwnhls 7C 16
Tamar Dr. B36: Cas B 1F 104
B76: Walm 2B 82
DY3: Sed 3F 74
Tamar Gro. WV6: Pert 5E 34
WV13: W'hall 7C 38
Tamarisk Cl. B29: W Cas 1B 142
Tamar Ri. DY8: Amb 1A 116
Tamar Rd. B77: Hock 4G 47
CV12: Bulk 7A 112
Tame Av. WS7: Burn 3K 17
WS10: W'bry 5H 55
Tame Bank B78: K'bry 3C 62
Tame Bri. WS5: Wals 5M 55
Tame Bri. Factory Est.
WS5: Wals 7B 56
Tamebridge Ind. Est.
B42: P Barr 5L 79
Tame Bridge Parkway Station (Rail)
.........................7M 55
Tame Cl. WS1: Wals 3L 55
Tame Ct. B78: Faz 1B 46
B79: Tam 4A 32
Tame Cres. B71: W Brom 3J 77
Tame Dr. WS3: Pels 8A 26
Tamedrive B78: Tam 5A 32
Tame Gro. WS11: Cann 1D 14
Tame Pk. Ind. Est. B77: Wiln ...3E 46
Tame Ri. B68: O'bry 1H 119
Tame Rd. B6: Witt 7A 80
B68: O'bry 1G 119
DY4: Tip 4C 76
Tame Rd. Ind. Est. B6: Witt 8A 80
Tamerton Rd. B32: Bart G 8K 119
Tameside Dr. B6: Witt 5M 79
B35: Cas V 8M 81
Tame St. B70: W Brom 1F 76
B77: Tam 6C 32
Tame St. WS1: Wals 3L 55
WV14: Bils 4M 53
Tame St. E. WS1: Wals 3M 55
Tame Valley Bus. Pk.
B77: Wiln 3E 46
Tame Valley Ind. Est.
B77: Wiln 2E 46
(not continuous)
Tame Way LE10: Hinc 1G 91
Tamora Cl. CV34: H'cte 6K 223
TAMWORTH 4B 32
Tamworth & District Indoor Bowls
Cen. 6J 33
Tamworth & Lichfield Coll.
WS13: Lich 2H 19
(off St John St.)
Tamworth Arts Cen. 4B 32
Tamworth Bus. Cen.
B77: Amin 6H 33
Tamworth Bus. Pk. B77: Amin ...6J 33
Tamworth Castle & Mus. 5B 32
Tamworth Cl. WS8: Bwnhls 7F 16
Tamworth F.C. 6C 32
Tamworth La. WS14: S'fen 2L 29
Tamworth Rd.
B46: Neth W, Over W 3G 85
(not continuous)
B75: Bass P 7B 44
B75: S Cold 2J 59
B76: Wis 7J 61
B77: Amin 4E 32
B77: Dost 3C 46
B77: Wiln 7C 32
(not continuous)
B78: Cliff, K'bry 8C 46
B78: Faz 1A 46
B78: Midd 7K 45
B78: Pole 8K 33
CV6: Cov 3J 129
CV7: Cor, Ker E 8G 109
(not continuous)
CV7: Fill, Old A 8A 86
CV9: Wood E 8J 47
WS14: Lich 4J 19
Tamworth Sailing Club 5B 62
Tamworth Sports Stadium 8F 32
Tamworth Station (Rail) 4C 32
Tamworth St. WS13: Lich 1H 19
Tanacetum Dr. WS5: Wals 6B 56
Tancred Cl. CV31: Lea S 4M 223
Tandy Ct. B14: K Hth 6M 143
Tandy Dr. B14: K Hth 6M 143
Tandy's La. DY10: Chad C, Harv,
Hillp 4K 159
Tanfield Cl. WV6: Tett 6H 35
Tanfield Rd. B33: Stech 6M 103
DY2: Dud 2H 97
Tanford Rd. B92: Sol 6C 124
Tanglewood Cl. B32: Quin 4H 119
B34: S End 4C 104
B60: B'wll 3G 189
Tanglewood Gro. DY3: Sed 7C 52
Tangmere Cl. WV6: Pert 4E 34
Tangmere Dr. B35: Cas V 7M 81
Tangmere Sq. B35: Cas V 6M 81
Tanhill B77: Wiln 2H 47
Tanhouse Av. B43: Gt Barr 2C 78
Tanhouse Farm Rd.
B92: Sol 7C 124
Tanhouse La. B63: Crad 3H 117
B98: Redd 2J 213
Tan La. DY13: Stour S 5F 182
Tanners Cl. B75: S Cold 2M 59
Tanners Ct. WS1: Wals 1L 55
TANNER'S GREEN 7A 166
Tanners Grn. La. B47: Wyt 7M 165
Tanners Grn La. B94: Earls 7B 166
Tanners Hill DY12: Bew 2A 156
Tanner's La. CV4: Tile H 1A 172
CV7: Berk, Tile H 1A 172
Tannery Cl. CV9: Ath 1L 65
WS2: Wals 6K 39
Tannery Ct. CV8: Ken 5F 198
Tanser Ct. CV22: Dunc 6J 205
Tansey B74: Four O 4F 42
Tansey Ct. DY5: P'ntt 2B 96
Tansey Cres. LE9: S Stan 7J 71
TANSEY GREEN 2B 96
Tansey Grn. Rd. DY5: P'ntt 8A 74
Tansley Cl. B93: Dorr 5F 168
Tansley Gro. B44: K'sdng 8M 57
Tansley Hill Av. DY2: Dud 1M 97
Tansley Hill Rd. DY2: Dud 1L 97
Tansley Rd. B44: K'sdng 1M 79
Tansley Vw.
WV2: Wolv 2D 52 (8L 7)
Tansy B77: Tam 6C 32
Tantallon Dr. B32: Bart G 8K 119
Tantany La. B71: W Brom 5J 77
Tantarra St. WS1: Wals 8M 39
(not continuous)
TANWOOD 7B 160
Tanwood Cl. B91: Sol 1B 168
B97: Redd 3A 220
Tanwood La. DY10: Chad C 8M 159
Tanworth Gro. B12: Bal H 3M 121
TANWORTH-IN-ARDEN 7G 193
Tanworth La. B90: Shir 2H 167
B94: Dan G 2K 215
B95: Blun G 3M 215
B98: Beo 2C 214

Tanyard—Threlfall Dr.

Tanyard WS13: Lich 1J 19
Tanyard Cl. B48: A'chu 3B 190
CV4: Tile H 8D 150
Tanyard La. B48: A'chu 3A 190
Tanyards B27: A Grn 6J 123
Tapcon Way CV2: Cov 4M 153
Tapestries Av. B70: W Brom 5G 77
Taplow Pl. WS11: Cann 5F 8
Tappinger Gro. CV8: Ken 4J 199
Tapster La. B94: Lapw 6E 194
(Church La.)
B94: Lapw 8G 195
(Yew Tree La.)
Tapton Cl. WS3: Blox 6J 25
TARDEBIGGE 2G 211
Tardebigge Ct. B97: Redd 3J 211
Tardebigge Ho. B60: B'gve 6B 188
(off Burcot La.)
Tarlington Rd. CV6: Cov 3L 151
Tarmac Rd. WV4: E'shll 4H 53
Tarn Cl. CV12: Bed 7G 111
Tarquin Cl. CV3: W'hall 2K 175
Tarragon Cl. CV2: Cov 8K 131
Tarragon Gdns. B31: Longb 7J 141
Tarrant B77: Wiln 1F 46
Tarrant Gro. B32: Harb 4M 119
Tarrant Wlk. CV2: W'grve S 4A 154
Tarrington Covert
B38: K Nor 1E 164
Tarry Hollow Rd. DY5: P'ntt 1B 96
Tarry Rd. B8: Salt 5E 102
Tarvin M. DY5: Brie H 8D 96
Taryn Dr. WS10: Darl 2D 54
Tasker St. B70: W Brom 5E 76
WS1: Wals 1K 55
Tasman Gro. WV6: Pert 4E 34
TAT BANK 3H 99
Tat Bank Rd. B68: O'bry 2G 99
B69: O'bry 2G 99
Tatnall Gro. CV34: Warw 1E 222
Tattle Bank CV47: Sou 6H 225
Taunton Av. WV10: F'hses 5D 22
Taunton Cl. B31: Longb 6J 141
Taunton Rd. B12: Bal H 5A 122
Taunton Way CV6: Cov 7A 130
Taverners Cl. WV12: W'hall 8C 24
Taverners Grn. B20: Hand 6F 78
Taverners La. CV9: Ath 2K 65
Tavistock Cl. B79: Tam 2C 32
Tavistock Rd. B27: A Grn 2J 145
Tavistock St. CV32: Lea S 8M 217
Tavistock Wlk. CV2: Cov 2J 153
Tavistock Way CV11: Nun 4L 89
Taw Cl. B36: Cas B 1F 104
Tay Cft. B37: F'bri 5J 105
Tay Gro. B38: K Nor 1F 164
B62: B'hth 1E 118
Taylor Av. CV32: Lill 7B 218
WS3: Blox 1K 39
Taylor Cl. CV8: Ken 3H 199
LE9: S Stan 7K 71
Taylor Ct. CV34: Warw 2D 222
Taylor Ho. WS2: Wals 2J 55
(off Oxford St.)
Taylor Rd. B13: Mose 4M 143
DY2: Neth 7L 97
WV4: E'shll 4F 52
Taylors La. B69: O'bry 2E 98
B71: W Brom 5K 77
B67: Smeth 4M 99
Taylors Orchard B23: Erd 5B 80
Taylor St. WV11: Wed 4K 37
Taylor Way B69: Tiv 1B 98
Taynton Covert B30: K Nor 6J 143
Tay Rd. B45: Fran 8H 141
CV6: Cov 3B 152
Taysfield Rd. B31: N'fld 3L 141
Taywood Dr. B10: Small H 2C 122
Teachers Cl. CV6: Cov 4A 152
Tea Gdn., The CV12: Bed 1E 130
Teal Bus. Pk. LE10: Hinc 2E 90
Tealby Gro. B29: S Oak 8G 121
Teal Cres. DY10: Kidd 6A 158
Teal Dr. B23: Erd 6B 80
LE10: Hinc 3G 91
Teal Gro. WS10: Mox 6B 54
Teall Ct. B27: A Grn 6J 123
Teall Rd. B8: Salt 4E 102
Teal Rd. B80: Stud 5L 221
Tean Cl. B11: Tys 6G 123
WS7: Burn 3K 17
Teasdale Way DY9: W'cte 5D 116
Teasel Cl. CV23: Brow 1D 180
Teasel Gro. WV10: F'stne 2H 23
Teasel Rd. WV11: Wed 4L 37
Teazel Av. B30: B'vlle 3D 142
Tebworth Cl. WV9: Pend 7M 21
Tedbury Cres. B23: Erd 3E 80
Tedder Rd. WS2: Wals 7F 38
Teddesley Ct. WS11: Cann 6D 8
Teddesley Gro. B33: Kitts G 5C 104
Teddesley St. WS4: Wals 6M 39
Teddesley Way WS12: Hunt 3C 8
Teddington Cl. B73: S Cold 7G 59
Teddington Gro. B42: P Barr 6K 79
Ted Pitts La. CV5: Alle 7H 129
Tedstone Rd. B32: Quin 4L 119
Teesdale Av. B34: Hodg H 3M 103
Teesdale Cl. WV1: Wolv 7G 37
Tees Gro. B38: K Nor 1F 164
Teeswater Cl. B60: Stoke H 3L 209
Teign B77: Hock 4G 47
Teignbank Cl. LE10: Hinc 7K 69
Teignbank Rd. LE10: Hinc 6J 69
Teignmouth Rd. B29: S Oak 7F 120
Telephone Rd. CV3: Cov 7J 153
Telfer Rd. CV6: Cov 2B 152
Telford Av. CV32: Lill 4B 218
WS6: Gt Wyr 6F 14
Telford Cl. B67: Smeth 8K 99
B71: W Brom 1G 77
WS2: Wals 4G 39
WS7: Burn 1H 17
Telford Ct. DY12: Bew 6B 156
(off Severn Side Ct.)
Telford Dr. DY12: Bew 6A 156
Telford Gdns. WV3: Wolv 2K 51
Telford Gro. WS12: Hed 2H 9
Telford Rd. B79: Tam 1M 31
CV7: Exh 1J 131
WS2: Wals 4G 39
Telford Way B66: Smeth 2M 99
Teme Av. DY11: Kidd 6H 157
Teme Gro. WV13: W'hall 7D 38
Teme Rd. B63: Crad 4H 117
DY8: Stourb 6M 115
Tempest St. B79: Tam 4A 32
WV2: Wolv 8D 36 (5K 7)
Templar Av. CV4: Tile H 8G 151
Templar Ind. Pk. CV4: Tile H 1H 173
Templars, The B69: O'bry 4E 98
CV34: Warw 4F 222
Templars' Flds. CV4: Canly 2H 173
Templars Wlk. WV13: W'hall 6A 38
Temple Av. B28: Hall G 3G 145
CV7: Bal C 3F 170
TEMPLE BALSALL 5C 170
Temple Bar WV13: W'hall 7A 38
Temple Cl. B98: Redd 5F 212
Temple Ct. B46: Col 8M 83
Templefield Gdns.
B9: Bord G 8C 102
Templefield Sq. B15: Edg 2H 121
Templefield St. B9: Bord G 8C 102
Temple Gro. CV34: Warw 4D 222
Temple Hill LE10: Wlvy 4L 113
Temple La. B93: Know 6A 170
Temple Mdws. Rd.
B71: W Brom 4L 77
Templemore Dr. B43: Gt Barr 2E 78
Temple Pas. B2: Birm 7K 101 (5F 4)
Templer Ct. CV11: Nun 6J 89
Temple Rd. B93: Dorr 6G 169
WV13: W'hall 6A 38
Temple Row B2: Birm 7K 101 (5F 4)
Temple Row W.
B2: Birm 7K 101 (4F 4)
Temple Sq. WV13: W'hall 6B 38
Temple St. B2: Birm 7K 101 (5F 4)
B70: W Brom 5J 77
CV21: Rugby 7C 180
DY3: Lwr G 6D 74
WV2: Wolv 8C 36 (5J 7)
WV14: Bils 4L 53
Templeton Cl. B93: Dorr 6G 169
Templeton Rd. B44: Gt Barr 7L 57
Temple Way B46: Col 8L 83
B69: Tiv 7C 76
Tenacre La. DY3: Up Gor 3E 74
TEN ACRES 1H 143
Ten Acres End B30: Stir 1H 143
Tenacres La. B98: Redd 6L 213
Ten Acres Works B30: Stir 1H 143
Ten Ashes La. B45: Coft H 5J 163
Tenbury Cl. B98: Redd 3J 213
WS2: Wals 6D 38
WS9: A'rdge 1J 41
Tenbury Ct. WV4: Penn 4K 51
Tenbury Gdns. WV4: Penn 5K 51
Tenbury Ho. B63: Hale 6A 118
(off Highfield La.)
Tenbury Rd. B14: K Hth 3K 143
Tenby Cl. CV12: Bed 8C 110
Tenby Ct. B29: W Cas 2C 142
(off Tugford Rd.)
Tenby Rd. B13: Mose 8D 122
Tenby St. B1: Birm 5H 101 (2B 4)
Tenby St. Nth.
B1: Birm 5H 101 (2B 4)
Tenby Twr. B31: N'fld 8A 142
Tenby Way DY13: Stour S 3E 182
Teneriffe Rd. CV6: Cov 8F 130
Tenlands Rd. B63: Hale 6M 117
Tenlons Rd. CV10: Nun 7F 88
Tenlons Rd. Ind. Est.
CV10: Nun 7F 88
Tennal Dr. B32: Harb 3M 119
Tennal Gro. B32: Harb 3M 119
Tennal La. B32: Harb 4L 119
Tennal Rd. B32: Harb 3L 119
Tennant Cl. CV21: Hillm 8E 180
Tennant St.
B15: Birm 8H 101 (8B 4)
CV11: Nun 6L 89
Tennis Ct. B30: K Nor 5D 142
Tennis Ct., The B15: Edg 4G 121
Tennis Ct. Flats B15: Edg 4G 121
Tennscore Av. WS6: C Hay 6E 14
Tennyson Av. B74: Four O 3F 42
B79: Tam 3A 32
CV22: Rugby 2L 205
CV34: Warw 5C 222
Tennyson Av. WS7: C Ter 8G 11
Tennyson Cl. CV8: Ken 5J 199
Tennyson Ho. B31: Longb 1A 164
B68: O'bry 5J 99
Tennyson Rd. B10: Small H 2E 122
B97: Redd 1C 220
CV2: Cov 6J 153
DY3: Lwr G 4A 74
LE10: Hinc 8H 69
WS3: Blox 1L 39
WV10: Bush 8G 23
WV12: W'hall 1E 38
Tennyson St. DY5: P'ntt 3D 96
Tennyson Way DY10: Kidd 3B 158
Ten Shilling Dr.
CV4: W'wd H 3E 172
Tenter Ct. B63: Hale 5B 118
Tenter Dr. B63: Hale 5B 118
Tenterfields B63: Hale 5B 118
Tenter St. CV9: Ath 1K 65
Tern Cl. WV4: E'shll 6D 52
Tern Gro. B38: K Nor 8E 142
Terrace, The B64: Crad H 1L 117
WV3: Wolv 8J 35
Terrace Rd. B15: Edg 6F 120
B19: Hock 2G 101
CV9: Ath 1K 65
Terrace St. B65: Row R 8B 98
DY5: Brie H 4E 96
WS10: W'bry 6G 55
Terry Av. CV32: Lea S 8J 217
Terry Cl. WS13: Lich 7F 12
Terry Dr. B76: Walm 8M 59
Terry Rd. CV1: Cov 7F 152
Terry's Cl. B98: Redd 4F 212
TERRY'S GREEN 1F 192
Terrys La. B24: Erd 6J 81
Terryspring Ct. B98: Redd 6E 212
(off West Av.)
Terry St. DY2: Dud 8K 75
Tessall La. B31: Longb 8H 141
(not continuous)
Tetbury Gro. B31: N'fld 6K 141
Tetley Av. WS4: Wals 5B 40
Tetley Rd. B11: S'hll 6E 122
Tetnall St. DY2: Dud 1K 97
TETTENHALL 5J 35
Tettenhall Rd. WV6: Wolv 5L 35
TETTENHALL WOOD 7G 35
Teviot Gdns. DY5: P'ntt 3A 96
WV8: Bilb 4G 21
Teviot Gro. B38: K Nor 1F 164
Teviot Twr. B19: Birm 4J 101
(off Mosborough Cres.)
Tewe Pl. WS13: Lich 3G 19
Tewkesbury Dr. CV12: Bed 6J 111
DY2: Neth 6K 97
Tewkesbury Rd. B20: Hand 8L 79
WS3: Blox 7E 24
Tewnalls La.
WS13: Elmh, Lich 5E 12
Tew Pk. Rd. B21: Hand 2E 100
Thackeray Cl. CV10: Gall C 5A 88
CV22: Rugby 2M 205
Thackeray Dr. B79: Tam 2A 32
Thackeray Rd. B30: B'vlle 4D 142
Thackhall St. CV2: Cov 5F 152
Thames Cl. CV12: Bulk 6A 112
DY5: P'ntt 2B 96
Thames Ct. B47: Wyt 7L 165
(off Chapel La.)
B73: S Cold 4H 59
Thames Gdns. WV14: Cose 8G 53
Thames Ho. DY10: Kidd 7L 157
Thames Rd. WS3: Blox 1K 39
Thames Twr. B7: Nech 4B 102
Thamley Rd. CV6: Cov 5A 152
Thane Cl. B80: Stud 5L 221
Thanet Cl. DY6: K'wfrd 3J 95
Thanet Gro. B42: P Barr 5J 79
Thatchers, The B62: B'hth 1E 118
Thatchings, The CV22: Dunc 6J 205
Thatchway Gdns. B38: K Nor 2E 164
Thaxted Rd. B33: Kitts G 6E 104
Theatre App.
B5: Birm 8L 101 (7G 5)
Theatre St. CV34: Warw 3D 222
Thebes Cl. CV5: Alle 1B 150
Theddingworth Cl. CV3: Bin 1L 175
Thelbridge Rd. B31: Longb 3L 163
Thelma Rd. DY4: Tip 4L 75
Thelma St. WS1: Wals 2K 55
Thelsford Way B92: Sol 1D 146
Theodore Cl. B17: Harb 5D 120
B69: O'bry 8E 76
Theresa Rd. B11: S'brk 2B 122
The Swallows Ind. Est.
B90: Shir 1K 167
Thetford Cl. DY4: Tip 4K 75
Thetford Gdns. WV11: Wed 3K 37
Thetford Rd. B42: Gt Barr 2H 79
Thetford Way WS5: Wals 6C 56
Thickett Cl. WS2: Wals 1H 55
Thicknall Dr. DY9: Pedm 7B 116
Thicknall La.
DY9: Clent, Hag 6M 137
Thicknall Ri. DY9: Hag 5A 138
Thickthorn Cl. CV8: Ken 6H 199
Thickthorn M. CV8: Ken 7H 199
Thickthorn Orchards
CV8: Ken 7H 199
Thimble Dr. B76: Walm 8M 59
THIMBLE END 8M 59
Thimble End Rd. B76: Walm 6M 59
Thimble La. B93: Know 3J 169
Thimble Mill La. B6: Aston 2B 102
B7: Nech 2B 102
Thimblemill Rd. B67: Smeth 5K 99
Thimbler Rd. CV4: Canly 2J 173
Thinktank 6M 101 (4K 5)
Third Av. B6: Witt 6M 79
B9: Bord G 7F 102
B29: S Oak 6J 121
DY6: P'ntt 1M 95
WS8: Bwnhls 8G 17
WV10: Bush 2E 36
Third Exhibition Av.
B40: Nat E C 5K 125
Third Rd. B61: Wild 6L 161
Thirlestane Cl. CV8: Ken 3J 199
Thirlmere CV21: Brow 2C 180
Thirlmere Av. CV11: Nun 3M 89
Thirlmere Cl. CV4: Tile H 6E 150
WS11: Cann 8E 8
WV6: Tett 1K 35
Thirlmere Dr. B13: Mose 1C 144
WV11: Ess 7A 24
Thirlmere Gro. WV6: Pert 5F 34
Thirlmere Ho. B15: Edg 6D 120
Thirlmere Rd. CV12: Bed 7G 111
DY13: Stour S 3F 182
LE10: Hinc 1G 91
WV6: Tett 1K 35
Thirlmere Wlk. DY5: Brie H 2B 116
Thirsk Cft. B36: Hodg H 1J 103
Thirsk Rd. CV3: Cov 4C 174
Thirsk Way B61: Cats 8B 162
Thirston Cl. WV11: Wed 4A 38
Thistle Cl. DY3: Sed 3F 74
Thistle Cft. WV11: Wed 4K 37
Thistledown Av. WS7: Burn 3G 17
Thistle Down Cl. B74: S'tly 7A 42
Thistledown Dr. WS12: Hth H 8J 9
WV10: F'stne 2G 23
Thistledown Rd. B34: S End 2C 104
Thistledown Wlk. DY3: Sed 8C 52
Thistle Grn. B38: K Nor 2E 164
Thistle Grn. Cl. B65: Row R 4M 97
Thistlegreen Rd. DY2: Neth 5L 97
Thistle Ho. B36: Hodg H 1K 103
Thistle La. B32: Bart G 1H 141
Thistle Way CV23: Brow 1D 180
Thistlewood Gro.
B93: Chad E 3B 196
Thistley Fld. E. CV6: Cov 3M 151
Thistley Fld. Nth. CV6: Cov 2A 152
Thistley Fld. Sth. CV6: Cov 3M 151
Thistley Fld. W. CV6: Cov 3M 151
Thistley Nook WS13: Lich 8G 13
Thomas Benson Pl.
B12: Birm 2M 121
Thomas Cres. B66: Smeth 4C 100
Thomas Greenway
WS13: Lich 7F 12
Thomas Guy Rd.
B70: W Brom 2E 76
B77: Tam, Wiln 7A 32
Thomas Guy Way B77: Two G 7K 31
B78: M Oak, Tam 7K 31
Thomas Hardy Ct. B79: Tam 2A 32
Thomas Ho. WS3: Blox 6K 25
Thomas King Ho. CV1: Cov 2F 6
Thomas Landsdail St.
CV3: Cov 8D 152 (8D 6)
Thomas La. St. CV6: Cov 8G 131
Thomas Mason Cl.
WV11: Wed 2K 37
Thomas Naul Cft.
CV4: Tile H 6F 150
Thomas Sharp St.
CV4: Tile H 2G 173
Thomas St. B6: Aston 3M 101
B66: Smeth 4B 100
B70: W Brom 7K 77
B77: Tam 5D 32
CV12: Bed 7G 111
CV32: Lea S 8A 218
WS2: Wals 7K 39
WV2: Wolv 1C 52 (7J 7)
THOMAS TOWN 6L 221
Thomas Wlk. B35: Cas V 6B 82
Thomas Way CV23: Long L 4G 179
Thompson Av. WV2: Wolv 2D 52
Thompson Cl. DY2: Neth 7H 97
WV13: W'hall 6A 38
Thompson Dr. B24: Erd 1F 102
Thompson Gdns. B67: Smeth 5M 99
Thompson Ho. DY4: Tip 1C 76
Thompson Rd. B67: Smeth 5M 99
B68: O'bry 5H 99
Thompsons Rd. CV7: Ker E 3L 129
Thompson St. WV13: W'hall 6A 38
WV14: Bils 4K 53
Thomson Av. B38: K Nor 8C 142
Thomson Cl. CV21: Rugby 3B 180
Thor Cl. WS11: Cann 4G 9
Thoresby B79: Tam 3L 31
Thoresby Cft. DY1: Dud 6F 74
Thorley's Hill WS15: Longd 3J 11
Thornberry Dr. DY1: Dud 1D 96
Thornberry Wlk. B7: Nech 3C 102
Thornbridge Av. B42: Gt Barr 2J 79
Thornbridge Gro.
WS9: Wals W 6F 26
Thorn Brook Ct. WS4: Wals 6M 39
(off Butts Rd.)
Thornbury Ct. WV6: Pert 6G 35
Thornbury La. B98: Redd 2J 213
Thornbury Rd. B20: Hand 7K 79
Thornby Av. B77: Wiln 1E 46
B91: Sol 4B 146
CV8: Ken 6G 199
Thornby Rd. B23: Erd 1C 80
Thorncliffe Cl. B97: Redd 3A 220
Thorncliffe Rd. B44: Gt Barr 7L 57
Thorncliffe Way CV10: Ans C 1L 87
Thorn Cl. CV21: Brow 3C 180
WS10: W'bry 5F 54
Thorncroft Way WS5: Wals 5B 56
Thorne Av. WV10: Bush 2E 36
Thorne Pl. B65: Row R 7C 98
Thorne Rd. WV13: W'hall 6A 38
THORNES 6L 27
Thornes Cft. WS9: Ston 5L 27
Thorne St. WV2: E'shll 2G 53
Thorneycroft La. WV10: Wolv 4G 37
Thorneycroft Pl. WV14: Bils 6B 54
Thorneycroft Rd. WV14: Bils 6A 54
Thorneyfield Rd. B90: Shir 6J 145
Thorney Rd. B74: S'tly 8M 41
CV2: Cov 3H 153
Thornfield Av. CV13: Stoke G 2E 68
Thornfield Cres. WS7: C Ter 1G 17
Thornfield Cft. DY3: Sed 2E 74
Thornfield Rd. B27: A Grn 7J 123
Thornfield Way LE10: Hinc 1L 91
Thorngrove Av. B91: Sol 1C 168
Thornham Way B14: K Hth 8K 143
Thornhill Dr. CV11: Nun 1B 112
Thornhill Gro. B21: Hand 1F 100
Thornhill Pk. B74: S'tly 1A 58
Thornhill Rd. B11: S'hll 6D 122
B21: Hand 2F 100
B63: Hale 6L 117
B74: S'tly 3A 58
B91: Sol 2C 146
B98: Redd 2L 213
CV1: Cov 4D 152
DY1: Dud 5J 75
DY5: Quar B 8E 96
WS12: Hed 2F 8
Thornhurst Av. B32: Quin 2L 119
Thornleigh DY3: Up Gor 4D 74
Thornleigh Trad. Est.
DY2: Dud 2G 97
Thornley Cl. B13: Mose 8A 122
CV31: Rad S 4F 224
WV11: Wed 8M 23
Thornley Cft. WS6: C Hay 8D 14
Thornley Gro. B76: Min 3C 82
Thornley Rd. WV11: Wed 8M 23
Thornley St.
WV1: Wolv 7D 36 (3K 7)
Thorn Rd. B30: B'vlle 2E 142
Thorns Av. DY5: Quar B 8E 96
Thornsett Gro. B90: Shir 3H 145
Thorns Leisure Cen. 1E 116
Thorns Rd. DY5: Quar B 2E 116
Thorn Stile Cl. CV32: Cubb 3E 218
Thornthwaite Cl. B45: Fran 7H 141
Thornton Cl. B69: Tiv 7C 76
CV5: E Grn 5C 150
CV34: Warw 8F 216
Thornton Dr. DY5: Brie H 8E 96
Thornton Ho. B19: Hock 4L 101
(off Ruddington Way)
Thornton Rd. B8: W End 4H 103
B90: M'path 3M 167
WV1: Wolv 8H 37
Thorntons Way CV10: Nun 6A 88
Thornton Way B77: Two G 1C 46
Thornwood Cl. B68: O'bry 4J 99
Thornycroft Rd. LE10: Hinc 1L 91
Thornyfield Cl. B90: Shir 6J 145
Thornyhurst La. WS14: Hilt 2A 28
Thorpe Av. WS7: C Ter 1D 16
Thorpe Cl. B75: S Cold 1J 59
WS7: C Ter 1D 16
Thorpe Ct. B91: Sol 3M 145
Thorpe Rd. WS1: Wals 2L 55
Thorpe St. WS7: C Ter 1D 16
Thorp St. B5: Birm 8K 101 (7F 4)
Threadneedle St. CV1: Cov 3D 152
Three Acres La. B90: Dic H 3F 166
Three Cnr. Cl. B90: Maj G 1E 166
Three Cornered Cl.
CV32: Cubb 3E 218
Three Leasows DY4: Tip 4C 76
THREE MAYPOLES 3H 167
Three Oaks Rd. B47: Wyt 5C 166
Three Pots Rd. LE10: Burb 5L 91
Three Shires Oak Rd.
B67: Smeth 7M 99
Three Spires Av. CV6: Cov 4A 152
Three Spires Ind. Est.
CV6: Longf 4G 131
Three Spires Junc. CV6: Cov 8E 130
Three Spires Shop. Cen.
WS13: Lich 1H 19
Three Tuns La. WV10: Oxl 7C 22
Three Tuns Pde. WV10: Oxl 7C 22
Three Ways CV35: Hase 7G 197
Threlfall Dr. DY12: Bew 5D 156

Threshers Dr.—Trident Pk.

Threshers Dr. WV12: W'hall 3D 38
Threshers Way WV12: W'hall . . .3D 38
Throckmorton Cl.
CV35: Hase 8F 196
Throckmorton Rd.
B98: Redd 2F 220
Throne Cl. B65: Row R 4C 98
Throne Cres. B65: Row R 4D 98
Throne Rd. B65: Row R 4C 98
Throstles Cl. B43: Gt Barr 2E 78
Thrushel Wlk. WV11: Wed 4J 37
Thrush Rd. B68: O'bry 7F 98
Thruxton Cl. B14: K Hth 6M 143
B98: Redd 6L 213
Thurcroft Cl. B8: W End 5F 102
Thuree Rd. B67: Smeth 7L 99
THURLASTON 6F 204
Thurlaston Dr. CV22: Dunc 3G 205
Thurlaston La. LE9: Earl S 1H 71
Thurleigh Cl. DY9: Pedm 7C 116
Thurlestone Rd. B31: Longb 2L 163
CV6: Cov 1M 151
Thurloe Cres. B45: Fran 8E 140
Thurlow Cl. CV9: Ath 7K 49
Thurlston Av. B92: Olton 5M 123
Thurlstone Dr. WV4: Penn 5M 51
Thurlstone Rd. WS3: Blox 6H 25
Thurmaston Ct.
CV32: Lea S 7M 217
Thurne B77: Wiln 1F 46
Thurnmill Rd. CV23: Long L . . .5J 179
Thursfield Rd. B71: W Brom 1L 77
CV32: Lill 6B 218
DY4: Tip 3A 76
Thurso B77: Amin 4E 32
Thurston Av. B69: O'bry 3F 98
Thurston Ct. *DY12: Bew 6B 156*
(off Severn Side S.)
Thynne St. B70: W Brom 7L 77
Tibbats Cl. B32: Bart G 6J 119
Tibberton Cl. B63: Hale 6C 118
B91: Sol 1A 168
WV3: Wolv 2K 51
Tibberton Ct. B60: B'gve 2L 209
Tibbets La. B17: Harb 5A 120
Tibbington Rd. DY4: Tip 2L 75
Tibbington Ter. DY4: Tip 2L 75
Tibbits Ct. CV34: Warw 3E 222
Tibbits Ho. *WS2: Wals 6K 39*
(off Burrowes St.)
Tibblestone B90: Dic H 4G 167
Tiber Cl. CV5: E Grn 5F 150
Tiberius Cl. B46: Col 8M 83
Tiber Way CV21: Rugby 2M 179
Tibland Rd. B27: A Grn 8J 123
Ticknall Cl. B97: Redd 4A 212
Tidbury Cl. B97: Redd 3C 220
TIDBURY GREEN 5E 166
Tiddington Cl. B36: Cas B 8B 82
Tideswell Cl. CV3: Bin 8A 154
Tideswell Rd. B42: Gt Barr 3J 79
Tidmarsh Cl. CV7: Bal C 3G 171
Tidmarsh Rd. CV35: Leek W 2G 217
Tidworth Cft. B14: K Hth 6A 144
Tierney Dr. DY4: Tip 3C 76
Tiffany La. WV9: Pend 7M 21
Tiffield Rd. B25: Yard 4J 123
Tigley Av. B32: Bart G 8K 119
Tilbury Cl. WV3: Wolv 1G 51
Tilbury Gro. B13: Mose 8K 121
Tildasley St. B70: W Brom 4H 77
Tildesley Dr. WV12: W'hall 4B 38
TILE CROSS 7C 104
Tile Cross Rd. B33: Kitts G 8D 104
Tile Cross Trad. Est.
B33: Kitts G 8D 104
Tiled Ho. La. DY5: P'ntt 4B 96
Tile Gro. B37: K'hrst 4G 105
TILE HILL 8D 150
Tile Hill La. CV4: Cov 7J 151
CV4: Tile H 8D 150
Tile Hill Station (Rail) 1D 172
Tilehill Wood Nature Reserve
. . . . .6D 150
Tilehouse B97: Redd 7D 212
TILEHOUSE GREEN 2F 168
Tilehouse Grn. La.
B93: Know 2F 168
Tilehouse La. B90: Tid G 5E 166
Tilehurst Dr. CV4: Tile H 7D 150
Tilesford Cl. B90: M'path 4A 168
Tilewood Av. CV5: E Grn 5E 150
Tilia Rd. B77: Amin 4G 33
Tiller Gro. B75: R'ley 5K 43
Tilley St. WS10: Darl 3E 54
Tillington Cl. B98: Redd 6L 213
Tillyard Cft. B29: S Oak 8C 120
Tilshead Cl. B14: K Hth 6L 143
Tilsley Gro. B23: Erd 4B 80
Tilston Dr. DY5: Brie H 8D 96
Tilton Rd. B9: Bord G 8C 102
(not continuous)
LE10: Burb 3L 91
Timbercombe Way
B21: Hand 1D 100
Timber Ct. CV22: Rugby 7C 180
Timberdine Cl. B63: Crad 3K 117
TIMBERHONGER 1D 208
Timberhonger La.
B61: U War 2E 208
Timberlake Cl. B90: M'path . . .3B 168
Timber La. DY13: Stour S 4H 183
Timberley Cft. B34: S End 2D 104
Timberley La. B34: S End 3C 104
(not continuous)
Timber Mill Ct. B17: Harb 3B 120
Timbers Way B11: S'brk 3A 122
B24: Erd 5M 81
Timbertree Cres. B64: Crad H . . .2L 117
Timbertree Rd. B64: Crad H . . .2L 117
Times Sq. Av. DY5: Brie H 7E 96
Timmins Cl. B91: Sol 4E 146
Timmis Cl. WV14: Cose 6H 53
Timms Rd. DY9: Lye 3C 116
Timon Vw. CV34: H'cte 6L 223
Timothy Gro. CV4: Tile H 8H 151
Timothy Rd. B69: Tiv 2C 98
Tinacre Hill WV6: Tett 7E 34
Tinchbourne St. DY1: Dud 8J 75
Tindal St. B12: Bal H 4M 121
Tink a Tank CV35: Leek W 3F 216
Tink-A-Tank CV34: Warw 3E 222
Tinker's Farm Gro.
B31: N'fld 6L 141
Tinker's Farm Rd. B31: N'fld . . .6L 141
Tinkers Grn. Rd. B77: Wiln 3F 46
Tinkers La. B94: H'ley H 2K 193
(not continuous)
B94: Lapw 8D 194
Tinmeadow Cres. B45: Redn . . .2J 163
Tinsley St. DY4: Tip 4E 76
Tintagel Cl. CV3: W'hall 4K 175
WV6: Pert 6F 34
Tintagel Dr. DY1: Dud 7E 74
Tintagel Gro. CV8: Ken 5H 199
Tintagel Way CV11: Nun 4A 90
WS9: A'rdge 3E 40
Tintern Cl. B61: B'gve 8L 187
B74: S'tly 2A 58
DY11: Kidd 3F 156
Tintern Ct. WV6: Pert 5E 34
Tintern Cres. WS3: Blox 6F 24
Tintern Ho. B32: Harb 4M 119
Tintern Rd. B20: Hand 8L 79
Tintern Vs. *B12: Bal H 4B 122*
(off Chesterton Rd.)
Tintern Way CV12: Bed 7J 111
WS3: Blox 7F 24
Tipperary Cl. B36: Hodg H 1L 103
Tipperary Wlk. B69: O'bry 2F 98
TIPPER'S HILL 3F 108
Tipper's Hill La. CV7: Fill 3D 108
Tipper Trad. Est. DY9: Lye 4G 117
Tippett Cl. CV11: Nun 2A 112
Tipping's Hill B97: Redd 4C 220
Tippity Grn. B65: Row R 5B 98
Tipps Stone Cl. DY4: Tip 5L 75
TIPTON 4K 75
Tipton Ind. Est. WV14: Cose 2K 75
Tipton Leisure Cen. 8A 54
Tipton Rd. B69: Tiv 6B 76
DY1: Dud 5L 75
DY3: Sed 2E 74
Tipton Station (Rail) 3M 75
Tipton St. DY3: Sed 2E 74
Tipton Swimming Cen. 4M 75
Tipton Trad. Est. WV14: Cose . . .2K 75
Tirley Rd. B33: Stech 4A 104
Tisdale Ri. CV8: Ken 3H 199
Titan Bus. Cen. CV34: Warw . . .5L 223
Titania Cl. B45: Fran 6H 141
Titan Way WS14: Lich 1M 19
Titchfield Cl. WV10: Bush 5E 22
Titford Cl. B69: O'bry 5F 98
Titford La. B65: Row R 5E 98
Titford Rd. B69: O'bry 5F 98
(not continuous)
Tithe Barn La. B94: H'ley H 4H 193
WS15: Gent 4J 21
Tithe Cl. CV13: Stoke G 3D 68
Tithe Cft. WV10: Wolv 6F 36
Tithe Rd. WV11: Wed 3K 37
Titterstone Rd. B31: Longb 1A 164
TITTON 8J 183
Titton La. DY13: Titt 8J 183
Tiverton Cl. DY6: K'wfrd 6M 95
Tiverton Dr. B71: W Brom 3J 77
CV11: Nun 4L 89
Tiverton Gro. *B67: Smeth 3M 99*
(off Dibble Rd.)
CV2: Cov 4K 153
Tiverton Rd. B29: S Oak 7F 120
B66: Smeth 4B 100
CV2: Cov 4K 153
Tiverton Road Pool & Fitness Cen.
. . . . .7F 120
Tiveycourt Rd. CV6: Cov 6G 131
TIVIDALE 8A 76
Tividale Rd. B69: Tiv 7M 75
Tividale St. DY4: Tip 6A 76
Tiviedale Rd. DY4: Tip 7M 75
Tivoli, The *B25: Yard 3K 123*
(off Church Rd.)
Tixall Rd. B28: Hall G 4E 144
Toadnest La. WV6: Pert 6A 34
Toberland WS2: Wals 2H 39
Tobruk Wlk. DY5: Brie H 6D 96
WV13: W'hall 8L 37
Tocil Cft. CV4: Canly 4K 173
Tocil Wood Nature Reserve . .6J 173
TOFT 7H 205
Toler Rd. CV11: Nun 4H 89
Tollard Cl. CV2: W'grve S 4M 153
TOLLBAR END 5J 175
Toll End Rd. DY4: Tip 2C 76
Tolley Rd. DY11: Kidd 8H 157
Tollgate Cl. B31: Longb 1M 163
Tollgate Dr. B20: Hand 2G 101
Tollgate Pct. B67: Smeth 3M 99
Toll Ga. Rd. CV47: Sou 4H 225
Toll Ho. Rd. B45: Redn 2J 163
Tollhouse Rd. B60: Stoke H 3L 209
Tollhouse Way B66: Smeth 2M 99
WV5: Wom 2E 72
Tolman Dr. B77: Tam 6D 32
Tolson Av. B78: Faz 1B 46
Tolson Cl. B77: Dost 4C 46
Tolworth Gdns.
WV2: Wolv 2E 52 (8M 7)
Tolworth Hall Rd. B24: Erd 6H 81
Tom Brown St. CV21: Rugby 5B 180
Tom Eatough Ct. LE9: Earl S 1G 71
Tom Ellis Ct. CV7: Exh 1F 130
Tomey Rd. B11: S'brk 4D 122
Tom Henderson Cl. CV3: Bin . . .2M 175
TOM HILL 5H 193
Tom Hill B94: Tan A 7G 193
Tomkinson Dr. DY11: Kidd 5H 157
Tomkinson Rd. CV10: Nun 5E 88
Tomlan Rd. B31: Longb 2C 164
Tomlinson Rd. B36: Cas B 8D 82
Tompstone Rd. B71: W Brom . . .1M 77
Tomson Av. CV6: Cov 4B 152
Toms Town La. B80: Stud 6L 221
Tom Ward Cl. CV3: Bin 2L 175
Tomwell Cl. CV47: Sou 4H 225
Tom Williams Way
B77: Two G 1C 46
Tonadine Cl. WV11: Wed 8A 24
Tonbridge Rd. B24: Erd 8G 81
CV3: Cov 3G 175
Tong Ct. WV1: Wolv 5C 36 (1J 7)
Tong St. WS1: Wals 8A 40
Tongue Av. B78: Faz 1A 46
Tookeys Dr. B96: A'wd B 8E 220
Topcroft Rd. B23: Erd 2F 80
Topfield Ho. B14: K Hth 8L 143
Top Fld. Wlk. B14: K Hth 7K 143
Topland Gro. B31: Longb 7J 141
Topp's Dr. CV12: Bed 8E 110
Topp's Heath CV12: Bed 8E 110
Top Rd. B61: Wild 4A 162
CV7: Barn 1A 132
Top Row DY12: Shat 2C 134
Topsham Cft. B14: K Hth 4K 143
Topsham Rd. B67: Smeth 3L 99
Torbay B77: Amin 4F 32
Torbay Rd. CV5: Cov 5J 151
Torcastle Cl. CV6: Cov 2F 152
Torc Av. B77: Amin 5E 32
Torcross Av. CV2: Cov 4J 153
Torfield WV8: Pend 7L 21
Tor Lodge Dr. WV6: Tett 7H 35
Toronto Gdns. B32: Harb 3L 119
Torpoint Cl. CV2: Cov 2J 153
Torrance Rd. CV21: Rugby 6M 179
Torre Av. B31: N'fld 7L 141
Torres Cl. CV34: Warw 5B 222
Torrey Gro. B8: W End 5J 103
Torridge B77: Hock 4G 47
Torridge Dr. WV11: Wed 4J 37
Torridon Cl. DY13: Stour S 2E 182
Torridon Cft. B13: Mose 6K 121
Torridon Rd. WV12: W'hall 8B 24
Torridon Way LE10: Hinc 8H 69
Torrington Av. CV4: Tile H 1D 172
Torrs Cl. B97: Redd 7D 212
Torside B77: Wiln 2H 47
TORTON 4B 184
Torton La. DY10: Tort 4B 184
DY11: Tort 4B 184
Tor Va. Rd. WV6: Tett 7G 35
Tor Way WS3: Pels 6M 25
Torwood Cl. CV4: W'wd H 3F 172
Totnes Cl. CV2: Cov 2J 153
Totnes Gro. B29: S Oak 7F 120
Totnes Rd. B67: Smeth 3M 99
Tottenham Cres. B44: K'sdng . . .7B 58
Touchstone Rd. CV34: H'cte 7L 223
Touchwood Hall Cl. B91: Sol 5C 146
Touchwood Shop. Cen.
B91: Sol 6C 146
Tourist Info. Cen.
Bewdley 6B 156
Birmingham 7J 101 (5C 4)
(Broad St.)
Birmingham 7L 101 (5G 5)
(Union St.)
Birmingham International
. . . . .5K 125
Bromsgrove 6A 188
Coventry 7D 152 (5D 6)
Dudley 8K 75
Kenilworth 5F 198
Kidderminster Town 4M 157
Kinver 6B 114
Lichfield 1H 19
Nuneaton 5J 89
Redditch 6E 212
Royal Leamington Spa
. . . . .1M 223
Rugby 6A 180
Solihull 6C 146
Tourist Info. Cen.
Warwick 3E 222
Wolverhampton 7C 36 (4J 7)
Worcester St. 7L 101 (6G 5)
Tove Ct. CV23: Long L 4H 179
Towbury Cl. B98: Redd 4F 220
Towcester Cft. B36: Hodg H . . .1K 103
Tower Bldgs. DY10: Kidd 3L 157
Tower Cft. B37: F'bri 5H 105
Tower Dr. B61: B'gve 3A 188
Tower Furlong CV23: Brow 1D 180
TOWER HILL 3H 79
Tower Hill B42: Gt Barr 3G 79
Tower Ri. B69: Tiv 2C 98
Tower Rd. B6: Aston 2M 101
(not continuous)
B69: Tiv 2B 98
B75: Four O 6H 43
CV12: Bed 7G 111
CV22: Rugby 8C 180
LE9: Earl S 1F 70
WS12: Hed 1F 8
Towers Cl. CV8: Ken 7F 198
DY10: Kidd 4B 158
Tower St. B19: Birm 4K 101 (1E 4)
(not continuous)
CV1: Cov 6C 152 (3C 6)
CV31: Lea S 2A 224
DY1: Dud 8J 75
DY3: Sed 8D 52
WS1: Wals 7L 39
WV1: Wolv 7D 36 (4K 7)
Tower Vw. Cres. CV10: Nun 6B 88
Tower Vw. Rd. WS6: Gt Wyr 1F 24
Tower Works Ind. Est.
WV3: Wolv 8A 36
Townend Rd. LE9: Barw 2A 70
Town End Sq. *WS1: Wals 7L 39*
(off Park St.)
Townend St. WS2: Wals 7L 39
Townesend Cl. CV34: Warw 8F 216
Townfields WS13: Lich 2G 19
(not continuous)
Townfields Cl. CV5: Alle 2H 151
Town Fold WS3: Pels 5A 26
Town Ga. Retail Pk.
DY1: Dud 7M 75
Town Hall Stop (MM) 6J 77
Townley Gdns. B6: Aston 8L 79
Townsend Av. B61: B'gve 5B 188
DY3: Sed 1D 74
Townsend Cft. CV3: Cov 2C 174
Townsend Dr. B76: Walm 2M 81
CV11: Nun 7M 89
Townsend Ho. B79: Tam 5A 32
Townsend La. CV23: Long L 4G 179
Townsend Pl. DY6: K'wfrd 3K 95
Townsend Rd. CV3: Cov 1C 174
CV21: Rugby 6D 180
LE9: S Stan 8K 71
Townsends Cl. CV11: Burt H 8G 91
Townsend Way
B1: Birm 6H 101 (4B 4)
Townshend Gro. B37: K'hrst 5F 104
Townson Rd. WV11: Wed 1A 38
Town Wall B77: Wiln 3F 46
Townwell Fold
WV1: Wolv 7C 36 (4H 7)
Town Wharf Bus. Pk.
WS2: Wals 8K 39
Town Yd. CV23: Brin 5M 155
WV13: W'hall 8A 38
Towpath Cl. B9: Birm 7B 102
Towyn Rd. B13: Mose 7D 122
Toy's La. B63: Crad 4J 117
Tozer St. DY4: Tip 2M 75
Traceys Mdw. B45: Redn 2G 163
Tractor Spares Ind. Est.
WV13: W'hall 7K 37
Trafalgar Cl. WS12: Hed 5L 9
Trafalgar Ct. B69: Tiv 8B 76
Trafalgar Gro. B25: Yard 3G 123
Trafalgar Ho. CV1: Cov 5A 6
Trafalgar Rd. B13: Mose 6M 121
B21: Hand 1E 100
B24: Erd 6F 80
B66: Smeth 5B 100
B69: Tiv 8B 76
Trafalgar Ter. B66: Smeth 5B 100
Trafford Cl. CV9: Ath 7K 49
Trafford Dr. CV10: Nun 4C 88
Trafford Pk., The B98: Redd 6F 212
Trafford Rd. LE10: Hinc 7M 69
Trajan Hill B46: Col 8M 83
Tram St. DY10: Kidd 4L 157
Tram Way B66: Smeth 2J 99
Tramway Cl. WS10: Darl 2E 54
WV14: Bils 2M 53
Tranter Av. B48: A'chu 4A 190
Tranter Cres. WS11: Hth H 7H 9
Tranter Rd. B8: W End 4G 103
Tranwell Cl. WV9: Pend 7M 21
TRAP'S GREEN 1F 214
Traquain Dr. DY1: Dud 6G 75
Travellers Cl. WS7: Burn 4G 17
Travellers Way B37: Chel W 6K 105
Treaford La. B8: W End 5H 103
Treasure Cl. B77: Amin 5E 32
Treddles La. B70: W Brom 6K 77
Tredington Cl. B29: W Cas 2A 142
B98: Redd 3H 221
Tredington Rd. CV5: E Grn 5F 150
Tree Acre Gro. B63: Crad 5J 117
Treedale Cl. CV4: Tile H 1D 172
Treeford Cl. B91: Sol 8M 145
Trees Rd. WS1: Wals 3M 55
Treeton Cft. B33: Yard 7A 104
Tree Tops WV5: Wom 1E 72
Treetops Dr. WV12: W'hall 4E 38
Trefoil B77: Amin 4H 33
Trefoil Cl. B29: W Cas 2A 142
(not continuous)
Treforest Rd. CV3: Cov 1J 175
Tregarron Rd. B63: Crad 4J 117
Tregea Ri. B43: Gt Barr 2C 78
Tregony Ri. WS14: Lich 3K 19
Tregorrick Rd. CV7: Exh 2G 131
Tregullan Rd. CV7: Exh 1H 131
Trehern Cl. B93: Know 4G 169
Treherne Rd. CV6: Cov 1B 152
Trehernes Dr. DY9: Pedm 8B 116
Trehurst Av. B42: Gt Barr 1J 79
Trejon Rd. B64: Crad H 1L 117
Trelawney Rd. CV7: Exh 2G 131
Tremaine Gdns.
WV10: Wolv 5D 36 (1L 7)
Tremelling Way CV7: Gun H . . .1F 108
Trenance Cl. WS14: Lich 2K 19
Trenance Rd. CV7: Exh 2G 131
Trenchard Cl. B75: S Cold 4M 59
Treneere Rd. CV7: Exh 1H 131
Trensale Av. CV6: Cov 5M 151
Trent Cl. DY8: Stourb 5A 116
WS7: Burn 3K 17
WV6: Pert 5E 34
Trent Ct. B73: S Cold 4H 59
Trent Cres. B47: Wyt 7L 165
Trent Dr. B36: Cas B 1F 104
Trentham Av. WV12: W'hall 4A 38
Trentham Cl. CV11: Nun 1M 111
WS11: Hth H 8H 9
Trentham Gdns. CV8: Ken 4J 199
Trentham Gro. B26: Yard 4L 123
Trentham Ri. WV2: E'shll 2F 52
Trentham Rd. CV1: Cov 5F 152
CV10: Harts 7A 66
Trent Ho. WS12: Hed 4J 9
Trent Pl. WS3: Blox 1K 39
Trent Rd. CV11: Nun 4K 89
CV12: Bulk 7A 112
LE10: Hinc 1G 91
WS3: Pels 8A 26
WS11: Cann 4E 8
Trent St. B5: Birm 7M 101 (6K 5)
Trent Twr. B7: Birm 5A 102 (1M 5)
Trent Valley Cotts.
WS13: S'hay 8M 13
Trent Valley Ind. Site
WS13: Lich 7K 13
Trent Valley Rd. WS13: Lich 1K 19
Trenville Av. B11: S'hll 4B 122
B12: Bal H 4B 122
Tresco Cl. B45: Fran 8E 140
TRESCOTT 2B 50
Trescott Rd. B31: N'fld 6K 141
B98: Redd 6F 212
Tresham Rd. B44: Gt Barr 8L 57
DY6: K'wfrd 1K 95
Tresillian Rd. CV7: Exh 1H 131
Tressel Cft. CV34: H'cte 7L 223
Trevanie Av. B32: Quin 3J 119
Trevelyan Ho. B37: Chel W 8J 105
Treville Cl. B98: Redd 6L 213
Treviscoe Cl. CV7: Exh 2G 131
Trevithick Cl. DY13: Stour S 5G 183
WS7: Burn 1J 17
Trevor Av. WS6: Gt Wyr 6G 15
Trevor Cl. CV4: Tile H 1D 172
Trevorne Cl. B12: Bal H 3M 121
Trevor Rd. LE10: Hinc 8M 69
WS3: Pels 5M 25
Trevor St. B7: Nech 3C 102
Trevor St. W. B7: Nech 3C 102
Trevor White Dr.
CV22: Rugby 8B 180
Trevose Av. CV7: Exh 2H 131
Trevose Cl. WS3: Blox 6F 24
Trevose Retreat B12: Bal H 4M 121
Trewern Dr. WS7: Chase 4F 16
Trewint Cl. CV7: Exh 1G 131
Trewman Cl. B76: Walm 1M 81
Treyamon Rd. WS5: Wals 2D 56
Treynham Cl. WV1: Wolv 8J 37
TRIANGLE 5H 17
Triangle, The B18: Hock 3E 100
CV5: Cov 5H 151
Trianon Rd. B60: B'gve 8C 188
Tribune Trad. Est.
CV21: Rugby 3A 180
Trickley Dr. B75: S Cold 3M 59
Tricorn Ho. B16: Edg . . .8G 101 (8A 4)
Trident Blvd. B35: Cas V 7B 82
Trident Bus. Pk. CV11: Nun 6K 89
Trident Cen. DY1: Dud 8J 75
Trident Cl. B23: Erd 2G 81
B76: Walm 2M 81
Trident Ct. B20: Hand 6G 79
B37: Mars G 1L 125
Trident Dr. B68: O'bry 4H 99
WS10: W'bry 6D 54
Trident Ho. B15: Birm . . .8J 101 (7C 4)
Trident Pk. CV34: Warw 5M 223

Trident Retail Pk.—Unketts Rd.

Trident Retail Pk.
B9: Birm .7A 102 (6M 5)
Trident Rd. B26: Birm A .5J 125
Trigen Ho. B90: Bly P .7M 167
Trigo Cft. B36: Hodg H .1L 103
TRIMPLEY .8C 134
Trimpley Cl. B93: Dorr .6E 168
Trimpley Dr. DY11: Kidd .2G 157
Trimpley Gdns. WV4: Penn .6L 51
Trimpley La. DY12: Bew .4D 156
DY12: Shat, Trim .3C 134
Trimpley Rd. B32: Bart G .1H 141
CV6: Cov .3C 152
DY11: Low H .8C 134
DY12: Trim .8C 134
Trinculo Gro. CV34: H'cte .7L 223
Trinder Rd. B67: Smeth .7K 99
Trindle Cl. DY2: Dud .8K 75
Trindle Rd. DY2: Dud .8K 75
Tring Ct. WV6: Wolv .5M 35
Trinity Cen. B64: Old H .7L 97
Trinity Chyd. CV1: Cov .4C 6
Trinity Cl. B92: Olton .8B 124
DY8: Word .7K 95
WS11: Cann .1E 14
WS14: Shens .3F 28
Trinity Ct. B6: Aston .8K 79
B60: B'gve .2B 210
B64: Old H .8L 97
CV21: Rugby .6B 180
DY10: Kidd .3A 158
LE10: Hinc .1J 91
WV3: Wolv .7A 36
WV13: W'hall .8L 37
Trinity Dr. B79: Tam .3K 31
Trinity Flds. DY10: Kidd .3M 157
Trinity Grange DY10: Kidd .2M 157
Trinity Gro. WS10: W'bry .6G 55
Trinity Hill B72: S Cold .4J 59
Trinity La. CV1: Cov .6C 152 (4C 6)
LE10: Hinc .1J 91
Trinity M. CV34: Warw .2F 222
Trinity Pk. B37: Mars G .6K 125
Trinity Pl. B72: S Cold .4J 59
Trinity Rd. B6: Aston .8K 79
B75: Four O .8H 43
B78: K'bry, Picc .3D 62
DY1: Dud .8J 75
DY8: Amb .1A 116
WV12: W'hall .3D 38
WV14: Bils .4M 53
(not continuous)
Trinity Rd. Nth. B70: W Brom .8K 77
(not continuous)
Trinity Rd. Sth.
B70: W Brom .8K 77
Trinity St. B64: Old H .8L 97
B67: Smeth .3A 100
B69: O'bry .4G 99
B70: W Brom .7K 77
CV1: Cov .6C 152 (4C 6)
CV32: Lea S .8M 217
DY5: Brie H .6D 96
Trinity Ter.
B11: S'brk .1A 122 (8M 5)
Trinity Vicarage Rd.
LE10: Hinc .1J 91
Trinity Wlk. CV11: Nun .6L 89
Trinity Way B70: W Brom .8K 77
Trinity Way Stop (MM) .8K 77
Trippleton Av. B32: Bart G .1H 141
Tristram Av. B31: N'fld .8B 142
Triton Cl. WS6: Gt Wyr .8F 14
Triton Pk. CV21: Rugby .1M 179
Trittiford Rd. B13: Mose .3B 144
Triumph B77: Glas .6E 32
Triumph Cl. CV2: Cov .6L 153
Triumph Ho. CV1: Cov .6C 6
Triumph Wlk. B36: Cas B .8G 83
Troilus Ct. CV34: H'cte .6M 223
Trojan B77: Glas .7E 32
Trojan Bus. Cen.
CV34: Warw .5L 223
Tromans Cl. B64: Crad H .2L 117
Tromans Ind. Est. DY2: Neth .6K 97
Troon B77: Amin .5H 33
Troon Cl. B75: S Cold .1K 59
WS3: Blox .6G 25
Troon Ct. WV6: Pert .4D 34
Troon Pl. DY8: Word .6J 95
Troon Way LE10: Burb .4K 91
Trossachs Rd. CV5: E Grn .6F 150
Trotter's La. B71: W Brom .2G 77
Troubridge Wlk. CV22: Bil .7J 179
Troughton Cres. CV6: Cov .4A 152
Trouse La. WS10: W'bry .6E 54
Troutbeck Av. CV32: Lea S .7J 217
Troutbeck Dr. DY5: Brie H .1B 116
Troutbeck Rd. CV5: E Grn .5F 150
Troy Bus. Pk. B96: Sam .6G 221
Troyes Cl. CV3: Cov .2D 174
Troy Gro. B14: K Hth .5K 143
Truck Stop Bus. Pk.
B11: Tys .4H 123
Truda St. WS1: Wals .2K 55
Trueman Cl. CV34: Warw .1E 222
TRUEMAN'S HEATH .2C 166
Trueman's Heath La.
B47: H'wd .2B 166
B90: Maj G .2B 166
Truggist La. CV7: Berk .1K 171
Truro Cl. B65: Row R .5E 98
CV11: Nun .4M 89
LE10: Hinc .5L 69
WS13: Lich .6H 13
Truro Dr. DY11: Kidd .3G 157
Truro Pl. WS12: Hth H .8J 9
Truro Rd. WS5: Wals .2D 56
Truro Twr. B16: Birm .7G 101
Truro Wlk. B37: Chel W .7G 105
Trussell Way CV22: Caw .1G 205
Trust Cotts. B96: Sam .8H 221
Trustin Cres. B92: Sol .1E 146
Tryan Rd. CV10: Nun .5E 88
Tryon Pl. WV14: Bils .3L 53
Tryst, The B61: L End .4B 188
TRYSULL .8C 50
Trysull Av. B26: Sheld .5C 124
Trysull Gdns. WV3: Wolv .2K 51
Trysull Holloway WV5: Try .5C 50
Trysull Rd. WV3: Wolv .2K 51
WV5: Wom .1E 72
Trysull Way DY2: Neth .6J 97
Tuckey Cl. LE9: Sap .1L 93
Tuckwell Cl. CV47: S'ton .1L 225
Tudbury Rd. B31: N'fld .5K 141
Tudman Cl. B76: Walm .2A 82
Tudor Av. CV5: E Grn .6F 150
Tudor Cl. B13: Mose .3M 143
B14: K Hth .8A 144
B73: New O .7D 58
CV7: Bal C .3G 171
WS6: C Hay .6E 14
WS7: Burn .3H 17
WS14: Lich .3M 19
Tudor Ct. B1: Birm .4B 4
B72: S Cold .4J 59
B74: Four O .7G 43
CV3: Cov .1C 174 (8B 6)
CV7: Exh .2E 130
CV34: Warw .4D 222
DY4: Tip .5A 76
WV11: Ess .6M 23
Tudor Cres. B77: Amin .5F 32
(not continuous)
CV9: Ath .8K 49
WV2: Wolv .3B 52
Tudor Cft. B37: F'bri .8F 104
Tudor Gdns. B23: Erd .6E 80
DY8: Stourb .4L 115
Tudor Grange Pk. .6A 146
Tudor Grange Sports Cen. .6B 146
Tudor Gro. B74: S'tly .1A 58
TUDOR HILL .3H 59
Tudor Hill B73: S Cold .3G 59
Tudor Ind. Est. B11: Tys .4H 123
Tudor La. CV47: Sou .6H 225
Tudor Pk. Ct. B74: Four O .6F 42
Tudor Pl. DY3: Up Gor .3E 74
Tudor Rd. B13: Mose .7M 121
B65: Row R .4C 98
B68: O'bry .5J 99
B73: S Cold .4H 59
CV10: Nun .3C 88
DY3: Up Gor .3E 74
DY12: Bew .2B 156
LE10: Hinc .7J 69
WS7: Burn .3J 17
WS12: Hed .1F 8
WV10: Wolv .5G 37
WV14: Bils .5B 54
Tudor Row *WS13: Lich .2H 19*
(off Wade St.)
Tudors Cl. B18: Small H .1C 122
Tudor St. B18: Win G .5D 100
DY4: Tip .5A 76
Tudor Ter. B17: Harb .3C 120
DY2: Dud .8L 75
Tudor Va. DY3: Up Gor .3E 74
Tudor Way B72: W Grn .7H 59
WS6: C Hay .8D 14
Tufnell Gro. B8: W End .2G 103
Tugford Rd. B29: W Cas .2C 142
Tuke Pl. WS13: Lich .8F 12
Tulips Gdns. B29: W Cas .2M 141
Tulip Tree Av. CV8: Ken .4H 199
Tulip Tree Ct. CV8: Ken .5H 199
Tulip Wlk. B37: Chel W .1J 125
Tulliver Cl. CV12: Bed .5H 111
Tulliver Rd. CV10: Nun .1J 111
Tulliver St. CV6: Cov .4B 152
Tulsi Cen. B19: Birm .5J 101 (1D 4)
Tulyar Cl. B36: Hodg H .1J 103
Tunnel Dr. B98: Redd .7E 212
Tunnel La.
B30: K Nor, K Hth .5H 143
Tunnel Rd. B70: W Brom .1G 77
CV10: Ansl .6J 87
Tunnel St. WV14: Cose .1J 75
Tunstall Rd. DY6: K'wfrd .4A 96
Turchill Dr. B76: Walm .1A 82
Turchil Rd. CV22: Caw .1G 205
Turchil Wlk. CV22: Caw .1G 205
Turf Cl. WS11: Nort C .5A 16
Turfpits La. B23: Erd .3D 80
Turf Pitts La. B75: Can .6M 43
(not continuous)
Turks Head Way B70: W Brom .7J 77
Turlands Cl. CV2: W'grve S .2A 154
Turley St. DY1: Dud .3G 75
Turls Hill Rd. DY3: Sed .1E 74
WV14: Cose .1G 75
Turls St. DY3: Sed .1E 74
Turnberry B77: Amin .4J 33
Turnberry Cl. WV6: Pert .4D 34
Turnberry Dr. CV11: Nun .1C 112
Turnberry Rd. B42: Gt Barr .1H 79
WS3: Blox .6F 24
Turner Av. WV14: Cose .7F 52
Turner Cl. CV12: Bed .5G 111
CV21: Hillm .1H 207
CV34: Warw .5B 222
WS11: Hth H .7K 9
Turner Dr. DY5: Quar B .2D 116
LE10: Hinc .6G 69
Turner Gro. WV6: Pert .5G 35
Turner Rd. CV5: Cov .6K 151
Turners Cft. B71: W Brom .1A 78
Turners Gro. DY3: Lwr G .5C 74
TURNER'S HILL .3B 98
Turner's Hill B65: Row R .3B 98
Turners Hill Rd. DY3: Lwr G .5C 74
Turner's La. DY5: Brie H .1C 116
Turner St. B11: S'brk .3A 122
B70: W Brom .5G 77
DY1: Dud .1H 97
DY3: Lwr G .6D 74
DY4: Tip .2M 75
Turney Rd. DY8: Stourb .3M 115
Turnham Grn. WV6: Pert .6E 34
Turnhouse Rd. B35: Cas V .5B 82
Turnley Rd. B34: S End .3C 104
Turnpike Cl. B11: S'brk .3A 122
CV7: Bal C .2H 171
Turnpike Dr. B46: Wat O .6J 83
Turnpike La. B97: Redd .5A 212
Turnstone Cl. CV23: Brow .1C 180
Turnstone Dr. WV10: F'stne .2H 23
Turnstone Rd. DY10: Kidd .8A 158
Turpin Ct. CV31: Lea S .3M 223
Turpin Ho. *CV21: Brow .2C 180*
(off Dovedale Cl.)
Turquoise Gro. WS11: Hth H .6J 9
Turton Cl. WS3: Blox .5G 25
Turton Rd. B70: W Brom .7H 77
DY4: Tip .8M 53
Turtons Cft. WV14: Cose .6H 53
Turton St. DY10: Kidd .1A 158
Turton Way CV8: Ken .5J 199
TURVES GREEN .8A 142
Turves Grn.
B31: Longb, N'fld .2M 163
Turves Green Leisure & Adult
Education Cen. .8A 142
Turville Cl. LE10: Burb .4M 91
Turville Rd. B20: Hand .8J 79
Tustin Gro. B27: A Grn .1J 145
Tutbury B77: Two G .2C 46
Tutbury Av. CV4: Canly .3L 173
WV6: Pert .6F 34
Tutbury Cl. WS11: Hth H .6J 9
Tutbury La. CV23: Bret, Brin .2K 177
Tutehill B77: Wiln .2H 47
Tuthill Furlong CV23: Brow .1D 180
TUTNALL .8F 188
Tutnall Cl. B60: Tutn .8F 188
Tutnall Dr. B94: H'ley H .3B 194
Tutnall Grange B60: Tutn .8G 189
Tutnall La. B60: Tutn .8F 188
Tutors Way DY10: Kidd .5L 157
Tuttle Hill CV10: Nun .2E 88
Tuttle Hill Ind. Est.
CV10: Nun .2E 88
Tuxford Cl.
WV10: Wolv .5E 36 (1M 7)
Twatling Rd.
B45: B Grn, Lick .7G 163
Tweedside Cl. LE10: Hinc .6M 69
Tweeds Well B32: Bart G .2H 141
Tweed Twr. B20: Hand .7K 79
Twelve O'Clock Ride
CV3: Bin, Bin W .7E 154
Twenty One Oaks CV9: Ath .3E 64
Twickenham Ct. DY8: Woll .2J 115
Twickenham Rd. B44: K'sdng .8B 58
Twickenham Way CV3: Bin .8B 154
Twiners Rd. B98: Redd .8F 212
TWO GATES .1C 46
Two Gates B63: Crad .4H 117
Two Gates Ind. Est.
B77: Wiln .2D 46
Two Gates La. B63: Crad .4J 117
Two Locks DY5: Brie H .5G 97
Two Oaks Av. WS7: C Ter .1C 16
Two Pike Leys CV23: Brow .1D 180
Two Trees Cl. B78: Hop .3J 31
Two Woods La. DY5: Brie H .8E 96
Twycross Gro. B36: Hodg H .2K 103
Twycross Rd. LE10: Burb .3M 91
Twycross Wlk. CV34: Warw .8D 216
Twydale Av. B69: Tiv .7C 76
Twyford Cl. WS9: A'rdge .4H 41
Twyford Ct. LE9: Barw .2B 70
Twyford Gro. WV11: Wed .2M 37
Twyford Rd. B8: W End .4J 103
Twyning Rd. B16: Edg .5D 100
B30: Stir .2H 143
Tybalt Cl. CV3: W'hall .4J 175
CV34: H'cte .5K 223
Tyber Dr. B20: Hand .6H 79
Tyberry Cl. B90: Shir .8G 145
TYBURN .6A 82
Tyburn Gro. B24: Erd .6K 81
Tyburn Rd. B24: Erd .8D 80
WV1: Wolv .8J 37
Tyburn Sq. B24: Erd .6K 81
Tyburn Trad. Est. B35: Cas V .7K 81
Tyebeams B34: S End .4C 104
Tye Gdns. DY9: Pedm .8B 116
Tyler Ct. B24: Erd .6F 80
Tyler Gdns. WV13: W'hall .8B 38
Tyler Gro. B43: Gt Barr .8G 57
Tyler Rd. WV13: W'hall .1A 54
Tylers Grn. B38: K Nor .7H 143
Tylers Gro. B90: M'path .3M 167
Tylney Cl. B5: Bal H .2K 121
CV3: Bin .7B 154
Tyndale Cres. B43: Gt Barr .6J 57
Tyndall Wlk. B32: Bart G .7G 119
Tyne Cl. B37: F'bri .5H 105
WS8: Bwnhls .7C 16
Tyne Ct. B73: S Cold .4H 59
Tynedale Cres. WV4: E'shll .6E 52
Tynedale Rd. B11: Tys .6F 122
Tyne Gro. B25: Yard .1K 123
Tynemouth Cl. CV2: Ald G .4K 131
Tyne Pl. DY5: Quar B .7F 96
Tynes, The B60: Stoke H .2L 209
Tyning Cl. WV9: Pend .7A 22
Tyninghame Av. WV6: Tett .3K 35
Tynings Cl. DY11: Kidd .8H 135
Tynings La. WS9: A'rdge .4G 41
Tynsall Av. B97: Redd .7M 211
Tynward Cl. CV3: Cov .4B 174
Tyrley Cl. WV6: Tett .7H 35
Tyrol Cl. DY8: Woll .4K 115
TYSELEY .4G 123
Tyseley Hill Rd. B11: Tys .5G 123
Tyseley Ind. Est. B11: Tys .4E 122
Tyseley La. B11: Tys .5G 123
Tyseley Station (Rail) .4G 123
Tysoe Cl. B94: H'ley H .3C 194
B98: Redd .7K 213
Tysoe Cft. CV3: Bin .1M 175
Tysoe Dr. B76: Walm .5M 59
Tysoe Rd. B44: K'sdng .2M 79
Tythbarn Leys CV23: Brow .1D 180
Tythe Barn Cl. B60: Stoke H .3K 209
Tythebarn Dr. DY6: W Hth .2G 95
Tythe Barn La. B90: Dic H .3E 166
(not continuous)
Tyzack Cl. DY5: Brie H .7C 96

U

UCI Cinema
Brierley Hill .7E 96
Shirley .2L 167
Tamworth .5C 32
Udall Rd. WV14: Cose .6K 53
Uffculme Rd. B30: Stir .1K 143
Uffmoor Est. B63: Hale .7L 117
UFFMOOR GREEN .4H 139
Uffmoor La.
B62: Roms, Hale .3K 139
B63: Hale .8L 117
Uffmoor Wood Nature Reserve
.2L 139
Ufton Cl. B90: Shir .6L 145
Ufton Cres. B90: Shir .6K 145
Ufton Cft. CV5: E Grn .6G 151
UGC Cinema
Bishopsgate St. .8H 101 (8B 4)
Bromsgrove St. .8L 101 (7G 5)
Rednal .1G 163
Ullapool Cl. B97: Redd .3D 220
ULLENHALL .6J 215
Ullenhall La.
B95: Oldb, Ullen .3D 214
B98: Beo .3C 214
Ullenhall Rd. B76: Walm .8M 59
B93: Know .3G 169
Ullenhall St. B95: Ullen .5J 215
Ullenwood B21: Hand .2D 100
Ulleries Rd. B92: Olton .7M 123
Ullrick Grn. B24: Erd .7F 80
Ullswater B77: Wiln .2G 47
Ullswater Av. CV11: Nun .3M 89
CV32: Lea S .7J 217
DY13: Stour S .3F 182
Ullswater Cl. B32: Bart G .7M 119
LE9: Earl S .2F 70
Ullswater Gdns. DY6: K'wfrd .3K 95
Ullswater Ho. B69: O'bry .4D 98
Ullswater Pl. WS11: Cann .8E 8
Ullswater Ri. DY5: Brie H .4D 96
Ullswater Rd. CV3: Bin .8L 153
CV12: Bed .7G 111
WV12: W'hall .8B 24
Ulster Cl. WS11: Cann .6G 9
Ulster Dr. DY6: K'wfrd .5L 95
Ulverley Ct. B92: Olton .1M 145
Ulverley Cres. B92: Olton .1M 145
ULVERLEY GREEN .1M 145
Ulverley Grn. Rd. B92: Olton .8L 123
Ulverscroft Rd. CV3: Cov .2C 174
Ulverston CV21: Brow .2D 180
Ulwine Dr. B31: N'fld .5M 141
UMBERSLADE .5L 193
Umberslade Bus. Cen.
B94: H'ley H .5L 193
Umberslade Children's Farm
.7J 193
Umberslade Rd. B29: S Oak .8F 120
B94: Earls, H'ley H .1H 193
B94: Tan A .4L 193
Uncle Ben's Cl. B69: O'bry .5F 98
Underhill Cl. B98: Redd .3F 220
CV3: Finh .6D 174
Underhill La. WV10: Bush .6F 22
Underhill Rd. B8: Salt .6F 102
DY4: Tip .3C 76
Underhill St. B69: O'bry .4G 99
Underhill Wlk. B69: O'bry .4G 99
Underley Cl. DY6: W Hth .2H 95
Underpass, The
B40: Nat E C .5K 125
Underwood Cl. B15: Edg .5D 120
B23: Erd .5C 80
B97: Redd .2A 220
Underwood Cres. LE9: Sap .1L 93
Underwood Dr. LE9: S Stan .8J 71
Underwood Rd. B20: Hand .4E 78
Unett Ct. B66: Smeth .4C 100
Unett St. B19: Hock .4J 101
(not continuous)
B66: Smeth .5C 100
Unett Wlk. B19: Birm .4J 101
Unicorn Av. CV5: E Grn .5E 150
Unicorn Hill B97: Redd .5D 212
Unicorn La. CV5: E Grn .5F 150
(not continuous)
Union Bldgs.
CV1: Cov .7C 152 (6C 6)
Union Cen. WS10: W'bry .7F 54
Union Cl. B77: Tam .6C 32
Union Dr. B73: Bold .7F 58
Union La. WV5: Try .8D 50
Union Mill St.
WV1: Wolv .7E 36 (4M 7)
Union Pas. B2: Birm .7L 101 (5G 5)
Union Pl. B29: S Oak .7H 121
CV6: Longf .4F 130
Union Rd. B6: Aston .1B 102
B69: O'bry .8E 76
B70: W Brom .7F 76
B90: Shir .7J 145
B91: Sol .5C 146
CV32: Lea S .8L 217
Union Row B21: Hand .1F 100
Union St. B2: Birm .7L 101 (5G 5)
B65: B'hth .8C 98
B70: W Brom .1K 99
B98: Redd .6F 212
CV22: Rugby .7A 180
DY2: Dud .8J 75
DY4: Tip .1M 75
(Attwell Rd.)
DY4: Tip .4M 75
(Unity Wlk.)
DY8: Stourb .4A 116
DY9: Lye .4E 116
DY10: Kidd .2L 157
WS1: Wals .7M 39
WS7: Chase .4E 16
WS10: W'bry .7F 54
WS11: Cann .3E 14
WV1: Wolv .7D 36 (4L 7)
WV13: W'hall .7A 38
WV14: Bils .4J 53
Union Wlk. CV31: Lea S .2A 224
Unisant Trad. Est. B64: Old H .7M 97
Unit Ind. Est. LE10: Hinc .3G 91
Unitt Dr. B64: Old H .1L 117
Unity Cl. WS10: Darl .5C 54
Unity Ho. CV1: Cov .2E 6
Unity Pl. B29: S Oak .7F 120
B69: O'bry .1G 99
Unity Wlk. DY4: Tip .4L 75
University of Aston
Chemical Engineering Building
.6M 101
Gem Sports Hall .6M 101
University of Birmingham
Edgbaston Pk. Rd. .4F 120
Selly Oak Campus .1D 142
University Rd. E. .5F 120
University of Central England
Bournville Campus .2E 142
Department of Art
.6K 101 (4E 4)
Gosta Green Campus
.5M 101 (1J 5)
Hamstead Campus .6E 78
Perry Barr Campus .6K 79
School of Jewellery
.5J 101 (2C 4)
Westbourne Campus .1G 121
University of Warwick
Gibbet Hill Campus .5K 173
Kirby Cnr. Rd. .3H 173
University Rd. .4J 173
University of Warwick Science Pk.
.3H 173
University of Wolverhampton
Molineux Rd. .6C 36 (2J 7)
St Peter's Sq. .7C 36 (3J 7)
University of Wolverhampton
(Walsall Campus) .2A 56
University Rd. CV4: Canly .4H 173
University Rd. E. B15: Edg .5F 120
University Rd. W. B15: Edg .5E 120
University Station (Rail) .5E 120
Unketts Rd. B67: Smeth .6L 99

Unwin Cres.—Victor Twr.

Unwin Cres. DY8: Stourb ... 4L 115
Upavon Cl. B35: Cas V ... 5A 82
Upfields WS7: Burn ... 2L 17
Upfields Cotts. WS7: Burn ... 2L 17
Upland Gro. B61: B'gve ... 4A 188
Upland Rd. B29: S Oak ... 7G 121
B61: B'gve ... 5A 188
Uplands B63: Hale ... 7K 117
CV2: Cov ... 4G 153
Uplands, The B67: Smeth ... 4M 99
Uplands Av. B65: Row R ... 6D 98
WV3: Wolv ... 1K 51
WV13: W'hall ... 8K 37
Uplands Cl. DY2: Dud ... 2M 97
WS15: Cann W ... 4F 10
Uplands Dr. DY3: Sed ... 1D 74
WV3: Wolv ... 1L 51
WV5: Wom ... 3G 73
Uplands Gro. WV13: W'hall ... 8J 37
Uplands Rd. B21: Hand ... 7D 78
DY2: Dud ... 2L 97
WV13: W'hall ... 8J 37
Upleadon Cl. B97: Redd ... 3A 220
Up. Abbey St. CV11: Nun ... 4H 89
Up. Ashley St. B62: B'hth ... 8C 98
Up. Balsall Heath Rd.
B12: Bal H ... 3M 121
UPPER BENTLEY ... 8H 211
Upper Bond St. LE10: Hinc ... 8K 69
Up. Brook St. WS2: Wals ... 8K 39
Upper Cape CV34: Warw ... 1D 222
Up. Castle St. WS10: Darl ... 1D 54
UPPER CATSHILL ... 8B 162
Up. Chapel St. B69: Tiv ... 7B 76
Up. Church La. DY4: Tip ... 1M 75
Up. Clifton Rd. B73: S Cold ... 4H 59
Upper Cl. B32: Bart G ... 6K 119
Up. Conybere St. B12: Birm ... 2M 121
Up. Crossgate Rd.
B98: Redd ... 1J 221
Up. Dean St.
B5: Birm ... 8L 101 (7G 5)
UPPER EASTERN GREEN ... 4D 150
Up. Eastern Grn. La.
CV5: E Grn ... 4C 150
Up. Ettingshall Rd.
WV14: Cose ... 1G 75
Up. Field Cl. B98: Redd ... 3J 213
Upperfield Way CV3: Bin ... 8A 154
(off Middlefield Dr.)
Up. Forster St. WS4: Wals ... 6M 39
Up. Gambolds La.
B60: Fins, S Prior ... 3C 210
UPPER GORNAL ... 4E 74
Up. Gough St.
B1: Birm ... 8K 101 (8E 4)
Upper Grn. WV6: Tett ... 4K 35
Up. Grosvenor Rd. B20: Hand ... 7H 79
Up. Grove St. CV32: Lea S ... 8L 217
Up. Gungate B79: Tam ... 4B 32
Upper Hall Cl. B98: Redd ... 7K 213
Up. Hall La. WS1: Wals ... 8L 39
Up. Highgate St. B12: Birm ... 2M 121
Up. High St. B64: Crad H ... 8K 97
WS10: W'bry ... 6F 54
Up. Hill St. CV1: Cov ... 6B 152 (3A 6)
CV32: Lea S ... 8A 218
Up. Holland Rd. B72: S Cold ... 5J 59
Up. Holly Wlk. CV32: Lea S ... 8A 218
Up. Keys Bus. Pk. WS12: Hed ... 6K 9
Up. Ladyes Hill CV8: Ken ... 3G 199
UPPER LADYES HILLS ... 3G 199
UPPER LANDYWOOD ... 1E 24
Up. Landywood La.
WS6: C Hay ... 8D 14
Up. Lichfield St.
WV13: W'hall ... 7A 38
Upper Mall CV32: Lea S ... 1M 223
(in Royal Priors Shop. Cen.)
Up. Mall E. B5: Birm ... 7L 101 (6H 5)
Up. Mall W. B5: Birm ... 7L 101 (6G 5)
UPPER MARLBROOK ... 7D 162
Up. Marshall St.
B1: Birm ... 8K 101 (7E 4)
Up. Meadow Rd. B32: Quin ... 4J 119
Up. Navigation St.
WS2: Wals ... 7K 39
Up. Norgrove Ho.
B97: Redd ... 8M 211
Upper Pk. CV3: W'hall ... 4K 175
Up. Portland St. B6: Aston ... 2A 102
Upper Pct. CV1: Cov ... 6C 152 (4B 6)
Upper Ride CV3: W'hall ... 4K 175
Up. Rosemary Hill CV8: Ken ... 4F 198
Up. Rushall St. WS1: Wals ... 8M 39
Up. Russell St. WS10: W'bry ... 7F 54
Up. St John St. WS14: Lich ... 2H 19
Up. St Mary's Rd.
B67: Smeth ... 8M 99
Up. Short St. WS2: Wals ... 8K 39
Up. Sneyd Rd. WV11: Ess ... 7B 24
Up. Spon St.
CV1: Cov ... 6A 152 (4A 6)
(not continuous)
Up. Spring La. CV8: Ken ... 2F 198
UPPER STOKE ... 5G 153
Up. Stone Cl. B76: Walm ... 5L 59
Upper St. WV6: Tett ... 4K 35
Up. Sutton St. B6: Aston ... 2M 101
Up. Thomas St. B6: Aston ... 2M 101
(not continuous)
Up. Trinity St.
B9: Birm ... 8A 102 (7L 5)
Up. Vauxhall WV1: Wolv ... 7A 36
Up. Villiers St. WV2: Wolv ... 3C 52
Up. Well St.
CV1: Cov ... 6C 152 (3B 6)
Up. William St.
B1: Birm ... 8J 101 (7C 4)
Up. York St.
CV1: Cov ... 8B 152 (7A 6)
Up. Zoar St.
WV3: Wolv ... 1B 52 (7G 7)
Upton Cl. B98: Redd ... 6M 213
Upton Ct. B23: Erd ... 6B 80
(off Alwynn Wlk.)
Upton Dr. CV11: Nun ... 1M 111
Upton Gdns. WV14: Bils ... 4J 53
Upton Gro. B33: Stech ... 8J 103
Upton La. CV13: Stoke G ... 2A 68
Upton Rd. B33: Stech ... 7J 103
CV22: Rugby ... 6K 179
DY10: Kidd ... 8M 135
Upton St. DY2: Neth ... 4J 97
UPTON WARREN ... 5G 209
Upton Warren Nature Reserve ... 6G 209
Upwey Av. B91: Sol ... 5A 146
USAM Trad. Est.
WV10: F'hses ... 7D 22
Usk Way B36: Cas B ... 1F 104
Usmere Rd. DY10: Kidd ... 8M 135
Utrillo Cl. CV5: Cov ... 6J 151
Uttoxeter Cl. WV6: Wolv ... 3B 36
Uxbridge Av. CV3: Cov ... 7J 153
Uxbridge Cl. DY3: Lwr G ... 6D 74
Uxbridge Ct. DY11: Kidd ... 4J 157
WS7: Chase ... 4E 16
WS12: Hed ... 4J 9
Uxbridge St. B19: Birm ... 4K 101
WS12: Hed ... 5J 9

V

Valbourne Rd. B14: K Hth ... 5J 143
Vale, The B11: S'hll ... 7C 122
B15: Edg ... 3G 121
CV3: Cov ... 1H 175
Vale Av. DY3: Up Gor ... 3D 74
WS9: A'rdge ... 6K 41
Vale Cl. B32: Bart G ... 6M 119
CV21: Hillm ... 1G 207
WS13: Lich ... 8H 13
Vale Head Dr. WV6: Tett ... 7G 35
Vale Ind. Est. DY11: Kidd ... 8J 157
Valencia Cft. B35: Cas V ... 5B 82
Valencia Rd. B60: B'gve ... 8C 188
CV3: Bin ... 7A 154
Valentine Cl. B74: S'tly ... 3M 57
Valentine Ct. B14: K Hth ... 8M 121
Valentine Rd. B14: K Hth ... 8L 121
B68: O'bry ... 7J 99
Valepits Rd. B33: Sheld ... 8C 104
Valerian B74: Four O ... 5F 42
Valerie Gro. B43: Gt Barr ... 1C 78
Vale Rd. DY2: Neth ... 5L 97
DY13: Stour S ... 6G 183
Vale Row DY3: Up Gor ... 4D 74
Vales Cl. B76: Walm ... 2L 81
Vale St. B71: W Brom ... 3L 77
DY3: Up Gor ... 4D 74
DY8: Amb ... 1A 116
WV2: E'shll ... 3G 53
Vale Vw. CV10: Nun ... 5E 88
WS9: A'rdge ... 5H 41
Valiant Ho. B35: Cas V ... 4B 82
Valiant Way B92: Sol ... 1C 146
Vallan Cft. B36: Hodg H ... 2M 103
Valley, The CV31: Rad S ... 5E 224
WS7: C Ter ... 1D 16
Valley Cl. B97: Redd ... 3A 220
DY11: Low H ... 1E 156
Valley Dr. CV21: Rugby ... 1A 180
Valley Farm Rd.
B45: Rubery ... 3F 162
Valley Grn. WS6: C Hay ... 7E 14
Valley Heritage Cen. & Mus. ... 3K 9
Valley La. B77: Wiln ... 2E 46
B94: Lapw ... 2K 195
WS13: Lich ... 1K 19
Valley Rd. B43: Gt Barr ... 2C 78
B61: B'hth ... 2L 187
B62: B'hth ... 1F 118
B64: Crad H ... 2L 117
B67: Smeth ... 6M 99
B74: S'tly ... 2M 57
B92: Sol ... 6C 124
B94: Earls ... 8G 167
CV2: Cov ... 3G 153
CV10: Gall C ... 5L 87
CV31: Rad S ... 5E 224
CV32: Lill ... 6B 218
DY3: Up Gor ... 3E 74
DY9: Lye ... 4F 116
WS3: Blox ... 1J 39
WS12: Haz ... 3A 10
WS12: Hed ... 3J 9
WV10: Wolv ... 4F 36
Valleyside WS3: Pels ... 7M 25
Valley Vw. DY12: Bew ... 3B 156
WS8: Bwnhls ... 2G 27
Valliant Cl. LE10: Burb ... 5L 91
Vanborough Wlk. DY1: Dud ... 7G 75
Vanbrugh Ct. WV6: Pert ... 6E 34
Van Diemans Rd. WV5: Wom ... 4E 72
Van Dyke Cl. CV5: Cov ... 6J 151
Van Gogh Cl. WS11: Hth H ... 7K 9
Vanguard B77: Wiln ... 3D 46
Vanguard Av. CV5: Cov ... 8J 151
Vanguard Cen. CV4: Canly ... 3J 173
Vanguard Cl. B36: Hodg H ... 1L 103
Vanguard Rd. B26: Birm A ... 5J 125
Vann Cl. B10: Small H ... 1C 122
(not continuous)
Vantage Point B70: W Brom ... 7J 77
(off Blacksmith Way)
Varden Cft. B5: Bal H ... 2K 121
Vardon Dr. CV3: Finh ... 5D 174
Vardon Way B38: K Nor ... 8D 142
Varley Rd. B24: Erd ... 5K 81
Varley Va. B24: Erd ... 5K 81
Varlins Way B38: K Nor ... 2D 164
Varney Av. B70: W Brom ... 7K 77
Vaughan Cl. B74: Four O ... 3F 42
Vaughan Gdns. WV8: Cod ... 5F 20
Vaughan Rd. WV13: W'hall ... 8K 37
Vaughan Trad. Est. DY4: Tip ... 5B 76
Vaughton Dr. B75: S Cold ... 3L 59
Vaughton St. B12: Birm ... 1M 121
Vaughton St. Sth. B5: Birm ... 1L 121
B12: Birm ... 1L 121
VAUXHALL ... 4B 102
Vauxhall Av. WV1: Wolv ... 7A 36
Vauxhall Bus. Pk. B7: Birm ... 4C 102
Vauxhall Cl. CV1: Cov ... 6E 152
Vauxhall Cres. B36: Cas B ... 8F 82
Vauxhall Gdns. DY2: Dud ... 2L 97
Vauxhall Gro.
B7: Birm ... 6B 102 (3M 5)
Vauxhall Ho. WV1: Wolv ... 7A 36
(off Upper Vauxhall)
Vauxhall Pl.
B7: Birm ... 6A 102 (3M 5)
Vauxhall Rd.
B7: Birm ... 6A 102 (3M 5)
DY8: Stourb ... 4A 116
Vauxhall St. CV1: Cov ... 6E 152
DY1: Dud ... 1H 97
Vauxhall Ter. B7: Birm ... 5B 102
Vauxhall Trad. Est. B7: Birm ... 5B 102
Vawdrey Cl. DY13: Stour S ... 8E 182
Vaynor Dr. B97: Redd ... 1D 220
Veasey Cl. CV11: Nun ... 6L 89
Vecqueray St. CV1: Cov ... 7E 152
Vector Ind. Pk. B71: W Brom ... 3J 77
Velsheda Rd. B90: Shir ... 7G 145
Venetia Rd. B9: Bord G ... 7C 102
Venice Ct. B13: Mose ... 7B 122
Venning Gro. B43: Gt Barr ... 2D 78
Ventnor Av. B19: Hock ... 2J 101
B36: Hodg H ... 2K 103
Ventnor Cl. B68: O'bry ... 2J 119
CV2: Cov ... 6L 153
Ventnor Rd. B92: Sol ... 6C 124
Ventnor St. CV10: Nun ... 3K 89
Ventura Pk. Rd. B78: Tam ... 5L 31
Ventura Retail Pk. B78: Tam ... 6A 32
Venture Ct. LE10: Hinc ... 1E 90
WV10: F'hses ... 4D 22
Venture Way
B7: Birm ... 5M 101 (1K 5)
Venus Bank DY12: Bew ... 6A 156
Vera Rd. B26: Yard ... 2L 123
Vera Roberts Way
DY11: Kidd ... 6H 157
Verbena Cl. B60: S Prior ... 8J 209
CV2: Cov ... 8H 131
Verbena Gdns.
B7: Birm ... 4A 102 (1M 5)
Verbena Rd. B31: N'fld ... 3M 141
Vercourt B74: Lit A ... 6B 42
Verden Av. CV34: Warw ... 5B 222
Verdi Ct. WS13: Lich ... 7J 13
Verdun Cl. CV31: W'nsh ... 7B 224
Verdun Cres. DY2: Dud ... 7M 75
Vere Rd. CV21: Hillm ... 8F 180
Vere St. B5: Birm ... 1K 121
Verity Wlk. DY8: Word ... 8L 95
Vermont Grn. WS11: Cann ... 6G 9
Vermont Gro. CV31: Lea S ... 3D 224
Verney Av. B33: Sheld ... 2D 124
Vernier Av. DY6: K'wfrd ... 4A 96
Vernon Av. B20: Hand ... 5F 78
CV22: Hillm ... 1E 206
DY4: Tip ... 5L 75
WS8: Bwnhls ... 1G 27
Vernon Cl. B62: B'hth ... 1C 118
B74: Four O ... 4E 42
B98: Redd ... 4G 213
CV1: Cov ... 6E 152
CV32: Lea S ... 6L 217
WV11: Ess ... 5M 23
WV13: W'hall ... 8L 37
Vernon Ct. B16: Edg ... 8E 100
B68: O'bry ... 2H 119
CV1: Cov ... 6E 152
DY13: Stour S ... 5G 183
Vernon Rd. B16: Edg ... 8D 100
B62: B'hth ... 1C 118
B68: O'bry ... 3J 99
DY13: Stour S ... 5G 183
WV14: Bils ... 3M 53
Vernons Ct. CV10: Nun ... 5E 88
Vernons La. CV10: Nun ... 5E 88
Vernons Pl. WV10: Share ... 1K 23
Vernon St. B70: W Brom ... 6E 76
WV14: Cose ... 7L 53
Vernon Trad. Est. B62: B'hth ... 1C 118
Vernon Way WS3: Blox ... 8D 24
Verona Cl. CV11: Nun ... 8A 90
Verona Rd. B60: B'gve ... 8C 188
Veronica Av. WV4: E'shll ... 4E 52
Veronica Cl. B29: W Cas ... 3M 141
Veronica Rd. DY6: K'wfrd ... 3A 96
Verstone Cft. B31: N'fld ... 7A 142
Verstone Rd. B90: Shir ... 5J 145
Verwood Cl. WV13: W'hall ... 8K 37
Vesey Cl. B46: Wat O ... 7H 83
B74: Four O ... 7F 42
Vesey Rd. B73: W Grn ... 8H 59
Vesey St. B4: Birm ... 5L 101 (2G 5)
Vestry Cl. B64: Old H ... 8M 97
Vestry Ct. DY8: Woll ... 3L 115
Viaduct Cl. CV21: Rugby ... 5D 180
Viaduct Dr. WV6: Wolv ... 3B 36
Viaduct St. B7: Birm ... 6A 102 (4M 5)
Vibart Rd. B26: Yard ... 1M 123
Vicarage Cl. B30: Stir ... 2J 143
B42: Gt Barr ... 2K 79
B60: B'gve ... 1B 210
B78: Dord ... 4M 47
CV9: Ath ... 2L 65
DY4: Tip ... 4L 75
DY5: Brie H ... 1C 116
WS8: Bwnhls ... 1G 27
(not continuous)
Vicarage Ct. DY7: Kinv ... 6A 114
LE9: Earl S ... 1F 70
Vicarage Cres. B97: Redd ... 6C 212
(Coppice Cl.)
B97: Redd ... 6D 212
(Vicarage Vw.)
DY10: Kidd ... 4M 157
Vicarage Dr. DY7: Kinv ... 6A 114
Vicarage Fld. CV34: Warw ... 1H 223
Vicarage Gdns. B65: B'hth ... 8C 98
B76: Walm ... 2M 81
CV8: Ken ... 7G 199
Vicarage Hill B78: Midd ... 8H 45
B94: Tan A ... 6E 192
CV23: Clift D ... 5E 180
Vicarage La. B46: Wat O ... 7H 83
CV7: Ash G ... 2C 130
CV22: Dunc ... 6K 205
CV35: Sher ... 8A 222
DY5: P'ntt ... 1D 96
Vicarage Pl. WS1: Wals ... 8L 39
Vicarage Prospect DY1: Dud ... 8H 75
Vicarage Ri. CV33: Bis T ... 8E 224
Vicarage Rd. B6: Aston ... 2A 102
(not continuous)
B14: K Hth ... 3J 143
B15: Edg ... 1F 120
B17: Harb ... 4B 120
B18: Hock ... 2G 101
B33: Stech ... 8L 103
B62: B'hth ... 8C 98
B67: Smeth ... 4M 99
B68: O'bry ... 5H 99
B71: W Brom ... 3K 77
B94: Earls ... 6J 167
B94: H'ley H ... 2E 194
CV8: S'lgh ... 3B 200
CV22: Rugby ... 6M 179
CV32: Lill ... 6B 218
DY3: Up Gor ... 4F 74
DY5: Brie H ... 2C 116
DY8: Amb ... 2A 116
DY8: Woll ... 2J 115
DY9: Lye ... 4F 116
DY10: Stone ... 7E 158
WS3: Pels ... 7A 26
WS8: Bwnhls ... 2F 26
WS10: W'bry ... 6F 54
WV2: Wolv ... 1D 52 (8L 7)
WV4: Penn ... 6K 51
WV11: Wed ... 3H 37
WV14: Cose ... 2J 75
Vicarage Rd. Sth. DY9: Lye ... 4E 116
Vicarage Rd. W. DY1: Dud ... 3H 75
Vicarage St. B68: O'bry ... 4H 99
CV11: Nun ... 5K 89
LE9: Earl S ... 1F 70
Vicarage Ter. WS2: Wals ... 1J 55
Vicarage Vw. B97: Redd ... 6D 212
Vicarage Wlk. WS1: Wals ... 8L 39
Vicar's Cl. WS13: Lich ... 1G 19
Vicar St. DY2: Dud ... 8J 75
DY3: Sed ... 1D 74
DY10: Kidd ... 3L 157
WS10: W'bry ... 6G 55
Vicars Wlk. DY9: W'cte ... 7E 116
Viceroy Cl. B5: Edg ... 3J 121
DY6: K'wfrd ... 4A 96
Victor Bus. Cen. B98: Redd ... 6H 213
Victor Cl. WV2: E'shll ... 3H 53
Victor Hodges Ho.
CV47: Sou ... 5H 225
Victoria Arc. B79: Tam ... 4B 32
WV1: Wolv ... 7C 36 (4J 7)
Victoria Av. B10: Small H ... 1D 122
B21: Hand ... 1F 100
B62: Quin ... 3F 118
Victoria Av. B66: Smeth ... 4A 100
CV21: Rugby ... 5M 179
WS3: Blox ... 8H 25
Victoria Bldgs. B16: Birm ... 6E 100
(off Barford Rd.)
Victoria Bus. Cen.
CV31: Lea S ... 2A 224
(off Neilston St.)
Victoria Bus. Pk.
CV31: Lea S ... 2A 224
(off Neilston St.)
Victoria Colonnade
CV31: Lea S ... 2M 223
(off Victoria Ter.)
Victoria Ct. B13: Mose ... 5M 121
B62: Quin ... 2G 119
(off Binswood Rd.)
B66: Smeth ... 3B 100
CV5: Cov ... 5K 151
DY5: Brie H ... 6D 96
DY10: Kidd ... 3M 157
WS11: Nort C ... 4B 16
Victoria Dr. B78: Faz ... 1A 46
Victoria Fold
WV1: Wolv ... 8C 36 (5H 7)
Victoria Gdns. B64: Old H ... 7M 97
WS13: Lich ... 3F 18
Victoria Gro. B18: Win G ... 5E 100
WV5: Wom ... 1G 73
Victoria Ho. B16: Birm ... 6A 4
WS3: Blox ... 1K 39
WS10: Darl ... 3C 54
(off Factory St.)
Victoria M. B45: B Grn ... 1K 189
B69: O'bry ... 6F 98
CV3: Bin ... 7L 153
CV34: Warw ... 2D 222
WS4: Wals ... 6A 40
Victoria New Works
WS10: Darl ... 1D 54
Victoria Pk. Rd.
B66: Smeth ... 4B 100
Victoria Pas. DY8: Stourb ... 4A 116
DY9: Hag ... 4A 138
WV1: Wolv ... 7C 36 (4J 7)
Victoria Pl. DY11: Kidd ... 6H 157
Victoria Rd. B6: Aston ... 2L 101
(not continuous)
B17: Harb ... 4B 120
B21: Hand ... 2E 100
B23: Erd ... 6D 80
B27: A Grn ... 7J 123
(not continuous)
B30: Stir ... 2G 143
B33: Stech ... 6K 103
B61: B'gve ... 6A 188
B61: D'frd ... 3F 186
B62: B'hth ... 8D 98
B64: Old H ... 7M 97
B68: O'bry ... 3J 99
B72: S Cold ... 4J 59
B79: Tam ... 4B 32
CV9: Man ... 3M 65
CV10: Harts ... 1B 88
CV31: Lea S ... 1L 223
DY3: Sed ... 1E 74
DY4: Tip ... 4M 75
DY5: Quar B ... 8G 97
LE10: Burb ... 4M 91
WS3: Pels ... 6A 26
WS10: Darl ... 3D 54
WV3: Wolv ... 2L 51
WV6: Tett ... 4L 35
WV10: Wolv ... 4F 36
WV11: Wed ... 3H 37
Victoria Sq. B2: Birm ... 7K 101 (5E 4)
WS13: Lich ... 3H 19
WV1: Wolv ... 7D 36 (4K 7)
Victoria St. B9: Small H ... 8D 102
B63: Hale ... 5A 118
B70: W Brom ... 4F 76
(Phoenix St.)
B70: W Brom ... 6J 77
(Price St.)
B98: Redd ... 5E 212
CV1: Cov ... 5E 152 (2F 6)
CV11: Nun ... 5J 89
CV21: Rugby ... 6L 179
CV31: Lea S ... 2L 223
CV34: Warw ... 2D 222
DY5: Brie H ... 6D 96
DY5: P'ntt ... 2C 96
DY6: W Hth ... 8H 73
DY8: Stourb ... 4A 116
LE10: Hinc ... 8K 69
WS10: W'bry ... 7E 54
WS11: Cann ... 5E 8
(Cemetery Rd.)
WS11: Cann ... 1D 14
(Newhall St.)
WS12: Hed ... 3J 9
WV1: Wolv ... 8C 36 (5J 7)
WV13: W'hall ... 6A 38
Victoria Ter. CV32: Lea S ... 2M 223
CV47: S'ton ... 1M 225
WS4: Wals ... 6A 40
Victor Rd. B18: Win G ... 3E 100
B92: Sol ... 6D 124
Victor St. WS1: Wals ... 2L 55
WS3: Pels ... 8A 26
Victor Twr. B7: Nech ... 3B 102

Victory Av.—Waring Rd.

Victory Av. B65: Row R ... 7B **98**
WS7: C Ter ... 2F **16**
WS10: Darl ... 5C **54**
Victory Cl. DY13: Stour S ... 7H **183**
WS12: Hed ... 5L **9**
Victory Ho. B13: Mose ... 5M **121**
Victory La. WS2: Wals ... 5G **39**
Victory Ri. B71: W Brom ... 4J **77**
Victory Rd. CV6: Cov ... 1E **152**
Victory Ter. B78: Faz ... 1B **46**
View Dr. DY2: Dud ... 1L **97**
Viewfield Av. WS12: Hed ... 2F **8**
Viewfield Cres. DY3: Sed ... 2D **74**
Viewlands Dr. WV6: Tett ... 7G **35**
View Point B69: Tiv ... 1B **98**
View St. WS12: Hed ... 3F **8**
VIGO
Tardebigge ... 6G **189**
Walsall Wood ... 6F **26**
Vigo Cl. WS9: Wals W ... 7F **26**
Vigo Pl. WS9: A'rdge ... 1F **40**
Vigo Rd. WS9: Wals W ... 7F **26**
Vigo Ter. WS9: Wals W ... 7F **26**
Viking B77: Wiln ... 2D **46**
Viking Ri. B65: Row R ... 5C **98**
Vilia Cl. LE10: Burb ... 5M **91**
Villa Cl. CV12: Bulk ... 8B **112**
Villa Cres. CV12: Bulk ... 8C **112**
VILLAGE, THE
Chaddesley Corbett ... 2L **185**
Hartlebury ... 7M **183**
Kingswinford ... 2L **95**
Village, The DY6: K'wfrd ... 2L **95**
Village M. CV22: Bil ... 1K **205**
Village M., The WV6: Tett ... 4J **35**
Village Rd. B6: Aston ... 8A **80**
Village Sq. B31: Longb ... 7J **141**
Village Wlk. WS10: W'bry ... 6H **55**
Village Way B76: Walm ... 1M **81**
WV14: Bils ... 4J **53**
Villa Park ... 8M **79**
Villa Rd. B19: Hock ... 2G **101**
CV6: Cov ... 3B **152**
Villa St. B19: Loz ... 2H **101**
(not continuous)
DY8: Amb ... 1A **116**
Villa Wlk. B19: Hock ... 3J **101**
Villebon Way CV31: W'nsh ... 7A **224**
Villette Gro. B14: Yard W ... 5C **144**
Villiers Av. WV14: Bils ... 2K **53**
Villiers Ho. *WV2: Wolv ... 2C 52*
(off Blakenhall Gdns.)
Villiers Pl. WV14: Bils ... 2K **53**
Villiers Rd. B60: B'gve ... 2K **209**
CV8: Ken ... 4H **199**
Villiers Sq. WV14: Bils ... 2K **53**
Villiers St. CV2: Cov ... 6G **153**
CV11: Nun ... 6H **89**
CV32: Lea S ... 8A **218**
DY10: Kidd ... 4A **158**
WS1: Wals ... 2L **55**
WV13: W'hall ... 7A **38**
Villiers Trad. Est.
WV2: Wolv ... 2B **52** (8G **7**)
Vimy Rd. B13: Mose ... 2B **144**
WS10: W'bry ... 5G **55**
Vimy Ter. WS10: W'bry ... 5G **55**
Vincent Cl. B12: Bal H ... 3M **121**
Vincent Dr. B15: Edg ... 6D **120**
Vincent Pde. B12: Bal H ... 3M **121**
Vincent Rd. B75: S Cold ... 2L **59**
Vincent St. B12: Bal H ... 4M **121**
(not continuous)
CV1: Cov ... 7B **152**
CV32: Lea S ... 8A **218**
WS1: Wals ... 2M **55**
Vincent Wyles Ho.
CV2: Cov ... 6L **153**
Vince St. B66: Smeth ... 6A **100**
Vinculum Way WV13: W'hall ... 1B **54**
Vine Av. B12: Bal H ... 4A **122**
Vinecote Rd. CV6: Longf ... 6F **130**
Vine Cres. B71: W Brom ... 3K **77**
Vine Gdns. B64: Old H ... 7M **97**
Vine La. B63: Hale ... 6B **118**
CV34: Warw ... 1E **222**
DY9: Clent ... 6F **138**
WS11: Cann ... 4D **14**
Vineries, The B27: A Grn ... 5K **123**
Vine St. B6: Aston ... 2B **102**
B97: Redd ... 5D **212**
CV1: Cov ... 5E **152** (2E **6**)
DY5: Brie H ... 4E **96**
DY8: Word ... 8L **95**
DY10: Kidd ... 1A **158**
Vine Ter. B17: Harb ... 4C **120**
Vineyard Cl. B18: Hock ... 2F **100**
Vineyard Rd. B31: N'fld ... 4M **141**
Vinnall Gro. B32: Bart G ... 1H **141**
Vintage Cl. B34: Stech ... 4A **104**
Violet Cl. CV2: Cov ... 6J **131**
CV12: Bed ... 7E **110**
CV23: Brow ... 1E **180**
Violet Cft. DY4: Tip ... 8C **54**
Violet La. DY9: Clent ... 5E **138**
Virage Pk. WS11: Cann ... 3F **14**
Virgin Active ... 6M **167**
Virginia Dr. WV4: Penn ... 5M **51**
Virginia Pl. CV10: Nun ... 6E **88**
Virginia Rd. CV1: Cov ... 6E **152**
Viscount Cen. CV4: Canly ... 3J **173**
Viscount Cl. B35: Cas V ... 7A **82**
CV31: Lea S ... 3M **223**
Viscount Dr. B35: Cas V ... 7B **82**
Viscount Ho. B26: Birm A ... 5J **125**
Viscount Rd. WS7: C Ter ... 8E **10**
Vista, The DY3: Sed ... 8D **52**
Vista Grn. B38: K Nor ... 8G **143**
(not continuous)
Vittle Dr. CV34: Warw ... 2D **222**
Vittoria St. B1: Birm ... 5J **101** (2C **4**)
B66: Smeth ... 3D **100**
Vivian Cl. B17: Harb ... 4C **120**
Vivian Rd. B17: Harb ... 4C **120**
Vixen Cl. B76: Walm ... 2K **81**
Vogue Cl. CV1: Cov ... 6E **152** (3F **6**)
Vowchurch Cl. B97: Redd ... 4A **212**
Voyager Dr. WS11: Cann ... 3F **14**
Vue Cinema ... 1D 102
(in Star City)
Vulcan Ind. Est. WS2: Wals ... 3J **39**
Vulcan Rd. B91: Sol ... 3C **146**
WS13: Lich ... 8L **13**
WV14: Bils ... 4M **53**
Vulcan Rd. Ind. Est.
B91: Sol ... 3C **146**
Vyrnwy Gro. B38: K Nor ... 1E **164**
Vyse St. B6: Aston ... 1B **102**
B18: Birm ... 4J **101** (1C **4**)

W

Wackrill Dr. CV32: Lill ... 6C **218**
Wadbarn B90: Dic H ... 4G **167**
Waddell Cl. WV14: Cose ... 7F **52**
Waddens Brook La.
WV11: Wed ... 4L **37**
Waddington Av. B43: Gt Barr ... 8E **56**
Wade Av. CV3: Cov ... 4B **174**
Wadebridge Dr. CV11: Nun ... 5L **89**
Wade Gro. CV34: Warw ... 7E **216**
Wades Cl. DY4: Tip ... 4L **75**
Wadesmill Lawns
WV10: Bush ... 5E **22**
Wade St. WS13: Lich ... 2H **19**
Wadham Cl. B65: Row R ... 3C **98**
Wadham Ho. B37: Chel W ... 6J **105**
Wadhurst Rd. B17: Edg ... 7B **100**
Wadley's Rd. B91: Sol ... 3M **145**
Waen Cl. DY4: Tip ... 1B **76**
Waggoners Cl. B60: Stoke H ... 3L **209**
CV8: Bubb ... 4J **201**
Waggoners La. B78: Hints ... 2D **44**
Waggon La.
DY10: Blak, C'hll, Hurc ... 6E **136**
Waggon St. B64: Old H ... 7M **97**
Waggon Wlk. B38: K Nor ... 1C **164**
(not continuous)
Wagoners Cl. B8: Salt ... 3F **102**
Wagon La. B92: Olton ... 5M **123**
Wagstaff Cl. WV14: Cose ... 1K **75**
Wagstaff Dr. CV10: Nun ... 2A **88**
Wainbody Av. Nth. CV3: Cov ... 4A **174**
Wainbody Av. Sth.
CV3: Finh ... 5M **173**
Waine Ho. WS8: Bwnhls ... 3G **27**
Wainrigg B77: Wiln ... 2H **47**
Wainwright Cl. DY6: W Hth ... 2G **95**
Wainwright St. B6: Aston ... 2A **102**
Waite Rd. WV13: W'hall ... 1L **53**
Wakefield Cl. B73: Bold ... 7G **59**
CV3: Bin ... 2M **175**
CV9: Hurl ... 5H **63**
Wakefield Ct. B13: Mose ... 7B **122**
B29: W Cas ... 2C 142
(off Abdon Av.)
Wakefield Gro. B46: Wat O ... 6H **83**
Wakeford Cl. CV10: Ridge L ... 6G **65**
Wakeford Rd. B31: N'fld ... 8C **142**
WAKE GREEN ... 7A **122**
Wake Grn. Pk. B13: Mose ... 7B **122**
Wake Grn. Rd. B13: Mose ... 6M **121**
DY4: Tip ... 8A **54**
Wake Gro. CV34: Warw ... 4B **222**
Wakehurst Cl. CV11: Nun ... 1M **111**
Wakelam Gdns. B43: Gt Barr ... 8D **56**
Wakelams Fold DY3: Gorn ... 6C **74**
Wakeley Hill WV4: Penn ... 5M **51**
Wakelin Rd. B90: Shir ... 2H **167**
Wakeman Ct. WV11: Ess ... 6M **23**
Wakeman Dr. B69: Tiv ... 1B **98**
Wakeman Gro. B33: Sheld ... 2D **124**
Wakes Cl. WV13: W'hall ... 8B **38**
Wakes Rd. WS10: W'bry ... 7G **55**
Walcot Cl. B75: Four O ... 6H **43**
Walcot Dr. B43: Gt Barr ... 3F **78**
Walcote Cl. LE10: Hinc ... 1F **90**
Walcot Gdns. WV14: Bils ... 5H **53**
Walcot Grn. B93: Dorr ... 7G **169**
Waldale Cl. WV11: Ess ... 8C **24**
Walden Gdns. WV4: Penn ... 3L **51**
Walden Rd. B11: Tys ... 6G **123**
Waldeve Gro. B92: Sol ... 1F **146**
Waldley Gro. B24: Erd ... 6J **81**
Waldon Wlk. B36: Cas B ... 1F **104**
Waldron Av. DY5: Brie H ... 7B **96**
Waldron Cl. WS10: W'bry ... 3F **54**
Waldrons Moor B14: K Hth ... 4J **143**
Walford Av. WV3: Wolv ... 1M **51**
Walford Dr. B92: Sol ... 6D **124**
Walford Grn. B32: Bart G ... 2H **141**
Walford Gro. CV34: Warw ... 8F **216**
Walford Pl. CV22: Hillm ... 1F **206**
Walford Rd. B11: S'brk ... 3B **122**
Walford St. B69: Tiv ... 7A **76**
Walford Wlk. B97: Redd ... 6E **212**
Walhouse Cl. WS1: Wals ... 7M **39**
Walhouse Rd. WS1: Wals ... 7M **39**
(not continuous)
Walhouse St. WS11: Cann ... 1E **14**
Walk, The DY3: Sed ... 8D **52**
Walker Av. B69: Tiv ... 2C **98**
DY5: Quar B ... 2D **116**
DY9: W'cte ... 6D **116**
WV10: Bush ... 1E **36**
Walker Dr. B24: Nech ... 1E **102**
DY10: Kidd ... 8A **136**
Walker Grange DY4: Tip ... 2M **75**
Walker Pl. WS3: Blox ... 1L **39**
Walker Rd. WS3: Blox ... 1K **39**
Walker's Cft. WS13: Lich ... 7J **13**
Walkers Fold WV12: W'hall ... 3D **38**
WALKER'S HEATH ... 7G **143**
Walkers Heath Rd.
B38: K Nor ... 8H **143**
Walkers Orchard CV8: S'lgh ... 3B **200**
Walkers Ri. WS12: Hed ... 1K **9**
Walkers Rd. B98: Redd ... 3L **213**
Walker's Ter. CV23: Brin ... 4K **155**
Walker St. DY2: Neth ... 5J **97**
DY4: Tip ... 2B **76**
Walkers Way CV8: Ken ... 7F **198**
B46: Col ... 3A **106**
CV12: Bed ... 8F **110**
Walk La. WV5: Wom ... 2G **73**
Walkmil Bus. Pk.
WS11: Cann ... 4D **14**
WALKMILL BRIDGE ... 4C **14**
Walkmill Dr. WR9: Wych ... 8D **208**
Walkmill La. WS11: Cann ... 4D **14**
Walkmill Way WS11: Cann ... 4D **14**
WALKWOOD ... 3C **220**
Walkwood Cres. B97: Redd ... 3C **220**
Walkwood Rd. B97: Redd ... 3C **220**
WALL ... 7D **18**
Wallace Cl. B69: O'bry ... 3D **98**
WS11: Nort C ... 4M **15**
Wallace Ct. CV34: Warw ... 2D **222**
WS6: C Hay ... 8D **14**
Wallace Ho. B69: O'bry ... 4D **98**
Wallace Ri. B64: Crad H ... 2L **117**
Wallace Rd. B29: S Oak ... 7H **121**
B69: O'bry ... 3D **98**
CV6: Cov ... 1A **152**
WS8: Bwnhls ... 1E **26**
WV14: Bils ... 6A **54**
Wall Av. B46: Col ... 4M **105**
Wallbank Rd. B8: W End ... 3G **103**
WALLBROOK ... 1K **75**
Wallbrook St. WV14: Cose ... 1K **75**
Wall Cft. WS9: A'rdge ... 2H **41**
Wall Dr. B74: Four O ... 5F **42**
Wall End Cl. WS2: Wals ... 2G **39**
Waller Cl. CV35: Leek W ... 2F **216**
Waller St. CV32: Lea S ... 7A **218**
Wallface B71: W Brom ... 2G **77**
WALL HEATH ... 1H **95**
Wallheath Cres. WS9: Ston ... 4L **27**
Wall Heath La. WS9: Ston ... 4M **27**
WALL HILL ... 5G **129**
Wall Hill Rd. CV5: Alle ... 5H **129**
CV7: Cor ... 2C **128**
Walling Cft. WV14: Cose ... 6H **53**
Wallingford Av. CV11: Nun ... 2M **89**
Wallington Cl. WS3: Blox ... 7H **25**
WALLINGTON HEATH ... 7G **25**
Wallington Heath WS3: Blox ... 7H **25**
Wallis Ct. B13: Mose ... 7B **122**
WALL LANE ... 7B **18**
Wall La. WS14: Wall ... 5D **18**
Wall Mus. ... 7D **18**
Wallows Ind. Est., The
DY5: Brie H ... 4D **96**
Wallows La. WS1: Wals ... 3J **55**
WS2: Wals ... 3J **55**
Wallows Pl. DY5: Brie H ... 4C **96**
Wallows Rd. DY5: Brie H ... 5C **96**
Wallows Wood DY3: Lwr G ... 5A **74**
Wallsgrove Cl. CV32: Lill ... 6B **218**
Wall's Rd. B60: S Prior ... 6J **209**
Wall St. WV1: Wolv ... 7H **37**
Wall Well B63: Hale ... 6M **117**
Wall Well La. B63: Hale ... 6M **117**
Wallwin Ct. CV34: Warw ... 3D **222**
Walmead Cft. B17: Harb ... 2M **119**
Walmer Gro. B23: Erd ... 4B **80**
Walmer Mdw. WS9: A'rdge ... 2H **41**
Walmers, The WS9: A'rdge ... 2H **41**
Walmers Wlk., The
B31: Longb ... 8K **141**
Walmer Way B37: Chel W ... 6J **105**
Walmesley Way B31: N'fld ... 6L **141**
WALMLEY ... 1M **81**
WALMLEY ASH ... 4M **81**
Walmley Ash La. B76: Walm ... 3B **82**
Walmley Ash Rd.
B76: Walm, Min ... 2M **81**
Walmley Cl. B63: Crad ... 2H **117**
B76: Walm ... 1M **81**
Walmley Rd. B76: Walm ... 5L **59**
Walney Cl. LE10: Hinc ... 8H **69**
Walnut Av. WV8: Bilb ... 6G **21**
Walnut Cl. B37: Chel W ... 8H **105**
CV10: Harts ... 1A **88**
CV10: Nun ... 3E **88**
DY9: Pedm ... 8B **116**
WS11: Cann ... 6F **8**
Walnut Cft. CV9: Bad E ... 1C **64**
Walnut Dr. B66: Smeth ... 4B **100**
CV32: Lill ... 6B **218**
WS11: Cann ... 7F **8**
WV3: Wolv ... 8K **35**
Walnut Gro. DY13: Stour S ... 5J **183**
WS14: Lich ... 2M **19**
Walnut Ho. B20: Hand ... 6F **78**
Walnut La. B60: Fins ... 1D **210**
WS10: W'bry ... 7G **55**
Walnut Rd. WS5: Wals ... 5A **56**
Walnut St. CV2: Cov ... 7H **131**
Walnut Tree Cl. CV8: Ken ... 6G **199**
Walnut Wlk. WS13: Lich ... 3E **18**
Walnut Way B31: Longb ... 1M **163**
CV22: Bil ... 8H **179**
Walpole St. WV6: Wolv ... 6A **36**
Walpole Wlk. B70: W Brom ... 8K **77**
WALSAL END ... 6A **148**
Walsal End La. B92: H Ard ... 6M **147**
WALSALL ... 8M **39**
Walsall Bus. Pk. WS9: A'rdge ... 6E **40**
Walsall Enterprise Pk.
WS2: Wals ... 1J **55**
Walsall FC ... 3K **55**
Walsall Gala Baths ... 7M **39**
Walsall Library & Mus. ... 7M 39
(off Tower St.)
Walsall Local History Cen. ... 5L **39**
Walsall New Firms Cen., The
WS1: Wals ... 1K **55**
Walsall Rd.
B42: Gt Barr, P Barr ... 8F **56**
B71: W Brom ... 2K **77**
B74: Four O ... 5D **42**
B74: Lit A ... 3C **42**
WS3: Pels ... 7A **26**
WS4: S'fld ... 8D **26**
WS5: Wals ... 5M **55**
WS6: Gt Wyr ... 4F **14**
WS9: A'rdge ... 6E **40**
WS9: Wals W ... 8D **26**
WS10: Darl ... 3D **54**
WS10: W'bry ... 7L **55**
WS11: Cann ... 1E **14**
WS11: Nort C ... 6M **15**
WS13: Lich, Pip ... 7A **18**
(not continuous)
WS14: Hilt, Lynn, Muck C, Wall
... 2K **27**
WV13: W'hall ... 7B **38**
Walsall Station (Rail) ... 8L **39**
Walsall St. B70: W Brom ... 6K **77**
CV4: Canly ... 2G **173**
WS10: Darl ... 2D **54**
WS10: W'bry ... 6F **54**
WV1: Wolv ... 8E **36** (5M **7**)
WV13: W'hall ... 8B **38**
WV14: Bils ... 3K **53**
WALSALL WOOD ... 5G **27**
Walsall Wood Rd.
WS9: A'rdge ... 7G **27**
Walsgrave Cl. B92: Sol ... 3D **146**
Walsgrave Dr. B92: Sol ... 2D **146**
Walsgrave Gdns.
CV2: W'grve S ... 2A **154**
WALSGRAVE ON SOWE ... 2A **154**
Walsgrave Retail Pk.
CV2: W'grve S ... 2B **154**
Walsgrave Rd. CV2: Cov ... 6F **152**
Walsgrave Triangle Bus. Pk.
CV2: W'grve S ... 8A **132**
Walsham Cft. B34: S End ... 4C **104**
Walsh Dr. B76: Walm ... 5M **59**
WALSHES, THE ... 8F **182**
Walshes Farm Cvn. Pk.
DY13: Stour S ... 7F **182**
Walsh Gro. B23: Erd ... 1D **80**
Walsh La. CV7: Mer ... 7L **127**
Walsingham Dr. CV10: Griff ... 1G **111**
Walsingham St. WS1: Wals ... 8A **40**
Walstead Cl. WS5: Wals ... 4C **56**
Walstead Rd. WS5: Wals ... 4M **55**
Walstead Rd. W. WS5: Wals ... 4L **55**
Walt Dene Cl. B43: Gt Barr ... 7E **56**
Walter Burden Ho.
B66: Smeth ... 6C **100**
Walter Cobb Dr. B73: W Grn ... 8G **59**
Walter Nash Rd. E.
DY11: Kidd ... 8G **157**
Walter Nash Rd. W.
DY11: Kidd ... 8G **157**
Walter Rd. B67: Smeth ... 3L **99**
WV14: Bils ... 6L **53**
Walters Cl. B31: Longb ... 3M **163**
Walter Scott Rd. CV12: Bed ... 8J **111**
Walters Rd. B68: O'bry ... 2G **119**
Walters Row DY1: Dud ... 8G **75**
Walter St. B7: Nech ... 3B **102**
B70: W Brom ... 7L **77**
WS3: Pels ... 8A **26**
Waltham Cl. B61: B'gve ... 8L **187**
Waltham Cres. CV10: Nun ... 5B **88**
Waltham Gro. B44: K'sdng ... 7B **58**
Waltham Ho. B38: K Nor ... 8G **143**
B70: W Brom ... 6K **77**
Walthamstow Ct. DY5: Brie H ... 8D **96**
Walton Av. B65: B'hth ... 1B **118**
Walton Cl. B63: Hale ... 7M **117**
B65: Row R ... 5A **98**
B98: Redd ... 6L **213**
CV3: Bin ... 2L **175**
CV11: Nun ... 2A **112**
DY10: Hartl ... 8C **184**
DY11: Kidd ... 7H **157**
DY13: Stour S ... 8D **182**
Walton Ct. B63: Hale ... 6M **117**
Walton Cres. WV4: E'shll ... 4E **52**
Walton Cft. B91: Sol ... 8B **146**
Walton Dr. DY9: Lye ... 4C **116**
Walton Gdns. WV8: Cod ... 5F **20**
Walton Gro. B30: K Nor ... 7H **143**
Walton Heath WS3: Blox ... 6F **24**
Walton Ho.
B16: Birm ... 7H **101** (6B **4**)
Walton La. DY10: Hartl ... 7D **184**
WALTON POOL ... 7G **139**
Walton Pool La. DY9: Clent ... 6F **138**
Walton Ri. DY9: Clent ... 6G **139**
Walton Rd. B61: B'gve ... 5B **188**
B68: O'bry ... 7H **99**
DY8: Amb ... 3A **116**
DY10: Hartl ... 7C **184**
WR9: Elm L ... 7C **184**
WS9: A'rdge ... 8G **27**
WS10: W'bry ... 7J **55**
WV4: E'shll ... 4E **52**
Walton St. DY4: Tip ... 4M **75**
Wanderers Av. WV2: Wolv ... 3C **52**
Wanderer Wlk. B36: Hodg H ... 8L **81**
Wandle Gro. B11: Tys ... 6G **123**
Wandsbeck B77: Wiln ... 1E **46**
Wandsworth Rd. B44: Gt Barr ... 6L **57**
Wanley Rd. CV3: Cov ... 3D **174**
Wannerton Rd. DY10: Blak ... 8H **137**
Wansbeck Gro. B38: K Nor ... 1E **164**
Wansbeck Wlk. DY3: Sed ... 3F **74**
Wansfell Cl. CV4: Tile H ... 2G **173**
Wanstead Gro. B44: K'sdng ... 8A **58**
Wantage Rd. B46: Col ... 8L **83**
WAPPENBURY ... 2M **219**
Wappenbury Cl. CV2: Cov ... 7J **131**
Wappenbury Rd. CV2: Cov ... 7K **131**
WAPPING
Beoley ... 3B **214**
Studley ... 4K **221**
Wapping La. B98: Beo ... 2B **214**
Warbage La. B61: D'frd ... 8F **160**
DY9: Belb ... 8F **160**
Warbank Cl. B48: A'chu ... 3A **190**
Warbler Pl. DY10: Kidd ... 7A **158**
Ward Cl. B8: W End ... 4G **103**
Warden Av. B73: Bold ... 1F **80**
WARD END ... 3G **103**
Ward End Cl. B8: Salt ... 3F **102**
Ward End Hall Gro.
B8: W End ... 3G **103**
Ward End Ho. B8: W End ... 3G **103**
Ward End Pk. Rd. B8: Salt ... 4F **102**
Wardend Rd. B8: W End ... 3G **103**
Warden Rd. B73: Bold ... 1F **80**
CV6: Cov ... 3B **152**
Wardens, The CV8: Ken ... 4J **199**
Wardens Av., The CV5: Alle ... 3H **151**
Ward Gro. CV34: Warw ... 2J **223**
WV4: E'shll ... 6E **52**
Wardle Cl. B75: Four O ... 5G **43**
Wardle Pl. WS11: Cann ... 4E **8**
Wardles La. WS6: Gt Wyr ... 7F **14**
Wardle St. B79: Tam ... 4A **32**
Wardle Way DY11: W'ley ... 6H **135**
Wardlow Cl. WV4: Penn ... 3B **52**
Wardlow Rd.
B7: Birm ... 4B **102** (1M **5**)
(not continuous)
Wardour Dr. B37: Chel W ... 7J **105**
Wardour Gro. B44: K'sdng ... 1C **80**
Ward Rd. WV4: Penn ... 4D **52**
WV8: Cod ... 6F **20**
Ward St. B19: Birm ... 5L **101** (1G **5**)
WS1: Wals ... 7M **39**
WS12: Hed ... 3F **8**
WV1: Wolv ... 7E **36** (4M **7**)
(not continuous)
WV2: E'shll ... 2H **53**
WV13: W'hall ... 6B **38**
WV14: Cose ... 1H **75**
Wareham Cl. WS3: Wals ... 4M **39**
Wareham Grn.
CV2: W'grve S ... 4A **154**
Wareham Ho. B28: Hall G ... 6E **144**
Wareham Rd. B45: Fran ... 7H **141**
Wareing Dr. B23: Erd ... 1D **80**
Ware Orchard CV23: Barby ... 7J **207**
Ware Rd. CV23: Barby ... 7J **207**
WARESLEY ... 8B **184**
Waresley Ct. Rd.
DY11: Hartl ... 8A **184**
Waresley Ho. Mans.
DY11: Ware ... 8B **184**
WARESLEY PARK ... 8A **184**
Waresley Pk. DY11: Ware ... 8A **184**
Waresley Rd. DY11: Hartl ... 8A **184**
Warewell Cl. WS1: Wals ... 7M **39**
Warewell St. WS1: Wals ... 8M **39**
Waring Cl. DY4: Tip ... 1L **75**
Waring Rd. DY4: Tip ... 1A **76**

Warings, The—Weaman St.

Warings, The WV5: Wom ... 5F **72**
WARING'S GREEN ... 1K **193**
Warings Grn. Rd.
B94: H'ley H ... 1K **193**
Waring Way CV22: Dunc ... 5K **205**
War La. B17: Harb ... 4B **120**
Warley Cft. B68: O'bry ... 1L **119**
Warley Hall Rd. B68: O'bry ... 1K **119**
Warley Rd. B68: O'bry ... 4J **99**
WARLEY WOODS ... 8L **99**
Warmington Cl. CV3: Bin ... 1L **175**
Warmington Dr. B73: S Cold ... 5H **59**
Warmington Gro.
CV34: Warw ... 1B **222**
Warmington Rd. B26: Sheld ... 4C **124**
B47: H'wd ... 3A **166**
Warmley Cl. B91: Sol ... 4D **146**
WV6: Wolv ... 4B **36**
Warmstry Rd. B60: B'gve ... 8D **188**
Warmwell Cl.
CV2: W'grve S ... 5M **153**
Warneford M. CV31: Lea S ... 2A **224**
Warner Cl. CV34: Warw ... 8D **216**
Warner Dr. DY5: Brie H ... 8D **96**
Warner Pl. WS3: Wals ... 3M **39**
Warner Rd. WS3: Wals ... 3M **39**
WS10: W'bry ... 7J **55**
WV8: Cod ... 6F **20**
Warner Row CV6: Cov ... 2G **153**
Warner St. B12: Birm ... 1A **122** (8L **5**)
Warners Wlk. B10: Small H ... 1C **122**
Warnford Wlk. WV4: Penn ... 3J **51**
Warple Rd. B32: Quin ... 4J **119**
Warren Av. B13: Mose ... 7M **121**
WV10: Wolv ... 4F **36**
Warren Cl. B94: Earls ... 1G **193**
CV8: Rytn D ... 8A **176**
CV32: Lea S ... 6M **217**
DY4: Tip ... 2M **75**
WS12: Haz ... 4A **10**
WS14: Lich ... 2L **19**
Warren Dr. B65: Row R ... 4M **97**
B93: Dorr ... 6G **169**
DY3: Sed ... 8C **52**
Warren Farm Rd.
B44: K'sdng ... 1M **79**
Warren Fld. CV8: Rytn D ... 8A **176**
Warren Gdns. DY6: K'wfrd ... 3J **95**
Warren Grn. CV4: Tile H ... 2F **172**
Warren Gro. B8: Salt ... 3E **102**
Warren Hill Rd. B44: K'sdng ... 3M **79**
Warren Ho. Ct. B76: Walm ... 8M **59**
Warren Ho. Wlk. B76: Walm ... 8M **59**
Warren La. B45: Lick ... 6H **163**
Warren Pl. WS8: Bwnhls ... 2G **27**
Warren Rd. B8: Salt ... 3E **102**
B30: Stir ... 2G **143**
B44: K'sdng ... 3A **80**
CV22: Hillm ... 8D **180**
WS7: Burn ... 4G **17**
Warrens Cft. WS5: Wals ... 4D **56**
Warrens End B38: K Nor ... 1F **164**
Warrens Hall Nature Reserve ... 3M **97**
Warrens Hall Rd. DY2: Dud ... 2K **97**
Warrington Cl. B76: Walm ... 8A **60**
Warrington Dr. B23: Erd ... 1D **80**
Warsash Cl. WV1: Wolv ... 1H **53**
WARSTOCK ... 6B **144**
Warstock La. B14: K Hth ... 4A **144**
Warstock Rd. B14: K Hth ... 6A **144**
Warston Av. B32: Bart G ... 7K **119**
WARSTONE ... 2B **24**
Warstone Cl. DY12: Bew ... 5D **156**
Warstone Ct.
B18: Birm ... 5J **101** (2C **4**)
Warstone Dr. B71: W Brom ... 5L **77**
Warstone La.
B18: Birm ... 5H **101** (2B **4**)
Warstone Mdws. DY12: Bew ... 4D **156**
Warstone M. B18: Birm ... 2C **4**
Warstone Pde. E.
B18: Birm ... 5H **101** (1B **4**)
Warstone Rd. WV10: Share ... 7A **14**
WV11: Ess ... 7A **14**
Warstones Cres. WV4: Penn ... 4K **51**
Warstones Dr. WV4: Penn ... 3J **51**
Warstones Gdns. WV4: Penn ... 3J **51**
Warstones Ho. WV4: Penn ... 3K **51**
Warstones Rd. WV4: Penn ... 6J **51**
Warstone Ter. B21: Hand ... 1E **100**
Warstone Twr. B36: Hodg H ... 1J **103**
Wartell Bank DY6: K'wfrd ... 2K **95**
Wartell Bank Ind. Est.
DY6: K'wfrd ... 2L **95**
Warton Cl. CV8: Ken ... 5J **199**
Warton La. B79: Wart ... 2M **49**
CV9: Gren ... 1E **48**
Warwards La. B29: S Oak ... 8G **121**
Warwell La. B26: Yard ... 3K **123**
WARWICK ... 3E **222**
Warwick Arts Cen. ... 5H **173**
Warwick Av. B60: B'gve ... 2A **210**
CV5: Cov ... 2A **174**
WS10: W'bry ... 5J **55**
WV6: Pert ... 6F **34**
WV13: W'hall ... 7D **38**
Warwick By-Pass CV35: Barf ... 8F **222**
CV35: Bud, Guys C, H Mag,
H Hill ... 6B **222**
Warwick Castle ... 3E **222**
Warwick Cl. B68: O'bry ... 7H **99**
B70: W Brom ... 2E **76**
B80: Stud ... 6K **221**
DY3: Lwr G ... 6D **74**
WS11: Cann ... 1F **14**
Warwick Ct. B13: Mose ... 7A **122**
B29: W Cas ... 2B **142**
B37: Chel W ... 7K **105**
B91: Sol ... 4B **146**
CV3: Cov ... 8B **6**
CV32: Lea S ... 8M **217**
Warwick Crest B15: Edg ... 2H **121**
Warwick Cft. B36: Hodg H ... 1J **103**
Warwick Dr. CV9: Ath ... 7K **49**
WV8: Cod ... 5E **20**
Warwick Gdns. B69: Tiv ... 7C **76**
CV10: Nun ... 6E **88**
LE10: Hinc ... 6L **69**
Warwick Gates Bus. Pk.
CV34: H'cte ... 6K **223**
Warwick Grange B91: Sol ... 2M **145**
Warwick Grn. CV12: Bulk ... 8C **112**
Warwick Gro. B92: Olton ... 8L **123**
Warwick Hall Gdns.
B60: B'gve ... 1A **210**
Warwick Ho. Ind. Pk.
CV47: Sou ... 7H **225**
Warwick La.
CV1: Cov ... 7C **152** (5C **6**)
Warwick New Rd.
CV32: Lea S ... 1J **223**
Warwick Pk. Ct.
B92: Olton ... 1M **145**
Warwick Parkway Station (Rail) ... 2A **222**
Warwick Pas.
B2: Birm ... 7L **101** (5G **5**)
Warwick Pl. CV32: Lea S ... 1K **223**
CV47: Sou ... 5H **225**
Warwick Racecourse ... 3C **222**
Warwick Rd. B6: Witt ... 7L **79**
(not continuous)
B11: S'hll ... 4C **122**
(not continuous)
B27: A Grn ... 5H **123**
B68: O'bry ... 2K **119**
B73: New O ... 7C **58**
B77: Amin ... 5E **32**
B91: Sol ... 4A **146**
B93: Chad E, Know ... 4J **169**
CV1: Cov ... 7C **152** (6B **6**)
CV3: Cov ... 1B **174** (8A **6**)
CV8: Ken ... 5F **198**
CV8: S'lgh ... 2B **200**
CV8: Wols ... 6F **176**
CV35: Leek W ... 2F **216**
CV47: Sou ... 6G **225**
DY2: Neth ... 6L **97**
DY8: Word ... 8K **95**
Warwick Rd. Trad. Est.
B11: S'hll ... 5D **122**
Warwick Row
CV1: Cov ... 7C **152** (6B **6**)
Warwickshire County Cricket Club
Edgbaston ... 4K **121**
Warwickshire Mus. ... 3E **222**
Warwickshire Yeomanry Mus. ... 3E **222**
Warwick Station (Rail) ... 2F **222**
Warwick St.
B12: Birm ... 8A **102** (8L **5**)
CV5: Cov ... 1M **173**
CV22: Rugby ... 6A **180**
CV32: Lea S ... 8L **217**
CV47: Sou ... 5H **225**
DY13: Stour S ... 4G **183**
WS4: Wals ... 6M **39**
WV1: Wolv ... 8E **36** (5M **7**)
WV14: Bils ... 4L **53**
Warwick Technology Pk.
CV34: Warw ... 4H **223**
Warwick Ter. CV32: Lea S ... 8L **217**
Warwick Wlk. WS9: A'rdge ... 8G **27**
Wasdale Cl. CV32: Lea S ... 8K **217**
Wasdale Dr. DY6: K'wfrd ... 3L **95**
Wasdale Rd. B31: N'fld ... 5M **141**
WS8: Clay ... 3D **26**
Waseley Hills Country Pk. ... 8C **140**
Waseley Hills Country Pk. Vis. Cen. ... 8C **140**
Waseley Rd. B45: Rubery ... 1E **162**
Washbourne Rd.
CV31: W'nsh ... 6A **224**
Washbrook La. CV5: Alle ... 7G **129**
WS11: Nort C ... 5J **15**
Washbrook Rd. B8: W End ... 3G **103**
WASHFORD ... 1L **221**
Washford Dr. B98: Redd ... 2J **221**
Washford Gro. B25: Yard ... 1H **123**
Washford Ind. Est.
B98: Redd ... 1L **221**
Washford La. B98: Redd ... 1K **221**
Washington Cen. DY2: Neth ... 6K **97**
Washington Cl. LE9: Barw ... 3A **70**
Washington Ct. B1: Birm ... 7D **4**
WV3: Wolv ... 8K **35**
Washington Dr. B20: Hand ... 6H **79**
Washington St.
B1: Birm ... 8J **101** (7D **4**)
DY2: Neth ... 6K **97**
DY11: Kidd ... 4J **157**
Washington St. Ind. Est.
DY2: Neth ... 6K **97**
Washington Wharf
B1: Birm ... 8J **101** (7D **4**)
Wash La. B25: Yard ... 2J **123**
WASHWOOD HEATH ... 3E **102**
Washwood Heath Rd.
B8: Salt ... 4D **102**
Wasperton Cl. B36: Cas B ... 1B **104**
CV3: Bin ... 1M **175**
Wassell Ct. B63: Hale ... 7L **117**
Wassell Dr. DY12: Bew ... 5C **156**
Wassell Gro. Bus. Cen.
DY9: Hag ... 7G **117**
Wassell Gro. La. DY9: Hag ... 1F **138**
Wassell Rd. B63: Hale ... 7L **117**
DY9: W'cte ... 7F **116**
WV14: Bils ... 2K **53**
Wassell Wood Nature Reserve ... 2C **156**
Waste La. CV6: Cov ... 8L **129**
CV7: Bal C ... 4L **171**
CV9: Ath, Gren ... 6E **48**
Wast Hill Gro. B38: K Nor ... 2F **164**
Wast Hills La. B38: Hopw ... 5D **164**
B48: Hopw ... 5D **164**
Waswater Ct. WV6: Pert ... 5F **34**
Watchbury Cl. B36: Cas B ... 8C **82**
Watch Cl. CV1: Cov ... 6B **152** (4A **6**)
Watchmaker Ct.
CV1: Cov ... 7B **152** (5A **6**)
Watchman Av. DY5: Quar B ... 2F **116**
Watchtower Rd.
DY13: Stour S ... 3K **183**
Watcombe Rd. CV2: Cov ... 1L **153**
Waterbridge La. WV5: Wom ... 2E **72**
Waterbrook Way WS11: Cann ... 3E **14**
Watercall Av. CV3: Cov ... 4C **174**
Water Dale WV3: Wolv ... 7L **35**
Waterdale B90: Ches G ... 4K **167**
WV5: Wom ... 4E **72**
Waterfall Cl. B66: Smeth ... 2L **99**
CV7: Mer ... 8J **127**
Waterfall La. B64: Old H ... 8A **98**
B65: B'hth ... 8A **98**
Waterfall La. Trad. Est.
B64: Old H ... 8A **98**
Waterfall Rd. DY5: Brie H ... 2C **116**
Waterfall Way LE9: Barw ... 4M **69**
Waterfield Cl. DY4: Tip ... 4J **75**
Waterfield Ho. WV5: Wom ... 2H **73**
Waterfield Way B26: Sheld ... 2C **124**
LE10: Burb ... 4H **91**
Waterford Ct. B23: Erd ... 5B **80**
Waterford Pl. B33: Kitts G ... 6D **104**
Waterford Rd. DY6: K'wfrd ... 2K **95**
Waterfront, The DY5: Brie H ... 5E **96**
Waterfront Bus. Pk.
DY5: Brie H ... 6D **96**
Waterfront E. DY5: Brie H ... 5E **96**
Waterfront Vw.
DY13: Stour S ... 6G **183**
Waterfront Way DY5: Brie H ... 5E **96**
WS2: Wals ... 7K **39**
Waterfront W. DY5: Brie H ... 5E **96**
Watergall Cl. CV47: Sou ... 6J **225**
Waterglade La. WV13: W'hall ... 8A **38**
Waterhaynes Cl.
B45: Rubery ... 3G **163**
Waterhead Cl. WV10: Bush ... 7G **23**
Waterhead Dr. WV10: Bush ... 7G **23**
Waterlaide Cl. DY11: Hartl ... 7A **184**
Waterlaide Rd. DY11: Hartl ... 7A **184**
Water La. B71: W Brom ... 2M **77**
Waterlilly Cl. WS12: Hed ... 6L **9**
Waterlinks Blvd. B6: Aston ... 2A **102**
Waterlinks Ho. B7: Birm ... 1K **5**
Waterloo Av. B37: F'bri ... 5H **105**
Waterloo Blvd. WS12: Hed ... 5L **9**
Waterloo Ct. CV34: Warw ... 1G **223**
Waterloo Ind. Est. B37: F'bri ... 4H **105**
Waterloo Pas. B2: Birm ... 7K **101**
Waterloo Pl. CV32: Lea S ... 8M **217**
Waterloo Rd. B14: K Hth ... 1L **143**
B25: Yard ... 3H **123**
B66: Smeth ... 6A **100**
DY12: Bew ... 3B **156**
LE10: Hinc ... 1J **91**
WV1: Wolv ... 7C **36** (3H **7**)
Waterloo Rd. Junc.
WV1: Wolv ... 7C **36** (3H **7**)
Waterloo St.
B2: Birm ... 7K **101** (5E **4**)
CV1: Cov ... 5E **152**
CV31: Lea S ... 2B **224**
DY1: Dud ... 1H **97**
DY4: Tip ... 4L **75**
DY10: Kidd ... 3L **157**
Waterloo St. E. DY4: Tip ... 4M **75**
Waterloo Ter.
WV1: Wolv ... 6B **36** (1G **7**)
Waterman Rd. CV6: Cov ... 4F **152**
Watermarque
B16: Birm ... 7H **101** (6A **4**)
Watermead Grange
WS8: Bwnhls ... 2E **26**
Watermeadow Dr. WS4: S'fld ... 8D **26**
Watermere WS4: S'fld ... 1D **40**
Water Mill Cl. B29: S Oak ... 6D **120**
Watermill Cl. WV10: F'hses ... 6D **22**
Water Mill Cres. B76: Walm ... 8M **59**
Water Mint Cl. WS12: Wim ... 5L **9**
WATER ORTON ... 6H **83**
Water Orton La. B76: Min ... 4D **82**
Water Orton Rd. B36: Cas B ... 1C **104**
Water Orton Station (Rail) ... 6G **83**
Water Rd. DY3: Gorn ... 7C **74**
Watersbridge Gdns.
CV10: Nun ... 8J **89**
Waters Dr. B74: Four O ... 6D **42**
Waters Edge, The
B1: Birm ... 7J **101** (6C **4**)
Waters End LE9: Barw ... 4A **70**
Watersfield Gdns.
CV31: Lea S ... 2C **224**
Waterside B15: Birm ... 8J **101** (8C **4**)
B43: Gt Barr ... 2E **78**
B78: Pole ... 3K **49**
CV6: Longf ... 3J **131**
Waterside Cl. B9: Birm ... 7C **102**
B24: Erd ... 4A **82**
Waterside Ct. B16: Birm ... 5A **4**
B77: Amin ... 4F **32**
CV31: Lea S ... 3B **224**
Waterside Dr. B18: Win G ... 4F **100**
CV21: Rugby ... 3C **180**
Waterside Est. DY2: Neth ... 6J **97**
Waterside Grange
DY10: Kidd ... 1L **157**
Waterside Ind.
Est. B65: Row R ... 5M **97**
WV2: E'shll ... 3G **53**
Waterside Orchard Cvn. Pk.
B48: Hopw ... 6B **164**
Waterside Pk. DY4: Tip ... 2D **76**
Waterside Vw. B18: Hock ... 4G **101**
DY5: Brie H ... 1B **116**
Waterside Way WS8: Bwnhls ... 7C **16**
WV9: Pend ... 6A **22**
Waters Mead Cl. WS12: Wim ... 5L **9**
Watersmeet Gro. CV2: Cov ... 3H **153**
Watersmeet Ho. B78: Faz ... 1B **46**
Watersmeet Rd. CV2: Cov ... 3H **153**
Waterson Cft. B37: Chel W ... 6K **105**
Water St. B3: Birm ... 6K **101** (3E **4**)
B70: W Brom ... 7K **77**
DY6: K'wfrd ... 2K **95**
WS7: C Ter ... 2E **16**
WV10: Wolv ... 6D **36** (1L **7**)
Waters Vw. WS3: Pels ... 4B **26**
Water Twr. La. CV8: Ken ... 3F **198**
Waterward Cl. B17: Harb ... 4C **120**
Waterway Ct. B14: Yard W ... 6C **144**
Waterways Dr. B69: O'bry ... 8E **76**
Waterways Gdns. DY8: Word ... 8L **95**
Waterworks Cotts.
B71: W Brom ... 2L **77**
Water Works Dr. B31: N'fld ... 4K **141**
Waterworks Rd. B16: Edg ... 8F **100**
Waterworks St. B6: Aston ... 1B **102**
Watery Ga. La. LE9: Thurl ... 1M **71**
(not continuous)
Watery La. B32: Quin ... 6G **119**
B46: Neth W ... 7C **84**
B48: A'chu, Hopw ... 6E **164**
(not continuous)
B67: Smeth ... 4A **100**
B93: Know ... 6L **169**
B94: Earls ... 5J **167**
B95: Ullen ... 6J **215**
B98: Redd ... 8G **213**
CV6: Cov ... 5A **130**
CV7: Cor ... 5E **128**
CV7: Ker E ... 5M **129**
CV8: Bubb ... 4G **201**
CV9: Bad E ... 7A **48**
CV35: Sher ... 8A **222**
DY4: Tip ... 4M **75**
(not continuous)
DY8: Word ... 7L **95**
DY9: Brme ... 2M **159**
DY13: Stour S ... 7H **183**
(not continuous)
WS1: Wals ... 2K **55**
(not continuous)
WS13: Chor ... 5H **11**
WS13: Lich ... 5J **13**
WS15: Gent ... 5H **11**
WV8: Cod ... 5G **21**
WV13: W'hall ... 6K **37**
Watery La. Ind. Est.
WV13: W'hall ... 6L **37**
Watery La. Middleway
B9: Birm ... 7B **102** (5M **5**)
WATFORD GAP ... 3F **42**
Watford Gap Rd. WS14: Lit H ... 2G **43**
Watford Rd. B30: K Nor ... 4F **142**
Wathan Av. WV14: Cose ... 7F **52**
Wathen Rd. CV32: Lea S ... 7A **218**
CV34: Warw ... 1E **222**
Watkins Gdns. B31: N'fld ... 6B **142**
Watkins Rd. WV12: W'hall ... 4C **38**
Watland Grn. B34: Stech ... 4A **104**
Watling Cl. LE10: Burb ... 4J **91**
Watling Ct. CV11: Nun ... 6L **89**
Watling Cres. CV23: Clift D ... 1J **181**
Watling Dr. LE10: Burb ... 5J **91**
Watling Rd. CV8: Ken ... 3H **199**
Watling St. B77: Two G, Wiln ... 1D **46**
B78: Dord ... 3K **47**
B78: Hints ... 4A **30**
CV9: Ath, Gren ... 6D **48**
Watling St. CV9: Man, With ... 2M **65**
CV10: Cald, Harts ... 5F **66**
CV10: Nun ... 7K **67**
CV11: Nun ... 8A **68**
CV23: Clift D, Hillm ... 1J **181**
WS8: Bwnhls ... 8D **16**
WS11: Cann, Four C, Nort C ... 2A **14**
(not continuous)
WS14: Lich, Muck C, Shens,
Wall, W'frd ... 7J **17**
Watling St. Bus. Pk.
WS3: Lit W ... 7A **16**
Watney Gro. B44: K'sdng ... 1C **80**
Watson Cl. B72: W Grn ... 7J **59**
CV34: Warw ... 8E **216**
Watson Rd. B8: W End ... 4F **102**
CV5: Cov ... 7K **151**
WS10: Mox ... 4A **54**
WV10: F'hses ... 7B **22**
WV14: Cose ... 7G **53**
Watson Rd. E. B7: Nech ... 2D **102**
Watsons Cl. DY2: Dud ... 1L **97**
Watson's Grn. Flds.
DY2: Dud ... 1M **97**
Watson's Grn. Rd. DY2: Dud ... 8L **75**
Watson Way CV7: Bal C ... 2J **171**
Watt Cl. B61: B'gve ... 8M **187**
Watt Ct. DY13: Stour S ... 4G **183**
Wattisham Sq. B35: Cas V ... 5A **82**
Wattis Rd. B67: Smeth ... 7A **100**
Wattle Grn. B70: W Brom ... 6F **76**
Wattle Rd. B70: W Brom ... 6F **76**
Watton Cl. WV14: Cose ... 8G **53**
Watton Grn. B35: Cas V ... 7A **82**
(not continuous)
Watton La. B46: Wat O ... 7J **83**
Wattons La. CV47: Sou ... 5H **225**
(not continuous)
Wattons Lodge CV47: Sou ... 5G **225**
Watton St. B70: W Brom ... 7K **77**
Watt Rd. B23: Erd ... 5E **80**
DY4: Tip ... 1B **76**
Watts Cl. DY4: Tip ... 4J **75**
Watts La. CV21: Hillm ... 1H **207**
Watts Rd. B10: Small H ... 1D **122**
B80: Stud ... 7L **221**
Watt St. B21: Hand ... 2D **100**
B66: Smeth ... 3B **100**
Wattville Av. B21: Hand ... 1C **100**
Wattville Rd.
B66: Hand, Smeth ... 2B **100**
Watwood Rd. B28: Hall G ... 6F **144**
B90: Hall G, Shir ... 6F **144**
Waugh Cl. B37: Chel W ... 7H **105**
Waugh Dr. B63: Hale ... 1K **139**
Wavebeck Ct. CV23: Long L ... 4H **179**
Waveley Rd. CV1: Cov ... 6A **152**
Wavell Rd. B8: Salt ... 4E **102**
DY5: Quar B ... 2F **116**
WS2: Wals ... 7E **38**
Wavendon Cl.
CV2: W'grve S ... 8M **131**
Waveney B77: Wiln ... 1E **46**
Waveney Av. WV6: Pert ... 5E **34**
Waveney Cl. LE10: Hinc ... 1G **91**
Waveney Cft. B36: Cas B ... 1F **104**
Waveney Gro. WS11: Cann ... 8B **8**
Wavenham Cl. B74: Four O ... 4E **42**
Wavere Ct. CV21: Brow ... 2D **180**
Waverhill Rd. B21: Hand ... 2F **100**
Waverley Av. B43: Gt Barr ... 5H **57**
CV11: Nun ... 8L **89**
Waverley Cl. DY10: Kidd ... 1M **157**
Waverley Cres. B62: Roms ... 5M **139**
WV2: Penn ... 3B **52**
WV4: E'shll ... 6F **52**
Waverley Edge CV8: Bubb ... 5H **201**
Waverley Gdns. WV5: Wom ... 2H **73**
Waverley Gro. B91: Sol ... 6M **145**
Waverley Rd. B10: Small H ... 2D **122**
CV8: Ken ... 6G **199**
CV21: Hillm ... 8G **181**
CV31: Lea S ... 3A **224**
WS3: Blox ... 7F **24**
WS10: Darl ... 3D **54**
Waverley Sq. CV11: Nun ... 1M **111**
Waverley St. DY2: Dud ... 1G **97**
Waverley Wlk. WS14: Lich ... 3H **19**
Waverton M. CV31: Lea S ... 3C **224**
Wavy Tree Cl. CV34: Warw ... 2D **222**
Waxland Rd. B63: Hale ... 7B **118**
Way Cft. DY11: Kidd ... 1G **183**
Wayfield Cl. B90: Shir ... 6J **145**
Wayfield Rd. B90: Shir ... 6J **145**
Wayford Dr. B72: W Grn ... 2K **81**
Wayford Glade WV13: W'hall ... 1M **53**
Wayford Gro. B8: W End ... 5H **103**
Waynecroft Rd. B43: Gt Barr ... 7E **56**
Wayside B37: Mars G ... 1F **124**
WV8: Pend ... 7L **21**
Wayside Acres WV8: Cod ... 7F **20**
Wayside Dr. B74: Lit A ... 6C **42**
B75: R'ley ... 6L **43**
Wayside Gdns. WV12: W'hall ... 5E **38**
Wayside Wlk. WS2: Wals ... 6G **39**
Waystone La. DY9: Belb ... 5D **160**
Wealden Hatch WV10: Bush ... 5E **22**
Wealdstone Dr. DY3: Lwr G ... 7D **74**
Weale Gro. CV34: Warw ... 8F **216**
Weaman St. B4: Birm ... 6L **101** (3G **5**)

Weates Yd.—Westhaven Dr.

Weates Yd. B27: A Grn 5J 123
Weatheroak Cl. B97: Redd 8A 212
WEATHEROAK HILL 8H 165
Weatheroak Hill B48: A'chu . . .8H 165
Weatheroak Rd. B11: S'hll 4C 122
Weather Oaks B17: Harb 4B 120
Weatheroaks B62: Quin 2G 119
WS9: Wals W 5H 27
Weaver Av. B26: Sheld 3B 124
B76: Walm 8A 60
Weaver Cl. DY5: P'ntt 3A 96
Weaver Ct. B75: R'ley 6L 43
Weaver Dr. CV23: Long L 5J 179
Weaver Gro. WV13: W'hall 7D 38
Weaver Rd. LE9: Earl S 1G 71
Weavers Cl. B97: Redd 5D 220
Weavers Hill B97: Redd 5D 220
Weavers Ri. DY2: Neth 6K 97
Weavers Wlk. CV6: Cov 1H 153
Weavers Wharf DY11: Kidd 3K 157
Weaving Gdns. WS11: Cann 8E 8
Webb Av. WV6: Pert 4E 34
Webbcroft Rd. B33: Stech 5L 103
Webb Dr. CV23: Brow 1D 180
Webb Ellis Bus. Pk.
CV21: Rugby 5B 180
Webb Ellis Rd. CV22: Rugby . . .7L 179
Webb La. B28: Hall G 3E 144
Webb Rd. DY4: Tip 2C 76
Webb St. CV10: Nun 6C 88
WV13: W'hall 7M 37
WV14: Cose 7J 53
Webbs Way LE9: S Stan 7K 71
WEBHEATH 8A 212
Webley Ri. WV10: Bush 5F 22
Webnor Ind. Est. WV2: E'shll . . .3G 53
Webster Av. CV8: Ken 3H 199
Webster Cl. B11: S'brk 3B 122
B72: W Grn 2H 81
Webster Rd. WS2: Wals 4K 39
WV13: W'hall 6A 38
Webster St. CV6: Cov 2E 152
Webster Wlk. WS11: Cann 5G 9
Webster Way B76: Walm 8A 60
Weddell Wynd WV14: Bils 8L 53
WEDDINGTON 2J 89
Weddington Ind. Est.
CV10: Nun 4J 89
Weddington La.
CV10: Cald, Nun 5G 67
Weddington Ter. CV10: Nun 4K 89
Wedgbury Way DY5: Brie H 8B 96
Wedge Ct. *WS1: Wals 8M 39*
(off Union St.)
Wedge St. WS1: Wals 7M 39
Wedgewood Av. B70: W Brom . . .2F 76
Wedgewood Cl.
CV2: W'grve S 1L 153
WS7: Burn 2J 17
WV5: Wom 2F 72
Wedgewood Ct. *WS4: S'fld 8C 26*
(off Green La.)
Wedgewood Ho. B37: F'bri 5H 105
Wedgewood Pl. B70: W Brom . . .2F 76
Wedgewood Rd. B32: Quin 4J 119
Wedge Woods CV5: Cov 1M 173
Wedgnock Grn. CV34: Warw . . .1D 222
Wedgnock Ind. Est.
CV34: Warw 8B 216
Wedgnock La. CV34: Warw 1C 222
Wedgwood Cl. WV1: Wolv 8G 37
Wedgwood Dr. B20: Hand 7H 79
Wedmore Rd. B73: Bold 8F 58
WEDNESBURY 7F 54
Wednesbury Great Western Street
Stop (MM) 7E 54
Wednesbury Leisure Cen. 6E 54
Wednesbury Mus. & Art Gallery
. . . . .7F 54
Wednesbury New Ent. Cen.
WS10: Mox 6C 54
Wednesbury Oak Rd.
DY4: Tip 8A 54
Wednesbury Parkway Stop (MM)
. . . . .7D 54
Wednesbury Rd. WS2: Wals 2J 55
Wednesbury Trad. Est.
WS10: W'bry 5E 54
WEDNESFIELD 4K 37
Wednesfield High Sports Cen.
. . . . .4L 37
Wednesfield Rd.
WV10: Wolv 6D 36 (2L 7)
WV13: W'hall 6A 38
Wednesfield Way
WV10: Wolv 5G 37
WV11: Wed 5G 37
Wednesfield Way Ind. Est.
WV11: Wed 5K 37
Wedon Cl. CV4: Tile H 2E 172
WEEFORD 5A 30
Weeford Dell B75: R'ley 6L 43
Weeford Dr. B20: Hand 5F 78
WEEFORD JUNC. 3K 29
Weeford Rd. B75: R'ley 7L 43
Weeford Sq. WS14: W'frd 5M 29
Weethley Ho. *B97: Redd 5A 212*
(off Lock Cl.)
Weights La. B97: Redd 2B 212
Weights La. Bus. Pk.
B97: Redd 1C 212
Weilerswist Dr.
CV31: W'nsh 5M 223
Weirbrook Cl. B29: W Cas 2B 142
Weland Cl. B46: Wat O 7H 83
Welbeck Av. LE10: Burb 5K 91
WV10: Bush 2D 36
Welbeck Cl. B62: Quin 4E 118
Welbeck Dr. DY11: Kidd 4H 157
WS4: Rus 2D 40
Welbeck Gro. B23: Erd 4B 80
Welbury Gdns. WV6: Wolv 4M 35
Welby Ga. CV7: Bal C 4H 171
Welby Rd. B28: Hall G 8F 122
Welch Cl. DY4: Tip 2B 76
Welches Cl. B31: N'fld 4B 142
Welch Ga. DY12: Bew 6A 156
Welcombe Dr. B76: Walm 2M 81
Welcombe Gro. B91: Sol 6M 145
Welcome Dr. B61: Cats 8A 162
Welcome St. CV9: Ath 1L 65
Welford Av. B26: Yard 1M 123
Welford Cl. B98: Redd 4F 220
Welford Gro. B74: Four O 6F 42
Welford Pl. CV6: Cov 2D 152
Welford Rd. B20: Hand 1G 101
B73: New O 8E 58
B77: Dost 4C 46
B90: Shir 5J 145
CV21: Rugby 5C 180
Welgarth Av. CV6: Cov 3L 151
Welham Cft. B90: M'path 3A 168
Welland Cl. CV23: Long L 4H 179
Welland Dr. DY8: Amb 1A 116
Welland Gro. B24: Erd 6J 81
WV13: W'hall 7C 38
Welland Rd. B63: Hale 7A 118
CV1: Cov 8F 152
Welland Way B76: Walm 2A 82
Well Cl. B36: Hodg H 1L 103
B97: Redd 4E 220
Wellcroft Rd. B34: S End 2A 104
Wellcroft St. WS10: W'bry 6F 54
Wellesbourne B79: Tam 1C 32
Wellesbourne Cl. B98: Redd . . .5E 212
WV3: Wolv 1H 51
Wellesbourne Dr.
WV14: Cose 2H 75
Wellesbourne Rd. B20: Hand . . .8H 79
CV5: E Grn 6G 151
Wellesbourne Twr. B5: Birm . . .1L 121
Wellesley Dr. DY4: Tip 4M 75
Wellesley Gdns. B13: Mose . . .8D 122
Wellesley Rd. B68: O'bry 3H 99
Wellfield Cl. CV7: Bal C 4K 171
WS11: Cann 2B 14
Wellfield Gdns. DY2: Dud 3L 97
Wellfield Rd. B28: Hall G 3H 145
WS9: A'rdge 1H 41
Wellhead La. B42: P Barr 7L 79
Wellhead Way B6: Witt 7L 79
Wellington Av. WV3: Wolv 2M 51
Wellington Cl. DY6: K'wfrd 5L 95
LE10: Burb 5L 91
Wellington Ct. B20: Hand 7J 79
B32: Harb 4M 119
B64: Old H 7M 97
(off Vine Gdns.)
DY11: Kidd 4J 157
Wellington Cres. B20: Hand 7H 79
Wellington Dr. WS11: Cann 8B 8
Wellington Gdns. CV1: Cov 7B 152
Wellington Gro. B91: Sol 3M 145
Wellington Ho. B32: Quin 5M 119
Wellington Ind. Est.
WV14: Cose 2J 75
Wellington Pas. B2: Birm 5F 4
Wellington Pl. WV13: W'hall . . .6M 37
Wellington Rd. B15: Edg 3H 121
B20: Hand 7H 79
B60: B'gve 1A 210
B67: Smeth 6A 100
CV32: Lill 6B 218
DY1: Dud 1H 97
DY4: Tip 5A 76
WS5: Wals 3C 56
WV14: Bils 2H 53
Wellington St. B18: Win G 3D 100
B64: Old H 7M 97
B66: Smeth 3D 100
B69: O'bry 3H 99
B71: W Brom 5J 77
B98: Redd 5E 212
CV1: Cov 5E 152 (2F 6)
WS2: Wals 2H 55
Wellington St. Sth.
B70: W Brom 5J 77
Wellington Ter. B19: Loz 2H 101
WV13: W'hall 6M 37
Wellington Twr. B31: N'fld 8A 142
Wellington Way B35: Cas V 7B 82
Well La. B5: Birm 7M 101 (6H 5)
B60: B'gve 7A 188
B94: Tan A 8G 193
LE10: Hinc 8K 69
WR9: Rush 7H 185
WS3: Blox 2L 39
WS6: Gt Wyr 8G 15
WV11: Wed 5J 37
Wellman Cft. B29: S Oak 8D 120
Wellman's Rd. WV13: W'hall . . .8C 38
Well Mdw. B45: Redn 3G 163
Wellmeadow Gro.
B92: H Ard 2A 148
Wellmead Wlk. B45: Rubery . . .1F 162
Well Pl. WS3: Blox 1L 39
Wells Av. WS10: Darl 3D 54
Wells Cl. CV10: Gall C 5M 87
DY4: Tip 8A 54
DY11: Kidd 3G 157
WS11: Cann 4E 8
WV6: Pert 5D 34
Wells Ct. B71: W Brom 1K 77
CV3: Cov 2F 174
DY2: Neth 4J 97
(off Meeting St.)
Wellsford Av. B92: Olton 5A 124
WELLS GREEN 4B 124
Wells Grn. Rd. B92: Olton 5M 123
Wells Grn. Shop. Cen.
B26: Sheld 5B 124
Well Spring Cl. CV9: Ath 1M 65
Wells Rd. B65: Row R 5E 98
B92: Sol 5C 124
DY5: Brie H 6B 96
WV4: Penn 4M 51
WV14: Bils 6L 53
Wells St. CV21: Rugby 6B 180
Wells Twr. B16: Birm 7G 101
Well St. B19: Birm 4J 101
CV1: Cov 6C 152 (3C 6)
WS10: Darl 3E 54
Wells Wlk. B37: Mars G 8G 105
Welney Gdns. WV9: Pend 6A 22
Welsby Av. B43: Gt Barr 2E 78
Welsh Cl. CV34: Warw 7E 216
Welsh Ho. Farm Rd.
B32: Quin, Harb 5M 119
Welshmans Hill B73: New O 7B 58
Welsh Rd. CV2: Cov 5H 153
CV32: Cubb 5E 218
CV33: Cubb, Off 8J 219
Welsh Rd. E. CV47: Sou 5J 225
Welton Cl. B76: Walm 7A 60
Welton Pl. CV22: Hillm 1D 206
Welton Rd. CV34: Warw 8D 216
Welwyndale Rd. B72: W Grn 3J 81
Welwyn Rd. LE10: Hinc 8M 69
Wembley Gro. B25: Yard 1J 123
Wembley La. WS7: C Ter 1D 16
Wembrook Cl. CV11: Nun 7K 89
Wembrook Ho. CV11: Nun 7L 89
Wembury B77: Amin 4E 32
Wem Gdns. WV11: Wed 3K 37
Wendell Crest WV10: Bush 5F 22
Wendiburgh St. CV4: Canly 2G 173
Wendover Dr. LE10: Hinc 5L 69
Wendover Ho. B31: Longb 1M 163
Wendover Ri. CV5: Cov 5J 151
Wendover Rd. B23: Erd 2C 80
B65: Row R 4A 98
WV4: E'shll 7F 52
Wendron Cl. B60: B'gve 7B 188
Wendron Gro. B14: K Hth 5K 143
Wenlock B77: Glas 6D 32
Wenlock Av. WV3: Wolv 1L 51
Wenlock Cl. B63: Hale 7K 117
DY3: Sed 2C 74
Wenlock Dr. B61: B'gve 4A 188
Wenlock Gdns. WS3: Wals 4L 39
Wenlock Rd. B20: Hand 8M 79
DY8: Amb 3B 116
Wenlock Way CV10: Nun 5B 88
DY13: Stour S 8E 182
Wenman St. B12: Bal H 3M 121
Wensley Cft. B90: Shir 3H 145
Wensleydale Av. LE9: Barw 4A 70
Wensleydale Cl. LE9: Barw 4A 70
Wensleydale Rd. B42: P Barr . . .3G 79
Wensley Rd. B26: Sheld 3M 123
Wensum Cl. LE10: Hinc 1H 91
Wentbridge Rd. WV1: Wolv 8J 37
Wentworth Av. B36: Cas B 1B 104
Wentworth Cl. LE10: Hinc 6L 69
WS7: Burn 2J 17
Wentworth Ct. B24: Erd 7F 80
B74: Four O 8H 43
Wentworth Dr. B60: B'wll 4G 189
B69: Tiv 2A 98
CV6: Cov 5B 130
CV11: Nun 8A 90
WS14: Lich 4K 19
Wentworth Ga. B17: Harb 3B 120
Wentworth Gro. WV6: Pert 4D 34
Wentworth Pk. Av.
B17: Harb 3B 120
Wentworth Ri. B62: Hale 5D 118
Wentworth Rd. B17: Harb 3A 120
B74: Four O 2G 59
B92: Olton 6M 123
CV22: Bil 8L 179
CV31: Lea S 3D 224
DY8: Woll 2K 115
WS3: Blox 5F 24
WV10: Bush 7E 22
Wentworth Way B32: Bart G . . .6M 119
Wenyon Cl. DY4: Tip 5B 76
Weoley Av. B29: S Oak 7C 120
WEOLEY CASTLE 8M 119
Weoley Castle 7A 120
Weoley Castle Rd.
B29: W Cas 8M 119
Weoley Hill B29: S Oak 1C 142
Weoley Pk. Rd. B29: S Oak 8B 120
WERGS 3F 34
Wergs Dr. WV6: Tett 2G 35
Wergs Hall Rd. WV6: Tett 8F 20
WV8: Cod 8F 20
Wergs Rd. WV6: Tett 3F 34
Werneth Gro. WS3: Blox 5G 25
Wesley Av. B63: Crad 1H 117
DY13: Stour S 8E 182
WS6: C Hay 6D 14
WV8: Bilb 7H 21
Wesley Cl. B64: Old H 8M 97
LE9: Sap 2L 93
WV5: Wom 4F 72
Wesley Ct. B16: Edg 6D 100
B64: Old H 1M 117
WS11: Cann 8E 8
WV13: W'hall 8L 37
Wesley Gro. WS10: W'bry 6E 54
Wesley Ho. *WS2: Wals 2J 55*
(off Oxford St.)
Wesley Pl. DY4: Tip 2C 76
WS12: Hed 2J 9
Wesley Rd. B23: Erd 4F 80
CV21: Hillm 1G 207
DY5: P'ntt 4B 96
WV8: Bilb 7H 21
WV12: W'hall 3C 38
Wesley's Fold WS10: Darl 3D 54
Wesley St. B69: O'bry 1G 99
B70: W Brom 6H 77
WV2: E'shll 3G 53
WV14: Bils 7L 53
Wesley Wlk. B60: B'gve 2L 209
LE10: Burb 4A 92
Wesley Way B77: Amin 5E 32
Wessenden B77: Wiln 2H 47
Wessex Cl. CV12: Bed 5G 111
WS8: Bwnhls 2F 26
Wessex Ct. B79: Shut 2M 33
Wessex Dr. WS11: Cann 7F 8
Wessex Rd. WV2: E'shll 3F 52
Wesson Gdns. B63: Hale 6A 118
Wesson Rd. WS10: Darl 1C 54
Westacre WV13: W'hall 8M 37
Westacre Cres. WV3: Wolv 1H 51
W. Acre Dr. DY5: Quar B 1F 116
Westacre Gdns. B33: Stech . . .6M 103
West Av. B20: Hand 5F 78
B36: Cas B 1D 104
B69: Tiv 2B 98
B98: Redd 6E 212
CV2: Cov 7G 153
CV7: Ker E 4A 130
CV12: Bed 7K 111
WV11: Wed 3J 37
West Blvd. B32: Quin, Bart G . . .3L 119
Westbourne Av.
B34: Hodg H 3L 103
WS6: C Hay 5E 14
WS11: Cann 7D 8
Westbourne Cl. B61: B'gve 8L 187
Westbourne Ct. *WS4: Wals 6A 40*
(off Lichfield Rd.)
Westbourne Cres. B15: Edg . . .1G 121
WS7: Burn 2H 17
Westbourne Gdns. B15: Edg . . .2G 121
Westbourne Gro. B21: Hand . . .2F 100
CV22: Bil 8M 179
Westbourne Rd. B15: Edg 2F 120
B21: Hand 8D 78
B62: B'hth 2E 118
B70: W Brom 7H 77
B92: Olton 1M 145
WS4: Wals 5M 39
WS10: Darl 2F 54
WV4: Penn 4A 52
Westbourne St. DY12: Bew 6B 156
WS4: Wals 6M 39
Westbourne Ter. B61: B'gve . . .8L 187
WEST BROMWICH 6K 77
West Bromwich Albion FC 8B 78
West Bromwich Central Stop (MM)
. . . . .7J 77
West Bromwich Crematorium
B71: W Brom 2A 78
W. Bromwich Parkway
B70: W Brom 6H 77
(Dartmouth St.)
B70: W Brom 8L 77
(Springfield Cres.)
W. Bromwich Ringway
B70: W Brom 6K 77
(New St.)
B70: W Brom 6J 77
(St Michael St.)
W. Bromwich Rd. WS1: Wals . . .3L 55
(not continuous)
W. Bromwich St. B69: O'bry 8F 76
WS1: Wals 1L 55
Westbrook Av. WS9: A'rdge 4E 40
Westbrook Ct. CV5: E Grn 5G 151
Westbrook Way WV5: Wom 4F 72
Westbury Av. WS10: W'bry 3F 54
Westbury Ct. CV34: Warw 2G 223
DY5: Brie H 7D 96
(off Lit. Potter St.)
Westbury Rd. B17: Edg 6B 100
CV5: Cov 4K 151
CV10: Nun 6D 88
WS10: W'bry 3F 54
Westbury St.
WV1: Wolv 7D 36 (3K 7)
West Cannock Way WS12: Hed . . .1K 9
WEST CHADSMOOR 3C 8
Westcliff Dr. CV34: Warw 7E 216
Westcliffe Dr. CV3: Cov 4B 174
Westcliffe Pl. B31: N'fld 5M 141
West Cl. LE10: Burb 2K 91
Westcombe Gro.
B32: Bart G 8G 119
W. Coppice Rd. WS8: Bwnhls . . .1C 26
Westcote Av. B31: Longb 7J 141
Westcote Cl. B92: Olton 7A 124
Westcotes CV4: Tile H 8H 151
Westcott Cl. DY6: K'wfrd 6M 95
Westcott Rd. B26: Yard 1A 124
West Ct. B60: B'gve 3M 209
WESTCROFT 7H 23
Westcroft Av. WV10: Bush 8G 23
Westcroft Gro. B38: K Nor 6C 142
Westcroft Rd. DY3: Sed 7B 52
WV6: Tett 3F 34
Westcroft Way B14: K Hth 8B 144
W. Cross Shop. Cen.
B66: Smeth 2K 99
W. Dean Cl. B62: Hale 5C 118
West Dr. B5: Edg 4J 121
B20: Hand 1H 101
B78: M Oak 7L 31
West End Av. B66: Smeth 2K 99
West End Ct. *CV34: Warw 3D 222*
(off Crompton St.)
Westerdale Cl. DY3: Sed 2G 75
Westerham Cl. B93: Know 3F 168
Westeria Cl. B36: Cas B 1C 104
Westering Parkway
WV10: Bush 5E 22
Westerings B20: Hand 7J 79
Western Av. B19: Loz 2J 101
B62: Hale 5E 118
DY3: Sed 1B 74
DY5: Brie H 7B 96
WS2: Wals 6D 38
Western Bus. Pk. B62: Hale . . .2B 118
Western By-Pass WS13: Lich . . .8E 12
Western Cl. WS2: Wals 6D 38
Western Ct. B9: Birm 7L 5
Western Hill Cl.
B96: A'wd B 8D 220
Western Rd. B18: Win G 5F 100
B24: Erd 6G 81
B64: Crad H 1L 117
B69: O'bry 4H 99
B73: W Grn 8G 59
DY8: Stourb 5M 115
DY9: Hag 5A 138
WS12: Hed 3H 9
Western Way DY11: Kidd 4G 157
WS10: Mox, W'bry 5C 54
Westfield Av. B14: K Hth 8B 144
Westfield Cl. B93: Dorr 7E 168
CV10: Nun 4K 89
Westfield Ct. LE10: Hinc 2H 91
Westfield Dr. WS9: A'rdge 3G 41
WV5: Wom 2F 72
Westfield Grange
B14: K Hth 8L 121
Westfield Gro. WV3: Wolv 1J 51
Westfield Hall B16: Edg 8C 100
Westfield Ho. B36: Cas B 2G 105
Westfield Mnr. B75: Four O 5G 43
Westfield Rd. B14: K Hth 1K 143
B15: Edg 1C 120
B27: A Grn 6H 123
B62: B'hth 8E 98
B67: Smeth 5M 99
CV22: Rugby 7M 179
CV47: Sou 6G 225
DY2: Dud 2K 97
DY3: Sed 8D 52
DY5: Quar B 1F 116
LE10: Hinc 2H 91
WV13: W'hall 1L 53
WV14: Bils 2H 53
Westfields B61: Cats 1M 187
B78: B'moor 1M 47
(Dexter Way)
B78: B'moor 1K 47
(Green La.)
Westford Gro. B28: Hall G 6E 144
West Ga. B1: Birm 6H 101
B16: Edg 6E 100
B69: O'bry 5E 98
Westgate B15: Edg 5E 120 (3B 4)
WS9: A'rdge 2D 40
WS12: Haz 3M 9
Westgate Cl. CV34: Warw 3D 222
DY3: Sed 2E 74
Westgate Ho. *CV34: Warw 3E 222*
(off Market St.)
Westgate Rd. CV21: Hillm 8E 180
Westgate Trad. Est.
WS9: A'rdge 3E 40
West Grn. WV4: Penn 4J 51
West Grn. Cl. B15: Edg 1H 121
W. Grove Av. B90: M'path 3M 167
Westgrove Ter. CV32: Lea S . . .1K 223
WEST HAGLEY 4A 138
Westhall Ga. WS3: Blox 7H 25
Westham Ho. B37: F'bri 5H 105
Westhaven Dr. B31: N'fld 2L 141

Westhaven Rd.—Whitley

Westhaven Rd. B72: S Cold 3J 59
Westhay Rd. B28: Hall G 2H 145
Westhead Rd. DY10: Cookl 5A 136
Westhead Rd. Nth.
DY10: Cookl 5A 136
WEST HEATH 8B 142
W. Heath Rd. B18: Win G 5D 100
B31: N'fld 7B 142
WEST HILL 3H 9
Westhill WV3: Wolv 7J 35
W. Hill Av. WS12: Hed 4H 9
Westhill Cl. B92: Olton 1L 145
West Hill Ct. B14: K Hth 5J 143
Westhill Rd. B38: K Nor 6F 142
CV6: Cov 3M 151
CV32: B'dwn 2A 218
West Holme B9: Birm 7C 102
Westholme Cft. B30: B'vlle 2E 142
Westhorpe Gro. B19: Birm 4J 101
Westhouse Gro. B14: K Hth ...5K 143
West Hyde LE10: Hinc 2F 90
Westland Av. WV3: Wolv 7M 35
West Land Cl. B23: Erd 4F 80
Westland Gdns. DY8: Amb 2M 115
WV3: Wolv 7A 36
Westland Rd. WV3: Wolv 7M 35
Westlands Est. DY8: Word 8L 95
Westlands Rd. B13: Mose 8A 122
B76: Walm 3M 81
Westland Wlk. B35: Cas V 7M 81
Westlea Rd. CV31: Lea S 3L 223
Westleigh Av. CV5: Cov 2M 173
Westleigh Rd. WV5: Wom 4F 72
Westley Brook Cl.
B26: Sheld 4B 124
Westley Cl. B28: Hall G 3H 145
West Leyes CV21: Rugby 6A 180
Westley Rd. B27: A Grn 6H 123
Westley St. B9: Birm ...7A 102 (6M 5)
DY1: Dud 1H 97
Westmead Av. B80: Stud 5L 221
Westmead Cres. B24: Erd 5J 81
W. Mead Dr. B14: K Hth 3L 143
Westmead Dr. B68: O'bry 5H 99
Westmede Cen. CV5: Cov 6J 151
West M. B44: Gt Barr 7K 57
West Midland Safari Pk. 6E 156
W. Mill Cft. B38: K Nor 2E 164
Westminster B37: K'hrst 4F 104
Westminster Av. WV4: Penn 4B 52
Westminster Cl. B61: B'gve ...8K 187
DY1: Dud 7G 75
Westminster Ct. B20: Hand 7H 79
B60: B'gve 7A 188
Westminster Dr. B14: K Hth ...3L 143
CV10: Nun 3B 88
LE10: Burb 5M 91
(not continuous)
Westminster Ind. Est.
DY2: Neth 7K 97
Westminster Rd. B20: Hand 7J 79
B29: S Oak 8G 121
B71: W Brom 8K 55
CV1: Cov 8B 152 (7A 6)
DY8: Word 7J 95
DY11: Kidd 3F 156
WS4: Rus 2B 40
WS11: Cann 3E 8
Westmore Way WS10: W'bry ...4K 55
Westmorland Av. CV10: Nun 5E 88
Westmorland Cl. B78: Tam 8A 32
Westmorland Ct.
B71: W Brom 2K 77
Westmorland Rd.
B71: W Brom 2K 77
CV2: Cov 5M 153
W. Oak Ho. CV4: W'wd H 3E 172
Weston Av. B11: S'brk 3C 122
Westonbirt Cl. CV8: Ken 3J 199
Weston Cl. B93: Dorr 7G 169
CV22: Dunc 5J 205
CV31: Lea S 3C 224
CV34: Warw 2F 222
LE10: Hinc 8G 69
WS1: Wals 3L 55
WS11: Hth H 8J 9
Weston Ct. B9: Birm 8A 102
(off Allcock St.)
CV21: Rugby 5C 180
WV1: Wolv 5C 36 (1J 7)
Weston Cres. WS9: A'rdge 4H 41
Weston Dr. DY4: Tip 7C 54
WS6: Gt Wyr 1E 24
WV14: Bils 5H 53
Weston Hall Rd.
B60: S Prior 8J 209
Weston Ho. B19: Hock 3L 101
WESTON IN ARDEN 6B 112
Weston Ind. Est. B11: Tys 5E 122
Weston La. B11: Tys 5E 122
CV8: Bubb 5H 201
CV12: Bulk 6B 112
Weston Rd. B19: Hock 2H 101
B67: Smeth 7M 99
WS13: Lich 8G 13
Weston St. CV1: Cov ...5D 152 (2E 6)
WS1: Wals 3L 55
Weston Ter. B19: Loz 1K 101
(off New Inn Rd.)
WESTON UNDER WETHERLEY
..........................2J 219
W. Orchards Shop. Cen.
CV1: Cov 6C 152 (4C 6)
Westover Rd. B20: Hand 5E 78
West Pk. CV4: Tile H 1F 172
West Pk. Av. B31: N'fld 7L 141
West Pk. Cl. WS9: A'rdge 4E 40
West Pk. Ct. WV1: Wolv 7A 36
West Pk. Rd. B67: Smeth 2K 99
West Pathway B17: Harb 3C 120
West Point B15: Edg 1C 120
Westport Cres.
WV11: Wed 4M 37
Westray Cl. B45: Fran 8E 140
Westray Dr. LE10: Hinc 8H 69
West Ridge CV5: Cov 4G 151
Westridge DY3: Sed 1C 74
Westridge Rd. B13: Mose 2C 144
West Ri. B75: S Cold 3J 59
West Rd. B6: Witt 7L 79
B43: Gt Barr 2E 78
B60: B'gve 8A 188
B63: Crad 3H 117
DY4: Tip 1B 76
West Rd. Sth. B63: Crad 3H 117
Westside Dr. B32: Bart G 8K 119
WEST SMETHWICK 2K 99
West St. B65: B'hth 8C 98
B77: Tam 6C 32
B79: Tam 4C 32
B98: Redd 6E 212
CV1: Cov 6E 152
CV23: Long L 4G 179
CV31: Lea S 2A 224
CV34: Warw 4D 222
DY3: Gorn 6D 74
DY5: Quar B 1F 116
DY8: Stourb 4M 115
LE9: Earl S 1F 70
WS3: Blox 2J 39
WS11: Cann 3E 14
WV10: Wolv 4C 36
West Vw. B8: W End 5J 103
CV10: Ans C 1L 87
West Vw. Ct. B75: S Cold 3L 59
West Vw. Dr. DY6: K'wfrd 4L 95
West Vw. Rd. B75: S Cold 3L 59
CV22: Rugby 7K 179
CV32: Cubb 4C 218
Westville Av. DY11: Kidd 4G 157
Westville Rd. WS2: Wals 6G 39
Westward Cl. B44: K'sdng 1M 79
West Way B31: Longb 2B 164
WS4: S'fld 7B 26
Westway CV21: Rugby 6A 180
Westwick Cl. WS9: Ston 5L 27
West Winds WV10: F'stne 2J 23
Westwood Av. B11: Tys 5D 122
DY8: Stourb 6J 115
Westwood Bus. Pk. B6: Witt 8B 80
CV4: W'wd H 3G 173
Westwood Cl. CV10: Nun 6E 88
Westwood Ct. B73: S'tly 5B 58
Westwood Cres. CV9: Ath 2K 65
Westwood Dr. B45: Redn 8H 141
Westwood Gro. B91: Sol 7M 145
WESTWOOD HEATH 3F 172
Westwood Heath Rd.
CV4: W'wd H 3C 172
Westwood Rd. B6: Witt 8A 80
B73: S'tly 5A 58
CV5: Cov 8A 152
CV9: Ath 1K 65
CV22: Hillm 2F 206
Westwoods Hollow
WS7: Burn 1H 17
Westwood St. DY5: Brie H 8A 96
Westwood Vw. B24: Erd 6J 81
Westwood Way
CV4: W'wd H 3E 172
Wetherby Cl. B36: Hodg H 1K 103
WV10: F'hses 5D 22
Wetherby Rd. B27: A Grn 7J 123
WS3: Blox 5G 25
Wetherell Way CV21: Brow 2C 180
Wetherfield Rd. B11: Tys 6G 123
Wexford Cl. DY1: Dud 7F 74
Wexford Rd. CV2: Cov 8K 131
Wexler Lofts B1: Birm 3B 4
Weybourne Rd. B44: Gt Barr 7L 57
Weycroft Rd. B23: K'sdng 2B 80
Weyhill Cl. WV9: Pend 7M 21
Weymoor Rd. B17: Harb 6A 120
Weymouth Cl. CV3: W'hall 4K 175
Weymouth Dr. B74: Four O 5F 42
Weymouth Ho. B79: Tam 5A 32
Whaley's Cft. CV6: Cov 1B 152
Wharf, The B1: Birm 7J 101 (6D 4)
Wharf App. WS9: A'rdge 2F 40
Wharf Cl. WS14: Lich 2J 19
Wharfdale Rd. B11: Tys 4G 123
Wharfedale Cl. DY6: W Hth 2H 95
Wharfedale St. WS10: W'bry 7F 54
Wharf Ind. Est., The
CV23: Stret F 2M 155
Wharf La. B60: Tard 8H 189
B91: Sol 3D 146
B94: Lapw 5C 194
WS8: Bwnhls 6G 17
Wharf Rd. B11: Tys 4H 123
B30: K Nor 7G 143
CV6: Cov 4F 152
Wharf Rd. Ind. Est.
B11: Tys 4H 123
Wharfside B69: O'bry 2F 98
Wharfside Leisure Complex
..........................4H 143
Wharfside St.
B1: Birm 8K 101 (7E 4)
Wharf St. B6: Aston 2A 102
B18: Hock 3G 101
CV34: Warw 2G 223
WV1: Wolv 8E 36 (5M 7)
Wharf Yd. LE10: Hinc 2G 91
Whar Hall Rd. B92: Sol 1E 146
Wharrington Cl. B98: Redd 1G 221
Wharrington Hill B98: Redd ...1G 221
Wharton Av. B92: Sol 2E 146
Wharton Rd. B66: Smeth 2C 100
Wharton St. B7: Nech 1D 102
Wharwell La. WS6: Gt Wyr 8G 15
Whatcote Grn. B92: Sol 1D 146
Whatecroft, The B17: Harb 3B 120
WHATELEY 6F 46
Whateley Av. WS3: Wals 3M 39
Whateley Ct. CV11: Nun 5H 89
Whateley Cres. B36: Cas B 1D 104
Whateley Grn. B36: Cas B 1C 104
B74: Four O 1G 59
Whateley Hall Cl.
B93: Know 2J 169
Whateley Hall Rd.
B93: Know 2H 169
Whateley La. B77: Hock 5F 46
B78: What 6F 46
Whateley Lodge Dr.
B36: Cas B 1C 104
Whateley Pl. WS3: Wals 3M 39
Whateley Rd. B21: Hand 1E 100
WS3: Wals 3M 39
Whateley's Dr. CV8: Ken 4G 199
Wheatcroft Av. DY12: Bew 5C 156
Wheatcroft Cl. B62: B'hth 1F 118
B75: R'ley 6L 43
B97: Redd 4A 212
WS7: Burn 4G 17
Wheatcroft Dr. B37: Chel W 8J 105
Wheatcroft Gro. DY2: Dud 8M 75
Wheatcroft Rd. B33: Yard 7M 103
Wheate Cft. CV4: Tile H 7F 150
Wheaten Cl. B37: Chel W 6K 105
Wheatfield Cl. B36: Cas B 2G 105
Wheatfield Rd. CV22: Bil 8J 179
Wheatfield Vw. B31: N'fld 3K 141
Wheatfield Way LE10: Hinc 6J 69
Wheat Hill WS5: Wals 1E 56
Wheathill Cl. CV32: Lea S 7L 217
WV4: Penn 6L 51
Wheatland Gro. WS9: A'rdge ...5H 41
Wheatlands, The WV6: Pert 6D 34
Wheatlands Cl. WS12: Hth H 8J 9
Wheatlands Cft. B33: Kitts G ...6E 104
Wheatley Cl. B68: O'bry 1K 119
B75: Four O 6J 43
B92: Sol 1E 146
Wheatley Grange B46: Col 3M 105
Wheatley Gro. WS6: Gt Wyr 7G 15
Wheatley Rd. B68: O'bry 1J 119
Wheatley St. B70: W Brom 6G 77
CV1: Cov 3E 6
(off White St.)
WV2: E'shll 3E 52
Wheatmill Cl. DY10: Blak 7H 137
Wheatmoor Ri. B75: S Cold 3L 59
Wheatmoor Rd. B75: S Cold 2M 59
Wheaton Cl. WV10: Oxl 2C 36
Wheaton Va. B20: Hand 6E 78
Wheatridge Cl. DY6: W Hth 1G 95
Wheatridge Rd.
B60: Stoke H 3K 209
Wheats Av. B17: Harb 6B 120
Wheatsheaf Cl. B75: R'ley 5L 43
Wheatsheaf La. B94: Lapw 8D 194
Wheatsheaf Rd. B16: Edg 7D 100
B69: Tiv 1A 98
WV8: Pend 8L 21
Wheatstone Cl. DY3: Sed 3E 74
Wheatstone Gro.
B33: Stech 4M 103
Wheat St. CV11: Nun 5J 89
Wheel Av. WV8: Cod 6F 20
Wheel Ct., The WV8: Cod 6F 20
Wheeler Cl. B93: Chad E 2B 196
WV8: Cod 5E 20
Wheeler Ho. B69: O'bry 2G 99
Wheeler Rd. WV11: Wed 1J 37
Wheeler's Fold
WV1: Wolv 7D 36 (4K 7)
Wheeler's Hill DY8: Stourb 3M 115
(off Lwr. High St.)
Wheelers La. B13: Mose 3L 143
B97: Redd 3C 212
Wheeler St. DY8: Stourb 4M 115
Wheeler St. Shop. Cen.
B19: Hock 3K 101
Wheeley Moor Rd.
B37: K'hrst 4G 105
Wheeley Rd. B48: A'chu 5J 189
B92: Sol 2D 146
Wheeley's La.
B15: Birm 1J 121 (8C 4)
Wheeley's Rd.
B15: Edg 2H 121 (8C 4)
Wheelfield WV8: Cod 6F 20
Wheel La. WS13: Lich 8F 12
Wheelock Cl. B74: S'tly 2M 57
Wheelwright Cl. B60: B'gve 3L 209
Wheelwright Ct. B24: Erd 7E 80
Wheelwright La. CV6: Cov 5C 130
CV7: Ash G 5C 130
Wheelwright Rd. B24: Erd 7E 80
Wheldrake Av. B34: S End 4C 104
Wheler Rd. CV3: Cov 1G 175
Whernside CV21: Brow 2C 180
Whernside Dr. WV6: Wolv 4A 36
Wherretts Well La. B91: Sol ...4E 146
Whetstone Cl. B15: Edg 4F 120
Whetstone Dr. CV21: Brow 2D 180
Whetstone Grn. WV10: Bush 8D 22
Whetstone Gro. WV10: Bush 1D 36
Whetstone La. WS9: A'rdge 5H 41
Whetstone Rd. WV10: Bush 1D 36
Whetty Bri. Rd. B45: Rubery ...3E 162
Whetty La. B45: Rubery 2E 162
Whichbury Ct. B65: Row R 5D 98
Whichcote Av. CV7: Mer 8J 127
Whichford Cl. B76: Walm 3K 81
Whichford Gro. B9: Bord G 7H 103
While Rd. B72: S Cold 5H 59
Whiley Cl. CV23: Clift D 4F 180
Whilmot Cl. WV10: F'stne 3H 23
Whimbrel Cl. CV23: Brow 1C 180
Whimbrel Gro. DY10: Kidd 8A 158
Whinberry Ri. DY5: P'ntt 8C 74
Whinchat Gro. DY10: Kidd 7A 158
Whinfield Rd. B61: D'frd 3H 187
Whinyates Ri. WS11: Cann 1F 14
Whisley Brook La.
B28: Hall G 7F 122
Whistler Gro. WV10: Bush 1G 37
Whiston Av. WV11: Wed 2A 38
Whiston Gro. B29: W Cas 1B 142
Whiston Ho. WS1: Wals 8M 39
WHITACRE HEATH 3D 84
Whitacre Heath Nature Reserve
...........................3B 84
Whitacre La. WS14: Lynn 2L 27
Whitacre Rd. B9: Bord G 6E 102
B93: Know 2H 169
CV11: Nun 5L 89
CV32: Lill 7A 218
Whitacre Rd. Ind. Est.
CV11: Nun 5L 89
Whitaker Rd. CV5: Cov 6J 151
Whitbourne Cl. B12: Bal H 4B 122
Whitburn Av. B42: P Barr 4G 79
Whitburn Cl. DY11: Kidd 4H 157
WV9: Pend 7A 22
Whitburn Rd. CV12: Bed 7C 110
Whitby Cl. WS3: Blox 6F 24
Whitby Rd. B12: Bal H 5A 122
Whitby Way WS11: Cann 1C 14
Whitchurch Cl. B98: Redd 3F 220
Whitchurch La. B90: Dic H 3G 167
Whitchurch Way CV4: Tile H ...1F 172
Whitcot Gro. B31: Longb 1M 163
White Bark Cl. WS12: Hed 1G 9
Whitebeam Cl. CV4: Tile H 8D 150
DY3: Lwr G 5C 74
WS8: Clay 3E 26
Whitebeam Cft. B38: K Nor 8E 142
Whitebeam Rd. B37: Chel W 1J 125
White City Rd. DY5: Quar B 8G 97
White Cl. DY9: Pedm 7C 116
Whitecrest B43: Gt Barr 7F 56
Whitecroft Rd. B26: Sheld 4C 124
White Falcon Ct. B91: Sol 7M 145
White Farm Rd. B74: Four O 4E 42
Whitefield Av. B17: Harb 3A 120
Whitefield Cl. CV4: W'wd H ...2D 172
WV8: Bilb 7H 21
Whitefields Cres. B91: Sol 7B 146
Whitefields Flats CV4: Canly ...5J 173
Whitefields Ga. B91: Sol 8A 146
Whitefields Rd. B91: Sol 8A 146
(not continuous)
Whitefriars Dr. B63: Hale 5A 118
CV22: Caw 8G 179
White Friars La.
CV1: Cov 7D 152 (6E 6)
Whitefriars Lodge Mus.
..................7E 152 (6F 6)
White Friars St.
CV1: Cov 7D 152 (5E 6)
Whitegate Dr. DY11: Kidd 6G 157
Whitegates Rd. WV14: Cose 6K 53
Whitehall WS13: Lich 1G 19
Whitehall Cl. CV10: Harts 7A 66
Whitehall Dr. B63: Hale 5B 118
DY1: Dud 7G 75
Whitehall Ind. Pk. DY4: Tip 4E 76
Whitehall Rd. B9: Small H 7D 102
B21: Hand 2G 101
B63: Hale 5B 118
B64: Crad H 1J 117
B70: W Brom 4E 76
CV21: Rugby 7B 180
DY4: Tip 4D 76
DY6: K'wfrd 3J 95
DY8: Stourb 7B 116
WS1: Wals 2L 55
WV4: Penn 5B 52
White Hart, The WS1: Wals 1L 55
(off Caldmore Grn.)
Whitehead Dr. B76: Min 3D 82
CV8: Ken 2J 199
Whitehead Gro. CV7: Bal C ...2H 171
Whitehead Rd. B6: Aston 2L 101
Whiteheads Ct.
CV32: Lea S 8M 217
White Heart Cvn. Pk.
DY7: Kinv 6A 114
White Heart Cl. DY12: Bew 2B 156
Whiteheath Ct. B69: O'bry 5E 98
(off Birchfield La.)
White Hill B31: N'fld 3B 142
DY7: Kinv 4A 114
Whitehill La. B29: W Cas 4A 142
Whitehill Rd. DY11: Kidd 6G 157
White Hollies WS3: Pels 5M 25
Whitehorse Cl. CV6: Longf 3H 131
White Horse Rd.
WS8: Bwnhls 7E 16
Whitehouse Av. WS10: Darl 2B 54
WS10: W'bry 6F 54
WV3: Wolv 1K 51
WV11: Wed 2M 37
White Ho. Cl. B91: Sol 6M 145
CV2: Cov 6J 153
WHITEHOUSE COMMON 2M 59
Whitehouse Comn. Rd.
B75: S Cold 1L 59
Whitehouse Ct. B75: S Cold 4M 59
Whitehouse Cres.
B75: S Cold 1L 59
CV10: Nun 6D 88
WS7: Burn 2H 17
WV11: Wed 8M 23
White Ho. Dr. B45: B Grn 8G 163
Whitehouse Dr. B66: Smeth ...2A 100
WS13: Lich 3F 18
WHITEHOUSE GATE 5E 98
White Ho. Grn. B91: Sol 6M 145
Whitehouse La. B98: Redd 6L 213
DY3: Swind 8A 72
DY7: Env 8A 72
WV8: Cod, Cod W 2B 20
White Ho. Pl. B45: Rubery 3F 162
Whitehouse Rd. B78: Dord 2M 47
DY10: Kidd 5K 157
White Ho's. La. WV10: F'stne ...3G 23
(not continuous)
Whitehouse St. B6: Aston 3M 101
DY4: Tip 7A 76
WS2: Wals 6K 39
WV14: Cose 1J 75
White Ho. Way B91: Sol 6A 146
Whitehouse Way WS9: A'rdge ...5F 40
Whitelaw Cres. CV5: Alle 3H 151
WHITEMOOR 4H 199
Whitemoor Dr. B90: M'path 2A 168
Whitemoor Rd. CV8: Ken 4G 199
Whitemoors Cl.
CV13: Stoke G 2E 68
Whitemoors Rd.
CV13: Stoke G 2E 68
White Oak Dr. DY6: K'wfrd 3J 95
WV3: Wolv 1J 51
Whitepits La. B48: A'chu 5M 191
Whitepoplars Cl. DY5: Brie H ...5C 96
White Pump La. B95: Ullen 4K 215
White Rd. B11: S'brk 2C 122
B32: Quin 3K 119
B67: Smeth 3L 99
White Row WV5: Try 8C 50
Whitesands Cl. B77: Amin 4E 32
Whites Dr. DY3: Sed 1E 74
Whiteside Cl. CV3: Bin 1M 175
Whiteslade Cl. B93: Know 2G 169
Whitesmiths Cl. DY3: Sed 1D 74
Whitesmiths Cft. B14: K Hth ...1L 143
Whites Rd. B71: W Brom 3J 77
Whites Row CV8: Ken 7G 199
WHITE STITCH 5J 127
Whitestitch La. CV7: Mer 6H 127
WHITESTONE 1M 111
Whitestone Rd. B63: Hale 3A 118
CV11: Nun 1A 112
White St. B12: Bal H 4A 122
CV1: Cov 6D 152 (3D 6)
WS1: Wals 1L 55
Whites Wood WV5: Wom 4G 73
Whitethorn Cl. WS12: Hed 1G 9
Whitethorn Cres. B74: S'tly 8K 41
Whitethorn Dr. CV32: Lill 7B 218
Whitethorn Rd. DY8: Word 8A 96
Whitewood Glade
WV12: W'hall 5E 38
Whitfield Rd. WS12: Hed 2J 9
Whitford Bri. Rd.
B60: S Prior 6M 209
Whitford Cl. B61: B'gve 1K 209
Whitford Dr. B90: M'path 2B 168
Whitford Gdns. B61: B'gve 7K 187
Whitford Rd. B61: B'gve 7K 187
(not continuous)
Whitgreave Av. WV10: Bush 1E 36
WV10: F'stne 2H 23
Whitgreave Ct. WV10: F'stne ...3H 23
Whitgreave St. B70: W Brom ...6E 76
Whiting B77: Two G 3D 46
Whitland Cl. B45: Redn 3H 163
Whitland Dr. B14: K Hth 6M 143
Whitlenge La. DY10: Hartl 7C 184
WHITLEY 3G 175

314 West Midlands Atlas

Whitley Av.—Windermere Way

Whitley Av. B77: Amin 4E 32
Whitley Cl. WV6: Tett 7H 35
Whitley Ct. B20: Hand 6E 78
CV3: Cov 2F 174
Whitley Ct. Rd. B32: Quin 3J 119
Whitley Dr. B74: S'tly 1A 58
Whitley St. WS10: W'bry 6E 54
Whitley Village CV3: Cov 2F 174
Whitlock Gro. B14: K Hth 4A 144
WHITLOCKS END 4E 166
Whitminster Av. B24: Erd 6H 81
Whitminster Cl. WV12: W'hall 5C 38
Whitmore Hill
WV1: Wolv 7C 36 (3H 7)
Whitmore Ho. WV6: Wolv 5A 36
WHITMORE PARK 8A 130
Whitmore Pk. Ind. Est.
CV6: Cov 8C 130
Whitmore Pk. Rd. CV6: Cov 6C 130
WHITMORE REANS 5A 36
Whitmore Rd. B10: Small H 1C 122
CV31: W'nsh 6A 224
DY8: Stourb 4K 115
Whitmore St. B18: Hock 4H 101
WS1: Wals 2K 55
WV1: Wolv 7D 36 (3K 7)
WHITNASH 5A 224
Whitnash Cl. CV7: Bal C 3G 171
Whitnash Gro. CV2: Cov 4K 153
Whitnash Rd. CV31: W'nsh 5B 224
Whitney Av. DY8: Woll 3K 115
Whittaker St. WV2: E'shll 3E 52
Whittall Dr. E. DY11: Kidd 8H 157
Whittall Dr. W. DY11: Kidd 8G 157
Whittall St. B4: Birm 6L 101 (3G 5)
Whittimere St. WS1: Wals 7M 39
Whittingham Gro.
WV11: Wed 3M 37
Whittingham Rd. B63: Hale 4A 118
WHITTINGTON
CV9 .....6H 49
DY7 .....7D 114
Whittington Cl. B14: K Hth 4L 143
B71: W Brom 1M 77
CV34: Warw 1H 223
Whittington Comn. Rd.
WS14: Lich 4M 19
Whittington Gro. B33: Yard 7M 103
Whittington Hall La.
DY7: Kinv 7D 114
Whittington Ho. *WS13: Lich 8L 13*
(off Hobs Rd.)
Whittington La. CV9: Whitt 7G 49
Whittington Oval B33: Yard 7A 104
Whittington Rd. DY8: Stourb 6K 115
Whittle Cl. CV3: Bin 1M 175
CV22: Bil 2K 205
Whittle Ct. CV32: Lea S 8B 218
Whittle Cft. B35: Cas V 6M 81
WHITTLEFORD 4B 88
Whittleford Gro. B36: Cas B 8C 82
Whittleford Rd. CV10: Nun 5C 88
Whittle Rd. LE10: Hinc 1E 90
Whittles Ct. DY11: Kidd 1H 157
Whitton St. WS10: Darl 3E 54
Whitville Cl. DY11: Kidd 2J 157
Whitwell Cl. B90: M'path 4A 168
Whitworth Av. CV3: Cov 8H 153
LE10: Hinc 2F 90
Whitworth Cl. WS10: Darl 2E 54
Whitworth Dr. B71: W Brom 8L 55
Whitworth Ind. Pk.
B9: Bord G 7C 102
WHOBERLEY 7K 151
Whoberley Av. CV5: Cov 6K 151
Whyle St. B63: Hale 5B 118
Whyley St. B70: W Brom 5G 77
Whyley Wlk. B69: O'bry 4G 99
Whynot Cl. B60: S Prior 7J 209
Whynot St. B63: Crad 4H 117
Wibert Cl. B29: S Oak 8G 121
Wichnor Rd. B92: Olton 4M 123
Wicket La. DY7: Stourt 8E 94
Wicketts Twr. B5: Edg 4J 121
Wickham Cl. CV6: Cov 7M 129
Wickham Ct. CV32: Lill 5B 218
Wickham Gdns. WV11: Wed 3H 37
Wickham Rd. B80: Stud 5M 221
Wickham Sq. B70: W Brom 7H 77
Wicklow Cl. B63: Hale 8K 117
Wickmans Dr. CV4: Tile H 7C 150
Wiclif Way CV10: Nun 6B 88
Widdecombe Cl. CV2: Cov 1K 153
Widdrington Rd.
CV1: Cov 4C 152 (1B 6)
Wideacre Dr. B44: Gt Barr 2L 79
Wide Acres B45: Fran 8F 140
Widgeon Gro. WV10: F'stne 2H 23
Widney Av. B29: S Oak 7C 120
WS9: A'rdge 8H 27
Widney Cl. B93: Ben H 4F 168
Widney Ho. Ind. Pk.
B97: Redd 5C 212
Widney La. B91: Sol 8L 145
Widney Mnr. Rd. B91: Sol 7C 146
Widney Manor Station (Rail)
.....1C 168
Widney Rd.
B93: Ben H, Know 4E 168
Wigford Rd. B77: Dost 4C 46
Wiggin Cotts. B17: Harb 4C 120
Wiggin Ho. WS3: Blox 6J 25
Wiggins Cft. B76: Walm 6M 59
Wiggins Hill Rd.
B76: Min, Wis 1F 82
Wigginsmill Rd.
WS10: W'bry 8D 54
Wiggin St. B16: Birm 6F 100
Wigginton Rd. B79: Tam 2B 32
Wight Cft. B36: Cas B 3H 105
Wightman Cl. LE9: S Stan 6K 71
WS14: Lich 3L 19
Wightman Rd. LE9: Barw 2C 70
Wightwick Bank WV6: Tett 8G 35
Wightwick Cl. WS3: Blox 8H 25
Wightwick Ct. WV6: Tett 7G 35
Wightwick Gro. WV6: Tett 7G 35
Wightwick Hall Rd. WV6: Tett 8E 34
Wightwick Leys WV6: Tett 7F 34
Wightwick Manor 8F 34
Wigland Way B38: K Nor 8G 143
Wigmore Gro. B44: K'sdng 1B 80
Wigmore La. B71: W Brom 1A 78
(not continuous)
Wigorn La. DY9: Pedm 1B 138
Wigorn Rd. B67: Smeth 8M 99
Wigston Hill CV9: Bax 4C 64
WIGSTON PARVA 8F 92
Wigston Rd. CV2: W'grve S 8M 131
CV21: Hillm 1G 207
Wike La. B96: Sam 8J 221
Wilberforce Way B92: Sol 2F 146
Wilbraham Rd. WS2: Wals 8J 39
Wilcote Gro. B27: A Grn 1J 145
Wilcox Av. WS12: Hed 2H 9
Wildacres DY8: Woll 3J 115
Wilday Cl. DY4: Tip 4A 76
Wildcroft Rd. CV5: Cov 7J 151
Wilde Cl. B14: K Hth 5K 143
WILDEN 3K 183
Wilden Cl. B31: N'fld 6J 141
Wilden Ind. Est.
DY13: Stour S 3J 183
Wilden La. DY10: Kidd 2K 183
DY11: Kidd 2K 183
DY13: Stour S 5J 183
Wilden Top Rd.
DY13: Stour S 5K 183
Wilderness La. B43: Gt Barr 7D 56
Wildey Rd. CV12: Bed 7D 110
Wildfell Rd. B27: A Grn 7K 123
Wild Goose La. B98: Redd 8K 213
WILDMOOR 5M 161
Wildmoor Cl. CV2: Ald G 5H 131
Wildmoor La.
B61: Cats, Wild 8A 162
Wildmoor Rd. B90: Shir 4H 145
Wildside Activity Cen. 4M 35
Wildtree Av. WV10: Bush 7G 23
Wileman's Cl. LE9: Earl S 3E 70
Wiley Av. WS10: Darl 3C 54
Wiley Av. Sth. WS10: Darl 4C 54
Wilf Bown Cl. LE9: Earl S 1H 71
Wilford Gro. B76: Walm 3B 82
B91: Sol 7B 146
Wilford Rd. B71: W Brom 3K 77
Wilhelmina Cl. CV32: Lea S 1L 223
Wilkes Av. WS2: Wals 7F 38
Wilkes Cl. WS3: Pels 6L 25
Wilkes Cft. DY3: Sed 2D 74
Wilkes Rd. WV8: Cod 5F 20
Wilkes St. B71: W Brom 2L 77
WV13: W'hall 8A 38
Wilkin, The WS8: Bwnhls 7C 16
Wilkin Rd. WS8: Bwnhls 7C 16
Wilkins Ho. *WS3: Blox 8G 25*
(off Sandbank)
Wilkinson Av. WV14: Bils 6L 53
Wilkinson Cl. B73: W Grn 7H 59
WS7: Burn 1H 17
Wilkinson Cft. B8: W End 3J 103
Wilkinson La. LE9: Elme 3E 70
Wilkinson Rd. WS10: Mox 4A 54
Wilkinson Way B46: Shu 7G 85
Wilkins Rd. WV14: Bils 2K 53
Wilks Grn. B21: Hand 6D 78
Willard Rd. B25: Yard 3J 123
Willaston Rd. B33: Sheld 2D 124
Willclare Rd. B26: Sheld 3A 124
Willcock Rd. WV2: Wolv 2E 52
Willday Dr. CV9: Ath 7K 49
WILLENHALL
CV3 .....3K 175
WV13 .....7B 38
Willenhall Ind. Est.
WV13: W'hall 6C 38
Willenhall La. CV3: Bin 3L 175
WS2: Wals 2F 38
WS3: Blox 2F 38
Willenhall La. Ind. Est.
WS3: Blox 1G 39
Willenhall Leisure Cen. 8B 38
Willenhall Library & Mus. 8B 38
Willenhall Rd. WS10: Darl 8D 38
WV1: Wolv 8G 37
WV13: W'hall 8G 37
WV14: Bils 3M 53
Willenhall St. WS10: Darl 1C 54
Willenhall Trad. Est.
WV13: W'hall 8A 38
Willerby Fold WV10: Bush 5F 22
Willersey Rd. B13: Mose 1D 144
Willes Ct. *B62: Quin 2G 119*
(off Binswood Rd.)
Willes Rd. B18: Win G 3E 100
CV31: Lea S 1A 224
CV32: Lea S 8A 218
Willes Ter. CV31: Lea S 1B 224
Willett Av. WS7: Chase 4E 16
Willett Rd. B71: W Brom 1L 77
Willetts Dr. B63: Crad 5H 117
Willetts Rd. B31: N'fld 8A 142
Willetts Way B64: Old H 7M 97
Willey Gro. B24: Erd 7H 81
William Arnold Cl. CV2: Cov 5G 153
William Batchelor Ho.
CV1: Cov 2C 6
William Beesley Cres.
CV11: Bram 3E 112
William Bentley Ct.
WV11: Wed 4J 37
William Booth La.
B4: Birm 5K 101 (2F 4)
William Bree Rd.
CV5: E Grn 4C 150
William Bristow Rd.
CV3: Cov 2E 174
William Bullock Cl.
DY13: Stour S 6F 182
William Coley Pl.
DY13: Stour S 8F 182
William Cook Rd.
B8: W End 4H 103
William Ct. B13: Mose 5M 121
B16: Edg 8E 100
William Cree Cl. CV8: Wols 6F 176
William Edward St.
B12: Birm 1M 121
William Grn. Rd.
WS10: W'bry 6J 55
William Groubb Cl. CV3: Bin 2L 175
William Harper Rd.
WV13: W'hall 8B 38
William Iliffe St. LE10: Hinc 2H 91
William Kerr Rd. DY4: Tip 4C 76
William Kirby Cl.
CV4: Tile H 8G 151
William McCool Cl.
CV3: Bin 1M 175
William McKee Cl. CV3: Bin 2L 175
William Malcolm Ho.
CV2: Cov 6L 153
William Morris Gro.
WS11: Cann 5E 8
William Rd. B31: N'fld 8M 141
B67: Smeth 6K 99
William's Cl. WV12: W'hall 4C 38
Williamson Av. WS12: Haz 5C 10
Williamson St.
WV3: Wolv 1B 52 (7G 7)
Williams Rd. CV31: Rad S 5E 224
William St. B15: Birm 8J 101 (8C 4)
B70: W Brom 4E 76
B97: Redd 5E 212
CV11: Nun 6L 89
CV12: Bed 7K 111
CV21: Rugby 6B 180
CV32: Lea S 1A 224
DY5: Brie H 6C 96
WS4: Wals 6M 39
William St. Nth.
B19: Birm 5K 101 (1F 4)
William St. W. B66: Smeth 2B 100
William Tarver Cl.
CV34: Warw 2G 223
William Thomson Ho.
CV1: Cov 1F 6
William Tolson's Ind. Est.
B78: Faz 1A 46
William Wiggin Av.
WS3: Blox 7H 25
Willingsworth Rd.
WS10: W'bry 8C 54
Willington Rd. B79: Tam 2B 32
Willington St. CV11: Nun 4G 89
Willingworth Cl. WV14: Cose 6G 53
Willis Gro. CV12: Bed 6J 111
Willis Pearson Av.
WV14: Bils 7M 53
Willis St. DY11: Kidd 4J 157
Willmore Gro. B38: K Nor 1F 164
Willmore Rd. B20: Hand 7K 79
Willmott Cl. B75: R'ley 6K 43
Willmott Rd. B75: R'ley 6K 43
Willoughby Av. CV8: Ken 6E 198
Willoughby Cl. CV3: Bin 1L 175
Willoughby Dr. B91: Sol 8B 146
Willoughby Gro. B29: W Cas 8A 120
Willoughby Pl. CV22: Hillm 1D 206
Willoughby Rd. B79: Tam 2L 31
Willow Av. B17: Edg 7A 100
WS7: Burn 3J 17
WS10: W'bry 5F 54
WV11: Wed 1G 37
Willow Bank WV3: Wolv 8J 35
Willowbank B78: Tam 8B 32
Willow Bank Rd. LE10: Hinc 2J 91
Willowbank Rd.
B93: Know 3F 168
Willowbrook Cl. LE10: Sharn 5J 93
Willow Brook Rd.
B48: A'chu 2A 190
Willowbrook Rd. CV8: Wols 5G 177
Willow Cl. B21: Hand 1D 100
B61: B'gve 7L 187
B64: Old H 8L 97
B78: K'bry 3D 62
CV10: Harts 2A 88
CV12: Bed 4G 111
CV31: W'nsh 7B 224
DY9: Hag 4M 137
LE10: Burb 4L 91
Willow Coppice B32: Bart G 8J 119
Willow Ct. B13: Mose 6A 122
B61: B'gve 6L 187
B66: Smeth 1K 99
CV34: H'cte 7L 223
WS14: Lich 4J 19
Willow Courtyard CV2: Cov 2K 153
Willowdale LE10: Hinc 2G 91
Willowdale Grange WV6: Tett 4L 35
Willowdene DY13: Stour S 6H 183
Willowdene Way LE9: Barw 3B 70
Willow Dr. B21: Hand 8C 78
B69: Tiv 2C 98
B90: Ches G 5K 167
WV8: Bilb 6H 21
Willow End DY9: W'cte 6D 116
Willowfield Dr. DY11: Kidd 1J 157
Willowfields Rd. CV11: Nun 8A 90
Willow Gdns. B16: Birm 5F 100
B61: B'gve 6L 187
CV47: Sou 5H 225
Willow Gro. CV4: Tile H 7H 151
WV11: Ess 6B 24
Willow Hgts. B64: Crad H 1A 118
Willowherb Cl. CV3: Bin 1M 175
WS5: Wals 6A 56
WS11: Hth H 7J 9
Willowherb Way B90: Dic H 4G 167
Willow Ho. B7: Birm 2M 5
CV32: Lea S 1K 223
Willow La. CV22: Rugby 7C 180
Willow Meer CV8: Ken 4H 199
Willow M. B29: S Oak 8B 120
Willow Pk. Dr. DY8: Stourb 7A 116
Willow Pk. Ind. Est.
CV13: Stoke G 2C 68
Willow Ri. DY5: Brie H 8C 96
Willow Rd. B30: B'vlle 1F 142
B43: Gt Barr 8F 56
B61: B'gve 6L 187
B91: Sol 7L 145
CV10: Nun 4E 88
DY1: Dud 5G 75
DY7: Kinv 6C 114
WV3: Wolv 1K 51
Willows, The B27: A Grn 7H 123
B47: H'wd 3A 166
B47: Wyt 2M 191
(off Hillcrest Pk.)
B74: Four O 7F 42
B76: Walm 7M 59
CV9: Ath 7L 49
CV12: Bed 7E 110
DY2: Neth 4L 97
DY13: Stour S 5H 183
WS11: Cann 8C 8
WV5: Wom 4F 72
Willowsbrook Rd. B62: B'hth 1F 118
Willows Cres. B12: Bal H 4K 121
Willow Sheets Mdw.
CV32: Cubb 3E 218
Willowside WS4: S'fld 1C 40
Willowsmere Dr. WS14: Lich 2M 19
Willows Rd. B12: Bal H 4L 121
WS1: Wals 8A 40
WS4: S'fld 1C 40
Willow Tree Cl. LE9: Barw 1B 70
WS13: Lich 7H 13
Willow Tree Dr. B45: B Grn 1K 189
Willow Tree Gdns.
CV21: Hillm 8G 181
Willow Wlk. B76: Walm 2M 81
CV7: Old A 8E 86
WS12: Hunt 1D 8
Willow Way B37: Chel W 7H 105
B80: Stud 7L 221
B97: Redd 5B 212
Wills Av. B71: W Brom 1H 77
Willsbridge Covert
B14: K Hth 7K 143
Wills Ho. B70: W Brom 7J 77
Willson Cft. B28: Hall G 6D 144
Wills St. B19: Loz 2H 101
Wills Way B66: Smeth 5C 100
Wilmcote Cl. B12: Bal H 3L 121
Wilmcote Ct. B61: B'gve 1K 209
Wilmcote Dr. B75: Four O 6H 43
Wilmcote Grn. CV5: E Grn 6G 151
Wilmcote Ho. *B97: Redd 5A 212*
(off Cardy Cl.)
Wilmcote Rd. B91: Sol 3M 145
Wilmcote Twr. B12: Birm 2M 121
Wilmhurst Rd. CV34: Warw 1C 222
Wilmington Rd. B32: Quin 3H 119
Wilmore La. B47: Wyt 5M 165
Wilmot Av. B46: Col 3M 105
Wilmot Cl. CV7: Bal C 1H 171
Wilmot Dr. B23: Erd 3G 81
DY4: Tip 3L 75
Wilmot Gdns. DY1: Dud 7G 75
Wilmott Cl. WS13: Lich 2F 18
WILNECOTE 2E 46
Wilnecote Gro. B42: P Barr 5K 79
CV31: Lea S 4B 224
Wilnecote La. B77: Wiln 7C 32
Wilnecote Leisure Cen. 3F 46
Wilnecote Station (Rail) 2D 46
Wilner's Vw. WS3: Pels 4M 25
Wilsford Cl. B14: K Hth 8K 143
WS4: S'fld 1C 40
Wilson Cl. CV22: Bil 7J 179
Wilson Dr. B75: S Cold 4A 60
(not continuous)
Wilson Grn. CV3: Bin 8M 153
Wilson Gro. CV8: Ken 5J 199
WS11: Hth H 7J 9
Wilson Rd. B19: Loz 1K 101
B66: Smeth 6B 100
B68: O'bry 1K 119
DY5: Brie H 5C 96
DY11: Hartl 8A 184
WV14: Cose 2J 75
Wilsons La. CV6: Longf 4F 130
CV7: Exh 3G 131
Wilsons Rd. B93: Know 3J 169
Wilson St. DY4: Tip 4A 76
WV1: Wolv 6D 36 (1K 7)
Wiltell Rd. WS14: Lich 3H 19
Wiltell Rd. Ind. Est.
WS14: Lich 3H 19
(off Wiltell Rd.)
Wilton Av. DY11: Kidd 2G 157
(not continuous)
Wilton Cl. DY3: Sed 2E 74
Wilton Rd. B11: S'hll 4B 122
B20: Hand 8H 79
B23: Erd 4G 81
CV7: Bal C 3H 171
Wilton St. B19: Loz 1K 101
Wiltshire Cl. CV5: E Grn 6H 151
CV12: Bed 6G 111
WS2: Wals 5K 39
Wiltshire Ct. *B29: W Cas 2C 142*
(off Tugford Rd.)
Wiltshire Dr. B63: Crad 2H 117
Wiltshire Way B71: W Brom 2J 77
WIMBLEBURY 6M 9
Wimblebury Rd.
WS12: Hed, Wim 5M 9
WS12: Hth H 8M 9
Wimbledon Dr. DY8: Stourb 7B 116
Wimborne Rd. WV10: Wolv 3G 37
Wimbourne Cl. CV10: Nun 4B 88
Wimbourne Dr.
CV2: W'grve S 5M 153
Wimbourne Rd. B16: Edg 6D 100
B76: Walm 5A 60
Wimhurst Mdw. WV10: Bush 5F 22
Wimperis Way B43: Gt Barr 5J 57
Wimpole Gro. B44: K'sdng 2B 80
Winbrook DY12: Bew 6A 156
Winbrook M. DY12: Bew 6A 156
Wincanton Cft. B36: Hodg H 1J 103
Winceby Pl. CV4: Tile H 8D 150
Winceby Rd. WV6: Pert 6F 34
Winchat Cl. CV3: Bin 8M 153
Winchcombe Cl. B92: Olton 7B 124
DY1: Dud 6E 74
Winchcombe Rd. B92: Olton 7B 124
Winchester Av. CV10: Nun 2J 89
DY11: Kidd 3G 157
Winchester Cl. B65: Row R 5E 98
DY9: Hag 3A 138
WS13: Lich 6J 13
Winchester Ct. *B74: Four O 7F 42*
(off Vesey Cl.)
CV22: Dunc 6J 205
Winchester Dr. B37: Chel W 7G 105
DY8: Stourb 6A 116
LE10: Burb 2A 92
Winchester Gdns. B31: N'fld 6A 142
Winchester Gro. B21: Hand 1C 100
Winchester M. WS9: A'rdge 5H 41
Winchester Ri. DY1: Dud 7G 75
Winchester Rd. B20: Hand 8K 79
B71: W Brom 1H 77
B78: Tam 6M 31
WS11: Cann 6G 9
WV10: F'hses 6C 22
Winchester St.
CV1: Cov 6E 152 (3F 6)
Winchfield Dr. B17: Harb 1M 119
Wincote Dr. WV6: Tett 5J 35
Wincrest Way B34: S End 4C 104
Windermere B77: Wiln 2G 47
Windermere Av. CV3: Bin 8L 153
CV5: E Grn 5E 150
CV11: Nun 2M 89
Windermere Cl. CV21: Brow 2C 180
LE9: Earl S 1F 70
Windermere Dr. B74: S'tly 6M 41
CV32: Lea S 7K 217
DY6: K'wfrd 3K 95
Windermere Ho. *B15: Edg 6D 120*
(off Vincent Rd.)
B69: O'bry 4D 98
DY10: Kidd 2L 157
Windermere Pl. WS11: Cann 8E 8
Windermere Rd. B13: Mose 8B 122
B21: Hand 7E 78
WV6: Tett 1K 35
Windermere Way
DY13: Stour S 3E 182

Windfall Ct.—Woodcock Cl.

Windfall Ct. B24: Erd 5K **81**
Winding Ho. La. CV6: Longf . . 5C **130**
CV7: Ash G, Longf 5C **130**
Winding Mill Nth.
DY5: Quar B 2E **116**
Winding Mill Sth.
DY5: Quar B 2E **116**
Windings, The WS13: Lich 8G **13**
Windlass Cft. B31: N'fld 4M **141**
Windleaves Rd. B36: Cas B . . . 1E **104**
Windley Cl. B19: Birm 4J **101**
Windley Ho. B73: New O 7C **58**
Windmill Av. B45: Rubery 1E **162**
B46: Col 2M **105**
Windmill Bank WS15: Gent 4G **11**
WV5: Wom 2G **73**
Windmill Cl. B31: N'fld 4C **142**
B79: Tam 1A **32**
CV8: Ken 3G **199**
DY13: Stour S 8F **182**
WS13: Lich 7F **12**
Windmill Ct. CV6: Cov 6G **131**
Windmill Cres. B66: Smeth 4C **100**
WV3: Wolv 8G **35**
Windmill Cft. CV32: Cubb 4D **218**
Windmill Dr. B97: Redd 3C **220**
Windmill End DY2: Neth 4L **97**
Windmill Gdns. B97: Redd 3A **220**
Windmill Gro. DY6: W Hth 1H **95**
Windmill Hill B31: N'fld 4B **142**
B63: Crad 3J **117**
CV32: Cubb 4D **218**
Windmill Hill, The CV5: Alle . . 2G **151**
Windmill Hill Community Nature Area
. . . . 1E **88**
Windmill Ind. Est. CV5: Alle . . 2F **150**
Windmill La. B66: Smeth 5B **100**
B93: Dorr 8F **168**
B94: H'ley H 8F **168**
B97: Redd 3B **220**
CV7: Bal C 5K **171**
CV7: Cor 3D **128**
CV9: Bax 3D **64**
CV10: Asty 4L **109**
CV22: Dunc 5G **205**
WS13: Lich 7G **13**
WS15: Gent 5G **11**
WV3: Wolv 8G **35**
Windmill Pk. CV7: Bal C 5K **171**
Windmill Pct. B66: Smeth 4B **100**
Windmill Rd. B90: Shir 7E **144**
CV6: Cov 6F **130**
CV7: Exh 1G **131**
CV9: Ath 8K **49**
CV10: Nun 2D **88**
CV31: Lea S 4M **223**
Windmill St. B1: Birm . . 8K **101** (8F **4**)
DY1: Dud 7G **75**
DY3: Up Gor 4D **74**
WS1: Wals 1L **55**
WS10: W'bry 6G **55**
Windmill Ter. WS10: W'bry . . . 6G **55**
Windmill Vw. DY1: Dud 2H **75**
Windridge Cl. CV3: W'hall . . . 3K **175**
Windridge Cres. B92: Sol . . . 1F **146**
Windrow, The WV6: Pert 5D **34**
Windrush Cl. B92: Olton 7A **124**
B97: Redd 3D **220**
Windrush Dr. LE10: Hinc 1G **91**
Windrush Gro. B29: S Oak . . . 1G **143**
Windrush Rd. B47: H'wd 2B **166**
WS11: Cann 3E **8**
Windrush Way
CV23: Long L 4H **179**
Windsor Arc.
B4: Birm 6L **101** (4G **5**)
Windsor Av. B68: O'bry 6G **99**
WS12: Hed 3H **9**
WV4: Penn 3L **51**
Windsor Cl. B31: Longb 3A **164**
B45: Fran 7G **141**
B63: Hale 6M **117**
B65: Row R 5C **98**
B79: Tam 2C **32**
DY3: Gorn 8B **74**
WS7: C Ter 8E **10**
Windsor Ct. B38: K Nor 8F **142**
CV4: Tile H 7H **151**
CV10: Nun 3E **88**
CV21: Rugby 6A **180**
CV32: Lea S 1M **223**
LE10: Burb 4A **92**
WS12: Hed 3H **9**
WS14: Lich 3H **19**
Windsor Cres. DY2: Dud 3K **97**
Windsor Dr. B24: Erd 4J **81**
B92: Sol 6B **124**
DY10: Kidd 2L **157**
DY13: Stour S 8F **182**
Windsor Gdns. B60: B'gve . . . 7A **188**
CV10: Nun 5E **88**
WV3: Wolv 2G **51**
WV8: Cod 6F **20**
Windsor Ga. WV12: W'hall . . . 5C **38**
Windsor Gro. DY8: Word 8L **95**
WS4: S'fld 7C **26**
Windsor Holloway
DY7: Kinv 7B **114**
Windsor Ho. B23: Erd 3F **80**
Windsor Ind. Est. B7: Birm . . . 4A **102**
Windsor Lodge B92: Olton . . . 1K **145**
Windsor Pl. B7: Birm . . 6A **102** (3M **5**)
B23: Erd 6E **80**
CV32: Lea S 1M **223**
Windsor Rd. B30: Stir 4H **143**
B36: Cas B 2F **104**
B63: Hale 5M **117**
B65: Row R 5C **98**
B68: O'bry 6G **99**
B71: W Brom 1H **77**
B73: New O 8D **58**
B78: Pole 1K **49**
B97: Redd 4D **212**
DY4: Tip 1A **76**
DY8: Stourb 6K **115**
WS6: C Hay 5E **14**
WV4: E'shll 4F **52**
WV5: Wom 3F **72**
Windsor St. B7: Birm . . 4M **101** (1K **5**)
B60: B'gve 7M **187**
B97: Redd 5D **212**
CV1: Cov 7B **152**
CV11: Nun 5H **89**
CV21: Rugby 6C **180**
CV32: Lea S 1M **223**
LE10: Burb 4M **91**
WS1: Wals 2L **55**
WV14: Bils 3J **53**
Windsor St. Sth.
B7: Birm 5A **102** (2L **5**)
Windsor Ter. B16: Edg 8F **100**
Windsor Vw. B32: Bart G 2H **141**
Windsor Wlk. WS10: Darl 1D **54**
Windsor Way WS4: Rus 2D **40**
Winds Point DY9: Hag 3A **138**
Windward Way B36: Cas B . . . 1F **104**
Windward Way Ind. Est.
B36: Cas B 1F **104**
WINDY ARBOUR 6H **199**
Windy Arbour CV8: Ken 4H **199**
Windy Mnr. Rd. B93: Know . . . 1D **168**
Windyridge Rd. B76: Walm . . . 3M **81**
Winfield Rd. CV11: Nun 4H **89**
Winfield St. CV21: Rugby 5D **180**
Winford Av. DY6: K'wfrd 5L **95**
Winforton Cl. B98: Redd 6L **213**
Wingate Cl. B30: K Nor 5F **142**
Wingate Ct. B74: Four O 5E **42**
Wingate Rd. WS2: Wals 7E **38**
Wing Cl. WS2: Wals 5F **38**
Wingfield Cl. B37: F'bri 6F **104**
Wingfield Ho. B37: K'hrst 4F **104**
Wingfield Rd. B42: Gt Barr 2J **79**
B46: Col 4M **105**
Wingfield Way CV6: Cov 7A **130**
Wingfoot Av. WV10: Bush 1E **36**
Wingfoot Way B24: Erd 8J **81**
Wingrave Cl. CV5: Alle 3G **151**
Wing Yip Cen. B7: Nech 3B **102**
Winifred Av. CV5: Cov 8A **152**
Winifride Ct. B17: Harb 4B **120**
Winkle St. B70: W Brom 5H **77**
Winleigh Rd. B20: Hand 7F **78**
Winnall Cl. WV14: Cose 7K **53**
Winnallthorpe CV3: W'hall . . . 3L **175**
Winn Ho. *WS2: Wals 6K 39*
(off Burrowes St.)
Winnie Rd. B29: S Oak 8E **120**
Winnington Rd. B8: W End . . . 2G **103**
Winnipeg Rd. B38: K Nor 1G **165**
Winrush Cl. DY3: Gorn 6D **74**
Winscar Cft. DY3: Lwr G 6E **74**
Winsford Av. CV5: Cov 5H **151**
Winsford Cl. B63: Hale 3A **118**
B76: Walm 6L **59**
CV7: Bal C 3G **171**
Winsford Ct. CV5: Cov 5J **151**
Winsham Gro. B21: Hand 1E **100**
Winsham Wlk. CV3: Finh 6C **174**
Winslow Av. B8: W End 5H **103**
Winslow Cl. B98: Redd 6M **213**
CV5: Cov 6H **151**
CV32: Lea S 8J **217**
Winslow Dr. WV6: Wolv 5M **35**
Winslow Ho. B29: S Oak 8B **120**
CV1: Cov 5A **6**
WINSON GREEN 4E **100**
Winson Green/ Outer Circle Station
(Rail) 2E **100**
Winson Grn. Rd. B18: Win G . . 4E **100**
Winson St. B18: Win G 5D **100**
Winspear Cl. CV7: Mer 8J **127**
Winstanley Rd. B33: Stech . . . 7K **103**
Winster Av. B93: Dorr 5E **168**
Winster Cl. CV7: Ker E 2A **130**
Winster Gro. B44: Gt Barr 7K **57**
Winster Gro. Ind. Est.
B44: Gt Barr 7K **57**
Winster Rd. B43: Gt Barr 1D **78**
WV1: Wolv 8H **37**
Winston Av. CV2: Cov 1K **153**
Winston Churchill Ct.
WV14: Bils 1J **53**
Winston Cl. CV2: Cov 1K **153**
Winston Cres. CV32: Lill 6C **218**
Winston Dr. B20: Hand 8H **79**
B62: Roms 5A **140**
Winstone Cl. B98: Redd 5G **213**
Winston Rd. DY3: Swind 7E **72**
DY11: Cau 3A **136**
Winterborne Gdns.
CV10: Nun 7F **88**
Winterbourne Cft.
B14: K Hth 8J **143**
Winterbourne Rd.
B91: Sol 5M **145**
Winter Cl. WS13: Lich 7K **13**
Winterdene CV7: Bal C 2H **171**
WINTERFOLD 1H **185**
Winterfold Cl. DY10: Kidd 3B **158**
Winterley Gdns. DY3: Sed 3E **74**
Winterley La. WS4: Rus 2C **40**
Winterton Rd. B44: K'sdng 6A **58**
CV12: Bulk 8C **112**
Winthorpe Dr. B91: Sol 1C **168**
Wintney Cl. B17: Harb 2A **120**
Winton Gro. B76: Walm 3A **82**
Wintour Wlk. B60: B'gve 2L **209**
Winward Rd. B98: Redd 8M **213**
Winwick Pl. CV22: Bil 1J **205**
Winwood Heath Rd.
B62: Roms 8K **139**
Winwood Rd. B65: Row R 6E **98**
Winwoods Gro. B32: Bart G . . . 1G **141**
Winyate Hill B98: Redd 7G **213**
WINYATES 6L **213**
Winyates Cen. B98: Redd 6L **213**
WINYATES GREEN 6M **213**
Winyates Way B98: Redd 4L **213**
Wirehill Dr. B98: Redd 8F **212**
Wiremill Cl. B44: Gt Barr 3L **79**
Wirral Rd. B31: N'fld 3M **141**
Wiseacre Cft. B90: Shir 7E **144**
Wise Gro. CV21: Hillm 7F **180**
CV34: Warw 7E **216**
Wiseman Gro. B23: Erd 8D **58**
Wisemore WS1: Wals 7L **39**
(not continuous)
Wise St. CV31: Lea S 2M **223**
Wise Ter. CV31: Lea S 2M **223**
WISHAW 7H **61**
Wishaw Cl. B90: Shir 7E **144**
B98: Redd 1G **221**
Wishaw Gro. B37: K'hrst 4F **104**
Wishaw La. B76: Curd 1G **83**
B76: Min, Wis 3D **82**
B78: Midd 1H **61**
Wisley Gro. CV8: Ken 4J **199**
Wisley Way B32: Harb 4M **119**
Wissage Ct. WS13: Lich 1K **19**
Wissage Cft. WS13: Lich 8J **13**
Wissage La. WS13: Lich 1K **19**
Wissage Rd. WS13: Lich 8J **13**
Wistaria Cl. B31: N'fld 3A **142**
Wisteria Cl. CV2: Cov 7H **131**
Wisteria Dr. WS5: Wals 5M **55**
WS8: Bwnhls 7C **16**
Wisteria Gro. B44: Gt Barr 7L **57**
Wistmans Cl. DY1: Dud 7E **74**
Wistwood Hayes WV10: Bush . . 5F **22**
Witham Cl. B76: Walm 8A **60**
Witham Cft. B91: Sol 8C **146**
Withdean Cl. B11: S'brk 4D **122**
Witherford Cl. B29: S Oak 1C **142**
Witherford Cft. B91: Sol 7K **145**
Witherford Way B29: S Oak . . . 1C **142**
WITHERLEY 1B **66**
Witherley Rd. CV9: Ath 1L **65**
Withern Way DY3: Gorn 6C **74**
Withers Rd. WV8: Bilb 6H **21**
Withers Way B71: W Brom 5K **77**
Withington Covert
B14: K Hth 7K **143**
Withington Gro.
B93: Ben H, Dorr 5E **168**
Withybed Cl. B48: A'chu 3A **190**
WITHYBED GREEN 3M **189**
Withybed La. B48: A'chu 3M **189**
WITHYBROOK 4M **133**
Withybrook Cl. CV2: Cov 7K **131**
Withybrook La.
CV7: Shil, Withy 4F **132**
Withybrook Rd. B90: Shir 1H **167**
CV12: Bulk 7D **112**
Withy Gro. B37: K'hrst 4F **104**
Withy Hill Rd. B75: S Cold 2M **59**
Withymere La. WV5: Wom 1J **73**
Withymoor Rd. DY2: Neth 5L **97**
DY8: Amb 2A **116**
WITHYMOOR VILLAGE 8D **96**
Withy Rd. WV14: Bils 6J **53**
Withy Rd. Ind. Est.
WV14: Bils 6J **53**
Withywood Cl. WV12: W'hall . . . 8C **24**
Witley Av. B63: Hale 5L **117**
B91: Sol 7C **146**
Witley Cl. DY11: Kidd 7H **157**
Witley Cres. B69: O'bry 4E **98**
Witley Farm Cl. B91: Sol 7C **146**
Witley Rd. B31: N'fld 7D **142**
Witley Way DY13: Stour S . . . 7A **182**
Witnell Rd. CV6: Cov 3C **152**
WITNELLS END 1C **134**
Witney Cl. B79: Tam 2M **31**
Witney Dr. B37: F'bri 7F **104**
Witney Gro. WV10: F'hses 6B **22**
Wittersham Ct. *WV13: W'hall . . 7B 38*
(off Birmingham St.)
WITTON 6M **79**
Witton Bank B62: Quin 2F **118**
Witton La. B6: Aston 8M **79**
B71: W Brom 1G **77**
Witton Lodge Rd. B23: Erd 2B **80**
Witton Rd. B6: Aston 1L **101**
WV4: Penn 3A **52**
Witton Station (Rail) 8M **79**
Witton St. DY8: Stourb 5L **115**
Wivelden Av.
DY13: Stour S 3K **183**
Wixford Cft. B34: S End 2A **104**
Wixford Gro. B90: Shir 7K **145**
Wobaston Rd. WV9: Pend 6K **21**
WV10: F'hses 5B **22**
Woburn B77: Glas 6D **32**
Woburn Av. WV12: W'hall 3B **38**
Woburn Cl. B61: B'gve 8K **187**
CV31: Lea S 3D **224**
LE10: Hinc 6L **69**
Woburn Cres. B43: Gt Barr 8D **56**
Woburn Dr. B62: Hale 2B **118**
CV10: Nun 7G **89**
DY5: Brie H 2B **116**
Woburn Gro. B27: A Grn 8J **123**
Woburn Ho. *B15: Edg 2J 121*
(off Woodview Dr.)
Wodehouse Cl. WV5: Wom 4E **72**
Wodehouse La. DY3: Sed 1J **73**
WV5: Wom 1J **73**
Woden Av. WV11: Wed 3J **37**
Woden Cl. WV5: Wom 2F **72**
Woden Cres. WV11: Wed 3J **37**
Woden Pas. WS10: W'bry 7F **54**
Woden Rd. WV10: Wolv 5E **36**
Woden Rd. E. WS10: W'bry 5H **55**
Woden Rd. Nth. WS10: W'bry . . . 4E **54**
Woden Rd. Sth. WS10: W'bry . . . 8F **54**
Woden Rd. W. WS10: Darl 5D **54**
WS10: W'bry 5D **54**
Wodensfield Twr. WV11: Wed . . . 4J **37**
Woden Way WV11: Wed 3J **37**
Wolcot Gro. B6: Witt 4M **79**
Wolds La. LE10: Wlvy 5L **113**
Wold Wlk. B13: Mose 3B **144**
Wolfe Rd. CV4: Tile H 2F **172**
Wolfsbane Dr. WS5: Wals 6A **56**
Wolfson Dr. B15: Edg 5D **120**
WOLLASTON 3K **115**
Wollaston Ct. DY8: Woll 3J **115**
WS1: Wals 7M 39
(off Lwr. Rushall St.)
Wollaston Cres. WV11: Wed . . . 3K **37**
Wollaston Rd. DY7: Stourt 2J **115**
DY8: Amb 2L **115**
Wollerton Gro. B75: S Cold 3M **59**
WOLLESCOTE 4F **116**
Wollescote Bus. Pk.
DY9: Lye 4F **116**
Wollescote Dr. B91: Sol 8B **146**
Wollescote Rd. DY9: W'cte 6C **116**
(not continuous)
Wolmer Rd. WV11: Wed 7M **23**
Wolseley B77: Glas 7F **32**
Wolseley Av. B27: A Grn 5K **123**
Wolseley Bank
WV10: Bush 2F **36**
Wolseley Cl. B36: Cas B 8G **83**
WV10: Bush 2F **36**
Wolseley Dr. B8: W End 2G **103**
Wolseley Ga. WV10: Bush 2F **36**
Wolseley Rd. B70: W Brom 2E **76**
WV14: Bils 2H **53**
Wolseley St. B9: Birm 7B **102**
(not continuous)
Wolsey Rd. CV22: Bil 4K **205**
WS13: Lich 7F **12**
WOLSTON 6G **177**
Wolston Bus. Pk.
CV8: Wols 4G **177**
Wolston Cl. B90: Shir 4H **145**
Wolston Ct. CV22: Dunc 3H **205**
Wolston La.
CV8: Rytn D, Wols 8C **176**
Wolston Way CV3: W'hall 3J **175**
WOLVERHAMPTON 7E **36** (3M **7**)
Wolverhampton Art Gallery & Mus.
. . . . *3K 7*
(off Lichfield St.)
Wolverhampton Race Course
. . . . 3A **36**
Wolverhampton Rd.
B68: O'bry 6G **99**
B69: O'bry 2D **98**
DY3: Sed 8D **52**
DY6: W Hth 8J **73**
DY7: Stourt 2E **114**
DY10: Cookl, Kidd, W'ley
. . . . 8A **136**
WS2: Wals 7G **39**
(not continuous)
WS3: Blox 8H **25**
WS3: Pels 6L **25**
WS6: C Hay 8B **14**
WS11: Cann 4B **14**
WV6: Nur 6A **34**
WV8: Cod 5F **20**
(not continuous)
WV10: Share 7A **14**
(Saredon Rd., not continuous)
WV10: Share 8B **14**
(Warstone Rd.)
WV10: Wolv 6F **36**
WV11: Ess 6M **23**
Wolverhampton Rd. E.
WV4: Penn 4D **52**
Wolverhampton Rd. Sth.
B32: Quin 2L **119**
Wolverhampton Rd. W.
WS2: Wals 7C **38**
WV13: W'hall 7C **38**
Wolverhampton Science Pk.
WV10: Wolv 3C **36**
Wolverhampton Sports Arena
. . . . 4A **36**
Wolverhampton Station (Rail)
. . . . 7D **36** (3L **7**)
Wolverhampton St. DY1: Dud . . 7H **75**
WS2: Wals 7K **39**
WS10: Darl 2B **54**
WV13: W'hall 8M **37**
WV14: Bils 3J **53**
Wolverhampton Wanderers FC
. . . . 6C **36** (2H **7**)
WOLVERLEY 6K **135**
Wolverley Av. DY8: Woll 3J **115**
WV4: Penn 4K **51**
Wolverley Cres. B69: O'bry 4D **98**
Wolverley Rd. B32: Bart G 1H **141**
B63: Hale 7M **117**
B92: Sol 7D **124**
DY11: Kidd 8H **135**
DY11: W'ley 6K **135**
Wolverson Cl. WV12: W'hall . . . 5C **38**
Wolverson Rd. WS9: Wals W . . . 5G **27**
Wolverton Cl. B98: Redd 7K **213**
Wolverton Rd. B37: Mars G . . . 2H **125**
B45: Redn 3J **163**
CV5: E Grn 6G **151**
DY2: Dud 8L **75**
Wolver Villa Farm Cvn. & Camping Pk.
LE10: Wlvy 7K **113**
WOLVEY 5K **113**
WOLVEY HEATH 3M **113**
Wolvey Rd. CV12: Bulk 7D **112**
LE10: Burb 6L **91**
WOMBOURNE 4F **72**
Wombourne Cl. DY3: Sed 1C **74**
Wombourne Ent. Pk.
WV5: Wom 4D **72**
Wombourne Leisure Cen. 2F **72**
Wombourne Pk. WV5: Wom 4F **72**
Wombourne Rd. DY3: Swind 7E **72**
Wombrook Bus. Cen.
WV5: Wom 3E **72**
Wombrook Dale WV5: Wom 3D **72**
Woodacre Rd. B24: Erd 5J **81**
Woodall Rd. B6: Aston 8M **79**
Woodall St. B64: Crad H 8J **97**
WS3: Blox 8J **25**
(not continuous)
Woodard Rd. DY4: Tip 2C **76**
Wood Av. DY3: Lwr G 5C **74**
WV11: Wed 3K **37**
Wood Bank B26: Yard 2L **123**
Woodbank LE10: Burb 2A **92**
Woodbank Dr. B61: Cats 1M **187**
Wood Bank Rd. WV3: Wolv 1G **51**
Woodbank Rd. DY3: Sed 2C **74**
Woodberrow La. B97: Redd 3D **220**
Woodberry Dr. B76: Walm 7A **60**
Woodberry Wlk.
B27: A Grn 6K **123**
Woodbine Av. B10: Small H . . . 1D **122**
Woodbine Cotts.
CV32: Lea S 1L **223**
Woodbine Cft. B26: Sheld 3A **124**
Woodbine St. CV32: Lea S 1L **223**
Woodbine Wlk. B37: Chel W . . . 7K **105**
Woodbourne B15: Edg 1D **120**
(not continuous)
Woodbourne Rd. B15: Edg 1B **120**
B17: Harb 1B **120**
B67: Smeth 7L **99**
Woodbridge Cl. WS3: Blox 6G **25**
WS4: S'fld 8D **26**
Woodbridge Ct.
CV21: Rugby 5B **180**
Woodbridge Rd. B13: Mose 6M **121**
Woodbrooke Gro. B31: N'fld . . . 3C **142**
Woodbrooke Rd. B30: B'vlle . . . 2D **142**
Woodbrook Ho. B37: Chel W . . . 7H **105**
Woodburn Cl. CV5: Cov 5H **151**
Woodburn Rd. B66: Smeth 2D **100**
Woodbury Cl. B62: B'hth 1F **118**
B97: Redd 3A **220**
DY5: Brie H 7E **96**
DY11: Hartl 8A **184**
Woodbury Dr. B45: B Grn 8G **163**
Woodbury Gro. B91: Sol 8B **146**
Woodbury Rd. B62: B'hth 1F **118**
B62: Quin 2F **118**
DY11: Kidd 7H **157**
DY13: Stour S 4F **182**
Woodbury Rd. Nth.
DY13: Stour S 4F **182**
Woodbury Rd. W.
DY13: Stour S 4F **182**
Woodchester DY9: Hag 5B **138**
Woodchester Rd. B93: Dorr 7E **168**
Woodchurch Grange
B73: Bold 1F **80**
Wood Cl. B46: Col 2M **105**
Woodclose Av. CV6: Cov 3M **151**
Woodclose Rd. B37: F'bri 6F **104**
Woodcock Cl. B31: Longb 8J **141**
B94: Tan A 6E **192**

Woodcock Gdns.—Worcester St.

Woodcock Gdns.
WV10: F'stne 2H **23**
WOODCOCK HILL 2L 141
Woodcock La. B27: A Grn 6K **123**
(not continuous)
B31: N'fld 2L **141**
Woodcock La. Nth.
B27: A Grn 5K **123**
Woodcock Sports Cen. *5M 101*
(off Woodcock St.)
Woodcock St.
B7: Birm 5M **101** (2J **5**)
Woodcombe Cl.
DY5: Brie H 2B **116**
Wood Comn. Grange
WS3: Pels 5M **25**
Woodcote Av. CV8: Ken 2D **198**
CV11: Nun 1M **89**
Woodcote Cl. B98: Redd 6L **213**
Woodcote Dr. B8: Salt 4F **102**
B93: Dorr 7H **169**
CV35: Leek W 2F **216**
WOODCOTE GREEN 4C 186
Woodcote La. B61: U War 3D **186**
CV35: Leek W 1E **216**
DY9: Belb 3D **186**
Woodcote Pl. B19: Loz 2J **101**
Woodcote Rd. B24: Erd 4K **81**
CV32: Lea S 6L **217**
CV34: Warw 1F **222**
WV6: Tett 5J **35**
Woodcote Way B18: Hock 4G **101**
B74: S'tly 3M **57**
Wood Ct. B20: Hand 7G **79**
B97: Redd 8C **212**
CV2: Cov 2J **153**
Woodcraft Cl. CV4: Tile H 7G **151**
Woodcroft B47: H'wd 3B **166**
Woodcroft Av. B20: Hand 6E **78**
B79: Tam 3B **32**
DY4: Tip 4J **75**
Woodcroft Cl. B60: B'wll 4F **188**
B64: Old H 1M **117**
WOODCROSS 7F 52
Woodcross La. WV14: Cose 7G **53**
Woodcross St. WV14: Cose 7F **52**
WOOD END
B94 . . . . .5F 192
CV2 . . . . .8J 131
CV7 . . . . .4G 109
CV9 . . . . .8J 47
WV11 . . . . .2J 37
Woodend B20: Hand 3E **78**
Woodend Cl. B97: Redd 7B **212**
Wood End Cft. CV4: Tile H 1E **172**
Wood End Dr. B45: B Grn 1G **189**
Wood End La. B24: Erd 6F **80**
B94: Tan A 3E **192**
CV7: Fill 5G **109**
WS13: Curb, Elmh, Frad 1F **12**
Woodend Pl. WV6: Tett 5H **35**
Wood End Rd. B24: Erd 6F **80**
WS5: Wals 1D **56**
WV11: Wed 2K **37**
Wood End Station (Rail) 5F 192
Woodend Way WS9: A'rdge 8H **27**
Woodfall Av. B30: K Nor 4F **142**
Woodfield DY9: Belb 1L **161**
(Bell Heath)
DY9: Belb 2D **160**
(Nash La.)
Woodfield Av. B64: Crad H 1K **117**
B69: O'bry 5G **99**
DY5: P'ntt 2B **96**
DY9: W'cte 7F **116**
WV4: Penn 3M **51**
Woodfield Cl. B74: Four O 1H **59**
B98: Redd 4G **213**
WS5: Wals 4E **56**
WS11: Nort C 2M **15**
Woodfield Cres. B12: Bal H 3A **122**
DY11: Kidd 4J **157**
Woodfield Dr. WS11: Nort C 2M **15**
Woodfield Hgts. WV6: Tett 5K **35**
Woodfield La. B62: Roms 1K **161**
DY9: Belb 1K **161**
Woodfield Rd. B12: Bal H 3A **122**
B13: K Hth 1M **143**
B91: Sol 3B **146**
CV5: Cov 1L **173**
DY3: Lwr G 5C **74**
LE10: Burb 3J **91**
Woodfields Dr. WS14: Lich 3L **19**
Woodfield Social & Sports Club
. . . . .3A 52
Woodfield St. DY11: Kidd 3J **157**
Woodfold Cft. WS9: A'rdge 2H **41**
Woodford Av. B36: Cas B 1B **104**
Woodford Cl. CV7: Ash G 4D **130**
CV10: Nun 5C **88**
WV9: Pend 7M **21**
Woodford Cres. WS7: Burn 2H **17**
Woodford End WS11: Cann 5F **8**
Woodford Grn. Rd.
B28: Hall G 1G **145**
Woodford La. CV10: Harts 5C **66**
WV5: Try, Wom 1C **72**
Woodford Way
WS12: Hth H 8J **9**
WV5: Wom 3D **72**
Woodfort Rd. B43: Gt Barr 2E **78**
WOODGATE
Bartley Green 1H **141**
Stoke Prior 8B **210**
Woodgate Bus. Pk.
B32: Bart G 7H **119**
Woodgate Dr. B32: Bart G 8G **119**
Woodgate Gdns.
B32: Bart G 7G **119**
Woodgate Ho. B97: Redd 5A **212**
Woodgate La. B32: Bart G 7G **119**
Woodgate Rd.
B60: S Prior, Lwr B 8A **210**
LE10: Burb 1A **92**
Woodgate Valley Country Pk.
. . . . .7H 119
Woodgate Valley Country Pk.
Vis. Cen. 7H 119
Woodgate Valley Urban Farm
B32: Bart G 7G **119**
Woodgate Way DY9: Belb 2E **160**
Woodglade Cft. B38: K Nor 7E **142**
WOOD GREEN 4H 55
Wood Grn. WS6: C Hay 4E **14**
Woodgreen Cl. B97: Redd 3A **220**
Woodgreen Cft. B68: O'bry 2J **119**
Wood Grn. Rd. B18: Win G 5D **100**
WS10: W'bry 5G **55**
Woodgreen Rd. B68: O'bry 2J **119**
Woodhall Cl. CV11: Nun 7A **90**
DY4: Tip 1A **76**
Woodhall Cft. B92: Olton 6M **123**
Woodhall Ho. *WS3: Blox* *1J 39*
(off Woodhall St.)
Woodhall Rd. WV4: Penn 5L **51**
Woodham Cl. B45: Fran 8E **140**
Woodhampton Cl.
DY13: Stour S 8F **182**
Woodhams Rd. CV3: W'hall 6J **175**
Woodhaven WS4: S'fld 8D **26**
Woodhaven WS11: Cann 4B **14**
WOOD HAYES 8J 23
Wood Hayes Cft. WV10: Bush . . .7J **23**
Wood Hayes Rd. WV10: Bush . . .7H **23**
WV11: Wed 8J **23**
Woodhill Cl. WV5: Wom 3F **72**
Wood Hill Dr. WV5: Wom 4F **72**
Wood Hill Ri. CV6: Cov 7D **130**
Wood Ho. WS1: Wals 2M **55**
Woodhouse Cl. CV3: Bin 1L **175**
Woodhouse Ct. DY5: Quar B 8G **97**
Woodhouse Fold WV11: Wed 4K **37**
Woodhouse La. B77: Amin 4G **33**
Woodhouse Orchard
DY9: Belb 2E **160**
Woodhouse Rd. B32: Quin 3L **119**
B60: S Prior 7K **209**
WV6: Tett 5H **35**
Woodhouse Rd. Nth.
WV6: Tett 5H **35**
WOODHOUSES 2M 17
Woodhouses La. WS7: Burn 3L **17**
Woodhouse Sports Cen. 5F 32
Woodhouses Rd. WS7: Burn 2A **18**
Woodhouse St. CV34: Warw . . .3D **222**
Woodhouse Way B64: Crad H 8J **97**
Woodhurst Cl. B77: Amin 4F **32**
Woodhurst Rd. B13: Mose 5A **122**
Wooding Cres. DY4: Tip 8B **54**
Woodington Rd. B75: S Cold 4A **60**
Woodland Av. CV5: Cov 2M **173**
DY1: Dud 6J **75**
DY5: Quar B 8G **97**
DY8: Hag 4M **137**
DY11: Kidd 2J **157**
LE10: Burb 3A **92**
WV6: Tett 6H **35**
Woodland Cl. DY9: Pedm 8D **116**
WS12: Hed 1H **9**
WV12: W'hall 3D **38**
Woodland Ct. WS12: Hunt 5C **8**
WS14: Shen W 2G **43**
Woodland Cres. WV3: Wolv 2K **51**
Woodland Dr. B45: B Grn 7G **163**
B66: Smeth 2L **99**
WS6: C Hay 5E **14**
Woodland Gro. B43: Gt Barr 6E **56**
DY3: Gorn 6B **74**
DY10: W'ley 6C **136**
Woodland Ri. B64: Crad H 1M **117**
B73: S Cold 5H **59**
Woodland Rd. B21: Hand 1C **100**
B31: N'fld 6B **142**
B61: D'frd 2F **186**
B62: B'hth 1D **118**
B77: Amin 6G **33**
B97: Redd 6B **212**
CV8: Ken 2H **199**
LE10: Hinc 8M **69**
WV3: Wolv 2K **51**
Wood Lands, The
B75: S Cold 3A **60**
Woodlands, The
B64: Crad H 2A **118**
CV9: Wood E 8J **47**
CV10: Harts 8A **66**
DY8: Stourb 7A **116**
DY11: Kidd 6H **157**
WS13: Lich 1K **19**
WV8: Cod 7G **21**
Woodlands Av. B46: Wat O 7H **83**
WS5: Wals 4E **56**
Woodlands Cen., The
WV12: W'hall 2E **38**
Woodlands Cl. B78: Dord 4A **48**
DY11: Hartl 7B **184**
Woodlands Cotts.
WV4: Penn 5L **51**
Woodlands Ct. CV3: Bin W 3D **176**
CV5: Cov 1A **174**
Woodlands Crematorium
B46: Col 4J **105**
Woodlands Cres. WS3: Pels 4M **25**
Woodlands Farm Rd.
B24: Erd 5M **81**
Woodlands La. B90: Shir 1H **167**
CV12: Bed 5E **110**
Woodlands Paddock
WV4: Penn 5L **51**
Woodlands Pk. CV9: Hurl 5J **63**
Woodlands Pk. Rd.
B30: B'vlle 3C **142**
Woodlands Rd. B8: Salt 5F **102**
B11: S'hll 6B **122**
B45: Rubery 2D **162**
CV3: Bin W 2D **176**
CV12: Bed 6E **110**
DY10: Cookl 5A **136**
WV5: Wom 4G **73**
Woodlands St. B66: Smeth 4C **100**
Woodlands Wlk. WV4: Penn 4L **51**
Woodlands Way
B37: Chel W 6K **105**
Woodland Way B78: B'moor 1M **47**
WS7: Burn 3G **17**
Wood La. B17: Harb 3A **120**
B20: Hand 7G **79**
B24: Erd 8G **81**
B32: Bart G 8G **119**
(not continuous)
B37: Mars G 1G **125**
B61: F'fld 7J **161**
B70: W Brom 6G **77**
B74: S'tly 8L **41**
B92: Bars 7L **147**
B94: Earls 7D **166**
CV7: Old A 7C **86**
CV7: Shil 4C **132**
CV10: Harts 1A **88**
CV13: High H 6K **67**
WS3: Pels 4M **25**
WS9: A'rdge 8M **27**
WS11: Cann 3A **14**
WS12: Hed 5J **9**
WS14: Foot 8B **28**
WV10: F'hses 8D **22**
WV12: W'hall 2E **38**
Wood La. Cl. WV12: W'hall 2E **38**
Woodlawn B91: Sol 5E **146**
Woodlawn Gro. DY6: K'wfrd 4K **95**
Woodlea Dr. B24: Erd 7F **80**
B91: Sol 4L **145**
Wood Leasow B32: Bart G 7K **119**
Wood Leaves B47: H'wd 1M **165**
Woodleigh Av. B17: Harb 5D **120**
Woodleigh Cl. B63: Hale 3A **118**
Woodleigh Ct. B38: K Nor 8F **142**
Woodleigh Rd. B72: W Grn 8J **59**
CV4: W'wd H 3F **172**
Woodleys, The B14: K Hth 5B **144**
Woodloes Av. Nth.
CV34: Warw 8E **216**
Woodloes Av. Sth.
CV34: Warw 8E **216**
Woodloes La. CV34: Guys C 6E **216**
CV35: Guys C 6E **216**
WOODLOES PARK 7E 216
Woodloes Rd. B90: Shir 1H **167**
Woodman Cl. B63: Hale 6C **118**
WS10: W'bry 5H **55**
Woodman Gro. B75: R'ley 6L **43**
Woodman La. DY9: Clent 5D **138**
WS6: C Hay 5E **14**
Woodman Rd. B14: K Hth 8A **144**
B63: Hale 6C **118**
Woodman Wlk. B23: Erd 4A **80**
Woodmeadow Rd.
B30: K Nor 6H **143**
Woodmill Mdw. CV8: Ken 3H **199**
Woodnorton Dr. B13: Mose 7L **121**
Woodnorton Rd. B65: Row R 7F **98**
Woodpecker Gro.
B36: Cas B 2G **105**
DY10: Kidd 7B **158**
Woodpecker Way
WS11: Hth H 6J **9**
Woodperry Av. B91: Sol 8C **146**
Wood Piece La. B98: Redd 2K **213**
Woodridge B6: Aston 8L **79**
Woodridge Av. B32: Quin 5H **119**
CV5: Alle 3G **151**
Woodridge Rd. B63: Hale 4A **118**
Wood Ridings WS13: Lich 8G **13**
Wood Rd. DY3: Lwr G 6C **74**
WV5: Wom 1H **73**
WV6: Tett 6H **35**
WV8: Cod 4D **20**
Woodroffe Wlk.
CV6: Longf 5G **131**
Woodrough Dr. B13: Mose 7M **121**
WOODROW
B98 . . . . .2H 221
DY10 . . . . .6L 159
Woodrow Cen. B98: Redd 2H **221**
(Bredon Ho.)
B98: Redd 1H **221**
(Eckington Cl.)
Woodrow Cl. B61: Cats 8M **161**
Woodrow Cres. B93: Know 4G **169**
Woodrow Dr. B98: Redd 3G **221**
Woodrow La. B61: Cats 8A **162**
DY10: Chad C, Harv 5J **159**
Woodrow Nth. B98: Redd 2G **221**
Woodrow Shop. Cen.
B98: Redd 2H **221**
Woodrow Sth. B98: Redd 2H **221**
Woodrow Wlk. B98: Redd 2G **221**
Woodruff Way WS5: Wals 5M **55**
Woodrush Dr. B47: H'wd 4A **166**
WOODS, THE 5J 55
Woods, The B14: K Hth 8M **121**
WOODS BANK 3D 54
Woods Bank Est., The
WS10: Darl 5D **54**
Woods Bank Ter.
WS10: Darl 4C **54**
Woods Ct. B77: Tam 6C **32**
Woods Cres. DY5: Quar B 8G **97**
Woods Cft. WS13: Lich 8G **13**
WOODSETTON 3F 74
Woodsetton Cl. DY1: Dud 3H **75**
Woodshill Av. B45: Lick 7G **163**
Woodshires Rd. B92: Olton 2L **145**
CV6: Longf 4F **130**
Woodsia Cl. CV23: Brow 1D **180**
WOODSIDE 3F 96
Wood Side WV11: Wed 1A **38**
Woodside B37: K'hrst 4E **104**
B74: Four O 7E **42**
CV7: Old A 8D **86**
CV9: Gren 8D **48**
Woodside Av. B97: Redd 7B **212**
Woodside Av. Nth.
CV3: Cov 3M **173**
Woodside Av. Sth.
CV3: Finh 5M **173**
Woodside Cl. CV9: Wood E 8J **47**
WS5: Wals 3D **56**
Woodside Cres. B93: Know 5H **169**
Wood Side Dr. B45: B Grn 1H **189**
Woodside Dr. B74: Lit A 4C **42**
Woodside Gro. WV8: Bilb 6H **21**
Woodside Ho. B34: S End 4E **104**
Woodside Ind. Est.
DY5: Brie H 4F **96**
Woodside Mobile Home Pk.
B94: Earls 2B **192**
Woodside Pk. CV8: Rytn D 3B **202**
CV21: Rugby 4A **180**
Woodside Pl. WS11: Cann 4E **8**
Woodside Rd. B29: S Oak 8G **121**
(not continuous)
DY2: Dud 3F **96**
WS5: Wals 3D **56**
Woodside Way B32: Bart G 1G **141**
B91: Sol 4L **145**
WS9: A'rdge 4H **41**
WV12: W'hall 2E **38**
Woods La. B64: Crad H 1J **117**
DY5: Brie H 2D **116**
Woodsome Gro. B23: Erd 2C **80**
Woodsorrel Rd. DY1: Dud 5F **74**
Woods Piece CV7: Ker E 3M **129**
Woodstile Cl. B75: R'ley 6K **43**
Woodstile Way B34: S End 3B **104**
Woodstock Cl. DY1: Dud 1G **97**
DY8: Word 8J **95**
LE10: Burb 3A **92**
WS5: Wals 6A **56**
Woodstock Cres. B93: Dorr 6F **168**
Woodstock Dr. B74: Four O 5D **42**
DY8: Word 8J **95**
WS12: Hunt 2C **8**
Woodstock Ho. B13: Mose 2A **144**
Woodstock Rd. B13: Mose 5A **122**
B21: Hand 1F **100**
CV3: Cov 2D **174**
CV11: Nun 8L **89**
WV1: Wolv 8H **37**
Woodston Gro. B91: Sol 1C **168**
Wood St. B16: Birm 7G **101**
CV9: Wood E 1H **63**
CV10: Nun 5F **88**
CV12: Bed 5G **111**
CV21: Rugby 4A **180**
CV32: Lea S 1A **224**
CV47: Sou 5H **225**
DY2: Dud 3F **96**
DY4: Tip 3L **75**
DY8: Woll 2K **115**
DY9: Lye 4F **116**
DY11: Kidd 3K **157**
LE9: Earl S 1E **70**
LE10: Hinc 8K **69**
WS10: Darl 3F **54**
WV4: E'shll 6G **53**
WV10: Wolv 4F **36**
WV13: W'hall 7A **38**
WV14: Bils 4K **53**
Wood St. Cl. LE10: Hinc 8K **69**
Wood Ter. B96: Sam 8H **221**
Woodthorne WV6: Tett 3H **35**
Woodthorne Cl. DY3: Gorn 7D **74**
Woodthorne Rd. WV6: Tett 3G **35**
Woodthorne Rd. Sth.
WV6: Tett 5G **35**
Woodthorne Wlk. DY6: K'wfrd . . .1L **95**
Woodthorpe Dr. DY9: W'cte . . .6D **116**
DY12: Bew 5A **156**
Woodthorpe Gdns.
B14: K Hth 4L **143**
Woodthorpe Rd. B14: K Hth . . .4K **143**
Woodvale Dr. B28: Hall G 5E **144**
Woodvale Rd. B28: Hall G 5E **144**
B32: Bart G 8G **119**
Woodview Dr. B15: Edg 2J **121**
Woodview Rd. CV9: Ath 2L **65**
Woodville Ct. *B23: Erd* *7E 80*
(off Gravelly Hill)
CV34: Warw 2F **222**
Woodville Gdns. DY3: Sed 8F **52**
Woodville Rd. B14: K Hth 1M **143**
B17: Harb 3A **120**
CV34: Warw 1E **222**
Woodward Cl. CV31: W'nsh . . .7A **224**
Woodward Pl. DY9: Lye 5C **116**
Woodward Rd. DY11: Kidd 6J **157**
Woodwards Cl. WS2: Wals 1H **55**
Woodwards Pl. WS2: Wals 1H **55**
Woodwards Rd. WS2: Wals 1H **55**
Woodward St. B71: W Brom 5L **77**
Woodway B24: Erd 4H **81**
Woodway Cl.
CV2: W'grve S 1M **153**
Woodway La.
CV2: W'grve S 1M **153**
WOODWAY PARK 8M 131
Woodway Wlk.
CV2: W'grve S 1L **153**
Woodwells Rd. B8: W End 4G **103**
Woody Bank WS6: C Hay 7E **14**
Woolacombe Lodge Rd.
B29: S Oak 7C **120**
Woolaston Rd. B98: Redd 1J **221**
Woolgrove St. CV6: Cov 6G **131**
Woolhope Cl. B98: Redd 6L **213**
Wooll St. CV21: Rugby 6A **180**
Woolmore Rd. B23: Erd 5C **80**
Woolpack, The CV34: Warw . . .3E **222**
Woolpack All.
WV1: Wolv 7C **36** (4J **7**)
Woolpack Cl. B65: Row R 5A **98**
Woolpack St.
WV1: Wolv 7C **36** (4J **7**)
Woolpack Way CV9: Ath 1K **65**
Woolwich Rd. CV11: Bram 3F **112**
Wooton Cl. B97: Redd 5A **212**
Wooton Ct. CV32: Lea S 7M **217**
Wooton Gro. B44: K'sdng 1C **80**
Wootton Av. WV11: Wed 2K **37**
Wootton Cl. DY5: Brie H 1B **116**
WS11: Hth H 7H **9**
WOOTTON GREEN 8G 149
Wootton Grn. La. CV7: Bal C . . .8G **149**
Wootton La. CV7: Bal C 8E **148**
Wootton Rd. B31: Longb 2A **164**
WV3: Wolv 2K **51**
Woottons Ct. WS11: Cann 8F **8**
Woottons Sq. WV14: Bils 7L **53**
Wootton St. CV12: Bed 6J **111**
Worcester Arc. *B2: Birm* *6G 5*
(off New St.)
Worcester Bar 7J 101 (6C 4)
Worcester Cl. B75: R'ley 6K **43**
CV5: Alle 2G **151**
DY9: Hag 4A **138**
LE9: Barw 2A **70**
WS11: Cann 1F **14**
WS13: Lich 6H **13**
Worcester Ct. CV6: Ald G 5H **131**
WV3: Wolv 3A **52**
Worcester Cross *DY10: Kidd* . . .*4L 157*
(off Ringway, The)
Worcester Grn. B71: W Brom . . .2J **77**
Worcester Gro. WV6: Pert 5D **34**
Worcester Ho. B36: Cas B 1G **105**
B63: Hale *6A 118*
(off Hill St.)
Worcester La. B75: R'ley 6K **43**
DY8: Stourb 8B **116**
DY9: Hag, Pedm 8B **116**
Worcester Ri. B29: S Oak 8H **121**
Worcester Rd. B6: Witt 7M **79**
B61: B'gve 1L **209**
B61: U War, Stoke H 6G **209**
B68: O'bry 1G **119**
CV8: Ken 6H **199**
DY2: Neth 6L **97**
DY9: Hag 6M **137**
DY10: Kidd 5L **157**
DY10: Shens 3C **184**
DY11: Kidd 1A **184**
DY13: Stour S, Titt 6H **183**
WR9: Wych 8E **208**
WV13: W'hall 7D **38**
Worcestershire County Mus.
. . . . .6M 183
Worcester Sq. B97: Redd 5E **212**
Worcester St. B2: Birm 6G **5**
CV21: Rugby 5A **180**
DY8: Stourb 5M **115**
DY10: Kidd 3L **157**
(not continuous)
DY13: Stour S 5G **183**
WV2: Wolv 8C **36** (6H **7**)

HOSPITALS and HOSPICES
covered by this atlas.

N.B. Where Hospitals and Hospices are not named on the map, the reference
given is for the road in which they are situated.

ACORNS CHILDREN'S HOSPICE 1E **142**
103 Oak Tree Lane
BIRMINGHAM
B29 6HZ
Tel: 0121 2484850

ACORNS CHILDREN'S HOSPICE (WALSALL) 4M **55**
Walstead Road
WALSALL
WS5 4NL
Tel: 01922 422500

ALEXANDRA HOSPITAL, THE 3J **221**
Woodrow Dri.
REDDITCH
B98 7UB
Tel: 01527 503030

BIRMINGHAM CHILDREN'S HOSPITAL
    (DIANA PRINCESS OF WALES HOSPITAL)
. . . . .6L **101** (3H **5**)
Steelhouse Lane
BIRMINGHAM
B4 6NH
Tel: 0121 3339999

BIRMINGHAM DENTAL HOSPITAL 6L **101** (3G **5**)
St Chad's Queensway
BIRMINGHAM
B4 6NN
Tel: 0121 2368611

BIRMINGHAM HEARTLANDS HOSPITAL 7H **103**
Bordesley Green East
BIRMINGHAM
B9 5ST
Tel: 0121 4242000

BIRMINGHAM NUFFIELD HOSPITAL, THE 4F **120**
22 Somerset Road
BIRMINGHAM
B15 2QQ
Tel: 0121 4562000

BIRMINGHAM WOMENS HOSPITAL 5D **120**
Metchley Park Road
BIRMINGHAM
B15 2TG
Tel: 0121 4721377

BLOXWICH HOSPITAL 1H **39**
Reeves Sreet
WALSALL
WS3 2JJ
Tel: 01922 858600

BRADBURY HOSPICE 7H **99**
494 Wolverhampton Road
OLDBURY
B68 8DG
Tel: 0121 5442712

BRAMCOTE HOSPITAL 2E **112**
Lutterworth Road
NUNEATON
CV11 6QL
Tel: 024 76388200

BUSHEY FIELDS HOSPITAL 2E **96**
Bushey Fields Rd.
DUDLEY
DY1 2LZ
Tel: 01384 457373

CANNOCK CHASE HOSPITAL 7D **8**
Brunswick Road
CANNOCK
WS11 5XY
Tel: 01543 572757

CITY HOSPITAL (BIRMINGHAM) 5F **100**
Dudley Road
BIRMINGHAM
B18 7QH
Tel: 0121 5543801

COMPTON HOSPICE 7J **35**
Compton Road West
WOLVERHAMPTON
WV3 9DH
Tel: 01902 774500

CORBETT HOSPITAL 2A **116**
Vicarage Rd.
STOURBRIDGE
DY8 4JB
Tel: 01384 456111

COVENTRY & WARWICKSHIRE HOSPITAL 5D **152** (2D **6**)
Stoney Stanton Road
COVENTRY
CV1 4FH
Tel: 024 76224055

DOROTHY PATTISON HOSPITAL 8H **39**
Alumwell Close
WALSALL
WS2 9XH
Tel: 01922 858000

EDWARD STREET HOSPITAL 6J **77**
Edward Street
WEST BROMWICH
B70 8NL
Tel: 0121 5537676

GEORGE ELIOT HOSPITAL 7H **89**
College Street
NUNEATON
CV10 7DJ
Tel: 024 76351351

GOOD HOPE HOSPITAL 3K **59**
Rectory Road
SUTTON COLDFIELD
B75 7RR
Tel: 0121 3782211

GOSCOTE HOSPITAL 1M **39**
Goscote Lane
WALSALL
WS3 1SJ
Tel: 01922 710710

GUEST HOSPITAL 6L **75**
Tipton Rd.
DUDLEY
DY1 4SE
Tel: 01384 456111

GULSON HOSPITAL 7E **152** (6F **6**)
Gulson Road
COVENTRY
CV1 2HR
Tel: 024 76552225

HAMMERWICH HOSPITAL 4H **17**
Hospital Rd.
BURNTWOOD
WS7 0EH
Tel: 01543 675754

HEATH LANE HOSPITAL 2K **77**
Heath Lane
WEST BROMWICH
B71 2BG
Tel: 0121 5531831

HIGHCROFT HOSPITAL 6D **80**
Fentham Road
BIRMINGHAM
B23 6AL
Tel: 0121 6235500

HILLCREST HOSPITAL 3J **221**
Quinneys Lane
REDDITCH
B98 7WG
Tel: 01527 500575

HINCKLEY & DISTRICT HOSPITAL 1K **91**
Mount Rd.
HINCKLEY
LE10 1AG
Tel: 01455 441800

HINCKLEY SUNNYSIDE HOSPITAL 4K **69**
Ashby Rd.
HINCKLEY
LE10 3DA
Tel: 01455 441922

HOSPITAL OF ST CROSS 8B **180**
Barby Road
RUGBY
CV22 5PX
Tel: 01788 572831

JOHN TAYLOR HOSPICE 4J **81**
76 Grange Road
BIRMINGHAM
B24 0DF
Tel: 0121 2552400

KEMP HOSPICE 6H **157**
58 Sutton Park Rd.
KIDDERMINSTER
DY11 6LF
Tel: 01562 861217

KIDDERMINSTER GENERAL HOSPITAL 4J **157**
Bewdley Rd.
KIDDERMINSTER
DY11 6RJ
Tel: 01562 823424

LITTLE ASTON BUPA HOSPITAL 4B **42**
Little Aston Hall Dri.
SUTTON COLDFIELD
B74 3UP
Tel: 0121 3532444

LITTLE BLOXWICH DAY HOSPICE 6K **25**
Stoney Lane
WALSALL
WS3 3DW
Tel: 01922 858735

LUCY BALDWIN HOSPITAL 4F **182**
Olive Gro.
STOURPORT-ON-SEVERN
DY13 8XZ
Tel: 01299 827327

MANOR HOSPITAL (WALSALL) 8J **39**
Moat Road
WALSALL
WS2 9PS
Tel: 01922 721172

MARY ANN EVANS HOSPICE .7G **89**
George Eliot Hospital
College Street
NUNEATON
CV10 7DJ
Tel: 024 76865440

MARY STEVENS HOSPICE 7B **116**
221 Hagley Rd.
STOURBRIDGE
DY8 2JR
Tel: 01384 443010

MIRAH HOUSE DAY HOSPITAL 4G **89**
Manor Court Avenue
NUNEATON
CV11 5HX
Tel: 024 76374434

MOSELEY HALL HOSPITAL 6L **121**
Alcester Road
BIRMINGHAM
B13 8JL
Tel: 0121 4424321

MOSSLEY DAY UNIT 8G **25**
Sneyd Lane
WALSALL
WS3 2LW
Tel: 01922 858680

MYTON HAMLET HOSPICE 2H **223**
Myton Lane
WARWICK
CV34 6PX
Tel: 01926 492518

NEW CROSS HOSPITAL (WOLVERHAMPTON) 4H **37**
Wolverhampton Road
WOLVERHAMPTON
WV10 0QP
Tel: 01902 307999

NORTHCROFT HOSPITAL 5D **80**
Reservoir Road
BIRMINGHAM
B23 6DW
Tel: 0121 3782211

NUNEATON PRIVATE BMI HOSPITAL 8J **89**
132 Coventry Road
NUNEATON
CV10 7AD
Tel: 024 76357500

PARKWAY BUPA HOSPITAL 4E **146**
1 Damson Parkway
SOLIHULL
B91 2PP
Tel: 0121 7041451

PENN HOSPITAL 5L **51**
Penn Road
WOLVERHAMPTON
WV4 5HN
Tel: 01902 444141

PRINCESS OF WALES COMMUNITY HOSPITAL 5A **188**
Stourbridge Rd.
BROMSGROVE
B61 0BB
Tel: 01527 488000

PRIORY HOSPITAL, THE 4H **121**
Priory Road
BIRMINGHAM
B5 7UG
Tel: 0121 4402323

QUEEN ELIZABETH HOSPITAL 5E **120**
Edgbaston
BIRMINGHAM
B15 2TH
Tel: 0121 6271627

QUEEN ELIZABETH PSYCHIATRIC HOSPITAL 5E **120**
Mindelsohn Way
BIRMINGHAM
B15 2QZ
Tel: 0121 678000

RIDGE HILL HOSPITAL 6L **95**
Brierly Hill Rd.
STOURBRIDGE
DY8 5ST
Tel: 01384 456111

ROWAN DAY HOSPITAL 5E **212**
Smallwood House
Church Green West
REDDITCH
B97 4BD
Tel: 01527 488621

ROWLEY REGIS COMMUNITY HOSPITAL 7B **98**
Moor Lane
ROWLEY REGIS
B65 8DA
Tel: 0121 6073465

ROYAL LEAMINGTON SPA REHABILITATION HOSPITAL ...5L **223**
Heathcote Lane
WARWICK
CV34 6SR
Tel: 01926 317700

ROYAL ORTHOPAEDIC HOSPITAL 4B **142**
Bristol Road South
BIRMINGHAM
B31 2AP
Tel: 0121 685 4000

RUGBY MYTON DAY HOSPICE 8B **180**
Barby Road
RUGBY
CV22 5PY
Tel: 01788 550085

RUSSELLS HALL HOSPITAL 2D **96**
Pensnett Rd.
DUDLEY
DY1 2HQ
Tel: 01384 456111

ST DAVID'S HOUSE (DAY HOSPITAL) 2G **73**
Planks La.
WOLVERHAMPTON
WV5 8DU
Tel: 01902 326001

ST MARY'S HOSPICE 8G **121**
176 Raddlebarn Road
BIRMINGHAM
B29 7DA
Tel: 0121 4721191

ST MICHAEL'S HOSPITAL (LICHFIELD) 1K **19**
Trent Valley Rd.
LICHFIELD
WS13 6EF
Tel: 01543 414555

ST MICHAEL'S HOSPITAL (WARWICK) 1D **222**
St. Michael's Road
WARWICK
CV34 5QW
Tel: 01926 406789

SANDWELL DISTRICT GENERAL HOSPITAL 4K **77**
Lyndon
WEST BROMWICH
B71 4HJ
Tel: 0121 5531831

SELLY OAK HOSPITAL 8F **120**
Raddlebarn Road
BIRMINGHAM
B29 6JD
Tel: 0121 6271627

SIR ROBERT PEEL HOSPITAL 7K **31**
Plantation La.
TAMWORTH
B78 3NG
Tel: 01827 263800

SOLIHULL HOSPITAL 5C **146**
Lode Lane
SOLIHULL
B91 2JL
Tel: 0121 4242000

SUTTON COLDFIELD COTTAGE HOSPITAL 5H **59**
Birmingham Road
SUTTON COLDFIELD
B72 1QH
Tel: 0121 255 4000

VICTORIA HOSPITAL 3G **19**
Friary Rd.
LICHFIELD
WS13 6QM
Tel: 01543 414926

WALSGRAVE HOSPITAL 3A **154**
Clifford Bridge Road
COVENTRY
CV2 2DX
Tel: 024 76602020

WARREN PEARL MARIE CURIE HOSPICE 5D **146**
911-913 Warwick Road
SOLIHULL
B91 3ER
Tel: 0121 2547800

WARWICK HOSPITAL 1E **222**
Lakin Road
WARWICK
CV34 5BW
Tel: 01926 495321

WARWICKSHIRE NUFFIELD HOSPITAL, THE 4L **217**
Old Milverton Lane
LEAMINGTON SPA
CV32 6RW
Tel: 01926 427971

WEST HEATH HOSPITAL 1C **164**
Rednal Road
BIRMINGHAM
B38 8HR
Tel: 0121 6271627

WEST MIDLANDS HOSPITAL 4K **117**
Colman Hill
HALESOWEN
B63 2AH
Tel: 01384 560123

WEST PARK REHABILITATION HOSPITAL 7A **36**
Park Road West
WOLVERHAMPTON
WV1 4PW
Tel: 01902 444000

WOLVERHAMPTON EYE INFIRMARY 7A **36**
Compton Road
WOLVERHAMPTON
WV3 9QR
Tel: 01902 307999

WOLVERHAMPTON NUFFIELD HOSPITAL 5J **35**
Wood Road
WOLVERHAMPTON
WV6 8LE
Tel: 01902 754177

WOODBOURNE PRIORY HOSPITAL 1C **120**
23 Woodbourne Road
Harborne
BIRMINGHAM
B17 8BY
Tel: 0121 4344343

WORDSLEY HOSPITAL 5L **95**
Stream Rd.
STOURBRIDGE
DY8 5QX
Tel: 01384 456111

WWW. Estate-Publications.co.uk

Local red book

01580 764225

st
Peter   Little Aston - B74 3AT